McDougal Littell

# Science

INTEGRATED COURSE

2

Earth's Atmosphere

Human Biology

Diversity of Living Things

Electricity and Magnetism

Motion and Forces

## INTEGRATED COURSE 2




**Acknowledgments:** Excerpts and adaptations from *National Science Education Standards* by the National Academy of Sciences. Copyright © 1996 by the National Academy of Sciences. Reprinted with permission from the National Academies Press, Washington, D.C.

Excerpts and adaptations from *Benchmarks for Science Literacy: Project 2061.* Copyright © 1993 by the American Association for the Advancement of Science. Reprinted with permission.





ISBN-13: 978-0-618-42301-9

ISBN-10: 0-618-42301-X 6 7 8 9 10 11 VJM 11 10 09 08 07

Internet Web Site: http://www.mcdougallittell.com

## Science Consultants

**Chief Science Consultant**

**James Trefil, Ph.D.** is the Clarence J. Robinson Professor of Physics at George Mason University. He is the author or co-author of more than 25 books, including *Science Matters* and *The Nature of Science.* Dr. Trefil is a member of the American Association for the Advancement of Science's Committee on the Public Understanding of Science and Technology. He is also a fellow of the World Economic Forum and a frequent contributor to *Smithsonian* magazine.

**Rita Ann Calvo, Ph.D.** is Senior Lecturer in Molecular Biology and Genetics at Cornell University, where for 12 years she also directed the Cornell Institute for Biology Teachers. Dr. Calvo is the 1999 recipient of the College and University Teaching Award from the National Association of Biology Teachers.

**Kenneth Cutler, M.S.** is the Education Coordinator for the Julius L. Chambers Biomedical Biotechnology Research Institute at North Carolina Central University. A former middle school and high school science teacher, he received a 1999 Presidential Award for Excellence in Science Teaching.

## Instructional Design Consultants

**Douglas Carnine, Ph.D.** is Professor of Education and Director of the National Center for Improving the Tools of Educators at the University of Oregon. He is the author of seven books and over 100 other scholarly publications, primarily in the areas of instructional design and effective instructional strategies and tools for diverse learners. Dr. Carnine also serves as a member of the National Institute for Literacy Advisory Board.

**Linda Carnine, Ph.D.** consults with school districts on curriculum development and effective instruction for students struggling academically. A former teacher and school administrator, Dr. Carnine also co-authored a popular remedial reading program.

**Sam Miller, Ph.D.** is a middle school science teacher and the Teacher Development Liaison for the Eugene, Oregon, Public Schools. He is the author of curricula for teaching science, mathematics, computer skills, and language arts.

**Donald Steely, Ph.D.** serves as principal investigator at the Oregon Center for Applied Science (ORCAS) on federal grants for science and language arts programs. His background also includes teaching and authoring of print and multimedia programs in science, mathematics, history, and spelling.

**Vicky Vachon, Ph.D.** consults with school districts throughout the United States and Canada on improving overall academic achievement with a focus on literacy. She is also co-author of a widely used program for remedial readers.

# Content Reviewers

**John Beaver, Ph.D.**
*Ecology*
Professor, Director of Science Education Center
College of Education and Human Services
Western Illinois University
Macomb, IL

**Donald J. DeCoste, Ph.D.**
*Matter and Energy, Chemical Interactions*
Chemistry Instructor
University of Illinois
Urbana-Champaign, IL

**Dorothy Ann Fallows, Ph.D., MSc**
*Diversity of Living Things, Microbiology*
Partners in Health
Boston, MA

**Michael Foote, Ph.D.**
*The Changing Earth, Life Over Time*
Associate Professor
Department of the Geophysical Sciences
The University of Chicago
Chicago, IL

**Lucy Fortson, Ph.D.**
*Space Science*
Director of Astronomy
Adler Planetarium and Astronomy Museum
Chicago, IL

**Elizabeth Godrick, Ph.D.**
*Human Biology*
Professor, CAS Biology
Boston University
Boston, MA

**Isabelle Sacramento Grilo, M.S.**
*The Changing Earth*
Lecturer, Department of the Geological Sciences
San Diego State University
San Diego, CA

**David Harbster, MSc**
*Diversity of Living Things*
Professor of Biology
Paradise Valley Community College
Phoenix, AZ

**Richard D. Norris, Ph.D.**
*Earth's Waters*
Professor of Paleobiology
Scripps Institution of Oceanography
University of California, San Diego
La Jolla, CA

**Donald B. Peck, M.S.**
*Motion and Forces; Waves, Sound, and Light; Electricity and Magnetism*
Director of the Center for Science Education (retired)
Fairleigh Dickinson University
Madison, NJ

**Javier Penalosa, Ph.D.**
*Diversity of Living Things, Plants*
Associate Professor, Biology Department
Buffalo State College
Buffalo, NY

**Raymond T. Pierrehumbert, Ph.D.**
*Earth's Atmosphere*
Professor in Geophysical Sciences (Atmospheric Science)
The University of Chicago
Chicago, IL

**Brian J. Skinner, Ph.D.**
*Earth's Surface*
Eugene Higgins Professor of Geology and Geophysics
Yale University
New Haven, CT

**Nancy E. Spaulding, M.S.**
*Earth's Surface, The Changing Earth, Earth's Waters*
Earth Science Teacher (retired)
Elmira Free Academy
Elmira, NY

**Steven S. Zumdahl, Ph.D.**
*Matter and Energy, Chemical Interactions*
Professor Emeritus of Chemistry
University of Illinois
Urbana-Champaign, IL

**Susan L. Zumdahl, M.S.**
*Matter and Energy, Chemical Interactions*
Chemistry Education Specialist
University of Illinois
Urbana-Champaign, IL

# Safety Consultant

**Juliana Texley, Ph.D.**
Former K–12 Science Teacher and School Superintendent
Boca Raton, FL

# English Language Advisor

**Judy Lewis, M.A.**
Director, State and Federal Programs for reading proficiency and high risk populations
Rancho Cordova, CA

## Teacher Panel Members

**Carol Arbour**
Tallmadge Middle School,
Tallmadge, OH

**Patty Belcher**
Goodrich Middle School,
Akron, OH

**Gwen Broestl**
Luis Munoz Marin Middle School,
Cleveland, OH

**Al Brofman**
Tehipite Middle School,
Fresno, CA

**John Cockrell**
Clinton Middle School,
Columbus, OH

**Jenifer Cox**
Sylvan Middle School,
Citrus Heights, CA

**Linda Culpepper**
Martin Middle School,
Charlotte, NC

**Kathleen Ann DeMatteo**
Margate Middle School,
Margate, FL

**Melvin Figueroa**
New River Middle School,
Ft. Lauderdale, FL

**Doretha Grier**
Kannapolis Middle School,
Kannapolis, NC

**Robert Hood**
Alexander Hamilton Middle School,
Cleveland, OH

**Scott Hudson**
Covedale Elementary School,
Cincinnati, OH

**Loretta Langdon**
Princeton Middle School,
Princeton, NC

**Carlyn Little**
Glades Middle School,
Miami, FL

**Ann Marie Lynn**
Amelia Earhart Middle School,
Riverside, CA

**James Minogue**
Lowe's Grove Middle School,
Durham, NC

**Joann Myers**
Buchanan Middle School,
Tampa, FL

**Barbara Newell**
Charles Evans Hughes Middle School,
Long Beach, CA

**Anita Parker**
Kannapolis Middle School,
Kannapolis, NC

**Greg Pirolo**
Golden Valley Middle School,
San Bernardino, CA

**Laura Pottmyer**
Apex Middle School,
Apex, NC

**Lynn Prichard**
Booker T. Washington Middle Magnet
School, Tampa, FL

**Jacque Quick**
Walter Williams High School,
Burlington, NC

**Stacy Rinehart**
Lufkin Road Middle School,
Apex, NC

**Robert Glenn Reynolds**
Hillman Middle School,
Youngstown, OH

**Theresa Short**
Abbott Middle School,
Fayetteville, NC

**Rita Slivka**
Alexander Hamilton Middle School,
Cleveland, OH

**Marie Sofsak**
B F Stanton Middle School,
Alliance, OH

**Nancy Stubbs**
Sweetwater Union Unified School District,
Chula Vista, CA

**Sharon Stull**
Quail Hollow Middle School,
Charlotte, NC

**Donna Taylor**
Okeeheelee Middle School,
West Palm Beach, FL

**Sandi Thompson**
Harding Middle School,
Lakewood, OH

**Lori Walker**
Audubon Middle School & Magnet Center,
Los Angeles, CA

## Teacher Lab Evaluators

**Andrew Boy**
W.E.B. DuBois Academy,
Cincinnati, OH

**Jill Brimm-Byrne**
Albany Park Academy,
Chicago, IL

**Gwen Broestl**
Luis Munoz Marin Middle School,
Cleveland, OH

**Al Brofman**
Tehipite Middle School,
Fresno, CA

**Michael A. Burstein**
The Rashi School,
Newton, MA

**Trudi Coutts**
Madison Middle School,
Naperville, IL

**Jenifer Cox**
Sylvan Middle School,
Citrus Heights, CA

**Larry Cwik**
Madison Middle School,
Naperville, IL

**Jennifer Donatelli**
Kennedy Junior High School,
Lisle, IL

**Melissa Dupree**
Lakeside Middle School,
Evans, GA

**Carl Fechko**
Luis Munoz Marin Middle School,
Cleveland, OH

**Paige Fullhart**
Highland Middle School,
Libertyville, IL

**Sue Hood**
Glen Crest Middle School,
Glen Ellyn, IL

**William Luzader**
Plymouth Community Intermediate School,
Plymouth, MA

**Ann Min**
Beardsley Middle School,
Crystal Lake, IL

**Aileen Mueller**
Kennedy Junior High School,
Lisle, IL

**Nancy Nega**
Churchville Middle School,
Elmhurst, IL

**Oscar Newman**
Sumner Math and Science Academy,
Chicago, IL

**Lynn Prichard**
Booker T. Washington Middle Magnet
School, Tampa, FL

**Jacque Quick**
Walter Williams High School,
Burlington, NC

**Stacy Rinehart**
Lufkin Road Middle School,
Apex, NC

**Seth Robey**
Gwendolyn Brooks Middle School,
Oak Park, IL

**Kevin Steele**
Grissom Middle School,
Tinley Park, IL

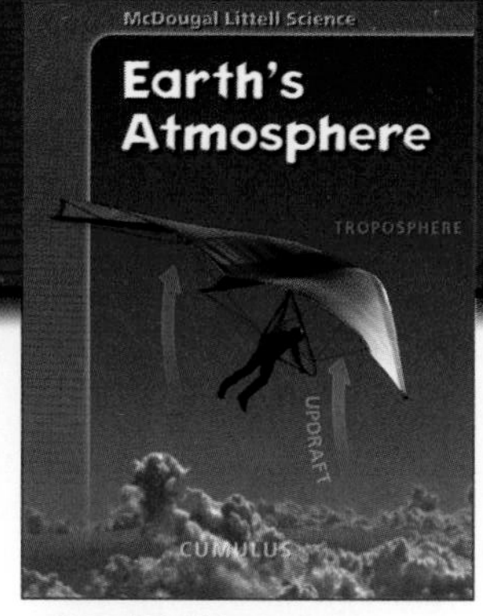


eEdition

UNIT A

# Earth's Atmosphere

## Unit Features

*What weather conditions do you see in the distance?* *page A40*

*What types of weather can move a house? page A76*

## 3 Weather Fronts and Storms A76

**the BIG idea**
The interaction of air masses causes changes in weather.

## 4 Climate and Climate Change A114

**the BIG idea**
Climates are long-term weather patterns that may change over time.



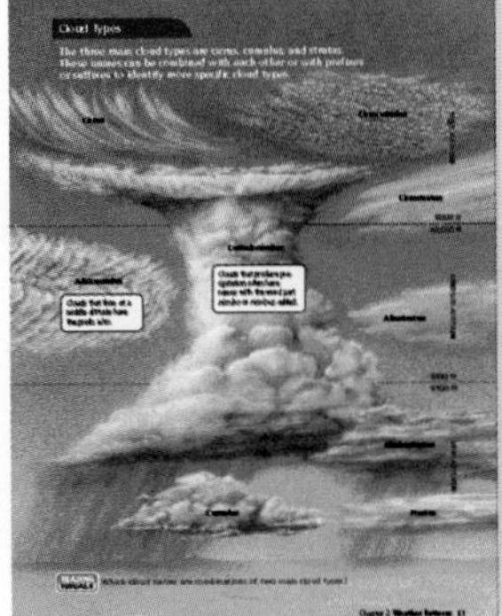

## Visual Highlights

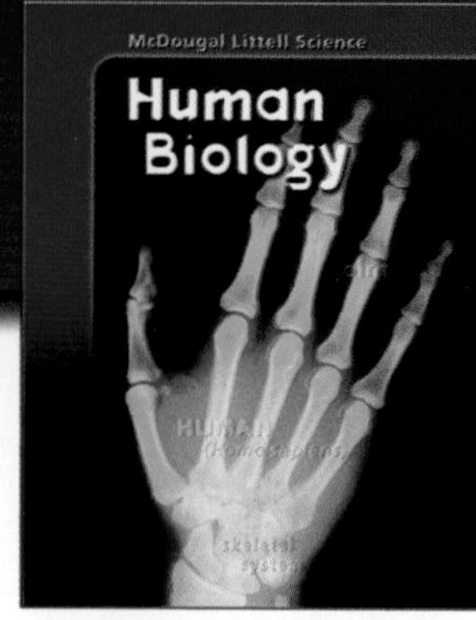


eEdition

UNIT B

# Human Biology

## Unit Features



## 1 Systems, Support, and Movement B6

the BIG idea

The human body is made up of systems that work together to perform necessary functions.



## 2 Absorption, Digestion, and Exchange B34

the BIG idea

Systems in the body obtain and process materials and remove waste.



*What materials does your body need to function properly?* *page B34*

*Red blood cells travel through a blood vessel. How do you think blood carries materials around your body? page B62*

## Visual Highlights

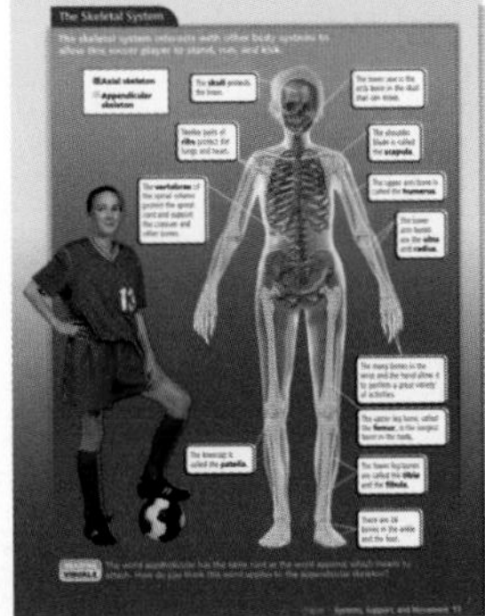

eEdition

UNIT C
# Diversity of Living Things

## Unit Features



## 1 Single-Celled Organisms and Viruses C6

**the BIG idea**

Bacteria and protists have the characteristics of living things, while viruses are not alive.



## 2 Introduction to Multicellular Organisms C40

**the BIG idea**

Multicellular organisms live in and get energy from a variety of environments.

*How does an organism get energy and materials from its environment?* *page C40*

## 3 Plants C82

the BIG idea

Plants are a diverse group of organisms that live in many land environments.



## 4 Invertebrate Animals C120

the BIG idea

Invertebrate animals have a variety of body plans and adaptations.



## 5 Vertebrate Animals C154

the BIG idea

Vertebrate animals live in most of Earth's environments.

## Visual Highlights

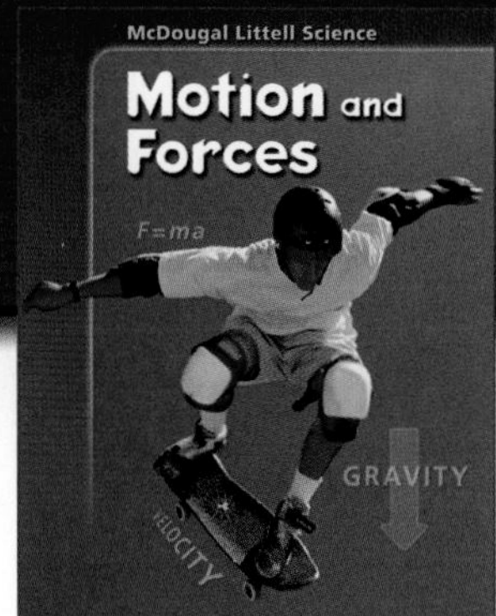


eEdition

UNIT D

# Motion and Forces

## Unit Features



## 1 Motion



**the BIG idea**
The motion of an object can be described and predicted.



## 2 Forces



**the BIG idea**
Forces change the motion of objects in predictable ways.

*What must happen for a team to win this tug of war? page D38*

What forces are acting on this snowboarder? on the snow? page D75

## Visual Highlights

McDougal Littell Science Electricity and Magnetism

eEdition

UNIT E
# Electricity and Magnetism

## Unit Features



## 1 Electricity E6

the BIG idea
Moving electric charges transfer energy.



## 2 Circuits and Electronics E40

the BIG idea
Circuits control the flow of electric charge.

*How can circuits control the flow of charge? page E40*

What force is acting on this compass needle? page E76



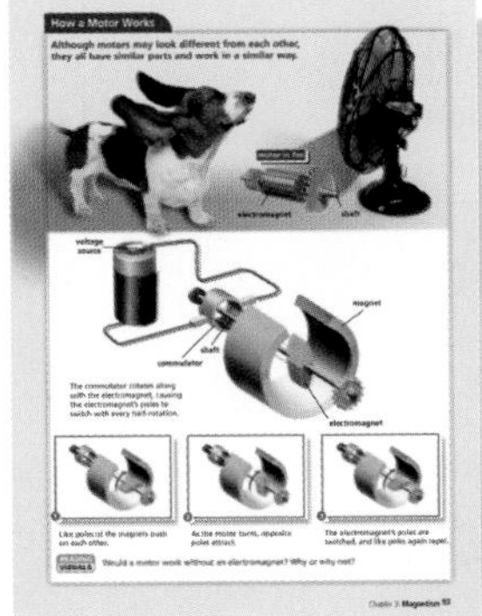

## Visual Highlights

# Features

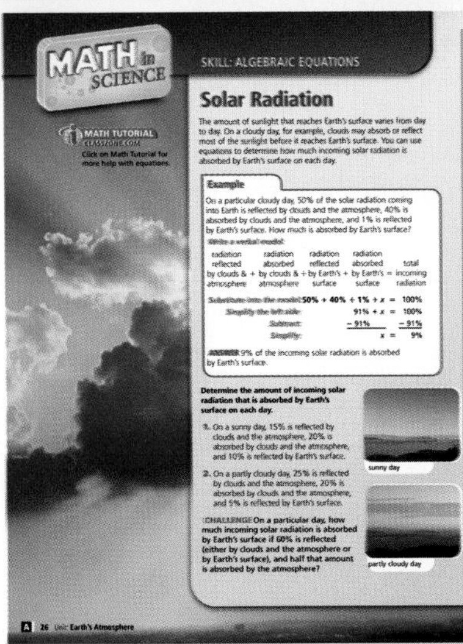

MATH in SCIENCE

SKILL: ALGEBRAIC EQUATIONS

## Solar Radiation

The amount of sunlight that reaches Earth's surface varies from day to day. On a cloudy day, for example, clouds may absorb or reflect most of the sunlight before it reaches Earth's surface. You can use equations to determine how much incoming solar radiation is absorbed by Earth's surface on each day.

MATH TUTORIAL
CLASSZONE.COM
Click on Math Tutorial for more help with equations.

**Example**

On a particular cloudy day, 50% of the solar radiation coming into Earth is reflected by clouds and the atmosphere, 40% is absorbed by clouds and the atmosphere, and 1% is reflected by Earth's surface. How much is absorbed by Earth's surface?

Write a verbal model:

radiation reflected by clouds & atmosphere + radiation absorbed by clouds & atmosphere + radiation reflected by Earth's surface + radiation absorbed by Earth's surface = total incoming radiation

Substitute into the model: $50\% + 40\% + 1\% + x = 100\%$

Simplify the left side: $91\% + x = 100\%$

Subtract: $-91\% \quad -91\%$

Simplify: $x = 9\%$

ANSWER 9% of the incoming solar radiation is absorbed by Earth's surface.

**Determine the amount of incoming solar radiation that is absorbed by Earth's surface on each day.**

1. On a sunny day, 15% is reflected by clouds and the atmosphere, 20% is absorbed by clouds and the atmosphere, and 10% is reflected by Earth's surface.
2. On a partly cloudy day, 25% is reflected by clouds and the atmosphere, 20% is absorbed by clouds and the atmosphere, and 5% is reflected by Earth's surface.

CHALLENGE **On a particular day, how much incoming solar radiation is absorbed by Earth's surface if 60% is reflected (either by clouds and the atmosphere or by Earth's surface), and half that amount is absorbed by the atmosphere?**

sunny day

partly cloudy day

A 26 Unit: Earth's Atmosphere

## Math in Science



## Think Science



## Connecting Sciences



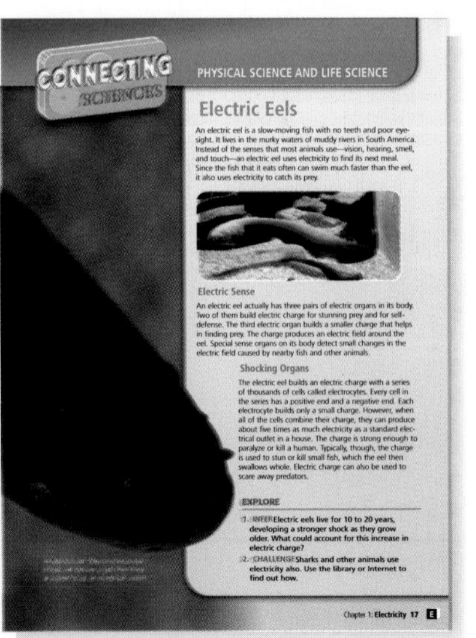

CONNECTING SCIENCES

PHYSICAL SCIENCE AND LIFE SCIENCE

## Electric Eels

An electric eel is a slow-moving fish with no teeth and poor eyesight. It lives in the murky waters of muddy rivers in South America. Instead of the senses that most animals use—vision, hearing, smell, and touch—an electric eel uses electricity to find its next meal. Since the fish that it eats often can swim much faster than the eel, it also uses electricity to catch its prey.

### Electric Sense

An electric eel actually has three pairs of electric organs in its body. Two of them build electric charge for stunning prey and for self-defense. The third electric organ builds a smaller charge that helps in finding prey. The charge produces an electric field around the eel. Special sense organs on its body detect small changes in the electric field caused by nearby fish and other animals.

### Shocking Organs

The electric eel builds an electric charge with a series of thousands of cells called electrocytes. Every cell in the series has a positive end and a negative end. Each electrocyte builds only a small charge. However, when all of the cells combine their charge, they can produce about five times as much electricity as a standard electrical outlet in a house. The charge is strong enough to paralyze or kill a human. Typically, though, the charge is used to stun or kill small fish, which the eel then swallows whole. Electric charge can also be used to scare away predators.

**EXPLORE**

1. INFER **Electric eels live for 10 to 20 years, developing a stronger shock as they grow older. What could account for this increase in electric charge?**
2. CHALLENGE **Sharks and other animals use electricity also. Use the library or Internet to find out how.**

Chapter 1: Electricity 17 E

## Science on the Job



## Extreme Science



## Frontiers in Science



## Timelines in Science



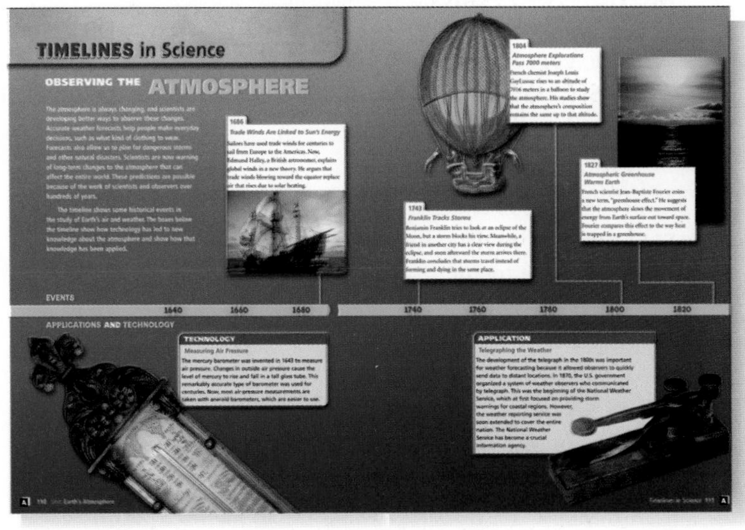

# Internet Resources @ ClassZone.com

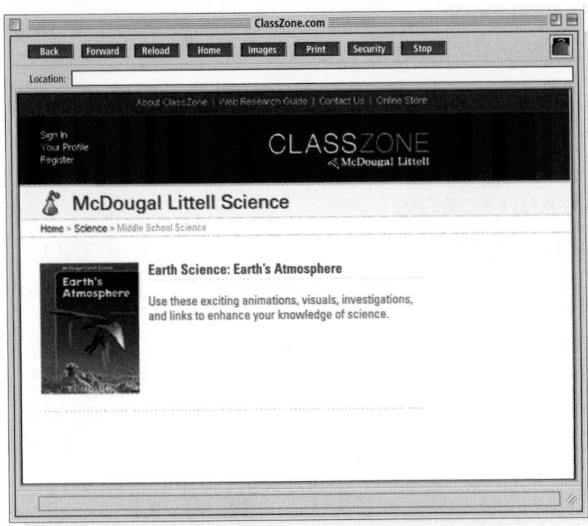


## Simulations



## Visualizations



## Career Centers

## Resource Centers

**EARTH'S ATMOSPHERE**
Resources for the following topics may be found at ClassZone.com: *Earth's Atmosphere, Ozone Layer, Air Pressure, Global Winds, Clouds, Lightning, Weather Safety, Weather and Weather Forecasting, Atmospheric Research, El Niño, Climate Zones, Climate and Climate Change, Global Warming.*

**HUMAN BIOLOGY**
Resources for the following topics may be found at ClassZone.com: *Skeletal System, Muscles, Respiratory System, Urinary System, Circulatory System, Blood Types, Lymphatic System, Skin, Current Medical Imaging Techniques, Senses, Nervous System, Endocrine System, Human Health, Nutrition, Fighting Disease.*

**DIVERSITY OF LIVING THINGS**
Resources for the following topics may be found at ClassZone.com: *Single-Celled Organisms and the Human Body, Bacteria, Viruses, Bee Dance, Plant Adaptations, Animal Adaptations, Fungi, Biodiversity Discoveries and Research, Plant Systems, Plant Evolution, Seeds, Extreme Seeds, Invertebrate Diversity, Worms, Mollusks, Arthropods, Fish, Amphibians, Reptiles, Mammals.*

**MOTION AND FORCES**
Resources for the following topics may be found at ClassZone.com: *Finding Position, Acceleration, Inertia, Moving Rocks, Newton's Laws of Motion, Momentum, Gravity, Gravitational Lenses, Friction, Forces, and Surfaces, Force and Motion Research, Work, Power, Machines in Everyday Objects, Artificial Limbs, Nanomachines, Robots.*

**ELECTRICITY AND MAGNETISM**
Resources for the following topics may be found at ClassZone.com: *Lightning and Lightning Safety, Electrochemical Cells, Electrical Safety, Electronics, Electronic and Computer Research, Magnetism, Dams and Electricity, Energy Use and Conservation.*

## Math Tutorials



## NSTA SciLinks

*Codes for use with the NSTA SciLinks site may be found on every chapter opener.*

## Content Review

*There is a content review for every chapter at ClassZone.com*

## Test Practice

*There is a standardized test practice for every chapter at ClassZone.com*

# Explore the Big Idea

*Chapter Opening Inquiry*

Each chapter opens with hands-on explorations that introduce the chapter's Big Idea.

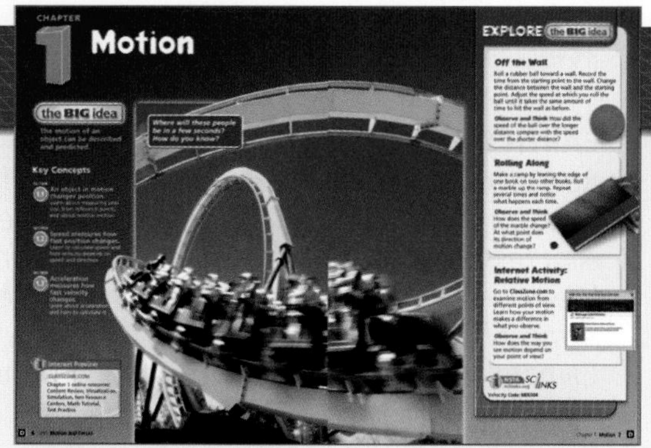

# Chapter Investigations

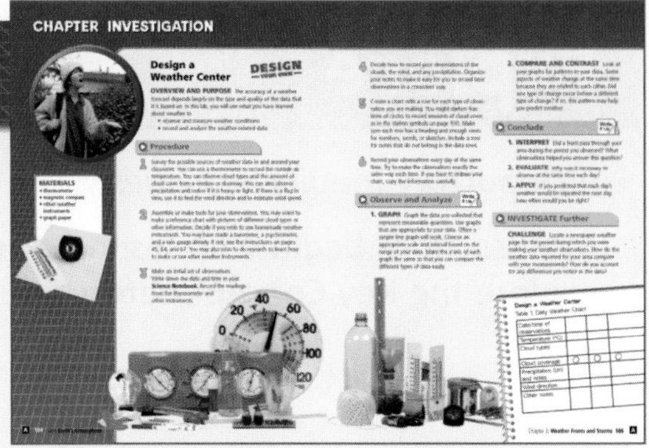
CHAPTER INVESTIGATION

Design a Weather Center

DESIGN YOUR OWN

Procedure

Observe and Analyze

Conclude

INVESTIGATE Further

*Full-Period Labs*

The Chapter Investigations are in-depth labs that let you form and test a hypothesis, build a model, or sometimes design your own investigation.



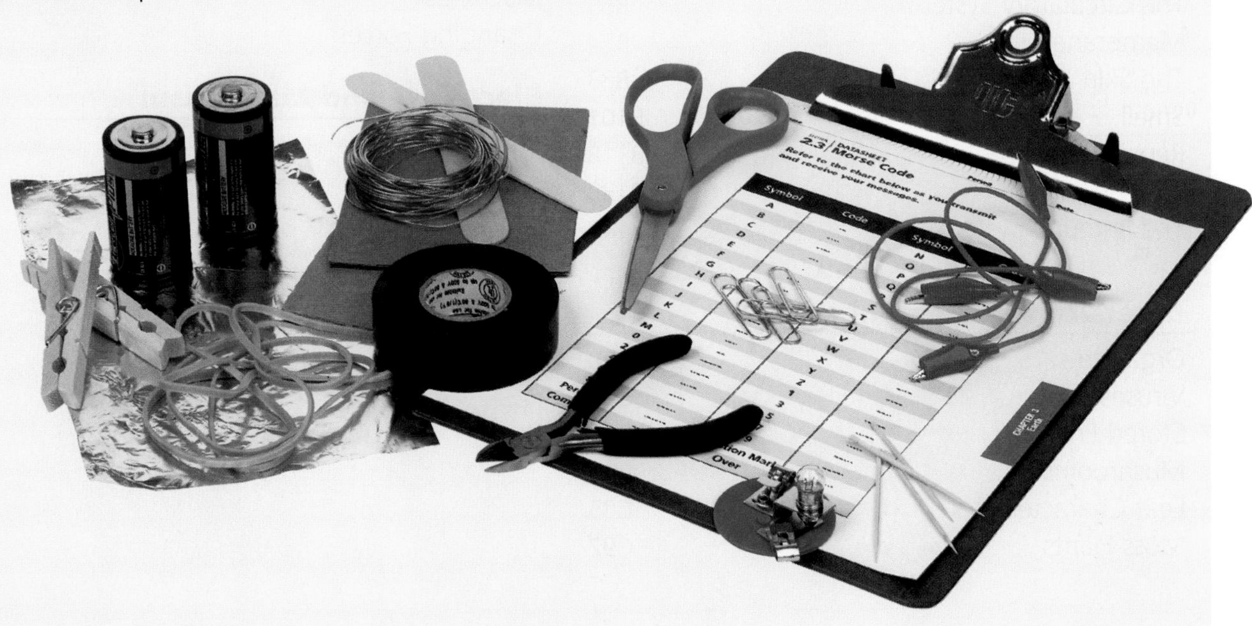

# Explore

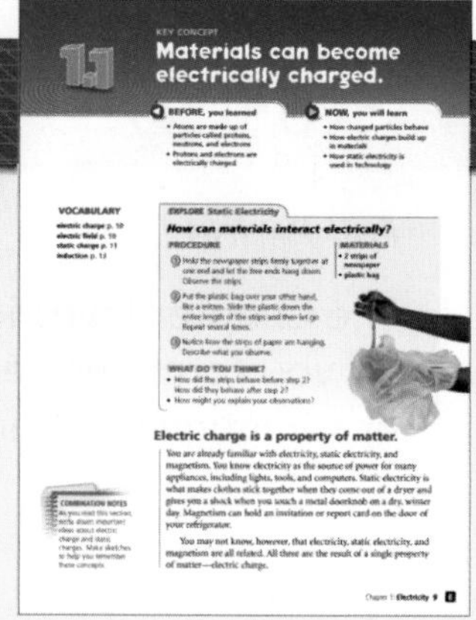

*Introductory Inquiry Activities*

Most sections begin with a simple activity that lets you explore the Key Concept before you read the section.

# Investigate

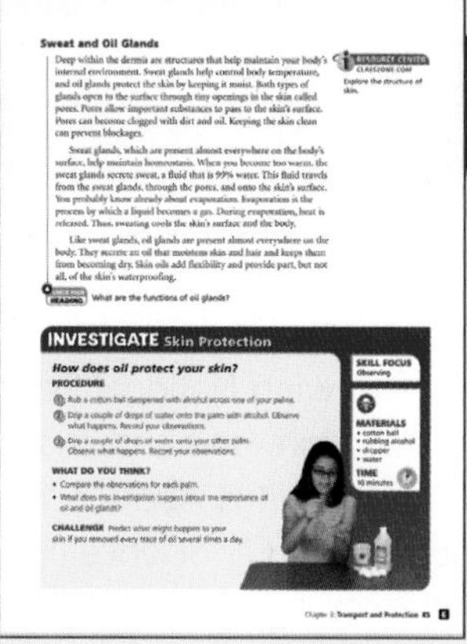

*Skill Labs*

Each Investigate activity gives you a chance to practice a specific science skill related to the content that you're studying.

# Standards and Benchmarks

Each unit addresses some of the learning goals described in the *National Science Education Standards* (NSES) and the Project 2061 *Benchmarks for Science Literacy.* The following National Science Education Standards are also addressed in the book introduction, unit and chapter features, and lab investigations in all the units: A.9 Understandings About Scientific Inquiry, E.6 Understandings About Science and Technology, F.5 Science and Technology in Society, G.1 Science as a Human Endeavor, G.2 Nature of Science, G.3 History of Science.

## National Science Education Standards

### Content Standards

**UNIT A Earth's Atmosphere**

| | |
|---|---|
| D.1.f | Water evaporates from Earth's surface; rises, cools, and condenses in the atmosphere; and falls as rain or snow. |
| D.1.h | The atmosphere is a mixture of the gases nitrogen and oxygen and small amounts of water vapor and other gases. |
| D.1.i | Clouds form when water vapor condenses. Clouds affect the weather. |
| D.1.j | Global patterns of motion in the atmosphere and the oceans and heat energy from oceans affect the weather. |
| D.2.a | The Earth processes we see today are similar to those that occurred in the past. |
| F.3.a | Processes of the Earth system, such as storms, can cause hazards that affect humans and wildlife. |
| F.3.b | Human activities can produce hazards and affect the speed of natural changes. |

**UNIT B Human Biology**

| | |
|---|---|
| C.1.a | Levels of organization for living systems include: cells, tissues, organs, organ systems, whole organisms, and ecosystems. |
| C.1.e | The human organism has systems that perform specific functions. |
| C.1.f | Some diseases are the result of infection by other organisms. |
| C.2.a | Reproduction is a characteristic of all living systems. |
| C.2.b | In many species, females produce eggs and males produce sperm. The egg and sperm come together to produce offspring with genetic material from both parents. |
| C.3.a | All organisms must be able to obtain and use resources, grow, reproduce, and maintain stable internal conditions. |
| C.3.b | Regulation of an organism's internal environment keeps conditions within the range required to survive. |
| F.1.c | Tobacco use increases the risk of illness. |
| F.1.d | Alcohol and other drugs can increase the risk of illness. |
| F.1.e | Food provides energy and nutrients for growth and development. |

**UNIT C Diversity of Living Things**

| | |
|---|---|
| C.1.b | All organisms are composed of cells—the basic unit of life. Most are single cells; others, including humans, are multicellular. |
| C.1.c | Cells perform the functions of life. They grow and divide. They take in nutrients for energy and materials. |
| C.1.d | Specialized cells perform specialized functions in multicellular organisms. |
| C.1.f | Some diseases are the result of the breakdown of structures or by infection by other organisms. |

| | |
|---|---|
| C.2.a | Reproduction is a characteristic of all living systems. Some organisms reproduce asexually. Others reproduce sexually. |
| C.2.b | In many species, females produce eggs and males produce sperm. The egg and sperm come together to produce offspring with genetic material from both parents. |
| C.3.a | All organisms must be able to obtain and use resources, grow, reproduce, and maintain stable internal conditions. |
| C.3.b | Regulation of an organism's internal environment keeps conditions within the range required to survive. |
| C.3.c | Behavior is one kind of response an organism makes. |
| C.4.c | Most energy in ecosystems enters as sunlight, gets transferred by producers into chemical energy, and passes from organism to organism as food. |
| C.5.a | Millions of species of animals, plants, and microorganisms are alive today. |
| F.1.e | Food provides energy and nutrients for growth and development. |

**UNIT D Motion and Forces**

| | |
|---|---|
| B.1.a | A substance has characteristic properties, such as density. |
| B.2.a | An object's motion is described by its position, direction of motion, and speed. That motion can be measured and shown on a graph. |
| B.2.b | An object will move in a straight line at a constant speed unless a force acts on it. |
| B.2.c | If more than one force acts on an object along a straight line, then the forces will reinforce or cancel each other. |
| B.3.a | Energy is often associated with heat, sound, and mechanical motion. Energy is transferred in many ways. |
| D.3.c | Gravity is the force that keeps planets in orbit around the Sun, governs motion within the solar system, holds us to Earth's surface, and produces tides. |
| E.6.c | Science and technology often work together. Science helps drive technology. Technology is used to improve scientific investigations. |
| E.6.d | Perfectly designed solutions do not exist. All technological solutions have trade-offs, such as cost, safety, and efficiency. |
| E.6.e | All designs have limits, including those having to do with material properties, safety, and environmental protection. |

**UNIT E Electricity and Magnetism**

| | |
|---|---|
| B.3.a | Energy is the property of substances that is often associated with electricity. Energy is transferred in many ways. |
| B.3.d | Circuits transfer electrical energy. Heat, light, sound, and chemical changes are produced. |
| B.3.e | In most chemical reactions, energy is transferred into or out of a system. Heat, light, motion, or electricity all might be involved in such transfers. |

# Process and Skill Standards

| | |
|---|---|
| A.1 | Identify questions that can be answered through scientific methods. |
| A.2 | Design and conduct a scientific investigation. |
| A.3 | Use appropriate tools and techniques to gather and analyze data. |
| A.4 | Use evidence to describe, predict, explain, and model. |
| A.5 | Think critically to find relationships between results and interpretations. |
| A.6 | Give alternative explanations and predictions. |
| A.7 | Communicate procedures and explanations. |
| A.8 | Use mathematics in scientific inquiry. |
| E.1 | Identify a problem to be solved. |
| E.2 | Design a solution or product. |
| E.3 | Implement the proposed solution. |
| E.4 | Evaluate the solution or design. |

# Project 2061 Benchmarks

## Content Benchmarks

### UNIT A Earth's Atmosphere

| | |
|---|---|
| 3.A.2 | Technologies are important in science because they let people gather, store, compute, and communicate large amounts of data. |
| 4.B.4 | Sunlight falls more intensely on different parts of Earth, and the pattern changes over the year. The differences in heating of Earth's surface produce seasons and other weather patterns. |
| 4.B.6 | The atmosphere can change suddenly when a volcano erupts or when Earth is struck by a huge rock from space. |
| 4.B.7 | Water is important in the atmosphere. Water evaporates from Earth's surface; rises and cools; condenses into rain or snow; and falls back to the surface. |
| 4.E.3 | Heat energy can move by the collision of particles, by the motion of particles, or by waves through space. |
| 11.B.1 | Models are often used to think about processes that cannot be observed directly or that are too vast or too dangerous to be changed directly. Models can be displayed on a computer and then changed to see what happens. |

### UNIT B Human Biology

| | |
|---|---|
| 6.A.1 | Human beings have body systems for diverse body functions |
| 6.C.2 | For the body to use food it must be digested and transported to cells. |
| 6.C.3 | Cells take in oxygen for combustion of food, and eliminate carbon dioxide. |
| 6.C.4 | Specialized cells and molecules identify and/or destroy microbes. |
| 6.B.1 | Fertilization occurs when a sperm cell enters an egg cell. |
| 6.B.3 | Cells divide and specialize as a fetus develops from the embryo. |
| 6.B.5 | Body changes occur as humans age. |
| 6.C.5 | Hormones are chemical messengers. |
| 6.C.6 | Interactions among senses, nerves, and the brain make learning possible. |
| 6.E.2 | Toxic substances, diet, and behavior may harm one's health. |
| 6.E.4 | White blood cells engulf invaders or produce antibodies. |

### UNIT C Diversity of Living Things

| | |
|---|---|
| 5.A.1 | One general distinction among organisms is between plants and animals. Many organisms are neither plants or animals. |
| 5.A.2 | Organisms have diverse body plans. |
| 5.A.3 | Organisms share similar features. |
| 5.B.2 | In sexual reproduction a specialized cell from a female joins one from a male. |
| 5.C.1 | All living things are made of cells. |
| 5.E.1 | Food provides organisms with fuel and materials. |
| 5.E.3 | Energy can change form in living things. |
| 6.B.3 | Patterns of human development are similar to those of other vertebrates. |
| 6.C.1 | Organs and organ systems are composed of cells and help provide basic needs. |
| 6.E.3 | Viruses, bacteria, fungi, and parasites may infect the human body. |

**UNIT D Motion and Forces**

| | |
|---|---|
| 4.B.3 | Everything on or near Earth is pulled toward Earth's center by the force of gravity. |
| 4.E.1 | Energy cannot be created or destroyed, but it can be changed from one form to another. |
| 4.E.4 | Energy appears in many different forms, including heat, chemical, mechanical, and gravitational. |
| 4.F.3 | An unbalanced force acting on an object changes its speed and/or direction of motion. |
| 4.G.1 | Every object exerts the force of gravity on every other object. |
| 4.G.2 | The sun's gravitational pull holds the earth and other planets in their orbits. The planets' gravity keeps their moons in orbit around them. |
| 8.B.4 | The use of robots has changed the nature of work in many fields, including manufacturing. |
| 10.A.1 | An object's motion is relative to some other object or point in space. |
| 10.B.1 | Newton's Laws describe motion everywhere in the universe. |
| 11.C.2 | A system may stay the same because no forces are acting on the system, or forces are acting on the system but they all cancel each other out. |

**UNIT E Electricity and Magnetism**

| | |
|---|---|
| 1.C.6 | Computers are important in science. |
| 3.A.2 | Technology is essential to science. |
| 3.A.3 | Engineers and others who work in design and technology use scientific knowledge to solve practical problems. |
| 4.G.3 | Electric currents and magnets can exert a force on each other. |
| 8.C.4 | Electrical energy can be produced from a variety of energy sources and can be transformed into almost any other form of energy. |
| 8.D.2 | The ability to code information as electric currents in wires has made communication many times faster than is possible by mail or sound. |
| 8.E.1 | Computers use digital codes containing only two symbols to perform all operations. |
| 9.A.6 | Numbers can be represented by using only 1s and 0s. |

# Process and Skill Benchmarks

| | |
|---|---|
| 1.A.3 | Some knowledge in science is very old and yet is still used today. |
| 1.B.1 | Design an investigation in which you collect evidence, reason logically, and use imagination to devise hypotheses. |
| 3.A.2 | Technology is essential to access outer space and remote locations, to collect, use, and share data, and to communicate. |
| 3.B.1 | Design requires taking constraints into account. |
| 9.B.3 | Use graphs to show the relationship between two variables. |
| 9.C.4 | Use graphs to show patterns and make predictions. |
| 11.A.2 | Think about things as systems by looking for the ways each part relates to others. |
| 11.B.1 | Use models to think about processes. |
| 11.C.4 | Use equations to summarize observed changes. |
| 11.D.2 | With complex systems, use summaries, averages, ranges, and examples. |
| 12.B.1 | Find what percentage one number is of another. |
| 12.B.2 | Use and compare numbers in equivalent forms such as decimals and percents. |
| 12.B.7 | Determine, use, and convert units. |
| 12.C.1 | Compare amounts proportionally. |
| 12.C.3 | Use and read measurement instruments. |
| 12.D.1 | Use tables and graphs to organize information and identify relationships. |
| 12.E.3 | Be skeptical of biased samples. |
| 12.E.4 | Recognize more than one way to interpret a given set of findings. |
| 12.E.5 | Criticize faulty reasoning. |

# Introducing Science

Scientists are curious. Since ancient times, they have been asking and answering questions about the world around them. Scientists are also very suspicious of the answers they get. They carefully collect evidence and test their answers many times before accepting an idea as correct.

In this book you will see how scientific knowledge keeps growing and changing as scientists ask new questions and rethink what was known before. The following sections will help get you started.

# What Is Science?

Science is the systematic study of all of nature, from particles too small to see to the human body to the entire universe. However, no individual scientist can study all of nature. Therefore science is divided into many different fields. For example, some scientists are biologists, others are geologists, and still others are chemists or astronomers.

All the different scientific fields can be grouped into three broad categories: life science, earth science, and physical science.

- Life science focuses on the study of living things; it includes the fields of cell biology, botany, ecology, zoology, and human biology.
- Earth science focuses on the study of our planet and its place in the universe; it includes the fields of geology, oceanography, meteorology, and astronomy.
- Physical science focuses on the study of what things are made of and how they change; it includes the fields of chemistry and physics.

## Integrated Science Course 2

Integrated Science pulls together units from the different categories of science to give you a broad picture of how scientists study nature. For example, scientists from the three broad categories might all study electricity, but from different points of view. You will learn in Unit A that a meteorologist might study the cloud types in which lightning forms. In Unit B, you will see how a biologist might study electrical signals within the human nervous system. In Unit E, you will learn how a physicist studies the magnetic fields formed by an electric current.

Even though science has many different fields, all scientists have similar ways of thinking and approaching their work. For example, scientists use instruments as well as their minds to look for patterns in nature. Scientists also try to find explanations for the patterns they discover. As you study each unit, you will in part focus on the patterns that scientists have found within that particular specialized branch. At the same time, as you move from one unit to another, you will be blending knowledge from the different branches of science together to form a more general understanding of our universe.

## Unifying Principles

As you learn, it helps to have a big picture of science as a framework for new information. McDougal Littell Science has identified unifying principles from each of the three broad categories of science: life science, earth science, and physical science. These unifying principles are described on the following pages. However, keep in mind that the broad categories of science do not have fixed borders. Earth science shades into life science, which shades into physical science, which shades back into earth science.

**the BIG idea**

Each chapter begins with a big idea. Keep in mind that each big idea relates to one or more of the unifying principles.

# What Is Life Science?

Life science is the study of the great variety of living things that have lived or now live on Earth. Life science includes the study of the characteristics and needs that all living things have in common. It is also a study of changes—both daily changes and those that take place over millions of years. Probably most important, in studying life science you will explore the many ways that all living things—including you—depend on Earth and its resources.

Living things, such as these birds, have certain characteristics that distinguish them from nonliving things. One important characteristic is the ability to grow. If all goes well, these warbler chicks will grow to become adult birds that can feed and take care of themselves.

# UNIFYING PRINCIPLES of Life Science

## All living things share common characteristics.

Despite the variety of living things on Earth, there are certain characteristics common to all. The basic unit of life is the **cell.** Any living thing, whether it has one cell or many, is described as an **organism.** All organisms are characterized by

- organization—the way that an organism's body is arranged
- growth—the way that an organism grows and develops over its lifetime
- reproduction—the way that an organism produces offspring like itself
- response—the ways an organism interacts with its surroundings

## All living things share common needs.

All living things have three basic needs: energy, materials, and living space. Energy enables an organism to carry out all the activities of life. The body of an organism needs water and other materials. Water is important because most of the chemical reactions in a cell take place in water. Organisms also require other materials. Plants, for example, need carbon dioxide to make energy-rich sugars, and most living things need oxygen. Living space is the environment in which an organism gets the energy and materials it needs.

## Living things meet their needs through interactions with the environment.

The **environment** is everything that surrounds a living thing. This includes other organisms as well as nonliving factors, such as rainfall, sunlight, and soil. Any exchange of energy or materials between the living and nonliving parts of the environment is an **interaction.** Plants interact with the environment by capturing energy from the Sun and changing that energy into chemical energy that is stored in sugar. Animals can interact with plants by eating the plants and getting energy from the sugars that the plants have made.

## The types and numbers of living things change over time.

A **species** is a group of living things so closely related that they can produce offspring together that can also reproduce. Scientists have named about 1.4 million different species. The great variety of species on Earth today is called **biodiversity.** Different species have different characteristics, or **adaptations,** that allow the members of that species to get their needs met in a particular environment. Over the millions of years that life has existed on Earth, new species have come into being and others have disappeared. The disappearance of a species is called **extinction.** Fossils of now extinct organisms is one way that scientists have of seeing how living things have changed over time.

# What Is Earth Science?

Earth science is the study of Earth's interior, its rocks and soil, its oceans, its atmosphere, and outer space. For many years, scientists studied each of these topics separately. They learned many important things. More recently, however, scientists have looked more and more at the connections among the different parts of Earth—its oceans, atmosphere, living things, and rocks and soil. Scientists have also been learning more about other planets in our solar system, as well as stars and galaxies far away. Through these studies they have learned much about Earth and its place in the universe.

When a wolf eats a rabbit, matter and energy move from one living thing into another. When a wolf drinks water warmed by the Sun, matter and energy move from Earth's waters into one of its living things.

# UNIFYING PRINCIPLES of Earth Science

## Heat energy inside Earth and radiation from the Sun provide energy for Earth's processes.

**Energy** is the ability to cause change. All of Earth's processes need energy to occur. Earth's interior is very hot. This heat energy moves up to Earth's surface, where it provides the energy to build mountains, cause earthquakes, and make volcanoes erupt. Earth also receives energy from the Sun as **radiation**—energy that travels across distances in the form of certain types of waves. Energy from the Sun causes winds to blow, ocean currents to flow, and water to move from the ground to the atmosphere and back again.

## Physical forces, such as gravity, affect the movement of all matter on Earth and throughout the universe.

What do the stars in a galaxy, the planet Earth, and your body have in common? For one thing, they are all made of matter. **Matter** is anything that has mass and takes up space. Rocks are matter. You are matter. Even the air around you is matter. Everything in the universe is also affected by the same physical forces. A **force** is a push or a pull. Forces affect how matter moves everywhere in the universe.

## Matter and energy move among Earth's rocks and soil, atmosphere, waters, and living things.

Think of Earth as a huge system, or an organized group of parts that work together. Within this system, matter and energy move among the different parts. The four major parts of Earth's system are the

- **atmosphere,** which includes all the air surrounding the solid planet
- **geosphere,** which includes all of Earth's rocks and minerals, as well as Earth's interior
- **hydrosphere,** which includes oceans, rivers, lakes, and every drop of water on or under Earth's surface
- **biosphere,** which includes all the living things on Earth

## Earth has changed over time and continues to change.

Events are always changing Earth's surface. Some events, such as the building or wearing away of mountains, occur over millions of years. Others, such as earthquakes, occur within seconds. A change can affect a small area or even the entire planet

# What Is Physical Science?

Physical science is the study of what things are made of and how they change. It combines the study of both physics and chemistry. Physics is the study of matter, energy, and forces, and it includes such topics as motion, light, and electricity and magnetism. Chemistry is the study of the structure and properties of matter. It focuses especially on how substances change into different substances.

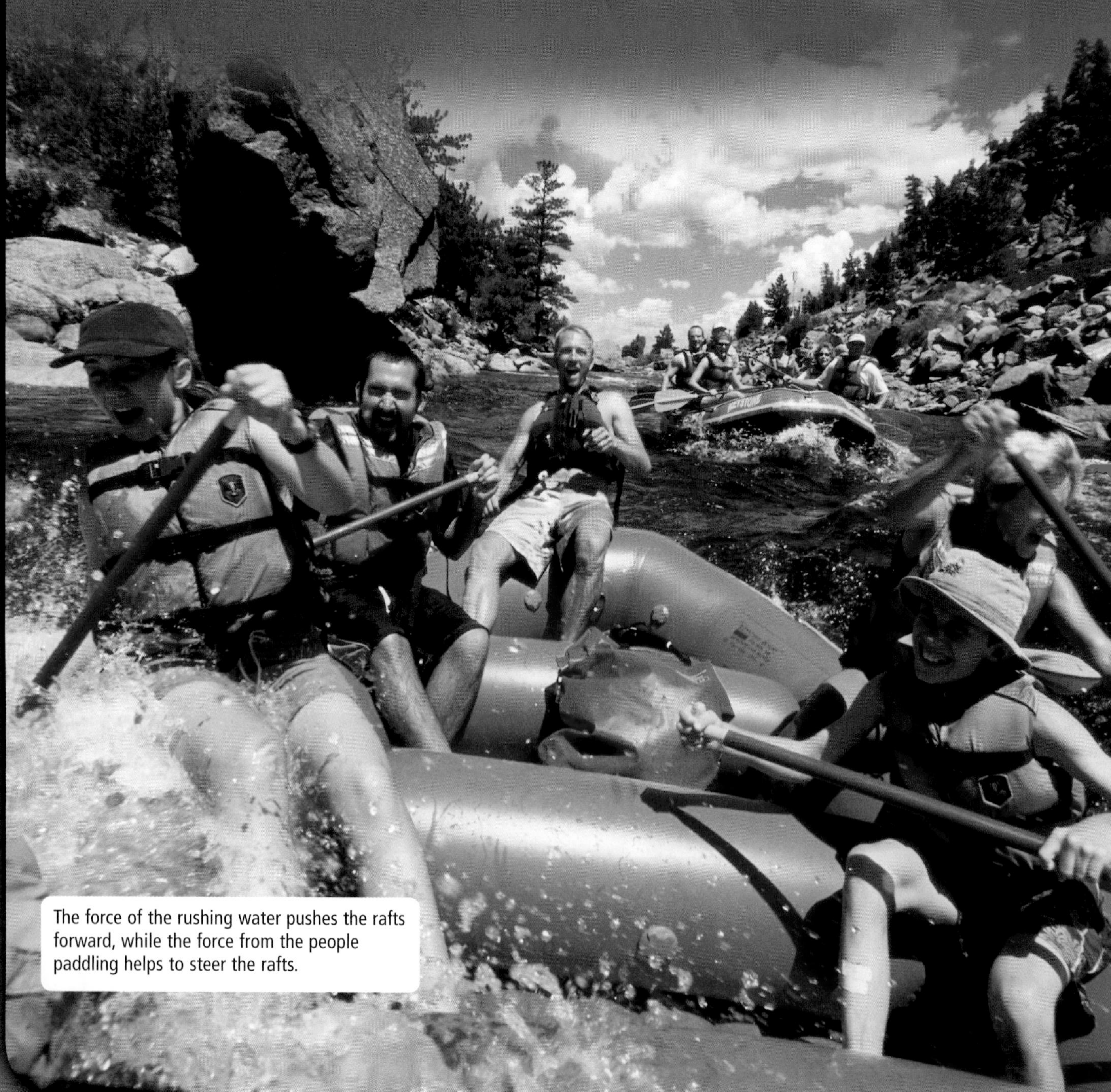

The force of the rushing water pushes the rafts forward, while the force from the people paddling helps to steer the rafts.

# UNIFYING PRINCIPLES of Physical Science

## Matter is made of particles too small to see.

The tiny particles that make up all matter are called **atoms.** Just how tiny are atoms? They are far too small to see even through a powerful microscope. In fact, an atom is about a million times smaller than the period at the end of this sentence. There are more than 100 basic kinds of matter called **elements.** The atoms of any element are all alike but different from the atoms of any other element. Everything around you is made of atoms and combinations of atoms.

## Matter changes form and moves from place to place.

You see objects moving and changing all around you. All changes in matter are the result of atoms moving and combining in different ways. Regardless of how much matter may change, however, under ordinary conditions it is never created or destroyed. Matter that seems to disappear merely changes into another form of matter.

## Energy changes from one form to another, but it cannot be created or destroyed.

All the changes you see around you depend on energy. Energy, in fact, means the ability to cause change. Using energy means changing energy. But energy is never created or destroyed, no matter how often it changes form. This fact is known as the **law of conservation of energy.** The energy you may think you've lost when a match has burned out has only been changed into other forms of energy that are less useful to you.

## Physical forces affect the movement of all matter on Earth and throughout the universe.

A **force** is a push or a pull. Every time you push or pull an object, you are applying a force to that object, whether or not the object moves. There are several forces—several pushes or pulls—acting on you right now. All these forces are necessary for you to do the things you do, even sitting and reading. **Gravity** keeps you on the ground. Gravity also keeps the Moon moving around Earth, and Earth moving around the Sun. **Friction** is the force that opposes motion. The friction between the bottoms of your shoes and the floor makes it possible for you to walk without slipping. Too much friction between a heavy box and the floor makes it hard to push the box across the floor.

# The Nature of Science

You may think of science as a body of knowledge or a collection of facts. More important, however, science is an active process that involves certain ways of looking at the world.

## Scientific Habits of Mind

**Scientists are curious.** They are always asking questions. A scientist who observes that the number of plants in a forest preserve has decreased might ask questions such as, "Are more animals eating the plants?" or "Has the way the land is used affected the numbers of plants?" Scientists around the world investigate these and other important questions.

**Scientists are observant.** They are always looking closely at the world around them. A scientist who studies plants often sees details such as the height of a plant, its flowers, and how many plants live in a particular area.

**Scientists are creative.** They draw on what they know to form a possible explanation for a pattern, an event, or a behavior that they have observed. Then scientists create a plan for testing their ideas.

**Scientists are skeptical.** Scientists don't accept an explanation or answer unless it is based on evidence and logical reasoning. They continually question their own conclusions as well as conclusions suggested by other scientists. Scientists trust only evidence that is confirmed by other people or methods.

A white-tailed deer feeds on many plants, including the trillium shown here.

By measuring the growth of this tree, a scientist can study interactions in the ecosystem.

## Science Processes at Work

You can think of science as a continuous cycle of asking and seeking answers to questions about the world. Although there are many processes that scientists use, scientists typically do each of the following:

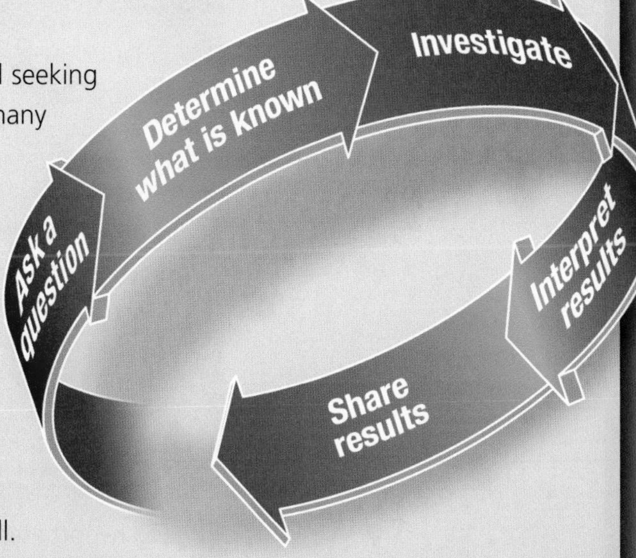


- Observe and ask a question
- Determine what is known
- Investigate
- Interpret results
- Share results

### Observe and Ask a Question

It may surprise you that asking questions is an important skill. A scientific investigation may start when a scientist asks a question. Perhaps scientists observe an event or a process that they don't understand, or perhaps answering one question leads to another.

### Determine What Is Known

When beginning an inquiry, scientists find out what is already known about a question. They study results from other scientific investigations, read journals, and talk with other scientists. A biologist who is trying to understand how the change in the number of deer in an area affects plants will study reports of censuses taken for both plants and animals.

## Investigate

Investigating is the process of collecting evidence. Two important ways of collecting evidence are observing and experimenting.

**Observing** is the act of noting and recording an event, a characteristic, a behavior, or anything else detected with an instrument or with the senses. For example, a scientist notices that plants in one part of the forest are not thriving. She sees broken plants and compares the height of the plants in one area with the height of those in another.

An **experiment** is an organized procedure during which all factors but the one being studied are controlled. For example, the scientist thinks the reason some plants in the forest are not thriving may be that deer are eating the flowers off the plants. An experiment she might try is to mark two similar parts of an area where the plants grow and then build a fence around one part so the deer can't get to the plants there. The fence must be constructed so the same amounts of light, air, and water reach the plants. The only factor that changes is contact between plants and the deer.

Close observation of the Colorado potato beetle led scientists to a biological pesticide that can help farmers control this insect pest.

Forming hypotheses and making predictions are two other skills involved in scientific investigations. A **hypothesis** is a tentative explanation for an observation or a scientific problem that can be tested by further investigation. For example, since at least 1900, Colorado potato beetles were known to be resistant to chemical insecticides. Yet the numbers of beetles were not as large as expected. It was hypothesized that bacteria living in the beetles' environment were killing many beetles. A **prediction** is an expectation of what will be observed or what will happen and can be used to test a hypothesis. It was predicted that certain bacteria would kill Colorado potato beetles. This prediction was confirmed when a bacterium called *Bt* was discovered to kill Colorado potato beetles and other insect pests.

## Interpret Results

As scientists investigate, they analyze their evidence, or data, and begin to draw conclusions. **Analyzing data** involves looking at the evidence gathered through observations or experiments and trying to identify any patterns that might exist in the data. Often scientists need to make additional observations or perform more experiments before they are sure of their conclusions. Many times scientists make new predictions or revise their hypotheses.

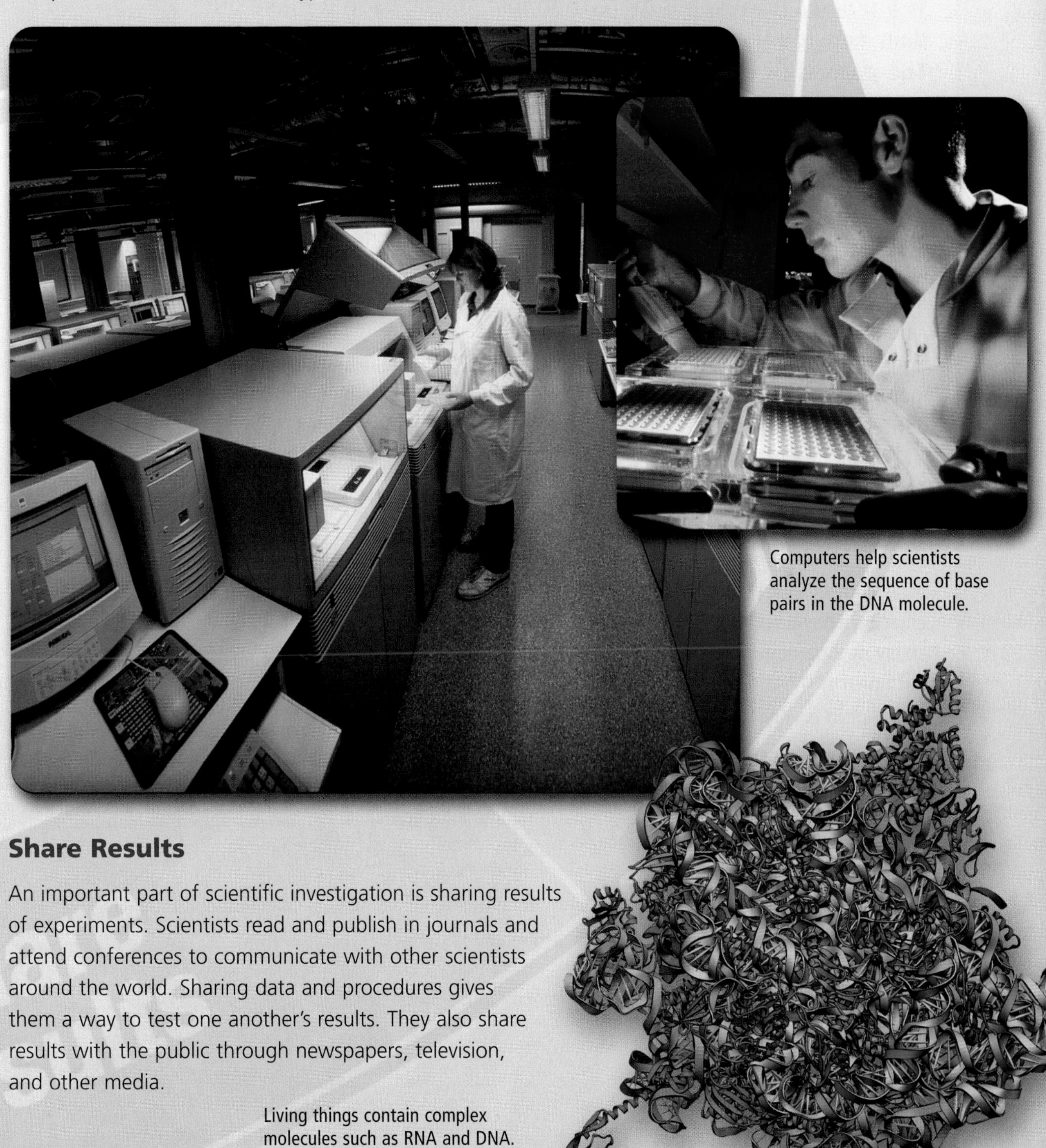

Computers help scientists analyze the sequence of base pairs in the DNA molecule.

## Share Results

An important part of scientific investigation is sharing results of experiments. Scientists read and publish in journals and attend conferences to communicate with other scientists around the world. Sharing data and procedures gives them a way to test one another's results. They also share results with the public through newspapers, television, and other media.

Living things contain complex molecules such as RNA and DNA. To study them, scientists often use models like the one shown here.

# The Nature of Technology

Imagine what life would be like without cars, computers, and cell phones. Imagine having no refrigerator or radio. It's difficult to think of a world without these items we call technology. Technology, however, is more than just machines that make our daily activities easier. Like science, technology is also a process. The process of technology uses scientific knowledge to design solutions to real-world problems.

## Science and Technology

Science and technology go hand in hand. Each depends upon the other. Even designing a device as simple as a toaster requires knowledge of how heat flows and which materials are the best conductors of heat. Scientists also use a number of devices to help them collect data. Microscopes, telescopes, spectrographs, and computers are just a few of the tools that help scientists learn more about the world. The more information these tools provide, the more devices can be developed to aid scientific research and to improve modern lives.

## The Process of Technological Design

Heart disease is among the leading causes of death today. Doctors have successfully replaced damaged hearts with hearts from donors. Medical engineers have developed pacemakers that improve the ability of a damaged heart to pump blood. But none of these solutions is perfect. Although it is very complex, the heart is really a pump for blood; thus, using technology to build a better replacement pump should be possible. The process of technological design involves many choices. In the case of an artificial heart, choices about how and what to develop involve cost, safety, and patient preference. What kind of technology will result in the best quality of life for the patient?

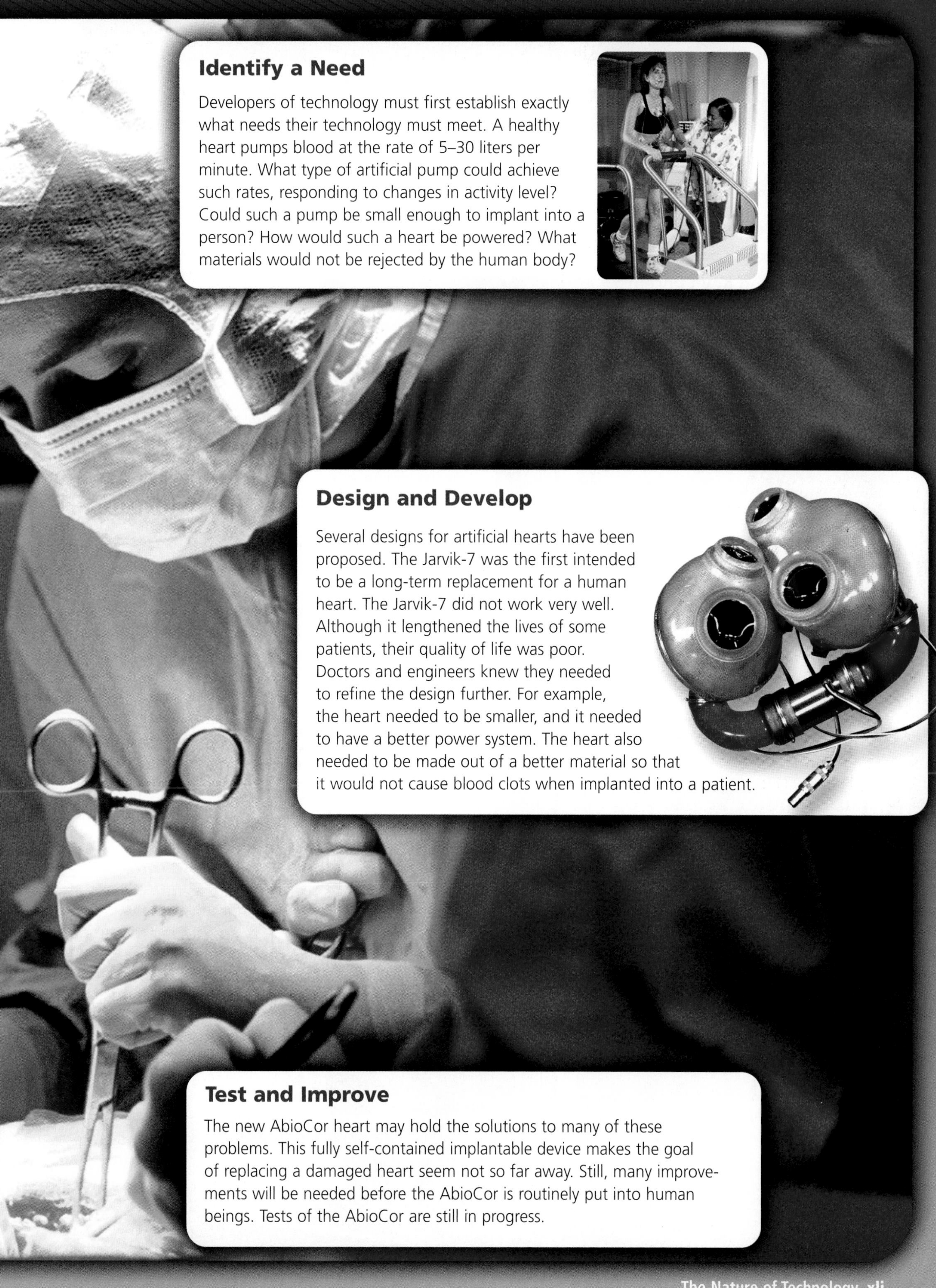

## Identify a Need

Developers of technology must first establish exactly what needs their technology must meet. A healthy heart pumps blood at the rate of 5–30 liters per minute. What type of artificial pump could achieve such rates, responding to changes in activity level? Could such a pump be small enough to implant into a person? How would such a heart be powered? What materials would not be rejected by the human body?

## Design and Develop

Several designs for artificial hearts have been proposed. The Jarvik-7 was the first intended to be a long-term replacement for a human heart. The Jarvik-7 did not work very well. Although it lengthened the lives of some patients, their quality of life was poor. Doctors and engineers knew they needed to refine the design further. For example, the heart needed to be smaller, and it needed to have a better power system. The heart also needed to be made out of a better material so that it would not cause blood clots when implanted into a patient.

## Test and Improve

The new AbioCor heart may hold the solutions to many of these problems. This fully self-contained implantable device makes the goal of replacing a damaged heart seem not so far away. Still, many improvements will be needed before the AbioCor is routinely put into human beings. Tests of the AbioCor are still in progress.

## Reading Text and Visuals

This book is organized to help you learn. Use these boxed pointers as a path to help you learn and remember the **Big Ideas** and **Key Concepts.**

**Take notes.**

Use the strategies on the **Getting Ready to Learn** page.

**Read the Big Idea.**

As you read **Key Concepts** for the chapter, relate them to **the Big Idea.**

CHAPTER 3

Transp
Protec

Systems function to transport materials and to defend and protect the body.

Key Concepts

SECTION

The circulatory system transports materials.
Learn how materials move through blood vessels.

SECTION

The immune system defends the body.
Learn about the body's defenses and responses to foreign materials.

SECTION

The integumentary system shields the body.
Learn about the structure of skin and how it protects the body.

Internet Preview
CLASSZONE.COM
Chapter 3 online resources: Content Review, two Visualizations, four Resource Centers, Math Tutorial, Test Practice

E 62 Unit: Human Biology

CHAPTER 3
Getting Ready to Learn

CONCEPT REVIEW
- The body's systems interact.
- The body's systems work to maintain internal conditions.
- The digestive system breaks down food.
- The respiratory system gets oxygen and removes carbon dioxide.

VOCABULARY REVIEW
**organ** p. 11
**organ system** p. 12
**homeostasis** p. 12
**nutrient** p. 45

CONTENT REVIEW
CLASSZONE.COM
Review concepts and vocabulary.

TAKING NOTES

MAIN IDEA AND DETAIL NOTES

Make a two-column chart. Write the main ideas, such as those in the blue headings, in the column on the left. Write details about each of those main heads in the column on the right.

VOCABULARY STRATEGY

Write each new vocabulary term in the center of a **frame game** diagram. Decide what information to frame it with. Use examples, descriptions, parts, sentences that use the term in context, or pictures. You can change the frame to fit each term.

See the Note-Taking Handbook on pages R45–R51.

SCIENCE NOTEBOOK

| MAIN IDEAS | DETAIL NOTES |
|---|---|
| 1. The circulatory system works with other body systems. | 1. Transports materials from digestive and respiratory systems to cells<br>2. Blood is fluid that carries materials and wastes<br>3. Blood is always moving through the body<br>4. Blood delivers oxygen and takes away carbon dioxide |

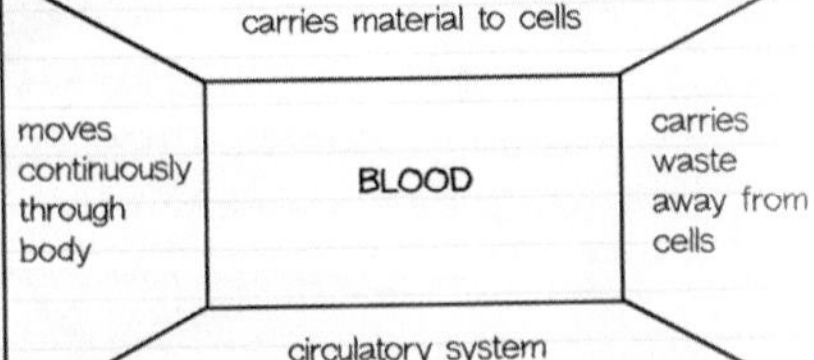


E 64 Unit: Human Biology

**Read each heading.**

See how it fits in the outline of the chapter.

KEY CONCEPT

# 3.1 The circulatory system transports materials.

**BEFORE, you learned**
- The urinary system removes waste
- The kidneys play a role in homeostasis

**NOW, you will learn**
- How different structures of the circulatory system work together
- About the structure and function of blood
- What blood pressure is and why it is important

**Remember what you know.**

Think about concepts you learned earlier and preview what you'll learn now.

**VOCABULARY**

**circulatory system** p. 65
**blood** p. 65
**red blood cell** p. 67
**artery** p. 69
**vein** p. 69
**capillary** p. 69

**EXPLORE The Circulatory System**

***How fast does your heart beat?***

**PROCEDURE**

1. Hold out your left hand with your palm facing up.
2. Place the first two fingers of your right hand on your left wrist below your thumb. Move your fingertips slightly until you can feel your pulse.
3. Use the stopwatch to determine how many times your heart beats in one minute.

**MATERIALS**
stopwatch

**WHAT DO YOU THINK?**
- How many times did your heart beat?
- What do you think you would find if you took your pulse after exercising?

**Try the activities.**

They will introduce you to science concepts.

## The circulatory system works with other body systems.

VOCABULARY
Add a frame game diagram for the term *circulatory system* to your notebook.

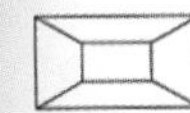

You have read that the systems in your body provide materials and energy. The digestive system breaks down food and nutrients, and the respiratory system provides the oxygen that cells need to release energy. Another system, called the **circulatory system,** transports products from the digestive and the respiratory systems to the cells.

Materials and wastes are carried in a fluid called **blood**. Blood moves continuously through the body, delivering oxygen and other materials to cells and removing carbon dioxide and other wastes from cells.

**Learn the vocabulary.**

Take notes on each term.

Chapter 3: **Transport and Protection** **65** E

# Reading Text and Visuals

## Read one paragraph at a time.

Look for a topic sentence that explains the main idea of the paragraph. Figure out how the details relate to that idea. One paragraph might have several important ideas; you may have to reread to understand.

## Answer the questions.

**Check Your Reading** questions will help you remember what you read.

## Study the visuals.

- Read the title.
- Read all labels and captions.
- Figure out what the picture is showing. Notice the information in the captions.

### Exchanging Oxygen and Carbon Dioxide

Like almost all living things, the human body needs oxygen to survive. Without oxygen, cells in the body die quickly. How does the oxygen you need get to your cells? Oxygen, along with other gases, enters the body when you inhale. Oxygen is then transported to cells throughout the body.

The air that you breathe contains only about 20 percent oxygen and less than 1 percent carbon dioxide. Almost 80 percent of air is nitrogen gas. The air that you exhale contains more carbon dioxide and less oxygen than the air that you inhale. It's important that you exhale carbon dioxide because high levels of it will damage, even destroy, cells.

In cells and tissues, proper levels of both oxygen and carbon dioxide are essential. Recall that systems in the body work together to maintain homeostasis. If levels of oxygen or carbon dioxide change, your brain or blood vessels signal the body to breathe faster or slower.

The photograph shows how someone underwater maintains proper levels of carbon dioxide and oxygen. The scuba diver needs to inhale oxygen from a tank. She removes carbon dioxide wastes with other gases when she exhales into the water. The bubbles you see in the water are formed when she exhales.

CHECK YOUR
READING

What gases are in the air that you breathe?

Gas Exchange

This scuba diver breathes the same mixture of gases present in air.

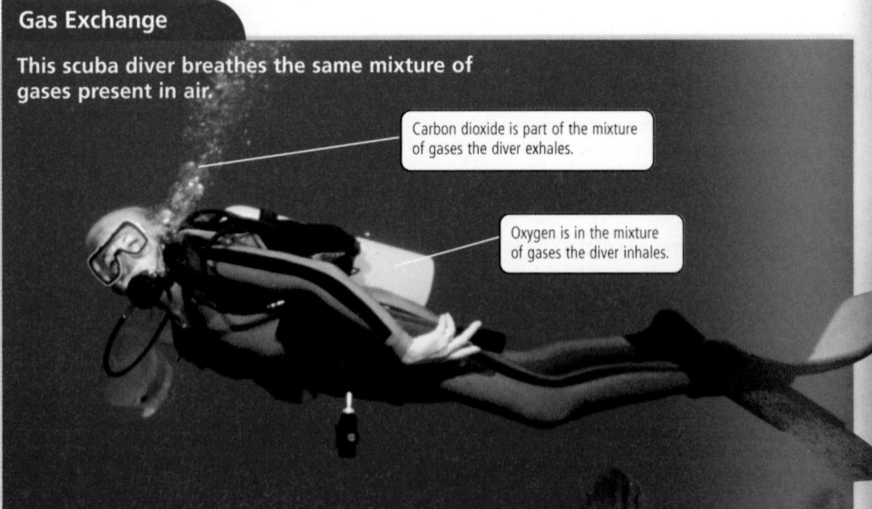
Carbon dioxide is part of the mixture of gases the diver exhales.
Oxygen is in the mixture of gases the diver inhales.

E 38 Unit: Human Biology

# Doing Labs

To understand science, you have to see it in action. Doing labs helps you understand how things really work.

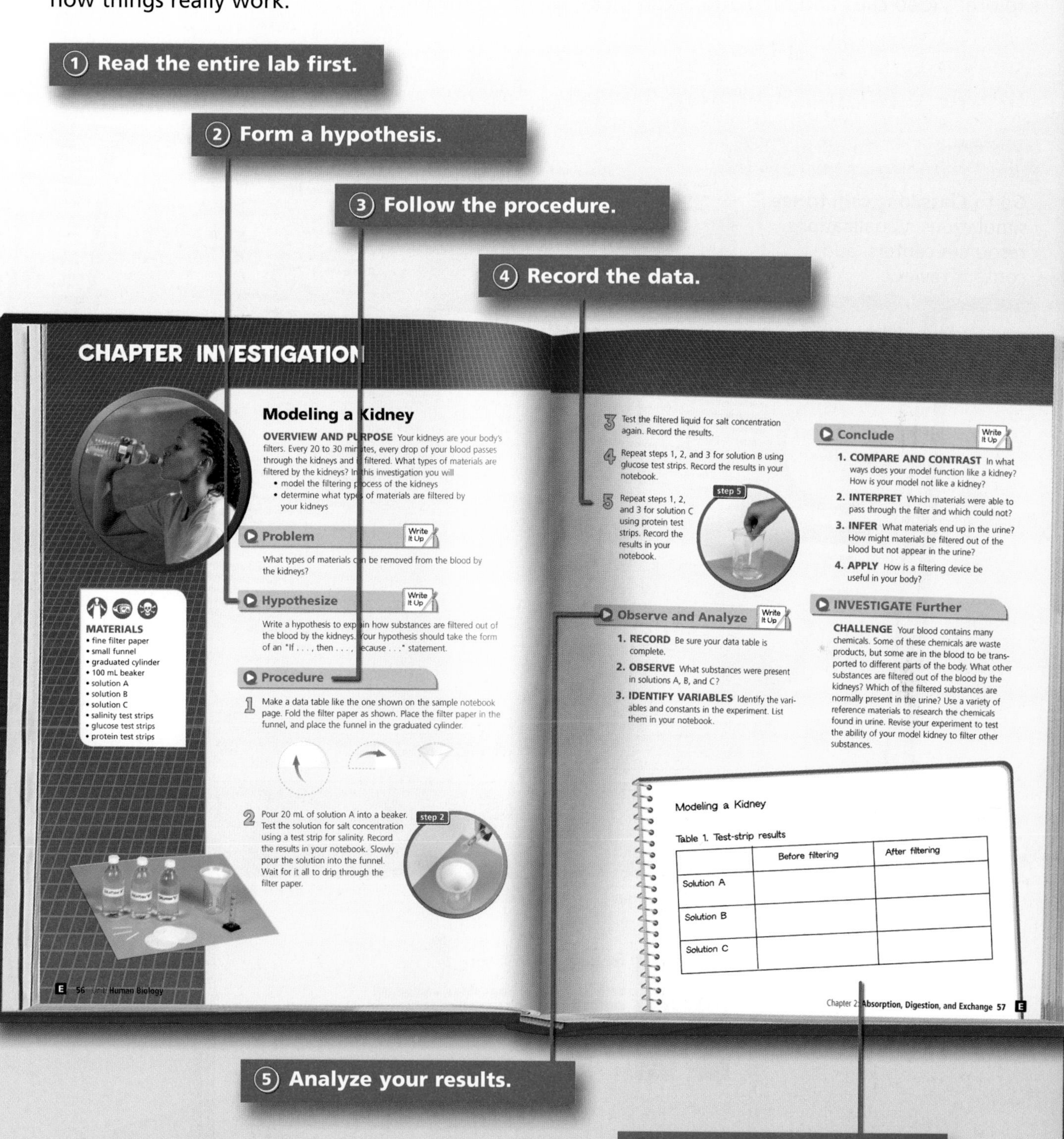

① Read the entire lab first.
② Form a hypothesis.
③ Follow the procedure.
④ Record the data.
⑤ Analyze your results.
⑥ Write your lab report.
CHAPTER INVESTIGATION
Modeling a Kidney
OVERVIEW AND PURPOSE Your kidneys are your body's filters. Every 20 to 30 minutes, every drop of your blood passes through the kidneys and is filtered. What types of materials are filtered by the kidneys? In this investigation you will
• model the filtering process of the kidneys
• determine what types of materials are filtered by your kidneys
Problem
What types of materials can be removed from the blood by the kidneys?
Hypothesize
Write a hypothesis to explain how substances are filtered out of the blood by the kidneys. Your hypothesis should take the form of an "If . . . , then . . . , because . . ." statement.
Procedure
1 Make a data table like the one shown on the sample notebook page. Fold the filter paper as shown. Place the filter paper in the funnel, and place the funnel in the graduated cylinder.
2 Pour 20 mL of solution A into a beaker. Test the solution for salt concentration using a test strip for salinity. Record the results in your notebook. Slowly pour the solution into the funnel. Wait for it all to drip through the filter paper.
step 2
MATERIALS
• fine filter paper
• small funnel
• graduated cylinder
• 100 mL beaker
• solution A
• solution B
• solution C
• salinity test strips
• glucose test strips
• protein test strips
3 Test the filtered liquid for salt concentration again. Record the results.
4 Repeat steps 1, 2, and 3 for solution B using glucose test strips. Record the results in your notebook.
5 Repeat steps 1, 2, and 3 for solution C using protein test strips. Record the results in your notebook.
step 5
Observe and Analyze
1. RECORD Be sure your data table is complete.
2. OBSERVE What substances were present in solutions A, B, and C?
3. IDENTIFY VARIABLES Identify the variables and constants in the experiment. List them in your notebook.
Conclude
1. COMPARE AND CONTRAST In what ways does your model function like a kidney? How is your model not like a kidney?
2. INTERPRET Which materials were able to pass through the filter and which could not?
3. INFER What materials end up in the urine? How might materials be filtered out of the blood but not appear in the urine?
4. APPLY How is a filtering device be useful in your body?
INVESTIGATE Further
CHALLENGE Your blood contains many chemicals. Some of these chemicals are waste products, but some are in the blood to be transported to different parts of the body. What other substances are filtered out of the blood by the kidneys? Which of the filtered substances are normally present in the urine? Use a variety of reference materials to research the chemicals found in urine. Revise your experiment to test the ability of your model kidney to filter other substances.
Write It Up
Modeling a Kidney
Table 1. Test-strip results
Before filtering
After filtering
Solution A
Solution B
Solution C
E 56 Unit: Human Biology
Chapter 2: Absorption, Digestion, and Exchange 57 E

# Using Technology

The Internet is a great source of information about up-to-date science. The ClassZone Website and SciLinks have exciting sites for you to explore. Video clips and simulations can make science come alive.

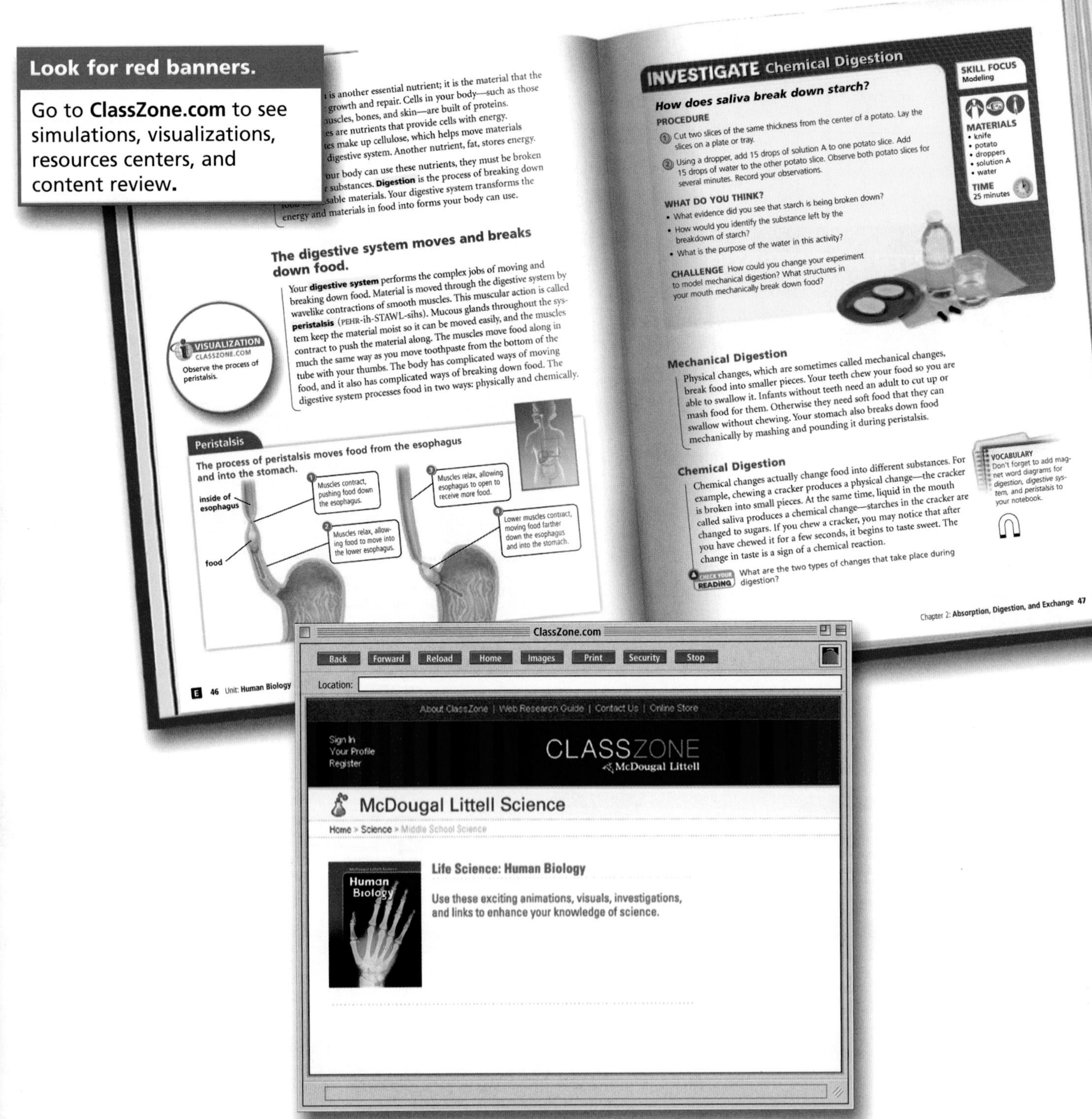

Look for red banners.
Go to **ClassZone.com** to see simulations, visualizations, resources centers, and content review.
The digestive system moves and breaks down food.
VISUALIZATION
CLASSZONE.COM
Observe the process of peristalsis.
Peristalsis
The process of peristalsis moves food from the esophagus and into the stomach.
inside of esophagus
food
Muscles contract, pushing food down the esophagus.
Muscles relax, allowing food to move into the lower esophagus.
Muscles relax, allowing esophagus to open to receive more food.
Lower muscles contract, moving food farther down the esophagus and into the stomach.
46 Unit: Human Biology
INVESTIGATE Chemical Digestion
How does saliva break down starch?
SKILL FOCUS
Modeling
MATERIALS
knife
potato
droppers
solution A
water
TIME
25 minutes
Mechanical Digestion
Chemical Digestion
VOCABULARY
Chapter 2: Absorption, Digestion, and Exchange 47
ClassZone.com
Back
Forward
Reload
Home
Images
Print
Security
Stop
Location:
About ClassZone | Web Research Guide | Contact Us | Online Store
Sign In
Your Profile
Register
CLASSZONE
McDougal Littell
McDougal Littell Science
Home > Science > Middle School Science
Life Science: Human Biology
Use these exciting animations, visuals, investigations, and links to enhance your knowledge of science.
Human Biology

FRONTIERS in Science

Surprising Senses

SCIENTIFIC AMERICAN FRONTIERS

SCIENTIFIC
AMERICAN
FRONTIERS
Learn more about how the brain and senses work. See the video "Sight of Touch."

2 Unit: Human Biology

**Watch the videos.**

See science at work in the **Scientific American Frontiers video.**

**Look up SciLinks.**

Go to **scilinks.org** to explore the topic.

UNIT A

# Earth's Atmosphere

TROPOSPHERE

UPDRAFT

CUMULUS

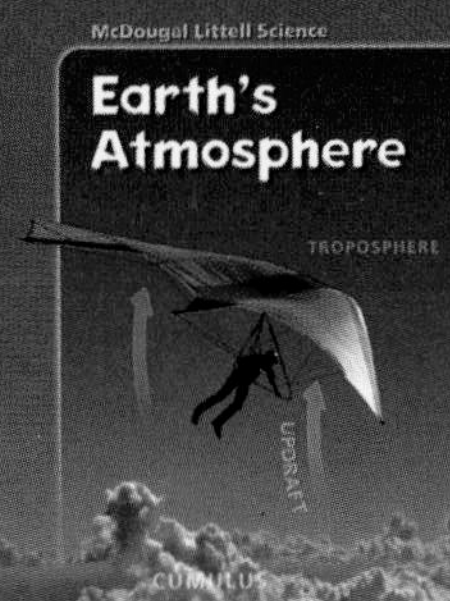

# Earth's Atmosphere Contents Overview

## Unit Features

FRONTIERS IN SCIENCE Dust in the Air 2
TIMELINES IN SCIENCE Observing the Atmosphere 110

## 1 Earth's Changing Atmosphere 6

the BIG idea

Earth's atmosphere is a blanket of gases that supports and protects life.

## 2 Weather Patterns 40

the BIG idea

Some features of weather have predictable patterns.

## 3 Weather Fronts and Storms 76

the BIG idea

The interaction of air masses causes changes in weather.

## 4 Climate and Climate Change 114

the BIG idea

Climates are long-term weather patterns that may change over time.

# DUST in the AIR

What happens around this beautiful island in the Caribbean when dust from an African storm travels thousands of kilometers across the ocean?

SCIENTIFIC AMERICAN FRONTIERS

Learn more about the scientists studying dust in the atmosphere. See the video "Dust Busting."

This map shows the path that dust travels from Africa, across the Atlantic Ocean, to the Caribbean—a distance of about 5000 kilometers (3000 mi).

## A Problem to Solve

Images from space show gigantic clouds of dust traveling from Africa thousands of kilometers across the Atlantic Ocean. Weather reports in the Caribbean warn listeners about African dust storms. Coral and manatees in Caribbean waters show signs of disease. Are these events connected?

Each year, natural events and human activities together send as much as 2 billion metric tons of material into the skies. Once dust enters the atmosphere, it moves with the other materials in the air.

But how do Earth's surface processes and the movement of air relate to diseased coral? Teams of scientists studied diseases in living things around the Caribbean. In addition, they examined satellite photographs and recorded when dust storms occurred. After analyzing these data, they hypothesized that materials in African dust were affecting living things in the Caribbean.

Satellite images show us how far dust can travel in the atmosphere. Experiments on air samples let scientists look at dust up close. Tests reveal that atmospheric dust includes many substances, including living material. As often happens in science, this new knowledge raises more questions. Could the living material in dust grow in a distant location? Could a fungus that lives in African soil end up in Caribbean waters?

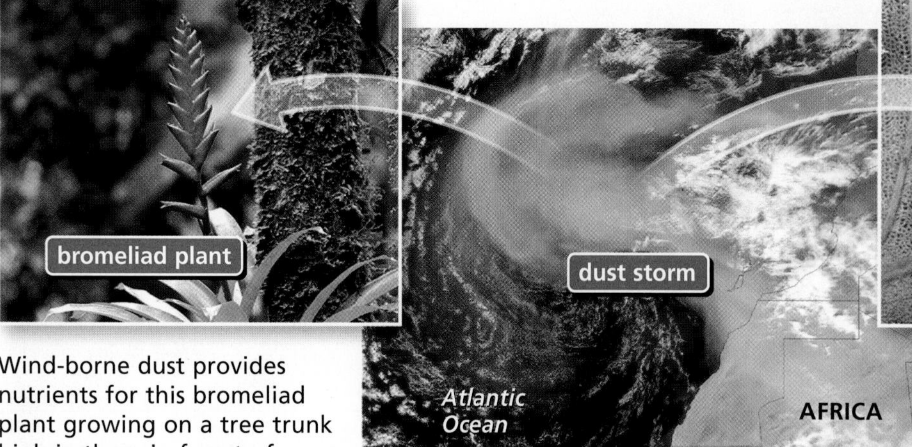

Wind-borne dust provides nutrients for this bromeliad plant growing on a tree trunk high in the rain forest of South America.

The huge dust storm shown in this satellite image carries both destructive fungus spores and life-sustaining nutrients across the Atlantic.

Fungus spores carried on dust particles have infected sea-fan corals growing on this reef near the island of St. John in the Caribbean Sea.

## Answers Hidden in Dust

To explore these questions, scientists in the Caribbean gather air samples during dust storms. They collect dust from high in the air and from locations closer to Earth's surface. To collect the samples, scientists pull air through a paper filter, trapping the dust. Once they have caught the dust, the scientists are ready to perform tests to see what's really in the tiny particles.

In the laboratory, researchers place dust samples on top of nutrients in petri dishes. Then they see if anything in the dust grows. Recent studies have shown that dust samples collected over the Caribbean contained African fungi and bacteria. More importantly, scientists saw that, even after their long voyage through the atmosphere, the living materials were able to grow.

### SCIENTIFIC AMERICAN FRONTIERS

**View the "Dust Busting" segment of your *Scientific American Frontiers* video to learn about the detective work that went into solving the mystery of sea-fan disease.**

**IN THIS SCENE FROM THE VIDEO** **Biologist Ginger Garrison shows diseased coral to host Alan Alda.**

**MYSTERY SOLVED** Sea fans are an important part of the Caribbean coral-reef community, but in the 1970s they began to die off. Recently marine biologist Garriet Smith was surprised to discover that a common soil fungus, called aspergillus, was killing the sea fans. But how could a soil fungus reach an undersea reef?

The answer came from geologist Gene Shinn, who knew that global winds carry dust from Africa to the Caribbean. When Shinn read about Smith's research, he hypothesized that aspergillus might be arriving with African dust. Shinn teamed up with Smith and biologist Ginger Garrison to test the hypothesis. They collected Caribbean air samples during an African dust event and cultured dust from the samples. Aspergillus grew in their very first cultures.

Dust from Africa also contains tiny bits of metals, such as iron. The soil and atmosphere in the Caribbean are enriched by iron carried in African dust. Beautiful plants called bromeliads get the iron they need directly from the atmosphere.

Unfortunately, some of the materials found in the dust samples could be harmful to living things, such as manatees and corals. One of the fungi found in Caribbean dust samples is *Aspergillus sydowii,* which may cause diseases in sea fans and other corals. In addition, the dust contains bacteria that may speed the growth of toxic red algae, which can be harmful to manatees and other ocean animals.

## Strong Connections

Dust storms affect the entire planet. On April 6–8, 2001, soils from the Gobi Desert in Mongolia and China blew into the air, creating a massive dust cloud. Satellite images showed the cloud traveling eastward. A few days later people in the western United States saw the sky turn a chalky white.

Such observations of atmospheric dust show us how events in one part of the planet can affect living and nonliving things thousands of kilometers away in ways we might not have imagined.

### UNANSWERED Questions

Tiny particles of atmospheric dust may have huge effects. Yet the more we learn about the makeup and nature of dust, the more questions we have.

- How do dust storms affect human health?
- What can dust tell us about climate change?
- How can we use information about dust storms to predict climate change?
- How do materials in dust change ecosystems?

## UNIT PROJECTS

**As you study this unit, work alone or with a group on one of these projects.**

### TV News Report

Prepare a brief news report on recent dust storms, using visuals and a script.

- Research dust storms that have occurred recently. Find out how they were related to the weather.
- Copy or print visuals, and write and practice delivering your report. Then make your presentation.

### Map the Dust

Make a map showing how dust arrives in your area or another location.

- Find out what the dust contains and how it moved there. Collect information from atlases, the Internet, newspapers, and magazines.
- Prepare your map, including all the areas you need to show. Include a key, a title, and a compass rose.

### Design an Experiment

Design an experiment to explore how the atmosphere has changed in the past or how it is changing today. Research the forms of evidence scientists gather about the state of our atmosphere.

- Pick one question to investigate in an experiment. Write a hypothesis.
- List and assemble materials for your experiment. Create a data table and write up your procedure.
- Demonstrate or describe your experiment for the class.

Learn about careers in meteorology.

CHAPTER

# Earth's Changing Atmosphere

## the BIG idea

Earth's atmosphere is a blanket of gases that supports and protects life.

## Key Concepts

SECTION

**1.1 Earth's atmosphere supports life.**
Learn about the materials that make up the atmosphere.

SECTION

**1.2 The Sun supplies the atmosphere's energy.**
Learn how energy from the Sun affects the atmosphere.

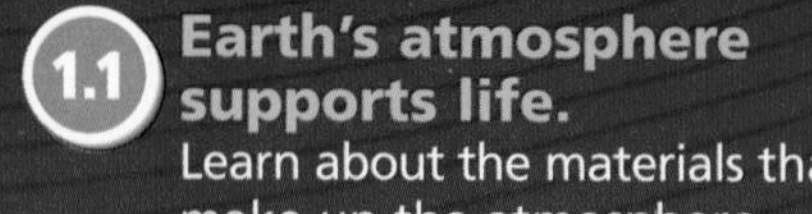

SECTION

**1.3 Gases in the atmosphere absorb radiation.**
Learn about the ozone layer and the greenhouse effect.

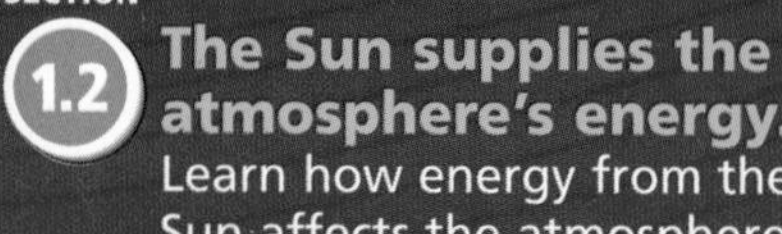

SECTION

**1.4 Human activities affect the atmosphere.**
Learn about pollution, global warming, and changes in the ozone layer.

**Internet Preview**

CLASSZONE.COM

Chapter 1 online resources: Content Review, two Visualizations, two Resource Centers, Math Tutorial, Test Practice

***What will make this kite soar?***

# EXPLORE the BIG idea

## How Heavy Is Paper?

Put a ruler on a table with one end off the edge. Tap on the ruler lightly and observe what happens. Then cover the ruler with a sheet of paper as shown. Tap again on the ruler and observe what happens.

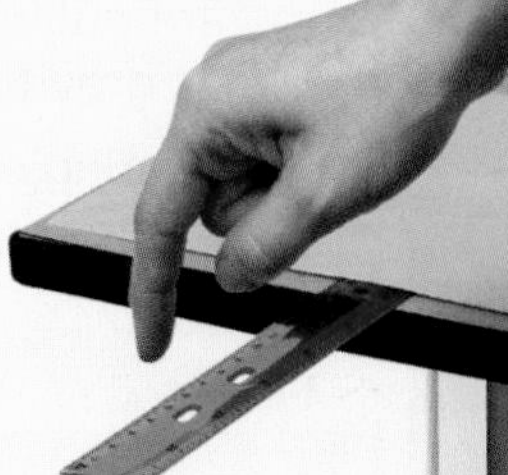

**Observe and Think**
What happened to the ruler when you tapped lightly on it with and without the sheet of paper? Was the paper heavy enough by itself to hold the ruler down?

## How Does Heating Affect Air?

Stretch the lip of a balloon over the neck of a small bottle. Next, fill a bowl with ice water and a second bowl with hot tap water. Place the bottle upright in the hot water. After 5 minutes, move the bottle to the cold water.

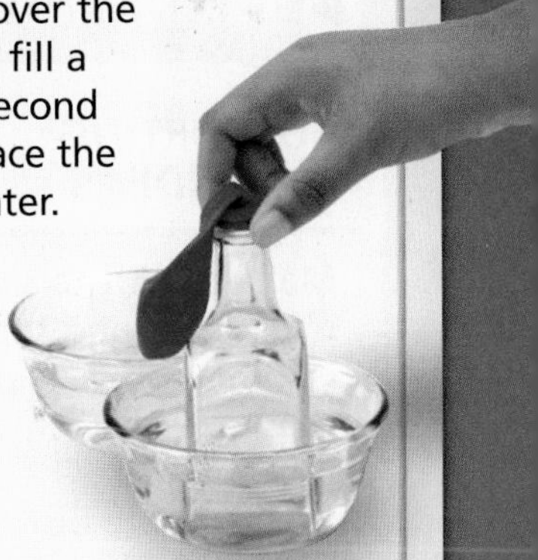

**Observe and Think** What changes did you observe in the balloon? What might have caused these changes?

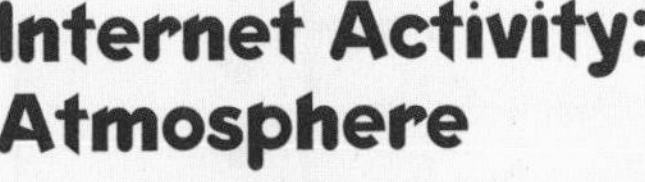

## Internet Activity: Atmosphere

Go to **ClassZone.com** to learn about Earth's atmosphere.

**Observe and Think** How does the thickness of the atmosphere compare with the height of a mountain or the altitude of the space shuttle in orbit?

NSTA scilinks.org SCILINKS
Composition of the Atmosphere **Code: MDL009**

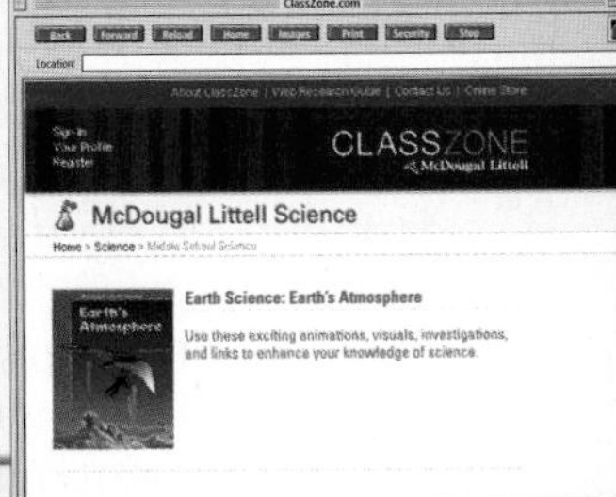

CHAPTER 1

# Getting Ready to Learn

## CONCEPT REVIEW

- Matter is made up of atoms.
- All things on or near Earth are pulled toward Earth by its gravity.
- Heating or cooling any material changes some of its properties.

## VOCABULARY REVIEW

*See Glossary for definitions.*

**atom**
**gas**
**gravity**
**mass**
**molecule**

**CONTENT REVIEW**
CLASSZONE.COM
Review concepts and vocabulary.

## TAKING NOTES

### SUPPORTING MAIN IDEAS

Make a chart to show main ideas and the information that supports them. Write each blue heading from the chapter in a separate box. In boxes below it, add supporting information, such as reasons, explanations, and examples.

### VOCABULARY STRATEGY

Write each new vocabulary term in the center of a **frame game** diagram. Decide what information to frame the term with. Use examples, descriptions, pictures, or sentences in which the term is used in context. You can change the frame to fit each term.

See the Note-Taking Handbook on pages R45–R51.

SCIENCE NOTEBOOK

The atmosphere makes life on Earth possible.

- Living things use gases in the air.
- The atmosphere keeps Earth warm.
- The atmosphere protects life.

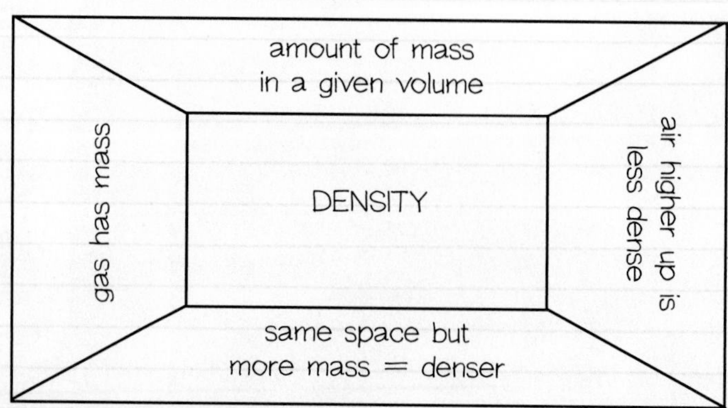

KEY CONCEPT

# Earth's atmosphere supports life.

**BEFORE, you learned**

- Living things need food, water, and air
- Matter can be solid, liquid, or gas

**NOW, you will learn**

- Why the atmosphere is important to living things
- What the atmosphere is made of
- How natural cycles affect the atmosphere

**VOCABULARY**

**atmosphere** p. 9
**altitude** p. 10
**density** p. 10
**cycle** p. 12

**EXPLORE Air Resistance**

### *How does air affect falling objects?*

**PROCEDURE**

1. Drop the washer from shoulder height.
2. Tape the metal washer to the center of the coffee filter. The filter will act as a parachute.
3. Drop the washer with the parachute from shoulder height.

**WHAT DO YOU THINK?**

- What difference did the parachute make?
- What do your results tell you about air?

**MATERIALS**

- metal washer
- coffee filter
- tape

## The atmosphere makes life on Earth possible.

**VOCABULARY**
Remember to make a frame game diagram for the term *atmosphere.*

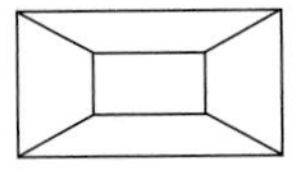

Every time you breathe in, your lungs fill with air, which is a mixture of gases. Your body uses materials from the air to help you stay alive. The **atmosphere** is a whole layer of air that surrounds Earth. The atmosphere supports life and protects it. The gases of the atmosphere keep Earth warm and transport energy to different regions of the planet. Without the atmosphere, the oceans would not exist, life would not survive, and the planet would be a cold, lifeless rock.

Even though the atmosphere is very important to life, it is surprisingly thin. If the solid part of Earth were the size of a peach, most of the atmosphere would be no thicker than the peach fuzz surrounding the fruit. The atmosphere is a small but important part of the Earth system.

CHECK YOUR READING How does the atmosphere make life possible? Find three examples in the text above.

## Characteristics of the Atmosphere

**INFER** This climber has reached the top of Mount Everest, 8850 m (29,000 ft) above sea level in Nepal. Why does he need an oxygen mask?

In 1862 two British balloonists reached the highest **altitude,** or distance above sea level, any human had ever reached. As their balloon rose to 8.8 kilometers (5.5 mi), one balloonist fainted and the other barely managed to bring the balloon back down. They found that the air becomes thinner as altitude increases.

The thickness or thinness of air is measured by its density. **Density** is the amount of mass in a given volume of a substance. If two objects take up the same amount of space, then the object with more mass has a greater density than the one with less mass. For example, a bowling ball has a higher density than a soccer ball.

The atmosphere's density decreases as you travel upward. The air on top of a mountain is less dense than the air at sea level. A deep breath of mountain air fills your lungs but contains less mass—less gas—than a deep breath of air at sea level. Higher up, at altitudes where jets fly, a breath of air would contain only about one-tenth the mass of a breath of air at sea level. The air farther above Earth's surface contains even less mass. There is no definite top to the atmosphere. It just keeps getting less dense as you get farther from Earth's surface. However, altitudes 500 kilometers (300 mi) or more above Earth's surface can be called outer space.

The decrease of density with greater altitude means that most of the mass of the atmosphere is close to Earth's surface. In fact, more than 99 percent of the atmosphere's mass is in the lowest 30 kilometers (20 mi).

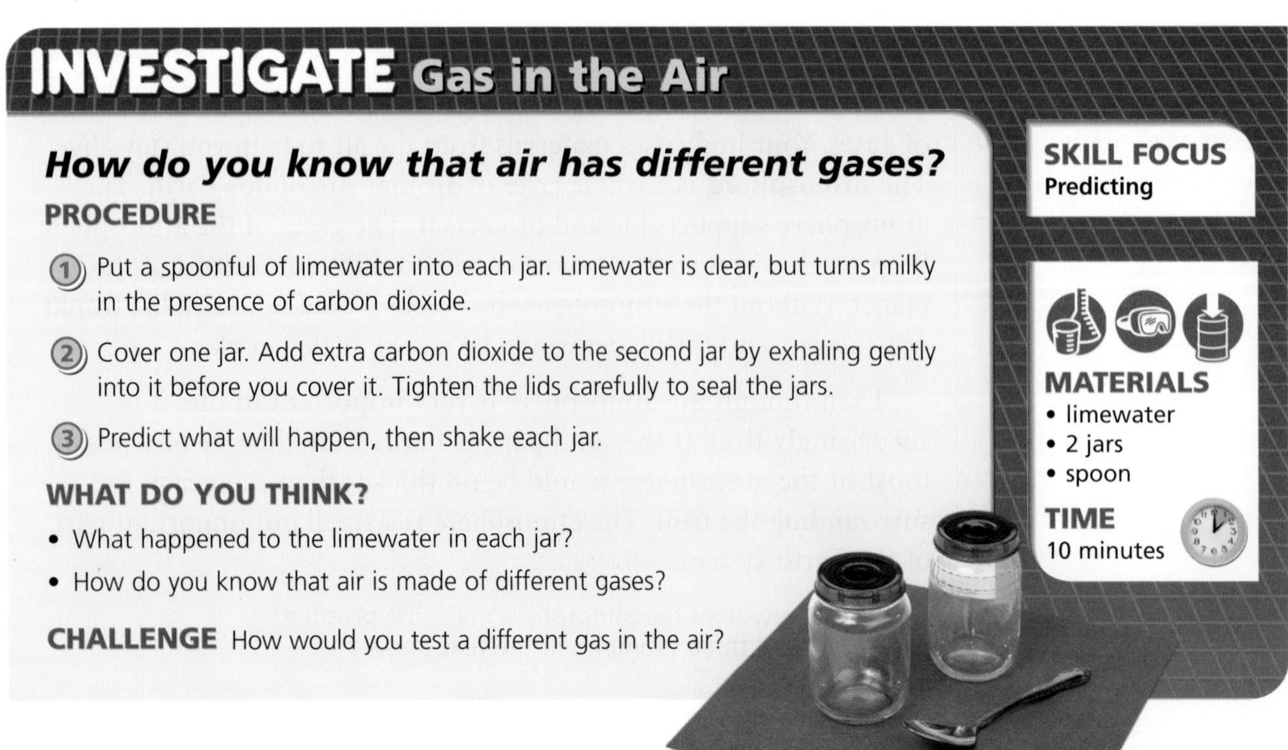

## INVESTIGATE Gas in the Air

### How do you know that air has different gases?

**PROCEDURE**

1. Put a spoonful of limewater into each jar. Limewater is clear, but turns milky in the presence of carbon dioxide.
2. Cover one jar. Add extra carbon dioxide to the second jar by exhaling gently into it before you cover it. Tighten the lids carefully to seal the jars.
3. Predict what will happen, then shake each jar.

**WHAT DO YOU THINK?**

- What happened to the limewater in each jar?
- How do you know that air is made of different gases?

**CHALLENGE** How would you test a different gas in the air?

**SKILL FOCUS**
Predicting

**MATERIALS**
- limewater
- 2 jars
- spoon

**TIME**
10 minutes

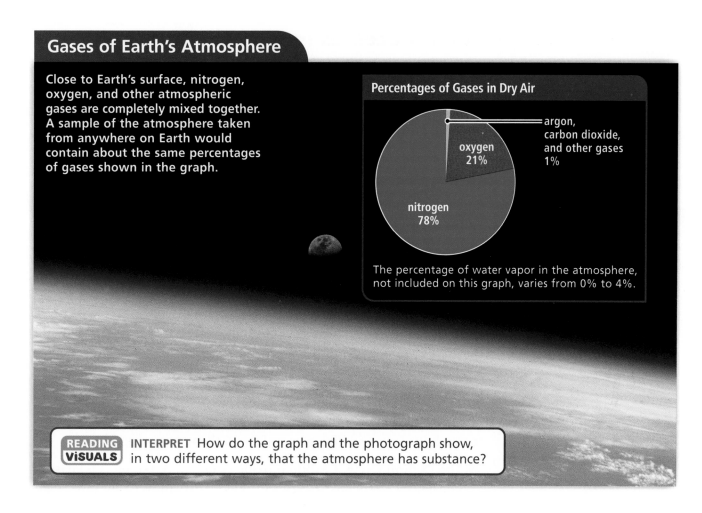

## Gases of Earth's Atmosphere

Close to Earth's surface, nitrogen, oxygen, and other atmospheric gases are completely mixed together. A sample of the atmosphere taken from anywhere on Earth would contain about the same percentages of gases shown in the graph.

**Percentages of Gases in Dry Air**



The percentage of water vapor in the atmosphere, not included on this graph, varies from 0% to 4%.

**READING VISUALS** INTERPRET How do the graph and the photograph show, in two different ways, that the atmosphere has substance?

## Materials in the Atmosphere

Most of the materials in the atmosphere are gases. However, the atmosphere also contains tiny particles of solid or liquid material such as dust, sea salt, and water droplets. Perhaps you have sat by an open window and noticed some of these particles on the window sill.

If you were to write a recipe for air, you would include nitrogen gas as the main ingredient. In dry air, about 78 percent of the gas is nitrogen. The next most common ingredient is oxygen gas, which makes up about 21 percent of the atmosphere. Argon, carbon dioxide, and other gases make up about 1 percent of the atmosphere. Unlike the amounts of nitrogen and other gases, the amount of water vapor varies a great deal. In some places at some times, water vapor can make up as much as 4 percent of the air.

**READING TIP**

As you read about the amounts of gases, find each gas on the graph above.

The atmosphere's gases provide materials essential for living things. Nitrogen promotes plant growth and is an important ingredient in the chemicals that make up living things. Oxygen is necessary for animals and plants to perform life processes. Plants use carbon dioxide and water to make food.

Which gas is the most common material in the air around you?

## Natural processes modify the atmosphere.

The exact amounts of some gases in the air change depending on location, time of day, season, and other factors. Water vapor, carbon dioxide, and other gases in the atmosphere are affected by both ongoing processes and sudden changes.

**SUPPORTING MAIN IDEAS**
Make a chart about processes that modify the atmosphere.

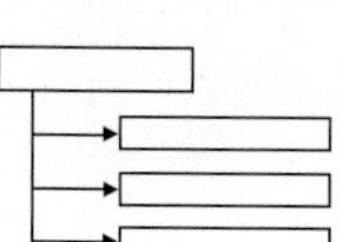

### Ongoing Processes

You and all other living things participate in ongoing processes. For example, each day you breathe in and out about 13,000 liters (3,000 gal) of air—about as much air as would fill five school buses. When you breathe, your body exchanges gases with the atmosphere. The air you inhale is a slightly different mixture of gases than the air you exhale.

Living things take part in a repeated process of gas exchange with the atmosphere. In addition, living things continually exchange materials in solid and liquid form with the environment. Processes like these that repeat over and over are called **cycles.**

Three of the most important cycles that affect the atmosphere are the carbon cycle, the nitrogen cycle, and the water cycle.

1. **The Carbon Cycle** Carbon dioxide ($CO_2$) and oxygen ($O_2$) gases constantly circulate, or cycle, among plants, animals, and the atmosphere. For example,
   - Animals inhale air, use some of its oxygen, and exhale air that has less oxygen but more carbon dioxide and water
   - Plants take in carbon dioxide and release oxygen as they make food in the process of photosynthesis
2. **The Nitrogen Cycle** Different forms of nitrogen cycle among the atmosphere, the soil, and living organisms. For example,
   - Tiny organisms remove nitrogen gas ($N_2$) from the air and transform it into other chemicals, which then enter the soil
   - Plants and animals use solids and liquids that contain nitrogen, which returns to the soil when the organisms die and decay
   - The soil slowly releases nitrogen back into the air as nitrogen gas
3. **The Water Cycle** Different forms of water ($H_2O$) cycle between Earth's surface and the atmosphere. For example,
   - Liquid water from oceans and lakes changes into gas and enters the atmosphere
   - Plants release water vapor from their leaves
   - Liquid water falls from the atmosphere as rain

**READING TIP**
In the diagrams on page 13, color is used to show particular materials.

is red.

is purple.

is aqua.

is blue.

## Cycles and the Atmosphere

**A tiger breathing, leaves decaying, trees growing—all are involved in cycles that affect our atmosphere. The diagrams to the right show how materials move in three important cycles.**

### 1 Carbon Cycle

- The tiger exhales carbon dioxide ($CO_2$). Carbon dioxide is taken in by the tree.
- The tree releases oxygen ($O_2$). Oxygen is taken in by the tiger.

### 2 Nitrogen Cycle

- Tiny organisms convert nitrogen gas ($N_2$) to other forms used by the tree.
- Decaying leaves release nitrogen gas ($N_2$) back into the atmosphere.

### 3 Water Cycle

- Water vapor ($H_2O$ gas) turns to liquid and rains down to Earth's surface.
- Water from the lake changes to gas and returns to the atmosphere.

**READING VISUALS** COMPARE AND CONTRAST How are the three cycles similar? How are they different?

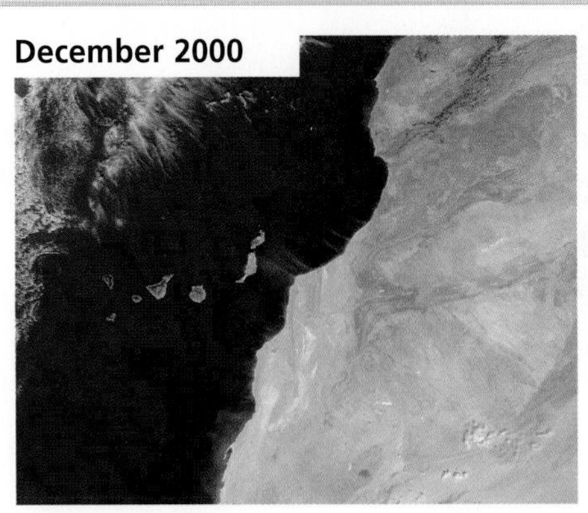


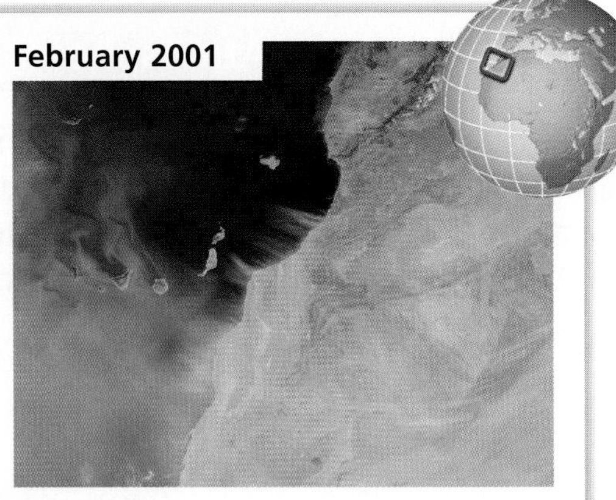


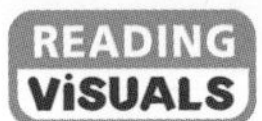


**COMPARE AND CONTRAST** These satellite images show northwestern Africa before and during a dust storm. How does the second image differ from the first?

**SUPPORTING MAIN IDEAS** Record information about the events that cause sudden changes in the atmosphere.

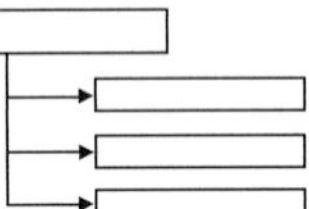

## Sudden Changes

In addition to ongoing processes, dramatic events may cause changes in the atmosphere. When sudden events occur, it takes time before the atmosphere is able to restore balance.

- **Volcanic Eruptions** Volcanoes shoot gases and huge amounts of ash into the atmosphere. Certain gases produce a haze that may affect the air for many months and lower temperatures worldwide.
- **Forest Fires** When forests burn, the carbon that makes up each tree combines with oxygen and enters the atmosphere as carbon dioxide. Wood ash also enters the atmosphere.
- **Dust Storms** Wind, water, or drought can loosen soil. Powerful windstorms may then raise clouds of this eroded soil, as in the second picture above. These storms add huge amounts of particles to the air for a time.

# 1.1 Review

### KEY CONCEPTS

1. How is the atmosphere important to living things?
2. What substances make up air?
3. Draw a diagram to show how one natural cycle affects the atmosphere.

### CRITICAL THINKING

4. **Apply** Give three examples from everyday life of how the atmosphere supports and protects life.
5. **Predict** How would the atmosphere in your area change if a disease killed all the plants?

### CHALLENGE

6. **Compare** Carbon dioxide enters the oceans from the air. Some carbon becomes stored in shells, and then in rocks. Eventually, it can be released back into the air by volcanoes in the form of carbon dioxide. How are these slow processes similar to the cycles shown on page 13?

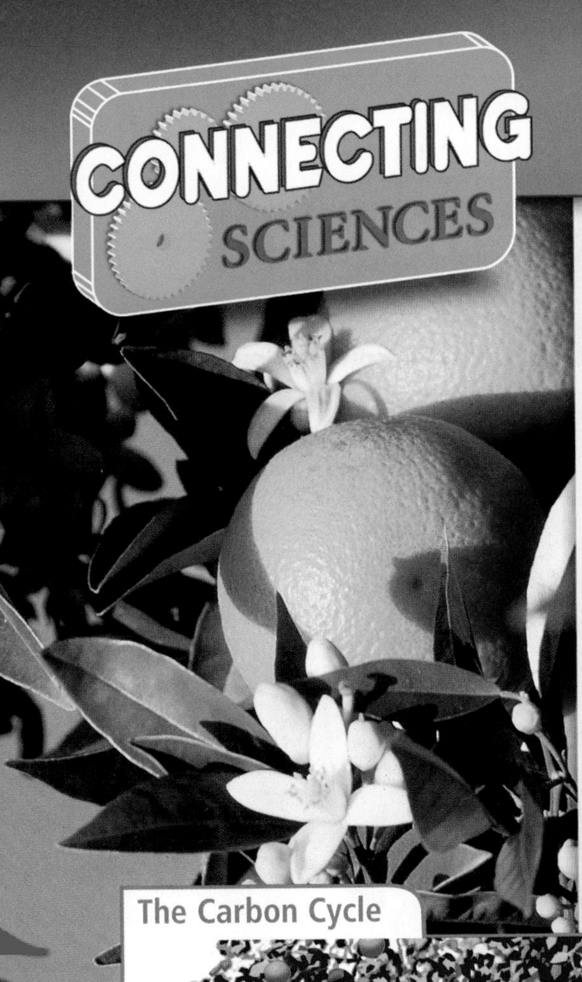
CONNECTING
SCIENCES

## EARTH SCIENCE AND PHYSICAL SCIENCE

# Carbon Cycle Chemistry

The atmosphere is keeping you alive. Every time you breathe, you take in the oxygen that you need to live. But that's not the end of the story. The food you eat would not exist without the carbon dioxide in the air that you, and every other animal on Earth, breathe out.

### A Closer Look at Oxygen and Carbon Dioxide

Gases in air are tiny molecules that are much too small to see, even if you look through a microscope. Chemists use diagrams to represent these molecules. Oxygen gas ($O_2$) is made of two atoms of oxygen, so a diagram of an oxygen gas molecule shows two red balls stuck together. A diagram of a carbon dioxide molecule ($CO_2$) looks similar, but it has one black carbon atom in addition to two red oxygen atoms.

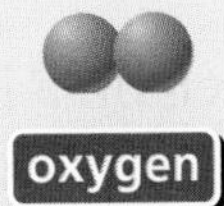

oxygen

carbon dioxide

The Carbon Cycle

1 The tree takes carbon from the air.
carbon in food
oxygen in air
carbon dioxide in air
2 You move carbon from food back into the air.

### The Carbon Connection

1. The orange tree takes in carbon dioxide from the air. Molecules of carbon dioxide are broken apart, and some carbon atoms become part of other more complex molecules in the growing orange.
2. You take carbon-containing molecules into your body when you eat the orange. Later, your body uses the food to carry out life processes. Some of the carbon atoms become part of carbon dioxide molecules, which you exhale into the air.

The carbon dioxide you exhale may be taken in again by the tree. This time, the carbon may become part of the trunk of the tree, and then return to the air when the tree dies and decays. Carbon keeps going around and around among living things and the atmosphere.

### EXPLORE

1. **COMPARE AND CONTRAST** What is the difference between a carbon dioxide molecule and an oxygen molecule?
2. **CHALLENGE** Draw a diagram showing how carbon can move into and out of the air when a tree grows and then later dies and decays.

KEY CONCEPT

# The Sun supplies the atmosphere's energy.

**BEFORE, you learned**

- The atmosphere supports and protects life
- The atmosphere contains a mixture of gases
- The atmosphere is affected by natural processes

**NOW, you will learn**

- How solar energy heats Earth's surface and atmosphere
- How the atmosphere moves heat energy around
- About the layers of the atmosphere

**VOCABULARY**

**radiation** p. 17
**conduction** p. 18
**convection** p. 19

**THINK ABOUT**

***Can you feel sunlight?***

If you have been on a hot beach, you have felt energy from sunlight. Perhaps you felt sunlight warming your skin or hot sand underneath your feet. It is easy to notice the energy of sunlight when it makes the ground or your skin warm. Where else does the energy from sunlight go?

## Energy from the Sun heats the atmosphere.

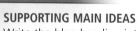

**SUPPORTING MAIN IDEAS**
Write the blue heading into your notes to begin a new chart. Add supporting details.

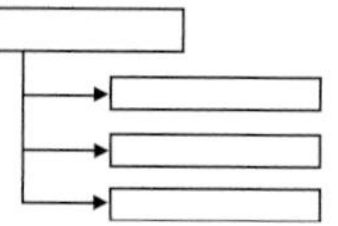

It may seem hard to believe, but almost all the energy around you comes from the Sun. That means that food energy, fires, and even the warmth of your own body can be traced back to energy from the Sun. A lot of this energy reaches Earth in a form you can see—visible light.

Two main things happen to the sunlight that reaches Earth. Some is reflected, or sent in a new direction. You see most of the objects around you by reflected light. The sand in the picture above looks light in color because it reflects much of the sunlight that hits it. Some of the sunlight that reaches Earth's surface is absorbed. The energy from this light heats the substance that absorbs it. The sand can become warm or even hot as it absorbs some of the sunlight that hits it. Some objects, such as the striped shirts above, have bright parts that reflect more light and dark parts that absorb more light.

What two things happen to the sunlight that reaches Earth?

The light that you can see is one type of radiation. **Radiation** (RAY-dee-AY-shuhn) is energy that travels across distances in the form of certain types of waves. Visible light and other types of radiation can be absorbed or reflected.

The diagram shows the average amounts of solar radiation, or radiation from the Sun, that are absorbed and reflected by Earth's atmosphere, clouds, and surface. Each arrow in the diagram represents 5 percent of the solar radiation that reaches Earth. As you can see, about 30 percent of the solar energy that reaches Earth is reflected. Clouds and snow-covered ground are white, so they reflect a lot of the radiation that hits them. Air also reflects some radiation. The energy of the reflected radiation goes back into outer space.

## Solar Radiation

**Arrows show the average global reflection and absorption of solar radiation.**

About 5% of solar energy is reflected by Earth's surface.

About 25% of solar energy is reflected by clouds and Earth's atmosphere.

About 20% of solar energy is absorbed by clouds and the atmosphere.

About 50% of solar energy is absorbed by Earth's surface.

*The atmosphere is much smaller than shown.*

The other 70 percent of solar radiation that reaches Earth is absorbed. Most of this energy is absorbed by oceans, landforms, and living things. The absorbed energy heats Earth's surface. In the same way, energy that is absorbed by gas molecules, clouds, and dust particles heats the atmosphere.

## INVESTIGATE Solar Radiation

### *How does reflection affect temperature?*

**PROCEDURE**

1. Cover the top of one cup with plastic wrap. Cover the second cup with paper. Secure the plastic wrap and paper with tape.
2. Poke a small slit in each cup's cover. Insert a thermometer through each slit.
3. Place the cups in direct sunlight. Record their temperature every minute for 15 minutes.

**WHAT DO YOU THINK?**

- How did the temperature change inside each cup?
- How did the coverings contribute to these changes?

**CHALLENGE** What does the paper represent in this model?

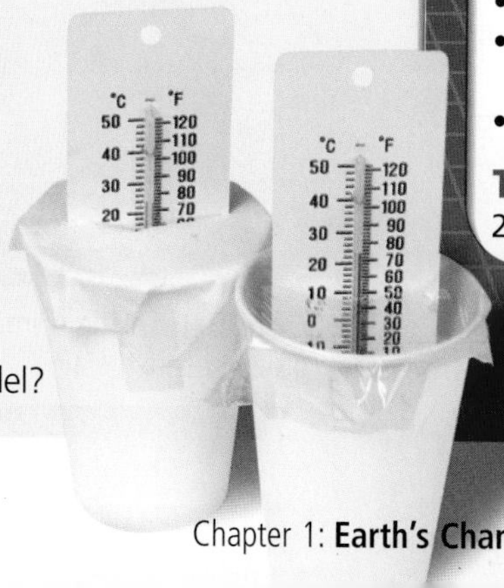

**SKILL FOCUS**
Measuring

**MATERIALS**
- 2 cups
- plastic wrap
- white paper
- tape
- 2 short thermometers
- watch

**TIME**
25 minutes

## The atmosphere moves energy.

If you walk along a sunny beach, you may be comfortably warm except for the burning-hot soles of your feet. The sand may be much hotter than the air. The sand absorbs solar energy all day and stores it in one place. The air also absorbs solar energy but moves it around and spreads it out. Radiation, conduction, and convection are processes that move energy from place to place.

**Radiation** You have already read that solar radiation warms a sandy beach. You may be surprised to learn that radiation also transfers energy from the sand to the air. Earth's surface gives off a type of invisible radiation, called infrared radiation, that can be absorbed by certain gases. The energy from the radiation warms the air. The air also gives off infrared radiation. You will read more about this cycle of radiation in Section 1.3.

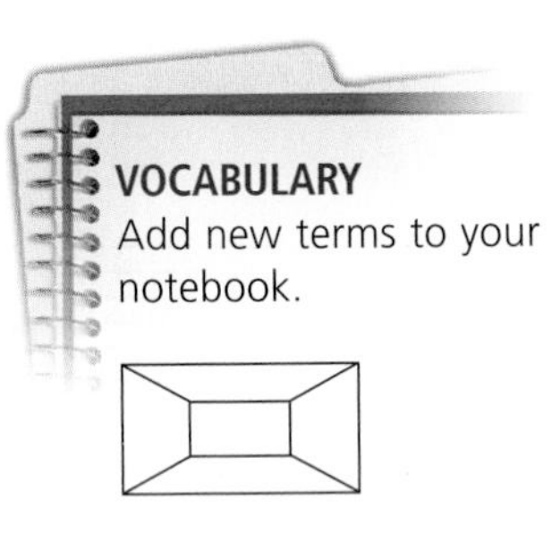
VOCABULARY
Add new terms to your notebook.

**Conduction** Another way that sand warms the air is through conduction. When you walk barefoot on a hot beach, rapidly moving molecules in the hot sand bump against molecules in your feet. This process transfers energy to your feet, which get hot. **Conduction** is the transfer of heat energy from one substance to another by direct contact. Earth's surface transfers energy to the atmosphere by conduction, such as when hot beach sand warms the air above it. Molecules of air can

### Transfer of Energy

**Radiation, conduction, and convection move energy from place to place.**

**warm air**
- Molecules move faster.
- Molecules are farther apart.
- Warm air is less dense.
- Warm air carries more energy than cool air.

**cool air**
- Molecules move slower.
- Molecules are closer together.
- Cool air is more dense.

1 **Radiation** Sunlight warms the ground.

2 **Conduction** The warm ground heats the air.

3 **Convection** Cool, dense air sinks downward and pushes warm air out of the way. Warm air carries energy upward.

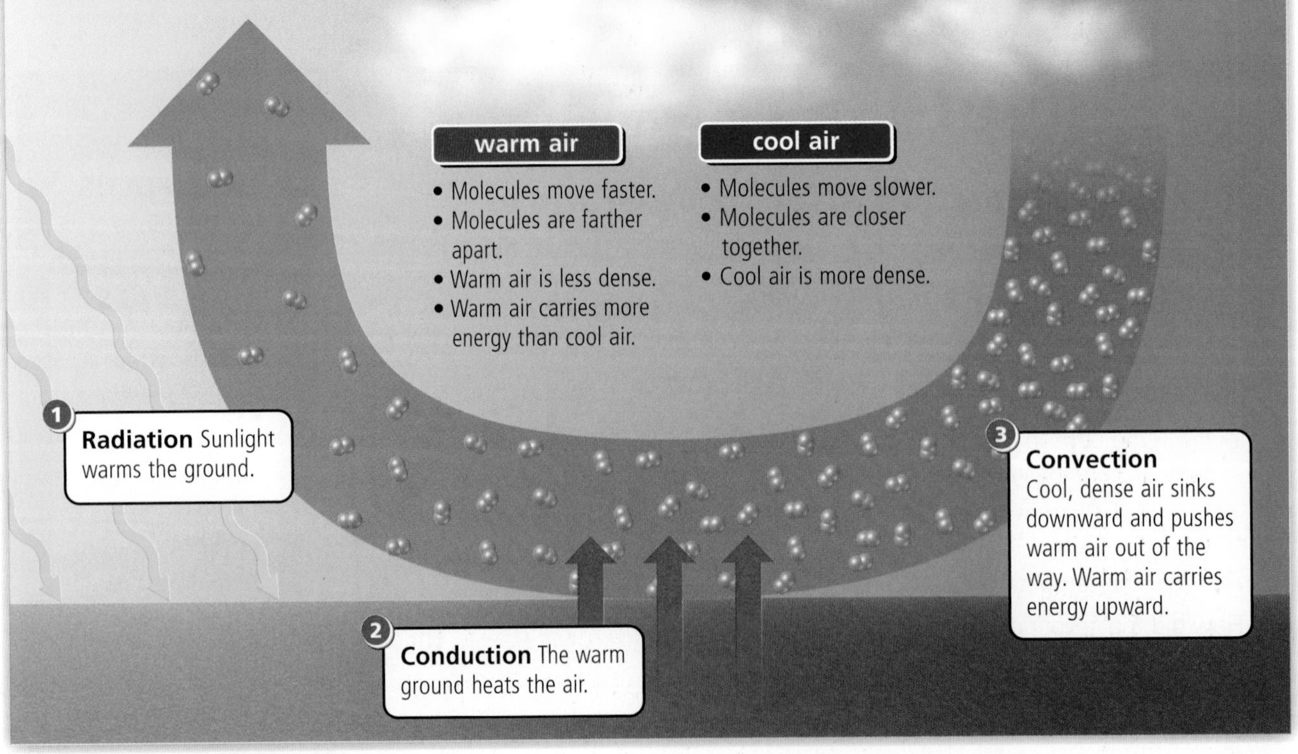

gain energy when they collide with molecules in grains of hot sand. The air just above the sand gets warm. Energy can also spread slowly through the air by conduction as air molecules bump into one another.

Moving hot air near the flames makes the mountain behind appear distorted.

**Convection** Heated air can move easily from place to place. When a heated liquid or gas moves, it carries energy along with it. **Convection** is the transfer of energy from place to place by the motion of gas or liquid. When scientists talk about convection in the atmosphere, they usually mean the motion of gases up and down rather than side to side. The heat energy comes from below and is moved upward. Think once more about the beach. First, radiation from the Sun warms the sand. Second, the hot sand conducts energy to the air. Third, the warm air carries energy upward in convection. Follow this cycle of radiation, conduction, and convection in the diagram on page 18.

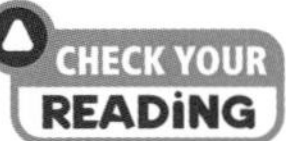
CHECK YOUR READING Compare conduction and convection. How are they similar?

Differences in density produce the motion of air convection. You have read that the atmosphere is less dense at higher altitudes. At any particular altitude, however, the density of air depends mostly on its temperature. Warm air has more energy, so the molecules move faster than they do in cool air. The motion makes the molecules collide more, so they stay farther apart. When there is more space between molecules, the air is less dense.

REMINDER
Density is the amount of mass in a given volume of a substance.

Imagine a box full of warm air and another box of the same size full of cool air. If you could see air molecules, you would find more molecules—more mass—in the box of cool air. Cool, dense air is heavier, so it tends to sink and push warm, less dense air upward.

As it moves upward, warm air carries energy away from the ground. The air can cool as it rises. Eventually, the air can become cool enough—dense enough—to sink back to the ground, where it may heat up again.

See radiation, conduction, and convection in action.

## The atmosphere has temperature layers.

Density is not the only characteristic of the atmosphere that changes with altitude. Different parts of the atmosphere absorb and move energy in different ways. As a result, the air's temperature changes with altitude. Scientists use the patterns of these temperature changes to define four layers of the atmosphere. To explore these layers, turn the page and ride an imaginary elevator up through the atmosphere.

## Temperature Layers

*Explore the atmosphere's temperature layers by riding an imaginary elevator up from the ground.*

**Thermosphere**
Continue through the thermosphere. The air thins out until you reach outer space.

**Mesosphere**
Reach the mesosphere after rising 50 km (31 mi) off the ground. You are now above 99.9% of the molecules of Earth's air.

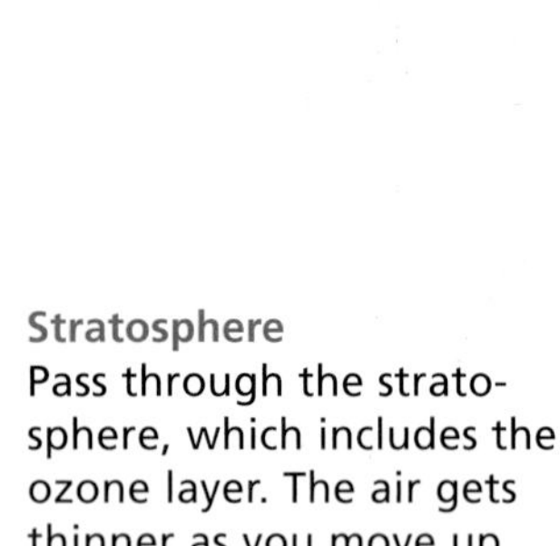

**Stratosphere**
Pass through the stratosphere, which includes the ozone layer. The air gets thinner as you move up through the atmosphere.

**Troposphere**
Board the elevator at ground level, which is also the bottom of the troposphere.

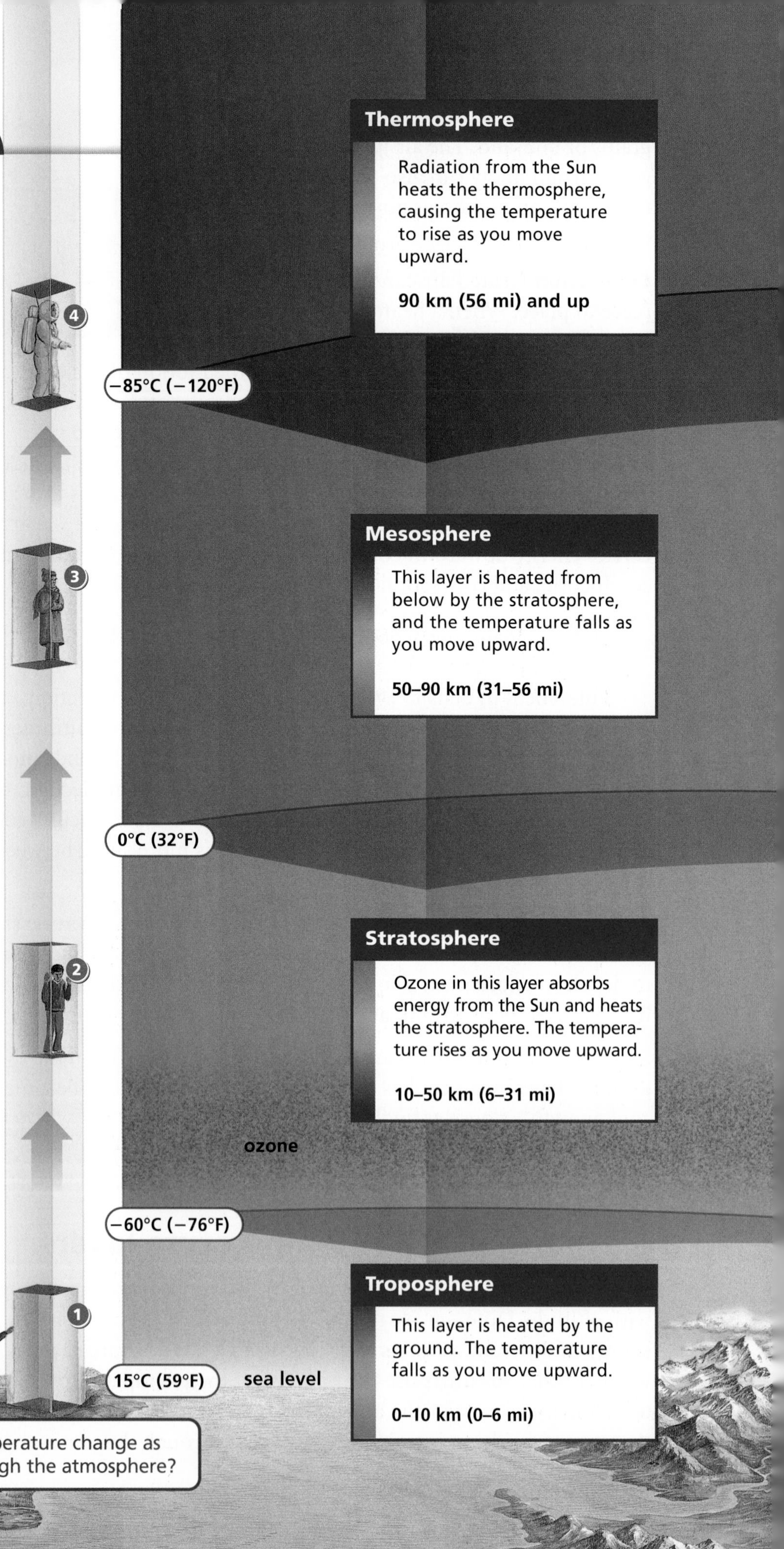

### Thermosphere

Radiation from the Sun heats the thermosphere, causing the temperature to rise as you move upward.

**90 km (56 mi) and up**

### Mesosphere

This layer is heated from below by the stratosphere, and the temperature falls as you move upward.

**50–90 km (31–56 mi)**

### Stratosphere

Ozone in this layer absorbs energy from the Sun and heats the stratosphere. The temperature rises as you move upward.

**10–50 km (6–31 mi)**

### Troposphere

This layer is heated by the ground. The temperature falls as you move upward.

**0–10 km (0–6 mi)**

**READING VISUALS** How does the temperature change as you move up through the atmosphere?

1. **Troposphere** (TROH-puh-SFEER) The layer of the atmosphere nearest Earth's surface is called the troposphere because convection seems to turn the air over. This layer contains about 80 percent of the total mass of the atmosphere, including almost all of the water vapor present in the atmosphere. The troposphere is warmed from below by the ground. The temperature is highest at ground level and generally decreases about 6.5°C for each kilometer you rise.

**READING TIP**

You can use the word parts to help you recall the temperature layers.

*tropo-* "turning"
*strato-* "spreading out"
*meso-* "middle"
*thermo-* "heat"

2. **Stratosphere** (STRAT-uh-SFEER) Above the troposphere lies a clear, dry layer of the atmosphere called the stratosphere. Within the stratosphere are molecules of a gas called ozone. These molecules absorb a type of solar radiation that is harmful to life. The energy from the radiation raises the temperature of the air. The temperature increases as you rise high in the stratosphere.

3. **Mesosphere** (MEHZ-uh-SFEER) The air in the mesosphere is extremely thin. In fact, this layer contains less than 0.1 percent of the atmosphere's mass. Most meteors that enter the atmosphere burn up within the mesosphere. The mesosphere, like the troposphere, is heated from below, so the temperature in the mesosphere decreases as you rise.

4. **Thermosphere** (THUR-muh-SFEER) The thermosphere starts about 90 kilometers (56 mi) above Earth's surface. It grows less and less dense over hundreds of kilometers until it becomes outer space. The air high in this layer becomes very hot because the molecules absorb a certain type of solar radiation. However, even the hottest air in this layer would feel cold to you because the molecules are so spread out that they would not conduct much energy to your skin. The temperature in the thermosphere increases as you rise.

How does the temperature change in each layer of the atmosphere?

# 1.2 Review

## KEY CONCEPTS

1. What two things happen to solar radiation that reaches Earth?
2. Describe the three processes that transport energy.
3. What characteristic do scientists use to define four layers of Earth's atmosphere?

## CRITICAL THINKING

4. **Draw Conclusions** How might a thick, puffy cloud reflect a different amount of the Sun's radiation than a thin, wispy one?
5. **Apply** Jet planes fly near the top of the troposphere. Is it more important to heat or to cool the passenger cabins? Explain your reasoning.

## CHALLENGE

6. **Analyze** Earth loses about the same amount of energy as it absorbs from the Sun. If it did not, Earth's temperature would increase. Does the energy move from Earth's surface and atmosphere out to space through radiation, conduction, or convection? Give your reasons.

KEY CONCEPT

# Gases in the atmosphere absorb radiation.

**BEFORE, you learned**

- Solar radiation heats Earth's surface and atmosphere
- Earth's surface and atmosphere give off radiation
- The ozone layer is in the stratosphere

**NOW, you will learn**

- More about how radiation and gases affect each other
- About the ozone layer and ultraviolet radiation
- About the greenhouse effect

**VOCABULARY**

**ultraviolet radiation** p. 23
**infrared radiation** p. 23
**ozone** p. 23
**greenhouse effect** p. 24
**greenhouse gas** p. 24

**EXPLORE Radiation**

### *Can you feel radiation?*

**PROCEDURE**

1. Turn on the lamp and wait for it to become warm. It gives off visible and infrared radiation.
2. Hold one hand a short distance from the bulb. Record your observations.
3. Turn the lamp off. The bulb continues to give off infrared radiation. Hold your other hand a short distance from the bulb.

**WHAT DO YOU THINK?**

- What did you see and feel?
- How did radiation affect each hand?

**MATERIALS**

- lamp

## Gases can absorb and give off radiation.

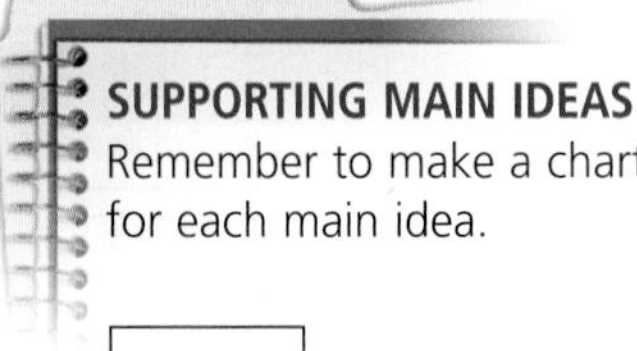

**SUPPORTING MAIN IDEAS**
Remember to make a chart for each main idea.

On a sunny day, objects around you look bright. Earth's atmosphere reflects or absorbs some sunlight, but allows most of the visible light to pass through to Earth's surface. A cloudy day is darker because clouds reflect and absorb much of the sunlight, so less light passes through to the ground.

The atmosphere can affect light in four ways. It can absorb light, reflect it, or let it pass through. Air can also emit, or give off, light. Although air does not emit much visible light, certain gases absorb and emit radiation that is similar to visible light.

List four ways that the atmosphere can affect light.

Just as there are sounds humans cannot hear, there are forms of radiation that humans cannot see. Sounds can be too high to hear. In a similar way, waves of **ultraviolet radiation** (UHL-truh-VY-uh-liht) have more energy than the light you can see. Ultraviolet radiation can cause sunburn and other types of damage. Sounds can also be too low for humans to hear. In a similar way, waves of **infrared radiation** (IHN-fruh-REHD) have less energy than visible light. Infrared radiation usually warms the materials that absorb it. Different gases in the atmosphere absorb these two different types of radiation.

## The ozone layer protects life from harmful radiation.

In Section 1.2, you read about a gas called ozone that forms in the stratosphere. An **ozone** molecule ($O_3$) is made of three atoms of the element oxygen. Your body uses regular oxygen gas ($O_2$), which has two atoms of oxygen. In the stratosphere, ozone and regular oxygen gases break apart and form again in a complex cycle. The reactions that destroy and form ozone normally balance each other, so the cycle can repeat endlessly. Even though ozone is mixed with nitrogen and other gases, the ozone in the stratosphere is called the ozone layer.

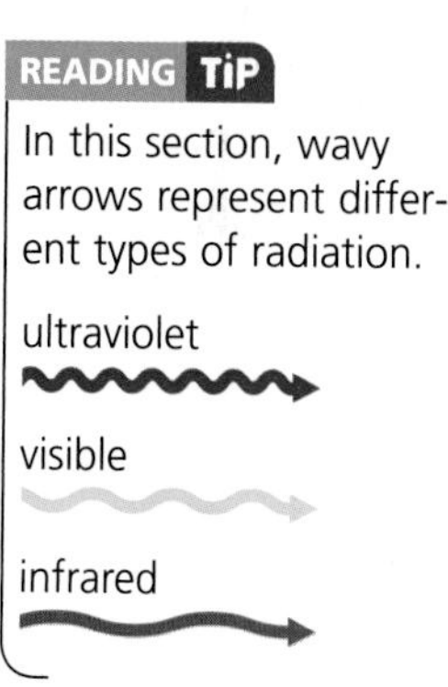

READING TIP
In this section, wavy arrows represent different types of radiation.
ultraviolet
visible
infrared


The ozone layer protects life on Earth by absorbing harmful ultraviolet radiation from the Sun. Too much ultraviolet radiation can cause sunburn, skin cancer, and damaged eyesight. Ultraviolet radiation can harm crops and materials such as plastic or paint. Ozone absorbs ultraviolet radiation but lets other types of radiation, such as visible light, pass through.

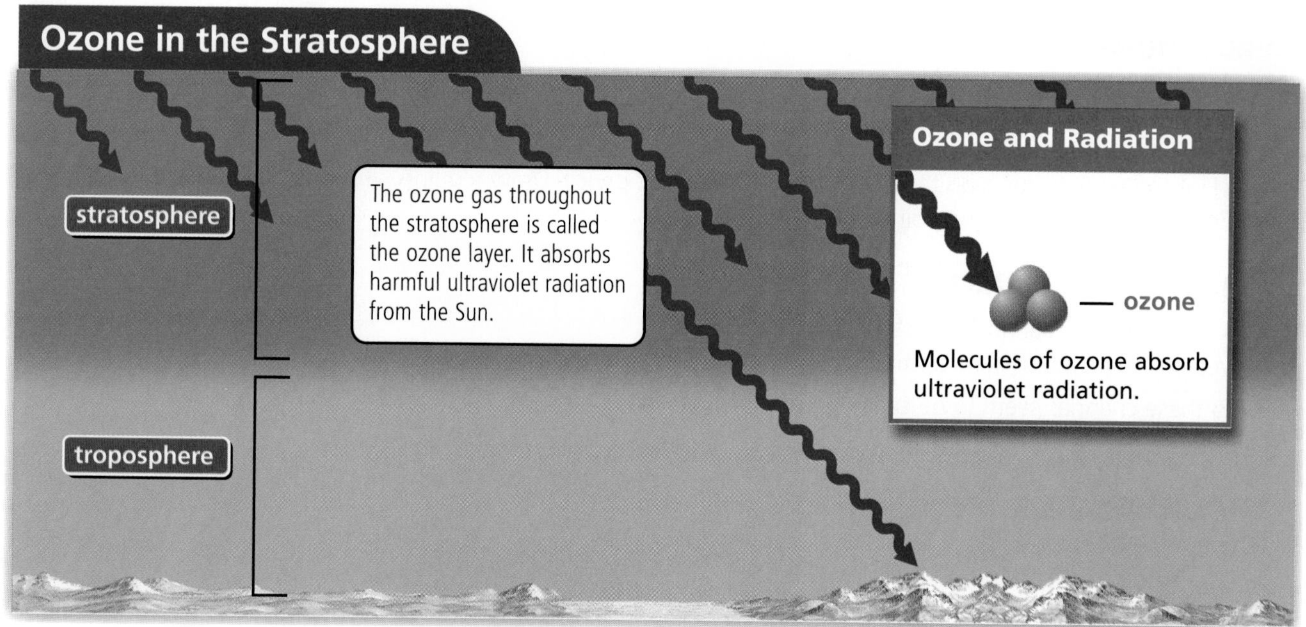

## The greenhouse effect keeps Earth warm.

See how the greenhouse effect works.

A jacket helps keep you warm on a cool day by slowing the movement of heat energy away from your body. In a similar way, certain gases in the atmosphere slow the movement of energy away from Earth's surface. The gases absorb and emit infrared radiation, which keeps energy in Earth's system for a while. This process was named the **greenhouse effect** because it reminded scientists of the way glass traps warmth inside a greenhouse.

Carbon dioxide, methane, water vapor, nitrous oxide, and other gases that absorb and give off infrared radiation are known as **greenhouse gases.** Unlike the glass roof and walls of a greenhouse, the greenhouse gases do not form a single layer. They are mixed together with nitrogen, oxygen, and other gases in the air. The atmosphere is densest in the troposphere—the lowest layer—so most of the greenhouse gas molecules are also in the troposphere.

**REMINDER**

Ozone absorbs ultraviolet radiation in the stratosphere. Greenhouse gases absorb and emit infrared radiation in the troposphere.

Radiation from the Sun, including visible light, warms Earth's surface, which then emits infrared radiation. If the atmosphere had no greenhouse gases, the infrared radiation would go straight through the atmosphere into outer space. Earth's average surface temperature would be only about –18°C (0°F). Water would freeze, and it would be too cold for most forms of life on Earth to survive.

# INVESTIGATE Greenhouse Gases

### *How have levels of greenhouse gases changed?*

Scientists have used ice cores from Antarctica to calculate prehistoric carbon dioxide levels and temperatures. The $CO_2$ data table has the results for you to plot.

**SKILL FOCUS**
Graphing

**MATERIALS**
- Carbon Dioxide Table
- regular pencil
- red pencil

**TIME**
30 minutes

#### PROCEDURE

1. Plot the $CO_2$ levels on the graph sheet using a regular pencil. Draw line segments to connect the points.
2. Plot the temperatures on the same graph using a red pencil. Draw red line segments to connect the points.

#### WHAT DO YOU THINK?

- How many times during the past 400,000 years were average temperatures in Antarctica above –56°C?
- Do these changes seem to be connected to changes in levels of carbon dioxide? Explain.

**CHALLENGE** Is it possible to tell from the graph whether temperature affected carbon dioxide levels or carbon dioxide levels affected temperature? Why or why not?

## The Greenhouse Effect

**Greenhouse gas molecules absorb and emit infrared radiation.**

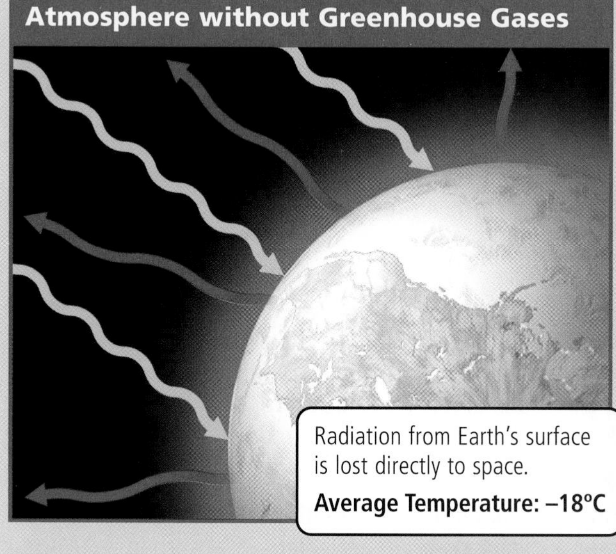
Atmosphere without Greenhouse Gases
Radiation from Earth's surface is lost directly to space.
Average Temperature: –18°C

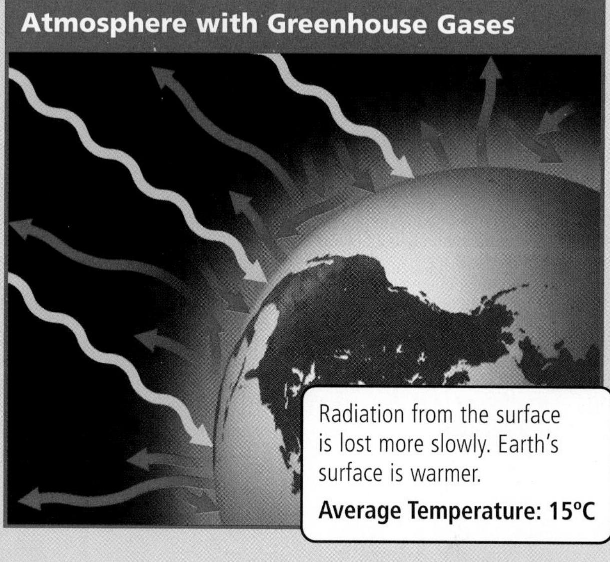
Atmosphere with Greenhouse Gases
Radiation from the surface is lost more slowly. Earth's surface is warmer.
Average Temperature: 15°C

sunlight infrared radiation

*The atmosphere is much thinner than shown here.*

Earth's atmosphere does have greenhouse gases. These gases absorb some of the infrared radiation emitted by Earth's surface. The greenhouse gases can then give off this energy as infrared radiation. Some of the energy is absorbed again by the surface, while some of the energy goes out into space. The greenhouse effect keeps Earth's average surface temperature around 15°C (59°F). The energy stays in Earth's system longer with greenhouse gases than without them. In time, all the energy ends up back in outer space. If it did not, Earth would grow warmer and warmer as it absorbed more and more solar radiation.

# 1.3 Review

### KEY CONCEPTS

1. Name and describe two of the ways gases can affect radiation.
2. What type of radiation does the ozone layer affect?
3. How do greenhouse gases keep Earth warm?

### CRITICAL THINKING

4. **Infer** What would happen if gases in the atmosphere absorbed visible light?
5. **Compare and Contrast** How are ozone and greenhouse gases alike? How are they different?

### CHALLENGE

6. **Predict** How would the temperature on Earth be affected if the amount of greenhouse gases in the atmosphere changed?

## SKILL: ALGEBRAIC EQUATIONS

# Solar Radiation

The amount of sunlight that reaches Earth's surface varies from day to day. On a cloudy day, for example, clouds may absorb or reflect most of the sunlight before it reaches Earth's surface. You can use equations to determine how much incoming solar radiation is absorbed by Earth's surface on each day.

**MATH TUTORIAL**
CLASSZONE.COM
Click on Math Tutorial for more help with equations.

### Example

On a particular cloudy day, 50% of the solar radiation coming into Earth is reflected by clouds and the atmosphere, 40% is absorbed by clouds and the atmosphere, and 1% is reflected by Earth's surface. How much is absorbed by Earth's surface?

***Write a verbal model:***

| radiation reflected by clouds & atmosphere | + | radiation absorbed by clouds & atmosphere | + | radiation reflected by Earth's surface | + | radiation absorbed by Earth's surface | = | total incoming radiation |
|---|---|---|---|---|---|---|---|---|

***Substitute into the model:*** $50\% + 40\% + 1\% + x = 100\%$

***Simplify the left side:*** $91\% + x = 100\%$

***Subtract:*** $-91\% \qquad -91\%$

***Simplify:*** $x = 9\%$

**ANSWER** 9% of the incoming solar radiation is absorbed by Earth's surface.

**Determine the amount of incoming solar radiation that is absorbed by Earth's surface on each day.**

1. On a sunny day, 15% is reflected by clouds and the atmosphere, 20% is absorbed by clouds and the atmosphere, and 10% is reflected by Earth's surface.
2. On a partly cloudy day, 25% is reflected by clouds and the atmosphere, 20% is absorbed by clouds and the atmosphere, and 5% is reflected by Earth's surface.

**CHALLENGE** On a particular day, how much incoming solar radiation is absorbed by Earth's surface if 60% is reflected (either by clouds and the atmosphere or by Earth's surface), and half that amount is absorbed by the atmosphere?

sunny day

partly cloudy day

KEY CONCEPT

# 1.4 Human activities affect the atmosphere.

**BEFORE, you learned**

- The atmosphere has gases that absorb and give off radiation
- The ozone layer absorbs ultraviolet radiation
- The greenhouse effect keeps Earth warm

**NOW, you will learn**

- What the types and effects of pollution are
- About the effect of human activities on greenhouse gases
- How the ozone layer is changing

**VOCABULARY**

**air pollution** p. 27
**particulate** p. 28
**fossil fuel** p. 28
**smog** p. 28

**EXPLORE Air Pollution**

### *Where does smoke go?*

**PROCEDURE**

1. Light the candle and let it burn for a minute or two. Observe the air around the candle.
2. Blow out the candle and observe the smoke until you cannot see it anymore.

**MATERIALS**

- candle in holder
- matches

**WHAT DO YOU THINK?**

- How far did the smoke from the candle travel?
- A burning candle produces invisible gases. Where do you think they went?

## Human activity can cause air pollution.

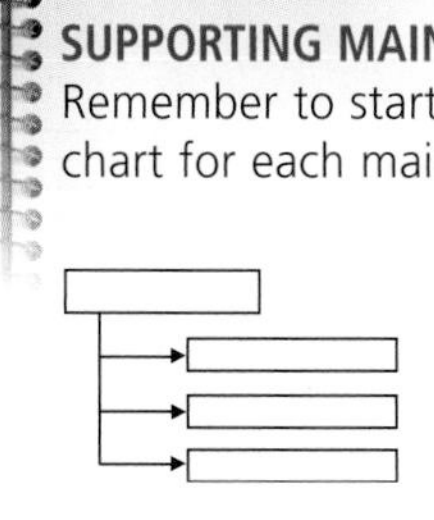

**SUPPORTING MAIN IDEAS**
Remember to start a new chart for each main idea.

If someone in your kitchen burns a piece of toast, and if a fan is blowing in the hallway, everyone in your home will smell the smoke. That means that everyone will breathe some air containing smoke. Smoke and other harmful materials that are added to the air are called **air pollution.** Outdoors, wind can spread air pollution from place to place the way a fan does within your home.

When toast burns, you may be able to see smoke. If smoke drifts in from another room, it may be too thin to see, but you may be able to smell it. There are other types of air pollution that you cannot see or smell. Like smoke, they can be spread around by wind. Air pollution from one place can affect a wide area. However, most types of pollution leave the air or become thin enough to be harmless after a time.

**CHECK YOUR READING** How is air pollution moved around?

## Types of Pollution

READING TIP

*Pollution* and *pollutant* have the same root, *pollute*—"to make unfit."

Scientists classify the separate types of air pollution, called pollutants, as either gases or particles. Gas pollutants include carbon monoxide, methane, ozone, sulfur oxides, and nitrogen oxides. Some of these gases occur naturally in the atmosphere. These gases are considered pollutants only when they are likely to cause harm. For example, ozone gas is good in the stratosphere but is harmful to breathe. When ozone is in the troposphere, it is a pollutant.

Particle pollutants can be easier to see than gas pollutants. **Particulates** are tiny particles or droplets that are mixed in with air. Smoke contains particulates. The wind can pick up other particulates, such as dust and dirt, pollen, and tiny bits of salt from the oceans. Some sources of pollutants are listed below.

CHECK YOUR READING What are the two types of pollutants? Give an example of each.

In cities and suburbs, most air pollution comes from the burning of fossil fuels such as oil, gasoline, and coal. **Fossil fuels** are fuels formed from the remains of prehistoric animals and plants. In London in the 1800s, burning coal provided much of the heat and energy for homes and factories. The resulting smoke and local weather conditions often produced a thick fog or cloud. The word **smog** describes this combination of smoke and fog. A newer type of air pollution is also called smog. Sunlight causes the fumes from gasoline, car exhaust, and other gases to react chemically. The reactions form new pollutants, such as ozone, which together are called smog. In cities, there can be enough smog to make a brownish haze.

### Sources of Pollution

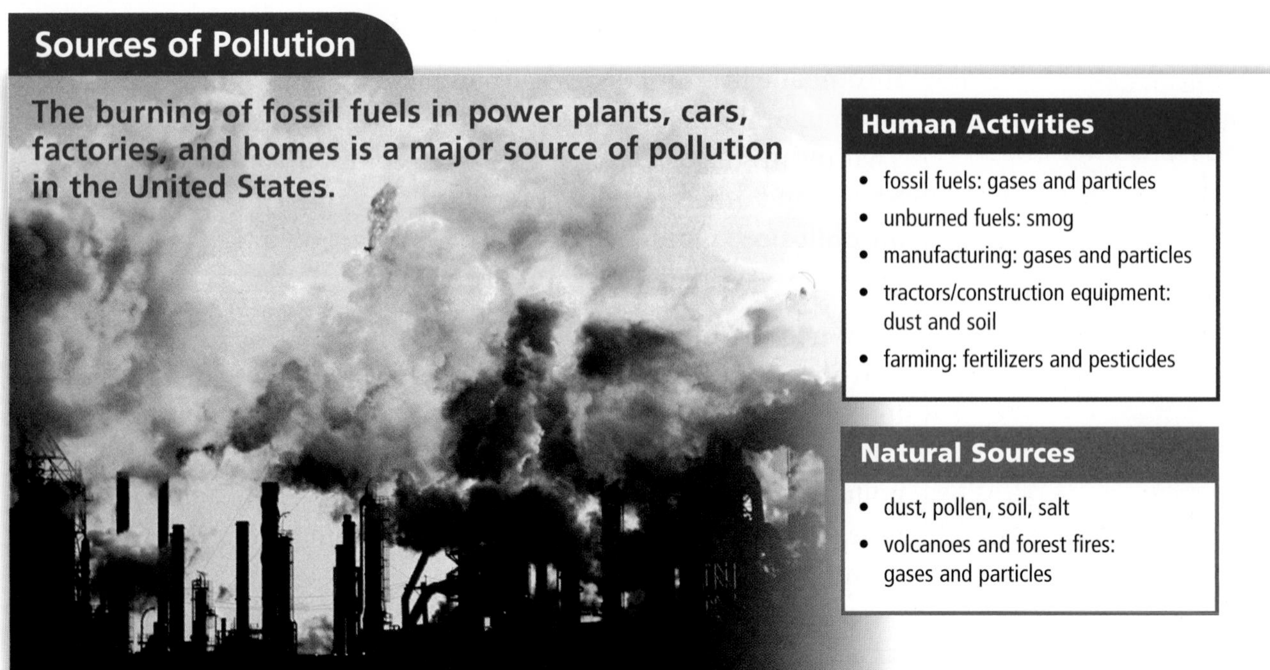

The burning of fossil fuels in power plants, cars, factories, and homes is a major source of pollution in the United States.
Human Activities
• fossil fuels: gases and particles
• unburned fuels: smog
• manufacturing: gases and particles
• tractors/construction equipment: dust and soil
• farming: fertilizers and pesticides
Natural Sources
• dust, pollen, soil, salt
• volcanoes and forest fires: gases and particles

## Effects of Pollution

Air pollution can cause health problems. Polluted air may irritate your eyes, nose, throat, and lungs. It can smell bad or make it hard to breathe. Gases or chemicals from particulates can move from your lungs to other parts of your body. Exercising in polluted air can be dangerous because you take more air into your lungs when you exercise. Over time, people who breathe polluted air can develop lung disease and other health problems. Air pollution can cause extra problems for young children, older adults, and people who suffer from asthma.

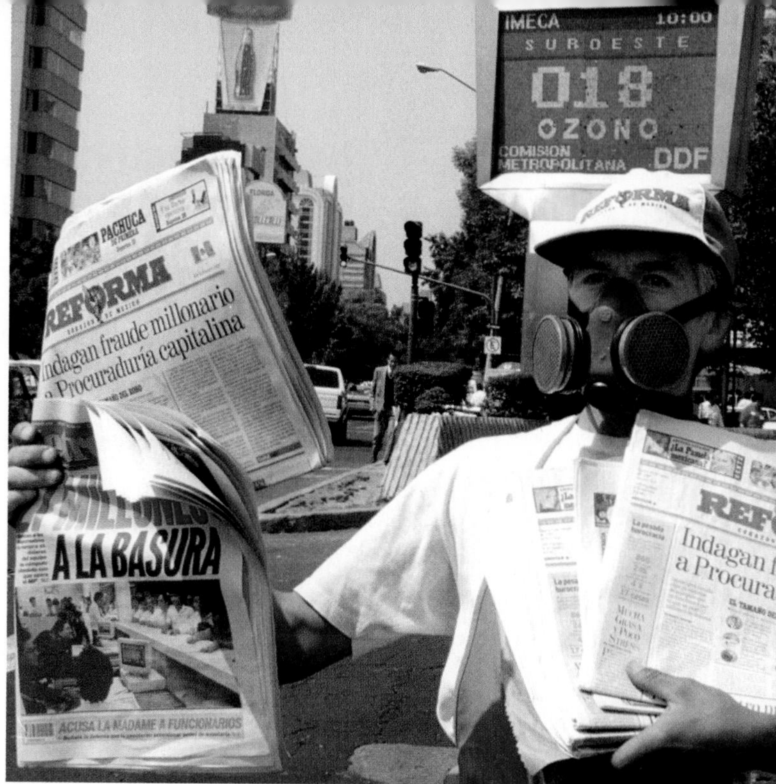


A man in Mexico City wears a gas mask while he sells newspapers. The green sign behind him warns people of a high ozone level.

Describe three of the ways in which pollution can affect people.

Particulates can stick to surfaces and damage plants, buildings, and other objects outdoors. Dusty air or a dust storm can darken the day and make it difficult to see. Particulates can be carried high into the atmosphere, where they can reflect or absorb sunlight and even affect the weather. Rain clears the air by removing particles and some polluting gases from the air. However, some pollutants are still harmful when rain moves them from the air to the ground, lakes, and oceans.

## Controlling Pollution

You may have experienced a smog or ozone alert. In some cities, smog becomes so bad that it is dangerous to exercise outdoors. Weather reports may include smog alerts so that people will know when to be careful. Cities may ask people not to drive cars when the weather conditions are likely to produce smog.

National, state, and local governments work together to reduce air pollution and protect people from its effects. Countries may come to agreements when the air pollution from one country affects another. Within the United States, Congress has passed laws to reduce air pollution. The Clean Air Act limits the amount of air pollution that factories and power plants are allowed to release. The act also sets rules for making car exhaust cleaner. The Environmental Protection Agency measures air pollution and works to enforce the laws passed by Congress.

## Human activities are increasing greenhouse gases.

A source of air pollution usually affects areas close to it. In contrast, some natural processes and human activities change the amounts of gases throughout Earth's atmosphere.

### Sources of Greenhouse Gases

REMINDER

Plants remove carbon dioxide from the air and store the carbon in solid forms.

You read in Section 1.1 how natural cycles move gases into and out of the atmosphere. Plant growth, forest fires, volcanoes, and other natural processes affect the amounts of carbon dioxide and other greenhouse gases in the atmosphere. The amounts of greenhouse gases then affect temperatures on Earth. In turn, the temperatures affect plant growth and other processes that produce or reduce greenhouse gases.

CHECK YOUR READING How do life and the atmosphere affect each other?

Most greenhouse gases occur naturally. They have helped keep temperatures within a range suitable for the plants and animals that live on Earth. However, human activities are producing greenhouse gases faster than natural processes can remove these gases from the

Greenhouse Gases from Human Activities
Carbon dioxide ($CO_2$)
Carbon dioxide comes largely from the use of fossil fuels in power plants, cars, factories, and homes.
Methane ($CH_4$)
Methane comes from cattle and other livestock, bacteria in rice fields, and landfills (waste disposal).
Nitrous oxide ($N_20$)
Nitrous oxide comes from fertilizers and chemical factories.

atmosphere. Some activities that produce greenhouse gases are shown on page 30. Water vapor is also a greenhouse gas, but the amount of water vapor in the air depends more on weather than on human activity.

## Global Warming

Many people are concerned about the amounts of greenhouse gases that humans are adding to the air. Carbon dioxide, for example, can stay in the atmosphere for more than 100 years, so the amounts keep adding up. The air contains about 30 percent more carbon dioxide than it did in the mid-1700s, and the level of carbon dioxide is now increasing about 0.4 percent per year.

How are carbon dioxide levels changing?

As the graph below shows, temperatures have risen in recent decades. Earth's atmosphere, water, and other systems work together in complex ways, so it is hard to know exactly how much greenhouse gases change the temperature. Scientists make computer models to understand the effects of greenhouse gases and explore what might happen in the future. The models predict that the average global temperature will continue to rise another 1.4–5.8°C (2.5–10.4°F) by the year 2100. This may not seem like a big change in temperature, but it can have big effects. Global warming can affect sources of food, the amount of water and other resources available, and even human health. You will read more about the possible effects of global warming in Chapter 4.

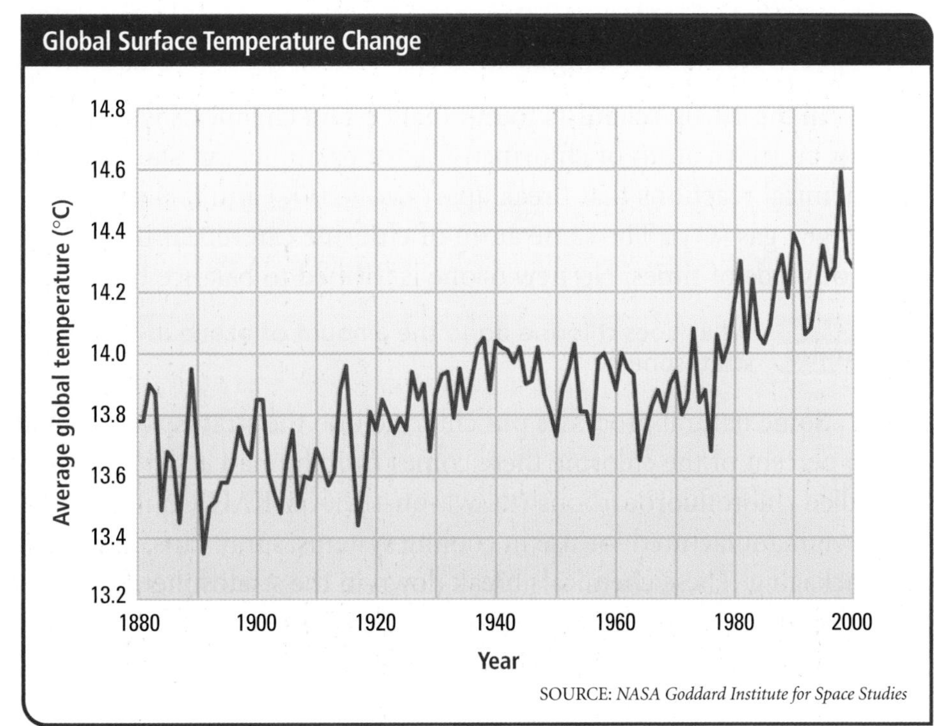


Earth's average temperature has risen over the last century.

This commuter is traveling to work without burning fossil fuels.

### Reducing Greenhouse Gases

Global warming is not a local issue. It affects the atmosphere around the entire planet. An international agreement to limit the amounts of greenhouse gases, called the Kyoto Protocol, would require developed nations to release no more greenhouse gases each year than they did in 1990. The Kyoto Protocol could take effect only if the nations releasing the most greenhouse gases accept the agreement. In 1990, more than one-third of the amount of greenhouse gases released came from the United States, which has not accepted the agreement.

New technologies may help fight the problem of global warming. Scientists are developing ways to heat and cool buildings, transport people and goods, and make products using less energy. Using less energy saves resources and money and it also reduces greenhouse gases. Scientists are also developing ways to produce energy without using any fossil fuels at all.

How can technology help reduce global warming?

## Human activities produce chemicals that destroy the ozone layer.

Examine the current state of the ozone layer.

At ground level, ozone is a pollutant, but at higher altitudes it benefits life. The ozone layer in the stratosphere protects living things by absorbing harmful ultraviolet radiation. You read in Section 1.3 that ozone is constantly being formed and broken apart in a natural cycle.

In the 1970s, scientists found that certain chemicals were disrupting this cycle. An atom of chlorine (Cl), for example, can start a series of chemical reactions that break apart ozone ($O_3$) and form regular oxygen gas ($O_2$). The same atom of chlorine can repeat this process thousands of times. No new ozone is formed to balance the loss.

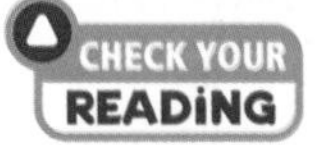


What does chlorine do to the amount of ozone in the stratosphere?

Some natural processes put chlorine into the stratosphere, but about 85 percent of the chlorine there comes from human activity. Chemicals called chlorofluorocarbons (KLAWR-oh-FLUR-oh-KAHR-buhnz) have been manufactured for use in cooling systems, spray cans, and foam for packaging. These chemicals break down in the stratosphere and release chlorine and other ozone-destroying chemicals.

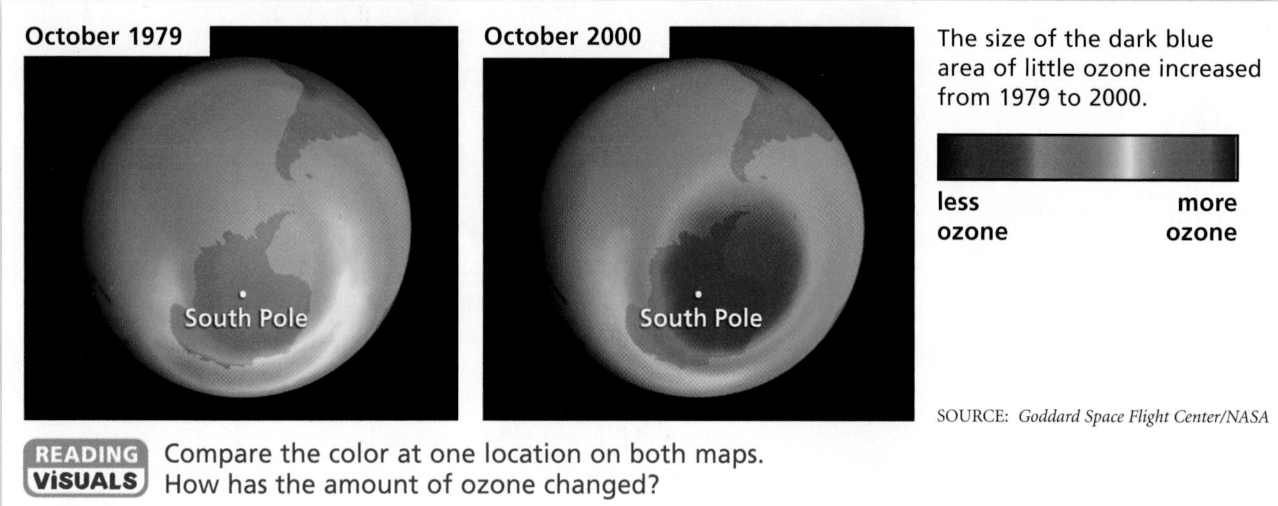


The size of the dark blue area of little ozone increased from 1979 to 2000.

SOURCE: *Goddard Space Flight Center/NASA*

**READING VISUALS** Compare the color at one location on both maps. How has the amount of ozone changed?

The amount of ozone in the stratosphere varies from place to place and changes with the seasons. Cold temperatures and sunshine make the ozone over Antarctica—the South Pole—especially sensitive to the chemicals that destroy ozone. The amount of ozone over Antarctica decreased by half from the 1970s to the mid-1990s. The maps above show the loss of ozone over Antarctica. Smaller but important changes were measured in other regions.

The ozone layer affects the whole world. Since 1987, more than 180 nations have signed an agreement called the Montreal Protocol. They have agreed on a plan to stop making and using chemicals that harm the ozone layer. Experts study the ozone layer and recommend changes to the agreement. The Montreal Protocol has been updated several times. Less harmful chemicals are now used instead of chlorofluorocarbons, but gases from past human activities are still in the ozone layer. If countries continue to follow the Montreal Protocol, ozone levels will return to normal in about 50 years.

## 1.4 Review

### KEY CONCEPTS

1. Describe two of the sources of air pollution.
2. What are three human activities that increase the levels of greenhouse gases?
3. How do human activities affect the ozone layer?

### CRITICAL THINKING

4. **Classify** List the following pollutants as either gases or particles: dust, ozone, pollen, carbon monoxide, methane.
5. **Predict** How might global warming affect the way you live in the future?

### CHALLENGE

6. **Synthesize** In North America, winds typically blow from west to east. Where might pollution from your community end up? Use a map to help you answer the question.

# Observing Particulates

**OVERVIEW AND PURPOSE** Many of us go through life unaware of particulates in the air, but allergy or asthma sufferers may become uncomfortably aware of high particulate levels. Certain particles, such as dust mite casings, can trigger asthma attacks. Particles that cling to surfaces can make them look dirty or even damage them. Some colors of surfaces may hide the dirt. In this investigation you will

- compare the number and types of particles that settle to surfaces in two different locations
- learn a method of counting particles

## Problem

How do the types and numbers of particles in two different locations compare?

## Hypothesize

You should decide on the locations in step 3 before writing your hypothesis. Write a hypothesis to explain how particulates collected at two different locations might differ. Your hypothesis should take the form of an "If . . . , then . . . , because . . ." statement.

**MATERIALS**
- 2 index cards
- ruler
- scissors
- transparent packing tape
- magnifying glass
- white paper
- black paper
- graph paper
- calculator

## Procedure

1. Use the ruler to mark on each index card a centered square that is 3 cm per side. Carefully cut out each square.

2. On each card, place a piece of tape so that it covers the hole. Press the edges of the tape to the card, but do not let the center of the tape stick to anything. You should have a clean sticky window when you turn the card over.

3. Choose two different collecting locations where you can safely leave your cards—sticky side up—undisturbed overnight. You might place them on outside and inside windowsills, on the ground and in a tree, or in different rooms.

4. Mark each card with your name, the date, and the location. Tape the cards in place or weigh them down so they will not blow away. Write your hypothesis. Collect your cards the next day.

## Observe and Analyze

Write It Up

1. **OBSERVE** Use the magnifying glass to inspect each card closely. Can you identify any of the particles? Try using white paper and black paper behind the card to help you see dark and light particles better. Describe and draw in your **Science Notebook** the types of particles from each card. How does the background affect the type or number of particles you see?
2. **RECORD** Make a data table like the one shown on the notebook page below. Then, place each card onto a piece of graph paper. Line up the top and left edges of each card's center square with the grid on the graph paper and tape the card down. Choose four graph-paper squares and count the number of visible particles in each square. Use the magnifying glass. Record your results on the data table.
3. **CALCULATE**

**AVERAGE** Calculate the average number of particles per square for each card.

$$\text{average} = \frac{\text{sum of particles in 4 squares}}{4}$$

**CONVERT** Use the formula below to convert from particles per square to particles per square centimeter. If your squares were half a centimeter wide, then use 0.5 cm in the denominator below.

$$\text{particles per cm}^2 = \text{particles per square} \times \left(\frac{\text{1 square}}{\text{width (in cm) of square}}\right)^2$$

## Conclude

Write It Up

1. **COMPARE** Compare the types of particles found on the cards. List similarities and differences. Compare the numbers of particles found on the cards.
2. **INTERPRET** Compare your results with your hypothesis. Do your data support your hypothesis?
3. **INFER** What can you infer about where the particles came from or how they reached each location? What evidence did you find to support these inferences?
4. **IDENTIFY LIMITS** What possible limitations or sources of error might have affected your results? Why was it necessary to average the number of particles from several squares?
5. **EVALUATE** Do you think the color of the graph paper affected the number of particles you were able to count?
6. **APPLY** What color would you choose for playground equipment in your area? Explain your choice.

## INVESTIGATE Further

**CHALLENGE** Design an experiment to find out how fast particles in one location are deposited.

Observing Particulates

Problem How do the types and numbers of particles in two different locations compare?

Hypothesize

Observe and Analyze

Table 1. Number of Particles

| | Number of Particles | | | | | | Notes |
|---|---|---|---|---|---|---|---|
| | Sq. 1 | Sq. 2 | Sq. 3 | Sq. 4 | Ave./ sq. | Ave./ $cm^2$ | |
| Card 1 | | | | | | | |
| Card 2 | | | | | | | |

Conclude

# 1 Chapter Review

## the BIG idea

**Earth's atmosphere is a blanket of gases that supports and protects life.**

## KEY CONCEPTS SUMMARY

### 1.1 Earth's atmosphere supports life.

The **atmosphere** is a thin layer surrounding Earth. Gases in the atmosphere provide substances essential for living things. Natural **cycles** and sudden changes affect the atmosphere.

**VOCABULARY**
**atmosphere** p. 9
**altitude** p. 10
**density** p. 10
**cycle** p. 12

### 1.2 The Sun supplies the atmosphere's energy.

Energy from the Sun moves through Earth's atmosphere in three ways.

radiation

convection

conduction

Density and temperature change with altitude. The layers, from top to bottom, are

- thermosphere
- mesosphere
- stratosphere
- troposphere

**VOCABULARY**
**radiation** p. 17
**conduction** p. 18
**convection** p. 19

### 1.3 Gases in the atmosphere absorb radiation.

Ozone molecules in the stratosphere absorb harmful ultraviolet radiation.

Greenhouse gases in the troposphere keep Earth warm by absorbing and emitting infrared radiation.

**VOCABULARY**
**ultraviolet radiation** p. 23
**infrared radiation** p. 23
**ozone** p. 23
**greenhouse effect** p. 24
**greenhouse gas** p. 24

### 1.4 Human activities affect the atmosphere.

Human activities have added pollutants and ozone-destroying chemicals to the atmosphere.

ozone

The amounts of greenhouse gases have been increasing and global temperatures are rising.

carbon dioxide

**VOCABULARY**
**air pollution** p. 27
**particulate** p. 28
**fossil fuel** p. 28
**smog** p. 28

## Reviewing Vocabulary

*Draw a word triangle for each of the vocabulary terms listed below. Define the term, use it in a sentence, and draw a picture to help you remember the term. A sample is shown below.*

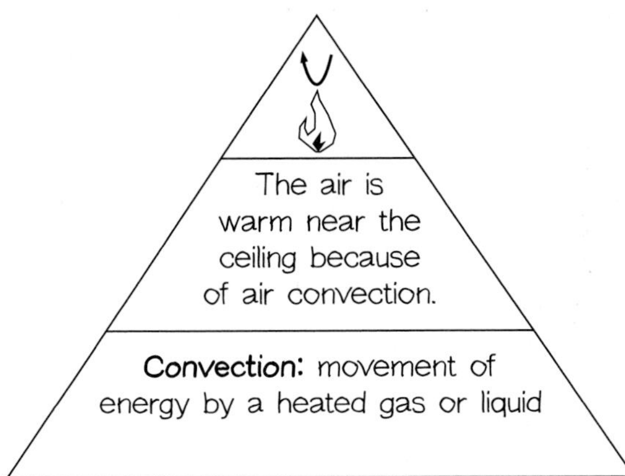

The air is warm near the ceiling because of air convection.
Convection: movement of energy by a heated gas or liquid


1. conduction
2. atmosphere
3. density
4. air pollution
5. altitude
6. radiation
7. cycle
8. particulate

## Reviewing Key Concepts

**Multiple Choice** *Choose the letter of the best answer.*

**9.** Which of the following represents a sudden change in Earth's atmosphere?
- **a.** the carbon cycle
- **b.** the nitrogen cycle
- **c.** a rain shower
- **d.** a dust storm

**10.** The gas that makes up the largest percentage of the atmosphere's substance is
- **a.** nitrogen
- **b.** oxygen
- **c.** water vapor
- **d.** carbon dioxide

**11.** Which of the cycles below involves oxygen gas?
- **a.** the carbon cycle
- **b.** the water cycle
- **c.** the density cycle
- **d.** the argon cycle

**12.** What process moves energy from Earth's surface to high in the troposphere?
- **a.** solar energy
- **b.** conduction
- **c.** convection
- **d.** the nitrogen cycle

**13.** In which of the atmosphere's layers does temperature decrease as the altitude increases?
- **a.** the troposphere and the stratosphere
- **b.** the troposphere and the mesosphere
- **c.** the stratosphere and the mesosphere
- **d.** the stratosphere and the thermosphere

**14.** What keeps Earth's surface warm?
- **a.** conduction
- **b.** the ozone layer
- **c.** convection
- **d.** the greenhouse effect

**15.** Which gas absorbs ultraviolet radiation?
- **a.** carbon dioxide
- **b.** methane
- **c.** ozone
- **d.** water vapor

**16.** Which type of pollution includes harmful droplets?
- **a.** particulate
- **b.** gas
- **c.** dust
- **d.** smoke

**Short Answer** *Write a short answer to each question.*

**17.** Explain why ozone is helpful to life in the stratosphere but harmful in the troposphere.

**18.** Describe three of the ways human activities affect the atmosphere.

**19.** Write a brief paragraph describing how the photograph below provides evidence that Earth's atmosphere is in motion.

## Thinking Critically

*Use the photographs to answer the next two questions.*

A

cold water hot water

B

In the demonstration pictured above, hot water has been tinted red with food coloring, and cold water has been tinted blue. View B shows the results after the divider has been lifted and the motion of the water has stopped.

**20. OBSERVE** Describe how the hot water and the cold water moved when the divider was lifted.

**21. APPLY** Use your understanding of density to explain the motion of the water.

**22. CALCULATE** The top of Mount Everest is 8850 meters above sea level. Which layer of the atmosphere contains the top of this mountain? Use the information from page 20 and convert the units.

**23. APPLY** Why is radiation from Earth's surface and atmosphere important for living things?

**24. PREDICT** Dust is often light in color, while soot from fires is generally dark. What would happen to the amounts of solar radiation reflected and absorbed if a large amount of light-colored dust was added to the air? What if a large amount of dark soot was added?

**25. IDENTIFY EFFECT** When weather conditions and sunlight are likely to produce smog, cities may ask motorists to refuel their cars at night instead of early in the day. Why would this behavior make a difference?

**26. COMPARE** How are the processes in the diagram on page 18 similar to those in the illustration below?

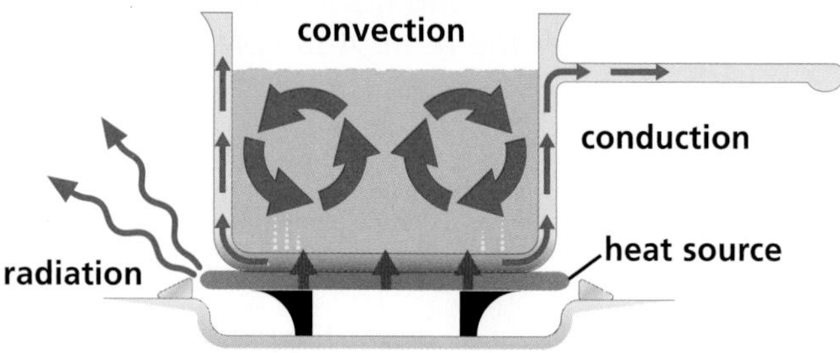


**27. CONNECT** Give an example from everyday life that shows that the atmosphere has substance.

**28. EVALUATE** If you had a choice between burning natural gas to cook or using electricity from a power plant, which would you choose? Explain the issues involved. **Hint:** Where does the power plant get energy?

## the BIG idea

**29. SYNTHESIZE** Write one or more paragraphs describing the specific ways that the atmosphere supports and protects life. In your description, use each of the terms below. Underline each term in your answer.

| carbon dioxide | solar radiation |
|---|---|
| water | ozone |
| oxygen | stratosphere |
| cycle | |

**30. APPLY** Look again at the photograph on pages 6–7. Now that you have finished the chapter, how would you change or add details to your answer to the question on the photograph?

## UNIT PROJECTS

If you are doing a unit project, make a folder for your project. Include in your folder a list of the resources you will need, the date on which the project is due, and a schedule to track your progress. Begin gathering data.

# Standardized Test Practice

## Interpreting Graphs

*The following three graphs show the amounts of three types of air pollutants released into the atmosphere in the United States each year from 1950 to 1990. Study the graphs closely and use the information to answer the first four questions.*

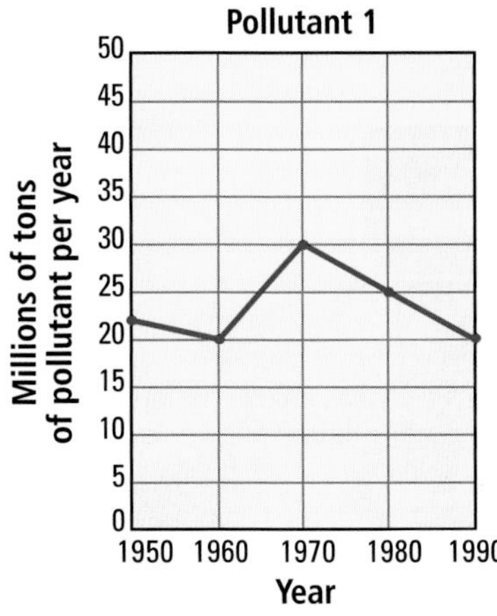


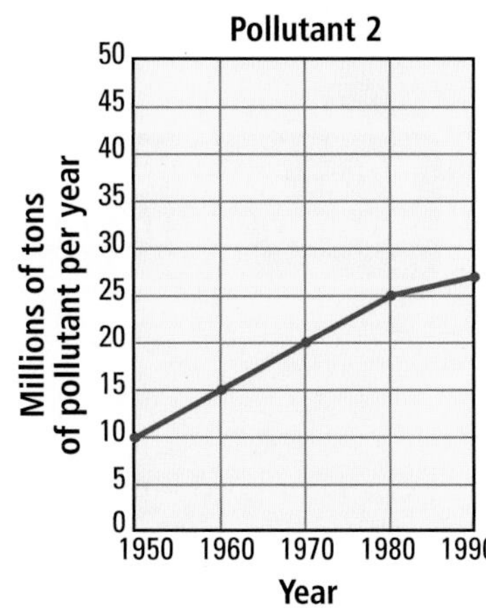


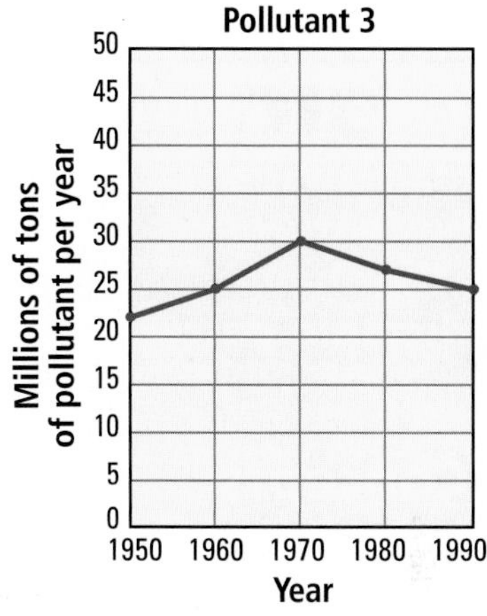


**1.** What conclusion can you make about pollutant 1?

**a.** The release of pollutant 1 has steadily decreased since 1970.
**b.** More pollutant 1 has been released since 1990.
**c.** More pollutant 1 has been released since 1970.
**d.** The release of pollutant 1 has not changed.

**2.** Based on the graph for pollutant 2, which of the following is true?

**a.** The release of pollutant 2 declined after 1950.
**b.** The release of pollutant 2 has increased since 1970.
**c.** The release of pollutant 2 declined and then rose.
**d.** About 15 million tons of pollutant 2 were released in 1990.

**3.** Compare the graphs for pollutants 1 and 2. Which of the following statements is supported by the graphs?

**a.** In 1950, more pollutant 1 was released than pollutant 2.
**b.** Since 1980, no pollutant 1 has been released.
**c.** In 1990, twice as much pollutant 2 was released as pollutant 1.
**d.** Since 1950, no pollutant 1 has been released.

**4.** About how many million tons of pollutant 3 entered the atmosphere in the United States in 1990?

**a.** 10
**b.** 15
**c.** 25
**d.** 30

## Extended Response

*Answer the next two questions in detail. Use in your answers some of the terms from the word box. In your answer, underline each term you use.*

| | | |
|---|---|---|
| oxygen | nitrogen | energy |
| water | air density | carbon dioxide |
| altitude | absorption | |

**5.** Luz builds a terrarium for her class science fair. She puts her pet slug in with the plants. She covers the terrarium with clear plastic that has vent holes. She places it in a sunlit window. How do the soil, plants, slug, sunlight, and plastic affect the air in Luz's terrarium?

**6.** Mile High Stadium in Denver, Colorado, makes bottled oxygen available to its players. Players at lower altitudes do not need extra oxygen. Explorers pack bottled oxygen when they climb tall mountains, such as Mount Everest. Explain why extra oxygen might be necessary for players in Mile High Stadium and climbers on tall mountains.

CHAPTER

# Weather Patterns

## the BIG idea

Some features of weather have predictable patterns.

## Key Concepts

SECTION

**The atmosphere's air pressure changes.**
Learn how air pressure changes and how it is measured.

SECTION

**The atmosphere has wind patterns.**
Learn how wind develops and about different types of wind.

SECTION

**Most clouds form as air rises and cools.**
Learn how water changes form in the atmosphere and about different types of clouds.

SECTION

**Water falls to Earth's surface as precipitation.**
Learn about the different types of precipitation and about acid rain.

### Internet Preview

CLASSZONE.COM

Chapter 2 online resources: Content Review, two Visualizations, four Resource Centers, Math Tutorial, Test Practice

*What weather conditions do you see in the distance?*

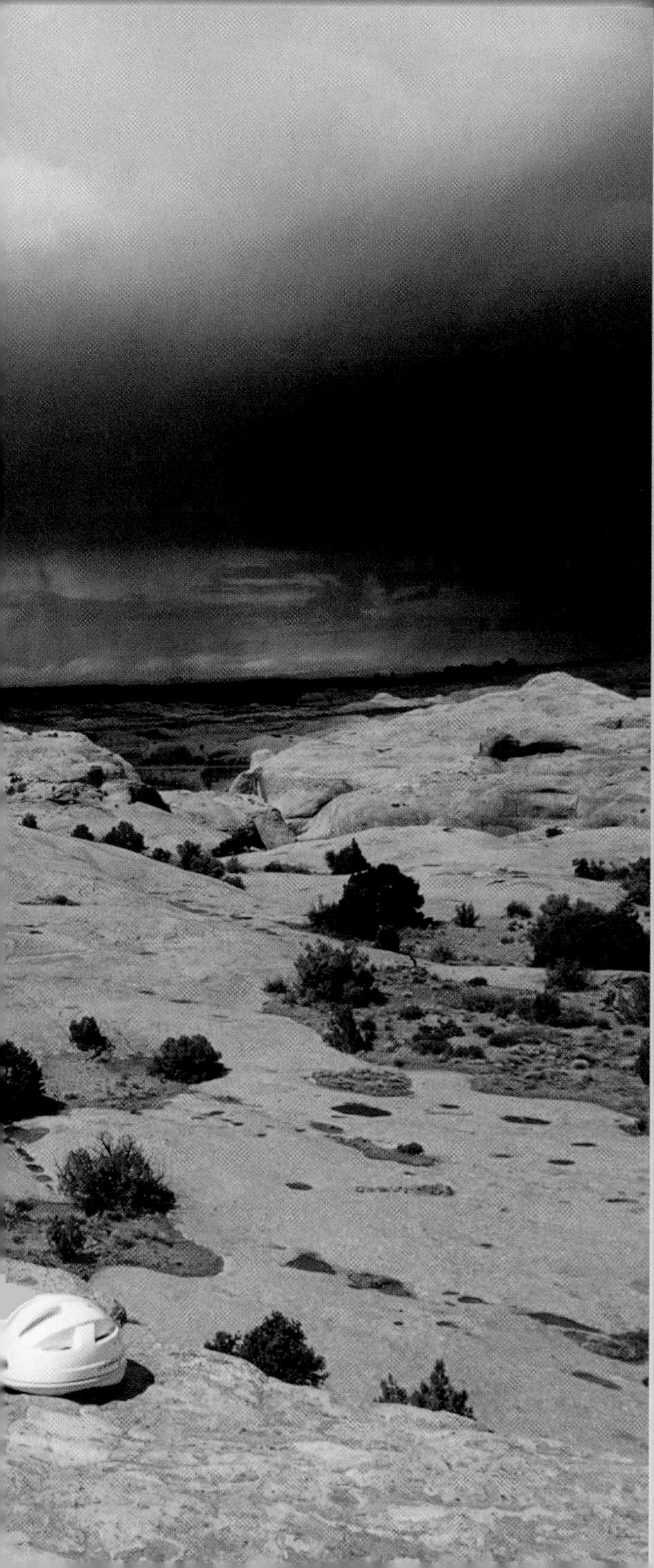

# EXPLORE the BIG idea

## Are You Stronger Than Air?

Line a wide-mouthed jar with a plastic bag. Secure the bag tightly with a rubber band. Reach in and try to pull the bag out of the jar.

**Observe and Think**
How easy was it to move the plastic bag? What was holding the bag in place?

## How Does Air Motion Affect Balloons?

Tie two balloons to a pencil 5 centimeters apart as shown. Gently blow air between the balloons.

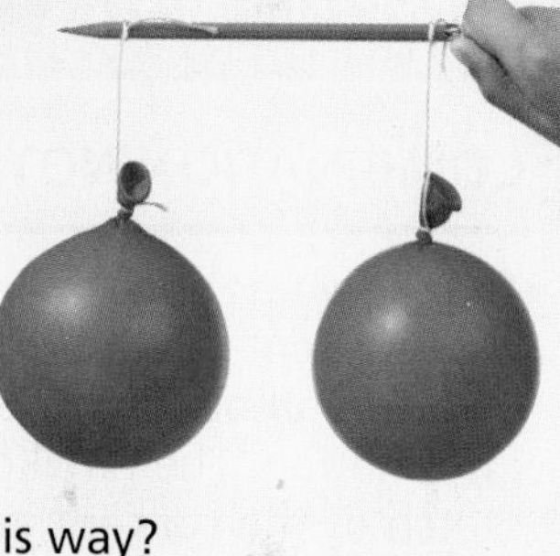

**Observe and Think**
How did the balloons move? Why did the air make them move this way?

## Internet Activity: Wind

Go to **ClassZone.com** to explore how breezes blowing over land and water change over the course of an entire day.

**Observe and Think**
What patterns can you see in winds that occur near water?

Atmospheric Pressure and Winds **Code: MDL010**

CHAPTER 2

# Getting Ready to Learn

## CONCEPT REVIEW

- The Sun supplies the atmosphere's energy.
- Energy moves throughout the atmosphere.
- Matter can be solid, liquid, or gas.

## VOCABULARY REVIEW

**atmosphere** p. 9
**altitude** p. 10
**density** p. 10
**convection** p. 19

Review concepts and vocabulary.

## TAKING NOTES

### COMBINATION NOTES

To take notes about a new concept, first make an informal outline of the information. Then make a sketch of the concept and label it so that you can study it later.

### VOCABULARY STRATEGY

Place each vocabulary term at the center of a **description wheel.** Write some words describing it on the spokes.

SCIENCE NOTEBOOK

NOTES

Air pressure
- is the force of air molecules pushing on an area
- pushes in all directions

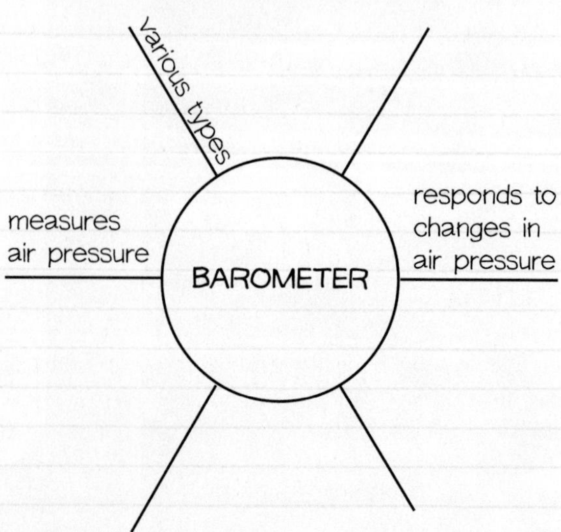


See the Note-Taking Handbook on pages R45–R51.

KEY CONCEPT

# The atmosphere's air pressure changes.

**BEFORE, you learned**

- Density is the amount of mass in a given volume of a substance
- Air becomes less dense as altitude increases
- Differences in density cause air to rise and sink

**NOW, you will learn**

- How the movement of air molecules causes air pressure
- How air pressure varies
- How differences in air pressure affect the atmosphere

**VOCABULARY**

**air pressure** p. 43
**barometer** p. 46

**EXPLORE Air Pressure**

### *What does air do to the egg?*

**PROCEDURE**

1. Set a peeled hard-boiled egg in the mouth of a bottle. Make sure that the egg can't slip through.
2. Light the matches. Remove the egg, and drop the matches into the bottle. Quickly replace the egg.
3. Watch carefully, and record your observations.

**MATERIALS**

- peeled hard-boiled egg
- glass bottle
- 2 wooden matches

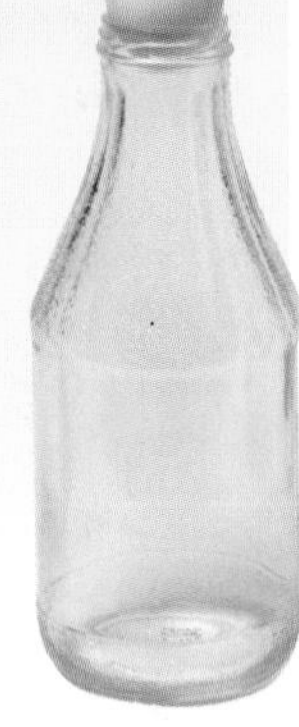

**WHAT DO YOU THINK?**

- What happened when you placed the egg back on top of the bottle?
- What can your observations tell you about the air in the bottle?

## Air exerts pressure.

Air molecules move constantly. As they move, they bounce off each other like rubber balls. They also bounce off every surface they hit. As you read this book, billions of air molecules are bouncing off your body, the book, and everything else around you.

Each time an air molecule bounces off an object, it pushes, or exerts a force, on that object. When billions of air molecules bounce off a surface, the force is spread over the area of that surface. **Air pressure** is the force of air molecules pushing on an area. The greater the force, the higher the air pressure. Because air molecules move in all directions, air pressure pushes in all directions.

**VOCABULARY**
Add a description wheel for *air pressure* to your notebook.

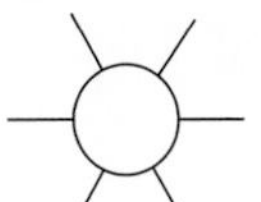

**CHECK YOUR READING** How does the number of air molecules relate to air pressure?

## Air pressure is related to altitude and density.

**COMBINATION NOTES**
Record details about how air pressure varies.

The air pressure at any area on Earth depends on the weight of the air above that area. If you hold out your hand, the force of air pushing down on your hand is greater than the weight of a bowling ball. So why don't you feel the air pushing down on your hand? Remember that air pushes in all directions. The pressure of air pushing down is balanced by the pressure of air pushing up from below.

Air pressure decreases as you move higher in the atmosphere. Think of a column of air directly over your body. If you stood at sea level, this column would stretch from where you stood to the top of the atmosphere. The air pressure on your body would be equal to the weight of all the air in the column. But if you stood on a mountain, the column of air would be shorter. With less air above you, the pressure would be lower. At an altitude of 5.5 kilometers (3.4 mi), air pressure is about half what it is at sea level.

**REMINDER**
Density is the amount of mass in a given volume of a substance.

Air pressure and density are related. Just as air pressure decreases with altitude, so does the density of air. Notice in the illustration that air molecules at sea level are closer together than air molecules over the mountain. Since the pressure is greater at sea level, the air molecules are pushed closer together. Therefore, the air at sea level is denser than air at high altitudes.

### Air Pressure and Density

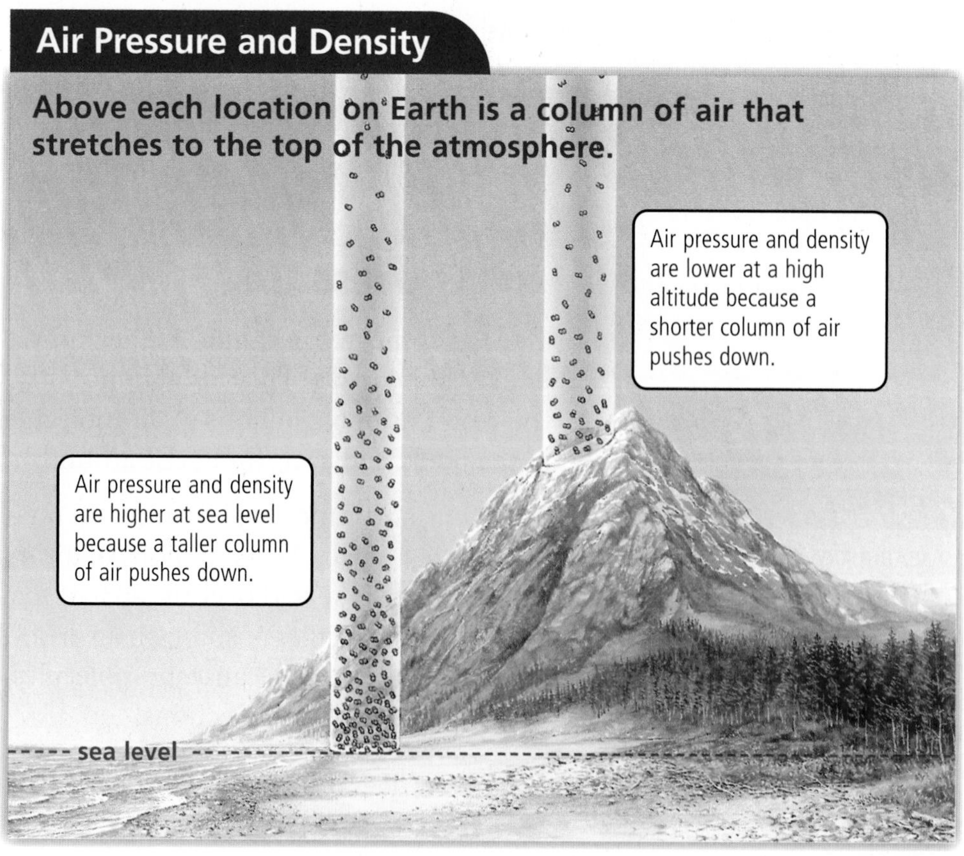

Above each location on Earth is a column of air that stretches to the top of the atmosphere.
Air pressure and density are lower at a high altitude because a shorter column of air pushes down.
Air pressure and density are higher at sea level because a taller column of air pushes down.
sea level

## Pressure and Air Motion

You've read that air pressure decreases as you move to higher altitudes. Air pressure also often varies in two locations at the same altitude. You can observe how such pressure differences affect air when you open a new can of tennis balls. You may hear a hiss as air rushes into the can. The air inside the sealed can of tennis balls is at a lower pressure than the air outside the can. When you break the seal, air moves from outside the can toward the lower pressure inside it.

Find out more about air pressure.

Air pressure differences in the atmosphere affect air in a similar way. If the air pressure were the same at all locations, air wouldn't move much. Because of differences in pressure, air starts to move from areas of higher pressure toward areas of lower pressure. The air may move only a short distance, or it may travel many kilometers. You will learn more about how air moves in response to pressure differences in Section 2.2.

**CHECK YOUR READING** How do differences in air pressure affect the movement of air?

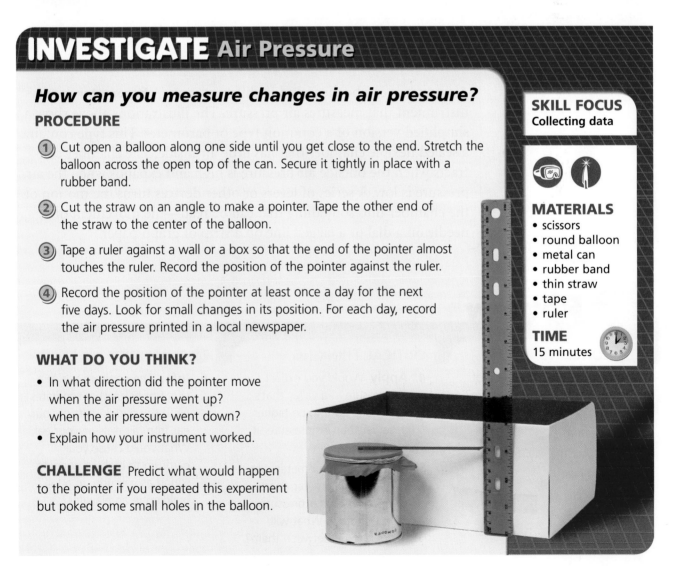

## INVESTIGATE Air Pressure

### *How can you measure changes in air pressure?*

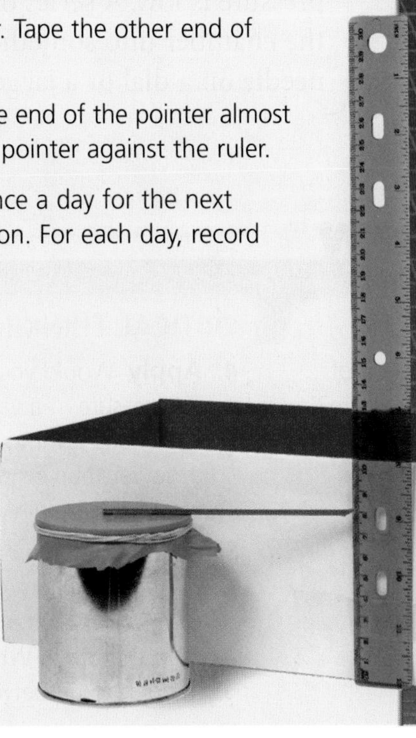

**SKILL FOCUS**
Collecting data

**MATERIALS**
- scissors
- round balloon
- metal can
- rubber band
- thin straw
- tape
- ruler

**TIME**
15 minutes

**PROCEDURE**

1. Cut open a balloon along one side until you get close to the end. Stretch the balloon across the open top of the can. Secure it tightly in place with a rubber band.
2. Cut the straw on an angle to make a pointer. Tape the other end of the straw to the center of the balloon.
3. Tape a ruler against a wall or a box so that the end of the pointer almost touches the ruler. Record the position of the pointer against the ruler.
4. Record the position of the pointer at least once a day for the next five days. Look for small changes in its position. For each day, record the air pressure printed in a local newspaper.

**WHAT DO YOU THINK?**

- In what direction did the pointer move when the air pressure went up? when the air pressure went down?
- Explain how your instrument worked.

**CHALLENGE** Predict what would happen to the pointer if you repeated this experiment but poked some small holes in the balloon.

## How a Barometer Works

### High Air Pressure

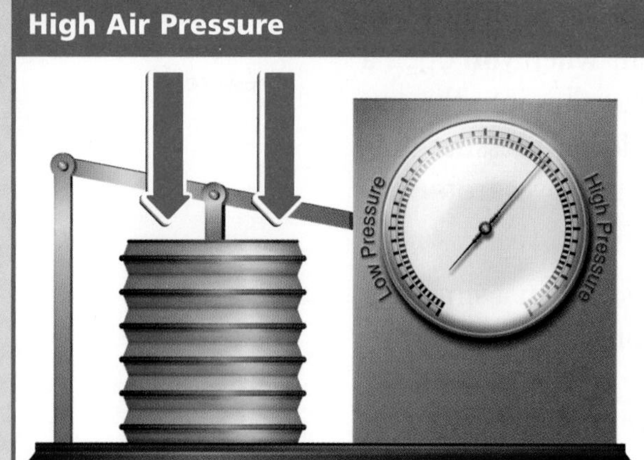


The flexible chamber on the barometer contracts when the air pressure increases.

### Low Air Pressure

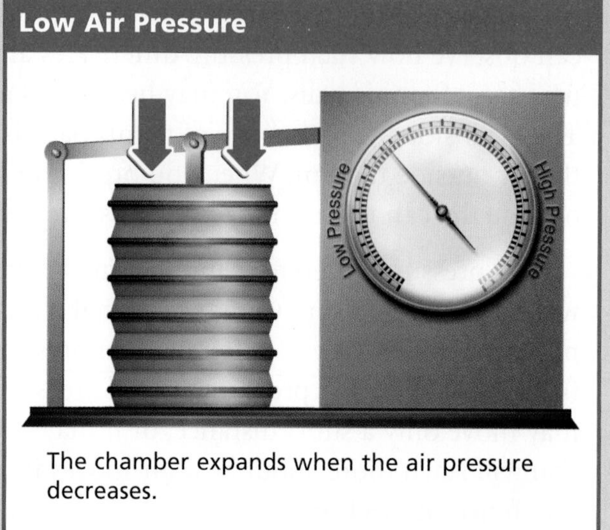


The chamber expands when the air pressure decreases.

**READING VISUALS** Which of these barometer readings would be the more likely one on a mountain? Explain why.

## Barometers and Air Pressure

Air pressure can be measured in different ways. A **barometer** is any instrument that measures air pressure. The illustrations above show a simplified version of a common type of barometer. This type contains a sealed flexible chamber that has little air inside. The chamber contracts when the outside air pressure is high and expands when the air pressure is low. A series of levers or other devices turns the motion of the chamber into something that can be read—the movement of a needle on a dial or a jagged line on a strip of graph paper.

# 2.1 Review

### KEY CONCEPTS

1. How does the movement of air molecules cause pressure?
2. How does altitude affect air pressure?
3. How is air density related to air pressure?

### CRITICAL THINKING

4. **Apply** Would you expect the air pressure in a valley that's below sea level to be higher or lower than air pressure at sea level? Explain.
5. **Predict** Two barometers are placed one kilometer apart. One shows higher pressure than the other. What will happen to air between them?

### CHALLENGE

6. **Infer** The eardrum is a thin sheet of tissue that separates air in the middle part of your ear from air outside your ear. What could cause your eardrum to make a popping sound as you ride up a tall building in an elevator?

KEY CONCEPT

# The atmosphere has wind patterns.

**BEFORE, you learned**

- Solar energy heats Earth's surface and atmosphere
- Differences in density cause air to move
- Air pressure differences set air in motion

**NOW, you will learn**

- About forces that affect wind
- About global winds
- About patterns of heating and cooling

**VOCABULARY**

**weather** p. 47
**wind** p. 47
**global wind** p. 48
**Coriolis effect** p. 49
**jet stream** p. 52
**monsoon** p. 54

**EXPLORE Solar Energy**

***How does Earth's shape affect solar heating?***

**PROCEDURE**

1. Place a globe on a desk in a darkened room.
2. Point a flashlight at the equator on the globe from a distance of about 15 centimeters. Keep the flashlight level. Observe the lighted area on the globe.
3. Keeping the flashlight level, raise it up and point it at the United States. Observe the lighted area.

**MATERIALS**

- globe
- flashlight
- ruler

**WHAT DO YOU THINK?**

- How were the two lighted areas different?
- What might have caused the difference?

## Uneven heating causes air to move.

On local news broadcasts, weather forecasters often spend several minutes discussing what the weather will be like over the next few days. **Weather** is the condition of Earth's atmosphere at a particular time and place. Wind is an important part of weather. You will read about other weather factors later in this chapter.

**Wind** is air that moves horizontally, or parallel to the ground. Remember that air pressure can differ from place to place at the same altitude. Uneven heating of Earth's surface causes such pressure differences, which set air in motion. Over a short distance, wind moves directly from higher pressure toward lower pressure.

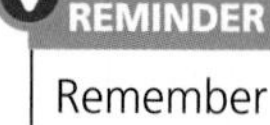

Remember that air pressure is the force that air molecules exert on an area.

What is the relationship between air pressure and wind?

View an animation of the Coriolis effect.

## How Wind Forms

1 Warmer air rises.
2 Cooler air sinks.

3 Wind moves across surface.

The illustration above shows a common pattern of air circulation caused by uneven heating of Earth's surface:

1. Sunlight strongly heats an area of ground. The ground heats the air. The warm air rises, and an area of low pressure forms.
2. Sunlight heats an area of ground less strongly. The cooler, dense air sinks slowly, and an area of high pressure forms.
3. Air moves as wind across the surface, from higher toward lower pressure.

When the difference in pressure between two areas is small, the wind may move too slowly to be noticeable. A very large pressure difference can produce wind strong enough to uproot trees.

**CHECK YOUR READING** What factor determines the strength of wind?

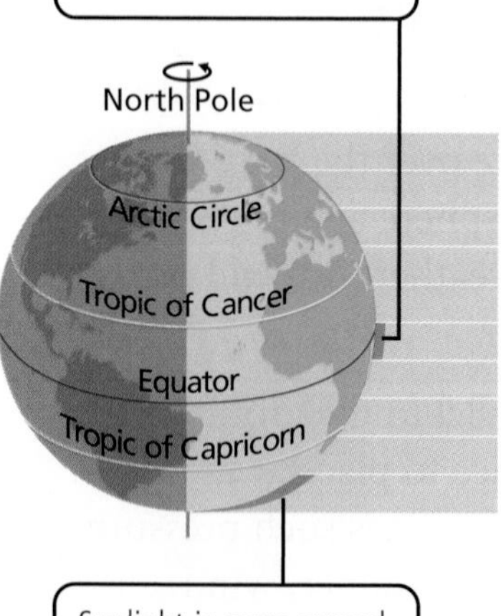

Sunlight is concentrated near the equator because it strikes the surface directly.
North Pole
Arctic Circle
Tropic of Cancer
Equator
Tropic of Capricorn
Sunlight is more spread out near the poles because it strikes at a lower angle.

The distance winds travel varies. Some winds die out quickly after blowing a few meters. In contrast, **global winds** travel thousands of kilometers in steady patterns. Global winds last for weeks.

Uneven heating between the equator and the north and south poles causes global winds. Notice in the illustration at left how sunlight strikes Earth's curved surface. Near the equator, concentrated sunlight heats the surface to a high temperature. Warm air rises, producing low pressure.

In regions closer to the poles, the sunlight is more spread out. Because less of the Sun's energy reaches these regions, the air above them is cooler and denser. The sinking dense air produces high pressure that sets global winds in motion.

## Earth's rotation affects wind direction.

If Earth did not rotate, global winds would flow directly from the poles to the equator. However, Earth's rotation changes the direction of winds and other objects moving over Earth. The influence of Earth's rotation is called the **Coriolis effect** (KAWR-ee-OH-lihs). Global winds curve as Earth turns beneath them. In the Northern Hemisphere, winds curve to the right in the direction of motion. Winds in the Southern Hemisphere curve to the left. The Coriolis effect is noticeable only for winds that travel long distances.

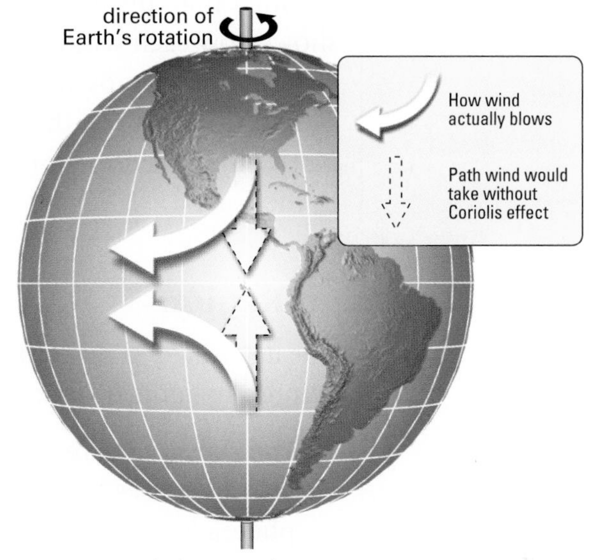


Because the Coriolis effect causes global winds to curve, they cannot flow directly from the poles to the equator. Instead, global winds travel along three routes in each hemisphere. These routes, which circle the world, are called global wind belts.

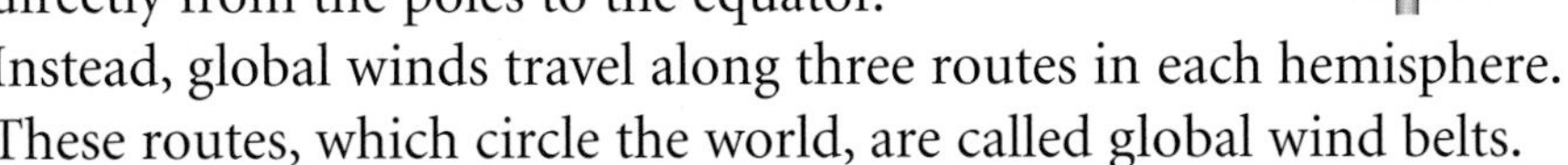

In which direction do winds curve in the Northern Hemisphere?

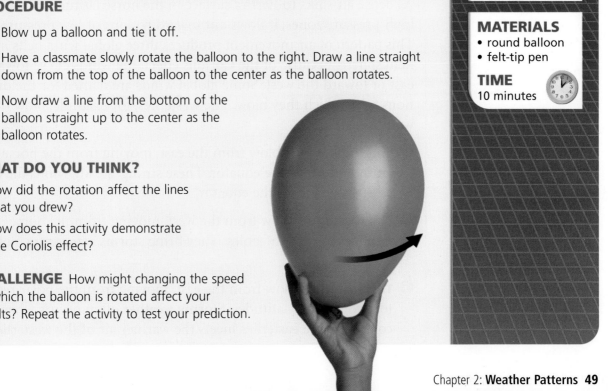

## INVESTIGATE Coriolis Effect

### How does Earth's rotation affect wind?

**SKILL FOCUS**
Modeling

**MATERIALS**
- round balloon
- felt-tip pen

**TIME**
10 minutes

**PROCEDURE**

1. Blow up a balloon and tie it off.
2. Have a classmate slowly rotate the balloon to the right. Draw a line straight down from the top of the balloon to the center as the balloon rotates.
3. Now draw a line from the bottom of the balloon straight up to the center as the balloon rotates.

**WHAT DO YOU THINK?**

- How did the rotation affect the lines that you drew?
- How does this activity demonstrate the Coriolis effect?

**CHALLENGE** How might changing the speed at which the balloon is rotated affect your results? Repeat the activity to test your prediction.

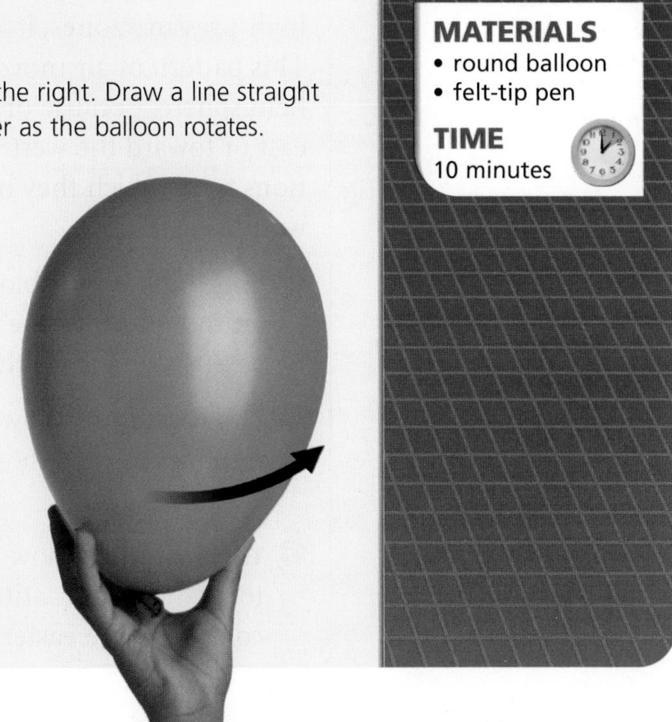

## Bands of calm air separate global wind belts.

Learn more about global winds.

Earth's rotation and the uneven heating of its surface cause a pattern of wind belts separated by calm regions. Each calm region is a zone of either high pressure or low pressure. The illustration on page 51 shows how each wind belt and the calm regions that border it form a giant loop of moving air. These loops are called circulation cells. The section of a cell that flows along Earth's surface is global wind. Notice that the direction of airflow changes from one circulation cell to the next.

### Calm Regions

The air usually stays calm in high-pressure and low-pressure zones. Winds are light, and they often change direction.

**READING TIP**

As you read about each region or wind belt, locate it in the diagram on page 51.

1. **The doldrums** are a low-pressure zone near the equator. There, warm air rises to the top of the troposphere, which is the atmosphere's lowest layer. Then the air spreads out toward the poles. The rising, moist air produces clouds and heavy rain. During the hottest months, heavy evaporation from warm ocean water in the region fuels tropical storms.

2. **The horse latitudes** are high-pressure zones located about 30° north and 30° south of the equator. Warm air traveling away from the equator cools and sinks in these regions. The weather tends to be clear and dry.

### Wind Belts

As dense air sinks to Earth's surface in the horse latitudes and other high-pressure zones, it flows out toward regions of low pressure. This pattern of air movement produces three global wind belts in each hemisphere. Because of the Coriolis effect, the winds curve toward the east or toward the west. Some global winds are named for the directions from which they blow. The westerlies, for example, blow from west to east.

3. **The trade winds** blow from the east, moving from the horse latitudes toward the equator. These strong, steady winds die out as they come near the equator.

4. **The westerlies** blow from the west, moving from the horse latitudes toward the poles. They bring storms across much of the United States.

5. **The easterlies** blow from the east, moving from the polar regions toward the mid-latitudes. Stormy weather often occurs when the cold air of the easterlies meets the warmer air of the westerlies.

## Global Winds

**Belts of global wind circle Earth. Because of the Coriolis effect, the winds in these belts curve to the east or the west. Between the global wind belts are calm areas of rising or falling air.**

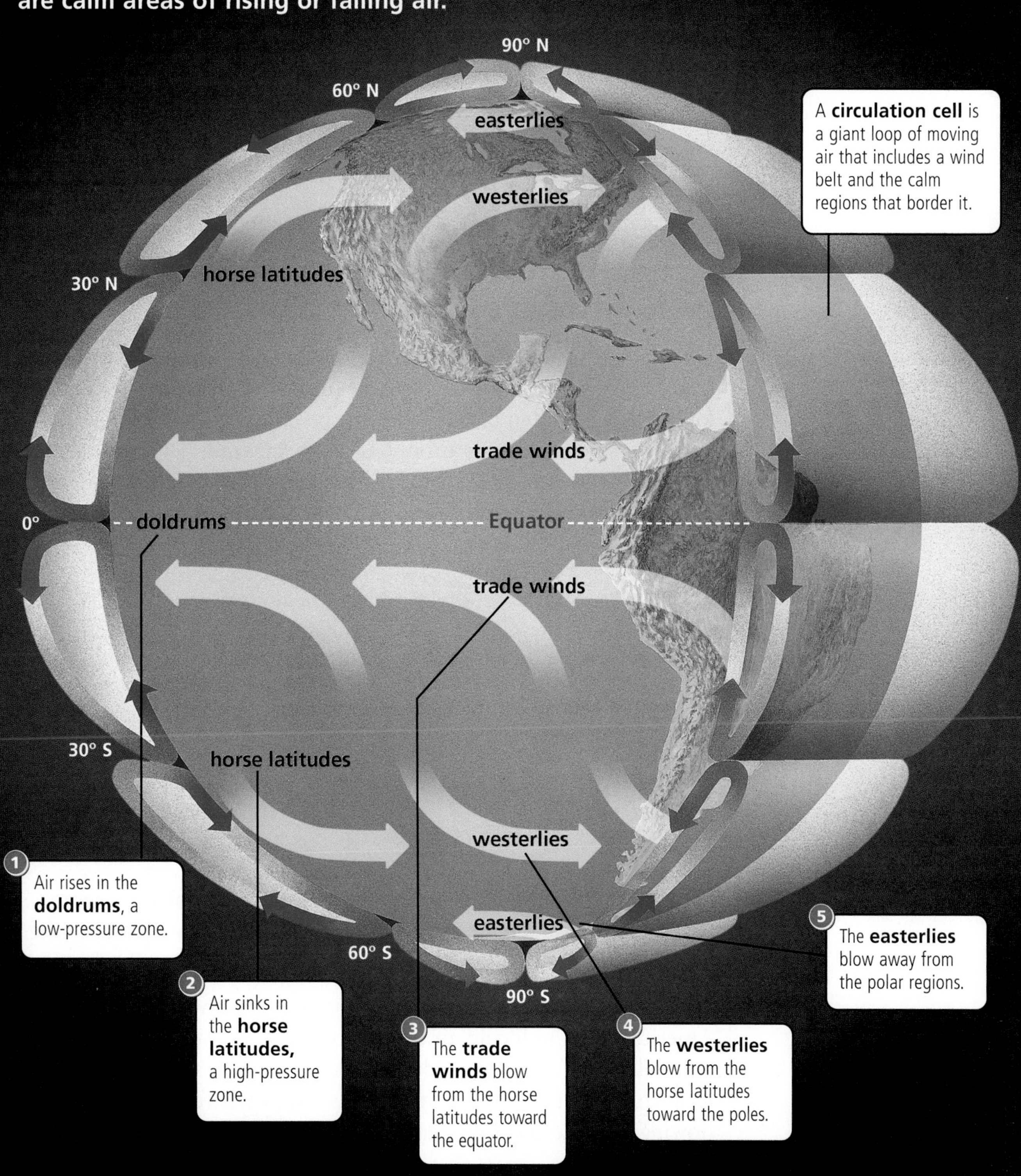

90° N
60° N
easterlies
westerlies
30° N
horse latitudes
trade winds
0°
doldrums
Equator
trade winds
30° S
horse latitudes
westerlies
easterlies
60° S
90° S
A **circulation cell** is a giant loop of moving air that includes a wind belt and the calm regions that border it.
1 Air rises in the **doldrums**, a low-pressure zone.
2 Air sinks in the **horse latitudes,** a high-pressure zone.
3 The **trade winds** blow from the horse latitudes toward the equator.
4 The **westerlies** blow from the horse latitudes toward the poles.
5 The **easterlies** blow away from the polar regions.

**READING VISUALS** What are the positions of the calm regions and the wind belts in the circulation cells?

### Effects of Wind on Travel

Before the invention of steam engines, sailors used to dread traveling through the doldrums and the horse latitudes. There often wasn't enough wind to move their sailing ships. A ship might stall for days or even weeks, wasting precious supplies of food and fresh water.

To avoid the calm regions, sailors sought out global wind belts. The trade winds got their name because traders used them to sail from east to west. For centuries, sailors relied on the trade winds to reach North America from Europe. They would return by sailing north to catch the westerlies and ride them across the Atlantic.

## Jet streams flow near the top of the troposphere.

**COMBINATION NOTES**
Record information about how jet streams flow and their effects on weather and travel.

Not all long-distance winds travel along Earth's surface. **Jet streams** usually flow in the upper troposphere from west to east for thousands of kilometers. Air often moves in jet streams at speeds greater than 200 kilometers per hour (124 mi/hr). Like global winds, jet streams form because Earth's surface is heated unevenly. Instead of following a straight line, jet streams loop north and south, as shown on the globe below.

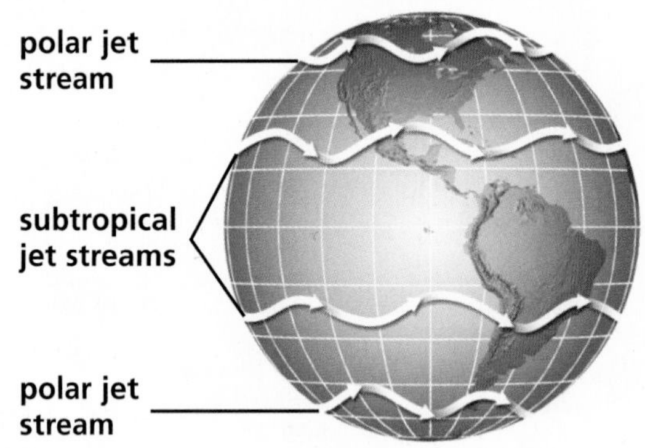


Jet streams flow in a wavy pattern from west to east around the world. They change positions during the year.

Each hemisphere usually has two jet streams, a polar jet stream and a subtropical jet stream. The polar jet streams flow closer to the poles in summer than in winter.

The polar jet stream has a strong influence on weather in North America. It can pull cold air down from Canada into the United States and pull warm air up toward Canada. In addition, strong storms tend to form along its loops. Scientists must know where the jet stream is flowing to make accurate weather predictions.

Jet streams also affect air-travel times. They usually flow 10 to 15 kilometers (6–9 mi) above Earth's surface. Since airplanes often fly at these altitudes, their travel times can be lengthened or shortened by the strong wind of a jet stream.

## Patterns of heating and cooling cause local winds and monsoons.

Have you ever noticed how the wind can change in predictable ways? For example, at the beach on a hot day you will often feel a cool breeze coming off the water. At night a breeze will flow in the opposite direction. The change in the breeze occurs because water and land heat up and cool down at different rates.

### Local Winds

Some winds change daily in a regular pattern. These local winds blow within small areas.

- Sea breezes and land breezes occur near shorelines. During the day, land heats up faster than water. The air over the land rises and expands. Denser ocean air moves into the area of low pressure, producing a sea breeze. As the illustration below shows, this pattern is reversed at night, when land cools faster than water. Warm air rises over the ocean, and cooler air flows in, producing a land breeze.

Sea Breeze
Warmer air rises over land during the day.
Cooler air blows in from water.
Land Breeze
Cooler air blows out from land.
Warmer air rises over water at night.

**REMINDER**
Red arrows stand for warmer air. Blue arrows stand for cooler air.

- Valley breezes and mountain breezes are caused by a similar process. Mountain slopes heat up and cool faster than the valleys below them. During the day, valley breezes flow up mountains. At night mountain breezes flow down into valleys.

**CHECK YOUR READING** How do mountains and bodies of water affect patterns of heating and cooling?

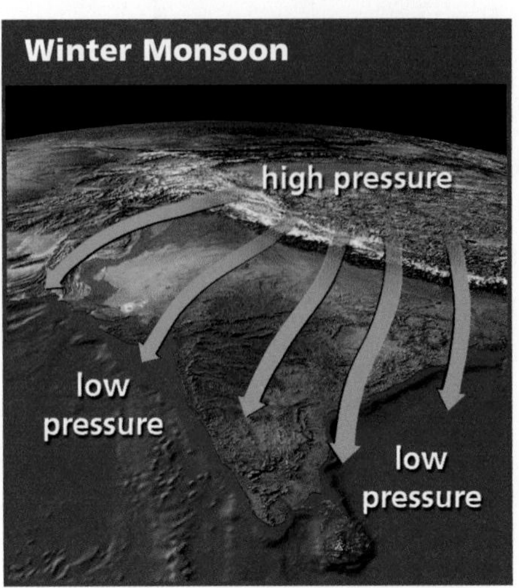


Dry air blows from the high-pressure area over the continent to the low-pressure areas over the ocean.

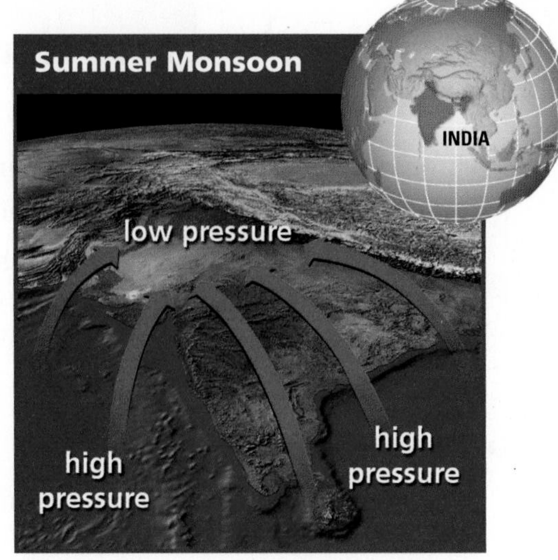


Moist air blows from the high-pressure areas over the ocean to the low-pressure area over the continent.

## Monsoons

**VOCABULARY**
Add a description wheel for *monsoon* to your notebook.

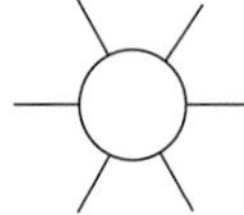

Winds that change direction with the seasons are called **monsoons.** Like sea breezes and land breezes, monsoons are caused by the different heating and cooling rates of land and sea. However, monsoons flow longer distances and affect much larger areas.

Winter monsoons occur in regions where the land becomes much cooler than the sea during winter. High pressure builds over the land, and cool, dry wind blows out toward the sea. During summer this pattern reverses as the land becomes much warmer than the sea. Moist wind flows inland, often bringing heavy rains. The most extreme monsoons occur in South Asia and Southeast Asia. Farmers there depend on rain from the summer monsoon to grow crops.

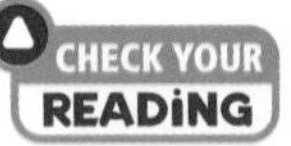
**CHECK YOUR READING** How do monsoon winds affect rainfall?

# 2.2 Review

### KEY CONCEPTS

1. How does the uneven heating of Earth's surface cause winds to flow?
2. How does Earth's rotation influence the movement of global winds?
3. Why do some winds change direction in areas where land is near water?

### CRITICAL THINKING

4. **Compare and Contrast** How are global winds and local winds similar? How are they different?
5. **Analyze** Make a table that shows the causes and effects of local winds and monsoons.

### CHALLENGE

6. **Predict** Suppose that a city is located in a valley between the sea and a mountain range. What kind of wind pattern would you predict for this area?

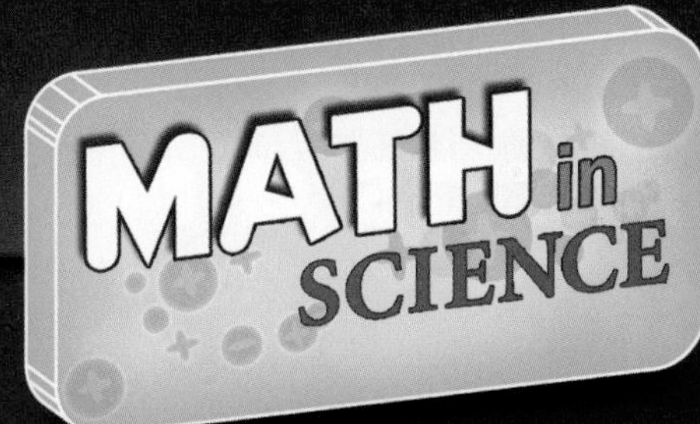


SKILL: ADDING MEASUREMENTS

# Navigate the Jet Stream

When an airplane is flying in the same direction as a jet stream, the airplane gets a boost in its speed. Pilots can save an hour or more if they fly with the jet stream. On the other hand, flying against the jet stream can slow an airplane down.

**MATH TUTORIAL**
CLASSZONE.COM

Click on Math Tutorial for more help with adding measures of time.

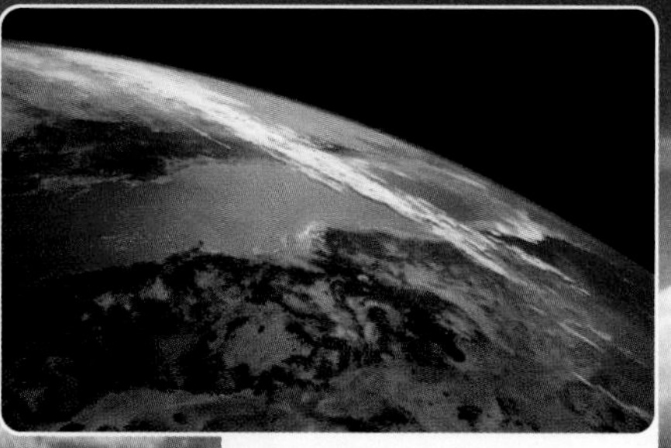

High clouds show the location of the jet stream in this satellite image.

## Example

To determine the total flight time between San Francisco and Chicago, with a stop in Denver, you need to add the hours and minutes separately. Set up the problem like this:

| | | |
|---|---|---|
| San Francisco to Denver: | 2 h | 10 min |
| Denver to Chicago: | 1 h | 45 min |
| Total flight time: | 3 h | 55 min |

**ANSWER** The total flight time is 3 hours 55 minutes.

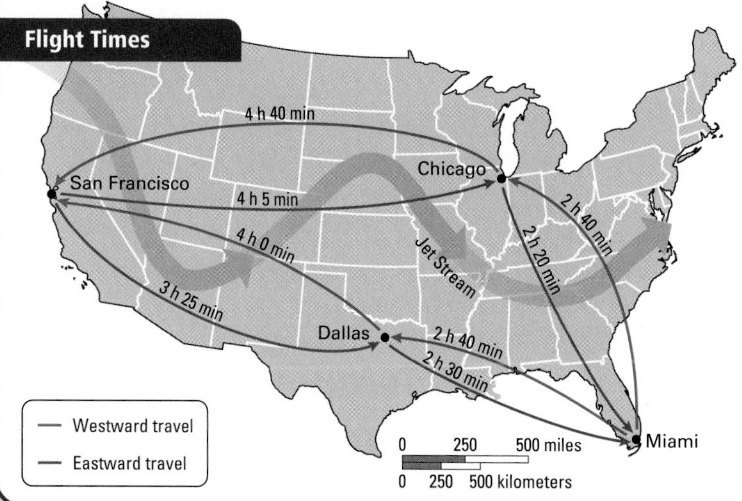


**Use the map to answer the following questions.**

1. What is the total flight time for an airliner flying from San Francisco to Miami through Chicago?
2. What is the total flight time for an airliner flying from San Francisco to Miami through Dallas?
3. How much time will the fastest possible trip from Miami to San Francisco take?
4. Compare the flight time from Chicago to San Francisco with the flight time from San Francisco to Chicago.

**CHALLENGE** What is the total flight time from Miami to San Francisco through Chicago? Convert minutes to hours if necessary.

KEY CONCEPT

# Most clouds form as air rises and cools.

**BEFORE, you learned**

- Water vapor circulates from Earth to the atmosphere
- Warm air is less dense than cool air and tends to rise

**NOW, you will learn**

- How water in the atmosphere changes
- How clouds form
- About the types of clouds

**VOCABULARY**

**evaporation** p. 56
**condensation** p. 56
**precipitation** p. 57
**humidity** p. 58
**saturation** p. 58
**relative humidity** p. 58
**dew point** p. 58

**EXPLORE Condensation**

### How does condensation occur?

**PROCEDURE**

1. Observe the air as a classmate breathes out.
2. Observe a mirror as a classmate breathes onto it.

**MATERIALS**

hand mirror

**WHAT DO YOU THINK?**

- What changes did you observe on the mirror?
- Why could you see water on the mirror but not in the air when your classmate breathed out?

## Temperature affects water in the air.

Water is always in the atmosphere. You may see water in solid form, such as falling snow. Water may also be present as liquid water droplets. Even if you can't see any water, it is still part of the air as water vapor, an invisible gas. When temperatures change, water changes its form.

- **Evaporation** is the process by which a liquid changes into a gas. For water to evaporate, it needs extra energy.
- **Condensation** is the process by which a gas, such as water vapor, changes into a liquid. Condensation occurs when moist air cools.

The picture on the left shows the processes of evaporation and condensation at work. Water in a teakettle absorbs heat. It gets enough energy to evaporate into water vapor. The invisible water vapor rises and escapes from the kettle. When the vapor hits the cooler air outside the kettle, it cools and condenses into tiny but visible water droplets.

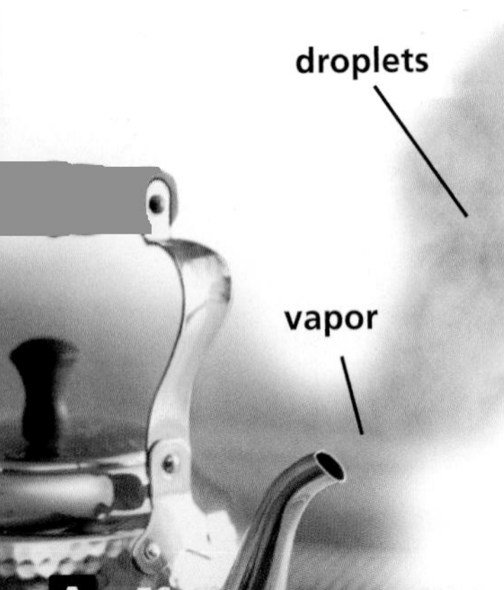

## Water in the Air

Vast amounts of Earth's water are recycled. The oceans hold most of the water. Water is also stored in lakes, rivers, and ice sheets; in plants; and underground. Energy from sunlight causes molecules to evaporate from the surface of a body of water. These molecules become part of the air in the form of water vapor.

As air rises in the atmosphere, it cools. The loss of heat causes water vapor to condense into tiny water droplets or ice crystals. If the droplets or crystals grow and become heavy enough, they fall as rain, snow, sleet, or hail. Any type of liquid or solid water that falls to Earth's surface is called **precipitation.** Earth's water goes through a never-ending cycle of evaporation, condensation, and precipitation.

**VOCABULARY**
Add a description wheel for *precipitation* to your notebook.

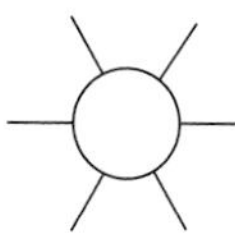

Water vapor can also condense on solid surfaces. Have you ever gotten your shoes wet while walking on grass in the early morning? The grass was covered with dew, which is water that has condensed on cool surfaces at night. If the temperature is cold enough, water vapor can change directly into a covering of ice, called frost.

**CHECK YOUR READING** Summarize the way water moves in the water cycle. For each part of the cycle, specify whether water exists as a gas, liquid, or solid.

### Water Cycle

1. Water evaporates from bodies of water.
2. Water vapor condenses to form clouds.
3. Water falls to Earth's surface as precipitation.

## Humidity and Relative Humidity

On a warm summer day, evaporation of moisture from your skin can help you feel comfortable. However, a lot of water vapor in the air can cause less moisture to evaporate from your skin. With less evaporation, the air will seem hotter and damper. **Humidity** is the amount of water vapor in air. Humidity varies from place to place and from time to time.

The illustration shows how humidity increases in a sealed container. As water molecules evaporate into the air, some start to condense and return to the water. For a while the air gains water vapor because more water evaporates than condenses. But eventually the air reaches **saturation,** a condition in which the rates of evaporation and condensation are equal. Any additional water that evaporates is balanced by water that condenses.

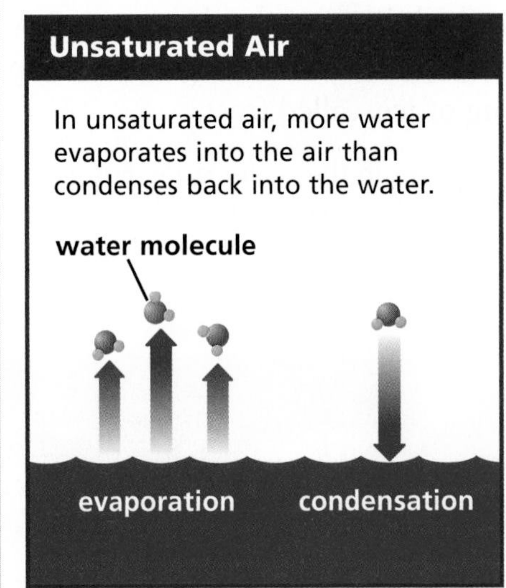

Unsaturated Air
In unsaturated air, more water evaporates into the air than condenses back into the water.
water molecule
evaporation
condensation

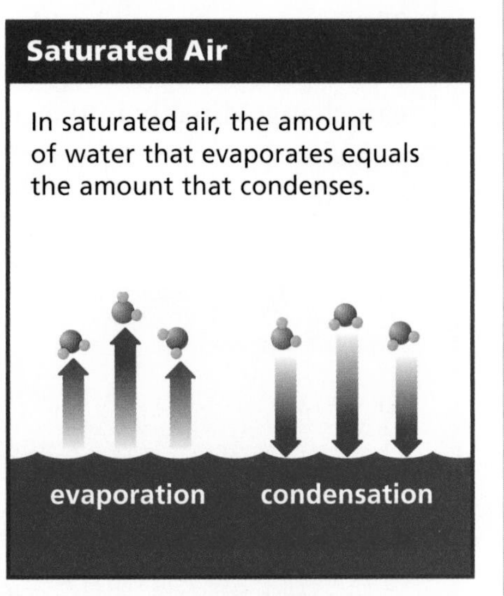

Saturated Air
In saturated air, the amount of water that evaporates equals the amount that condenses.
evaporation
condensation

**READING TIP**

*Relative* means "considered in comparison with something else."

The amount of water vapor in air at saturation depends on the temperature of the air. The warmer air is, the more water vapor it takes to saturate it. Scientists use this principle to describe the humidity of air in two different ways: relative humidity and dew point.

**Relative humidity** compares the amount of water vapor in air with the maximum amount of water vapor that can be present at that temperature. For example, air with 50 percent relative humidity has half the amount of water needed for saturation. If the amount of water vapor in air stays the same, relative humidity will decrease as the air heats up and increase as the air cools.

**Dew point** is the temperature at which air with a given amount of water vapor will reach saturation. For example, air with a dew point of 26°C (79°F) will become saturated if it cools to 26°C. The higher the dew point of air, the more water vapor the air contains.

## Water vapor condenses and forms clouds.

Clouds are made of condensed water vapor. As warm air rises in the atmosphere, it cools. When the air cools to its dew point—the temperature at which air reaches saturation—water vapor condenses into tiny droplets or ice crystals. These droplets and crystals are so light that they either float as clouds on rising air or fall very slowly.

Rising warm air can produce clouds. Water vapor begins to condense when the air cools to its dew point.

Recall how dew condenses on grass. Water must condense on something solid. There are no large solid surfaces in the air. However, the air is filled with tiny particles such as dust, smoke, and salt from the ocean. Water vapor condenses on these particles.

## INVESTIGATE Condensation

### *How does a cloud form?*

**PROCEDURE**

1. Add a spoonful of water to the bottle to increase the humidity inside it.
2. Lay the bottle on its side. Light a match, blow it out, and then stick the match into the bottle for a few seconds to let smoke flow in. Replace the cap.
3. Squeeze the bottle quickly and then release it. Observe what happens when the bottle is allowed to expand.

**WHAT DO YOU THINK?**

- What happened to the water vapor inside the bottle when you squeezed the bottle and then let it expand?
- How did the smoke affect what happened to the water vapor?

**CHALLENGE** How would the cloud change if you raised or lowered the temperature inside the bottle?

**SKILL FOCUS**
Observing

**MATERIALS**
- clear 1-liter plastic bottle with cap
- water at room temperature
- tablespoon
- matches

**TIME**
10 minutes

Observe different types of clouds.

## Characteristics of Clouds

If you watch the sky over a period of time, you will probably observe clouds that do not look alike. Clouds have different characteristics because they form under different conditions. The shapes and sizes of clouds are mainly determined by air movement. For example, puffy clouds form in air that rises sharply or moves straight up and down. Flat, smooth clouds covering large areas form in air that rises gradually.

Location affects the composition of clouds. Since the troposphere gets colder with altitude, clouds that form at high altitudes are made of tiny ice crystals. Closer to Earth's surface, clouds are made of water droplets or a mixture of ice crystals and water droplets.

**CHECK YOUR READING** How are clouds that form at high altitudes different from clouds that form close to Earth's surface?

**COMBINATION NOTES** Record information about the three main cloud types.

In the illustration on page 61, notice that some cloud names share word parts. That is because clouds are classified and named according to their altitudes, the ways they form, and their general characteristics. The three main types of clouds are cirrus, cumulus, and stratus. These names come from Latin words that suggest the clouds' appearances.

- ***Cirrus*** (SEER-uhs) means "curl of hair." Cirrus clouds appear feathery or wispy.
- ***Cumulus*** (KYOOM-yuh-luhs) means "heap" or "pile." Cumulus-type clouds can grow to be very tall.
- ***Stratus*** (STRAT-uhs) means "spread out." Stratus-type clouds form in flat layers.

Word parts are used to tell more about clouds. For example, names of clouds that produce precipitation contain the word part *nimbo-* or *nimbus.* Names of clouds that form at a medium altitude have the prefix *alto-*.

cirrus clouds

## Cirrus Clouds

Cirrus clouds form in very cold air at high altitudes. Made of ice crystals, they have a wispy or feathery appearance. Strong winds often blow streamers or "tails" off cirrus clouds. These features show the direction of the wind in the upper troposphere. You will usually see cirrus clouds in fair weather. However, they can be a sign that a storm is approaching.

## Cloud Types

**The three main cloud types are cirrus, cumulus, and stratus. These names can be combined with each other and with other word parts to identify more specific cloud types.**

cirrus

cirrocumulus

high altitude

cumulonimbus

cirrostratus

6000 m
20,000 ft

Clouds that produce precipitation often have names containing the word part *nimbo-* or *nimbus*.

altocumulus

Clouds that form at a medium altitude have names with the prefix *alto-*.

altostratus

medium altitude

2000 m
6500 ft

nimbostratus

low altitude

cumulus

stratus

READING VISUALS Which cloud names are combinations of names of two main cloud types?

READING TIP

As you read each description of a main cloud type, look back at the visual on page 61. Notice the different clouds that have the main cloud type as part of their names.

## Cumulus Clouds

cumulus clouds

Cumulus clouds are puffy white clouds with darker bases. They look like cotton balls floating in the sky. There are several varieties of cumulus clouds. Usually they appear in the daytime in fair weather, when warm air rises and its water vapor condenses. Cooler air sinks along the sides of the clouds, keeping cumulus clouds separate from one another.

cumulonimbus clouds

If cumulus clouds keep growing taller, they can produce showers. The precipitation usually lasts less than half an hour because there are spaces between the clouds. The tallest clouds are cumulonimbus clouds, or thunderheads. These clouds produce thunderstorms that drop heavy rainfall. A cumulonimbus cloud can tower 18 kilometers (11 mi) above Earth's surface. By comparison, jet planes usually fly at about 10 kilometers (6 mi). Strong high-altitude winds often cause the top of the cloud to jut out sharply.

How are cumulonimbus clouds different from other cumulus clouds?

## Stratus Clouds

stratus clouds

Have you ever noticed on some days that the whole sky looks gray? You were looking at stratus clouds. They form in layers when air cools over a large area without rising or when the air is gently lifted. Stratus clouds are smooth because they form without strong air movement.

Some low stratus clouds are so dark that they completely block out the Sun. These clouds produce steady, light precipitation—unlike the brief showers that come from cumulus clouds. Stratus clouds that form at high altitudes are much thinner than low stratus clouds. You can see the Sun and the Moon through them. The ice crystals in high stratus clouds can make it seem as if there's a circle of colored light around the Sun or the Moon.

This fog formed around Castleton Tower in Utah. The land cooled overnight, causing water vapor in the air above it to condense.

## Fog

Fog is a cloud that rests on the ground or a body of water. Like stratus clouds, fog has a smooth appearance. It usually forms when a surface is colder than the air above it. Water vapor in the air condenses as it cools, forming a thick mist. Fog on land tends to be heaviest at dawn, after the ground has cooled overnight. It clears as the ground is heated up by sunlight.

Fog can look beautiful rolling over hills or partly covering structures such as bridges. However, it often makes transportation dangerous by limiting visibility. In the United States close to 700 people die each year in automobile accidents that occur in dense fog.

# 2.3 Review

### KEY CONCEPTS

1. Describe the three forms in which water is present in the atmosphere.
2. How does altitude affect the composition of clouds?
3. How are clouds classified?

### CRITICAL THINKING

4. **Summarize** Describe the main characteristics of cirrus, cumulus, and stratus clouds.
5. **Draw Conclusions** Why might cumulonimbus clouds be more likely to form on sunny days than on days with little sunlight?

### CHALLENGE

6. **Apply** Imagine that the sky has turned very cloudy after a hot morning. You notice that the bread in your sandwich is soggy and the towels on the towel rack won't dry. Explain why these things are happening. Use the following terms in your answer: *condensation, evaporation, relative humidity.*

# CHAPTER INVESTIGATION

## Relative Humidity

**OVERVIEW AND PURPOSE** Finding out the relative humidity can help you predict how comfortable you will feel on a hot day or whether dew will form on the ground. You can use a psychrometer to measure relative humidity. A psychrometer is a device made from two thermometers—one with a wet bulb and the other with a dry bulb. In this activity you will

- make a milk-carton psychrometer
- use it to measure the relative humidity of the air at two locations in your school

### Problem

Which location will have the greater relative humidity?

### Hypothesize

Write a hypothesis in "If . . . , then . . . , because . . ." form to answer the problem.

**MATERIALS**

- 2 thermometers
- cotton or felt cloth
- 3 rubber bands
- plastic bowl
- water at room temperature
- scissors
- pint milk carton
- ruler
- Relative Humidity Chart

### Procedure

1. Make a table like the one shown on the sample notebook page to record your data.

2. Check the two thermometers that you are using in this experiment to make sure they read the same temperature. Wrap a piece of cotton or felt cloth around the bulb of one thermometer. Hold the cloth in place with a rubber band as shown in the photograph. Dip this wet-bulb thermometer into a bowl of room-temperature water until the cloth is soaked.

3. Use scissors to cut a small hole in one side of the milk carton, 2 centimeters from the bottom of the carton. Place the wet-bulb thermometer on the same side as the hole that you made in the milk carton, and attach it with a rubber band. Push the tail of the cloth through the hole. Attach the dry-bulb thermometer as shown.

step 3

4. Fill the carton with water to just below the hole so that the cloth will remain wet. Empty the bowl and place the completed psychrometer inside it.

5. Write "science room" under the heading "Location 1" in your data table. Take your first readings in the science classroom about 10 minutes after you set up your psychrometer. Read the temperatures on the two thermometers in degrees Celsius. Record the temperature readings for the first location in the first column of your table.

6. Choose a second location in your school, and identify it under the heading "Location 2" in the data table. Take a second set of temperature readings with your psychrometer in this location. Record the readings in the second column of your table.

7. Subtract the wet-bulb reading from the dry-bulb reading for each location. Record this information in the third row of your data table.

8. Use the relative humidity table your teacher provides to find each relative humidity (expressed as a percentage). In the left-hand column, find the dry-bulb reading for location 1 that you recorded in step 5. Then find in the top line the number you recorded in step 7 (the difference between the dry-bulb and wet-bulb readings). Record the relative humidity in the last row of your data table. Repeat these steps for location 2.

## Observe and Analyze

Write It Up

1. **RECORD OBSERVATIONS** Draw the setup of your psychrometer. Be sure your data table is complete.
2. **IDENTIFY** Identify the variables and constants in this experiment. List them in your **Science Notebook.**
3. **COMPARE** How do the wet-bulb readings compare with the dry-bulb readings?
4. **ANALYZE** If the difference between the temperature readings on the two thermometers is large, is the relative humidity high or low? Explain why.

## Conclude

1. **INTERPRET** Answer the question in the problem. Compare your results with your hypothesis.
2. **IDENTIFY LIMITS** Describe any possible errors that you made in following the procedure.
3. **APPLY** How would you account for the differences in relative humidity that you obtained for the two locations in your school?

## INVESTIGATE Further

**CHALLENGE** Use the psychrometer to keep track of the relative humidity in your classroom over a period of one week. Make a new chart to record your data. What do you notice about how the changes in relative humidity relate to the weather conditions outside?

Relative Humidity

Problem Which location will have the greater relative humidity?

Hypothesize

Observe and Analyze

Table 1. Relative Humidity at Two Locations

| | Location 1 | Location 2 |
|---|---|---|
| | | |
| Dry-bulb temperature | | |
| Wet-bulb temperature | | |
| Difference between dry-bulb and wet-bulb readings | | |
| Relative humidity | | |

Conclude

KEY CONCEPT

# Water falls to Earth's surface as precipitation.

**BEFORE, you learned**

- Water moves between Earth's surface and the atmosphere
- Water vapor condenses into clouds

**NOW, you will learn**

- How precipitation forms
- How precipitation is measured
- About acid rain

**VOCABULARY**

**freezing rain** p. 68
**sleet** p. 68
**hail** p. 68
**acid rain** p. 70

THINK ABOUT

***Why does steam from a shower form large drops?***

When you run a hot shower, the bathroom fills up with water vapor. The vapor condenses into tiny droplets that make it seem as if you are standing in fog. You may also see larger drops running down cool surfaces, such as a mirror. Why do some drops fall while others remain suspended?

## Precipitation forms from water droplets or ice crystals.

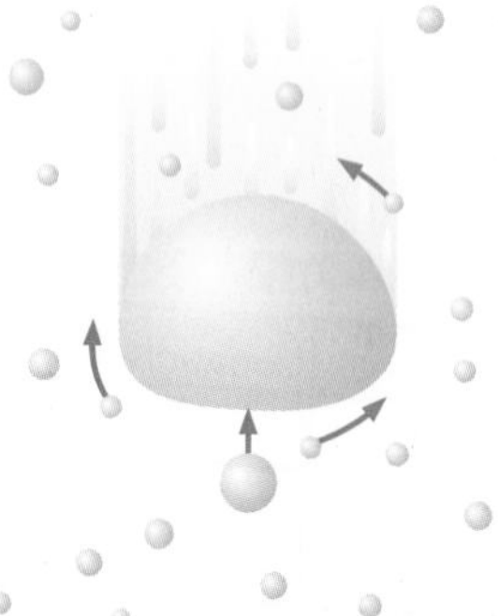

Water droplets combining to form a raindrop

All precipitation comes from clouds. For example, rain occurs when water droplets in a cloud fall to the ground. Then why doesn't every cloud produce precipitation? Cloud droplets are much smaller than a typical raindrop. They weigh so little that it takes only a slight upward movement of air to hold them up. In order for rain to fall from a cloud and reach Earth's surface, the cloud droplets must become larger and heavier.

One way that precipitation can form is through the combining of cloud droplets. The tiny droplets of water move up and down in clouds. Some collide with each other and combine, forming slightly bigger droplets. As the droplets continue to combine, they grow larger and larger. Eventually they become heavy enough to fall. It takes about a million droplets to make a single raindrop.

Another way that precipitation can form is through the growth of ice crystals. When the temperature inside a cloud is below freezing, water vapor changes into tiny ice crystals. The crystals grow by collecting more water vapor or by colliding and merging with one another. When the crystals become heavy enough, they fall from the cloud. Snow isn't the only type of precipitation that forms this way. Most rain in the United States actually starts out as falling ice crystals. Before the crystals reach the ground, they melt in a layer of warm air.

**CHECK YOUR READING** How do cloud droplets become large enough to fall as precipitation?

## Measuring Precipitation

Scientists use a rain gauge to measure rainfall. A funnel or opening at the top of the gauge allows rain to flow into a cylinder. By measuring the water collected, you can find out how much rain fell in a storm or over a period of time.

**READING TIP** A gauge (gayj) is an instrument used for measuring or testing.

Snow depth can be measured with a long ruler. Because the amount of water in snow varies, scientists use a special gauge to find out how much water the snow contains. A built-in heater melts the snow so that it can be measured just like rain.

# INVESTIGATE Precipitation

### *How much rain falls during a storm?*

**PROCEDURE**

1. Cut off the top third of the bottle. Set this part aside.
2. Put some gravel at the bottom of the bottle to keep it from tipping over. Add water to cover the gravel. Draw a horizontal line on the bottle at the top of the water. Use a ruler to mark off centimeters on the bottle above the line that you drew. Now take the part of the bottle that you set aside and turn it upside down. Fit it inside the bottle to create a funnel.
3. Place the bottle outside when a rainstorm is expected. Make sure that nothing will block rain from entering it. Check your rain gauge after 24 hours. Observe and record the rainfall.

**WHAT DO YOU THINK?**

- How much rain fell during the time period?
- How do the measurements compare with your observations?

**CHALLENGE** Do you think you would measure the same amount of rain if you used a wider rain gauge? Explain.

**SKILL FOCUS**
Measuring

**MATERIALS**
- scissors
- 1-liter plastic bottle
- gravel
- water
- permanent marker
- ruler

**TIME**
15 minutes

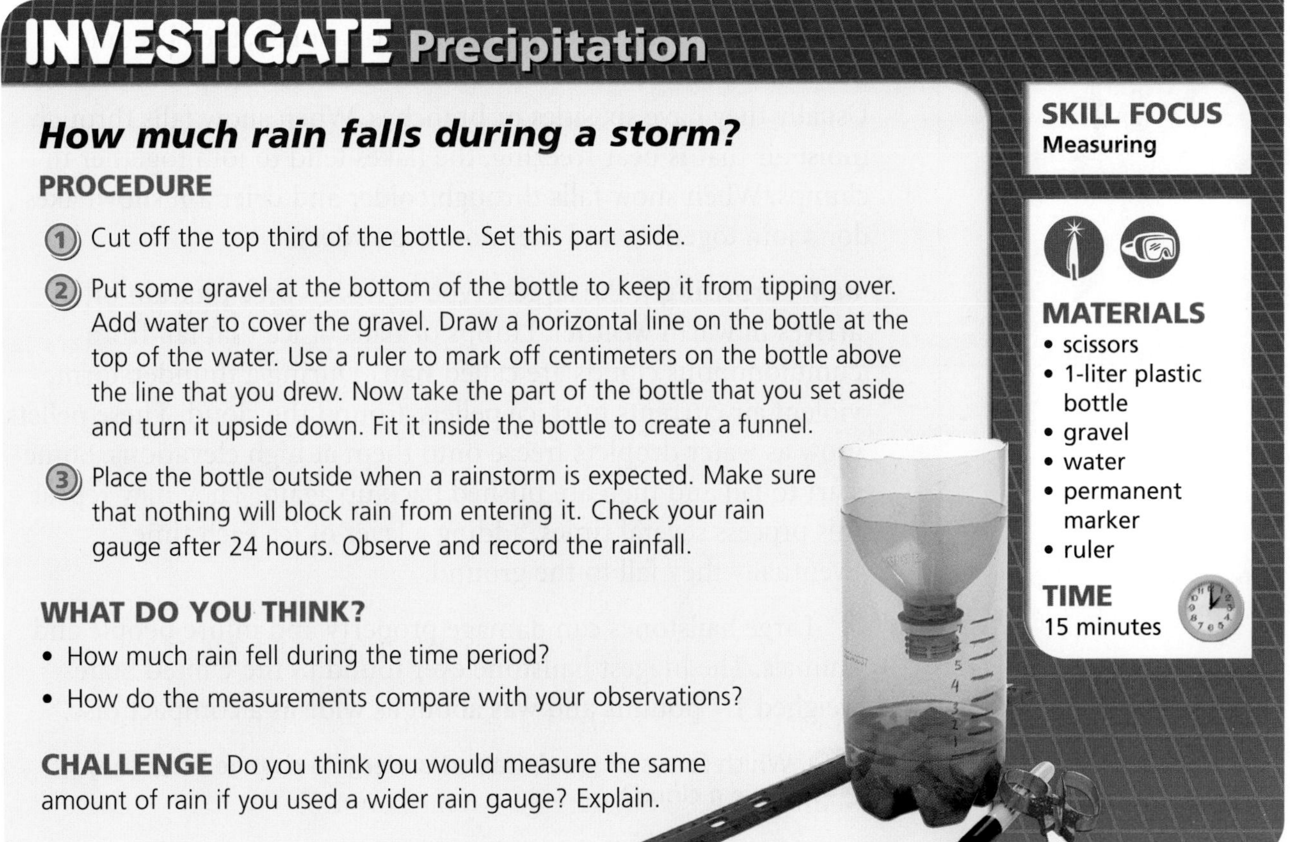

When you watch weather reports on television, you often see storm systems passing across a weather map. Some of these images are made with Doppler radar. The radar shows which areas are getting precipitation and how fast it is falling. Forecasters use this information to estimate the total amount of precipitation an area will receive.

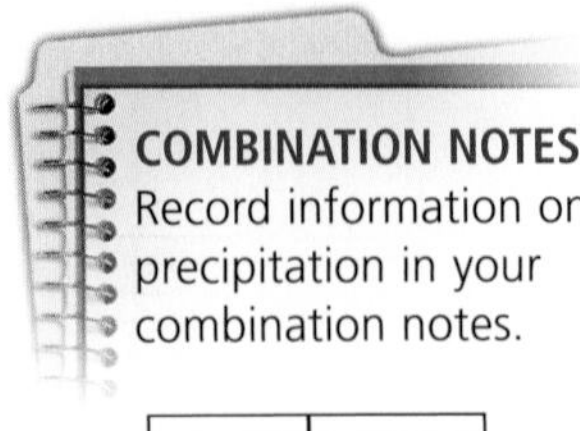


## Types of Precipitation

Precipitation reaches Earth's surface in various forms. Some precipitation freezes or melts as it falls through the atmosphere.

1. **Rain and Drizzle** Rain is the most common type of precipitation. Raindrops form from liquid cloud droplets or from ice crystals that melt as they fall. A light rain with very small drops is called drizzle. Drizzle usually comes from stratus clouds, which don't have enough air movement to build up larger raindrops.

2. **Freezing Rain** Raindrops may freeze when they hit the ground or other surfaces in cold weather. **Freezing rain** covers surfaces with a coating of ice. During an ice storm, roads become slippery and dangerous. The weight of ice can also bring down trees and power lines.

3. **Sleet** When rain passes through a layer of cold air, it can freeze before hitting the ground. The small pellets of ice that form are called **sleet.**

Most snowflakes have six branches or sides.

4. **Snow** As ice crystals grow and merge in clouds, they become snowflakes. Snowflakes come in many different shapes and sizes. Usually they have six sides or branches. When snow falls through moist air that is near freezing, the flakes tend to join together in clumps. When snow falls through colder and drier air, snowflakes don't join together, and the snow is powdery.

5. **Hail** Surprisingly, the largest type of frozen precipitation often arrives in warm weather. Lumps or balls of ice that fall from cumulonimbus clouds are called **hail.** During a thunderstorm, violent air currents hurl ice pellets around the cloud. These pellets grow as water droplets freeze onto them at high elevations. Some start to fall and then are pushed back up again. They may repeat this process several times, adding a layer of ice each time. Eventually they fall to the ground.

   Large hailstones can damage property and injure people and animals. The biggest hailstone ever found in the United States weighed 1.7 pounds and was about as wide as a compact disc.

Which forms of precipitation undergo a change after they leave a cloud?

## How Precipitation Forms

**All precipitation forms from water droplets or ice crystals in clouds. Some precipitation freezes or melts after it falls from the clouds.**

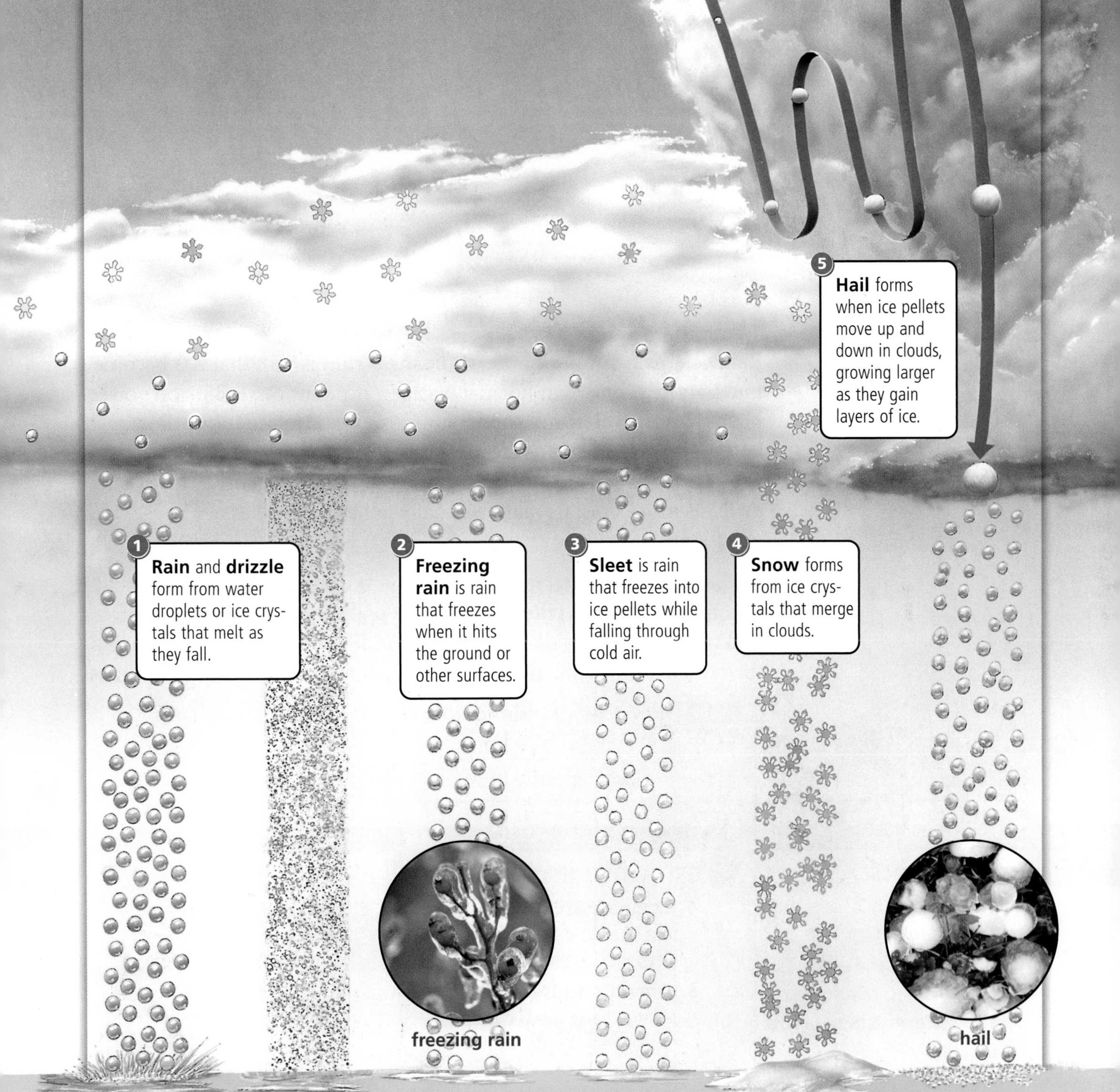

5 **Hail** forms when ice pellets move up and down in clouds, growing larger as they gain layers of ice.
1 **Rain** and **drizzle** form from water droplets or ice crystals that melt as they fall.
2 **Freezing rain** is rain that freezes when it hits the ground or other surfaces.
3 **Sleet** is rain that freezes into ice pellets while falling through cold air.
4 **Snow** forms from ice crystals that merge in clouds.
freezing rain
hail

**READING VISUALS** What forms of precipitation occur most often where you live?

These trees have few needles because acid rain has damaged the trees.

## Precipitation can carry pollution.

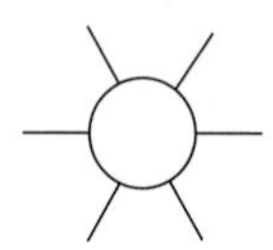

**VOCABULARY**
Add a description wheel for *acid rain* to your notebook.

Rainwater is naturally a little acidic. **Acid rain** is rain that has become much more acidic than normal because of pollution. Factories, power plants, automobiles, and some natural sources release sulfur dioxide and nitrogen oxides into the air. These gases can combine with water vapor to form sulfuric acid and nitric acid. The acids mix with cloud droplets or ice crystals that eventually fall to Earth's surface as precipitation.

Because wind can blow air pollution hundreds of kilometers, acid rain may fall far from the source of the pollution. Acid rain harms trees and raises the acidity of lakes, making it difficult for fish to live in them. Acid rain also damages the surfaces of buildings and sculptures.

**CHECK YOUR READING** How does acid rain form? Your answer should mention water vapor.

## 2.4 Review

### KEY CONCEPTS

1. What are the two ways that rain can form?
2. How are rain and snow measured?
3. What human activities cause acid rain?

### CRITICAL THINKING

4. **Compare and Contrast** How are sleet and freezing rain similar? How are they different?
5. **Draw Conclusions** When a large hailstone is cut open, four layers can be seen. What conclusions can you draw about the formation of the hailstone?

### CHALLENGE

6. **Predict** Temperatures in a cloud and on the ground are below freezing. A warmer layer of air lies between the cloud and the ground. What type of precipitation do you predict will occur? Explain.

# Caught Inside a Thunderhead

In 1959, engine failure forced Lieutenant Colonel William Rankin to eject from his plane at a high altitude. When his parachute opened, he thought he was out of danger. However, he soon realized that he was caught inside a cumulonimbus cloud during a fierce thunderstorm.

As Rankin hung by his parachute, violent air movement inside the cloud tossed him "up, down, sideways, clockwise." The rain was so heavy that he feared he would drown in midair. Lightning flashed all around him. Rankin finally landed 40 minutes after his adventure began. He had many injuries, including bruises from hailstones. Fortunately, none of the storm's lightning had struck him.

## Where Lightning Strikes

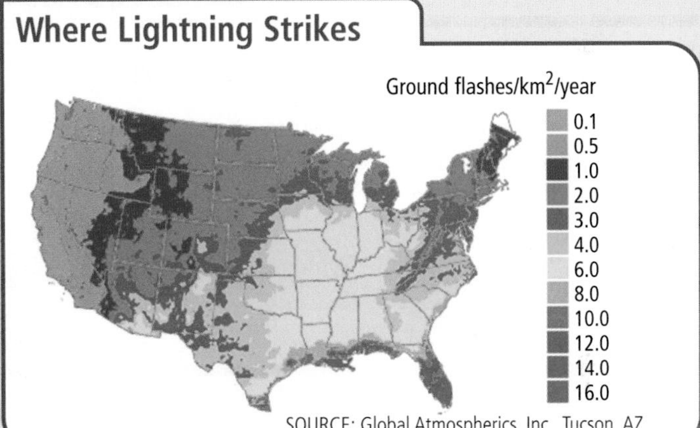


SOURCE: Global Atmospherics, Inc., Tucson, AZ

### Water, Wind, Hail, and Lightning

- A cumulonimbus cloud, or thunderhead, can rise to over 18 kilometers above Earth's surface. That's about twice the elevation of Mount Everest.
- A cumulonimbus cloud may contain 500,000 tons of water.
- Thunderstorm clouds cause 8 million lightning flashes each day.

### EXPLORE

1. **ANALYZE** Find where you live on the map. Use the color key to figure out how often lightning strikes each square kilometer in your area.
2. **CHALLENGE** Use information from the Resource Center to propose an explanation for the pattern of lightning frequencies shown on the map.

Learn more about lightning.

Lightning flashes to the ground from a thunderhead, or cumulonimbus cloud.

# Chapter Review

## the BIG idea

**Some features of weather have predictable patterns.**

## KEY CONCEPTS SUMMARY

### 2.1 The atmosphere's air pressure changes.

Air pressure is the force of air molecules pushing on an area. Air pressure decreases as you move higher in the atmosphere. Air pressure can also differ in two locations at the same altitude.

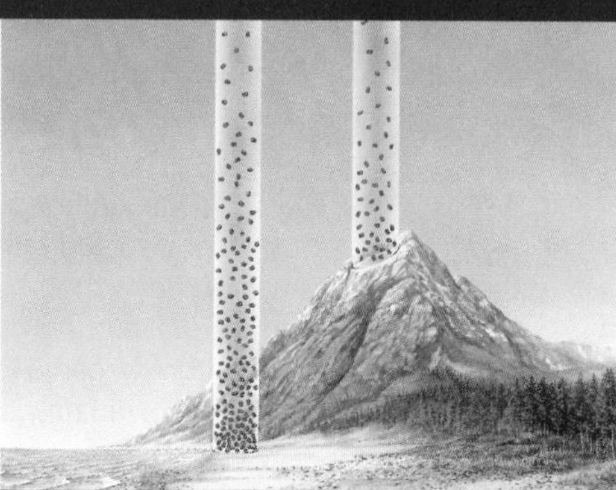

**VOCABULARY**
**air pressure** p. 43
**barometer** p. 46

### 2.2 The atmosphere has wind patterns.

Wind blows from areas of high pressure toward areas of low pressure. Earth's rotation causes long-distance winds to curve.

**area of high pressure** → *wind direction* → **area of low pressure**

**VOCABULARY**
**weather** p. 47
**wind** p. 47
**global wind** p. 48
**Coriolis effect** p. 49
**jet stream** p. 52
**monsoon** p. 54

### 2.3 Most clouds form as air rises and cools.

Clouds are made of tiny water droplets or ice crystals that condense from water vapor in rising air.

**VOCABULARY**
**evaporation** p. 56
**condensation** p. 56
**precipitation** p. 57
**humidity** p. 58
**saturation** p. 58
**relative humidity** p. 58
**dew point** p. 58

### 2.4 Water falls to Earth's surface as precipitation.

Water droplets in clouds merge to form raindrops.

Ice crystals in clouds can form snow, rain, and other types of precipitation.

**VOCABULARY**
**freezing rain** p. 68
**sleet** p. 68
**hail** p. 68
**acid rain** p. 70

## Reviewing Vocabulary

*Write a definition of each term. Use the meaning of the underlined root to help you.*

| Word | Root Meaning | Definition |
|---|---|---|
| EXAMPLE air pressure | to apply force | the force of air molecules pushing on an area |
| **1.** barometer | weight | |
| **2.** saturation | to fill | |
| **3.** global wind | sphere | |
| **4.** monsoon | season | |
| **5.** evaporation | steam | |
| **6.** condensation | thick | |
| **7.** humidity | moist | |
| **8.** precipitation | thrown down | |

## Reviewing Key Concepts

**Multiple Choice** *Choose the letter of the best answer.*

**9.** The movement of air molecules causes

**a.** air density **c.** humidity
**b.** air pressure **d.** relative humidity

**10.** Winds curve as they move across Earth's surface because of

**a.** the Coriolis effect **c.** humidity
**b.** air pressure **d.** relative humidity

**11.** Jet streams generally flow toward the

**a.** north **c.** east
**b.** south **d.** west

**12.** Condensation increases with greater

**a.** relative humidity **c.** air pressure
**b.** air temperature **d.** wind speed

**13.** Any type of liquid or solid water that falls to Earth's surface is called

**a.** precipitation **c.** a monsoon
**b.** dew **d.** humidity

**14.** What are low-altitude clouds composed of?

**a.** snowflakes **c.** water droplets
**b.** raindrops **d.** water vapor

**15.** Clouds made of ice crystals form under conditions of

**a.** strong winds **c.** low humidity
**b.** high altitude **d.** high pressure

**16.** Which type of cloud is most likely to bring thunderstorms?

**a.** stratus **c.** cumulonimbus
**b.** altostratus **d.** cirrus

**17.** Over short distances wind blows toward areas of

**a.** high pressure **c.** low temperature
**b.** high density **d.** low pressure

**18.** The doldrums and the horse latitudes are both regions of

**a.** high air pressure **c.** heavy rains
**b.** light winds **d.** low temperatures

**19.** As altitude increases, air pressure usually

**a.** decreases **c.** varies more
**b.** increases **d.** varies less

**Short Answer** *Write a short answer to each question.*

**20.** What causes land breezes to flow at night?

**21.** Why does hair take longer to dry after a shower on days with high relative humidity?

**22.** How does air pressure affect air density?

**23.** Why are dust and other particles necessary for precipitation?

**24.** How did global wind belts and calm regions affect transportation in the past?

## Thinking Critically

The soil in this terrarium was soaked with water two weeks ago. Then the box was sealed so that no moisture could escape. Use the diagram to answer the next six questions.

25. **IDENTIFY EFFECTS** How does sunlight affect conditions inside the terrarium?

26. **ANALYZE** Draw a diagram of the water cycle inside the terrarium.

27. **INFER** What do the water drops on the glass indicate about the temperatures inside and outside the terrarium?

28. **PREDICT** Explain how long you think the plants will live without being watered.

29. **PREDICT** What would happen if you placed the terrarium on top of a block of ice?

30. **HYPOTHESIZE** How would conditions inside the terrarium change if there were a hole in one side of it?

31. **COMPARE AND CONTRAST** How are sea breezes and monsoon winds alike, and how are they different?

32. **PREDICT** A cumulus cloud is growing taller. What will happen to the density of the air beneath it? Explain.

33. **INFER** Imagine that a group of factories and power plants lies 200 kilometers to the west of a forest where trees are dying. Describe three steps in a process that could be causing the trees to die.

**IDENTIFY EFFECTS** Write the type of precipitation that would form under each set of conditions.

| Conditions | Precipitation |
|---|---|
| **34.** above-freezing air inside a cloud and freezing air beneath it | |
| **35.** above-freezing air beneath a cloud and freezing temperatures on the ground | |
| **36.** below-freezing air inside a cloud and above-freezing temperatures in the air beneath it and on the ground | |
| **37.** below-freezing air inside a cloud and beneath it | |
| **38.** ice pellets hurled around by air currents inside a cloud | |

## the BIG idea

39. **APPLY** Look again at the photograph on pages 40–41. Now that you have finished the chapter, how would you change your response to the question on the photograph?

40. **WRITE** Write one or more paragraphs explaining how energy from the Sun influences the weather. In your discussion, include at least three of the following topics:
    - global wind belts
    - high- and low-pressure areas
    - local winds
    - monsoons
    - the water cycle
    - cloud formation

## UNIT PROJECTS

If you need to do an experiment for your unit project, gather the materials. Be sure to allow enough time to observe results before the project is due.

# Standardized Test Practice

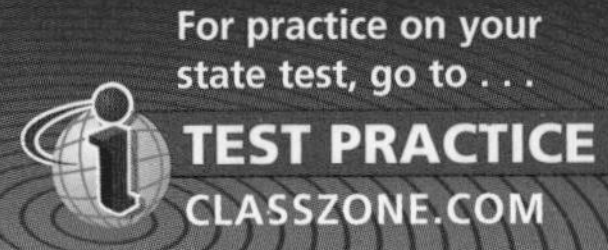


## Analyzing a Diagram

*This diagram shows the water cycle. Use it to answer the questions below.*

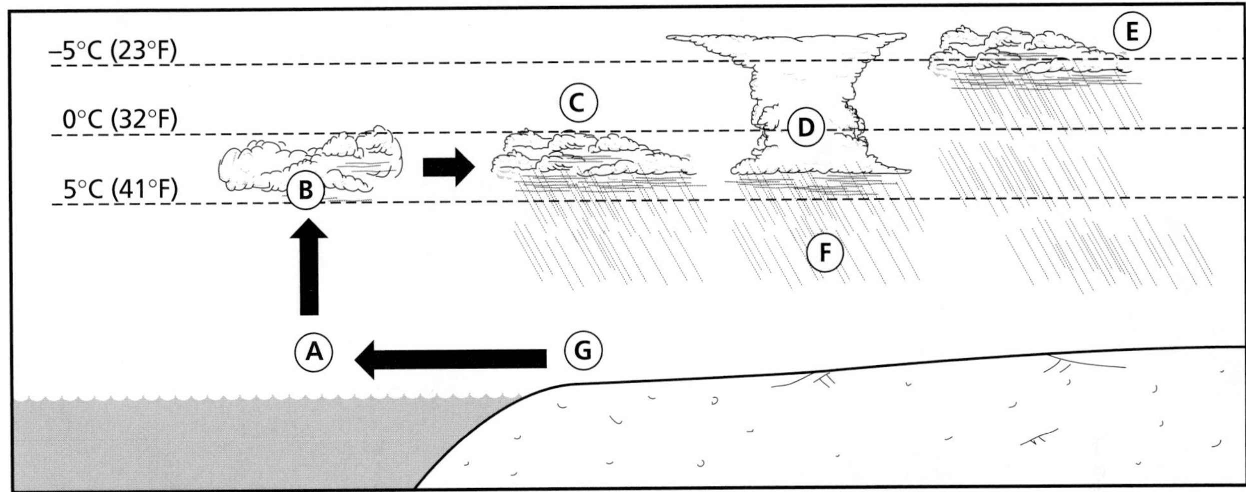


**1.** Where is evaporation occurring?

**a.** A
**b.** D
**c.** F
**d.** G

**2.** Where is condensation occurring?

**a.** A
**b.** B
**c.** F
**d.** G

**3.** Where is precipitation shown?

**a.** A
**b.** C
**c.** E
**d.** F

**4.** Where is hail most likely to form?

**a.** C
**b.** D
**c.** E
**d.** F

**5.** From which cloud will precipitation fall as snow and then turn to rain?

**a.** B
**b.** C
**c.** D
**d.** E

**6.** Which is the best estimate for the temperature in B?

**a.** 8°C (46°F)
**b.** 3°C (37°F)
**c.** –3°C (27°F)
**d.** –8°C (17°F)

**7.** What does the arrow pointing up between A and B indicate?

**a.** the movement of moisture
**b.** the direction of the wind
**c.** a low pressure area
**d.** a reflection off the water

## Extended Response

*Answer the two questions below in detail. Include some of the terms shown in the word box. In your answers underline each term you use.*

| low air pressure | cool air | west |
|---|---|---|
| high air pressure | warm air | east |
| Coriolis effect | | |

**8.** Whenever Richard rides in an elevator to the top of a skyscraper, he feels a pop inside his ears. Explain what is happening in the air to produce the pop in Richard's ears.

**9.** Winds tend to blow from west to east across the United States. If Earth spun in the other direction, how might the winds across the United States be different? Use the terms *east, west,* and *Coriolis effect* in your answer.

# CHAPTER 3 Weather Fronts and Storms

## the BIG idea

The interaction of air masses causes changes in weather.

What types of weather can move a house?

## Key Concepts

SECTION

**Weather changes as air masses move.**
Learn about air masses, fronts, and high- and low-pressure systems.

SECTION

**Low-pressure systems can become storms.**
Learn about hurricanes and winter storms.

SECTION

**Vertical air motion can cause severe storms.**
Learn about thunderstorms, lightning, and tornadoes.

SECTION

**Weather forecasters use advanced technologies.**
Learn about different types of weather data and how forecasters predict weather.

### Internet Preview

CLASSZONE.COM

Chapter 3 online resources: Content Review, two Visualizations, two Resource Centers, Math Tutorial, Test Practice

# EXPLORE the BIG idea

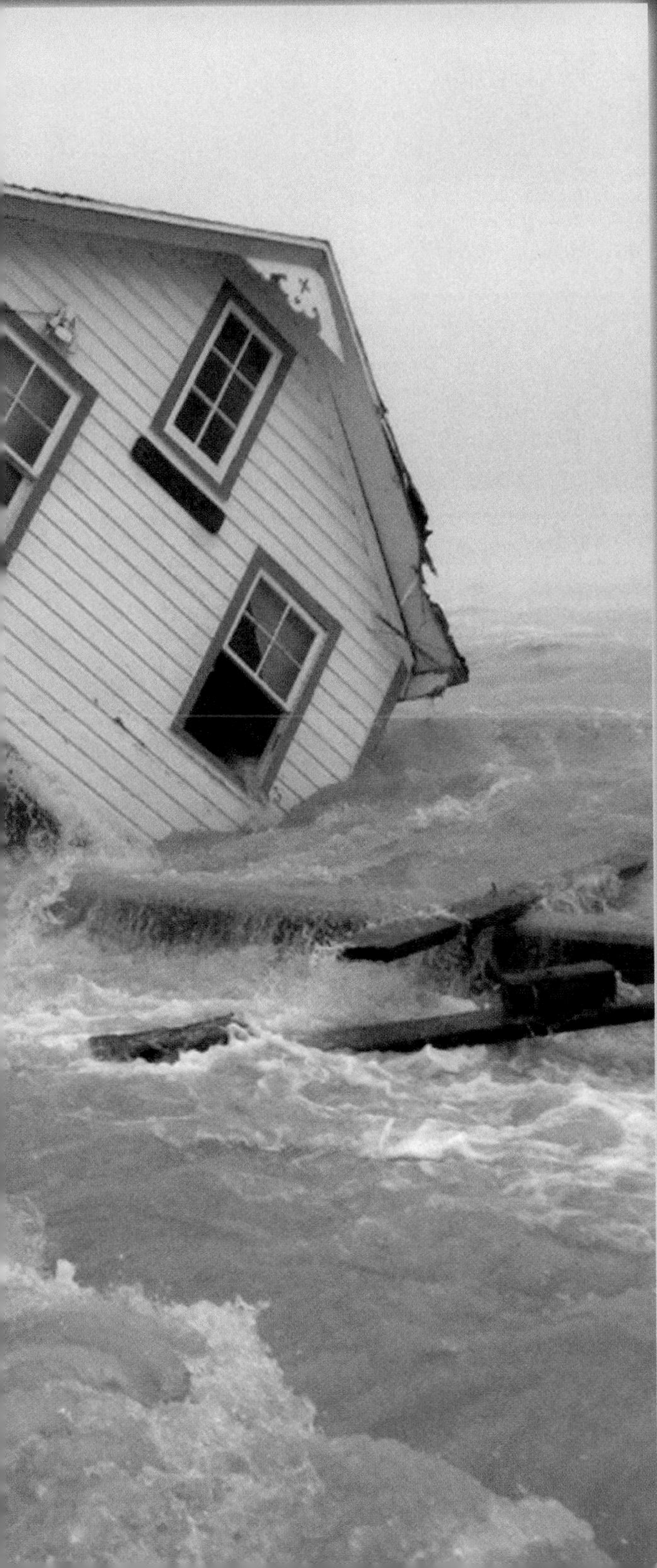

## How Does Cold Air Move?

Hold one hand near the top of a refrigerator door and the other hand near the bottom. Open the refrigerator door just a little bit.

**Observe and Think**
How did each hand feel before and after you opened the door? How did the air move?

## How Does Weather Move?

Collect newspaper weather maps for three consecutive days. Identify at least one flagged line on a map (identifying a weather front) and track the line's movement over the three days.

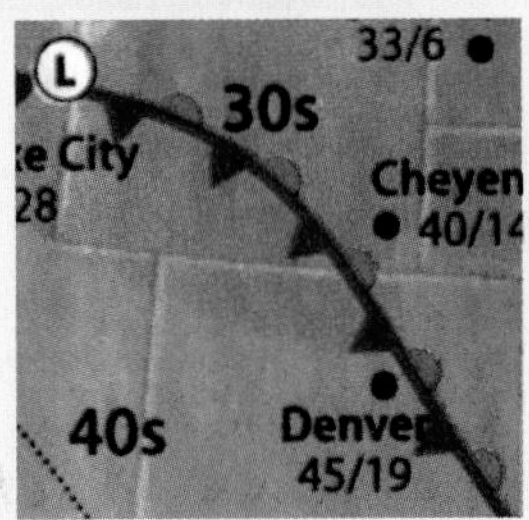


**Observe and Think**
What type of weather did you find each day where the line passed? Why did this line move the way it did?

## Internet Activity: Weather Safety

Go to **ClassZone.com** to find information about weather safety. Find out the types of dangerous weather that may affect your region.

**Observe and Think**
What can you do ahead of time to be ready for severe weather?

Severe Weather **Code: MDL011**

CHAPTER 3

# Getting Ready to Learn

## CONCEPT REVIEW

- Air temperature decreases as you rise in the troposphere.
- Temperature affects air density.
- Pressure differences make air move.
- Uneven heating of Earth's surface produces winds.
- Clouds form as air rises, expands, and cools.

## VOCABULARY REVIEW

**altitude** p. 10

**convection** p. 19

**evaporation** p. 56

**condensation** p. 56

**relative humidity** p. 58

CONTENT REVIEW
CLASSZONE.COM

Review concepts and vocabulary.

## TAKING NOTES

### MAIN IDEA WEB

Write each new blue heading—a main idea—in a box. Then put notes with important terms and details into boxes around the main idea.

### VOCABULARY STRATEGY

Draw a **word triangle** diagram for each new vocabulary term. In the bottom row write and define the term. In the middle row, use the term correctly in a sentence. At the top, draw a small picture to help you remember the term.

See the Note-Taking Handbook on pages R45–R51.

SCIENCE NOTEBOOK

Marine air masses form over water.

Continental air masses form over land.

Air masses are large bodies of air.

Tropical air masses are warm.

Polar air masses are cold.

Yesterday the temperature fell as a cold front passed us.

**front**: the boundary between two air masses

KEY CONCEPT

# Weather changes as air masses move.

 **BEFORE, you learned**

- Air pressure changes with location and altitude
- Water vapor in the atmosphere condenses when air rises

 **NOW, you will learn**

- What air masses are
- What happens when air masses meet
- How pressure systems affect the weather

**VOCABULARY**

**air mass** p. 79
**front** p. 82
**high-pressure system** p. 84
**low-pressure system** p. 85

**EXPLORE Air Masses**

### *How does an air mass form?*

**PROCEDURE**

1. Put ice into one bowl and warm water into a second bowl. Leave the third bowl empty.
2. Place each bowl in a different box and cover the box with plastic wrap. Wait a few minutes.
3. Put your hand into each box in turn.

**WHAT DO YOU THINK?**

- How would you describe the air in each box?
- Which box's air feels the most humid? Why?

**MATERIALS**

- 3 bowls
- ice
- warm water
- 3 shoeboxes
- plastic wrap

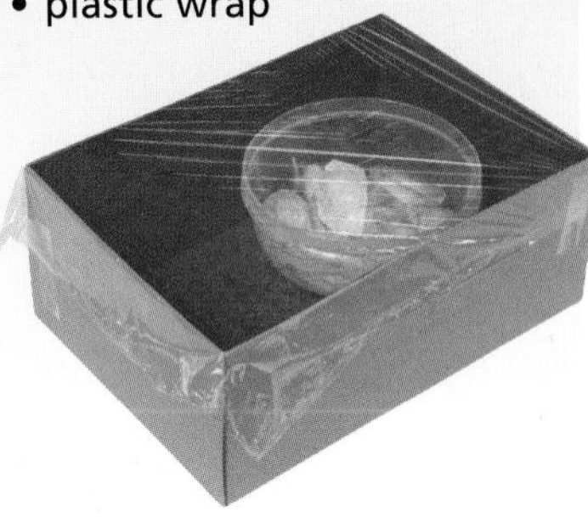

## Air masses are large bodies of air.

**MAIN IDEA WEB**
Organize important terms and details about air masses.

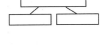

You have probably experienced the effects of air masses—one day is hot and humid, and the next day is cool and pleasant. The weather changes when a new air mass moves into your area. An **air mass** is a large volume of air in which temperature and humidity are nearly the same in different locations at the same altitude. An air mass can cover many thousands of square kilometers.

An air mass forms when the air over a large region of Earth sits in one place for many days. The air gradually takes on the characteristics of the land or water below it. Where Earth's surface is cold, the air becomes cold. Where Earth's surface is wet, the air becomes moist. As an air mass moves, it brings its temperature and moisture to new locations.

Explain how the weather can change with the arrival of a new air mass. Your answer should include two ways that weather changes.

## North American Air Masses

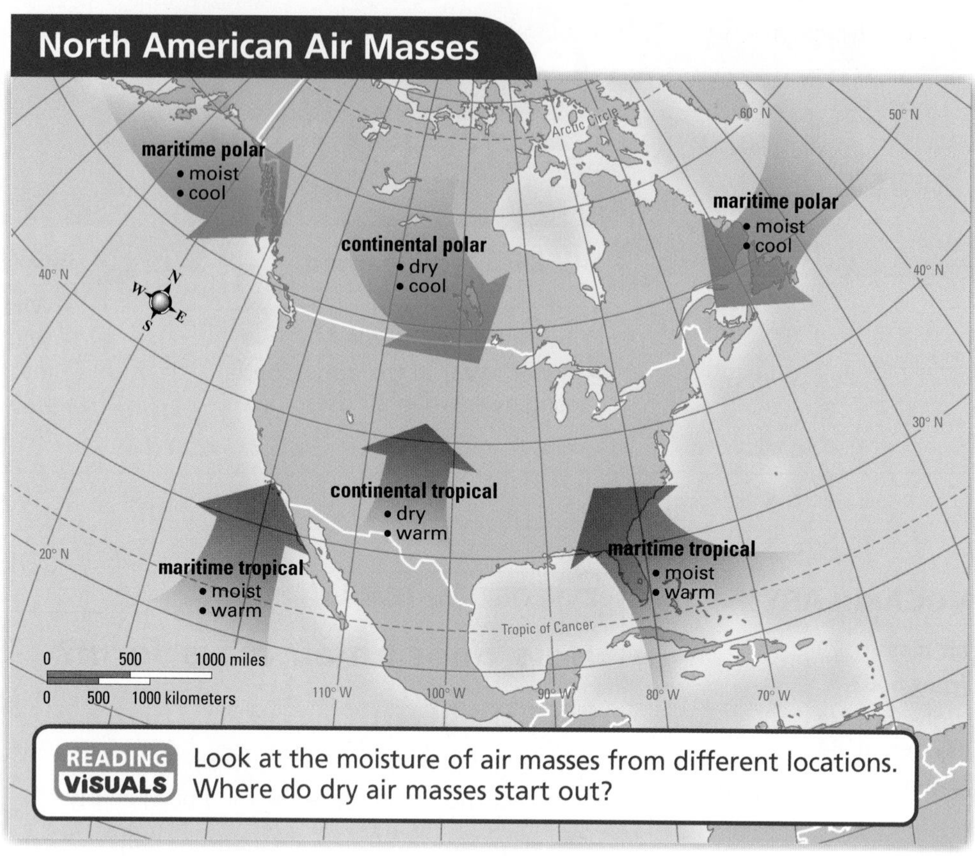


**READING VISUALS** Look at the moisture of air masses from different locations. Where do dry air masses start out?

## Characteristics of an Air Mass

Some regions of Earth's surface, such as those shown in the map above, produce air masses again and again. The characteristics of an air mass depend on the region where it forms. A hot desert produces dry, hot air masses, while cool ocean waters produce moist, cool air masses. Scientists classify air masses into categories according to the characteristics of regions. Each category name is made of two words—one for moisture, one for temperature.

The first word of an air mass's category name tells whether the air mass formed over water or dry land. It describes the moisture of the air mass.

- **Continental** air masses form over land. Air becomes dry as it loses its moisture to the dry land below it.
- **Maritime** (MAR-ih-TYM) air masses form over water. Air becomes moist as it gains water vapor from the water below it.

**READING TIP**

The word *maritime* has the same root as the word *marine*. Both come from the Latin word *mare*, which means "sea."

The second word of a category name tells whether an air mass formed close to the equator. It describes the air mass's temperature.

- **Tropical** air masses form near the equator. Air becomes warm as it gains energy from the warm land or water.
- **Polar** air masses form far from the equator. Air becomes cool as it loses energy to the cold land or water.

The combination of words gives the characteristics of the air mass. A maritime tropical air mass is moist and warm, while a continental polar air mass is dry and cold.

What can you tell from each word of an air mass's name?

## Movement of an Air Mass

Air masses can travel away from the regions where they form. They move with the global pattern of winds. In most of the United States, air masses generally move from west to east. They may move along with the jet stream in more complex and changing patterns.

When an air mass moves to a new region, it carries along its characteristic moisture and temperature. As the air moves over Earth's surface, the characteristics of the surface begin to change the air mass. For example, if a continental polar air mass moves over warm water, the air near the surface will become warmer and gain moisture. These changes begin where the air touches the surface. It may take days or weeks for the changes to spread upward through the entire air mass. An air mass that moves quickly may not change much. If it moves quickly enough, a continental polar air mass can move cold air from northern Canada all the way to the southern United States.

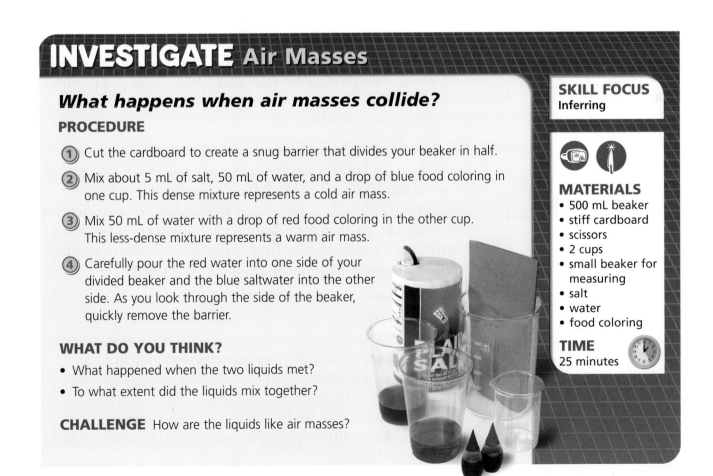

## INVESTIGATE Air Masses

### *What happens when air masses collide?*

**PROCEDURE**

1. Cut the cardboard to create a snug barrier that divides your beaker in half.
2. Mix about 5 mL of salt, 50 mL of water, and a drop of blue food coloring in one cup. This dense mixture represents a cold air mass.
3. Mix 50 mL of water with a drop of red food coloring in the other cup. This less-dense mixture represents a warm air mass.
4. Carefully pour the red water into one side of your divided beaker and the blue saltwater into the other side. As you look through the side of the beaker, quickly remove the barrier.

**WHAT DO YOU THINK?**

- What happened when the two liquids met?
- To what extent did the liquids mix together?

**CHALLENGE** How are the liquids like air masses?

**SKILL FOCUS**
Inferring

**MATERIALS**
- 500 mL beaker
- stiff cardboard
- scissors
- 2 cups
- small beaker for measuring
- salt
- water
- food coloring

**TIME**
25 minutes

## Weather changes where air masses meet.

When a new air mass moves over your area, you can expect the weather to change. Perhaps you have heard a weather forecaster talk about fronts. A **front** is a boundary between air masses. The weather near a front can differ from the weather inside the rest of an air mass. As one air mass pushes another, some of the air at the boundary will be pushed upward. Clouds can form in this rising air. The weather often becomes cloudy or stormy as a front passes. Afterward, you experience the temperature and humidity of the air mass that has moved in.

MAIN IDEA WEB
Organize the notes you take about fronts.

### Fronts and Weather

Different types of fronts produce different patterns of weather. When a cold, dense air mass pushes warmer air, it produces a cold front. When a warm air mass pushes colder air, it produces a warm front. These names tell you which way the temperature will change but not how much it will change. A cold front can turn a heat wave into normal summer weather or turn cold winter air into very cold weather.

How would the weather change if a cold front moved into your area?

1. **Cold fronts** can move into regions quickly. As you can see on page 83, a cold front is steeper than the other types of fronts. As a mass of cold, dense air moves forward, warmer air ahead of it is pushed upward. Water vapor in the warm air condenses as the air rises. Cold fronts often produce tall cumulonimbus clouds and precipitation. Brief, heavy storms are likely. After the storms, the air is cooler and often very clear.

See how the air moves in warm fronts and cold fronts.

2. **Warm fronts** move more slowly than cold fronts. Warm air moves gradually up and over a mass of denser and colder air. Moisture in the warm air condenses all along the sloping front, producing cloud-covered skies. As a warm front approaches, you may first see high cirrus clouds, then high stratus clouds, then lower and lower stratus clouds. Often, a warm front brings many hours of steady rain or snow. After the front passes, the air is warmer.

3. **Stationary fronts** occur when air masses first meet or when a cold or warm front stops moving. For a while, the boundary between the air masses stays in the same location—it stays stationary. The air in each air mass can still move sideways along the front or upward. The upward air motion may produce clouds that cover the sky, sometimes for days at a time. When the front starts moving, it becomes a warm front if the warm air advances and pushes the cold air. If the cold air moves forward instead, the front becomes a cold front.

## Fronts and Weather

**As fronts move across Earth's surface, they produce changes in the weather.**

### 1 Cold Front

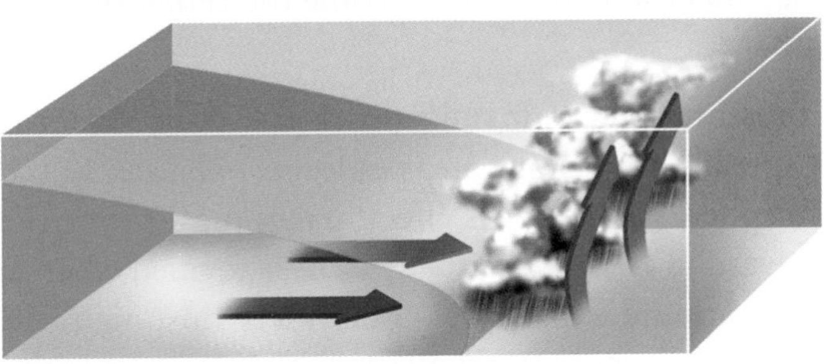

A **cold front** forms when a cold air mass pushes a warm air mass and forces the warm air to rise. As the warm air rises, its moisture condenses and forms tall clouds.

Triangles show the direction that a cold front moves.

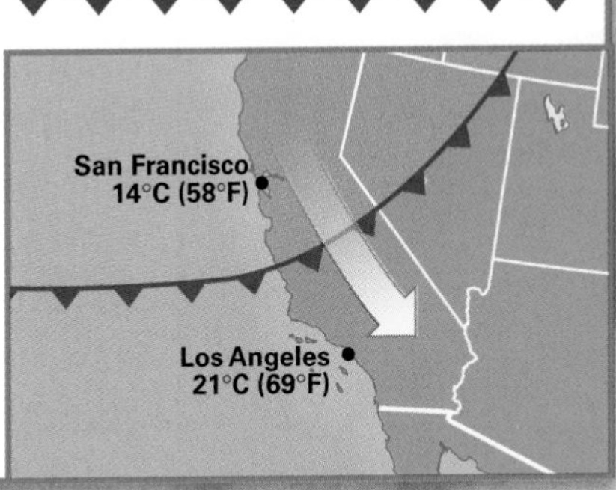


### 2 Warm Front

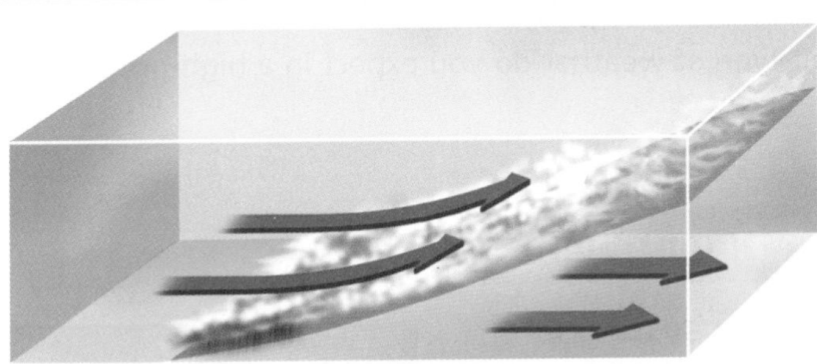

A **warm front** forms when a warm air mass pushes a cold air mass. The warm air rises slowly over the cold air and its moisture condenses into flat clouds.

Semicircles show the direction that a warm front moves.

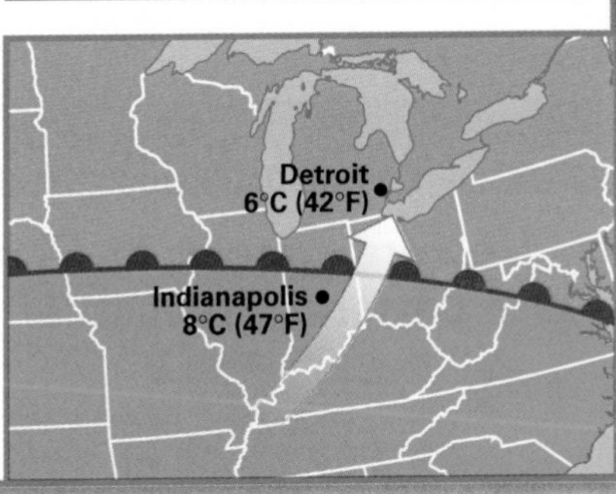


### 3 Stationary Front

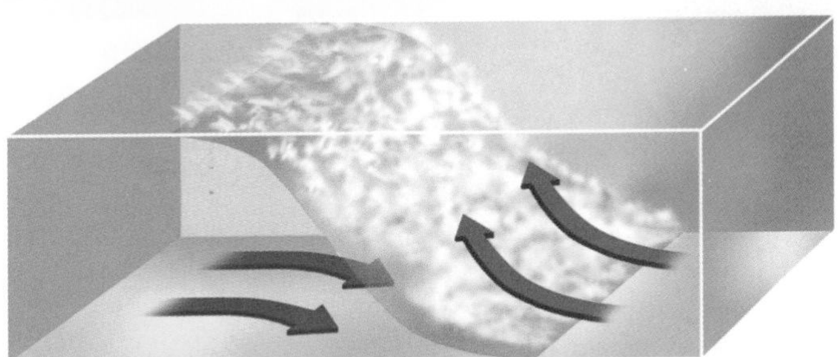

A **stationary front** occurs when two air masses push against each other without moving. A stationary front becomes a warm or cold front when one air mass advances.

Alternating triangles and semicircles show a stationary front.

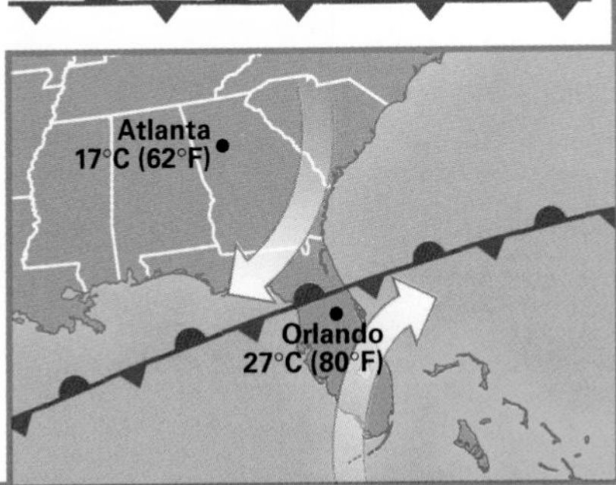


READING VISUALS **PREDICT** Which city will the cold front affect next?

## High-Pressure Systems

You may have seen the letters H and L on a weather map. These letters mark high-pressure centers and low-pressure centers, often simply called highs and lows. Each center is the location of the highest or lowest pressure in a region. The pressure differences cause air to move in ways that may make a high or low become the center of a whole system of weather.

> **READING TIP**
> A *system* includes different parts that work together.

At a high-pressure center, air sinks slowly down. As the air nears the ground, it spreads out toward areas of lower pressure. In the Northern Hemisphere, the Coriolis effect makes the air turn clockwise as it moves outward. A **high-pressure system** is formed when air moves all the way around a high-pressure center. Most high-pressure systems are large and change slowly. When a high-pressure system stays in one location for a long time, an air mass may form. The air—and resulting air mass—can be warm or cold, moist or dry.

A high-pressure system generally brings clear skies and calm air or gentle breezes. This is because as air sinks to lower altitudes, it warms up a little bit. Water droplets evaporate, so clouds often disappear.

**CHECK YOUR READING** What type of weather do you expect in a high-pressure system?

### Weather Systems in the Northern Hemisphere

**High-pressure systems and low-pressure systems produce patterns of weather across Earth's surface.**

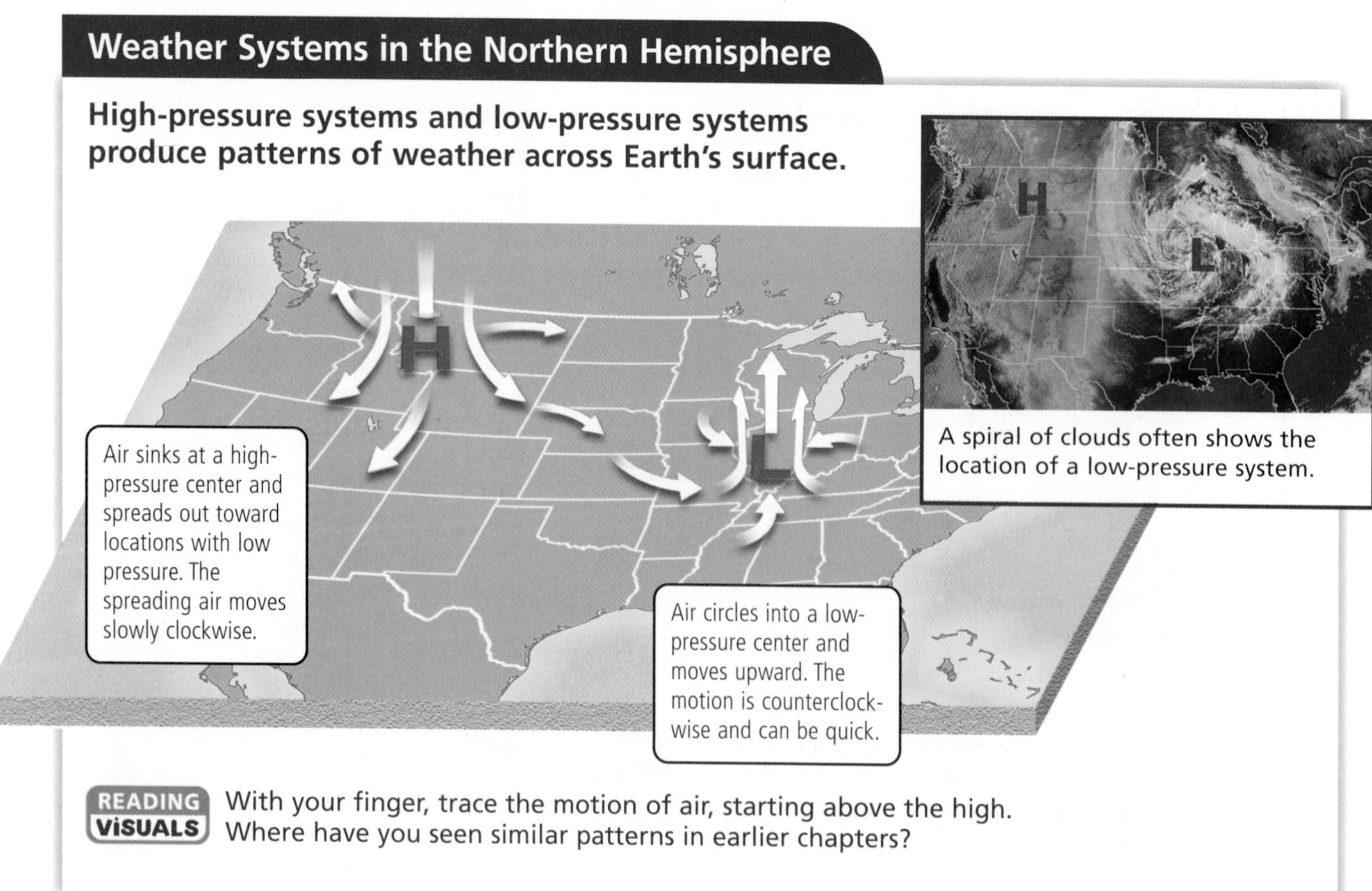

H
L
Air sinks at a high-pressure center and spreads out toward locations with low pressure. The spreading air moves slowly clockwise.
Air circles into a low-pressure center and moves upward. The motion is counterclockwise and can be quick.
H
L


A spiral of clouds often shows the location of a low-pressure system.

**READING VISUALS** With your finger, trace the motion of air, starting above the high. Where have you seen similar patterns in earlier chapters?

## Low-Pressure Systems

A small area of low pressure can also develop into a larger system. A **low-pressure system** is a large weather system that surrounds a center of low pressure. It begins as air moves around and inward toward the lowest pressure and then up to higher altitudes. The upward motion of the air lowers the air pressure further, and so the air moves faster. The pattern of motion strengthens into a low-pressure weather system. The rising air produces stormy weather. In the Northern Hemisphere, the air in a low-pressure system circles in a counterclockwise direction.

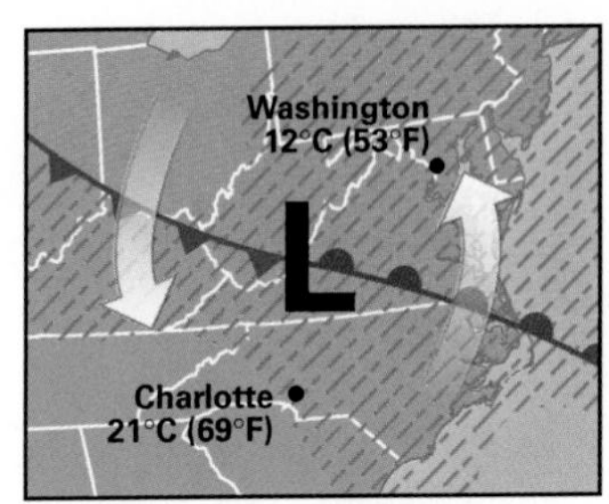


A low-pressure system can develop wherever there is a center of low pressure. One place this often happens is along a boundary between a warm air mass and a cold air mass. The diagram shows an example of this process.

- Part of the boundary between the air masses moves south and becomes a cold front.
- Part of the boundary moves north and becomes a warm front.
- A center of low pressure forms where the ends of the two fronts meet.

The low-pressure center and fronts become parts of a whole system of weather. Rising air at the fronts and at the low can cause very stormy weather.

The diagram on page 84 shows how air moves between pressure centers. Air moves down, out, and around a high-pressure center. Then it swirls around and into a low-pressure center and moves upward. Highs and lows affect each other as they move across the surface. Large weather systems generally move with the pattern of global winds—west to east over most of North America. But, within a weather system, winds can blow in different directions.

## 3.1 Review

### KEY CONCEPTS

1. What are the two characteristics of an air mass that you need to know in order to classify it?
2. What happens when a warmer air mass pushes a cooler air mass?
3. What type of weather system brings calm, clear weather?

### CRITICAL THINKING

4. **Compare and Contrast** Explain how air moves differently in low- and high-pressure systems.
5. **Apply** If the weather becomes stormy for a short time and then becomes colder, which type of front has passed?

### CHALLENGE

6. **Synthesize** You check a barometer and observe that the air pressure has been dropping all day. Is tonight's weather more likely to be calm or stormy?

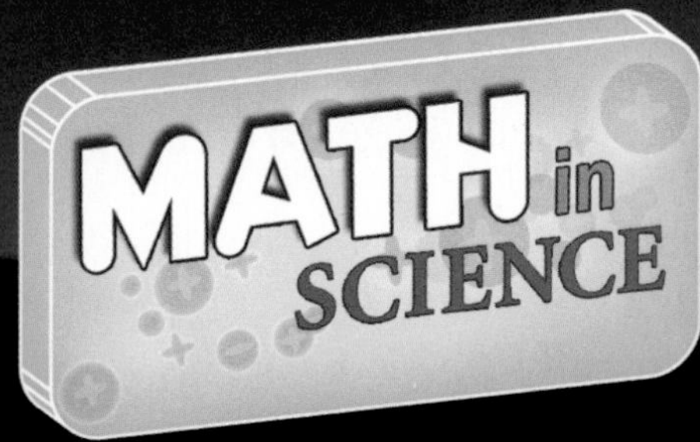


SKILL: DETERMINING RATES

# Movement of a Front

Click on Math Tutorial for more help with rates as ratios.

Scientists measure the speeds of weather fronts to forecast weather conditions. The speed at which a front moves is an example of a rate. A rate can be written as a ratio. For example, the rate of a front that moves a distance of 500 kilometers in 1 day can be written as follows:

500 kilometers : 1 day

The map below shows the movement of a cold front over four consecutive days. Use the map scale to determine the distance that the front moves on each day.

## Cold Front Movement

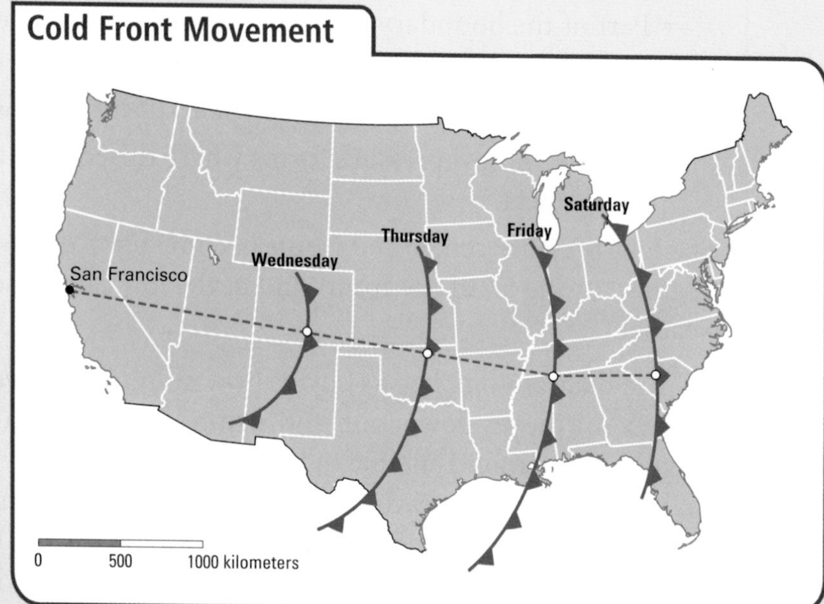


**Answer the following questions.**

1. What was the front's rate of movement between Wednesday and Thursday? Express your answer as a ratio.

   ? : 1 day

2. What was the front's rate of movement between Friday and Saturday? Express your answer as a ratio.
3. What was the mean rate of the front's movement from Wednesday to Saturday? Remember, *mean* means "average." Express your answer as a ratio.

**CHALLENGE** Use the rate from Wednesday to Saturday to estimate the day on which the front must have moved through San Francisco.

KEY CONCEPT

# Low-pressure systems can become storms.

**BEFORE, you learned**

- Moving air masses cause changes in weather
- A low-pressure system brings stormy weather

**NOW, you will learn**

- How hurricanes develop
- About the dangers of hurricanes
- About different types of winter storms

**VOCABULARY**

**tropical storm** p. 87
**hurricane** p. 87
**storm surge** p. 89
**blizzard** p. 90

**EXPLORE Hurricanes**

***What things make hurricanes lose strength?***

**PROCEDURE**

1. Crumple a piece of paper, then flatten it out. Crumple and flatten it out again.
2. Spin the top on the flattened paper. Count the seconds until it stops spinning.
3. Spin the top on a smooth surface. Count the seconds until it stops spinning.

**MATERIALS**

- sheet of paper
- top

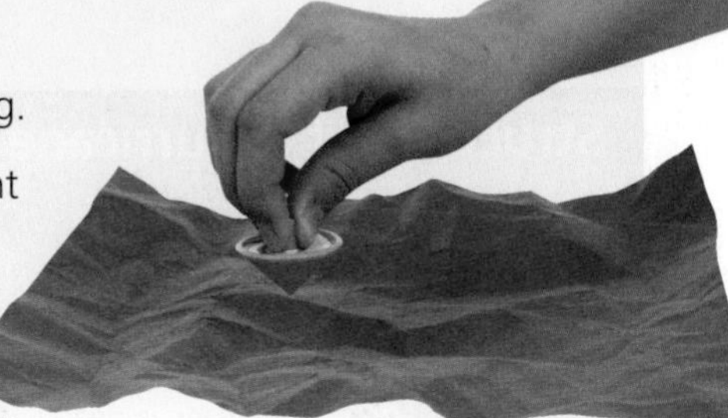

**WHAT DO YOU THINK?**

How does the texture of the surface affect the rate at which the top loses energy?

## Hurricanes form over warm ocean water.

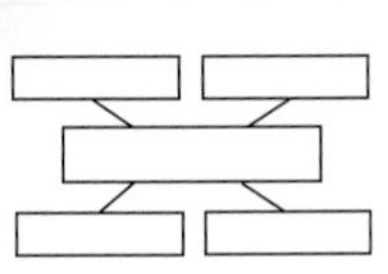

MAIN IDEA WEB
Remember to make notes about hurricanes.

Near the equator, warm ocean water provides the energy that can turn a low-pressure center into a violent storm. As water evaporates from the ocean, energy moves from the ocean water into the air. This energy makes warm air rise faster. Tall clouds and strong winds develop. As winds blow across the water from different directions into the low, the Coriolis effect bends their paths into a spiral. The winds blow faster and faster around the low, which becomes the center of a storm system.

A **tropical storm** is a low-pressure system that starts near the equator and has winds that blow at 65 kilometers per hour (40 mi/h) or more. A **hurricane** (HUR-ih-KAYN) is a tropical low-pressure system with winds blowing at speeds of 120 kilometers per hour (74 mi/h) or more—strong enough to uproot trees. Hurricanes are called typhoons or cyclones when they form over the Indian Ocean or the western Pacific Ocean.

## Formation of Hurricanes

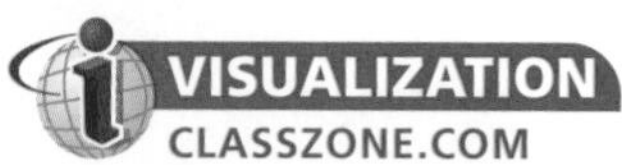

**VISUALIZATION**
CLASSZONE.COM
Watch the progress of a hurricane.

In the eastern United States, hurricanes most often strike between August and October. Energy from warm water is necessary for a low-pressure center to build into a tropical storm and then into a hurricane. The ocean water where these storms develop only gets warm enough—26°C (80°F) or more—near the end of summer.

Tropical storms and hurricanes generally move westward with the trade winds. Near land, however, they will often move north, south, or even back eastward. As long as a storm stays above warm water, it can grow bigger and more powerful. As soon as a hurricane moves over land or over cooler water, it loses its source of energy. The winds lose strength and the storm dies out. If a hurricane moves over land, the rough surface of the land reduces the winds even more.

The map below shows the progress of a storm. The tropical storm gained energy and became a hurricane as it moved westward. When the hurricane moved north, the storm lost energy and was called a tropical storm again as its winds slowed.

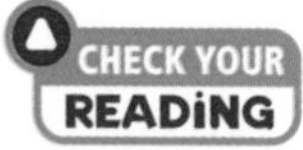

**CHECK YOUR READING** What is the source of a hurricane's energy?

### Structure of a Hurricane

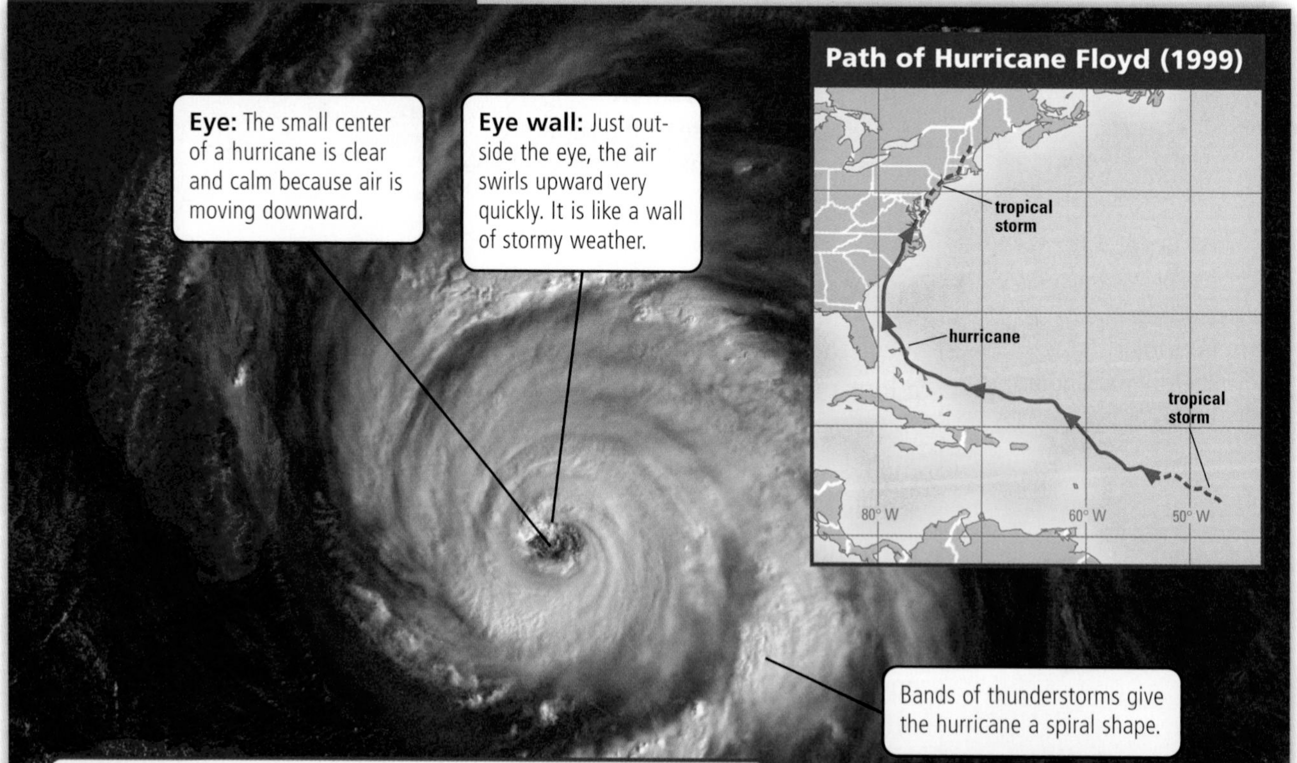

**Eye:** The small center of a hurricane is clear and calm because air is moving downward.
**Eye wall:** Just outside the eye, the air swirls upward very quickly. It is like a wall of stormy weather.
Bands of thunderstorms give the hurricane a spiral shape.
Path of Hurricane Floyd (1999)
tropical storm
hurricane
tropical storm
80° W
60° W
50° W

**READING VISUALS** Compare this computer-colored image with the map. What does green represent?

At the center of a hurricane is a small area of clear weather, 20–50 kilometers (10–30 mi) in diameter, called the eye. The storm's center is calm because air moves downward there. Just around the eye, the air moves very quickly around and upward, forming a tall ring of cumulonimbus clouds called the eye wall. This ring produces very heavy rains and tremendous winds. Farther from the center, bands of heavy clouds and rain spiral inward toward the eye.

**SAFETY TIPS**

**HURRICANES**

- Before a storm, prepare a plan to leave the area. Gather emergency supplies.
- Listen to weather reports for storm updates.
- Secure loose objects outside, and cover windows.
- If ordered to evacuate, leave immediately.
- During a storm, stay indoors and away from windows.
- After a storm, be aware of power lines, hanging branches, and flooded areas.

## Effects of Hurricanes

A hurricane can pound a coast with huge waves and sweep the land with strong winds and heavy rains. The storms cause damage and dangerous conditions in several ways. Hurricane winds can lift cars, uproot trees, and tear the roofs off buildings. Hurricanes may also produce tornadoes that cause even more damage. Heavy rains from hurricanes may make rivers overflow their banks and flood nearby areas. When a hurricane moves into a coastal area, it often pushes a huge mass of ocean water known as a **storm surge.** In a storm surge, the sea level rises several meters, backing up rivers and flooding the shore. A storm surge can be destructive and deadly. Large waves add to the destruction. A hurricane may affect an area for a few hours or a few days, but the damage may take weeks or even months to clean up.

**CHECK YOUR READING** What are the effects of hurricanes? Make a list for your answer.

The National Hurricane Center helps people know when to prepare for a hurricane. The center puts out a tropical-storm or hurricane watch when a storm is likely to strike within 36 hours. People may be evacuated, or moved away for safety, from areas where they may be in danger. As the danger gets closer—24 hours or less—the center issues a tropical-storm or hurricane warning. The warning stays in effect until the danger has passed.

**COMPARE AND CONTRAST** These pictures show a shoreline in North Carolina before and after Hurricane Fran in 1996. Compare the houses, road, and water in the two pictures.

## Winter storms produce snow and ice.

Most severe winter storms in the United States are part of low-pressure systems. Unlike hurricanes, the systems that cause winter storms form when two air masses collide. A continental polar air mass that forms over snow-covered ground is especially cold, dry, and dense. It can force moist air to rise very quickly, producing a stormy low-pressure system.

The National Weather Service (NWS) alerts people to dangerous weather. The NWS issues a winter storm watch up to 48 hours before a storm is expected. A winter storm warning means that dangerous conditions are already present or will affect an area shortly.

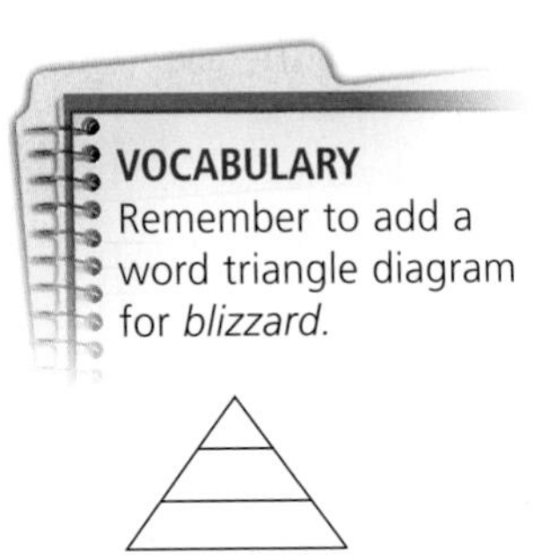

VOCABULARY
Remember to add a word triangle diagram for *blizzard*.


**Blizzards** Strong winds can blow so much snow into the air at once that it becomes difficult to see and dangerous to travel. **Blizzards** are blinding snowstorms with winds of at least 56 kilometers per hour (35 mi/h) and low temperatures—usually below –7°C (20°F). Blizzards occur in many parts of the northern and central United States. Wind and snow can knock down trees and power lines. Without heat, buildings can become very cold, and water in pipes may freeze. Schools, hospitals, and businesses may have to close. Deep, heavy snow on top of a building may cause the roof to cave in.

**Lake-Effect Snowstorms** Some of the heaviest snows fall in the areas just east and south of the Great Lakes. Cold air from the northwest gains moisture and warmth as it passes over the Great Lakes. Over cold land, the air cools again and releases the moisture as snow. The lake effect can cover areas downwind of the Great Lakes with clouds and snow even when the rest of the region has clear weather.

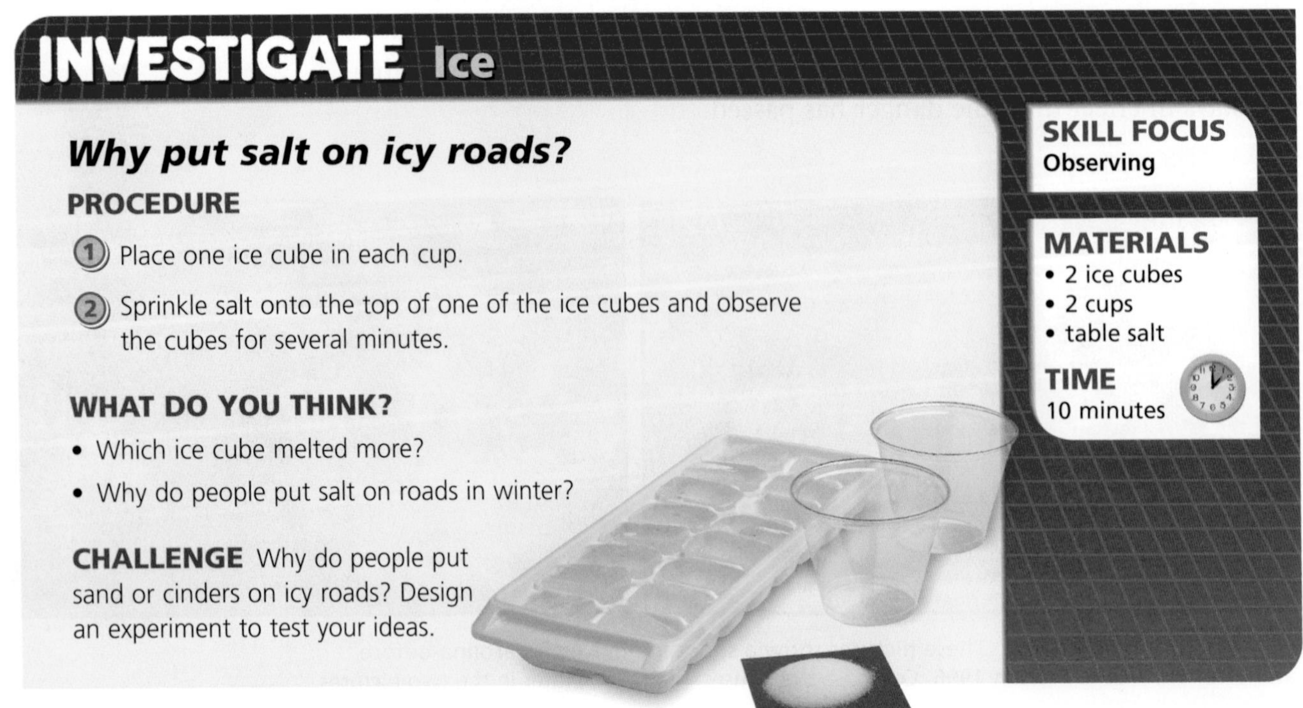

## INVESTIGATE Ice

### *Why put salt on icy roads?*

**PROCEDURE**

1. Place one ice cube in each cup.
2. Sprinkle salt onto the top of one of the ice cubes and observe the cubes for several minutes.

**WHAT DO YOU THINK?**

- Which ice cube melted more?
- Why do people put salt on roads in winter?

**CHALLENGE** Why do people put sand or cinders on icy roads? Design an experiment to test your ideas.

**SKILL FOCUS**
Observing

**MATERIALS**
- 2 ice cubes
- 2 cups
- table salt

**TIME**
10 minutes

## SAFETY TIPS

### WINTER STORMS

- Before a storm, prepare emergency kits for home and car.
- Listen to weather reports for updates.
- If caught in a storm, find or make a shelter and try to stay dry.
- If you are in a car or truck, make sure the exhaust pipe is clear and open a window a little bit.
- Use a colored cloth, fire, or light to help rescuers find you.
- Exercise a little to keep warm and keep blood flowing to your fingers and toes.
- If at home, stay inside even if there is no heat or power. Wear layers of clothing.

**Ice Storms** When rain falls onto freezing-cold ground, conditions can become dangerous. The cold rain freezes as it touches the ground and other surfaces. This freezing rain covers everything with heavy, smooth ice. The ice-covered roads become slippery and dangerous. Drivers may find it hard to steer and to stop their cars. Branches or even whole trees may break from the weight of ice. Falling branches can block roads, tear down power and telephone lines, and cause other damage. Damage from ice storms can sometimes shut down entire cities.

What type of precipitation occurs in each type of winter storm?

## 3.2 Review

### KEY CONCEPTS

1. Where and when do hurricanes form?
2. In what two ways can hurricanes cause floods?
3. List three of the possible dangers from winter storms.

### CRITICAL THINKING

4. **Compare and Contrast** What are the differences between the eye and the eye wall of a hurricane?
5. **Compare** What do hurricanes and winter storms have in common?

### CHALLENGE

6. **Apply** If the wind is blowing from the west and the conditions are right for lake-effect snow, will the snow fall to the north, south, east, or west of a lake? Drawing a diagram may help you work out an answer.

KEY CONCEPT

# Vertical air motion can cause severe storms.

**BEFORE, you learned**

- Fronts produce changes in weather
- Rising moist air can produce clouds and precipitation

**NOW, you will learn**

- How thunderstorms develop
- About the effects of thunderstorms
- About tornadoes and their effects

**VOCABULARY**

**thunderstorm** p. 92
**tornado** p. 95

**EXPLORE Lightning**

### *Does miniature lightning cause thunder?*

**PROCEDURE**

1. Use a thumbtack to attach the eraser to the center of a piece of foil.
2. Rub the foam tray quickly back and forth several times on the wool. Set the tray down.
3. Using the eraser as a handle, pick up the foil and set it onto the tray. Slowly move your finger close to the foil.

**WHAT DO YOU THINK?**

What happened when you touched the foil?

**MATERIALS**

- thumbtack
- eraser
- aluminum foil
- plastic foam tray
- wool fabric

## Thunderstorms form from rising moist air.

If you have ever shuffled your shoes on a carpet, you may have felt a small shock when you touched a doorknob. Electrical charges collected on your body and then jumped to the doorknob in a spark of electricity.

In a similar way, electrical charges build up near the tops and bottoms of clouds as pellets of ice move up and down through the clouds. Suddenly, a charge sparks from one part of a cloud to another or between a cloud and the ground. The spark of electricity, called lightning, causes a bright flash of light. The air around the lightning is briefly heated to a temperature hotter than the surface of the Sun. This fast heating produces a sharp wave of air that travels away from the lightning. When the wave reaches you, you hear it as a crack of thunder. A **thunderstorm** is a storm with lightning and thunder.

**VOCABULARY**
Put new terms into a word triangle diagram.

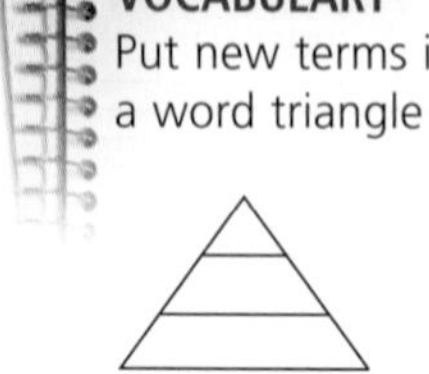

**CHECK YOUR READING** Is thunder a cause or an effect of lightning?

## Formation of Thunderstorms

Thunderstorms get their energy from humid air. When warm, humid air near the ground moves vertically into cooler air above, the rising air, or updraft, can build a thunderstorm quickly.

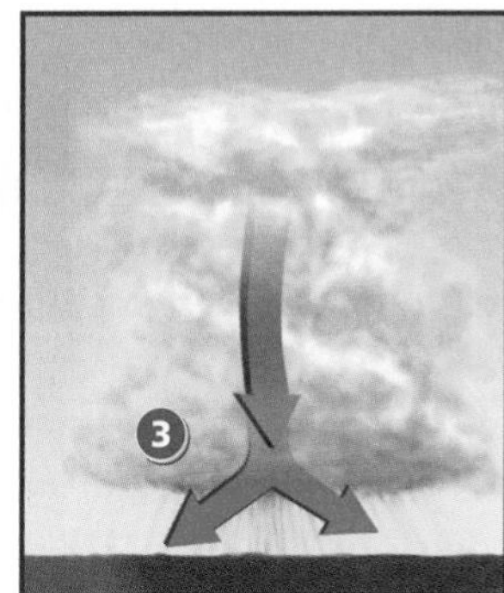


1. Rising humid air forms a cumulus cloud. The water vapor releases energy when it condenses into cloud droplets. This energy increases the air motion. The cloud continues building up into the tall cumulonimbus cloud of a thunderstorm.
2. Ice particles form in the low temperatures near the top of the cloud. As the ice particles grow large, they begin to fall and pull cold air down with them. This strong downdraft brings heavy rain or hail—the most severe stage of a thunderstorm.
3. The downdraft can spread out and block more warm air from moving upward into the cloud. The storm slows down and ends.

Thunderstorms can form at a cold front or within an air mass. At a cold front, air can be forced upward quickly. Within an air mass, uneven heating can produce convection and thunderstorms. In some regions, the conditions that produce thunderstorms occur almost daily during part of the year. In Florida, for example, the wet land and air warm up during a long summer day. Then, as you see in the diagram, cool sea breezes blow in from both coasts of the peninsula at once. The two sea breezes together push the warm, humid air over the land upward quickly. Thunderstorms form in the rising air.

In contrast, the summer air along the coast of California is usually too dry to produce thunderstorms. The air over the land heats up, and a sea breeze forms, but there is not enough moisture in the rising warm air to form clouds and precipitation.

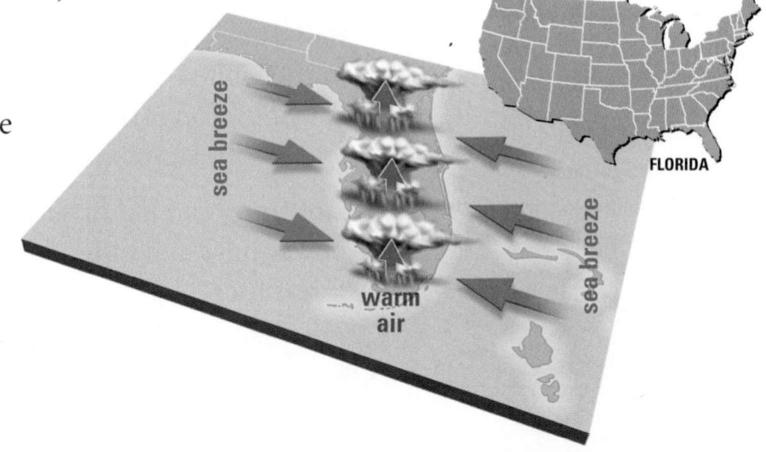

# INVESTIGATE Updrafts

## *How do updrafts form?*

**PROCEDURE**

1. Set up the cardboard, the cups, the container, and the cool water as shown in the photograph. Wait for the water to become still.
2. Use the eyedropper to place 2–3 drops of coloring at the bottom of the water.
3. Slide a cup of hot water (about 70°C) beneath the food coloring.

**WHAT DO YOU THINK?**

In what ways was the motion of the water like the air in a thunderstorm?

**CHALLENGE** How could you observe updrafts in air?

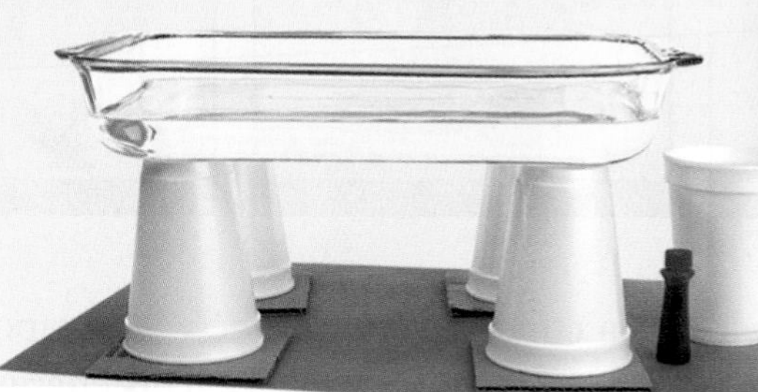

**SKILL FOCUS**
Inferring

**MATERIALS**

- 4 cardboard squares
- 5 foam cups
- clear container
- cool water
- food coloring
- eyedropper
- hot tap water

**TIME**
20 minutes

## Effects of Thunderstorms

A thunderstorm may provide cool rain at the end of a hot, dry spell. The rain can provide water for crops and restore lakes and streams. However, thunderstorms are often dangerous.

**Flash floods** can be strong enough to wash away people, cars, and even houses. One thunderstorm can produce millions of liters of rain. If a thunderstorm dumps all its rain in one place, or if a series of thunderstorms dump rain onto the same area, the water can cover the ground or make rivers overflow their banks.

**Winds** from a thunderstorm can be very strong. They can blow in bursts that exceed 270 kilometers per hour (170 mi/hr). Thunderstorm winds once knocked down a stretch of forest in Canada that was about 16 kilometers (10 mi) wide and 80 kilometers (50 mi) long. Thunderstorms can also produce sudden, dangerous bursts of air that move downward and spread out.

**Hail** causes nearly $1 billion in damage to property and crops in the United States every year. Hail can wipe out entire fields of a valuable crop in a few minutes. Large hailstones can damage roofs and kill livestock.

**Lightning** can kill or seriously injure any person it hits. It can damage power lines and other equipment. Lightning can also spark dangerous forest fires.

**SAFETY TIPS**

**THUNDERSTORMS**

- Stay alert when storms are predicted or dark, tall clouds are visible.
- If you hear thunder, seek shelter immediately and stay there for 30 minutes after the last thunder ends.
- Avoid bodies of water, lone trees, flagpoles, and metal objects.
- Stay away from the telephone, electrical appliances, and pipes.
- If flash floods are expected, move away from low ground.
- Do not try to cross flowing water, even if it looks shallow.

**CHECK YOUR READING** In what ways are thunderstorms dangerous? Did any surprise you?

## Tornadoes form in severe thunderstorms.

Under some conditions, the up-and-down air motion that produces tall clouds, lightning, and hail may produce a tornado. A **tornado** is a violently rotating column of air stretching from a cloud to the ground. A tornado moves along the ground in a winding path underneath the cloud. The column may even rise off the ground and then come down in a different place.

**READING TIP**

A spinning column of air is not called a tornado unless it touches the ground. If it touches water instead, it is called a waterspout.

You cannot see air moving. A tornado may become visible when water droplets appear below the cloud in the center of the rotating column. A tornado may lift dust and debris from the ground, so the bottom of the column becomes visible, as you see in the photographs below. Water droplets and debris may make a tornado look like an upright column or a twisted rope.

**CHECK YOUR READING** What makes a tornado become visible?

More tornadoes occur in North America than anywhere else in the world. Warm, humid air masses move north from the Gulf of Mexico to the central plains of the United States. There, the warm air masses often meet cold, dense air and form thunderstorms. In the spring, the winds in this region often produce the conditions that form tornadoes. A thunderstorm may form a series of tornadoes or even a group of tornadoes all at once.

### Tornado Formation

As a tornado forms, a funnel cloud seems to stretch down from the cloud above.

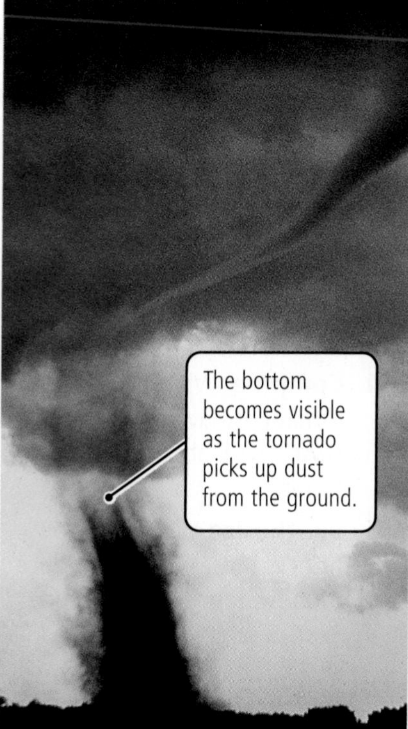

The bottom becomes visible as the tornado picks up dust from the ground.

The tornado moves along the ground before it dies out.

## Effects of Tornadoes

The powerful winds of a tornado can cause damage as the bottom of the tornado moves along the ground. Tornado winds can also pick up and slam dirt and small objects into buildings or anything else in the tornado's path.

The most common tornadoes are small and last only a few minutes. Their winds may be strong enough to break branches off trees, damage chimneys, and tear highway billboards. A typical path along the ground may be 100 meters (300 ft) wide and 1.5 kilometers (1 mi) long.

Larger tornadoes are less common but have stronger winds and last longer. About 20 percent of tornadoes are strong enough to knock over large trees, lift cars off the ground, and tear the roofs off houses. Very few—about 1 percent of all tornadoes—are violent enough to lift or completely demolish sturdy buildings. These huge tornadoes may last more than two hours. You can find more details about tornadoes in the Appendix.

**SAFETY TIPS**

**TORNADOES**

- Listen for tornado warnings when severe weather is predicted.
- If you are in a car or mobile home, get out and go into a sturdy building or a ditch or depression.
- Go to the basement if possible.
- Avoid windows and open areas.
- Protect your head and neck.

## Paths of Tornadoes

A tornado moves along with its thunderstorm. It travels at the same pace and weaves a path that is impossible to predict. A tornado may appear suddenly and then disappear before anyone has time to report it. However, the conditions that form tornadoes may persist, so citizens' reports are still useful. The National Weather Service issues a tornado watch when the weather conditions might produce tornadoes. A tornado warning is issued when a tornado has been detected.

# 3.3 Review

### KEY CONCEPTS

1. What conditions produce thunderstorms?
2. How can rain from thunderstorms become dangerous?
3. How do tornadoes cause damage?

### CRITICAL THINKING

4. **Compare** What do hail and tornadoes have in common? **Hint:** Think about how each forms.
5. **Synthesize** Which type of front is most likely to produce thunderstorms and tornadoes? Explain why.

### CHALLENGE

6. **Compare and Contrast** If you saw the photograph above in a newspaper, what details would tell you that the damage was due to a tornado and not a hurricane?

SKILL: EVALUATING HYPOTHESES

# What Type of Weather Buried This Truck?

This picture was taken soon after a weather event partly buried this truck in Britannia Beach, British Columbia.

## Observations and Inferences

One observer made this analysis.

a. The truck, the tree, and two fences in the background were partly buried by sand and stones.

b. No stones are visible inside the truck.

c. The rounded stones must have come from an ocean or river.

d. The tree near the truck has green leaves. The wind must have been too weak to tear off the leaves.

e. The area is near the Pacific Ocean. It is far from the equator. There is a very large island between the location and the ocean.

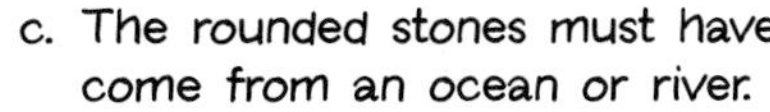

## Hypotheses

The observer made the following hypotheses.

a. A storm surge carried sand and stones from the Pacific Ocean. The material covered a large area. The truck floated, so it was not filled with material.

b. A tornado picked up the truck with other material. It dumped everything together, and the material partly buried the truck, fences, and tree.

c. Thunderstorms produced a flash flood that carried sand and stones from a riverbed to this area. The flood receded and left material that covered the area.

d. The truck was parked on a pile of snow during a blizzard. When the snow melted, the area under the truck collapsed and the truck sank into the ground.

A waterway leads south and west from Britannia Beach to a bay, around an island, to the Pacific Ocean.

## Evaluate Each Hypothesis

Review each hypothesis and think about whether the observations support it. Some facts may rule out some hypotheses. Some facts may neither support nor weaken some hypotheses.

**CHALLENGE** How could you model one or more of the hypotheses with a toy truck, sand, and a basin of water?

KEY CONCEPT

# Weather forecasters use advanced technologies.

**BEFORE, you learned**

- Weather changes when air masses move
- High-pressure systems bring fair weather
- Fronts and low-pressure systems bring stormy weather

**NOW, you will learn**

- How weather data are collected
- How weather data are displayed
- How meteorologists forecast the weather

**VOCABULARY**

**meteorologist** p. 98
**isobar** p. 101

**EXPLORE Weather Maps**

### *What does a weather map show?*

**PROCEDURE**

1. Look at the weather outside. Write down the conditions you observe.
2. Use the map to check the weather conditions for your region.

**WHAT DO YOU THINK?**

- What symbols on the map do you recognize?
- How does the information on the weather map compare with the weather you observed outside?

**MATERIALS**

newspaper weather map

## Weather data come from many sources.

Looking at the weather outside in the morning can help you decide what to wear. Different things give you clues to the current weather. If you see plants swaying from side to side, you might infer that it is windy. If you see a gray sky and wet, shiny streets, you might decide to wear a raincoat.

You might also check a weather report to get more information. A weather report can show conditions in your area and also in the region around you. You can look for weather nearby that might move into your area during the day. More detailed predictions of how the weather will move and change may be included in a weather report by a meteorologist. A **meteorologist** (MEE-tee-uh-RAHL-uh-jihst) is a scientist who studies weather.

**VOCABULARY**
Make a word triangle for *meteorologist.*

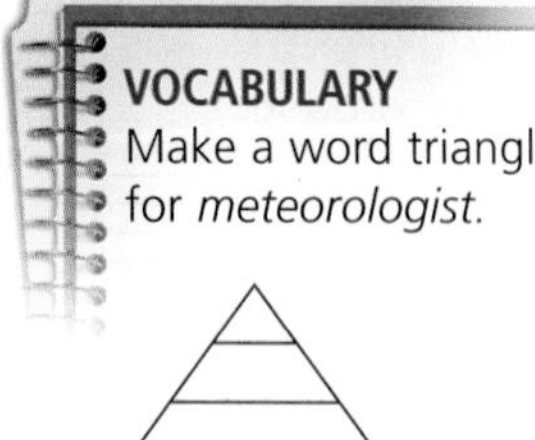

What information can a weather report show?

In order to predict the weather, meteorologists look at past and current conditions. They use many forms of technology to gather data. The illustration below shows how weather information is gathered. For example, radar stations and satellites use advanced technologies to gather data for large areas at a time.

Learn more about weather forecasting and your local weather.

Instruments within the atmosphere can make measurements of local weather conditions. Newer instruments can make measurements frequently and automatically and then report the results almost instantly. Instruments are placed in many ground stations on land and weather buoys at sea. Instruments can also be carried by balloons, ships, and planes. These instruments report a series of measurements along a path within the atmosphere.

## Collection of Weather Data

**Instruments that gather weather data use many technologies and can be found in many places.**

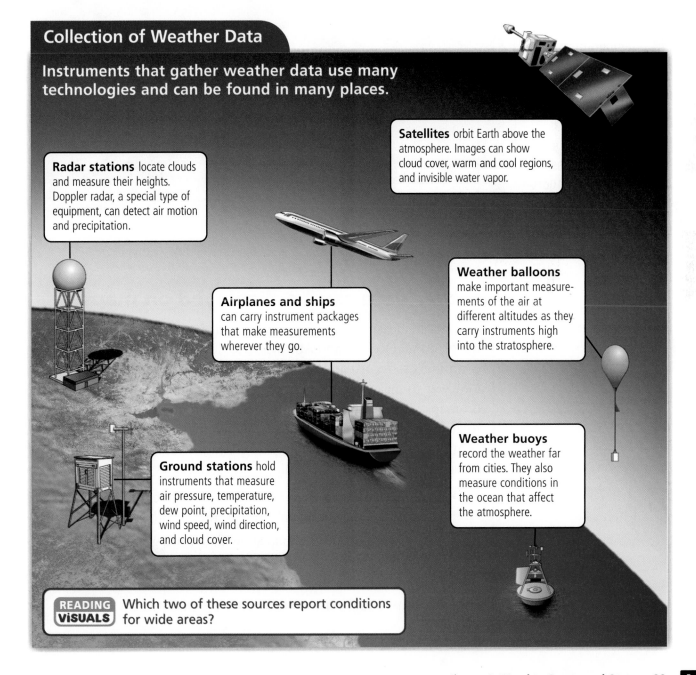

**Satellites** orbit Earth above the atmosphere. Images can show cloud cover, warm and cool regions, and invisible water vapor.

**Radar stations** locate clouds and measure their heights. Doppler radar, a special type of equipment, can detect air motion and precipitation.

**Weather balloons** make important measurements of the air at different altitudes as they carry instruments high into the stratosphere.

**Airplanes and ships** can carry instrument packages that make measurements wherever they go.

**Weather buoys** record the weather far from cities. They also measure conditions in the ocean that affect the atmosphere.

**Ground stations** hold instruments that measure air pressure, temperature, dew point, precipitation, wind speed, wind direction, and cloud cover.

**READING VISUALS** Which two of these sources report conditions for wide areas?

## Information on a Weather Map

**Meteorologists use maps to display a lot of weather information at once.**

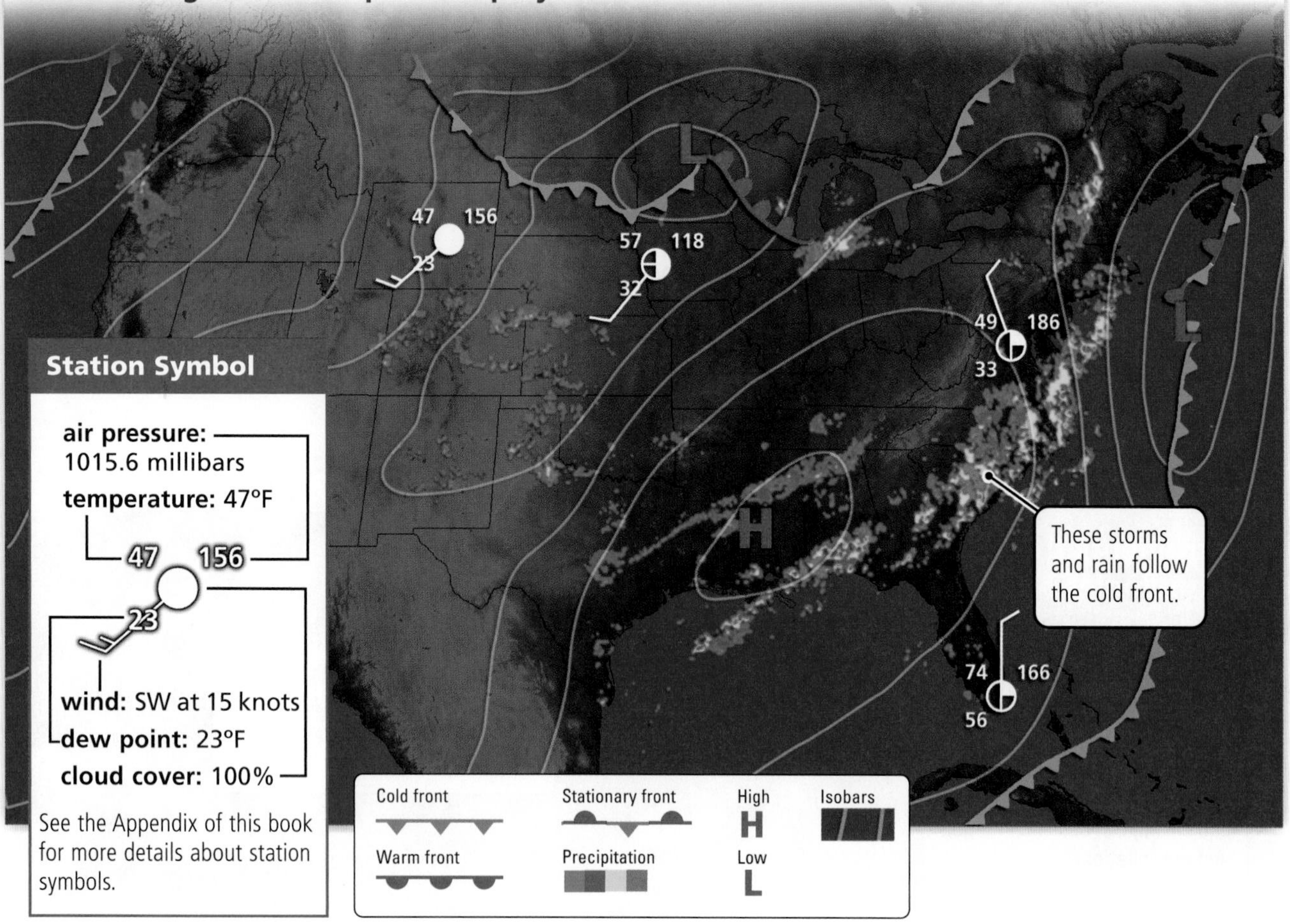

47 156
23
57 118
32
49 186
33
74 166
56
L
L
H

These storms and rain follow the cold front.

**Station Symbol**

**air pressure:** 1015.6 millibars
**temperature:** 47°F
47 156
23
**wind:** SW at 15 knots
**dew point:** 23°F
**cloud cover:** 100%

See the Appendix of this book for more details about station symbols.

Cold front
Warm front
Stationary front
Precipitation
High H
Low L
Isobars

# Weather data can be displayed on maps.

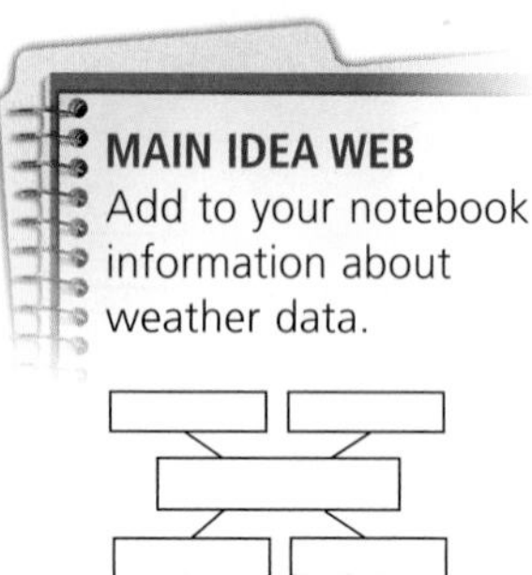

MAIN IDEA WEB
Add to your notebook information about weather data.

Automatic measurements from many sources constantly pour in to the National Oceanic and Atmospheric Administration. Scientists use computers to record and use the enormous amount of data gathered. One way to make the information easier to understand is to show it on maps. A single map can show many different types of data together to give a more complete picture of the weather. The map above combines information from ground stations with Doppler radar measurements of precipitation.

- Precipitation is shown as patches of blue, green, yellow, and red. The colors indicate the amounts of rain or other precipitation.
- Station symbols on the map show data from ground stations. Only a few stations are shown.
- Symbols showing fronts and pressure patterns are added to the map to make the overall weather patterns easier to see.

How is information from Doppler radar shown?

Computer programs are used to combine information from many ground stations. The resulting calculations give the highs, lows, and fronts that are marked on the map. The cold front near the East Coast has triangles to show that the front is moving eastward. This cold front produced the heavy rain that is visible in the Doppler radar data.

## Air Pressure on Weather Maps

The map below shows conditions from the same date as the map on page 100. Thin lines represent air pressure. An **isobar** (EYE-suh-BAHR) is a line that connects places that have the same air pressure. Each isobar represents a different air pressure value. All the isobars together, combined with the symbols for highs and lows, show the patterns of air pressure that produce weather systems.

**READING TIP**

*Iso-* means "equal," and *bar* means "pressure."

Each isobar is labeled with the air pressure for that whole line in units called millibars (MIHL-uh-BAHRZ). A lower number means a lower air pressure. As you read earlier, differences in pressure cause air to move. Meteorologists use isobars to understand air motion.

Sometimes air-pressure measurements are listed in inches of mercury. This unit comes from an old type of barometer that measures how high the air pressure pushes a column of mercury, a liquid metal. Computer-controlled instruments are used more often today, but the measurements may be converted to inches of mercury.

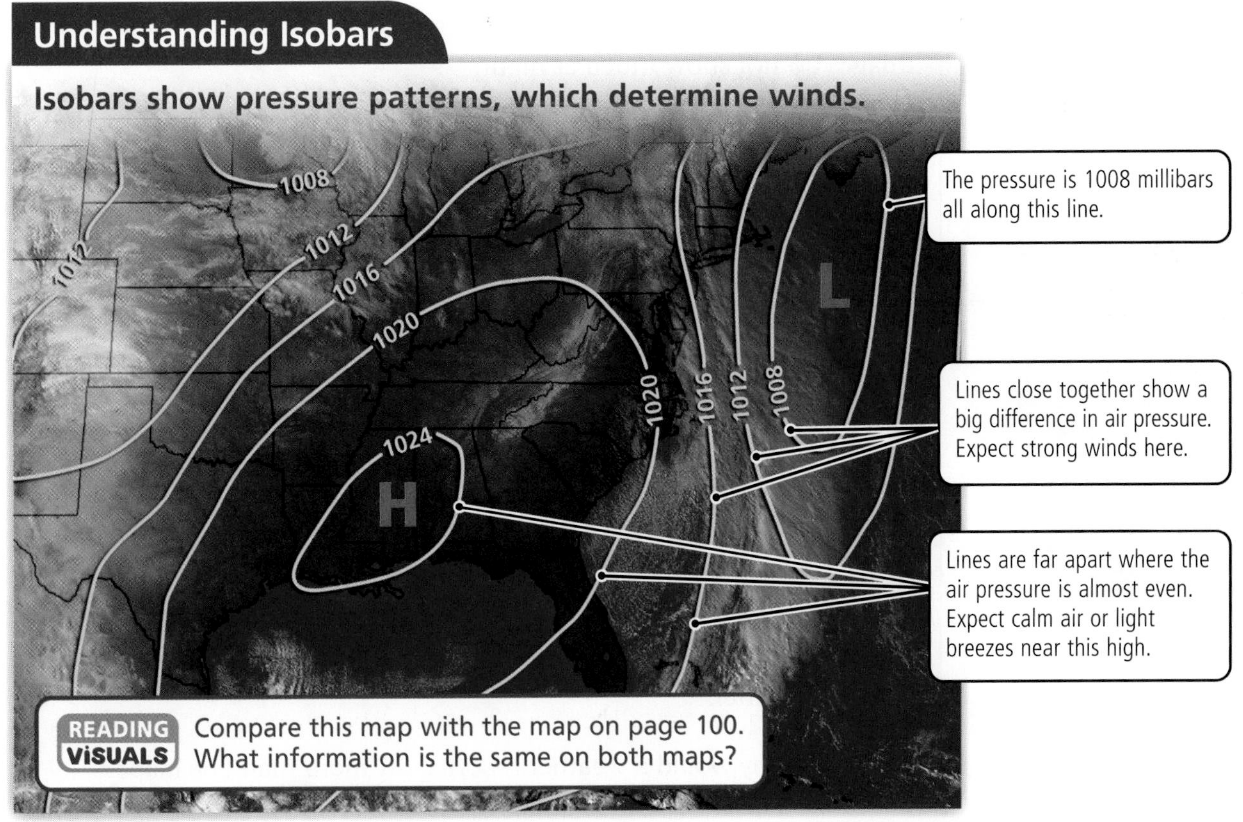

Understanding Isobars
Isobars show pressure patterns, which determine winds.
1008
1012
1012
1016
1020
1024
1020
1016
1012
1008
L
H
The pressure is 1008 millibars all along this line.
Lines close together show a big difference in air pressure. Expect strong winds here.
Lines are far apart where the air pressure is almost even. Expect calm air or light breezes near this high.
READING VISUALS Compare this map with the map on page 100. What information is the same on both maps?

## Satellite Images

**Visible Light**

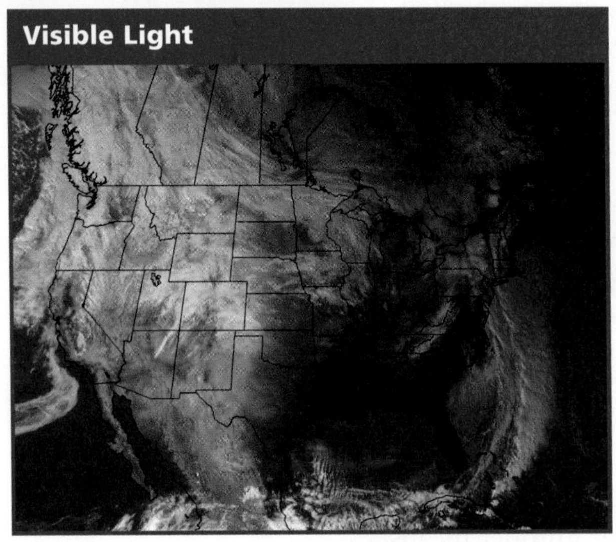

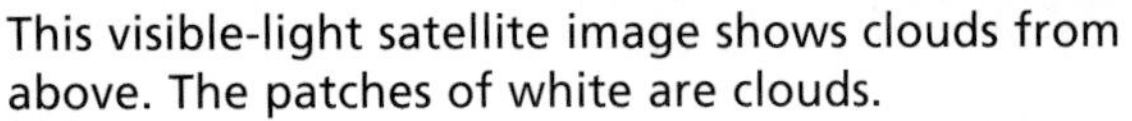

This visible-light satellite image shows clouds from above. The patches of white are clouds.

**Infrared Radiation**

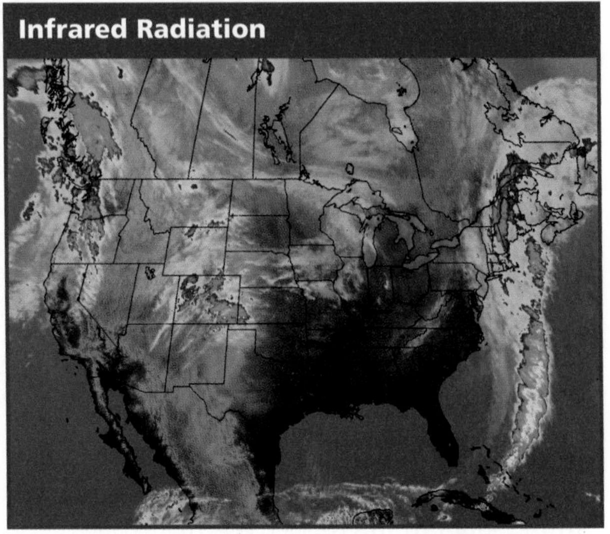

This infrared satellite image also shows clouds, but uses colors to show where there are tall clouds.

**READING VISUALS** Find a location on these maps and the map on page 100. What were the weather conditions?

## Satellite Images and Special Maps

Satellites take different types of images from space. Some images record the visible light that reflects off clouds and Earth's surface. Clouds and snow-covered land look white in sunlight. Unfortunately, visible-light images do not show much at night.

Another type of image shows infrared radiation given off by the warm surface and cooler clouds. These infrared images can show cloud patterns even at night because objects with different temperatures show up differently. Air temperatures change with altitude, so infrared images also show which clouds are low and which are high or tall. You can see in the maps above how visible and infrared satellite images show similar clouds but different details. Outlines of the states have been added to make the images easier to understand.

The colors on this map represent different ranges of temperature (°F).

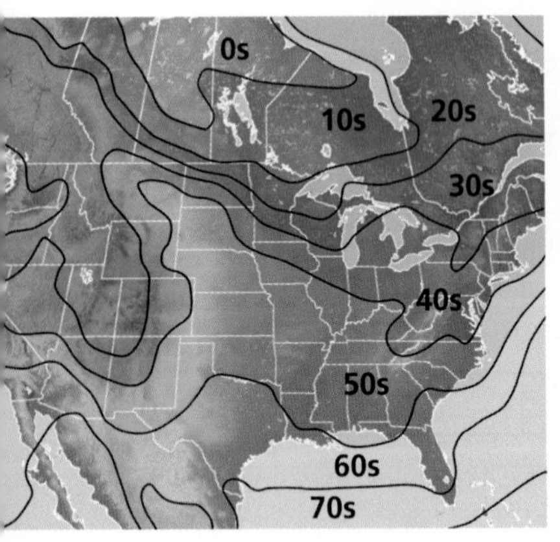


Data from ground stations and other sources can be used to make other types of maps. The map at left shows the pattern of temperatures on the same date as the images above and the map on page 100. Other maps may show winds or amounts of pollution. A map can be made to show any type of measurement or weather prediction. Different types of maps are often used together to give a more complete picture of the current weather.

**CHECK YOUR READING** Why would a weather report show more than one map?

## Forecasters use computer models to predict weather.

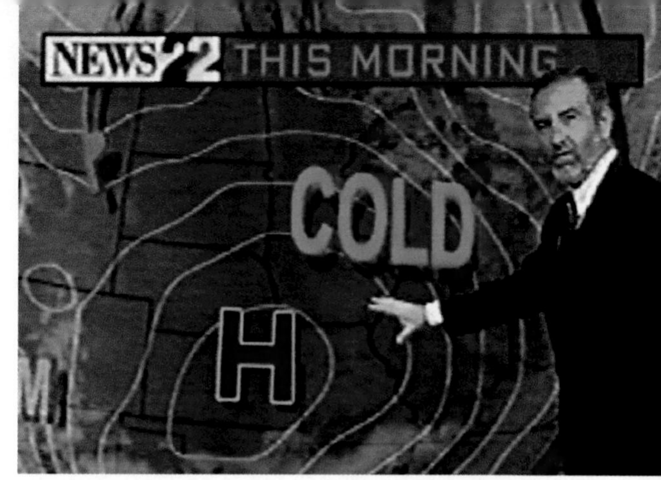


Forecasters use maps and satellite images to communicate weather conditions and predictions.

Instruments can only measure the current weather conditions. Most people want to know what the weather will be like in the future.

Forecasters can make some predictions from their own observations. If they see cirrus clouds above and high stratus clouds to the west, they might infer that a warm front is approaching. They would predict weather typical for a warm front—more clouds, then rain, and eventually warmer weather. If they also have information from other places, the forecasters might be able to tell where the warm front is already and how fast it is moving. They might be able to predict how soon it will arrive and even how warm the weather will be after the front passes.

Computers have become an important tool for forecasting weather. When weather stations send in data, computers can create maps right away. Computer models combine many types of data to forecast what might happen next. Different computer models give different types of forecasts. Scientists study the computer forecasts, then apply their knowledge and experience to make weather predictions.

Forecasting the weather is complicated. As a result, some forecasts are more dependable than others. The farther in advance a forecast is made, the more time there is for small differences between the predicted and the actual weather to add up. For this reason, short-range forecasts—up to three days in advance—are the most accurate. Forecasts of fast-changing weather, such as severe storms, are less accurate far in advance. It is best to watch for new predictions close to the time the storm is forecast.

# 3.4 Review

### KEY CONCEPTS

1. List three of the sources of weather data.
2. What does a map with isobars show?
3. How do meteorologists use computers?

### CRITICAL THINKING

4. **Draw Conclusions** Why do meteorologists not combine all their weather information into one map?
5. **Analyze** How is the information from radar and satellites different from the information from ground stations?

### CHALLENGE

6. **Apply** Suppose you are planning an afternoon picnic a week in advance. Fair weather is forecast for that day, but a storm is expected that night. What will you do? Explain your reasoning.

# CHAPTER INVESTIGATION

## Design a Weather Center

DESIGN — YOUR OWN —

**OVERVIEW AND PURPOSE** The accuracy of a weather forecast depends largely on the type and quality of the data that it is based on. In this lab, you will use what you have learned about weather to

- observe and measure weather conditions
- record and analyze the weather-related data

**MATERIALS**
- thermometer
- magnetic compass
- other weather instruments
- graph paper

### Procedure

1. Survey the possible sources of weather data in and around your classroom. You can use a thermometer to record the outside air temperature. You can observe cloud types and the amount of cloud cover from a window or doorway. You can also observe precipitation and notice if it is heavy or light. If there is a flag in view, use it to find the wind direction and to estimate wind speed.

2. Assemble or make tools for your observations. You may want to make a reference chart with pictures of different cloud types or other information. Decide if you wish to use homemade weather instruments. You may have made a barometer, a psychrometer, and a rain gauge already. If not, see the instructions on pages 45, 64, and 67. You may also wish to do research to learn how to make or use other weather instruments.

3. Make an initial set of observations. Write down the date and time in your **Science Notebook.** Record the readings from the thermometer and other instruments.

4 Decide how to record your observations of the clouds, the wind, and any precipitation. Organize your notes to make it easy for you to record later observations in a consistent way.

5 Create a chart with a row for each type of observation you are making. You might darken fractions of circles to record amounts of cloud cover, as in the station symbols on page 100. Make sure each row has a heading and enough room for numbers, words, or sketches. Include a row for notes that do not belong in the data rows.

6 Record your observations every day at the same time. Try to make the observations exactly the same way each time. If you have to redraw your chart, copy the information carefully.

## Observe and Analyze

Write It Up

1. **GRAPH** Graph the data you collected that represent measurable quantities. Use graphs that are appropriate to your data. Often a simple line graph will work. Choose an appropriate scale and interval based on the range of your data. Make the *x*-axis of each graph the same so that you can compare the different types of data easily.
2. **COMPARE AND CONTRAST** Look at your graphs for patterns in your data. Some aspects of weather change at the same time because they are related to each other. Did one type of change occur before a different type of change? If so, this pattern may help you predict weather.

## Conclude

Write It Up

1. **INTERPRET** Did a front pass through your area during the period you observed? What observations helped you answer this question?
2. **EVALUATE** Why was it necessary to observe at the same time each day?
3. **APPLY** If you predicted that each day's weather would be repeated the next day, how often would you be right?

## INVESTIGATE Further

**CHALLENGE** Locate a newspaper weather page for the period during which you were making your weather observations. How do the weather data reported for your area compare with your measurements? How do you account for any differences you notice in the data?

Design a Weather Center

Table 1. Daily Weather Chart

| Date/time of observations | | | |
|---|---|---|---|
| Temperature (°C) | | | |
| Cloud types | | | |
| Cloud coverage | ○ | ○ | ○ |
| Precipitation (cm) and notes | | | |
| Wind direction | | | |
| Other notes | | | |

# 3 Chapter Review

## the BIG idea

**The interaction of air masses causes changes in weather.**

## KEY CONCEPTS SUMMARY

### 3.1 Weather changes as air masses move.

**Air masses** meet and produce **fronts,** which can bring lowered pressure and stormy weather. Fronts can be cold, warm, or stationary.

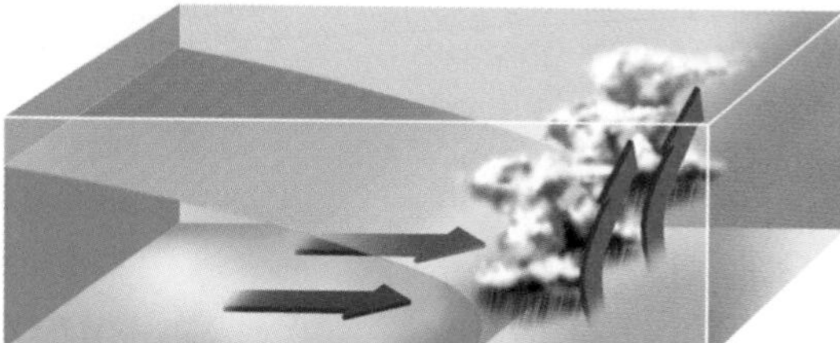

**VOCABULARY**
**air mass** p. 79
**front** p. 82
**high-pressure system** p. 84
**low-pressure system** p. 85

### 3.2 Low-pressure systems can become storms.

**Hurricanes** and winter storms develop from low-pressure systems.

Hurricanes form over warm ocean water.

**VOCABULARY**
**tropical storm** p. 87
**hurricane** p. 87
**storm surge** p. 89
**blizzard** p. 90

### 3.3 Vertical air motion can cause severe storms.

Rising moist air can produce **thunderstorms.** The up-and-down motion of air in a thunderstorm can produce a **tornado.**

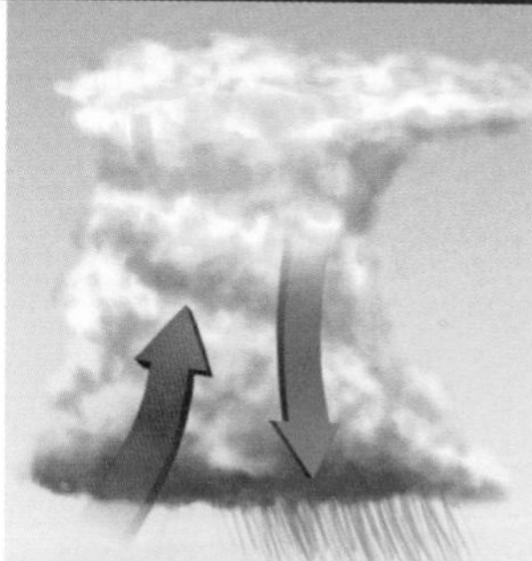

**VOCABULARY**
**thunderstorm** p. 92
**tornado** p. 95

### 3.4 Weather forecasters use advanced technologies.

Weather information comes from many sources.

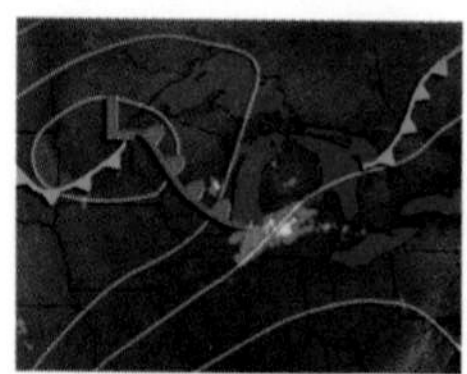

**Meteorologists** use weather data and computer models to forecast weather.

**VOCABULARY**
**meteorologist** p. 98
**isobar** p. 101

## Reviewing Vocabulary

*Describe each term below, using the related term as part of the description.*

| Term | Related Term | Description |
|---|---|---|
| EXAMPLE<br>hurricane | low-pressure system | a low-pressure system in the tropics with winds at least 120 km/h |
| **1.** front | air mass | |
| **2.** low-pressure system | low-pressure center | |
| **3.** storm surge | hurricane | |
| **4.** tropical storm | low-pressure system | |
| **5.** air mass | humidity | |
| **6.** thunderstorm | convection | |
| **7.** tornado | thunderstorm | |
| **8.** blizzard | low-pressure system | |

## Reviewing Key Concepts

**Multiple Choice** *Choose the letter of the best answer.*

**9.** What qualities are nearly the same at different locations in a single air mass?
- **a.** temperature and pressure
- **b.** temperature and humidity
- **c.** air pressure and wind speed
- **d.** air pressure and humidity

**10.** Which is the name for an air mass that forms over the ocean near the equator?
- **a.** maritime tropical
- **b.** maritime polar
- **c.** continental tropical
- **d.** continental polar

**11.** A meteorologist is a scientist who
- **a.** predicts meteor showers
- **b.** studies maps
- **c.** studies the weather
- **d.** changes the weather

**12.** An isobar shows locations with the same
- **a.** temperature
- **b.** rainfall
- **c.** air pressure
- **d.** wind speed

**13.** Which is produced when a warm air mass pushes a colder air mass?
- **a.** a stationary front
- **b.** a cold front
- **c.** a warm front
- **d.** a thunderstorm

**14.** Which can be measured in inches of mercury?
- **a.** air pressure
- **b.** temperature
- **c.** hail
- **d.** lightning

**15.** Which source provides measurements for just one location?
- **a.** ground station
- **b.** radar station
- **c.** weather balloon
- **d.** satellite

**16.** Compared with warm fronts, cold fronts are
- **a.** faster moving
- **b.** less dense
- **c.** more cloudy
- **d.** less steep

**17.** Which statement is usually true of high-pressure systems in North America?
- **a.** They bring fair weather.
- **b.** They change quickly.
- **c.** The air in them is cold and dense.
- **d.** The air in them moves counterclockwise.

**18.** Thunderstorms often begin with the rising of
- **a.** cool, dry air
- **b.** cool, humid air
- **c.** warm, dry air
- **d.** warm, humid air

**19.** What is the relationship between lightning and thunder?
- **a.** They have separate causes.
- **b.** They have the same cause.
- **c.** Lightning causes thunder.
- **d.** Thunder causes lightning.

**Short Answer** *Write a short answer to each question.*

**20.** Why are hurricanes in the eastern United States more likely in autumn than in spring?

**21.** What causes lake-effect snow?

**22.** In what four ways can thunderstorms be dangerous?

## Thinking Critically

*Use this weather map to answer the next six questions. The numbers under each city name are the highest and the lowest temperature for the day in degrees Fahrenheit.*

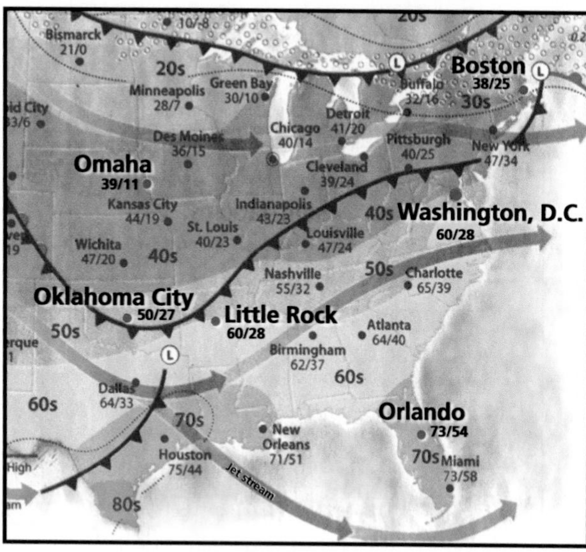


**23. INFER** Name and describe the air mass that has moved south to Omaha from Canada.

**24. IDENTIFY EFFECTS** How are two low-pressure systems affecting the weather near Boston?

**25. PREDICT** Explain whether Washington, D.C., or Orlando is more likely to have a big change in weather in the next two days.

**26. COMPARE AND CONTRAST** Explain the difference in temperature between Oklahoma City and Little Rock.

**27. PREDICT** How will the weather in Little Rock change in the next day or two?

**28. APPLY** Does this map indicate that it is hurricane season? Explain your reasoning.

**29. CONNECT** Describe today's weather and explain what fronts and pressure systems might be influencing it.

**30. COMPARE AND CONTRAST** Use a Venn diagram to compare images from visible light and infrared radiation.

**PREDICT** *For each set of conditions listed in the chart, write a weather prediction.*

| Conditions | Prediction |
|---|---|
| **31.** A cold front is moving into an area that has warm, moist air. | |
| **32.** A warm front is moving into an area that has cold, dense air. | |
| **33.** A cool sea breeze is blowing inland, causing warm, humid air to rise. | |
| **34.** Air pressure is falling and the temperature is rising. | |
| **35.** Air pressure is increasing and the temperature is steady. | |
| **36.** A thunderstorm is developing spinning winds at its center. | |
| **37.** A low-pressure center is over the Atlantic Ocean where the water temperature is above 27°C (81°F). | |
| **38.** Cold air is pushing warm air where the air is 2°C (36°F) and the ground is -3°C (27°F). | |

**39. COMPARE** How is the air motion in the eye of a hurricane similar to the air motion at a high-pressure center?

**40. EVALUATE** Which type of storm is most dangerous? Explain your reasoning.

## the BIG idea

**41. APPLY** Look again at the photograph on pages 76–77. Now that you have finished the chapter, how would you change your response to the question on the photograph?

**42. SEQUENCE** Draw a storyboard with at least four sketches to show how cool, sunny weather might change into warm, rainy weather.

## UNIT PROJECTS

Check your schedule for your unit project. How are you doing? Be sure that you have placed data or notes from your research in your project folder.

## Analyzing a Map

*Use this weather map to answer the questions below.*

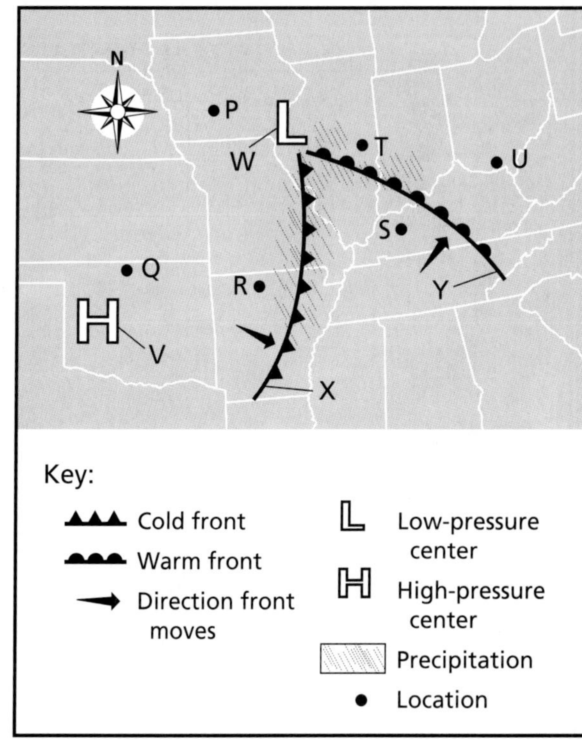


**1.** Which letter labels a cold front?

**a.** Q  **c.** X
**b.** U  **d.** Y

**2.** Which word best describes the general movement of the fronts?

**a.** to the north  **c.** clockwise
**b.** to the east  **d.** counterclockwise

**3.** A warm front occurs where warm air moves into colder air. Which of these locations is probably warmest?

**a.** R  **c.** T
**b.** S  **d.** U

**4.** Temperatures usually change quickly near a front and more slowly away from a front. The temperature at Q is 10°C (50°F). The temperature at S is 20°C (68°F). Which is the best estimate for the temperature at R?

**a.** 6°C (43°F)  **c.** 20°C (68°F)
**b.** 11°C (52°F)  **d.** 24°C (75°F)

**5.** If the fronts continue to move as shown, which location will get warmer soon?

**a.** Q  **c.** S
**b.** R  **d.** T

**6.** Low pressure often brings stormy weather, and high pressure often brings fair weather. Which of these locations is most likely to have clear skies?

**a.** Q  **c.** S
**b.** R  **d.** U

## Extended Response

*Use the map above to answer the two questions below in detail. Include some of the terms shown in the word box. Underline each term you use in your answers.*

| cold front | humid | west |
|---|---|---|
| warm front | east | prevailing winds |

**7.** Along which front on the weather map above would you expect to find cumulonimbus clouds? Explain why.

**8.** The weather system shown on the map above is in the continental United States. In which direction do you expect it to move? Explain why.

# TIMELINES in Science

## OBSERVING THE ATMOSPHERE

The atmosphere is always changing, and scientists are developing better ways to observe these changes. Accurate weather forecasts help people make everyday decisions, such as what kind of clothing to wear. Forecasts also allow us to plan for dangerous storms and other natural disasters. Scientists are now warning of long-term changes to the atmosphere that can affect the entire world. These predictions are possible because of the work of scientists and observers over hundreds of years.

The timeline shows some historical events in the study of Earth's air and weather. The boxes below the timeline show how technology has led to new knowledge about the atmosphere and show how that knowledge has been applied.

**1686**

*Trade Winds Are Linked to Sun's Energy*

Sailors have used trade winds for centuries to sail from Europe to the Americas. Now, Edmund Halley, a British astronomer, explains global winds in a new theory. He argues that trade winds blowing toward the equator replace air that rises due to solar heating.

**EVENTS**

1640 1660 1680

**APPLICATIONS AND TECHNOLOGY**

**TECHNOLOGY**

**Measuring Air Pressure**

The mercury barometer was invented in 1643 to measure air pressure. Changes in outside air pressure cause the level of mercury to rise and fall in a tall glass tube. This remarkably accurate type of barometer was used for centuries. Now, most air-pressure measurements are taken with aneroid barometers, which are easier to use.

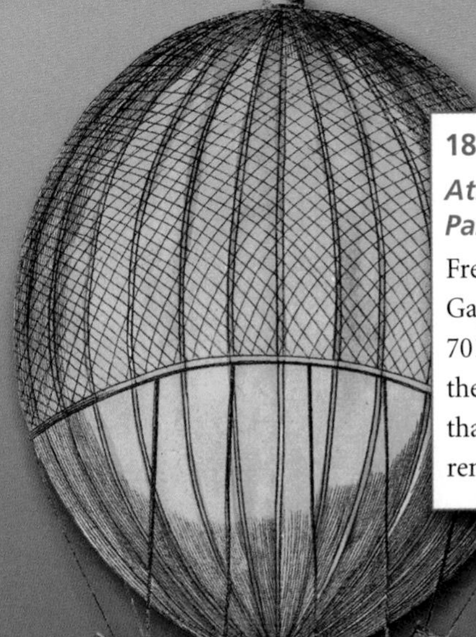

1804

*Atmosphere Explorations Pass 7000 Meters*

French chemist Joseph Louis Gay-Lussac rises to an altitude of 7016 meters in a balloon to study the atmosphere. His studies show that the atmosphere's composition remains the same up to that altitude.

1827

*Atmospheric Greenhouse Warms Earth*

French scientist Jean-Baptiste Fourier coins a new term, "greenhouse effect." He suggests that the atmosphere slows the movement of energy from Earth's surface out toward space. Fourier compares this effect to the way heat is trapped in a greenhouse.

1743

*Franklin Tracks Storms*

Benjamin Franklin tries to look at an eclipse of the Moon, but a storm blocks his view. Meanwhile, a friend in another city has a clear view during the eclipse, and soon afterward the storm arrives there. Franklin concludes that storms travel instead of forming and dying in the same place.

1740 1760 1780 1800 1820

## APPLICATION

### Telegraphing the Weather

The development of the telegraph in the 1800s was important for weather forecasting because it allowed observers to quickly send data to distant locations. In 1870, the U.S. government organized a system of weather observers who communicated by telegraph. This was the beginning of the National Weather Service, which at first focused on providing storm warnings for coastal regions. However, the weather reporting service was soon extended to cover the entire nation. The National Weather Service has become a crucial information agency.

## 1942
### *Pilots Find Jet Streams*
Wartime pilots discover very fast winds called jet streams at high altitudes. Pilots find that the jet streams are like narrow rivers of air moving at speeds that average 180 kilometers per hour (110 mi/h).

## 1918
### *Storm Fronts Explained*
Norway's Jacob Bjerknes explains how large storm systems develop at the boundaries between masses of air. He calls the boundaries "fronts," comparing them to battlefronts between armies.

## 1958
### *Greenhouse Gas Monitored*
Carbon dioxide and other greenhouse gases are measured at Mauna Loa Observatory on the Big Island of Hawaii, 11,000 feet above sea level. Accurate measurements can be obtained from this location because it is far from cities and other human influences.

1900 1920 1940 1960

## TECHNOLOGY
### Picturing the Weather
Ground-based weather stations cannot collect data from high altitudes or from areas between stations. The development of weather technology helped fill the gaps. In the 1930s, weather balloons carried instruments to different altitudes. In 1953, the development of Doppler radar showed raindrop sizes and speeds. Scientists later began using Doppler radar to measure precipitation for a wide area all at once.

In 1960, weather satellites began to provide images of weather from space. Satellites can show hurricanes long before they hit the shore. Fifteen years later, scientists began to use instruments on satellites to detect radiation other than visible light. Infrared cameras showed clouds at night and made detailed measurements that improved forecasts.

**1985**

***Hole Found in Ozone Layer***

Using data from a ground-based instrument in Antarctica, scientists discover a large area where the protective layer of ozone is very thin. They call it the ozone hole. The discovery confirms earlier predictions that certain industrial chemicals can result in ozone destruction.

**RESOURCE CENTER**
CLASSZONE.COM
Learn more about current research on the atmosphere.

**1980** **2000**

## APPLICATION

### Computer Modeling

Scientists use computers not only to collect data but also to make models of the atmosphere. Models show how the atmosphere changed in the past and how it may change in the future. As computers become faster and better, the models can be made more detailed and therefore more reliable.

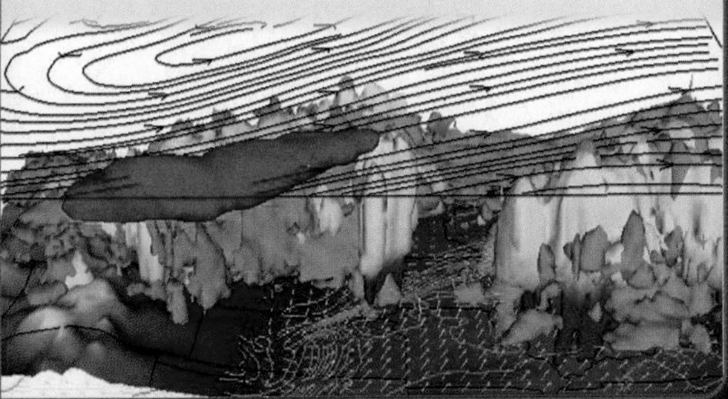

## INTO THE FUTURE

With frequent measurements of much of Earth's atmosphere, scientists can now understand a lot more about weather. Supercomputers let scientists make models of ordinary weather and complicated storms.

In the future, scientists will better understand the way the oceans and the atmosphere affect one another. They will make models of complex patterns that involve long-term changes in the oceans and the atmosphere.

Researchers will use models of Earth's past weather to understand the changes happening today. They will make more detailed predictions about future changes. People will be able to make better decisions about human activities that affect Earth's atmosphere. Researchers will continue to improve and use their understanding of the atmospheres of other worlds to understand Earth.

## ACTIVITIES

### Reliving History

Ancient peoples made simple weather instruments, such as wind vanes. You can make a wind vane and then map the wind directions in your neighborhood.

Push a straight pin through the middle of a drinking straw and then into an eraser at the end of a pencil. Tape a square of cardboard vertically to one end of the straw. Put a small piece of clay on the other end so that the wind vane is balanced. The straw will turn so that the clay end of the straw points into the wind.

Use your wind vane and a magnetic compass to find the wind direction in several places in your neighborhood. Record the results on a copy of a map. Do you notice any patterns?

### Writing About Science

Suppose scientists learn to control the weather. What factors have to be considered in choosing the weather? Write a conversation in which opposing viewpoints are debated.

CHAPTER

# Climate and Climate Change

## the BIG idea

Climates are long-term weather patterns that may change over time.

## Key Concepts

SECTION

**Climate is a long-term weather pattern.**
Learn about the main factors that affect climate and about seasons.

SECTION

**Earth has a variety of climates.**
Learn about different categories of climate.

SECTION

**Climates can change suddenly or slowly.**
Learn about climate changes caused by natural events and human activity.

**Internet Preview**

CLASSZONE.COM

Chapter 4 online resources: Content Review, Simulation, four Resource Centers, Math Tutorial, Test Practice

***What evidence of different types of climate can you see in this photo?***

## Why Are Climates Different?

Look at a newspaper weather map. Find some cities that usually have very different weather from the weather in your area.

**Observe and Think**
Where are those cities located on the map? Are they north or south of your location? What geographical differences might help make the weather in those cities different from the weather in your area?

## How Do Microclimates Form?

Go outside with a thermometer and take temperature readings in four different places. Repeat your observations at a later time of day.

**Observe and Think**
What temperature readings did you observe? Did the readings stay the same later in the day?

## Internet Activity: El Niño

Go to **ClassZone.com** to find out information about El Niño.

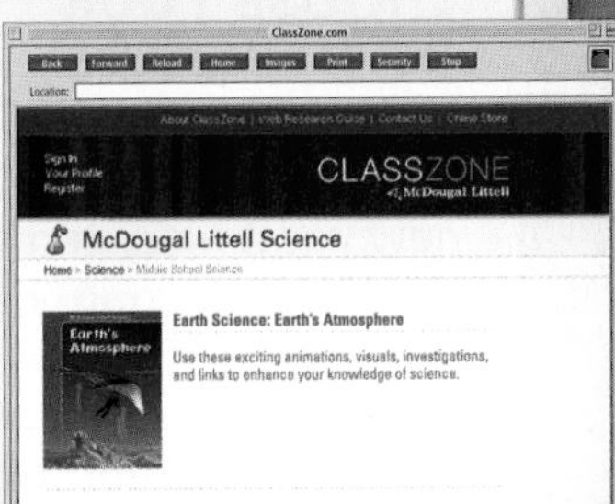


**Observe and Think**
How does El Niño affect temperature and precipitation patterns in your region?

What Is Climate? **Code: MDL012**

CHAPTER 4

# Getting Ready to Learn

## CONCEPT REVIEW

- Earth's atmosphere supports life.
- In a system that consists of many parts, the parts usually influence one another.
- Human activities are increasing greenhouse gases.

## VOCABULARY REVIEW

**altitude** p. 10
**greenhouse gas** p. 24
**weather** p. 47
**precipitation** p. 57

CONTENT REVIEW
CLASSZONE.COM
Review concepts and vocabulary.

## TAKING NOTES

### MAIN IDEA AND DETAIL NOTES

Make a two-column chart. Write the main ideas, such as those in the blue headings, in the column on the left. Write details about each of those main ideas in the column on the right.

### CHOOSE YOUR OWN STRATEGY

Take notes about new vocabulary terms, using one or more of the strategies from earlier chapters—**frame game, description wheel,** or **word triangle.** Feel free to mix and match the strategies, or use an entirely different vocabulary strategy.

See the Note-Taking Handbook on pages R45–R51.

SCIENCE NOTEBOOK

| MAIN IDEAS | DETAIL NOTES |
| --- | --- |
| 1. Latitude affects climate. | 1. Places close to the equator are usually warmer than places close to the poles.<br>1. Latitude has the same effect in both hemispheres. |
| 2. Altitude affects climate. | 2. Temperature decreases with altitude.<br>2. Altitude can overcome the effect of latitude on temperature. |

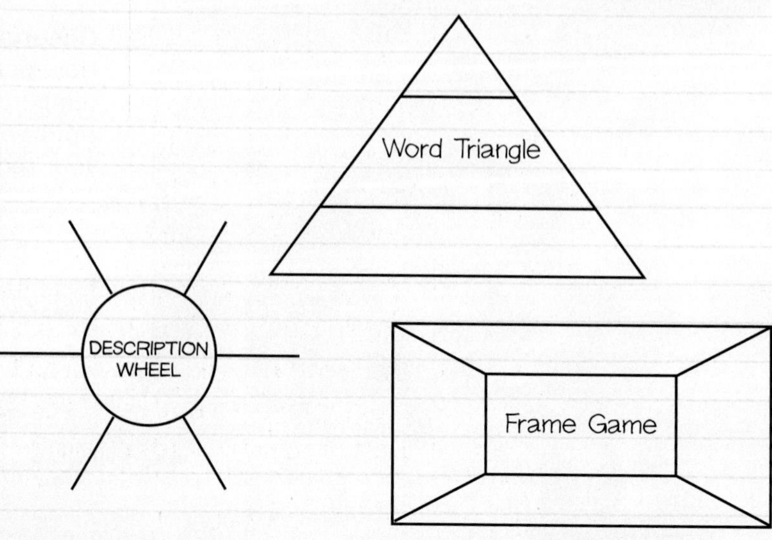

KEY CONCEPT

# Climate is a long-term weather pattern.

**BEFORE, you learned**

- The Sun's energy heats Earth's surface unevenly
- The atmosphere's temperature changes with altitude
- Oceans affect wind flow

**NOW, you will learn**

- How climate is related to weather
- What factors affect climate
- About seasonal patterns of temperature and precipitation

**VOCABULARY**

**climate** p. 117
**latitude** p. 118
**marine climate** p. 120
**continental climate** p. 120
**ocean current** p. 121
**season** p. 122

**EXPLORE Solar Energy**

## *How does the angle of light affect heating?*

**PROCEDURE**

1. Tape a black square over the bulb of each thermometer. Then tape the thermometers to the cardboard tube as shown.
2. Place the arrangement on a sunny windowsill or under a lamp. One square should directly face the light. Record the temperatures.
3. Wait 10 minutes. Record the temperature changes.

**WHAT DO YOU THINK?**

- How did the temperature readings change?
- How did the angle of light affect the amount of heat absorbed?

**MATERIALS**

- tape
- 2 black paper squares
- 2 thermometers
- 1 cardboard tube from a paper towel roll
- sunny windowsill or lamp

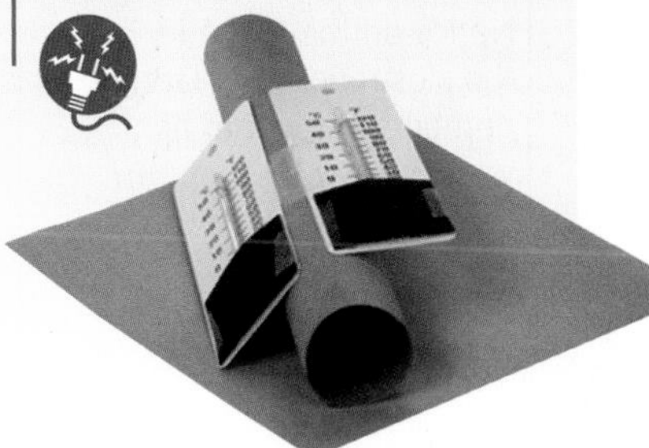

## Geography affects climate.

You can check your current local weather simply by looking out a window. Weather conditions may not last very long; they can change daily or even hourly. In contrast, the climate of your area changes over much longer periods of time. **Climate** is the characteristic weather conditions in a place over a long period. Climate influences the kind of clothes you own, the design of your home, and even the sports you play.

All parts of weather make up climate, including wind, humidity, and sunshine. However, meteorologists usually focus on patterns of temperature and precipitation when they classify climates. Four key geographical factors affect temperature and precipitation: latitude, altitude, distance from large bodies of water, and ocean currents.

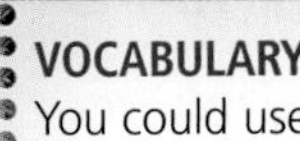

**VOCABULARY**
You could use a frame game diagram to take notes about the term *climate*.

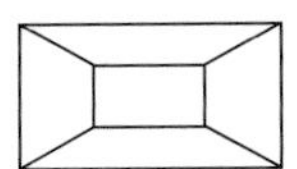

## Latitude and Temperature

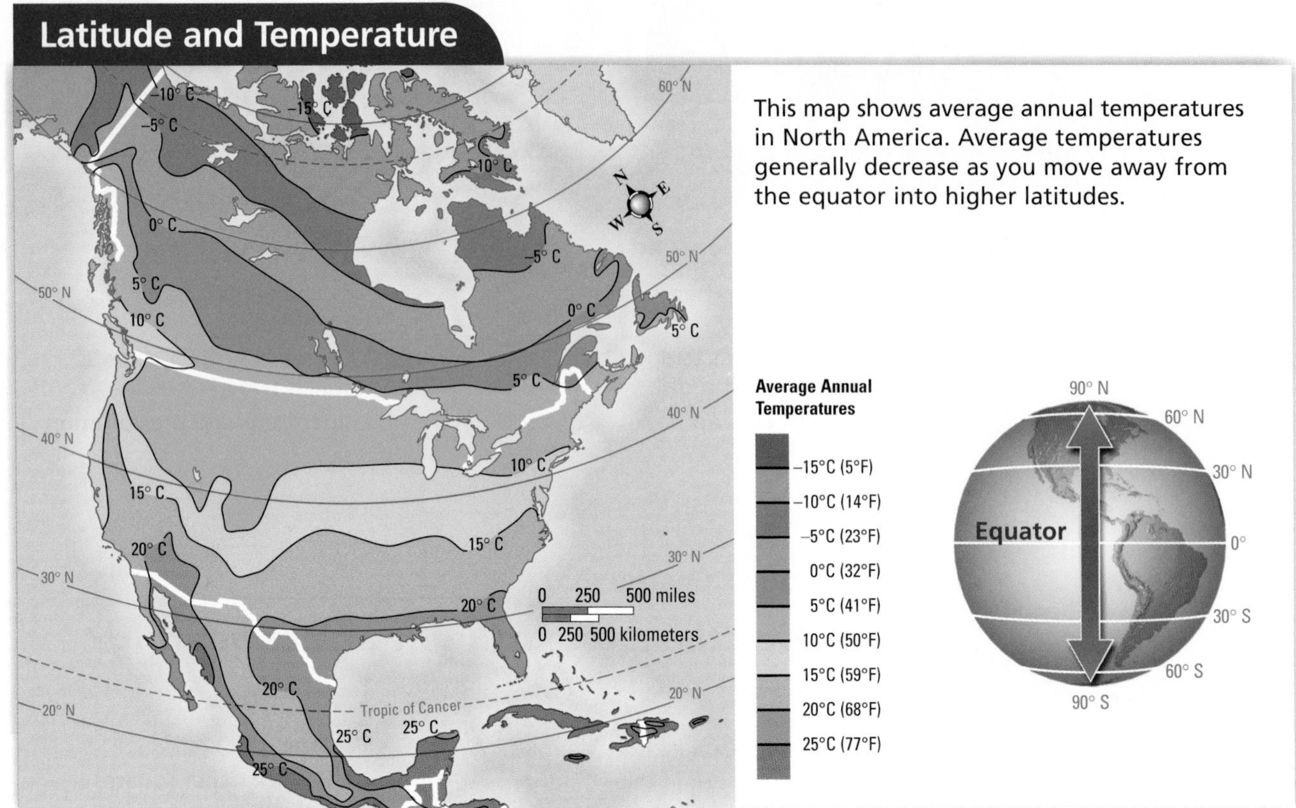


This map shows average annual temperatures in North America. Average temperatures generally decrease as you move away from the equator into higher latitudes.

## Latitude

**READING TIP**

Notice on the globe in the illustration that latitude numbers get higher as you move away from the equator.

One factor that affects temperature is latitude. **Latitude** is the distance in degrees north or south of the equator, which is 0°. Each degree equals 1/360 of the distance around the world.

As you read in Chapter 2, the Sun heats Earth's curved surface unevenly. Sunlight strikes Earth's surface directly near the equator. Near the poles, sunlight strikes the surface at a lower angle, so it is more spread out. In addition, the polar regions receive little or no solar energy during winter.

Because of this pattern of uneven heating, average annual temperatures generally decrease as you move closer to the poles. For example, Belém, Brazil, which is almost on the equator, has an average temperature of about 26°C (79°F). Qaanaaq, Greenland, located close to the North Pole, has an average temperature of only –11°C (12°F).

Latitude has the same effect on temperature in both hemispheres. Suppose one city is located at 45° N and another city is located at 45° S. The first city is in the Northern Hemisphere, and the second is in the Southern Hemisphere. However, they are both nearly 5000 kilometers (3100 mi) from the equator, so they would receive about the same amount of sunlight over a year.

What is the connection between latitude and temperature?

## Altitude

Altitude, the height above sea level, is another geographical factor that affects temperature. If you rode a cable car up a mountain, the temperature would decrease by about 6.5°C (11.7°F) for every kilometer you rose in altitude. Why does it get colder as you move higher up? The troposphere is mainly warmed from below by Earth's surface. As convection lifts the warmed air to higher altitudes, the air expands and cools.

Even at the equator, a mountain peak can be covered with snow and ice.

snow line

Temperatures are too cold above this elevation for trees to grow.

tree line

Because altitude changes sharply on a mountain, different climates can exist within a small area.

Altitude increases can overcome the effect of lower latitudes on temperature. The temperature at the peak of a tall mountain is low regardless of the mountain's latitude. One example is Mount Stanley, near the border of Uganda and the Democratic Republic of the Congo in central Africa. Although it lies just a short distance from the equator, Mount Stanley has ice sheets and a permanent covering of snow. Notice in the illustration how one mountain can have several types of climates.

Explore the effects of latitude and altitude.

## INVESTIGATE Heating and Cooling Rates

### *How quickly do soil and water heat and cool?*

**SKILL FOCUS**
Comparing

**PROCEDURE**

1. Mark a line 3 centimeters from the top of each cup. Fill one cup to the line with water and the other with soil. Place a thermometer into the contents of each cup. Wait 2 minutes. Record the temperature in each cup.
2. Place the cups side by side in bright sunlight or under a lamp. Wait 10 minutes. Record the temperature in each cup.
3. Move the cups into a shaded area to cool. Wait 10 minutes. Record the temperature in each cup.

**WHAT DO YOU THINK?**

- Which heats up faster, soil or water?
- Which cools faster?
- How might the heating and cooling rates of inland areas compare with those of coastal areas?

**CHALLENGE** Will adding gravel to the soil change your results? Repeat the activity to test your prediction.

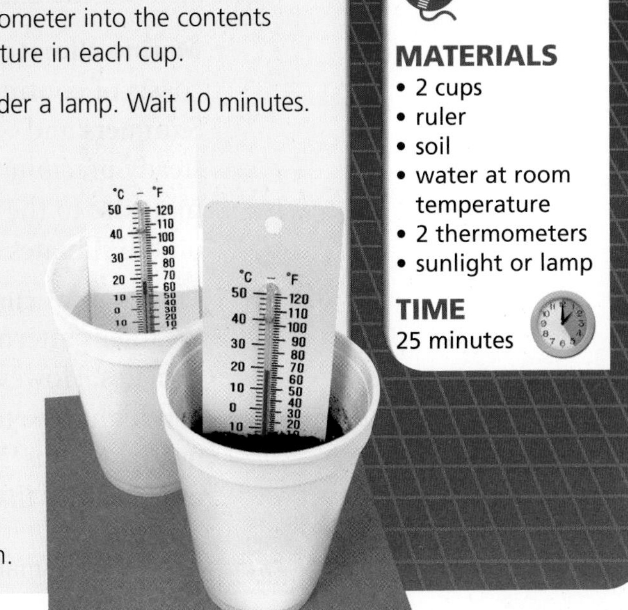

**MATERIALS**
- 2 cups
- ruler
- soil
- water at room temperature
- 2 thermometers
- sunlight or lamp

**TIME**
25 minutes

## How Oceans Affect Climate

**Regions near oceans have milder temperatures than inland regions at the same latitudes.**

45° N

35° N

PACIFIC OCEAN

**Portland:**
**Latitude:** 45.6° N

Minneapolis:
**Latitude:** 44.9° N

**Portland (Marine Climate)**

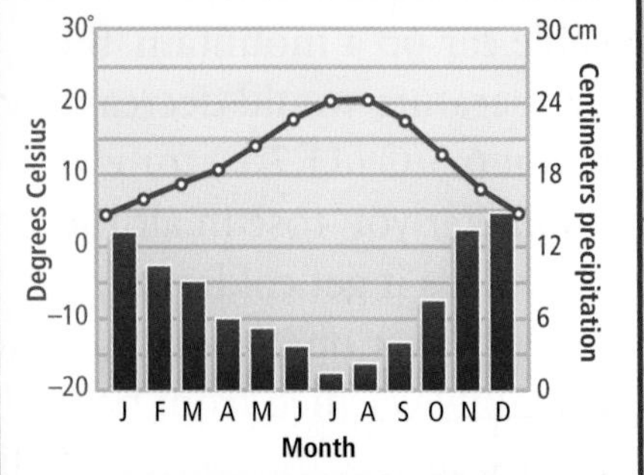

Degrees Celsius: 30°, 20, 10, 0, −10, −20

Centimeters precipitation: 30 cm, 24, 18, 12, 6, 0

J F M A M J J A S O N D

Month

**Minneapolis (Continental Climate)**

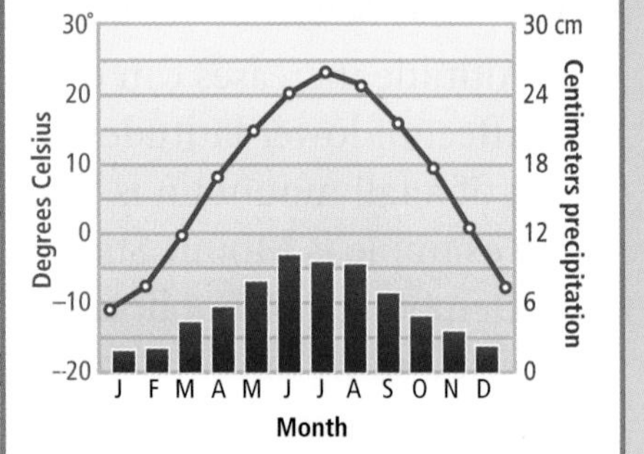

Degrees Celsius: 30°, 20, 10, 0, −10, −20

Centimeters precipitation: 30 cm, 24, 18, 12, 6, 0

J F M A M J J A S O N D

Month

SOURCE: National Climatic Data Center

**READING VISUALS** The bars in the graphs show average precipitation, and the lines show average temperature. Compare each of these patterns in the two cities.

## Large Bodies of Water

Land heats up and cools off faster than water. Because oceans and large lakes slow down heating and cooling of the air, coastal regions tend to have milder temperatures than areas far inland. Large bodies of water also affect precipitation. Climates influenced by these factors are called marine and continental climates.

- **Marine climates** occur near the ocean, usually along the west coasts of continents. Temperatures do not drop very far at night. Summers and winters are mild. Many marine climates receive steady precipitation because winds blowing off the ocean bring moisture to the atmosphere. Large lakes can have a similar effect on the climates near their shores.
- **Continental climates** occur in the interior of continents. Weather patterns vary in the different types of continental climates. However, most have large differences between daytime and nighttime temperatures because they lack the influence of nearby oceans. For the same reason, winter months are usually much colder than summer months.

How are marine climates different from continental climates?

## Ocean Currents

**Ocean currents** are streams of water that flow through oceans in regular patterns. They influence climates by transferring energy from one part of an ocean to another. In general, warm-water currents carry warmth from the tropics to higher latitudes, where they help keep coastal regions warm. Cold-water currents have the opposite effect. They cool coastal regions by carrying cold water from polar regions toward the equator.

**VOCABULARY**
A description wheel would be a good choice for taking notes about the term *ocean current*.

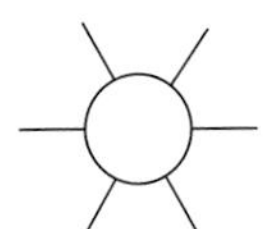

The illustration below shows the paths of ocean currents in the North Atlantic. Find the Gulf Stream on the illustration. The Gulf Stream is a major warm-water current. As the waters that feed the Gulf Stream pass near the Caribbean Sea and the Gulf of Mexico, the concentrated solar rays that strike there warm its water. Water flowing in the Gulf Stream can be 6°C to 10°C (11–18°F) warmer than the surrounding water. The Gulf Stream warms the winds that blow over it. In turn, those winds warm coastal regions.

Like altitude, ocean currents can overcome the effects of latitude. For example, London, England, has an average annual temperature of nearly 11°C (52°F). Natashquan, a town in eastern Canada at about the same latitude and altitude, has an average annual temperature of only 1°C (34°F). London's milder climate is the result of an ocean current carrying warm water to Europe's west coast.

### Ocean Currents

**Ocean currents can cause two places at the same latitude to have different climates.**

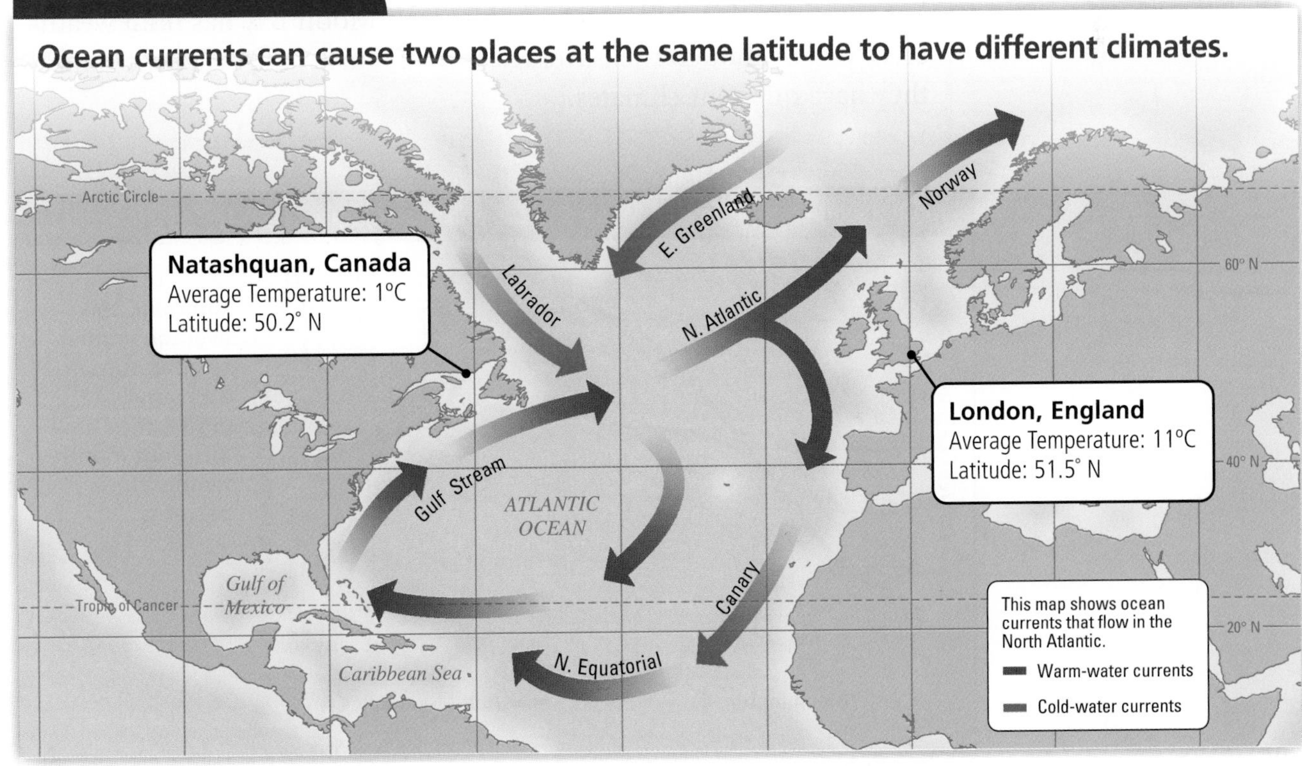

## Seasonal changes are part of climate.

What marks the change of seasons where you live? In the Midwest and New England, there are four distinct seasons. Mild spring and autumn months come between hotter summers and colder winters. In Florida and other southern states, the seasonal changes are much less extreme. **Seasons** are periods of the year associated with specific weather conditions, such as cold temperatures or frequent rain. These periods are part of the overall pattern that makes up a climate.

### Temperature Patterns

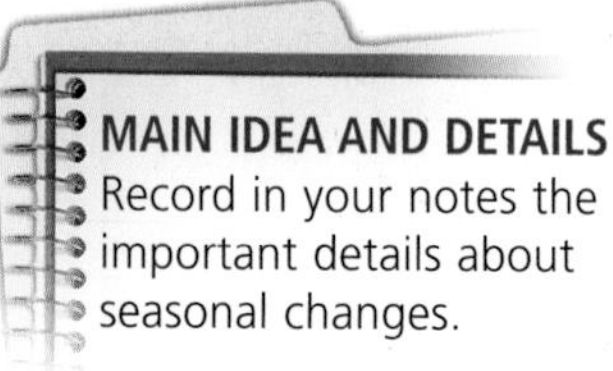

**MAIN IDEA AND DETAILS** Record in your notes the important details about seasonal changes.

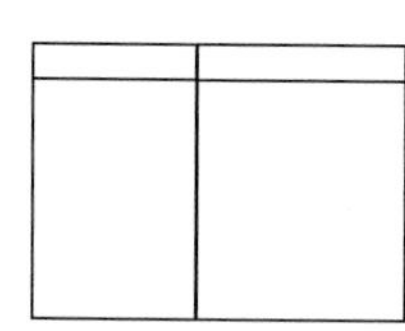

Seasons occur because the amounts of energy that the Northern Hemisphere and the Southern Hemisphere receive from the Sun change over the course of a year. Winter begins in the Northern Hemisphere around December 21, when the daytime is shortest. Summer begins around June 21, when the daytime is longest. Spring begins around March 21, and autumn begins around September 22. On the first day of spring and of autumn, day and night are equal in length. There are 12 hours of daylight and 12 hours of darkness.

**CHECK YOUR READING** Which seasons have the longest and the shortest periods of daytime?

Temperature patterns are an important feature of climate. The graph below shows the average monthly temperatures in Half Moon Bay, California, and Bloomington, Indiana. Each city has an average annual temperature of about 12°C (54°F). However, Bloomington has hot summers and cold winters, while Half Moon Bay has mild weather all year. Although their average annual temperatures are the same, they have different climates.

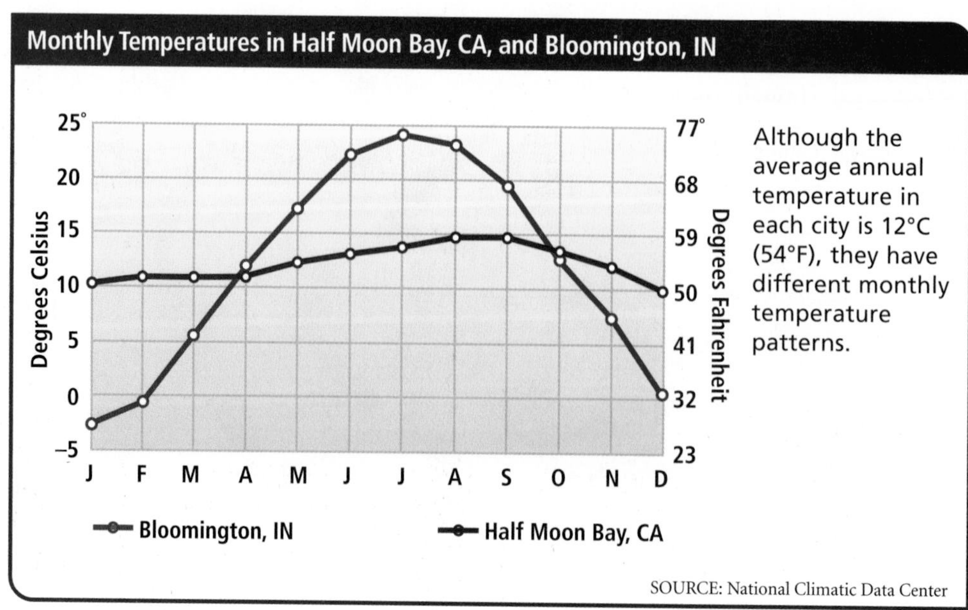


Although the average annual temperature in each city is 12°C (54°F), they have different monthly temperature patterns.

These photos show the same rice fields in India at different times of the year.

## Precipitation Patterns

Like temperature patterns, seasonal patterns of precipitation vary among different climates. For example, Connecticut's precipitation is distributed fairly evenly throughout the year. In contrast, nearly half of Montana's precipitation falls during May, June, and July. Many tropical regions have wet and dry seasons. These regions stay warm all year long, but certain months are much rainier than other months.

The seasonal pattern of precipitation can determine the types of plants that grow in a region and the length of the growing season. Although Montana is a fairly dry state, much of its precipitation falls during the growing season. This pattern allows the state to be a major grain producer.

## 4.1 Review

### KEY CONCEPTS

1. Explain the difference between climate and weather.
2. Make a chart showing how latitude, altitude, large bodies of water, and ocean currents affect climate.
3. How does the length of daytime change with each season?

### CRITICAL THINKING

4. **Predict** How would a region's climate change if a cold-water ocean current stopped flowing past it?
5. **Identify Cause** What geographical factors might cause a region to have a narrow temperature range and mild weather all year?

### CHALLENGE

6. **Infer** Suggest specific climate characteristics that might make the owners of a vacation resort decide to advertise the average annual temperature rather than provide temperature averages for each month or season.

## ARCHITECT

# Climate and Architecture

When architects design houses, office towers, and other buildings, they think about how the climate will affect the structures and the people who will use them. For example, when planning a house for a cold climate, an architect will consider ways to keep warm air inside. He or she might call for energy-efficient glass in the windows, thick insulation in walls, and an extra set of inside doors to close off entryways.

### Snow

Snow is very heavy. Because of snow's weight, architects usually design slanted roofs on houses built in snowy climates. The sharper the slant, the easier snow slides off. This church was built in Norway around 1150.

### Heat

In the 1960s, Houston wanted to get a major league baseball team. City officials asked architects to design a stadium suitable for Houston's hot, rainy climate. They created the first domed, air-conditioned ballpark, the Astrodome.

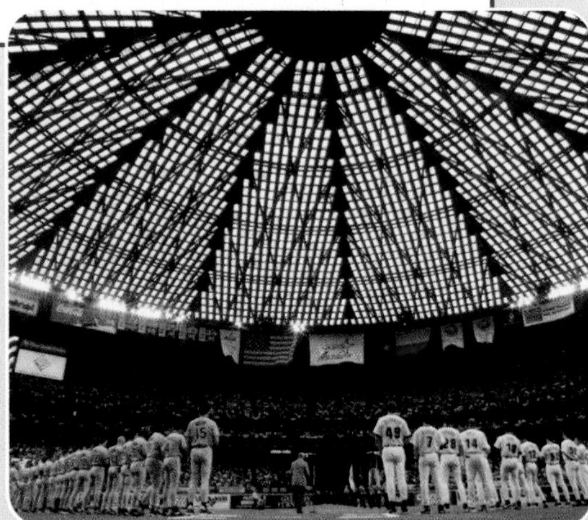

### Floods

Intense rains and high winds combine to make floods common in many places. To protect themselves, some people who live on the shores of large rivers, lakes, and oceans build their homes on stilts. This home is in the Northern Territory of Australia. It was designed by the architect Glenn Murcutt and completed in 1994.

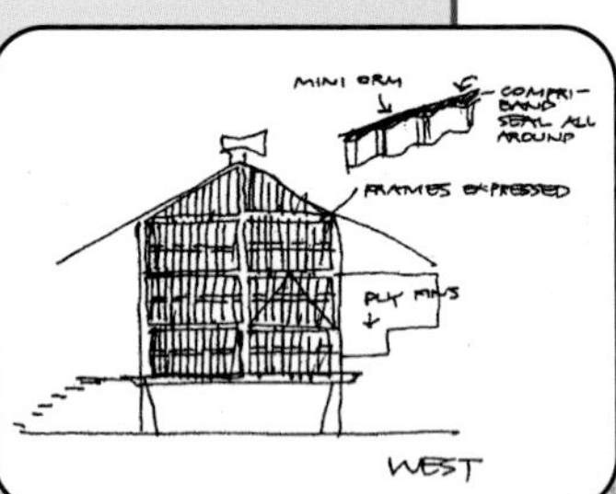


### EXPLORE

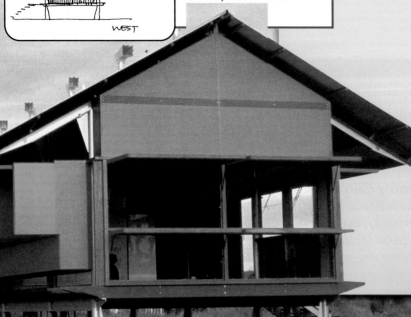

1. **ANALYZING** Bring to class photos of buildings located in various climate regions. Discuss whether the architecture reflects the influence of the climate.
2. **CHALLENGE** Use building blocks to make a model of a house for a warm climate in which the wind usually blows from the west. Place doors, windows, and walls to get the best flow of air through the house. To check the airflow, dust your model with a light powder. Blow lightly and note how much powder moves.

KEY CONCEPT

# Earth has a variety of climates.

**BEFORE, you learned**

- The main factors that affect climate are latitude, altitude, distance from large bodies of water, and ocean currents
- Seasonal changes in temperature and precipitation are part of climate

**NOW, you will learn**

- How scientists classify climates
- About the characteristics of different climate zones
- How natural features and human activity affect climate

**VOCABULARY**

**climate zone** p. 125
**microclimate** p. 128
**urban heat island** p. 128
**rain shadow** p. 129

**THINK ABOUT**

### *What does ground cover reveal about climate?*

For trees and bushes to grow, they must have enough precipitation and at least a few months of mild temperatures each year. Lichens and some small plants can grow in harsher climates. The photograph shows typical ground cover along Greenland's rocky coast. What does the ground cover tell you about Greenland's long-term weather patterns?

## Scientists have identified six major climate zones.

Classification systems can help you see patterns. For example, communities are often classified as cities, towns, and villages. This classification system organizes communities on the basis of size. Two cities in different parts of a country might have more in common than a village and a nearby city.

To show patterns in climate data, scientists have developed systems for classifying climates. A **climate zone** is one of the major divisions in a system for classifying the climates of different regions based on characteristics they have in common. The most widely used system groups climates by temperature and precipitation. The six major climate zones of this classification system are (1) humid tropical, (2) dry, (3) moist mid-latitude with mild winters, (4) moist mid-latitude with severe winters, (5) polar, and (6) highland.

Find out more about climate zones.

The chart on page 127 summarizes information about the different climate zones. Each climate zone has a specific set of characteristics. For example, humid tropical climates are hot and rainy. Many areas close to the equator have this type of climate.

Notice that most of the climate zones are further divided into subclimates. When scientists identify a subclimate, they choose one characteristic that makes it different from other subclimates within the same climate zone. For example, the humid tropical climate zone includes tropical wet climates and tropical wet and dry climates. The difference between them is that tropical wet climates have abundant rainfall every month, while tropical wet and dry climates have a few months of dry weather.

The climate map below shows that many regions scattered throughout the world have similar climates. When you use the map, keep in mind that climates do not change suddenly at the borders of the colored areas. Instead, each climate gradually blends into neighboring ones.

**READING TIP**

The colors on the map below correspond to the colors in the chart on page 127. As you read descriptions on the chart, look back to the map to find examples.

## World Climates

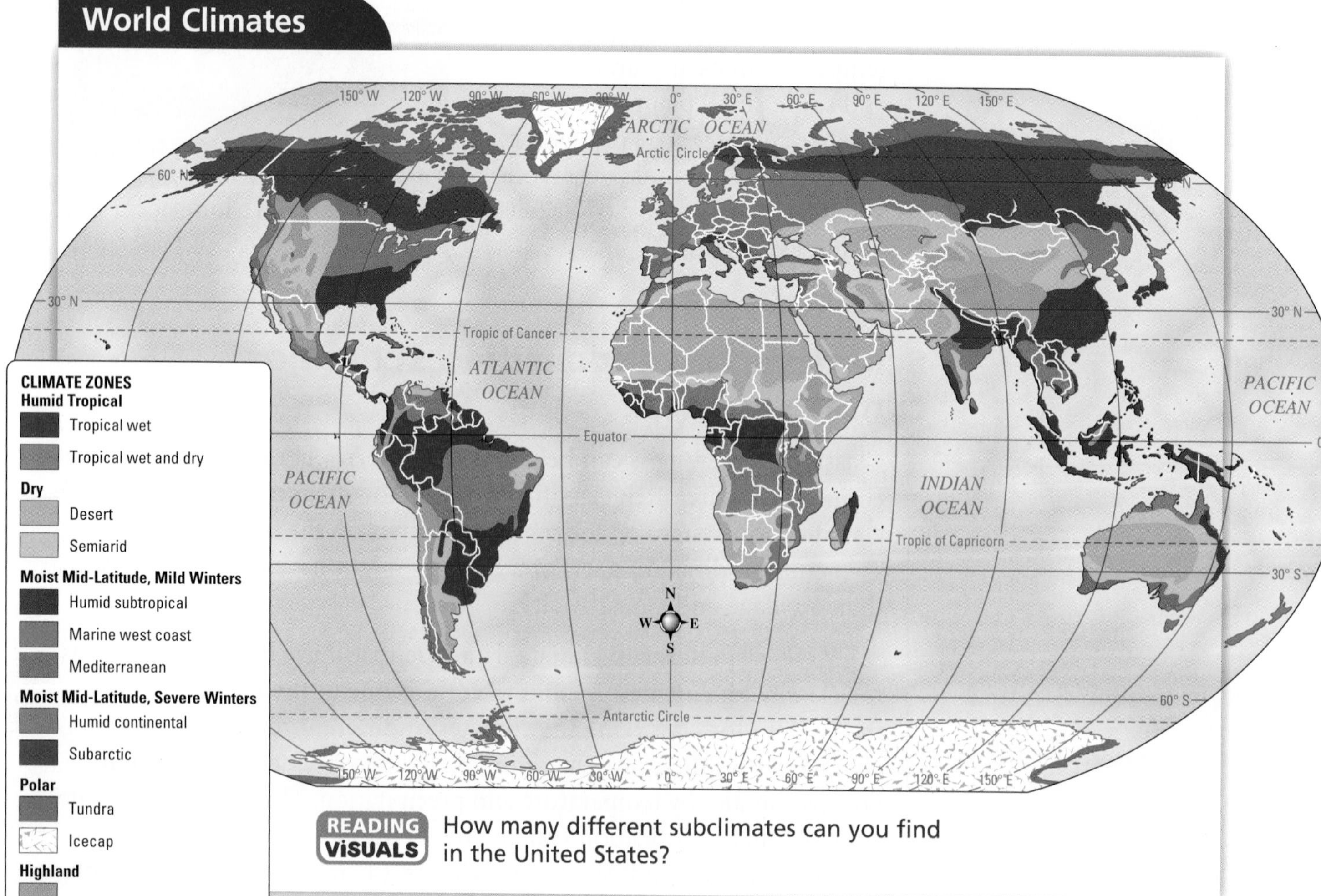


**READING VISUALS** How many different subclimates can you find in the United States?

## Climate Classification

| Climate Zone | Subclimate | Description |
|---|---|---|
| **Humid tropical** | **Tropical wet**<br>Example: Amazon rain forest in South America | Temperatures remain high throughout the year. Rising hot, humid air causes heavy cloud cover and abundant rainfall, with no dry season. Annual rainfall usually is more than 2.5 meters (8 ft). |
| | **Tropical wet and dry**<br>Example: Miami, Florida | Like tropical wet climates, these climates are hot and rainy, but they have a dry season in winter. |
| **Dry** | **Desert**<br>Example: Phoenix, Arizona | Precipitation is infrequent and scanty—usually less than 20 centimeters (8 in.) per year. Deserts include the hottest places on Earth, but they can be cool, especially at night. In most deserts high daytime temperatures lead to rapid evaporation, which increases the dryness. |
| | **Semiarid**<br>Example: Denver, Colorado | These regions are found next to deserts. They have wider temperature ranges than deserts and are not as dry. Most of the Great Plains region in North America is semiarid. |
| **Moist mid-latitude with mild winters** | **Humid subtropical**<br>Example: Charlotte, North Carolina | Summers are hot and muggy. Winters are usually mild. Precipitation is fairly even throughout the year. |
| | **Marine west coast**<br>Example: Seattle, Washington | These regions have mild temperatures year-round and steady precipitation. Low clouds and fog are common. |
| | **Mediterranean**<br>Example: San Francisco, California | Dry summers and mild, wet winters are typical of these regions. Some coastal areas have cool summers and frequent fog. |
| **Moist mid-latitude with severe winters** | **Humid continental**<br>Example: Des Moines, Iowa | These regions have hot summers and cold winters. Precipitation is fairly even throughout the year. Snow covers the ground for 1 to 4 months in winter. |
| | **Subarctic**<br>Example: Fairbanks, Alaska | Temperatures usually stay below freezing for 6 to 8 months each year. Summers are brief and cool. The amount of precipitation is low, but snow remains on the ground for long periods because of the cold. |
| **Polar** | **Tundra**<br>Example: Barrow, Alaska | The average temperature of the warmest month is below 10°C (50°F). A deep layer of soil is frozen year-round. During summer a shallow layer at the surface thaws out and turns muddy. |
| | **Icecap**<br>Example: Antarctica | The surface is permanently covered with ice and snow. Temperatures rarely rise above freezing, even in summer. |
| **Highland** | **Highland**<br>Example: Rocky Mountains | Because temperature drops as altitude increases, mountain regions can contain many climates. Tall mountains may have a year-round covering of ice and snow at their peaks. |

Tropical wet

Desert

Marine west coast

Humid continental

Tundra

## Natural features and human activity can affect local climates.

The climate map on page 126 shows three subclimates in Madagascar, a large island off the east coast of Africa. But if you went to Madagascar, you would probably notice a greater variety of climates. A meadow might be warmer than a nearby wooded area, and a city block might be warmer than a meadow.

**READING TiP**

You can use word parts to help you recall the meaning of climate terms. The prefix *sub-* can indicate a part of a larger unit. The prefix *micro-* means "very small."

The climates of smaller areas within a subclimate are called **microclimates.** The area of a microclimate can be as large as a river valley or smaller than a garden. Forests, beaches, lakes, valleys, hills, and mountains are some of the features that influence local climates. For example, sea breezes often make beaches cooler than nearby inland areas on warm afternoons.

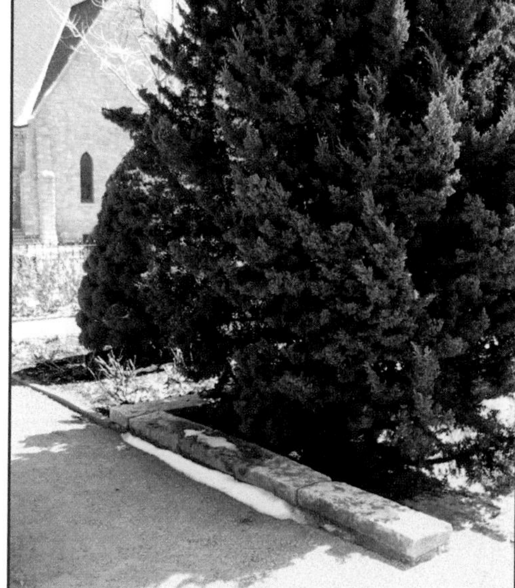

Shade from the tree produces a cooler microclimate where snow takes longer to melt.

### Urban Heat Islands

Humans create artificial surfaces that can also affect local climates. Cities are usually warmer than surrounding rural areas. The warmer body of air over a city is called an **urban heat island.** At certain times the air temperature may be as much as 12°C (22°F) higher in a large city than in the nearby countryside. The following factors contribute to this effect:

- During the day, buildings and streets absorb more solar energy than do grass, trees, and soil. These artificial surfaces release the additional stored energy at night, which warms the air over a city.
- Evaporation of moisture helps cool areas. Because artificial surfaces absorb less water than most natural surfaces, there is less cooling from evaporation in cities than in rural areas.
- Cities use a lot of energy for cooling, transportation, and other activities. The use of energy releases heat into the atmosphere.

How do cities influence local temperature?

## How Rain Shadows Form

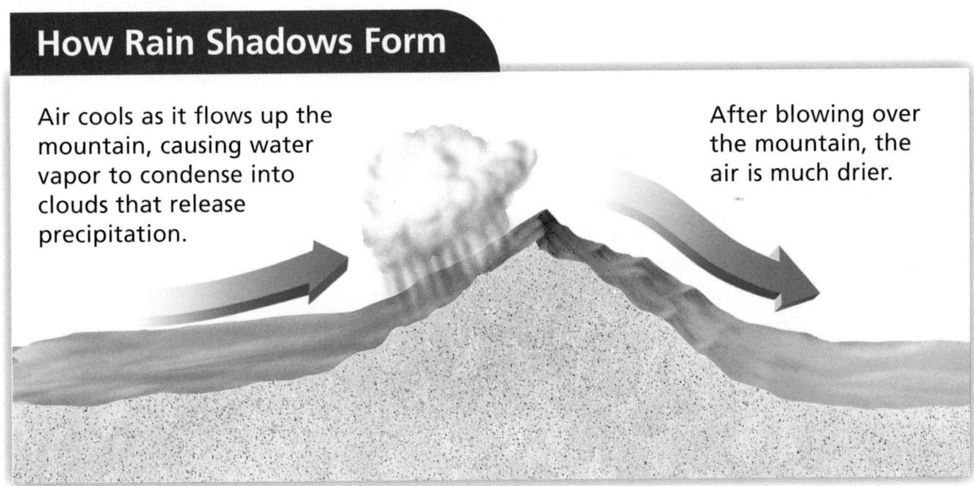

Air cools as it flows up the mountain, causing water vapor to condense into clouds that release precipitation.
After blowing over the mountain, the air is much drier.


## Rain Shadows

Mountains have a strong effect on climate in places where steady winds blow inland from oceans. The illustration above shows how mountains can affect precipitation:

- Air is forced to rise as it flows over a mountain.
- As the air rises and cools, it condenses into clouds. Areas near the side of a mountain that faces wind may get heavy precipitation.
- After passing over the mountain, the air is much drier because it has lost moisture through condensation and precipitation.

The dry area on the downwind side of a mountain where this process occurs is called a **rain shadow.** Mountains do not affect only local climates. Many dry climate zones that extend over large regions are found in the rain shadows of mountain ranges.

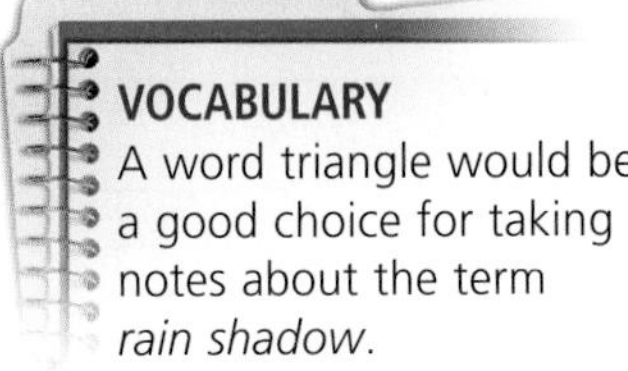

**VOCABULARY**
A word triangle would be a good choice for taking notes about the term *rain shadow*.

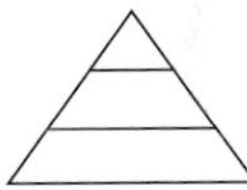

# 4.2 Review

### KEY CONCEPTS

1. What two weather characteristics do meteorologists usually focus on when they determine climate zones?
2. Why do highland climate zones contain more than one climate?
3. How do mountains affect precipitation patterns?

### CRITICAL THINKING

4. **Compare and Contrast** How are tundra and icecap subclimates similar? How are they different?
5. **Infer** In which climates would you expect to find the most vacation resorts? Explain.

### CHALLENGE

6. **Apply** What is the subclimate of the region where you live? What microclimates exist in your local area?

# CHAPTER INVESTIGATION

## Microclimates

**OVERVIEW AND PURPOSE** Microclimates are local variations within a region's climate. Natural and artificial features such as beaches, hills, wooded areas, buildings, and pavement can cause such variations. Even trees planted around a house or parking lot may influence the climate of that small area. In this lab, you will use what you have learned about weather and climate to

- measure weather factors, such as air temperature, in two different microclimates
- discover how natural and artificial features affect local climate

### Problem

How do natural and artificial features affect the climate of a small area?

### Hypothesize

Write a hypothesis to explain how you expect the microclimates of two nearby locations to be affected by the different natural and artificial features in those areas. Your hypothesis should take the form of an "If . . . , then . . . , because . . ." statement. You should complete steps 1–3 of the procedure before writing your hypothesis.

**MATERIALS**

- 2 thermometers
- 2 other weather instruments of the same kind

### Procedure

1. Work in a group of four students. You will use a thermometer to record air temperature. Choose another weather instrument that you have made or that is available to you. You might use a psychrometer to measure relative humidity, a barometer to measure air pressure, or an anemometer to measure wind speed.

2. Make data tables similar to the ones in the sample notebook page. The label in the second row of each table should identify what you will measure with the instrument you chose in step 1.

3. Go outside the school with your teacher, taking your instruments and notebook. Choose two locations near the school with different features for your group to study. For example, you might choose a grassy area and a paved area, or one area with trees and another area without trees.

4 Divide your group into two pairs. Each pair of students should have one thermometer and the other instrument you have chosen. You and your partner will study one location. The other pair will study the second location.

5 Decide ahead of time how you will control for variables. For example, both pairs might take measurements at a set height above the ground.

6 Draw pictures of the location you are studying in your notebook. Write a description of the natural and artificial features in this area.

7 Set up the instruments in your location. Record the air temperature. Take follow-up readings five and ten minutes later. Take a reading with the other weather instrument each time you take a temperature reading.

8 Record data gathered by the other two members of your group in your data table. Calculate the average temperature for each location. Then calculate the average reading for the other weather factor that you measured.

## Observe and Analyze

Write It Up

1. **IDENTIFY VARIABLES AND CONSTANTS** Identify the variables and constants in the investigation. List these factors in your **Science Notebook.**
2. **COMPARE AND CONTRAST** Which average measurements in the two locations were the same? What differences did your investigations reveal? For example, was one area cooler or less windy than the other?

## Conclude

Write It Up

1. **INFER** Answer the question posed in the problem.
2. **INTERPRET** Compare your results with your hypothesis. Did the results support your hypothesis? Did the natural and artificial features have the effects you expected?
3. **EVALUATE** What were the limitations of your instruments? What other sources of error could have affected the results?
4. **APPLY** How could you apply the results of your investigation to help you make landscaping or building decisions? For example, what could you do to make a picnic area more comfortable?

## INVESTIGATE Further

**CHALLENGE** Return to the locations you investigated at the same time of day on three consecutive days. Take readings with the same weather instruments that you used before. Are these new readings consistent with the patterns you observed on the first day? If not, how would you alter your earlier conclusions?

Microclimates

Problem How do natural and artificial features affect the climate of a small area?

Hypothesize

Observe and Analyze

Table 1. Weather Factors Within Microclimates

| Time (min) | Location 1 | | Location 2 | |
|---|---|---|---|---|
| | Temp (°C) | Wind Speed | Temp (°C) | Wind Speed |
| 0 | | | | |
| 5 | | | | |
| 10 | | | | |

Conclude

KEY CONCEPT

# Climates can change suddenly or slowly.

**BEFORE, you learned**

- Earth absorbs and reflects solar energy
- Greenhouse gases help keep Earth warm
- Human activities are contributing to global warming

**NOW, you will learn**

- How climates can cool when particles block sunlight
- About climate changes that repeat over time
- How climates may change because of global warming

**VOCABULARY**

**ice age** p. 135
**El Niño** p. 136

THINK ABOUT

***How do particles affect light?***

If you shine a light through foggy air, you may notice that the beam of light is dimmer than usual. The droplets, or liquid particles, that make up fog block some of the light from reaching objects in the beam's path. Which natural events can suddenly add many particles to the atmosphere?

## Climates cool when particles block sunlight.

Our atmosphere contains many particulates—tiny solid and liquid particles mixed in with air. Particulates block some of the Sun's energy, preventing it from reaching Earth's surface. Occasionally a natural event will suddenly release enormous amounts of particulates. Such an event may cause a temporary change in climates around the world.

Large volcanic eruptions can send huge clouds of gas and dust into the stratosphere. When these clouds enter the stratosphere, they spread out and drift around the world. Volcanoes affect global climate mainly by releasing sulfur dioxide gas. The gas combines with water to form sulfuric acid droplets, which block sunlight. Because Earth absorbs less solar energy, average global temperatures may decrease for up to several years.

How can a sudden release of particles affect climate?

In 1991, Mount Pinatubo erupted in the Philippines. The eruption, one of the largest of the last century, affected climates for about two years. During the summer of 1992, parts of North America were more than 3°C (5.4°F) cooler than usual. Over that entire year, global temperatures dropped by 0.5°C (0.9°F).

The eruption of Mount Pinatubo in 1991 affected temperatures around the world for about two years.

The impact of rocky objects from space can also release particles into the atmosphere. Earth is often hit by space objects. Most are too small to have much of an effect. However, objects 3 kilometers (2 mi) in diameter strike Earth about once every million years. These powerful collisions can suddenly change climates.

When a large space object strikes Earth, it explodes and leaves behind a crater, or pit, in the surface. The explosion throws dust into the atmosphere. The largest impacts may have raised so much dust that temperatures around the world dropped sharply for months. They may also have caused changes in the atmosphere by setting off forest fires. A space object that hit Earth 65 million years ago blasted out a crater about 200 kilometers (120 mi) in diameter in what is now Mexico. Many scientists think that climate changes following this impact led to the extinction of the dinosaurs and other species.

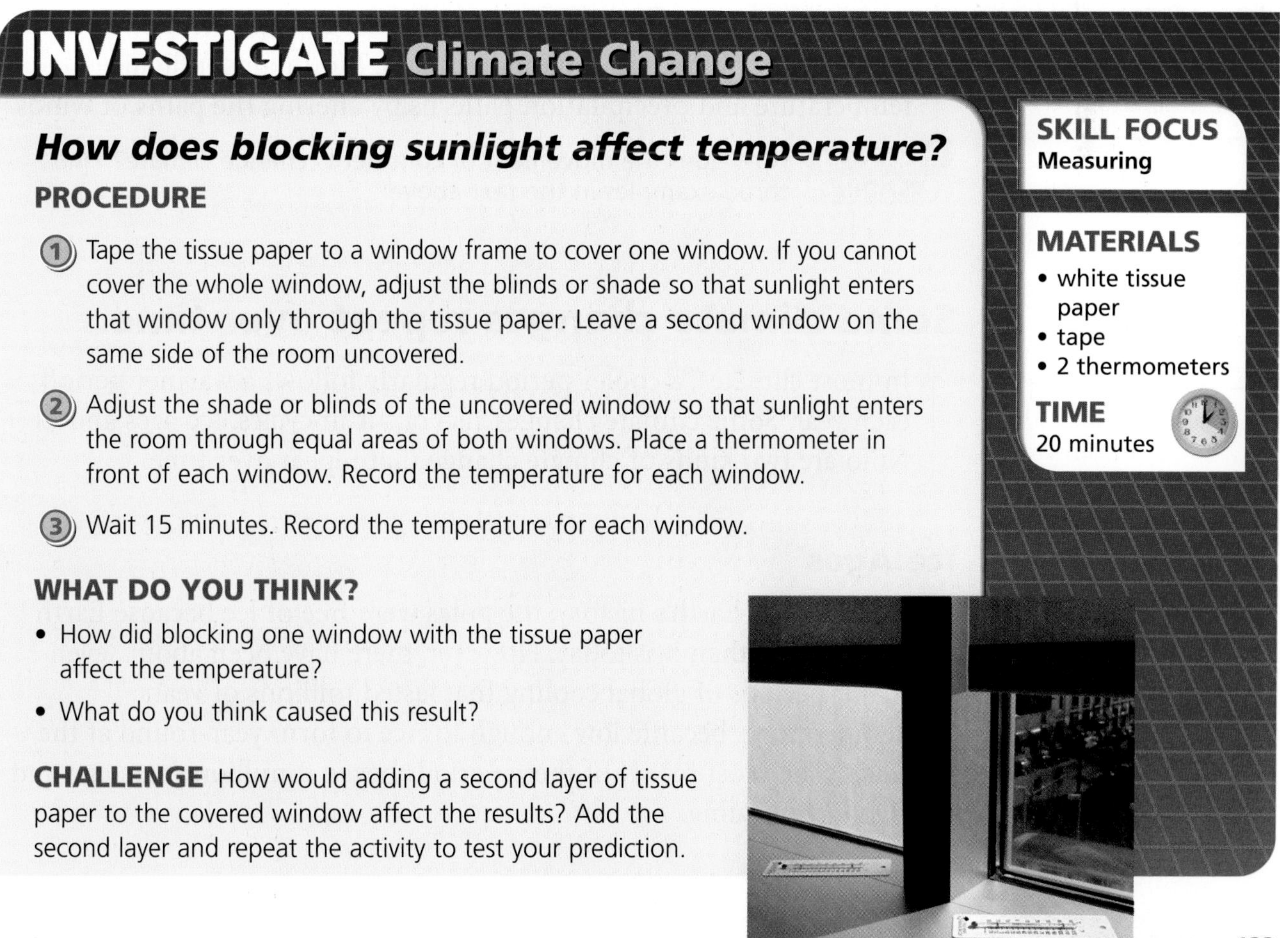

## INVESTIGATE Climate Change

### *How does blocking sunlight affect temperature?*

**PROCEDURE**

1. Tape the tissue paper to a window frame to cover one window. If you cannot cover the whole window, adjust the blinds or shade so that sunlight enters that window only through the tissue paper. Leave a second window on the same side of the room uncovered.
2. Adjust the shade or blinds of the uncovered window so that sunlight enters the room through equal areas of both windows. Place a thermometer in front of each window. Record the temperature for each window.
3. Wait 15 minutes. Record the temperature for each window.

**WHAT DO YOU THINK?**

- How did blocking one window with the tissue paper affect the temperature?
- What do you think caused this result?

**CHALLENGE** How would adding a second layer of tissue paper to the covered window affect the results? Add the second layer and repeat the activity to test your prediction.

**SKILL FOCUS**
Measuring

**MATERIALS**
- white tissue paper
- tape
- 2 thermometers

**TIME**
20 minutes

## Climates change as continents move.

Climates can change suddenly for brief periods after a volcanic eruption. In contrast, the movement of continents causes steady climate changes over many millions of years. The maps below show two stages of this movement in the distant past.

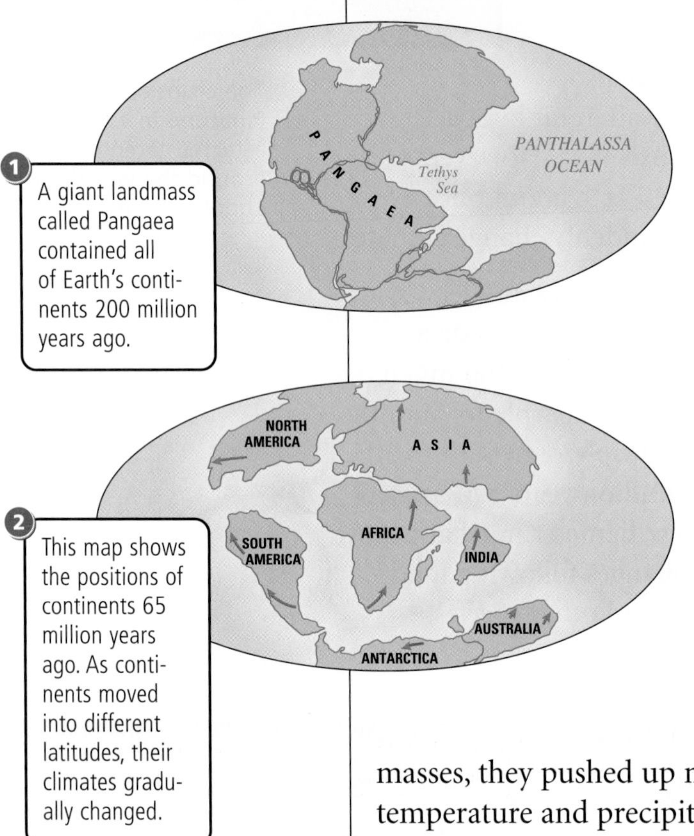


1 A giant landmass called Pangaea contained all of Earth's continents 200 million years ago.

2 This map shows the positions of continents 65 million years ago. As continents moved into different latitudes, their climates gradually changed.

1 Earth's continents were once joined together in a gigantic landmass called Pangaea (pan-JEE-uh). This giant landmass began to break up about 200 million years ago.

2 By 65 million years ago, the continents had moved closer to their present positions. As the continents moved, their climates gradually changed in different ways. Some continents cooled as they moved toward higher latitudes. Other continents grew warmer as they moved toward the equator.

The movement of continents had other effects on climate. As they drifted apart, the continents changed the paths of ocean currents that help warm coastal regions. When landmasses collided with other landmasses, they pushed up mountain ranges. Mountains influence temperature and precipitation patterns by altering the paths of winds.

**CHECK YOUR READING** How does the movement of continents change climate? Find three examples in the text above.

## Some climate changes repeat over time.

In most climates, a cooler period regularly follows a warmer period each year. Some climate changes also occur in cycles. Ice ages and El Niño are two kinds of climate change that repeat over time.

### Ice Ages

Learn more about climate change.

For much of Earth's history, the poles were free of ice because Earth was warmer than it is today. However, there have been about seven major periods of global cooling that lasted millions of years. Temperatures became low enough for ice to form year-round at the poles. The most recent of these periods began 2 million years ago and is still continuing.

## How Ice Expands in an Ice Age

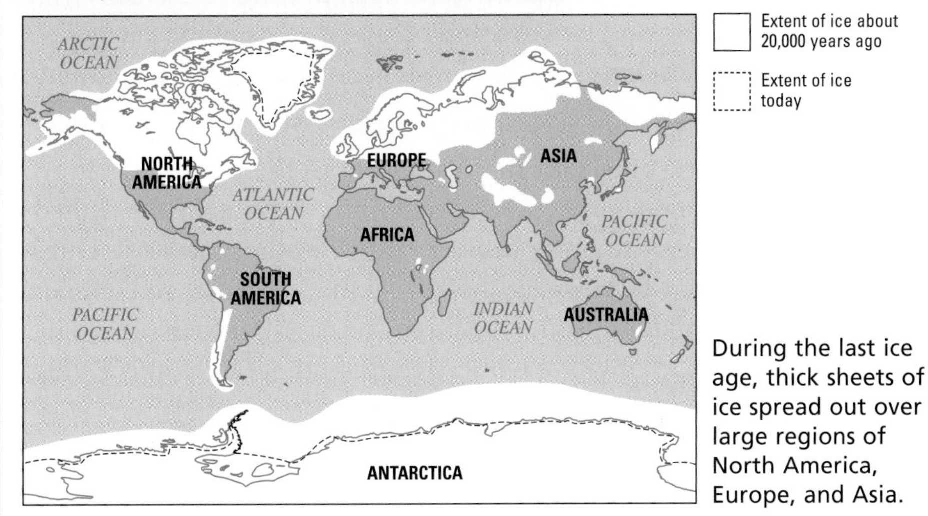


During the last ice age, thick sheets of ice spread out over large regions of North America, Europe, and Asia.

During major periods of global cooling, there are times when polar ice expands. **Ice ages** are periods in which huge sheets of ice spread out beyond the polar regions. The map above shows how far the ice sheets reached in the last ice age, which ended between 14,000 and 10,000 years ago. These sheets were several kilometers thick and covered nearly a third of Earth's land area.

**MAIN IDEA AND DETAILS**
Record in your notes the important details about ice ages.

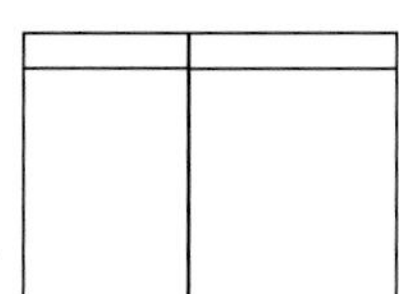

Ice ages usually last tens of thousands of years. They are separated by warmer periods in which ice sheets shrink back toward the poles. We are living in one of these warmer periods. Average global temperatures are now 5°C to 10°C (9–18°F) higher than they were during the last ice age. Only Greenland and Antarctica have large ice sheets today.

Various sources of evidence show that ice ages occurred. Scientists study polar ice and the ocean floor to estimate past changes in temperature. Geological features that formed during ice ages, such as scratches on rocks, can reveal the movement of ice sheets. Some of the evidence also provides clues about what causes ice ages. Most scientists think that there are two main causes:

- Ice ages are closely linked to changes in how Earth moves around the Sun. These changes may have caused ice sheets to grow by altering the temperature patterns of the seasons.
- As you learned in Chapter 1, carbon dioxide is a greenhouse gas. Levels of carbon dioxide in the atmosphere dropped during ice ages. Lower carbon dioxide levels may have caused global cooling by weakening the greenhouse effect.

Other factors probably play a role in the development of ice ages. Scientists are still trying to understand how different factors work in combination to cause global cooling.

## El Niño

The oceans are closely connected to climate. **El Niño** (ehl NEEN-yoh) is a disturbance of wind patterns and ocean currents in the Pacific Ocean. It usually occurs every 3 to 7 years and lasts for 12 to 18 months.

El Niño causes temporary climate changes in many parts of the world. It can cause unusually dry conditions in the western Pacific region and unusually heavy rainfall in South America. In the United States, El Niño tends to bring heavier rainfall to the Southeast. During winter, storms may be stronger than usual in California, and temperatures are often milder in some northern states. All of these unusual conditions follow changes in wind strength and ocean temperatures.

1. **Normal Year** Strong trade winds normally push warm water toward the western Pacific, where an area of low pressure develops. The rising warm air condenses into clouds that release heavy rain. Cooler water flows near the west coast of South America.
2. **El Niño Year** Weak trade winds allow warm water to flow back toward the central and eastern Pacific. The clouds and heavy rain also shift eastward, toward South America. The effects of El Niño vary, depending on how much warming occurs in the eastern Pacific.

### How El Niño Forms

**Weak trade winds during El Niño cause changes in ocean temperature and precipitation.**

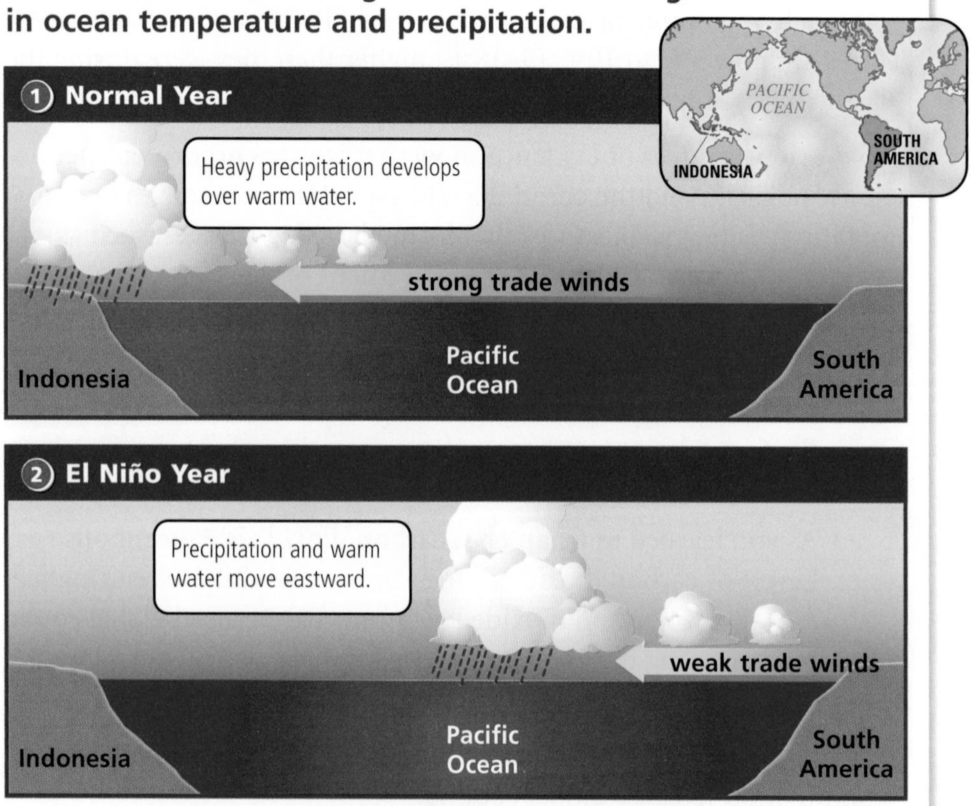

**READING TIP**

In the diagrams, color is used to show ocean temperature. **Red** means warmer water. **Blue** means cooler water.

1983

2002

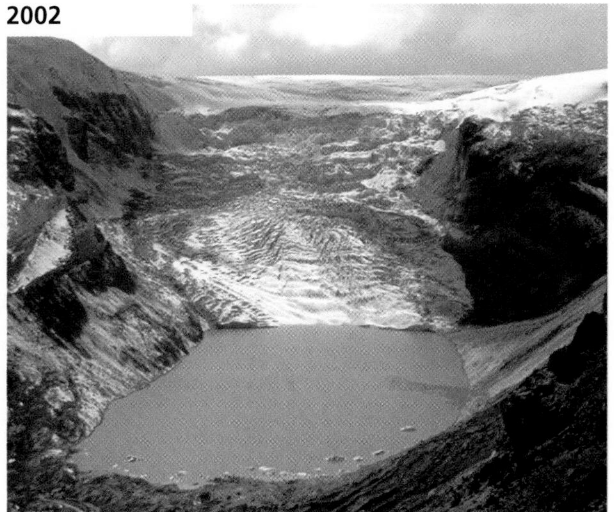

This ice sheet on a mountain in Peru has shrunk 820 meters (2690 ft) in 19 years.

## Human activities are changing climate.

Most climate experts predict that by 2100, there will be a rise in global temperature of 1.4°C to 5.8°C (2.5–10.4°F). As you read in Chapter 1, human activities release greenhouse gases. Higher levels of greenhouse gases in the atmosphere cause global warming. Earth hasn't warmed so rapidly at any time in at least the last 10,000 years. Even a small temperature increase could have a great impact on climate.

REMINDER

Remember that greenhouse gases are gases that absorb infrared energy.

### Predictions of Climate Change

Although scientists expect all land areas to warm up by 2100, the rate of warming will be uneven. The greatest warming is expected to occur in the high latitudes of the Northern Hemisphere. The increase in Greenland's temperature, for example, may be two or three times the global average. Higher temperatures have recently started to melt the ice sheet that covers much of Greenland. Ice is also melting in the Arctic Ocean and on mountains in many parts of the world.

The effects of global warming on precipitation will also vary. Scientists predict an overall increase in precipitation, because more water will evaporate from Earth's warmer surface. Precipitation will tend to fall more heavily in short periods of time, which will increase flooding. However, some areas where water is already scarce may get even less precipitation. Lower precipitation in those areas will make droughts more frequent and severe.

CHECK YOUR READING Summarize how global warming is expected to affect temperature and precipitation.

MAIN IDEA AND DETAILS
Record in your notes the important details about the impact of global warming.

## Impact of Global Warming

Global warming affects many of Earth's systems. Because these systems work together in complex ways, it is difficult to predict the full impact of global warming. Most climate scientists predict that global warming will probably cause the following changes.

**Sea Levels** As temperatures warm, the oceans will expand. They will also gain additional water from melting ice. Scientists expect the average sea level to rise 9 to 88 centimeters (4–35 in.) over the next century. Higher sea levels will damage coastal regions and increase flooding. These problems could be severe in small island nations.

**Wildlife** Global warming will endanger many plant and animal species by altering natural habitats. Some species will die out or move to cooler areas. Other species, such as warm-water fishes, will benefit from an expansion of their habitats.

Find out more about the effects of global warming.

**Agriculture** Changes in temperature and precipitation can affect crops and livestock. If Earth warms more than a few degrees Celsius, most of the world's agriculture will be harmed. More moderate warming will help agriculture in some regions by lengthening the growing season. However, even moderate warming will harm agriculture in other regions.

**Human Health** Warmer temperatures could increase heat-related deaths and deaths from some diseases, such as malaria, especially in areas near the equator. On the other hand, deaths caused by extreme cold could decrease at higher latitudes.

Some scientists predict more dangerous changes beyond 2100 if humans continue to add greenhouse gases to the atmosphere at current levels. However, the harmful effects of global warming can be limited if we reduce emissions of greenhouse gases.

## 4.3 Review

### KEY CONCEPTS

1. How can volcanic eruptions and impacts of large objects from space change climate?
2. What changes in climate occur during an ice age?
3. Give two examples of ways in which global warming will probably affect life on Earth.

### CRITICAL THINKING

4. **Connect** What is the connection between latitude, the movement of continents, and climate change?
5. **Compare and Contrast** Compare and contrast the effects of El Niño and ice ages on climate.

### CHALLENGE

6. **Infer** Discuss why some countries might be more reluctant than others to take steps to reduce levels of greenhouse gases.

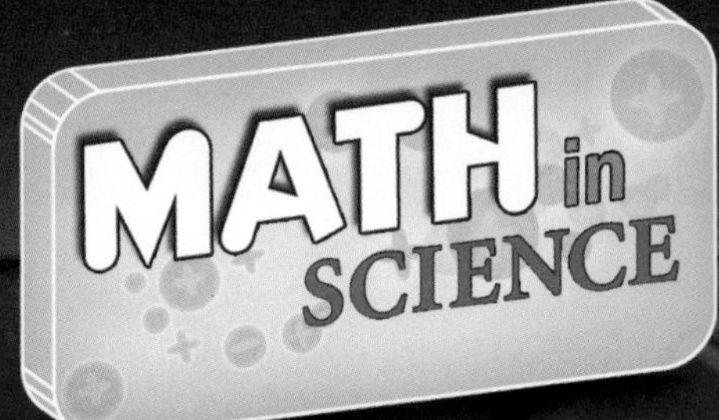


MATH TUTORIAL

CLASSZONE.COM

Click on Math Tutorial for more help with interpreting line graphs.

## SKILL: INTERPRETING LINE GRAPHS

# Carbon Dioxide Levels

Since the 1950s, carbon dioxide levels have been measured in air samples collected at the Mauna Loa Observatory in Hawaii. The graphs below show the carbon dioxide data plotted in two different ways. In the graph on the left, the scale showing carbon dioxide levels starts at 0 parts per million (ppm) and goes up to 400 ppm. The graph on the right offers a close-up view of the same data. The scale on the right-hand graph is broken to focus on the values from 310 ppm to 380 ppm.

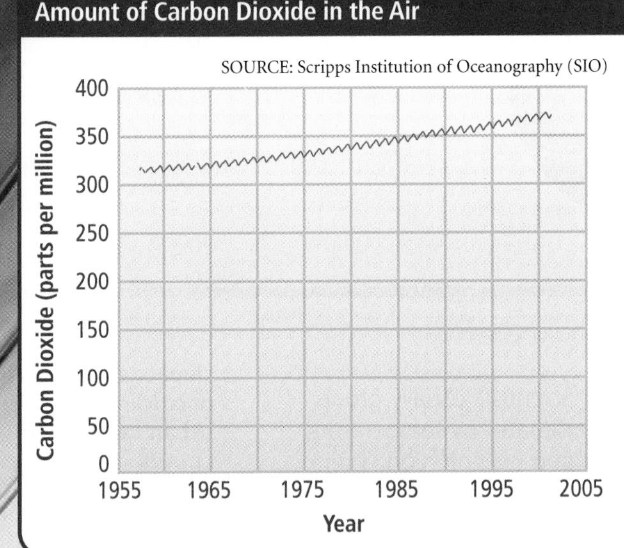


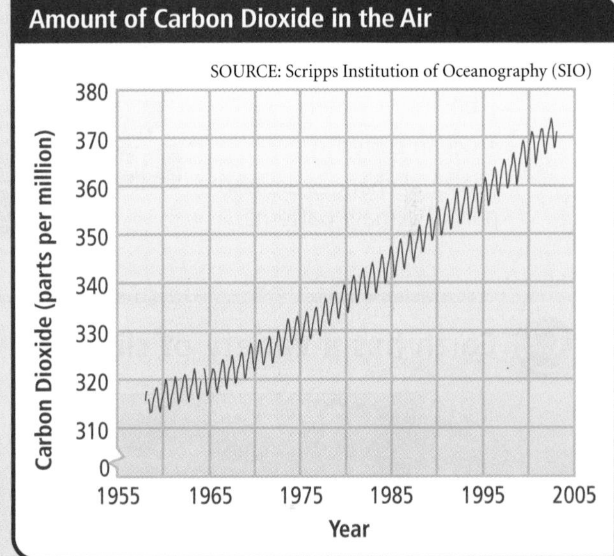

**Use the graphs to answer the following questions.**

1. What was the carbon dioxide level at the beginning of 1995?
2. The data show a 17 percent increase in the carbon dioxide level in the air from 1958 through 2001. Which graph shows this increase more clearly? Why?
3. In both graphs, the line that shows carbon dioxide levels is jagged, because carbon dioxide levels rise and fall regularly as the seasons change. In some years, the seasonal rise and fall is greater than in other years. Which graph emphasizes these variations more? Why?

**CHALLENGE** The carbon dioxide level in the air starts falling in May or June each year and continues to fall through October. What do you think causes this change to occur?

# 4 Chapter Review

## the BIG idea

**Climates are long-term weather patterns that may change over time.**

## KEY CONCEPTS SUMMARY

### 4.1 Climate is a long-term weather pattern.

The main factors that influence climate are

- latitude
- altitude
- distance from large bodies of water
- ocean currents

Seasonal changes are also part of climate patterns.

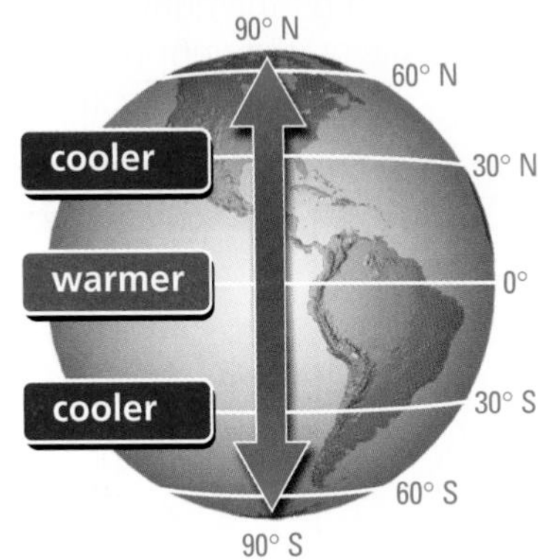

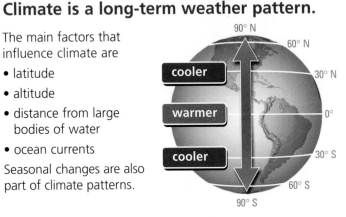

Temperatures usually decrease as latitude increases.

**VOCABULARY**
**climate** p. 117
**latitude** p. 118
**marine climate** p. 120
**continental climate** p. 120
**ocean current** p. 121
**season** p. 122

### 4.2 Earth has a variety of climates.

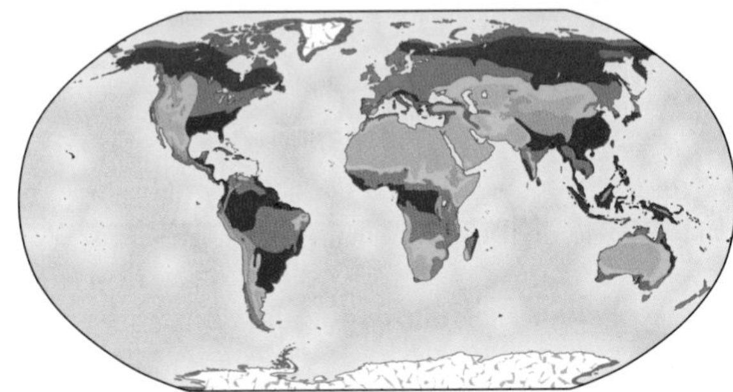

Each color on the map shows a different subclimate.

Scientists usually group climates by temperature and precipitation. There are six major climate zones. Climate zones can be divided into subclimates. Microclimates are smaller areas within subclimates.

**VOCABULARY**
**climate zone** p. 125
**microclimate** p. 128
**urban heat island** p. 128
**rain shadow** p. 129

### 4.3 Climates can change suddenly or slowly.

Natural events, such as eruptions of volcanoes, can change climate. Human activities that release greenhouse gases are also changing climate.

**VOCABULARY**
**ice age** p. 135
**El Niño** p. 136

## Reviewing Vocabulary

*Make a magnet word diagram for each of the vocabulary terms listed below. Write the term in the magnet. Write other terms or ideas related to it on the lines around the magnet.*

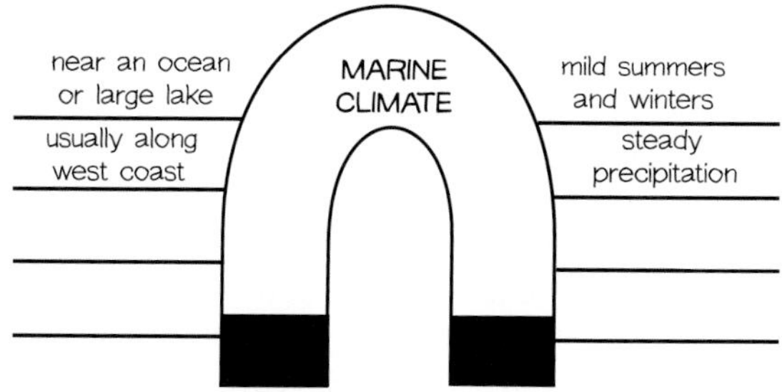


1. continental climate
2. ocean current
3. microclimate
4. urban heat island
5. rain shadow
6. ice age

## Reviewing Key Concepts

**Multiple Choice** *Choose the letter of the best answer.*

**7.** Compared with weather patterns, climate patterns are more

**a.** severe **c.** local
**b.** long-term **d.** unusual

**8.** Climates are usually classified by

**a.** plant cover and animal life
**b.** altitude and latitude
**c.** bodies of water and ocean currents
**d.** temperature and precipitation

**9.** Which latitude receives the least amount of solar energy?

**a.** 30° N **c.** 30° S
**b.** 0° **d.** 90° S

**10.** What is El Niño?

**a.** a change in wind patterns and ocean currents
**b.** an increase in carbon dioxide levels
**c.** a decrease in global temperature
**d.** a change in solar energy

**11.** Which effect is a likely result of global warming?

**a.** fewer droughts
**b.** lower sea levels
**c.** more flooding
**d.** more cold-related deaths

**12.** Volcanoes can cool the climate by

**a.** increasing wind speeds
**b.** using up Earth's energy
**c.** releasing gas and particles
**d.** raising air pressure

**13.** A large coastal city probably has cooler summers than a city at the same latitude that is

**a.** on a mountain **c.** near a volcano
**b.** much smaller **d.** far inland

**14.** Which carries warmth from the tropics toward the polar regions?

**a.** urban heat islands
**b.** warm-water currents
**c.** cold-water currents
**d.** trade winds

**15.** Several different climates can exist within a small area in

**a.** marine climates
**b.** continental climates
**c.** polar climates
**d.** highland climates

**16.** Day and night are equal in length on the first day of

**a.** spring **c.** winter
**b.** summer **d.** El Niño

**Short Answer** *Write a short answer to each question.*

**17.** How can changes caused by the movement of continents affect climate?

**18.** Identify the two main causes of ice ages.

**19.** Describe how a space object might have helped kill off the dinosaurs.

**20.** How is the climate of a city usually different from the climate of a nearby rural area?

## Thinking Critically

*Use the climate graphs to answer the next four questions.*

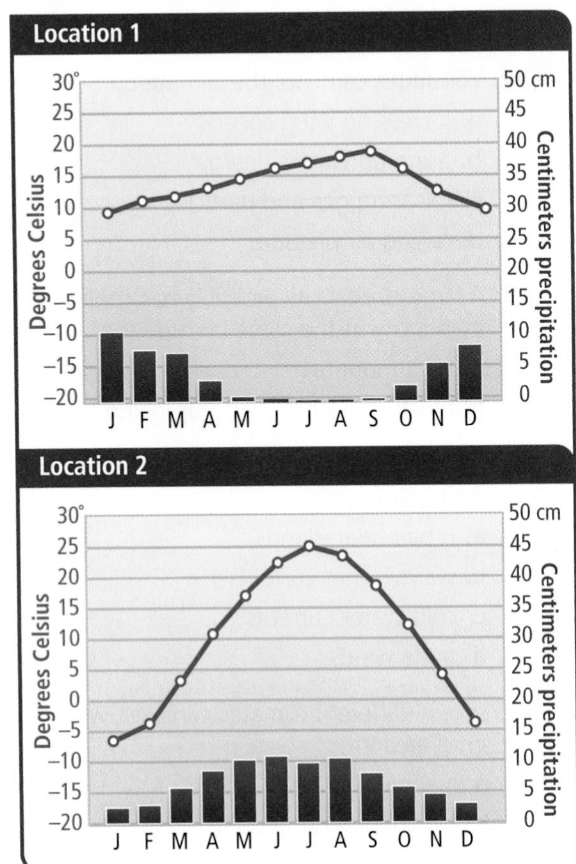


21. **COMPARE AND CONTRAST** Compare and contrast the seasonal precipitation patterns shown in the graphs.

22. **COMPARE AND CONTRAST** Contrast the seasonal temperature patterns shown in the graphs.

23. **HYPOTHESIZE** Which of the four main geographical factors that affect climate is the most likely cause of the difference in temperature patterns in the two locations? Explain.

24. **SYNTHESIZE** Suppose you want to plant a crop that requires a long growing season. Which location would you choose? Why?

25. **IDENTIFY EFFECTS** Describe the possible effect on the microclimate of a city if people planted grass lawns on the roofs of buildings.

26. **SYNTHESIZE** Would you expect to find a greater variety of climates on a tall mountain at 10° N or at 65° N? Explain.

27. **APPLY** In the evening after a hot summer day, the temperature at a beach stays higher longer than it does farther inland. Explain why this happens.

28. **APPLY** Both Kathmandu, Nepal, and Fuzhou, China, are located at about 25° N. Kathmandu is far inland and high in the mountains. Fuzhou is a seaport. How would you expect their climates to differ?

29. **PREDICT** What might be the impact of global warming in the area where you live?

## the BIG idea

30. **APPLY** Look again at the photograph on pages 114–115. Now that you have finished the chapter, how would you change your response to the question on the photograph?

31. **EVALUATE** Describe a place that has what you consider to be a perfect climate. Explain how the following geographical factors affect the climate of that place:
    - latitude
    - altitude
    - distance from large bodies of water
    - ocean currents

## UNIT PROJECTS

Evaluate all the data, results, and information in your project folder. Prepare to present your project.

## Analyzing Data

*The following tables show the average temperatures in four cities and the temperature characteristics of four climate zones. Use the information in the tables to answer the questions below.*

| City | Avg. Temperature in Coldest Month | Avg. Temperature in Warmest Month |
|---|---|---|
| Miami, Florida | 20°C | 29°C |
| Minneapolis, Minnesota | -11°C | 23°C |
| Little Rock, Arkansas | 4°C | 28°C |
| Barrow, Alaska | -26°C | 4°C |

| Climate Zone | Characteristics |
|---|---|
| Polar | Average temperature of warmest month is below 10°C. |
| Moist mid-latitude with severe winters | Average temperature of coldest month is below -2°C. |
| Moist mid-latitude with mild winters | Average temperature of coldest month is between -2°C and 18°C. |
| Humid tropical | Average temperature of every month is greater than 18°C. |

**1.** What is the average temperature in Miami in the coldest month?

**a.** −11°C
**b.** 4°C
**c.** 20°C
**d.** 29°C

**2.** What is the average temperature in Little Rock in the warmest month?

**a.** 4°C
**b.** 23°C
**c.** 28°C
**d.** 29°C

**3.** Which city has a moist mid-latitude climate with mild winters?

**a.** Miami
**b.** Minneapolis
**c.** Little Rock
**d.** Barrow

**4.** Which city has a humid tropical climate?

**a.** Miami
**b.** Minneapolis
**c.** Little Rock
**d.** Barrow

**5.** Which city has a moist mid-latitude climate with severe winters?

**a.** Miami
**b.** Minneapolis
**c.** Little Rock
**d.** Barrow

**6.** In which climate zone would Little Rock be if its average temperature in the coldest month were 10° colder?

**a.** polar
**b.** moist mid-latitude with severe winters
**c.** moist mid-latitude with mild winters
**d.** humid tropical

## Extended Response

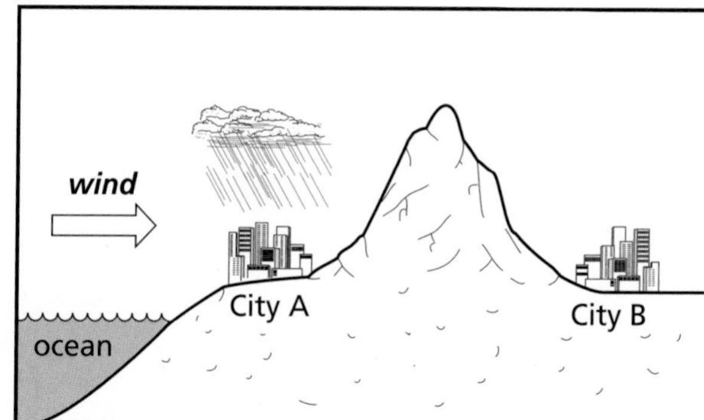


*Use information in the diagram to answer the two questions below in detail.*

**7.** City A receives 165 centimeters of rain each year. Explain why its climate is so moist. Use the words *wind, evaporate, condense,* and *precipitation* in your answer.

**8.** City B receives an average of 22 centimeters of rain each year. Explain why city B is much drier than city A. Use the term *rain shadow* in your answer.

UNIT B

# Human Biology

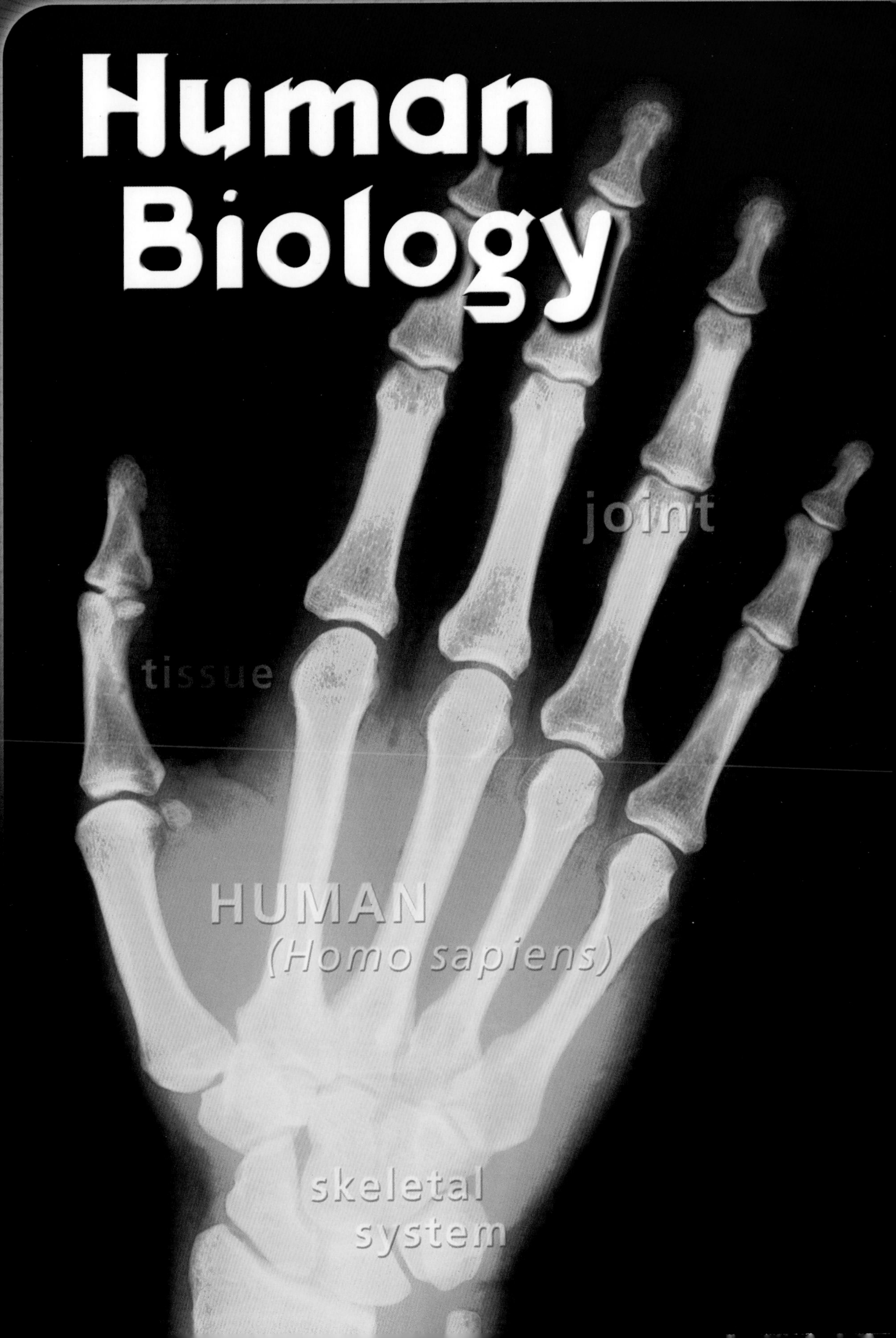

joint

tissue

HUMAN
*(Homo sapiens)*

skeletal
system

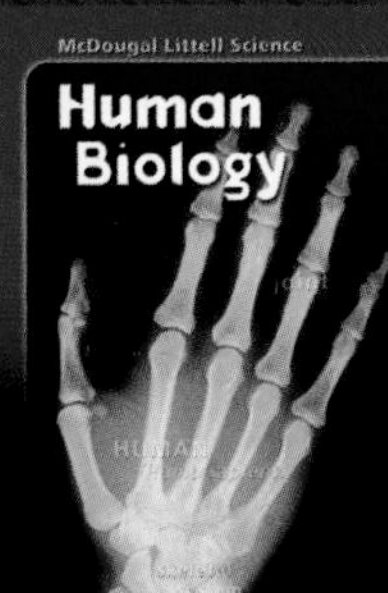

# Human Biology
# Contents Overview

## Unit Features

FRONTIERS IN SCIENCE Surprising Senses 2
TIMELINES IN SCIENCE Seeing Inside the Body 94

## 1 Systems, Support, and Movement 6

the BIG idea

The human body is made up of systems that work together to perform necessary functions.

## 2 Absorption, Digestion, and Exchange 34

the BIG idea

Systems in the body obtain and process materials and remove waste.

## 3 Transport and Protection 62

the BIG idea

Systems function to transport materials and to defend and protect the body.

## 4 Control and Reproduction 98

the BIG idea

The nervous and endocrine systems allow the body to respond to internal and external conditions.

## 5 Growth, Development, and Health 130

the BIG idea

The body develops and maintains itself over time.

# Surprising Senses

SCIENTIFIC AMERICAN FRONTIERS

Learn more about how the brain and senses work. See the video "Sight of Touch."

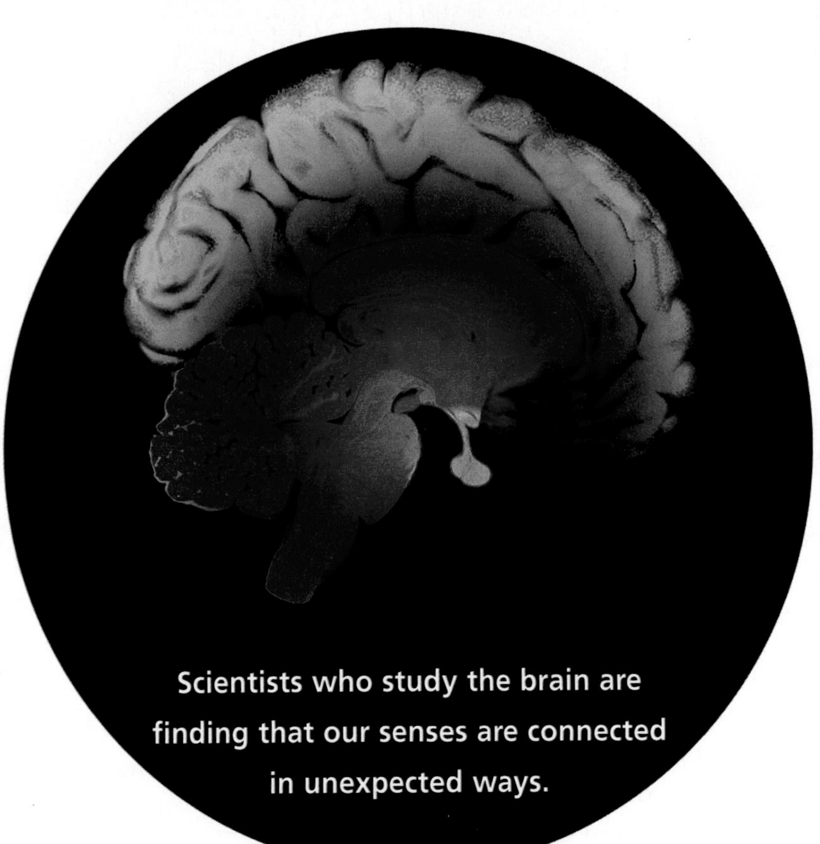

Scientists who study the brain are finding that our senses are connected in unexpected ways.

## Senses and the Brain

One of the great mysteries still unsolved in science is what happens inside the brain. What is a thought? How is it formed? Where is it stored? How do our senses shape our thoughts? There are far more questions than answers. One way to approach questions about the brain is to study brain activity at times when the body is performing different functions.

Most advanced brain functions happen in the part of the brain called the cerebral cortex (suh-REE-bruhl KOR-tehks). That's where the brain interprets information from the senses. The cerebral cortex has many specialized areas. Each area controls one type of brain activity. Scientists are mapping these areas. At first, they studied people with brain injuries. A person with an injury to one area might not be able to speak. Someone with a different injury might have trouble seeing or hearing. Scientists mapped the areas in which damage seemed to cause each kind of problem.

Now scientists have even more tools to study the brain. One tool is called functional magnetic resonance imaging, or FMRI. Scientists put a person into a machine that uses radio waves to produce images of the person's brain. Scientists then ask the person to do specific activities, such as looking at pictures of faces or listening for specific sounds. The FMRI images show what parts of the person's brain are most active during each activity.

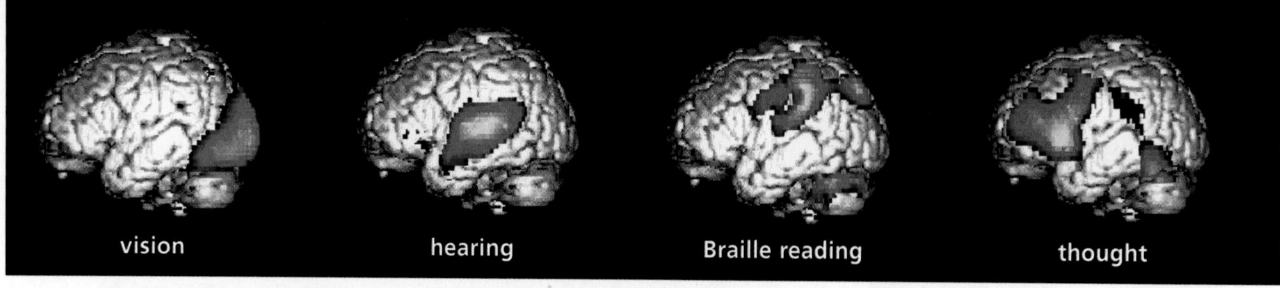


**The PET scans show areas of the brain active during particular tasks. Braille is a textured alphabet read by the fingers. Braille reading activates areas associated with touch, vision, hearing, and thought.**

## Double Duty

Using FMRI and other tools, scientists have identified the parts of the cerebral cortex that are responsible for each of the senses. The vision area is located at the back of the brain. The smell, taste, touch, and hearing areas are all close together in the middle part of the brain.

People don't usually use just one sense at a time. Scientists have found some unexpected connections. In one study, Marisa Taylor-Clarke poked the arms of some volunteers with either one or two pins. Then she asked them how many pins they felt. Taylor-Clarke found that people who looked at their arms before the test did better than those who didn't. FMRI showed that the part of their brains responsible for touch was also more active when they used their sense of sight.

These connections in the brain show up even when one sense doesn't work. Many people who have hearing impairments read lips to understand what other people are saying. Scientists using FMRI discovered that these people use the part of the brain normally used for hearing to help them understand what they see. This is even true for people who have never been able to hear.

## Scrambled Senses

Some people have more connections between their senses than most people have. They may look at numbers and see colors, or associate smells with shapes. Some even get a taste in their mouths when they touch something. All these are examples of synesthesia (sin-uhs-THEE-zhuh). About 1 in 200 people have some kind of synesthesia.

### SCIENTIFIC AMERICAN FRONTIERS

**View the "Sight of Touch" segment of your Scientific American Frontiers video to learn about another example of connections between the senses.**

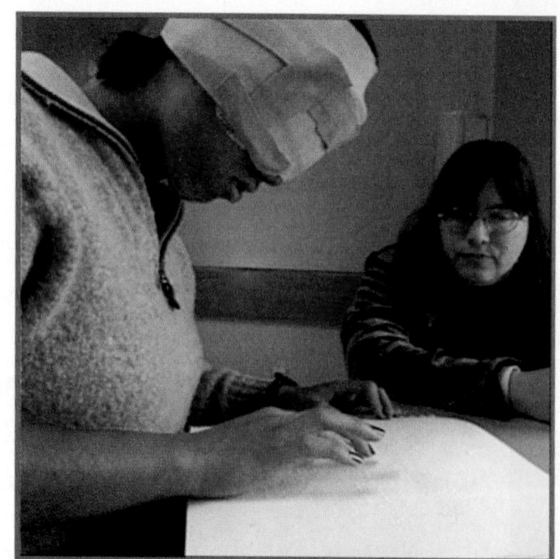

**IN THIS SCENE FROM THE VIDEO** Michelle, a research subject, reads Braille with her fingers after wearing a blindfold for three days.

**SEEING BY TOUCHING** Many blind people read using Braille, a system of raised dots used to represent letters. Some, such as Braille proofreader Gil Busch, can read Braille at astonishing speeds. Scientist Alvaro Pascual-Leone used MRI to study Gil's brain. The visual area of Gil's brain was active while he read Braille.

Gil has been blind since birth, so his brain has had a long time to adjust. Pascual-Leone wanted to know whether the brain could rewire itself in a shorter time. He asked volunteer Michelle Geronimo to wear a blindfold for a week. During that time, she learned to read Braille and experienced the world as a blind person does. At the end of the week, Pascual-Leone was able to demonstrate that Michelle's brain had rewired itself, too. Her visual center was active when she read Braille.

FMRI has made it possible for scientists to learn more about synesthesia. One group of scientists studied people who saw colors when they heard words. FMRI showed that the visual areas of their brains were active along with the hearing areas. (For most people, only the hearing area would be active.)

But why does synesthesia happen? Some scientists think that people with synesthesia have more connections between areas of their brains. Every person has extra connections when they're born, but most people lose many of them in childhood. Perhaps people with synesthesia keep theirs. Another theory suggests that their brains are "cross-wired," so information goes in unusual directions.

**Some people with synesthesia see this colorful pattern when they hear a dog bark.**

As scientists explore synesthesia and other connections between the senses, they learn more about how the parts of the brain work together. The human body is complex. And the brain, along with the rest of the nervous system, has yet to be fully understood.

## UNANSWERED Questions

Scientists have learned a lot about how senses are connected. Their research leads to new questions.

- How does information move between different areas of the brain?
- How and why does the brain rewire itself?
- How does cross-wired sensing (synesthesia) happen?

## UNIT PROJECTS

**As you study this unit, work alone or in a group on one of the projects below.**

### Your Body System

Create one or several models showing important body systems.

- Draw the outline of your own body on a large piece of craft paper.
- Use reference materials to help you place everything correctly. Label each part.

### The Brain: "Then and Now"

Compare and contrast past and present understandings of the brain.

- One understanding is that each part of the brain is responsible for different body functions. This understanding has changed over time.
- Research the history of this idea.
- Prepare diagrams of then and now. Share your presentation.

### Design an Experiment

Design an experiment that will test one of the senses. You should first identify a problem question you want to explore.

- The experiment may include a written introduction, materials procedure, and a plan for recording and presenting outcomes.
- Prepare a blank written experiment datasheet for your classmates to use.

Learn more about careers in neurobiology.

# 1 Systems, Support, and Movement

## the BIG idea

The human body is made up of systems that work together to perform necessary functions.

## Key Concepts

SECTION 1.1 **The human body is complex.**
Learn about the parts and systems in the human body.

SECTION 1.2 **The skeletal system provides support and protection.**
Learn how the skeletal system is organized and what it does.

SECTION 1.3 **The muscular system makes movement possible.**
Learn about the different types of muscles and how they work.

***What systems make it possible for this racer to move so fast?***

### Internet Preview

CLASSZONE.COM

Chapter 1 online resources: Content Review, two Simulations, three Resource Centers, Math Tutorial, Test Practice

## How Many Bones Are in Your Hand?

Use a pencil to trace an outline of your hand on a piece of paper. Feel the bones in your fingers and the palm of your hand. At points where you can bend your fingers and hand, draw a circle. Each circle represents a joint where two bones meet. Draw lines to represent the bones in your hand.

**Observe and Think** How many bones did you find? How many joints?

## How Does It Move?

The bones in your body are hard and stiff, yet they move smoothly. The point where two bones meet and move is called a joint. There are probably many objects in your home that have hard parts that move against each other: a joystick, a hinge, a pair of scissors.

**Observe and Think** What types of movement are possible when two hard objects are attached to each other? What parts of your body produce similar movements?

## Internet Activity: The Human Body

Go to **ClassZone.com** to explore the different systems in the human body.

**Observe and Think** How are the systems in the middle of the body different from those that extend to the outer parts of the body?

Tissues and Organs **Code: MDL044**

CHAPTER 1

# Getting Ready to Learn

## CONCEPT REVIEW

- The cell is the basic unit of living things.
- Systems are made up of interacting parts that share matter and energy.
- In multicellular organisms cells work together to support life.

## VOCABULARY REVIEW

*See Glossary for definitions.*

**cell**
**system**

Review concepts and vocabulary.

## TAKING NOTES

### MAIN IDEA WEB

Write each new blue heading in a box. Then write notes in boxes around the center box that give important terms and details about that blue heading.

### VOCABULARY STRATEGY

Write each new vocabulary term in the center of a **four square** diagram. Write notes in the squares around each term. Include a definition, some features, and some examples of the term. If possible, write some things that are not examples of the term.

See the Note-Taking Handbook on pages R45–R51.

SCIENCE NOTEBOOK

The cell is the basic unit of living things.

Tissues are groups of similar cells that function together.

The body has cells, tissues, and organs.

Organs are groups of tissues working together.

| Definition | Features |
|---|---|
| Group of cells that work together | A level of organization in the body |
| **Examples** | **Nonexamples** |
| connective tissue, like bone | individual bone cells |

TISSUE

KEY CONCEPT

# The human body is complex.

**BEFORE, you learned**

- All living things are made of cells
- All living things need energy
- Living things meet their needs through interactions with the environment

**NOW, you will learn**

- About the organization of the human body
- About different types of tissues
- About the functions of organ systems

**VOCABULARY**

**tissue** p. 10
**organ** p. 11
**organ system** p. 12
**homeostasis** p. 12

**THINK ABOUT**

### *How is the human body like a city?*

A city is made up of many parts that perform different functions. Buildings provide places to live and work. Transportation systems move people around. Electrical energy provides light and heat. Similarly, the human body is made of several systems. The skeletal system, like the framework of a building, provides support. The digestive system works with the respiratory system to provide energy and materials. What other systems in your body can you compare to a system in the city?

## The body has cells, tissues, and organs.

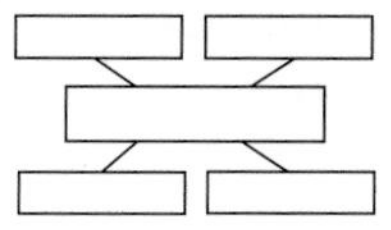

**MAIN IDEA WEB**
As you read this section, complete the main idea web begun on page 8.

Your body is made of many parts that work together as a system to help you grow and stay healthy. The basic level of organization in your body is the cell. Next come tissues, then individual organs, and then systems that are made up of organs. The highest level of organization is the organism itself. You can think of the body as having five levels of organization: cells, tissues, organs, organ systems, and the organism. Although these levels seem separate from one another, they all work together.

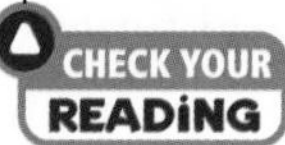


What are five levels of organization in your body?

# INVESTIGATE Systems

## How do the systems in your body interact?

**SKILL FOCUS**
Predicting

**MATERIALS**
large sheet of paper

**TIME**
20 minutes

**PROCEDURE**

1. Work with other classmates to make a list of everyday activities.
2. Discuss how your body responds to each task. Record your ideas.
3. Identify and count the systems in your body that you think are used to perform the task.
4. Have someone from your group make a chart of the different activities.

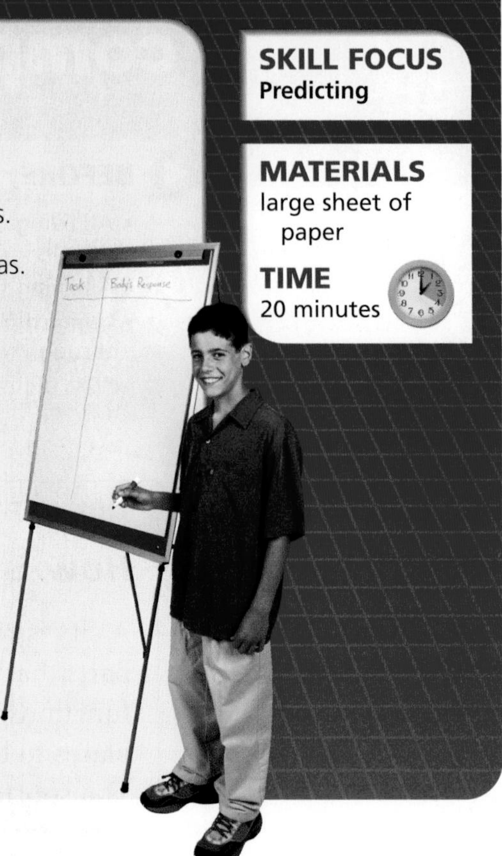


**WHAT DO YOU THINK?**

- Which systems did you name, and how did they work together to perform each activity?
- When you are asleep, what activities does your body perform?

**CHALLENGE** How could you make an experiment that would test your predictions?

## Cells

The cell is the basic unit of life. Cells make up all living things. Some organisms, such as bacteria, are made of only a single cell. In these organisms the single cell performs all of the tasks necessary for survival. That individual cell captures and releases energy, uses materials, and grows. In more complex organisms, such as humans and many other animals and plants, cells are specialized. Specialized cells perform specific jobs. A red blood cell, for example, carries oxygen from the lungs throughout the body.

## Tissues

A **tissue** is a group of similar cells that work together to perform a particular function. Think of a tissue as a brick wall and the cells within it as the individual bricks. Taken together, the bricks form something larger and more functional. But just as the bricks need to be placed in a certain way to form the wall, cells must be organized in a tissue.

How are cells related to tissues?

The human body contains several types of tissues. These tissues are classified into four main groups according to their function: epithelial tissue, nerve tissue, muscle tissue, and connective tissue.

- Epithelial (ehp-uh-THEE-lee-uhl) tissue functions as a boundary. It covers all of the inner and outer surfaces of your body. Each of your internal organs is covered with a layer of epithelial tissue.
- Nerve tissue functions as a messaging system. Cells in nerve tissue carry electrical impulses between your brain and the various parts of your body in response to changing conditions.
- Muscle tissue functions in movement. Movement results when muscle cells contract, or shorten, and then relax. In some cases, such as throwing a ball, you control the movement. In other cases, such as the beating of your heart, the movement occurs without conscious control.
- Connective tissue functions to hold parts of the body together, providing support, protection, strength, padding, and insulation. Tendons and ligaments are connective tissues that hold bones and muscles together. Bone itself is another connective tissue. It supports and protects the soft parts of your body.

## Organs

Groups of different tissues make up organs. An **organ** is a structure that is made up of two or more types of tissue that work together to carry out a function in the body. For example, the heart that pumps blood around your body contains all four types of tissues. As in cells and tissues, the structure of an organ relates to its function. The stomach's bag-shaped structure and strong muscular walls make it suited for breaking down food. The walls of the heart are also muscular, allowing it to function as a pump.

### Levels of Organization

**The human body can be studied at different levels of organization.**

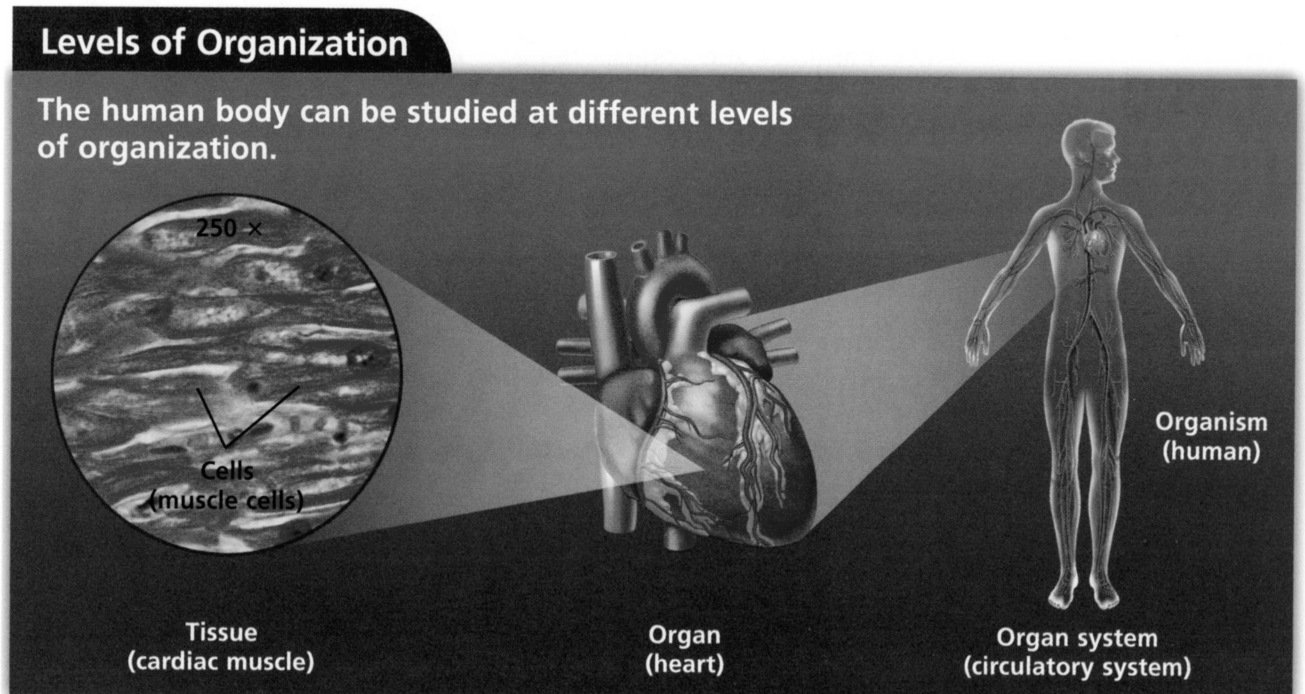

## Organ Systems

An **organ system** is a group of organs that together perform a function that helps the body meet its needs for energy and materials. For example, your stomach, mouth, throat, large and small intestines, liver, and pancreas are all part of the organ system called the digestive system. The body is made up of many organ systems. In this unit, you will read about these systems. They include the skeletal, muscular, respiratory, digestive, urinary, circulatory, immune, nervous, and reproductive systems. Together, these systems allow the human organism to grow, reproduce, and maintain life.

## The body's systems interact with one another.

READING TIP

**VOCABULARY**
The word *homeostasis* contains two word roots. *Homeo* comes from a root meaning "same." *Stasis* comes from a root meaning "stand still" or "stay."

The ability of your body to maintain internal conditions is called **homeostasis** (HOH-mee-oh-STAY-sihs). Your body is constantly regulating such things as your body temperature, the amount of sugar in your blood, even your posture. The processes that take place in your body occur within a particular set of conditions.

The body's many levels of organization, from cells to organ systems, work constantly to maintain the balance needed for the survival of the organism. For example, on a hot day, you may sweat. Sweating keeps the temperature inside your body constant, even though the temperature of your surroundings changes.

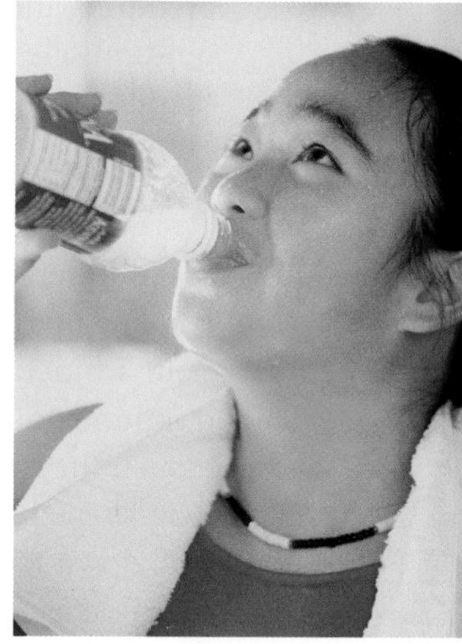

**INFER** This student is drinking water after exercising. Why is it important to drink fluids after you sweat?

# 1.1 Review

**KEY CONCEPTS**

1. Draw a diagram that shows the relationship among cells, tissues, organs, and organ systems.
2. Make a chart of the four basic tissue groups that includes names, functions, and examples.
3. Identify three functions performed by organ systems.

**CRITICAL THINKING**

4. **Apply** How does drinking water after you sweat help maintain homeostasis?
5. **Compare and Contrast** Compare and contrast the four basic tissue groups. How would all four types of tissue be involved in a simple activity, like raising your hand?

**CHALLENGE**

6. **Apply** Describe an object, such as a car, that can be used as a model of the human body. Explain how the parts of the model relate to the body.

**Think SCIENCE**

SKILL: INFERRING

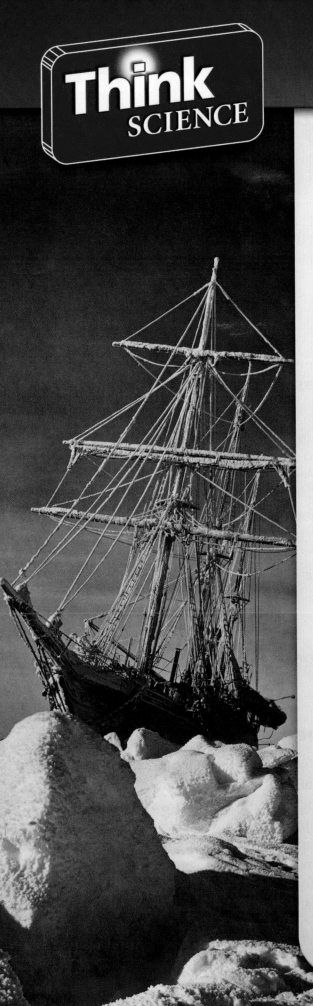

# What Does the Body Need to Survive?

In 1914, Ernest Shackleton and 27 men set sail for Antarctica. Their goal was to cross the continent by foot and sled. The crew never set foot on Antarctica. Instead, the winter sea froze around their ship, crushing it until it sank. They were stranded on floating ice, over 100 miles from land. How long could they survive? How would their bodies respond? What would they need to stay alive?

You can make inferences in answer to any of these questions. First you need to recall what you know. Then you need new evidence. What was available to the explorers? Did they save supplies from their ship? What resources existed in the environment?

## Prior Knowledge

- The human body needs air, water, and food.
- The human body needs to maintain its temperature. The body can be harmed if it loses too much heat.

## Observations

Several of Shackleton's explorers kept diaries. From the diaries we know the following:

- The crew hunted seals and penguins for fresh meat.
- The temperature was usually below freezing.
- Tents and overturned lifeboats sheltered the crew from the wind.
- Their clothes were made of thick fabric and animal skins and furs.
- They melted snow and ice in order to have fresh water.

## Make Inferences

**On Your Own** Describe how the explorers met each of the needs of the human body.

**As a Group** How long do you think these 28 men could have survived these conditions? Use evidence and inferences in your answer.

**CHALLENGE** How might survival needs differ for sailors shipwrecked in the tropics compared to the Antarctic?

Learn more about Shackleton's expedition.

KEY CONCEPT

# The skeletal system provides support and protection.

### BEFORE, you learned

- The body is made of cells, tissues, organs, and systems
- Cells, tissues, organs, and organ systems work together
- Systems in the body interact

### NOW, you will learn

- About different types of bone tissue
- How the human skeleton is organized
- How joints allow movement

### VOCABULARY

**skeletal system** p. 14
**compact bone** p. 15
**spongy bone** p. 15
**axial skeleton** p. 16
**appendicular skeleton** p. 16

### EXPLORE Levers

## *How can a bone act as a lever?*

### PROCEDURE

1. A lever is a stiff rod that pivots about a fixed point. Hold the bag in your hand and keep your arm straight, like a lever. Move the bag up and down.
2. Move the handles of the bag over your elbow. Again hold your arm straight and move the bag up and down.
3. Now move the bag to the top of your arm and repeat the procedure.

### MATERIALS

sports bag

### WHAT DO YOU THINK?

- At which position is it easiest to move the bag?
- At which position does the bag move the farthest?
- How does the position of a load affect the action of a lever?

## Bones are living tissue.

**MAIN IDEA WEB**
Make a web of the important terms and details about the main idea: *Bones are living tissue.*

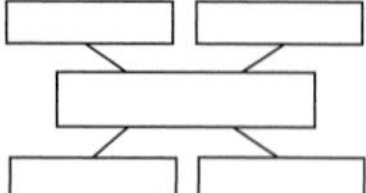

Every movement of the human body is possible because of the interaction of muscles with the **skeletal system.** Made up of a strong connective tissue called bone, the skeletal system serves as the anchor for all of the body's movement, provides support, and protects soft organs inside the body. Bones can be classified as long bones, short bones, irregular bones, and flat bones. Long bones are found in the arms and legs. Short bones are found in the feet and hands. Irregular bones are found in the spine. Flat bones are found in the ribs and skull.

You might think that bones are completely solid and made up of dead tissue. They actually are made of both hard and soft materials.

Like your heart or skin, bones are living tissue. Bones are not completely solid, either; they have spaces inside. The spaces allow blood carrying nutrients to travel throughout the bones. Because bones have spaces, they weigh much less than they would if they were solid.

RESOURCE CENTER
CLASSZONE.COM

Explore the skeletal system.

## Two Types of Bone Tissue

Every bone is made of two types of bone tissue: compact bone and spongy bone. The hard compact bone surrounds the soft spongy bone. Each individual bone cell lies within a bony web. This web is made up mostly of minerals containing calcium.

**Compact Bone** Surrounding the spongy, inner layer of the bone is a hard layer called **compact bone.** Compact bone functions as the basic supportive tissue of the body, the part of the body you call the skeleton. The outer layer of compact bone is very hard and tough. It covers the outside of most bones.

**Spongy Bone** Inside the bone, the calcium network is less dense. This tissue is called **spongy bone.** Spongy bone is strong but lightweight. It makes up most of the short, flat, and irregular bones found in your body. It also makes up the ends of long bones.

## Marrow and Blood Cells

Within the spongy bone tissue is marrow, the part of the bone that produces blood cells. The new blood cells travel from the marrow into the blood vessels that run throughout the bone. The blood brings nutrients to the bone cells and carries waste materials away.

### A Close Look at Bone

**All bone, like the long bone shown here, is made up of compact bone tissue and spongy bone tissue.**

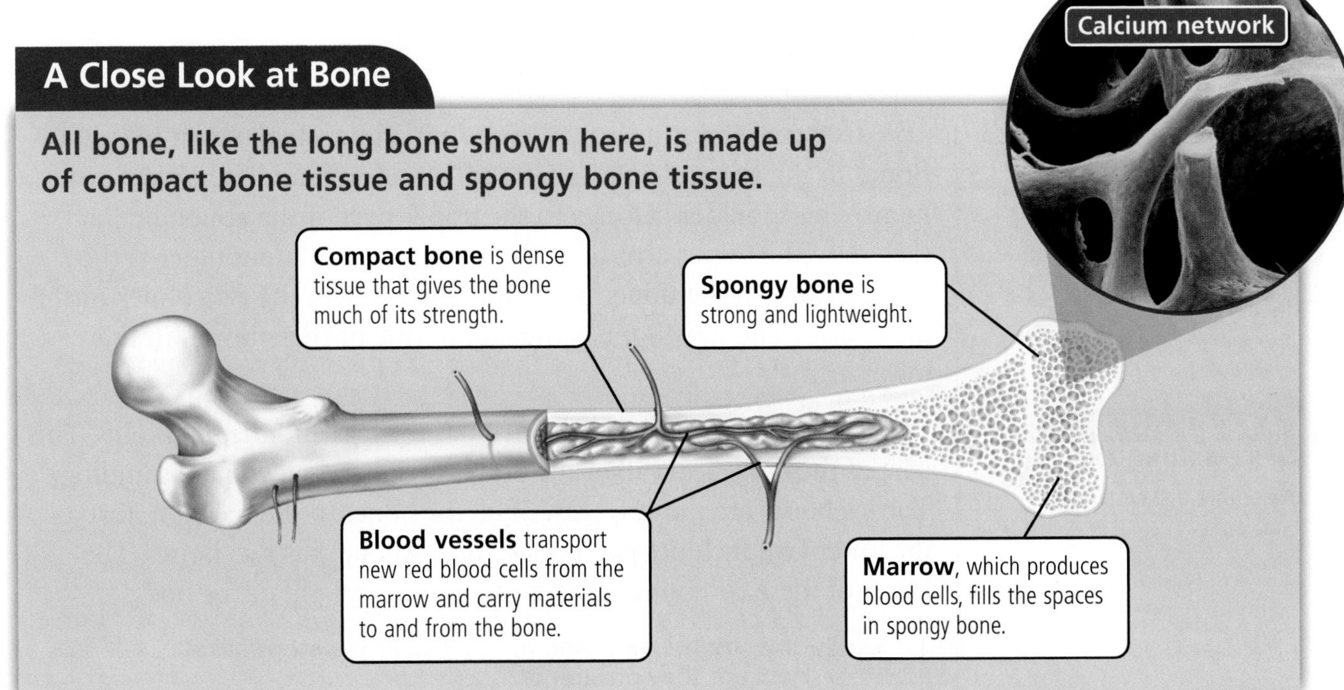
Calcium network
**Compact bone** is dense tissue that gives the bone much of its strength.
**Spongy bone** is strong and lightweight.
**Blood vessels** transport new red blood cells from the marrow and carry materials to and from the bone.
**Marrow**, which produces blood cells, fills the spaces in spongy bone.

## The skeleton is the body's framework.

Like the frame of a building, the skeleton provides the body's shape. The skeleton also works with other systems to allow movement. Scientists have identified two main divisions in the skeleton. These are the axial (AK-see-uhl) skeleton, which is the central part of the skeleton, and the appendicular (AP-uhn-DIHK-yuh-luhr) skeleton. Bones in the appendicular skeleton are attached to the axial skeleton. The diagram on page 17 labels some of the important bones in your skeleton.

### The Axial Skeleton

**VOCABULARY**
Remember to add four squares for *axial skeleton* and *appendicular skeleton* to your notebook.

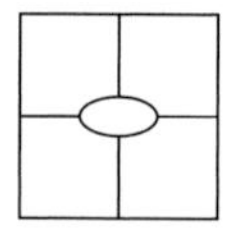

Imagine a line straight down your back. You can think of that line as an axis. Sitting, standing, and twisting are some of the motions that turn around the axis. The **axial skeleton** is the part of the skeleton that forms the axis. It provides support and protection. In the diagram, parts of the axial skeleton are colored in red.

The axial skeleton includes the skull, or the cranium (KRAY-nee-uhm). The major function of the cranium is protection of the brain. Most of the bones in the cranium do not move. The skull connects to the spinal column in a way that allows the head to move up and down as well as right and left.

Your spinal column makes up the main portion of the axial skeleton. The spinal column is made up of many bones called vertebrae. The many bones allow flexibility. If you run your finger along your back you will feel the vertebrae. Another set of bones belonging to the axial skeleton are the rib bones. The ribs function to protect the soft internal organs, such as the heart and lungs.

### The Appendicular Skeleton

The diagram shows the bones in the appendicular skeleton in yellow. Bones in the **appendicular skeleton** function mainly to allow movement. The shoulder belongs to the upper part of the appendicular skeleton. The upper arm bone that connects to the shoulder is the longest bone in the upper body. It connects with the two bones of the lower arm. The wristbone is the end of one of these bones in the lower arm.

Assemble a skeleton.

The lower part of the body includes the legs and the hip bones. This part of the body bears all of the body's weight when you are standing. The leg bones are the strongest of all the bones in the skeleton. Just as the lower arm includes two bones, the lower leg has two bones. The larger of these two bones carries most of the weight of the body.

How are the axial and appendicular skeletons alike? How are they different?

## The Skeletal System

**The skeletal system interacts with other body systems to allow this soccer player to stand, run, and kick.**

**axial skeleton**
**appendicular skeleton**
The **skull** protects the brain.
The lower jaw is the only bone in the skull that can move.
Twelve pairs of **ribs** protect the lungs and heart.
The shoulder blade is called the **scapula**.
The **vertebrae** of the spinal column protect the spinal cord and support the cranium and other bones.
The upper arm bone is called the **humerus**.
The lower arm bones are the **ulna** and **radius**.
13
The many bones in the wrist and the hand allow the hand to perform a great variety of activities.
The upper leg bone, called the **femur**, is the longest bone in the body.
The kneecap is called the **patella**.
The lower leg bones are called the **tibia** and the **fibula**.
There are 26 bones in the ankle and the foot.

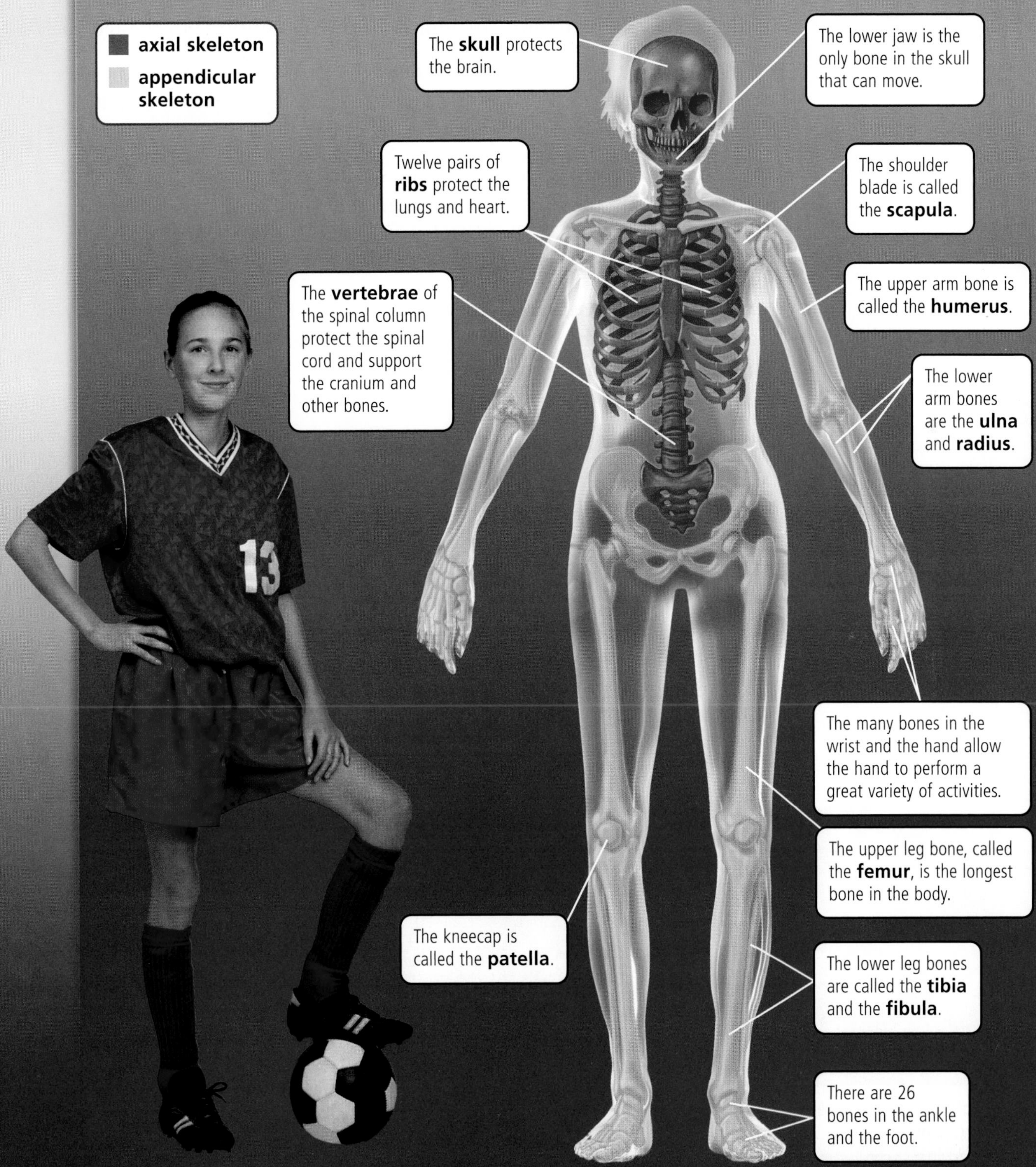

**READING VISUALS** The word *appendicular* has the same root as the word *append,* which means to attach. How do you think this word applies to the appendicular skeleton?

## The skeleton changes as the body develops and ages.

**MAIN IDEA WEB** Make a web of the important terms and details about the main idea: *The skeleton changes as the body develops and ages.*

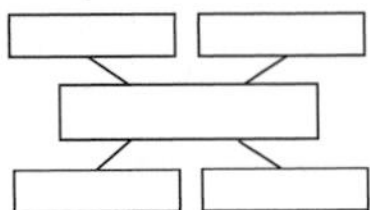

You will remember that bones are living tissue. During infancy and childhood, bones grow as the rest of the body grows. Bones become harder as they stop growing. In adulthood, bones continue to change.

**Infancy** The skull of a newborn is made up of several bones that have spaces between them. As the brain grows, the skull also grows. During the growth of the skull, the spaces between the bones close.

**Childhood** Bone growth occurs at areas called growth plates. These growth plates are made of cartilage, a firm, flexible connective tissue. The length and shape of bones is determined by growth plates. Long bones grow at the ends of the bone surrounding growth plates.

**Adolescence** At the end of adolescence (AD-uhl-EHS-uhns) bones stop growing. The growth plate is the last portion of the bone to become hard. Once growth plates become hard, arms and legs stop growing and the skull plates fuse.

**REMINDER**

Density is the ratio of mass over volume. Bone density is a measure of the mass of a bone divided by the bone's volume.

**Adulthood** Even after bones stop growing, they go through cycles in which old bone is broken down and new bone is formed. As people age, more bone is broken down than is formed. This can lead to a decrease in bone mass, which causes a decrease in bone density. The strength of bones depends upon their density. As people age, their bone density may decrease. Bones that are less dense may break more easily. Many doctors recommend that adults over a certain age get regular bone density tests.

### Test of Bone Density

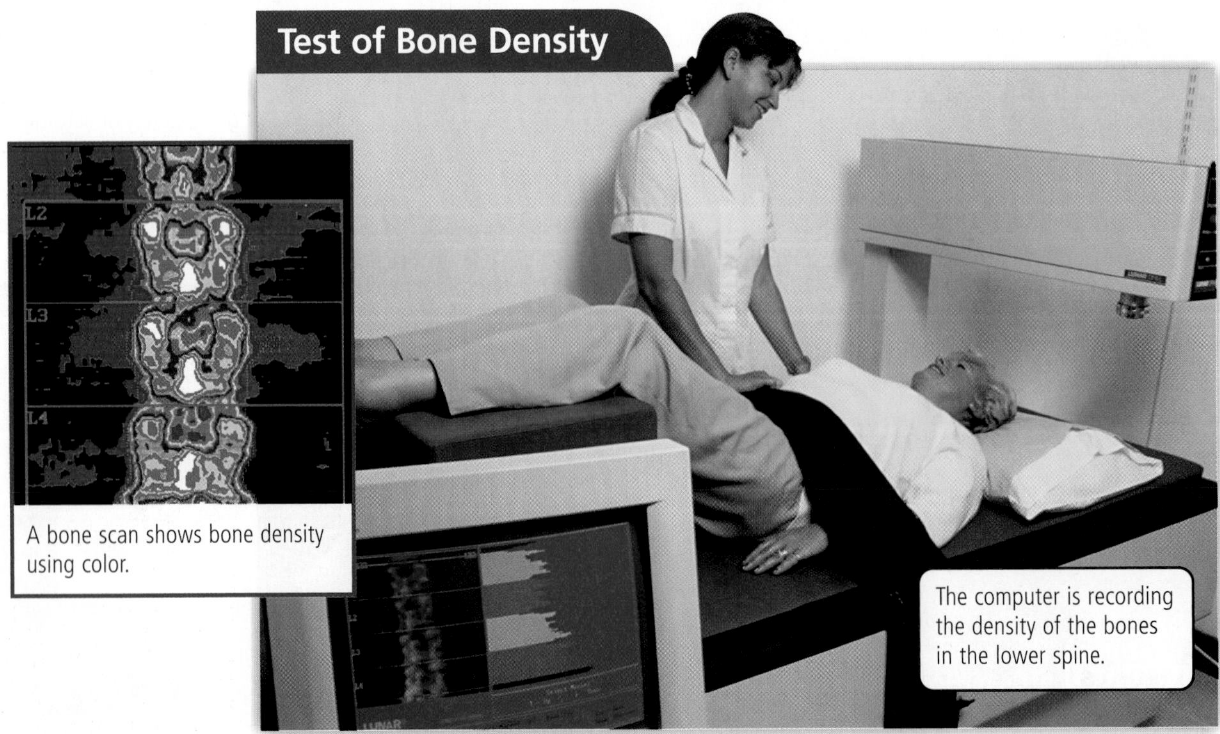


A bone scan shows bone density using color.

The computer is recording the density of the bones in the lower spine.

## Joints connect parts of the skeletal system.

A joint is a place at which two parts of the skeletal system meet. There are three types of joints: immovable, slightly movable, and freely movable.

**Immovable and Slightly Movable Joints** An immovable joint locks bones together like puzzle pieces. The bones of your skull are connected by immovable joints. Slightly movable joints are able to flex slightly. Your ribs are connected to your sternum by slightly movable joints.

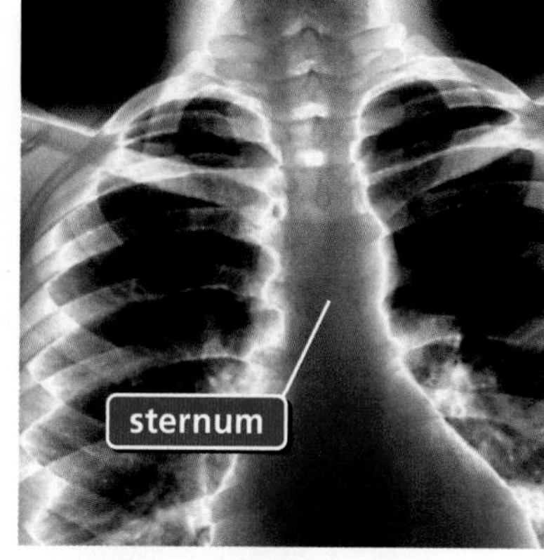

The sternum is an example of a slightly movable joint.

**Freely Movable Joints** Freely movable joints allow your body to bend and to move. Tissues called ligaments hold the bones together at movable joints. Other structures inside the joint cushion the bones and keep them from rubbing together. The entire joint also is surrounded by connective tissue.

Movable joints can be classified by the type of movement they produce. Think about the movement of your arm when you eat an apple. Your arm moves up, then down, changing the angle between your upper and lower arms. This is angular movement. The joint that produces this movement is called a hinge joint.

## INVESTIGATE Movable Joints

### How can you move at joints?

**PROCEDURE**

1. Perform several activities that involve your joints. Twist at the waist. Bend from your waist to one side. Reach into the air with one arm. Open and close your mouth. Push a book across your desk. Lift the book.
2. Record each activity and write a note describing the motion that you feel at each joint.
3. Try to see how many different ways you can move at joints.

**WHAT DO YOU THINK?**

- How was the motion you felt similar for each activity? How was it different?
- Based on your observations, identify two or more ways that joints move.

**CHALLENGE** Draw a diagram showing how you think each joint moves. How might you classify different types of joints based upon the way they move?

**SKILL FOCUS**
Observing

**MATERIALS**
book

**TIME**
20 minutes

## Movable Joints

**The joints in the elbow and hip allow different types of movement.**

**Angular movement (elbow)**

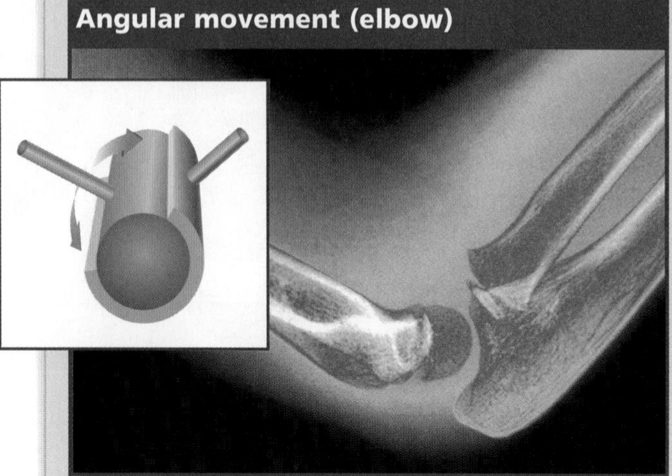

**Rotational movement (hip)**

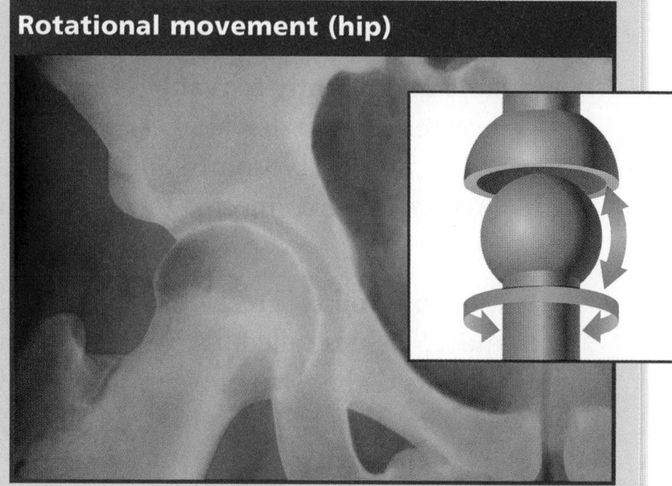

**READING VISUALS** INFER How do the structure and shape of each joint allow bones to move?

Your arm can also rotate from side to side, as it does when you turn a doorknob. Rotational movement like this is produced by a pivot joint in the elbow. You can also rotate your arm in a circle, like the motion of a softball pitcher winding up and releasing a ball. The joint in the shoulder that produces this type of rotational movement is called a ball-and-socket joint.

Joints also produce gliding movement. All joints glide, that is, one bone slides back and forth across another. In some cases, as with the joints in your backbone, a small gliding movement is the only movement the joint produces.

# 1.2 Review

### KEY CONCEPTS

1. What are the functions of the two types of bone tissue?
2. What are the main divisions of the human skeleton?
3. Name three types of movement produced by movable joints and give an example of each.

### CRITICAL THINKING

4. **Infer** What function do immovable joints in the skull perform? Think about the different stages of development in the human body.
5. **Analyze** Which type of movable joint allows the most movement? How does the joint's shape and structure contribute to this?

### CHALLENGE

6. **Classify** The joints in your hand and wrist produce three different types of movement. Using your own wrist, classify the joint movement of the fingers, palm, and wrist. Support your answer.

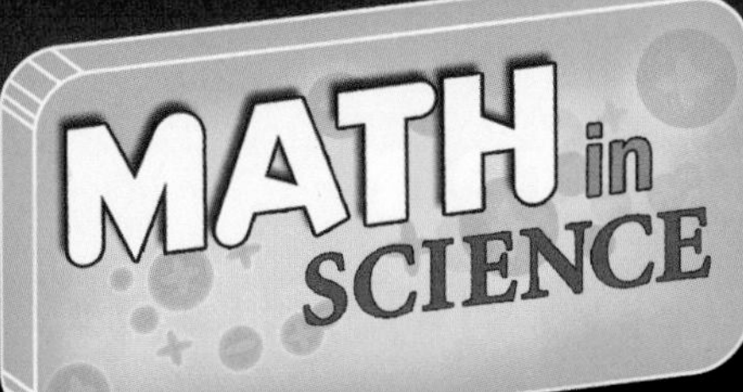


## SKILL: COMPARING RATES

# Rates of Production

**MATH TUTORIAL**

CLASSZONE.COM

Click on Math Tutorial for more help with unit rates.

Where do red blood cells come from? They are produced inside bone marrow at the center of long bones. An average of about 200 billion red blood cells per day are produced by a healthy adult. When a person produces too few red blood cells, a condition called anemia may occur. Doctors study rates of blood cell production to diagnose and treat anemia.

A rate is a ratio that compares two quantities of different units. The number of cells produced per 24 hours is an example of a rate.

### Example

A healthy adult produces red blood cells at a rate greater than 166 billion cells per 24 hours. Suppose a man's body produces 8 billion red blood cells per 1 hour. Would he be considered anemic?

**(1)** Write the two rates as fractions.

$\frac{8}{1}$ $\frac{166}{24}$

**(2)** Simplify the fractions, so that the denominators are both 1. To simplify, divide the numerator by the denominator.

$\frac{8}{1}$ $\frac{6.9}{1}$

**(3)** Compare the two whole numbers. Is the first number $<$, $>$, or $=$ to the second number?

$8 > 6.9$

**ANSWER** The rate is greater than 6.9. The patient is not anemic.

**Compare the following rates to see if they indicate that a person is anemic or normal.**

1. For women, a normal rate is about 178 billion red blood cells per day. A certain woman produces 6 billion red blood cells per hour. Is her rate low or healthy?
2. Suppose a different woman produces 150 million (not billion) red blood cells per minute. How does that rate compare to 178 billion cells per day? Is it $<$, $>$, or $=$ to it?
3. Suppose a certain man is producing 135 million red blood cells per minute. Is that rate low or healthy?

**CHALLENGE** In the example above of a man producing 166 billion cells per day, calculate the percentage by which the rate would need to increase to bring it up to the average count of 200 billion per day.

KEY CONCEPT

# The muscular system makes movement possible.

**BEFORE, you learned**

- There are different types of bone tissue
- The human skeleton has two separate divisions
- Joints function in several different ways

**NOW, you will learn**

- About the functions of muscles
- About the different types of muscles and how they work
- How muscles grow and heal

**VOCABULARY**

**muscular system** p. 23
**skeletal muscle** p. 24
**voluntary muscle** p. 24
**smooth muscle** p. 24
**involuntary muscle** p. 24
**cardiac muscle** p. 24

**EXPLORE Muscles**

***How do muscles change as you move?***

**PROCEDURE**

1. Sit on a chair with your feet on the floor.
2. Place your hand around your leg. Straighten one leg as shown in the photograph.
3. Repeat step 2 several times.

**WHAT DO YOU THINK?**

- How did your muscles change during the activity?
- Record your observations.
- What questions do you have about the muscular system?

## Muscles perform important functions.

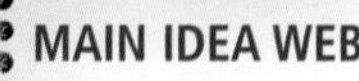

**MAIN IDEA WEB**
Make a web for the main idea: *Muscles perform important functions.*

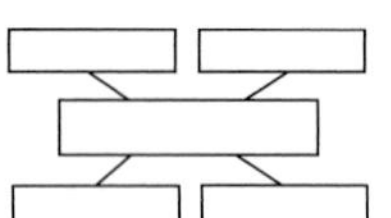

Every movement of your body—from the beating of your heart, to the movement of food down your throat, to the blinking of your eyes—occurs because of muscles. Some movements are under your control, and other movements seem to happen automatically. However, muscles do more than produce movement. They perform other functions as well. Keeping body temperature stable and maintaining posture are two additional functions of muscles.

CHECK YOUR READING What are three functions that muscles perform?

## Movement

The **muscular system** works with the skeletal system to allow movement. Like all muscles, the muscles that produce movement are made up of individual cells called muscle fibers. These fibers contract and relax.

RESOURCE CENTER
CLASSZONE.COM
Discover more about muscles.

Most of the muscles involved in moving the body work in pairs. As they contract, muscles shorten, pulling against bones. It may surprise you to know that muscles do not push. Rather, a muscle on one side of a bone pulls in one direction, while another muscle relaxes. Muscles are attached to bones by stretchy connective tissue.

## Maintaining Body Temperature

Earlier you read that processes within the body require certain conditions, such as temperature and the right amount of water and other materials. The balance of conditions is called homeostasis. One of the functions of the muscular system is related to homeostasis. Muscles function to maintain body temperature.

When muscles contract, they release heat. Without this heat from muscle contraction, the body could not maintain its normal temperature. You may have observed the way your muscles affect your body temperature when you shiver. The quick muscle contractions that occur when you shiver release heat and raise your body temperature.

How do muscles help maintain homeostasis?

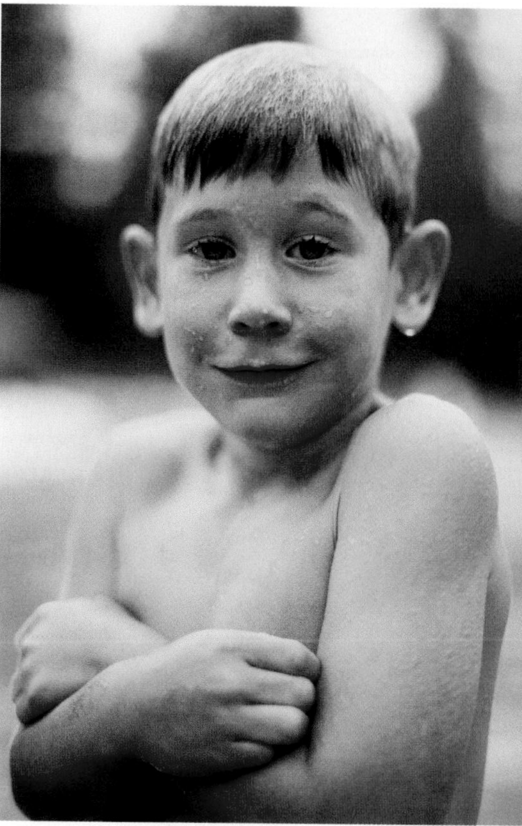
Muscles contract during shivering, raising body temperature.

## Maintaining Posture

Have you ever noticed that you stand up straight without thinking about it, even though gravity is pulling your body down? Most muscles in your body are always a little bit contracted. This tension, or muscle tone, is present even when you are sleeping. The muscles that maintain posture relax completely only when you are unconscious.

Try standing on the balls of your feet for a few moments, or on one leg. When you are trying to balance or hold one position for any length of time, you can feel different muscles contracting and relaxing. Your muscles make constant adjustments to keep you sitting or standing upright. You don't have to think about these tiny adjustments; they happen automatically.

## Your body has different types of muscle.

Your body has three types of muscle. All three types of muscle tissue share certain characteristics. For example, each type of muscle contracts and relaxes. Yet all three muscle types have different functions, and different types of muscle are found in different locations.

### Skeletal Muscle

The muscles that are attached to your skeleton are called **skeletal muscles.** Skeletal muscle performs voluntary movement—that is, movement that you choose to make. Because they are involved in voluntary movement, skeletal muscles are also called **voluntary muscles.**

READING TIP

The root of the word *voluntary* comes from the Latin root *vol-*, meaning "wish." In the word *involuntary* the prefix *in-* suggests the meaning "unwished for." *Involuntary movement* means movement you can't control.

Skeletal muscle, like all muscle, is made of long fibers. The fibers are made up of many smaller bundles, as a piece of yarn is made up of strands of wool. One type of bundle allows your muscles to move slowly. Those muscles are called slow-twitch muscles. Another type of bundle allows your muscles to move quickly. These are called fast-twitch muscles. If you were a sprinter, you would want to develop your fast-twitch muscles. If you were a long distance runner, you would develop your slow-twitch muscles.

What does it mean that skeletal muscles are voluntary muscles?

### Smooth Muscle

**Smooth muscle** is found inside some organs, such as the intestines and the stomach. Smooth muscles perform automatic movement and are called **involuntary muscles.** In other words, smooth muscles work without your knowing it. You have no control over their movement. For example, smooth muscles line your stomach wall and push food through your digestive system. Smooth muscle fibers are not as long as skeletal muscle fibers. Also, unlike skeletal muscles, smooth muscles are not fast-twitch. Smooth muscles contract slowly.

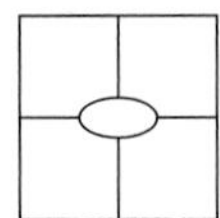

VOCABULARY

Remember to add four squares for *involuntary muscles* and *voluntary muscles* to your notebook. Note differences in the two diagrams.

### Cardiac Muscle

Your heart is made of **cardiac muscle.** Like smooth muscle, cardiac muscle moves without conscious control. Each cardiac muscle cell has a branched shape. The cells of the heart connect in a chain. These chains form webs of layered tissue that allow cardiac cells to contract together and make the heart beat. Just like the smooth muscle cells, the cardiac muscle cells contract slowly, except in emergencies.

Compare and contrast the three types of muscle described: skeletal, smooth, and cardiac.

Muscle Tissue
The marchers in this band are using all three different types of muscle tissue.
250 ×
Cardiac muscle allows the hearts of the band members to pump blood as they march to the beat of the music.
150 ×
Smooth muscle in the air passages of the lungs allows the band members to breathe as they play their instruments.
360 ×
Skeletal muscle moves the legs of these marchers.
READING VISUALS
Which movements of these band members are voluntary, and which are involuntary?

## Skeletal muscles and tendons allow bones to move.

Skeletal muscles are attached to your bones by strong tissues called tendons. The tendons on the end of the muscle attach firmly to the bone. As the fibers in a muscle contract, they shorten and pull the tendon. The tendon, in turn, pulls the bone and makes it move.

You can feel your muscles moving your bones. Place your left arm, stretched out flat, in front of you on a table. Place the fingers of your right hand just above your left elbow. Bend your elbow and raise and lower your left arm. You are contracting your biceps. Can you feel the muscle pull on the tendon?

The dancers in the photograph are using many sets of muscles. The diagrams show how muscles and tendons work together to move bones. Muscles are shown in red. Notice how each muscle crosses a joint. Most skeletal muscles do. One end of the muscle attaches to one bone, crosses a joint, then attaches to a second bone. As the muscle contracts, it pulls on both bones. This pulling produces movement—in the case of these dancers, very exciting movement.

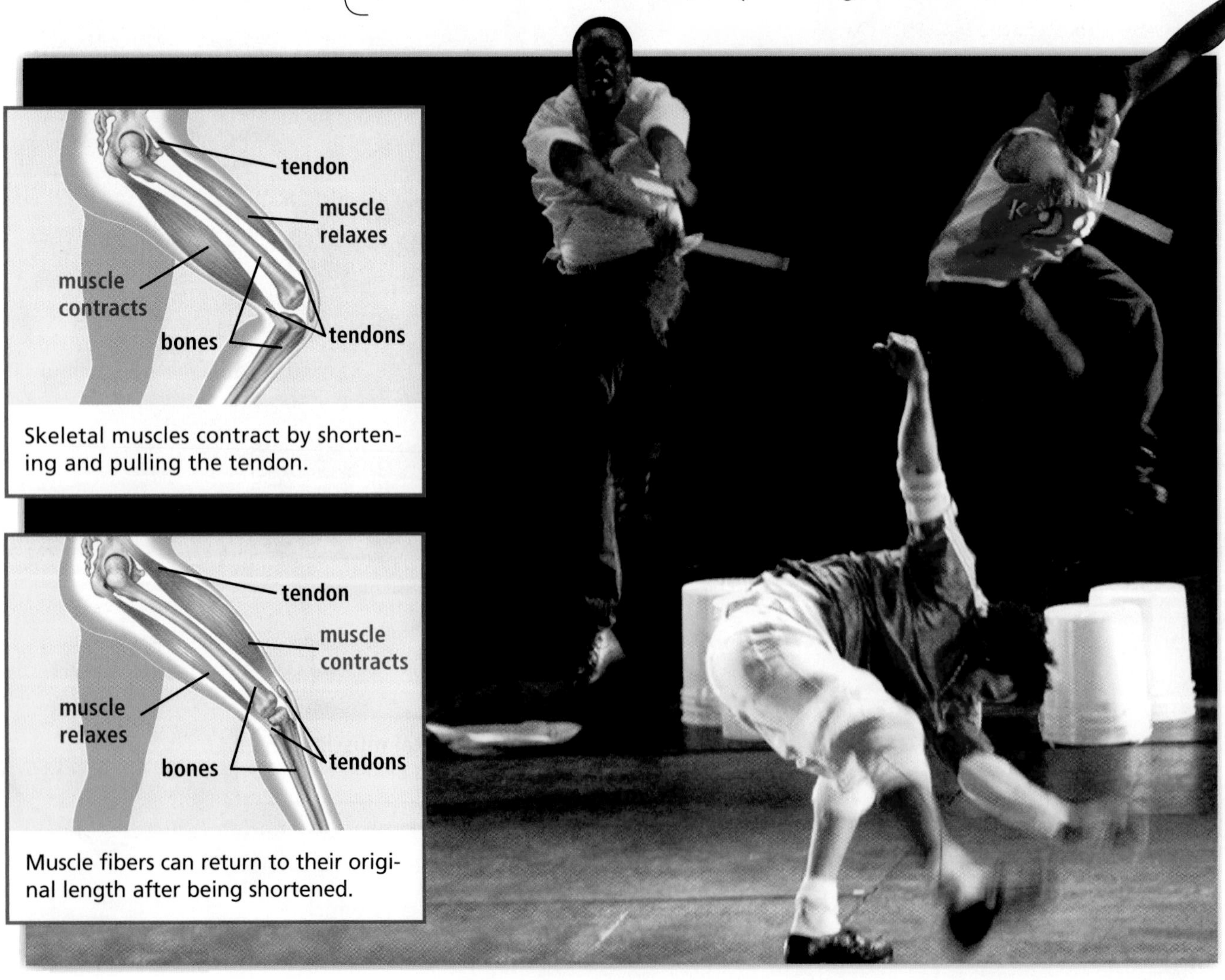


Skeletal muscles contract by shortening and pulling the tendon.



Muscle fibers can return to their original length after being shortened.

## Muscles grow and heal.

**Developing Muscles** An infant's muscles cannot do very much. A baby cannot lift its head, because the neck muscles are not strong enough to support it. For the first few months of life, a baby needs extra support, until the neck muscles grow strong and can hold up the baby's head.

The rest of the skeletal muscles also have to develop and strengthen. During infancy and childhood and into adolescence, humans develop muscular coordination and become more graceful in their movements. Coordination reaches its natural peak in adolescence but can be further improved by additional training.

**Exercise and Muscles** When you exercise regularly, your muscles may get bigger. Muscles increase in size with some types of exercise, because their cells reproduce more rapidly in response to the increased activity. Exercise also stimulates growth of individual muscle cells, making them larger.

Stretching your muscles before exercise helps prevent injury.

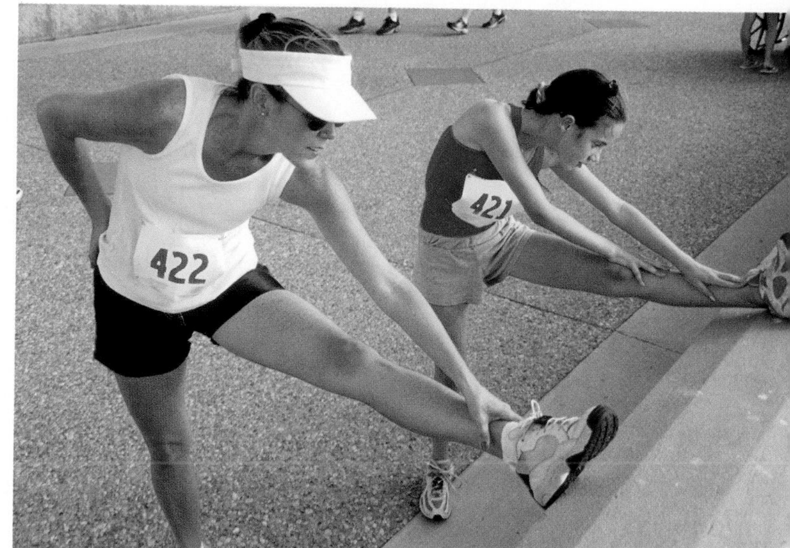


You may have experienced sore muscles during or after exercising. During exercise, chemicals can build up in the muscles and make them cramp or ache. The muscle soreness you feel a day or so after exercise is caused by damage to the muscle fibers. The muscle fibers have been overstretched or torn. Such injuries take time to heal, because the body must remove injured cells, and new ones must form.

## 1.3 Review

### KEY CONCEPTS

1. What are the three main functions of the muscular system?
2. Make a rough outline of a human body and label places where you could find each of the three types of muscles.
3. Explain why you may be sore after exercise.

### CRITICAL THINKING

4. **Apply** You are exercising and you begin to feel hot. Explain what is happening in your muscles.
5. **Analyze** Describe what happens in your neck muscles when you nod your head.

### CHALLENGE

6. **Infer** The digestive system breaks down food and transports materials. How are the short length and slow movement of smooth muscle tissues in the stomach and intestines related to the functions of these organs?

# CHAPTER INVESTIGATION

## A Closer Look at Muscles

**OVERVIEW AND PURPOSE** You use the muscles in your body to do a variety of things. Walking, talking, reading the words on this page, and scratching your head are all actions that require muscles. How do your muscles interact with your bones? In this investigation you will

- examine chicken wings to see how the muscles and the bones interact
- compare the movement of the chicken wing with the movement of your own bones and muscles

### Problem

What are some characteristics of muscles?

### Hypothesize

Write a hypothesis to propose how muscles interact with bones. Your hypothesis should take the form of an "If . . . , then . . . , because . . ." statement.

**MATERIALS**
- uncooked chicken wing and leg (soaked in bleach)
- paper towels
- dissection tray
- scissors

### Procedure

1. Make a data table like the one shown on the sample notebook page. Put on your protective gloves. Be sure you are wearing gloves whenever you touch the chicken.

2. Obtain a chicken wing from your teacher. Rinse it in water and pat dry with a paper towel. Place it in the tray.

3. Extend the wing. In your notebook, draw a diagram of the extended wing. Be sure to include any visible external structures. Label the following on your diagram: lower limb, upper joint, and the wing tip.

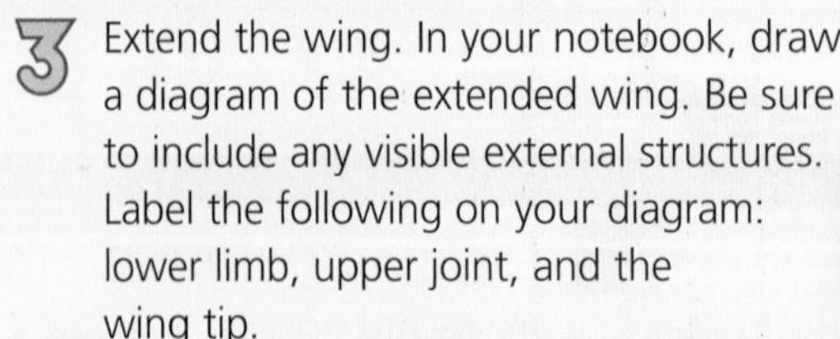
step 3

4. Use scissors to remove the skin. Use caution so that you cut only through the skin. Peel back the skin and any fat so you can examine the muscles.

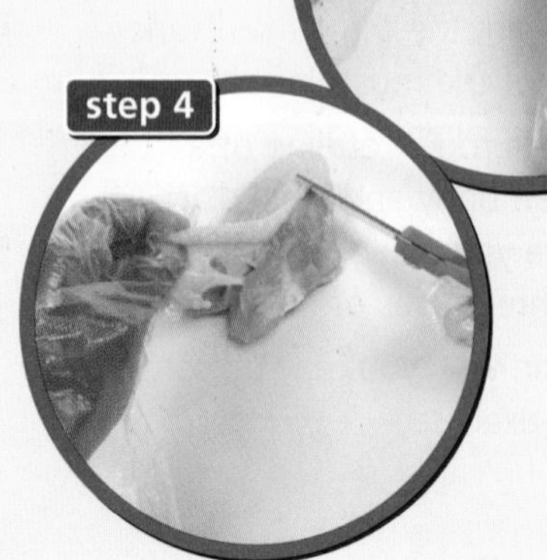
step 4

5 The muscles are the pink tissues that extend from one end of the bone to the other. Locate these in the upper wing and observe the way they move when you move the wing. Record your observations in your notebook.

6 Repeat this procedure for the muscles in the lower wing. In your notebook, draw a diagram of the muscles in the chicken wing.

7 There are also tendons in the chicken wing. These are the shiny white tissues at the end of the muscles. Add the tendons to your diagram.

8 Dispose of the chicken wing and parts according to your teacher's instructions. **Be sure to wash your hands well.**

## Observe and Analyze

1. **RECORD** Write a brief description of how the bones and muscles work together to allow movement.
2. **EVALUATE** What difficulties, if any, did you encounter in carrying out this experiment?

## Conclude

1. **INTERPRET** How does the chicken wing move when you bend it at the joint?
2. **OBSERVE** What happens when you pull on one of the wing muscles?
3. **COMPARE** Using your diagram of the chicken wing as an example, locate the same muscle groups in your own arm. How do they react when you bend your elbow?
4. **APPLY** What role do the tendons play in the movement of the muscles or bones?

## INVESTIGATE Further

**CHALLENGE** Using scissors, carefully remove the muscles and the tendons from the bones. Next find the ligaments, which are located between the bones. Add these to your diagram. Describe how you think ligaments function.

### A Closer Look at Muscles

**Problem** What are some characteristics of muscles?

Table 1. Observations

| Draw your diagrams | Write your observations |
|---|---|
| Extended wing | Muscles in the upper wing |
| Muscles in the wing | Muscles in the lower wing |

# 1 Chapter Review

## the BIG idea

**The human body is made up of systems that work together to perform necessary functions.**

### KEY CONCEPTS SUMMARY

#### 1.1 The human body is complex.

You can think of the body as having five levels of organization: cells, tissues, organs, organ systems, and the whole organism itself. The different systems of the human body work together to maintain homeostasis.

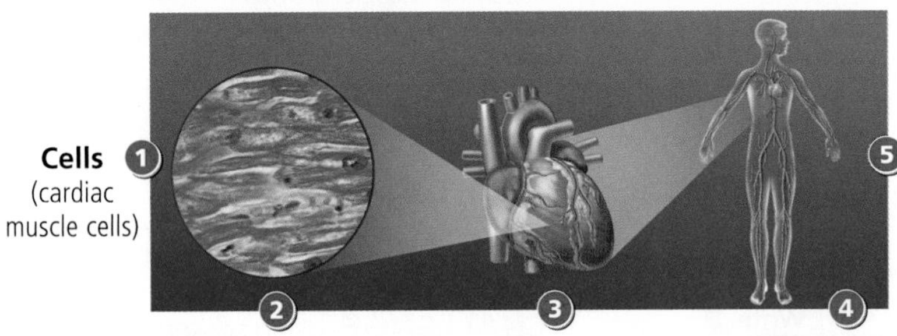


**VOCABULARY**
**tissue** p. 10
**organ** p. 11
**organ system** p. 12
**homeostasis** p. 12

#### 1.2 The skeletal system provides support and protection.

Bones are living tissue. The skeleton is the body's framework and has two main divisions, the **axial skeleton** and the **appendicular skeleton**. Bones come together at joints.

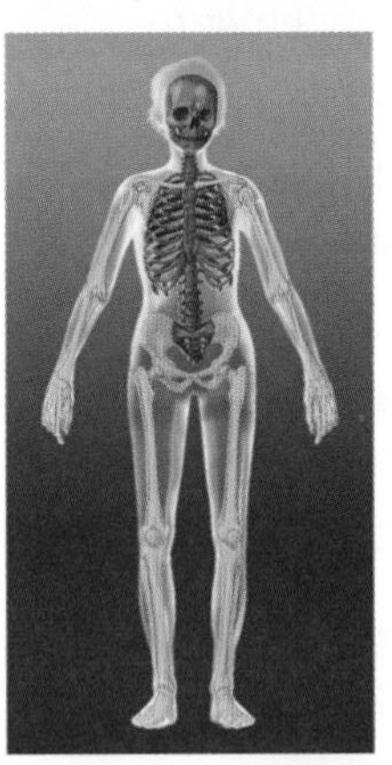

**VOCABULARY**
**skeletal system** p. 14
**compact bone** p. 15
**spongy bone** p. 15
**axial skeleton** p. 16
**appendicular skeleton** p. 16

#### 1.3 The muscular system makes movement possible.

| Types of muscle | Function |
|---|---|
| skeletal muscle, voluntary | moves bones, maintains posture, maintains body temperature |
| smooth muscle, involuntary | moves internal organs, such as the intestines |
| cardiac muscle, involuntary | pumps blood throughout the body |

**VOCABULARY**
**muscular system** p. 23
**skeletal muscle** p. 24
**voluntary muscle** 24
**smooth muscle** p. 24
**involuntary muscle** p. 24
**cardiac muscle** p. 24

## Reviewing Vocabulary

*In one or two sentences describe how the vocabulary terms in each of the following pairs of words are related. Underline each vocabulary term in your answer.*

1. cells, tissues
2. organs, organ systems
3. axial skeleton, appendicular skeleton
4. skeletal muscle, voluntary muscle
5. smooth muscle, involuntary muscle
6. compact bone, spongy bone

## Reviewing Key Concepts

**Multiple Choice** *Choose the letter of the best answer.*

7. Which type of tissue carries electrical impulses from your brain?
   - **a.** epithelial tissue
   - **b.** muscle tissue
   - **c.** nerve tissue
   - **d** connective tissue

8. Connective tissue functions to provide
   - **a.** support and strength
   - **b.** messaging system
   - **c.** movement
   - **d.** heart muscle

9. Bone cells lie within a network made of
   - **a.** tendons
   - **b.** calcium
   - **c.** marrow
   - **d.** joints

10. The marrow produces
    - **a.** spongy bone
    - **b.** red blood cells
    - **c.** compact bone
    - **d.** calcium

11. Which bones are part of the axial skeleton?
    - **a.** skull, shoulder blades, arm bones
    - **b.** skull, spinal column, leg bones
    - **c.** shoulder blades, spinal column, and hip bones
    - **d.** skull, spinal column, ribs

12. Bones of the skeleton connect to each other at
    - **a.** tendons
    - **b.** ligaments
    - **c.** joints
    - **d.** muscles

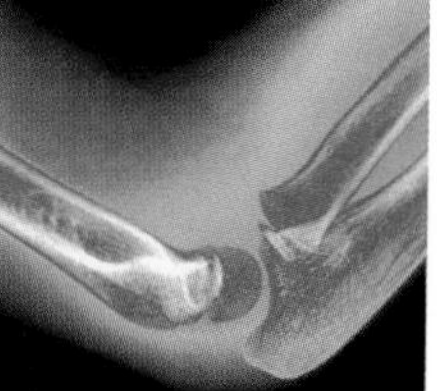

13. How do muscles contribute to homeostasis?
    - **a.** They keep parts of the body together.
    - **b.** They control the amount of water in the body.
    - **c.** They help you move.
    - **d.** They produce heat when they contract.

14. Cardiac muscle is found in the
    - **a.** heart
    - **b.** stomach
    - **c.** intestines
    - **d.** arms and legs

15. The stomach is made up of
    - **a.** cardiac muscle
    - **b.** skeletal muscle
    - **c.** smooth muscle
    - **d.** voluntary muscle

**Short Answer** *Write a short answer to each question.*

16. What is the difference between spongy bone and compact bone?
17. The root word *homeo* means "same," and the root word *stasis* means "to stay." How do these root words relate to the definition of *homeostasis*?
18. Hold the upper part of one arm between your elbow and shoulder with your opposite hand. Feel the muscles there. What happens to those muscles as you bend your arm?

## Thinking Critically

19. **PROVIDE EXAMPLES** What are the levels of organization of the human body from simple to most complex? Give an example of each.

20. **CLASSIFY** There are four types of tissue in the human body: epithelial, nerve, muscle, and connective. How would you classify blood? Explain your reasoning.

21. **CONNECT** A clam shell is made of a calcium compound. The material is hard, providing protection to the soft body of a clam. It is also lightweight. Describe three ways in which the human skeleton is similar to a seashell. What is one important way in which it is different?

*Use the diagram below to answer the next two questions*

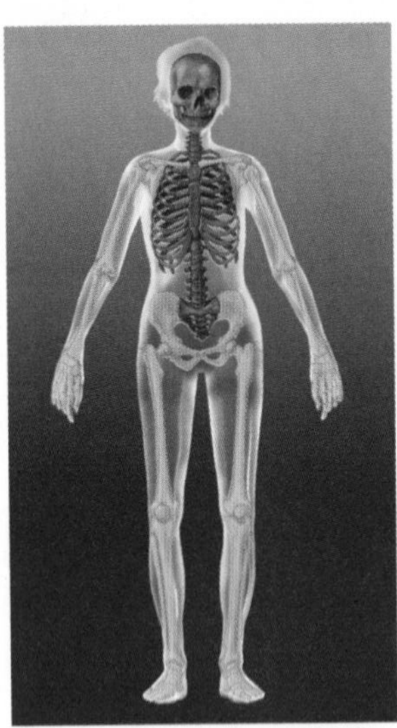

22. **SYNTHESIZE** Identify the types of joints that hold together the bones of the skull and sternum. How do these types of joints relate to the function of the skull and sternum?

23. **SYNTHESIZE** The human skeleton has two main divisions. Which skeleton do the arms and legs belong to? How do the joints that connect the arms to the shoulders and the legs to the hips relate to the function of this skeleton?

24. **COMPARE AND CONTRAST** How is the skeletal system of your body like the framework of a house or building? How is it different?

25. **SUMMARIZE** Describe three important functions of the skeleton.

26. **APPLY** The joints in the human body can be described as producing three types of movement. Relate these three types of movement to the action of brushing your teeth.

27. **COMPARE AND CONTRAST** When you stand, the muscles in your legs help to keep you balanced. Some of the muscles on both sides of your leg bones contract. How does this differ from how the muscles behave when you start to walk?

28. **INFER** Muscles are tissues that are made up of many muscle fibers. A muscle fiber can either be relaxed or contracted. Some movements you do require very little effort, like picking up a piece of paper. Others require a lot of effort, like picking up a book bag. How do you think a muscle produces the effort needed for a small task compared with a big task?

## the BIG idea

29. **INFER** Look again at the picture on pages 6–7. Now that you have finished the chapter, how would you change or add details to your answer to the question on the photograph?

30. **SUMMARIZE** Write a paragraph explaining how skeletal muscles, bones, and joints work together to allow the body to move and be flexible. Underline the terms in your paragraph.

## UNIT PROJECTS

If you are doing a unit project, make a folder for your project. Include in your folder a list of resources you will need, the date on which the project is due, and a schedule to track your progress. Begin gathering data.

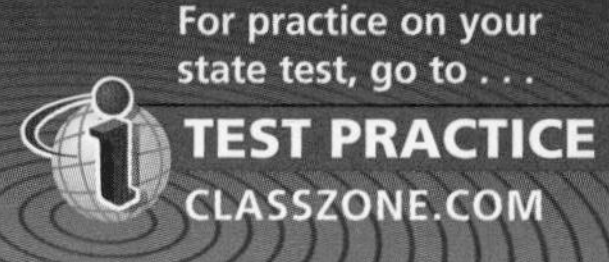


## Interpreting Diagrams

The action of a muscle pulling on a bone can be compared to a simple machine called a lever. A lever is a rod that moves about a fixed point called the fulcrum. Effort at one end of the rod can move a load at the other end. In the human body, a muscle supplies the effort needed to move a bone—the lever. The joint is the fulcrum, and the load is the weight of the body part being moved. There are three types of levers, which are classified according to the position of the fulcrum, the effort, and the load.

*Read the text and study the diagrams, and then choose the best answer for the questions that follow.*

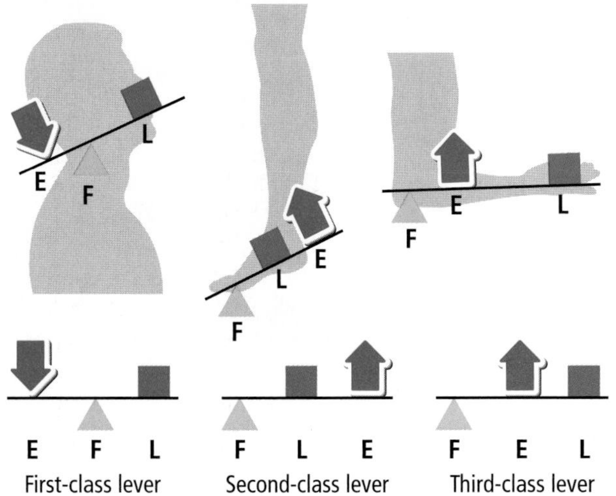


1. In a first-class lever
   **a.** the load is at end of the lever opposite the fulcrum
   **b.** the load is between the effort and the fulcrum
   **c.** the fulcrum is between the load and the effort
   **d.** the effort and load are on the same side

2. What is true of all levers?
   **a.** The fulcrum must be located at the center of a lever.
   **b.** The force of the load and effort point in the same direction.
   **c.** The load and effort are on the same side of the fulcrum.
   **d.** The lever exerts a force in a direction opposite the weight of the load.

3. The lever represents what structure in the human body?
   **a.** a joint
   **b.** a bone
   **c.** a muscle
   **d.** a ligament

4. The main point of the diagram is to show
   **a.** how bones work
   **b.** that there are three types of joints and how they are classified as levers
   **c.** where to apply a force
   **d.** the forces involved in moving parts of the body

## Extended Response

*Use the diagrams above and terms from the word box to answer the next question. Underline each term you use in your answer.*

| fulcrum | load | effort | rod |
|---|---|---|---|
| bone | muscle | joint | |

5. Suppose you had a heavy box to lift. Your first thought might be to bend over, stretch out your arms, and grab the box. Your body would be acting as a simple machine. Identify the type of lever this is and the parts of this machine.

6. A doctor would advise you not to lift a heavy object, like a box, simply by bending over and picking it up. That action puts too much strain on your back. It is better to bend your knees, hold the box close to your body, and then lift. How does this way of lifting change how you are using your body?

CHAPTER

# Absorption, Digestion, and Exchange

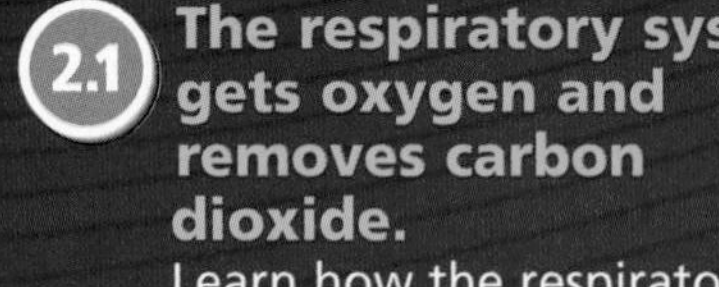

Systems in the body obtain and process materials and remove waste.

What materials does your body need to function properly?

## Key Concepts

SECTION

**2.1 The respiratory system gets oxygen and removes carbon dioxide.**
Learn how the respiratory system functions.

SECTION

**2.2 The digestive system breaks down food.**
Learn how the digestive system provides cells with necessary materials.

SECTION

**2.3 The urinary system removes waste materials.**
Learn how the urinary system removes wastes.

**Internet Preview**

CLASSZONE.COM

Chapter 2 online resources: Content Review, two Visualizations, two Resource Centers, Math Tutorial, Test Practice.

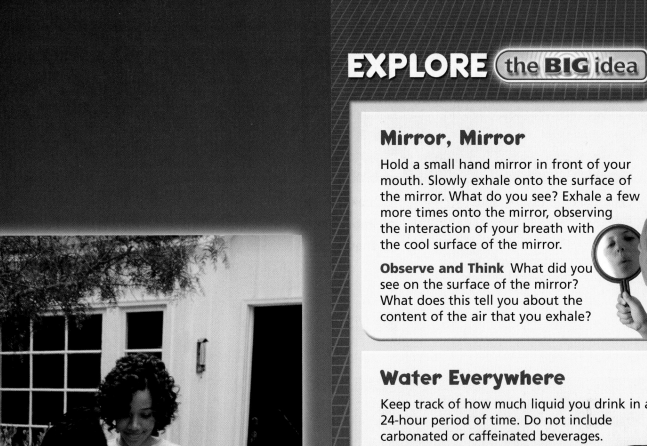

## Mirror, Mirror

Hold a small hand mirror in front of your mouth. Slowly exhale onto the surface of the mirror. What do you see? Exhale a few more times onto the mirror, observing the interaction of your breath with the cool surface of the mirror.

**Observe and Think** What did you see on the surface of the mirror? What does this tell you about the content of the air that you exhale?

## Water Everywhere

Keep track of how much liquid you drink in a 24-hour period of time. Do not include carbonated or caffeinated beverages. Water, juice, and milk can count. Add up the number of ounces of liquid you drink in that period of time.

**Observe and Think** How many ounces did you drink in one day? Do you drink fluids only when you feel thirsty?

## Internet Activity: Lung Movement

Go to **ClassZone.com** to watch a visualization of lung and diaphragm movement during respiration. Observe how movements of the diaphragm and other muscles affect the lungs.

**Observe and Think** How do the diaphragm and lungs move during inhalation? during exhalation? Why do movements of the diaphragm cause the lungs to move?

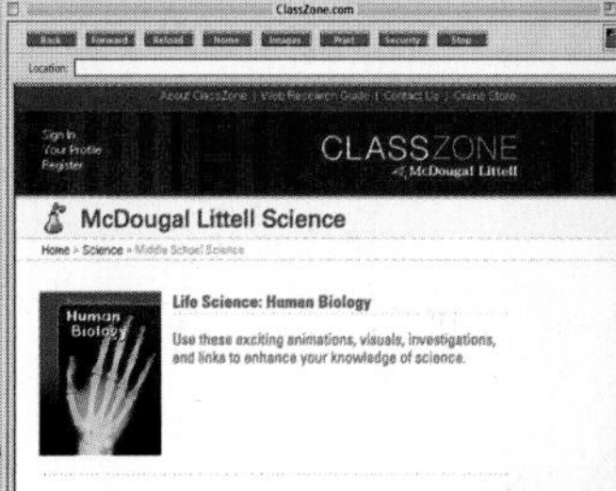

Digestion **Code: MDL045**

CHAPTER 2

# Getting Ready to Learn

## CONCEPT REVIEW

- Cells make up tissues, and tissues make up organs.
- The body's systems interact.
- The body's systems work to maintain internal conditions.

## VOCABULARY REVIEW

**homeostasis** p. 12

**smooth muscle** p. 24

**energy** *See Glossary.*

Review concepts and vocabulary.

## TAKING NOTES

### OUTLINE

As you read, copy the blue headings on your paper in the form of an outline. Then add notes in your own words that summarize what you read.

SCIENCE NOTEBOOK

THE RESPIRATORY SYSTEM GETS OXYGEN AND REMOVES CARBON DIOXIDE.

A. Your body needs oxygen.
   1. Oxygen is used to release energy
   2. Oxygen is in air you breathe

B. Structures in the respiratory system function together
   1. nose, throat, trachea
   2. lungs

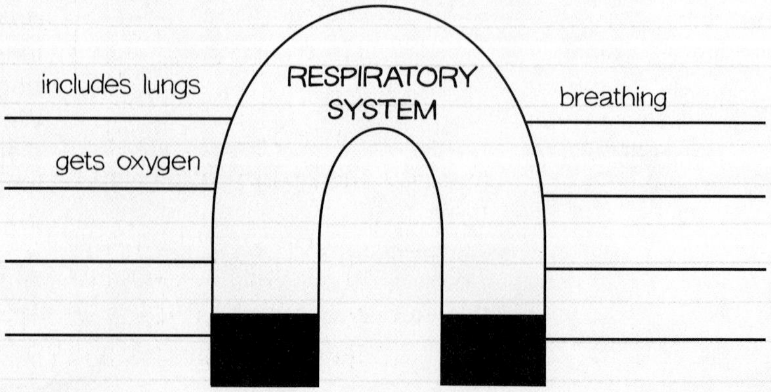

### VOCABULARY STRATEGY

Think about a vocabulary term as a **magnet word** diagram. Write the other terms or ideas related to that term around it.

RESPIRATORY SYSTEM

includes lungs

gets oxygen

breathing

See the Note-Taking Handbook on pages R45–R51.

KEY CONCEPT

# The respiratory system gets oxygen and removes carbon dioxide.

**BEFORE, you learned**

- Cells, tissues, organs, and organ systems work together
- Organ systems provide for the body's needs
- Organ systems are important to the body's survival

**NOW, you will learn**

- About the structures of the respiratory system that function to exchange gases
- About the process of cellular respiration
- About other functions of the respiratory system

**VOCABULARY**

**respiratory system** p. 37
**cellular respiration** p. 39

**EXPLORE Breathing**

***How do your ribs move when you breathe?***

**PROCEDURE**

1. Place your hands on your ribs.
2. Breathe in and out several times, focusing on what happens when you inhale and exhale.
3. Record your observations in your notebook.

**WHAT DO YOU THINK?**

- What movement did you observe?
- Think about your observations. What questions do you have as a result of your observations?

## Your body needs oxygen.

During the day, you eat and drink only a few times, but you breathe thousands of times. In fact, breathing is a sign of life. The body is able to store food and liquid, but it is unable to store very much oxygen. The **respiratory system** is the body system that functions to get oxygen from the environment and remove carbon dioxide and other waste products from your body. The respiratory system interacts with the environment and with other body systems.

**VOCABULARY**
Make a word magnet diagram for the term *respiratory system.*

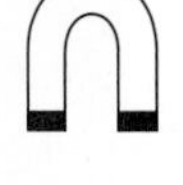

The continuous process of moving and using oxygen involves mechanical movement and chemical reactions. Air is transported into your lungs by mechanical movements, and oxygen is used during chemical reactions that release energy in your cells.

CHECK YOUR READING What are the two main functions of your respiratory system?

## Exchanging Oxygen and Carbon Dioxide

Like almost all living things, the human body needs oxygen to survive. Without oxygen, cells in the body die quickly. How does the oxygen you need get to your cells? Oxygen, along with other gases, enters the body when you inhale. Oxygen is then transported to cells throughout the body by red blood cells.

The air that you breathe contains only about 20 percent oxygen and less than 1 percent carbon dioxide. Almost 80 percent of air is nitrogen gas. The air that you exhale contains more carbon dioxide and less oxygen than the air that you inhale. It's important that you exhale carbon dioxide because high levels of it will damage, even destroy, cells.

In cells and tissues, proper levels of both oxygen and carbon dioxide are essential. Recall that systems in the body work together to maintain homeostasis. If levels of oxygen or carbon dioxide change, your nervous system signals the need to breathe faster or slower.

The photograph shows how someone underwater maintains proper levels of carbon dioxide and oxygen. The scuba diver needs to inhale oxygen from a tank. She removes carbon dioxide wastes with other gases when she exhales into the water. The bubbles you see in the water are formed when she exhales.

CHECK YOUR
READING

What gases are in the air that you breathe?

### Gas Exchange

**This scuba diver breathes the same mixture of gases present in air.**

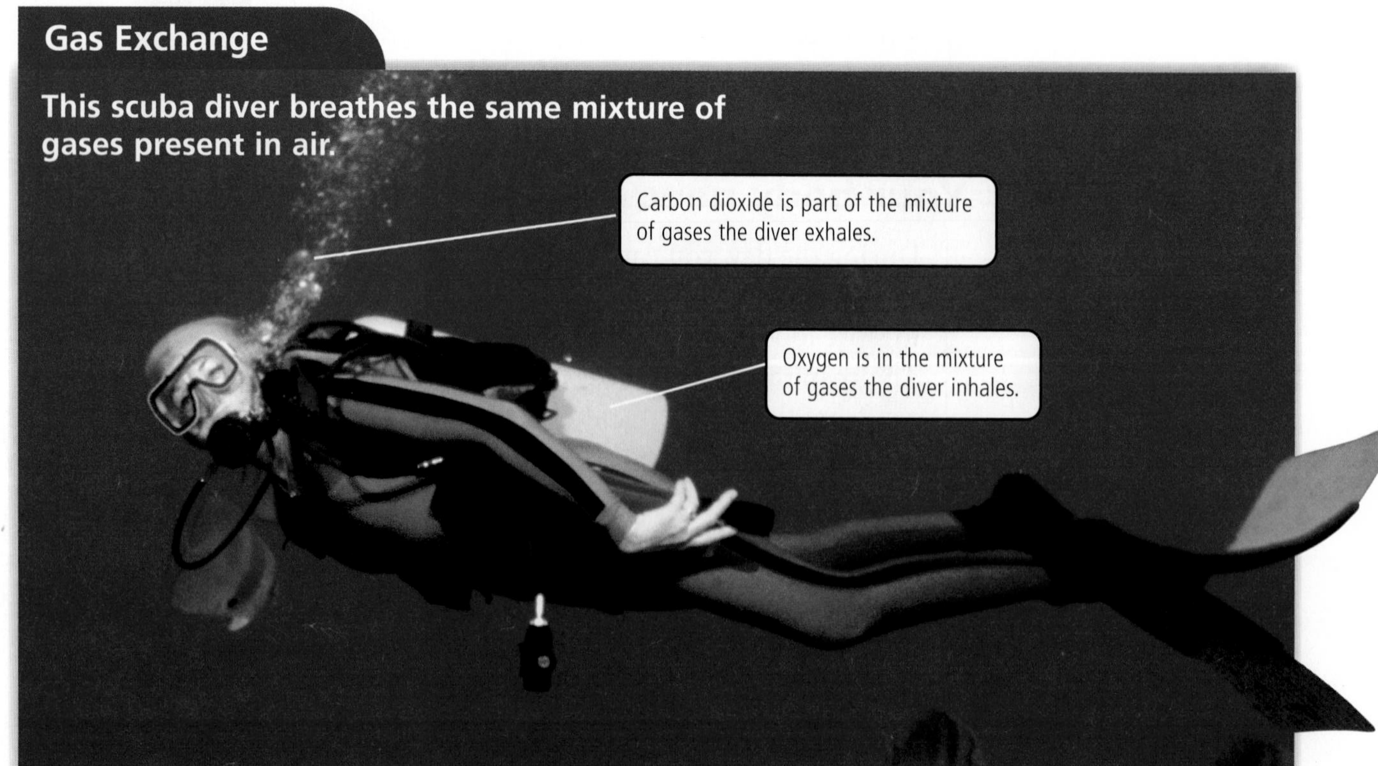
Carbon dioxide is part of the mixture of gases the diver exhales.
Oxygen is in the mixture of gases the diver inhales.

# INVESTIGATE Lungs

## How does air move in and out of lungs?

**SKILL FOCUS**
Making Models

**MATERIALS**
- one medium balloon
- 1-L clear plastic bottle with labels removed
- duct tape

**TIME**
15 minutes

**PROCEDURE**

1. Create a model of your lungs as shown. Insert an uninflated balloon into the top of the plastic bottle. While squeezing the bottle to force out some air, stretch the end of the balloon over the lip of the bottle. The balloon should still be open to the outside air. Tape the balloon in place with duct tape to make a tight seal
2. Release the bottle so that it expands back to its normal shape. Observe what happens to the balloon. Squeeze and release the bottle several times while observing the balloon. Record your observations.

**WHAT DO YOU THINK?**

- Describe, in words, what happens when you squeeze and release the bottle.
- How do you think your lungs move when you inhale? when you exhale?

**CHALLENGE** Design an addition to your model that could represent a muscle called the diaphragm. What materials do you need? How would this work? Your teacher may be able to provide additional materials so you can test your model. Be sure to come up with a comprehensive list of materials as well as a specific diagram.

## Cellular Respiration

Inside your cells, a process called **cellular respiration** uses oxygen in chemical reactions that release energy. The respiratory system works with the digestive and circulatory systems to make cellular respiration possible. Cellular respiration requires glucose, or sugars, which you get from food, in addition to oxygen, which you get from breathing. These materials are transported to every cell in your body through blood vessels. You will learn more about the digestive and circulatory systems later in this unit.

**VOCABULARY**
Add a magnet diagram for *cellular respiration* to your notebook. Include the word *energy* in your diagram.

During cellular respiration, your cells use oxygen and glucose to release energy. Carbon dioxide is a waste product of the process. Carbon dioxide must be removed from cells.

What three body systems are involved in cellular respiration?

## Structures in the respiratory system function together.

**OUTLINE**
Add *Structures in the respiratory system function together* to your outline. Be sure to include the six respiratory structures in your outline.

I. Main idea
  A. Supporting idea
    1. Detail
    2. Detail
  B. Supporting idea

The respiratory system is made up of many structures that allow you to move air in and out of your body, communicate, and keep out harmful materials.

**Nose, Throat, and Trachea** When you inhale, air enters your body through your nose or mouth. Inside your nose, tiny hairs called cilia filter dirt and other particles out of the air. Mucus, a sticky liquid in your nasal cavity, also helps filter air by trapping particles such as dirt and pollen as air passes by. The nasal cavity warms the air slightly before it moves down your throat toward a tubelike structure called the windpipe, or trachea (TRAY-kee-uh). A structure called the epiglottis (EHP-ih-GLAHT-ihs) keeps air from entering your stomach.

**Lungs** The lungs are two large organs located on either side of your heart. When you inhale, air enters the throat, passes through the trachea, and moves into the lungs through structures called bronchial tubes. Bronchial tubes branch throughout the lungs into smaller and smaller tubes. At the ends of the smallest tubes, air enters tiny air sacs called alveoli. The walls of the alveoli are only one cell thick. In fact, one page in this book is much thicker than the walls of the alveoli. Oxygen passes from inside the alveoli through the thin walls and diffuses into the blood. At the same time, carbon dioxide waste passes from the blood into the alveoli.

Through which structures does oxygen move into the lungs?

**Ribs and Diaphragm** If you put your hands on your ribs and take a deep breath, you can feel your ribs expand. The rib cage encloses a space inside your body called the thoracic (thuh-RAS-ihk) cavity. Some ribs are connected by cartilage to the breastbone or to each other, which makes the rib cage flexible. This flexibility allows the rib cage to expand when you breathe and make room for the lungs to expand and fill with air.

A large muscle called the diaphragm (DY-uh-FRAM) stretches across the floor of the thoracic cavity. When you inhale, your diaphragm contracts and pulls downward, which makes the thoracic cavity expand. This movement causes the lungs to push downward, filling the extra space. At the same time, other muscles draw the ribs outward and expand the lungs. Air rushes into the lungs, and inhalation is complete. When the diaphragm and other muscles relax, the process reverses and you exhale.

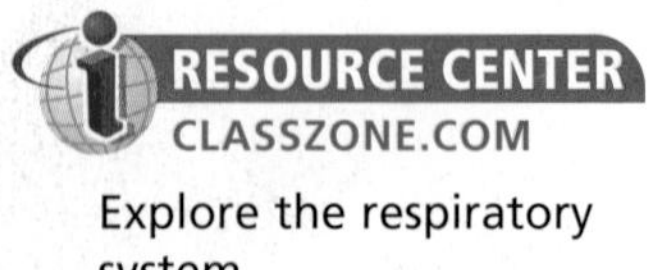

Explore the respiratory system.

Describe how the diaphragm and the rib cage move.

## Respiratory System

**The structures in the respiratory system allow this flutist to play music.**

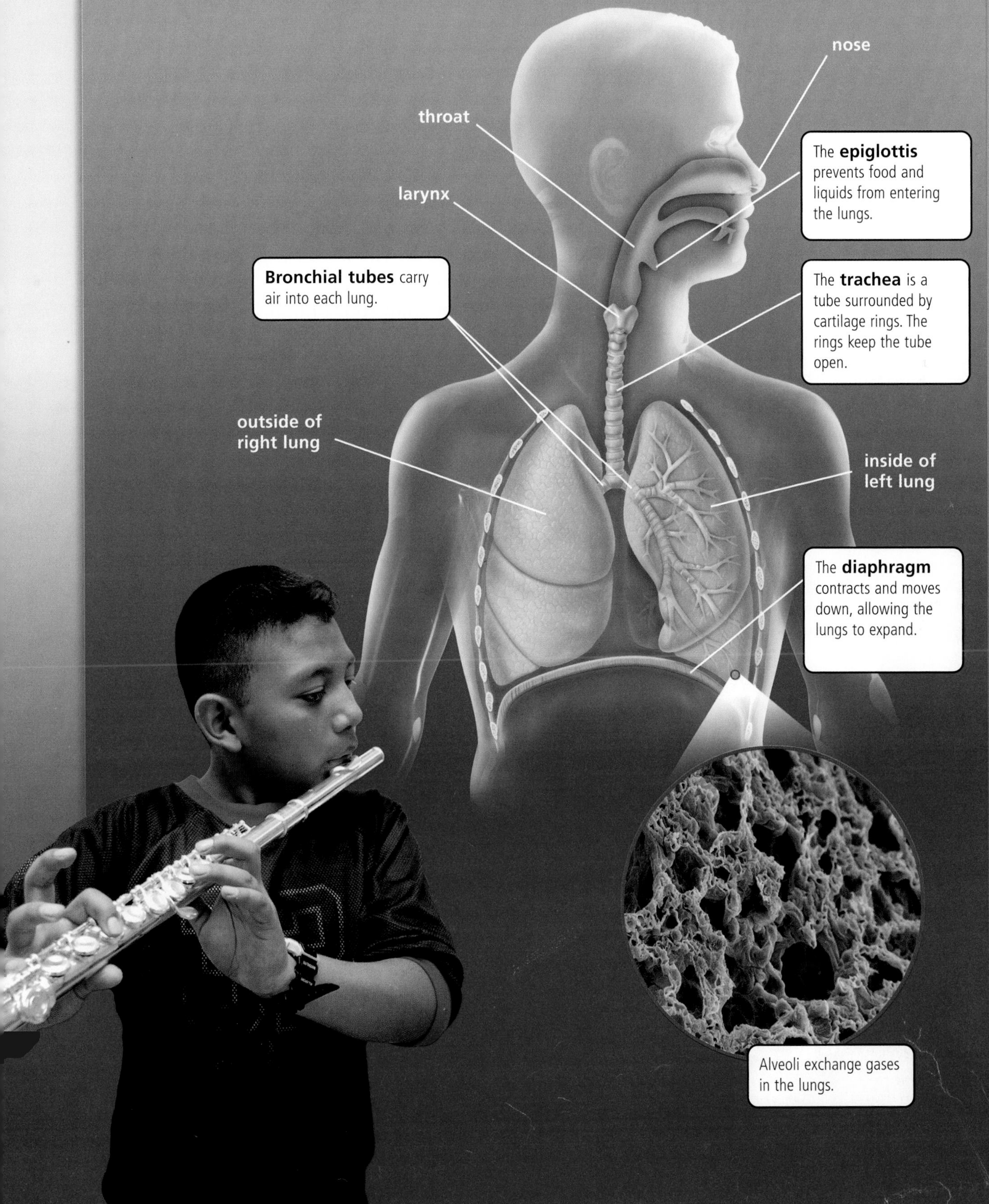

nose

throat

larynx

The **epiglottis** prevents food and liquids from entering the lungs.

**Bronchial tubes** carry air into each lung.

The **trachea** is a tube surrounded by cartilage rings. The rings keep the tube open.

outside of right lung

inside of left lung

The **diaphragm** contracts and moves down, allowing the lungs to expand.

Alveoli exchange gases in the lungs.

## The respiratory system is also involved in other activities.

In addition to providing oxygen and removing carbon dioxide, the respiratory system is involved in other activities of the body. Speaking and singing, along with actions such as sneezing, can be explained in terms of how the parts of the respiratory system work together.

### Speech and Other Respiratory Movements

If you place your hand on your throat and hum softly, you can feel your vocal cords vibrating. Air moving over your vocal cords allows you to produce sound, and the muscles in your throat, mouth, cheeks, and lips allow you to form sound into words. The vocal cords are folds of tissue in the larynx. The larynx, sometimes called the voice box, is a two-inch, tube-shaped organ about the length of your thumb, located in the neck, at the top of the trachea. When you speak, the vocal cords become tight, squeeze together, and force air from the lungs to move between them. The air causes the vocal cords to vibrate and produce sound.

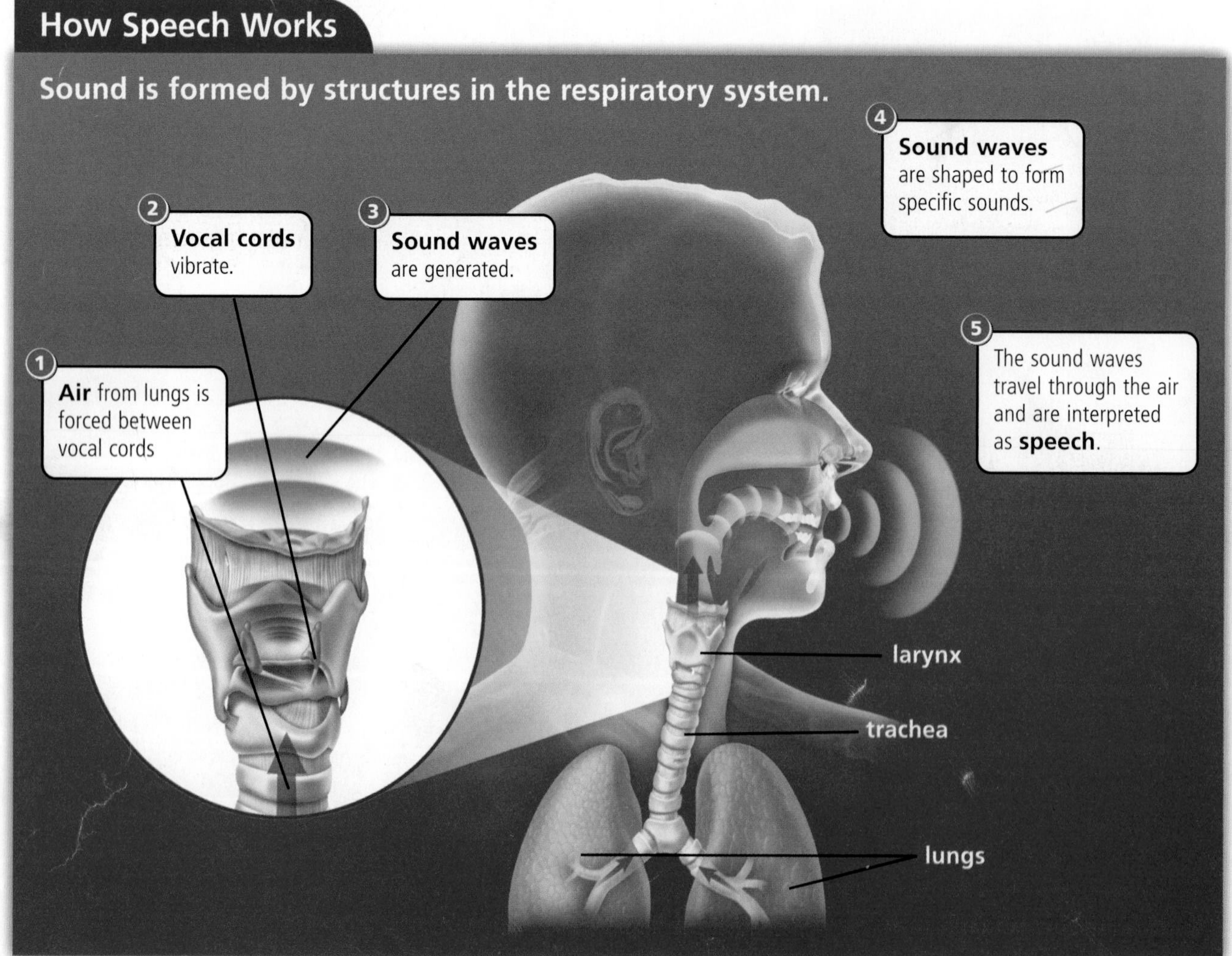
How Speech Works
Sound is formed by structures in the respiratory system.
1 Air from lungs is forced between vocal cords
2 Vocal cords vibrate.
3 Sound waves are generated.
4 Sound waves are shaped to form specific sounds.
5 The sound waves travel through the air and are interpreted as speech.
larynx
trachea
lungs

Some movements of the respiratory system allow you to clear particles out of your nose and throat or to express emotion. The respiratory system is involved when you cough or sneeze. Sighing, yawning, laughing, and crying also involve the respiratory system.

Sighing and yawning both involve taking deep breaths. A sigh is a long breath followed by a shorter exhalation. A yawn is a long breath taken through a wide-open mouth. Laughing and crying are movements that are very similar to each other. In fact, sometimes it's difficult to see the difference between laughing and crying.

The respiratory system also allows you to hiccup. A hiccup is a sudden inhalation that makes the diaphragm contract. Several systems are involved when you hiccup. Air rushes into the throat, causing the diaphragm to contract. When the diaphragm contracts, the air passageway between the vocal cords closes. The closing of this passageway produces the sound of the hiccup. Hiccups can be caused by eating too fast, sudden temperature changes, and stress.

## Water Removal

Hiccups, coughs, yawns, and all other respiratory movements, including speaking and breathing, release water from your body into the environment. Water is lost through sweat, urine, and exhalations of air. When it is cold enough outside, you can see your breath in the air. That is because the water vapor you exhale condenses into larger droplets when it moves from your warm body to the cold air.

Water leaves your body through your breath every time you exhale.

# 2.1 Review

### KEY CONCEPTS

1. How is oxygen used by your body's cells?
2. What are the structures in the respiratory system and what do they do?
3. In addition to breathing, what functions does the respiratory system perform?

### CRITICAL THINKING

4. **Sequence** List in order the steps that occur when you exhale.
5. **Compare and Contrast** How is the air you inhale different from the air you exhale?

### CHALLENGE

6. **Hypothesize** Why do you think a person breathes more quickly when exercising?

SCIENCE on the JOB

## YOGA INSTRUCTOR

# Breathing and Yoga

If you're reading this, you must be breathing. Are you thinking about how you are breathing? Yoga instructors help their students learn deep, slow breathing. The practice of yoga uses an understanding of the respiratory system as a tool for healthy exercise.

nostrils

lungs

diaphragm muscle

### Abdominal Breathing

Yoga instructors tell students to slowly expand and release the diaphragm:

- The diaphragm is a muscle below the lungs.
- When the muscle contracts, air enters into the lungs.
- When it relaxes, air is pushed out of the lungs.

### Nostril Breathing

An important aspect of breathing is removing wastes from the body:

- Yoga instructors teach students to inhale through the nostrils and exhale through the mouth.
- The nostrils filter dust and other particles, keeping dirt out of the lungs.
- The nostrils also warm the air as it enters the body.

### Full Lung Breathing

Yoga instructors help students breathe in slowly so that first the abdomen expands, then the rib cage area, and finally the upper chest by the shoulders. When students exhale, they collapse the diaphragm, then release the chest, and lastly relax the shoulders.

## EXPLORE

1. **APPLY** Try one of the three breathing methods described. Start by taking a few slow deep breaths; then try the yoga breathing. Count to 4 as you inhale, and to 4 again breathing out. How do you feel after each breath?
2. **CHALLENGE** Choose one of the breathing methods above. Describe what happens to air each time you inhale and exhale. Draw or write your answer.

KEY CONCEPT

# 2.2 The digestive system breaks down food.

**BEFORE, you learned**

- The respiratory system takes in oxygen and expels waste
- Oxygen is necessary for cellular respiration
- The respiratory system is involved in speech and water removal

**NOW, you will learn**

- About the role of digestion in providing energy and materials
- About the chemical and mechanical process of digestion
- How materials change as they move through the digestive system

**VOCABULARY**

**nutrient** p. 45
**digestion** p. 46
**digestive system** p. 46
**peristalsis** p. 46

**EXPLORE Digestion**

### *How does the digestive system break down fat?*

**PROCEDURE**

1. Using a dropper, place 5 mL of water into a test tube. Add 5 mL of vegetable oil. Seal the test tube with a screw-on top. Shake the test tube for 10 seconds, then place it in a test tube stand. Record your observations.
2. Drop 5 mL of dish detergent into the test tube. Seal the tube. Shake the test tube for 10 seconds, then place in the stand. Observe the mixture for 2 minutes. Record your observations.

**WHAT DO YOU THINK?**

- What effect does detergent have on the mixture of oil and water?
- How do you think your digestive system might break down fat?

**MATERIALS**

- water
- graduated cylinders
- test tube with cap
- vegetable oil
- test tube stand
- liquid dish detergent

## The body needs energy and materials.

**OUTLINE**
Remember to add *The body needs energy and materials* to your outline.

I. Main idea
  A. Supporting idea
    1. Detail
    2. Detail
  B. Supporting idea

After not eating for a while, have you ever noticed how little energy you have to do the simplest things? You need food to provide energy for your body. You also need materials from food. Most of what you need comes from nutrients within food. **Nutrients** are important substances that enable the body to move, grow, and maintain homeostasis. Proteins, carbohydrates, fats, and water are some of the nutrients your body needs.

You might not think of water as a nutrient, but it is necessary for all living things. More than half of your body is made up of water.

Protein is another essential nutrient; it is the material that the body uses for growth and repair. Cells in your body—such as those composing muscles, bones, and skin—are built of proteins. Carbohydrates are nutrients that provide cells with energy. Carbohydrates make up cellulose, which helps move materials through the digestive system. Another nutrient, fat, stores energy.

Before your body can use these nutrients, they must be broken into smaller substances. **Digestion** is the process of breaking down food into usable materials. Your digestive system transforms the energy and materials in food into forms your body can use.

## The digestive system moves and breaks down food.

Observe the process of peristalsis.

Your **digestive system** performs the complex jobs of moving and breaking down food. Material is moved through the digestive system by wavelike contractions of smooth muscles. This muscular action is called **peristalsis** (PEHR-ih-STAWL-sihs). Mucous glands throughout the system keep the material moist so it can be moved easily, and the muscles contract to push the material along. The muscles move food along in much the same way as you move toothpaste from the bottom of the tube with your thumbs. The body has complicated ways of moving food, and it also has complicated ways of breaking down food. The digestive system processes food in two ways: physically and chemically.

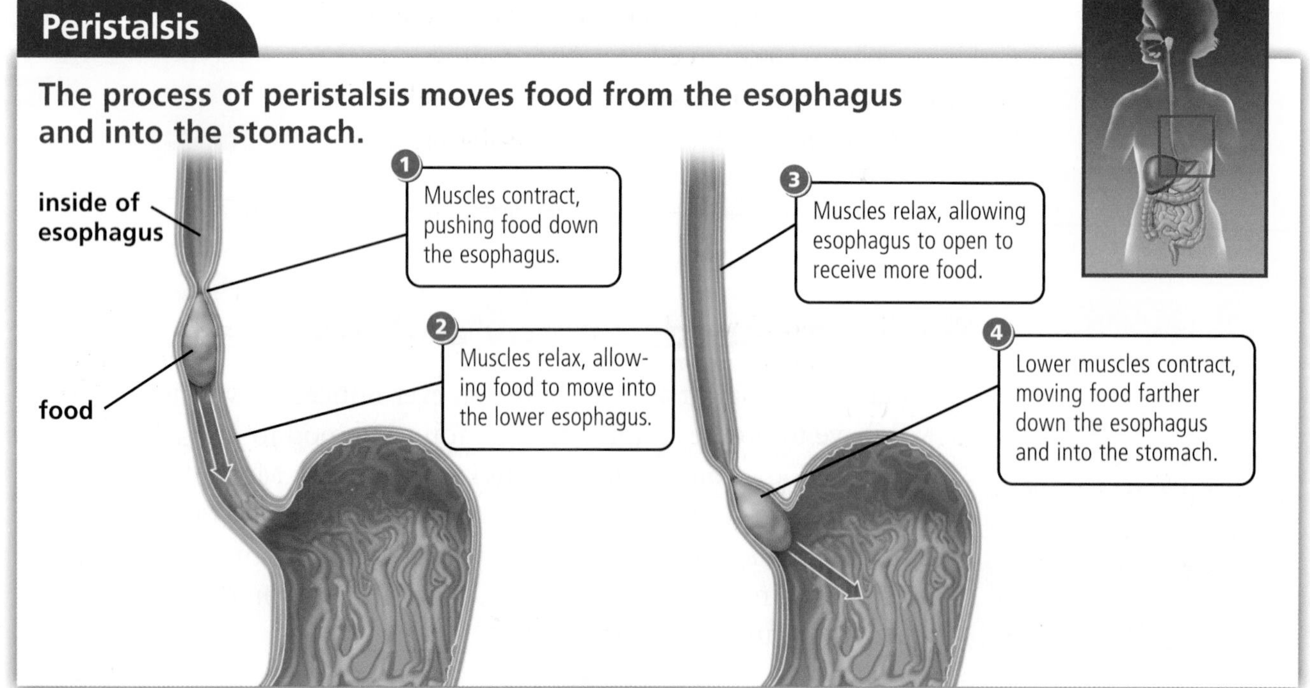

Peristalsis
The process of peristalsis moves food from the esophagus and into the stomach.
inside of esophagus
food
1 Muscles contract, pushing food down the esophagus.
2 Muscles relax, allowing food to move into the lower esophagus.
3 Muscles relax, allowing esophagus to open to receive more food.
4 Lower muscles contract, moving food farther down the esophagus and into the stomach.

# INVESTIGATE Chemical Digestion

## How does saliva affect starch?

SKILL FOCUS
Making Models

### PROCEDURE

1. Cut two slices of the same thickness from the center of a potato. Lay the slices on a plate or tray.
2. Using a dropper, add 15 drops of solution A to one potato slice. Add 15 drops of water to the other potato slice. Observe both potato slices for several minutes. Record your observations.

### WHAT DO YOU THINK?

- What evidence did you see that starch is being broken down?
- How would you identify the substance left by the breakdown of starch?
- What is the purpose of the water in this activity?

**CHALLENGE** How could you change your experiment to model mechanical digestion? What structures in your mouth mechanically break down food?

**MATERIALS**
- cooked potato slices
- droppers
- solution A
- water

**TIME**
25 minutes

## Mechanical Digestion

Physical changes, which are sometimes called mechanical changes, break food into smaller pieces. You chew your food with your teeth so you are able to swallow it. Infants without teeth need an adult to cut up or mash food for them. They need soft food that they can swallow without chewing. Your stomach also breaks down food mechanically by mashing and pounding it during peristalsis.

## Chemical Digestion

Chemical changes actually change food into different substances. For example, chewing a cracker produces a physical change—the cracker is broken into small pieces. At the same time, liquid in the mouth called saliva produces a chemical change—starches in the cracker are changed to sugars. If you chew a cracker, you may notice that after you have chewed it for a few seconds, it begins to taste sweet. The change in taste is a sign of a chemical reaction.

What are the two types of changes that take place during digestion?

**VOCABULARY**
Don't forget to add magnet word diagrams for *digestion, digestive system,* and *peristalsis* to your notebook.

## Materials are broken down as they move through the digestive tract.

The digestive system contains several organs. Food travels through organs in the digestive tract: the mouth, esophagus, stomach, small intestine, and large intestine. Other organs, such as the pancreas, liver, and gall bladder, release chemicals that are necessary for chemical digestion. The diagram on page 49 shows the major parts of the entire digestive system.

**READING TIP**

As you read about the digestive tract, look at the structures on page 49.

**Mouth and Esophagus** Both mechanical and chemical digestion begin in the mouth. The teeth break food into small pieces. The lips and tongue position food so that you can chew. When food is in your mouth, salivary glands in your mouth release saliva, which softens the food and begins chemical digestion. The tongue pushes the food to the back of the mouth and down the throat while swallowing.

**CHECK YOUR READING** What part does the mouth play in digestion?

When you swallow, your tongue pushes food down into your throat. Food then travels down the esophagus to the stomach. The muscle contractions of peristalsis move solid food from the throat to the stomach in about eight seconds. Liquid foods take about two seconds.

**Stomach** Strong muscles in the stomach further mix and mash food particles. The stomach also uses chemicals to break down food. Some of the chemicals made by the stomach are acids. These acids are so strong that they could eat through the stomach itself. To prevent this, the cells of the stomach's lining are replaced about every three days, and the stomach lining is coated with mucus.

Villi allow broken-down nutrients to be absorbed into your bloodstream.

**Small Intestine** Partially digested food moves from the stomach to the small intestine. There, chemicals released by the pancreas, liver, and gallbladder break down nutrients. Most of the nutrients broken down in digestion are absorbed in the small intestine. Structures called villi are found throughout the small intestine. These structures contain folds that absorb nutrients from proteins, carbohydrates, and fats. Once absorbed by the villi, nutrients are transported by the circulatory system around the body. You will read more about the circulatory system in Chapter 3.

**Large Intestine** In the large intestine, water and some other nutrients are absorbed from the digested material. Most of the solid material then remaining is waste material, which is compacted and stored. Eventually it is eliminated through the rectum.

**CHECK YOUR READING** Where in your digestive system does mechanical digestion occur?

## Digestive System

**As food moves through the digestive tract, structures of the digestive system break it down and absorb necessary materials.**

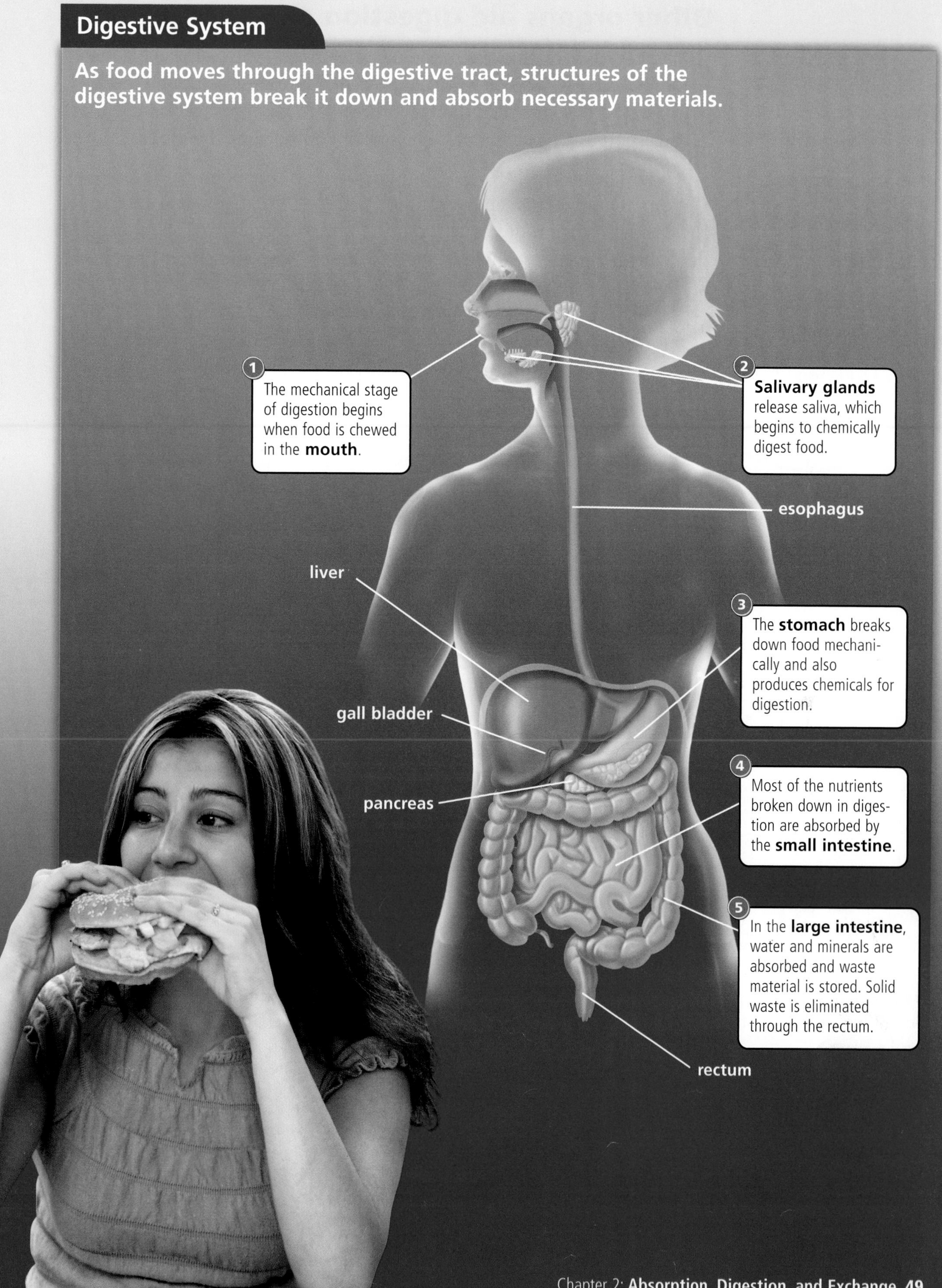

1 The mechanical stage of digestion begins when food is chewed in the **mouth**.
2 **Salivary glands** release saliva, which begins to chemically digest food.
esophagus
liver
3 The **stomach** breaks down food mechanically and also produces chemicals for digestion.
gall bladder
pancreas
4 Most of the nutrients broken down in digestion are absorbed by the **small intestine**.
5 In the **large intestine**, water and minerals are absorbed and waste material is stored. Solid waste is eliminated through the rectum.
rectum

## Other organs aid digestion and absorption.

The digestive organs not in the digestive tract—the liver, gallbladder, and pancreas—also play crucial roles in your body. Although food does not move through them, all three of these organs aid in chemical digestion by producing or concentrating important chemicals.

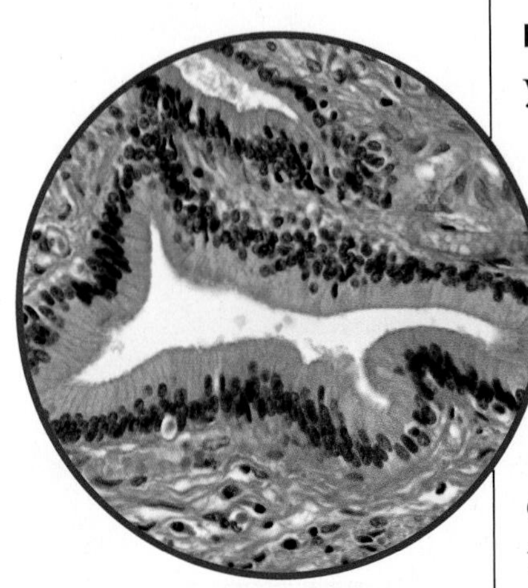

Bile is transferred from the liver to the gallbladder and small intestines through the bile duct.

**Liver** The liver—the largest internal organ of the body—is located in your abdomen, just above your stomach. Although you can survive losing a portion of your liver, it is an important organ. The liver filters blood, cleansing it of harmful substances, and stores unneeded nutrients for later use in the body. It produces a golden yellow substance called bile, which is able to break down fats, much like the way soap breaks down oils. The liver also breaks down medicines and produces important proteins, such as those that help clot blood if you get a cut.

**Gallbladder** The gallbladder is a tiny pear-shaped sac connected to the liver. Bile produced in the liver is stored and concentrated in the gallbladder. The bile is then secreted into the small intestine.

**Pancreas** Located between the stomach and the small intestine, the pancreas produces chemicals that are needed as materials move between the two. The pancreas quickly lowers the acidity in the small intestine and breaks down proteins, fats, and starch. The chemicals produced by the pancreas are extremely important for digesting and absorbing food substances. Without these chemicals, you could die of starvation, even with plenty of food in your system. Your body would not be able to process and use the food for energy without the pancreas.

How does the pancreas aid in digestion?

## 2.2 Review

### KEY CONCEPTS

1. List three of the functions of the digestive system.
2. Give one example each of mechanical digestion and chemical digestion.
3. How does your stomach process food?

### CRITICAL THINKING

4. **Apply** Does an antacid deal with mechanical or chemical digestion?
5. **Apply** You have just swallowed a bite of apple. Describe what happens as the apple moves through your digestive system. Include information about what happens to the material in the apple.

### CHALLENGE

6. **Compare and Contrast** Describe the roles of the large and the small intestines. How are they similar? How are they different?

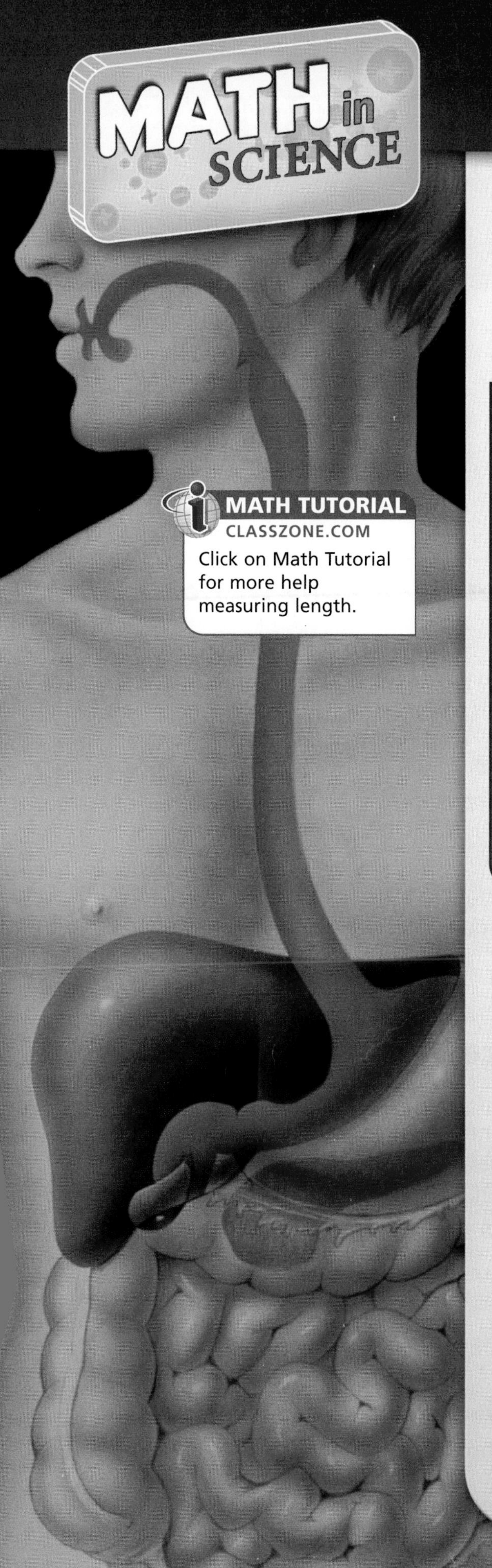


MATH TUTORIAL
CLASSZONE.COM
Click on Math Tutorial for more help measuring length.

SKILL: CHOOSING UNITS OF LENGTH

# Internal Measurement

It wouldn't be useful if someone told you the length of your tongue in meters, or the length of a tooth in centimeters. To be meaningful, these measurements must be given in appropriate units.

## Example

Your esophagus is about the length of your forearm. Choose the appropriate units to measure its length. Would meters, centimeters, or millimeters be most appropriate?

**(1)** Look at your arm from your wrist to your elbow. It is about the same as a rolling pin. You don't need to measure your forearm to see that a meter would be too large a unit. One meter is about the height of a lab table.

**(2)** Look at the ruler in the picture. Compare your arm to the centimeters shown and the millimeters.

**(3)** You can measure your arm with either unit, but if you wiggle a bit, the count of millimeters is thrown off.

**ANSWER** Centimeters are the most appropriate units.

**Answer the following questions.**

**1.** If you uncoiled a human intestine, its length would be about equal to that of 2 cars parked end to end. What would be appropriate units to use to measure that?

**2.** What units would you use to measure the length of your tongue? The length of a tooth?

**3.** The large intestine is actually shorter than the small intestine. The small intestine is about the length of a small bus, and the large is about as long as a car's back seat. Tell the units you would choose for each. Explain why.

**CHALLENGE** Your stomach when empty is about the size of your clenched fist. To measure its volume (the space it takes up), what units would you use?



The ruler shows 20 centimeters (cm). There are 10 millimeters (mm) in each centimeter.

KEY CONCEPT

# The urinary system removes waste materials.

**BEFORE, you learned**

- The digestive system breaks down food
- Organs in the digestive system have different roles

**NOW, you will learn**

- How different body systems remove different types of waste
- Why the kidneys are important organs
- About the role of the kidneys in homeostasis

**VOCABULARY**

**urinary system** p. 53
**urine** p. 53

**EXPLORE** Waste Removal

### *How does the skin get rid of body waste?*

**PROCEDURE**

1. Place a plastic bag over the hand you do not use for writing and tape it loosely around your wrist.
2. Leave the bag on for five minutes. Write down the changes you see in conditions within the bag.

**WHAT DO YOU THINK?**

- What do you see happen to the bag?
- How does what you observe help explain the body's method of waste removal?

**MATERIALS**

- plastic bag
- tape
- stopwatch

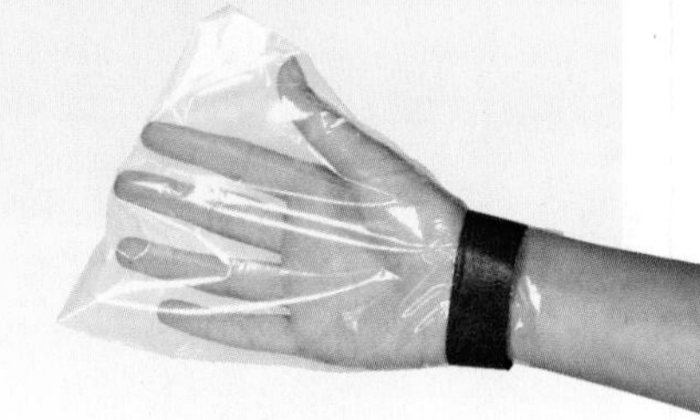

## Life processes produce wastes.

**OUTLINE**
Add *Life processes produce wastes* to your outline. Include four ways the body disposes of waste products.

I. Main idea
  A. Supporting idea
    1. Detail
    2. Detail
  B. Supporting idea

You have read that the respiratory system and the digestive system provide the body with energy and materials necessary for important processes. During these processes, waste materials are produced. The removal of these wastes is essential for the continuing function of body systems. Several systems in your body remove wastes.

- The urinary system disposes of liquid waste products removed from the blood.
- The respiratory system disposes of water vapor and waste gases from the blood.
- The digestive system disposes of solid waste products from food.
- The skin releases wastes through sweat glands.

What are four ways the body disposes of waste products?

## The urinary system removes waste from the blood.

If you have observed an aquarium, you have seen a filter at work. Water moves through the filter, which removes waste materials from the water. Just as the filter in a fish tank removes wastes from the water, structures in your urinary system filter wastes from your blood.

As shown in the diagram, the **urinary system** contains several structures. The kidneys are two organs located high up and toward the rear of the abdomen, one on each side of the spine. Kidneys function much as the filter in the fish tank does. In fact, the kidneys are often called the body's filters. Materials travel in your blood to the kidneys. There, some substances are removed, and others are returned to the blood.

After the kidneys filter chemical waste from the blood, the liquid travels down two tubes called ureters (yu-REE-tuhrz). The ureters bring the waste to the bladder, a storage sac with a wall of smooth muscle. The lower neck of the bladder leads into the urethra, a tube that carries the liquid waste outside the body. Voluntary muscles at one end of the bladder allow a person to hold the urethra closed until he or she is ready to release the muscles. At that time, the bladder contracts and sends the liquid waste, or **urine,** out of the body.

**VOCABULARY**
Add a magnet diagram for *urinary system* to your notebook. Include in your diagram information about how kidneys function.

### Urinary System

**The urinary system transports wastes out of the body.**

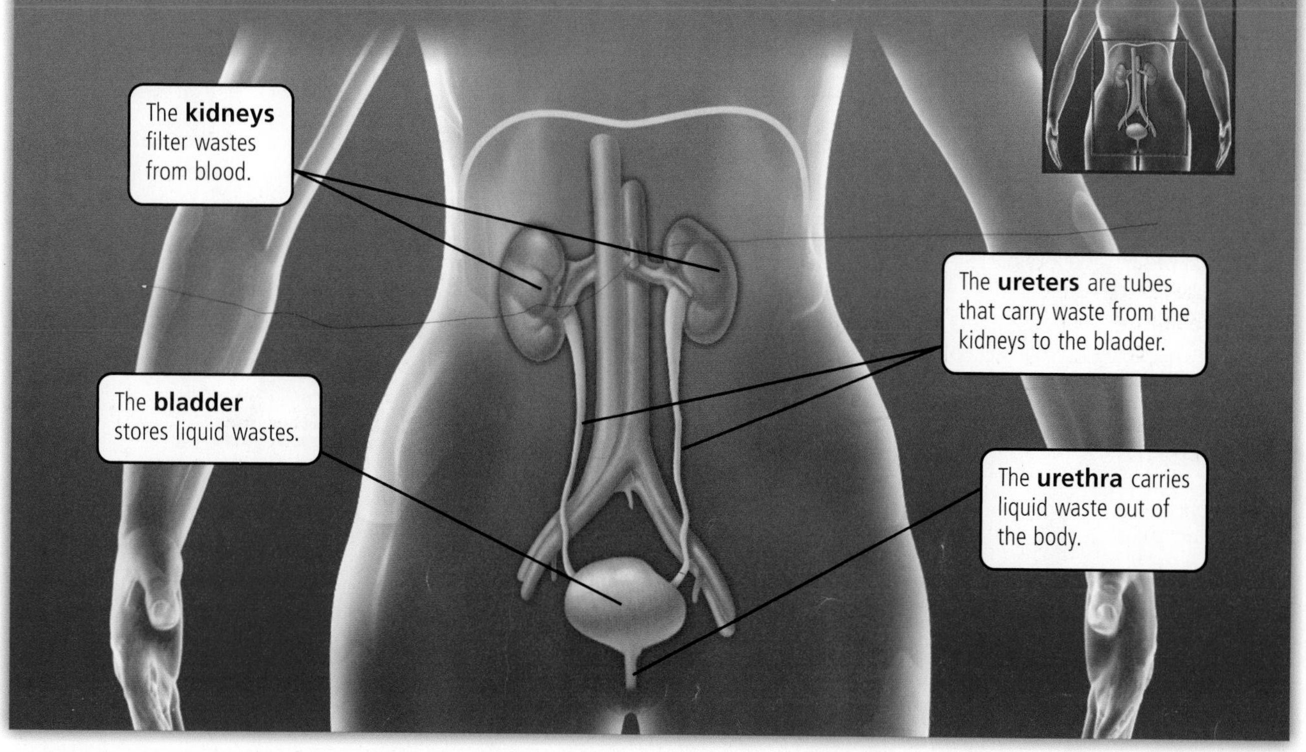

The **kidneys** filter wastes from blood.

The **ureters** are tubes that carry waste from the kidneys to the bladder.

The **bladder** stores liquid wastes.

The **urethra** carries liquid waste out of the body.

## The kidneys act as filters.

Find out more about the urinary system.

At any moment, about one quarter of the blood leaving your heart is headed toward your kidneys to be filtered. The kidneys, which are about as long as your index finger—only 10 centimeters (3.9 in.) long—filter all the blood in your body many times a day.

### The Nephron

Inside each kidney are approximately one million looping tubes called nephrons. The nephron regulates the makeup of the blood.

1. Fluid is filtered from the blood into the nephron through a structure called the glomerulus (gloh-MEHR-yuh-luhs). Filtered blood leaves the glomerulus and circulates around the tubes that make up the nephron.
2. As the filtered fluid passes through the nephron, some nutrients are absorbed back into the blood surrounding the tubes. Some water is also filtered out in the glomerulus, but most water is returned to the blood.
3. Waste products travel to the end of the nephron into the collecting duct. The remaining liquid, now called urine, passes out of the kidney and into the ureters.

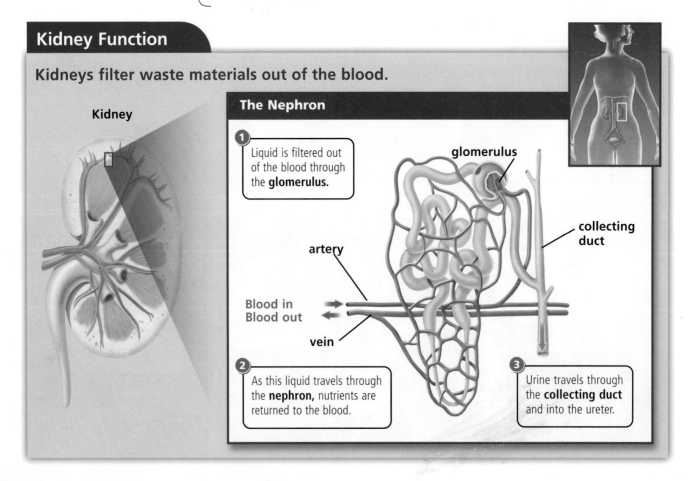

#### Kidney Function

**Kidneys filter waste materials out of the blood.**

Kidney

**The Nephron**

1 Liquid is filtered out of the blood through the **glomerulus.**

glomerulus

collecting duct

artery

Blood in

Blood out

vein

2 As this liquid travels through the **nephron,** nutrients are returned to the blood.

3 Urine travels through the **collecting duct** and into the ureter.

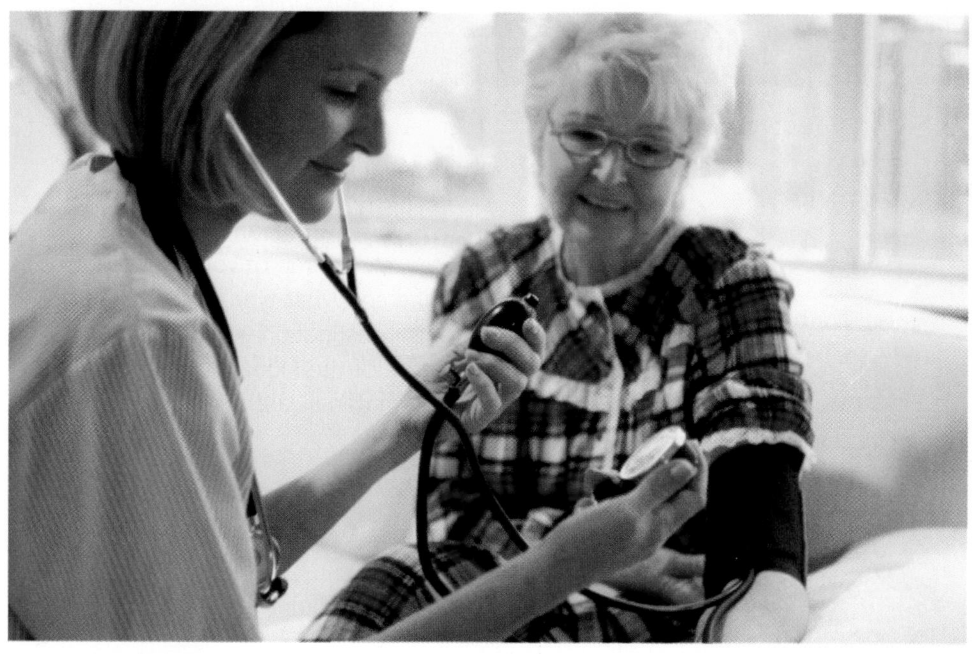

The amount of water in your body affects your blood pressure. Excess water increases blood pressure.

## Water Balance

The kidneys not only remove wastes from blood, they also regulate the amount of water in the body. You read in Chapter 1 about the importance of homeostasis—a stable environment within your body. The amount of water in your cells affects homeostasis. If your body contains too much water, parts of your body may swell. Having too little water interferes with cell processes.

About one liter of water leaves the body every day. The kidneys control the amount of water that leaves the body in urine. Depending on how much water your body uses, the kidneys produce urine with more or less water.

How do your kidneys regulate the amount of water in your body?

### KEY CONCEPTS

1. Describe the four organ systems that remove waste and explain how each removes waste.
2. Describe the function of four organs in the urinary system.
3. Describe homeostasis and explain why the kidneys are important to homeostasis.

### CRITICAL THINKING

4. **Connect** Make a word web with the term *kidney* in the center. Add details about kidney function to the web.

### CHALLENGE

5. **Synthesize** Explain why you may become thirsty on a hot day. Include the term *homeostasis* in your explanation.

# CHAPTER INVESTIGATION

## Modeling a Kidney

**OVERVIEW AND PURPOSE** Your kidneys are your body's filters. Every 20 to 30 minutes, every drop of your blood passes through the kidneys and is filtered. What types of materials are filtered by the kidneys? In this investigation you will

- model the filtering process of the kidneys
- determine what types of materials are filtered by your kidneys

### Problem

What types of materials can be removed from the blood by the kidneys?

### Hypothesize

Write a hypothesis to explain how substances are filtered out of the blood by the kidneys. Your hypothesis should take the form of an "If . . . , then . . . , because . . ." statement.

**MATERIALS**
- fine filter paper
- small funnel
- graduated cylinder
- 100 mL beaker
- solution A
- solution B
- solution C
- salinity test strips
- glucose test strips
- protein test strips

### Procedure

1 Make a data table like the one shown on the sample notebook page. Fold the filter paper as shown. Place the filter paper in the funnel, and place the funnel in the graduated cylinder.

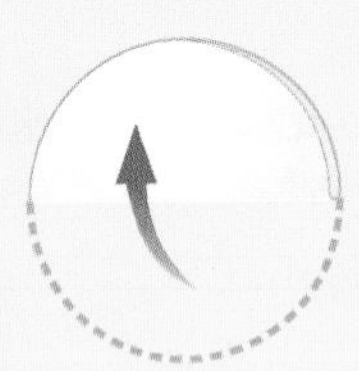

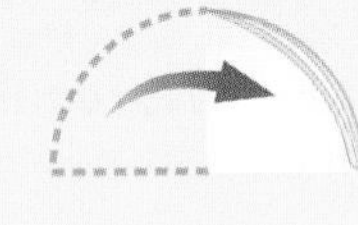

2 Pour 20 mL of solution A into a beaker. Test the solution for salt concentration using a test strip for salinity. Record the results in your notebook. Slowly pour the solution into the funnel. Wait for it all to drip through the filter paper.

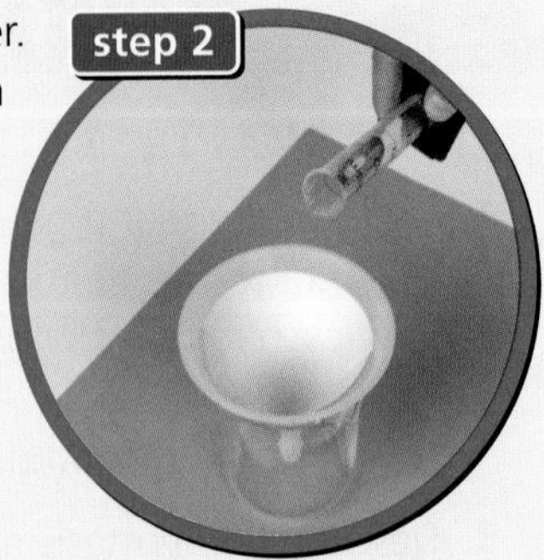

3 Test the filtered liquid for salt concentration again. Record the results.

4 Repeat steps 1, 2, and 3 for solution B using glucose test strips. Record the results in your notebook.

5 Repeat steps 1, 2, and 3 for solution C using protein test strips. Record the results in your notebook.

## Observe and Analyze

Write It Up

1. **RECORD** Be sure your data table is complete.
2. **OBSERVE** What substances were present in solutions A, B, and C?
3. **IDENTIFY VARIABLES** Identify the variables and constants in the experiment. List them in your notebook.

## Conclude

1. **COMPARE AND CONTRAST** In what ways does your model function like a kidney? How is your model not like a kidney?
2. **INTERPRET** Which materials were able to pass through the filter and which could not?
3. **INFER** What materials end up in the urine? How might materials be filtered out of the blood but not appear in the urine?
4. **APPLY** How could a filtering device be useful in your body?

## INVESTIGATE Further

**CHALLENGE** Your blood contains many chemicals. Some of these chemicals are waste products, but some are in the blood to be transported to different parts of the body. What other substances are filtered out of the blood by the kidneys? Which of the filtered substances are normally present in the urine? Use a variety of reference materials to research the chemicals found in urine. Revise your experiment to test the ability of your model kidney to filter other substances.

Modeling a Kidney

Table 1. Test-strip results

| | Before filtering | After filtering |
|---|---|---|
| Solution A | | |
| Solution B | | |
| Solution C | | |

# 2 Chapter Review

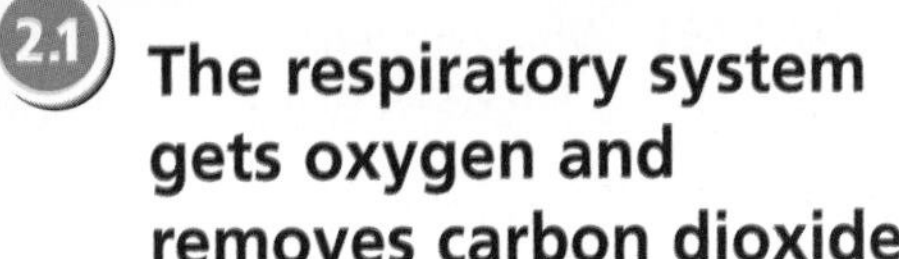


**Systems in the body obtain and process materials and remove waste.**

## KEY CONCEPTS SUMMARY

### 2.1 The respiratory system gets oxygen and removes carbon dioxide.

- Your body needs oxygen
- Structures in the respiratory system function together
- Your respiratory system is involved in other functions

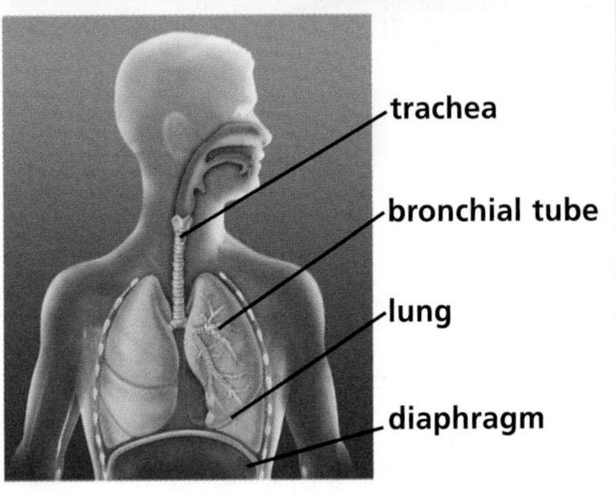


**VOCABULARY**
**respiratory system** p. 37
**cellular respiration** p. 39

### 2.2 The digestive system breaks down food.

| Structure | Function |
|---|---|
| Mouth | chemical and mechanical digestion |
| Esophagus | movement of food by peristalsis from mouth to stomach |
| Stomach | chemical and mechanical digestion; absorption of broken-down nutrients |
| Small intestine | chemical digestion; absorption of broken-down nutrients |
| Large intestine | absorption of water and broken-down nutrients, elimination of wastes |

**VOCABULARY**
**nutrient** p. 45
**digestion** p. 46
**digestive system** p. 46
**peristalsis** p. 46

### 2.3 The urinary system removes waste materials.

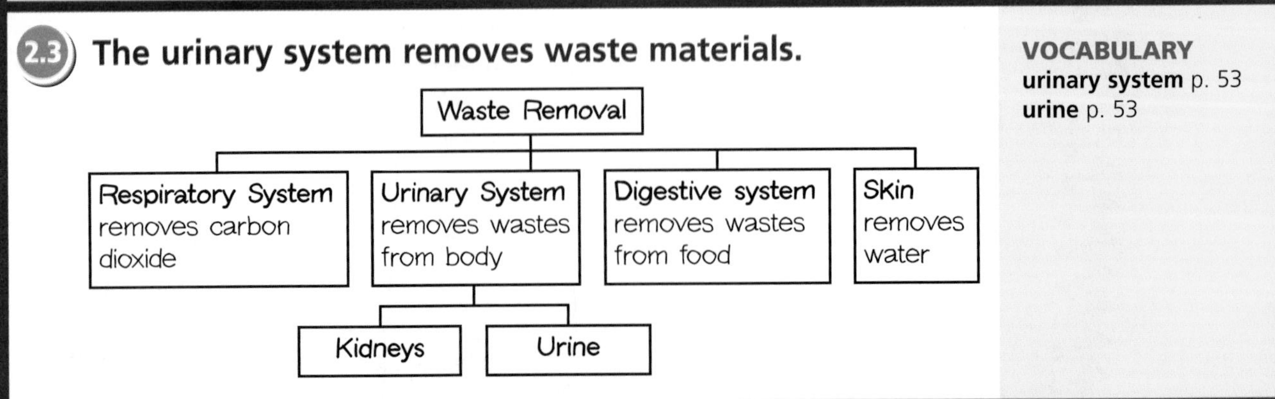


**VOCABULARY**
**urinary system** p. 53
**urine** p. 53

## Reviewing Vocabulary

*Copy the chart below and write the definition for each word. Use the meaning of the word's root to help you.*

| Word | Root Meaning | Definition |
|---|---|---|
| EXAMPLE: rib cage | to arch over | bones enclosing the internal organs of the body |
| 1. respiration | to breathe | |
| 2. nutrient | to nourish | |
| 3. digestion | to separate | |
| 4. peristalsis | to wrap around | |

## Reviewing Key Concepts

**Multiple Choice** *Choose the letter of the best answer.*

**5.** Which system brings oxygen into your body and removes carbon dioxide?
- **a.** digestive system
- **b.** urinary system
- **c.** respiratory system
- **d.** muscular system

**6.** Which body structure in the throat keeps air from entering the stomach?
- **a.** trachea
- **b.** epiglottis
- **c.** lungs
- **d.** alveoli

**7.** Oxygen and carbon dioxide are exchanged through structures in the lungs called
- **a.** bronchial tubes
- **b.** alveoli
- **c.** cartilage
- **d.** villi

**8.** Carbon dioxide is a waste product that is formed during which process?
- **a.** cellular respiration
- **b.** peristalsis
- **c.** urination
- **d.** circulation

**9.** Carbohydrates are nutrients that
- **a.** make up most of the human body
- **b.** make up cell membranes
- **c.** enable cells to grow and repair themselves
- **d.** are broken down for energy

**10.** Which is *not* a function of the digestive system?
- **a.** absorb water from food
- **b.** absorb nutrients from food
- **c.** filter wastes from blood
- **d.** break down food

**11.** Which is an example of a physical change?
- **a.** teeth grind cracker into smaller pieces
- **b.** liquids in mouth change starches to sugars
- **c.** bile breaks down fats
- **d.** stomach breaks down proteins

**12.** Where in the digestive system is most water absorbed?
- **a.** kidneys
- **b.** stomach
- **c.** large intestine
- **d.** esophagus

**13.** Chemical waste is filtered from the blood in which structure?
- **a.** alveoli
- **b.** kidney
- **c.** stomach
- **d.** villi

**14.** The kidneys control the amount of
- **a.** oxygen that enters the blood
- **b.** blood cells that leave the body
- **c.** urine that is absorbed by the body
- **d.** water that leaves the body

**Short Answer** *Write a short answer to each question.*

15. Draw a sketch that shows how the thoracic cavity changes as the diaphragm contracts and pulls downward.

16. What are two products that are released into the body as a result of cellular respiration?

17. Through which organs does food pass as it travels through the digestive system?

18. What is the function of the urinary system?

## Thinking Critically

19. **SUMMARIZE** Describe how gas exchange takes place inside the lungs.

20. **SYNTHESIZE** Summarize what happens during cellular respiration. Explain how the digestive system and the respiratory system are involved.

21. **ANALYZE** When there is a lot of dust or pollen in the air, people may cough and sneeze. What function of the respiratory system is involved?

22. **INFER** When you exhale onto a glass surface, the surface becomes cloudy with a thin film of moisture. Explain why this happens.

23. **COMPARE AND CONTRAST** Where does mechanical digestion take place? How is it different from chemical digestion?

24. **PREDICT** People with stomach disease often have their entire stomachs removed and are able to live normally. Explain how this is possible. Would a person be able to live normally without the small intestine? Explain your answer.

25. **APPLY** An athlete drinks a liter of water before a basketball game and continues to drink water during the game. Describe how the athlete's body is able to maintain homeostasis during the course of the game.

26. **INTERPRET** Use the diagram of the nephron shown below to describe what happens to the blood as it travels through the vessels surrounding the nephron.

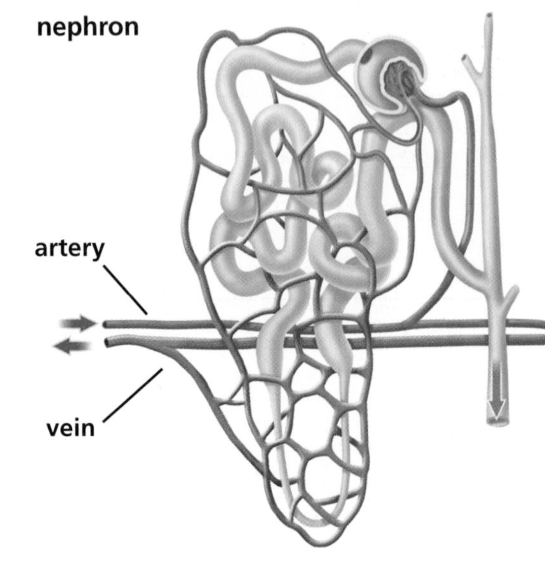


## the BIG idea

27. **INFER** Look again at the picture on pages 34–35. Now that you have finished the chapter, how would you change or add details to your answer to the question on the photograph?

28. **SYNTHESIZE** Write a paragraph explaining how the respiratory system, the digestive system, and the urinary system work together with the circulatory system to eliminate waste materials from the body. Underline these terms in your paragraph.

## UNIT PROJECTS

Check your schedule for your unit project. How are you doing? Be sure that you've placed data or notes from your research in your project folder.

## Analyzing Data

The bar graph below shows respiration rates.

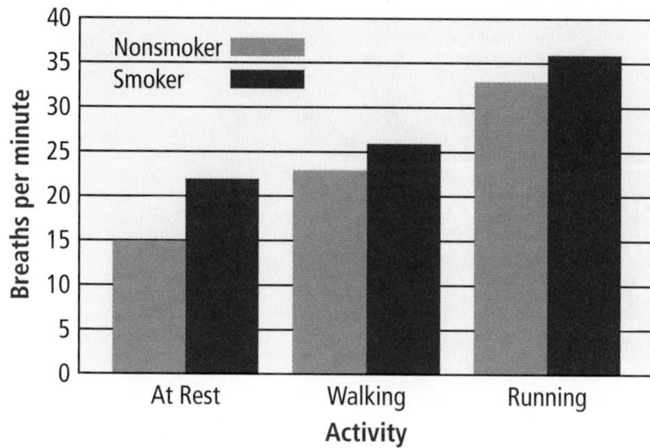


*Use the graph to answer the questions below.*

**1.** What is the best title for this graph?

**a.** Respiration Rates of Smokers and Nonsmokers
**b.** Cigarettes Smoked During Exercise
**c.** Activities Performed by Smokers and Nonsmokers
**d.** Blood Pressure Levels of Smokers and Nonsmokers.

**2.** How many breaths per minute were taken by a nonsmoker at rest?

**a.** 15 breaths per minute
**b.** 22 breaths per minute
**c.** 26 breaths per minute
**d.** 33 breaths per minute

**3.** For the nonsmokers, by how much did the respiration rate increase between resting and running?

**a.** 15 breaths per minute
**b.** 18 breaths per minute
**c.** 23 breaths per minute
**d.** 33 breaths per minute

**4.** Which statement is *not* true?

**a.** The nonsmoker at rest took more breaths per minute than the smoker at rest.
**b.** The nonsmoker took more breaths per minute running than walking.
**c.** The smoker took more breaths per minute than the nonsmoker while walking.
**d.** The nonsmoker took fewer breaths per minute than the smoker while running.

**5.** Which statement is the most logical conclusion to draw from the data in the chart?

**a.** Smoking has no effect on respiration rate.
**b.** Increased activity has no effect on respiration rate.
**c.** There is no difference in the respiration rates between the smoker and the nonsmoker.
**d.** Smoking and activity both cause an increase in respiration rate.

## Extended Response

**6.** Tar, which is a harmful substance found in tobacco smoke, coats the lining of the lungs over time. Based on the information in the graph and what you know about the respiratory system, write a paragraph describing how smoking cigarettes affects the functioning of the respiratory system.

**7.** Ads for cigarettes and other tobacco products have been banned from television. However, they still appear in newspapers and magazines. These ads make tobacco use look glamorous and exciting. Using your knowledge of the respiratory system, design an ad that discourages the use of tobacco products. Create a slogan that will help people remember how tobacco affects the health of the respiratory system.

CHAPTER

# Transport and Protection

## the BIG idea

Systems function to transport materials and to defend and protect the body.

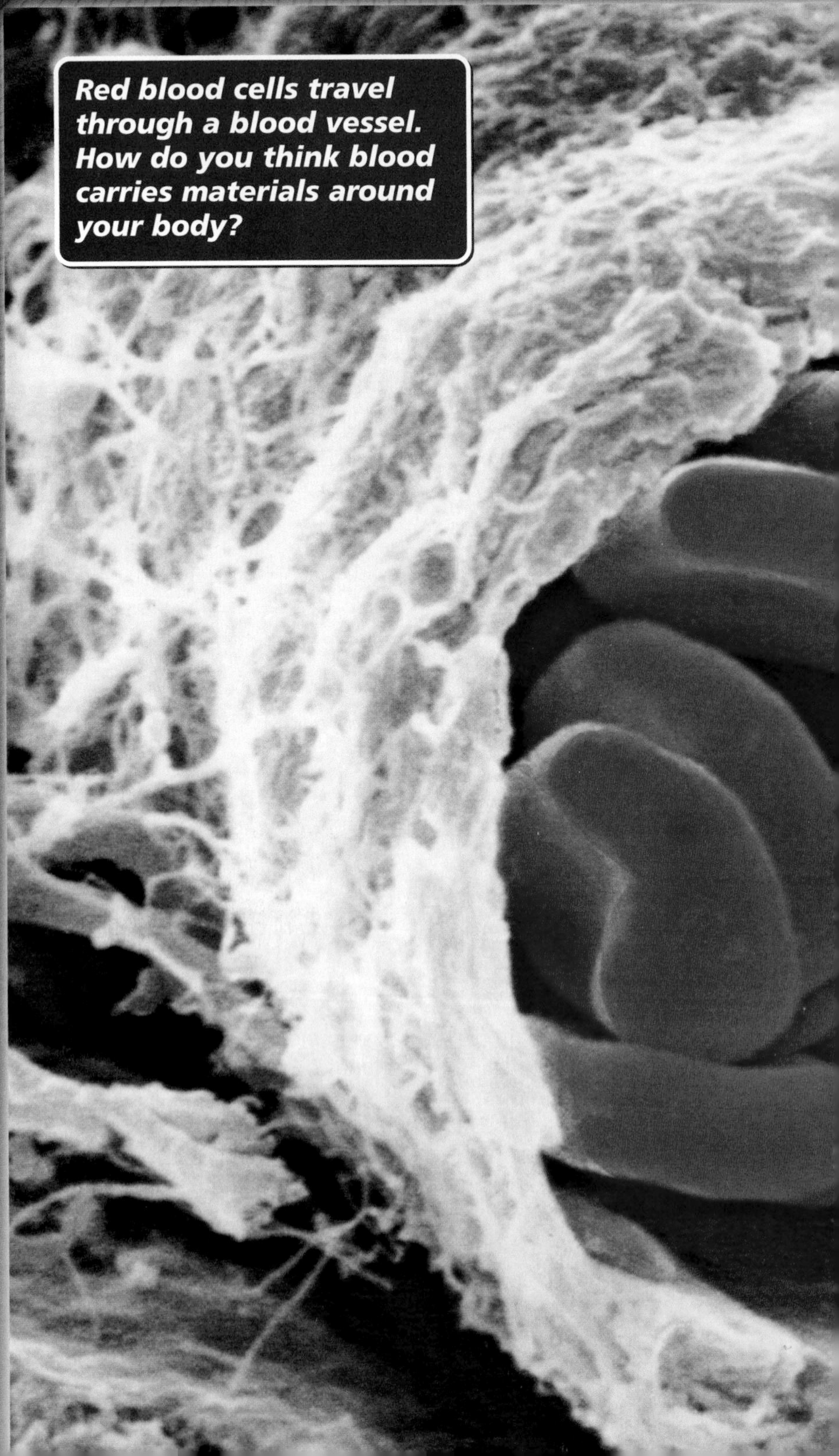

Red blood cells travel through a blood vessel. How do you think blood carries materials around your body?

## Key Concepts

SECTION

**The circulatory system transports materials.**
Learn how materials move through blood vessels.

SECTION

**The immune system defends the body.**
Learn about the body's defenses and responses to foreign materials.

SECTION

**The integumentary system shields the body.**
Learn about the structure of skin and how it protects the body.

**Internet Preview**

CLASSZONE.COM

Chapter 3 online resources: Content Review, two Visualizations, four Resource Centers, Math Tutorial, Test Practice

## Blood Pressure

Fill a small, round balloon halfway full with air. Tie off the end. Gently squeeze the balloon in your hand. Release the pressure. Squeeze again.

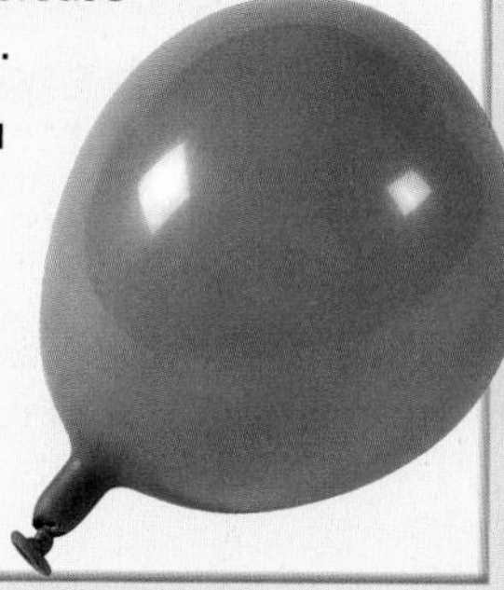

**Observe and Think** As you squeeze your hand, what happens to the air in the balloon? What happens as you release the pressure?

## Wet Fingers

Dip your finger into a cup of room-temperature water. Then hold the finger up in the air and note how it feels.

**Observe and Think** How does your finger feel now compared with the way it felt before you dipped it?

## Internet Activity: Heart Pumping

Go to **ClassZone.com** to learn about how the heart pumps blood. See how the circulatory system interacts with the respiratory system.

**Observe and Think** Where does the blood go after it leaves the right side of the heart? the left side of the heart?

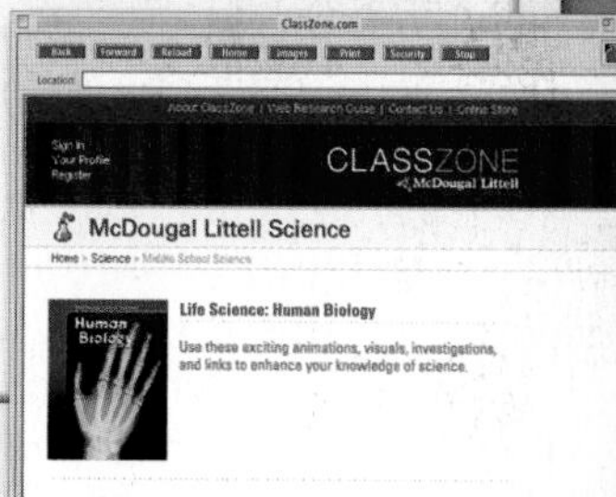

Immune System **Code: MDL046**

CHAPTER 3

# Getting Ready to Learn

## CONCEPT REVIEW

- The body's systems interact.
- The body's systems work to maintain internal conditions.
- The digestive system breaks down food.
- The respiratory system gets oxygen and removes carbon dioxide.

## VOCABULARY REVIEW

**organ** p. 11
**organ system** p. 12
**homeostasis** p. 12
**nutrient** p. 45

Review concepts and vocabulary.

## TAKING NOTES

### MAIN IDEA AND DETAIL NOTES

Make a two-column chart. Write the main ideas, such as those in the blue headings, in the column on the left. Write details about each of those main heads in the column on the right.

### VOCABULARY STRATEGY

Write each new vocabulary term in the center of a **frame game** diagram. Decide what information to frame it with. Use examples, descriptions, parts, sentences that use the term in context, or pictures. You can change the frame to fit each term.

See the Note-Taking Handbook on pages R45–R51.

SCIENCE NOTEBOOK

| MAIN IDEAS | DETAIL NOTES |
| --- | --- |
| 1. The circulatory system works with other body systems. | 1. Transports materials from digestive and respiratory systems to cells<br>2. Blood is fluid that carries materials and wastes<br>3. Blood is always moving through the body<br>4. Blood delivers oxygen and takes away carbon dioxide |

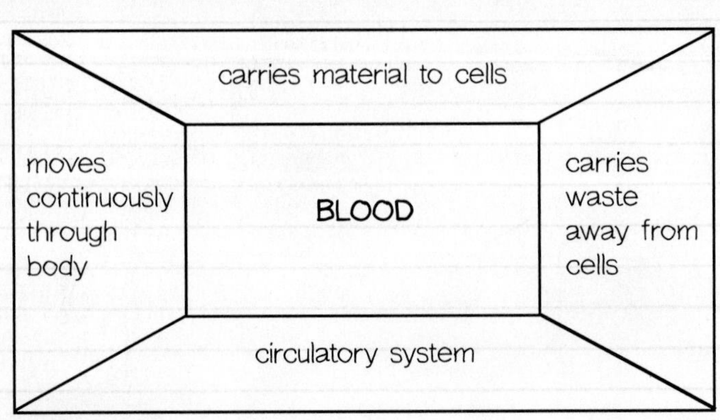

KEY CONCEPT

# The circulatory system transports materials.

**BEFORE, you learned**

- The urinary system removes waste
- The kidneys play a role in homeostasis

**NOW, you will learn**

- How different structures of the circulatory system work together
- About the structure and function of blood
- What blood pressure is and why it is important

**VOCABULARY**

**circulatory system** p. 65
**blood** p. 65
**red blood cell** p. 67
**artery** p. 69
**vein** p. 69
**capillary** p. 69

**EXPLORE** The Circulatory System

### *How fast does your heart beat?*

**PROCEDURE**

1. Hold out your left hand with your palm facing up.
2. Place the first two fingers of your right hand on your left wrist below your thumb. Move your fingertips slightly until you can feel your pulse.
3. Use the stopwatch to determine how many times your heart beats in one minute.

**WHAT DO YOU THINK?**

- How many times did your heart beat?
- What do you think you would find if you took your pulse after exercising?

**MATERIALS**

stopwatch

## The circulatory system works with other body systems.

**VOCABULARY**
Add a frame game diagram for the term *circulatory system* to your notebook.

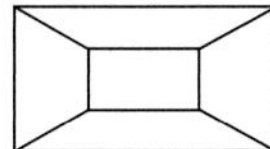

You have read that the systems in your body provide materials and energy. The digestive system breaks down food and nutrients, and the respiratory system provides the oxygen that cells need to release energy. Another system, called the **circulatory system,** transports materials from the digestive and the respiratory systems to the cells.

Materials and wastes are carried in a fluid called **blood**. Blood moves continuously through the body, delivering oxygen and other materials to cells and removing carbon dioxide and other wastes from cells.

## Structures in the circulatory system function together.

Find out more about the circulatory system.

In order to provide the essential nutrients and other materials that your cells need, your blood must keep moving through your body. The circulatory system, which is made up of the heart and blood vessels, allows blood to flow to all parts of the body. The circulatory system works with other systems to provide the body with this continuous flow of life-giving blood.

### The Heart

The heart is the organ that pushes blood throughout the circulatory system. The human heart actually functions as two pumps—one pump on the right side and one on the left side. The right side of the heart pumps blood to the lungs to receive oxygen, and the left side pumps blood to the entire body. The lungs receive oxygen when you inhale and remove carbon dioxide when you exhale. Inside the lungs, the respiratory system interacts with the circulatory system.

**The Heart**

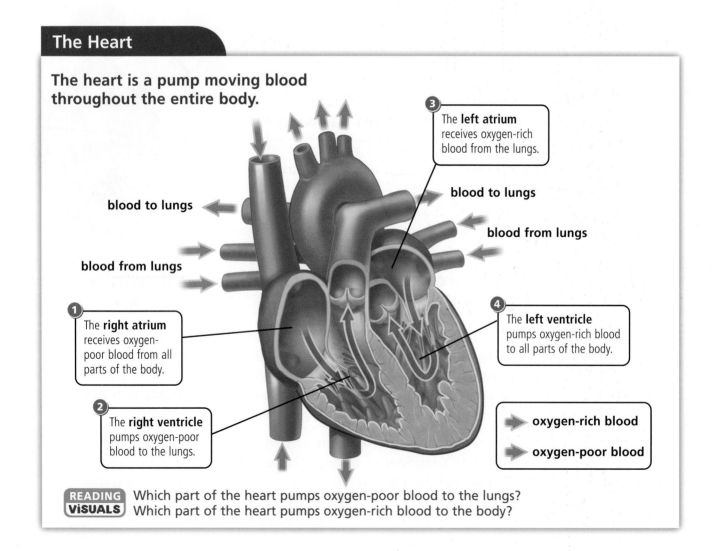

**The heart is a pump moving blood throughout the entire body.**

blood to lungs

blood from lungs

blood to lungs

blood from lungs

1 The **right atrium** receives oxygen-poor blood from all parts of the body.

2 The **right ventricle** pumps oxygen-poor blood to the lungs.

3 The **left atrium** receives oxygen-rich blood from the lungs.

4 The **left ventricle** pumps oxygen-rich blood to all parts of the body.

oxygen-rich blood

oxygen-poor blood

**READING VISUALS** Which part of the heart pumps oxygen-poor blood to the lungs? Which part of the heart pumps oxygen-rich blood to the body?

Each side of the heart is divided into two areas called chambers. Oxygen-poor blood, which is blood from the body with less oxygen, flows to the right side of your heart, into a filling chamber called the right atrium. With each heartbeat, blood flows from the right atrium into a pumping chamber, the right ventricle, and then into the lungs. There the blood releases carbon dioxide waste and absorbs oxygen.

After picking up oxygen, blood is pushed back to the heart, filling another chamber, which is called the left atrium. Blood moves from the left atrium to the left ventricle, a pumping chamber, and again begins its trip out to the rest of the body. Both oxygen-poor blood and oxygen-rich blood are red. However, oxygen-rich blood is a much brighter and lighter shade of red than is oxygen-poor blood. The diagram on page 66 shows oxygen-poor blood in blue, so that you can tell where in the circulatory system oxygen-poor and oxygen-rich blood are found.

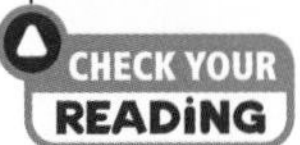

Summarize the way blood moves through the heart. Remember, a summary contains only the most important information.

## Blood

The oxygen that your cells need in order to release energy must be present in blood to travel through your body. Blood is a tissue made up of plasma, red blood cells, white blood cells, and platelets. About 60 percent of blood is plasma, a fluid that contains proteins, glucose, hormones, gases, and other substances dissolved in water.

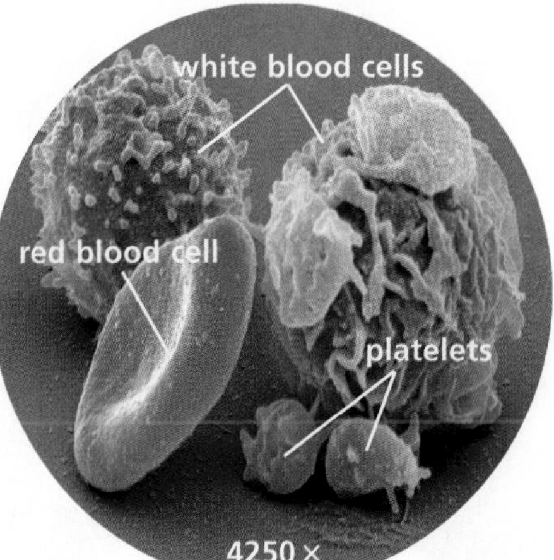

Blood is made mostly of plasma, which transports red blood cells, white blood cells, and platelets.

White blood cells help your body fight infection by attacking disease-causing organisms. **Red blood cells** are more numerous than white blood cells and have a different function. They pick up oxygen in the lungs and transport it throughout the body. As red blood cells travel through the circulatory system, they deliver oxygen to other cells.

Platelets are large cell fragments that help form blood clots when a blood vessel is injured. You know what a blood clot is if you've observed a cut or a scrape. The scab that forms around a cut or scrape is made of clotted blood. After an injury such as a cut, platelets nearby begin to enlarge and become sticky. They stick to the injured area of the blood vessels and release chemicals that result in blood clotting. Blood clotting keeps blood vessels from losing too much blood.

What are the four components that make up blood?

## Circulatory System

**The circulatory system allows blood to flow continuously throughout the body. The runner depends on a constant flow of oxygen-rich blood to fuel his cells.**

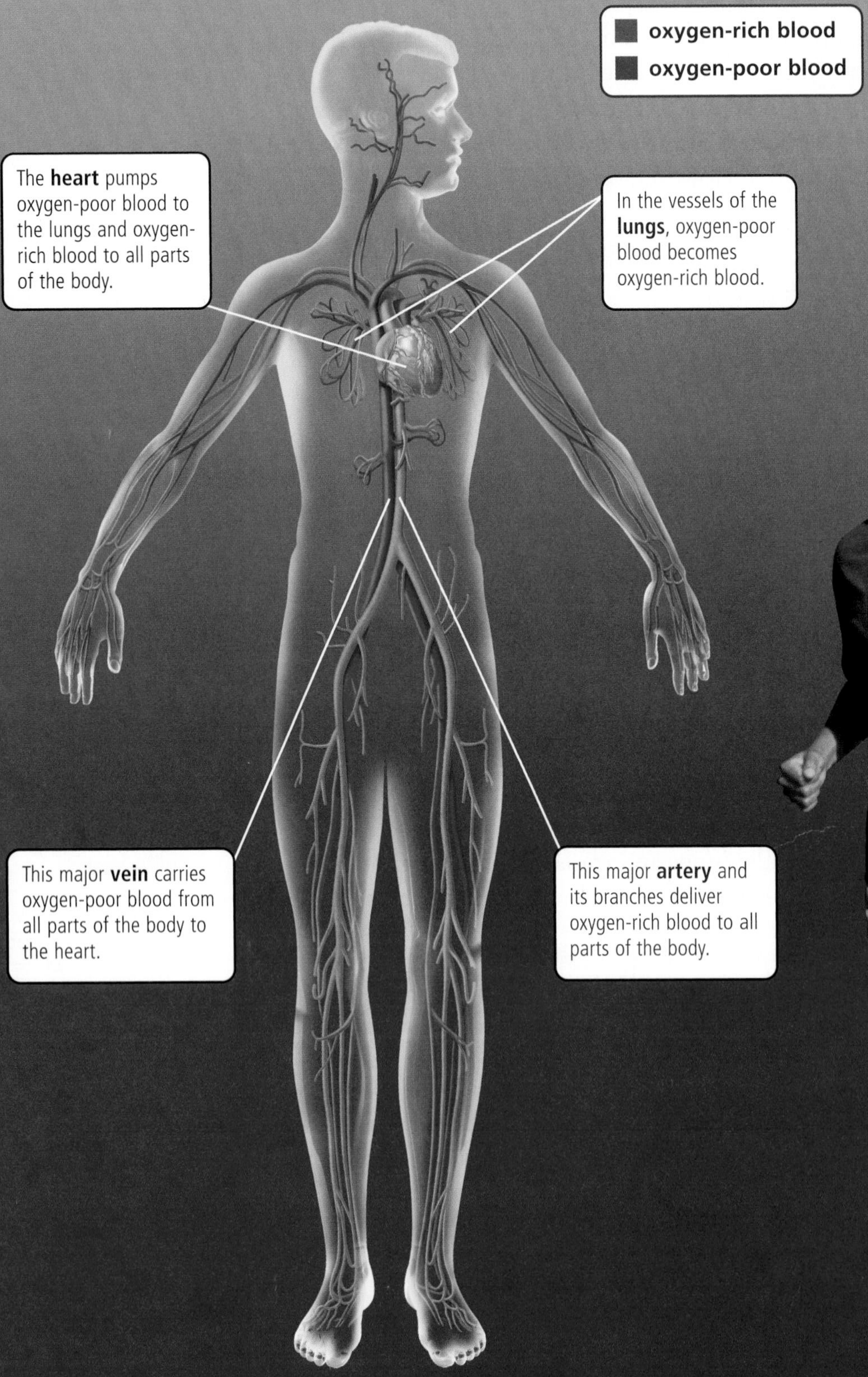

oxygen-rich blood
oxygen-poor blood

The **heart** pumps oxygen-poor blood to the lungs and oxygen-rich blood to all parts of the body.

In the vessels of the **lungs**, oxygen-poor blood becomes oxygen-rich blood.

This major **vein** carries oxygen-poor blood from all parts of the body to the heart.

This major **artery** and its branches deliver oxygen-rich blood to all parts of the body.

As blood travels through blood vessels, some fluid is lost. This fluid, called lymph, is collected in lymph vessels and returned to veins and arteries. As you will read in the next section, lymph and lymph vessels are associated with your immune system. Sometimes scientists refer to the lymph and lymph vessels as the lymphatic system. The lymphatic system helps you fight disease.

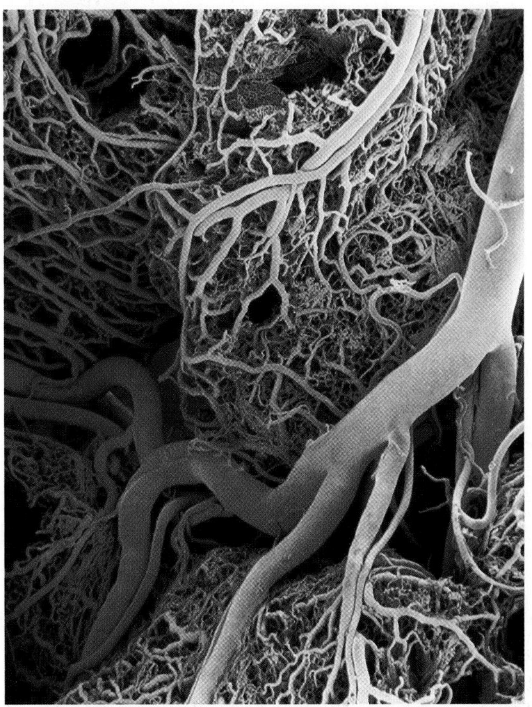
Arteries, capillaries, and veins form a complex web to carry blood to all the cells in the body (30×).

## Blood Vessels

Blood moves through a network of structures called blood vessels. Blood vessels are tube-shaped structures that are similar to flexible drinking straws. The structure of blood vessels suits them for particular functions. **Arteries**, which are the vessels that take blood away from the heart, have strong walls. An artery wall is thick and elastic and can handle the tremendous force produced when the heart pumps. **Veins** are blood vessels that carry blood back to the heart. The walls of veins are thinner than those of arteries. However, veins are generally of greater diameter than are arteries.

Most arteries carry oxygen-rich blood away from the heart, and most veins carry oxygen-poor blood back to the heart. However, the pulmonary blood vessels are exceptions. Oxygen-poor blood travels through the two pulmonary arteries, one of which goes to each lung. The two pulmonary veins carry oxygen-rich blood from the lungs to the heart.

Veins and arteries branch off into very narrow blood vessels called capillaries. **Capillaries** connect arteries with veins. Through capillaries materials are exchanged between blood and tissues. Oxygen and materials from nutrients move from the blood in the arteries to the body's tissues through tiny openings in the capillary walls. Waste materials and carbon dioxide move from the tissues' cells through the capillary walls and into the blood in the veins.

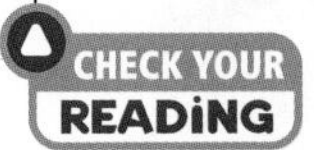

Compare and contrast arteries, veins, and capillaries.

## Blood exerts pressure on blood vessels.

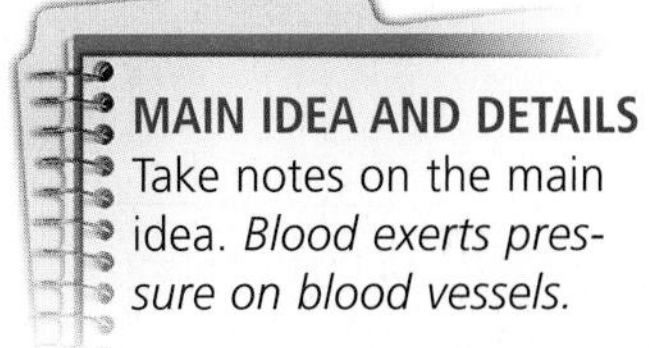

MAIN IDEA AND DETAILS
Take notes on the main idea. *Blood exerts pressure on blood vessels.*


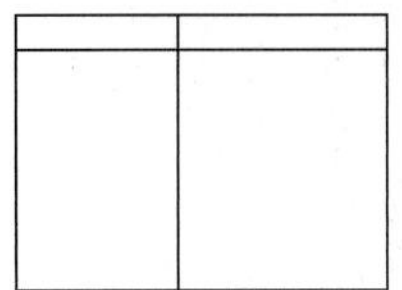

As you have read, the contractions of the heart push blood through blood vessels. The force produced when the heart contracts travels through the blood, putting pressure on the blood vessels. This force is called blood pressure. Compare a vessel to a plastic bag filled with water.

If you push down at the center of the bag, you can see the water push out against the sides of the bag.

The heart pushes blood in a similar way, exerting pressure on the arteries, veins, and capillaries in the circulatory system. It is important to maintain healthy blood pressure so that materials in blood get to all parts of your body. If blood pressure is too low, some of the cells will not get oxygen and other materials. On the other hand, if blood pressure is too high, the force may weaken the blood vessels and require the heart to work harder to push blood through the blood vessels. High blood pressure is a serious medical condition, but it can be treated.

The circulatory system can be considered as two smaller systems: one, the pulmonary system, moves blood to the lungs; the other, the systemic system, moves blood to the rest of the body. Blood pressure is measured in the systemic part of the circulatory system.

You can think of blood pressure as the pressure that blood exerts on the walls of your arteries at all times. Health professionals measure blood pressure indirectly with a device called a sphygmomanometer (SFIHG-moh-muh-NAHM-ih-tuhr).

Blood pressure is expressed with two numbers—one number over another number. The first number refers to the pressure in the arteries when the heart contracts. The second number refers to the pressure in the arteries when the heart relaxes and receives blood from the veins.

## Blood Pressure

**Blood pressure allows materials to travel to all parts of your body.**

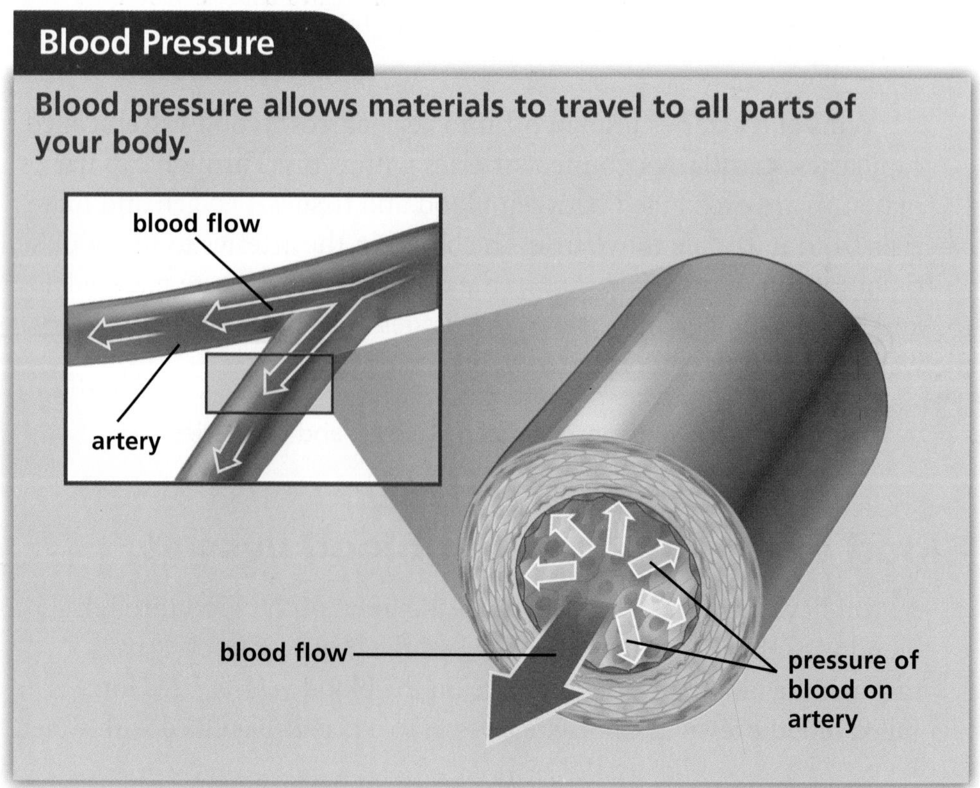

## There are four different blood types.

Each red blood cell has special proteins on its surface. One group of surface proteins determines blood type. There are two blood-type proteins, A and B. A person whose blood cells have the A proteins has type A blood. One with cells having B proteins has type B blood. Some people have both proteins—type AB blood. Other people have neither protein, a type of blood referred to as type O.

Maybe you, or someone you know, has had a blood transfusion, a procedure in which one person receives blood donated by another. Knowing blood type is important for transfusions. As you will learn in the next section, the body has structures that protect it from unknown substances. They are part of an immune system that recognizes and protects cells and molecules that are "self" from those that are unrecognized, or "nonself." The body attacks unrecognized substances, including those in donated blood.

The blood used for transfusions is usually the same type as the blood type of the receiver, but sometimes other blood types are used. The diagram shows which blood types are compatible. Because the cells in type O blood have neither protein, the immune system of someone with A, B, or AB blood will not attack O blood cells. A person with type O blood, however, cannot receive any other blood type because that person's immune system would attack A or B surface proteins.

**Blood Type Compatibility**

| Blood Type | Can Donate Blood To | Can Receive Blood From |
|---|---|---|
| A | A, AB | A, O |
| B | B, AB | B, O |
| AB | AB | A, B, AB, O |
| O | A, B, AB, O | O |

People can donate blood to others.

RESOURCE CENTER
CLASSZONE.COM

Learn more about blood types.

CHECK YOUR READING Why is it important to know your blood type?

# 3.1 Review

### KEY CONCEPTS

1. What are the functions of the two sides of the heart?
2. What is the primary function of red blood cells?
3. Why can both high and low blood pressure be a problem?

### CRITICAL THINKING

4. **Apply** List three examples of the circulatory system working with another system in your body.
5. **Compare and Contrast** Explain why blood pressure is expressed with two numbers.

### CHALLENGE

6. **Identify Cause and Effect** You can feel the speed at which your heart is pumping by pressing two fingers to the inside of your wrist. This is your pulse. If you run for a few minutes, your pulse rate is faster for a little while, then it slows down again. Why did your pulse rate speed up and slow down?

# CHAPTER INVESTIGATION

## Heart Rate and Exercise

**OVERVIEW AND PURPOSE** In this activity, you will calculate your resting, maximum, and target heart rates. Then you will examine the effect of exercise on heart rate. Before you begin, read through the entire investigation.

### MATERIALS

- notebook
- stopwatch
- calculator
- graph paper

### Procedure

1. Make a data table like the one shown on the sample notebook page.

2. Measure your resting heart rate. Find the pulse in the artery of your neck, just below and in front of the bottom of your ear, with the first two fingers of one hand. Do not use your thumb to measure pulse since the thumb has a pulse of its own. Once you have found the pulse, count the beats for 30 seconds and multiply the result by 2. The number you get is your resting heart rate in beats per minute. Record this number in your notebook.

step 2

3. Calculate your maximum heart rate by subtracting your age from 220. Record this number in your notebook. Your target heart rate should be 60 to 75 percent of your maximum heart rate. Calculate and record this range in your notebook.

4. Someone who is very athletic or has been exercising regularly for 6 months or more can safely exercise up to 85 percent of his or her maximum heart rate. Calculate and record this rate in your notebook.

5. Observe how quickly you reach your target heart rate during exercise. Begin by running in place at an intensity that makes you breathe harder but does not make you breathless. As with any exercise, remember that if you experience difficulty breathing, dizziness, or chest discomfort, stop exercising immediately.

step 5

6 Every 2 minutes, measure your heart rate for 10 seconds. Multiply this number by 6 to find your heart rate in beats per minute and record it in your notebook. Try to exercise for a total of 10 minutes. After you stop exercising, continue recording your heart rate every 2 minutes until it returns to the resting rate you measured in step 2.

## Observe and Analyze

Write It Up

1. **GRAPH DATA** Make a line graph of your heart rate during and after the exercise. Graph the values in beats per minute versus time in minutes. Your graph should start at your resting heart rate and continue until your heart rate has returned to its resting rate. Using a colored pencil, shade in the area that represents your target heart-rate range.
2. **ANALYZE DATA** How many minutes of exercising were needed for you to reach your target heart rate of 60 to 75 percent of maximum? Did your heart rate go over your target range?
3. **INTERPRET DATA** How many minutes after you stopped exercising did it take for your heart rate to return to its resting rate? Why do you think your heart rate did not return to its resting rate immediately after you stopped exercising?

## Conclude

Write It Up

1. **INFER** Why do you think that heart rate increases during exercise?
2. **IDENTIFY** What other body systems are affected when the heart rate increases?
3. **PREDICT** Why do you think that target heart rate changes with age?
4. **CLASSIFY** Create a table comparing the intensity of different types of exercise, such as walking, skating, bicycling, weight lifting, and any others you might enjoy.

## INVESTIGATE Further

**CHALLENGE** Determine how other exercises affect your heart rate. Repeat this investigation by performing one or two of the other exercises from your table. Present your data, with a graph, to the class.

### Heart Rate and Exercise

Resting heart rate:

Maximum heart rate:

Target heart rate (60–75% of maximum):

Target heart rate (85% of maximum):

Table 1. Heart Rate During and After Exercise

| Time (minutes) | 0 | 2 | 4 | 6 | 8 | 10 | 12 | 14 | 16 | 18 | 20 |
|---|---|---|---|---|---|---|---|---|---|---|---|
| Heart rate (beats per minute) | | | | | | | | | | | |

KEY CONCEPT

# The immune system defends the body.

**BEFORE, you learned**

- The circulatory system works with other systems to fuel the body cells
- Structures in the circulatory system work together
- Blood pressure allows materials to reach all parts of the body

**NOW, you will learn**

- How foreign material enters the body
- How the immune system responds to foreign material
- Ways that the body can become immune to a disease

**VOCABULARY**

**pathogen** p. 74
**immune system** p. 75
**antibody** p. 75
**antigen** p. 78
**immunity** p. 80
**vaccine** p. 80
**antibiotic** p. 81

**EXPLORE Membranes**

### *How does the body keep foreign particles out?*

**PROCEDURE**

1. Place a white cloth into a sandwich bag and seal it. Fill a bowl with water and stir in several drops of food coloring.
2. Submerge the sandwich bag in the water. After five minutes, remove the bag and note the condition of the cloth.
3. Puncture the bag with a pin. Put the bag back in the water for five minutes. Remove the bag and note the condition of the cloth.

**WHAT DO YOU THINK?**

- How does a puncture in the bag affect its ability to protect the cloth?

**MATERIALS**

- white cloth
- zippered sandwich bag
- large bowl
- water
- food coloring
- small pin

## Many systems defend the body from harmful materials.

**MAIN IDEA AND DETAILS**
Add the main idea *Many systems defend the body from harmful materials* to your chart along with detail notes.

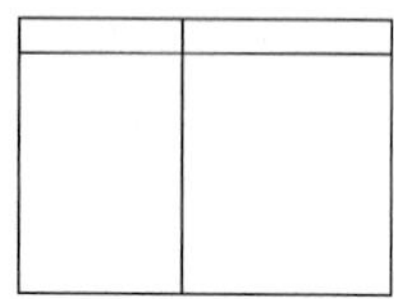

You might not realize it, but you come into contact with harmful substances constantly. Because your body has ways to defend itself, you don't even notice. One of the body's best defenses is to keep foreign materials from entering in the first place. The integumentary (ihn-TEHG-yu-MEHN-tuh-ree), respiratory, and digestive systems are the first line of defense against **pathogens,** or disease-causing agents. Pathogens can enter through your skin, the air you breathe, and even the food you eat or liquids you drink.

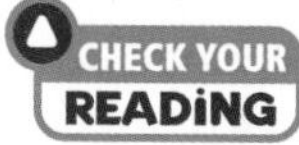


Which systems are your first line of defense against pathogens?

**Integumentary System Defenses** Most of the time, your skin functions as a barrier between you and the outside world. The physical barrier the skin forms is just one obstacle for pathogens and other foreign materials. The growth of pathogens on your eyes can be slowed by substances contained in tears. The millions of bacteria cells that live on the skin can also kill pathogens. A common way pathogens can enter the body is through a cut. The circulatory system is then able to help defend the body because blood contains cells that respond to foreign materials.

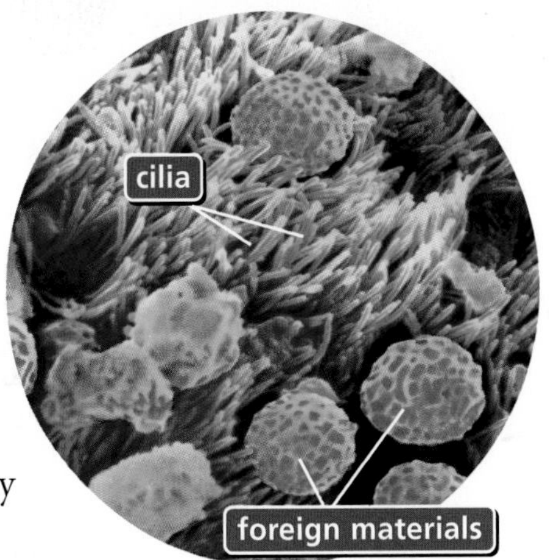


Cilia are hairlike protrusions that trap materials entering your respiratory system (600×).

**Respiratory System Defenses** Sneezing and coughing are two ways the respiratory system defends the body from harmful substances. Cilia and mucus also protect the body. Cilia are tiny, hairlike protrusions in the nose and the lungs that trap dust particles present in the air. Mucus is a thick and slippery substance found in the nose, throat, and lungs. Like the cilia, mucus traps dirt and other particles. Mucus contains substances similar to those in tears that can slow the growth of pathogens.

**Digestive System Defenses** Some foreign materials manage to enter your digestive system, but many are destroyed by saliva, mucus, enzymes, and stomach acids. Saliva in your mouth helps kill bacteria. Mucus protects the digestive organs by coating them. Pathogens can also be destroyed by enzymes produced in the liver and pancreas or by the acids in the stomach.

## The immune system has response structures.

Sometimes foreign materials manage to get past the first line of defense. When this happens, the body relies on the **immune system** to respond. This system functions in several ways:

- Tissues in the bone marrow, the thymus gland, the spleen, and the lymph nodes produce white blood cells, which are specialized cells that function to destroy foreign organisms.
- Some white blood cells produce a nonspecific response to injury or infection.
- Some white blood cells produce proteins called **antibodies,** which are part of a specific immune response to foreign materials.

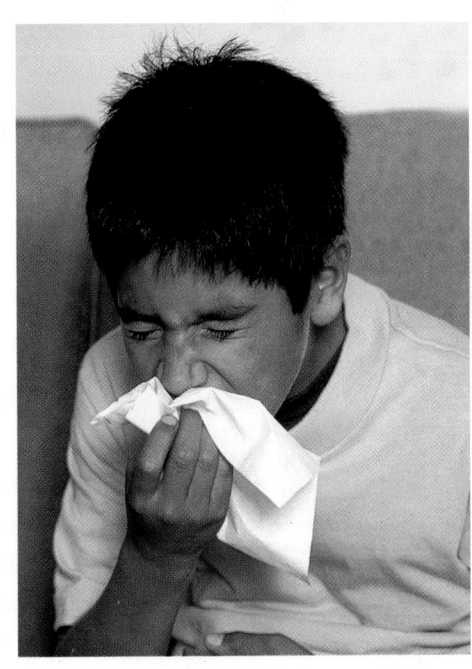

Sneezing helps to expel foreign substances from the body.

### White Blood Cells

The immune system has specialized cells called white blood cells that recognize foreign materials in the body and respond. The number of white blood cells in the blood can increase during an immune response. These cells travel through the circulatory system and the lymphatic system to an injured or infected area of the body. White blood cells leave the blood vessels and travel into the damaged tissue, where the immune response takes place.

### The Lymphatic System

RESOURCE CENTER
CLASSZONE.COM

Learn more about the lymphatic system.

The lymphatic system transports pathogen-fighting white blood cells throughout the body, much as the circulatory system does. The lymphatic system carries lymph, and the circulatory system carries blood. Both fluids transport similar materials, such as white blood cells.

Lymph is the fluid left in the tissues by the circulatory system. It moves through lymph vessels, which are similar to veins. However, the lymphatic system has no pump like the heart to move fluid. Lymph drifts through the lymph vessels when your skeletal muscles contract or when your body changes position. As it moves, it passes through lymph nodes, which filter out pathogens and store white blood cells and antibodies. Because lymph nodes filter out pathogens, infections are often fought in your lymph nodes, causing them to swell when you get sick.

How does the lymphatic system help the immune system?

## The immune system responds to attack.

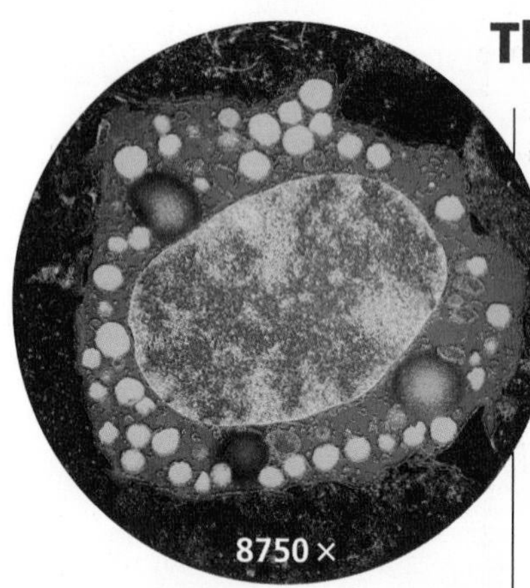


The mast cell above is an important part of the immune system.

Certain illnesses can cause symptoms such as coughing, sneezing, and fever. These symptoms make you uncomfortable when you are sick. But in fact, most symptoms are the result of the immune system's response to foreign materials in the body.

The immune system responds in two ways. The white blood cells that first respond to the site of injury or infection attack foreign materials in a nonspecific response. Some of these cells attack foreign materials and produce chemicals that help other white blood cells work better. The second part of the response is very specific to the types of pathogens invading the body. These white blood cells produce antibodies specific to each pathogen and provide your body with immunity.

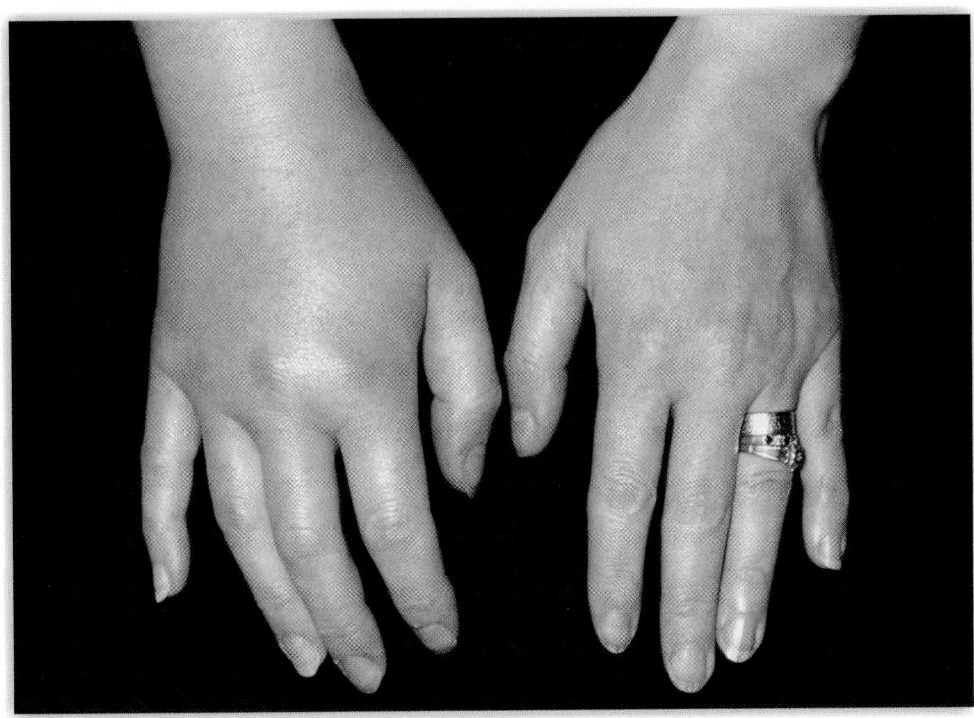

Wasp stings cause an immediate immune response. The area of the sting swells up and increases in temperature while your body battles the injury.

## Nonspecific Response

Swelling, redness, and heat are some of the symptoms that tell you that a cut or scrape has become infected by foreign materials. They are all signs of inflammation, your body's first defense reaction against injuries and infections.

When tissue becomes irritated or damaged, it releases large amounts of histamine (HIHS-tuh-meen). Histamine raises the temperature of the tissues and increases blood flow to the area. Increased blood flow, which makes the injured area appear red, allows antibodies and white blood cells to arrive more quickly for battle. Higher temperatures improve the speed and power of white blood cells. Some pathogens cannot tolerate heat, so they grow weaker. The swelling caused by the production of histamine can be a small price to pay for this chemical's important work.

When a foreign material affects more than one area of your body, many tissues produce histamine. As a result, the temperature of your whole body rises. Any temperature above 37 degrees Celsius (98.6°F) is considered a fever, but only temperatures hot enough to damage tissues are dangerous. Trying to lower a high fever with medication is advisable in order to avoid tissue damage. When you have a small fever, lowering your body temperature might make you more comfortable, but it will not affect how long you stay sick.

What causes a fever when you are sick?

## Specific Response

Specific immune responses differ from nonspecific responses in two ways. First, specific responses are triggered by antigens. An **antigen** is a chemical marker on a cell's surface that indicates whether the cell is from your body or is a foreign material. When the body detects a foreign antigen, specific immune responses occur. Second, a specific immune response provides protection from future exposure to the same material. Three major types of white blood cells—phagocytes, T cells, and B cells—function together in a specific response.

**Phagocytes and T Cells** Phagocytes ingest and break down foreign materials. Small pieces of the foreign materials are incorporated into the surface of the phagocyte's cell membrane. These foreign particles contain antigens that are detected as foreign by T cells. The T cells

### Immune Response

**When pathogens invade the body, several types of white blood cells function together to identify and attack foreign materials.**

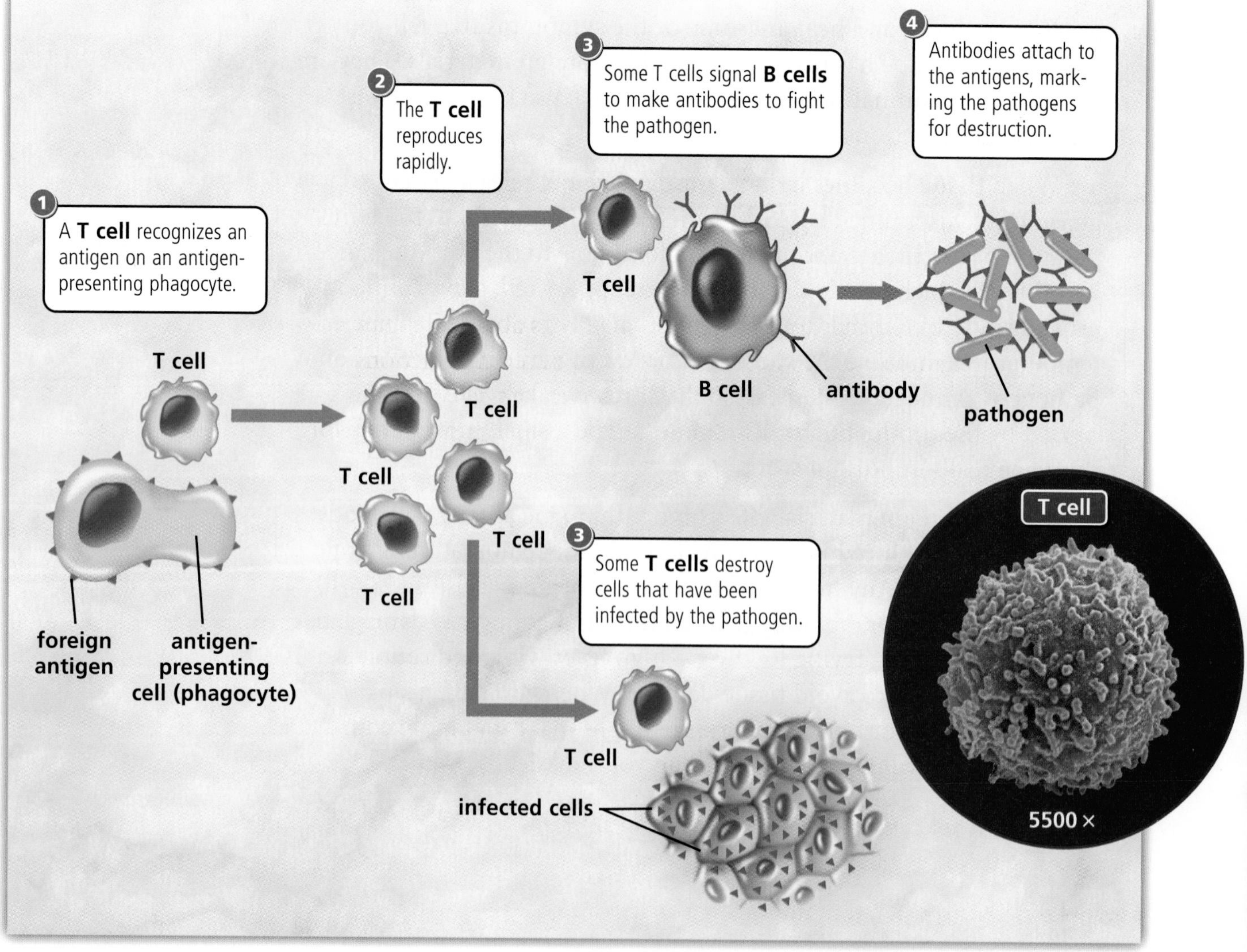

1. A **T cell** recognizes an antigen on an antigen-presenting phagocyte.
2. The **T cell** reproduces rapidly.
3. Some T cells signal **B cells** to make antibodies to fight the pathogen.
4. Antibodies attach to the antigens, marking the pathogens for destruction.

3. Some **T cells** destroy cells that have been infected by the pathogen.

T cell
foreign antigen
antigen-presenting cell (phagocyte)
T cell
T cell
T cell
T cell
T cell
T cell
B cell
antibody
pathogen
T cell
infected cells
T cell
5500 ×

# INVESTIGATE Antibodies

## How do antibodies stop pathogens from spreading?

**SKILL FOCUS**
Making models

**MATERIALS**
- plastic containers with lids
- masking tape

**TIME**
15 minutes

### PROCEDURE

1. Your teacher will hand out plastic lids, each labeled with the name of a different pathogen. You will see plastic containers spread throughout the room. There is one container in the room with the same label as your lid.
2. At the signal, find the plastic container with the pathogen that has the same label as your lid and wait in place for the teacher to tell you to stop. If you still haven't found the matching container when time is called, your model pathogen has spread.
3. If your pathogen has spread, write its name on the board.

### WHAT DO YOU THINK?

- Which pathogens spread?
- What do you think the lid and container represent? Why?
- How do antibodies identify pathogens?

**CHALLENGE** Why do you think it is important for your body to identify pathogens?

respond by dividing rapidly. Some types of T cells attack the materials with the foreign antigens, whereas others have different functions. Because antigens that differ from those on a person's cells and provoke an immune response are found on pathogens, the human immune system is necessary for survival in a germ-filled world.

**B Cells** After T cells divide, B cells that recognize the same foreign antigen are activated and divide rapidly. After several days, many of these B cells begin to produce antibodies that help destroy pathogens. Antibodies attach to the foreign antigens, marking the pathogens for killer T cells or other cells and chemicals that can destroy pathogens.

Some B cells do not make antibodies but remain in the body as a form of immune system memory. If the same pathogen enters the body again, the immune system can respond much more quickly. B cells that recognize the foreign antigen already exist, and antibodies will be produced more quickly.

CHECK YOUR READING Why is it important for the body to store B cells?

### Development of Immunity

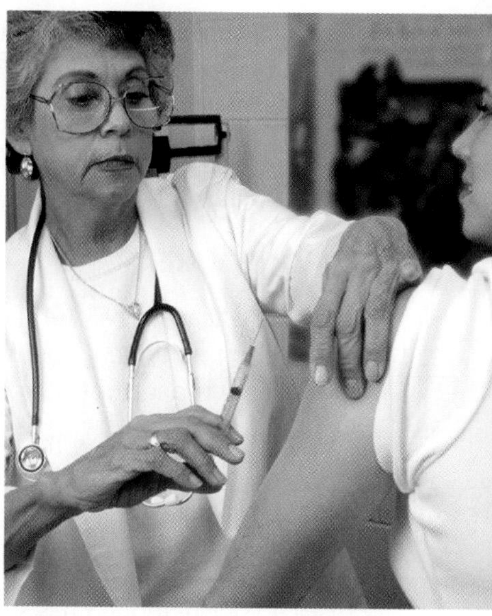

COMPARE A doctor gives a girl a vaccination. Is getting a vaccination an example of passive or active immunity?

After your body has destroyed a specific pathogen, B cells that fight that pathogen remain in your system. If the same pathogen were to enter your body again, your immune system would almost certainly destroy it before you became ill. This resistance to a sickness is called **immunity.**

Immunity takes two forms: passive and active. When babies are first born, they have only the immune defenses transferred to them by their mothers. They have not had the chance to develop antibodies of their own. This type of immunity is called passive immunity. Antibodies are not produced by the person's own body but given to the body from another source. Babies develop their own antibodies after a few months.

You have active immunity whenever your body makes its own antibodies. Your body will again fight against any specific pathogen you have developed antibodies against. For example, it is most unlikely that you will get chicken pox twice.

What is the difference between active and passive immunity?

## Most diseases can be prevented or treated.

Given enough time, your immune system will fight off most diseases. However, some infections can cause significant and lasting damage before they are defeated by the body's defenses. Other infections are so strong that the immune system cannot successfully fight them. Medical advances in the prevention and treatment of diseases have reduced the risks of many serious illnesses.

### Vaccination

Another way to develop an immunity is to receive a **vaccine.** Vaccines contain small amounts of weakened or dead pathogens that stimulate an immune response. Your B cells are called into action to create antibodies as if you were fighting the real illness. The pathogens are usually weakened or dead so that you will not get sick, yet they still enable your body to develop an active immunity.

Today we have vaccines for many common pathogens. Most children who are vaccinated will not get many diseases that their great grandparents, grandparents, and even parents had. Vaccinations can be administered by injection or by mouth. Babies are not the only ones who get them, either. You can be vaccinated at any age.

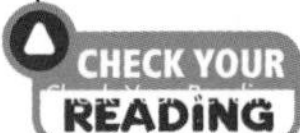


Why don't vaccinations usually make you sick?

## Treatment

Not all diseases can be prevented, but many of them can be treated. In some cases, treatments can only reduce the symptoms of the disease while the immune system fights the disease-causing pathogens. Other treatments attack the pathogens directly.

In some cases, treatment can only prevent further damage to body tissues by a pathogen that cannot be cured or defeated by the immune system. The way in which a disease is treated depends on what pathogen causes it. Many bacterial infections can be treated with antibiotics. **Antibiotics** are medicines that block the growth and reproduction of bacteria. You may have taken antibiotics when you have had a disease such as strep throat or an ear infection. Other types of medicine can help fight infections caused by viruses, fungi, and parasites.

**Types of Pathogens**

| Disease | Pathogen |
|---|---|
| Colds, chicken pox, hepatitis, AIDS, influenza, mumps, measles, rabies | virus |
| Food poisoning, strep throat, tetanus, tuberculosis, acne, ulcers, Lyme disease | bacteria |
| Athlete's foot, thrush, ringworm | fungus |
| Malaria, parasitic pneumonia, pinworm, scabies | parasites |

# 3.2 Review

### KEY CONCEPTS

1. Make a chart showing three ways that foreign material enters the body and how the immune system defends against each type of attack.
2. What are white blood cells and what is their function in the body?
3. What are two ways to develop immunity?

### CRITICAL THINKING

4. **Compare and Contrast** Make a chart comparing B cells and T cells. Include an explanation of the function of antibodies.
5. **Apply** Describe how your immune system responds when you scrape your knee.

### CHALLENGE

6. **Hypothesize** Explain why, even if a person recovers from a cold, that person could get a cold again.

SKILL: MAKING A LINE GRAPH

MATH TUTORIAL
CLASSZONE.COM
Click on Math Tutorial for more help making line graphs.

# Pollen Counts

Every year, sometime between July and October, in nearly every state in the United States, the air will fill with ragweed pollen. For a person who has a pollen allergy, these months blur with tears. Linn County, Iowa, takes weekly counts of ragweed and non-ragweed pollen.

**Weekly Pollen Counts, Linn County, Iowa**

| | Jul. 29 | Aug. 5 | Aug. 12 | Aug. 19 | Aug. 26 | Sept. 2 | Sept. 9 | Sept. 16 | Sept. 23 | Sept. 30 | Oct. 7 |
|---|---|---|---|---|---|---|---|---|---|---|---|
| Ragweed (Grain/$m^3$) | 0 | 9 | 10 | 250 | 130 | 240 | 140 | 25 | 20 | 75 | 0 |
| Non-Ragweed (Grain/$m^3$) | 10 | 45 | 15 | 50 | 100 | 50 | 40 | 10 | 20 | 25 | 0 |

## Example

A line graph of the data will show the pattern of increase and decrease of ragweed pollen in the air.

**(1)** Begin with a quadrant with horizontal and vertical axes.

**(2)** Mark the weekly dates at even intervals on the horizontal axis.

**(3)** Starting at 0 on the vertical axis, mark even intervals of 50 units.

**(4)** Graph each point. Connect the points with line segments.

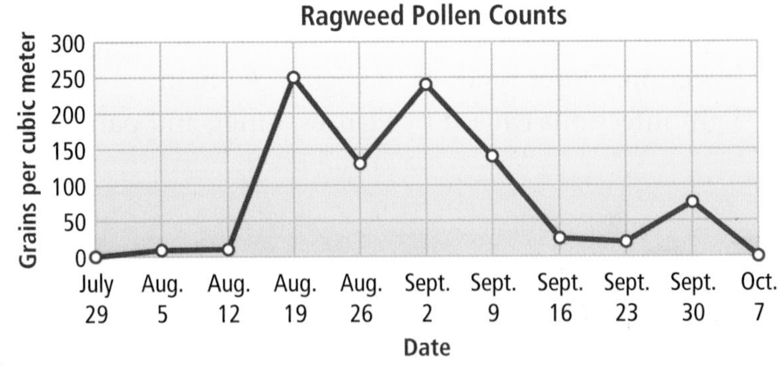


**Complete and present your graph as directed below.**

1. Use graph paper to make your own line graph of the non-ragweed pollen in Linn County.
2. Write some questions that can be answered by comparing the two graphs. Trade questions with a partner.
3. Which weeks have the highest pollen counts in Linn County?

**CHALLENGE** Try making a double line graph combining both sets of data in one graph.

The pollen of *Ambrosia artemisiifolia* (common ragweed) sets off a sneeze.

KEY CONCEPT

# The integumentary system shields the body.

**BEFORE, you learned**

- The body is defended from harmful materials
- Response structures fight disease
- The immune system responds in many ways to illness

**NOW, you will learn**

- About the functions of the skin
- How the skin helps protect the body
- How the skin grows and heals

**VOCABULARY**

**integumentary system** p. 83
**epidermis** p. 84
**dermis** p. 84

**EXPLORE The Skin**

### *What are the functions of skin?*

**PROCEDURE**

1. Using a vegetable peeler, remove the skin from an apple. Take notes on the characteristics of the apple's peeled surface. Include observations on its color, moisture level, and texture.
2. Place the apple on a dry surface. After fifteen minutes, note any changes in its characteristics.

**WHAT DO YOU THINK?**

- What is the function of an apple's skin? What does it prevent?
- What does this experiment suggest about how skin might function in the human body?

**MATERIALS**

- vegetable peeler
- apple

## Skin performs important functions.

**MAIN IDEA AND DETAILS**
Start a two-column chart with the main idea *Skin performs important functions.* Add detail notes about those functions.

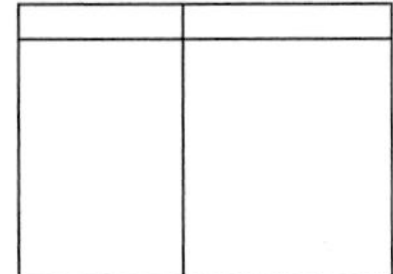

Just as an apple's skin protects the fruit inside, your skin protects the rest of your body. Made up of flat sheets of cells, your skin protects the inside of your body from harmful materials outside. The skin is part of your body's **integumentary system** (ihn-TEHG-yu-MEHN-tuh-ree), which also includes your hair and nails.

Your skin fulfills several vital functions:

- Skin repels water.
- Skin guards against infection.
- Skin helps maintain homeostasis.
- Skin senses the environment.

## Skin Structure

**When you look at your hand, you only see the outer layer of skin. The skin has many structures to protect your body.**

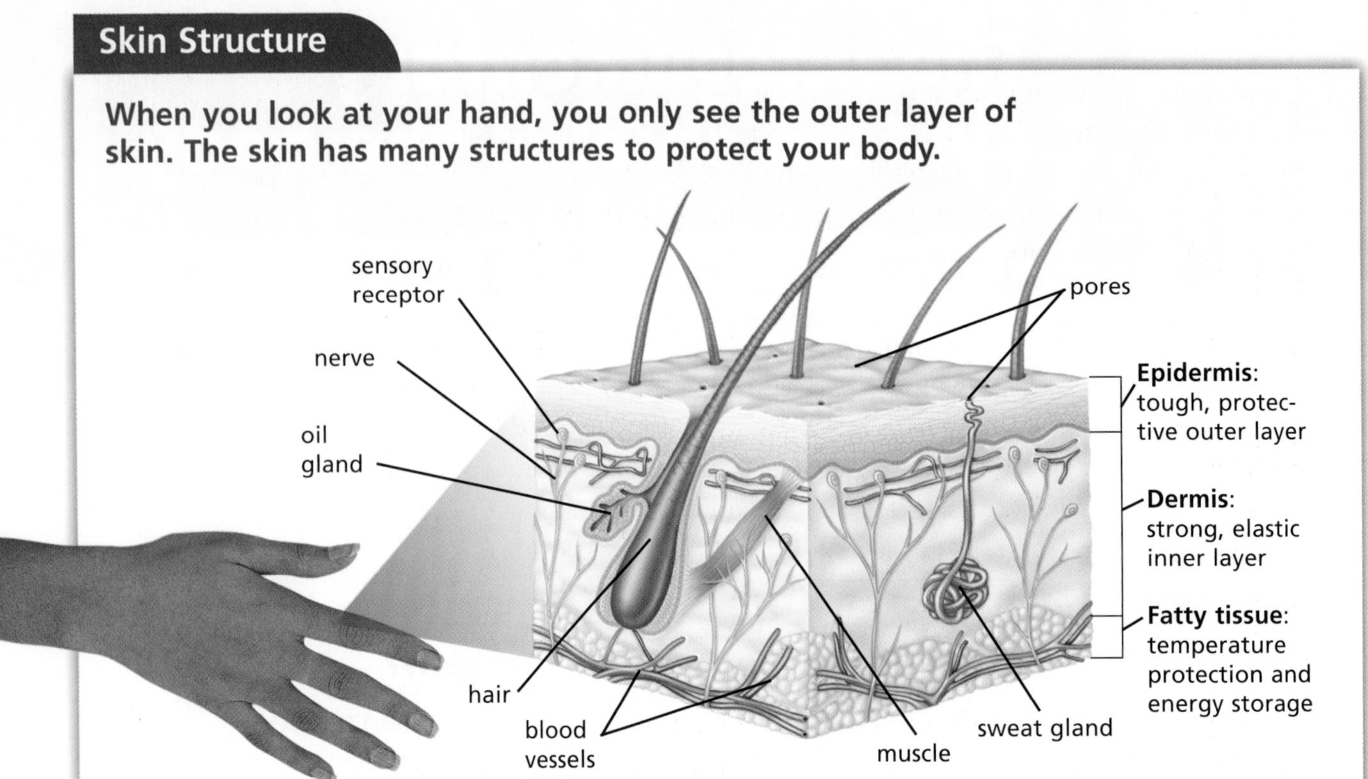


# The structure of skin is complex.

Have you ever looked closely at your skin? Your skin is more complex than it might at first seem. It does more than just cover your body. The skin is made up of many structures, which perform many different jobs.

## Dermis and Epidermis

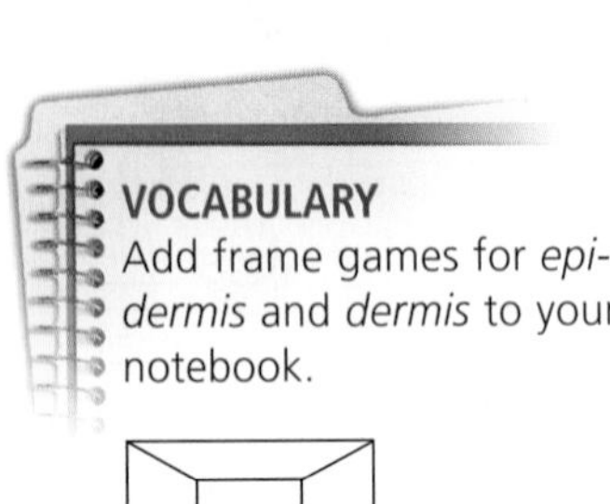

VOCABULARY
Add frame games for *epidermis* and *dermis* to your notebook.

As you can see in the diagram above, human skin is composed of two layers: an outer layer, called the **epidermis,** and an inner layer, called the **dermis.** The cells of the epidermis contain many protein fibers that give the skin tough, protective qualities. These cells are formed in the deepest part of the epidermis. Skin cells move upward slowly as new cells form below them. Above new cells, older cells rub off. The surface cells in the epidermis are dead but form a thick, waterproof layer about 30 cells deep.

The dermis, the inner layer of skin, is made of tissue that is strong and elastic. The structure of the dermis allows it to change shape instead of tear when it moves against surfaces. The dermis is rich in blood vessels, which supply oxygen and nutrients to the skin's living cells. Just beneath the dermis lies a layer of fatty tissue. This layer protects the body from extremes in temperature, and it stores energy for future use. Also in the dermis are structures that have special functions, including sweat and oil glands, hair, nails, and sensory receptors.

## Sweat and Oil Glands

Deep within the dermis are structures that help maintain your body's internal environment. Sweat glands help control body temperature, and oil glands protect the skin by keeping it moist. Both types of glands open to the surface through tiny openings in the skin called pores. Pores allow important substances to pass to the skin's surface. Pores can become clogged with dirt and oil. Keeping the skin clean can prevent blockages.

Explore the structure of skin.

Sweat glands, which are present almost everywhere on the body's surface, help maintain homeostasis. When you become too warm, the sweat glands secrete sweat, a fluid that is 99% water. This fluid travels from the sweat glands, through the pores, and onto the skin's surface. You probably know already about evaporation. Evaporation is the process by which a liquid becomes a gas. During evaporation, heat is released. Thus, sweating cools the skin's surface and the body.

Like sweat glands, oil glands are present almost everywhere on the body. They secrete an oil that moistens skin and hair and keeps them from becoming dry. Skin oils add flexibility and provide part, but not all, of the skin's waterproofing.

**CHECK YOUR READING** What are the functions of oil glands?

# INVESTIGATE Skin Protection

### *How does oil protect your skin?*

**PROCEDURE**

1. Rub a cotton ball dampened with alcohol across one of your palms. Alcohol removes the oil from the surface of your skin.
2. Drip a couple of drops of water onto the palm with alcohol. Observe what happens. Record your observations.
3. Drip a couple of drops of water onto your other palm. Observe what happens. Record your observations.

**WHAT DO YOU THINK?**

- Compare the observations for each palm.
- What does this investigation suggest about the importance of oil and oil glands?

**CHALLENGE** Predict what might happen to your skin if you removed every trace of oil several times a day.

**SKILL FOCUS**
Observing

**MATERIALS**
- cotton ball
- rubbing alcohol
- dropper
- water

**TIME**
10 minutes

## Hair and Nails

In addition to your skin, your integumentary system includes your hair and nails. Many cells in your hair and nails are actually dead but continue to perform important functions.

The hair on your head helps your body in many ways. When you are outside, it shields your head from the Sun. In cold weather, it traps heat close to your head to keep you warmer. Your body hair works the same way, but it is much less effective at protecting your skin and keeping you warm.

Fingernails and toenails protect the tips of the fingers and toes from injury. Both are made of epidermal cells that are thick and tough. They grow from the nail bed, which continues to manufacture cells as the cells that form the nail bond together and grow.

**CHECK YOUR READING** What are the functions of hair and nails?

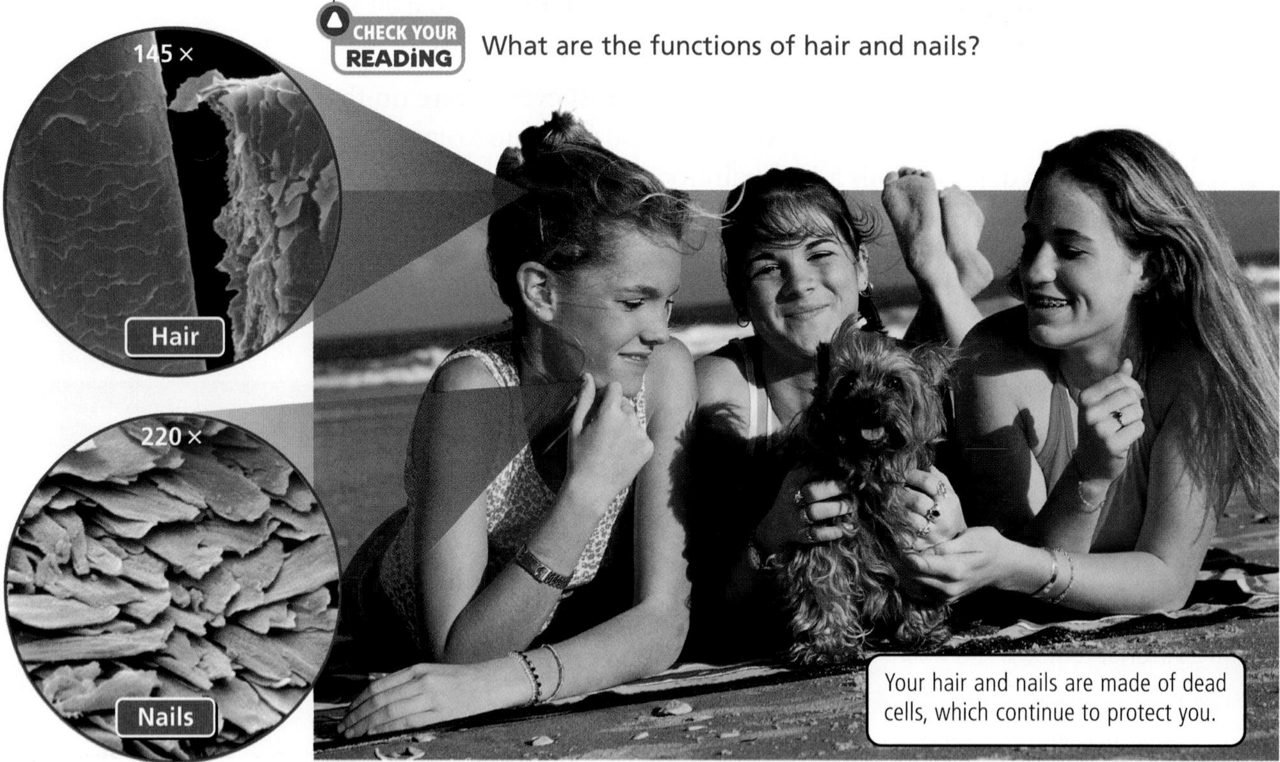

Your hair and nails are made of dead cells, which continue to protect you.

## Sensory Receptors

How does your body know when you are touching something too hot or too cold? You get that information from sensory receptors attached to the nerves. These receptors are actually part of the nervous system, but they are located in your skin. Your skin contains receptors that sense heat, cold, pain, touch, and pressure. These sensors help protect the body. For example, temperature receptors sense when an object is hot. If it is too hot and you touch it, pain receptors send signals to your brain telling you that you have been burned.

**CHECK YOUR READING** What are the five types of sensory receptors in skin?

## The skin grows and heals.

As a person grows, skin also grows. As you have noticed if you have ever had a bruise or a cut, your skin is capable of healing. Skin can often repair itself after injury or illness.

### Growth

As your bones grow, you get taller. As your muscles develop, your arms and legs become thicker. Through all your body's growth and change, your skin has to grow, too.

Most of the growth of your skin occurs at the base of the epidermis, just above the dermis. The cells there grow and divide to form new cells, constantly replacing older epidermal cells as they die and are brushed off during daily activity. Cells are lost from the skin's surface all the time: every 2 to 4 weeks, your skin surface is entirely new. In fact, a percentage of household dust is actually dead skin cells.

**Healing Skin**

**Small injuries to the skin heal by themselves over time.**

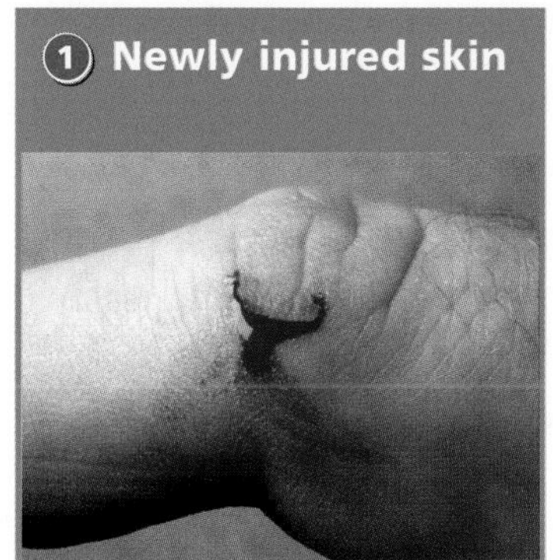


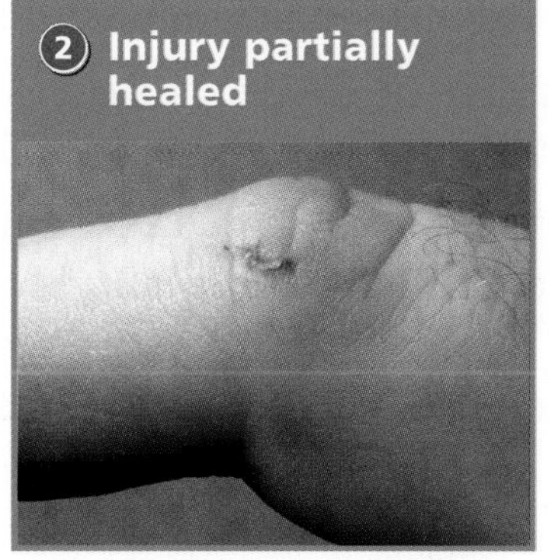


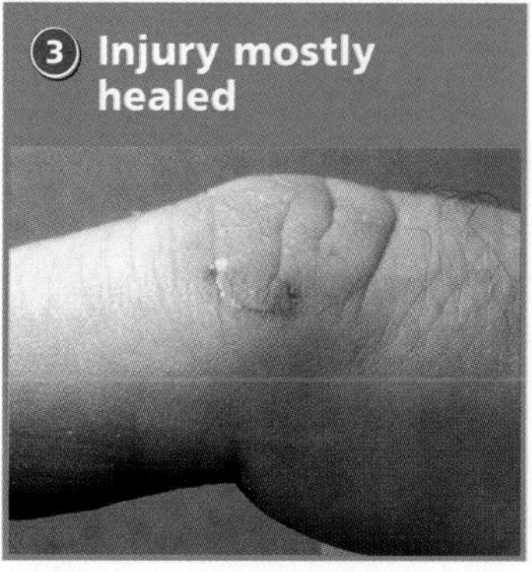


READING VISUALS How do you think small injuries to the skin heal?

### Injuries and Healing

You have probably experienced some injuries to your skin, such as blisters, burns, cuts, and bruises. Most such injuries result from the skin's contact with the outside world, such as a concrete sidewalk. In simple injuries, the skin can usually repair itself.

Explore how the skin heals.

Burns can be serious injuries. They can be caused by heat, electricity, radiation, or certain chemicals. In mild cases—those of first-degree burns—skin merely becomes red, and the burn heals in a day or two. In severe cases—those of second-degree and third-degree burns—the body loses fluids, and death can result from fluid loss, infection, and other complications.

Sunburns are usually minor first-degree burns, but that does not mean they cannot be serious. Rays from the Sun can burn and blister the skin much as a hot object can. Repeated burning can increase the chance of skin cancer. Specialized cells in the skin make a pigment that absorbs the Sun's ultraviolet rays and helps prevent tissue damage. These cells produce more of the skin pigment melanin when exposed to the Sun. The amount of melanin in your skin determines how dark your skin is.

Severe cold can damage skin as well. Skin exposed to cold weather can get frostbite, a condition in which the cells are damaged by freezing. Mild frostbite often heals just as well as a minor cut. In extreme cases, frostbitten limbs become diseased and have to be amputated.

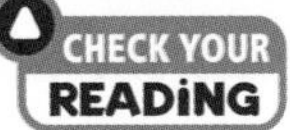

What types of weather can damage your skin?

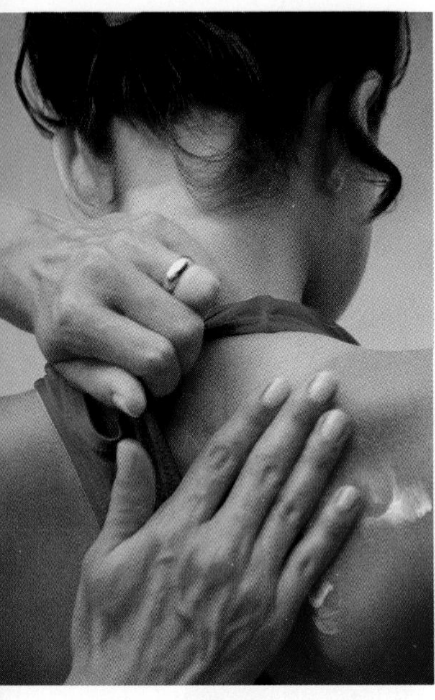
Wearing sunblock when you are outside protects your skin from harmful rays from the Sun.

## Protection

Your skin is constantly losing old cells and gaining new cells. Although your skin is always changing, it is still important to take care of it.

- Good nutrition supplies materials the skin uses to maintain and repair itself. By drinking water, you help your body, and thus your skin, to remain moist and able to replace lost cells.
- Appropriate coverings, such as sunblock in summer and warm clothes in winter, can protect the skin from weather damage.
- Skin also needs to be kept clean. Many harmful bacteria cannot enter the body through healthy skin, but they should be washed off regularly. This prevents them from multiplying and then entering the body through small cuts or scrapes.

# 3.3 Review

### KEY CONCEPTS

1. List four functions of the skin.
2. How do the epidermis and dermis protect the body?
3. Make your own diagram with *How skin grows and repairs itself* at the center. Around the center, write at least five facts about skin growth and healing.

### CRITICAL THINKING

4. **Apply** Give three examples from everyday life of sensory receptors in your skin reacting to changes in your environment.
5. **Connect** Describe a situation in which sensory receptors could be critical to survival.

### CHALLENGE

6. **Infer** Exposure to sunlight may increase the number of freckles on a person's skin. Explain the connection between sunlight, melanin, and freckles.

A spray-on polymer creates an artificial outer skin to help heal surface wounds on an arm.

GROWING NEW SKIN

# Artificial Skin

Skin acts like a barrier, keeping our insides in and infections out. Nobody can survive without skin. But when a large amount of skin is severely damaged, the body cannot work fast enough to replace it. In some cases there isn't enough undamaged skin left on the body for transplanting. Using skin from another person risks introducing infections or rejection by the body. The answer? Artificial skin.

## Here's the Skinny

To make artificial skin, scientists start with cells in a tiny skin sample. Cells from infants are used because infant skin-cell molecules are still developing, and scientists can manipulate the molecules to avoid transplant rejection. The cells from just one small sample of skin can be grown into enough artificial skin to cover 15 basketball courts. Before artificial skin, badly burned victims didn't have much chance to live. Today, 96 out of 100 burn victims survive.

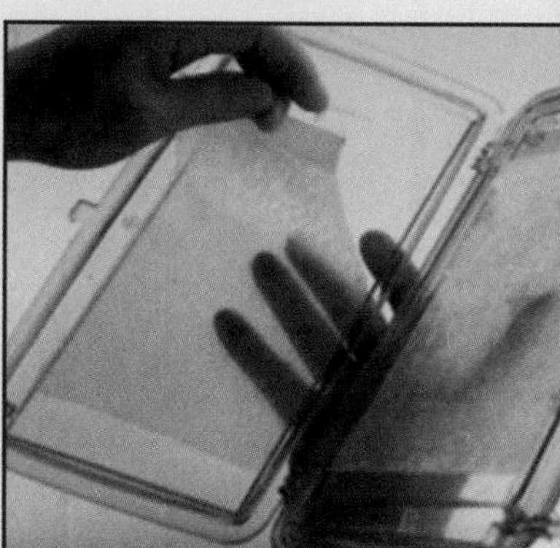

A surgeon lifts a layer of artificial skin. The skin is so thin, a newspaper could be read behind it.

## What's Next?

- Scientists are hoping to be able to grow organs using this technology. Someday artificially grown livers, kidneys, and hearts may take the place of transplants and mechanical devices.
- A self-repairing plastic skin that knits itself back together when cracked has been developed. It may someday be used to create organs or even self-repairing rocket and spacecraft parts.
- Artificial polymer "skin" for robots is being developed to help robots do delicate work such as microsurgery or space exploration.

Robot designer David Hanson has developed the K-bot, a lifelike face that uses 24 motors to create expressions.

## EXPLORE

1. **COMPARE AND CONTRAST** Detail the advantages and disadvantages of skin transplanted from another place on the body and artificial skin.
2. **CHALLENGE** Artificial skin is being considered for applications beyond those originally envisioned. Research and present a new potential application.

# 3 Chapter Review

## the BIG idea

**Systems function to transport materials and to defend and protect the body.**

### 3.1 The circulatory system transports materials.

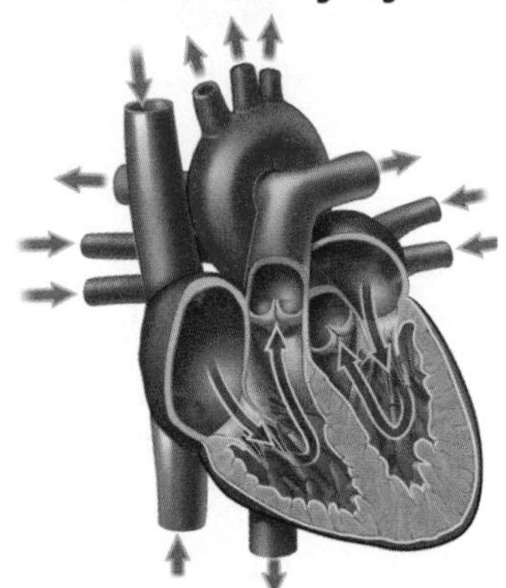

The heart, blood vessels, and blood of the circulatory system work together to transport materials from the digestive and respiratory systems to all cells. The blood exerts pressure on the walls of the blood vessels as the heart keeps the blood moving through the body.

**VOCABULARY**
**circulatory system** p. 65
**blood** p. 65
**red blood cell** p. 67
**artery** p. 69
**vein p.** 69
**capillary** p. 69

### 3.2 The immune system defends the body.

The immune system defends the body from pathogens. White blood cells identify and attack pathogens that find their way inside the body. The immune system responds to attack with inflammation, fever, and development of immunity.

**Types of Pathogens**

| Disease | Pathogen |
|---|---|
| colds, chicken pox, hepatitis, AIDS, influenza, mumps, measles, rabies | virus |
| food poisoning, strep throat, tetanus, tuberculosis, acne, ulcers, Lyme disease | bacteria |
| athlete's foot, thrush, ring worm | fungus |
| malaria, parasitic pneumonia, pinworm, scabies | parasites |

**VOCABULARY**
**pathogen** p. 74
**immune system** p. 75
**antibody** p. 75
**antigen** p. 78
**immunity** p. 80
**vaccine** p. 80
**antibiotic** p. 81

### 3.3 The integumentary system shields the body.

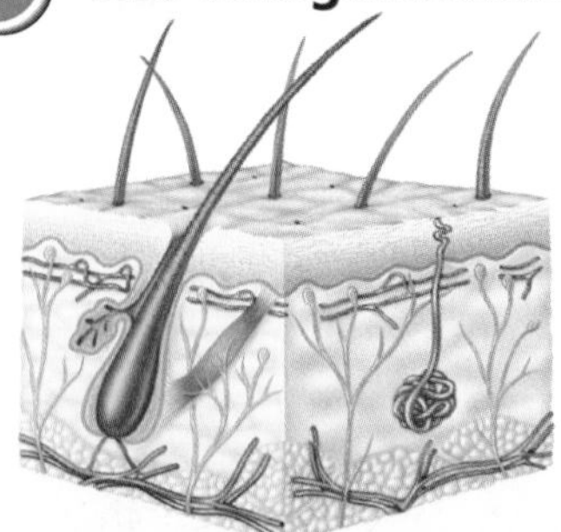

The skin protects the body from harmful materials in the environment, and allows you to sense temperature, pain, touch, and pressure. In most cases the skin is able to heal itself after injury.

**VOCABULARY**
**integumentary system** p. 83
**epidermis** p. 84
**dermis** p. 84

## Reviewing Vocabulary

*Draw a word triangle for each of the terms below. Write a term and its definition in the bottom section. In the middle section, write a sentence in which you use the term correctly. In the top section, draw a small picture to illustrate the term.*

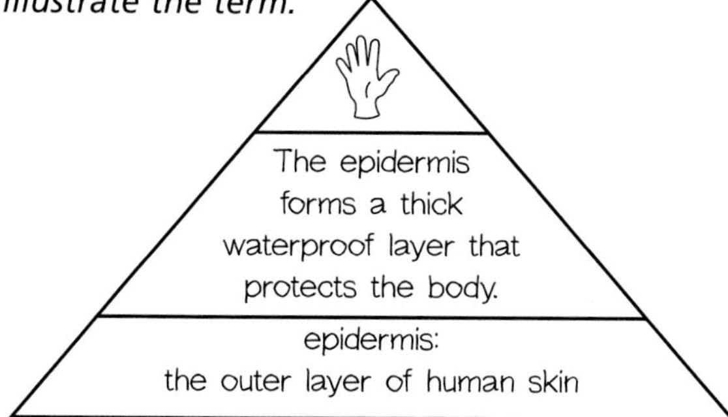

The epidermis forms a thick waterproof layer that protects the body.
epidermis:
the outer layer of human skin


**1.** capillary

**2.** blood

**3.** dermis

**4.** antigen

*Write a sentence describing the relationship between each pair of terms.*

**5.** pathogen, antibody

**6.** artery, vein

**7.** immunity, vaccine

## Reviewing Key Concepts

**Multiple Choice** *Choose the letter of the best answer.*

**8.** Which chamber of the heart pumps oxygen-poor blood into the lungs?
- **a.** right atrium
- **b.** right ventricle
- **c.** left atrium
- **d.** left ventricle

**9.** Which structures carry blood back to the heart?
- **a.** veins
- **b.** capillaries
- **c.** arteries
- **d.** platelets

**10.** The structures in the blood that carry oxygen to the cells of the body are the
- **a.** plasma
- **b.** platelets
- **c.** white blood cells
- **d.** red blood cells

**11.** High blood pressure is unhealthy because it
- **a.** does not exert enough pressure on your arteries
- **b.** causes your heart to work harder
- **c.** does not allow enough oxygen to get to the cells in your body
- **d.** causes your veins to collapse

**12.** Which category of pathogens causes strep throat?
- **a.** virus
- **b.** bacteria
- **c.** fungus
- **d.** parasite

**13.** Which of the following is a function of white blood cells?
- **a.** destroying foreign organisms
- **b.** providing your body with nutrients
- **c.** carrying oxygen to the body's cells
- **d.** forming a blood clot

**14.** Which makes up the integumentary system?
- **a.** a network of nerves
- **b.** white blood cells and antibodies
- **c.** the brain and spinal cord
- **d.** the skin, hair, and nails

**15.** Which structure is found in the epidermis layer of the skin?
- **a.** pores
- **b.** sweat glands
- **c.** hair follicles
- **d.** oil glands

**16.** The layer of fatty tissue below the dermis protects the body from
- **a.** cold temperatures
- **b.** bacteria
- **c.** sunburn
- **d.** infection

**Short Answer** *Write a short answer to each question.*

**17.** What are platelets? Where are they found?

**18.** What are antibodies? Where are they found?

**19.** What special structures are found in the dermis layer of the skin?

## Thinking Critically

20. **COMPARE AND CONTRAST** How do the functions of the atria and ventricles of the heart differ? How are they alike? Use this diagram of the heart as a guide.

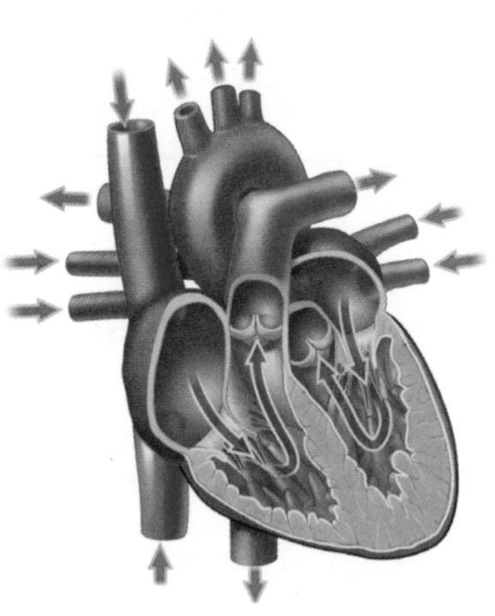

21. **APPLY** Veins have one-way valves that prevent the blood from flowing backwards. Most arteries do not have valves. Explain how these structures help the circulatory system function.

22. **PROVIDE EXAMPLES** Describe three structures in the body that help prevent harmful foreign substances from entering the body.

23. **IDENTIFY CAUSE** HIV is a virus that attacks and destroys the body's T cells. Why is a person who is infected with HIV more susceptible to infection and disease?

24. **APPLY** You fall and scrape your knee. How does the production of histamines aid the healing of this injury?

25. **ANALYZE** Describe how the structure of the epidermis helps protect the body from disease.

26. **SYNTHESIZE** Explain how sweat glands, oil glands, and hair help your body maintain homeostasis.

27. **HYPOTHESIZE** People with greater concentrations of melanin in their skin are less likely to get skin cancer than people who have lesser concentrations of melanin. Write a hypothesis explaining why this is so.

*Answer the next six questions by listing the main structures and functions of the systems shown in the graphic organizer.*

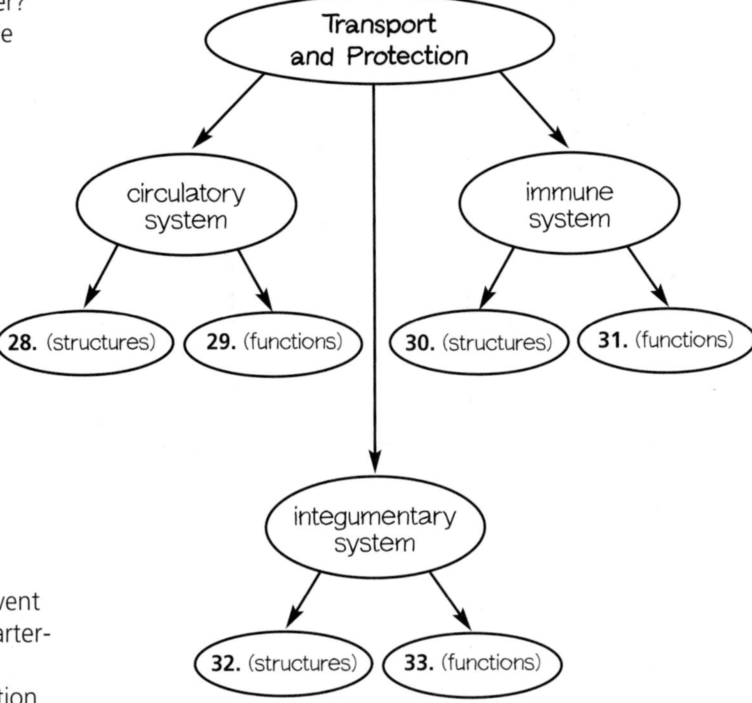


## the BIG idea

34. **INFER** Look again at the picture on pages 62–63. Now that you have finished the chapter, how would you change or add details to your answer to the question on the photograph?

35. **SYNTHESIZE** Write a paragraph explaining how the integumentary system and the immune system work together to help your body maintain its homeostasis. Underline these terms in your paragraph.

## UNIT PROJECTS

If you need to create graphs or other visuals for your project, be sure you have grid paper, poster board, markers, and other supplies.

# Standardized Test Practice

For practice on your state test, go to . . .
TEST PRACTICE
CLASSZONE.COM

## Analyzing Data

*Choose the letter of the best answer.*

This chart shows the amount of time a person can stay in sunlight without burning, based on skin type and use of a sunscreen with the SPF shown.

**Minimum Sun Protection Factors (SPF)**

| Skin Type | 1 hr | 2 hr | 3 hr | 4 hr | 5 hr |
|---|---|---|---|---|---|
| Very Fair/ Sensitive | 15 | 30 | 30 | 45 | 45 |
| Fair/Sensitive | 15 | 15 | 30 | 30 | 45 |
| Fair | 15 | 15 | 15 | 30 | 30 |
| Medium | 8 | 8 | 15 | 15 | 30 |
| Dark | 4 | 8 | 8 | 15 | 15 |

**1.** What is the least SPF that a person with very fair skin should use while exposed to the sun?

**a.** 8
**b.** 15
**c.** 30
**d.** 45

**2.** If a person with a medium skin type is exposed to sunlight for 5 hours, which SPF should be used?

**a.** 4
**b.** 8
**c.** 15
**d.** 30

**3.** Which skin type requires SPF 30 for three hours of sun exposure?

**a.** fair/sensitive
**b.** fair
**c.** medium
**d.** dark

**4.** Based on the data in the chart, which statement is a reasonable conclusion?

**a.** People with a fair skin type are less prone to UV damage than those with a dark skin type.
**b.** The darker the skin type, the more SPF protection a person needs.
**c.** A person with a fair skin type does not need as much SPF protection as a person with a medium skin type.
**d.** If exposure to sunlight is longer, then a person needs a higher SPF for protection.

**5.** If a person normally burns after 10 minutes with no protection, an SPF 2 would protect that person for 20 minutes. How long would the same person be protected with SPF 15?

**a.** 1 hour
**b.** $1\frac{1}{2}$ hours
**c.** 2 hours
**d.** $2\frac{1}{2}$ hours

## Extended Response

**6.** UV index levels are often broadcast with daily weather reports. A UV index of 0 to 2 indicates that it would take an average person about 60 minutes to burn. A UV index level of 10 indicates that it would take the average person about 10 minutes to burn. Write a paragraph describing some variable conditions that would affect this rate. Include both environmental as well as conditions that would apply to an individual.

**7.** Sun protection factors are numbers on a scale that rate the effectiveness of sunscreen. Without the use of sunscreen, UV rays from the Sun can cause sunburns. People who spend time in sunlight without protection, or who get repeated burns are at a higher risk of developing deadly forms of skin cancer. Based on the information in the table and your knowledge of the layers of the skin, design a brochure encouraging people to protect their skin from sunlight. Include in your brochure the harmful effects on your skin and ways to protect your skin from harmful UV rays.

# TIMELINES in Science

## SEEING INSIDE the Body

What began as a chance accident in a darkened room was only the beginning. Today, technology allows people to produce clear and complete pictures of the human body. From X-rays to ultrasound to the latest computerized scans, accidental discoveries have enabled us to study and diagnose the inner workings of the human body.

Being able to see inside the body without cutting it open would have seemed unthinkable in the early 1890s. But within a year of the discovery of the X-ray in 1895, doctors were using technology to see through flesh to bones. In the time since then, techniques for making images have advanced to allow doctors to see soft tissue, muscle, and even to see how body systems work in real time. Many modern imaging techniques employ X-ray technology, while others employ sound waves or magnetic fields.

**1895**

***Accidental X-Ray Shows Bones***

Working alone in a darkened lab to study electric currents passing through vacuum tubes, William Conrad Roentgen sees a mysterious light. He puts his hand between the tubes and a screen, and an image appears on the screen—a skeletal hand! He names his discovery the X-ray, since the images are produced by rays behaving like none known before them. Roentgen uses photographic paper to take the first X-ray picture, his wife's hand.

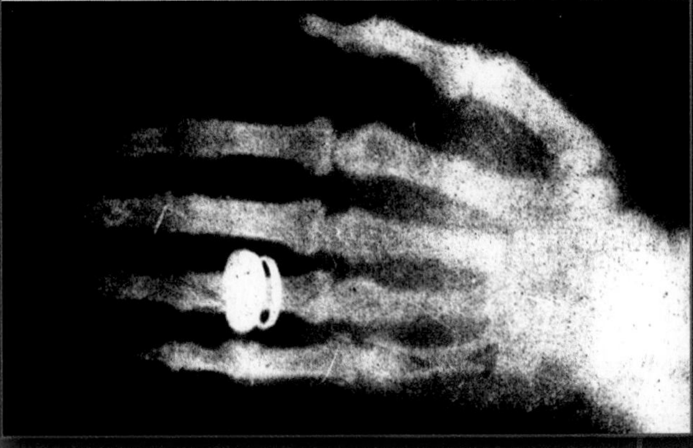

### EVENTS

1880 1890

### APPLICATIONS AND TECHNOLOGY

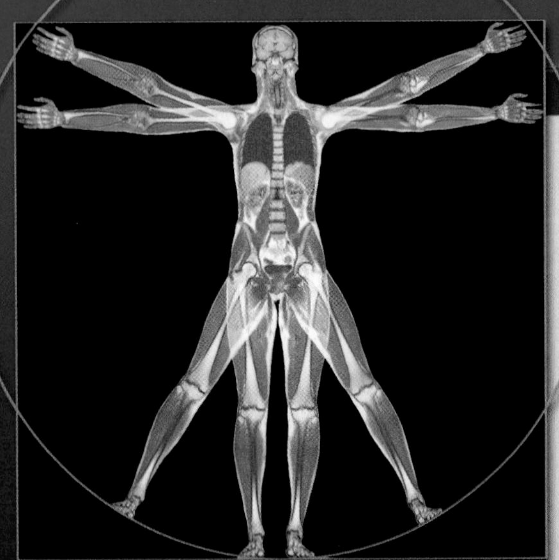

**APPLICATION**

**Doctor Detectives**

Within a year of Roentgen's discovery, X-rays were used in medicine for examining patients. By the 1920s, their use was wide-spread. Modern day X-ray tubes are based on the design of William Coolidge. Around 1913, Coolidge developed a new X-ray tube which, unlike the old gas tube, provides consistent exposure and quality. X-ray imaging changed the practice of medicine by allowing doctors to look inside the body without using surgery. Today, X-ray images, and other technologies, like the MRI used to produce the image at the left, show bones, organs, and tissues.

**1914–1918**

***Radiologists in the Trenches***

In World War I field hospitals, French physicians use X-ray technology to quickly diagnose war injuries. Marie Curie trains the majority of the female X-ray technicians. Following the war, doctors return to their practices with new expertise.

**1898**

***Radioactivity***

Building on the work of Henri Becquerel, who in 1897 discovers "rays" from uranium, physicist Marie Curie discovers radioactivity. She wins a Nobel Prize in Chemistry in 1911 for her work in radiology.

**1955**

***See-Through Smile***

X-ray images of the entire jaw and teeth allow dentist to check the roots of teeth and wisdom teeth growing below the gum line.

1900 1910 1950

## APPLICATION

### Better Dental Work

Throughout the 1940s and 1950s dentists began to use X-rays. Photographing teeth with an X-ray allows cavities or decay to show up as dark spots on a white tooth. Photographing below the gum line shows dentists the pattern of growth of new teeth. By 1955, dentists could take a panoramic X-ray, one which shows the entire jaw. In the early years of dental X-rays, little was known about the dangers of radiation. Today, dentists cover a patient with a lead apron to protect them from harmful rays.

**1976**

### *New Scans Show Blood Vessels*

The first computerized tomography (CT) systems scan only the head, but whole-body scanners follow by 1976. With the CT scan, doctors see clear details of blood vessels, bones, and soft organs. Instead of sending out a single X-ray, a CT scan sends several beams from different angles. Then a computer joins the images, as shown in this image of a heart.

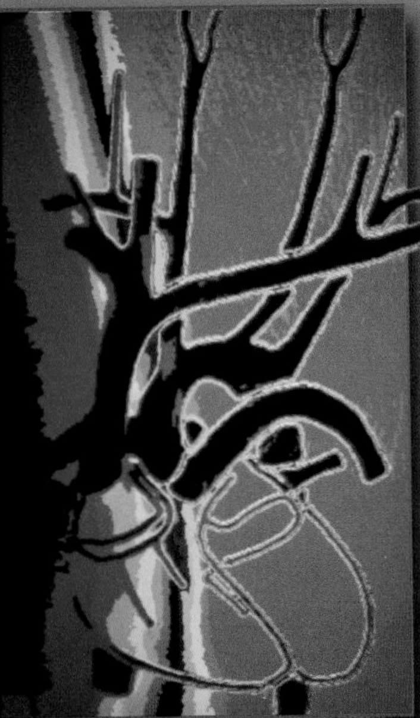

**1977**

### *Minus the X-ray*

Doctors Raymond Damadian, Larry Minkoff, and Michael Goldsmith, develop the first magnetic resonance imaging (MRI). They nick-name the new machine "The Indomitable," as everyone told them it couldn't be done. MRI allows doctors to "see" soft tissue, like the knee below, in sharp detail without the use of X-rays.

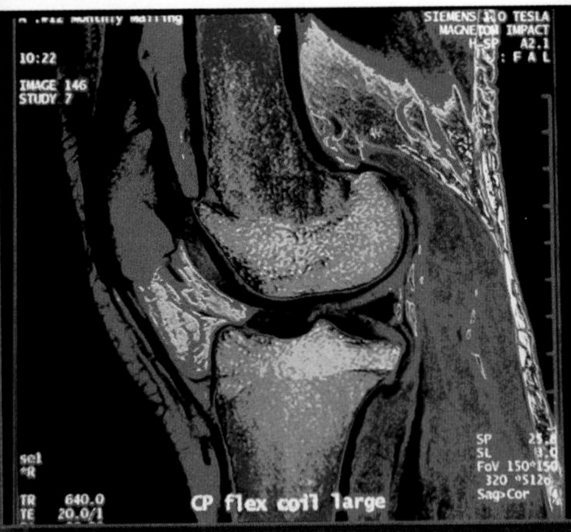


**1973**

### *PET Shows What's Working*

The first positron emission tomography machine is called PET Scanner 1. It uses small doses of radioactive dye which travel through a patient's bloodstream. A PET scan then shows the distribution of the dye.

1960 1970 1980

## TECHNOLOGY

### Ultrasound: Moving Images in Real Time

Since the late 1950s, Ian Donald's team in Scotland had been viewing internal organs on a TV monitor using vibrations faster than sound. In 1961, while examining a female patient, Donald noticed a developing embryo. Following the discovery, ultrasound imaging became widely used to monitor the growth and health of fetuses. Ultrasound captures images in real-time, showing movement of internal tissues and organs. Ultrasound uses high frequency sound waves to create images of organs or structures inside the body. Sound waves are bounced back from organs, and a computer converts the sound waves into moving images on a television monitor.

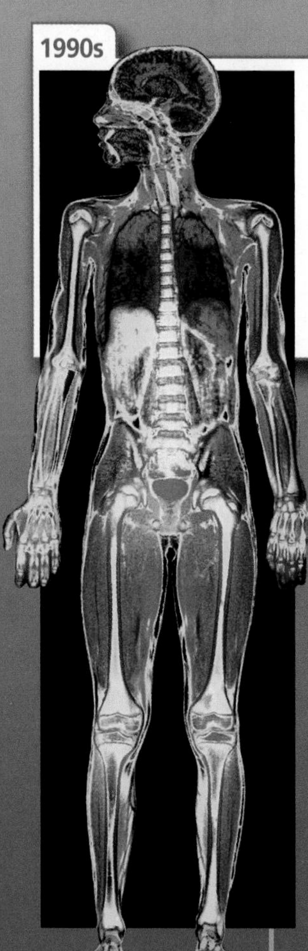

1990s

*Filmless Images*

With digital imaging, everything from X-rays to MRIs is now filmless. Data move directly into 3-D computer programs and shared databases.

2003

*Multi-Slice CT*

By 2003, 8- and 16-slice CT scanners offer detail and speed. A multi-slice scanner reduces exam time from 45 minutes to under 10 seconds.

RESOURCE CENTER
CLASSZONE.COM

Find more on advances in medical imaging.

1990 2000

## TECHNOLOGY

### 3-D Images and Brain Surgery

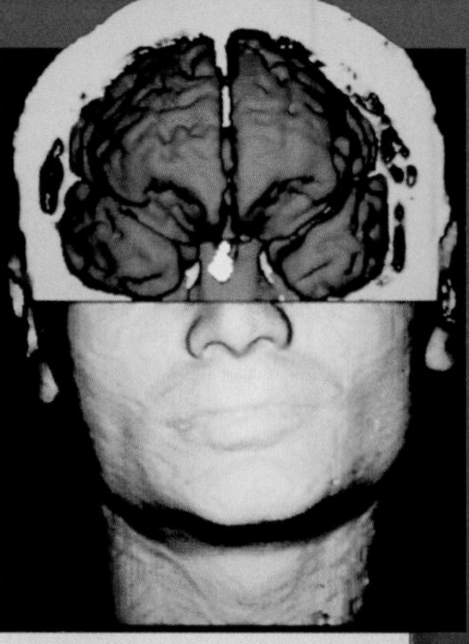

In operating rooms, surgeons are beginning to use another type of 3-D ultrasound known as interventional MRI. They watch 3-D images in real time and observe details of tissues while they operate. These integrated technologies now allow scientists to conduct entirely new types of studies. For example, 3-D brain images of many patients with one disease—can now be integrated into a composite image of a "typical" brain of someone with that disease.

## INTO THE FUTURE

Although discovered over 100 years ago X-rays are certain to remain a key tool of health workers for many years. What will be different in the future? Dentists have begun the trend to stop using film images, and rely on digital X-rays instead. In the future, all scans may be viewed and stored on computers. Going digital allows doctors across the globe to share images quickly by email.

Magnetic resonance imaging has only been in widespread use for about 20 years. Look for increased brain mapping—ability to scan the brain during a certain task. The greater the collective data on brain-mapping, the better scientists will understand how the brain works. To produce such an image requires thousands of patients and trillions of bytes of computer memory.

Also look for increased speed and mobile MRI scanners, which will be used in emergency rooms and doctor's offices to quickly assess internal damage after an accident or injury.

## ACTIVITIES

### Writing About Science: Brochure

Make a chart of the different types of medical imaging used to diagnose one body system. Include an explanation of how the technique works and list the pros and cons of using it.

### Reliving History

X-rays use radioactivity which can be dangerous. You can use visible light to shine through thin materials that you don't normally see through. Try using a flashlight to illuminate a leaf. Discuss or draw what you see.

CHAPTER

# Control and Reproduction

## the BIG idea

**The nervous and endocrine systems allow the body to respond to internal and external conditions.**

## Key Concepts

SECTION

**The nervous system responds and controls.**
Learn how the senses help the body get information about the environment.

SECTION

**The endocrine system helps regulate body conditions.**
Learn the functions of different hormones.

SECTION

**The reproductive system allows the production of offspring.**
Learn about the process of reproduction.

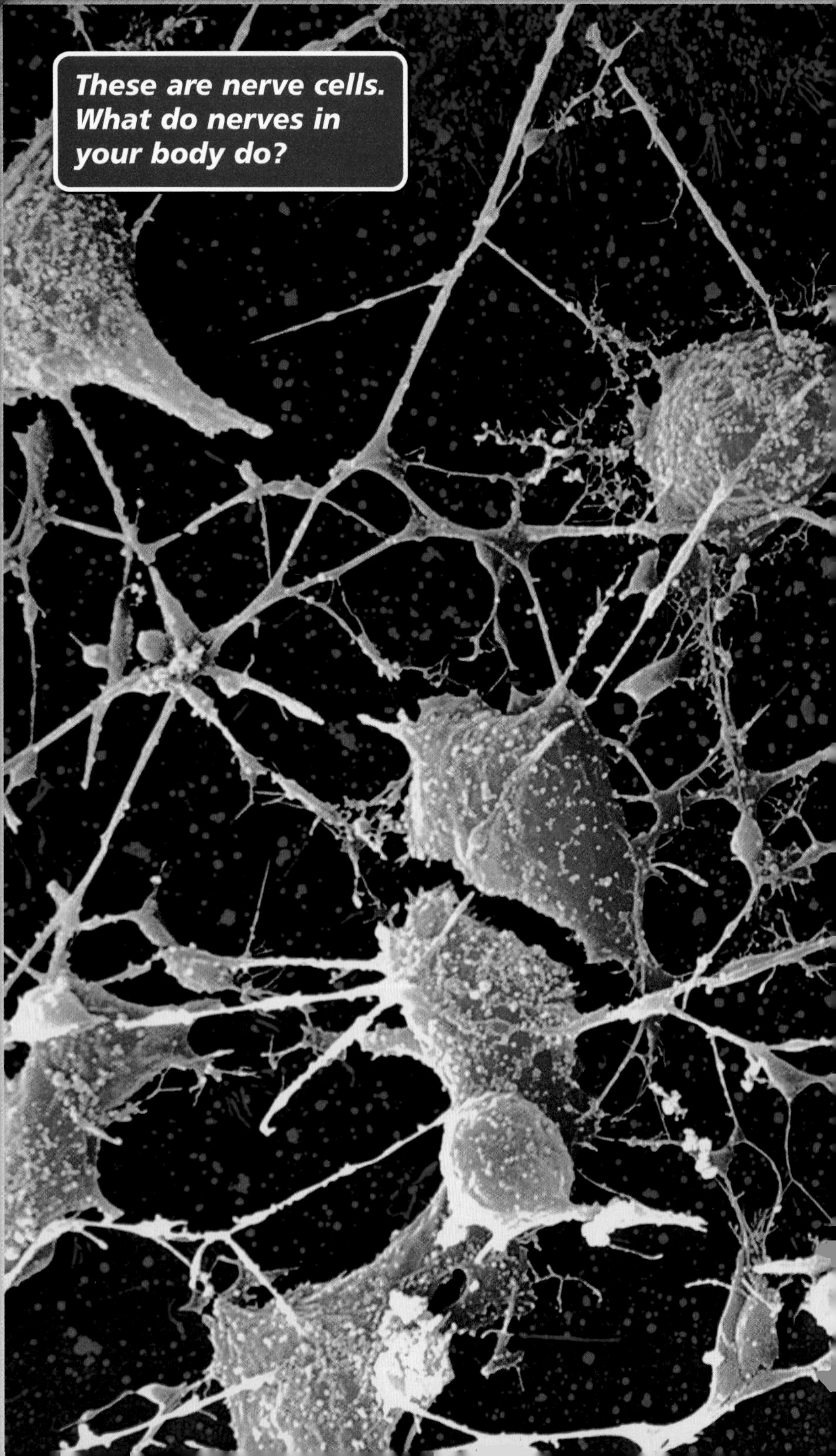

*These are nerve cells. What do nerves in your body do?*

**Internet Preview**

CLASSZONE.COM

Chapter 4 online resources: Content Review, Visualization, three Resource Centers, Math Tutorial, Test Practice

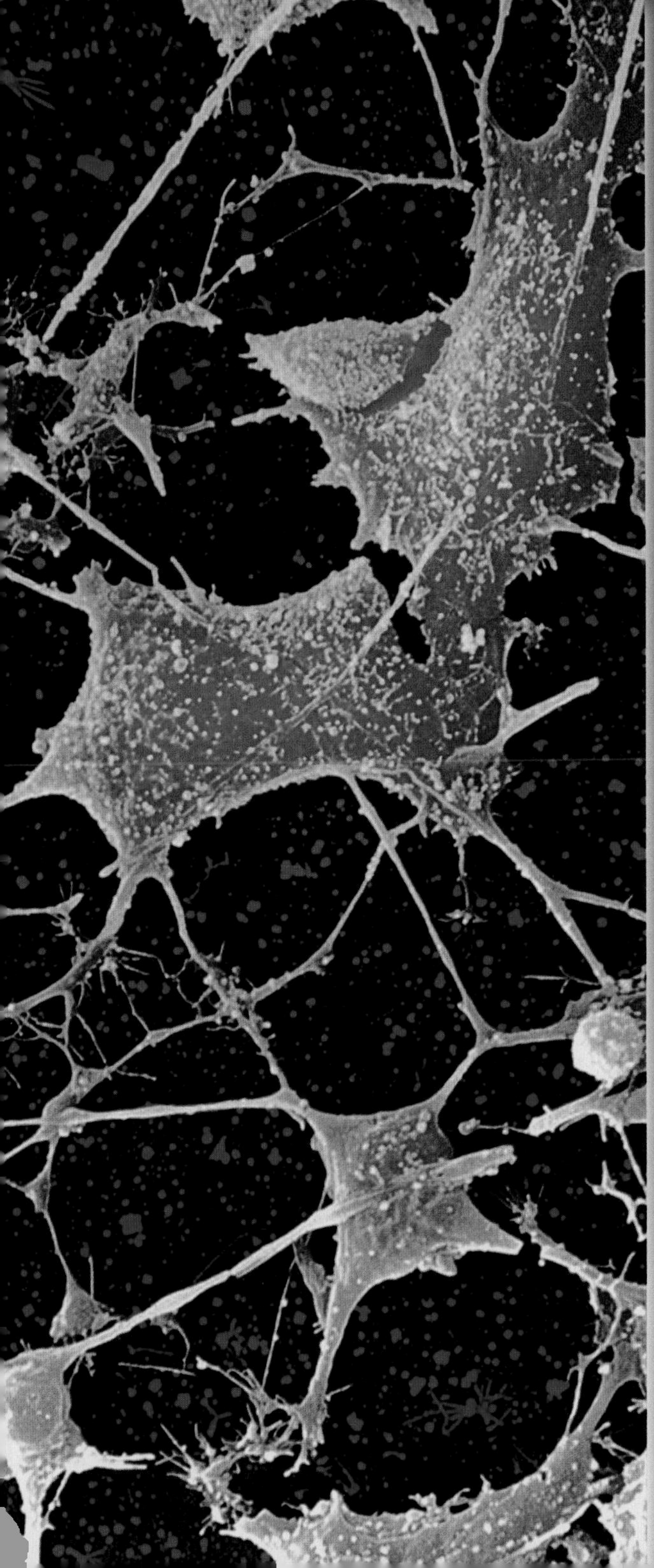

# EXPLORE the BIG idea

## Color Confusion

Make a list of six colors using a different color marker or colored pencil to write each one. Make sure not to write the color name with the same color marker or pencil. Read the list out loud as fast as you can. Now try quickly saying the color of each word out loud.

**Observe and Think** Did you notice a difference between reading the words in the list and saying the colors? If so, why do you think that is?

## Eggs

Examine a raw chicken egg. Describe the appearance of the outside shell. Break it open into a small dish and note the different parts inside. Wash your hands when you have finished.

**Observe and Think** If this egg had been fertilized, which part do you think would have served as the food for the growing chicken embryo? Which part would protect the embryo from impact and serve to cushion it?

## Internet Activity: The Senses

Go to **ClassZone.com** to learn how the senses allow the body to respond to external conditions. See how each sense sends specific information to the brain.

**Observe and Think** How do the different senses interact with one another?

Reproductive System **Code: MDL047**

CHAPTER 4

# Getting Ready to Learn

## CONCEPT REVIEW

- The circulatory system transports materials.
- The immune system responds to foreign materials.
- The integumentary system protects the body.

## VOCABULARY REVIEW

**homeostasis** p. 12
**circulatory system** p. 65
**immune system** p. 75
**integumentary system** p. 83

CLASSZONE.COM
Review concepts and vocabulary.

## TAKING NOTES

### CHOOSE YOUR OWN STRATEGY

Take notes using one or more of the strategies from earlier chapters—**main idea webs, outlines,** or **main idea and detail notes.** You can also use other note-taking strategies that you might already know.

### VOCABULARY STRATEGY

Place each vocabulary term at the center of a **description wheel** diagram. Write some words describing it on the spokes.

See the Note-Taking Handbook on pages R45–R51.

SCIENCE NOTEBOOK

Main Idea Web

Main Idea and Detail Notes

Outline
I. Main Idea
A. Supporting idea
1. Detail
2. Detail
B. Supporting idea

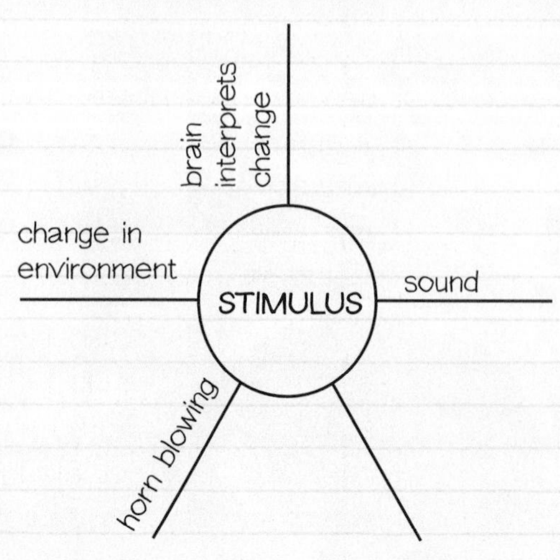

KEY CONCEPT

# The nervous system responds and controls.

**BEFORE, you learned**

- The body can respond to the presence of foreign materials
- The body is defended from harmful materials
- The immune system responds to pathogens in many ways

**NOW, you will learn**

- How the body's senses help monitor the environment
- How the sensory organs respond to stimuli
- How the nervous system works with other body systems

**VOCABULARY**

**stimulus** p. 102
**central nervous system** p. 104
**neuron** p. 105
**peripheral nervous system** p. 106
**autonomic nervous system** p. 107
**voluntary nervous system** p. 107

**EXPLORE Smell**

### *Can you name the scent?*

**PROCEDURE**

1. With a small group, take turns smelling the 3 mystery bags given to you by your teacher.
2. In your notebook, write down what you think is inside each bag without showing the people in your group.
3. Compare your answers with those in your group and then look inside the bags.

**MATERIALS**

three small paper bags

**WHAT DO YOU THINK?**

- Did you know what was in the bags before looking inside? If so, how did you know?
- What are some objects that would require more than a sense of smell to identify?

## Senses connect the human body to its environment.

**CHOOSE YOUR OWN STRATEGY**
Use a strategy from an earlier chapter to take notes on the main idea. *Senses connect the human body to its environment.*

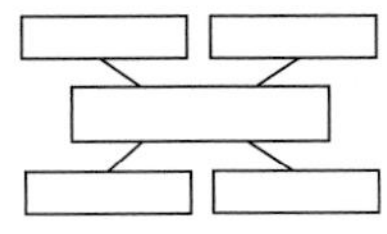

To maintain homeostasis and to survive, your body must constantly monitor the environment in which you live. This involves organs that interact so closely with the nervous system that they are often considered extensions of the nervous system. These are your sense organs. They give you the ability to see, smell, touch, hear, and taste.

Each of the senses can detect a specific type of change in the environment. For example, if you have begun to cross the street but suddenly hear a horn blowing, you may stop and step back onto the curb. Your sense of hearing allowed your brain to perceive that a car was coming and thus helped you to protect yourself.

The sound of the horn is a **stimulus.** A stimulus is a change in your environment that you react to, such as a smell, taste, sound, feeling, or sight. Your brain interprets any such change. If it did not, the information detected by the senses would be meaningless.

## Sight

If you have ever tried to find your way in the dark, you know how important light is for seeing. Light is a stimulus. You are able to detect it because your eyes, the sense organs of sight, capture light and help turn it into an image, which is processed by the brain.

Light enters the eye through the lens, a structure made of transparent tissue. Muscles surrounding the lens change its shape so the lens focuses light. Other muscles control the amount of light that enters the eye by altering the size of the pupil, a dark circle in the center of the eye. To reduce the amount of light, the area around the pupil, called the iris, contracts, making the pupil smaller, thus allowing less light to enter. When the iris relaxes, more light can enter the eye.

At the back of the eye, the light strikes a layer called the retina. Among the many cells of the retina are two types of receptors, called rods and cones. Rods detect changes in brightness, while cones are sensitive to color.

### Sight

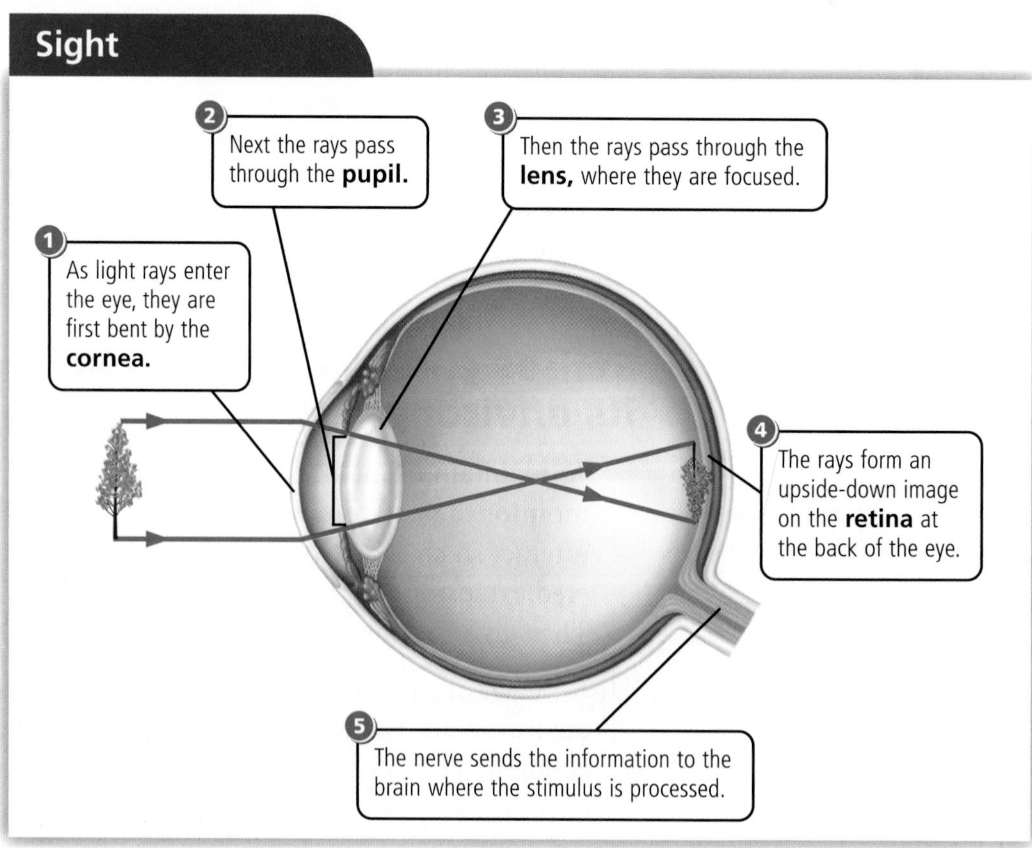

1 As light rays enter the eye, they are first bent by the **cornea.**
2 Next the rays pass through the **pupil.**
3 Then the rays pass through the **lens,** where they are focused.
4 The rays form an upside-down image on the **retina** at the back of the eye.
5 The nerve sends the information to the brain where the stimulus is processed.

## Hearing

Your eyes perceive light waves, but your ears detect a different type of stimulus, sound waves. Sound waves are produced by vibrations. A reed on a clarinet vibrates, and so do your vocal cords. So does a bell after it has been hit by a mallet. The motion causes changes in the air that surrounds the bell. These changes can often be detected by the ear as sound, although many vibrations are too low or high to be heard by humans.

Sound waves enter the ear and are funneled into the auditory canal, a tube-shaped structure that ends at the eardrum. The eardrum vibrates when the sound waves strike it, and it transmits some of the vibrations to a tiny bone called the stirrup. Pressure caused by vibrations from the stirrup causes fluid in the ear to move. The movement of the fluid results in signals sent to the brain that are interpreted as sound.

How are vibrations involved in hearing?

### Hearing

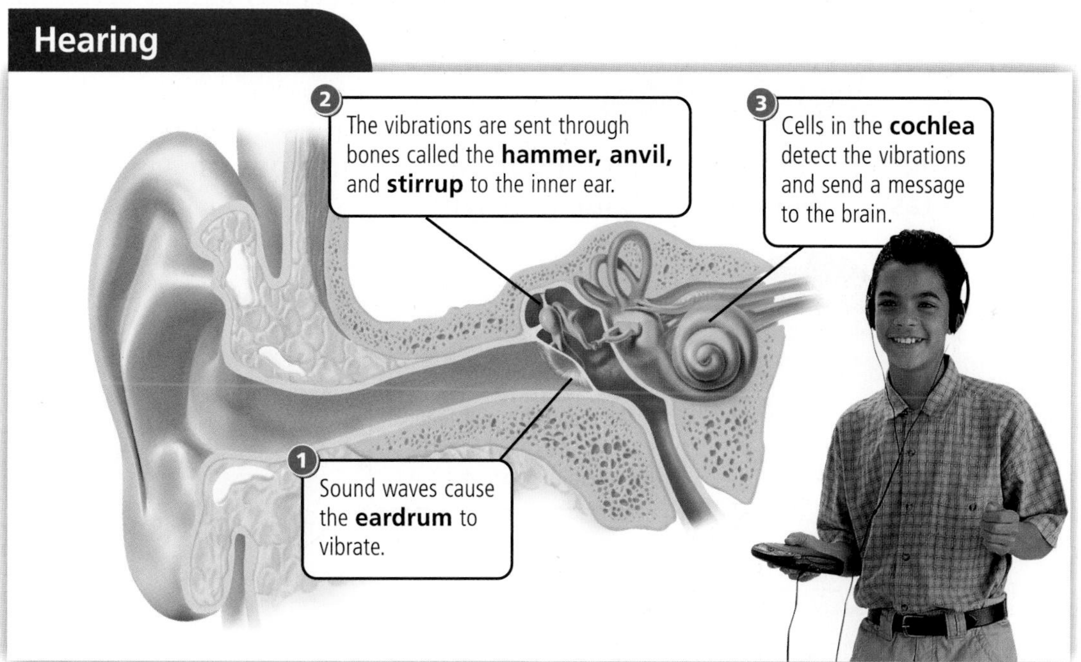

2 The vibrations are sent through bones called the **hammer, anvil,** and **stirrup** to the inner ear.
3 Cells in the **cochlea** detect the vibrations and send a message to the brain.
1 Sound waves cause the **eardrum** to vibrate.

## Touch

The sense of touch depends on tiny sensory receptors in the skin. Without these you wouldn't be able to feel pressure, temperature, or pain. Nerves near the top of the inner layer of your skin, or dermis, sense textures, like smooth glass or rough concrete. Nerves deeper in the dermis sense pressure. Other receptors in the dermis sense how hot or cold an object is and can thus help protect you from burning yourself. The sense of touch is important in alerting your brain to danger. Though you might wish that you couldn't feel pain, it serves a critical purpose. Without it, you could harm your body without realizing it.

## Smell

Whereas sight, touch, and hearing involve processing physical information from the environment, the senses of smell and taste involve detecting chemical information. Much as taste receptors sense chemicals in food, scent receptors sense chemicals in the air. High in the back of your nose, a patch of tissue grows hairlike fibers covered in mucus. Molecules enter your nose, stick to the mucus, and then bind to receptors in the hairlike fibers. The receptors send an impulse to your brain, and you perceive the scent.

## Taste

Your tongue is covered with small sensory structures called taste buds, which are also found in the throat and on the roof of the mouth. Each taste bud includes about 100 sensory cells. The receptors are specialized to detect four general tastes: sweet, sour, bitter, and salty. The thousands of tastes you experience are also partially due to sense organs in your nose. That is why when you have a cold, your ability to taste decreases.

### Taste

**Taste receptors on the tongue sense four types of taste: sweet, bitter, sour, and salty.**

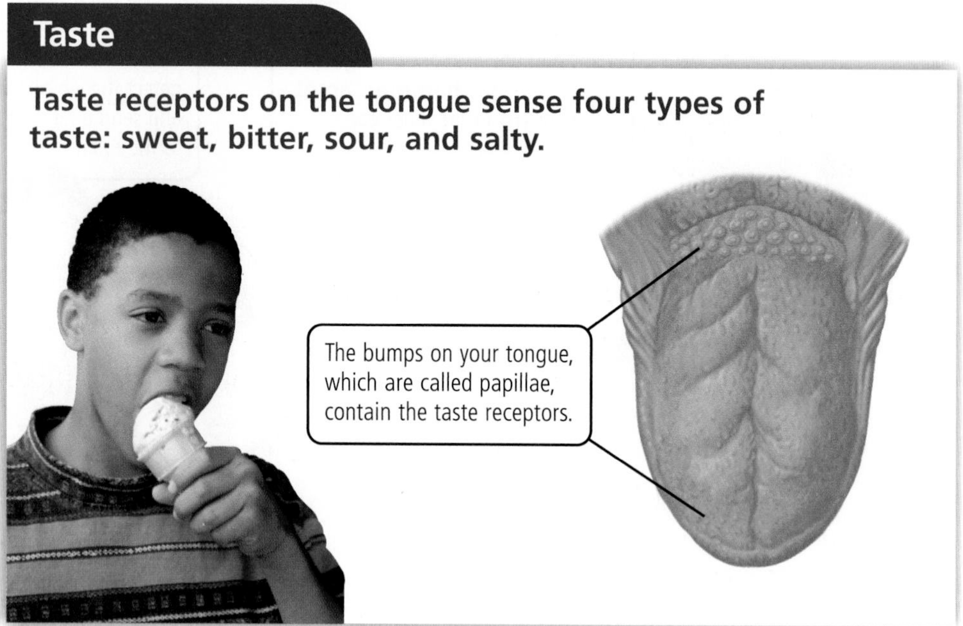

The bumps on your tongue, which are called papillae, contain the taste receptors.

## The central nervous system controls functions.

Explore the nervous system.

The **central nervous system** consists of the brain and spinal cord. The brain is located in and protected by the skull, and the spinal cord is located in and protected by the spine. The central nervous system communicates with the rest of the nervous system through electrical signals sent through nerve cells. Impulses travel very quickly, some as fast as 90 meters (295 ft) per second. That's like running almost the entire length of a soccer field in one second.

## The Brain

Different areas of the brain control different functions.

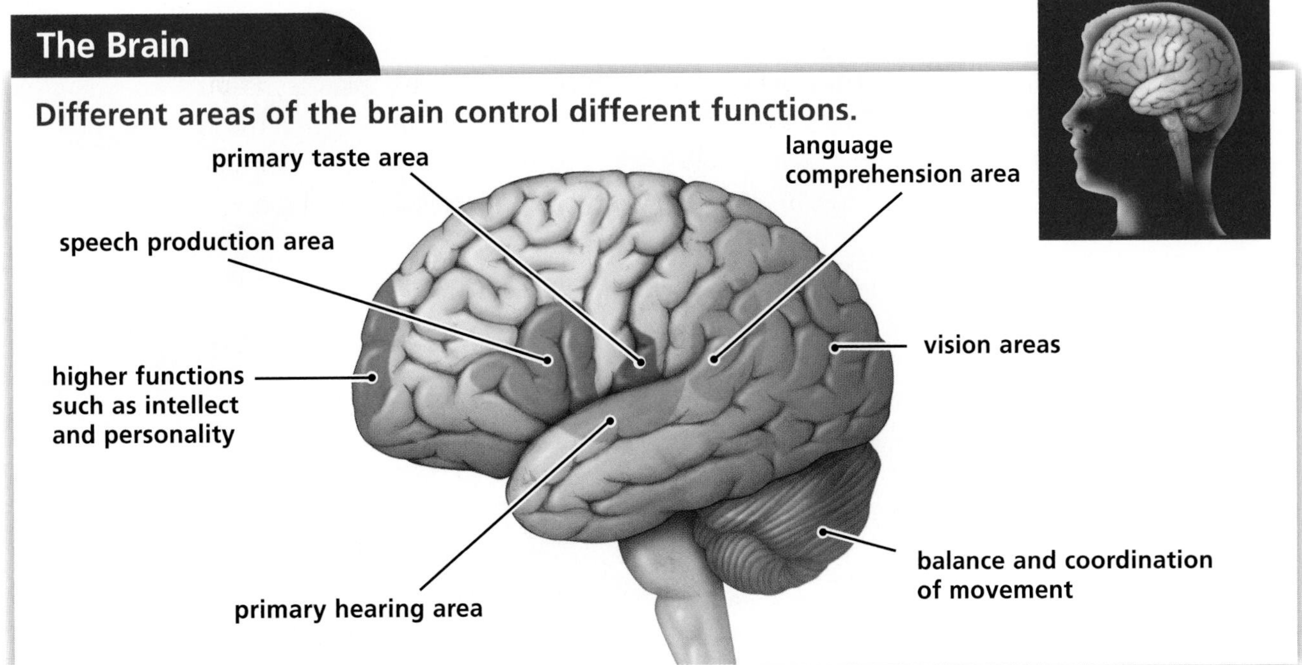


## Brain

The average adult brain contains nearly 100 billion nerve cells, called **neurons.** The brain directly controls voluntary behavior, such as walking and thinking. It also allows the body to control most involuntary responses such as heartbeat, blood pressure, fluid balance, and posture.

**VOCABULARY**
Be sure to make a description wheel for the term *neuron.*

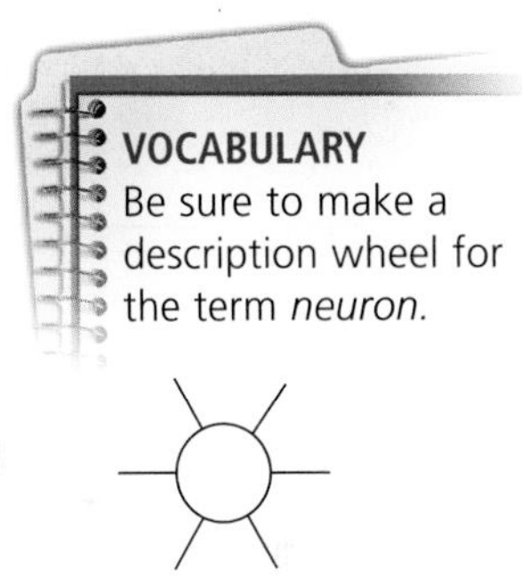

As you can see in the diagram, every area of the brain has a specific function, although many functions involve more than one area. For example, certain areas in the brain process and perceive senses, while other areas help you stand up straight. The lower part of the brain, called the brain stem, controls activities such as breathing and vomiting.

## Spinal Cord

The spinal cord is about 44 centimeters (17 in.) long and weighs about 35–40 grams (1.25–1.4 oz). It is the main pathway for information, connecting the brain and the nerves throughout your body. The spinal cord is protected and supported by the vertebral column, which is made up of small bones called vertebrae. The spinal cord itself looks like a double-layered tube with an outer layer of nerve fibers wrapped in tissue, an inner layer of nerve cell bodies, and a central canal that runs the entire length of the cord. Extending from the spinal cord are 31 pairs of nerves, which send sensory impulses into the spinal cord, which in turn sends them to the brain. In a similar way, spinal nerves send impulses to muscles and glands.

Describe the functions performed by the central nervous system.

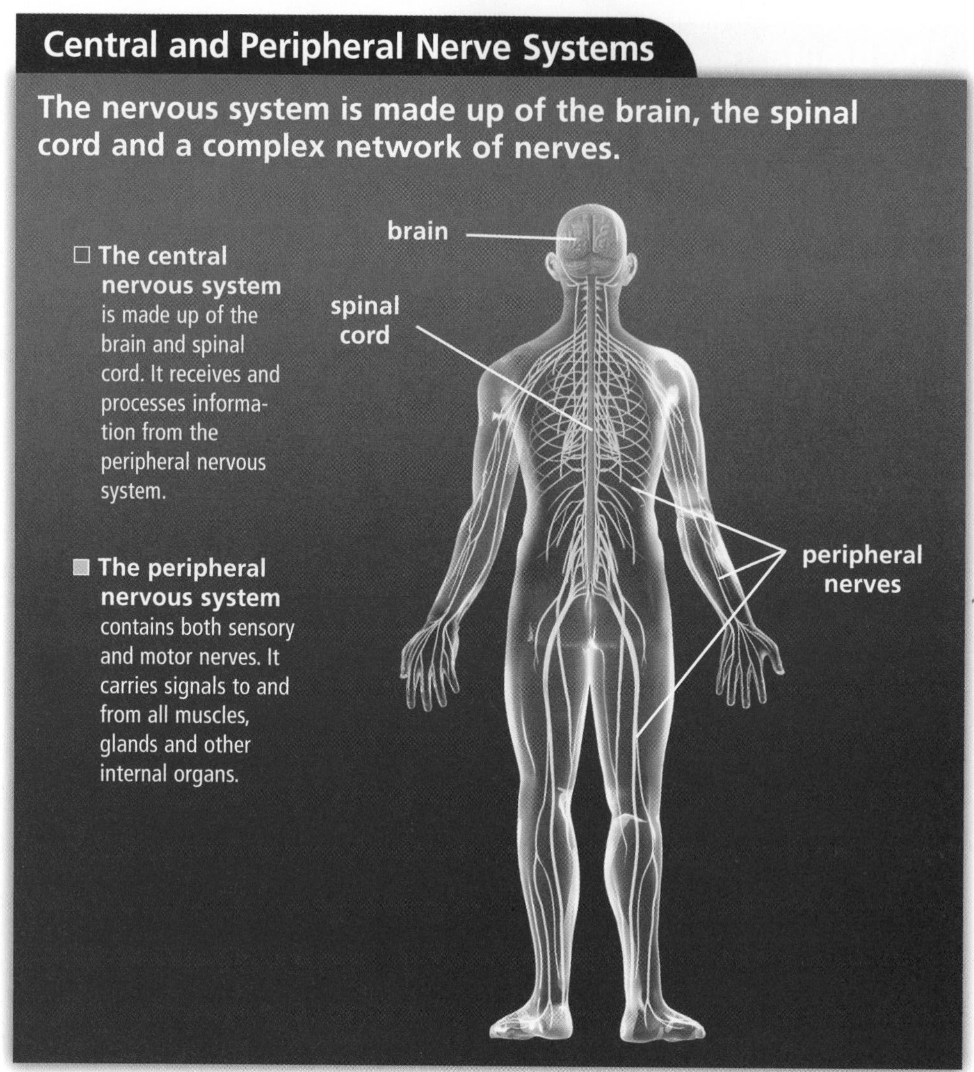

Central and Peripheral Nerve Systems
The nervous system is made up of the brain, the spinal cord and a complex network of nerves.
The central nervous system is made up of the brain and spinal cord. It receives and processes information from the peripheral nervous system.
The peripheral nervous system contains both sensory and motor nerves. It carries signals to and from all muscles, glands and other internal organs.
brain
spinal cord
peripheral nerves


## The peripheral nervous system is a network of nerves.

Nerves, which are found throughout the body, are often referred to all together as the **peripheral nervous system.** Both sensory and motor nerves are parts of the peripheral nervous system. Sensory nerves receive information from the environment—such as heat or cold—and pass the information to the central nervous system. Motor nerves send signals to your muscles that allow you to move. The peripheral nervous system carries information for both voluntary and involuntary responses.

Involuntary responses of the body are necessary for your survival. In times of danger, there is no time to think. The body must respond immediately. In less stressful situations, the body maintains activities like breathing and digesting food. These functions go on without conscious thought. They are controlled by part of the peripheral nervous system called the autonomic (AW-tuh-NAHM-ihk) nervous system.

The **autonomic nervous system** controls the movement of the heart, the smooth muscles in the stomach, the intestines, and the glands. The autonomic nervous system has two distinct functions: to conserve and store energy and to respond quickly to changes. You can think of the autonomic nervous system as having a division that performs each of these two main functions.

Each division is controlled by different locations on the spinal cord, or within the brain and the brain stem. The cerebellum, which is located at the rear of the brain, coordinates balance and related muscle activity. The brain stem, which lies between the spinal cord and the rest of the brain, controls heartbeat, respiration, and the smooth muscles in the blood vessels.

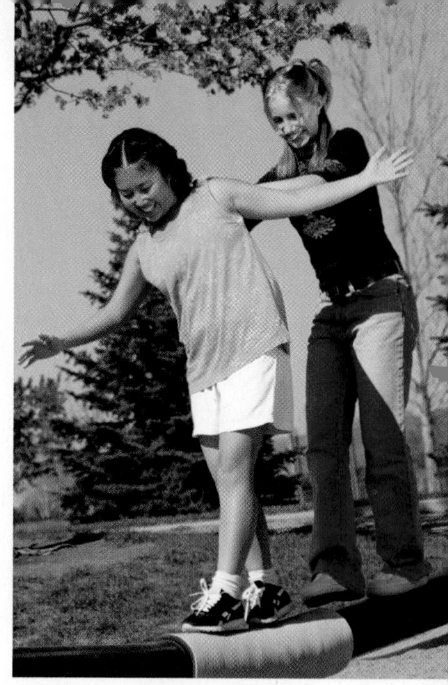

The autonomic nervous system responds quickly to changes in balance.

When you are under stress, one part of the autonomic nervous system causes what is called the "fight or flight response." Rapid changes in your body prepare you either to fight the danger or to take flight and run away from the danger. The response of your nervous system is the same, whether the stress is a real danger, like falling off a skateboard, or a perceived danger, like being worried or embarrassed.

The **voluntary nervous system** monitors movement and functions that can be controlled consciously. Every movement you think about is voluntary. The voluntary nervous system controls the skeletal muscles of the arms, the legs, and the rest of the body. It also controls the muscles that are responsible for speech and the senses.

What is the difference between the voluntary and the autonomic nervous systems?

## 4.1 Review

### KEY CONCEPTS

1. Make a chart of five senses that includes a definition and a stimulus for each sense.
2. Explain the process by which you hear a sound.
3. What are two body systems with which the nervous system interacts? How do these interactions take place?

### CRITICAL THINKING

4. **Classify** Determine if the following actions involve the autonomic or the voluntary nervous system: chewing, eye blinking, jumping at a loud noise, and riding a bike.
5. **Apply** Describe what messages are sent by the nervous system when you go outside wearing a sweater on a hot day.

### CHALLENGE

6. **Hypothesize** When people lose their sense of smell, their sense of taste is often affected as well. Why do you think the ability to taste would be decreased by the loss of the ability to smell?

# Are You a Supertaster?

**OVERVIEW AND PURPOSE** Do you think broccoli tastes bitter? If so, you might be extra sensitive to bitter tastes. In this investigation you will

- examine the surface of your tongue to find a possible connection between the bumps you find there and your sensitivity to bitter flavors
- calculate the average number of papillae in your class

Make sure to do this investigation in the cafeteria since you will be placing food coloring on your tongue.

**MATERIALS**
- blue food coloring
- paper cup
- 1 cotton swab
- 1 reinforcement circle for ring-binder paper
- paper towel or napkin
- 1 sheet of white paper

## Problem

How can you tell if you are a supertaster?

## Hypothesize

Write a hypothesis to explain how you might tell if you are a supertaster. Your hypothesis should take the form of an "If . . . , then . . . , because . . ." statement.

## Procedure

1. Make a data table in your **Science Notebook** like the one shown on page 109.

2. Put a few drops of blue food coloring into a paper cup.

3. Use a paper towel or a napkin to pat your tongue thoroughly dry.

4. Dip the tip of a cotton swab into the blue food coloring, and use it to paint the first 2 centimeters of your tongue.

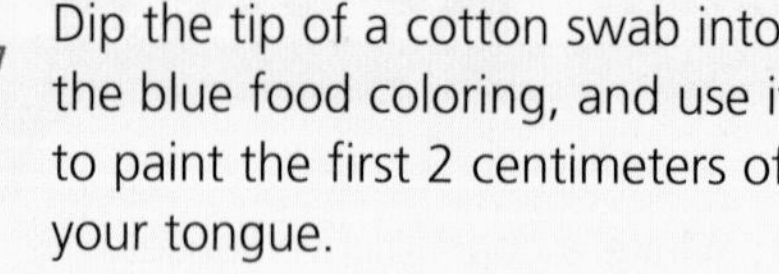

5 Press a piece of white paper firmly onto the painted surface of your tongue, and then place the paper on your desk.

6 Place a notebook reinforcement circle on the blue area.

7 You should see white circles in a field of blue. The white circles are the bumps on your tongue called fungiform papillae, which contain taste buds. Count the number of white circles inside the reinforcement circle. There may be many white circles crammed together that vary in size, or just a few. If there are just a few, they may be larger than the ones on someone who has many white circles close together. If there are too many to count, try to count the number in half of the circle and multiply this number by 2. Record your total count in your data table.

## Observe and Analyze

Write It Up

1. **OBSERVE** What did you observe while looking at the tongue print? Is the surface the same all over your tongue?

2. **CALCULATE** Record the number of papillae within the reinforcement circle of all the students in your class.

**AVERAGE** Calculate the average number of papillae counted in the class.

$$\text{average} = \frac{\text{sum of papillae in class}}{\text{number of students}}$$

## Conclude

1. **INTERPRET** How do the number of fungiform papillae on your tongue compare with the number your partner counted?
2. **INFER** Do you think there is a relationship between the number of fungiform papillae and taste? If so, what is it?
3. **IDENTIFY** What foods might a supertaster not like?
4. **APPLY** Do you think that there are other taste perceptions besides bitterness that might be influenced by the number of fungiform papillae that an individual has? Why do you think so?

## INVESTIGATE Further

**CHALLENGE** Calculate the area in square millimeters inside the reinforcement circle, and use this value to express each person's papillae count as a density (number of papillae per square millimeter).

### Are You a Supertaster?

Table 1. Papillae

| Name | Number of papillae |
|---|---|
| | |
| | |
| | |
| | |

KEY CONCEPT

# The endocrine system helps regulate body conditions.

**BEFORE, you learned**

- Many body systems function without conscious control
- The body systems work automatically to maintain homeostasis
- Homeostasis is important to an organism's survival

**NOW, you will learn**

- About the role of hormones
- About the functions of glands
- How the body uses feedback mechanisms to help maintain homeostasis

**VOCABULARY**

**endocrine system** p.110
**hormone** p.111
**gland** p.111

**THINK ABOUT**

***How does your body react to surprise?***

In a small group, determine how your body responds to a surprising situation. Have one student in the group pretend he or she is responding to a surprise. The other group members should determine how the body reacts physically to that event. How do your respiratory system, digestive system, circulatory system, muscle system, and skeletal system react?

CHOOSE YOUR OWN STRATEGY
Begin taking notes on the main idea: *Hormones are the body's chemical messengers.* Use a strategy from an earlier chapter or one of your own. Include a definition of *hormone* in your notes.

## Hormones are the body's chemical messengers.

Imagine you're seated on a roller coaster climbing to the top of a steep incline. In a matter of moments, your car drops one hundred feet. You might notice that your heart starts beating faster. You grab the seat and notice that your palms are sweaty. These are normal physical responses to scary situations. The **endocrine system** controls the conditions in your body by making and releasing chemicals that are transported thoughout the body. Most responses of the endocrine system are controlled by the autonomic nervous system.

**Hormones** are chemicals that are made in one organ, travel through the blood, and produce an effect in target cells. Target cells have structures that allow them to respond to the chemical. Many hormones, as you can see in the table below, affect all the cells in the body.

Because hormones are made at one location and function at another, they are often called chemical messengers. In order for a hormone to have an effect, it binds to receptors on the surface of or inside the cells. There the hormone begins the chemical changes that cause the target cells to function in a specific way. All of the functions of the endocrine system work automatically, without your conscious control.

The individuals on this roller coaster are experiencing a burst of the hormone adrenaline.

Different types of hormones perform different jobs. Some of these jobs are to control the production of other hormones, to regulate the balance of chemicals such as glucose and salt in your blood, or to produce responses to changes in the environment. Some hormones are made only during specific times in a person's life. For example, hormones that control the development of sexual characteristics are not produced in significant amounts during childhood. During adolescence, high levels of these hormones cause major changes in a person's body.

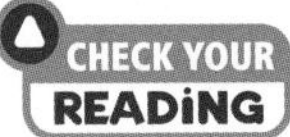


How are hormones like messengers?

**Hormones**

| Name | Where produced | Produces responses in |
|---|---|---|
| Growth hormone | pituitary gland | all body cells |
| Antidiuretic hormone | pituitary gland | kidneys |
| Thyroxine | thyroid gland | all body cells |
| Cortisol | adrenal glands | all body cells |
| Adrenaline | adrenal glands | heart, lungs, stomach, intestines, glands |
| Insulin | pancreas | all body cells |
| Testosterone (males) | testes | all body cells |
| Estrogen (females) | ovaries | all body cells |

## Glands produce and release hormones.

Learn more about the endocrine system.

The main structures of the endocrine system are groups of specialized cells called **glands.** Many glands in the body produce hormones and release them into your circulatory system. As you can see in the illustration on page 113, endocrine glands can be found in many parts of your body. However, all hormones move from the cells in which they are produced to cause effects in target cells.

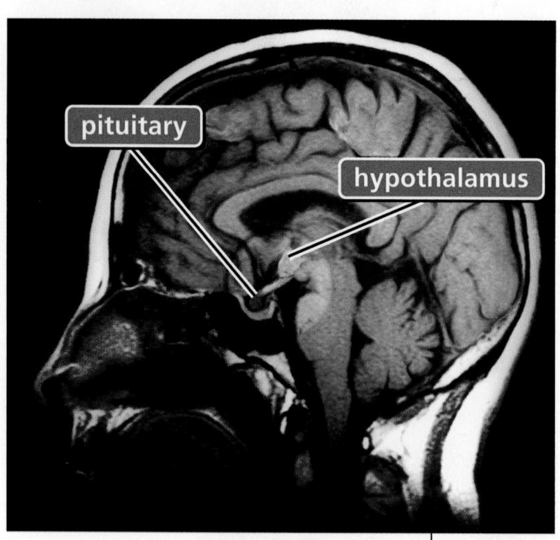

The hypothalamus and the pituitary are important endocrine glands.

**Pituitary Gland** The pituitary (pih-TOO-ih-TEHR-ee) gland can be thought of as the director of the endocrine system. The pituitary gland is the size of a pea and is located at the base of the brain—right above the roof of your mouth. Many important hormones are produced in the pituitary gland, including hormones that control growth, sexual development, and the absorption of water into the blood by the kidneys.

**Hypothalamus** The hypothalamus (HY-poh-THAL-uh-muhs) is attached to the pituitary gland and is the primary connection between the nervous and endocrine systems. All of the secretions of the pituitary gland are controlled by the hormones produced in the hypothalamus.

**Pineal Gland** The pineal (PIHN-ee-uhl) gland is a tiny organ about the size of a pea. It is buried deep in the brain. The pineal gland is sensitive to different levels of light and the hormone it produces is essential to rhythms such as sleep, body temperature, reproduction, and aging.

**Thyroid Gland** You can feel your thyroid gland if you place your hand on the part of your throat called the Adam's apple and swallow. What you feel is the cartilage surrounding your thyroid gland. The thyroid releases hormones necessary for growth and metabolism. The tissue of the thyroid is made of millions of tiny pouches, which store the thyroid hormones. The thyroid gland also produces the hormone calcitonin, which is involved in the regulation of calcium in the body.

**Thymus** The thymus is located in your chest. It is relatively large in the newborn baby and continues to grow until puberty. Following puberty, it gradually decreases in size. The thymus helps the body fight disease by controlling the production of white blood cells called T cells.

**Adrenal Glands** The adrenal glands are located on top of your kidneys. The adrenal glands secrete about 30 different hormones that regulate carbohydrate, protein, and fat metabolism and water and salt levels in your body. Some other hormones produced by the adrenal glands help you fight allergies. Roller coaster rides, loud noises, or stress can activate your adrenal glands to produce adrenaline, the hormone that makes your heart beat faster.

**Pancreas** The pancreas is part of both the digestive and the endocrine systems. The pancreas secretes two hormones, insulin and glucagon. These hormones regulate the level of glucose in your blood. The pancreas sits beneath the stomach and is connected to the small intestine.

**Ovaries and Testes** The ovaries and testes secrete hormones that control sexual development.

**Other Organs** Some organs that are not considered part of the endocrine system do produce important hormones. The kidneys secrete a hormone that regulates the production of red blood cells. This hormone is secreted whenever the oxygen level in your blood decreases. Once the hormone has stimulated the red bone marrow to produce more red blood cells, the oxygen level of the blood increases. The heart produces two hormones that help regulate blood pressure. These hormones, secreted by one of the chambers of the heart, stimulate the kidneys to remove more salt from the blood.

Which glands and organs are part of the endocrine system?

## Endocrine System

**The endocrine system is made of a group of glands. These glands produce and release hormones, or chemical messengers.**

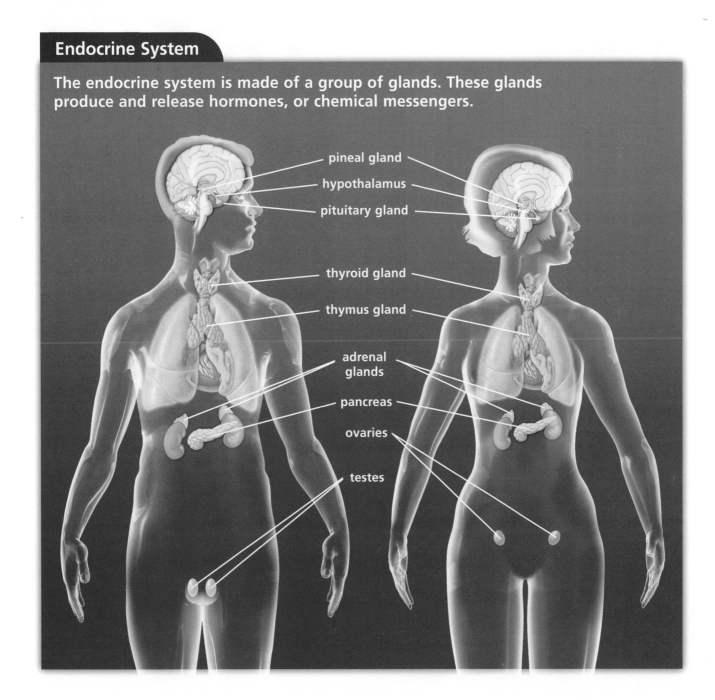

pineal gland
hypothalamus
pituitary gland
thyroid gland
thymus gland
adrenal glands
pancreas
ovaries
testes

# INVESTIGATE Response to Exercise

## How does your body temperature change when you exercise?

**PROCEDURE**

1. Working in groups of two, read all the instructions in this activity first. Appoint one person to be the subject and one person to be the timer and note taker. Using a mercury-free thermometer, have the subject take his or her temperature. Record the temperature in your notebook.
2. While staying seated the subject begins to do sitting-down jumping jacks. The subject does the jumping jacks for 1 minute and then immediately takes his or her temperature. Continue this procedure for a total of 3 times, measuring the temperature after each minute of exercise.

**WHAT DO YOU THINK?**

- How did the subject's temperature change while exercising?
- What factors may contribute to the rate at which the temperature changed in each person?
- How did the subject's physical appearance change from the beginning of the activity to the end?

**CHALLENGE** Graph the results on a line graph, with temperature on the *x*-axis and time on the *y*-axis.

**SKILL FOCUS**
Observing

**MATERIALS**
- stopwatch or timing device
- notebook
- graph paper
- mercury-free thermometer
- rubbing alcohol or plastic thermometer covers

**TIME**
30 minutes

## Control of the endocrine system includes feedback mechanisms.

As you might recall, the cells in the human body function best within a specific set of conditions. Homeostasis (HOH-mee-oh-STAY-sihs) is the process by which the body maintains these internal conditions, even though conditions outside the body may change. The endocrine system is very important in maintaining homeostasis.

Why is homeostasis important?

Because hormones are powerful chemicals capable of producing dramatic changes, their levels in the body must be carefully regulated. The endocrine system has several levels of control. Most glands are regulated by the pituitary gland, which in turn is controlled by the hypothalamus, part of the brain. The endocrine system helps maintain homeostasis through the action of negative feedback mechanisms.

## Negative Feedback

Most feedback mechanisms in the body are called negative mechanisms, because the final effect of the response is to turn off the response. An increase in the amount of a hormone in the body feeds back to inhibit the further production of that hormone.

The production of the hormone thyroxine by the thyroid gland is an example of a negative feedback mechanism. Thyroxine controls the body's metabolism, or the rate at which the cells in the body release energy by cellular respiration. When the body needs energy, the thyroid gland releases thyroxine into the blood to increase cellular respiration. However, the thyroid gland is controlled by the pituitary gland, which in turn is controlled by the hypothalamus. Increased levels of thyroxine in the blood inhibit the signals from the hypothalamus and the pituitary gland to the thyroid gland. Production of thyroxine in the thyroid gland decreases.

### Negative and Positive Feedback

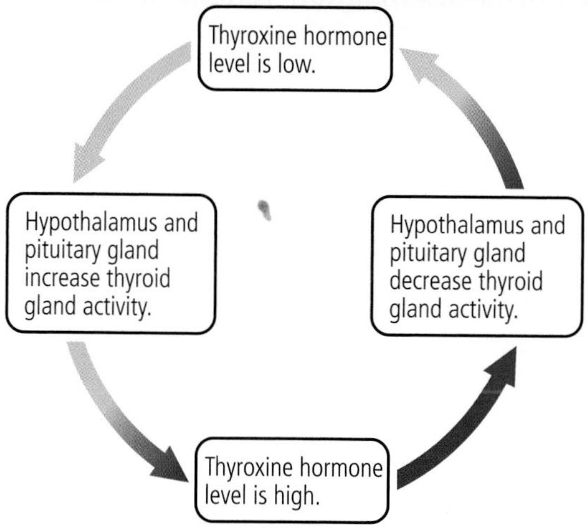

Thyroxine hormone level is low.

Hypothalamus and pituitary gland increase thyroid gland activity.

Thyroxine hormone level is high.

Hypothalamus and pituitary gland decrease thyroid gland activity.

**Negative feedback** The process shown here regulates levels of thyroid hormone. Feedback keeps conditions within a narrow range to maintain homeostasis.

white blood cell

red blood cell

fibrin

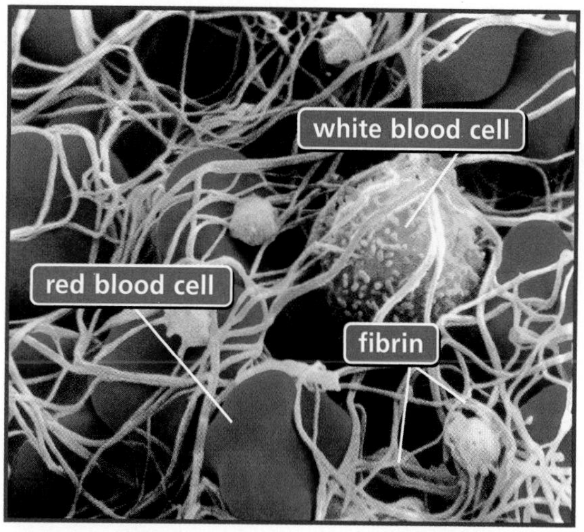

**Positive feedback** These red blood cells are surrounded by fibrin, a protein that allows them to clot.

## Positive Feedback

Some responses of the endocrine system, as well as other body systems, are controlled by positive feedback. The outcome of a positive feedback mechanism is not to maintain homeostasis, but to produce a response that continues to increase. Most positive feedback mechanisms result in extreme responses that are necessary under extreme conditions.

For example, when you cut yourself, the bleeding is controlled by positive feedback. First, the damaged tissue releases a chemical signal.

The signal starts a series of chemical reactions that lead to the formation of threadlike proteins called fibrin. The fibrin causes the blood to clot, filling the injured area. Other examples of positive feedback include fever, the immune response, puberty, and the process of childbirth.

What is the difference between negative and positive feedback?

## Balanced Hormone Action

In the body, the action of one hormone is often balanced by the action of another. When you ride a bicycle, you are able to ride in a straight line, despite bumps and dips in the road, by making constant steering adjustments. If the bicycle is pulled to the right, you adjust the handlebars by turning a tiny bit to the left.

Some hormones maintain homeostasis in the same way that you steer your bicycle. The pancreas, for example, produces two hormones. One hormone, insulin, decreases the level of sugar in the blood. The other hormone, glucagon, increases sugar levels in the blood. The balance of the levels of these hormones maintains stable blood sugar between meals.

## Hormone Imbalance

Because hormones regulate critical functions in the body, too little or too much of any hormone can cause serious disease. When the pancreas produces too little insulin, sugar levels in the blood can rise to dangerous levels. Very high levels of blood sugar can damage the circulatory system and the kidneys. This condition, known as diabetes mellitus, is often treated by injecting synthetic insulin into the body to replace the insulin not being made by the pancreas.

### KEY CONCEPTS

1. List three different jobs that hormones perform.
2. Draw an outline of the human body. Add the locations and functions of the pituitary, thyroid, adrenal, and pineal glands to your drawing.
3. What is the function of a negative feedback mechanism?

### CRITICAL THINKING

4. **Analyze** Explain why hormones are called chemical messengers.
5. **Analyze** List two sets of hormones that have opposing actions. How do the actions of these hormones help maintain homeostasis?

### CHALLENGE

6. **Connect** Copy the diagram below and add three more stimuli and the resulting feedback mechanisms.

CONNECTING SCIENCES

## CONNECTING LIFE AND PHYSICAL SCIENCE

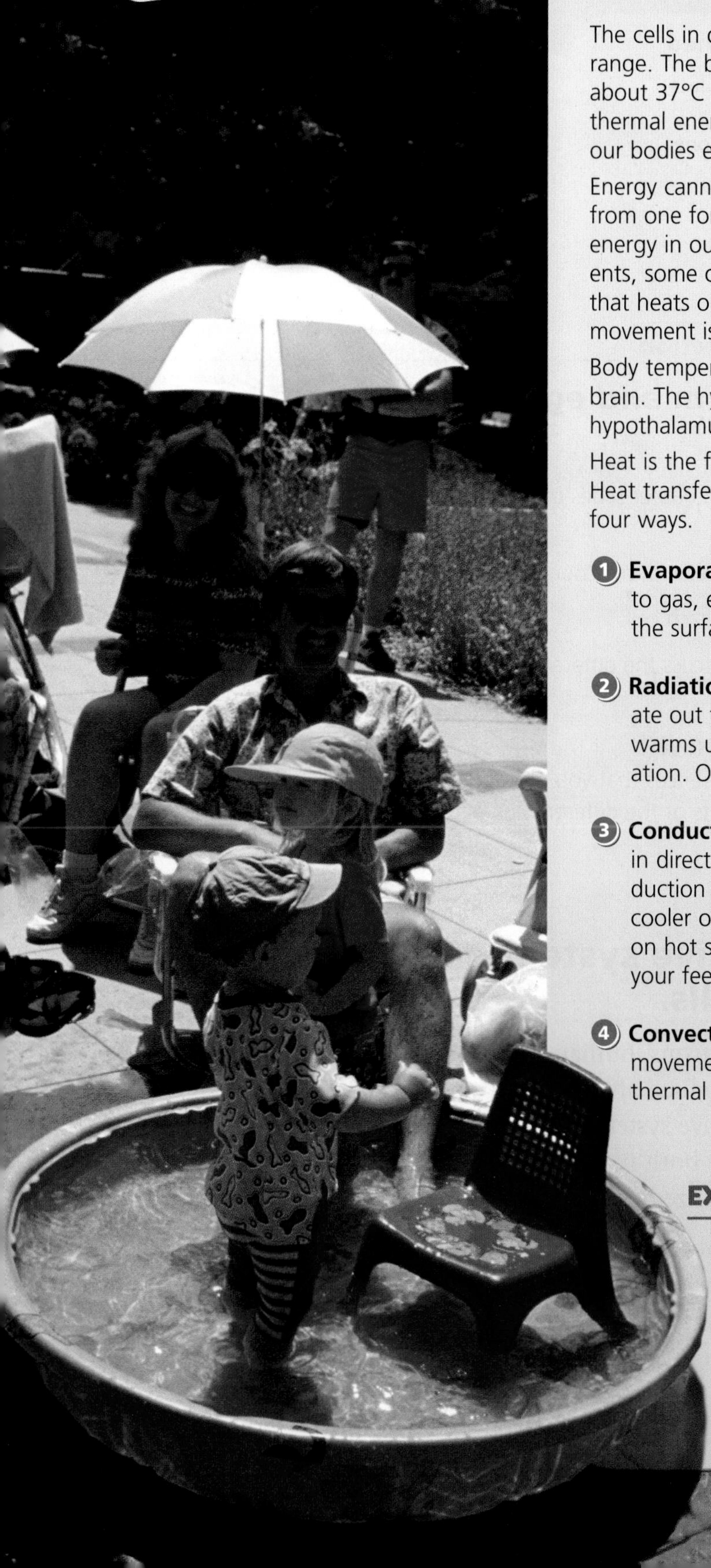

# Heating and Cooling

The cells in our bodies can survive only within a limited temperature range. The body must maintain a constant core temperature at about 37°C (98.6°F). Body temperature is a measure of the average thermal energy in the body. To keep a constant temperature range, our bodies either lose or gain thermal energy.

Energy cannot be created or destroyed, but it can be transferred from one form or place to another. The major source of thermal energy in our bodies is food. When our bodies break down nutrients, some of the chemical energy is released as thermal energy that heats our bodies. Also, some of the kinetic energy from muscle movement is converted into thermal energy.

Body temperature is controlled by the hypothalamus region of the brain. The hypothalamus controls the rate of nutrient use. The hypothalamus also controls shivering and sweating.

Heat is the flow of energy from a warmer to a cooler object. Heat transfer between the body and its surroundings occurs in four ways.

1. **Evaporation:** When water evaporates, or changes from liquid to gas, energy is required. When perspiration evaporates from the surface of our skin, we lose thermal energy as heat.

2. **Radiation:** Heat transfer also occurs through waves that radiate out from a warm object or area. Sitting in the sunshine warms us because we gain thermal energy from the Sun's radiation. Our warm bodies can also radiate energy into cooler air.

3. **Conduction:** When two objects are in direct contact, heat flows by conduction from the warmer to the cooler object. If you stand barefoot on hot sand, heat quickly flows into your feet by conduction.

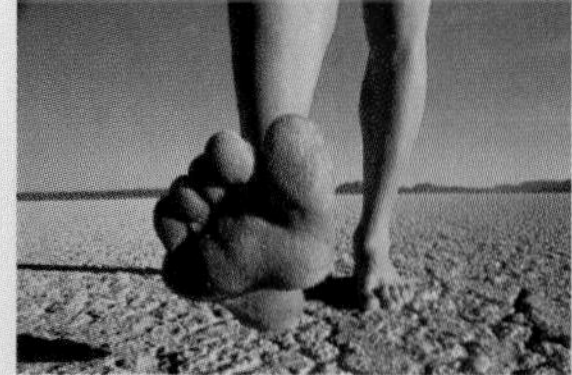

4. **Convection:** In convection, heat transfer occurs through the movement of particles in a gas or liquid. Your body loses some thermal energy because of convection in the air around you.

### EXPLORE

1. **CONNECT** What are some behaviors that help you lose or gain thermal energy?
2. **CHALLENGE** Choose a behavior that either warms or cools your body. Draw a diagram and label it with the types of heat transfer that are occurring.

KEY CONCEPT

# The reproductive system allows the production of offspring.

**BEFORE, you learned**

- Some hormones regulate sexual development
- Glands release hormones

**NOW, you will learn**

- About specialized cells and organs in male and female reproductive systems
- About fertilization
- About the development of the embryo and fetus during pregnancy

**VOCABULARY**

**menstruation** p. 119
**fertilization** p. 121
**embryo** p. 121
**fetus** p. 122

**EXPLORE Reproduction**

***How are sperm and egg cells different?***

**PROCEDURE**

1. From your teacher, gather slides of egg cells and sperm cells.
2. Put each slide under a microscope.
3. Draw a sketch of each cell.
4. With a partner, discuss the differences that you observed.

**WHAT DO YOU THINK?**

- What were the differences that you observed?
- What are the benefits of the different characteristics for each cell?

**MATERIALS**

- slides of egg and sperm cells
- microscope
- paper
- pencil

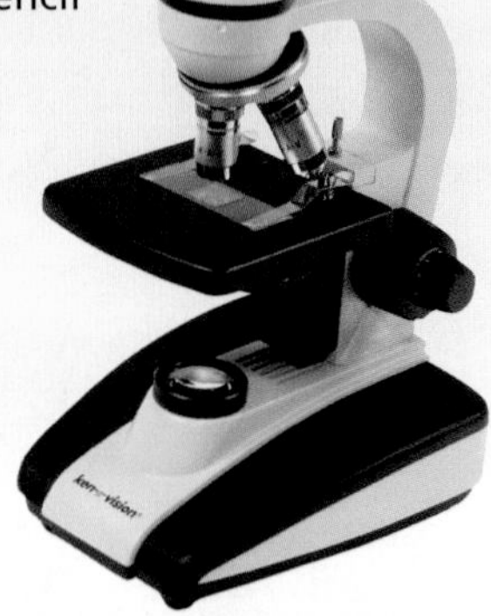

## The reproductive system produces specialized cells.

**CHOOSE YOUR OWN STRATEGY**
Begin taking notes on the idea that the reproductive system produces specialized cells. You might use an outline or another strategy of your choice.

Like all living organisms, humans reproduce. The reproductive system allows adults to produce offspring. Although males and females have different reproductive systems, both systems share an important characteristic. They both make specialized cells. In any organism or any system, a specialized cell is a cell that takes on a special job.

In the female these specialized cells are called egg cells. In the male they are called sperm cells. In the reproductive system, each specialized cell provides genetic material. Genetic material contains the information that an organism needs to form, develop, and grow.

Both the male and female reproductive systems rely on hormones from the endocrine system. The hormones act as chemical messengers that signal the process of sexual development. Sexual development includes the growth of reproductive organs and the development of sexual characteristics. Once mature, the reproductive organs produce hormones to maintain secondary sexual characteristics.

## The Female Reproductive System

The female reproductive system has two functions. The first is to produce egg cells, and the second is to protect and nourish the offspring until birth. The female has two reproductive organs called ovaries. Each ovary contains on average hundreds of egg cells. About every 28 days, the pituitary gland releases a hormone that stimulates some of the eggs to develop and grow. The ovaries then produce hormones that get the uterus ready to receive the egg.

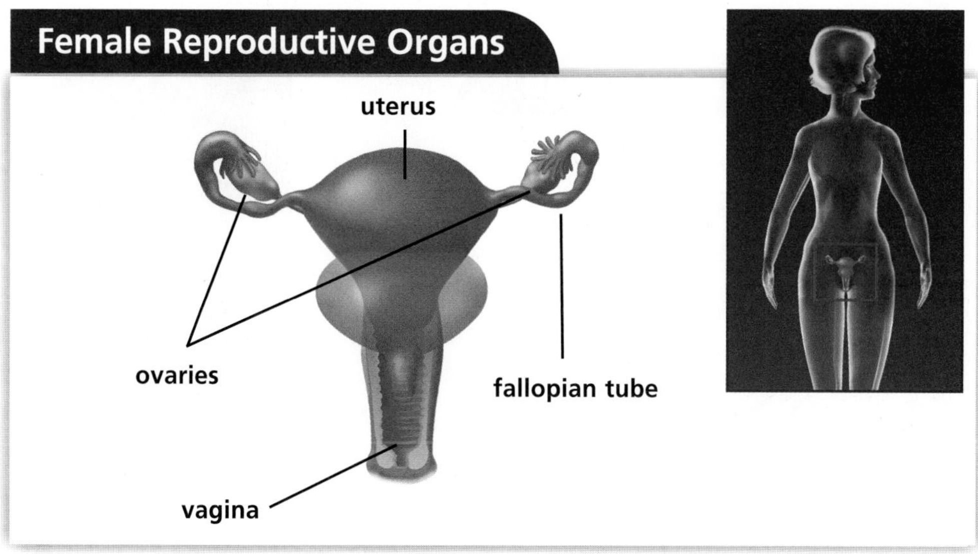


## Menstruation

After an egg cell develops fully, another hormone signals the ovary to release the egg. The egg moves from the ovary into a fallopian tube. Within ten to twelve hours, the egg cell may be fertilized by a sperm cell and move to the uterus. Once inside the thick lining of the uterus, the fertilized egg cell rapidly grows and divides.

However, if fertilization does not occur within 24 hours after the egg cell leaves the ovary, both the egg and the lining of the uterus begin to break down. The muscles in the uterus contract in a process called **menstruation.** Menstruation is the flow of blood and tissue from the body through a canal called the vagina over a period of about five days.

Where does the egg travel after it leaves the ovary?

### The Male Reproductive System

**Testes** The organs that produce sperm are called the testes (TEHS-teez). Inside the testes are tiny, coiled tubes hundreds of feet long. Sperm are produced inside these coiled tubes. The testes release a hormone that controls the development of sperm. This hormone is also responsible for the development of physical characteristics in men such as facial hair and a deep voice.

**Sperm** Sperm cells are the specialized cells of the male reproductive system. Males start producing sperm cells sometime during adolescence. The sperm is a single cell with a head and a tail. The sperm's head is filled with chromosomes, and the tail functions as a whip, making the sperm highly mobile. The sperm travel from the site of production, the testes, through several different structures of the reproductive system. While they travel, the sperm mix with fluids. This fluid is called semen and contains nutrients for the sperm cells. One drop of semen contains up to several million sperm cells.

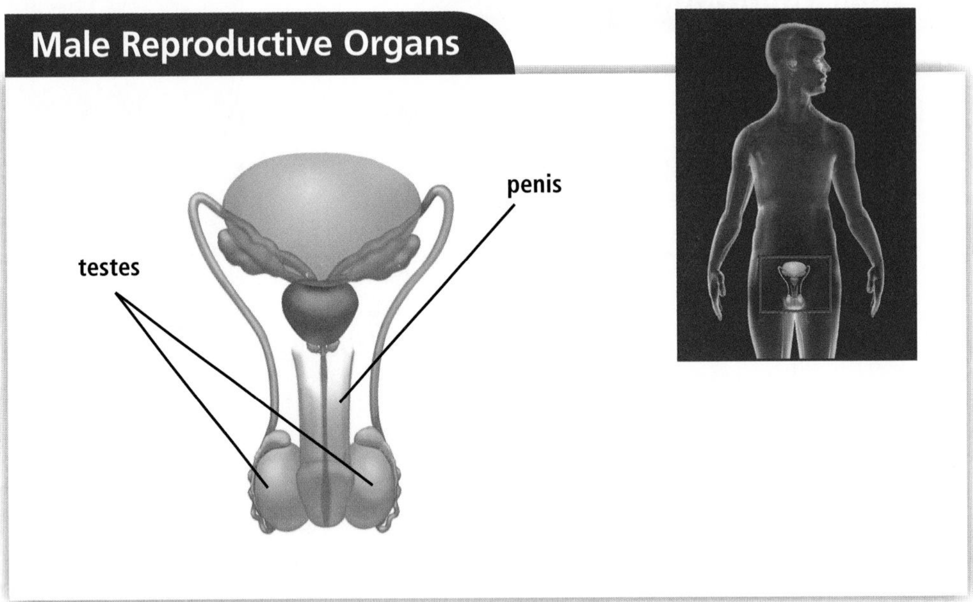


## The production of offspring includes fertilization, pregnancy, and birth.

Follow an egg from fertilization to implantation.

Each sperm cell, like each egg cell, has half of the genetic material needed for a human being to grow and develop. During sexual intercourse, millions of sperm cells leave the testes. The sperm cells exit the male's body through the urethra, a tube that leads out of the penis. The sperm cells enter the female's body through the vagina. Next they travel into the uterus and continue on to the fallopian tube.

## Fertilization

**Fertilization** occurs when one sperm cell joins the egg cell. The fallopian tube is the site of fertilization. Immediately, chemical changes in the egg's surface prevent any more sperm from entering. Once inside the egg, the genetic material from the sperm combines with the genetic material of the egg cell. Fertilization is complete.

The fertilized egg cell then moves down the fallopian tube toward the uterus. You can trace the path of the egg cell in the diagram on this page. It divides into two cells. Each of those cells divides again, to form a total of four cells. Cell division continues, and a ball of cells forms, called an **embryo** (EM-bree-OH). Within a few days, the embryo attaches itself to the thickened, spongy lining of the uterus in a process called implantation.

**VOCABULARY**
Be sure to add the description wheels for the terms *fertilization* and *embryo* to your notebook.

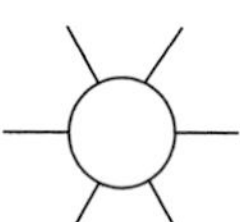

### Fertilization

**The egg moves down the fallopian tube following fertilization. Its final destination is the uterus.**

1 Egg is released from ovary.

2 Fertilization occurs.

3 Fertilized egg begins to divide.

4 Dividing egg continues down fallopian tube.

5 Embryo moves towards the uterus.

6 Embryo implants in lining of uterus.

fallopian tube

ovary

uterus

**READING VISUALS** Where does fertilization occur?

## Pregnancy

The nine months of pregnancy can be divided into three periods of about the same length. Each period marks specific stages of development. In the first week following implantation, the embryo continues to grow rapidly. Both the embryo and the uterus contribute cells to a new, shared organ called the placenta. The placenta has blood vessels that lead from the mother's circulatory system to the embryo through a large tube called the umbilical cord. Oxygen and nutrients from the mother's body will move through the placenta and umbilical cord to the growing embryo.

**Uterus and Placenta**

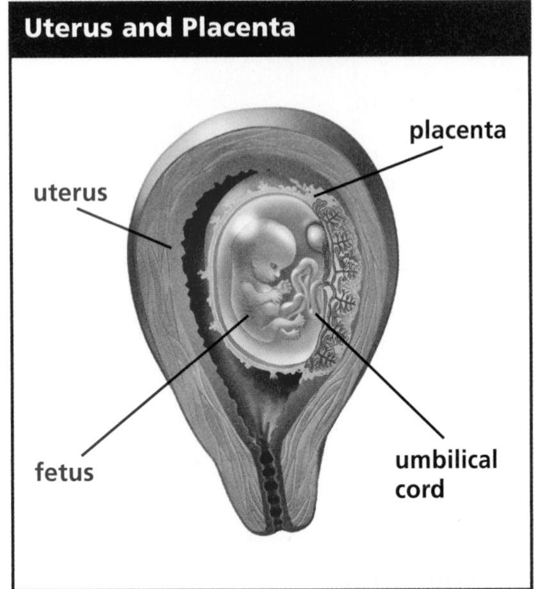


Around the eighth week of pregnancy, the developing embryo is called a **fetus.** The fetus begins to have facial features, major organ systems, and the beginnings of a skeleton. The fetus develops the sexual traits that are either male or female. In the twelfth week, the fetus continues to grow and its bones develop further. In the last twelve weeks, the fetus and all of its organ systems develop fully.

Describe the development of an embryo and fetus at two weeks, eight weeks, and twelve weeks.

## Labor and Delivery

At the end of pregnancy, the fetus is fully developed and is ready to be born. The birth of a fetus is divided into three stages; labor, delivery of the fetus, and delivery of the placenta.

The first stage of birth begins with muscular contractions of the uterus. These contractions initially occur at intervals of 10 to 30 minutes and last about 40 seconds. They happen continually until the muscular contractions are occurring about every 2 minutes.

The second stage of birth is delivery. With each contraction, the opening to the uterus expands until it becomes wide enough for the mother's muscles to push the fetus out. During delivery the fetus is pushed out of the uterus, through the vagina, and out of the body. The fetus is still connected to the mother by the umbilical cord.

The umbilical cord is cut shortly after the fetus is delivered. Within minutes after birth, the placenta separates from the uterine wall and the mother pushes it out with more muscular contractions.

What happens during each of the three stages of birth?

## Growth of the Fetus

**An embryo grows and develops from a cluster of cells to a fully formed fetus.**

**4-day blastula**

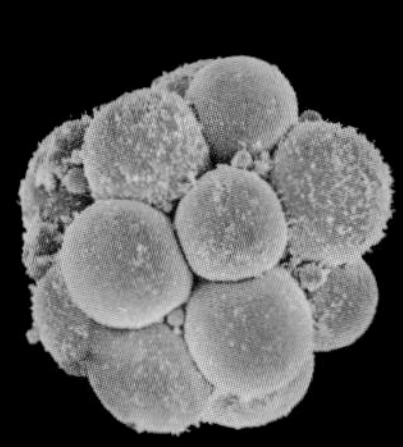

magnification 620x

- Embryo has 16 cells
- Not yet implanted in the uterus

**5-week embryo**

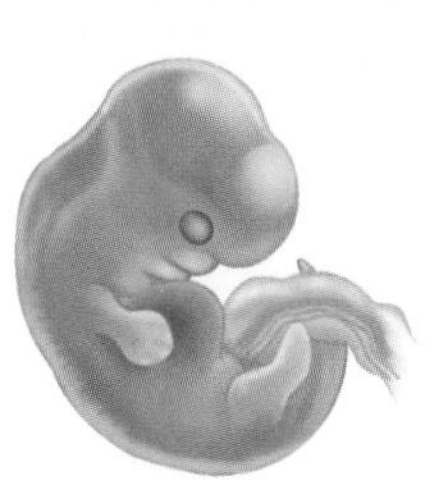

size < 1 cm

- Heart is beating
- Beginning of eyes, arms and legs are visible

**8-week fetus**

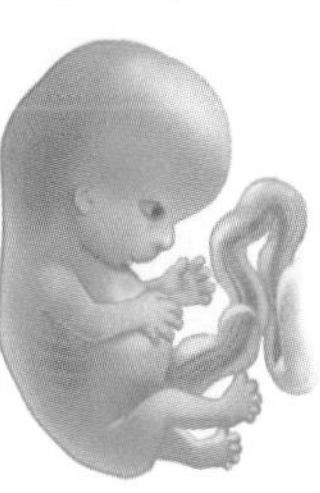

size 2–3 cm

- Embryo is now called a fetus
- Has all basic organs and systems

**16-week fetus**

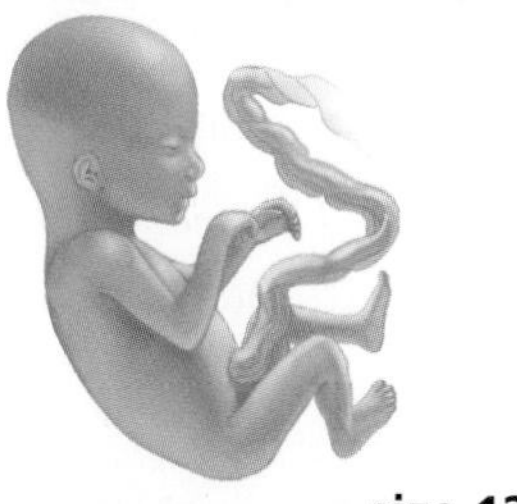

size 12 cm

- Can move around in the womb
- Hair, eyelashes and eyebrows are growing

**7–8 month fetus** shown in this composite image is about 35–40 cm in length and weighs about 1.5–2.3 kg. The fetus usually gains at least 1 kg during the final month of pregnancy.

These twins provide an example of offspring born in a multiple birth.

## Multiple Births

Do you have any friends who are twins or triplets? Perhaps you and your brothers or sisters are twins or triplets. The birth of more than one offspring is called a multiple birth. Multiple births are relatively uncommon in humans.

Identical twins are produced when a single fertilized egg divides in half early in embryo development. Each half then forms one complete organism, or twin. Such twins are always of the same sex, look alike, and have identical blood types. Approximately 1 in 29 of twin births, or 4 in every 1000 of all births, is a set of identical twins.

Twins that are not identical are called fraternal twins. Fraternal twins are produced when two eggs are released at the same time and are fertilized by two different sperm. Consequently, fraternal twins may be as similar or different from each other as siblings born at different times. Fraternal twins can be the same sex or different sexes.

Why are some twins identical and some are not?

### KEY CONCEPTS

1. Describe the function of the male reproductive system and the two main functions of the female reproductive system.
2. Identify two roles hormones play in making egg cells available for fertilization.
3. How is an embryo different from a fetus?

### CRITICAL THINKING

4. **Sequence** Describe the sequence of events that occurs between fertilization and the stage called implantation.
5. **Analyze** Detail two examples of hormones interacting with the reproductive system, one involving the male system and one involving the female system.

### CHALLENGE

6. **Synthesize** Describe the interaction between the endocrine system and the reproductive system.

MATH in SCIENCE

MATH TUTORIAL

CLASSZONE.COM

Click on Math Tutorial for more help with solving proportions.

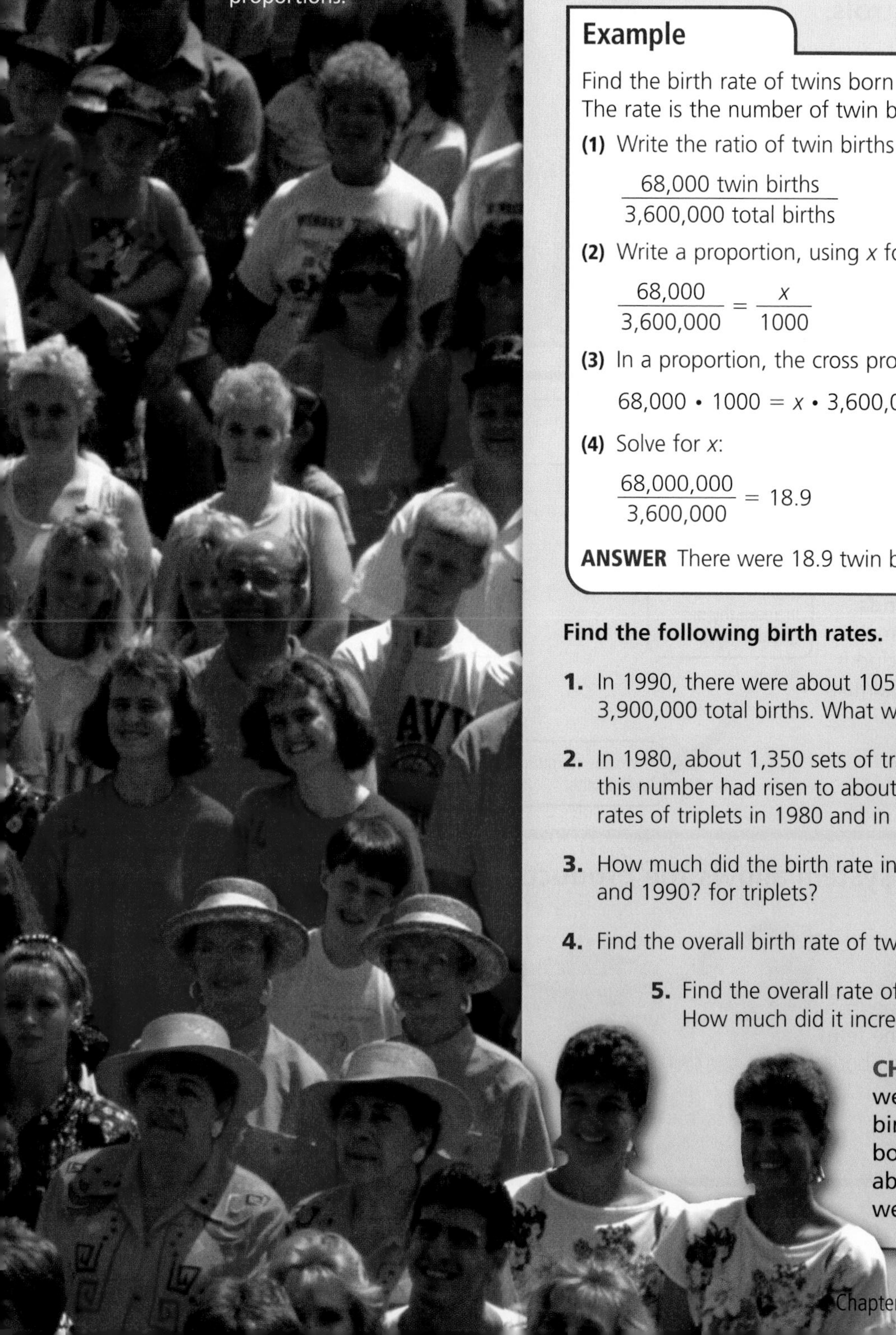

## SKILL: SOLVING PROPORTIONS

# Twins and Triplets

Is the number of twins and triplets on the rise? Between 1980 and 1990, twin births in The United States rose from roughly 68,000 to about 105,000. In 1980, there were about 3,600,000 births total. To convert the data to birth rates, you can use proportions. A proportion is an equation. It shows two ratios that are equivalent.

### Example

Find the birth rate of twins born in The United States for 1980. The rate is the number of twin births per 1000 births.

**(1)** Write the ratio of twin births to total births for that year.

$$\frac{68{,}000 \text{ twin births}}{3{,}600{,}000 \text{ total births}}$$

**(2)** Write a proportion, using $x$ for the number you need to find.

$$\frac{68{,}000}{3{,}600{,}000} = \frac{x}{1000}$$

**(3)** In a proportion, the cross products are equal, so

$$68{,}000 \cdot 1000 = x \cdot 3{,}600{,}000$$

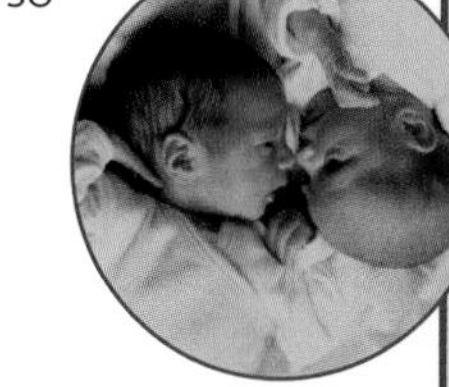

**(4)** Solve for $x$:

$$\frac{68{,}000{,}000}{3{,}600{,}000} = 18.9$$

**ANSWER** There were 18.9 twin births for every 1000 births in 1980.

**Find the following birth rates.**

1. In 1990, there were about 105,000 twin births and about 3,900,000 total births. What was the birth rate of twins?
2. In 1980, about 1,350 sets of triplets were born, and by 1990, this number had risen to about 6,750. What were the birth rates of triplets in 1980 and in 1990?
3. How much did the birth rate increase for twins between 1980 and 1990? for triplets?
4. Find the overall birth rate of twins and triplets in 1980.
5. Find the overall rate of twin and triplet births in 1990. How much did it increase between 1980 and 1990?

**CHALLENGE** In 1989, there were about 4 million total births, and the rate of triplets born per million births was about 700. How many triplets were born?

# 4 Chapter Review

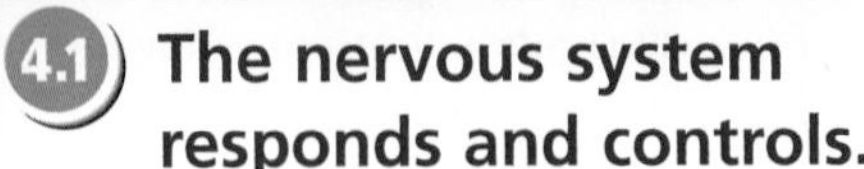

**The nervous and endocrine systems allow the body to respond to internal and external conditions.**

## KEY CONCEPTS SUMMARY

### 4.1 The nervous system responds and controls.

- The nervous system connects the body with its environment using different senses: sight, touch, hearing, smell, and taste. Central nervous system includes the brain, the control center, and the spinal cord.
- The peripheral nervous system includes the autonomic and voluntary systems

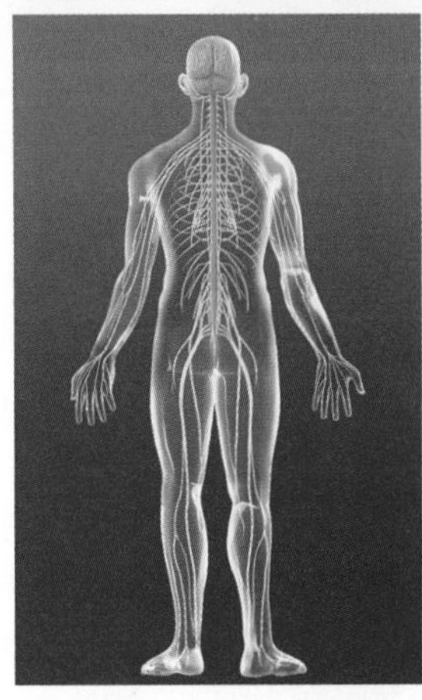

**VOCABULARY**
**stimulus** p. 102
**central nervous system** p. 104
**neuron** p.105
**peripheral nervous system** p. 106
**autonomic nervous system** p. 107
**voluntary nervous system** p. 107

### 4.2 The endocrine system helps regulate body conditions.

The body has chemical messengers called **hormones** that are regulated by the **endocrine system. Glands** produce and release hormones. The endocrine system includes feedback systems that maintain homeostasis.

Thyroxine hormone level is low.

Hypothalamus and pituitary gland increase thyroid gland activity.

Thyroxine hormone level is high.

Hypothalamus and pituitary gland decrease thyroid gland activity.

**VOCABULARY**
**endocrine system** p. 110
**hormone** p. 111
**gland** p. 111

### 4.3 The reproductive system allows the production of offspring.

The female produces eggs, and the male produces sperm. Following **fertilization** the fetus develops over a period of about nine months.

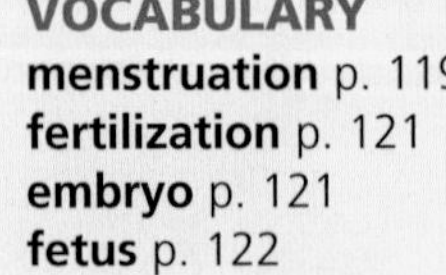

**VOCABULARY**
**menstruation** p. 119
**fertilization** p. 121
**embryo** p. 121
**fetus** p. 122

## Reviewing Vocabulary

*Make a frame for each of the vocabulary words listed. Write the word in the center. Decide what information to frame it with. Use definitions, examples, descriptions, parts, or pictures.*

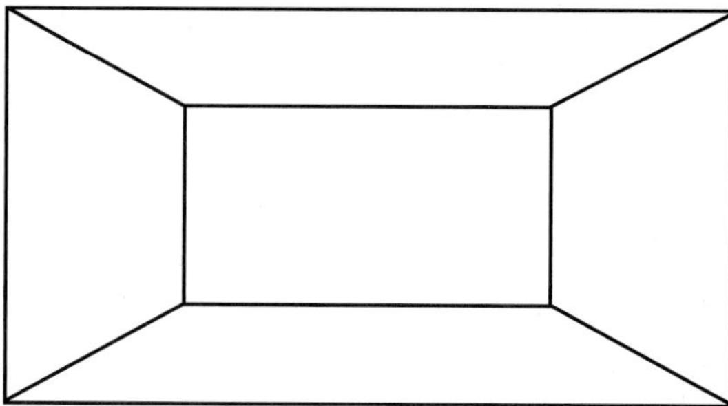

1. stimulus
2. neurons
3. hormones
4. fertilization
5. embryo

## Reviewing Key Concepts

**Multiple Choice** *Choose the letter of the best answer.*

6. Which is a stimulus?
   - **a.** a car horn blowing
   - **b.** jumping at a loud noise
   - **c.** taste buds on the tongue
   - **d.** turning on a lamp

7. Light enters the eye through
   - **a.** the lens
   - **b.** the auditory canal
   - **c.** the olfactory epithelium
   - **d.** the taste buds

8. Which senses allow you to process chemical information?
   - **a.** sight and smell
   - **b.** taste and smell
   - **c.** touch and hearing
   - **d.** hearing and taste

9. What conserves energy and responds quickly to change?
   - **a.** central nervous system
   - **b.** spinal cord
   - **c.** autonomic nervous system
   - **d.** voluntary nervous system

10. Which is not regulated by hormones?
    - **a.** production of white blood cells
    - **b.** physical growth
    - **c.** blood pressure
    - **d.** sexual development

11. Which gland releases hormones that are necessary for growth and metabolism?
    - **a.** thymus
    - **b.** pituitary gland
    - **c.** pancreas
    - **d.** pineal gland

12. Eggs develop in the female reproductive organ called
    - **a.** an ovary
    - **b.** a fallopian tube
    - **c.** a uterus
    - **d.** a vagina

13. The joining of one sperm cell and one egg cell is an event called
    - **a.** menstruation
    - **b.** fertilization
    - **c.** implantation
    - **d.** birth

14. A cluster of cells that is formed by fertilization is called the
    - **a.** testes
    - **b.** urethra
    - **c.** ovary
    - **d.** embryo

15. The period in which a fetus and all of its systems develop fully is the
    - **a.** first three months
    - **b.** second three months
    - **c.** third three months
    - **d.** pregnancy

**Short Answer** *Write a short answer to each question.*

16. List the parts of the body that are controlled by the autonomic nervous system.
17. What is a negative feedback mechanism? Give an example.
18. How are fertilization and menstruation related?

## Thinking Critically

*Use the diagram to answer the following two questions.*

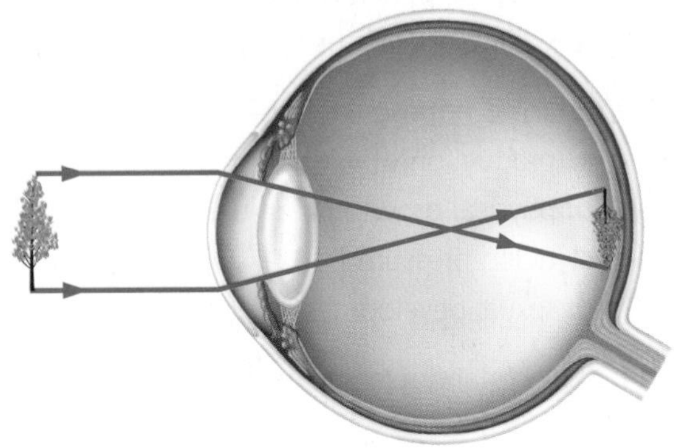

19. **SUMMARIZE** Use the diagram of the eye to describe how images are formed on the retina.

20. **COMPARE AND CONTRAST** How is the image that forms on the retina like the object? How is it different? Explain how the viewer interprets the image that forms on the retina.

21. **APPLY** A person steps on a sharp object with a bare foot and quickly pulls the foot back in pain. Describe the parts of the nervous system that are involved in this action.

22. **ANALYZE** Explain why positive feedback mechanisms do not help the body maintain homeostasis. Give an example.

23. **CONNECT** Copy the concept map and add the following terms to the correct box: brain, spinal cord, autonomic.

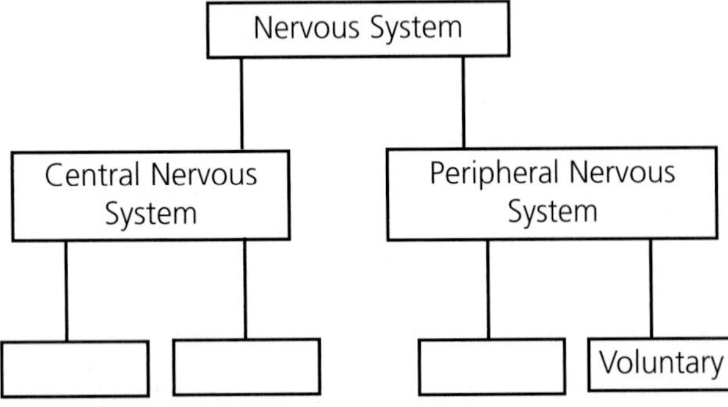


24. **DRAW CONCLUSIONS** A person who is normally very active begins to notice a significant decrease in energy level. After visiting a doctor, tests results show that one of the endocrine glands is not secreting enough of its hormone. Which gland could this be? Explain your answer.

25. **SUMMARIZE** Describe the events that occur during the female's 28-day menstrual cycle. Include in your answer how hormones are involved in the cycle.

26. **COMPARE AND CONTRAST** How are the functions of the ovaries and the testes alike? How are their functions different?

## the BIG idea

27. **INFER** Look again at the picture on pages 98–99. Now that you have finished the chapter, how would you change or add details to your answer to the question on the photograph?

28. **SYNTHESIZE** How does the nervous system interact with the endocrine and reproductive systems? Give examples that support your answer.

## UNIT PROJECTS

If you need to do an experiment for your unit project, gather the materials. Be sure to allow enough time to observe results before the project is due.

# Standardized Test Practice

For practice on your state test, go to . . . TEST PRACTICE CLASSZONE.COM

## Analyzing Data

This chart shows some of the stages of development of a typical fetus.

| Week of Pregnancy | Approximate Length of Fetus (cm) | Developmental Changes in the Fetus |
|---|---|---|
| 6 | 1 | Primitive heartbeat |
| 10 | 3 | Face, fingers, and toes are formed |
| 14 | 8.5 | Muscle and bone tissue have developed |
| 18 | 14 | Fetus makes active movements |
| 24 | 30 | Fingerprints and footprints forming |
| 28 | 37.5 | Rapid brain development |
| 36 | 47.5 | Increase in body fat |
| 38 | 50 | Fetus is considered full term |

*Use the chart to answer the questions below.*

**1.** What is the approximate length of the fetus at 10 weeks?

**a.** 1 cm
**b.** 2 in.
**c.** 3 cm
**d.** 3 in.

**2.** At about which week of development does the fetus begin to make active movements?

**a.** week 10
**b.** week 14
**c.** week 18
**d.** week 24

**3.** At about which week of development does the fetus reach a length of about 30 cm?

**a.** week 18
**b.** week 24
**c.** week 36
**d.** week 38

**4.** Which statement is true?

**a.** Between weeks 28 and 38, the fetus grows at an average of a little over a centimeter per week.
**b.** The fetus begins to develop fingerprints at about week 28.
**c.** During week 10, the length of the fetus is about 7.5 cm
**d.** The fetus is about 12.5 cm long when muscle and bone tissue develop.

**5.** Between which two weeks of development does the greatest overall increase in length usually take place?

**a.** weeks 6 and 10
**b.** weeks 10 and 14
**c.** weeks 14 and 18
**d.** weeks 24 and 28

## Extended Response

**6.** A pregnancy lasts about 42 weeks, roughly 9 months. The development of the fetus can be broken down into three stages, each 14 weeks long. These stages are referred to as trimesters. Briefly describe changes in length and development that occur during each of these stages.

**7.** The endocrine system and the nervous system have similar functions. Compare and contrast the two systems including the terms in the box. Underline each term in your answer.

| homeostasis | autonomic system | hormones |
|---|---|---|
| feedback | smooth muscles | |

CHAPTER

# Growth, Development, and Health

The body develops and maintains itself over time.

## Key Concepts

SECTION

**The human body changes over time.**
Learn about the different stages of human development.

SECTION

**Systems in the body function to maintain health.**
Learn about what a body needs to be healthy.

SECTION

**5.3 Science helps people prevent and treat disease.**
Learn how to help prevent the spread of disease.

*How do people change as they grow?*

**Internet Preview**

CLASSZONE.COM

Chapter 5 online resources: Content Review, Visualization, three Resource Centers, Math Tutorial, Test Practice

# EXPLORE the BIG idea

## How Much Do You Exercise?

In your notebook, create a chart to keep track of your exercise for a week. Each time you exercise, write down the type of activity and the amount of time you spend. If possible, measure your heart rate during the activity.

**Observe and Think** How does the exercise affect your heart rate? If you exercised regularly, what would be the effect on your heart rate while you were resting?

## How Safe Is Your Food?

Almost all food that you buy in a store is dated for freshness. Look at the labels of various foods including cereal, juice, milk, eggs, cheese, and meats.

**Observe and Think** Why do you think some foods have a longer freshness period than others? What types of problems could you have from eating food that is past date?

## Internet Activity: Human Development

Go to **ClassZone.com** to watch a movie of a person aging.

**Observe and Think** In what ways does a person's face change as he or she ages?

Human Development **Code: MDL048**

CHAPTER 5

# Getting Ready to Learn

## CONCEPT REVIEW

- The integumentary system protects the body.
- The immune system fights disease.
- A microscope is an instrument used to observe very small objects.

## VOCABULARY REVIEW

**nutrient** p. 45

**pathogen** p. 74

**antibiotic** p. 81

**hormone** p. 111

**CONTENT REVIEW**
CLASSZONE.COM

Review concepts and vocabulary.

## TAKING NOTES

### CONTENT FRAME

Make a content frame for each main idea. Include the following columns: *Topic, Definition, Detail,* and *Connection.* In the first column, list topics about the title. In the second column, define the topic. In the third column, include a detail about the topic. In the fourth column, add a sentence that connects that topic to another topic in the chart.

### CHOOSE YOUR OWN STRATEGY

For each new vocabulary term, take notes by choosing a strategy from earlier chapters—**four square, magnet word, frame game,** or **description wheel.** Or, use a strategy of your own.

See the Note-Taking Handbook on pages R45–R51.

**SCIENCE NOTEBOOK**

| The human body develops and grows. | | | |
|---|---|---|---|
| Topic | Definition | Detail | Connection |
| Childhood | Period after infancy and before sexual maturity. | Children depend on parents, but learn to do things for themselves, such as get dressed. | Adults do not have to depend on parents; they are independent and can care for others. |

Four Square

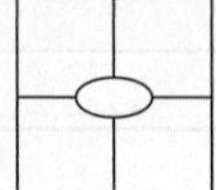

Frame Game

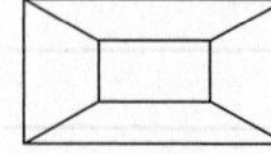

Magnet Word

Description Wheel

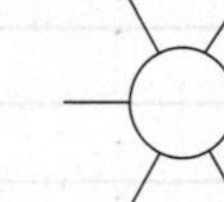

KEY CONCEPT

# The human body changes over time.

**BEFORE, you learned**

- Living things grow and develop
- The digestive system breaks down nutrients in food
- Organ systems interact to keep the body healthy

**NOW, you will learn**

- About four stages of human development
- About the changes that occur as the body develops
- How every body system interacts constantly with other systems to keep the body healthy

**VOCABULARY**

**infancy** p. 134
**childhood** p. 134
**adolescence** p. 135
**adulthood** p. 136

**EXPLORE Growth**

### *Are there patterns of growth?*

**PROCEDURE**

1. Measure the circumference of your wrist by using the measuring tape as shown. Record the length. Now measure the length from your elbow to the tip of your middle finger. Record the length.
2. Create a table and enter all the data from each person in the class.

**MATERIALS**

- flexible tape measure
- graph paper

**WHAT DO YOU THINK?**

- How does the distance between the elbow and the fingertip compare with wrist circumference?
- Do you see a pattern between the size of one's wrist and the length of one's forearm?

**CONTENT FRAME**

Make a content frame for the first main idea: *The human body develops and grows.* List the red headings in this section in the topics column.

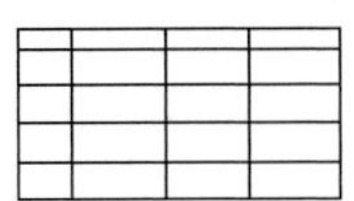

## The human body develops and grows.

Have you noticed how rapidly your body has changed over the past few years? Only five years ago you were a young child in grade school. Today you are in middle school. How has your body changed? Growth is both physical and emotional. You are becoming more responsible and socially mature. What are some emotional changes that you have noticed?

Human development is a continuous process. Although humans develop at different rates, there are several stages of development common to human life. In this section we will describe some of the stages, including infancy, childhood, adolescence, and adulthood.

## Infancy

The stage of life that begins at birth and ends when a baby begins to walk is called **infancy.** An infant's physical development is rapid. As the infant's body grows larger and stronger, it also learns physical skills. When you were first born, you could not hold up your head. But as your muscles developed, you gained the ability to hold up your head, to roll over, to sit, to crawl, to stand, and finally to walk. You also learned to use your hands to grasp and hold objects.

Infants also develop thinking skills and social skills. At first, they simply cry when they are uncomfortable. Over time, they learn that people respond to those cries. They begin to expect help when they cry. They learn to recognize the people who care for them. Smiling, cooing, and eventually saying a few words are all part of an infant's social development.

Nearly every body system changes and grows during infancy. For example, as the digestive system matures, an infant becomes able to process solid foods. Changes in the nervous system, including the brain, allow an infant to see more clearly and to better control parts of her or his body.

The Apgar score is used to evaluate the newborn's condition after delivery.

**Apgar Score**

| Quality | 0 points | 1 point | 2 points |
|---|---|---|---|
| Appearance | Completely blue or pale | Good color in body, blue hands or feet | Completely pink or good color |
| Pulse | No heart rate | <100 beats per minute | >100 beats per minute |
| Grimace | No response to airway suction | Grimace during suctioning | Grimace, cough/ sneeze with suction |
| Activity | Limp | Some arm and leg movement | Active motion |
| Respiration | Not breathing | Weak cry | Good, strong cry |

## Childhood

The stage called **childhood** lasts for several years. Childhood is the period after infancy and before the beginning of sexual maturity. During childhood, children still depend very much upon their parents. As their bodies and body systems grow, children become more able to care for themselves. Although parents still provide food and other needs, children perform tasks such as eating and getting dressed. In addition, children are able to do more complex physical tasks such as running, jumping, and riding a bicycle.

Childhood is also a time of mental and social growth. During childhood a human being learns to talk, read, write, and communicate in other ways. Along with the ability to communicate come social skills such as cooperation and sharing. A child learns to interact with others.

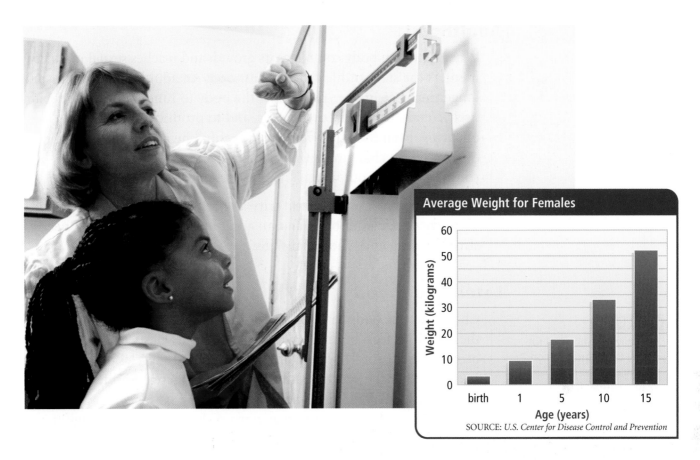

**Average Weight for Females**

Weight (kilograms): 0, 10, 20, 30, 40, 50, 60

Age (years): birth, 1, 5, 10, 15

SOURCE: *U.S. Center for Disease Control and Prevention*

## Adolescence

The years from puberty to adulthood are called **adolescence** (AD-uhl-EHS-uhns). Childhood ends when the body begins to mature sexually. This process of physical change is called puberty. Not all people reach puberty at the same age. For girls, the changes usually start between ages eight and fourteen; for boys, puberty often begins between ages ten and sixteen.

**VOCABULARY**
Choose a strategy from earlier chapters or one of your own to take notes on the term *adolescence*.

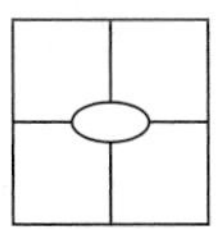

The human body changes greatly during adolescence. As you learned in Chapter 4, the endocrine system produces chemicals called hormones. During adolescence, hormones signal parts of the reproductive system to mature. At this stage a person's sexual organs become ready for reproduction. These changes are accompanied by other changes. Adolescents develop secondary sexual characteristics. Boys may notice their voices changing. Girls begin developing breasts. Boys and girls both begin growing more body hair.

Probably the change that is the most obvious is a change in height. Boys and girls grow taller by an average of 10 centimeters (3.9 in.) per year during adolescence. Most adolescents eat more as they grow. Food provides materials necessary for growth.

What are some of the ways the body changes during adolescence?

## Adulthood

When a human body completes its growth and reaches sexual maturity, it enters the stage of life called **adulthood.** An adult's body systems no longer increase in size. They allow the body to function fully, to repair itself, to take care of its own needs, and to produce and care for offspring. Even though a person reaches full height early in adulthood, other physical changes, as well as mental and social development, continue throughout life.

Mental and emotional maturity are important parts of adulthood. To maintain an adult body and an adult lifestyle, an individual needs strong mental and emotional skills.

## Later Adulthood

READING TIP

You may find it helpful to review the information on the skeletal and muscular system in Chapter 1.

Changes in the body that you might think of as aging begin at about the age of 30. Skin begins to wrinkle and lose its elasticity. Eyesight becomes increasingly poor, hair loss begins, and muscles decrease in strength. After the age of 65, the rate of aging increases. Internal organs become less efficient. Blood vessels become less elastic. The average blood pressure increases and may remain slightly high. Although the rate of breathing usually does not change, lung function decreases slightly. Body temperature is harder to regulate. However, one can slow the process of aging by a lifestyle of exercise and healthy diet.

# Systems interact to maintain the human body.

It's easy to observe the external changes to the body during growth and development. Inside the body, every system interacts constantly with other systems to keep the whole person healthy throughout his or her lifetime. For example, the respiratory system constantly sends oxygen to the blood cells of the circulatory system. The circulatory system transports hormones produced by the endocrine system.

Your body systems also interact with the environment outside your body. Your nervous system monitors the outside world through your senses of taste, smell, hearing, vision, and touch. It allows you to respond to your environment. For example, your nervous system allows you to squint if the sun is too bright or to move indoors if the weather is cold. Your endocrine system releases hormones that allow you to have an increased heart rate and send more blood to your muscles if you have to respond to an emergency.

# INVESTIGATE Life Expectancy

## *How has life expectancy changed over time?*

In this activity, you will look for trends in the changes in average life expectancy over the past 100 years.

**SKILL FOCUS**
Graphing

**MATERIALS**
- graph paper
- computer graphing program

**TIME**
30 minutes

### PROCEDURE

1. Using the following data, create a bar graph to chart changes in life expectancy in the U.S. over the last 100 years.

**Life Expectancy 1900–2000**

| Year | 1900 | 1910 | 1920 | 1930 | 1940 | 1950 | 1960 | 1970 | 1980 | 1990 | 2000 |
|---|---|---|---|---|---|---|---|---|---|---|---|
| Average Life Expectancy (years) | 47.3 | 50.0 | 54.1 | 59.7 | 62.9 | 68.2 | 69.7 | 70.8 | 73.7 | 75.4 | 76.9 |

SOURCE: National Center for Health Statistics

2. Study the graph. Observe any trends that you see. Record them in your notebook.

### WHAT DO YOU THINK?

- In general, what do these data demonstrate about life expectancy?
- Between which decades did average life expectancy increase the most?

**CHALLENGE** Using a computer program, create a table and bar graph to chart the data shown above.

Every part of your daily life requires interactions among your body systems. Even during sleep body systems cooperate. When you sleep, your nervous system allows your muscular system to keep your heart pumping and your lungs breathing. The heart pumps blood through your circulatory system, which has received oxygen from your respiratory system. All this cooperation takes place even while you are sleeping. Your endocrine system releases growth hormone during your sleep, allowing your bones and muscles to grow. The activity of neurons in your brain changes when you fall asleep.

Keeping the body healthy is complex. The digestive and urinary systems eliminate solid and liquid wastes from the body. The circulatory and respiratory systems remove carbon dioxide gas. As you will learn in the next section, a healthy diet and regular exercise help the body to stay strong and function properly.

**CHECK YOUR READING** Name three systems that interact as your body grows and maintains itself.

READING VISUALS COMPARE AND CONTRAST How do the interactions of your body system change when you are active and when you rest?

When body systems fail to work together, the body can become ill. Stress, for example, can affect all the body systems. Some types of stress, such as fear, can be a healthy response to danger. However, if the body experiences stress over long periods of time, serious health problems such as heart disease, headaches, muscle tension, and depression can arise.

All stages of life include different types of stress. Infants and children face stresses as they learn to become more independent and gain better control over their bodies. Adolescents can be challenged by school, by the changes of puberty, or by being socially accepted by their peers. Adults may encounter stress in their jobs or with their families. The stress of aging can be very difficult for some older adults.

## 5.1 Review

### KEY CONCEPTS

1. Make a development timeline with four sections. Write the names of the stages in order under each section. Include a definition and two details.
2. List a physical characteristic of each stage of development.
3. Give an example of an activity that involves two or more body systems.

### CRITICAL THINKING

4. **Compare and Contrast** Make a chart to compare and contrast the infancy and childhood stages of development.
5. **Identify Cause and Effect** How is the endocrine system involved in adolescence?

### CHALLENGE

6. **Synthesis** How does each of the body systems described change as a human being develops from infancy to older adulthood?

## STAGE MAKEUP ARTIST

# Aging the Face

In a movie, characters may go through development stages of a whole lifetime in just over an hour. An actor playing such a role will need to look both older and younger than he or she really is. Makeup artists have a toolbox full of techniques to make the actor look the part.

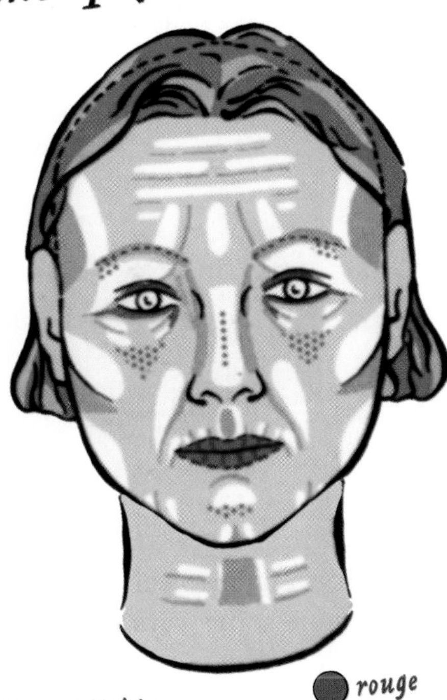


### Hair

As humans go through adulthood, their hair may lose the pigments that make it dark. Makeup artists color hair with dyes or even talcum powder. Wigs and bald caps, made of latex rubber, cover an actor's real hair. Eyebrows can be colored or aged by rubbing them with makeup.

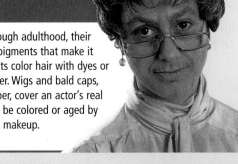

### Features

For a bigger-looking nose or extra skin around the neck, makeup artists use foam rubber, or layers of liquid rubber, and, sometimes, wads of paper tissue to build up facial features. For example, building up the cheekbones with layers of latex makes the cheeks appear sharper, less rounded, and more hollow.

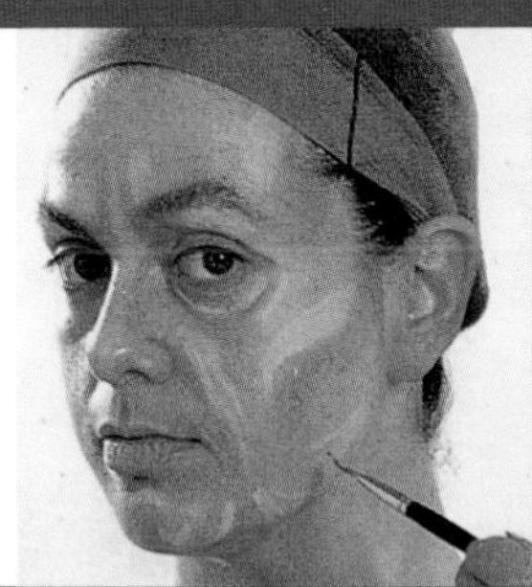

### Skin

To make wrinkles or scars, makeup artists use light-colored makeup for the raised highlights and dark-colored makeup for lower shadows and spots.

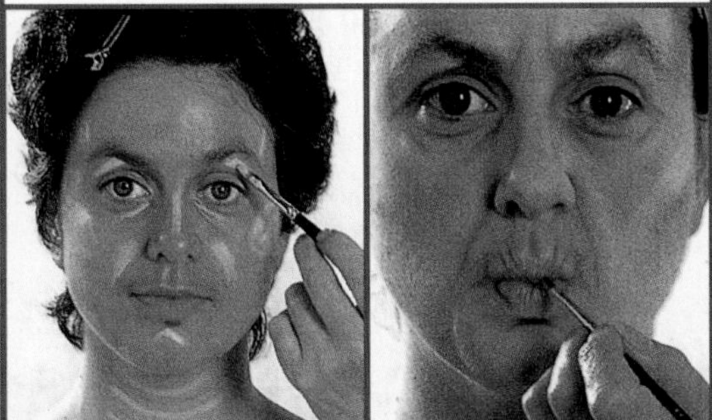

### EXPLORE

1. **COMPARE** Look at photos of an older relative at three different stages of life, at about ten years apart. Describe how you might apply makeup to your own face if you were to portray this person's life in three movie scenes. What changes do you need to show?
2. **CHALLENGE** Research to find an image of a character portrayed in a movie by an actor who looked very different in real life. From the picture, describe how the effect was achieved.

KEY CONCEPT

# Systems in the body function to maintain health.

**BEFORE, you learned**

- Human development involves all the body systems
- The human body continues to develop throughout life
- Every body system interacts constantly with other systems to keep the body healthy

**NOW, you will learn**

- About the role of nutrients in health
- Why exercise is needed to keep body systems healthy
- How drug abuse, eating disorders, and addiction can affect the body

**VOCABULARY**

**nutrition** p. 140
**addiction** p. 146

THINK ABOUT

### *What is health?*

If you went online and searched under the word *health,* you would find millions of links. Clearly, health is important to most people. You may be most aware of your health when you aren't feeling well. But you know that clean water, food, exercise, and sleep are all important for health. Preventing illness is also part of staying healthy. How would you define health? What are some ways that you protect your health?

## Diet affects the body's health.

What makes a meal healthy? The choices you make about what you eat are important. Nutrients from food are distributed to every cell in your body. You use those nutrients for energy and to maintain and build new body tissues. **Nutrition** is the study of the materials that nourish your body. It also refers to the process in which the different parts of food are used for maintenance, growth, and reproduction. When a vitamin or other nutrient is missing from your diet, illness can occur. Your body's systems can function only when they get the nutrients they need.

VOCABULARY
Choose a strategy from an earlier chapter, such as a magnet word diagram, for taking notes on the term *nutrition*. Or use any strategy that you think works well.

CHECK YOUR READING How is nutrition important to health?

This family is enjoying a healthy meal that includes proteins, carbohydrates, and fats.

## Getting Nutrients

Discover more about human health.

In order to eat a healthy diet, you must first understand what good nutrition is. There are six classes of nutrients: carbohydrates, proteins, fats, vitamins, minerals, and water. All of these nutrients are necessary for your body cells to carry out the chemical reactions that sustain life.

**Proteins** are molecules that build tissues used for growth and repair. Proteins provide the building blocks for many important hormones. Good sources of proteins are poultry, red meat, fish, eggs, nuts, beans, grains, soy, and milk. Protein should make up at least 20 percent of your diet.

**Carbohydrates** are the body's most important energy source and are found in starch, sugar, and fiber. Fiber provides little energy, but is important for regular elimination. Natural sugars such as those found in fruits and vegetables are the best kinds of sugars for your body. Carbohydrates are found in bread and pasta, fruits, and vegetables. Carbohydrates should make up about 40 to 50 percent of your diet.

**Fats** are essential for energy and should account for about 10 to 15 percent of your diet. Many people eliminate fats from their diet in order to lose weight. But a certain amount of fat is necessary. Fats made from plants have the greatest health benefits. For example, olive oil is better for you than the oil found in butter.

**Vitamins and minerals** are needed by your body in small amounts. Vitamins are small molecules that regulate body growth and development. Minerals help build body tissues. While some vitamins can be made by your body, most of them are supplied to the body in food.

**Water** is necessary for life. A human being could live for about a month without food, but only about one week without water. Water has several functions. Water helps regulate your body temperature through evaporation when you sweat and breathe. Without water, important materials such as vitamins and other nutrients could not be transported around the body. Water helps your body get rid of the waste products that move through the kidneys and pass out of the body in urine. Urine is composed mostly of water.

To make sure your body can function and maintain itself, you need to drink about two and one half liters, or about eight glasses, of water every day. You also get water when you eat foods with water in them, such as fresh fruit and vegetables.

**Vitamins and Minerals**

| Vitamin or Mineral | Recommended Daily Allowance |
|---|---|
| Vitamin A | 0.3 to 1.3 mg |
| Niacin | 6–18 mg |
| Vitamin $B_2$ | 0.5–1.6 mg |
| Vitamin $B_6$ | 0.5–2.0 mg |
| Vitamin C | 15–120 mg |
| Vitamin E | 6–19 mg |
| Calcium | 500–1300 mg |
| Phosphorus | 460–1250 mg |
| Potassium | 1600–2000 mg |
| Zinc | 3–13 mg |
| Magnesium | 80–420 mg |
| Iron | 7–27 mg |

Source: National Institutes of Health

## Understanding Nutrition

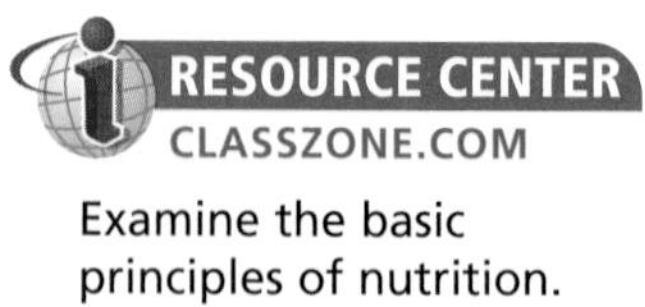


Examine the basic principles of nutrition.

Ever wonder what the word *lite* really means? What do labels saying that food is fresh or natural or organic mean? Not all advertising about nutrition is reliable. It is important to know what the labels on food really mean. Groups within the government, such as the United States Department of Agriculture, have defined terms that are used to describe food products. For example, if a food label says the food is "all natural," that means it does not contain any artificial flavor, color, or preservative.

Another example is the term *low-fat*. That label means that the food provides no more than 3 grams of fat per serving. The word *organic* means that the produce has been grown using no human-made fertilizers or chemicals that kill pests or weeds. It also means that livestock has been raised on organic feed and has not been given antibiotics or growth hormones. It takes some effort and a lot of reading to stay informed, but the more you know, the better the choices you can make.

# INVESTIGATE Food Labels

## *What are you eating?*

**SKILL FOCUS**
Analyzing

**MATERIALS**
nutrition labels

**TIME**
30 minutes

**PROCEDURE**

1. Gather nutrition labels from the following products: a carbonated soft drink, a bag of fresh carrots, canned spaghetti in sauce, potato chips, plain popcorn kernels, unsweetened applesauce, and fruit juice. Look at the percent of daily values of the major nutrients, as shown on the label for each food.
2. Make a list of ways to evaluate a food for high nutritional value. Include such criteria as nutrient levels and calories per serving.
3. Examine the nutrition labels and compare them with your list. Decide which of these foods would make a healthy snack.

**WHAT DO YOU THINK?**

- How does serving size affect the way you evaluate a nutritional label?
- What are some ways to snack and get nutrients at the same time?

**CHALLENGE** Design a full day's food menu that will give you all the nutrients you need. Use snacks as some of the foods that contribute these nutrients.

**Spaghetti**
IN TOMATO SAUCE WITH CHEESE

**Nutrition Facts**
Serving Size: 1 cup (252g)
Servings Per Container: about 2

| Amount Per Serving | |
|---|---|
| Calories 210 | Calories from Fat 20 |
| | % Daily Value* |
| **Total Fat** 2g | 3% |
| Saturated Fat 1g | 5% |
| **Cholesterol** 5mg | 2% |
| **Sodium** 1,020 mg | 43% |
| **Total Carbohydrate** 41g | 14% |
| Dietary Fiber 3g | 12% |
| Sugars 14g | |
| **Protein** 7g | |
| Vitamin A 10% | Vitamin C 0% |
| Calcium 4% | Iron 10% |

* Percent Daily Values are based on a 2,000 calorie diet. Your daily values may be higher or lower depending on your calorie needs.

## Exercise is part of a healthy lifestyle.

Regular exercise allows all your body systems to stay strong and healthy. You learned that your lymphatic system doesn't include a structure like the heart to pump its fluid through the body. Instead, it relies on body movement and strong muscles to help it move antibodies and white blood cells. Exercise is good for the lymphatic system.

### Exercise

When you exercise, you breathe harder and more quickly. You inhale and exhale more air, which exercises the muscles of your respiratory system and makes them stronger. Exercise also brings in extra oxygen. Oxygen is necessary for cellular respiration, which provides energy to other body systems. The circulatory system is strengthened by exercise. Your heart becomes stronger the more it is used. The skeletal system grows stronger with exercise as well. Studies show that older adults who lift weights have stronger bones than those who do not. In addition, physical activity can flush out skin pores by making you sweat, and it reduces the symptoms of depression.

By eating healthy meals and exercising, you help your body to grow and develop.

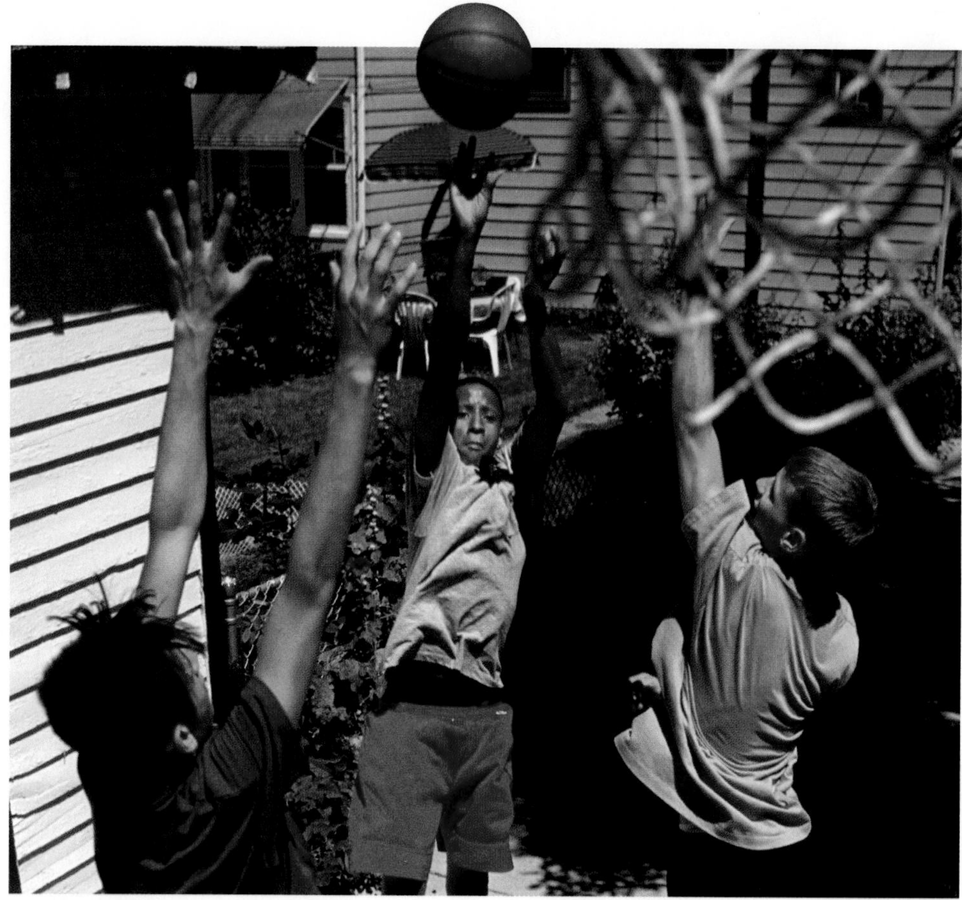

### Lifestyle

The lifestyles of many people involve regular exercise. Some lifestyles, however, include more sitting still than moving. A lifestyle that is sedentary, associated mostly with sitting down, can harm a person's health. Muscles and bones that are not exercised regularly can begin to break down. Your body stores unused energy from food as fat. The extra weight of body fat can make it harder for you to exercise. Therefore, it is harder to use up energy or to strengthen your skeletal, muscular, and immune systems. Researchers have also made connections between excess body fat and heart disease and diabetes.

How does lifestyle affect health?

**CONTENT FRAME**
Make a content frame for the main idea: *Drug abuse, addiction, and eating disorders cause serious health problems.*

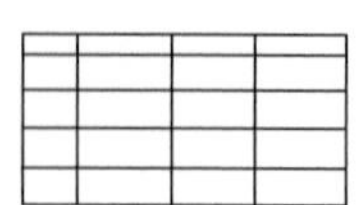

## Drug abuse, addiction, and eating disorders cause serious health problems.

Every day, you make choices that influence your health. Some choices can have more serious health risks, or possibilities for harm, than others. You have the option to make healthy choices for yourself. Making unhealthy decisions about what you put into your body can lead to drug abuse, addiction, or eating disorders.

## Drug Abuse

A drug is any chemical substance that you take in to change your body's functions. Doctors use drugs to treat and prevent disease and illness. The use of a drug for any other reason is an abuse of that drug. Abuse can also include using too much of a substance that is not harmful in small amounts. People abuse different drugs for different reasons. Drugs often do allow an individual to feel better for the moment. But they can also cause serious harm to an individual's health.

**Tobacco** Nicotine, the drug in tobacco, increases heart rate and blood pressure and makes it seem as if the user has more energy. Nicotine is also a poison; in fact, some farmers use it to kill insects. Tobacco smoke contains thousands of chemicals. Tar and carbon monoxide are two harmful chemicals in smoke. Tar is a sticky substance that is commonly used to pave roads. Carbon monoxide is one of the gases that cars release in their exhaust. People who smoke or chew tobacco have a higher risk of cancer, and smokers are also at risk for heart disease.

**Compounds Found in Unfiltered Tobacco Smoke**

| Compound | Amount in First-Hand Smoke (mg per cigarette) | Amount in Second-Hand Smoke (mg per cigarette) |
|---|---|---|
| Nicotine | 1–3 | 2.1–46 |
| Tar | 15–40 | 14–30 |
| Carbon monoxide | 14–23 | 27–61 |
| Benzene | 0.012–0.05 | 0.4 |
| Formaldehyde | 0.07–0.1 | 1.5 |
| Hydrogen cyanide | 0.4–0.5 | 0.014–11 |
| Phenol | 0.08–0.16 | 0.07–0.25 |

Source: U.S. Department of Health and Human Services

**Alcohol** Even a small amount of alcohol can affect a person's ability to think and reason. Alcohol can affect behavior and the ability to make decisions. Many people are killed every year, especially in automobile accidents, because of choices they made while drinking alcohol. Alcohol abuse damages the heart, the liver, the nervous system, and the digestive system.

**Other Drugs** Some drugs, such as cocaine and amphetamines, can make people feel more energetic and even powerful because they stimulate parts of the nervous system and speed up the heart. These drugs are very dangerous. They can cause heart attacks, and long-term use may cause brain damage.

Drugs called narcotics also affect the nervous system. Instead of stimulating it, however, they decrease its activity. Narcotics are prescribed by doctors to relieve pain and to help people sleep. Because narcotics work by decreasing the function of nerves in some brain regions, large amounts of these drugs can cause the heart and lungs to stop. Abuse of narcotics can also lead to addiction.

Students can be active in protesting drug abuse.

## Addiction

Drug abuse can often lead to addiction. **Addiction** is an illness in which a person becomes dependent on a substance or behavior. Repeated use of drugs such as alcohol, tobacco, and narcotics can cause the body to become physically dependent. When a person is dependent on a drug, taking away that drug can cause withdrawal. If affected by withdrawal, a person may become physically ill, sometimes within a very short period of time. Symptoms of withdrawal from some types of drugs can include fever, muscle cramps, vomiting, and hallucinations.

Another type of addiction can result from the effect produced by a drug or even a behavior. Although physical dependency may not occur, a person can become emotionally dependent. Gambling, overeating, and risk-taking are some examples of addictive behaviors. Someone who suffers from an addiction can be treated and can work to live a healthy life, but most addictions never go away completely.

## Eating Disorders

An eating disorder is a condition in which people continually eat too much or too little food. One example of an eating disorder is anorexia nervosa. People with this disorder eat so little and exercise so hard that they become unhealthy. No matter how thin they are, they believe they need to be thinner. People with anorexia do not receive necessary nutrients because they don't eat. When the energy used by the body exceeds the energy taken in from food, tissues in the body are broken down to provide fuel. Bones and muscles, including the heart, can be damaged, and the person can die.

## 5.2 Review

### KEY CONCEPTS

1. How do nutrients affect health?
2. Explain the effects of exercise on the respiratory and circulatory systems.
3. Make a chart showing the effects of tobacco, alcohol, and other drugs on the body.

### CRITICAL THINKING

4. **Explain** How would you define health? Write your own definition.
5. **Synthesize** Explain how water can be considered a nutrient. Include a definition of *nutrient* in your explanation.

### CHALLENGE

6. **Apply** You have heard about a popular new diet. Most of the foods in the diet are fat-free, and the diet promises fast weight loss. How might this diet affect health? Explain your answer.

MATH in SCIENCE

## SKILL: CHOOSING A DATA DISPLAY

MATH TUTORIAL
CLASSZONE.COM
Click on Math Tutorial for more help with choosing a data display.

# Pumping Up the Heart

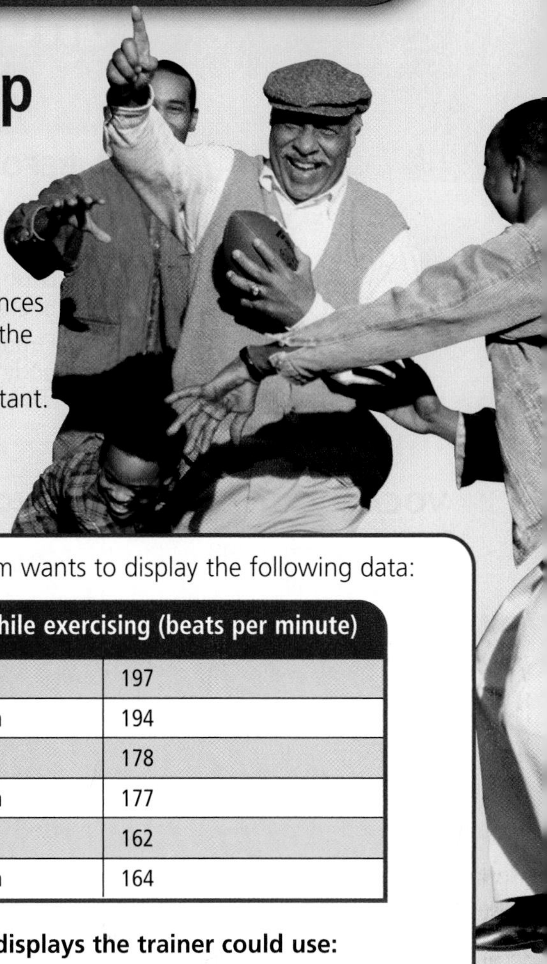

Heart rates differ with age, level of activity, and fitness. To communicate the differences clearly, you need to display the data visually. Choosing the appropriate display is important.

### Example

The fitness trainer at a gym wants to display the following data:

| Maximum heart rate while exercising (beats per minute) | | |
|---|---|---|
| Age 21 | Men | 197 |
| | Women | 194 |
| Age 45 | Men | 178 |
| | Women | 177 |
| Age 65 | Men | 162 |
| | Women | 164 |

**Here are some different displays the trainer could use:**

- A bar graph shows how different categories of data compare. Data can be broken into 2 or even 3 bars per category.
- A line graph shows how data changes over time.
- A circle graph represents data as parts of a whole.

**ANSWER** The fitness trainer wants to show heart rate according to both age and gender, so a double bar graph would be the clearest.

What would be an appropriate way to display data in the following situations?

**1.** A doctor wants to display how a child's average heart rate changes as the child grows.

**2.** A doctor wants to display data showing how a person's resting heart rate changes the more the person exercises.

**3.** A scientist is studying each type of diet that the people in an experiment follow. She will show what percentage of the people with each diet had heart disease.

**CHALLENGE** Describe a situation in which a double line graph is the most appropriate data display.

KEY CONCEPT

# Science helps people prevent and treat disease.

**BEFORE, you learned**

- Good nutrition and exercise help keep the body healthy
- Drug abuse can endanger health
- Eating disorders can affect the body's health

**NOW, you will learn**

- About some of the causes of disease
- How diseases can be treated
- How to help prevent the spread of disease

**VOCABULARY**

**microorganism** p. 148
**bacteria** p. 149
**virus** p. 149
**resistance** p. 153

**EXPLORE The Immune System**

### *How easily do germs spread?*

**PROCEDURE**

1. Early in the day, place a small amount of glitter in the palm of one hand. Rub your hands together to spread the glitter to both palms. Go about your day normally.
2. At the end of the day, examine your environment, including the people around you. Where does the glitter show up?

**MATERIALS**
glitter

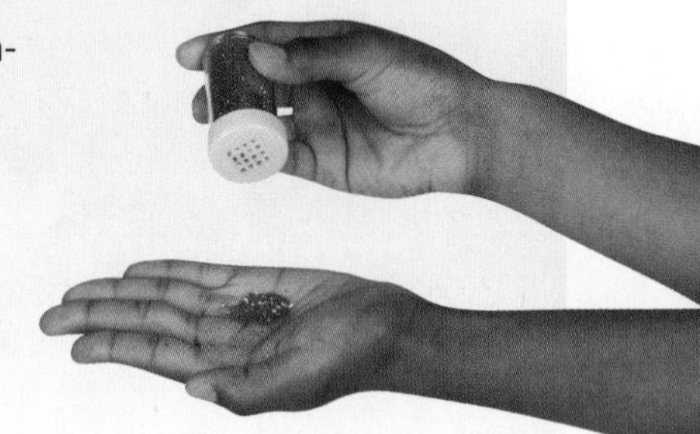

**WHAT DO YOU THINK?**

- How easily did the glitter transfer to other people and objects?
- What do you think this might mean about how diseases might spread?

## Scientific understanding helps people fight disease.

Disease is a change that disturbs the normal functioning of the body's systems. If you have ever had a cold, you have experienced a disease that affected your respiratory system. What are the causes of disease? Many diseases are classified as infectious diseases, or diseases that can be spread. Viruses, bacteria, and other pathogens cause infectious disease. The organisms that cause sickness are called **microorganisms.**

Before the invention of the microscope, people didn't know about microorganisms that cause disease. They observed that people who lived near each other sometimes caught the same illness, but they didn't understand why. Understanding disease has helped people prevent and treat many illnesses.

**VOCABULARY**
Remember to choose a strategy from earlier chapters or one of your own to take notes on the term *microorganism.*

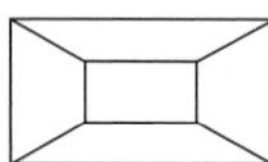

## The germ theory describes some causes of disease.

In the 1800s, questions about the causes of some diseases were answered. Scientists showed through experiments that diseases could be caused by very small living things. In 1857, French chemist Louis Pasteur did experiments that showed that microorganisms caused food to decay. Later, Pasteur's work and the work of Robert Koch and Robert Lister contributed to the germ theory. Pasteur's germ theory states that some diseases, called infectious diseases, are caused by germs.

### Bacteria and Viruses

Germs are the general name given to organisms that cause disease. **Bacteria** (bak-TEER-ee-uh) are single-celled organisms that live almost everywhere. Within your intestines, bacteria function to digest food. Some bacteria, however, cause disease. Pneumonia (nu-MOHN-yuh), ear infections (ihn-FEHK-shuhnz), and strep throat can be caused by bacteria.

Explore ways to fight disease.

**Viruses** do not fit all parts of the definition of living things. For example, they must enter and exist inside living cells in order to reproduce. Stomach flu, chicken pox, and colds are sicknesses caused by viruses. Both bacteria and viruses are examples of pathogens, agents that cause disease. The word *pathogen* comes from the Greek *pathos*, which means "suffering." Other pathogens include yeasts, fungi, and protists.

### Treating Infectious Diseases

Diseases caused by bacteria can be treated with medicines that contain antibiotics. An antibiotic is a substance that can destroy bacteria. The first antibiotics were discovered in 1928 when a scientist named Alexander Fleming was performing experiments on bacteria. Fleming found mold growing on his bacteria samples. While most of the petri dish was covered with bacterial colonies, the area around the mold was clear. From this observation, Fleming concluded that a substance in the mold had killed the bacteria.

Fleming had not intended to grow mold in his laboratory, but the accident led to the discovery of penicillin. Since the discovery of penicillin, many antibiotics have been developed. Antibiotics have saved the lives of millions of people.

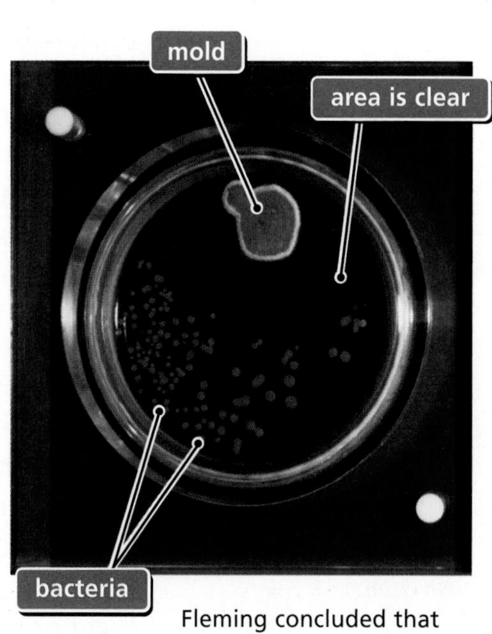


Fleming concluded that something in the mold had killed the bacteria.

## Infectious diseases spread in many ways.

READING TIP

As you read the text on this page, notice how each pathogen shown on p. 151 spreads.

One of the best ways to protect your health is by being informed and by avoiding pathogens. Pathogens can be found in many places, including air, water, and on the surfaces of objects. By knowing how pathogens travel, people are able to limit the spreading of disease.

### Food, Air, and Water

Sometimes people get sick when they breathe in pathogens from the air. The viruses that cause colds can travel through air. If you cover your mouth when you sneeze or cough, you can avoid sending pathogens through the air. Pathogens also enter the body in food or water. Washing fruits and vegetables and cooking meats and eggs kills bacteria. Most cities in the United States add substances, such as chlorine, to the supply of public water. These substances kill pathogens. Boiling water also kills pathogens. People sometimes boil water if their community loses power or experiences a flood. Campers need to boil or filter water taken from a stream before they use it.

### Contact with Animals

Animals can also carry organisms that cause disease. The animal itself does not cause the illness, but you can become sick if you take in the pathogen that the animal carries. Lyme disease, for example, is caused by bacteria that inhabit ticks. The ticks are not the cause of illness, but if an infected tick bites you, you will get Lyme disease.

A deadly central nervous system infection called rabies can also come from animal contact. The virus that causes rabies is found in the saliva of an infected animal, such as a bat, raccoon, or opossum. If that animal bites you, you may get the disease. A veterinarian can give your pet an injection to prevent rabies. You can get other infections from pets. These infections include worms that enter through your mouth or nose and live in your intestines. You can also get a skin infection called ringworm, which is actually a fungus rather than a worm.

### Person-to-Person Contact

Most of the illnesses you have had have probably been passed to you by another person. Even someone who does not feel sick can have pathogens on his or her skin. If you touch that person or if that person touches something and then you touch it, the pathogens will move to your skin. If the pathogens then enter your body through a cut or through your nose, mouth, or eyes, they can infect your body. The simplest way to avoid giving or receiving pathogens is to wash your hands often and well.

## Pathogens and Disease

### Infectious diseases are caused by microorganisms.

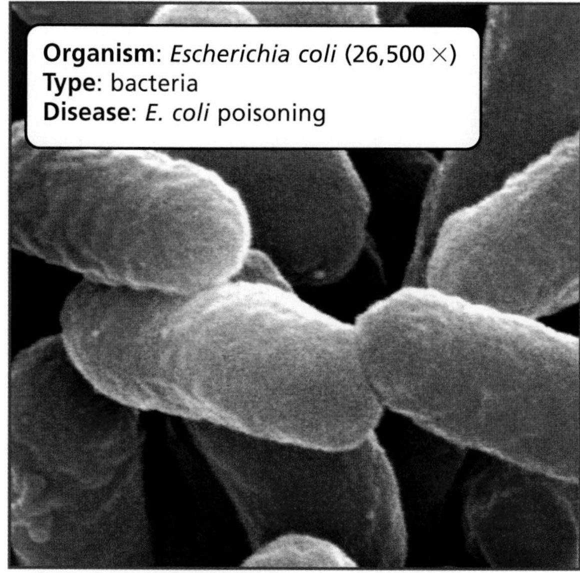

**Organism**: *Escherichia coli* (26,500 ×)
**Type**: bacteria
**Disease**: *E. coli* poisoning


**Spread**: contaminated food or water

**Prevention**: handwashing, thoroughly cooking meat, boiling contaminated water, washing fruits and vegetables, drinking only pasteurized milk, juice, or cider

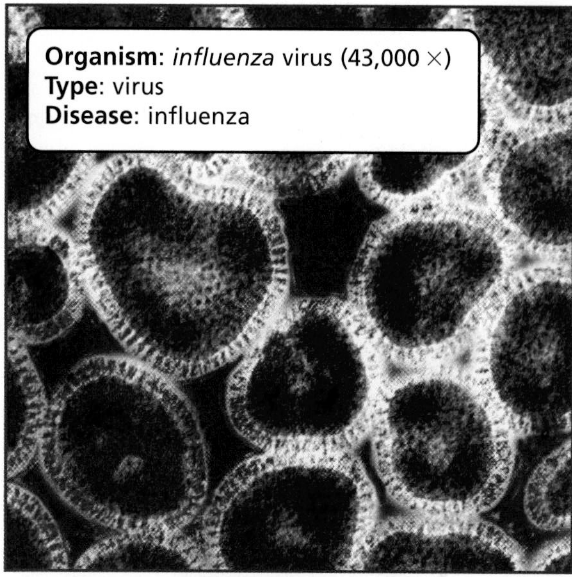

**Organism**: *influenza* virus (43,000 ×)
**Type**: virus
**Disease**: influenza


**Spread**: inhaling virus from sneezes or coughs of infected person

**Prevention**: vaccination

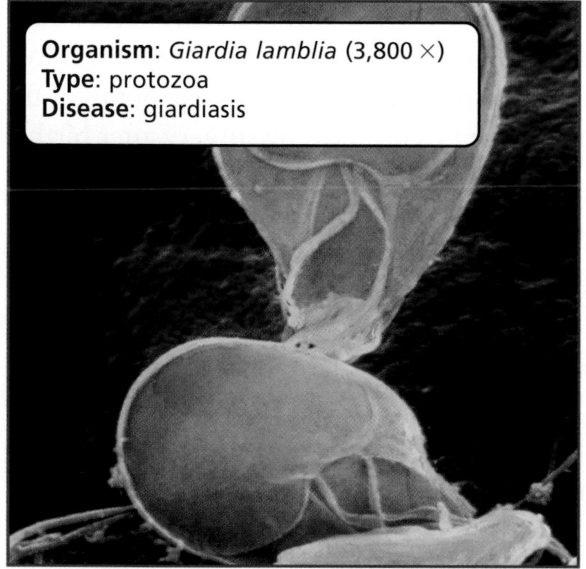

**Organism**: *Giardia lamblia* (3,800 ×)
**Type**: protozoa
**Disease**: giardiasis


**Spread**: contaminated food or water, close contact with infected person

**Prevention**: handwashing, thoroughly cooking meat, boiling contaminated water, washing fruits and vegetables, drinking only pasteurized milk, juice, or cider

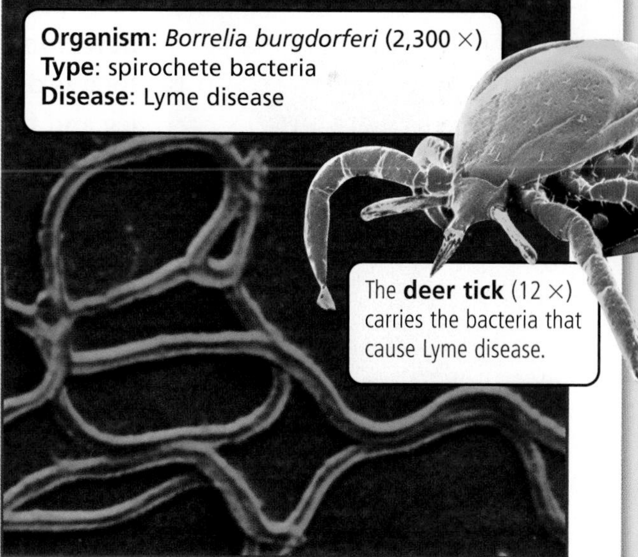

**Organism**: *Borrelia burgdorferi* (2,300 ×)
**Type**: spirochete bacteria
**Disease**: Lyme disease
The **deer tick** (12 ×) carries the bacteria that cause Lyme disease.


**Spread**: tick bite

**Prevention**: wear light-colored clothing, tuck pants into socks or shoes, check for ticks after outdoor activities, use repellents containing DEET

How can people prevent each of these pathogens from spreading?

## Noninfectious diseases are not contagious.

Noninfectious diseases are diseases that cannot be spread by pathogens. They are not contagious. People are born with some of these, and others can develop during life.

### Diseases Present at Birth

Some diseases present at birth are inherited. Genes, which act as instructions for your cells, are inherited from your parents. Some forms of a gene produce cells that do not function properly. Most genetic disorders are due to recessive forms of a gene, which means that while both parents carry the defective form, neither one has the disorder. Cystic fibrosis and sickle cell disease are diseases inherited this way.

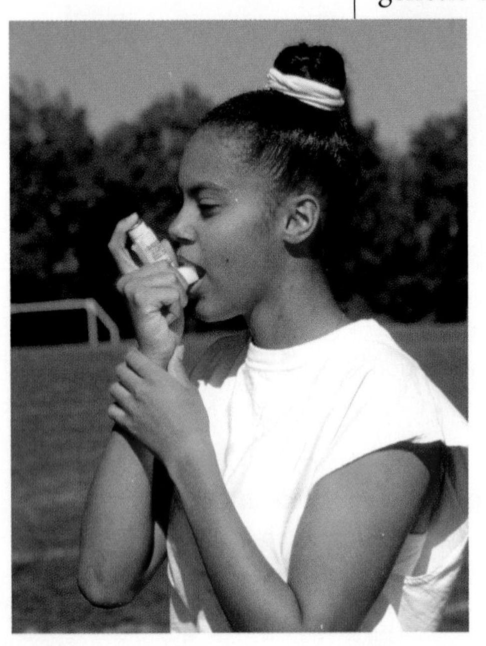

Asthma is a noncontagious disease often present at birth.

The symptoms of some genetic diseases may not be present immediately at birth. Huntington's disease, even though it is an inherited condition, does not begin to produce symptoms until a person reaches adulthood. Other genes can increase the chances of developing a disease later in life, such as cancer or diabetes, but the pattern of inheritance is complex.

The process of human development is complex. Some diseases present at birth may involve both inherited factors and development. Talipes, a disorder commonly known as clubfoot, is due to the improper development of the bones of the leg and foot. Talipes can be corrected by surgery after birth.

### Diseases in Later Life

Some diseases, including heart disease, certain forms of cancer, and many respiratory disorders, have much less to do with genetics and more to do with environment and lifestyle. You have learned about the ways in which you can lead a healthy lifestyle. Good nutrition, exercise, and avoiding substances that can damage the body systems not only increase the length of life, but also the quality of life.

While people with family histories of cancer are at higher risk of getting it, environmental factors can influence risk as well. Tar and other chemicals from cigarettes can damage the lungs, in addition to causing cancer. Much is still not known about the causes of cancer.

**CHECK YOUR READING** Name a noninfectious disease that is present at birth and one that may occur later in life.

## Scientists continue efforts to prevent and treat illness.

In spite of all that scientists have learned, disease is still a problem all over the world. Illnesses such as AIDS and cancer are better understood than they used to be, but researchers must still find ways to cure them.

Scientists work hard to fight disease.

Even though progress is sometimes slow, it does occur. Better education has led to better nutrition. The use of vaccines has made some diseases nearly extinct. However, new types of illness sometimes appear. AIDS was first identified in the 1980s and spread quickly before it was identified. More recently, the West Nile virus appeared in the United States. This virus is transmitted by infected mosquitoes and can cause the brain to become inflamed. Efforts to control the disease continue.

Antibiotics fight pathogens, but they can also lead to changes in them. When an antibiotic is used too often, bacteria can develop **resistance,** which means that the strain of bacteria is no longer affected by the drug. Once a strain of bacteria has developed resistance, the resistance will be passed on to new generations of the bacteria. This means that a particular antibiotic will not stop that particular bacterial infection.

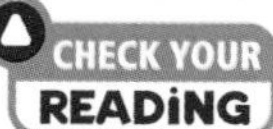

CHECK YOUR READING Describe the advantages and disadvantages of using an antibiotic when you are sick.

## 5.3 Review

### KEY CONCEPTS

1. Define microorganism and explain how microorganisms can affect health.
2. What is an antibiotic?
3. Make a chart showing ways that infectious diseases spread and ways to keep them from spreading.

### CRITICAL THINKING

4. **Connect** Make a list of things you can do to avoid getting Lyme disease or the West Nile virus.
5. **Apply** How does washing your hands before eating help protect your health?

### CHALLENGE

6. **Synthesize** How can nutrition help in the prevention of disease? Use these terms in your answer: *nutrients, pathogens,* and *white blood cells.*

# CHAPTER INVESTIGATION

## Cleaning Your Hands

**OVERVIEW AND PURPOSE** Your skin cells produce oils that keep the skin moist. This same layer of oil provides a nutrient surface for bacteria to grow. When you wash your hands with soap, the soap dissolves the oil and the water carries it away, along with the bacteria. In this activity you will

- sample your hands for the presence of bacteria
- test the effectiveness of washing your hands with water compared with washing them with soap and water

### Problem

Write It Up

Is soap effective at removing bacteria?

### Hypothesize

Write It Up

Write a hypothesis explaining how using soap affects the amount of bacteria on your hands. Your hypothesis should take the form of an "If . . . , then . . . , because . . ." statement.

**MATERIALS**

- 3 covered petri dishes with sterile nutrient agar
- soap
- marker
- tape
- hand lens

### Procedure

1. Make a data table in your **Science Notebook** like the one shown on page 155.
2. Obtain three agar petri dishes. Be careful not to open the dishes accidentally.
3. Remove the lid from one dish and gently press two fingers from your right hand onto the surface of the agar. Close the lid immediately. Tape the dish closed. Mark the tape with the letter *A*. Include your initials and the date.

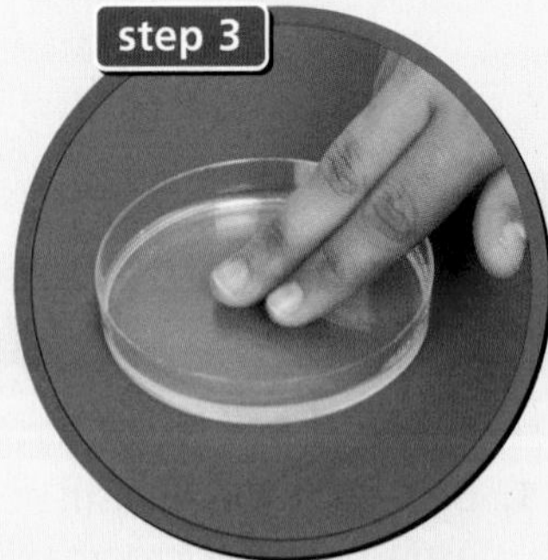

4 Wash your hands in water and let them air-dry. Open the second dish with your right hand and press two fingers of your left hand into the agar. Close the lid immediately. Tape and mark the dish *B*, as in step 3.

5 Wash your hands in soap and water and let them air-dry. Open the third dish with one hand and press two fingers of the other hand into the agar. Close the lid immediately. Tape and mark the dish *C*, as in step 3.

6 Place the agar plates upside down in a dark, warm place for two to three days. **Caution:** Do not open the dishes. Wash your hands.

## Observe and Analyze

Write It Up

1. **OBSERVE** Use a hand lens to observe the amounts of bacterial growth in each dish, and record your observations in Table 1. Which dish has the most bacterial growth? the least growth?
2. **OBSERVE** Is there anything you notice about the bacterial growth in each dish other than the amount of bacterial growth?
3. Return the petri dishes to your teacher for disposal. **Caution:** Do not open the dishes. Wash your hands thoroughly with warm water and soap when you have finished.

## Conclude

Write It Up

1. **INFER** Why is it necessary to air-dry your hands instead of using a towel?
2. **INFER** Why is it important to use your right hand in step 3 and your left hand in step 4?
3. **INTERPRET** Compare your results with your hypothesis. Do your observations support your hypothesis?
4. **EVALUATE** Is there much value in washing your hands simply in water?
5. **EVALUATE** How might the temperature of the water you used when you washed your hands affect the results of your experiment?
6. **EVALUATE** Given the setup of your experiment, could you have prepared a fourth sample, for example to test the effectiveness of antibacterial soap?

## INVESTIGATE Further

**CHALLENGE** It is hard to tell which products are best for washing hands without testing them. Design an experiment to determine which cleans your hands best: baby wipes, hand sanitizer, regular soap, or antibacterial soap.

Cleaning Your Hands

Table 1. Observations

| Petri Dish | Source | Amount of Bacteria |
|---|---|---|
| A | hand | |
| B | hand washed with water | |
| C | hand washed with soap and water | |

# Chapter Review

## the BIG idea

**The body develops and maintains itself over time.**

## KEY CONCEPTS SUMMARY

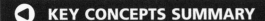

### The human body changes over time.

Your body changes throughout your entire life. Some changes are physical and some are emotional. The stages of life are infancy, childhood, adolescence, adulthood, and later adulthood. All the different systems in the body interact to maintain your health.

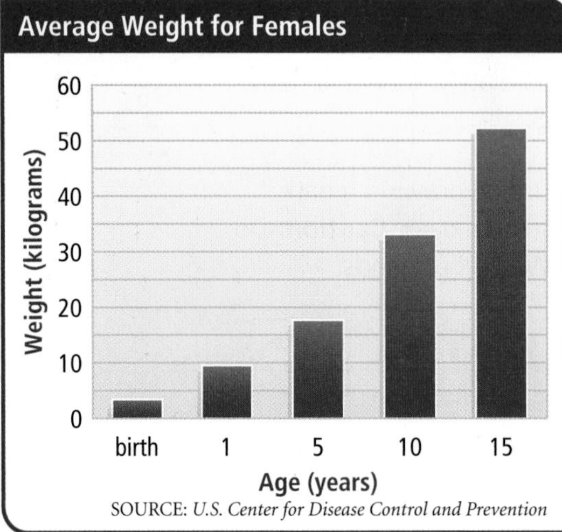


**VOCABULARY**
**infancy** p. 134
**childhood** p. 134
**adolescence** p. 135
**adulthood** p. 136

**5.2**

### Systems in the body function to maintain health.

Your diet affects your health. Important nutrients include proteins, carbohydrates, fats, vitamins, minerals, and water. Water is also essential to healthy living. Exercise is another ingredient to a healthy life. Problems that can interfere with a healthy life are drug abuse, addiction, and eating disorders.

**VOCABULARY**
**nutrition** p. 140
**addiction** p. 146

### Science helps people prevent and treat disease.

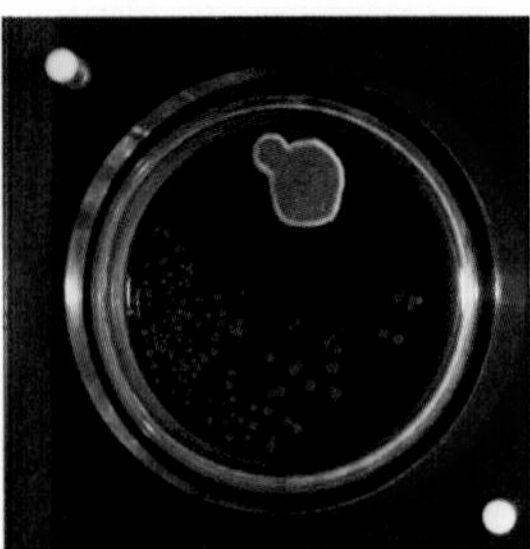

- Science helps people fight disease.
- Antibiotics are used to fight diseases caused by bacteria.
- Infectious disease can spread in many ways including food, air, water, insects, other animals, and person-to-person contact.
- Noninfectious diseases are not contagious. Some noninfectious diseases are present at birth and others occur in later life.

**VOCABULARY**
**microorganism** p. 148
**bacteria** p. 149
**virus** p. 149
**resistance** p. 153

## Reviewing Vocabulary

*Make a frame for each of the vocabulary words listed below. Write the word in the center. Decide what information to frame it with. Use definitions, examples, descriptions, parts, or pictures.*

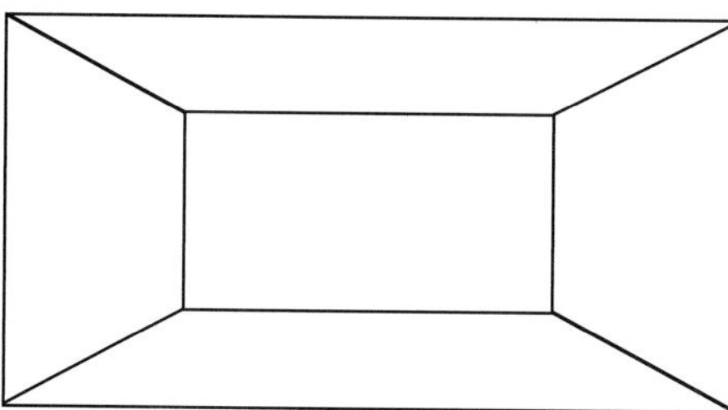

**1.** infancy
**2.** childhood
**3.** adolescence
**4.** adulthood

## Reviewing Key Concepts

**Multiple Choice** *Choose the letter of the best answer.*

**5.** The stage of life known as infancy ends when an infant
- **a.** begins to cry
- **b.** learns to walk
- **c.** holds up his head
- **d.** sees more clearly

**6.** The process in which the body begins to mature sexually is called
- **a.** adolescence
- **b.** adulthood
- **c.** nutrition
- **d.** puberty

**7.** Which nutrients are the main sources of energy for the body?
- **a.** fats and carbohydrates
- **b.** water and protein
- **c.** fats and proteins
- **d.** water and carbohydrates

**8.** Which is *not* a benefit of regular exercise?
- **a.** flushed-out skin pores
- **b.** stronger skeletal system
- **c.** increased body fat
- **d.** strengthened heart

**9.** A sedentary life style is associated with
- **a.** a stronger immune system
- **b.** more sitting than moving
- **c.** regular exercise
- **d.** an eating disorder

**10.** The chemical found in tobacco that increases heart rate and blood pressure is
- **a.** cocaine
- **b.** narcotics
- **c.** tar
- **d.** nicotine

**11.** Which term includes all of the others?
- **a.** bacteria
- **b.** fungus
- **c.** virus
- **d.** pathogen

**12.** An example of a disease caused by bacteria is
- **a.** an ear infection
- **b.** stomach flu
- **c.** chicken pox
- **d.** a cold

**13.** Which statement about viruses is true?
- **a.** Viruses function to digest food.
- **b.** Viruses are one-celled organisms.
- **c.** Viruses need living cells to reproduce.
- **d.** Examples of viruses are fungi and yeasts.

**14.** A substance that can destroy bacteria is called
- **a.** a vitamin
- **b.** a pathogen
- **c.** an antibiotic
- **d.** a mold

**15.** Lyme disease is spread through
- **a.** drinking unfiltered water
- **b.** uncooked meats
- **c.** the bite of a dog
- **d.** the bite of a tick

**Short Answer** *Write a short answer to each question.*

**16.** In your own words, define *nutrition.*

**17.** What are pathogens? Give three examples.

**18.** Explain what happens if antibiotics are used too often.

## Thinking Critically

19. **ANALYZE** Why do you think crying is an example of a social skill that develops during infancy?

20. **ANALYZE** Describe one physical, one mental, and one social change that a ten-year-old boy might experience over the next five years.

21. **EVALUATE** Explain why a diet that doesn't contain any fat would be unhealthy.

22. **APPLY** Explain why people who live sedentary lifestyles should get more exercise.

23. **SYNTHESIZE** Discuss why doctors recommend that women avoid alcohol and tobacco use during pregnancy.

24. **COMPARE AND CONTRAST** People who overeat and then quickly try to lose weight are bulimic. How is bulimia like anorexia? How does it differ?

25. **ANALYZE** Explain why Pasteur's work was important in the understanding of disease.

26. **HYPOTHESIZE** In 1854 a disease called cholera spread through the city of London. Most of the people who contracted the disease lived near the city's various water pumps. What might you hypothesize about the cause of the disease? How could you prevent people from contracting the disease in the future?

BROAD STREET

Ⓟ Pump Ⓟ Contaminated pump • Cholera death

27. **PROVIDE EXAMPLES** What are some ways that a person can prevent noninfectious diseases such as cancer or diabetes?

## the BIG idea

28. **INFER** Look again at the picture on pages 130–131. Now that you have finished the chapter, how would you change or add details to your answer to the question on the photograph?

29. **SUMMARIZE** Write one or more paragraphs explaining how lifestyle can lead to a healthy body and a longer life. Include these terms in your description.

| | |
|---|---|
| nutrition | alcohol |
| exercise | infectious disease |
| germs | noninfectious disease |
| tobacco | |

## UNIT PROJECTS

Evaluate all the data, results, and information from your project folder. Prepare to present your project.

For practice on your state test, go to . . .
TEST PRACTICE
CLASSZONE.COM

## Analyzing Data

The table below presents information about causes of death in the United States.

**Leading Causes of Death in the United States**

| 2000 | | 1900 | |
|---|---|---|---|
| **Cause of Death** | **Percent of Deaths** | **Cause of Death** | **Percent of Deaths** |
| heart disease | 31% | pneumonia* | 12% |
| cancer | 23% | tuberculosis* | 11% |
| stroke | 9% | diarrhea* | 11% |
| lung disease | 5% | heart disease | 6% |
| accident | 4% | liver disease | 5% |
| pneumonia* | 4% | accident | 4% |
| diabetes | 3% | cancer | 4% |
| kidney disease | 1% | senility | 2% |
| liver disease | 1% | diphtheria* | 2% |

* infectious disease

*Use the table to answer the questions below.*

**1.** What was the leading cause of death in 1900?
- **a.** heart disease
- **b.** cancer
- **c.** pneumonia
- **d.** tuberculosis

**2.** Which infectious disease was a leading cause of death both in 1900 and 2000?
- **a.** tuberculosis
- **b.** diphtheria
- **c.** stroke
- **d.** pneumonia

**3.** Which was the leading noninfectious cause of death in both 1900 and 2000?
- **a.** pneumonia
- **b.** cancer
- **c.** heart disease
- **d.** accidents

**4.** Which cause of death showed the greatest increase between 1900 and 2000?
- **a.** heart disease
- **b.** cancer
- **c.** liver disease
- **d.** pneumonia

**5.** Which statement is true?
- **a.** The rate of infectious disease as a leading cause of death increased from 1900 to 2000.
- **b.** The rate of infectious disease as a leading cause of death decreased from 1900 to 2000.
- **c.** The rate of noninfectious disease as a leading cause of death decreased from 1900 to 2000.
- **d.** The rate of noninfectious disease as a leading cause of death remained the same.

**6.** The percent of deaths caused by heart disease in 2000 was how much greater than in 1900?
- **a.** 37%
- **b.** 31%
- **c.** 25%
- **d.** 6%

## Extended Response

**7.** Write a paragraph explaining the change in the number of deaths due to infectious diseases from 1900 to 2000. Use the information in the data and what you know about infectious disease in your description. Use the vocabulary words in the box in your answer.

| bacterium | virus | pathogen |
|---|---|---|
| antibiotic | resistance | microorganism |

**8.** The spread of infectious disease can be controlled in many different ways. Write a paragraph describing how the spread of infectious disease may be limited. Give at least two examples and describe how these diseases can be prevented or contained.

UNIT C

# Diversity of Living Things

ANIMALS

fungi

adaptations

PLANTS

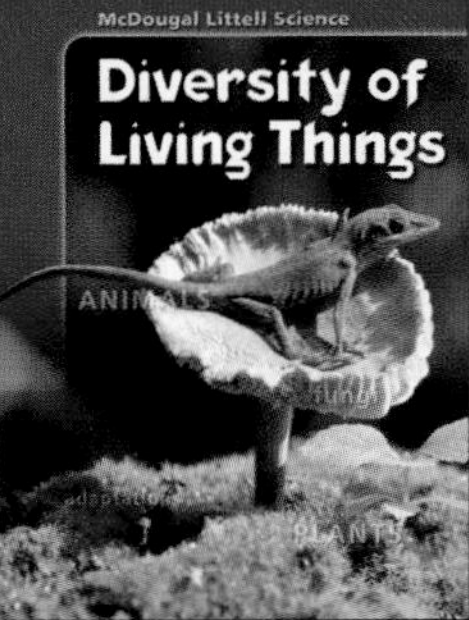

# Diversity of Living Things Contents Overview

## Unit Features

FRONTIERS IN SCIENCE Chilling Changes 2
TIMELINES IN SCIENCE Discoveries in Biodiversity 78

## 1 Single-Celled Organisms and Viruses 6

the BIG idea

Bacteria and protists have the characteristics of living things, while viruses are not alive.

## 2 Introduction to Multicellular Organisms 40

the BIG idea

Multicellular organisms live in and get energy from a variety of environments.

## 3 Plants 82

the BIG idea

Plants are a diverse group of organisms that live in many land environments.

## 4 Invertebrate Animals 120

the BIG idea

Invertebrate animals have a variety of body plans and adaptations.

## 5 Vertebrate Animals 154

the BIG idea

Vertebrate animals live in most of Earth's environments.

# Chilling Changes

How do organisms survive in this chilly Arctic landscape? Scientists are studying how organisms have adapted to the extreme cold of Earth's northern climates.

Learn more about how living things respond to freezing temperatures in the video "Frozen Alive."

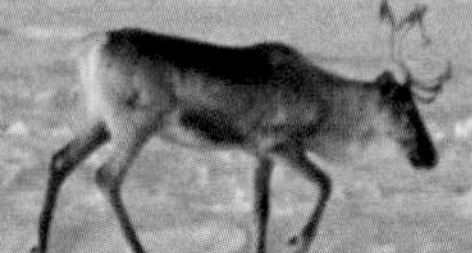

Caribou search for lichen and small plants to eat in northern Alaska.

Lichen find materials and living space on rocks in frozen environments.

## When Life Chills Out

When faced with the approach of winter, some animals hurry up, and some slow down. You may have seen animals getting a move on, migrating to warmer places. Other animals stay alive at home by hibernating, or entering a sleep-like state. Hibernation conserves energy until spring by slowing down many body processes. But what happens when an organism's body temperature dips below freezing?

Ice formation inside an organism's body is one of the most serious, and potentially damaging, threats to winter survival. If ice forms inside cells, it can damage the cell's operation and tear holes in the cell membrane, almost certainly leading to death.

An arctic ground squirrel peers above snow-covered ground in Alaska.

Some animals and plants take cold weather survival to an extreme. Some frogs and insects can allow their bodies to freeze solid. Some fish have fluids in their bodies that can *cool* below the freezing point of water and still flow. How do they do it?

Scientists studying survivors of extreme cold are not just learning about the ways organisms respond in the wild. Research on cold weather survival helps scientists understand problems faced by human society. Growing crops year-round and using bacteria to clean up pollution in a frozen environment are two examples. There are two main responses that allow living things to live in a subfreezing world.

Arctic woolly bear caterpillars may take many years to grow to full size.

When the caterpillar reaches full size, it forms a cocoon and changes into a moth.

## Avoid Ice, or Tolerate It

Organisms can either avoid the forming of ice or tolerate it. Some animals, like a fish called a flounder, produce antifreeze proteins in their bodies. The proteins keep ice from forming in the blood and other fluids. The fluids thicken but still flow. They never turn to ice crystals. Scientists call this response freeze-avoidance.

Other organisms—including some frogs, many types of insects, and some trees—do allow ice to form inside their bodies. In these organisms, ice forms, but only in the spaces outside the cells. Freeze-tolerant organisms pump fluid out of their cells. Specialized proteins located outside of the cells encourage ice to form there, rather than inside the cells.

Perhaps the champion of freeze tolerance is a small Arctic insect called the Arctic woolly bear caterpillar. It is only active for a few weeks out of the year, during the brief Arctic summer. It can take this caterpillar up to fifteen years to mature into a moth!

Temperatures during Arctic winters often fall as low as −70°C. Because the ground is frozen year-round, the caterpillars cannot burrow. Instead, their bodies freeze solid in winter, shutting down nearly all of their cellular activity and

**SCIENTIFIC AMERICAN FRONTIERS**

**View the "Frozen Alive" segment of your Scientific American Frontiers video to see how scientists studying fish and frogs have begun to solve the mysteries of life surviving a freeze.**

**IN THIS SCENE FROM THE VIDEO** How do the frog's systems start up again, after being shut down during freezing?

**WHAT BRINGS ON THE THAW?** Ken Storey collects wood frogs. The frogs have an automatic response to cold temperatures, which allows Ken and his team to keep them in a freezer without killing them. Storey and his team know the "what" of freeze tolerance. They want to learn the "how." How does the frog stay alive during and after shutdown? Storey expects that the thawing process works in the usual way, that the frogs will begin to warm from the outside in. Instead he finds that internal organs begin the thaw. The liver is the first organ to activate. It produces glucose or sugar, which then gets other cells, those in the heart, to begin their work.

expending almost no energy. Scientists have known for centuries that some insects can freeze over the winter, but only recently have they begun to understand exactly how insects' bodies change to allow them to freeze and thaw.

Scientist Ken Storey has discovered a set of genes that turn on, like a switch, in response to freezing temperatures. These genes are called master control genes, because they have the ability to turn other genes in the body on or off. In the case of freeze-tolerant animals, master control genes first turn off nearly all the genes in the body. Arctic woolly bear caterpillars have many thousands of genes, but during the winter most of those genes are turned off. Keeping genes turned off is an adaptation that helps the caterpillar conserve energy throughout the winter.

## Is It Really Extreme?

Organisms have adapted to a wide variety of environments. The Arctic woolly bear caterpillar is suited to life near the Arctic Circle. Some organisms must be able to survive in the exact opposite—the extreme heat of deserts. Others thrive in extremely salty conditions. Some plants and bacteria can even live in places with dangerously high levels of poisonous chemicals.

An environment doesn't have to be extreme to present challenges to the organisms that live there. Animals in a forest or meadow still need to find food and shelter, avoid predators, and respond to changes. The organisms living in any environment face a unique set of challenges.

### UNANSWERED Questions

As scientists learn more about how animals survive in extremely cold climates, they also uncover additional questions:

- Do animals respond to temperature or a lack of light?
- How do cellular processes that halt during the winter get started up again?
- Can scientists grow freeze resistant crops?

## UNIT PROJECTS

**As you study this unit, work alone or in a group on one of the projects listed below. Use the bulleted steps to guide your project.**

### Museum Exhibit

Plan a museum exhibit showing different ways in which animals respond to extreme environments.

- Research three to five types of organisms and find out what kind of environmental changes these organisms face.
- Design, make visuals, and write text to accompany your exhibit.

### Grow a Fast Plant

Observe the entire life cycle of a plant in less than six weeks. Record your observations in a journal.

- Gather information and any materials necessary to grow and care for fast plants. Obtain fast plant seeds and plant them.
- Observe the plant for a few minutes every day. Make notes in your journal, and write weekly summaries.

### Local Field Study

Report on organisms that live in your local area.

- Identify three organisms you see on a regular basis and learn more about how they survive throughout the year.
- Pick one plant or animal and observe it for a few minutes once a week in the morning and in the late afternoon. How does it change over time?

Learn more about careers in zoology.

CHAPTER

# Single-Celled Organisms and Viruses

## the BIG idea

Bacteria and protists have the characteristics of living things, while viruses are not alive.

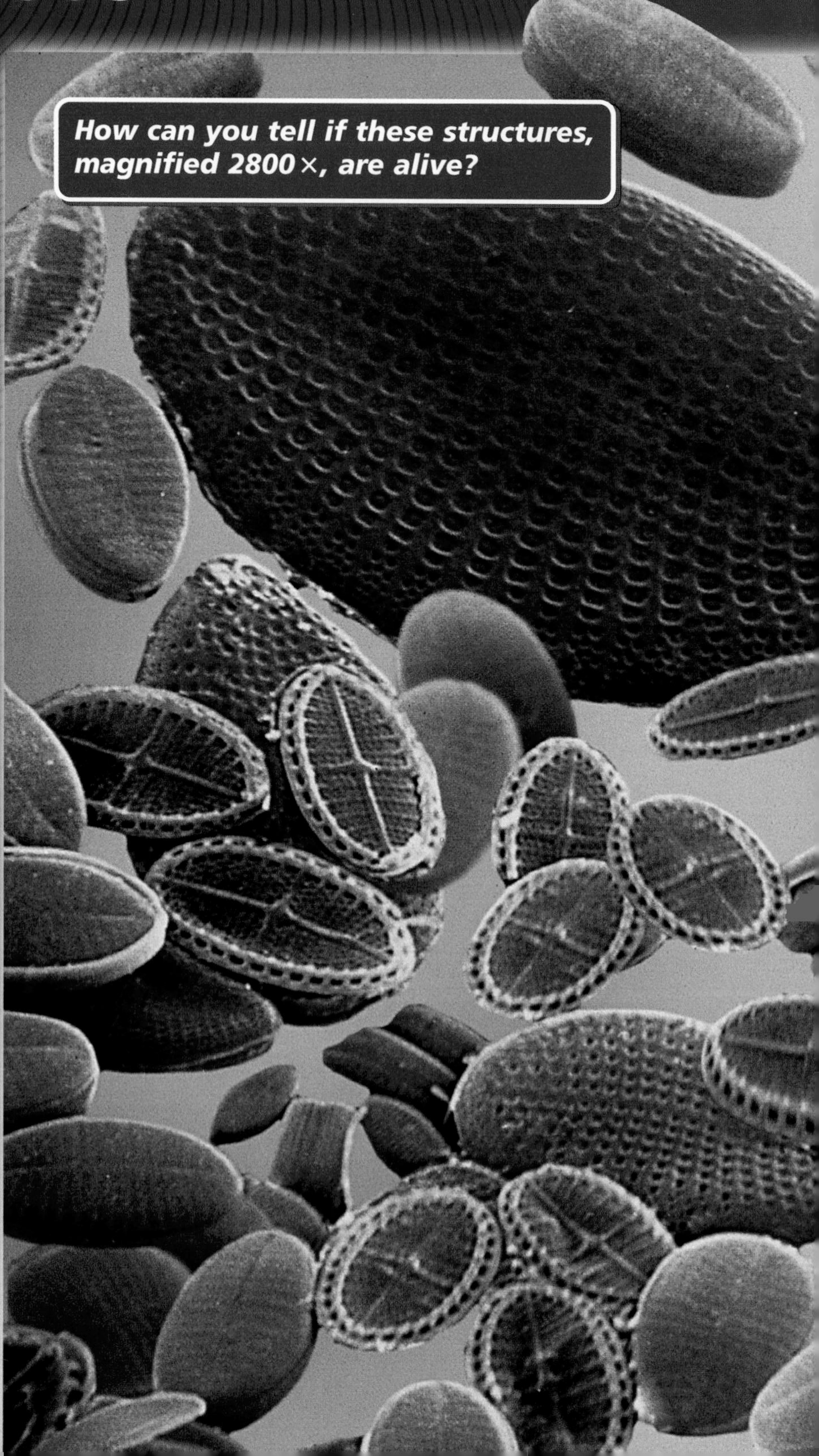

How can you tell if these structures, magnified 2800×, are alive?

## Key Concepts

SECTION

**Single-celled organisms have all the characteristics of living things.**
Learn about characteristics shared by all living things.

SECTION

**Bacteria are single-celled organisms without nuclei.**
Learn about the characteristics of bacteria and archaea.

SECTION

**Viruses are not alive but affect living things.**
Learn about the structure of viruses and how they affect cells.

SECTION

**Protists are a diverse group of organisms.**
Learn about protists and how they affect the environment.

**Internet Preview**

CLASSZONE.COM

Chapter 1 online resources: Content Review, two Visualizations, three Resource Centers, Math Tutorial, Test Practice.

## Where Can You Find Microscopic Life?

Make a list of places where you might find living things that are too small to be seen by your unaided eye. Then use a hand lens, magnifying glass, or microscope, to investigate some of the places on your list.

**Observe and Think** What do you think microscopic organisms look like? Why can microscopic life be found in so many places?

## How Quickly Do Bacteria Multiply?

Tape a funnel to the top of a two-liter bottle. Place one bean in the funnel. After one minute, drop two more beans into the funnel. Continue adding beans to the bottle every minute, adding twice as many beans as you did before. When it is time to add 64 beans, use 1/8 of a cup, and then continue to double the amounts.

**Observe and Think** How long did it take to fill the bottle?

## Internet Activity: Microscopic Life and You

Go to **ClassZone.com** to learn about the single-celled organisms.

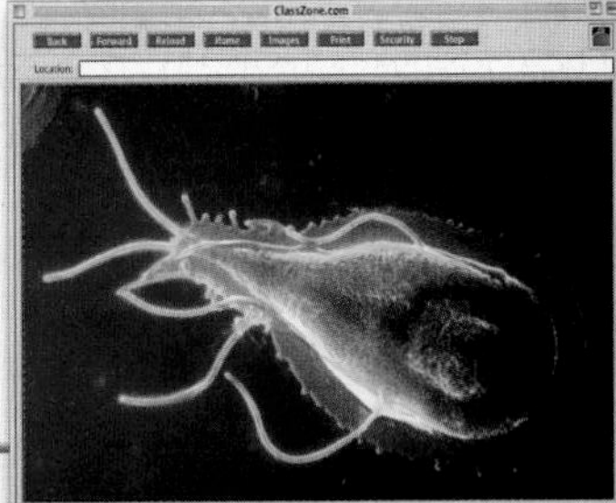

**Observe and Think** What types of organisms live in the human body?

Kingdom Protista **Code: MDL039**

CHAPTER 1

# Getting Ready to Learn

## CONCEPT REVIEW

- All living things interact with their environment to meet their needs.
- The cell is the fundamental unit of life.

## VOCABULARY REVIEW

*See Glossary for definitions.*

**cell**
**matter**
**molecule**
**organism**
**species**

Review concepts and vocabulary.

## TAKING NOTES

### MAIN IDEA WEB

Write each new blue heading in a box. Then write notes in boxes around the center box that give important terms and details about that blue heading.

### VOCABULARY STRATEGY

Place each vocabulary term at the center of a **description wheel diagram.** Write some words describing it on the spokes.

SCIENCE NOTEBOOK

They are organized, with an outside and an inside.

They increase in size.

Living things share common characteristics.

They reproduce and form other organisms like themselves.

They respond to changes in the environment.

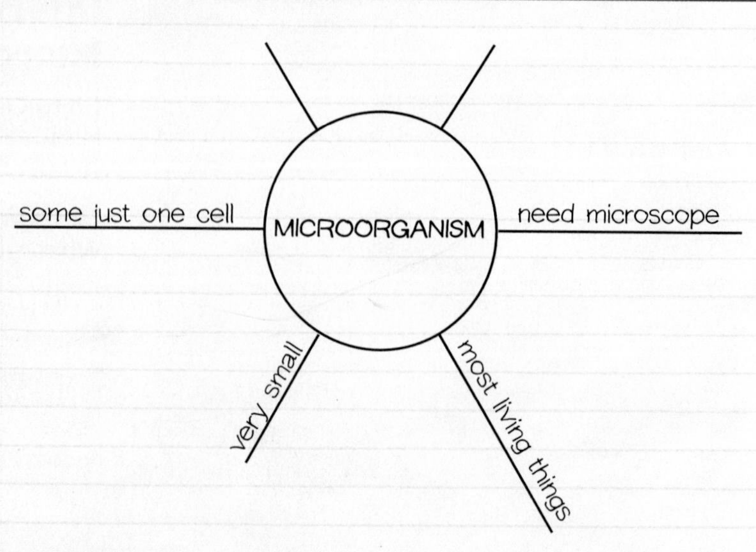


See the Note-Taking Handbook on pages R45–R51.

KEY CONCEPT

# Single-celled organisms have all the characteristics of living things.

**BEFORE, you learned**

- All living things are made of cells
- Organisms respond to their environment
- Species change over time

**NOW, you will learn**

- About the various sizes of organisms
- About characteristics that are shared by all living things
- About needs shared by all organisms

**VOCABULARY**

**microorganism** p. 10
**kingdom** p. 11
**binary fission** p. 12
**virus** p. 14

**EXPLORE Organisms**

### *What living things are in the room with you?*

**PROCEDURE**

1. Make a list of all the living things that are in your classroom.
2. Compare your list with the lists of your classmates. Make one list containing all the living things your class has identified.

**MATERIALS**

- paper
- pencil

**WHAT DO YOU THINK?**

- How did you identify something as living?
- Were you and your classmates able to see all the living things on your list?

## Living things come in many shapes and sizes.

**MAIN IDEA WEB**
Make a web of the important terms and details about the main idea: *Living things come in many shapes and sizes.*

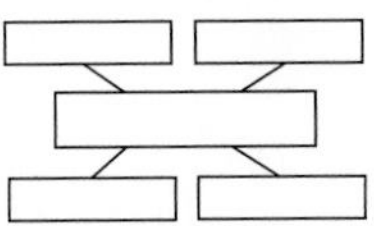

You can spot mushrooms in many places while walking through a forest. Scientists have discovered mushrooms that come from the same individual fungus more than 5 kilometers (3 miles) apart in an Oregon forest. Most of this honey mushroom fungus is below ground, stretching over an area covering more than 1600 football fields. This mushroom is one of the largest known living things on Earth.

Many other living things share the soil in the Oregon forest. Earthworms, insects, and many other organisms that are too small to be seen with a naked eye, also live there. For every living thing that is large enough to be seen, there are often countless numbers of smaller living things that share the same living space.

The honey mushroom fungus is one example of an organism. You, too, are an organism, and tiny bacteria living inside your body are also organisms. In fact, any living thing can be called an organism.

When you think of living things, you probably begin with those you can observe—plants, animals, and fungi such as mushrooms. However, most living things are too small to observe without a microscope. Even the tiniest organisms are made of cells. Very small organisms are called **microorganisms.** Many microorganisms are made of just one cell.

**READING TIP**

The prefix *micro-* means "very small." Therefore, *microscope* means "very small scope" and *microorganism* means "very small organism."

**CHECK YOUR READING** Compare and contrast the words *microorganism* and *organism.*

A visitor to a mangrove swamp forest can find an amazing variety of organisms. The mangrove trees themselves are the most obvious organisms. Roots from these trees grow above and below the muddy bottom of the forest. Other organisms live in almost every part of the mangrove tree.

## Six Kingdoms of Life

| Mostly Microscopic Kingdoms | Mostly Multicellular Kingdoms |
|---|---|
| • archaea<br>• bacteria<br>• protists | • animals<br>• fungi<br>• plants |

A single drop of water from a mangrove swamp may be living space for many microorganisms. The circled photograph on page 10 was taken using a microscope, and shows an amoeba that may be found in the water of the swamp. Larger organisms, such as manatees and fish, swim around the roots of mangrove trees. Birds, such as tri-colored herons and roseate spoonbills, use the branches.

Scientists divide the organisms they identify into groups called **kingdoms.** This unit will cover all of the kingdoms of life, listed in the table on page 10. You are already familiar with plants and animals. Fungi are another kingdom. Fungi include mushrooms found in a forest. The other three kingdoms are composed of mostly microscopic life. You will learn more about microscopic organisms later in this chapter.

**VOCABULARY**
Add a description wheel for *kingdom* to your notebook. The spokes of your wheel should include examples from the six kingdoms.

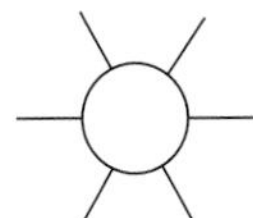

## Living things share common characteristics.

All living things—from the microorganisms living in a mangrove swamp to the giant organisms living in the open ocean—share similar characteristics. Living things are organized, grow, reproduce, and respond to the environment.

**READING TIP**
As you read about the four characteristics of all living things, note the examples of how single-celled organisms meet these four standards.

### Organization

Cells are the basic unit of all living things. Cells, like all living things, have an inside and an outside. The boundary separating the inside from the outside of an individual cell is called the cell membrane. Within some cells, another structure called the nucleus is also surrounded by a membrane.

In this chapter, you will read about organisms made of a single cell. Some types of single-celled organisms contain a nucleus and some do not. All single-celled organisms contain everything they need to survive within their one cell. These cells are able to get energy from complex molecules, to move, and to sense their environment. The ability to perform these and other functions is part of their organization.

### Growth

Living things increase in size. Organisms made of one cell do not grow as large as organisms made of many cells. But all living things need to get energy. All living things also need to obtain materials to build new structures inside cells or replace worn-out cell parts. As a result, individual cells grow larger over time.

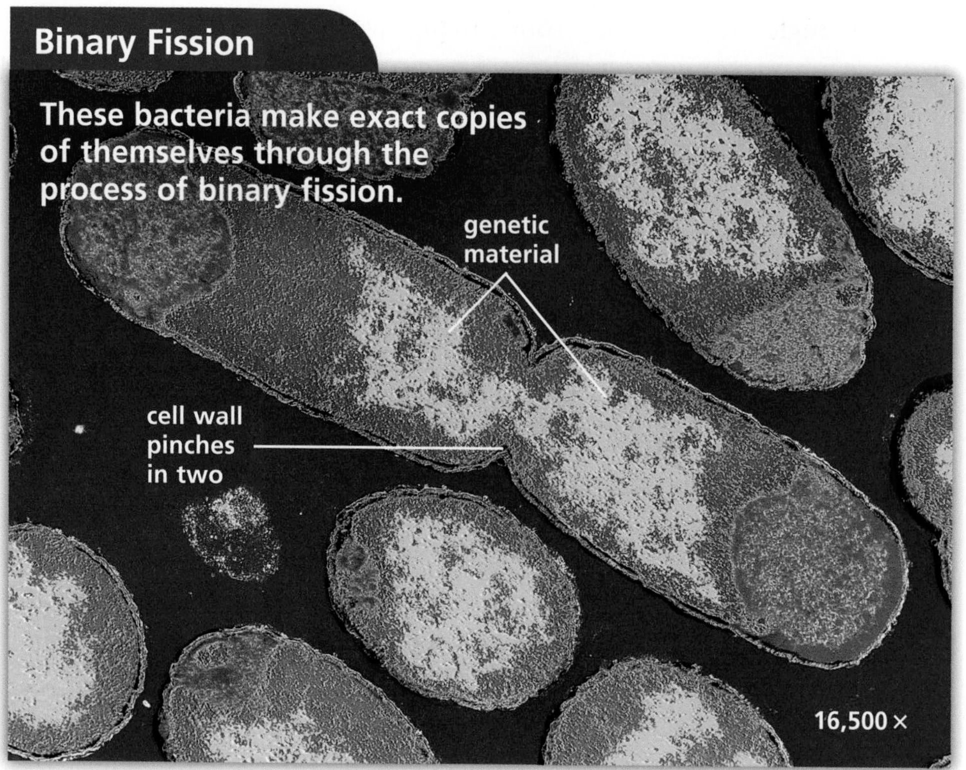

Binary Fission
These bacteria make exact copies of themselves through the process of binary fission.
genetic material
cell wall pinches in two
16,500 ×


## Reproduction

Living things reproduce, forming other organisms like themselves. Every organism contains genetic material, which is a code contained in a special molecule called DNA. The code contains characteristics of the individual organism. In order to reproduce, an organism must make a copy of this material, which is passed on to its offspring.

Observe the process of binary fission.

Some single-celled organisms reproduce by a process called **binary fission.** In binary fission, material from one cell separates into two cells. The genetic material of the original cell first doubles so that each daughter cell has an exact copy of the DNA of the original cell. You might say that single-celled organisms multiply by dividing. One cell divides into 2 cells, 2 cells divide into 4, 4 into 8, 16, 32, 64, and so on. In some cells, binary fission can take place as often as every 20 minutes.

Describe how a single-celled organism is organized, grows, and reproduces.

## Response

Organisms respond to changes in the environment. Even microscopic organisms respond to conditions such as light, temperature, and touch. The ability to respond allows organisms to find food, avoid being eaten, or perform other tasks necessary to survive.

# INVESTIGATE Microorganisms

## How do these organisms respond to their environment?

**PROCEDURE**

1. Place a drop of the hydra culture on a microscope slide. Using the microscope, find a hydra under medium power and sketch what you see.
2. Add a drop of warm water to the culture on the slide. How does the hydra respond? Record your observations.
3. Add a drop of the daphnia culture. Record your observations.

**WHAT DO YOU THINK?**

- Which observations, if any, indicate that hydras respond to their environment?
- Daphnia are organisms. What is the relationship between hydra and daphnia?

**CHALLENGE** What other experiments could you do to observe the responses of hydra or daphnia to their environment?

**SKILL FOCUS**
Observing

**MATERIALS**
- microscope
- slide
- hydra culture
- daphnia culture
- water

**TIME**
30 minutes

## Living things need energy, materials, and living space.

Have you ever wondered why you need to eat food, breathe air, and drink water? All living things need energy and materials. For most organisms, water and air are materials necessary for life.

Food supplies you with energy. You—like all living things—need energy to move, grow, and develop. All animals have systems for breaking down food into usable forms of energy and materials. Plants have structures that enable them to transform sunlight into usable energy. Some microorganisms transform sunlight, while others need to use other organisms as sources of energy.

Most of the activities of living things take place in water. Water is also an ingredient for many of the reactions that take place in cells. In addition, water helps support an organism's body. If you add water to the soil around a wilted plant, you will probably see the plant straighten up as water moves into its cells.

Materials in the air include gases such as carbon dioxide and oxygen. Many of the processes that capture and release energy involve these gases. Some organisms—such as those found around hydrothermal vents—use other chemicals to capture and release energy.

## Viruses are not alive.

Sometimes it's not easy to tell the difference between a living and a nonliving thing. A **virus** has genetic material enclosed in a protein shell. Viruses have many of the characteristics of living things, including genetic material. However, a virus is not nearly as complex as a cell and is not considered a living thing.

**Rotavirus**

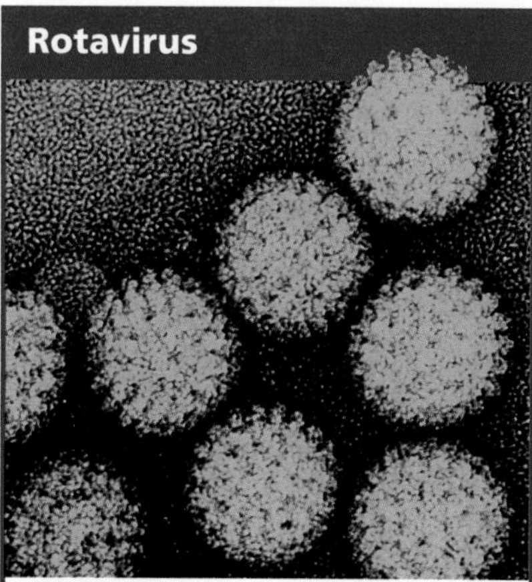

These viruses contain DNA but do not grow or respond to their environment. 570,000×

**Animal Cell**

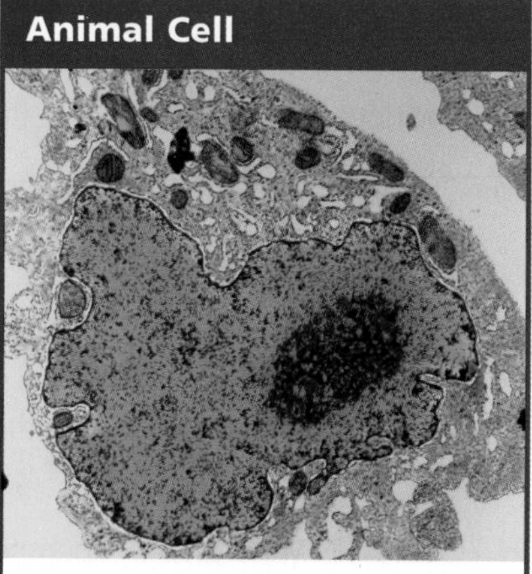

Animal cells grow, reproduce, and respond to external conditions. 4800×

For example, animal cells have structures that allow them to get materials or energy from their environment. Virus particles do not grow once they have formed, and they do not take in any energy. Animal cells can make copies of their genetic material and reproduce by dividing in two. Viruses are able to reproduce only by "taking over" a cell and using that cell to make new viruses. Animal cells also have many more internal structures than viruses. Viruses usually contain nothing more than their genetic material and a protein coat.

## 1.1 Review

### KEY CONCEPTS

1. Give examples of organisms that are very large and organisms that are very small.
2. Name four characteristics that all living things share.
3. Name three things that living things must obtain to survive.

### CRITICAL THINKING

4. **Synthesize** Give examples of how a common animal, such as a dog, is organized, grows, responds, and reproduces.
5. **Predict** In a certain lake, would you expect there to be more organisms that are large enough to see or more organisms that are too small for you to see? Why?

### CHALLENGE

6. **Design** Try to imagine the different structures that a single-celled organism needs to survive in pond water. Then use your ideas to design your own single-celled organism.

MATH in SCIENCE

MATH TUTORIAL
CLASSZONE.COM

Click on Math Tutorial for more help with interpreting line graphs.

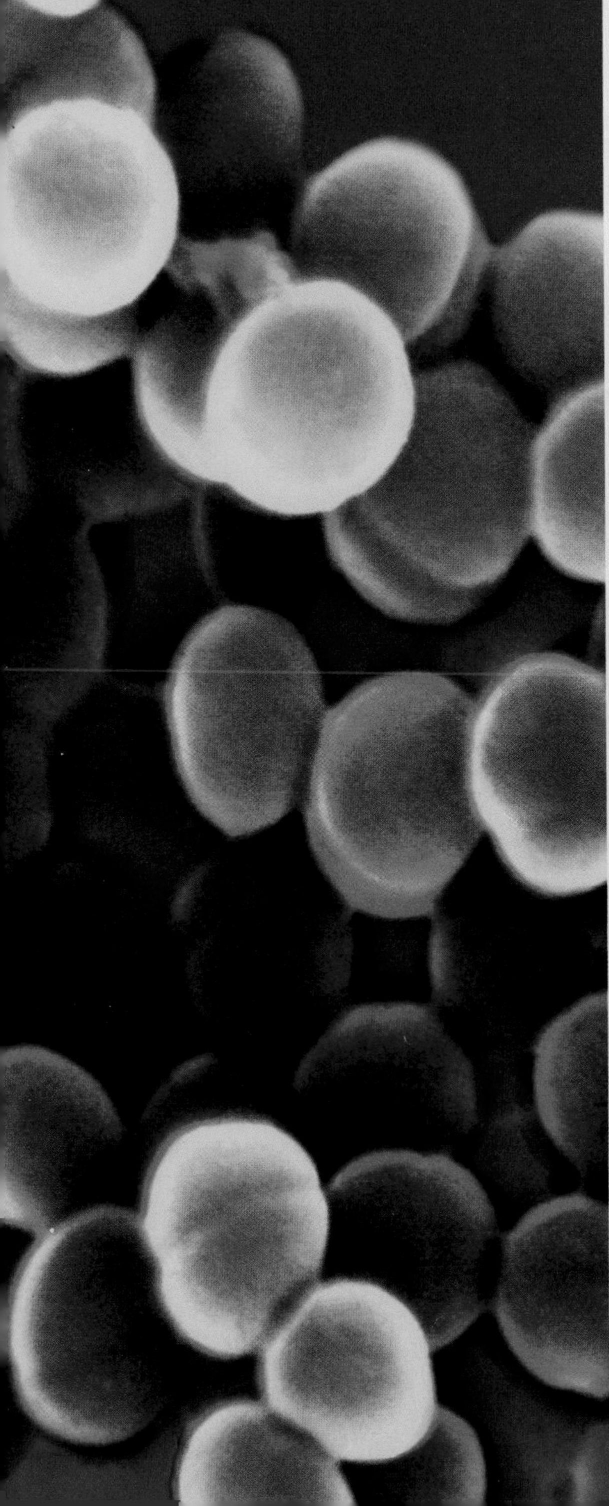

## SKILL: MAKING A LINE GRAPH

# Graphing Growth

If you hold marbles in your hand and drop them into a bowl one at a time, each drop into the bowl adds the same amount. If you plot this growth on a line graph, you will have a straight line.

By contrast, a bacterial colony's growth expands exponentially as it grows. All the bacteria divide in two. Every time all the bacteria divide, the colony doubles in size.

### EXAMPLE

Compare the two types of growth on a graph.

**Graph 1.** Suppose the marble collection begins with one marble, and after every hour, one marble is added.

The graph shows: $x + 1 = y$
The slope of the line stays the same at each interval.

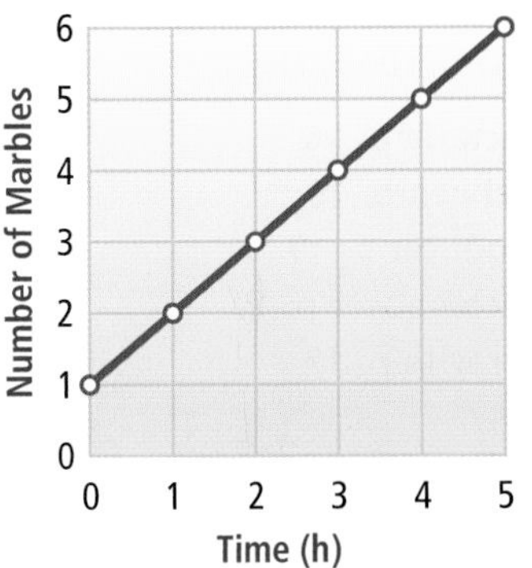


**Graph 2.** Suppose a bacterial colony begins with one bacterium, and every hour, a bacterial cell divides, forming two bacteria.

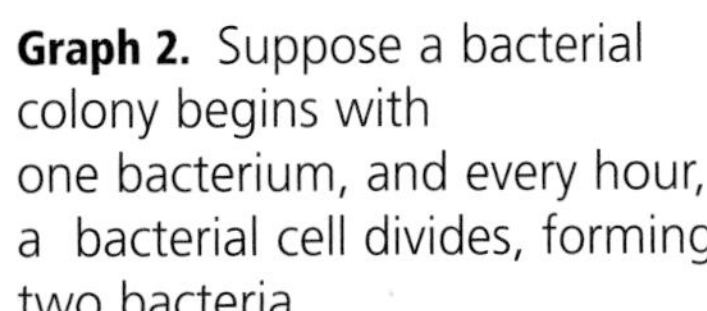

The graph shows: $2^x = y$
The slope gets steeper at each interval.

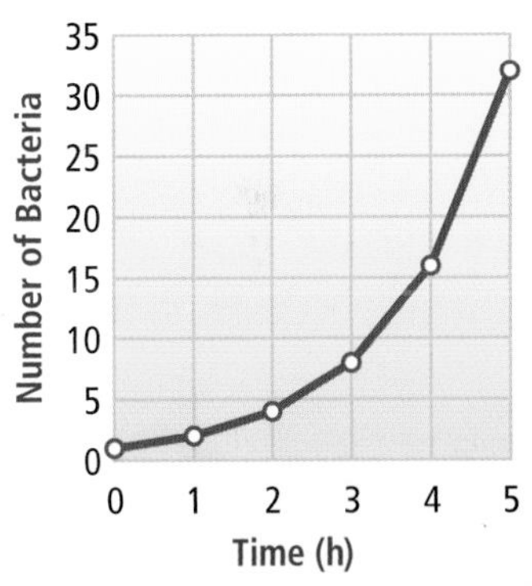


**Examine the graphs and answer the questions.**

1. How many marbles are in the collection after 3 h? How many bacteria are in the colony after 3 h?
2. After 7 h, what number of marbles would show in graph 1? Name the coordinates for this point. What number of bacteria would be shown in graph 2? Name the coordinates.
3. Copy the two graphs on graph paper. Extend each graph to 10 h. Plot the growth according to the pattern or formula given.

**CHALLENGE** Suppose each bacterium lives for 10 h. How many bacteria will be in the colony after 20 h?

KEY CONCEPT

# Bacteria are single-celled organisms without nuclei.

**BEFORE, you learned**

- Organisms come in all shapes and sizes
- All living things share common characteristics
- Living things may be divided into six kingdoms

**NOW, you will learn**

- About the simplest living things
- About bacteria and archaea
- That bacteria may help or harm other organisms

**VOCABULARY**

**bacteria** p. 16
**archaea** p. 18
**producer** p. 19
**decomposer** p. 19
**parasite** p. 19

**THINK ABOUT**

### *Where are bacteria?*

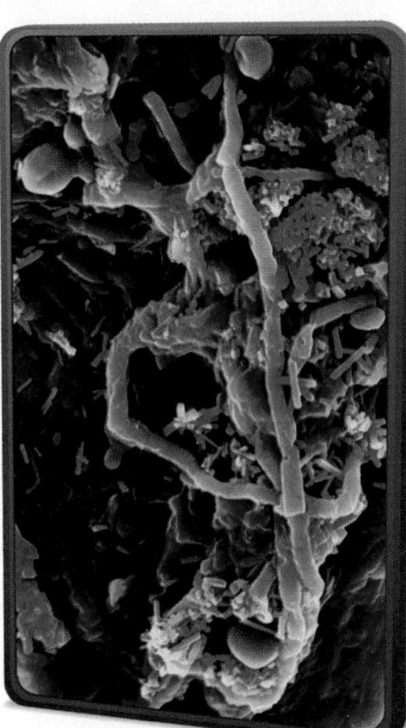

Bacteria are the simplest form of life. But that doesn't mean they're not important or numerous. As you look about the room you're sitting in, try to think of places where you might find bacteria. In fact, bacteria are on the walls, in the air, on the floor, and on your skin. It's hard to think of a place where you wouldn't find bacteria. The photograph shows a magnification of bacteria living on a sponge. The bacteria are magnified 580×. There are hundreds of millions of bacteria on your skin right now. There are trillions of bacteria that live inside your intestines and help you digest food.

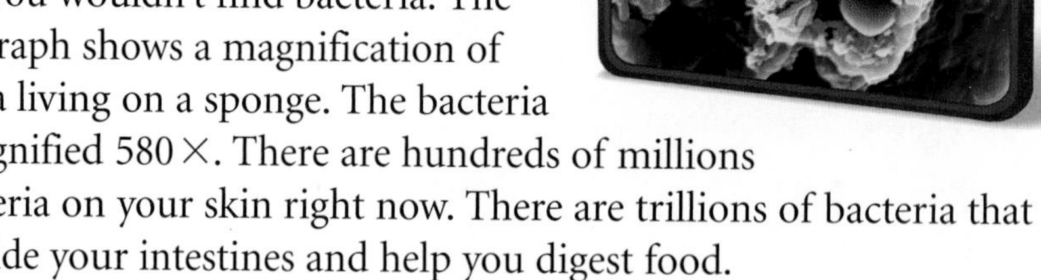

## Bacteria and archaea are the smallest living things.

**MAIN IDEA WEB**
Make a web of the important terms and details about the main idea: *Bacteria and archaea are the smallest living things.* Be sure to include how bacteria are classified.

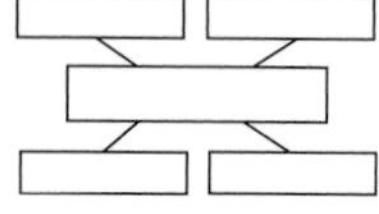

The names of the organisms belonging in the kingdoms Archaea and Bacteria are probably unfamiliar. Yet you actually encounter these organisms every day. Bacteria are everywhere: on your skin, in the ground, in puddles and ponds, in the soil, and in the sea. About 300 species of bacteria are living in your mouth right now.

**Bacteria** are the simplest kind of life known on Earth. All bacteria are composed of just one cell without a nucleus. Their genetic material is contained in loops within the cell. A bacterium reproduces using binary fission.

## Bacteria

**All bacteria are single cells without nuclei.**

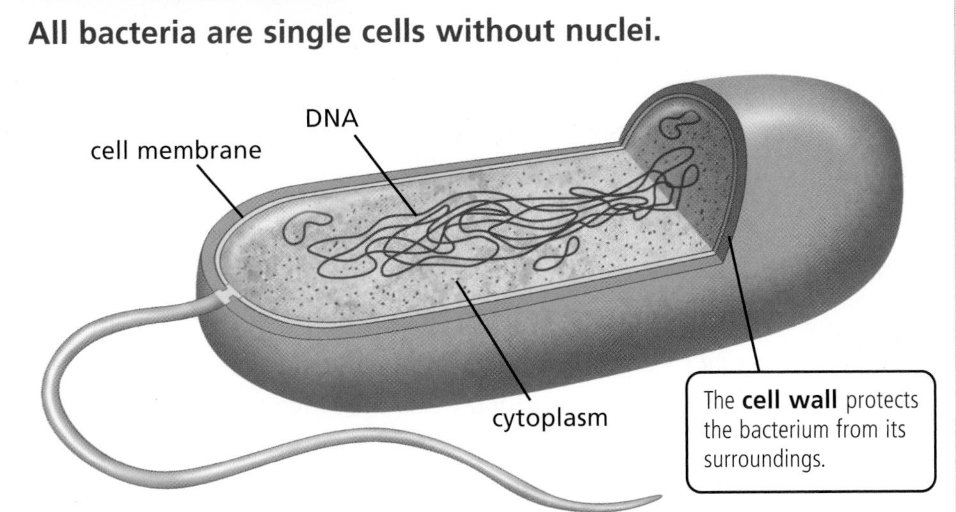
DNA
cell membrane
cytoplasm
The **cell wall** protects the bacterium from its surroundings.

Bacterial cells are different from the cells of other organisms. A bacterial cell is about 1/10 to 1/20 the size of a typical cell from organisms such as animals, plants, fungi, or protists. These four groups include organisms made up of cells with true nuclei. The nucleus is a structure that is enclosed by a membrane and that holds the genetic material.

**READING TIP**
The plural of *bacterium* is *bacteria,* and the plural of *nucleus* is *nuclei.*

Despite their small size, bacteria are simple only when compared with more complex cells. Bacteria are much more complex than viruses, because they have many internal structures that viruses do not have. For example, one important feature of most bacteria is a covering called a cell wall, which surrounds and protects the soft cell membrane like a rain jacket. Bacterial cells contain many large molecules and structures that are not found in viruses.

**Spiral Bacteria**

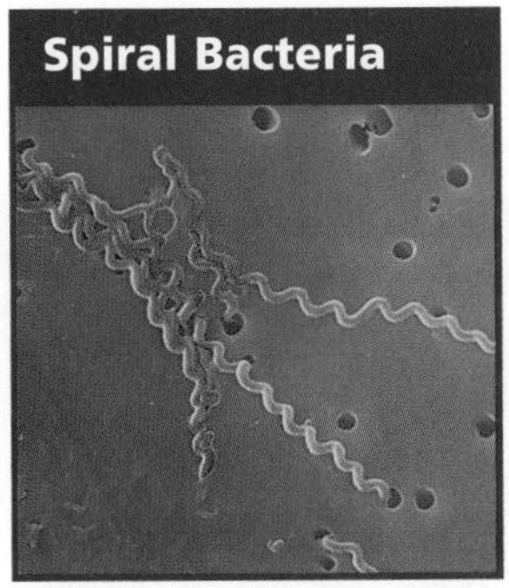

**Rod Bacteria**

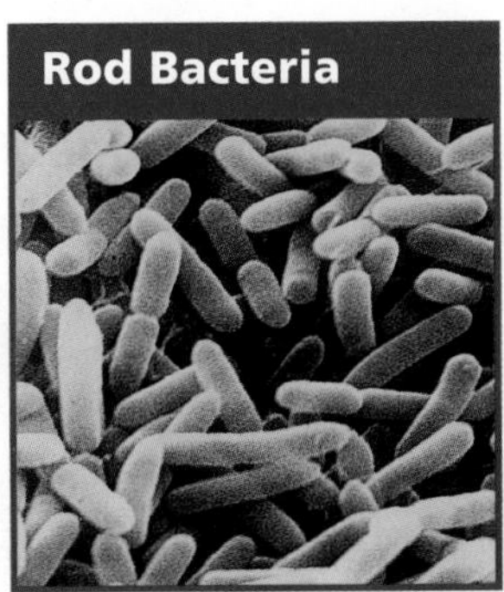

**Round Bacteria**

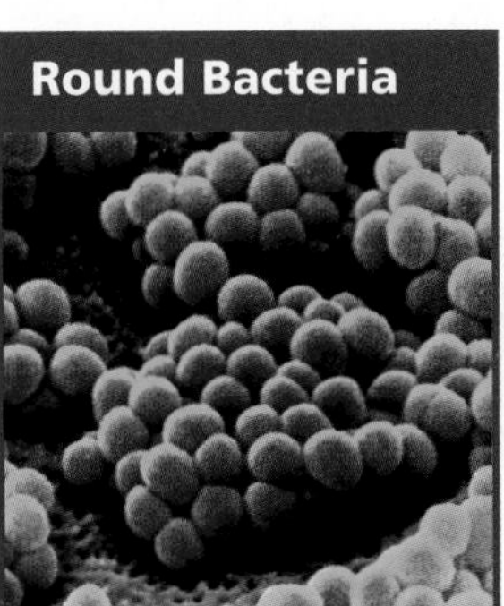

Scientists often classify bacteria by their external shapes.

- Spiral-shaped bacteria occur in single strands.
- Rod-shaped bacteria may occur singly or in chains.
- Round-shaped bacteria may occur singly or in pairs, chains, or clusters.

CHECK YOUR READING

Name two features that all bacteria share.

## Archaea and bacteria are found in many environments.

Find out more about the many different types of bacteria.

Two types of single-celled organisms do not have nuclei. Bacteria are the most common and can be found in nearly every environment. Archaea are similar in size to bacteria, but share more characteristics with the cells of complex organisms like plants and animals.

### Archaea

**Archaea** (AHR-kee-uh) are single-celled organisms that can survive in the largest range of environments. These environments may be very hot, very cold, or contain so much of a substance such as salt that most living things would be poisoned. As a result, scientists often group archaea according to where they live.

**Methanogens** take their name from methane, the natural gas they produce. These archaea die if they are exposed to oxygen. They may live in the dense mud of swamps and marshes, and in the guts of animals such as cows and termites.

READING TIP

The word halophile is formed using the root word *halo-* which means "salt," and the suffix *–phile* which means "love." Therefore, a *halophile* is a "salt lover."

**Halophiles** live in very salty lakes and ponds. Some halophiles die if their water is not salty enough. When a salty pond dries up, so do the halophiles. They can survive drying and begin dividing again when water returns to the pond.

**Thermophiles** are archaea that thrive in extreme heat or cold. They may live in hot environments such as hot springs, near hot vents deep under the sea, or buried many meters deep in the ice.

### Archaea

**Archaea are organisms that can live in extreme environments.**

**Methanogens**

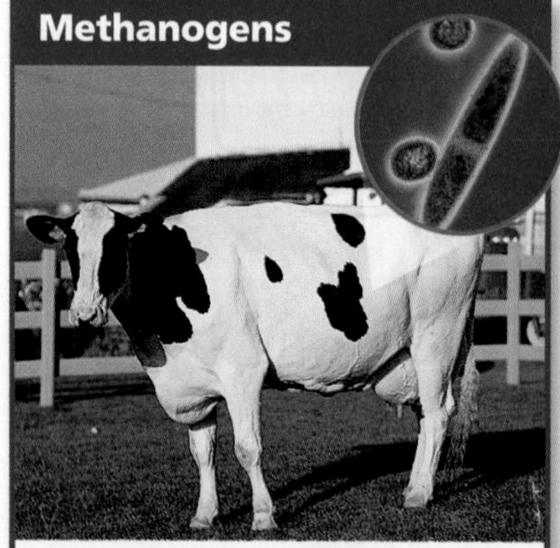

Methanogens may be found in a cow's stomach where they help with digestion.

**Halophiles**

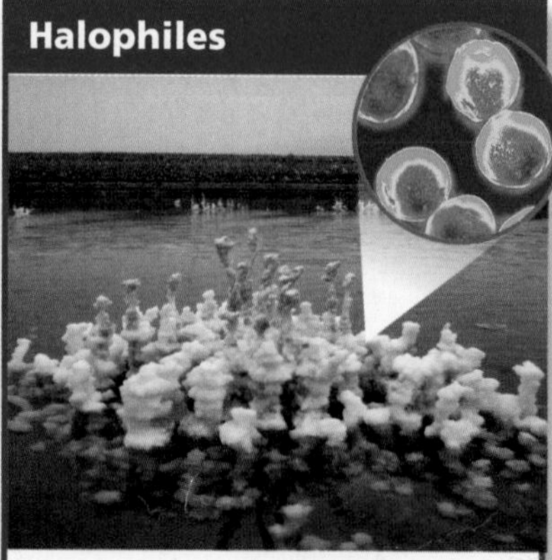

Halophiles can be found in extremely salty bodies of water such as the Dead Sea.

**Thermophiles**

Thermophiles may be found in hot geysers such as this one in Yellowstone National Park.

## Bacteria

Most single-celled organisms without a nucleus are classified as bacteria. Bacteria are found in almost every environment and perform a variety of tasks. Some bacteria contain chlorophyll. Using sunlight for energy, these bacteria are an important food source in oceans. These bacteria also release oxygen gas, which animals need to breathe.

**CHECK YOUR READING** What are some common traits of bacteria and archaea?

Bacteria without chlorophyll perform different tasks. Some bacteria break down parts of dead plants and animals to help recycle matter. Some bacteria release chemicals into the environment, providing a food source for other organisms. Scientists often group bacteria by the roles they play in the environment. Three of the most common roles are listed below.

Bacteria that transform energy from sunlight into energy that can be used by cells are called **producers.** These bacteria are a food source for organisms that cannot make their own food.

**Decomposers** get energy by breaking down materials in dead or decaying organisms. Decomposers help other organisms reuse materials found in decaying matter.

Some bacteria live in a very close relationship either inside or on the surface of other organisms. Some of these bacteria may have no effect on their host organisms or host cells. Some bacteria help their hosts. Other bacteria are **parasites,** organisms that harm their hosts.

**VOCABULARY**
Be sure to add description wheels for *producer, decomposer,* and *parasite* to your notebook.

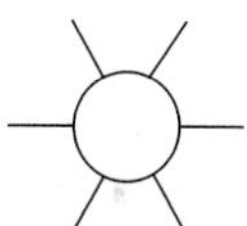

### Bacteria

**Three roles bacteria play in the environment are shown below.**

**Producers**

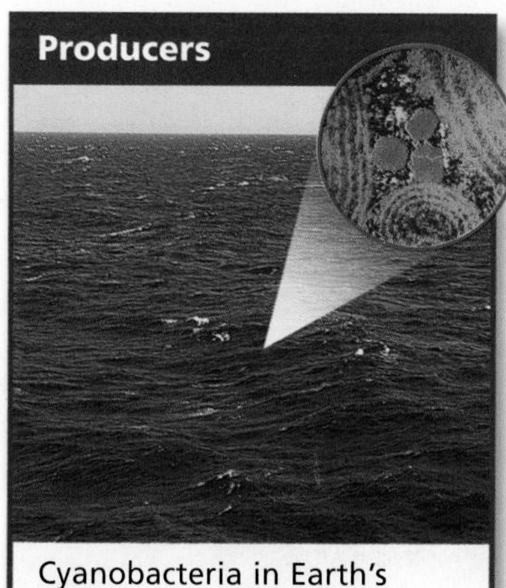

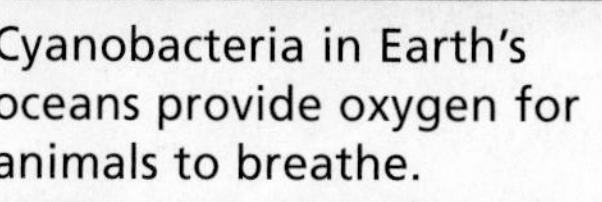

Cyanobacteria in Earth's oceans provide oxygen for animals to breathe.

**Decomposers**

Some bacteria break down dead wood into materials used by other organisms.

**Parasites**

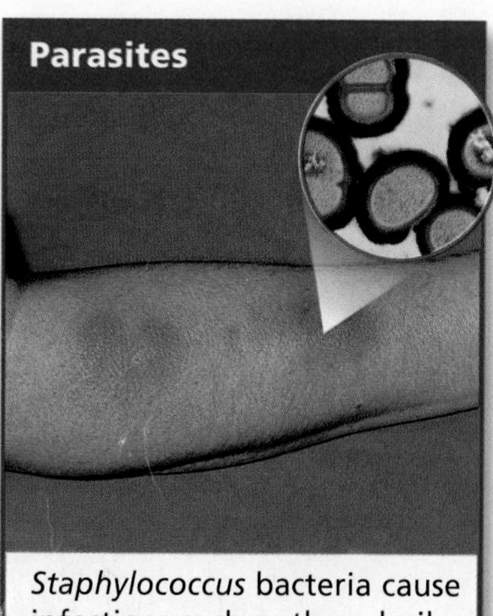

*Staphylococcus* bacteria cause infections such as these boils in humans.

## Bacteria may help or harm other organisms.

Some bacteria, such as producers and decomposers, are helpful to other organisms. But other bacteria can be harmful. These bacteria can cause diseases in animals and plants.

### Helpful Bacteria

One shovelful of ordinary soil contains trillions of bacteria, and every fallen leaf or dead animal is covered with bacteria. These bacteria break down the matter in dead bodies and waste materials. These broken-down materials are then available for other organisms to build their bodies.

Cities use bacteria to break down sewage. Bacteria in sewage-treatment plants live on the material dissolved in liquid sewage. These bacteria help make the water clean enough to be released into rivers or oceans. Other bacteria are used to clean up oil spills by decomposing oil suspended on the ocean's surface.

Bacteria can also change materials that do not come from living things and make them available for other organisms. For example, some bacteria can convert nitrogen gas to nitrogen compounds. This process, called nitrogen fixation, makes nitrogen available to plants in a form that is useful to them. Plants use this nitrogen in making proteins, which are an important part of every cell.

Helpful Bacteria
Bacteria inside the root nodules of soybean plants convert nitrogen into a form the plant can use.
bacteria inside nodules
nodules on roots

Like bacteria, certain types of archaea are helpful to other organisms. Animals that eat plants such as grass often depend on archaea. Methanogens help break down the cellulose in cell walls. Termites and cows are two examples of animals that can digest cellulose because of the archaea in their stomachs.

Name two helpful roles that bacteria can play in the environment.

## Harmful Bacteria

Not all bacteria are helpful to other organisms. Scientists first discovered that bacteria cause some diseases in the late 1800s. Much of the scientific research into harmful bacteria developed because bacteria cause disease in humans. Tuberculosis, cholera, and infant diarrhea are examples of disease caused by bacteria. Bacteria also may cause disease in many other animals and in plants.

Bacteria can cause the symptoms of disease in three ways.

- They can invade parts of the body, multiplying in body tissues and dissolving cells.
- They can poison the body with chemicals they produce and release.
- They can poison the body with chemicals that are part of the bacteria themselves.

Bacterial wilt caused disease in this pumpkin.

One way to fight bacterial disease is with vaccinations. Vaccines help individual organisms prepare to fight diseases they might encounter in the future. Humans, as well as cats and dogs, get vaccinations for bacterial diseases.

# 1.2 Review

### KEY CONCEPTS

1. Explain why bacteria are classified as living cells but viruses are not.
2. Name two main groups of bacteria.
3. Describe three ways that bacteria affect other organisms.

### CRITICAL THINKING

4. **Visualize** Draw a diagram of a bacterium. Label the parts of the cell.
5. **Predict** Where in your neighborhood would you find most of the bacteria that cause decomposition?

### CHALLENGE

6. **Analyze** Parasitic bacteria do not usually kill their hosts, at least not quickly. For a parasite, why is it better not to kill the host?

# CHAPTER INVESTIGATION

## Bacteria

**OVERVIEW AND PURPOSE** People routinely wash themselves to keep clean. You probably take a bath or shower every day, and you also wash your hands. Your hands may appear to be perfectly clean, but appearances can be deceiving. Your hands pick up bacteria from the objects you touch. You cannot see or feel these microscopic organisms, but they are there, on your skin. In this activity you will

- sample bacteria in your environment
- sample bacteria on your hands

### Problem

Do you pick up bacteria from your environment?

### Hypothesize

Write a hypothesis about whether bacteria in your environment are transferred to your skin. Your hypothesis should take the form of an "If . . . , then . . . , because . . ." statement.

**MATERIALS**

- 3 covered petri dishes with sterile nutrient agar
- marker
- tape
- everyday object, like a coin or eraser
- sterile cotton swab
- hand lens

*for Challenge:*

- 1 covered petri dish with sterile nutrient agar
- sterile swab

### Procedure

1. Make a data table in your **Science Notebook** like the one shown on page 23.

2. Obtain three agar petri dishes. Be careful not to accidentally open the dishes.

3. Remove the lid from one dish and gently press two fingers onto the surface of the agar. Close the lid immediately. Tape the dish closed. Mark the tape with the letter A. Include your initials and the date. Mark your hand as the source in Table 1. Wash your hands.

step 3

4 Choose a small object you handle every day, such as a coin or an eraser. Remove the lid from the second petri dish and swipe the object across the agar. You can instead use a sterile swab to rub on the object, and then swipe the swab across the agar. Close the lid immediately. Tape and mark the dish B, as in step 3. Include the source in Table 1.

5 Choose an area of the classroom you have regular contact with, for example, the top of your desk or the classroom door. Use a clean swab to rub the area and then swipe the swab across the agar of the third petri dish. Tape and mark the dish as C, following the instructions in step 3. Dispose of the swab according to your teacher's instructions.

step 5

6 Place the agar plates upside down in a dark, warm place for two to three days. **CAUTION: Do not open the dishes. Wash your hands when you have finished.**

## Observe and Analyze

Write It Up

1. **OBSERVE** Observe the dishes with the hand lens. You may want to pull the tape aside, but do not remove the covers. Include a description of the bacteria in Table 1. Are the bacteria in one dish different from the others?
2. **OBSERVE** Observe the amounts of bacterial growth in each dish and record your observations in Table 1. Describe the amount of growth in relative terms, using words such as *most, least,* or *moderate.* Which dish has the most bacterial growth? the least growth?
3. Return the petri dishes to your teacher for disposal. **CAUTION: Do not open the dishes. Wash your hands thoroughly with warm water and soap when you have finished.**

## Conclude

1. **INFER** Why is it necessary for the agar to be sterile before you begin the experiment?
2. **INFER** What function does the agar serve?
3. **INTERPRET** Compare your results with your hypothesis. Do your observations support your hypothesis?
4. **IDENTIFY LIMITS** What limits are there in making a connection between the bacteria in dish A and those in dishes B and C?
5. **EVALUATE** Why is it important to keep the petri dishes covered?
6. **APPLY** Why is it important to use separate petri dishes for each sample?

## INVESTIGATE Further

**CHALLENGE** Contamination can be a problem in any experiment involving bacteria, because bacteria are everywhere. Obtain a petri dish from your teacher. Swipe a sterile swab on the agar and place the agar plate upside down in a dark, warm place for two to three days. Do the results of this test make you reevaluate your other lab results?

Bacteria

Table 1. Observations of Bacteria

| Petri Dish | Source | Description of Bacteria | Amount of Bacteria |
|---|---|---|---|
| A | hand | | |
| B | | | |
| C | | | |

KEY CONCEPT

# Viruses are not alive but affect living things.

**BEFORE, you learned**

- Most organisms are made of a single cell
- Living things share common characteristics
- Viruses are not living things

**NOW, you will learn**

- About the structure of viruses
- How viruses use a cell's machinery to reproduce
- How viruses affect host cells

**VOCABULARY**

**host cell** p. 26

**EXPLORE Viruses**

### *How were viruses discovered?*

**PROCEDURE**

1. Fill a small container with mixed sesame seeds and salt.
2. Holding the sieve over the paper plate, pour the mixture into the sieve.
3. Gently shake the sieve until nothing more falls through.
4. Using a hand lens, examine the material that fell through the sieve and the material that stayed in the sieve.

**MATERIALS**

- small container
- sesame seeds
- table salt
- small kitchen sieve
- paper plate
- hand lens

**WHAT DO YOU THINK?**

- What is the most important difference between the particles that got through the sieve and the particles that remained behind?
- How could you change your sieve to make it not let through both kinds of particles?

## Viruses share some characteristics with living things.

**MAIN IDEA WEB**
Remember to make a web of the important terms and details about the main idea: *Viruses share some characteristics with living things.*

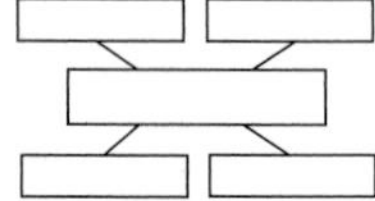

In the late 1800s, scientists such as Louis Pasteur showed that some small organisms can spoil food and cause disease. Once the cause was found, scientists looked for ways to prevent spoilage and disease. One method of prevention they found was removing these harmful organisms from liquids.

Bacteria may be removed from liquids by pouring the liquid through a filter, like a coffee filter or a sieve. To remove bacteria, a filter must have holes smaller than one millionth of a meter in diameter.

# INVESTIGATE Viruses

## *How do infections spread?*

**SKILL FOCUS**
Analyzing

**MATERIALS**
- paper cup
- sample liquid
- solution A
- solution B

**TIME**
30 minutes

### PROCEDURE

1. Get a cup of sample liquid from your teacher. Pour half the liquid from your cup into the cup of a classmate, then pour the same amount back into the original cup. Your cup should then contain a mixture of the liquids from both cups.
2. Repeat step 1 with at least two other classmates.
3. Drop one drop of solution A into your paper cup. If it changes color, you are "infected." If you were "infected," add drops of solution B until your liquid turns clear again. Count how many drops it takes to "cure" you.

### WHAT DO YOU THINK?

- If you were "infected," can you figure out who "infected" you?
- If you were not "infected," is it possible for anyone who poured liquid into your cup to be "infected"?

**CHALLENGE** Only one person in your class started out with an "infection." Try to figure out who it was.

When a filter had removed all of the harmful organisms from a liquid, the liquid no longer caused any illnesses. This method worked when there was only bacteria in the liquid. Sometimes filtering did not prevent disease. Something much smaller than bacteria was in the liquid. Scientists called these disease-causing particles viruses, from the Latin word for "slimy liquid" or "poison."

**RESOURCE CENTER**
CLASSZONE.COM

Learn more about viruses.

**CHECK YOUR READING** How does the size of viruses compare with the size of bacteria?

Scientists have learned much about viruses, and can even make images of them with specialized microscopes. Viruses consist of genetic material contained inside a protective protein coat called a capsid. The protein coat may be a simple tube, such as the coat of an ebola virus, or have many layers, such as the smallpox virus shown on page 26.

Viruses may come in many shapes and sizes, but all viruses consist of a capsid and genetic material. Viruses are able to use living cells to get their DNA copied and so can produce new viruses, a characteristic that makes them similar to living things. Also the protein coat is similar to a cell's outer membrane. But viruses do not grow, and viruses do not respond to changes in their environment. Therefore, viruses are not living organisms.

## Virus

**All viruses, including this smallpox virus, contain genetic material surrounded by a capsid.**

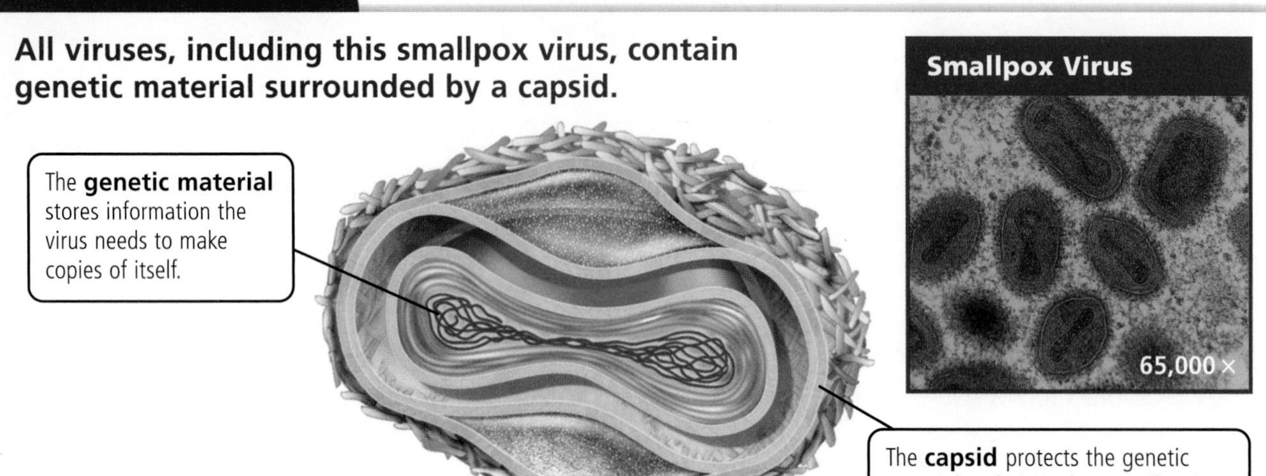

The **genetic material** stores information the virus needs to make copies of itself.
Smallpox Virus
65,000 ×
The **capsid** protects the genetic material and gives shape to the virus.

## Viruses multiply inside living cells.

See how viruses infect and multiply within bacteria.

Remember that all living things reproduce. Viruses cannot reproduce by themselves, which is one of the ways they are different from living things. However, viruses can use materials within living cells to make copies of themselves. The cells that viruses infect in order to make copies are called **host cells.** Despite their tiny size, viruses have the ability to cause a lot of damage to cells of other organisms.

One of the best studied viruses infects bacteria. It's called a bacteriophage (bak-TEER-ee-uh-FAYJ), which comes from the Latin for "bacteria eater." Some of the steps that a bacteriophage goes through to multiply are shown in the illustration on page 27.

1. **Attachment** The virus attaches to the surface of a bacterium.
2. **Injection** The virus injects its DNA into the bacterium.
3. **Production** Using the same machinery used by the host cell for copying its own DNA, the host cell makes copies of the viral DNA.
4. **Assembly** New viruses assemble from the parts that have been created.
5. **Release** The cell bursts open, releasing 100 or more new viruses.

Viruses have proteins on their surfaces that look like the proteins that the host cell normally needs. The virus attaches itself to special sites on the host that are usually reserved for these proteins.

Not every virus makes copies in exactly the same way as the bacteriophage. Some viruses stay inside their host cells. Others use the host cell as a factory that produces new viruses one at a time. These viruses may not be as harmful to the infected organism because the host cell is not destroyed.

## Making New Viruses

**Viruses, such as this bacteriophage, use cells to make new viruses.**

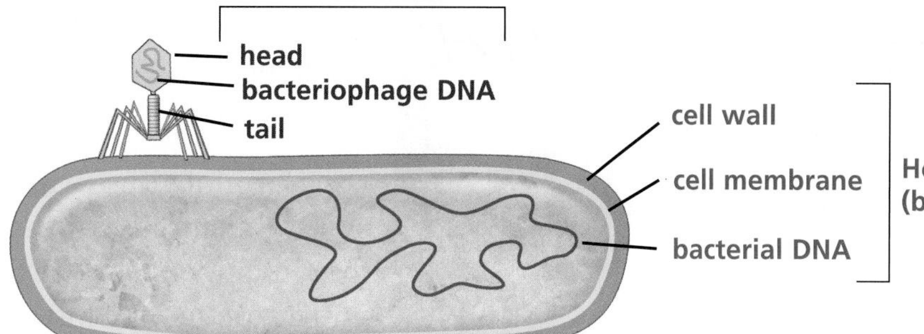

**1 Attachment**
The bacteriophage virus attaches to a bacterium.

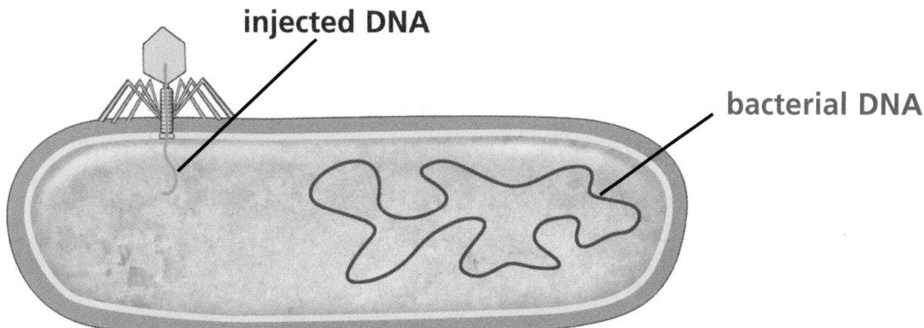


**2 Injection**
The virus injects its DNA into the host cell.

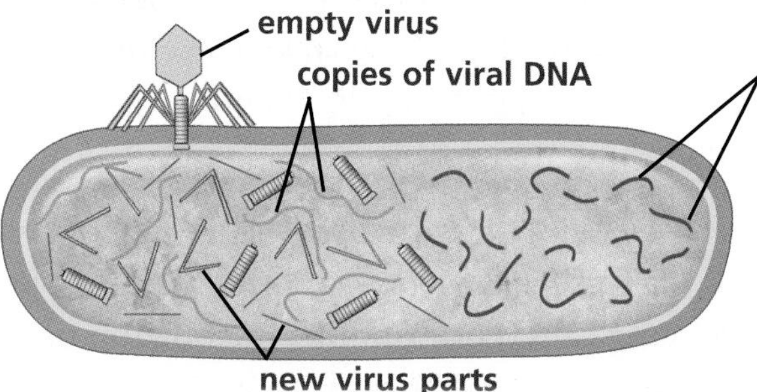


**3 Production**
The viral DNA uses the host cell's machinery to break down the host cell's DNA and produce the parts of new viruses.

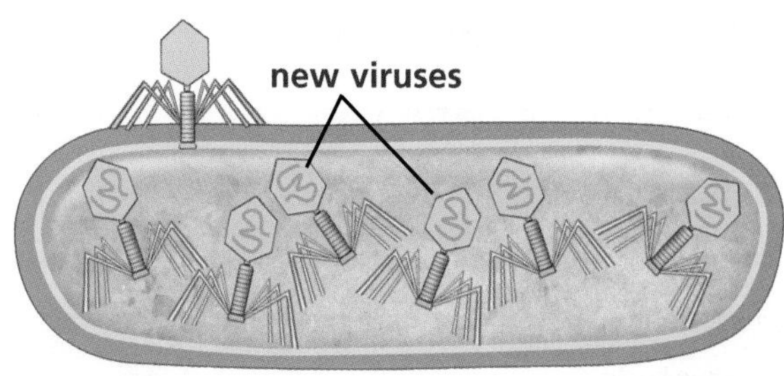


**4 Assembly**
The parts assemble into new viruses.

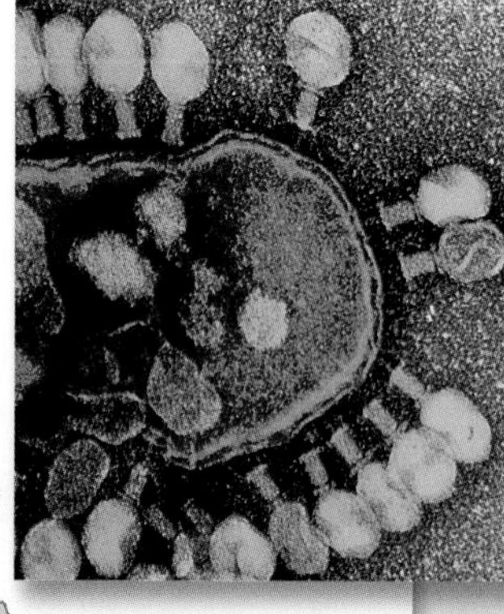

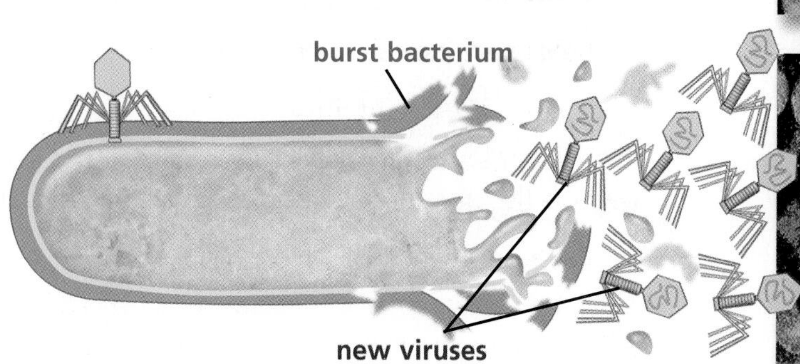


**5 Release**
The host cell breaks apart and new viruses that are able to infect other host cells are released.

Rows of hospital beds are filled with Massachusetts influenza patients in 1918.

## Viruses may harm host cells.

A host cell does not often benefit from providing living space for a virus. The virus uses the cell's material, energy, and processes. In many cases, after a virus has made many copies of itself, the new viruses burst out of the host cell and destroy it.

Harmful viruses cause huge problems. Viruses that cause diseases such as polio, smallpox, diphtheria, or AIDS have had a major impact on human history. About 25 million people died of influenza in an outbreak that occurred just after World War I.

In the photograph, nurses work to ease the symptoms of infected patients. The most infectious patients were enclosed in tents. Others were made as comfortable as possible on beds outside. Since viruses such as influenza can spread quickly, the camp was isolated from the rest of the community.

Plant viruses can stunt plant growth and kill plants. When plant viruses invade crop plants, they can cause much economic damage, decreasing food production. Plants, animals, bacteria, and all other living things are capable of being infected by viruses.

Today, scientists are discovering ways to use viruses in a positive way. Scientists use viruses to insert certain pieces of genetic material into living cells. For example, the portion of genetic material that allows some marine organisms to produce a chemical that glows can be inserted into tissue samples to help scientists study the samples.

# 1.3 Review

### KEY CONCEPTS

1. What are the two parts that every virus has?
2. Why are viruses not considered to be living things?
3. Explain how copies of viruses are produced.

### CRITICAL THINKING

4. **Compare and Contrast** What features do viruses and cells have in common? How are they different?
5. **Explain** Summarize the steps by which a bacteriophage makes new viruses.

### CHALLENGE

6. **Synthesize** What characteristics of viruses can make them so dangerous to humans and other living organisms?

## TULIPOMANIA

# The Virus and the Tulip

The people of Holland around the 1620s were trading fortunes and farmland for one beautiful flower. Tulips had arrived from Turkey by way of Vienna, and interest in the flower spread through Holland like a fever. In a frenzy called "tulipomania," collectors paid as much as 5400 guilders, the price of a city house, for just one tulip bulb—but not any ordinary tulip.

### Broken Flower Bulbs

Tulip traders searched for tulips with patterns, stripes, or feathery petals. These plants were called broken bulbs. Within a field of colored tulips, suddenly an odd or patterned flower grew. Once a color break showed up, it stayed with that flower's line into each new generation, until the line died off. And die off it did. The patterned petals were caused by a virus inside the plant, and the virus caused the flowers to weaken. The blooms got smaller in each generation.

### The Mystery Source

While the trade in tulips rose, growers tried many tricks to produce the crazy patterns. Still, the broken bulbs grew rarely and randomly, or so it seemed. Viruses weren't discovered until 300 years later. Scientists then figured out that a virus had caused the broken bulbs.

**A small leaf-eating insect called an aphid had carried the virus from plant to plant.**



### Back Down to the Ground

Like any goldrush, tulipomania crashed. People lost fortunes and fought over claims. In 1637, the government stopped all trading. Today, tulips with striped and feathery patterns grow around the world, but the patterns observed are not caused by viruses. Still, every now and then, a strange looking bulb appears. Instead of prizing it, growers remove it. They don't want a field of virus-infested, weakened plants.

**Patterns in these tulips are part of the genetic make-up of the flowers.**

### EXPLORE

1. **OBSERVE** Look at tulips in a garden catalog, and find breeds with patterns. Observe the tulip closely. Draw or paint the modern flower and label its name.
2. **CHALLENGE** Viruses can produce sickness, but they have other effects too. Do research on viruses to list some effects of viruses that have value to scientists, doctors, or other people.

KEY CONCEPT

# Protists are a diverse group of organisms.

**BEFORE, you learned**

- Organisms are grouped into six kingdoms
- Bacteria are single-celled organisms without a nucleus
- Viruses are not living things

**NOW, you will learn**

- About characteristics of protists
- About the cell structure of protists
- How protists get their energy

**VOCABULARY**

**algae** p. 31
**plankton** p. 33
**protozoa** p. 34

**THINK ABOUT**

***Where can protists be found?***

Protists include the most complex single-celled organisms found on Earth. Fifty million years ago, a spiral-shelled protist called a nummulitid was common in some oceans. Even though its shell was the size of a coin, the organism inside was microscopic and single celled. When the organism died, the shells accumulated on the ocean floor. Over millions of years, the shells were changed into the rock called limestone. This limestone was used to build the great pyramids of Egypt. Some of the most monumental structures on Earth would not exist without organisms made of just a single cell.

## Most protists are single celled.

When Anton van Leeuwenhoek began using one of the world's first microscopes, he looked at pond water, among other things. He described, in his words, many "very little animalcules." Some of the organisms he saw probably were animals—microscopic but multicellular animals. However, many of the organisms Leeuwenhoek saw moving through the pond water had only a single cell. Today, more than 300 years later, scientists call these single-celled organisms protists.

Protists include all organisms with cells having nuclei and not belonging to the animal, plant, or fungi kingdoms. In other words, protists may be considered a collection of leftover organisms. As a result, protists are the most diverse of all the kingdoms.

# INVESTIGATE Protists

## What lives in pond water?

**SKILL FOCUS**
Observing

**MATERIALS**
- dropper
- pond water
- slide
- cover slip
- hand lenses
- microscope

**TIME**
40 minutes

### PROCEDURE

1. Using a dropper, place one small drop of pond water in the center of a slide. Try to include some of the material from the bottom of the container.
2. Gently place a cover slip on the drop of water.
3. Observe the slide with a hand lens first.
4. Starting with low power, observe the slide with a microscope. Be sure to follow microscope safety procedures as outlined by your teacher. Carefully focus up and down on the water. If you see moving organisms, try to follow them by gently moving the slide.

### WHAT DO YOU THINK?

- Describe and draw what you could see with the hand lens.
- Describe and draw what you could see with the microscope.
- Compare your observations with those of other students.

**CHALLENGE** Choose one organism that moves and observe it for some time. Describe its behavior.

Most protists are single-celled, microscopic organisms that live in water. However, protists also include some organisms with many cells. These many-celled organisms have simpler structures than animals, plants, or fungi. They also have fewer types of cells in their bodies.

Why are protists considered the most diverse group of organisms?

The group of protists you're probably most familiar with is seaweeds. At first glance, seaweed looks like a plant. On closer inspection scientists see that it has a simpler structure. Some seaweeds called kelp can grow 100 meters long.

The name **algae** applies to both multicellular protists and single-celled protists that use sunlight as an energy source. Both seaweed and diatoms are types of algae. Slime molds are another type of multicellular protist.

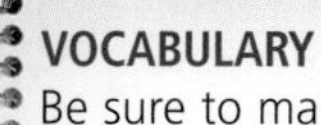

**VOCABULARY**
Be sure to make a description wheel for *algae* and add to it as you read this section.

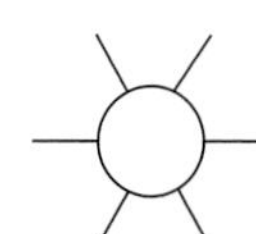

Given the many different types of organisms grouped together as protists, it is no surprise that protists play many roles in their environments. Algae are producers. They obtain energy from sunlight. Their cells provide food for many other organisms. These protists also produce oxygen, which is beneficial to many other organisms. Both of these roles are similar to those played by plants. Other protists act as parasites and can cause disease in many organisms, including humans.

## Diversity of Protists

**Protists come in a variety of shapes and sizes.**

**Euglena**

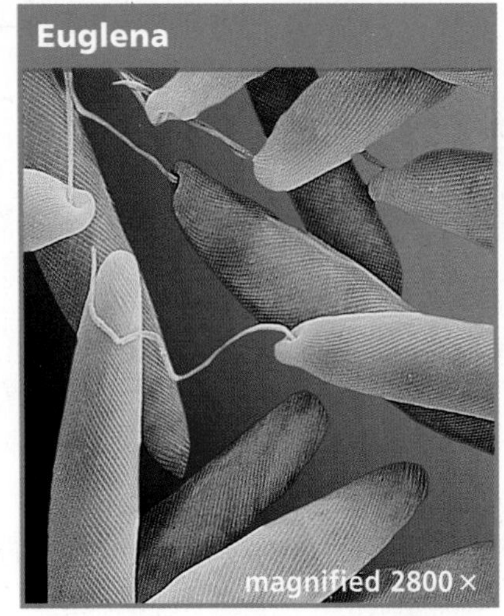

magnified 2800 ×

**Diatoms**

magnified 65 ×

**Seaweed**

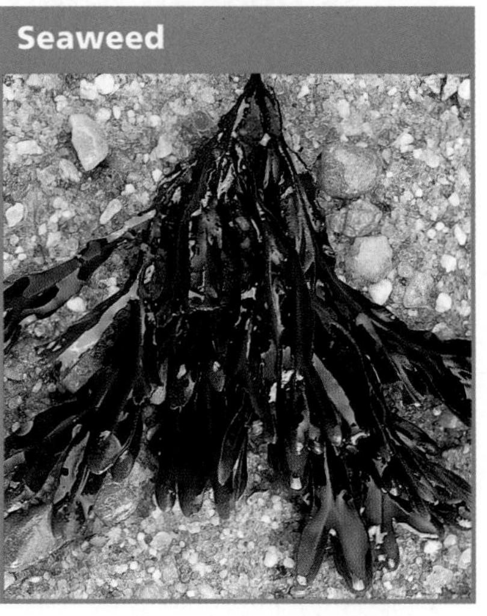

Protists live in any moist environment, including both freshwater and saltwater, and on the forest floor. Some protists move around in the water, some simply float in place, and some stick to surfaces. The photographs above show a small sample of the large variety of organisms that are called protists.

**MAIN IDEA WEB**
Remember to make a web of the important terms and details about the main idea: *Protists obtain their energy in three ways.* Include examples of each method of obtaining energy.

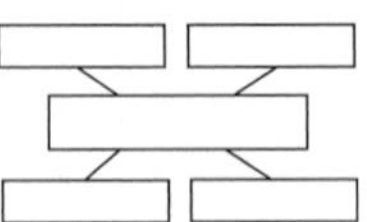

Seaweed is a multicellular protist that floats in the water and can be found washed up on beaches. Slime molds are organisms that attach to surfaces, absorbing nutrients from them. Diatoms are single-celled algae that float in water and are covered by hard shells. Euglena are single-celled organisms that can move like animals but also get energy from sunlight.

## Protists obtain their energy in three ways.

Protists can be classified by their way of getting energy. Some protists capture sunlight and convert it to usable energy. Another group of protists gets its energy from eating other organisms. A third group gets energy by absorbing materials and nutrients from its environment.

Some protists, such as the euglena in the upper left photograph, can even switch from one mode of life to another. They swim rapidly through pond water like animals. If they receive enough sunlight, they look green and make their own food like plants. But if they are left in the dark long enough, they absorb nutrients from their environment like fungi.

Explain how the organisms in the photographs above get their energy.

## Algae

Plantlike protists, called algae, get energy from sunlight. Like plants, they use the Sun's energy, water, and carbon dioxide from the air or water. Algae contain chlorophyll, a green pigment that they use to capture the Sun's energy. In the process of transforming energy from sunlight, algae release oxygen gas into the air. This important process, which is called photosynthesis, also takes place in plants and some bacteria. Organisms that perform photosynthesis also supply much of the food for other organisms.

Diatoms are examples of single-celled algae. Like all algae, a diatom contains a nucleus which holds its genetic material. Diatoms also have chloroplasts, which are the energy-producing centers that contain chlorophyll.

### Algae

**Algae are plantlike protists. *Chlamydomonas* is an example of single-celled algae.**

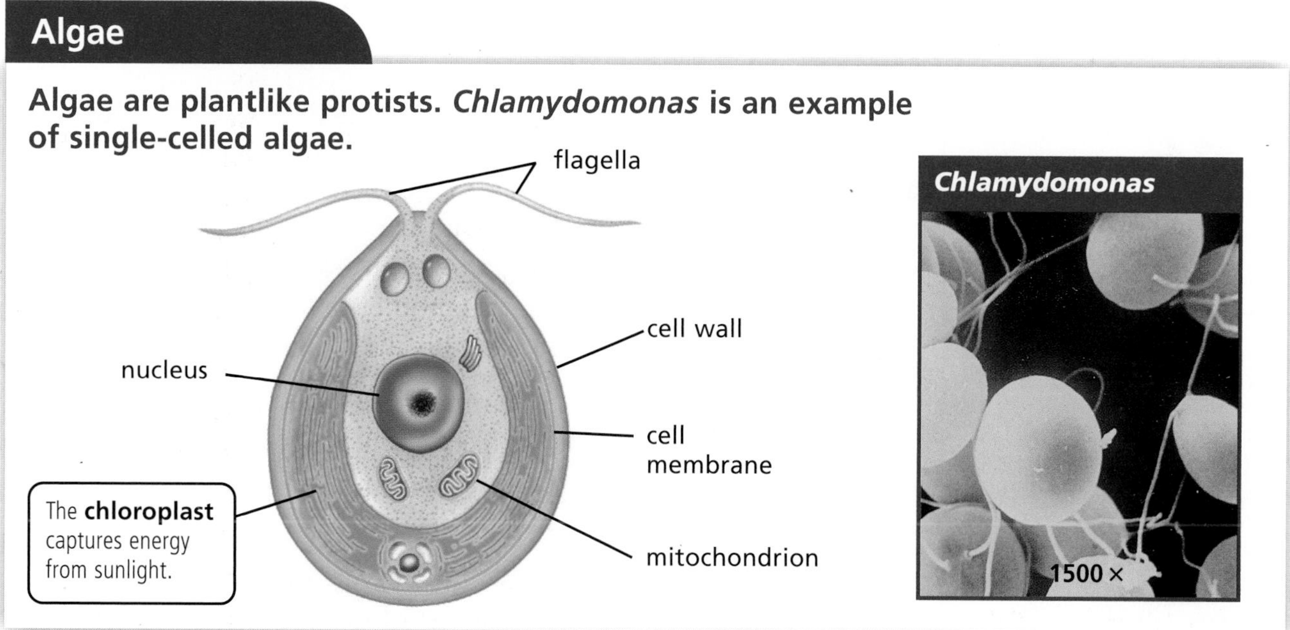


Another type of algae, called volvox, are microscopic colonies of nearly identical cells. These cells, arranged in a hollow ball, look like some single-celled algae. Sometimes cells break off from the hollow ball to form new colonies. The new colonies will eventually escape the parent colony. Colonial organisms such as volvox are the simplest kind of multicellular organisms. Seaweed is another example of multicellular algae.

All organisms that drift in water are called **plankton.** Plankton include the young of many animals and some adult animals, as well as protists. Plankton that perform photosynthesis are called phytoplankton (plantlike plankton). Phytoplankton include algae and the cyanobacteria you learned about earlier. Phytoplankton live in all of the world's oceans and produce most of the oxygen animals breathe.

## Protozoa

**Protozoa, such as this *Paramecium*, are animal-like protists.**

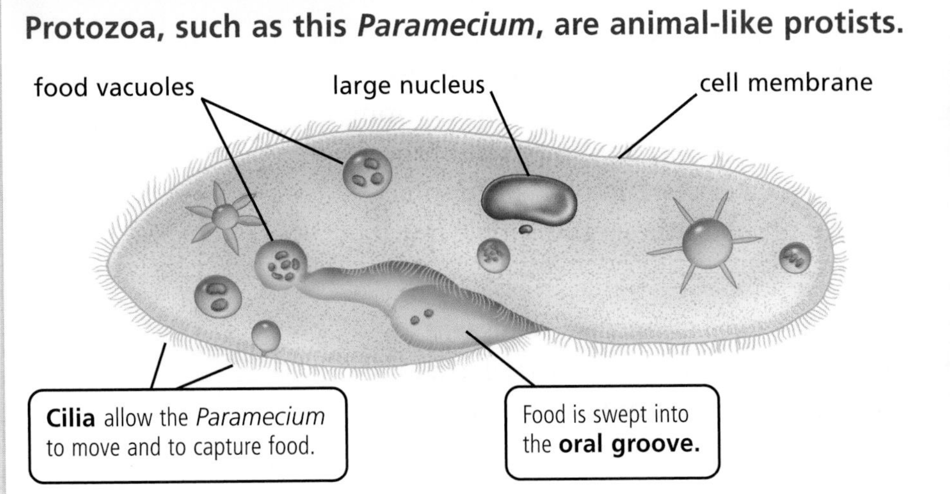

food vacuoles
large nucleus
cell membrane
**Cilia** allow the *Paramecium* to move and to capture food.
Food is swept into the **oral groove.**

*Paramecium*
40×

### Protozoa

Protists that eat other organisms, or decaying parts of other organisms, are animal-like protists, or **protozoa.** They include many forms, all single-celled. Protozoa cannot use sunlight as a source of energy and they must move around to obtain the energy they need to survive. Certain chemicals in protozoa can recognize when a particle of food is nearby. The food particle is usually another organism or a part of one. The protozoan ingests the food and breaks it down to obtain energy.

Some animal-like protists swim rapidly, sweeping bacteria or other protists into a groove that looks like a mouth. One example, called a paramecium, is shown above. A paramecium moves about using thousands of short wavy strands called cilia.

Another group of protozoa swim with one or more long whiplike structures called flagella. A third group of protozoa has very flexible cells. Organisms such as the amoeba oozes along surfaces. When it encounters prey, the amoeba spreads out and wraps around its food.

A number of protists live as parasites, some of which cause disease in animals, including humans. One of the world's most significant human diseases, malaria, is caused by a protist. A mosquito carries the parasite from human to human. When the mosquito bites an infected human, it sucks up some of the parasite in the blood. When that same mosquito bites another human, it passes on some of the parasite. Within a human host, the parasite goes through a complex life cycle, eventually destroying red blood cells.

**REMINDER**

A parasite is an organism that lives inside or on another organism and causes the organism harm.

**CHECK YOUR READING** How do protozoa and algae differ in the way they obtain energy?

## Decomposers

Protists that absorb food from their environment can be called funguslike protists. These protists take in materials from the soil or from other organisms and break materials down in order to obtain energy. They are called decomposers.

The term *mold* refers to many organisms that produce a fuzzy-looking growth. Most of the molds you might be familiar with, like bread mold, are fungi. But three groups of protists are also called molds. These molds have structures that are too simple to be called fungi, and they are single celled for a portion of their lives. One example of a funguslike protist is water mold, which forms a fuzzy growth on food. This food may be decaying animal or plant tissue or living organisms. Water molds live mainly in fresh water.

Slime molds live on decaying plants on the forest floor. One kind of slime mold consists of microscopic single cells that ooze around, eating bacteria. When their food is scarce, however, many of the cells group together to produce a multicellular colony. The colony eventually produces a reproductive structure to release spores. Wind can carry spores about, and they sprout where they land.

A walk in a moist forest might give you a chance to see a third kind of mold. This organism looks like a fine net, like lace, several centimeters across, on rotting logs. These slime molds are not multicellular, but instead one giant cell with many nuclei. They are the plasmodial slime molds.

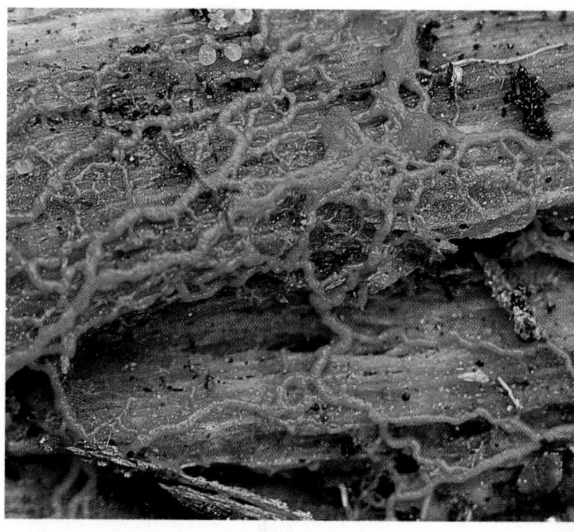

Plasmodial slime mold may grow on decaying wood after a period of rainy weather.

How do funguslike protists get energy?

## 1.4 Review

### KEY CONCEPTS

1. What are two characteristics of protists?
2. What feature do all protists have in common?
3. What are the three different types of protists?

### CRITICAL THINKING

4. **Provide Examples** Some protists are dependent on other organisms and cannot live independently. Other protists are independent and have organisms that depend on them. Give an example of each.

### CHALLENGE

5. **Hypothesize** Scientists are considering reclassifying protists into many kingdoms. How might they decide how many kingdoms to use and how to place organisms within these kingdoms?

# Chapter Review

## the BIG idea

**Bacteria and protists have the characteristics of living things, while viruses are not alive.**

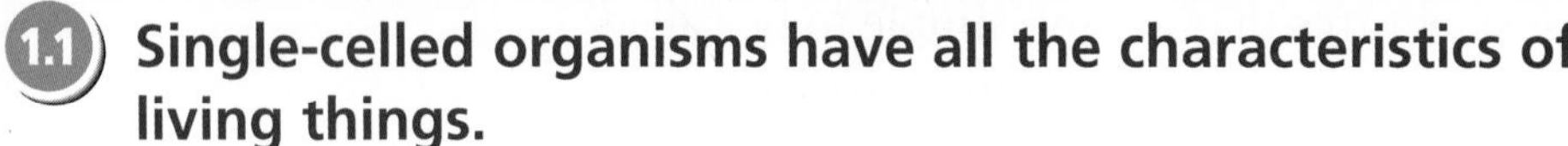


### 1.1 Single-celled organisms have all the characteristics of living things.

Scientists divide organisms into six **kingdoms.** All living things, including **microorganisms,** are organized, grow, reproduce, and respond to the environment.

Plants

Animals

Protists

Fungi

Archaea

Bacteria

**VOCABULARY**
**microorganism** p. 10
**kingdom** p. 11
**binary fission** p. 12
**virus** p. 14

### 1.2 Bacteria are single-celled organisms without nuclei.

- Bacteria and archaea are the smallest living things.
- Archaea and bacteria are found in many environments.
- Bacteria may help or harm other organisms.

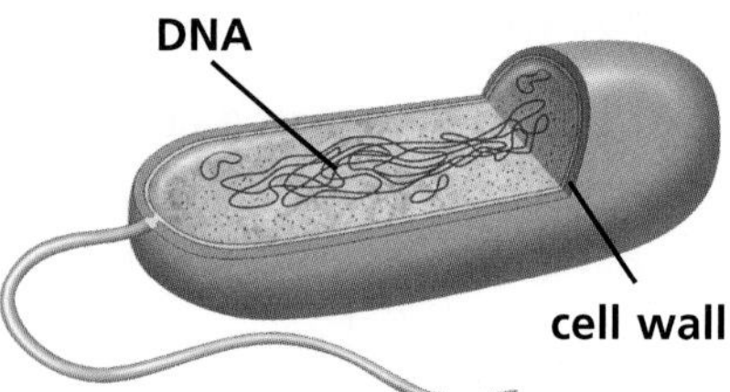


**VOCABULARY**
**bacteria** p. 16
**archaea** p. 18
**producer** p. 19
**decomposer** p. 19
**parasite** p. 19

### 1.3 Viruses are not alive but affect living things.

A virus consists of genetic material enclosed in a protein coat. Viruses cannot reproduce on their own, but they use materials within living cells to make copies of themselves.

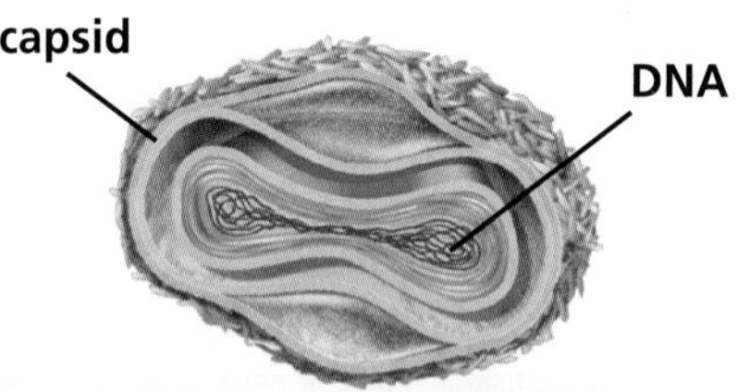


**VOCABULARY**
**host cell** p. 26

### 1.4 Protists are a diverse group of organisms.

Plantlike **algae** get energy from sunlight.

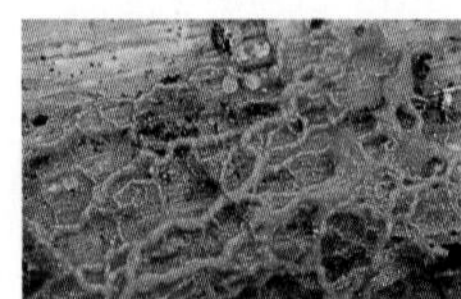
Funguslike protists are decomposers.

**Protozoa,** or animal-like protists, eat other organisms.

**VOCABULARY**
**algae** p. 31
**plankton** p. 33
**protozoa** p. 34

## Reviewing Vocabulary

*Draw a triangle for each of the terms listed below. Define the term, use it in a sentence, and draw a picture to help you remember the term. An example is completed for you.*

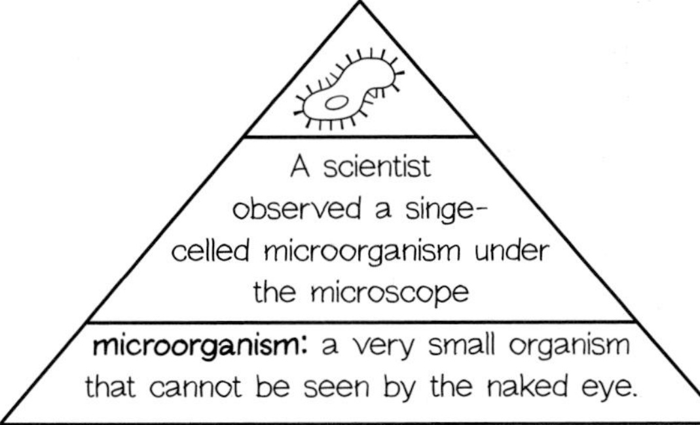

A scientist observed a singe-celled microorganism under the microscope
microorganism: a very small organism that cannot be seen by the naked eye.

1. binary fission
2. producer
3. virus
4. host cell

*Describe how the vocabulary terms in the following pairs of words are related to each other. Explain the relationship in a one- or two-sentence answer. Underline each vocabulary term in your answers.*

5. archaea, bacteria
6. microorganism, organism
7. decomposers, parasite
8. protists, algae

## Reviewing Key Concepts

**Multiple Choice** *Choose the letter of the best answer.*

9. Which group is *not* a microscopic kingdom?
   - **a.** fungi
   - **b.** bacteria
   - **c.** archaea
   - **d.** protists

10. What happens in binary fission?
    - **a.** DNA is combined into one cell.
    - **b.** The daughter cells differ from the parent cell.
    - **c.** Material from one cell is divided into two cells.
    - **d.** One cell divides into four exact cells.

11. Which is a characteristic of a virus?
    - **a.** obtains energy from sunlight
    - **b.** responds to light and temperature
    - **c.** doesn't contain DNA
    - **d.** reproduces only within cells

12. Which is the simplest type of organism on Earth?
    - **a.** protists
    - **b.** bacteria
    - **c.** viruses
    - **d.** parasites

13. Which statement about bacteria is *not* true?
    - **a.** Bacteria reproduce using binary fission.
    - **b.** Bacteria do not have a nucleus.
    - **c.** Bacteria do not contain genetic material.
    - **d.** Bacteria are either rod-, round-, or spiral-shaped.

14. Archaea that can survive only in extreme temperatures are the
    - **a.** methanogens
    - **b.** halophiles
    - **c.** thermophiles
    - **d.** bacteria

15. A fluid containing weakened disease-causing viruses or bacteria is
    - **a.** a filter
    - **b.** a diatom
    - **c.** a bacteriophage
    - **d.** a vaccine

16. Which group of protists are decomposers?
    - **a.** diatoms
    - **b.** molds
    - **c.** protozoa
    - **d.** plankton

17. Which obtains energy by feeding on other organisms?
    - **a.** amoeba
    - **b.** algae
    - **c.** phytoplankton
    - **d.** mushroom

**Short Answer** *Write a short answer to each question.*

18. Briefly describe the characteristics that all living things share.

19. How are some bacteria harmful to humans?

20. What are plankton?

## Thinking Critically

21. **APPLY** Imagine you are a scientist on location in a rain forest in Brazil. You discover what you think might be a living organism. How would you be able to tell if the discovery is a living thing?

22. **COMMUNICATE** What process is shown in this photograph? Describe the sequence of events in the process shown.

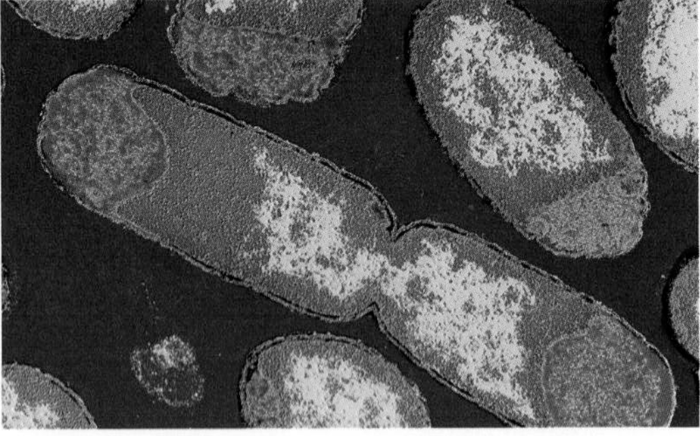

23. **CLASSIFY** Why are archaea classified in a separate kingdom from bacteria?

24. **ANALYZE** Why are some bacteria considered "nature's recyclers"? Explain the role that these bacteria play in the environment.

25. **CALCULATE** A bacterium reproduces every hour. Assuming the bacteria continue to reproduce at that rate, how many bacteria will there be after 10 hours? Explain how you know.

26. **HYPOTHESIZE** A student conducts an experiment to determine the effectiveness of washing hands on bacteria. He rubs an unwashed finger across an agar plate, then washes his hands and rubs the same finger across a second plate. What hypothesis might the student make for this experiment? Explain.

27. **COMPARE AND CONTRAST** Describe three ways that viruses differ from bacteria.

28. **ANALYZE** A scientist has grown cultures of bacteria on agar plates for study. Now the scientist wants to grow a culture of viruses in a laboratory for study. How might this be possible? Give an example.

29. **PROVIDE EXAMPLES** How are protists both helpful and harmful to humans? Give examples in your answer.

## the BIG idea

30. **INFER** Look again at the picture on pages 6–7. Now that you have finished the chapter, how would you change or add details to your answer to the question on the photograph?

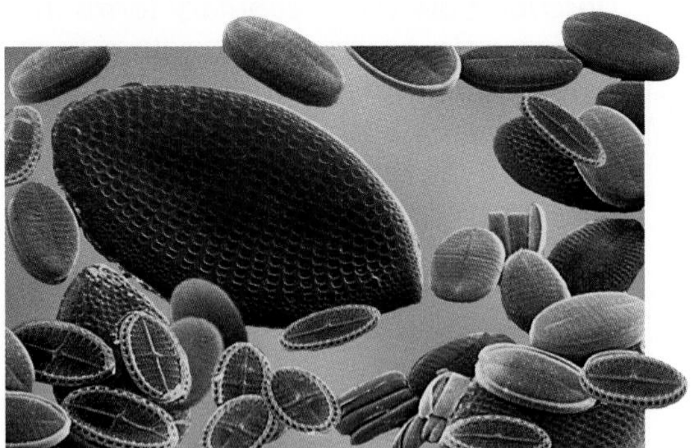

## UNIT PROJECTS

If you are doing a unit project, make a folder for your project. Include in your folder a list of resources you will need, the date on which the project is due, and a schedule to track your progress. Begin gathering data.

## Analyzing Data

The graph below shows growth rates of bacteria at different temperatures.

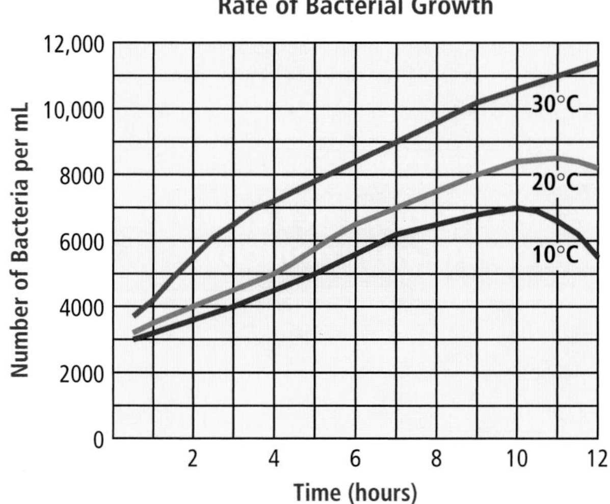


*Choose the letter of the best answer.*

1. At which temperature did growth of bacteria occur at the greatest rate?
   **a.** 0°C
   **b.** 10°C
   **c.** 20°C
   **d.** 30°C

2. Which statement is true about the growth rate of bacteria at 10°C?
   **a.** Bacteria grew rapidly at first, then declined after 6 hours.
   **b.** Bacteria growth increased at a steady rate.
   **c.** Bacteria grew slowly, then declined rapidly after 10 hours.
   **d.** Bacteria showed neither an increase nor decrease in growth rate.

3. What is the concentration of bacteria at a temperature of 20°C after 4 hours?
   **a.** about 5000 per mL
   **b.** about 6000 per mL
   **c.** about 7000 per mL
   **d.** about 8000 per mL

4. During which hour was the concentration of bacteria at 20°C the greatest?
   **a.** hour 2
   **b.** hour 4
   **c.** hour 8
   **d.** hour 10

5. Which conclusion can be drawn from the data in the graph?
   **a.** The rate of bacterial growth is the greatest at the highest temperature.
   **b.** The rate of bacterial growth is the least at the highest temperature.
   **c.** The rate of bacterial growth is the greatest at the lowest temperature.
   **d.** The rate of bacterial growth does not change depending on temperature.

6. How much did the rate of bacterial growth increase between 2 hours and 8 hours at 30°C?
   **a.** 2000 per mL
   **b.** 4000 per mL
   **c.** 6000 per mL
   **d.** 8000 per mL

## Extended Response

7. A scientist wants to test the effect of temperature on the same bacteria shown in the graph at higher temperatures. The scientist tests the growth rate of bacteria at 50°C, 75°C, and 100°C. Based on the information in the graph and your knowledge of bacteria, what results might the scientist get? Explain your reasoning.

8. Antibiotics are drugs that are used to inhibit the growth of bacterial infections. A scientist wants to test the ability of three different antibiotics to control the growth of a certain type of bacteria. The scientist has isolated the bacteria in test tubes. Each antibiotic is prepared in a tablet form. Design an experiment that will test the effectiveness of the antibiotic tablets on the bacteria. Your experiment should include a hypothesis, a list of materials, a procedure, and a method of recording data.

CHAPTER

# Introduction to Multicellular Organisms

## the BIG idea

Multicellular organisms live in and get energy from a variety of environments.

### Key Concepts

SECTION

**Multicellular organisms meet their needs in different ways.**
Learn about specialized cells, tissues, and organs.

SECTION

**Plants are producers.**
Learn how plants get energy and respond to the environment.

SECTION

**Animals are consumers.**
Learn how animals get energy and how they interact with the environment.

SECTION

**Most fungi are decomposers.**
Learn about fungi and how they get energy.

**Internet Preview**

CLASSZONE.COM

Chapter 2 online resources: Content Review, Visualization, four Resource Centers, Math Tutorial, Test Practice

***How does an organism get energy and materials from its environment?***

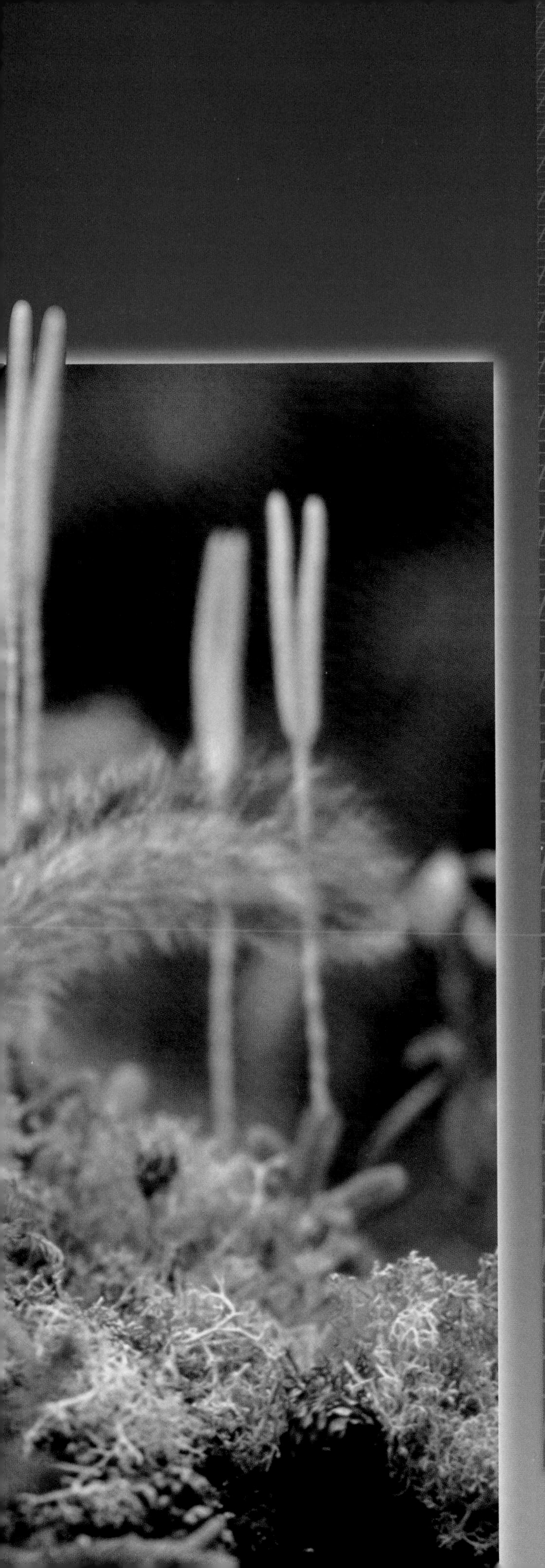

# EXPLORE the BIG idea

## Where Does It Come From?

Think about the things you use every day. Just like any other organism, you depend on the environment to meet your needs. The food you eat comes from plants and animals. Also, much of what you use is made of materials processed from living matter.

**Observe and Think** Identify three nonfood items you come into contact with every day. Where does the material for these products come from?

## How Can a Multicellular Organism Reproduce on Its Own?

Take an old potato and cut it in half, making sure that there are eyes on both halves. Plant each half in a pot of soil. Water the pots once a day. After two weeks, remove the potato halves from the pots and examine.

**Observe and Think** What happened to the potato halves?

## Internet Activity: Bee Dance

Go to **ClassZone.com** to explore how bees communicate.

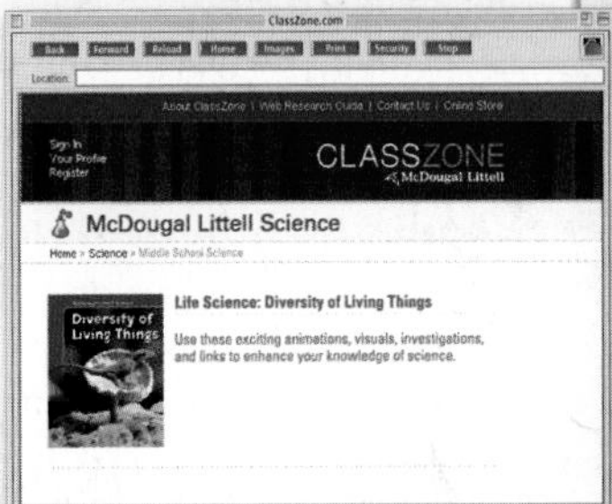


**Observe and Think** What type of information can a bee communicate to other bees in a hive?

Animal Behavior **Code: MDL040**

CHAPTER 2

# Getting Ready to Learn

## CONCEPT REVIEW

- Living things are organized, grow, respond, and reproduce.
- Protists get energy in three different ways.
- Single-celled organisms reproduce when the cell divides.

## VOCABULARY REVIEW

**kingdom** p. 11

**producer** p. 19

**decomposer** p. 19

*See Glossary for definitions.*

**adaptation, DNA, genetic material**

CONTENT REVIEW
CLASSZONE.COM

Review concepts and vocabulary.

## TAKING NOTES

### MAIN IDEA AND DETAILS

Make a two-column chart. Write the main ideas, such as those in the blue headings, in the column on the left. Write details about each of those main ideas in the column on the right.

### VOCABULARY STRATEGY

Write each new vocabulary term in the center of a **four square** diagram. Write notes in the squares around each term. Include a definition, some characteristics, and some examples of the term. If possible, write some things that are not examples of the term.

See the Note-Taking Handbook on pages R45–R51.

SCIENCE NOTEBOOK

| MAIN IDEAS | DETAILS |
|---|---|
| Plants respond to their environment. | 1. Plants respond to different stimuli.<br>2. A stimulus is something that produces a response. |

| Definition | Characteristics |
|---|---|
| Group of same type of cells performing similar functions | Cells are similar. Different tissues do different jobs. |
| **TISSUE** | |
| **Examples** | **Nonexamples** |
| skin tissue<br>nerve tissue<br>muscle tissue | a simple cell |

KEY CONCEPT

# Multicellular organisms meet their needs in different ways.

**BEFORE, you learned**

- Organisms get energy and materials from the environment
- All organisms are organized, grow, respond, and reproduce
- Differences in genetic material lead to diversity

**NOW, you will learn**

- About the functions of cells in multicellular organisms
- How multicellular organisms are adapted to different environments
- About sexual reproduction

**VOCABULARY**

**tissue** p. 44
**organ** p. 44
**sexual reproduction** p. 48
**meiosis** p. 48
**fertilization** p. 48

THINK ABOUT

***Why is teamwork important?***

For any team to be successful, it is important for people to work well together. Within a team, each person has a different role. For example, the team in this restaurant includes people to greet diners and seat them, people to buy and cook the food, and people to take food orders and serve the food. By dividing different jobs among different people, a restaurant can serve more customers at the same time. What would happen in a large restaurant if the diners were seated, cooked for, and served by the same person?

## Multicellular organisms have cells that are specialized.

MAIN IDEA AND DETAILS
Make a chart and add notes about the main idea: *Multicellular organisms have cells that are specialized.*

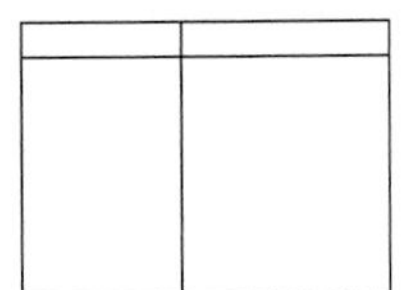

In single-celled organisms, all the functions of life are performed by one cell. These functions include getting energy and materials, removing wastes, and responding to changes in the environment. In multicellular organisms, however, different jobs are done by different cells—the cells are specialized. A blood cell carries oxygen. A nerve cell sends and receives signals. Just as the different jobs of running a restaurant are divided among different people, in multicellular organisms different functions are divided among different cells.

In this chapter, you will read about plants, animals, and fungi. These three kingdoms are made up almost entirely of multicellular organisms. The cells in multicellular organisms are organized in ways that enable them to survive and reproduce.

# INVESTIGATE Specialization

## What are some advantages of specialization?

**SKILL FOCUS**
Making Models

**MATERIALS**
- two boxes, each containing 20 paper clips, 2 pieces of paper, and 1 pencil

**TIME**
10 minutes

**PROCEDURE**

1. Form into two teams,each representing an organism. The single-celled team will be made up of just one person; the multicellular team will be made up of three. Each team obtains a box of materials from the teacher.
2. Each team must do the following tasks as quickly as possible: make a paper-clip chain, write the alphabet on both sides of one piece of paper, and make a paper airplane from the second piece of paper. The members of the three-person team must specialize, each person doing one task only.

**WHAT DO YOU THINK?**

- What are some advantages to having each person on the three-person team specialize in doing a different job?
- Why might efficiency be a factor in the activities done by cells in a multicellular organism?

**CHALLENGE** Suppose the "life" of the multicellular team depended on the ability of one person to make a paper airplane. How would specialization be a disadvantage if that person were not at school?

## Levels of Organization

For any multicellular organism to survive, different cells must work together. The right type of cell must be in the right place to do the work that needs to be done.

Organization starts with the cell. Cells in multicellular organisms are specialized for a specific function. In animals, skin cells provide protection, nerve cells carry signals, and muscle cells produce movement. Cells of the same type are organized into **tissue,** a group of cells that work together. For example, what you think of as muscle is muscle tissue, made up of many muscle cells.

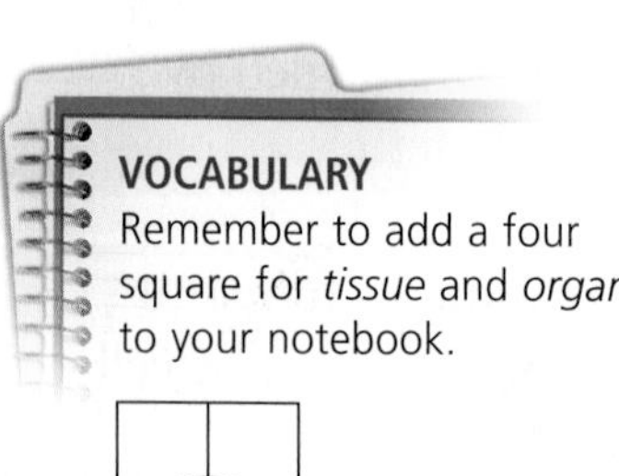

**VOCABULARY**
Remember to add a four square for *tissue* and *organ* to your notebook.

A structure that is made up of different tissues is called an **organ.** Organs have particular functions. The heart is an organ that functions as a pump. It has muscle tissue, which pumps the blood, and nerve tissue, which signals when to pump. Different organs that work together and have a common function are called an organ system. A heart and blood vessels are different organs that are both part of a circulatory system. These organs work together to deliver blood to all parts of a body. Together, cells, tissues, organs, and organ systems form an organism.

## Organ Systems and the Organism

In almost all multicellular organisms, different organ systems take care of specific needs. Here are a few examples of organ systems found in many animals:

- nervous system enables a response to changing conditions
- muscular system produces movement and supplies heat
- respiratory system takes in oxygen and releases carbon dioxide
- circulatory system delivers oxygen and removes carbon dioxide
- digestive system breaks down food into a usable form

Organ systems allow multicellular organisms to obtain large amounts of energy, process large amounts of materials, respond to changes in the environment, and reproduce.

**REMINDER**
A system is a group of objects that interact, sharing energy and matter.

**CHECK YOUR READING** How are the functions of organ systems related to the needs of an organism? Give an example.

Different organ systems work together. For example, the respiratory system works with the circulatory system to deliver oxygen and remove carbon dioxide. When an animal such as a turtle breathes in, oxygen is brought into the lungs. Blood from the circulatory system picks up the oxygen, and the heart pumps the oxygen-rich blood out to the cells of the body. As oxygen is delivered, waste carbon dioxide is picked up. The blood is pumped back to the lungs. The carbon dioxide is released when the turtle breathes out. More oxygen is picked up when the turtle breathes in.

### Organ Systems

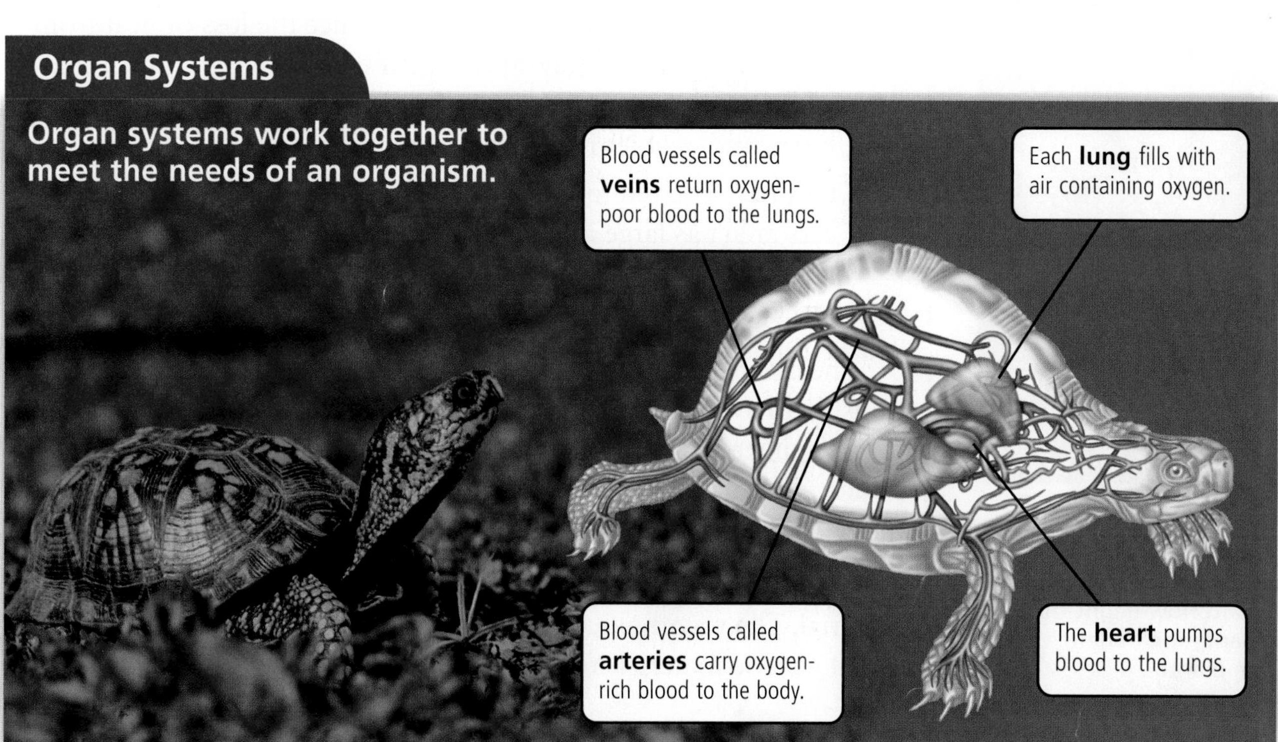

Organ systems work together to meet the needs of an organism.
Blood vessels called **veins** return oxygen-poor blood to the lungs.
Each **lung** fills with air containing oxygen.
Blood vessels called **arteries** carry oxygen-rich blood to the body.
The **heart** pumps blood to the lungs.

## Multicellular organisms are adapted to live in different environments.

READING TIP

*Offspring* is a word used to describe the new organisms produced by reproduction in any organism. Think of it as meaning "to spring off."

All organisms have characteristics that allow them to survive in their environment. An adaptation is any inherited characteristic that increases the chance of an organism's surviving and producing offspring that also reproduce. An adaptation may have to do with the way an organism gets its energy or processes materials. An adaptation may relate to the shape or structure of an organism's body. An adaptation can even be a form of behavior.

The text above mentions different types of adaptations. Name three.

When most multicellular organisms reproduce, the offspring are not exact copies of the parents. There are differences. If a particular difference gives an organism an advantage over other members in its group, then that difference is referred to as an adaptation. Over time, the organism and its offspring do better and reproduce more.

You are probably familiar with the furry animal called a fox. Different species of fox have different adaptations that enable them to survive in different environments. Here are three examples:

- **Fennec** The fennec is a desert fox. Its large ears are an adaptation that helps the fox keep cool in the hot desert. As blood flows through the vessels in each ear, heat is released. Another adaptation is the color of its fur, which blends in with the desert sand.
- **Arctic fox** The Arctic fox lives in the cold north. Its small ears, legs, and nose are adaptations that reduce the loss of heat from its body. Its bluish-gray summer fur is replaced by a thick coat of white fur as winter approaches. Its winter coat keeps the fox warm and enables it to blend in with the snow.
- **Red fox** The red fox is found in grasslands and woodlands. Its ears aren't as large as those of the fennec or as small as those of the Arctic fox. Its body fur is reddish brown tipped in white and black, coloring that helps it blend into its environment.

**INFER** The strong odor of the rafflesia flower attracts flies into the plant. How might this adaptation benefit the plant?

The diversity of life on Earth is due to the wide range of adaptations that have occurred in different species. An elephant has a trunk for grasping and sensing. A female kangaroo carries its young in a pouch. The largest flower in the world, the rafflesia flower, is almost a meter wide, blooms for just a few days, and smells like rotting meat.

Adaptations are the result of differences that can occur in genetic material. The way multicellular organisms reproduce allows for a mixing of genetic material. You will read about that next.

## Adaptations in Different Environments

**Fennec**

**Habitat**: warm; Sahara Desert and Saudi Arabia

**Size**: about 40 cm (15 in.), 1.25 kg (2.7 lb)

**Arctic Fox**

**Habitat**: cold; Northern Eurasia and North America

**Size**: about 50 cm (20 in.), 4 kg (9 lb)

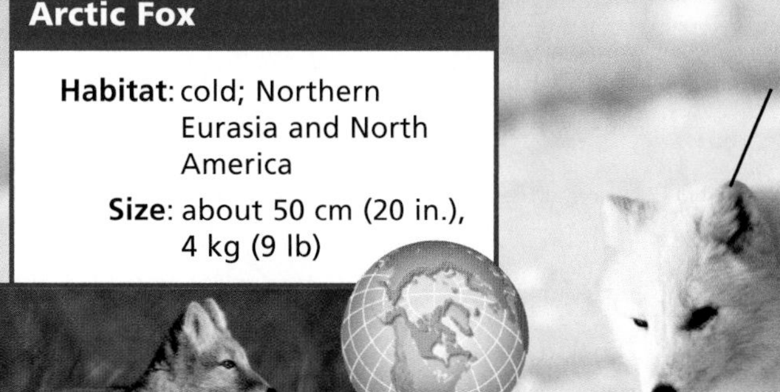


**Red Fox**

**Habitat**: moderate; North and Central America, Eurasia

**Size**: about 65 cm (25 in.), 6 kg (13 lb)

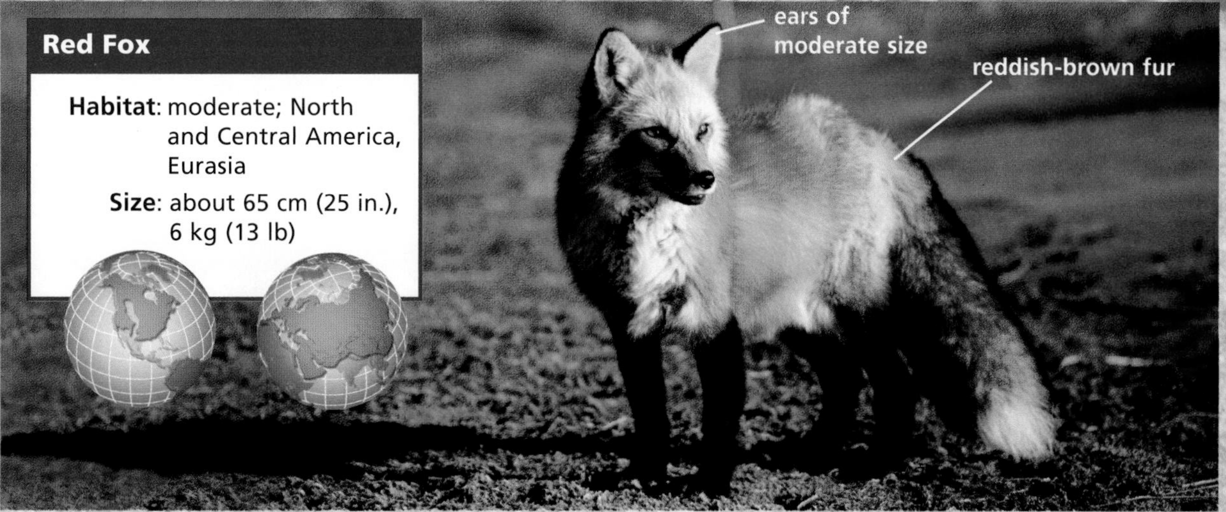


**READING VISUALS** Foxes are hunters that feed on small animals. How might the coat color of each fox contribute to its survival?

## Sexual reproduction leads to diversity.

Most multicellular organisms reproduce sexually. In **sexual reproduction,** the genetic material of two parents comes together, and the resulting offspring have genetic material from both. Sexual reproduction leads to diversity because the DNA in the offspring is different from the DNA in the parents.

One copy of DNA in cell after meiosis

Two different cellular processes are involved in sexual reproduction. The first is **meiosis** (my-OH-sihs), a special form of cell division that produces sperm cells in a male and egg cells in a female. Each sperm or egg cell contains only one copy of DNA, the genetic material. Most cells contain two copies of DNA.

The second process in sexual reproduction is **fertilization.** Fertilization occurs when the sperm cell from the male parent combines with the egg cell from the female parent. A fertilized egg is a single cell with DNA from both parents. Once the egg is fertilized, it divides. One cell becomes two, two cells become four, and so on. As the cells divide, they start to specialize, and different tissues and organs form.

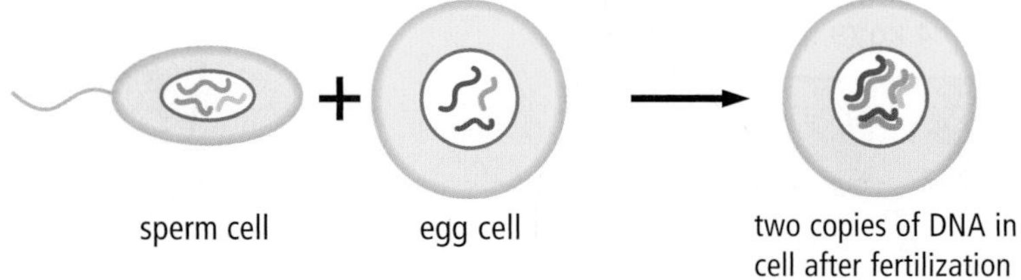


Differences in genetic material and in the environment produce differences in offspring. Whether a tulip flower is red or yellow depends on the genetic material in its cells. How well the tulip grows depends on conditions in the environment as well as genetic materials.

**Sexual Reproduction** The fertilized eggs of a salamander contain genetic material from two parents.

**Asexual Reproduction** The buds of a sea coral have the same genetic material as the parent.

Most reproduction that occurs in multicellular organisms is sexual reproduction. However, many multicellular organisms can reproduce by asexual reproduction. With asexual reproduction, a single parent produces offspring.

Budding is a form of asexual reproduction. In budding, a second organism grows off, or buds, from another. Organisms that reproduce asexually can reproduce more often. Asexual reproduction limits genetic diversity within a group because offspring have the same genetic material as the parent.

**CHECK YOUR READING** How do offspring produced by sexual reproduction compare with offspring produced by asexual reproduction?

With sexual reproduction, there is an opportunity for new combinations of characteristics to occur in the offspring. Perhaps these organisms process food more efficiently or reproduce more quickly. Or perhaps they have adaptations that allow them to survive a change in their environment. In the next three sections, you will read how plants, animals, and fungi have adapted to similar environments in very different ways.

# 2.1 Review

## KEY CONCEPTS

1. How do specialized cells relate to the different levels of organization in a multicellular organism?
2. What is an adaptation? Give an example.
3. What two cellular processes are involved in sexual reproduction?

## CRITICAL THINKING

4. **Compare and Contrast** How does the genetic diversity of the offspring differ in sexual reproduction versus asexual reproduction?
5. **Predict** If fertilization occurred without meiosis, how many copies of DNA would be in the cells of the offspring?

## CHALLENGE

6. **Synthesize** Do you consider the different levels of organization in a multicellular organism an adaptation? Explain your reasoning.

SKILL: USING CIRCLE GRAPHS

# Making Data Visual

A circle graph is a good way to see part-to-whole relationships. To use data presented in a circle graph, do the following:

Click on Math Tutorial for more help interpreting circle graphs.

## Example

Suppose, at a waterhole in a game preserve, researchers observed ten animals throughout the day. What fraction of the sightings were giraffes?

**(1)** The circle graph shows the data for the sightings. The whole circle represents the total sightings, 10.

**(2)** 3 of the 10 equal parts are shaded for giraffes.

**(3)** Write "3 out of 10" as a fraction $\frac{3}{10}$.

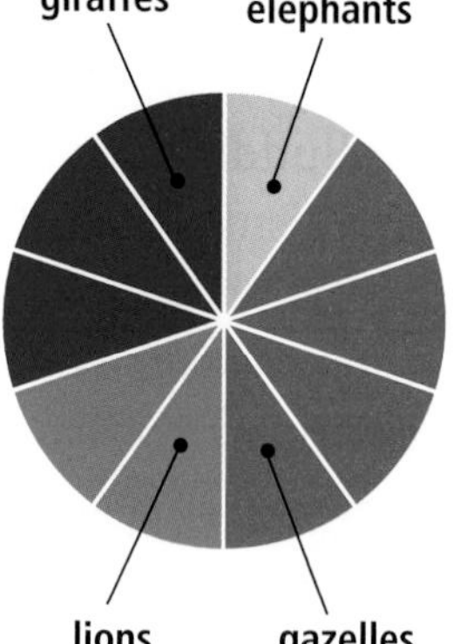


**ANSWER** Giraffes $= \frac{3}{10}$ of the sightings.

**Answer the following questions.**

1. What fraction of the sightings were lions?
2. What fraction of the sightings were gazelles?
3. Which animal did the researchers observe in greatest number?
4. Which animal did they observe in the least number? How many sightings occurred for that animal?
5. What fraction of the total does that animal represent?
6. If the researchers had seen one hundred animals, and the graph looked the same as it does, how many giraffe sightings would their graph represent?

**CHALLENGE** You also record the nighttime visitors: first, 2 young elephants; then a lioness with 2 thirsty cubs; then a giraffe, followed by a hyena and 3 gazelles. Calculate the fraction of the night's population that is represented by each type of animal. Use the fractions to draw a circle graph of the data on "Night Sightings at the Waterhole." Shade and label the graph with the types of animals.

KEY CONCEPT

# 2.2 Plants are producers.

**BEFORE, you learned**

- Multicellular organisms have tissues, organs, and systems
- Organisms have adaptations that can make them suited to their environment
- Sexual reproduction leads to genetic diversity

**NOW, you will learn**

- How plants obtain energy
- How plants store energy
- How plants respond to their environment

**VOCABULARY**

**photosynthesis** p. 52
**autotroph** p. 52
**cellular respiration** p. 53
**stimulus** p. 55

**EXPLORE Stored Energy**

### *In what form does a plant store energy?*

**PROCEDURE**

1. Obtain pieces of potato, celery, and pear that have been placed in small plastic cups.
2. Place a few drops of the iodine solution onto the plant material in each cup. The iodine solution will turn dark blue in the presence of starch. It does not change color in the presence of sugar.

**MATERIALS**

- pieces of potato, celery, and pear
- 3 plastic cups
- iodine solution
- eye dropper

**WHAT DO YOU THINK?**

- Observing each sample, describe what happened to the color of the iodine solution after a few minutes.
- Starch and sugars are a source of energy for a plant. What do your observations suggest about how different plants store energy?

## Plants capture energy from the Sun.

**MAIN IDEA AND DETAILS** Add the main idea *plants capture energy from the Sun* to your notebook and fill in details on photosynthesis and stored energy.

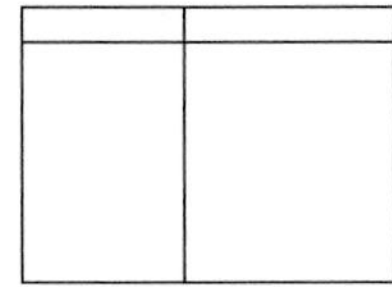

If you stand outside on a warm, sunny day, you may see and feel energy from the Sun. Without the Sun's energy, Earth would be a cold, dark planet. The Sun's heat and light provide the energy almost all organisms need to live.

However, energy from the Sun cannot drive cell processes directly. Light energy must be changed into chemical energy. Chemical energy is the form of energy all organisms use to carry out the functions of life. Plants are an important part of the energy story because plants capture energy from the Sun and convert it to chemical energy.

## Producing Sugars

**READING TIP**

The roots for *photosynthesis* are *photo-*, which means "light," and *synthesis*, which means "to put together." Together they mean "put together by light."

Plants capture energy from sunlight and convert it to chemical energy through the process of **photosynthesis.** The plant takes in water and carbon dioxide from the environment and uses these simple materials to produce sugar, an energy-rich compound that contains carbon. Oxygen is also produced. Plants are referred to as producers because they produce energy-rich carbon compounds using the Sun's energy.

The cells, tissues, and organ systems in a plant work together to supply the materials needed for photosynthesis. Most photosynthesis takes place in the leaves. The leaves take in carbon dioxide from the air, and the stems support the leaves and hold them up toward the Sun. The roots of the plant anchor it in the soil and supply water. The sugars produced are used by the plant for energy and as materials for growth.

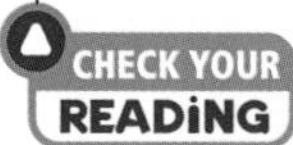


What is the product of photosynthesis?

Another name for a plant is **autotroph** (AW-tuh-TRAHF). Autotroph means self-feeder. Plants do not require food from other organisms. Plants will grow if they have energy from the Sun, carbon dioxide from the air, and water and nutrients from the soil.

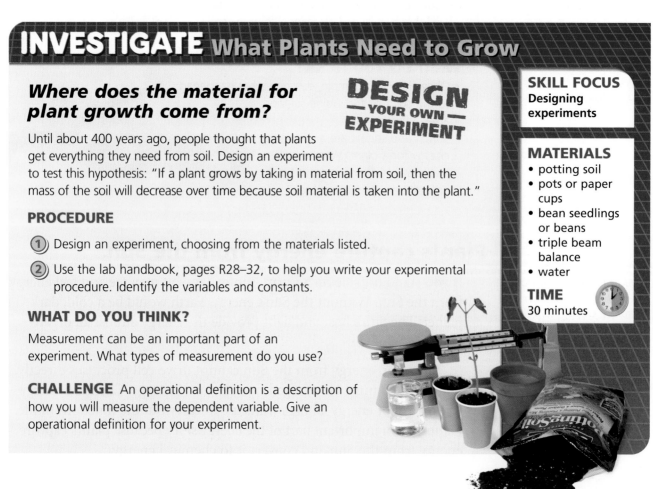

## INVESTIGATE What Plants Need to Grow

### Where does the material for plant growth come from?

**DESIGN — YOUR OWN — EXPERIMENT**

Until about 400 years ago, people thought that plants get everything they need from soil. Design an experiment to test this hypothesis: "If a plant grows by taking in material from soil, then the mass of the soil will decrease over time because soil material is taken into the plant."

**PROCEDURE**

1. Design an experiment, choosing from the materials listed.
2. Use the lab handbook, pages R28–32, to help you write your experimental procedure. Identify the variables and constants.

**WHAT DO YOU THINK?**

Measurement can be an important part of an experiment. What types of measurement do you use?

**CHALLENGE** An operational definition is a description of how you will measure the dependent variable. Give an operational definition for your experiment.

**SKILL FOCUS**
Designing experiments

**MATERIALS**
- potting soil
- pots or paper cups
- bean seedlings or beans
- triple beam balance
- water

**TIME**
30 minutes

## Storing and Releasing Energy

Plants are not the only organisms that capture energy through photosynthesis. Algae and certain bacteria and protists also use photosynthesis. Plants are different from single-celled producers, however. Plants are multicellular organisms with parts of their bodies specialized for storing energy-rich material. Single-celled producers can store very little energy.

Only part of the energy captured by a plant is used as fuel for cellular processes. Some of the sugar produced is used as building material, enabling the plant to grow. The remaining sugar is stored. Often the sugars are stored as starches. Starch is an energy-rich compound made of many sugars. Starches can store a lot of chemical energy. When a plant needs energy, the starches are broken back down into sugars and energy is released. **Cellular respiration** is the process by which a cell uses oxygen to break down sugars to release the energy they hold.

Some plants, such as carrots and beets, store starch in their roots. Other plants, including rhubarb, have stems adapted for storing starch. A potato is a swollen, underground stem called a tuber. Tubers have buds—the eyes of the potato—that can sprout into new plants. The starch stored in the tuber helps the new sprouts survive.

What is the original source of a plant's stored energy?

# Plants are adapted to different environments.

Almost everywhere you look on land, you'll see plants. Leaves, stems, and roots are adaptations that enable plants, as producers, to live on land. Not all plants, however, look the same. Just as there are many different types of land environments, there are many different types of plants that have adapted to these environments.

Grasses are an example of plants that grow in several environments. Many grasses have deep roots, produce seeds quickly, and can grow in areas with a wide range of temperatures and different amounts of precipitation. Grasses can survive drought, fires, freezing temperatures, and grazing. As long as the roots of the plant survive, the grasses will grow again. Grasses are found in the Arctic tundra, as well as in temperate and tropical climates.

Now compare trees to grasses. If the leaves and stems of a tree die away because of fire or drought, often the plant will not survive. Because of their size, trees require a large amount of water for photosynthesis. A coniferous (koh-NIHF-uhr-uhs) tree, like the pine, does well in colder climates. It has needle-shaped leaves that stay green throughout the year, feeding the plant continually. A deciduous (dih-SIHJ-oo-uhs) tree, like the maple, loses its leaves when temperatures turn cold. The maple needs a long growing season and plenty of water for new leaves to grow.

Learn more about plant adaptations.

Plants have reproductive adaptations. It may surprise you to learn that flowering plants living on cold, snowy mountaintops have something in common with desert plants. When rain falls in the desert, wildflower seeds sprout very quickly. Within a few weeks, the plants grow, flower, and produce new seeds that will be ready to sprout with the next rainy season. The same thing happens in the mountains, where the snow may thaw for only a few weeks every summer. Seeds sprout, flowers grow, and new seeds are produced—all before the snow returns. You will read more about plant reproduction in Chapter 3.

Some plants have adaptations that protect them. Plants in the mustard family give off odors that keep many plant-eating insects away. Other plants, such as poison ivy and poison oak, produce harmful chemicals. The nicotine in a tobacco plant is a poison that helps to keep the plant from being eaten.

Name two different types of adaptations plants have.

Some adaptations plants have relate to very specific needs. For example, the Venus flytrap is a plant that grows in areas where the soil lacks certain materials. The leaves of the Venus flytrap fold in the middle and have long teeth all around the edges. When an insect lands on an open leaf, the two sides of the leaf fold together. The teeth form a trap that prevents the captured insect from escaping. Fluids given off by the leaf digest the insect's body, providing materials the plant can't get from the soil.

**ANALYZE** An insect provides nutrients that this Venus flytrap cannot get from the soil. Is this plant still a producer? Ask yourself where the plant gets its energy.

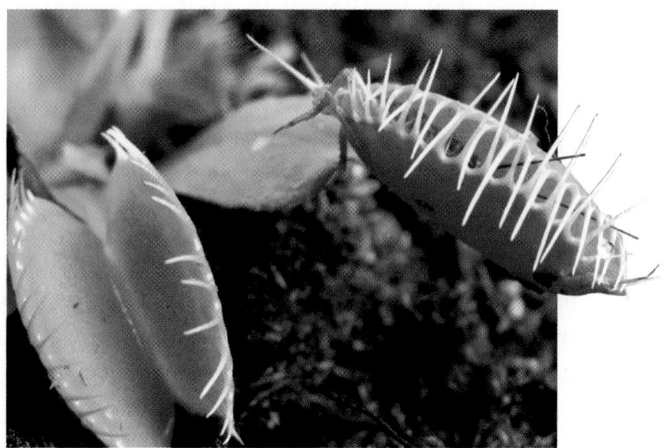

Plant roots always grow downward and stems always grow upward. All plants respond to gravity as a stimulus.

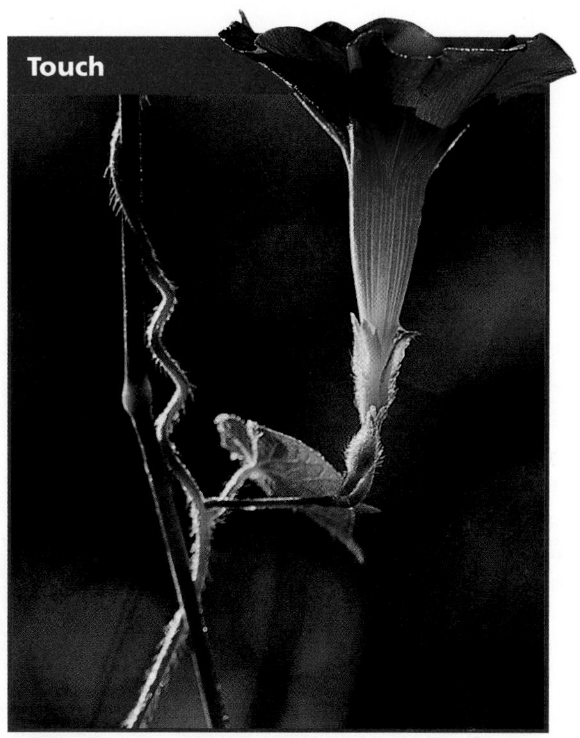


The tendril of a climbing plant grows around a nearby object. The plant responds to touch as a stimulus.

## Plants respond to their environment.

During a hot afternoon, parts of the flower known as the Mexican bird of paradise close. As the Sun goes down, the flower reopens. The plant is responding to a stimulus, in this case, sunlight. A **stimulus** is something that produces a response from an organism. Plants, like all organisms, respond to stimuli in their environment. This ability helps them to survive and grow.

**VOCABULARY** Make a four square for the term *stimulus* in your science notebook.

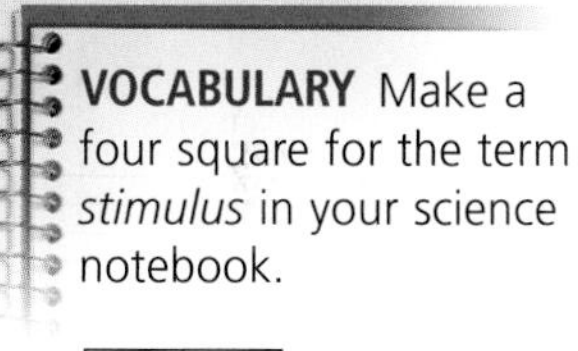

### Gravity

Gravity is the force that keeps you bound to Earth and gives you a sense of up and down. All plants respond to gravity. They also have a sense of up and down—roots grow down and stems grow up. Suppose you place a young seedling on its side, so that its roots and stems stretch out to the side. In a very short time, the tip of the root will begin to turn down, and the tip of the stem will turn up.

### Touch

Many plants also respond to touch as a stimulus. Peas, morning glories, tropical vines, and other climbing plants have special stems called tendrils. Tendrils respond to the touch of a nearby object. As the tendrils grow, they wrap around the object. The twining of tendrils around a fence or another plant helps raise a plant into the sunlight.

## How Plants Respond to Light

**Auxin, a hormone, is a chemical substance that stimulates cell growth and makes plant stems bend toward light.**

1. The presence of sunlight stimulates the production of auxin at the tip of the stem.
2. Auxin moves to cells on the dark side of the plant.
3. Cells with high levels of auxin grow longer than other cells, causing the plant to bend.

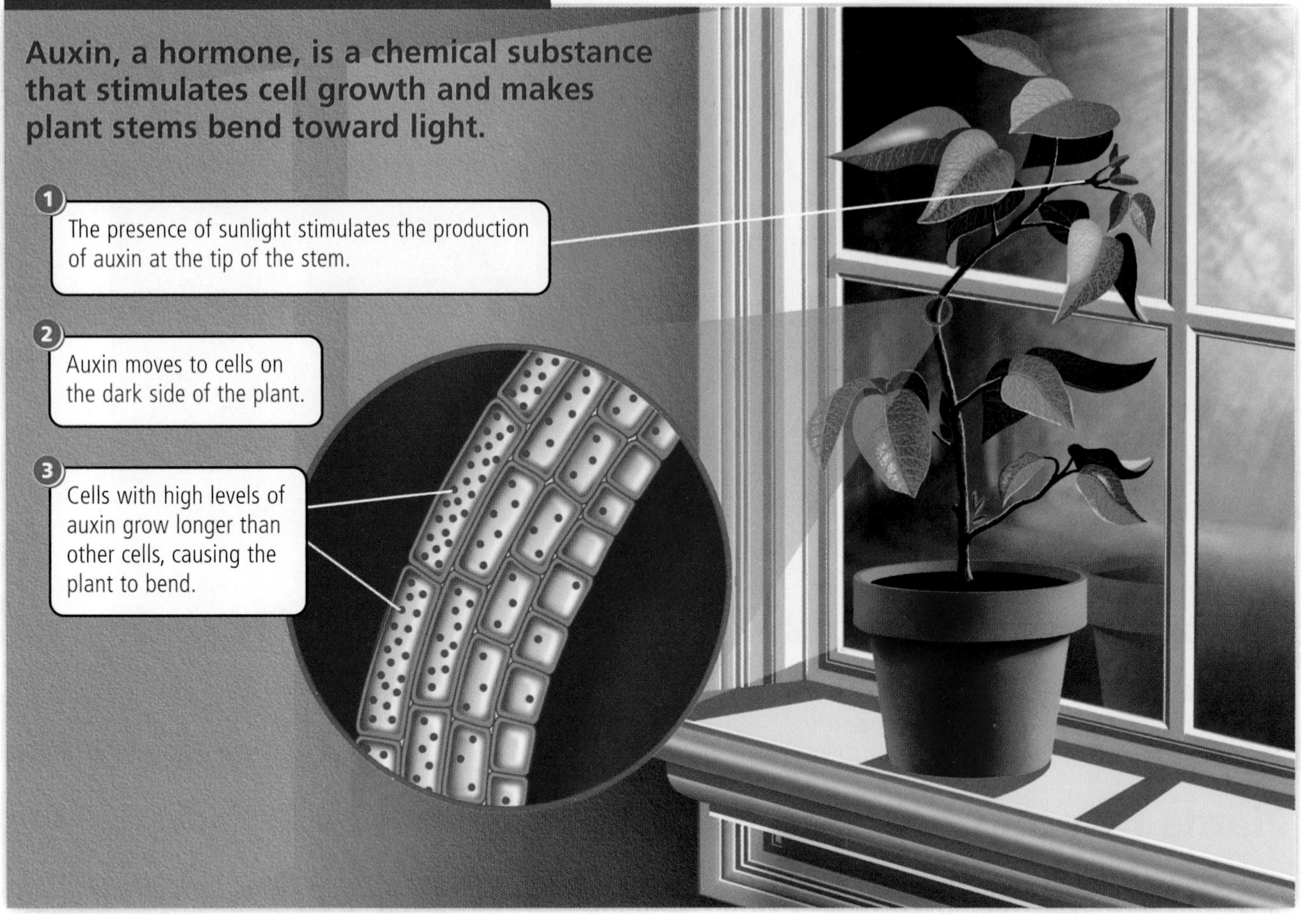

## Light

**READING TIP**

The words *stimulus, stimuli,* and *stimulate* all have the same root, meaning "to provoke or encourage action."

Light is a powerful stimulus for plants. You can see that stems and leaves grow toward light by placing an indoor plant near a window. After several days, the tips of the stems start to bend toward the window. What happens if you turn the plant around so that those stems reach into the room? The stems will bend as they continue to grow, turning back toward the light.

Plants respond to light with the help of a hormone. A hormone is a chemical substance that is produced in one part of an organism and travels to a different part where it produces a reaction. Hormones act as chemical messengers. They allow an organism to respond to changes in its body or to changes in the environment around it.

Examine how plants respond to different stimuli.

Auxin (AWK-sihn), a plant hormone that stimulates cell growth, is produced at the tip of a plant stem. Auxin moves away from light. As a result, the cells on the darker side of a plant stem contain more auxin than those on the lighter side. Higher levels of auxin in plant cells on the darker side cause those cells to grow longer. The longer cells cause the plant stem to bend, moving the tip of the stem toward the light.

## Plants respond to seasonal changes.

Most regions of the world go through seasonal changes every year. For example, during the summer in North America, temperatures rise and the days get longer. As winter approaches, temperatures go down and the days become shorter. These types of seasonal changes have an effect on plants.

For plants, a shorter period of daylight will affect the amount of sunlight available for photosynthesis. Shorter days cause many plants to go into a state of dormancy. When plants are dormant, they temporarily stop growing and so require less energy.

In temperate climates, the approach of winter causes the leaves of deciduous trees to die and drop to the ground. The trees enter a state of dormancy during which their growth is slowed. Other plants, such as wild cornflowers, do not survive the change. New cornflowers will grow the following season, from seeds left behind.

CHECK YOUR READING What stimulus causes a deciduous plant to respond by dropping its leaves?

For many plants, reproduction is also affected by seasonal changes. For some plants, the amount of daylight is a factor. A few plants, such as rice and ragweed, produce flowers only in autumn or winter, when days are short. They are short-day plants. Long-day plants flower in late spring and summer, when days are long. Lettuce, spinach, and irises are long day-plants. You will read more about plants in Chapter 3.

## 2.2 Review

### KEY CONCEPTS

1. What process makes a plant a producer, and what does a plant produce?
2. Name three stimuli that plants respond to, and give examples of how a plant responds.
3. How do seasonal changes affect plants? Give an example.

### CRITICAL THINKING

4. **Give Examples** Give three examples of ways that plants are adapted to their environments. How do these adaptations benefit the plant?

### CHALLENGE

5. **Apply** Some experiments suggest that the hormone auxin is involved in the twining of tendrils. Use what you know about auxin to explain how it might cause tendrils to twine around anything they touch. Draw a diagram.

KEY CONCEPT

# Animals are consumers.

**BEFORE, you learned**

- Plants are producers
- Plants have adaptations for capturing and storing energy
- Plants respond to different stimuli

**NOW, you will learn**

- How animals obtain energy
- How animals process food
- About different ways animals respond to their environment

**VOCABULARY**

**consumer** p. 58
**heterotroph** p. 58
**behavior** p. 62
**predator** p. 63
**prey** p. 63
**migration** p. 64
**hibernation** p. 64

**THINK ABOUT**

***What can you tell from teeth?***

Many animals have teeth. Teeth bite, grind, crush, and chew. A fox's sharp biting teeth capture small animals that it hunts on the run. A horse's teeth are flat and strong—for breaking down the grasses it eats. Run your tongue over your own teeth. How many different shapes do you notice? What can the shape of teeth suggest about the food an animal eats?

## Animals obtain energy and materials from food.

You probably see nonhuman animals every day, whether you live in a rural area or a large city. If the animals are wild animals, not somebody's pet, then chances are that what you see these animals doing is moving about in search of food.

Animals are consumers. A **consumer** is an organism that needs to get energy from another organism. Unlike plants, animals must consume food to get the energy and materials they need to survive. Animals are heterotrophs. A **heterotroph** (HEHT-uhr-uh-TRAHF) is an organism that feeds on, or consumes, other organisms. By definition, animals are, quite simply, multicellular organisms that have adaptations that allow them to take in and process food.

**READING TIP**

The meaning of *heterotroph* is opposite to that of *autotroph*. The root *hetero-* means "other." *Heterotroph* means "other-feeder," or "feeds on others."

## Obtaining Food

**Food is a source of energy and materials for animals.**

**Simple feeding** Some animals, such as corals, can filter food from their environment.

**Complex feeding** Many animals, such as bats, actively search for and capture food.

Animals need food and have many different ways of getting it. For some animals, feeding is a relatively simple process. An adult coral simply filters food from the water as it moves through the coral's body. Most animals, however, must search for food. Grazing animals, such as horses, move along from one patch of grass to another. Other animals must capture food. Most bats use sound and hearing to detect the motion of insects flying at night. Its wings make the bat able to move through the air quickly and silently.

### What Animals Eat

Just about any type of living or once-living material is a source of food for some animal. Animals can be grouped by the type of food they eat.

- Herbivores (HUR-buh-VAWRS) feed on plants or algae.
- Carnivores (KAHR-nuh-VAWRS) feed on other animals.
- Omnivores (AWM-nuh-VAWRS) feed on both plants and animals.

Another group are those animals that feed on the remains of once-living animals. Many insects do, as do some larger animals, such as vultures. Other animals, such as worms, act as decomposers.

**MAIN IDEA AND DETAILS**
Make a chart about the main idea: *Animals obtain energy and materials from food.* Include *herbivore, carnivore,* and *omnivore* in the details.

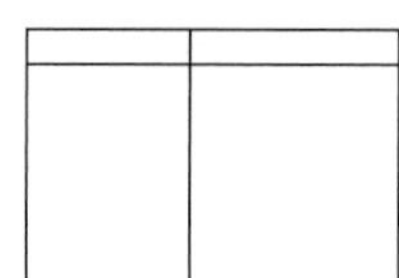

**CHECK YOUR READING** Describe how herbivores, carnivores, and omnivores get their energy.

Different species of animals have adapted in different ways to take advantage of all the energy-rich material in the environment. To get energy and materials from food, all animals must first break the food down—that is, they must digest it.

## Processing Food

RESOURCE CENTER
CLASSZONE.COM

Find out more about animal adaptations.

Energy is stored in complex carbon compounds in food. For the cells in an animal to make use of the energy and materials stored in this food, the large complex compounds must be broken back down into simpler compounds.

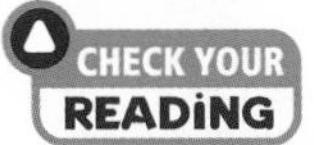

CHECK YOUR READING How must food be changed so an animal gets energy?

Digestion is the process that breaks food down into pieces that are small enough to be absorbed by cells. A few animals, such as sponges, are able to take food particles directly into their cells. Most animals, however, take the food into an area of their body where the materials are broken down. Cells absorb the materials they need. Animals such as jellyfish have a single opening in their bodies where food is brought into a central cavity, or gut. The unused materials are released through the same opening.

A digestive system uses both physical and chemical activity to break down food. Many animals have a tubelike digestive system. Food is brought in at one end of the animal, the mouth, and waste is released at the other end. As food moves through the system, it is continually broken down, releasing necessary materials called nutrients to the cells.

## INVESTIGATE Owl Pellets

### *What does an owl eat, and how well does it digest its food?*

**PROCEDURE**

1. Get an owl pellet from your teacher. Open the foil and place the pellet in a tray.
2. Use a needle tool and tweezers to sort through the materials in the pellet and separate them.
3. When you have finished, dispose of the materials according to your teacher's instructions, and wash your hands.

**WHAT DO YOU THINK?**

- What can you tell about what an owl eats from looking at the remains in the pellet?
- What materials are not digested?

**CHALLENGE** Use the bone identification key to identify what the owl ate.

**SKILL FOCUS**
Inferring

**MATERIALS**
- owl pellet
- needle tool
- tweezers
- tray
- *for Challenge:* bone identification key

**TIME**
30 minutes

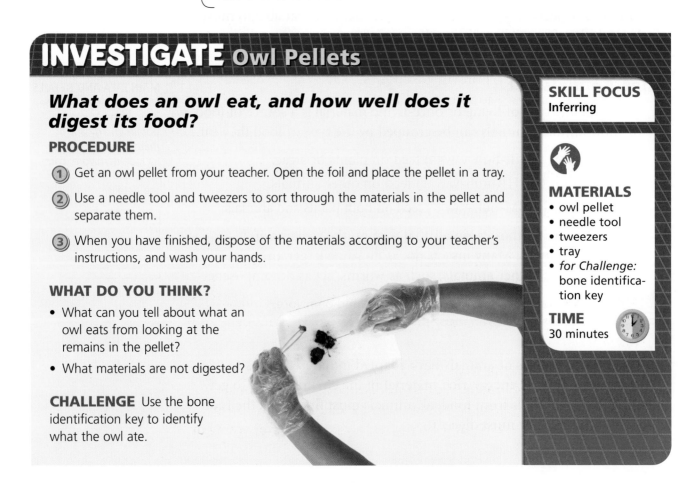

## Obtaining Oxygen

**Animals need oxygen to release the energy in food.**

**Grasshopper**

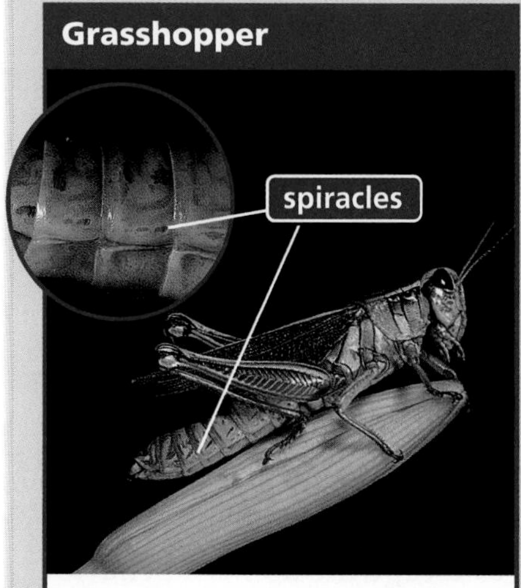


Most insects take in oxygen through body openings called spiracles.

**Bass**

Fish have gills, which pick up dissolved oxygen as water flows over them.

**Tiger**

This yawning tiger, like many animals, gets oxygen by inhaling air into its lungs.

## Releasing and Storing Energy

Animals obtain energy from sugars and other carbon compounds the same way plants do, through the process of cellular respiration. As you read in Section 2.2, cellular respiration is a process in which energy is released when sugars are broken down inside a cell. The process requires both oxygen and water.

What is the function of cellular respiration?

Many animals take in water in the same way they take in food, through the digestive system. Oxygen, however, is often taken in through a respiratory system. In many animals, the respiratory system delivers oxygen to the blood, and the blood carries oxygen to the cells.

Animals have different structures for obtaining oxygen. Many insects take in oxygen through spiracles, tiny openings in their bodies. Fish have gills, structures that allow them to pick up oxygen dissolved in the water. Other air-breathing animals take in oxygen through organs called lungs.

Most animals do not feed continuously, so they need to be able to store materials from food in their tissues or organs. Many animals, including humans, take in large amounts of food at one time. This gives an animal time to do other activities, such as caring for young or looking for more food.

## Animals interact with the environment and with other organisms.

Animals, as consumers, must obtain food, as well as water, from their environment. An animal's body has many adaptations that allow it to process food. These can include digestive, respiratory, and circulatory systems. Also important are the systems that allow animals to interact with their environment to obtain food. In many animals, muscle and skeletal systems provide movement and support. A nervous system allows the animal to sense and respond to stimuli.

Animals respond to many different types of stimuli. They respond to sights, sounds, odors, light, or a change in temperature. They respond to hunger and thirst. They also respond to other animals. Any observable response to a stimulus is described as a **behavior.** A bird's drinking water from a puddle is a behavior. A lion's chasing an antelope is a behavior, just as the antelope's running to escape the lion is a behavior.

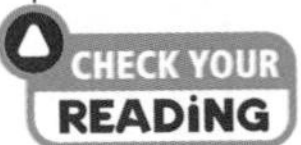

What is a behavior and how does it relate to a stimulus?

Some behaviors are inherited, which means they are present at birth. For example, a spider can weave a web without being shown. Other behaviors are learned. For example, the young lion in the photograph learns that a porcupine is not a good source of food.

All behaviors fall into one of three general categories:

- individual behaviors
- interactions between animals of the same species
- interactions between animals of different species

**ANALYZE** Do you consider the defensive behavior of a porcupine an adaptation?

Individual behaviors often involve meeting basic needs. Animals must find food, water, and shelter. They sleep. They groom themselves. Animals also respond to changes in their environment. A lizard may warm itself in the morning sunlight and then move into the shade when the Sun is high in the sky.

For macaques, grooming is both an individual and a social behavior. Here a mother grooms her young.

Interactions that occur between animals of the same species are often described as social behaviors. Basic social behaviors include those between parents and offspring and behaviors for attracting a mate. Within a group, animals of the same species may cooperate by working together. Wolves hunt in packs and bees maintain a hive. Behaviors among animals of the same species can also be competitive. Animals often compete for a mate or territory.

What are some ways that animals of the same species cooperate and compete?

Interactions that occur between animals of different species often involve the search for food. A **predator** is an animal that hunts other animals for food. Predators have behaviors that allow them to search for and capture other organisms. A cheetah first stalks an antelope, then chases it down, moving as fast as 110 kilometers per hour.

An animal that is hunted by another animal as a source of food is the **prey.** Behaviors of prey animals often allow them to escape a predator. An antelope may not be able to outrun a cheetah, but antelopes move in herds. This provides protection for the group since a cheetah will kill only one animal. Other animals, such as the pufferfish and porcupine, have defensive behaviors and structures.

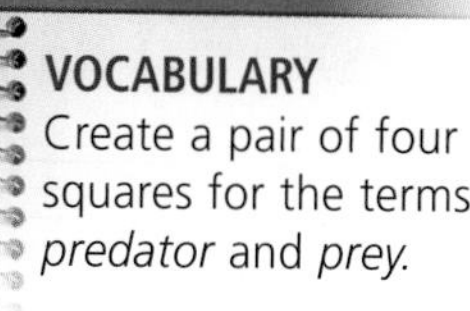

VOCABULARY
Create a pair of four squares for the terms *predator* and *prey.*


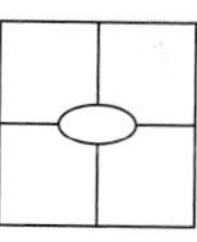

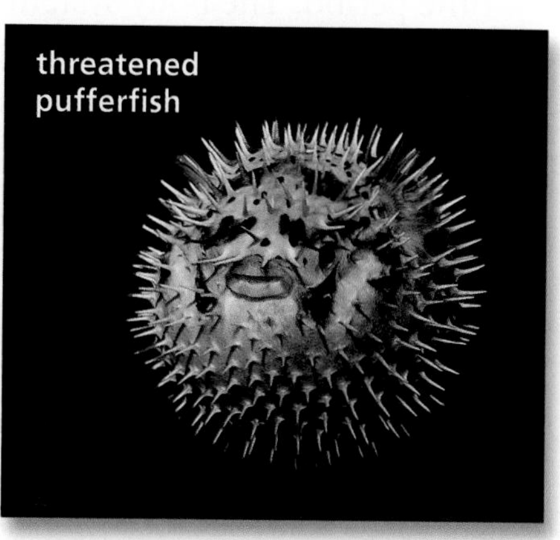


Animals of different species can also interact in cooperative ways. Tickbirds remove ticks from the skin of an impala. This behavior provides food for the bird and provides relief for the impala. Sometimes animals take advantage of the behavior of other animals. Many animals eat the remains of prey left over after a predator has finished feeding.

## Animals respond to seasonal changes.

monarch butterfly

Animals, like plants, are affected by seasonal changes in their environment. Certain types of food may not be available all year round. A region might go through periods of drought. Some animals do not do well in extreme heat or cold. Unlike plants, animals can respond to seasonal changes by changing their location. **Migration** is the movement of animals to a different region in response to changes in the environment.

Each spring, millions of monarch butteflies begin to fly north from Mexico and parts of southern California. They first migrate to the southern United States, where the females lay eggs on milkweed plants. The new generation will travel further north and then lay eggs, too. Summer monarchs live as butterflies for only three to five weeks. After three or four generations, the last generation reaches the northern United States and Canada. Monarchs cannot survive the winter temperatures of the north, so the last generation of butterflies makes the long journey back to Mexico and California in the fall. These buttteflies will live eight or nine months. The fall migration route is shown on the map.

CANADA
ROCKY MTNS.
UNITED STATES
MEXICO

Monarch butterflies migrate each winter to California and Mexico.

Not all animals migrate in response to seasonal changes. Many nonmigratory animals do change their behaviors, however. For example, when winter cold reduces the food supply, some animals hibernate. **Hibernation** is a sleeplike state that lasts for an extended time period. The body systems of a hibernating animal slow down, so the animal needs less energy to survive. Many animals, including frogs, turtles, fish, and some types of insects, hibernate. You will learn more about different types of animals in Chapters 4 and 5.

## 2.3 Review

### KEY CONCEPTS

1. In what way are animals consumers?
2. Name three body systems that relate to how an animal gets its energy.
3. What is a behavior?

### CRITICAL THINKING

4. **Give Examples** Identify three categories of animal behavior and give an example of each.
5. **Analyze** How is migration similar to hibernation? How is it different?

### CHALLENGE

6. **Analyze** Scientists often look at feeding patterns as a flow of energy through the living parts of the environment. Describe the flow of energy as it relates to plants, herbivores, and carnivores.

## WILDLIFE PHOTOGRAPHER

# An Animal's World

Have you ever watched a TV documentary, or flipped through the pages of a magazine and wondered, "How did the photographer ever get that picture?" For a wildlife photographer, understanding animal behavior is essential.

### Cover and Protection

Photographers use camera traps and blinds. A blind, made of branches, is built upwind of an animal gathering place. Steve Winter has built camera traps, where a hidden camera emits a beam of light when an animal steps into it.

### Specialized Gear

Certain environments—such as snow and cold, swamp and mud, or sea water—present challenges to a person with a camera. Underwater photographers need to use scuba gear to swim with animals like the Caribbean reef shark.

### Behavior

To photograph an endangered species like the jaguar, a photographer must learn animal behavior. Steve Winter and a team of scientists used dogs with keen scent-tracking to find jaguars who are active mostly at night. They learned that jaguars have a favorite scratching tree—perfect photo opportunity!

## EXPLORE

1. **OBSERVE** With or without a camera, find a spot where you are likely to find wildlife. Sit as still as possible and wait. What animals do you observe? What do they do?
2. **CHALLENGE** Interview a photographer about digital photogra-

KEY CONCEPT

# Most fungi are decomposers.

**BEFORE, you learned**
- All organisms interact with the environment
- Plants transform sunlight into chemical energy
- Animals get energy by eating other organisms

**NOW, you will learn**
- How fungi get energy and materials
- About different types of fungi
- How fungi interact with other organisms

**VOCABULARY**

**hyphae** p. 67
**spore** p. 67
**lichen** p. 70

**EXPLORE Mushrooms**

### *What does a mushroom cap contain?*

**PROCEDURE**

1. Carefully cut the stem away from the mushroom cap, as near the cap as possible.
2. Place the mushroom cap on white paper and cover it with a plastic cup. Leave overnight.
3. Carefully remove the cup and lift the mushroom cap straight up.
4. Use a hand lens to examine the mushroom cap and the print it leaves behind.

**WHAT DO YOU THINK?**
- How does the pattern in the mushroom cap compare with the mushroom print?
- What made the print?

**MATERIALS**
- fresh store-bought mushrooms
- sharp knife
- clear plastic cup
- paper
- hand lens

## Fungi absorb materials from the environment.

**MAIN IDEA AND DETAILS**
Don't forget to make a main idea chart with detail notes on the main idea: *Fungi absorb materials from the environment.*

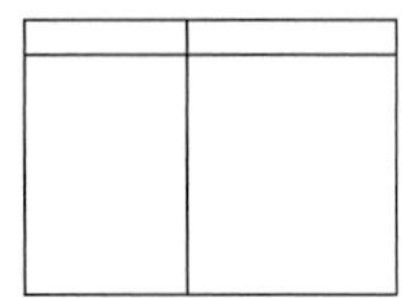

Plants are producers; they capture energy from the Sun and build complex carbon compounds. Animals are consumers; they take in complex carbon compounds and use them for energy and materials. Fungi (FUHN-jy), at least most fungi, are decomposers. Fungi break down, or decompose, the complex carbon compounds that are part of living matter. They absorb nutrients and leave behind simpler compounds.

Fungi are heterotrophs. They get their energy from living or once-living matter. They, along with bacteria, decompose the bodies of dead plants and animals. They also decompose materials left behind by organisms, such as fallen leaves, shed skin, and animal droppings.

## Characteristics of Fungi

Except for yeasts, most fungi are multicellular. The cells of a fungus have a nucleus and a thick cell wall, which provides support. Fungi are different from plants and animals in their organization. Plants and animals have specialized cells, which are usually organized into tissues and organs. Multicellular fungi don't have tissues or organs. Instead, a typical fungus is made up of a reproductive body and network of cells that form threadlike structures called **hyphae** (HY-fee).

**READING TIP**

The root of the word *hyphae* means "web." Look at the diagram below to see their weblike appearance.

A mass of hyphae, like the one shown in the diagram below, is called a mycelium (my-SEE-lee-uhm). The hyphae are just one cell thick. This means the cells in the mycelium are close to the soil or whatever substance the fungus is living in. The cells release chemicals that digest the materials around them, and then absorb the nutrients they need. As hyphae grow, openings can form between the older cells and the new ones. This allows nutrients to flow back to the older cells, resulting in what seems like one huge cell with many nuclei.

## Reproduction

Fungi reproduce with spores, which can be produced either asexually or sexually. A **spore** is a single reproductive cell that is capable of growing into a new organism. The mushrooms that you buy at the store are the spore-producing structures of certain types of fungi. These spore-producing structures are reproductive bodies of mushrooms. A single mushroom can produce a billion spores.

### Parts of a Fungus

**The mycelium makes up a large part of a multicellular fungus.**

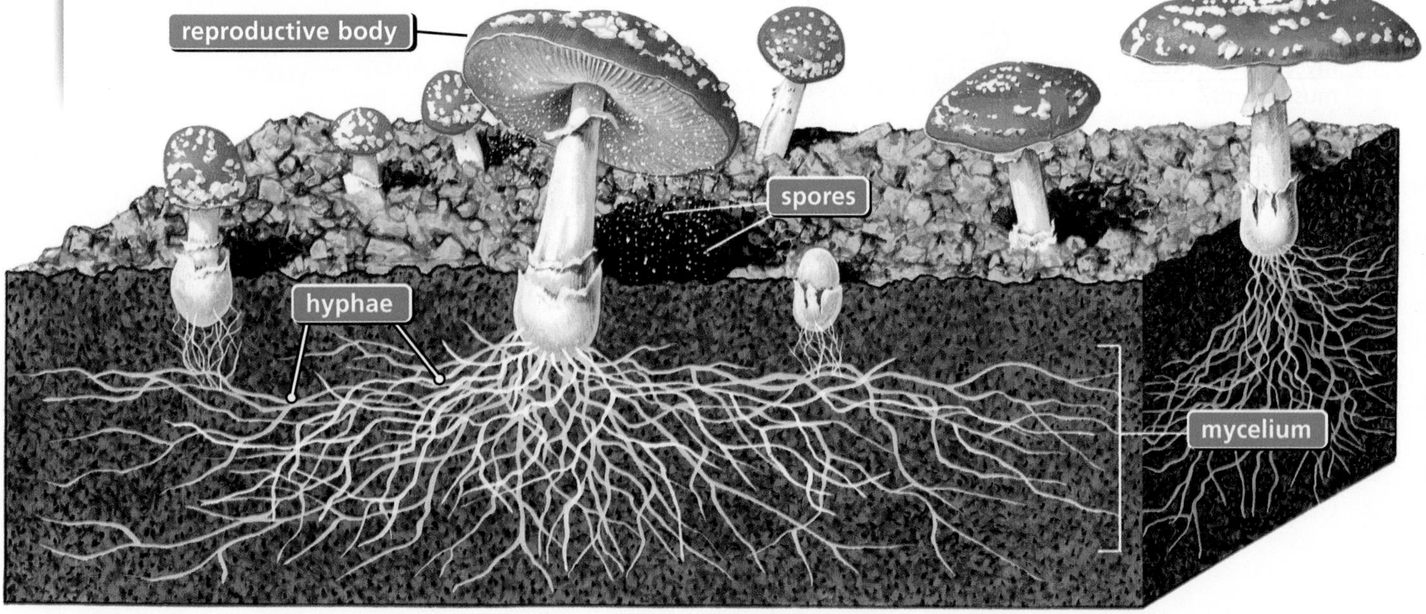

Learn more about different types of fungi.

Spores are released into the air and spread by the wind. Because they're so small and light, the wind can carry spores long distances. Scientists have found spores 160 kilometers above Earth's surface. Some spores have a tough outer covering that keeps the reproductive cell from drying out. Such spores can survive for many years. If the parent fungus dies, the spores may remain and grow when conditions are right.

Fungi reproduce in other ways. For example, a multicellular fungi can reproduce asexually when hyphae break off and form a new mycelium. Yeasts, which are single-celled fungi, reproduce asexually by simple cell division or by budding. Yeasts can also produce spores.

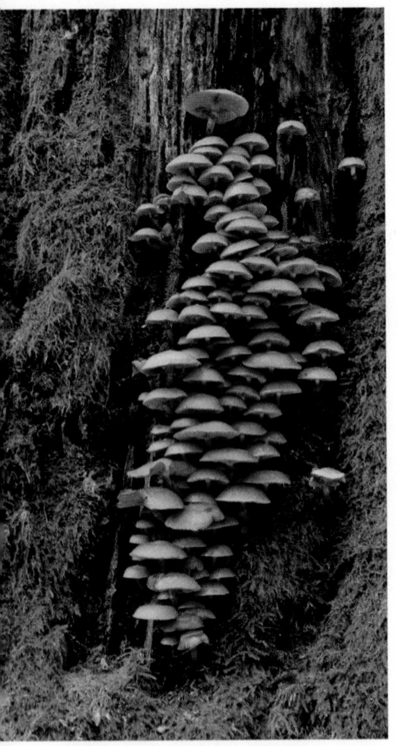

**INFER** Where is the mycelium of these mushrooms?

## Fungi include mushrooms, molds, and yeasts.

A convenient and simple way to study fungi is to look at their forms. They are mushrooms, molds, and yeasts. You are probably familiar with all of them. The mushrooms on your pizza are a fungus. So is the mold that grows if you leave a piece of pizza too long in the refrigerator. The crust of the pizza itself rises because of the activity of yeast.

### Mushrooms

What we call a mushroom is only a small part of a fungus. A single mushroom you buy in the store could have grown from a mycelium that fills an area 30 meters across. When you see a patch of mushrooms, they are probably all part of a single fungus.

For humans, some mushrooms are edible and some are poisonous. A toadstool is a poisonous mushroom. The cap of a mushroom is where the spores are produced. Both the cap and the stalk it grows on are filled with hyphae.

What is produced in a mushroom cap?

### Molds

What we call mold, that fuzzy growth we sometimes see on food, is the spore-producing part of another form of fungus. The hyphae of the mold grow into the food, digesting it as they grow. Not all food molds are bad. Different species of the fungus *Penicillium* are used in the production of Brie, Camembert, and blue cheeses. Some species of the *Aspergillus* fungus are used to make soy sauce.

One interesting application of a mold is the use of the fungus *Trichoderma.* This mold grows in soil. The digestive chemicals it produces are used to give blue jeans a stonewashed look.

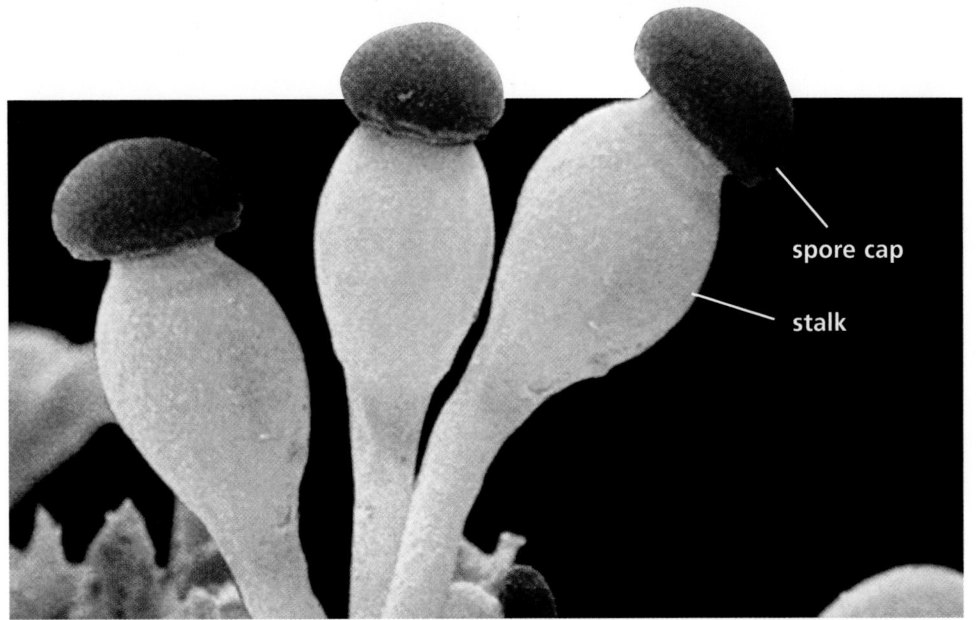


*Pilobolus* reacts to sunlight as a stimulus. The bend in the stalk will cause the spore cap to fly off.

Many molds cause disease. Fungal molds cause athlete's foot. Molds also affect plants. They are the cause of Dutch elm disease and the powdery white mildews that grow on plants. Compounds made from molds are also used to treat disease. Penicillin is an antibiotic that comes from the *Penicillium* fungus. It is used to fight bacterial diseases, such as pneumonia.

Molds reproduce with spores, which are typically carried by moving air. The "hat thrower" fungus *Pilobolus*, however, has an interesting adaptation for spreading spores. *Pilobolus* grows in animal droppings. It has a spore-containing cap—its hat—that grows on top of a stalk. The stalk responds to light as a stimulus and bends toward the Sun. As the stalk bends, water pressure builds up, causing the spore cap to shoot off, like a tiny cannonball. A spore cap can be thrown up to two meters away. If the spore caps land in grass, then cows and other grazing animals will eat the caps as they graze. A new cycle begins, with more *Pilobolus* being dispersed in the animal's droppings.

## Yeasts

Yeasts are single-celled fungi. Some species of fungi exist in both yeast form and as multicellular hyphae. Yeasts grow in many moist environments, including the sap of plants and animal tissues. They also grow on moist surfaces, including shower curtains. Certain yeasts grow naturally on human skin. If the yeast begins to reproduce too rapidly, it can cause disease.

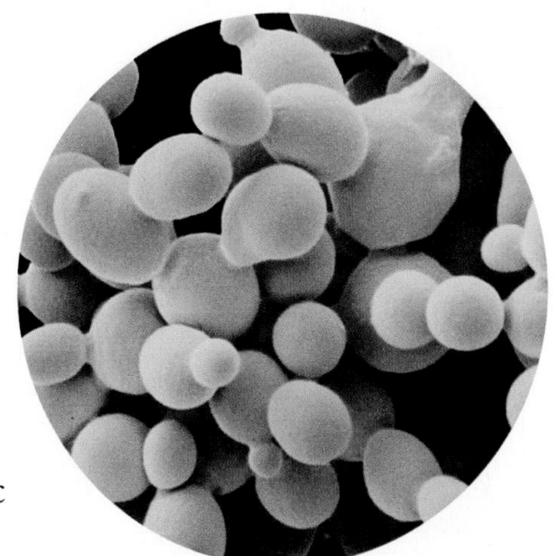

Yeasts are single-celled fungi.

Yeasts are used in many food products. The activity of yeast cells breaking down sugars is what makes bread rise. The genetic material of the yeast *Saccharomyces cerevisiae* has been carefully studied by scientists. The study of this organism has helped scientists understand how genetic material controls the activities of a cell.

## Fungi can be helpful or harmful to other organisms.

Fungi have a close relationship to the environment and all living things in the environment. Fungi, along with bacteria, function as the main decomposers on Earth. The digestive chemicals that fungi release break down the complex compounds that come from living matter, dead matter, or the waste an organism leaves behind. A fungus absorbs what it needs to live and leaves behind simpler compounds and nutrients. These are then picked up again by plants, as producers, to start the cycle over again. Fungi also live in the sea, recycling materials for ocean-living organisms.

What beneficial role do fungi play in the environment?

The threadlike hyphae of a fungus can grow into and decompose the material produced by another organism. This means that fungi can be helpful, for example, by releasing the nutrients in a dead tree back into the soil. Or fungi can be harmful, for example, attacking the tissues of a plant, such as the Dutch elm.

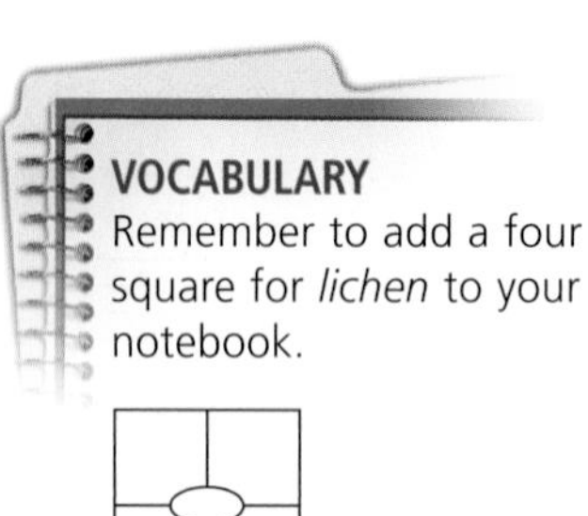

**VOCABULARY**
Remember to add a four square for *lichen* to your notebook.

Most plants interact with fungi in a way that is helpful. The hyphae surround the plant roots, providing nutrients for the plant. The plant provides food for the fungus. Some fungi live together with single-celled algae, a network referred to as a **lichen** (LY-kuhn). The hyphae form almost a sandwich around the algae, which produce sugars and other nutrients the fungus needs.

### Lichen

**A lichen is formed by a close association between algae and fungi.**

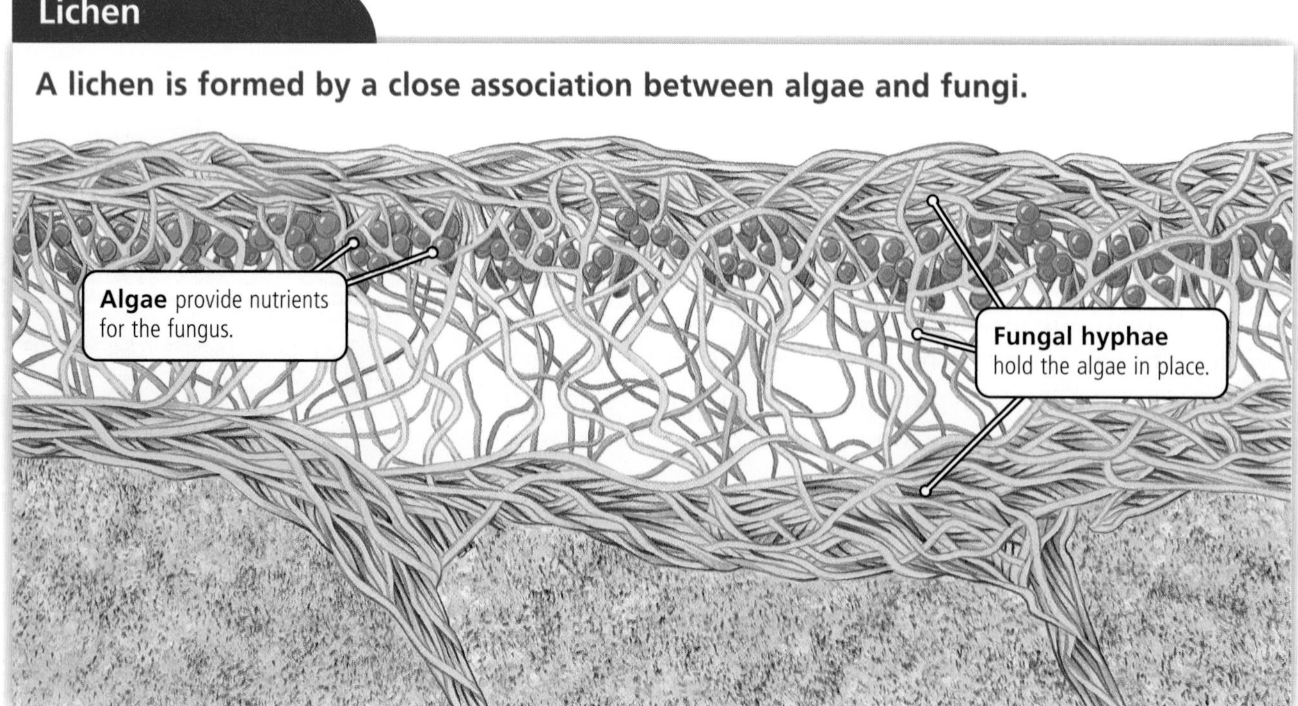
**Algae** provide nutrients for the fungus.
**Fungal hyphae** hold the algae in place.

Lichens can live just about anywhere. Lichens are found in the Arctic and in the desert. They can even grow on bare rock. The hyphae can break the rock down, slowly, and capture the particles of newly formed soil. This eventually prepares the ground for new plant growth.

On the harmful side, many fungi produce toxins, harmful chemicals. In 1845, a fungus infected Ireland's potato crop, causing the population of Ireland to drop from 8 million to about 4 million. Many people died from disease. Others died from starvation because of the loss of the important food crop. And hundreds of thousands of Irish left Ireland, many emigrating to the United States. Today, several fungal diseases are spreading through the world's banana crops.

Name some ways fungi can be harmful to organisms.

The toxic quality of a fungus can be put to good use, as in the case of the antibiotic penicillin. The photographs show what happens when a bacterium comes in contact with penicillin. The antibiotic prevents the bacterial cells from making new cell walls when they divide. This causes the cells to break open and the bacteria to die.

**Bacterium before penicillin**

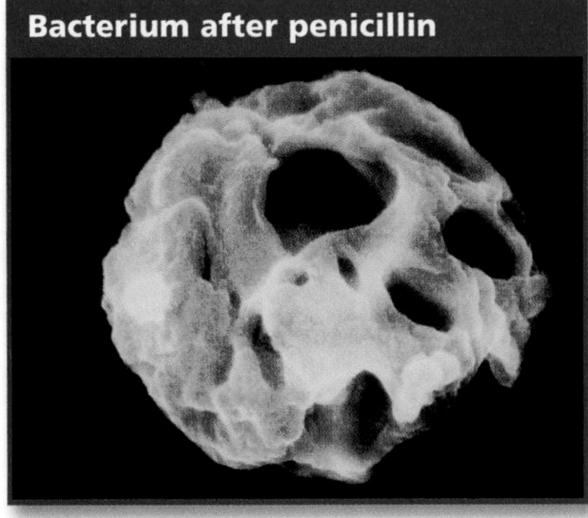


Penicillin is an antibiotic drug made from compounds taken from a species of the *Penicillium* fungus.

# 2.4 Review

## KEY CONCEPTS

1. Describe the structure of a fungus.
2. How do fungi reproduce?
3. Describe two relationships between fungi and other organisms.

## CRITICAL THINKING

4. **Analyze** Scientists used to classify fungi as plants. Today, scientists say that fungi are more like animals than plants. How are fungi like plants? How are they like animals?
5. **Predict** What might change in an environment where there were no fungi?

## CHALLENGE

6. **Connect** Think of at least one way your life is affected by fungi in each of their three main forms: mushrooms, molds, and yeast. Are these effects beneficial or harmful to you?

# CHAPTER INVESTIGATION

## What Do Yeast Cells Use for Energy?

**OVERVIEW AND PURPOSE** Yeasts are tiny one-celled fungi that require food, water, and a warm place to grow. When they have a food source, they release carbon dioxide gas as a waste product. Yeast is used to make foods such as bread. In this activity, you will

- observe the activity of yeast
- draw conclusions about the effect of three materials on the activity of yeast

### Problem

How do sugar, salt, and sweetener affect the growth of yeast?

### Hypothesize

Write a hypothesis to explain how sugar, sweetener, and salt affect the activity of yeast in bread dough. Your hypothesis should take the form of an "If . . ., then . . ., because . . ." statement.

**MATERIALS**
- baking sheet
- flour
- measuring cups
- measuring spoons
- sugar
- artificial sweetener
- salt
- quick-rise yeast
- warm water
- metric ruler
- marker
- clothespins
- clear plastic straws

### Procedure

1. Make a data table like the one shown on page 73. Label four sheets of notebook paper *A, B, C,* and *D.*

2. Spread a very thin layer of flour over the baking sheet. Measure $\frac{1}{4}$ cup of flour and place it on the baking sheet as a mound. Repeat three times, forming separate mounds. Label the mounds *A, B, C,* and *D.*

3 Add 3 teaspoons of sugar to mound A. Add 3 tsp of sweetener to mound B. Add 3 tsp of salt to mound C. Add nothing to mound D.

4 Add $\frac{1}{4}$ tsp of the quick-rise yeast to each of the mounds. Slowly add 1 tsp of warm water to each mound to moisten the mixture. Spread a pinch of flour over your hands and knead the mounds by hand. Add water, 1 tsp at a time until the mixture has the consistency of dough. If the mixture gets too sticky, add more flour. Knead well and form each mound into a ball. Wash your hands thoroughly when you are finished. Do not taste or eat the dough.

5 Push 2 straws into each ball of dough, making sure the dough reaches at least 3 cm into the straws.

step 5

6 Squeeze the end of each straw to push the dough from the ends. Place a clothespin on the end of each straw closest to the dough. Fold and tape the other end. Mark both edges of the dough on the straw. Stand each straw upright on the appropriate piece of paper labeled *A, B, C,* or *D.*

step 6

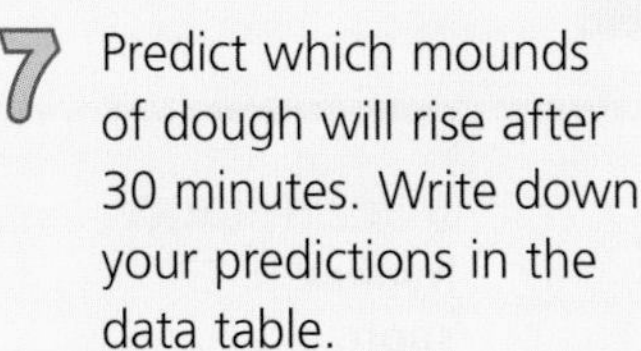

7 Predict which mounds of dough will rise after 30 minutes. Write down your predictions in the data table.

8 After 30 minutes, measure the amount the dough has risen in each straw. Write down the results in the data table.

## Observe and Analyze

Write It Up

1. **OBSERVE** In which mounds did the dough rise?
2. **OBSERVE** Did any of the remaining mounds of dough change? Explain.
3. **INFER** What was the purpose of using two straws for each of the mounds?

## Conclude

1. **INTERPRET** Which is the most likely source of energy for yeast: salt, sugar, or sweetener? How do you know?
2. **INTERPRET** Compare your results with your hypothesis. How does your data support or disprove your hypothesis?
3. **LIMITATIONS** What limitations or sources of error could have affected your results?
4. **CONNECT** How would you account for the air spaces that are found in some breads?
5. **APPLY** Would you predict that breads made without yeast contain air spaces?

## INVESTIGATE Further

**CHALLENGE** Design an experiment in which you can observe the production of carbon dioxide by yeast.

### What Do Yeast Cells Use for Energy?

Table 1. Observations of Dough Rising

| Mound | Prediction | Results |
|---|---|---|
| A. sugar and yeast | | |
| B. sweetener and yeast | | |
| C. salt and yeast | | |
| D. yeast | | |

# 2 Chapter Review

## the BIG idea

**Multicellular organisms live in and get energy from a variety of environments.**

## KEY CONCEPTS SUMMARY

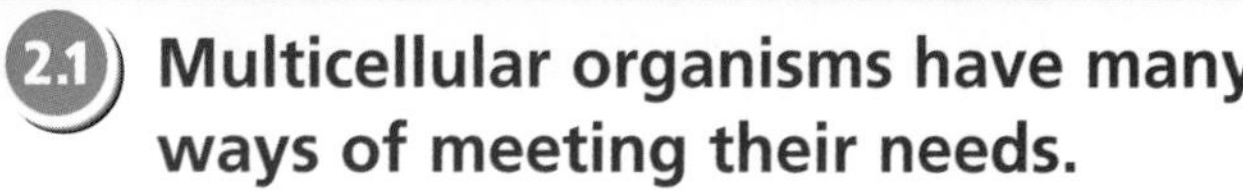

### 2.1 Multicellular organisms have many ways of meeting their needs.

- The bodies of multicellular organisms have different levels of organization.
- Multicellular organisms have a wide range of adaptations.
- Multicellular organisms reproduce by sexual reproduction. Some also reproduce asexually.

**VOCABULARY**
**tissue** p. 44
**organ** p. 44
**sexual reproduction** p. 48
**meiosis** p. 48
**fertilization** p. 48

### 2.2 Plants are producers.

Plants capture energy from the Sun and store it as sugar and starch. Plants are adapted to many environments. They respond to stimuli in the environment.

**VOCABULARY**
**autotroph** p. 52
**photosynthesis** p. 52
**cellular respiration** p. 53
**stimulus** p. 55

### 2.3 Animals are consumers.

Animals consume food to get energy and materials. Animals are adapted to many enviroments. They interact with the environment and with other organisms.

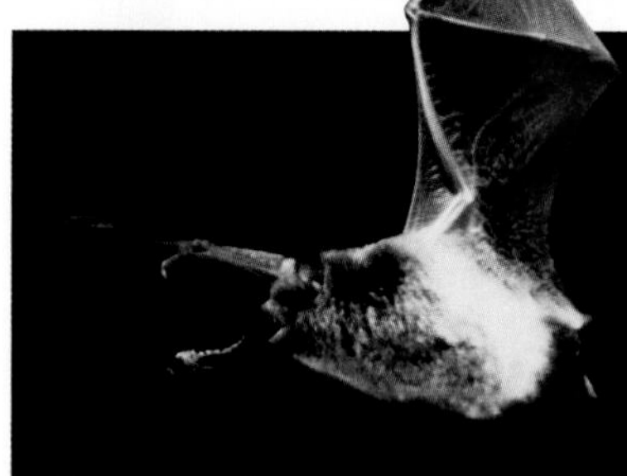

**VOCABULARY**
**consumer** p. 58
**heterotroph** p. 58
**behavior** p. 62
**predator** p. 63
**prey** p. 64
**migration** p. 64
**hibernation** p. 64

### 2.4 Most fungi are decomposers.

Fungi absorb energy from their surroundings. Fungi include mushrooms, molds, and yeasts. They affect people and other organisms in both helpful and harmful ways.

**VOCABULARY**
**hyphae** p. 67
**spore** p. 67
**lichen** p. 70

## Reviewing Vocabulary

*Draw a Venn diagram for each pair of terms. Put at least one shared characteristic in the overlap area, and put at least one difference in the outer circles.*

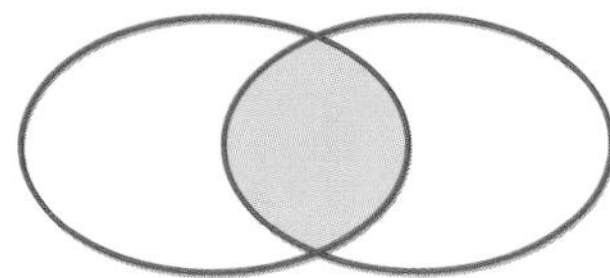

1. tissue, organ
2. autotroph, heterotroph
3. photosynthesis, cellular respiration
4. predator, prey
5. producer, consumer
6. migration, hibernation

## Reviewing Key Concepts

**Multiple Choice** *Choose the letter of the best answer.*

7. Which body system transports materials such as nutrients and oxygen throughout an animal's body?
   - **a.** respiratory system
   - **b.** circulatory system
   - **c.** digestive system
   - **d.** nervous system

8. An example of an adaptation is
   - **a.** a change in climate that increases plant growth
   - **b.** the movement of a group of animals to an area that has more food and water
   - **c.** a change in location of a squirrel's nest
   - **d.** the ability of a plant to resist fungal disease better than other plants

9. Plants capture the Sun's energy through which process?
   - **a.** reproduction
   - **b.** cellular respiration
   - **c.** photosynthesis
   - **d.** digestion

10. Plants produce auxin in response to which stimulus?
    - **a.** light
    - **b.** gravity
    - **c.** temperature
    - **d.** touch

11. A plant is best described as
    - **a.** a herbivore
    - **b.** an omnivore
    - **c.** a carnivore
    - **d.** a producer

12. A carnivore is best described as an animal that
    - **a.** eats plants
    - **b.** eats plants and other animals
    - **c.** eats other animals
    - **d.** makes its own food

13. Mushrooms produce
    - **a.** spores
    - **b.** buds
    - **c.** mold
    - **d.** yeast

14. Fungi and algae together form
    - **a.** hyphae
    - **b.** mushrooms
    - **c.** lichen
    - **d.** mold

**Short Answer** *Write a short answer to each question.*

15. Write a short paragraph comparing sexual reproduction with asexual reproduction. How are they the same? How are they different?

16. Write a short paragraph to explain how the sugars and starches stored in plant tissue are important to the survival of animals.

17. Write a short paragraph to explain how fungi are dependent on plants and animals for their energy.

## Thinking Critically

*The diagram below shows a woodland food web. Each arrow starts with a food source and points to a consumer. Use the diagram to answer the next six questions.*

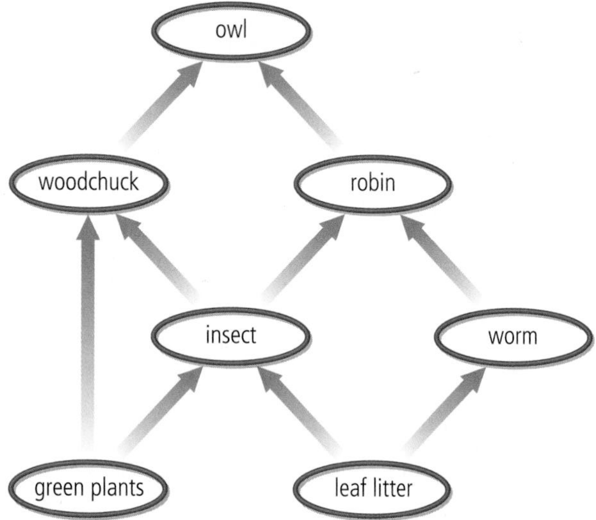


18. **ANALYZE** What is the original source of energy for all the animals in the food web? Explain your reasoning.

19. **CLASSIFY** Identify the consumers in this food web.

20. **CLASSIFY** Identify the animals in the food web as either herbivores, carnivores, omnivores, or decomposers.

21. **EVALUATE** Does an omnivore have an advantage over carnivores and herbivores in finding food?

22. **ANALYZE** What role does the worm play in the food web, and why it is important?

23. **PREDICT** How might this food web change over the course of a year, and how would that affect the feeding activity of animals in the food web?

24. **CONNECT** A woodchuck is sometimes referred to as a groundhog. Many people celebrate February 2 as groundhog day. The legend is that if a groundhog emerges from its burrow on this day and sees its shadow, then there will be six more weeks of winter. The groundhog is emerging from a long sleeplike state. What is this behavior, and how does it benefit the animal?

25. **ANALYZE** Do you think the defensive behavior of a porcupine or pufferfish is an adaptation? Explain your reasoning.

26. **SYNTHESIZE** A plant responds to gravity, touch, and light as stimuli. How does this relate to a plant being a producer?

27. **SYNTHESIZE** How are the cells of multicellular organisms like those of single-celled organisms? How are they different?

28. **ANALYZE** What quality of asexual reproduction makes a fungal disease spread so quickly.

## the BIG idea

29. **SYNTHESIZE** Look again at the photograph on pages 40–41. Plants, animals, and fungi are pictured there. How do these organisms get energy and materials from the environment?

30. **SUMMARIZE** Write a short paragraph to describe how matter and energy move between members of the kingdoms of plants, animals, and fungi. Use the words in the box below. Underline the terms in your answer.

| photosysnthesis | consumer |
|---|---|
| producer | decomposer |

## UNIT PROJECTS

By now you should have completed the following items for your unit project.

- questions that you have asked about the topic
- schedule showing when you will complete each step of your project
- list of resources including Web sites, print resources, and materials

## Interpreting Diagrams

The diagram shows the feeding relationships between certain animals and plants in a forest environment. The size of the bars represent the relative numbers of each organism. The arrow shows the flow of energy between these groups of organisms.

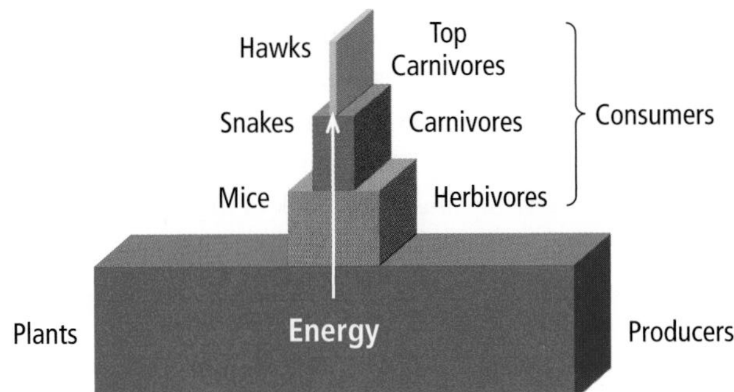


**Feeding Relationships Among Plants and Animals**

*Use the diagram to answer the questions below.*

**1.** Which is the largest group of organisms in the forest?

**a.** plants

**b.** mice

**c.** snakes

**d.** hawks

**2.** Most energy in the forest comes from

**a.** top carnivores

**b.** carnivores

**c.** herbivores

**d.** plants

**3.** Which description best fits the snake?

**a.** a producer that feeds upon mice

**b.** a consumer that is eaten by mice

**c.** a consumer that feeds upon mice

**d.** a consumer that feeds upon plants

**4.** A hawk is a top carnivore that feeds upon both snakes and mice. Which of the following best describes a top carnivore?

**a.** a carnivore that feeds upon other carnivores

**b.** a carnivore that feeds upon both carnivores and herbivores

**c.** a consumer that gets its energy from producers

**d.** a producer that supplies energy to consumers

**5.** Which statement best summarizes the diagram?

**a.** The energy in a forest environment flows one way, from producers to consumers.

**b.** Consumers don't need as much energy as producers.

**c.** Energy in a forest environment goes from plants to animals and then back to plants.

**d.** The number of producers depends on the number of consumers.

## Extended Response

**6** The diagram above shows the relative number of organisms at each level of a forest environment and the flow of energy from the producers to the consumers. Describe what happens to the amount of energy going from the producer level into the different levels of consumers. Not all the energy produced at a given level is available to organisms in the next level. What has happened to that energy? Use the words in the word box in your answer. Underline the words.

| producer | energy |
|---|---|
| consumer | food |

**7.** How would the number of plants, snakes, and hawks be affected if some disease were to reduce the numbers of mice in the forest?

# DISCOVERIES IN Biodiversity

Scientists have discovered new species in the treetops of tropical forests and in the crannies of coral reefs. The quest to catalog the types and numbers of living things, the biodiversity of Earth, began in the late 1600s. A wave of naturalists set sail from Europe to the Americas and to Africa to find specimens of living things.

In the late 19th century, biologists reached agreement on a system for naming and classifying each new species. The mid-20th century brought an understanding of DNA and how it could be used to compare one species with another. Now new organisms could be pinpointed with precision. To this day, millions of undiscovered species lie deep in the unexplored ocean, in tropical forests, and even in heavily trafficked U.S. cities. A large concentration of Earth's known species now live in named and protected biodiversity "hotspots."

1670

### *Merian Illustrates from Life*

In her day, it was typical to work from preserved specimens, but Maria Merian draws from life. Shown below is her illustration of the Legu Lizard she observes in South America. In 1670, she publishes a richly illustrated book of insects, the first to describe the process of metamorphosis.

## EVENTS

1670

## APPLICATIONS AND TECHNOLOGY

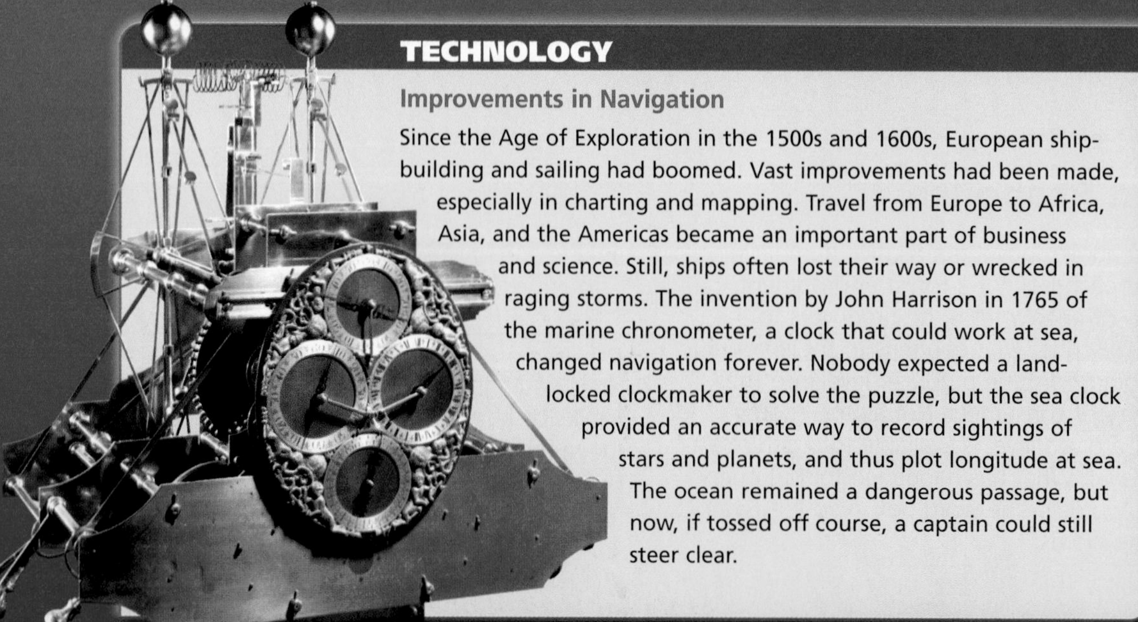

### TECHNOLOGY

#### Improvements in Navigation

Since the Age of Exploration in the 1500s and 1600s, European shipbuilding and sailing had boomed. Vast improvements had been made, especially in charting and mapping. Travel from Europe to Africa, Asia, and the Americas became an important part of business and science. Still, ships often lost their way or wrecked in raging storms. The invention by John Harrison in 1765 of the marine chronometer, a clock that could work at sea, changed navigation forever. Nobody expected a landlocked clockmaker to solve the puzzle, but the sea clock provided an accurate way to record sightings of stars and planets, and thus plot longitude at sea. The ocean remained a dangerous passage, but now, if tossed off course, a captain could still steer clear.

**1775**

### *A Catalog of Living Things*

In 1775 Carl Linnaeus completed a book called *Systema Naturae.* His book outlines a system to organize and name plants and animals. The naming system gave scientists a precise and consistent method for sharing discoveries.

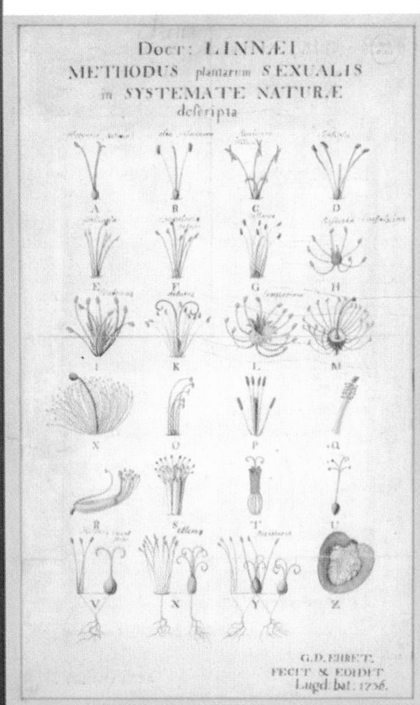

**1859**

### *Naturalists in the Amazon*

Henry Walter Bates travels from England to the Amazon rainforest in South America with Alfred Russell Wallace. Bates sails home in 1859, bringing over 14,000 specimens, mostly insects. About 8000 of Bates's finds are new discoveries. Wallace loses his collection in a shipwreck.

**1889**

### *Naming Discoveries*

At the height of discovering new species, conflicts arise over who gets to name living things. In 1889, a conference settles the matter. The first person to publish a description of an organism has the right to claim the discovery and to name it.

1770 1780 1860 1870 1880

## TECHNOLOGY

### Living Things Too Small to See

Before the 1600s, scientists were unable to see microorganisms. Anton van Leeuwenhoek, a drapery maker who made microscopes in his spare time, was one of the first to observe these tiny organisms. He made the first observation of bacteria, and viewed lake water through a microscope like the one shown to the far right. Others used microscopes to draw detailed close-ups, such as an insect's compound eye shown here.

### 1970

#### *The Bacteria Kingdom Divides*

Dr. Carl Woese discovers that bacterialike organisms living in places with extremely high temperatures have genetic material very different from bacteria. Woese suggests a new kingdom or domain called archaebacteria, which is later shortened to Archaea.

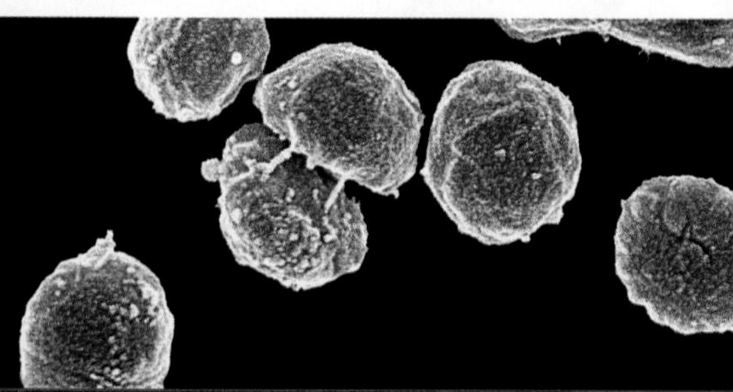

### 1990

#### *Diver, SCUBA Pioneer, Heads Research*

Dr. Sylvia Earle is the first woman to serve as chief scientist at the National Oceanic and Atmospheric Administration (NOAA). Earle uses SCUBA diving and discovers many new fish and marine species—especially new seaweeds in the Gulf of Mexico. Here she shows a sample to a student in a submersible vehicle.

### 1974

#### *Fogging the Rainforest*

Terry Erwin spouts plumes of insecticide into trees and discovers thousands of new insects species in the rainforest canopy. Erwin uses an organic insecticide that does not harm other parts of the ecosystem. Erwin spreads ground sheets or big funnels around a tree, sprays, and, after an hour or so catches the fallen insects, which look like jewels.

1970 1980 1990

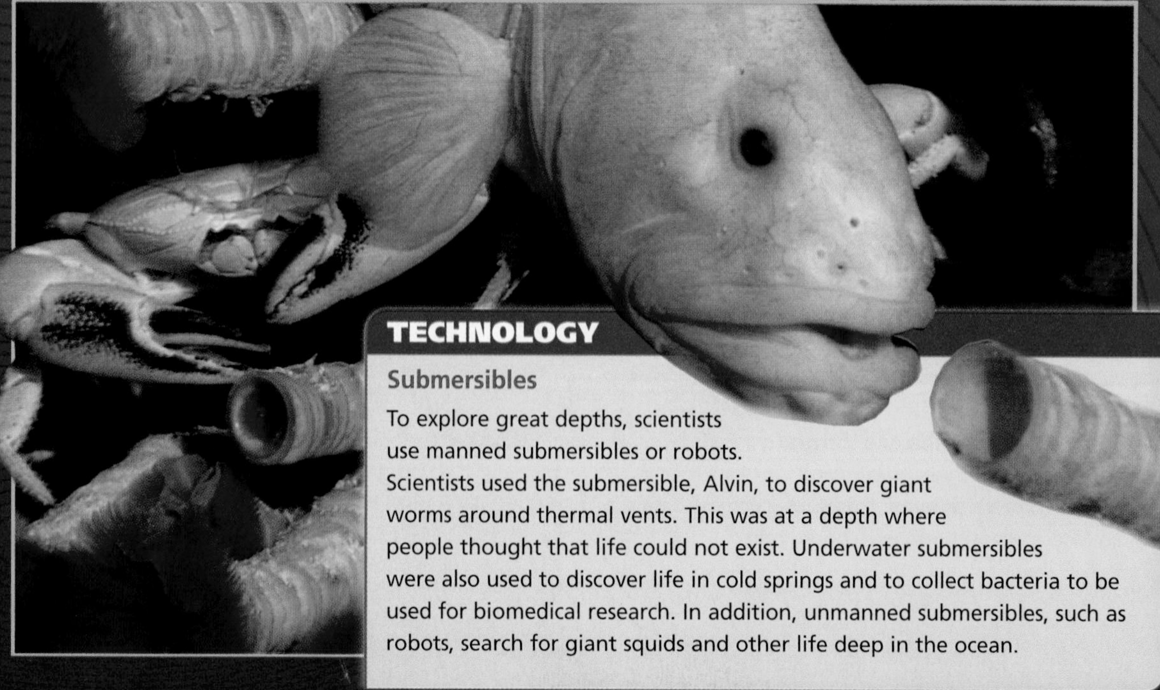

### TECHNOLOGY

#### Submersibles

To explore great depths, scientists use manned submersibles or robots. Scientists used the submersible, Alvin, to discover giant worms around thermal vents. This was at a depth where people thought that life could not exist. Underwater submersibles were also used to discover life in cold springs and to collect bacteria to be used for biomedical research. In addition, unmanned submersibles, such as robots, search for giant squids and other life deep in the ocean.

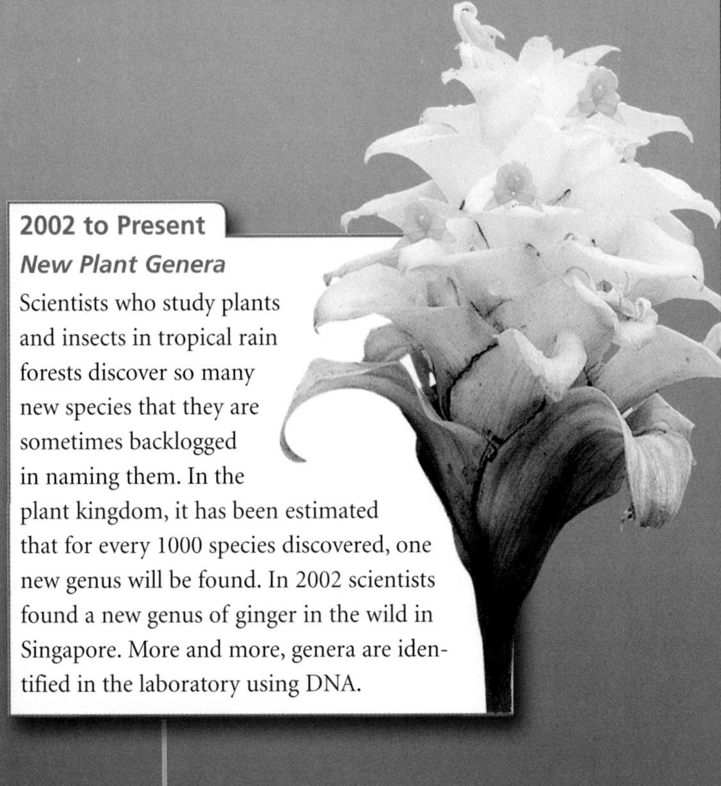

### 2002 to Present

***New Plant Genera***

Scientists who study plants and insects in tropical rain forests discover so many new species that they are sometimes backlogged in naming them. In the plant kingdom, it has been estimated that for every 1000 species discovered, one new genus will be found. In 2002 scientists found a new genus of ginger in the wild in Singapore. More and more, genera are identified in the laboratory using DNA.

**RESOURCE CENTER**
CLASSZONE.COM
Read about current biodiversity discoveries and research.

2000

## INTO THE FUTURE

Although scientists have explored most of the continents, little is known about what life is like in the more remote areas. Deep-sea exploration, for example, is only just beginning, and big surprises surface with each expedition. Technology will continue to delve deeper toward the floor of deep oceans with underwater robotics, manned submersibles, and better mapping and imaging systems.

Science will increasingly rely on organizing the growing data on biodiversity. Currently, scientists who study one area of life mostly share data with others in the same field. For example, scientists studying plants share their data with other botanists. An effort to create global databases to share information about all species is beginning to bring together this data. Databases that catalogue the genes of living things are being created. The better we know the genetic profile of various species, the better we can identify and compare them.

In addition, the attention to the health of biodiversity hotspots and ecosystems everywhere may help stop extinction, the dying off of a whole species. Extinction decreases the diversity of living things, and scientists have recognized that Earth's biodiversity plays a big role in keeping ecosystems healthy.

## APPLICATION

### Biodiversity Hotspots

In 1988, British ecologist Norman Mike Myers creates a list of 18 areas that he calls biodiversity "hotspots." In 2000, Myers and others increase the number of hotspots to 25. How does an area get to be called a hotspot? It has to have a large number of species that exist only in that location and it has to be a region in great danger of habitat loss. Hotspots cover only 1.5 % of the Earth's surface yet they contain 44 percent of all species of higher plants and 35 percent of all land vertebrates. Scientists place most of their effort in discovering new species in these hotspots.

cold  hot

## ACTIVITIES

### Writing About Science: Documentary

Research one hotspot and report on the diverse species living there. Note any legal steps or other efforts to conserve biodiversity in that area.

### Reliving History

Devise an animal classification system based on a criterion such as habitat, diet, or behavior. What are the strengths and weaknesses of your system?

CHAPTER

# Plants

## the BIG idea

Plants are a diverse group of organisms that live in many land environments.

How does such a large tree get what it needs to survive?

## Key Concepts

SECTION

**Plants are adapted to living on land.**
Learn about plant characteristics and structures.

SECTION

**Most mosses and ferns live in moist environments.**
Learn about how mosses and ferns live and reproduce.

SECTION

**Seeds and pollen are reproductive adaptations.**
Learn about seeds, pollen, and gymnosperms.

SECTION

**Many plants reproduce with flowers and fruit.**
Learn about flowers, fruit, and angiosperms.

### Internet Preview

CLASSZONE.COM

Chapter 3 online resources: Content Review, Simulation, Visualization, four Resource Centers, Math Tutorial, Test Practice

# EXPLORE the BIG idea

## How Are Plants Alike, How Are They Different?

Find samples of plants in your area. Draw or take pictures of them for your science notebook. Note each plant's shape, size, and the environment where you found it.

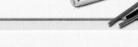

**Observe and Think** Do all plants have leaves? Do all plants have flowers?

## How Are Seeds Dispersed?

Make a model of a seed with wings, such as a seed from a maple tree. Fold a strip of paper in half the long way and then unfold it. Cut a little less than halfway along the fold. Refold the uncut part of the paper and bend out the two cut strips so they look like wings. Put a paper clip on the bottom of the folded part. Drop your seed.

**Observe and Think** How does having seeds with wings benefit a plant?

## Internet Activity: Sprouting Seeds

Go to **ClassZone.com** to watch a time-lapse video of a seed sprouting.

**Observe and Think** If plants come from seeds, where do seeds come from?

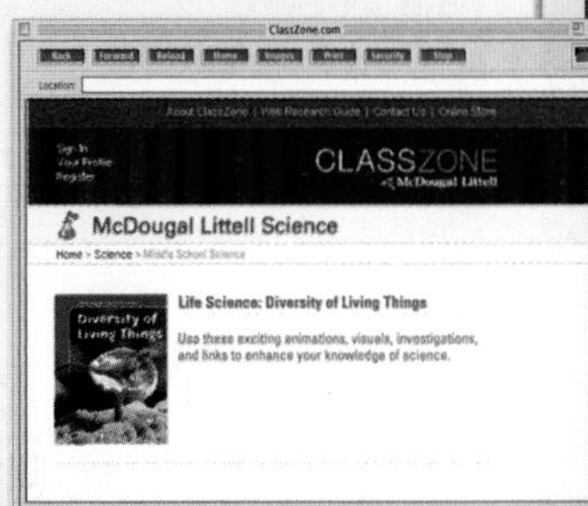

Plant Kingdom **Code: MDL041**

CHAPTER 3

# Getting Ready to Learn

## CONCEPT REVIEW

- All organisms get water and other materials from the environment.
- Plants have specialized tissues with specific functions.
- Plants are producers.

## VOCABULARY REVIEW

**meiosis** p. 48

**fertilization** p. 48

**photosynthesis** p. 52

**spore** p. 67

**cycle** *See Glossary.*

**CONTENT REVIEW**

CLASSZONE.COM

Review concepts and vocabulary.

## TAKING NOTES

### MIND MAP

Write each main idea, or blue heading, in an oval; then write details that relate to each other and to the main idea. Organize the details so that each spoke of the web has notes about one part of the main idea.

### VOCABULARY STRATEGY

Draw a **word triangle** diagram for each new vocabulary term. On the bottom line, write and define the term. Above that, write a sentence that uses the term correctly. At the top, draw a small picture to remind you of the definition.

See the Note-Taking Handbook on pages R45–R51.

SCIENCE NOTEBOOK

cells have a nucleus

cells have cell walls

two-part life cycle

producers

PLANTS SHARE COMMON CHARACTERISTICS

multicellular

live on land

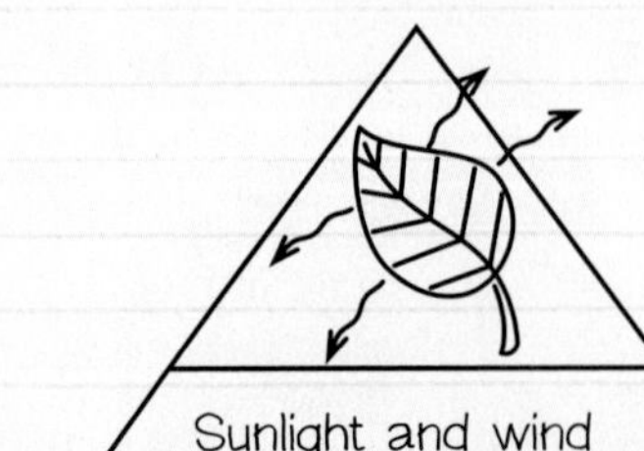

Sunlight and wind can cause transpiration.

Transpiration: the movement of water vapor out of a plant and into the air

KEY CONCEPT

# Plants are adapted to living on land.

**BEFORE, you learned**

- All organisms have certain basic needs and characteristics
- The bodies of multicellular organisms are organized
- Plants are producers

**NOW, you will learn**

- About plant diversity
- About common characteristics of plants
- How the bodies of plants are organized

**VOCABULARY**

**vascular system** p. 87
**transpiration** p. 88

**EXPLORE Leaf Characteristics**

### *What is a leaf?*

**PROCEDURE**

1. Examine the leaf your teacher gives you carefully. Try to notice as many details as you can.
2. Make a drawing of both sides of your leaf in your notebook. Label as many parts as you can and write down your ideas describing each part's function.
3. Compare your diagram and notes with those of your classmates.

**MATERIALS**

- assorted leaves
- hand lens

**WHAT DO YOU THINK?**

- What characteristics did most or all of your leaves have?
- How would you describe your leaf to someone who could not see it?

## Plants are a diverse group of organisms.

**MIND MAP**
Make a mind map for the first main idea: *Plants are a diverse group of organisms.*

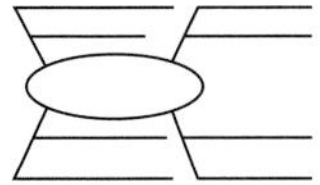

Plants are nearly everywhere. Walk through a forest, and you're surrounded by trees, ferns, and moss. Drive along a country road, and you pass fields planted with crops like cotton or wheat. Even a busy city has tree-lined sidewalks, grass-covered lawns, and weeds growing in vacant lots or poking through cracks in the pavement.

Earth is home to an amazing variety of plant life. Plants come in all shapes and sizes, from tiny flowers no bigger than the head of a pin to giant trees taller than a 12-story building. Plants are found in all types of environments, from the icy Arctic to the steamy tropics.

## Diversity of Plants

**Plant species live in a variety of environments and have a wide range of features.**

**Orchids**

Seed pods of the vanilla orchid are used to flavor food.

**Horsetails**

Horsetails have a distinctive shape and texture.

**Bristlecone Pine**

Bristlecone pines are some of the oldest trees on Earth.

## Plants share common characteristics.

Scientists estimate that at least 260,000 different species of plants live on Earth today. The photographs on this page show three examples of plants that are very different from one another.

Orchids are flowering plants that mostly grow in tropical rain forests. To get the sunlight they need, many orchids grow not in the soil but on the trunks of trees. Horsetails are plants that produce tiny grains of a very hard substance called silica. Sometimes called scouring rushes, these plants were once used to scrub clean, or scour, dishes and pots. Bristlecone pine trees live on high mountain slopes in North America, where there is little soil and often high winds. These trees grow very slowly and can live for several thousand years.

**READING TIP**

The word *species* comes from a root word meaning "kind" or "type." In science, *species* is a classification for a group of organisms that are so similar that members of the group can breed and produce offspring that can also reproduce.

You can see from these three examples that plant species show great diversity. Despite how different an orchid is from a horsetail and a bristlecone pine, all three plants share certain characteristics. These are the characteristics that define a plant as a plant:

- Plants are multicellular organisms.
- A plant cell has a nucleus and is surrounded by a cell wall.
- Plants are producers. They capture energy from the Sun.
- Plant life cycles are divided into two stages, or generations.

**CHECK YOUR READING** What characteristics are shared by all plants?

## Plant parts have special functions.

You could say that a plant lives in two worlds. The roots anchor a plant in the ground. Aboveground, reaching toward the Sun, are stems and leaves. Together, stems and leaves make up a shoot system. These two systems work together to get a plant what it needs to survive.

**REMINDER**

Plants, like animals, have several levels of oranization. The root system and shoot system are organ systems.

A plant's root system can be as extensive as the stems and leaves that you see aboveground. Roots absorb water and nutrients from the soil. These materials are transported to the leaves through the stems. The leaves use the materials, along with carbon dioxide from the air, to make sugars and carbohydrates. The stems then deliver these energy-rich compounds back to the rest of the plant.

**CHECK YOUR READING** What are two plant systems, and what are their functions?

### Transporting Water and Other Materials

Stems serve as the pathway for transporting water, nutrients, and energy-rich compounds from one part of a plant to another. In most plants, the materials move through a **vascular system** (VAS-kyuh-lur) that is made up of long, tubelike cells. These tissues are bundled together and run from the roots to the leaves. A vascular bundle from the stem of a buttercup plant is shown.

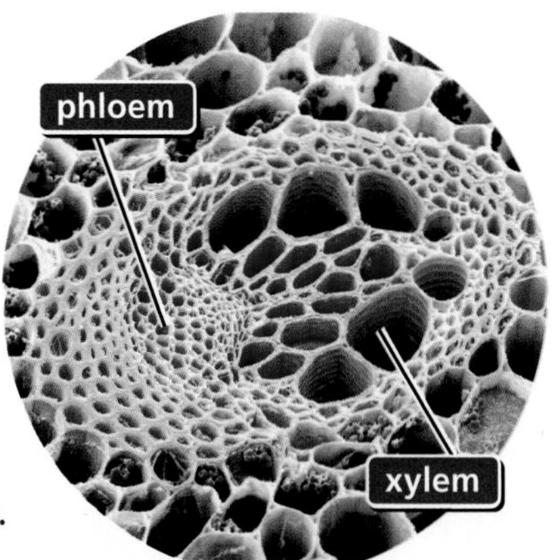


This vascular bundle has been magnified 113×.

Transport is carried out by two types of tissue. Xylem (ZY-luhm) is a tissue that carries water and dissolved nutrients up from the roots. Phloem (FLOH-em) is a tissue that transports energy-rich materials down from the leaves. Xylem cells and phloem cells are long and hollow, like pipes. The xylem cells are a little larger than the phloem cells. Both tissues include long fibers that help support the plant body, as well as cells that can store extra carbohydrates for energy.

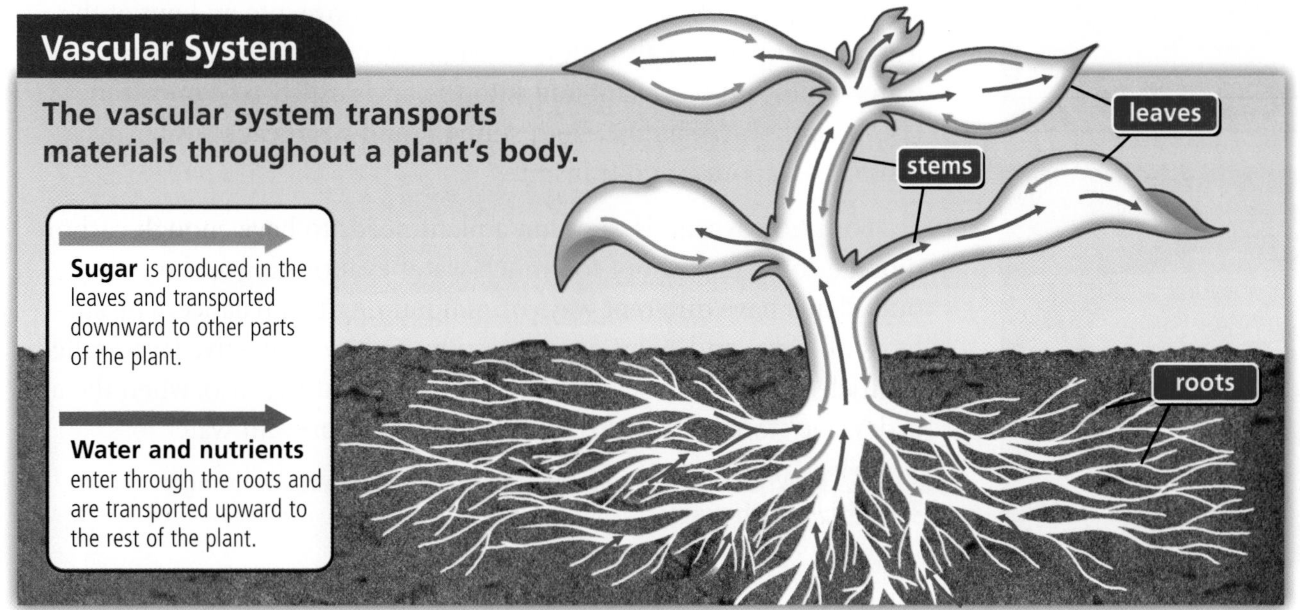

Vascular System
The vascular system transports materials throughout a plant's body.
Sugar is produced in the leaves and transported downward to other parts of the plant.
Water and nutrients enter through the roots and are transported upward to the rest of the plant.
leaves
stems
roots

## Making Sugars

Plants produce sugars through the process of photosynthesis. Photosynthesis is a series of chemical reactions that capture light energy from the Sun and convert it into chemical energy stored in sugar molecules. The starting materials needed are carbon dioxide, water, and light. The end products are sugars and oxygen. The chemical reactions for photosynthesis can be summarized like this:

**carbon dioxide + water + sunlight → sugars + oxygen**

Photosynthesis takes place in chloroplasts, structures that contain chlorophyll. Chlorophyll absorbs the sunlight that the chloroplasts need to produce the reaction. Most chloroplasts in a plant are located in leaf cells. As you can see from the illustration on page 89, the structure of the leaf is specialized for capturing light energy and producing sugar.

What is photosynthesis, and why is it important?

The upper surface of the leaf, which is turned toward the Sun, has layers of cells filled with chloroplasts. Vascular tissue located toward the center of the leaf brings in water and nutrients and carries away sugars and other carbohydrates. Tiny openings at the bottom of the leaf, called stomata (STOH-muh-tuh), lead to a network of tiny spaces where gases are stored. The carbon dioxide gas needed for photosynthesis comes in through the stomata, and oxygen gas moves out. This process is called gas exchange.

**Open Stomata**

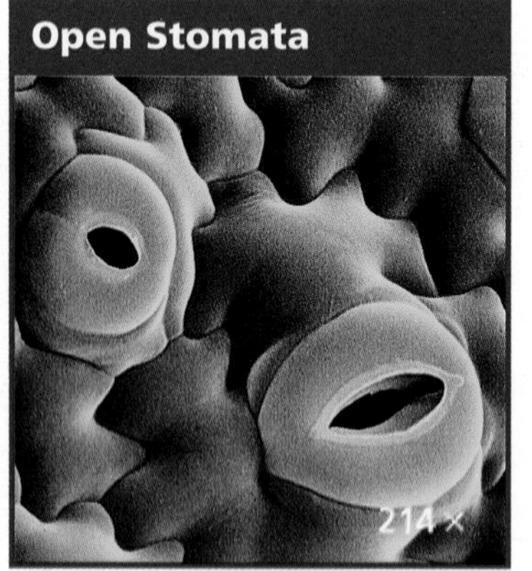


**Closed Stomata**

## Controlling Gas Exchange and Water Loss

For photosynthesis to occur, a plant must maintain the balance of carbon dioxide and water in its body. Carbon dioxide gas from the air surrounding a plant enters through the stomata in its leaves. Open stomata allow carbon dioxide and oxygen to move into and out of the leaf. These openings also allow water to evaporate. The movement of water vapor out of a plant and into the air is called **transpiration** (TRAN-spuh-RAY-shuhn). Both sunlight and wind cause water in leaves to evaporate and transpire.

For photosynthesis to occur, a plant needs to have enough carbon dioxide come in without too much water evaporating and moving out. Plants have different ways of maintaining this balance. The surfaces of leaves and stems are covered by a waxy protective layer, called a cuticle. The cuticle keeps water from evaporating. Also, when the air is dry, the stomata can close. This can help to prevent water loss.

What are two ways plants have to keep from losing too much water?

# Inside a Leaf

**The leaf is an organ that produces sugars. It is made up of different types of cells and tissues.**

Cells at the surface produce a waxy cuticle that keeps the leaf from losing water.
Most chloroplasts are located in cells of the upper layer of the leaf.
Xylem transports water and nutrients up from the roots.
Phloem transports energy-rich compounds made in the leaf down to other parts of the plant.
Carbon dioxide, oxygen, and water vapor move into and out of the leaf through stomata.

**READING VISUALS** How is the top of a leaf different from the bottom of a leaf?

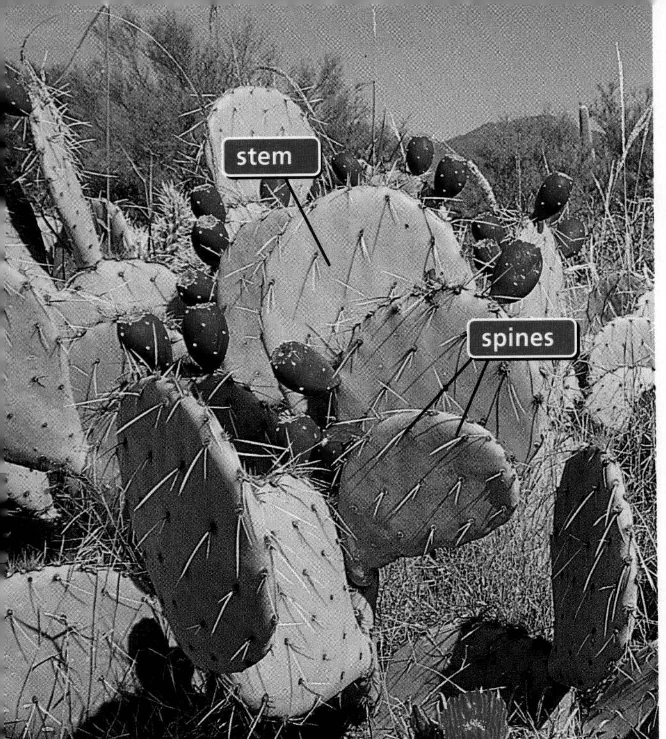


**APPLY** Plant stems branch as they grow. Do cactus plants have branches?

The stomata are an adaptation that allows a plant to adjust to daily changes in its environment. Plants can respond to hot, dry weather by keeping their stomata closed. Stomata can be open during the night, when evaporation is less likely to occur. Most plants have stomata.

Some species of plants have special adaptations for survival in a particular environment. For example, a cactus plant has adaptations that allow it to survive in a desert. The spines of a cactus are actually modified leaves. A plant with regular leaves would lose too much water through transpiration. In cacti, most photosynthesis occurs in the thick fleshy stem, where the cactus also stores water and carbon dioxide gas.

## Plants grow throughout their lifetimes.

Plants grow as long as they live. This is true for plants that live for only one season, such as sunflowers, and for plants that can live for many years, such as trees. Plants grow bigger when cells at the tips of their roots and stems divide and multiply more rapidly than other plant cells do. A plant's roots and stems can grow longer and thicker and can branch, or divide. However, only stems grow leaves. Leaves grow from buds produced by growth tissue in a plant's stems. The bud of an oak tree is shown on page 91.

Plant stems are structures with more than one function. You have read that a plant's stem includes its vascular system, which allows the plant to transport materials between its leaves and roots. Long stiff fibers in the tissues of the vascular system provide support and give the plant shape. Plant stems can also store the sugars produced by photosynthesis. Many plants, including broccoli, celery, and carrots, convert sugars into starch and then store this energy-rich material in their stems or roots.

What are three functions of plant stems?

### Plants with Soft Stems

Learn more about plant systems.

The soft stems and leaves of many wildflowers, garden flowers, and vegetables die when the environment they live in becomes too cold or too dry. This type of plant survives by using the carbohydrates stored in its roots. Then, when the environment provides it with enough warmth, water, and sunlight, the plant will grow new, soft, green stems and leaves.

## Plant Growth

Plants, such as these oak trees, grow most when there is enough warmth, water, and sunlight.

The tips of the shoots produce buds, which become new leaves and stems.

### Plants with Woody Stems

Some plants, such as trees and shrubs, have tough, thick stems that do not die each year. These stems keep growing longer and thicker. As the stems grow, they develop a type of tough xylem tissue that is not found in soft stems. This tough xylem tissue is called wood. The growing tissues in woody stems are located near the outer surface of the stem, right under the bark. This means that, for a tree like one of the oaks in the photograph above, the center of the trunk is the oldest part of the plant.

## 3.1 Review

### KEY CONCEPTS

1. What characteristics do all plants have in common?
2. How does the structure of a leaf relate to its function?
3. What tissues move materials throughout a plant?

### CRITICAL THINKING

4. **Summarize** Describe how the structure of a leaf allows a plant to control the materials involved in photosynthesis.
5. **Analyze** Do you think the stems of soft-stemmed plants have chloroplasts? How about woody-stemmed plants? Explain your reasoning. Hint: Think about the color of each.

### CHALLENGE

6. **Evaluate** Scientists who study the natural world say that there is unity in diversity. How does this idea apply to plants?

KEY CONCEPT

# Most mosses and ferns live in moist environments.

**BEFORE, you learned**

- All plants share common characteristics
- The body of a plant has specialized parts
- Plants grow throughout their lifetimes

**NOW, you will learn**

- About the first plants
- About reproduction in nonvascular plants, such as mosses
- About reproduction in vascular plants, such as ferns

**EXPLORE Moss Plants**

### *What do moss plants look like?*

**PROCEDURE**

1. Use a hand lens to examine a moss plant. Look for different structures and parts you can identify.
2. Draw a diagram of the moss plant in your notebook. Label parts you identified and parts you would like to identify.
3. Write a brief description of each part's function.

**MATERIALS**

- live moss plant
- hand lens

**WHAT DO YOU THINK?**

- How would you describe a moss plant to someone who had never seen one?
- How does a moss plant compare with the other plants you are familiar with?

## Plant species adapted to life on land.

Evidence indicates that life first appeared on Earth about 3.8 billion years ago. Tiny single-celled and multicellular organisms lived in watery environments such as warm shallow seas, deep ocean vents, and ponds. Fossil evidence suggests that plant life did not appear on land until about 475 million years ago. The ancestors of the first plants were among the first organisms to move onto land.

What did these plantlike organisms look like? Scientists think they looked much like the green algae you can find growing in watery ditches or shallow ponds today. Both green algae and plants are autotrophs, or producers. Their cells contain chloroplasts that enable them to convert the Sun's light energy into the chemical energy stored in sugars.

Explore plant evolution.

## The First Plants

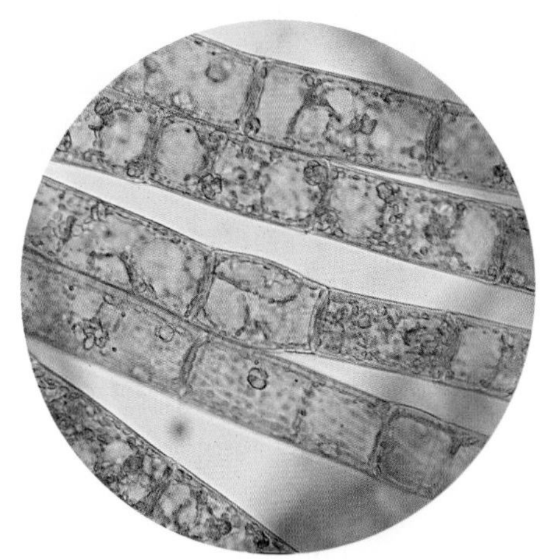

Scientists think the first plants shared a common ancestor with green algae, shown here magnified about 80×.

Suppose that hundreds of millions of years ago, the area now occupied by your school was a shallow pond full of tiny, floating organisms that could photosynthesize. The Sun overhead provided energy. The pond water was full of dissolved nutrients. The organisms thrived and reproduced, and over time the pond became crowded. Some were pushed to the very edges of the water. Then, after a period of dry weather, the pond shrank. Some organisms at the edge were no longer in the water. The ones that were able to survive were now living on land.

Scientists think that something like this took place in millions of watery environments over millions of years. Those few organisms that were stranded and were able to survive became ancestors to the first plants. Life on land is very different from life in water. The first plants needed to be able to get both nutrients and water from the land. There is no surrounding water to provide support for the body or to keep body tissues from drying out. However, for organisms that survived, life on land had many advantages. There is plenty of carbon dioxide in the air and plenty of direct sunlight.

Why is having plenty of sunlight and water an advantage for a plant? Your answer should mention photosynthesis.

## Mosses and Ferns

Among the first plants to live on Earth were the ancestors of the mosses and ferns you see today. Both probably evolved from species of algae that lived in the sea and in freshwater. Mosses are simpler in structure than ferns. Mosses, and two closely related groups of plants known as liverworts and hornworts, are descended from the first plants to spread onto the bare rock and soil of Earth. Ferns and their relatives appeared later.

This diorama shows what a forest on Earth might have looked like about 350 million years ago.

# INVESTIGATE Capturing the Sun's Energy

**SKILL FOCUS**
Measuring

### *How much sunlight reaches an organism living in water?*

**PROCEDURE**

1. Thread the string through the holes in the button so that the button hangs flat. Fill the empty bottle with clean water.
2. Look down through the top of the bottle. Lower the button into the water until it either disappears from view or reaches the bottom. Have a classmate measure how far the button is from the surface of the water.
3. Add two spoonfuls of kelp granules to the water. Repeat step 2.

**WHAT DO YOU THINK?**

- How did the distance measured the second time compare with your first measurement?
- Why might a photosynthetic organism living on land get more sunlight than one living in water?

**CHALLENGE** What do the kelp granules in this experiment represent? What does that suggest about the advantages of living on land?

**MATERIALS**
- white button
- string
- empty clear plastic bottle
- water
- ruler
- kelp granules
- tablespoon

**TIME**
20 minutes

## Mosses are nonvascular plants.

Moss plants have adaptations for life on land. For example, each moss cell, like all plant cells, is surrounded by a thick wall that provides it with support. Moss cells also have special storage areas for water and nutrients. Mosses do not grow very large, but they have simple structures that function like roots, stems, and leaves. These adaptations help moss plants survive on land, while algae survive only in water.

If you look closely at a clump of moss, you will see that it is actually made up of many tiny, dark green plants. Mosses belong to a group called nonvascular plants. Nonvascular plants do not have vascular tissue. Water and nutrients simply move through nonvascular plants' bodies cell by cell. A plant can get enough water this way as long as its body is no more than a few cells thick.

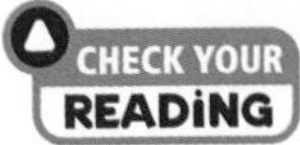


What limits the size of moss plants?

Water also plays a part in the reproductive cycle of a moss plant. In the first part of the cycle, the moss grows and maintains itself, producing the male and female structures needed for sexual reproduction. If conditions are right and there is enough water, the plant enters a spore-producing stage, the second part of the cycle.

## Mosses reproduce with spores.

Mosses, ferns, and fungi all reproduce with spores. Spores are an important adaptation that allowed the ancestors of these organisms to reproduce on land. A spore is a single reproductive cell that is protected by a hard, watertight covering. The covering prevents the cell from drying out. Spores are small and can be transported through the air. This means offspring from spores can grow in places that are distant from the parent organisms.

The green moss plants you are familiar with have grown from spores. They represent the first generation. Within a clump of moss are both male and female reproductive structures. When conditions are right, these structures produce sperm and eggs. Fertilization can occur only if water is present because the tiny moss sperm move by swimming. A layer of water left by rain is one way sperm can move to the eggs on another part of the plant.

The fertilized egg grows into a stalk with a capsule on the end—the second generation of the plant. The stalk and capsule grow from the female moss plant. Inside the capsule, the process of meiosis produces thousands of tiny spores. When the spores are released, as shown in the photograph, the cycle can begin again.

**REMINDER**

Sexual reproduction involves two processes: fertilization and meiosis.

### Moss Releasing Spores

**IDENTIFY** Point out the two generations of the moss plant shown here.

Mosses, like other plants, can also reproduce asexually. A small piece of a moss plant can separate and can grow into a new plant, or new plants can branch off from old ones. Asexual reproduction allows plants to spread more easily than sexual reproduction. However, the genetic material of the new plants is the same as that of the parent. Sexual reproduction increases genetic diversity and the possibility of new adaptations.

Compare and contrast sexual and asexual reproduction. Your answer should mention *genetic material.*

## Ferns are vascular plants.

Ferns, and two closely related groups of plants known as horsetails and club mosses, were the first plants on Earth with vascular systems. The tubelike tissue of a vascular system moves water through a plant's body quickly and effectively. Because of this transport system, vascular plants can grow much larger than nonvascular plants. Vascular tissue also provides support for the weight of a larger plant.

The presence of vascular tissue has an effect on the development of roots, stems, and leaves. The root system can branch out more, anchoring a larger plant as well as providing water and nutrients. Vascular tissue moves materials more efficiently and gives extra support. The stems can branch out and more leaves can grow. This results in more sugars and other materials needed for energy and growth.

**Nonvascular**

Liverworts are tiny nonvascular plants. The liverworts shown here are life-size.

**Vascular**

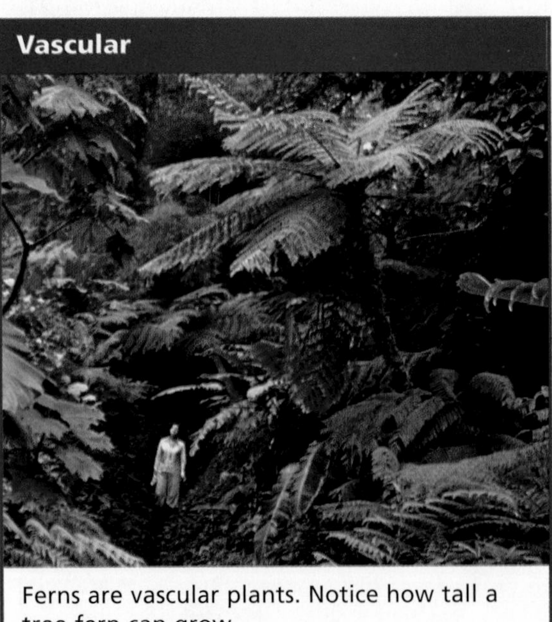

Ferns are vascular plants. Notice how tall a tree fern can grow.

**READING VISUALS** COMPARE AND CONTRAST How do the penny and the person help to show that the tree ferns are much larger than the liverworts?

## Ferns reproduce with spores.

You may have seen ferns growing in the woods or in a garden. The leaves of ferns, called fronds, are often included in a flower bouquet. The next time you have a chance to look at a fern frond, take a look at the back. You will probably see many small clusters similar to those shown to the right. The clusters are full of spores.

As fern fronds grow, they produce clusters of spores on the back of the fronds.

Ferns, like mosses, have a two-part life cycle. In ferns, spores grow into tiny structures that lie very close to the ground. You would have to look closely to find these structures on the ground, for they are usually smaller than the size of your thumbnail. Within these structures are the sperm- and egg-producing parts of the fern plant. This is the first generation of the plant. Like mosses, the sperm of a fern plant need water to swim to the egg. So fertilization occurs only when plenty of moisture is present.

The second part of a fern life cycle is the plant with fronds that grows from the fertilized egg. As the fronds grow, the small egg-bearing part of the plant dies away. The fronds produce clusters, and cells within those clusters undergo meiosis and produce spores. The more the fern grows, the more clusters and spores it produces. The spores, when they are released, spread through the air. If conditions are right where the spores land, they grow into new fern plants and a new cycle begins. This is sexual reproduction. Ferns, like mosses, also reproduce asexually. New ferns branch off old ones, or pieces separate from the plant and grow.

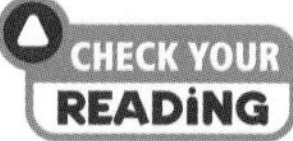


Explain one way that sexual reproduction in ferns is similar to reproduction in mosses. Explain one way it is different.

## 3.2 Review

### KEY CONCEPTS

1. For the ancestors of the first plants, what were some advantages to living on land?
2. What are three adaptations that make mosses able to live on land?
3. What are two characteristics you can observe that distinguish vascular plants from nonvascular plants?

### CRITICAL THINKING

4. **Synthesize** Vascular plants such as ferns can grow bigger and taller than nonvascular plants such as mosses. Does this mean they can also capture more sunlight? Explain your answer.
5. **Compare** Make a chart that shows how the life cycles of mosses and ferns are different, and how they are similar.

### CHALLENGE

6. **Evaluate** Consider the conditions that are needed for mosses and ferns to reproduce sexually. Sexual reproduction increases genetic diversity within a group of plants, while asexual reproduction does not. Explain why asexual reproduction is still important for both moss and fern plants.

KEY CONCEPT

# Seeds and pollen are reproductive adaptations.

**BEFORE, you learned**

- Plant species evolved from algaelike ancestors
- Mosses are nonvascular plants that reproduce with spores
- Ferns are vascular plants that reproduce with spores

**NOW, you will learn**

- How some plants reproduce with pollen and seeds
- About the advantages of pollen and seeds

**VOCABULARY**

**seed** p. 98
**embryo** p. 98
**germination** p. 99
**pollen** p. 100
**gymnosperm** p. 102

**THINK ABOUT**

***Is a seed alive?***

A lotus is a type of pond lily that is commonly found in water gardens. The plants take root in the bottom of a pond. A plant scientist in California experimented with lotus seeds from China that were over 1000 years old. The scientist made a small opening in the hard covering of each seed and planted the seeds in wet soil. Some of the seeds sprouted and grew. What made it possible for these seeds to survive for such a long time? Is a seed alive?

## Seeds are an important adaptation.

Spores are one adaptation that made it possible for plants to reproduce on land. Seeds are another. A **seed** is a young plant that is enclosed in a protective coating. Within the coating are enough nutrients to enable the plant to grow. Seeds and spores can both withstand harsh conditions. Seed plants, however, have several survival advantages over seedless plants. These advantages make it possible for seed plants to spread into environments where seedless plants are less likely to survive.

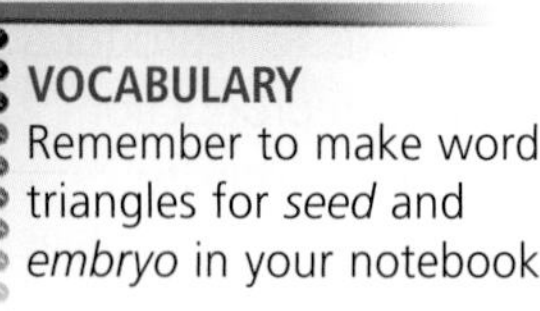

VOCABULARY
Remember to make word triangles for *seed* and *embryo* in your notebook.

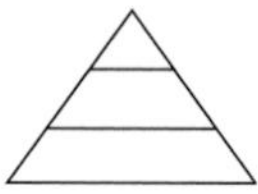

In all plants, fertilization brings about the growth of the next generation of the plant, beginning with an embryo. An **embryo** (EHM-bree-OH) is the immature form of an organism that has the potential to grow and develop. In seed plants, the embryo is protected. The seed coat protects the immature plant until conditions are right for it to grow.

An embryo can remain inside a seed for a long time without growing. When moisture, temperature, and other conditions are right, a seed will start to grow. **Germination** (JUR-muh-NAY-shuhn) is the beginning of growth of a new plant from a spore or a seed. If you've ever planted a seed that sprouted, you've observed germination.

What is germination?

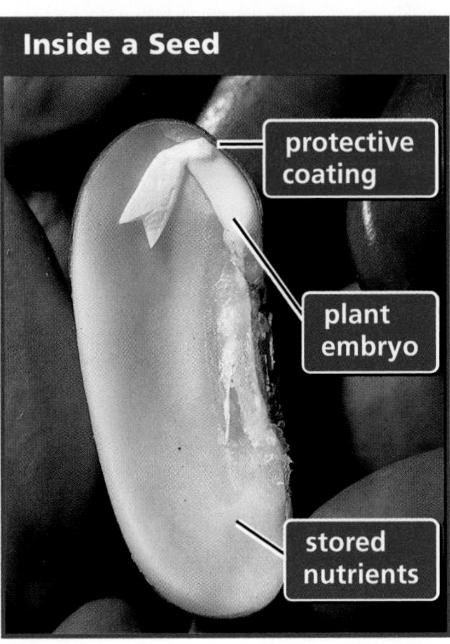


When a seed germinates, it takes in water from its surroundings. As the embryo begins to grow, it uses the stored nutrients in the seed for energy and materials. The nutrients need to last until the new plant's roots and shoots can start to function.

## Some plants reproduce with seeds.

In most places, plants that reproduce with seeds are common and easy to see. Trees, bushes, flowers, and grasses are all seed plants. It's a bit harder to find plants that reproduce with spores, such as mosses or ferns. Why are there so many more seed plants in the world? The diagram below shows some of the differences and similarities between seeds and spores.

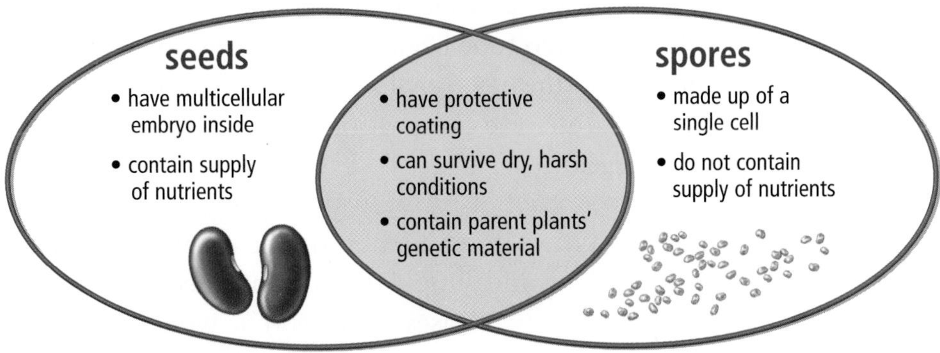


One important difference between a seed and a spore is that the seed contains a multicellular organism. If you look closely at the photograph above you can see the tiny leaves at the top of the embryo, with the root below. Spores are just a single cell. Seeds can be spread by wind, animals, or water. Spores are mostly carried by the wind. The sperm of seed plants, unlike the sperm of mosses and ferns, do not need water to reach the egg. One important similarity between a seed and a spore is that both can grow into a new plant.

Name three ways seeds are different from spores.

Learn more about seeds.

## Pine trees reproduce with pollen and seeds.

Seed plants, such as pine trees, do not have swimming sperm. Instead, they have pollen. A **pollen** grain is a small multicellular structure that holds a sperm cell. It has a hard outer covering to keep the sperm from drying out. Pollen grains can be carried from one plant to another by wind, water, or by animals such as insects, bats, or birds. The process of pollination is completed when a pollen grain attaches to the part of a plant that contains the egg and releases the sperm.

**READING TIP**

As you read the numbered paragraphs on this page, follow the numbers on the labels of the diagram on page 101.

The life cycle of a pine tree provides an example of how seed plants reproduce.

1. The reproductive structures of a pine tree are the pinecones. Meiosis occurs in the pine cones, producing sperm and egg cells. Each tree has separate male and female cones.

Pinecones release lots of pollen into the air.

2. In male cones, the sperm cells are contained in pollen grains, which are released into the air. In female cones, the egg cells are enclosed in protective compartments within the cone scales.

3. The female cone produces a sticky substance. When a pollen grain lands, it sticks. A pollen tube begins to grow from the pollen grain through the scale to the egg. Fertilization occurs when the pollen tube reaches the protective compartment and sperm travel through it to one of the eggs.

4. The fertilized egg grows into an embryo. The compartment, with its protective covering and supply of nutrients, becomes the seed. The pinecone eventually releases its seeds. The winged seeds can float through the air and may be carried long distances by the wind. If the seed lands on the ground and germinates, it can become a new pine tree.

In the life cycle of a pine tree, meiosis and fertilization occur completely within the tissue of the mature plant. Fertilization doesn't require an outside source of water. The sperm cells in a pollen grain and the egg cells in a cone scale represent the first generation of the plant. The seed and the tree that grows from the seed represent the second generation.

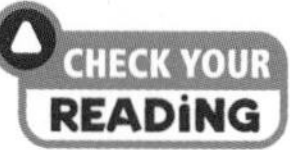


What do pollen grains and cone scales contain?

## Life Cycle of a Pine Tree

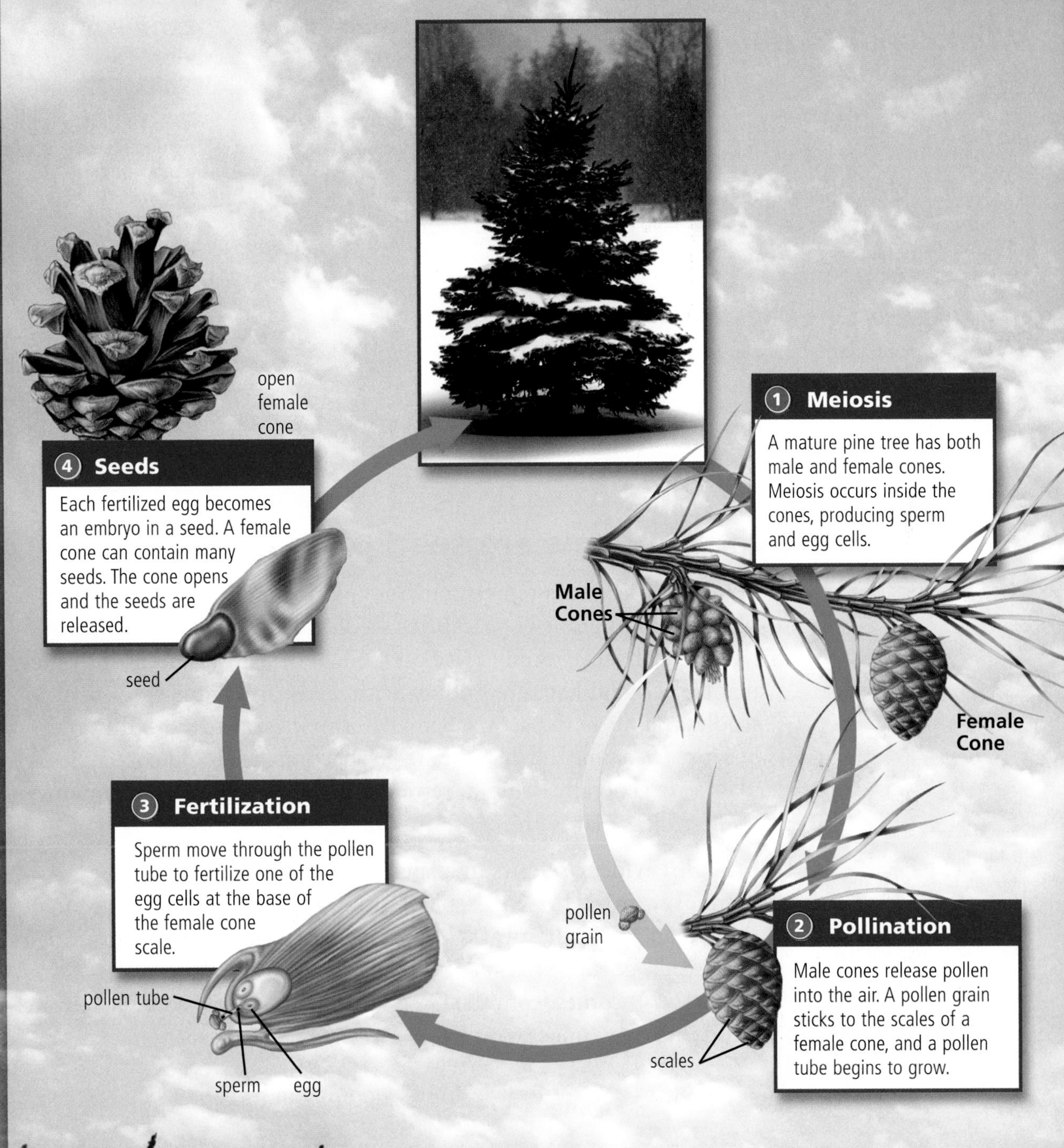

1 Meiosis
A mature pine tree has both male and female cones. Meiosis occurs inside the cones, producing sperm and egg cells.
Male Cones
Female Cone
2 Pollination
Male cones release pollen into the air. A pollen grain sticks to the scales of a female cone, and a pollen tube begins to grow.
pollen grain
scales
3 Fertilization
Sperm move through the pollen tube to fertilize one of the egg cells at the base of the female cone scale.
pollen tube
sperm
egg
4 Seeds
Each fertilized egg becomes an embryo in a seed. A female cone can contain many seeds. The cone opens and the seeds are released.
seed
open female cone

**READING VISUALS** Use the definition of a cycle to predict what happens after seeds are released from pinecones.

# INVESTIGATE Pinecones

## *What conditions make a pinecone open?*

**PROCEDURE**

1. Place your pinecone in the beaker of water. Observe any changes that take place. Leave the cone in the water until the changes stop.
2. Remove the cone from the water and place it on a paper towel to dry. Observe any changes that take place as the cone dries.

**WHAT DO YOU THINK?**

- What did you observe when the cone was in the water?
- What happened when the cone dried out?

**CHALLENGE** Try this procedure on cones from different plant species.

**SKILL FOCUS**
Observing

**MATERIALS**
- dried, open pinecones
- beaker of water
- paper towels

**TIME**
20 minutes

## Gymnosperms are seed plants.

Pollen and seeds are reproductive adaptations. They did not appear in plants until millions of years after seedless plants such as mosses and ferns had already begun to live on land. Today, however, most of the plant species on Earth reproduce with seeds, and many species of seedless plants have become extinct. Some scientists think this is because over time Earth's climate has become drier and cooler. Seed plants are generally better at reproducing in dry, cool environments than seedless plants are.

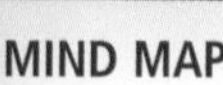

**MIND MAP**
Make a mind map for the main idea that *gymnosperms are seed plants.* Don't forget to include the definition of a gymnosperm in your mind map.

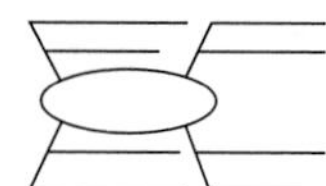

Fossil evidence shows that species of seed plants in the **gymnosperm** (JIHM-nuh-SPURM) group have existed on Earth for more than 250 million years. Plants classified as gymnosperms produce seeds, but the seeds are not enclosed in fruit. The word *gymnosperm* comes from the Greek words for "naked seed." There are four types of gymnosperms living on Earth today.

**CHECK YOUR READING** What is distinctive about gymnosperm seeds?

### Conifers

The conifers, or cone-bearing trees, are the type of gymnosperm you are probably most familiar with. The conifers include pine, fir, spruce, hemlock, cypress, and redwood trees. Many conifers are adapted for living in cold climates, where there is relatively little water available. Their leaves are needle-shaped and have a thick cuticle. This prevents the plant from losing much water to transpiration. Conifers can also keep their needles for several years, which means the plants can produce sugars all year.

Ginkgo trees like this one are gymnosperms that do not produce cones. Their seeds are exposed to the environment.

## Other Gymnosperms

The other types of living gymnosperms are cycads, gnetophytes (NEE-toh-fyts), and ginkgoes. These three types of gymnosperms appear to be quite different from one another. Cycads are palmlike plants that are found in tropical areas. They produce cones for seeds. Many cycads produce poisonous compounds. Gnetophytes are another type of tropical gymnosperm that produces cones. Chemicals taken from certain gnetophyte plants have been used to treat cold symptoms for thousands of years.

Ginkgoes are gymnosperms with fleshy seeds that hang from their branches. Ginkgoes are often grown in parks and along streets, but you will not often see them with seeds. People avoid putting male and female ginkgo trees together because the seed coat of a ginkgo produces a particularly foul smell.

# 3.3 Review

### KEY CONCEPTS

1. How are seeds different from spores?
2. How does fertilization in seed plants differ from fertilization in seedless plants?
3. Seed plants are found in environments where seedless plants are not. List at least two reasons why.

### CRITICAL THINKING

4. **Compare and Contrast** What is the difference between a spore and a pollen grain? In what ways are spores and pollen grains similar?
5. **Hypothesize** Gymnosperms produce a lot of pollen, and most of it blows away, never fertilizing an egg. Why might this characteristic help a plant species survive?

### CHALLENGE

6. **Analyze** Like all plants, a pine tree has a two-part life cycle. Look again at the diagram on page 101, and then make a new version of it in your notebook. Your version should show where in the life cycle each generation begins and ends. Hint: reread the text on page 100.

# CHAPTER INVESTIGATION

## Which Seeds Will Grow?

**OVERVIEW AND PURPOSE** Many of the foods you eat come from seed plants. What seeds or parts of seed plants have you eaten lately? What seeds can you find outside in your neighborhood? What conditions do the seeds from these plants need to grow? In this investigation, you will

- plant a variety of seeds
- observe differences in germination and growth among seeds planted in similar conditions

### Problem

Write It Up

How successfully will a variety of seeds germinate in conditions that can be provided in your classroom?

### Hypothesize

Read through all of the steps of the procedure and then write a hypothesis. Your hypothesis should explain what you think will happen when your class plants its collection of seeds and observes their growth for at least ten days. Your hypothesis should take the form of an "If . . . , then . . . , because . . ." statement.

**MATERIALS**
- assorted seeds
- potting soil
- paper cups
- water
- paper towels
- labels

### Procedure

1. Make a data table in your **Science Notebook** like the one shown on page 105.

2. Examine the seeds you will use in this investigation. Try to identify them. Record your observations in the data table.

step 2

3 Use the materials provided to plant the seeds. Remember that the planting conditions should be the same for each of the seeds. Label each container.

4 Decide where you will keep your seeds while they are growing and how often you will check and water them. Be sure to keep the growing conditions for all of the seeds the same. Wash your hands.

5 Observe your seeds for at least ten days. Check and water them according to the plan you made.

## Observe and Analyze

Write It Up

1. In your **Science Notebook**, draw and label a diagram showing how you planted the seeds, the materials you used, and the place where they are being kept.
2. Each time you check on your seeds, record your observations in your data table.
3. **IDENTIFY** Which seeds germinated? What differences in growth and development did you observe in the different types of seeds?

## Conclude

Write It Up

1. **INTERPRET** Compare your results with your hypothesis. Did your data support your hypothesis?
2. **INFER** What patterns or similarities did you notice in the seeds that grew most successfully?
3. **IDENTIFY LIMITS** What unexpected factors or problems might have affected your results?
4. **APPLY** Use your experience to tell a young child how to grow a plant from a seed. What type of seeds would you suggest? Write directions for planting and caring for seeds that a younger child could understand.

## INVESTIGATE Further

**CHALLENGE** Some seeds need special conditions, such as warmth or a certain amount of moisture, before they will germinate. Design an experiment in which you test just one type of seed in a variety of conditions to learn which results in the most growth. Include a hypothesis, a materials list, and a procedure when you write up your experiment.

Which Seeds Will Grow?

Table 1. Observations of Seeds

| Seed | Observations |
|---|---|
| Kidney bean | sprouted March 3 |
| Popcorn | |
| Sunflower | |
| Rice | |
| | |

EXTREME SCIENCE



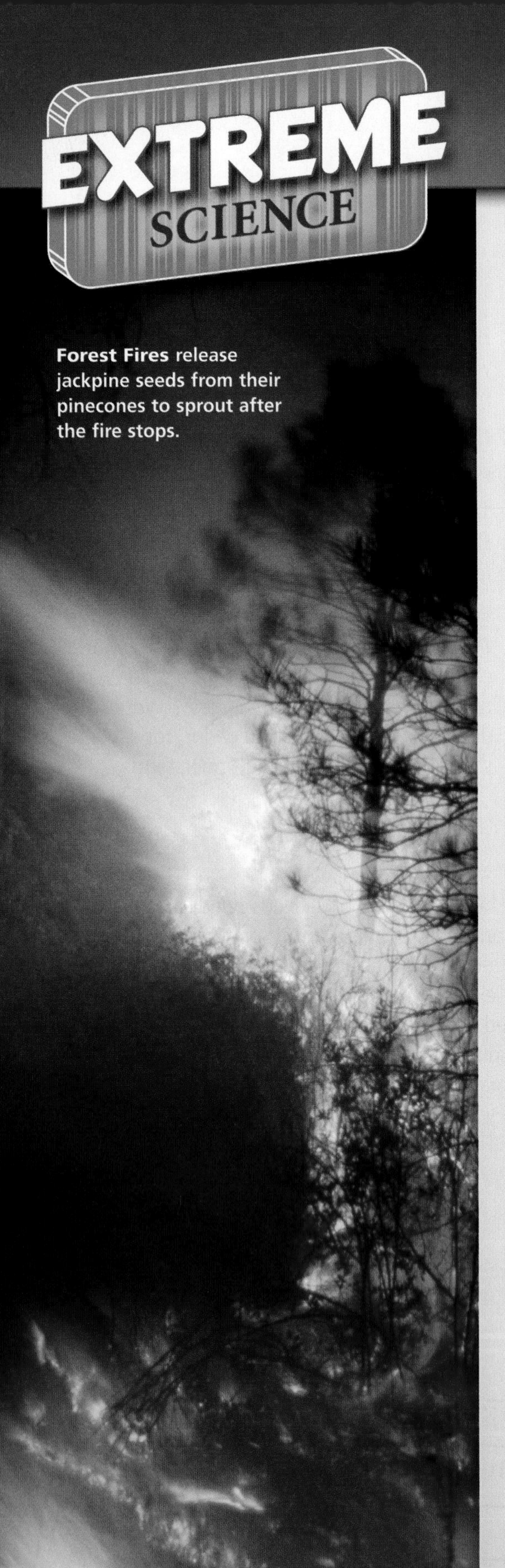

**Forest Fires** release jackpine seeds from their pinecones to sprout after the fire stops.

# Seed Survivors

Not only can seeds survive harsh conditions, but sometimes harsh conditions actually make it possible for seeds to grow into new plants.

## Forest Fires

Jackpine seeds are locked inside pinecones by a sticky resin. The pinecones survive hot forest fires that melt the resin and release the seeds. In fact, without the high temperatures from fires, the seeds would never get the chance to germinate and grow into jackpine trees.

## Bomb Damage

In 1940, during World War II, the British Museum was firebombed. People poured water over the burning museum and its contents. In the museum were silk-tree seeds collected in China and brought to the museum in 1793. After the firebombing 147 years later, the seeds sprouted.

## Dodo Digestion

Seeds of Calvaria trees, which live on the island of Mauritius have very hard outer shells. The outer shell must be softened before the seeds can sprout. Hundreds of years ago, dodo birds ate the Calvaria fruits. Stones and acids in the birds' digestive tract helped soften the seed. After the dodo birds deposited them, the softened seeds would sprout. Dodo birds went extinct in 1681, and no young Calvaria trees grew. In 1975, only about 13 Calvaria trees remained. Recently, scientists have used artificial means to grind and break down the Calvaria seed cover and foster new tree growth.

## EXPLORE

1. **INFER** Why do you think the silk tree seeds sprouted? Think about how the seeds' environment changed.
2. **CHALLENGE** If you were a scientist who wanted to help the Calvaria trees make a comeback, what methods might you try for softening the seeds?

Find out more about extreme seeds.

KEY CONCEPT

# Many plants reproduce with flowers and fruit.

**BEFORE, you learned**

- Seed plants do not have swimming sperm
- Gymnosperms reproduce with pollen and seeds

**NOW, you will learn**

- About flowers and fruit
- About the relationship between animals and flowering plants
- How humans need plants

**VOCABULARY**

**angiosperm** p. 107
**flower** p. 108
**fruit** p. 108

**EXPLORE Fruit**

### What do you find inside fruit?

**PROCEDURE**

1. Place the apple on a paper towel. Carefully cut the apple in half. Find the seeds.
2. Place the pea pod on a paper towel. Carefully split open the pea pod. Find the seeds.
3. Both the apple and the pea pod are examples of fruits. In your notebook, draw a diagram of the two fruits you examined. Label the fruit and the seeds.

**MATERIALS**

- apple
- paper towel
- plastic knife
- pea pod

**WHAT DO YOU THINK?**

- How many seeds did you find?
- What part of an apple do you eat? What part of a pea?

## Angiosperms have flowers and fruit.

**MIND MAP**
Make a mind map diagram for the main idea: *Angiosperms have flowers and fruit.*

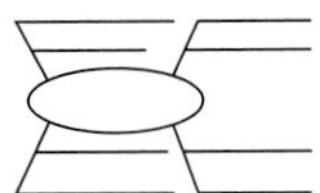

Have you ever eaten peanuts, grapes, strawberries, or squash? Do you like the way roses smell, or how spider plants look? All of these plants are angiosperms, or flowering plants. An **angiosperm** (AN-jee-uh-SPURM) is a seed plant that produces flowers and fruit. Most of the species of plants living now are angiosperms. The grasses at your local park are angiosperms. Most trees whose leaves change color in the fall are angiosperms.

The sperm of a flowering plant are protected in a pollen grain and do not need an outside source of water to reach the eggs. The eggs develop into embryos that are enclosed within seeds. Both generations of angiosperms and gymnosperms occur within a single plant.

The reproductive cycles of angiosperms and gymnosperms are alike in many ways. Both angiosperms and gymnosperms have separate male and female reproductive structures. In some species, male and female parts grow on the same plant, but in others there are separate male and female plants.

**VOCABULARY**
Remember to add word triangles for *flower* and *fruit* to your notebook.

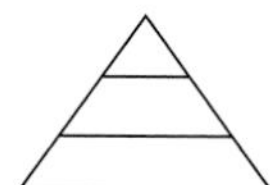

An important difference between angiosperms and gymnosperms is that in angiosperms, the sperm and egg cells are contained in a flower. The **flower** is the reproductive structure of an angiosperm. Egg cells develop in a part of the flower called an ovary. Once the eggs are fertilized and the seed or seeds form, the ovary wall thickens and the ovary becomes a **fruit.**

**CHECK YOUR READING** What reproductive structures do angiosperms have that gymnosperms do not?

The diagram on page 109 shows the life cycle of one type of angiosperm, a cherry tree. As you read the numbered paragraphs below, follow the numbers on the labels in the diagram.

1. The reproductive structures of a cherry tree are its flowers. The anther is the male part. The pistil is the female part. Meiosis in the anther produces sperm cells enclosed within pollen grains. Meiosis in the ovary of the pistil produces egg cells.
2. The pollen grains are released. When a pollen grain is caught on the pistil of a flower, a pollen tube starts to grow. Within the ovary one of the egg cells matures.
3. Fertilization occurs when the pollen tube reaches the ovary and a sperm fertilizes the egg. The fertilized egg grows into an embryo and develops a seed coat. The ovary develops into a fruit.
4. The fruit may fall to the ground or it may be eaten by animals. If the seed inside lands in a place where it can germinate and survive, it will grow into a new cherry tree.

**CHECK YOUR READING** What is the flower's role in the sexual reproduction of an angiosperm?

Many flowering plants also reproduce asexually. New shoots can grow out from the parent plant. For example, strawberries and spider plants can reproduce by sending out shoots called runners. New plants grow from the runners, getting nutrients from the parent until the roots of the new plant are established. Plants can spread quickly this way. This form of asexual reproduction allows plants to reproduce even when conditions are not right for the germination of seeds.

## Life Cycle of a Cherry Tree

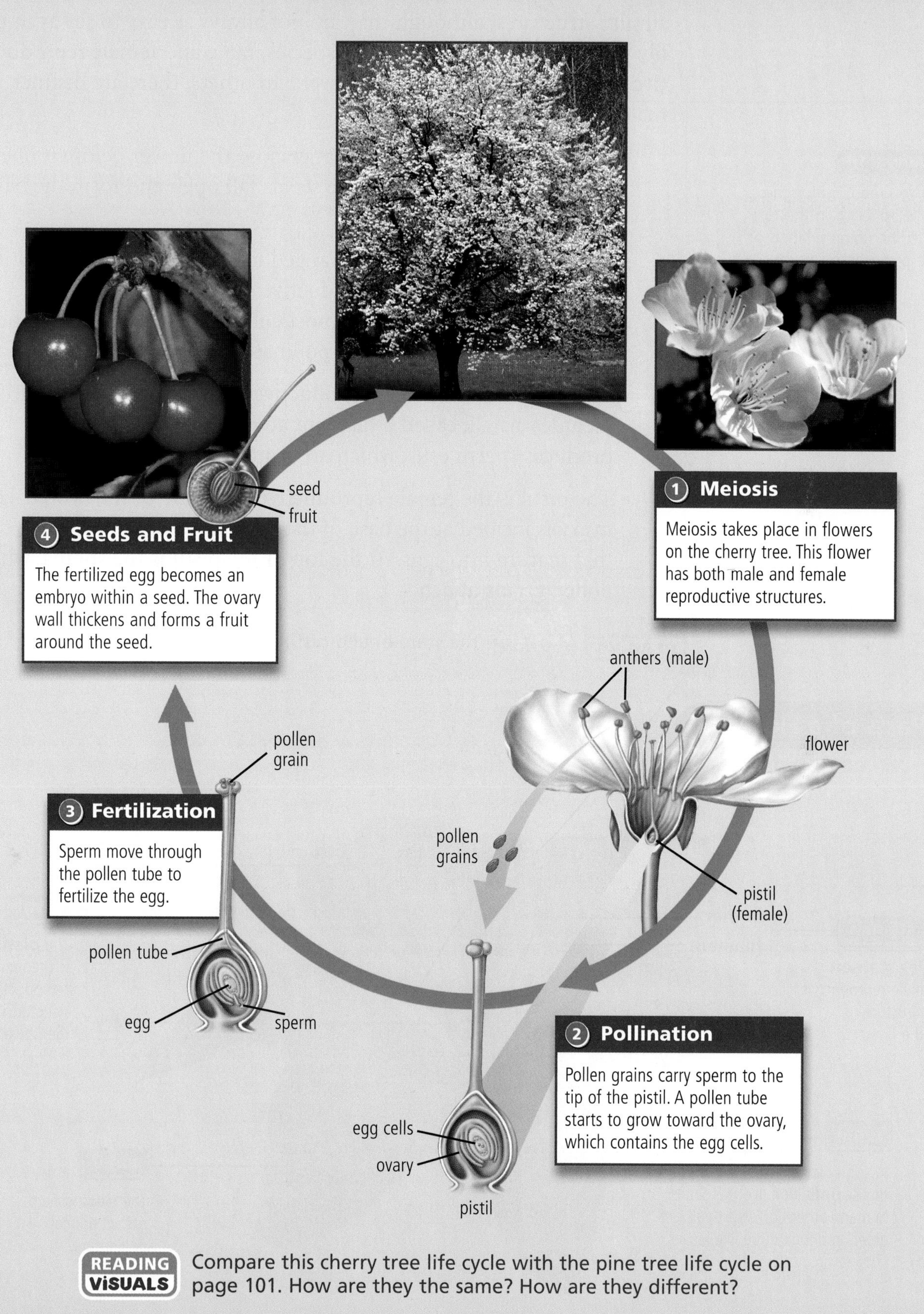

seed
fruit
4 Seeds and Fruit
The fertilized egg becomes an embryo within a seed. The ovary wall thickens and forms a fruit around the seed.
1 Meiosis
Meiosis takes place in flowers on the cherry tree. This flower has both male and female reproductive structures.
anthers (male)
flower
pollen grain
3 Fertilization
Sperm move through the pollen tube to fertilize the egg.
pollen grains
pistil (female)
pollen tube
egg
sperm
2 Pollination
Pollen grains carry sperm to the tip of the pistil. A pollen tube starts to grow toward the ovary, which contains the egg cells.
egg cells
ovary
pistil

**READING VISUALS** Compare this cherry tree life cycle with the pine tree life cycle on page 101. How are they the same? How are they different?

## Flowers

Flowers vary in size, shape, color, and fragrance. They all have some similar structures, although they are not always as easy to see as in the lily pictured below. Also, in some species, male and female reproductive structures are on different flowers. In others, there are distinct male and female plants.

**READING TIP**

As you read, match the bulleted items in the text with the colored labels on the photograph below.

- Sepals are leafy structures that enclose the flower before it opens. When the flower blooms, the sepals fall open and form the base of the flower.
- Petals are leafy structures arranged in a circle around the pistil. The petals open as the reproductive structures of the plant mature. Petals are often the most colorful part of a flower. The petals help to attract animal pollinators.
- The stamen is the male reproductive structure of a flower. It includes a stalk called a filament and the anther. The anther produces sperm cells, which are contained in pollen grains.
- The pistil is the female reproductive structure of the flower. The ovary is located at the base of the pistil and contains the egg cells that mature into eggs. At the top of the pistil is the stigma, where pollen grains attach.

**CHECK YOUR READING** What are the stamen and pistil?

### Parts of a Flower

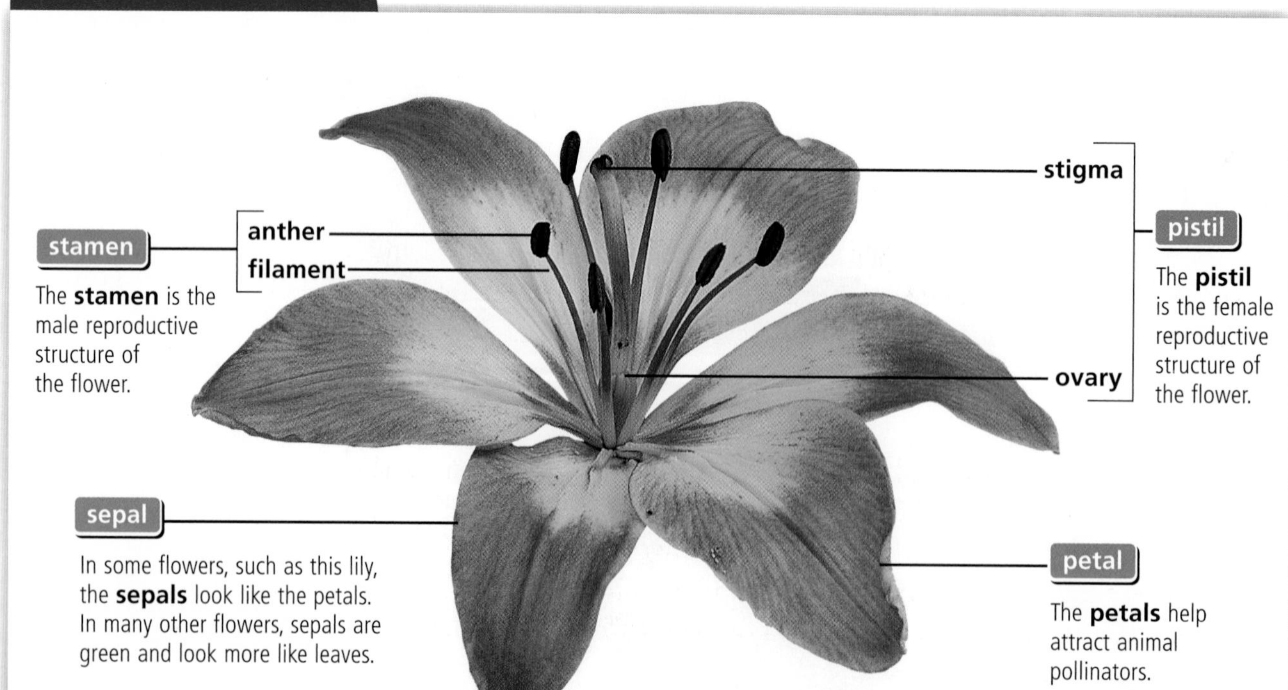
stigma
pistil
The **pistil** is the female reproductive structure of the flower.
ovary
anther
filament
stamen
The **stamen** is the male reproductive structure of the flower.
sepal
In some flowers, such as this lily, the **sepals** look like the petals. In many other flowers, sepals are green and look more like leaves.
petal
The **petals** help attract animal pollinators.

# INVESTIGATE Flower Parts

## What parts of a flower can you identify?

**SKILL FOCUS**
Observing

**MATERIALS**
- assorted flowers
- hand lens

**TIME**
15 minutes

**PROCEDURE**

1. Examine the flower you are given. Try to notice as many details as you can. Draw a diagram of the flower in your notebook and label its parts.
2. Carefully take your flower apart. Sort the parts. Draw and label one example of each part in your notebook.

**WHAT DO YOU THINK?**

- Which of the parts of a flower labeled in the diagram on page 110 did you find in your flower?
- Based on your experience, what would you look for if you were trying to decide whether a structure on an unfamiliar plant was a flower?

### Fruit

A fruit is a ripened plant ovary. Some ovaries contain more than one seed, such as an apple. Some contain only one seed, like a cherry. Apples and cherries are called fleshy fruits, because they have juicy flesh. The corn you eat as corn on the cob is a fleshy fruit. There are also dry fruits. Peanuts, walnuts, and sunflowers are dry fruits. The shells of dry fruits help protect the seeds. Some dry fruits, like the winged fruit of a maple tree or the feathery tip of a dandelion seed, have structures that allow the seeds to be carried by the wind.

## Animals spread both pollen and seeds.

Reproduction in many types of flowering plants includes interactions between plants and animals. The plants are a source of food for the animal. The animals provide a way to transport pollen and seeds. As they eat, animals move pollen from flower to flower and seeds from place to place.

Have you ever watched a honeybee collect nectar from a flower? Nectar is a sweet sugary liquid located at the bottom of the flower. As the bee crawls around in the flower, reaching down for the nectar, it rubs against the anthers and picks up pollen grains. When the bee travels to another flower, some of that pollen rubs off onto the pistil of the second flower.

How do bees benefit from the flowers they pollinate?

An animal that pollinates a flower is called a pollinator. Bees and other insects are among the most important pollinators. Bees depend on nectar for food, and they collect pollen to feed their young. Bees recognize the colors, odors, and shapes of flowers. Thousands of species of plants are pollinated by bees, including sunflowers and lavender.

**READING TIP**

The word *pollinate* means "to transfer pollen from an anther to a stigma." Note the differences in spelling between *pollen* and *pollinate, pollinator.*

The relationship between angiosperms and their pollinators can be highly specialized. Sometimes the nectar is located in a tube-shaped flower. Only certain animals, for example hummingbirds with long, slender beaks, can pollinate those flowers. Some flowers bloom at night. These flowers attract moths and bats as pollinators. Night-blooming flowers are usually pale, which means they are visible at night. Also, they may give off a strong scent to attract animal pollinators.

The advantage of animal pollination is that the pollen goes to where it is needed most. The pollen collected by a bee has a much better chance of being brought to another flower. By comparison, pollen grains that are spread by the wind are blown in all directions. Each grain has only a small chance of landing on another flower. Wind-pollinated plants produce a lot more pollen than plants that are pollinated by animals.

What is the advantage of animal pollination over wind pollination?

Compare the different ways seeds are dispersed.

The fruits produced by angiosperms help to spread the seeds they contain. Some seeds, like dandelion and maple seeds, are carried by the wind. Many seeds are scattered by fruit-eating animals. The seeds go through the animal's digestive system and are eventually deposited on the ground with the animal's waste. Wide scattering of seeds ensures that some seeds will land in an area with enough resources and room to grow.

Animals eat fleshy fruit and distribute the seeds with their waste.

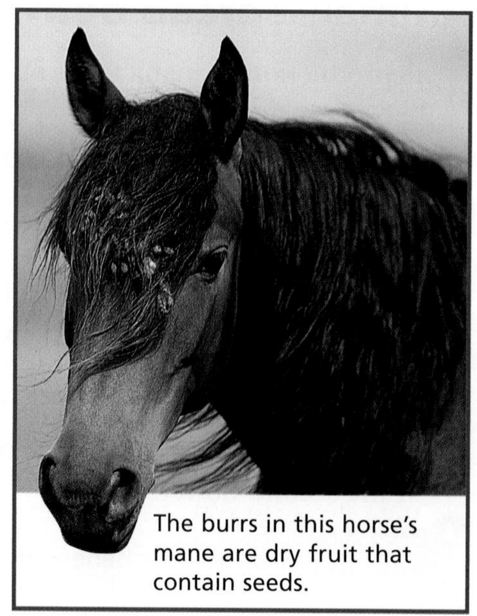

The burrs in this horse's mane are dry fruit that contain seeds.

Animals also help to scatter some types of dry fruits—not by eating them, but by catching them on their fur. Have you ever tried to pet a dog that has run through a grassy field? You might have noticed burrs stuck in the animal's fur. The seeds of many grasses and wildflowers produce dry fruits that are covered with spines or have pointed barbs. Seeds protected by these types of dry fruits stick to fur. The seeds travel along with the animal until the animal rubs them off.

## Humans depend on plants for their survival.

Without plants, humans and all other animals would not be able to live on Earth. After plants adapted to life on land, it became possible for animals to live on land as well. Land animals rely on plants for food and oxygen. Many animals live in or near plants. Plants also supply materials humans use every day.

### Food and Oxygen

All organisms must have energy to live. For animals, that energy comes from food. Plants, especially angiosperms, are the ultimate source of food for all land animals. Plants capture energy from the Sun to make sugars and other carbohydrates. Those same energy-rich materials are then consumed by animals as food. Even animals that eat other animals depend on plants for survival, because plants may provide food for the animals they eat.

Photosynthesis, the process that plants use to produce sugars and carbohydrates, also produces oxygen. The oxygen in the air you breathe is the product of the photosynthetic activity of plants and algae. Animals, including humans, need oxygen to release the energy stored in food.

Plants capture light energy from the Sun and store it in sugars and other carbohydrates.

### Energy Resources and Soil

Plants are an important source of many natural resources. Natural gas and coal are energy resources that formed deep underground from the remains of plants and other organisms. Natural gas and coal are important fuels for many purposes, including the generation of electricity.

Even the soil under your feet is a natural resource associated with plants. Plant roots can break down rock into smaller and smaller particles to form soil. When plants die, their bodies decay and add richness to the soil.

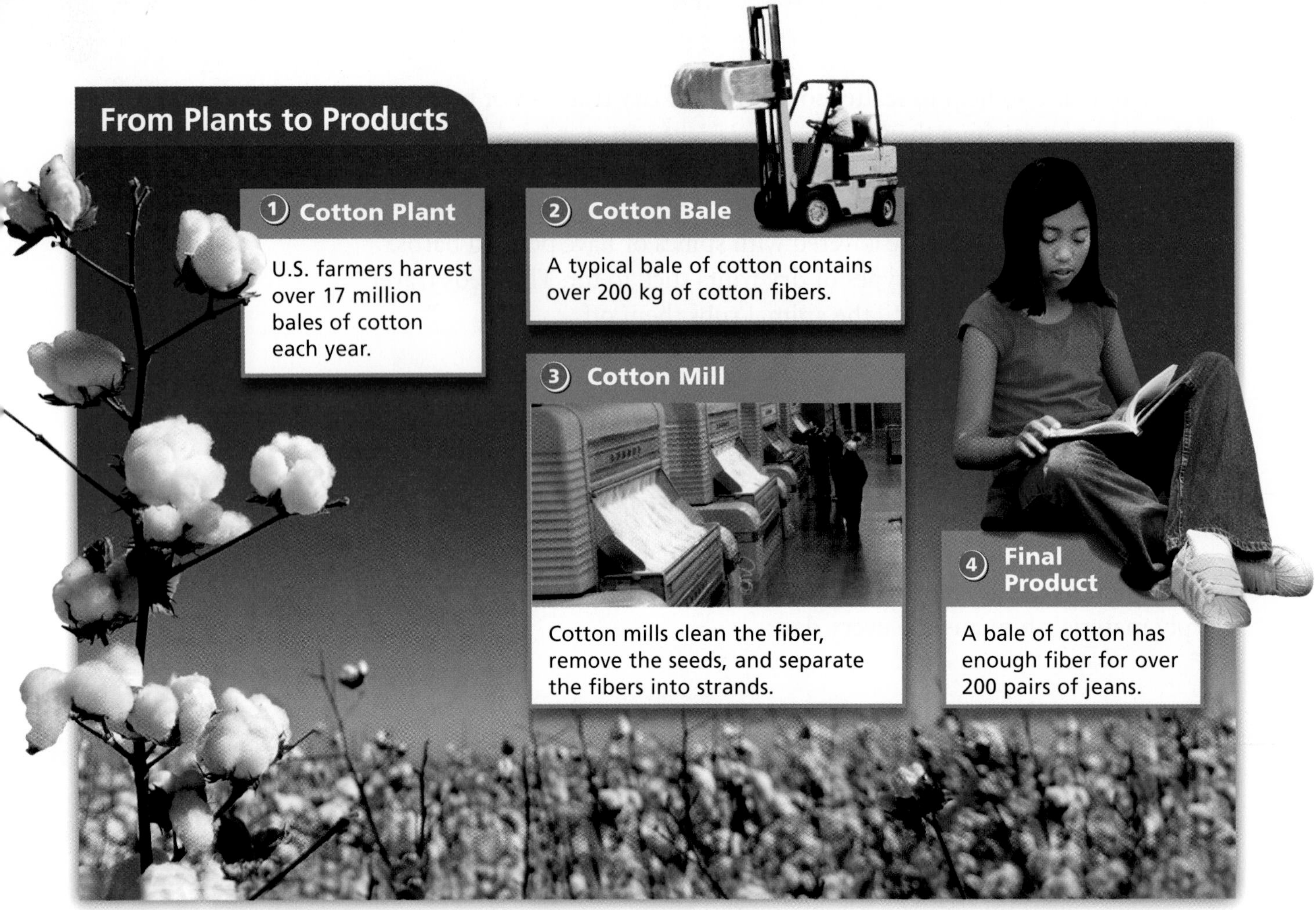

## From Plants to Products

**1 Cotton Plant**

U.S. farmers harvest over 17 million bales of cotton each year.

**2 Cotton Bale**

A typical bale of cotton contains over 200 kg of cotton fibers.

**3 Cotton Mill**

Cotton mills clean the fiber, remove the seeds, and separate the fibers into strands.

**4 Final Product**

A bale of cotton has enough fiber for over 200 pairs of jeans.

### Other Products

Plant materials are part of many products people use every day. Plants provide the wood used to build houses and the wood pulp used to make paper for books like the one you are reading. The cotton in blue jeans comes from plants. So do many dyes that are used to add color to fabrics. Aspirin and many other medicines made by drug companies today are based on chemicals originally found in plants.

**KEY CONCEPTS**

1. How do flowers relate to fruit?
2. How are animals involved in the life cycles of some flowering plants?
3. List three ways that humans depend upon plants.

**CRITICAL THINKING**

4. **Predict** If you observed three plants in a forest—a moss, a fern, and a flowering plant—which would have the most insects nearby? Why?
5. **Connect** Draw an apple like the one shown on page 107. Label three parts of the fruit and explain from which part of an apple flower each part grew.

**CHALLENGE**

6. **Synthesize** There are more species of flowering plants on Earth than species of mosses, ferns, or cone-bearing plants such as pine trees. How do you think the different ways spores, pollen, and seeds are spread affect the genetic diversity of different types of plants? Explain your reasoning.

## SKILL: USING GRIDS TO ESTIMATE

Click on Math Tutorial for more help with perimeter and area.

# Chloroplast Math

You can't count the number of chloroplasts in a leaf very easily, but you can estimate the number. For example, if you know the number of chloroplasts in a small area, you can estimate the number of chloroplasts in a whole leaf.

### Example

Suppose you are studying how lilacs make food from sunlight. You read that there are 50 million chloroplasts for every square centimeter of a leaf. You want to know the number in a whole leaf.

**(1)** Cover the leaf with centimeter grid paper.

**(2)** Count the number of whole squares covering the leaf.
7

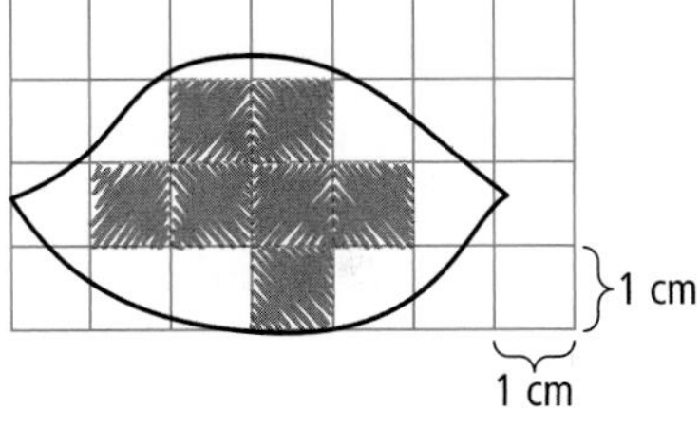


**(3)** Match pairs or sets of partly covered squares, that add up to a whole square.
7 + 5 = 12

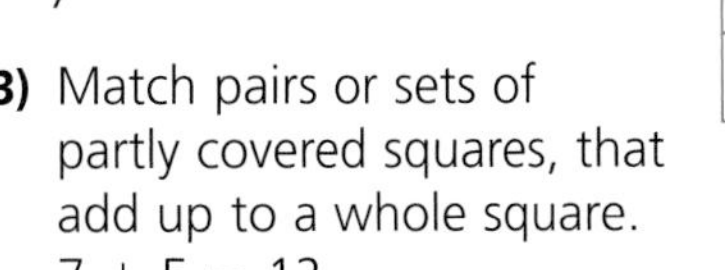

**(4)** Add on any remaining 0.5 (half), 0.025 (quarter), or 0.75 (three-quarters) of a square.
12 + .5 = 12.5

**(5)** Finally, multiply the number of squares by the number of chloroplasts in one square.

**ANSWER** 50,000,000 × 12.5 = 625,000,000.

**Give estimates for the following amounts.**

1. Trace the beech leaf shown on this page onto a sheet of centimeter grid paper. What is the leaf's approximate area in $cm^2$?
2. About how many chloroplasts are in this beech leaf?
3. A eucalyptus leaf is long and thin. Suppose a healthy leaf is 1.5 centimeters wide and 6 centimeters long. Estimate its area. Hint: Make a sketch.

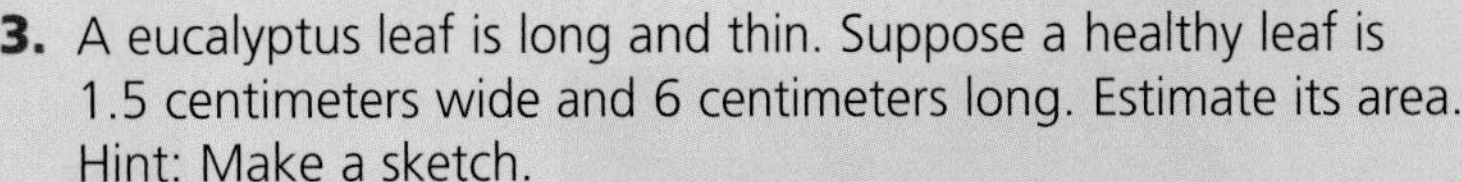

4. What is the approximate number of chloroplasts in the eucalyptus leaf described above?

**CHALLENGE** Collect two leaves. Trace the leaves on centimeter grid paper. Label each tracing with its name, estimated area, and its approximate number of chloroplasts.

# 3 Chapter Review

## the BIG idea

**Plants are a diverse group of organisms that live in many land environments.**

## KEY CONCEPTS SUMMARY

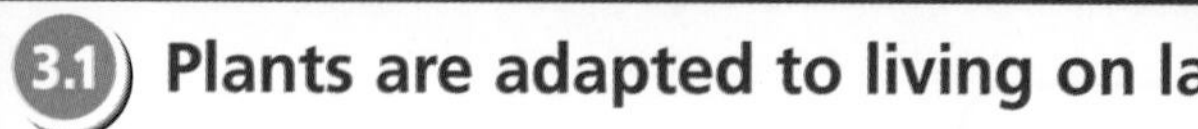

### 3.1 Plants are adapted to living on land.

All plants share common characteristics. The parts of a plant are specialized to get water and nutrients from the soil, gases from the air, and energy from the Sun. Plants have tissues, organs, and organ systems.

**VOCABULARY**
**vascular system** p. 87
**transpiration** p. 88

### 3.2 Most mosses and ferns live in moist environments.

The ancestors of present-day mosses and ferns were among the first land plants. Mosses are small nonvascular plants. Ferns are larger vascular plants. Both reproduce with spores and need moisture for a sperm to reach an egg.

### 3.3 Seeds and pollen are reproductive adaptations.

**Gymnosperms**, such as the pine tree, reproduce with **pollen** and seeds.

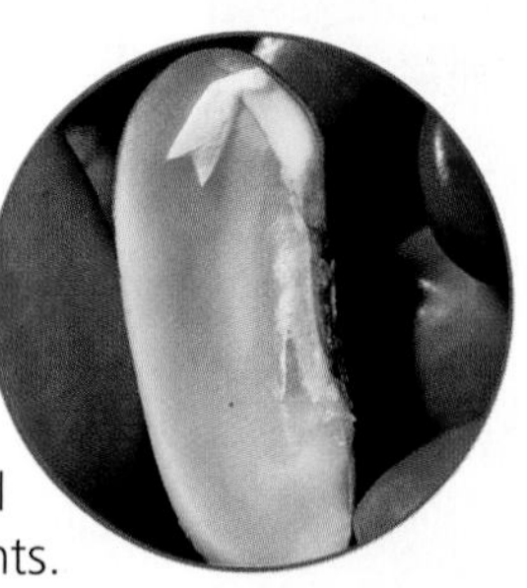

**Seeds** provide protection for the young plant as well as a supply of nutrients.

**VOCABULARY**
**seed** p. 98
**embryo** p. 98
**germination** p. 99
**pollen** p. 100
**gymnosperm** p. 102

### 3.4 Many plants reproduce with flowers and fruit.

**Angiosperms** use flowers and fruit to reproduce. **Flowers** produce pollen and contain the plant's reproductive structures.

**Fruit** develops after pollination and contains seeds. Animals eat fruit and transport seeds to new locations.

**VOCABULARY**
**angiosperm** p. 107
**flower** p. 108
**fruit** p. 108

## Reviewing Vocabulary

*Write a statement describing how the terms in each pair are related to each other.*

1. transpiration, cuticle
2. spores, seeds
3. seed, embryo
4. flower, fruit

*The table below shows Greek (G.) and Latin (L.) words that are roots of words used in this chapter.*

| | |
|---|---|
| angeion (G.) | vessel or holder |
| gymnos (G.) | naked |
| sperma (G.) | seed |
| germinatus (L.) | sprout |
| pollen (L.) | fine flour |

*Describe how these word roots relate to the definitions of the following words.*

5. angiosperm
6. gymnosperm
7. germination
8. pollen

## Reviewing Key Concepts

**Multiple Choice** *Choose the letter of the best answer.*

9. Which of these is a characteristic of only some plants?
   a. They produce sugars.
   b. They are multicellular.
   c. They have a vascular system.
   d. They have a two-stage life cycle.

10. Which part of a plant anchors it in the soil?
    a. shoot system
    b. root system
    c. vascular system
    d. growth tissue

11. Which plant system transports water to different parts of the plant?
    a. vascular
    b. leaf
    c. stomata
    d. cuticle

12. Which part of a leaf does *not* allow transpiration?
    a. stomata
    b. cell wall
    c. stem
    d. cuticle

13. Which of these structures do mosses and ferns reproduce with?
    a. seeds
    b. growth tissue
    c. spores
    d. pollen

14. How are mosses different from ferns, pine trees, and flowering plants?
    a. Mosses reproduce through sexual reproduction.
    b. Mosses need moisture to reproduce.
    c. Mosses produce sugar through photosynthesis.
    d. Mosses have no vascular tissue.

15. What do seeds have that spores and pollen do not?
    a. a supply of nutrients
    b. a reproductive cell
    c. a protective covering
    d. a way to be transported

**Short Answer** *Write a short answer to each question.*

16. What are three ways plants are important to humans?

17. Explain how the bat in these photographs is interacting with the flower. How might the activity benefit the plant?

## Thinking Critically

*The next four questions refer to the labeled parts of the diagram of the leaf below.*

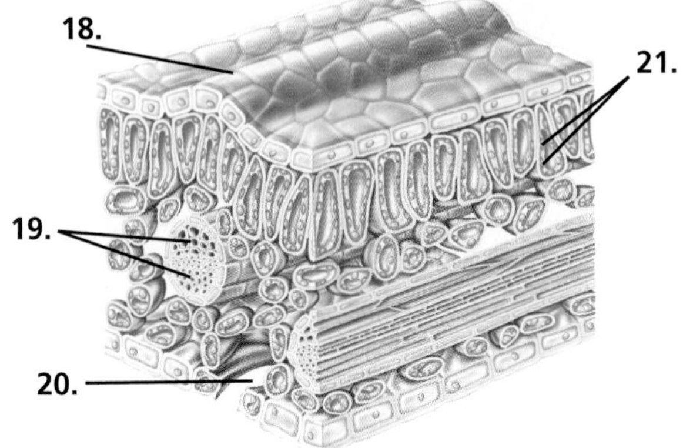


18. **CLASSIFY** Identify the layer that covers a leaf. What function does it serve, and why is that function important?

19. **CLASSIFY** What are the two tissues shown here, how do they function, and what system do they belong to?

20. **PREDICT** Identify the structure and predict what would happen to this structure if the air around the plant was very hot and dry.

21. **ANALYZE** What are these structures? What is their function? What are the advantages of having more of them at the top of the leaf than at the bottom?

22. **COMMUNICATE** A leaf is made up of different tissues and specialized cells. What is the main function of a leaf? How does the organization of tissues and cells in a leaf help it to carry out this function? Include the following terms in your answer: *sunlight*, *energy*, *oxygen gas*, *carbon dioxide gas*, *water*, and *sugar*.

23. **CLASSIFY** What is the name of the group of plants pine trees belong to? What group of plants do cherry trees belong to? Which of the two groups is more widespread?

24. **CONNECT** You or someone you know may be allergic to pollen that is in the air during some plants' growing seasons. What is the advantage of a plant producing so much pollen?

25. **SUMMARIZE** Copy and complete the table below, indicating which reproductive structures are part of the life cycles of mosses, ferns, pine trees, and cherry trees. The first row is done.

| | moss | fern | pine tree | cherry tree |
|---|---|---|---|---|
| sperm | ✓ | ✓ | ✓ | ✓ |
| egg | | | | |
| pollen | | | | |
| seed | | | | |
| cone | | | | |
| flower | | | | |
| fruit | | | | |

26. **SYNTHESIZE** Plants were among the first organisms to live on land. Name at least two ways that plants made land habitable for animals. In what way did animals help plants to spread farther onto the land?

27. **INFER** Describe how a plant might reproduce asexually. Explain one advantage and one disadvantage asexual reproduction might have for the plant you described.

## the BIG idea

28. **SUMMARIZE** Look again at the photograph on pages 82-83. Now that you have finished the chapter, how would you change or add details to your answer to the question on the photograph?

29. **SYNTHESIZE** Think of three different types of plants that you have seen. Use what you know about those plants as supporting evidence in a paragraph you write on one of these topics:

*Plants are a diverse group of organisms.*

*Plants share common characteristics.*

## UNIT PROJECTS

Check your schedule for your unit project. How are you doing? Be sure that you have placed data or notes from your research in your project folder.

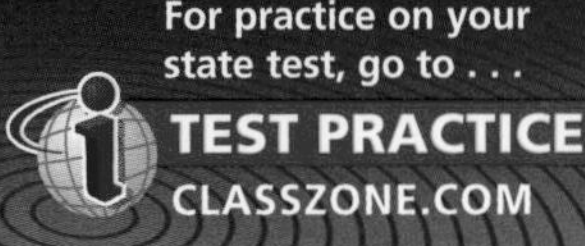


## Analyzing Data

A pesticide is a material that kills pests, such as insects. A plant specialist wants to know if a new pesticide has any effect on the production of oranges. Grove A is planted using the same pesticide that was used in previous years. The new pesticide is used in grove B. Both groves have the same number of orange trees. The bar graph shows the data for one season.

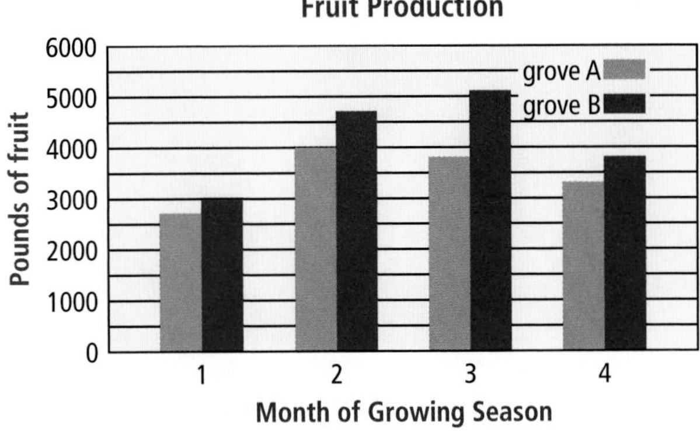


*Choose the letter of the best response.*

**1.** About how many pounds of fruit were grown in grove A during month 1 of the growing season?

**a.** about 2000 lb
**b.** about 2700 lb
**c.** about 3000 lb
**d.** about 3500 lb

**2.** During which month in the growing season was the most fruit produced?

**a.** month 1
**b.** month 2
**c.** month 3
**d.** month 4

**3.** About how many pounds of fruit were produced altogether by both groves in month 2?

**a.** about 4000 lb
**b.** about 4700 lb
**c.** about 5000 lb
**d.** about 8700 lb

**4.** Comparing the production in both groves, during which month was there the least amount of difference in the number of pounds of fruit produced?

**a.** month 1
**b.** month 2
**c.** month 3
**d.** month 4

**5.** Based on the data in the graph, what might the plant specialist conclude about the effectiveness of the new pesticide used in grove B?

**a.** The pesticide is effective only after three months of growth.
**b.** The pesticide does not have any effect on orange production.
**c.** The pesticide used in grove A is more effective than the pesticide used in grove B.
**d.** The pesticide increases the overall production of oranges throughout the growing season.

## Extended Response

**6.** Pesticides are intended to kill insects that harm the growth of a plant. However, not all insects are harmful. Insects often pollinate the flowers of fruit trees. Pollination leads to fertilization of the flower, and fruit grows from the fertilized flower. Describe what might happen if a pesticide kills insects that are pollinators. What effect might such a pesticide have on the flowers of the plant and on its fruit?

**7.** Pesticides are only one factor that affect the growth of plants and the number of flowers or fruit the plant produces. Write a paragraph that names some other factors that may affect plant growth. Include environmental factors and factors that are controlled by humans.

CHAPTER

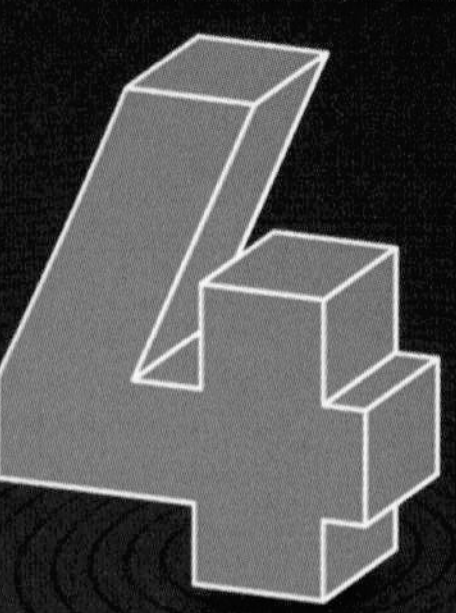

# Invertebrate Animals

## the BIG idea

Invertebrate animals have a variety of body plans and adaptations.

How does this jellyfish find food and eat?

## Key Concepts

SECTION

**Most animals are invertebrates.**
Learn about sponges and other invertebrates.

SECTION

**Cnidarians and worms have different body plans.**
Learn how the body plans of cnidarians are different from those of worms.

SECTION

**Most mollusks have shells, and echinoderms have spiny skeletons.**
Learn about how mollusks and echinoderms meet their needs.

SECTION

**Arthropods have exoskeletons and joints.**
Learn about insects, crustaceans, and arachnids.

**Internet Preview**

CLASSZONE.COM

Chapter 4 online resources: Content Review, Visualization, four Resource Centers, Math Tutorial, Test Practice

## Worm-Watching

Find a worm and observe it for a while in its natural environment. How much can you learn about how a worm meets its needs by watching it for a short time? Record your observations in your notebook.

**Observe and Think**
What body parts can you identify on a worm? How would you describe a worm's activities and behavior?

## Insects and You

Think about times when you have seen or noticed insects. Make a list of your experiences in your notebook. Then, start keeping a list of all the insects you see for the next week. How long do you think this list will be?

**Observe and Think** How many different types of insects did you see? Where did you see them? What characteristics do you think insects share?

## Internet Activity: Invertebrate Diversity

Go to **ClassZone.com** to learn more about different types of invertebrates.

**Observe and Think**
Of every 20 animal species on Earth, 19 are invertebrates. How many types of invertebrates can you name?

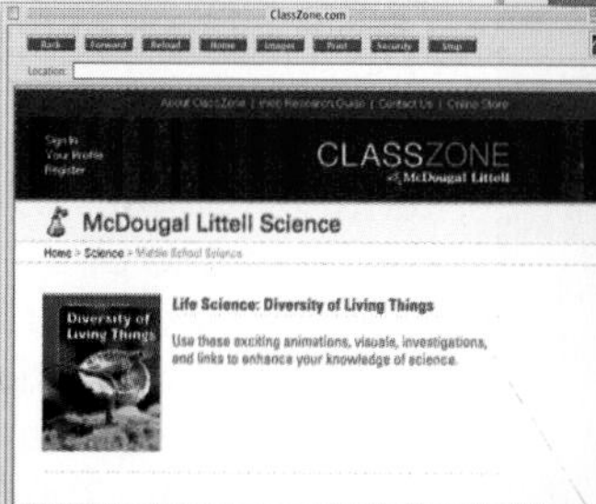

Sponges **Code: MDL042**

CHAPTER 4

# Getting Ready to Learn

## CONCEPT REVIEW

- All animals need energy, materials, and living space.
- Animals get energy and materials from food.
- Animals have different adaptations and behaviors for meeting their needs.

## VOCABULARY REVIEW

**predator** p. 63

**prey** p. 63

**adaptation** *See Glossary.*

Review concepts and vocabulary.

## TAKING NOTES

### COMBINATION NOTES

To take notes about a new concept, first make an informal outline of the information. Then make a sketch of the concept and label it so you can study it later. Use arrows to connect parts of the concept when appropriate.

SCIENCE NOTEBOOK

Notes

Sponges are simple animals

- no organs
- attached to one place
- remove food from water

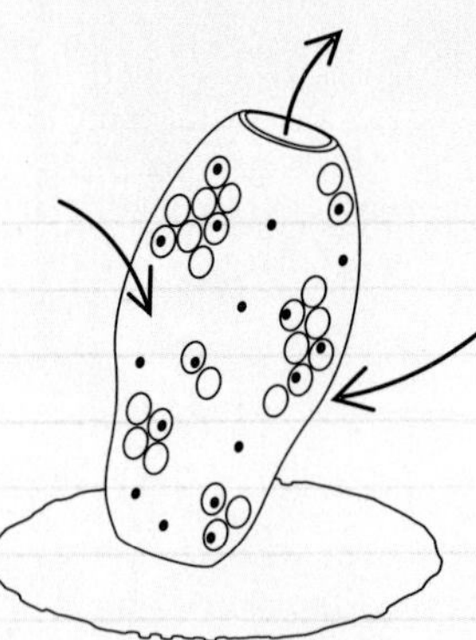

### CHOOSE YOUR OWN STRATEGY

For each new vocabulary term, take notes by choosing one of the strategies from earlier chapters—**description wheel, four square,** or **word triangle.** You can also use other vocabulary strategies that you might already know.

Description Wheel

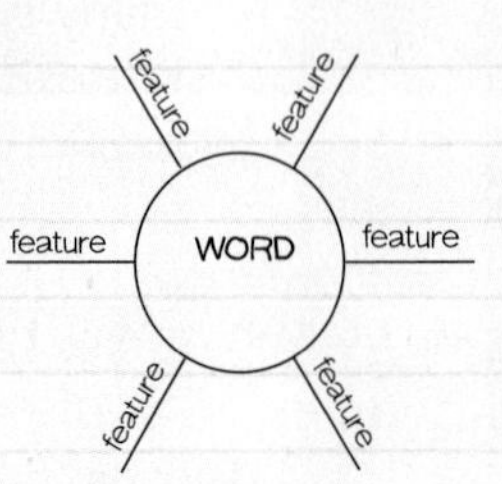


Four Square

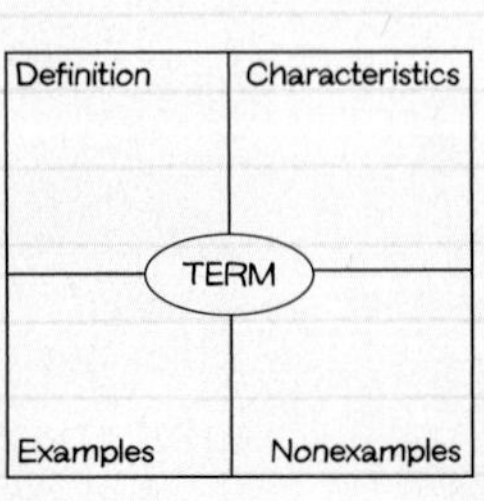


Word Triangle

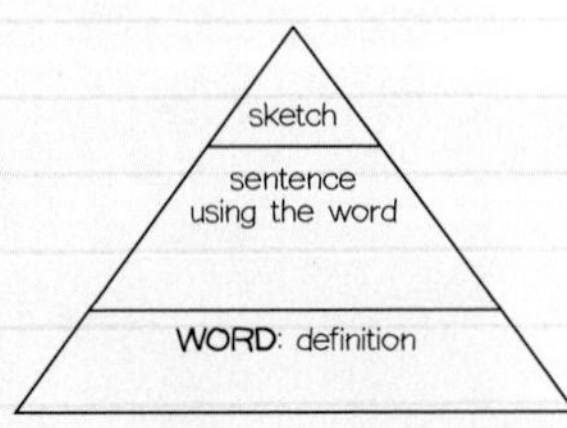


See the Note-Taking Handbook on pages R45–R51.

KEY CONCEPT

# Most animals are invertebrates.

**BEFORE, you learned**

- Animals are consumers; they get food from the environment
- Most animals have body systems, including tissues and organs
- Animals interact with the environment and other animals

**NOW, you will learn**

- About the diversity of invertebrates
- About six groups of invertebrates
- How sponges get energy

**VOCABULARY**

**invertebrate** p. 123
**sponge** p. 125
**sessile** p. 125
**larva** p. 126

**THINK ABOUT**

### *What makes an animal an animal?*

A sponge is an animal. It has no head, eyes, ears, arms, or legs. A sponge doesn't have a heart or a brain or a mouth. It doesn't move. Typically, it spends its life attached to the ocean floor. Many people used to think that sponges were plants that had adapted to life in the water. Scientists, however, classify them as animals. How might you decide if the organism in the photograph is an animal?

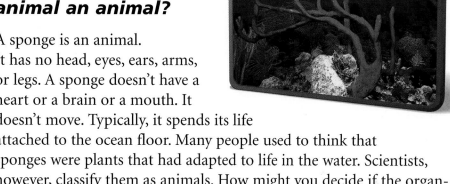

## Invertebrates are a diverse group of organisms.

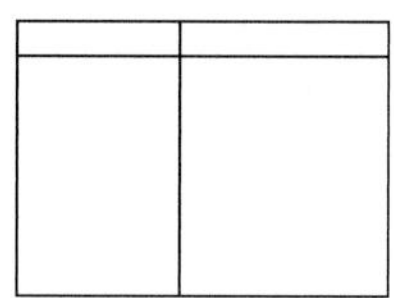

**COMBINATION NOTES** Make notes and diagrams for the first main idea: *Invertebrates are a diverse group of organisms.* Include a sketch of a member of each group.

About one million invertebrate species live on Earth. **Invertebrates** are animals that do not have backbones. In fact, invertebrates do not have any bone tissue at all. Invertebrates can be found just about everywhere, from frozen tundra to tropical forests. Some invertebrates live in water, while others survive in deserts where there is almost no water. Many invertebrates live inside other organisms.

Most invertebrate animals are small. Crickets, oysters, sea stars, earthworms, ants, and spiders are some examples of invertebrates. The fact that invertebrates do not have backbones for support tends to limit their size. However, some ocean-dwelling invertebrates can be quite large. For example, the giant squid can grow to 18 meters (59 ft) in length and can weigh over 450 kilograms (992 lb).

# INVESTIGATE Invertebrates

## *Which types of invertebrates live near you?*

**SKILL FOCUS**
Observing

**MATERIALS**
- potato
- knife
- spoon
- masking tape

**TIME**
20 minutes

**PROCEDURE**

1. Cut the potato in half lengthwise. Scoop out a hole and carve a channel so it looks like the photograph below.
2. Put the two halves back together and wrap them with masking tape. Leave the channel uncovered. It is the entrance hole.
3. Take the potato trap outside and bury it upright in soil, with the entrance hole sticking out of the ground. Wash your hands.
4. Collect the potato the next day. Remove the masking tape and look inside.

**WHAT DO YOU THINK?**

- Observe the contents of the potato. Record your observations.
- Would you classify the contents of the potato as living or nonliving? Do you think they are animals or plants?

**CHALLENGE** Predict how your observations would be different if you buried the potato in a different place.

In this chapter, you will learn about six groups of invertebrates:

- **Sponges** are the simplest invertebrates. They live in water. They filter food from the water that surrounds them.
- **Cnidarians** also live in water. Animals in this group have a central opening surrounded by tentacles. They take in food and eliminate waste through this opening. Jellyfish, sea anemones, hydras, and corals are cnidarians.
- **Worms** are animals with soft, tube-shaped bodies and a distinct head. Some worms live inside other animals. Others live in the water or on land.
- **Mollusks** have a muscular foot that allows them to move and hunt for food. Some mollusks live on land. Others live in water. Clams, snails, and octopuses are mollusks.
- **Echinoderms** are water animals that have a central opening for taking in food. Sea stars and sand dollars are echinoderms.
- **Arthropods** are invertebrates that are found on land, in the water, and in the air. They have legs. Some have wings. Insects, spiders, crabs, and millipedes are arthropods.

## Sponges are simple animals.

**Sponges** are the simplest multicellular animals on Earth. These invertebrates are **sessile** (SEHS-EEL) organisms, which means they live attached to one spot and do not move from place to place. Most live in the ocean, although some live in fresh water. Sponges have no tissues or organs. The body of a sponge is made up of a collection of cells. The cells are organized into a body wall, with an outside and an inside. Sponges are adapted to feed continuously. They feed on plankton and other tiny organisms that live in the water.

**VOCABULARY**
Make a description wheel for *sponge*. Include information on its specialized cells.

### Specialized Cells

A sponge meets its needs with cells specialized for different functions. Pore cells along the body wall create tiny openings throughout the body. The pores lead into larger canals and sometimes a central opening, where cells with tiny hairs, or flagella, move water through the sponge. As water moves out, more water enters, as shown in the diagram below. Specialized cells filter out food particles and oxygen. Other specialized cells digest the food.

What adaptations does a sponge have for obtaining food?

### Feeding in Sponges

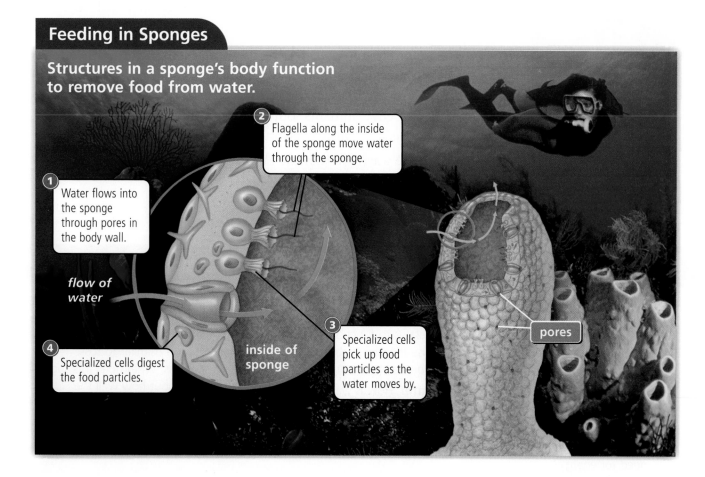

**Structures in a sponge's body function to remove food from water.**

1 Water flows into the sponge through pores in the body wall.

2 Flagella along the inside of the sponge move water through the sponge.

3 Specialized cells pick up food particles as the water moves by.

4 Specialized cells digest the food particles.

*flow of water*

inside of sponge

pores

Another adaptation sponges have are structures that make the body stiff. Most sponges have spicules (SPIHK-yoolz), which are needlelike spines made of hard minerals such as calcium or silicon. Spicules help give the sponge its shape and provide support. In some sponges, spicules stick out from the body. This may make the sponge less likely to become a source of food for other animals.

## Reproduction

Sponges can reproduce asexually. Buds form alongside the parent sponge or the buds break off and float away. Tiny sponges can float quite a distance before they attach to the ocean floor or some underwater object and start to grow.

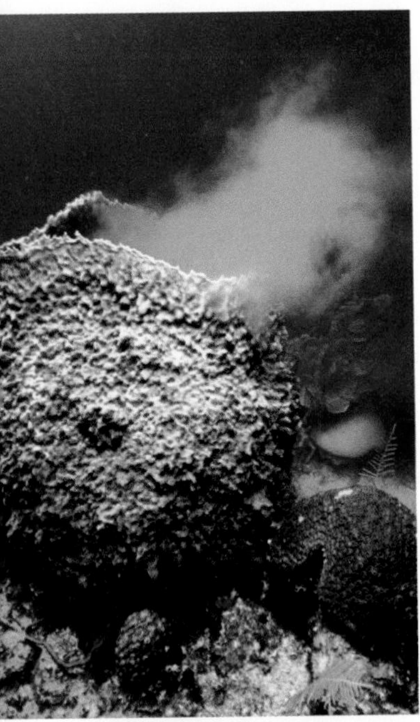
This basket sponge is releasing microscopic larvae into the water.

Sponges also reproduce sexually, as most multicellular organisms do. In sponges, sperm are released into the water. In some sponges, the eggs are released too. In this case, fertilization occurs in the water. In other sponges, the eggs are contained in specialized cells in the body wall. Sperm enter the sponge to fertilize the eggs.

A fertilized egg becomes a larva. A **larva** is an immature form—an early stage—of an organism that is different from the parent. Sponge larvae are able to swim. They move away from the parent and will grow into a sponge once they attach to some underwater surface. Then they become sessile, like their parents.

Sponges provide a good starting point for studying other invertebrates. There are many different types of invertebrates, with a wide range of body structures and behaviors. Invertebrates have adapted to many different environments. But the sponge is a simple organism that has changed very little over time. Sponges today look very similar to fossil sponges that are millions of years old.

# 4.1 Review

### KEY CONCEPTS

1. Make a table with six columns. Write the name of an invertebrate group above each column. Fill in the table with a characteristic and an example for each group.
2. What does it mean that sponges are sessile?
3. How do sponges meet their need for energy?

### CRITICAL THINKING

4. **Apply** Give two examples of how structure in a sponge relates to function. You should use the words *flagella* and *spicule* in your answer.
5. **Infer** How is water involved in the reproductive cycle of a sponge?

### CHALLENGE

6. **Analyze** Sponges have lived on Earth for hundreds of millions of years. Sponges today look very similar to fossil sponges. What does this suggest about how well the simple structure of a sponge meets its needs? Do species always change over time?

MATH in SCIENCE

## SKILL: LINE SYMMETRY

MATH TUTORIAL
CLASSZONE.COM

Click on Math Tutorial for more help with line symmetry.

# Mirror, Mirror

A pattern or shape that has *line symmetry* contains a mirror image of its parts on either side of a straight line. Think about the shapes of a sea star or a butterfly.

### Example

If you were to cut these shapes out of flat paper, you could fold the paper along a line of symmetry. The two halves would match.

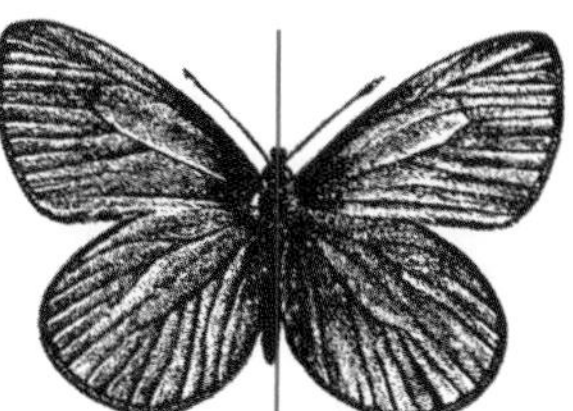

Some shapes have more than one line of symmetry. The shapes of most anemones and sea stars can fold along two, three, or more lines of symmetry.

**Sketch each shape. Then draw any lines of symmetry. If there are none, write "zero."**

1) 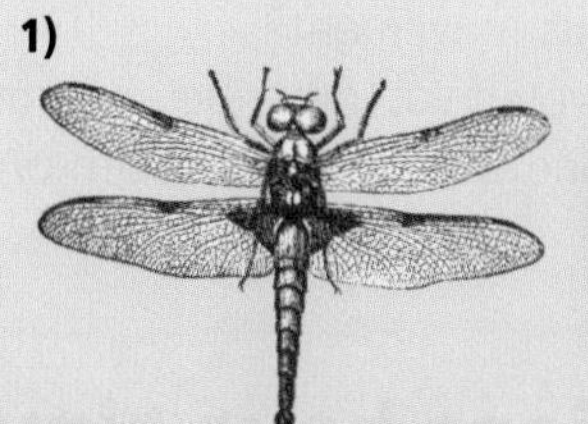

2) 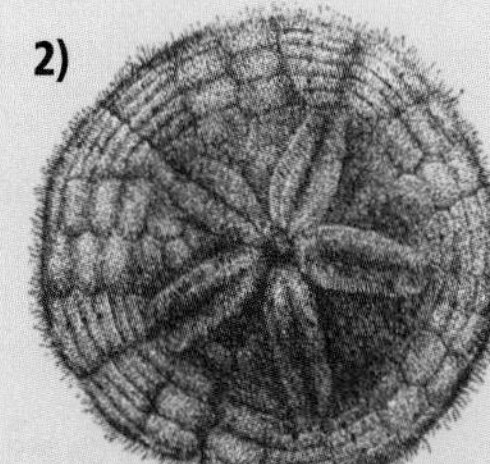

3) 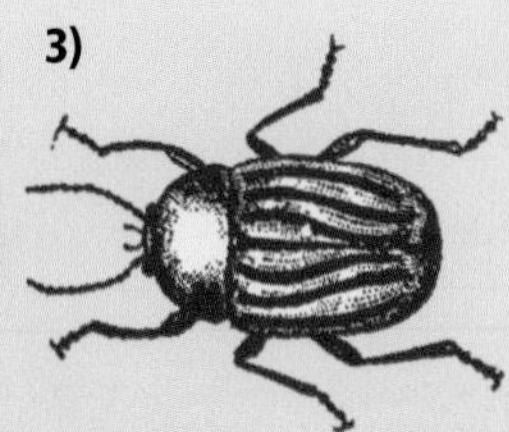

4) 

5) 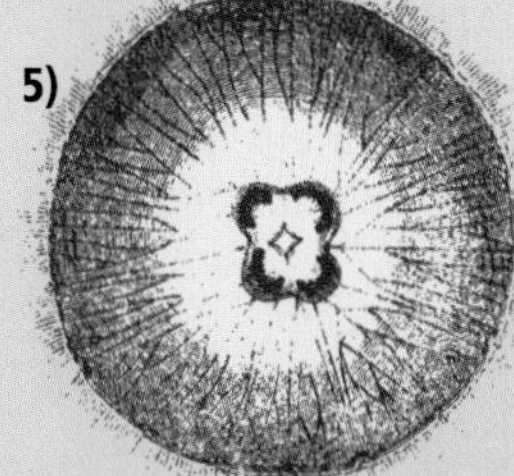

**CHALLENGE** Write out the uppercase letters of the alphabet *A* to *Z*. For each letter, write whether it has zero, one, or two lines of symmetry.

KEY CONCEPT

# Cnidarians and worms have different body plans.

**BEFORE, you learned**

- Invertebrates are a diverse group of animals
- Sponges are sessile organisms
- Sponges meet their needs with simple bodies and specialized cells

**NOW, you will learn**

- About body systems in cnidarians
- About body symmetry and feeding patterns
- About body systems in worms

**VOCABULARY**

**cnidarian** p. 128
**tentacle** p. 128
**mobile** p. 130

**EXPLORE Worm Movement**

### How does body shape affect movement?

**PROCEDURE**

1. Put a thin layer of soil on the tray and gently place the worm on it. Use the spray bottle to keep the soil and your hands moist.
2. Draw a sketch of the worm and try to identify the parts of its body.
3. Record your observations of its movement.
4. Follow your teacher's instructions in handling the worm and materials at the end of the lab. Wash your hands.

**MATERIALS**

- worm
- tray
- soil
- spray bottle filled with distilled water

**WHAT DO YOU THINK?**

- How does the shape of a worm's body affect its movement?
- How would you describe a worm to someone who has never seen one?

## Cnidarians have simple body systems.

**COMBINATION NOTES**
Make notes and diagrams for the main idea: *Cnidarians have simple body systems.*

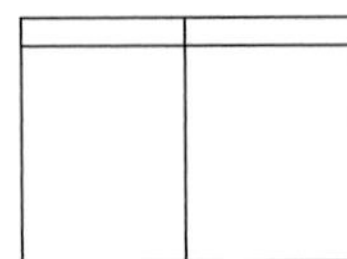

**Cnidarians** (ny-DAIR-ee-uhnz) are invertebrates. Like sponges, cnidarians are found only in water. This group includes jellyfish, corals, sea anenomes, and small freshwater organisms called hydras. Most cnidarians feed on small plankton, fish, and clams. Many cnidarians are sessile for most of their lives. Like sponges, cnidarians have adaptations that allow them to pull food in from the water that surrounds them.

All cnidarians have **tentacles,** fingerlike extensions of their body that reach into the water. Other animals have tentacles, but the tentacles of cnidarians have specialized stinging cells. The tentacles, with their stinging cells, are an adaptation that enables cnidarians to capture prey.

## Stinging Cells in Cnidarians

Jellyfish have specialized cells on their tentacles.

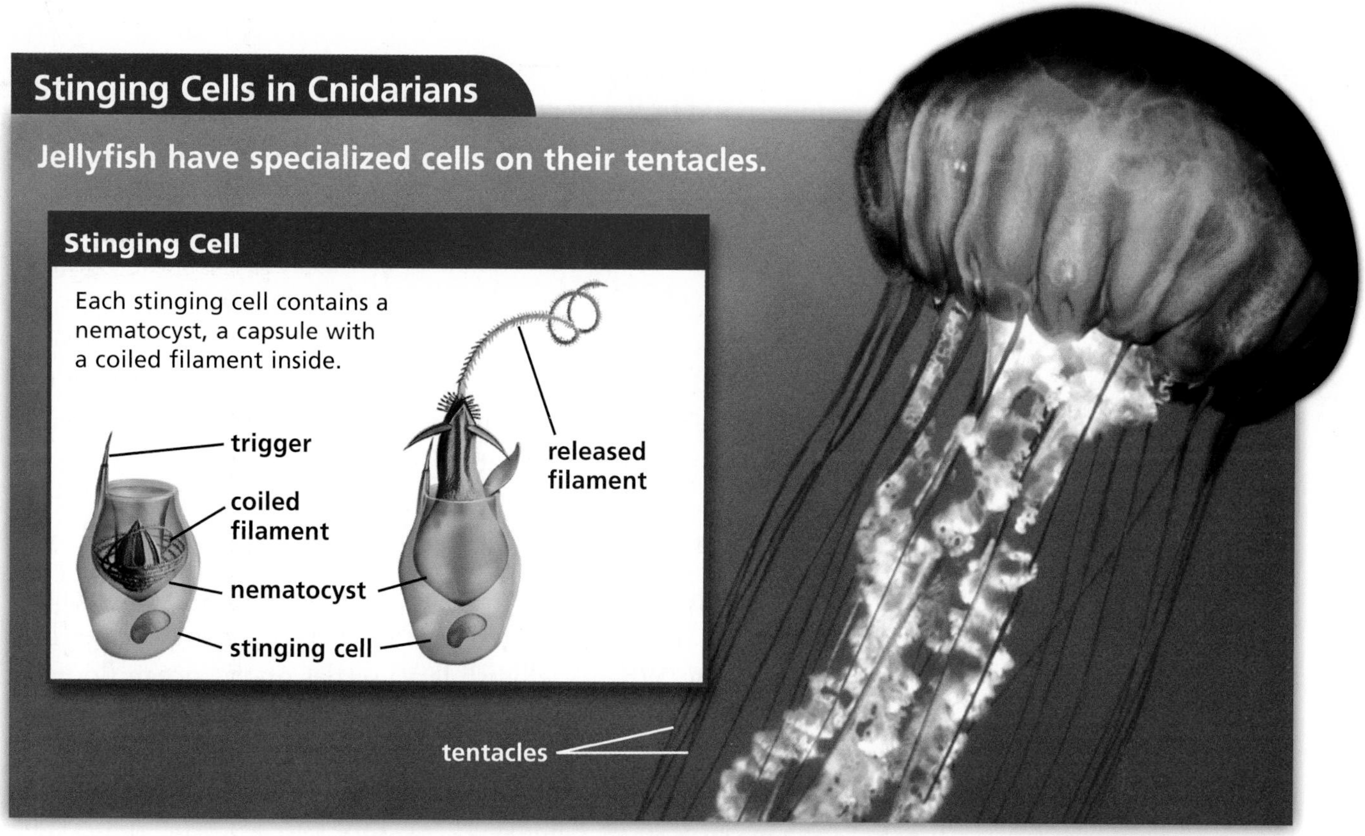

### Stinging Cell

Each stinging cell contains a nematocyst, a capsule with a coiled filament inside.



Each stinging cell has a nematocyst (NEHM-uh-tuh-SIHST), a capsule that holds a barbed filament. The filament is like a tiny hollow tube coiled up inside the capsule. When prey comes into contact with the stinger cell, the filament is released. Sometimes this stinger wraps itself around the prey. In most species of cnidarians, the stinger stabs the prey and releases a poison from its tip. These stingers are what produce the sting of a jellyfish. Stinging cells have a second function. They protect cnidarians from predators.

**READING TIP** Refer to the diagram above as you read the description of a nematocyst and its structure.

**CHECK YOUR READING** Describe how the structure of a nematocyst allows it to function in capturing food and providing protection.

## Tissues and Body Systems

A cnidarian's body is made up of flexible layers of tissue. These tissues, along with specialized cells, make up its body systems. The tissues are organized around a central opening where food is taken in and wastes are released. The tentacles bring the prey into this opening. The opening leads into a cavity, a gut, where the food is digested.

Cnidarians have a simple muscle system for movement. Even though cnidarians are sessile during most of their lives, they still move their bodies. Cnidarians bend from side to side and extend their tentacles. Adult jellyfish swim. The movement is produced by muscle cells that run around and along the sides of its body. When the muscle cells shorten, or contract, they produce movement.

When cnidarians move, they interact with the environment. They sense and respond to the prey that come in contact with their tentacles. This behavior is the result of a simple nervous system. Cnidarians have a network of nerve cells, a nerve net that extends throughout their bodies.

**VOCABULARY**
Choose a strategy from earlier chapters, such as a four square, or one of your own to take notes on the term *mobile.*

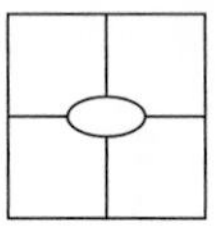

## Reproduction

Cnidarians reproduce both sexually and asexually, and water plays a role in both processes. Buds produced by asexual reproduction are carried away from the sessile parent by water. In sexual reproduction, sperm are carried to the egg. Fertilization results in a free-swimming larva. The larva, if it survives, develops into an adult.

Jellyfish are cnidarians with a life cycle that includes several stages. A jellyfish's body, or form, is different at each stage, as you can see in the diagram below. When a jellyfish larva settles on the ocean floor, it grows into a form called a polyp. The polyp, which is sessile, develops disk-shaped buds that stack up like a pile of plates. The buds, once they are released, are called medusas. Each medusa is an adult jellyfish. In the medusa stage, jellyfish are **mobile,** which means they can move their bodies from place to place.

### Jellyfish Life Cycle

**Jellyfish have a two-part life cycle that includes both a mobile and a sessile form.**

Young Medusa

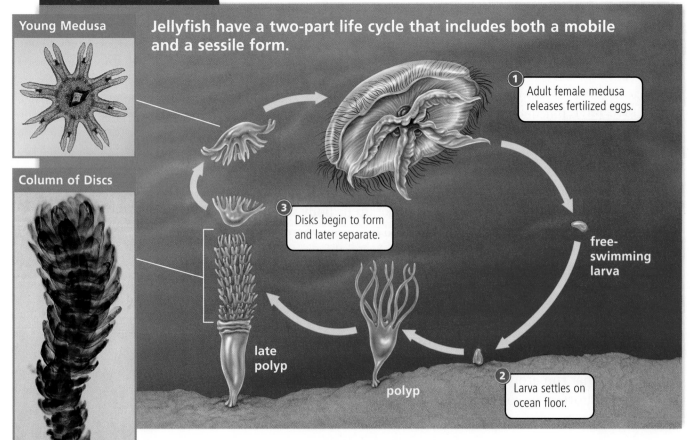

Column of Discs

1 Adult female medusa releases fertilized eggs.

free-swimming larva

2 Larva settles on ocean floor.

polyp

late polyp

3 Disks begin to form and later separate.

Radial Symmetry

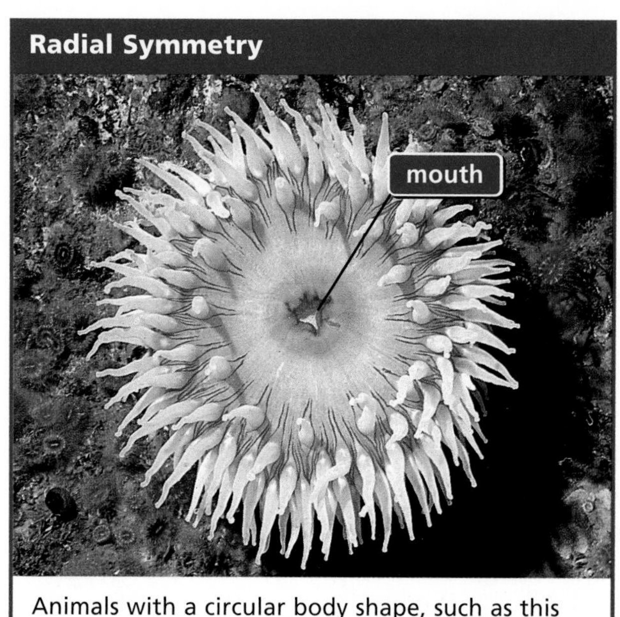


Animals with a circular body shape, such as this sea anemone, have radial symmetry.

Bilateral Symmetry

Animals with identical right and left sides, such as this butterfly, have bilateral symmetry.

## Animals have different body plans.

Scientists sometimes use the term *body plan* to describe the shape of an animal's body. Most cnidarians have a body plan with radial symmetry. This means the body is organized around a central point, a mouthlike opening that leads into a gut. You can see from the diagram of the jellyfish life cycle on page 130 that both the polyp and medusa have radial symmetry.

A radial body plan allows a sessile organism, such as the sea anemone shown in the photograph above, to capture food from any direction. A radial body plan also affects how a mobile animal moves. A jellyfish medusa moves forward by pushing down on the water. It has to stop moving to change direction.

Most animals, including worms, butterflies, birds, and humans, have a body plan with bilateral symmetry. One half looks just like the other, as you can see in the photograph of the butterfly above. You can recognize a bilaterally symmetrical shape because there is only one way to draw a line dividing it into two equal halves.

**READING TIP**

The root of the word *radial* means "ray," like the spoke of a wheel. The roots of the word *bilateral* are *bi-*, meaning "two," and *lateral,* meaning "side."

Animals with bilateral symmetry have a forward end where the mouth is located. This is the animal's head. The animal moves forward, head first, in search of food. A bilateral body shape works well in animals that are mobile. Food enters at one end, and is processed as it moves through the body. Once all the nutrients have been absorbed, the remaining wastes are released at the other end.

Describe how radial symmetry and bilateral symmetry affect an animal's feeding behaviors.

## Most worms have complex body systems.

RESOURCE CENTER
CLASSZONE.COM

Learn more about the many types of worms.

Some worms have simple bodies. Others have well-developed body systems. Worms have a tube-shaped body, with bilateral symmetry. In many worms, food enters at one end and is processed as it moves through a digestive tract. Worms take in oxygen, dissolved in water, through their skin. Because of this, worms must live in moist environments. Many live in water.

### Segmented Worms

Segmented worms have bodies that are divided into individual compartments, or segments. These worms are referred to as annelids (AN-uh-lihdz), which means "ringed animals." One annelid you might be familiar with is the earthworm. As the diagram below shows, an earthworm's segments can be seen on the outside of its body.

An earthworm has organs that are organized into body systems. The digestive system of an earthworm includes organs for digestion and food storage. It connects to the excretory system, which removes waste. Earthworms pass soil through their digestive system. They digest decayed pieces of plant and animal matter from the soil and excrete what's left over. A worm's feeding and burrowing activity adds nutrients and oxygen to the soil.

Name two body systems found in earthworms.

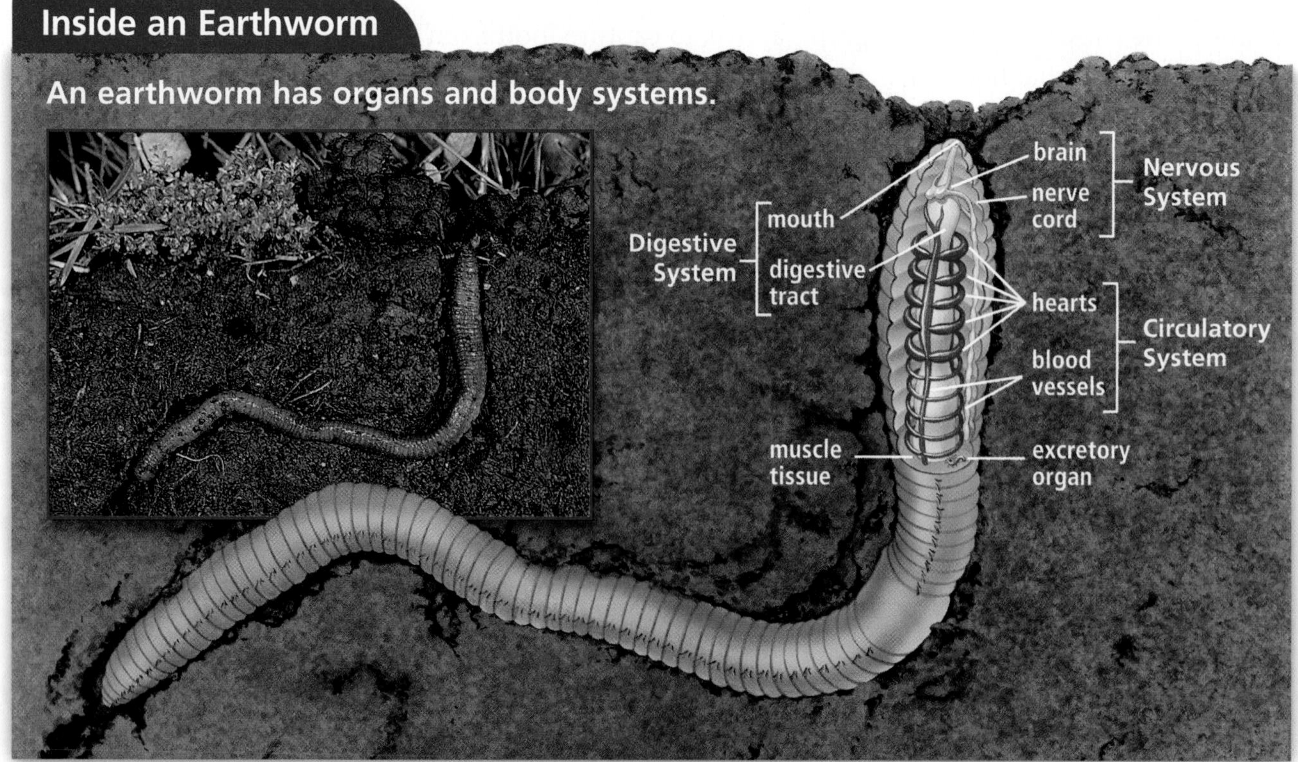

Earthworms have several layers of muscle tissue in their body wall. Hairlike bristles on the segments help to anchor a worm in the soil as it moves. The nervous system includes a brain and a nerve cord that runs through the body. An earthworm can detect strong light and vibrations in the soil. These stimuli signal danger to a worm. An earthworm also has a circulatory system. It is made up of several hearts that pump blood through blood vessels.

Some annelids reproduce asexually, while others reproduce sexually. There are no distinct male or female worms. Earthworms, for example, carry both male and female reproductive structures. To reproduce, two worms exchange sperm. The sperm fertilize eggs the worms carry in their bodies. The eggs are laid and later hatch into larvae.

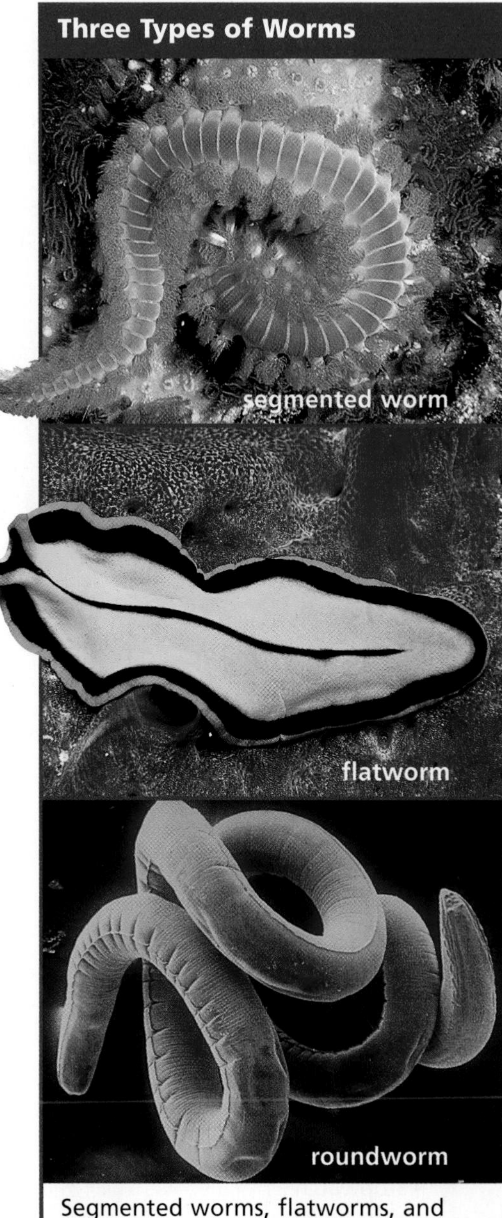


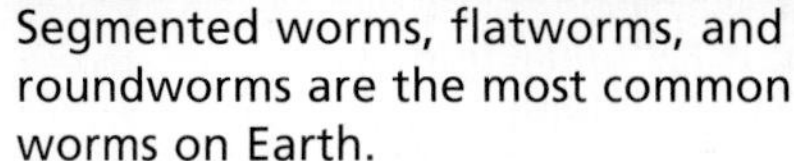
Segmented worms, flatworms, and roundworms are the most common worms on Earth.

## Flatworms and Roundworms

Flatworms are the worms with the simplest bodies. Some are so small and flat that they move with cilia, not muscles. These flatworms absorb nutrients directly through the skin. Many flatworms live as parasites, feeding off other organisms. For example, tapeworms are flatworms that infect humans and other animals. The tapeworm has no need for a digestive system because it gets digested nutrients from its host.

Roundworms are found just about everywhere on Earth. The bodies of roundworms are more complex than those of flatworms. They have muscles to move with, and a nervous system and digestive system. Some roundworms are important decomposers on land and in the water.

# 4.2 Review

### KEY CONCEPTS

1. What adaptation do cnidarians have for capturing prey?
2. What is the difference between radial symmetry and bilateral symmetry?
3. Pick two systems found in an earthworm and describe how they work together.

### CRITICAL THINKING

4. **Predict** How might having sense organs located at the front end of the body benefit an animal?
5. **Infer** Would the food of a jellyfish medusa be different from the food of a polyp? Support your answer.

### CHALLENGE

6. **Compare and Contrast** Describe how the different body symmetries of cnidarians and segmented worms affect their movement and feeding behaviors.

# CHAPTER INVESTIGATION

## Worm Behavior

**OVERVIEW AND PURPOSE** Earthworms do not have eyes, so they cannot see. An earthworm needs an environment that provides it with moisture, food, and protection from predators. How do worms gather information about their surroundings? How do they respond to changes in their environment? In this investigation you will

- observe worm behavior
- predict how worms will respond to surfaces with different textures

### Problem

How is worm behavior affected by environmental conditions?

### Hypothesize

You should complete steps 1–9 in the procedure before writing your hypothesis. Write a hypothesis to explain how worms will respond to different surface textures in an environment. Your hypothesis should take the form of an "If . . . , then . . . , because . . ." statement.

**MATERIALS**

- aquarium
- potting soil
- coarse sand
- small beaker
- distilled water
- spray bottle
- filter paper
- 5 or more worms
- 2 containers, one for untested worms and one for tested worms
- stopwatch
- *for Challenge* flashlight

### Procedure

1. Make a data table in your **Science Notebook** like the one shown on page 135.

2. Cover one half of the bottom of the aquarium with potting soil and the other half with sand.

3. Fill the beaker with 250 mL of distilled water and use it to fill the spray bottle. Spray all the water over the potting soil so it is evenly moistened.

4. Repeat step 3, but this time moisten the sand. Refill the spray bottle.

step 5

5. Place a piece of filter paper in the middle of the aquarium so it is half on the soil and half on the sand, as shown.

step 6

6. Put on your gloves. Spray your hands with water. Gently remove one worm and observe it until you can tell which end is its head.

7. Start the stopwatch as you place the worm on the middle of the filter paper. Note which part of the aquarium the worm's head points toward.

8. Observe the worm's behavior for two minutes and then remove it carefully from the aquarium and place it in the container for tested worms.

9. Write your observations in your data table. State your hypothesis.

10. Fix the sand, soil, and paper in the aquarium so they are arranged as they were for the first worm. Then repeat steps 6–9 with at least four more worms.

11. Return the worms to their original living place. Wash your hands.

## Observe and Analyze

Write It Up

1. **OBSERVE** What behaviors suggest that worms get information about their surroundings?
2. **OBSERVE** What evidence did you see to suggest that worms respond to information they get about their surroundings?
3. **INTERPRET DATA** What patterns did you notice in the behavior of the worms you tested?

## Conclude

Write It Up

1. **INTERPRET** Compare your results with your hypothesis. Does your data support your hypothesis?
2. **IDENTIFY LIMITS** What sources of error could have affected your investigation?
3. **EVALUATE** Based on your observations and evidence, what conclusions can you draw about the connection between worm behavior and environmental conditions?

## INVESTIGATE Further

**CHALLENGE** Worms respond to light as a stimulus. Design an experiment to test the reaction of worms to the presence of light.

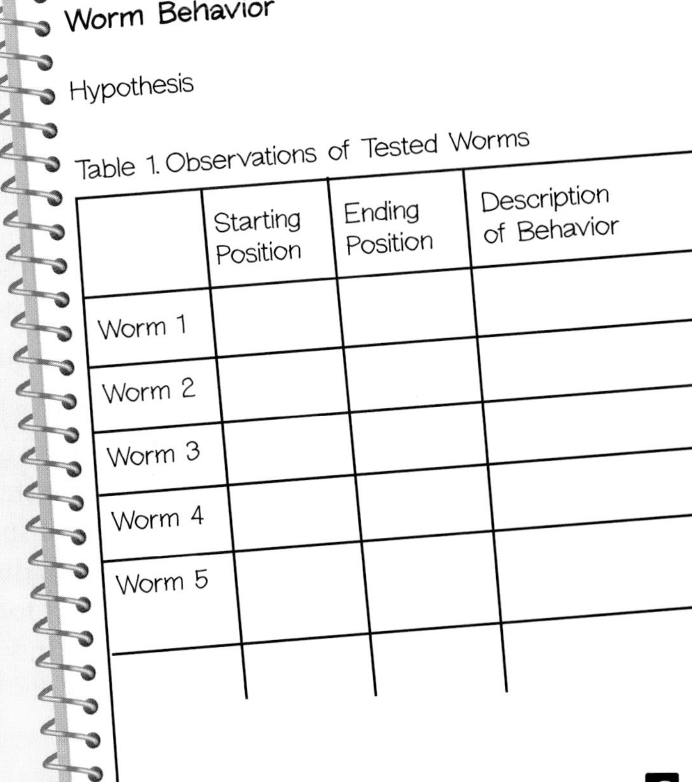
Worm Behavior

Hypothesis

Table 1. Observations of Tested Worms

| | Starting Position | Ending Position | Description of Behavior |
|---|---|---|---|
| Worm 1 | | | |
| Worm 2 | | | |
| Worm 3 | | | |
| Worm 4 | | | |
| Worm 5 | | | |
| | | | |

KEY CONCEPT

# Most mollusks have shells, and echinoderms have spiny skeletons.

**BEFORE, you learned**

- Body shape affects how animals move and behave
- Cnidarians have radial symmetry and simple body systems
- Worms have bilateral symmetry and segmented body systems

**NOW, you will learn**

- About different types of mollusks and their features
- About different types of echinoderms and their features

**VOCABULARY**

**mollusk** p. 136
**gill** p. 137
**lung** p. 137
**echinoderm** p. 139

**THINK ABOUT**

***How does a snail move?***

Snails belong to a group of mollusks called gastropods. The name means "belly foot." Snails are often put into aquariums to clean up the algae that can build up along the walls of the tank. If you get a chance, look at a snail moving along the glass walls of an aquarium, observe how it uses its foot to move. How would you describe the action of the snail's foot?

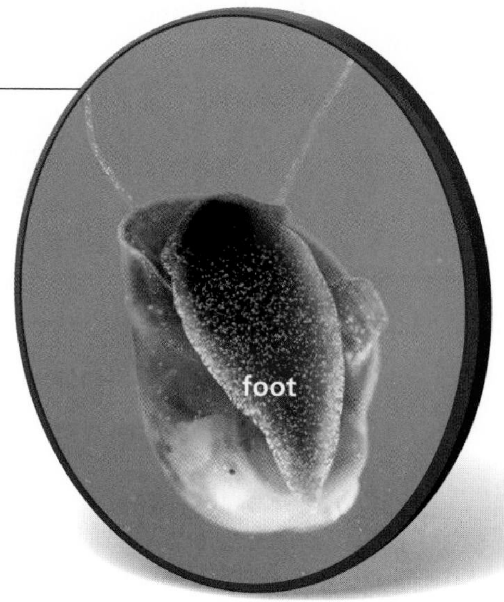


## Mollusks are soft-bodied animals.

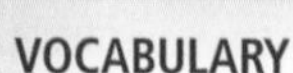

**VOCABULARY**
Choose a strategy from earlier chapters, such as a word triangle, or one of your own to take notes on the term *mollusk*.

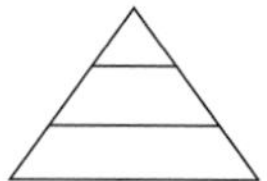

One characteristic that is shared by all **mollusks** is a soft body. Many of these invertebrate animals also have an outer shell to protect their body. Oysters, clams, snails, and mussels are all mollusks. So are octopuses, squids, and slugs. Mollusks live on land and in freshwater and saltwater environments. You will read about three groups of mollusks: bivalves, gastropods, and cephalopods.

Most mollusks have well-developed organ systems. They have muscles, a digestive system, a respiratory system, a circulatory system, and a nervous system with sensory organs. Mollusks reproduce sexually, and in most species there are distinct male and female organisms. Two adaptations distinguish mollusks as a group. First, all mollusks have a muscular foot. A mollusk's head is actually attached to its foot. Second, all mollusks have a mantle, a layer of folded skin that protects its internal organs.

## Bivalves

Bivalves are named for a hard shell that is made up of two matching halves. Clams, mussels, scallops, and oysters are all bivalves. The shell, when it is closed, completely encloses the body. If you've ever seen a raw oyster, you know that a bivalve's body looks like a mass of tissue. Bivalves do not have a distinct head, but they do have a mouth and sensory organs. The scallop shown in the photograph has light-sensitive organs that look like tiny eyes.

**Bivalve**

Most of this blue-eyed scallop's body is inside its two-part shell.

Bivalves are filter feeders, they filter food from the surrounding water. To move, a bivalve balances upright, opens its shell, and extends its foot. The animal moves by pushing the foot in and out. The foot is also used for burrowing, digging down into the sand.

The invertebrates you've studied so far—sponges, cnidarians, and worms—take in oxygen all along the surface of their bodies. A bivalve takes in oxygen through a pair of gills. A **gill** is an organ that filters dissolved oxygen from water. The gill is an adaptation that allows an organism to take in a lot of oxygen in just one area of its body. It is made up of many folds of tissue that create a large surface area. Blood picks up the oxygen and moves it to the rest of the animal's body. In most bivalves, the gills also filter food from the water.

Discover more about mollusks.

What are the two functions of gills and how do those functions relate to where bivalves live?

## Gastropods

Gastropods are the most diverse group of mollusks. Some, such as snails and slugs, live on land. Many live in water, for example, conches, whelks, and periwinkles. Many gastropods are protected by a spiral-shaped shell. To protect itself, a gastropod withdraws into the shell.

**Gastropod**

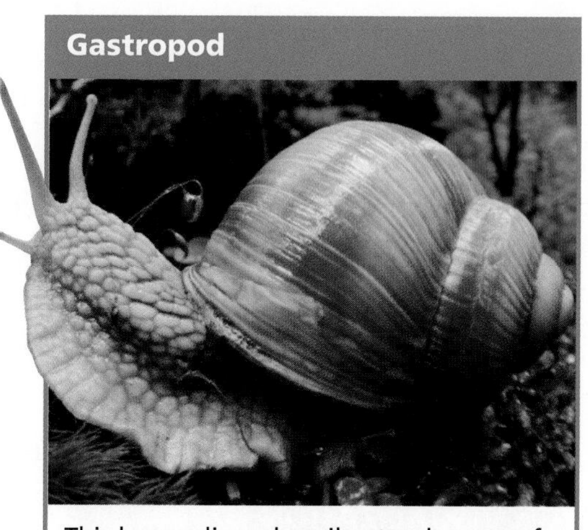

This brown-lipped snail extends most of its body out of its shell when it moves.

The gastropod's head is located at the end of its foot. The head has eyes and specialized tentacles for sensing. Many gastropods have a cutting mouth part, called a radula, that shreds their food. Some gastropods eat animals, but most feed on plants and algae. Gastropods that live in water have gills. Some gastropods that live on land have lungs. A **lung** is an organ that absorbs oxygen from the air. Like gills, lungs have a large surface area.

## INVESTIGATE Mollusks and Echinoderms

### *How do mollusk shells compare with echinoderm skeletons?*

**PROCEDURE**

1. Closely observe the mollusk shells and skeletons of sea stars and sand dollars you are given.
2. Examine the shape and texture of each. Sort them by their characteristics.

**WHAT DO YOU THINK?**

How are the shells and skeletons the same? How are they different?

**CHALLENGE** Based on your observations, what can you infer about the bodies of living mollusks, sea stars, and sand dollars?

**SKILL FOCUS**
Observing

**MATERIALS**
Selection of mollusk shells, sea stars, and sand dollars

**TIME**
15 minutes

## Cephalopods

Cephalopods (SEHF-uh-luh-PAHDZ) live in saltwater environments. Octopuses, squids, and chambered nautiluses are cephalopods. Among mollusks, cephalopods have the most well-developed body systems.

**Cephalopods**

This Maori octopus has a well-developed head attached to a foot with eight tentacles.

Cephalopods have a brain and well-developed nerves. They have a pair of eyes near their mouth. The foot, which surrounds the mouth, has tentacles for capturing prey. The mantle is adapted to push water forcefully through a tube-shaped structure called a siphon. This produces a jet of water that moves the animal. Gills take in oxygen, which is picked up by blood vessels and pumped through the body by three hearts.

Octopuses and squids do not have protective shells. They do have protective behaviors, however. Some can change body color to match their surroundings. Some release dark clouds of inklike fluid into the water, to confuse their predators. The lack of a shell lets them move freely through the water.

The nautilus is the only cephalopod that has a shell. The shell is made up of separate compartments, or chambers. The nautilus itself lives in the outermost chamber. The inner chambers are filled with gas, which makes the animal better able to float. The chambered shell also provides the soft-bodied nautilus with protection from predators.

Watch how different cephalopods move.

How is the foot of a cephalopod adapted for hunting?

## Mollusks show a range of adaptations.

You might not think that a clam would belong to the same group as an octopus. These organisms look very different from one another. They also interact with the environment in different ways. The great variety of mollusks on Earth today provides a good example of how adaptations within a group can lead to great diversity. A good example of this is the range of adaptations shown in the shape and function of a mollusk's foot.

The foot of the bivalve is a simple muscular structure that moves in and out of its shell. The foot allows a bivalve to crawl along the ocean floor and to bury itself in the sand. Gastropods have a head at the end of the foot, which runs the length of the body. Muscles in the foot produce ripples that allow the gastropod to glide over a surface as it searches for food. In cephalopods, the foot has tentacles to pull food into its mouth. The tentacles also help some cephalopods move along the ocean floor.

**COMPARE** How does the foot of this clam compare with the foot of an octopus?

## Echinoderms have unusual adaptations.

**Echinoderms** are a group of invertebrates that live in the ocean. In their adult form, their bodies have radial symmetry. Sea stars, sea urchins, sea cucumbers, and sand dollars belong to this group. Echinoderms feed off the ocean floor as they move along. An echinoderm's mouth is located at the center of the body, on the underside. Some echinoderms, such as sea urchins and sand dollars, filter food from their surroundings. Others, such as sea stars, are active predators that feed on clams, snails, and even other echinoderms.

**COMBINATION NOTES**
Remember to take notes and make sketches for the main idea: *Echinoderms have unusual adaptations.*

### Spines and Skeletons

Echinoderm means "spiny-skinned." Some of the more familiar echinoderms have long, sharp spines, like the sea urchin in the photograph at the bottom of this page. However, some echinoderm species, such as sea cucumbers, have spines that are very small.

One unusual adaptation that echinoderms have is a type of skeleton. Remember that echinoderms are invertebrates, they have no bone tissue. The echinoderm skeleton is made up of a network of stiff, hard plates. The plates lie just under the surface of the echinoderm's skin. Some echinoderms, such as sea stars, have skeletons with loosely connected plates and flexible arms. In other echinoderms, such as sand dollars, the plates grow close together, so the skeleton does not allow for much flexibility.

This purple sea urchin has very obvious spines.

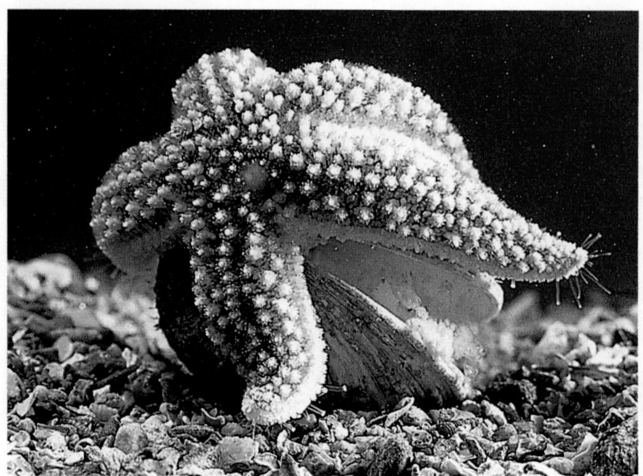

This sea star has captured a bivalve and is using its tube feet to open the shell.

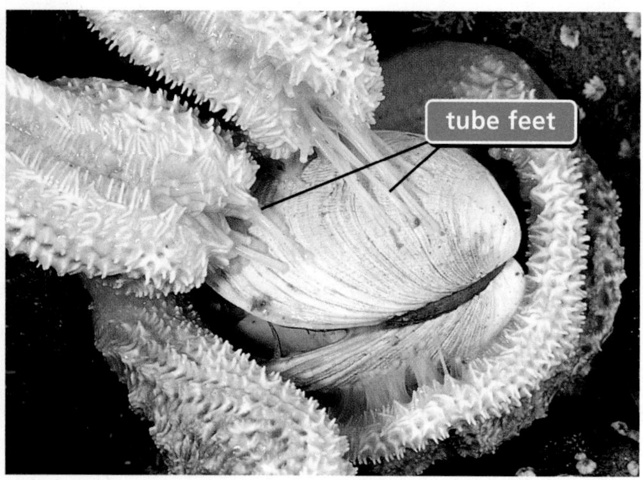


This sea star's arms have been pulled up to show how its tube feet are attached to the bivalve's shell.

### Water Vascular System and Tube Feet

Another adaptation that is unique to echinoderms is a water vascular system. This system is made up of water-filled tubes that radiate out from the center of the echinoderm's body. Tiny openings along the upper surface of the echinoderm's body feed water into these tubes. At the base of the tubes is a series of tube feet.

Muscles attached to the top of each tube can close the tube off, producing suction at the base of the tube. The tube feet stick to the ocean floor, allowing the echinoderm to pull itself along. The tube feet can also be used for hunting prey. For example, a sea star can surround a clam or oyster with its body, as shown in the photograph on the left. The tube feet pull the shell open. Then, the sea star's stomach is pushed out through its mouth and into the bivalve's shell, where it begins to digest the bivalve's body. Not all echinoderms eat other animals. Some, like sea urchins, feed off algae on the ocean floor.

## 4.3 Review

#### KEY CONCEPTS

1. What two features do all mollusks have?
2. What are two features all echinoderms have?
3. What are two functions of tube feet in echinoderms?

#### CRITICAL THINKING

4. **Analyze** For mollusks and echinoderms, what are the advantages and disadvantages of having a shell or spiny skeleton?
5. **Compare and Contrast** Compare the foot of mollusks with the tube feet of echinoderms.

#### CHALLENGE

6. **Analyze** Animals with lungs or gills can be larger than animals that take in oxygen through their skin. What feature do both lungs and gills have that affect the amount of oxygen they can absorb? What role does the circulatory system play?

The common sea star *(Asterias rubeus)* can regrow a missing arm. Its main prey is the mussel.

## SKILL: EVALUATING CONCLUSIONS

# Eating Well

Common sea stars have five arms. When one arm is missing, sea stars are, amazingly, able to grow another. Scientists interested in this amazing ability designed an experiment to see how having four arms instead of five affects a sea star's ability to consume prey. The sea stars use tube feet on each arm to pry open the shells of mussels and eat the animals' insides.

Scientists, working in 1999 and 2000, examined common sea stars caught in fishing gear. The study divided them into two groups: one group with five arms and one group with only four arms. Each sea star was tested to see how well it could open and eat a mussel.

## Observations

Scientists made these observations:

a. Most of the sea stars with all five arms opened and ate a mussel.
b. Fewer than half of the sea stars with four arms opened and ate a mussel.
c. All the sea stars that opened a mussel took about 13 hours to finish eating it.

## Conclusions

Here are some conclusions about sea stars eating mussels:

a. Common sea stars are most likely to feed successfully if they have all their arms.
b. A common sea star with only four arms will starve.
c. Common sea stars eat slowly regardless of how many arms they have.
d. Common sea stars with only four arms choose mussels that are difficult to open.

## Evaluate the Conclusions

**On Your Own** Think about each observation that the scientists noted. Do they support the conclusions? Do some observations support one conclusion but not another? If a conclusion is not supported, what extra observations would you need to make?

**With a Partner** Compare your thinking with your partner's thinking. Do you both agree with the conclusions?

**CHALLENGE** Why do you think the sea stars with only four arms were less likely to open and eat a mussel?

KEY CONCEPT

# Arthropods have exoskeletons and joints.

**BEFORE, you learned**

- Mollusks are invertebrates with soft bodies, some have shells
- Echinoderms have spiny skeletons
- Different species adapt to the same environment in different ways

**NOW, you will learn**

- About different groups of arthropods
- About exoskeletons in arthropods
- About metamorphosis in arthropods

**VOCABULARY**

**arthropod** p. 142
**exoskeleton** p. 143
**molting** p. 143
**insect** p. 145
**metamorphosis** p. 146

**EXPLORE Arthropods**

***What are some characteristics of arthropods?***

**PROCEDURE**

1. Observe the pillbugs in their container. Draw a sketch of a pillbug.
2. Gently remove the pillbugs from their container and place them in the open end of the box. Observe and make notes on their behavior for several minutes.
3. Return the pillbugs to their container.

**MATERIALS**

- clear container
- shoebox with half of cover removed
- pillbugs
- hand lens

**WHAT DO YOU THINK?**

- Describe some of the characteristics you noticed about pillbugs.
- Are pillbugs radially or bilaterally symmetrical?

## Most invertebrates are arthropods.

**COMBINATION NOTES**
Make notes and diagrams for the main idea: *Most invertebrates are arthropods.*

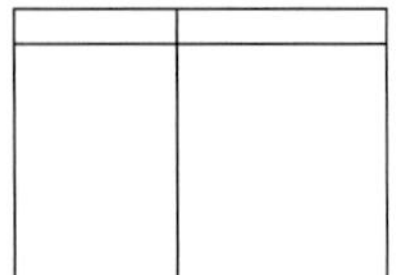

There are more species of arthropods than there are any other type of invertebrate. In fact, of all the animal species classified by scientists, over three-quarters are arthropods. An **arthropod** is an invertebrate that has a segmented body covered with a hard outer skeleton. Arthropods can have many pairs of legs and other parts that extend from their body. Insects are arthropods, as are crustaceans such as the shrimp and arachnids such as the spider.

Fossil evidence shows that arthropods first appeared on land about 420 million years ago, around the same time as plants. Arthropods are active animals that feed on all types of food. Many arthropods live in water, but most live on land.

The exoskeleton of this crayfish completely covers its body.

RESOURCE CENTER
CLASSZONE.COM

Find out more about the diversity of arthropods.

## Exoskeletons and Jointed Parts

One adaptation that gives arthropods the ability to live in many different environments is the exoskeleton. An **exoskeleton** is a strong outer covering, made of a material called chitin. The exoskeleton completely covers the body of an arthropod. In a sense, an exoskeleton is like a suit of armor that protects the animal's soft body. For arthropods living on land, the exoskeleton keeps cells, tissues, and organs from drying out.

What are two functions of an exoskeleton?

A suit of armor is not much good unless you can move around in it. The arthropod's exoskeleton has joints, places where the exoskeleton is thin and flexible. There are joints along the different segments of the animal's body. An arthropod body typically has three sections: a head at one end, a thorax in the middle, and an abdomen at the other end. Legs are jointed, as are other parts attached to the body, such as antennae and claws. Muscles attach to the exoskeleton around the joints, enabling the arthropod to move.

COMPARE How does the shape of this cicada's molted exoskeleton compare to the shape of its body?

The exoskeleton is like a suit of armor in one other way. It doesn't grow. An arthropod must shed its exoskeleton as it grows. This process is called **molting.** For an arthropod, the times when it molts are dangerous because its soft body is exposed to predators.

## Complex Body Systems

Arthropods have well-developed body systems. They have a nervous system with a brain and many different sensory organs. Their digestive system includes a stomach and intestines. Arthropods have an open circulatory system, which means the heart moves blood into the body directly. There are no blood vessels. Arthropods reproduce sexually. An arthropod has either a male or a female reproductive system.

## Three Major Groups of Arthropods

**Scientists have named at least ten groups of arthropods, but most arthropod species belong to one of three groups: insects, crustaceans, or arachnids.**

### Insects

- Includes beetles, bees, wasps, ants, butterflies, moths, and grasshoppers
- 3 pairs of legs, 3 body segments, 1 pair of antennae
- Most live on land

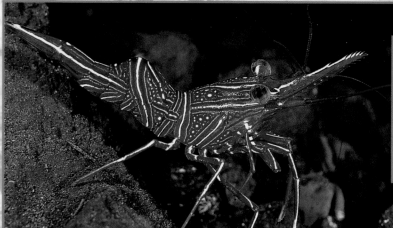

### Crustaceans

- Includes shrimp, crabs, lobsters, barnacles, and pill bugs
- Number of body segments and pairs of legs varies, 2 pairs of antennae
- Most live in water; some live on land

### Arachnids

- Includes spiders, ticks, mites, and scorpions
- 4 pairs of legs, 2 body segments, no antennae
- Most live on land

**READING VISUALS** What body features can you see that are shared by all of these arthropods?

## Parts of an Insect's Body

**Adult insects have three body segments and six jointed legs.**

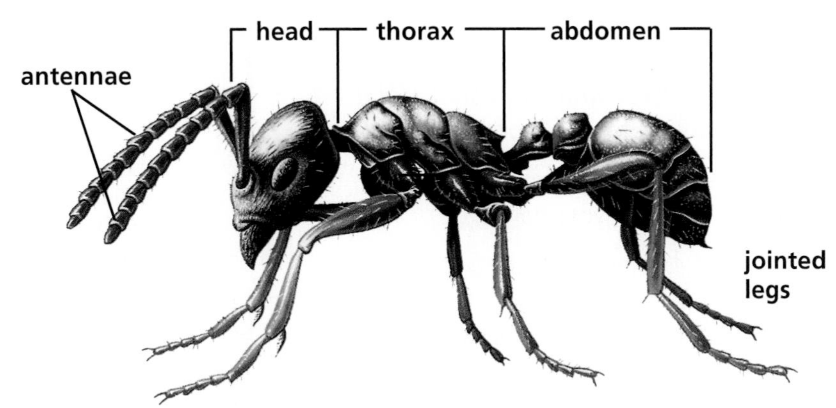


READING TIP

The word *insect* relates to its body being **in sect**ions. Note the three sections in the diagram of the ant.

## Insects are six-legged arthropods.

Scientists have so far identified over 700,000 insect species. **Insects** are arthropods that as adults have three body segments, a pair of antennae, and six legs attached to the middle segment, the thorax. Insect species have adapted to all sorts of environments and live on every continent. Most insects live on land. These insects obtain oxygen through spiracles, small openings in their exoskeleton.

CHECK YOUR READING What are two characteristics all adult insects share?

VOCABULARY

Don't forget to take notes on the term *insect,* using a strategy from an earlier chapter or one that you already know.

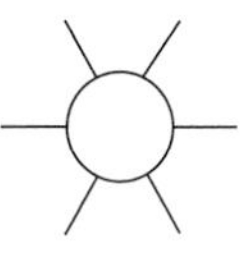

Insects show great diversity in appearance. Many species have adaptations in color and shape that allow them to blend into their environments. For example, a stick insect is the same color and shape as a twig. Insect bodies also have different adaptations. Many insects have compound eyes and antennae, which are sensory organs. Many insects fly, having one or two pairs of wings.

Many insects are herbivores. And many insect species have mouth parts adapted for feeding on specific plants. A butterfly, for example, has a tubelike mouth that can reach into a flower to get nectar. Insects that feed on flowers often help the plants reproduce because the insects carry pollen from flower to flower. Other insects harm the plants they feed on. A grasshopper has jawlike mouth parts that crush parts of a plant. Many plants have defensive adaptations, such as poisons in leaves and stems, to keep insects from eating them.

Some insects, for example, ants, termites, and some bees, are social insects. They must live in groups in order to survive. Members of the group work together to gather food, maintain the nest, and care for the offspring. Often with social insects, just one female, called a queen, produces and lays eggs.

# INVESTIGATE Insect Metamorphosis

## How often do mealworms molt?

**SKILL FOCUS**
Observing

**MATERIALS**
- glass jar
- lid with air holes
- oat bran
- potato
- carrot
- mealworms
- *for Challenge:* petri dish tweezers

**TIME**
20 minutes

### PROCEDURE

1. Prepare the jar for the mealworms. Fill it halfway with oat bran for food. Place a slice of potato and a piece of carrot on top for moisture.
2. In your notebook, note how many mealworms you have. Carefully place the mealworms inside the jar and close the lid. Wash your hands.
3. Without opening the jar, look for signs of activity every day. Once a week, open the container and pour some of the contents into a tray. Examine this sample for molted exoskeletons. Then return it to the jar. Replace the vegetables and add new oats as needed. Wash your hands.

### WHAT DO YOU THINK?

- What changes did you observe in the mealworms?
- Did you see any sign of other stages of development?

**CHALLENGE** Use tweezers and a petri dish to collect the molted exoskeletons. How do the number of molts compare to the number of worms? Estimate how often the worms molt.

All insects can reproduce sexually. Females lay eggs, often a large number of eggs. The queen honey bee can lay over a million eggs in her lifetime. Many insect eggs have a hard outer covering. This adaptation protects the egg from drying out and can allow hatching to be delayed until conditions are right.

During their life cycle, insects undergo a process in which their appearance and body systems may change dramatically. This process is called **metamorphosis.** There are three stages to a complete metamorphosis. The first stage is the larva, which spends its time eating. The second stage is the pupa. During this stage, the insect body develops within a protective casing. The final stage is the adult, which is capable of going on to produce a new generation.

**READING TIP**
The word *metamorphosis* means "many changes."

**CHECK YOUR READING** What happens to an insect during metamorphosis?

Not all insects go through complete metamorphosis. Some insects, such as grasshoppers, have a simple metamorphosis. When a young grasshopper hatches from an egg, its form is similar to an adult's, just smaller. A grasshopper grows and molts several times before reaching adult size.

1 A female mosquito lays a mass of eggs on the surface of the water.

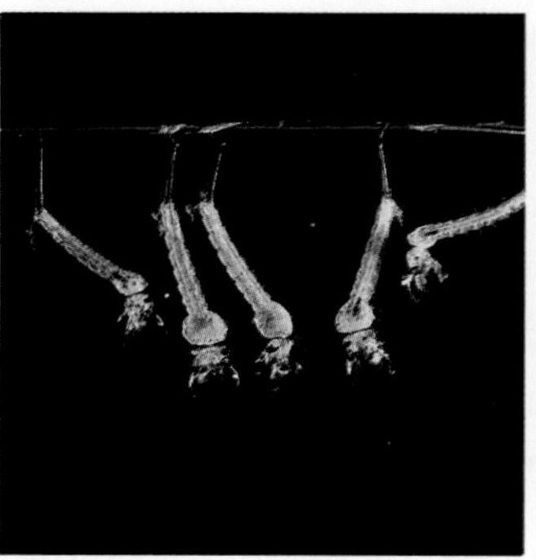

2 Each egg develops into a larva that swims head down, feeding on algae.

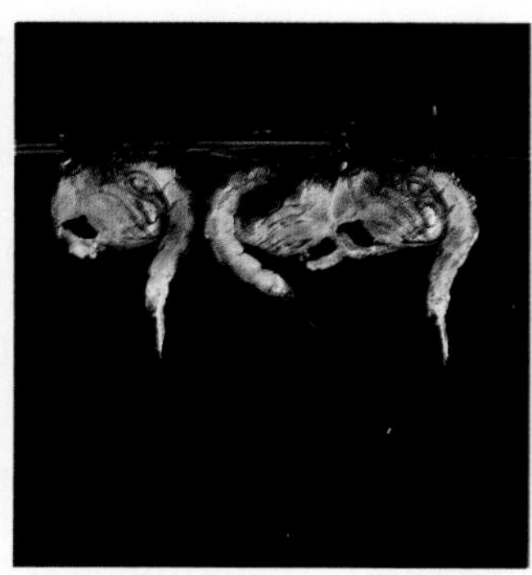

3 The larva develops into a pupa. Inside, the body of the insect matures.

4 At the adult stage, the mosquito leaves the water and flies away.

You have probably seen many insects in their larval form. A caterpillar is a larva; so is an inchworm. Often the larval form of an insect lives very differently from its adult form. A mosquito, for example, begins its life in the water. The larva swims about, feeding on algae. The pupa forms at the water's surface. The developing mosquito is encased in a protective covering. The adult form of the mosquito, the flying insect, leaves the water. The female is a parasite that feeds off the blood of other animals.

## Crustaceans live in water and on land.

Most crustacean species live in the water. Several of these, including the Atlantic lobster and the Dungeness crab, are used by people as a source of food. Crustaceans are important to the ocean food web. Tiny crustaceans such as krill and copepods are a food source for many other animals, including other invertebrates, fish, and whales. Some species of crustaceans live in freshwater and a few, such as pill bugs, live on land.

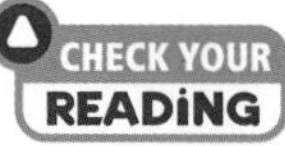


Where do most crustaceans live?

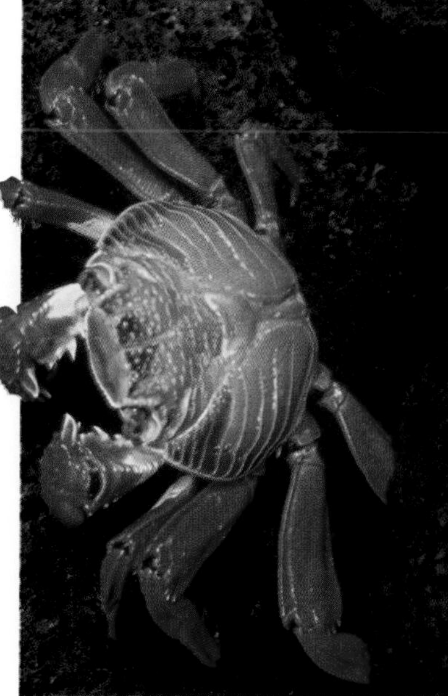

**IDENTIFY** How many pairs of legs does this crab have?

Crustaceans have three or more pairs of legs and two pairs of sensory antennae. Many of the larger, water-living crustaceans, such as crabs, have gills. Most crustaceans, like other arthropods, have a circulatory system that includes a heart but no blood vessels. Crustaceans reproduce sexually. Their young hatch from eggs.

The eating habits of crustaceans vary. Lobsters and shrimp eat plants and small animals. Many crustaceans are scavengers, feeding off the remains of other organisms. Some, such as barnacles, are filter feeders. The larval form of a barnacle is free swimming. However, as an adult this arthropod attaches itself to a rock or another hard surface, such as a mollusk's shell or the hull of a ship. It uses its tentacles to capture food from the surrounding water.

## Arachnids are eight-legged arthropods.

This mite is an arachnid that lives in dust. This micrograph shows it magnified 150×.

Spiders, mites, ticks, and scorpions belong to a group called the arachnids. Like all arthropods, arachnids have an exoskeleton, jointed limbs, and segmented bodies. But the bodies of arachnids have some characteristics that distinguish them from other arthropods. Arachnids always have four pairs of legs and only two body segments. Arachnids do not have antennae.

Some arachnids, including ticks and chigger mites, are parasites. Other arachnids, such as spiders and scorpions, are predators. Recall that predators get their food by capturing and consuming other animals. Predatory arachnids kill their prey by stinging them, biting them, or injecting them with venom.

The spiders are the largest group of arachnids. Many spiders have a unique adaptation for capturing their prey. They produce an extremely strong material, called silk, inside their bodies and use the silk to make webs for capturing food. The spider spins strands of silk out from tubes called spinnerets at the rear of its abdomen. It weaves the strands into a nearly invisible web. The web serves as a net for catching insects and other small organisms that the spider eats. This adaptation allows web-building spiders to wait for their prey to come to them. Other invertebrates, such as silkworms, produce silk, but they do not weave webs.

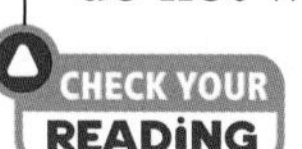


How is the way some spiders capture prey unusual?

Some arachnids obtain oxygen through spiracles, as insects do. However, certain species of spiders have a unique type of respiratory organ referred to as book lungs. Book lungs are like moist pockets with folds. They are located inside the animal's abdomen.

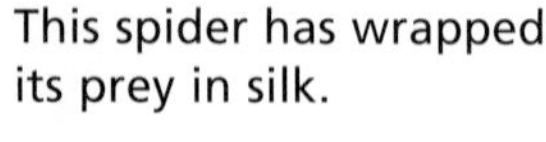

This spider has wrapped its prey in silk.

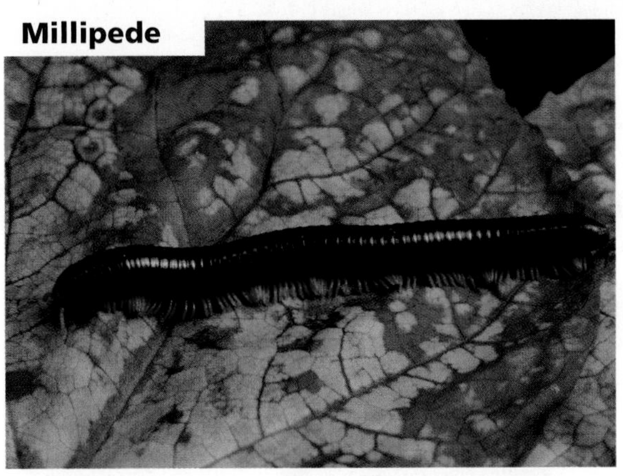

READING VISUALS COMPARE AND CONTRAST With their long segmented bodies, a millipede and a centipede look very similar. How are they different?

## Millipedes and centipedes are arthropods.

At first glance, the members of two other arthropod groups look similar. Both centipedes and millipedes have long, segmented bodies and many legs. However, animals from these groups differ in their body features and their behavior.

Millipedes are arthropods with two pairs of walking legs on each body segment. Millipedes move rather slowly and eat decaying leaves and plant matter. When disturbed, many millipedes emit a foul odor that can be harmful to predators.

Centipedes can move more quickly. They have one pair of walking legs per body segment. They have antennae and jawlike mouthparts. Many centipedes also have pincers on their rearmost segment. Centipedes are predators. They can use their jaws and pincers to paralyze prey and protect themselves from predators.

## 4.4 Review

### KEY CONCEPTS

1. Describe the characteristics of insects, crustaceans, and arachnids.
2. What is molting and how does it relate to an exoskeleton?
3. Name three arthropods and the adaptations they have for feeding.

### CRITICAL THINKING

4. **Analyze** How does the form of an exoskeleton relate to its function?
5. **Connect** Mosquitoes can spread disease, such as the West Nile virus. People are advised not to leave open containers of water in the yard. How does standing water contribute to an increase in the number of mosquitoes?

### CHALLENGE

6. **Evaluate** Many plant-eating insects live less than a year. An adult will lay eggs in the fall and then die as winter comes. The eggs hatch the next spring. How does the life cycle of the insect fit in with the life cycle of plants? What role does the egg play in the survival of the insect species in this case?

# 4 Chapter Review

**the BIG idea**

**Invertebrate animals have a variety of body plans and adaptations.**

## KEY CONCEPTS SUMMARY

### 4.1 Most animals are invertebrates.

**Invertebrates** are a diverse group of animals. Species of invertebrates live in almost every environment.

**Sponges** are simple invertebrates that have several types of specialized cells.

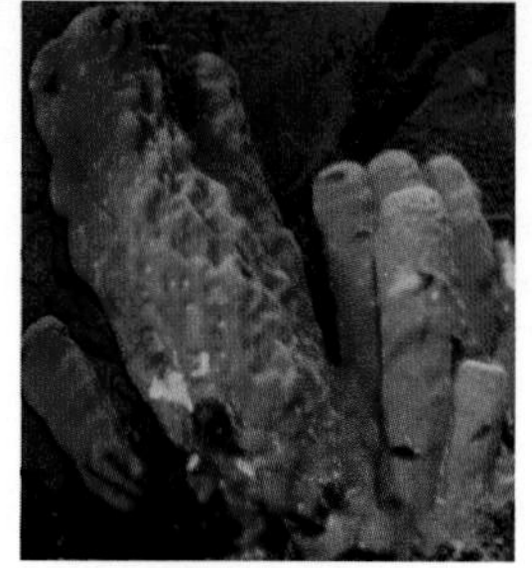

**VOCABULARY**
**invertebrate** p. 123
**sponge** p. 125
**sessile** p. 125
**larva** p. 126

### 4.2 Cnidarians and worms have different body plans.

**Cnidarians** have simple bodies with specialized cells and tissues.

Most **worms** have organs and complex body systems.

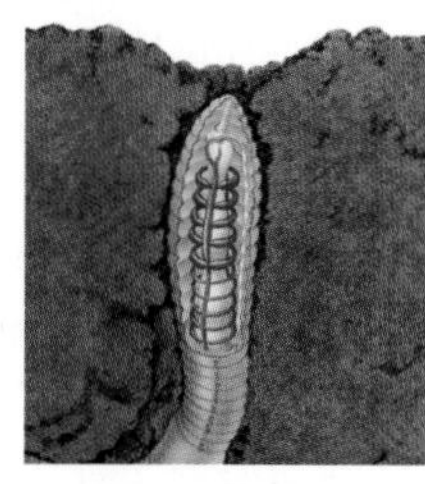

**VOCABULARY**
**cnidarian** p.128
**tentacle** p. 128
**mobile** p. 130

### 4.3 Most mollusks have shells, and echinoderms have spiny skeletons.

**Mollusks** include bivalves, gastropods, and cephalopods.

**Echinoderms** have a water vascular system and tube feet.

**VOCABULARY**
**mollusk** p. 136
**gill** p. 137
**lung** p. 137
**echinoderm** p. 139

### 4.4 Arthropods have exoskeletons and joints.

**Arthropods**, which include insects, crustaceans, and arachnids, are the most abundant and diverse group of animals.

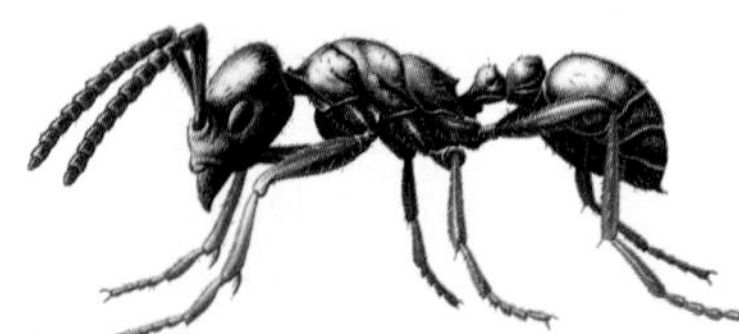

**VOCABULARY**
**arthropod** p. 142
**exoskeleton** p. 143
**molting** p. 143
**insect** p. 145
**metamorphosis** p. 146

## Reviewing Vocabulary

*Copy and complete the chart below.*

| Word | Definition | Example |
|---|---|---|
| 1. mollusk | | clam, snail, squid |
| 2. arthropod | invertebrate with jointed legs, segmented body, and an exoskeleton | |
| 3. | ocean-dwelling animal with spiny skeleton | sea star |
| 4. sessile | | sponge |
| 5. larva | | caterpillar |
| 6. metamorphosis | | caterpillar changing into a butterfly |
| 7. molting | process by which an arthropod sheds its exoskeleton | |
| 8. | arthropod with three body segments, one pair of antennae, and six legs | grasshopper, mosquito, beetle |

## Reviewing Key Concepts

**Multiple Choice** *Choose the letter of the best answer.*

**9.** Which of the following groups of animals is the most abundant?

**a.** worms
**b.** mollusks
**c.** echinoderms
**d.** arthropods

**10.** In what way are all invertebrates alike?

**a.** They do not have backbones.
**b.** They live in the ocean.
**c.** They are predators.
**d.** They have a closed circulatory system.

**11.** Sponges bring food into their bodies through a

**a.** system of pores
**b.** water vascular system
**c.** mouth
**d.** digestive tract

**12.** Which group of invertebrates has a mantle?

**a.** echinoderms
**b.** crustaceans
**c.** cnidarians
**d.** mollusks

**13.** Bivalves, cephalopods, and gastropods are all types of

**a.** echinoderms
**b.** mollusks
**c.** crustaceans
**d.** cnidarians

**14.** As they grow, arthropods shed their exoskeleton in a process called

**a.** metamorphosis
**b.** symmetry
**c.** molting
**d.** siphoning

**15.** Which invertebrate animals always have three body segments: a head, a thorax, and an abdomen?

**a.** segmented worms
**b.** adult insects
**c.** arachnids
**d.** echinoderms

**16.** Which group of invertebrates have a water vascular system and tube feet?

**a.** echinoderms
**b.** crustaceans
**c.** cnidarians
**d.** mollusks

**Short Answer** *Write a short answer to each question.*

**17.** Describe the stages in the life cycle of an insect that has complete metamorphosis.

**18.** Explain one advantage and one disadvantage an exoskeleton has for an organism.

**19.** Is a spider an insect? Explain.

## Thinking Critically

20. **CLASSIFY** What characteristics does a sponge have that make it seem like a plant? What characteristic makes a sponge an animal?

21. **PROVIDE EXAMPLES** Arthropods are the most diverse and abundant group of animals on Earth. Give three examples of arthropod features that enable them to be active in their environment.

22. **INFER** Worms have a tube-shaped body with openings at either end. How does this body plan relate to the way a worm obtains its food and processes it?

23. **COMPARE** Jellyfish go through a life cycle that involves different stages of development. Insects also go through different stages of development in a process called metamorphosis. What are some similarities between metamorphosis in a mosquito, for example, and a jellyfish life cycle? Use the terms in the table below in your answer.

| larva | polyp | medusa |
|---|---|---|
| pupa | adult | mobile |
| sessile | | |

*Refer to the chart below as you answer the next three questions.*

**Invertebrate Species by Group**

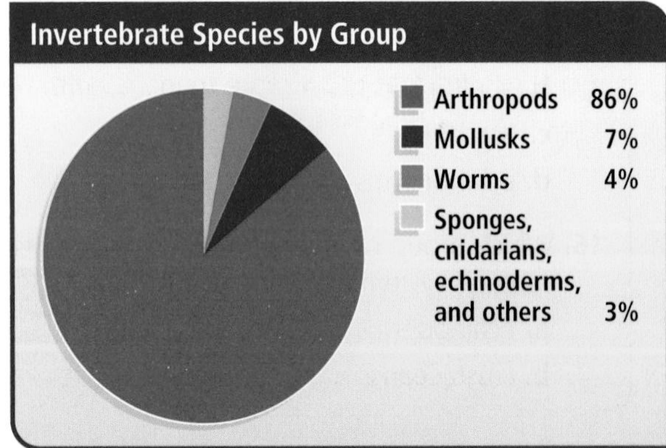


24. **APPLY** What percentage of invertebrate species are arthropods?

25. **CALCULATE** What is the combined percentage of all other invertebrate species, not including arthropods?

26. **APPLY** How could you modify this pie chart to show that insects, crustaceans, and arachnids are types of arthropods?

27. **APPLY** A sea star has a radial body plan. A spider has a bilateral body plan. How does the shape of these animal's bodies affect how they capture their food?

28. **COMPARE AND CONTRAST** How are the three main groups of arthropods similar? How are they different?

29. **SYNTHESIZE** Animal bodies need support as well as protection. What structures do the bodies of a sponge, a bivalve, and an insect have for protection and support? Use the terms in the table below in your answer.

| spicule | shell | exoskeleton |
|---|---|---|

30. **PREDICT** Many people think of insects as pests, but some species of insects are important pollinators for many flowering plants. Also, many animals eat insects. What problems would humans face if Earth's insect species became extinct?

## the BIG idea

31. **INFER** How does a cnidarian such as the jellyfish in the photograph on pages 120–121 respond to its environment? Is the diver in the photograph in danger? Explain your answer.

32. **COMPARE AND CONTRAST** Make a chart showing the key features of the body plans of three different invertebrate animal groups. For each group, identify one characteristic that is an adaptation.

## UNIT PROJECTS

If you need to create graphs or other visuals for your project, be sure you have grid paper, poster board, markers, or other supplies.

# Standardized Test Practice

For practice on your state test, go to . . .
TEST PRACTICE
CLASSZONE.COM

## Analyzing Data

Reef-building corals are invertebrates that live in clear, warm ocean water. As a coral grows, it produces a hard external skeleton. If many generations of corals grow near each other over a long period of time, their accumulated skeletons form a structure called a reef. Many ocean life-forms live in and around coral reefs. This table shows the maximum growth rates of five species of reef-building corals.

| Species | Rate of Growth (mm per year) | Number of Years to Grow a 1400-m Reef |
|---|---|---|
| A | 143 | 9,790 |
| B | 99 | 14,100 |
| C | 120 | 11,700 |
| D | 100 | 14,000 |
| E | 226 | 6,190 |

*Choose the letter of the best response*

**1.** Which has the fastest rate of growth?
- **a.** Species C
- **b.** Species B
- **c.** Species D
- **d.** Species E

**2.** What is the growth rate for Species B ?
- **a.** 99 mm per year
- **b.** 120 mm per year
- **c.** 143 mm per year
- **d.** 14,100 mm per year

**3.** Which takes the shortest amount of time to grow to 1400 meters?
- **a.** Species B
- **b.** Species C
- **c.** Species D
- **d.** Species E

**4.** Which have about the same rate of growth?
- **a.** Species A and C
- **b.** Species B and D
- **c.** Species C and E
- **d.** Species D and E

**5.** How many years does it take Species A to grow into a 1400-m reef?
- **a.** 143
- **b.** 226
- **c.** 9790
- **d.** 14,000

**6.** Based on the information in the table, which statement is true?
- **a.** Coral species with the fastest growth rates take the greatest amount of time to grow.
- **b.** Coral species with the slowest growth rates take the least amount of time to grow.
- **c.** Coral species have different rates of growth that affect how long it takes them to grow.
- **d.** Coral species that grow more than 100 mm per year take the longest to grow.

## Extended Response

**7.** Corals are cnidarians. They are sessile animals that live attached to one place. Other ocean-dwelling animals are mobile and can move about their environment. Crustaceans like the lobster are mobile, so are mollusks like the octopus. How does being sessile or mobile affect the feeding behaviors of an animal? Do you think the bodies and systems of sessile animals are going to be different from those of mobile animals? Use some of the terms in the word box in your answer.

| | | |
|---|---|---|
| digestive system | sessile | mobile |
| nervous system | filter | mouth |
| muscle tissue | food | sensory organs |

CHAPTER

# Vertebrate Animals

## the BIG idea

Vertebrate animals live in most of Earth's environments.

## Key Concepts

SECTION

**Vertebrates are animals with endoskeletons.**
Learn how most of the vertebrates on Earth are fish.

SECTION

**Amphibians and reptiles are adapted for life on land.**
Learn how most amphibians hatch in water and most reptiles hatch on land.

SECTION

**Birds meet their needs on land, in water, and in the air.**
Learn how adaptations for flight affect how birds meet their needs.

SECTION

**Mammals live in many environments.**
Learn about mammals' many adaptations.

**Internet Preview**

CLASSZONE.COM

Chapter 5 online resources: Content Review, Visualization, five Resource Centers, Math Tutorial, Test Practice.

***What do these penguins have in common with this seal?***

# EXPLORE the BIG idea

## What Animals Live Near You?

Make a list of animals you think live in your neighborhood. Remember that some animals are small! Organize the animals on your list into groups.

**Observe and Think** Where do you think you would see the most animals? What about the widest variety?

## How Is a Bird Like a Frog?

Fish, frogs, snakes, birds, dogs, and humans are all vertebrate animals. Choose two vertebrates and quickly sketch their body plans, including their skeletons.

**Observe and Think**
Where do you think each animal's brain, heart, and stomach are located?

## Internet Activity: Where in the World?

Go to **ClassZone.com** to learn more about the distribution of reptiles and amphibians across the world.

**Observe and Think**
In what area of the world do the greatest number of species live? the least? What features of these animals might help explain the pattern of distribution?

Bird Characteristics **Code: MDL043**

CHAPTER 5

# Getting Ready to Learn

## CONCEPTS REVIEW

- All living things have common needs.
- Plants and some invertebrates have adaptations for life on land.
- Most multicellular organisms can reproduce sexually.

## VOCABULARY REVIEW

**migration** p. 64
**embryo** p. 98
**gill** p. 137
**lung** p. 137
**exoskeleton** p. 143

CONTENT REVIEW
CLASSZONE.COM
Review concepts and vocabulary.

## TAKING NOTES

### CHOOSE YOUR OWN STRATEGY

Take notes using one or more of the strategies from earlier chapters – **main idea webs, main idea and details, mind maps**, or **combination notes**. You can also use other note-taking strategies that you may already know.

### VOCABULARY STRATEGY

Think about a vocabulary term as a **magnet word** diagram. Write other terms and ideas related to that term around it.

See the Note-Taking Handbook on pages R45–R51.

SCIENCE NOTEBOOK

Main Idea Web

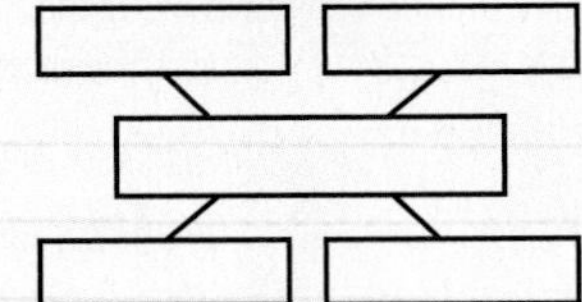

Main Idea and Details

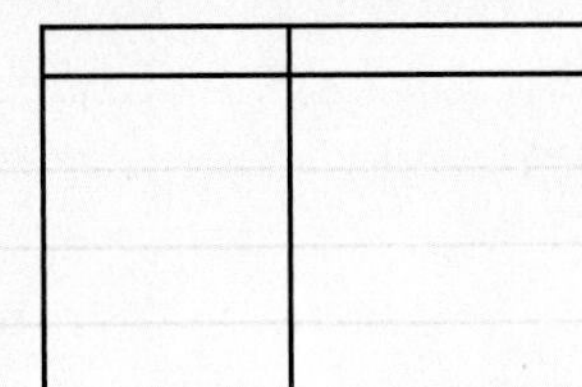

Mind Map

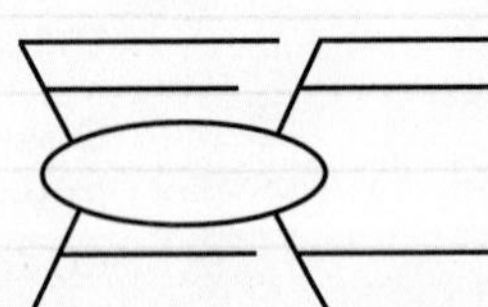

ENDOTHERM

bird

mammal

transforms food into heat

hair, feathers, blubber

shivers, sweats, pants

active in cold environments

KEY CONCEPT

# Vertebrates are animals with endoskeletons.

**BEFORE, you learned**

- Most animals are invertebrates
- Animals have adaptations that suit their environment
- Animals get energy by consuming food

**NOW, you will learn**

- About the skeletons of vertebrate animals
- About the characteristics of fish
- About three groups of fish

**VOCABULARY**

**vertebrate** p. 157
**endoskeleton** p. 157
**scale** p. 161

**EXPLORE Streamlined Shapes**

***How does a fish's shape help it move?***

**PROCEDURE**

1. Place your hand straight up and down in a tub of water. Keep your fingers together and your palm flat.
2. Move your hand from one side of the tub to the other, using your palm to push the water.
3. Move your hand across the tub again, this time using the edge of your hand as if you were cutting the water.

**MATERIALS**
tub of water

**WHAT DO YOU THINK?**

- In which position was the shape of your hand most like the shape of a fish's body?
- How might the shape of a fish's body affect its ability to move through water?

## Vertebrate animals have backbones.

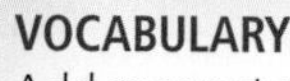

VOCABULARY
Add magnet word diagrams for *vertebrate* and *endoskeleton* to your notebook.

If you asked someone to name an animal, he or she would probably name a vertebrate. Fish, frogs, snakes, birds, dogs, and humans are all **vertebrates,** or animals with backbones. Even though only about 5 percent of animal species are vertebrates, they are among the most familiar and thoroughly studied organisms on Earth.

Vertebrate animals have muscles, a digestive system, a respiratory system, a circulatory system, and a nervous system with sensory organs. The characteristic that distinguishes vertebrates from other animals is the **endoskeleton,** an internal support system that grows along with the animal. Endoskeletons allow more flexibility and ways of moving than exoskeletons do.

## Vertebrate Skeleton and Muscles

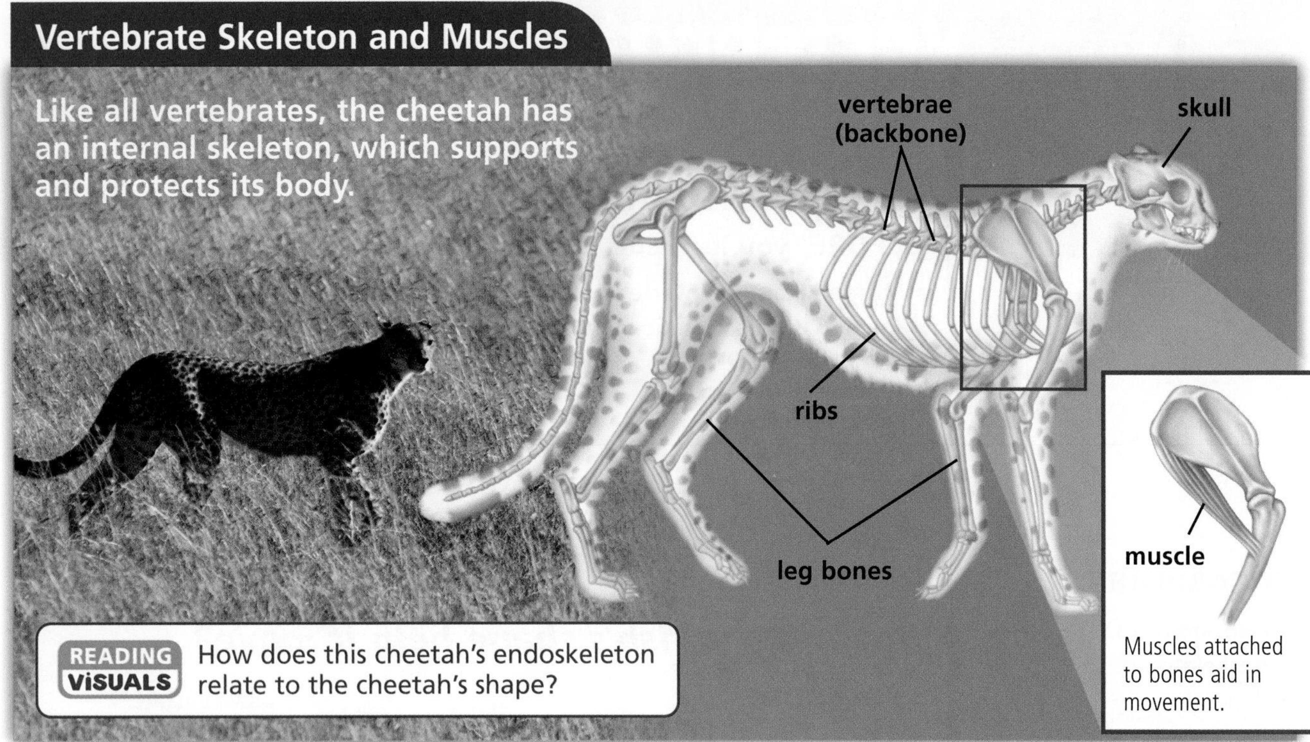

Like all vertebrates, the cheetah has an internal skeleton, which supports and protects its body.
vertebrae (backbone)
skull
ribs
leg bones
muscle
READING VISUALS How does this cheetah's endoskeleton relate to the cheetah's shape?

Muscles attached to bones aid in movement.

Vertebrates are named for specialized bones called vertebrae. These bones are located in the middle of each vertebrate animal's central body segment. Together, the vertebrae are sometimes called a backbone. The vertebrae support muscles and surround the spinal cord, which connects the animal's brain to its nerves. Other bones, such as the ribs and skull, protect organs like the heart, lungs, and brain.

What is one function of the endoskeleton for vertebrate animals?

## Most vertebrates are fish.

**NOTETAKING STRATEGY**
Choose a strategy from an earlier chapter to take notes on the idea that most vertebrates are fish. Be sure to include information on adaptations to water.

Fish are the most diverse group of vertebrate animals. There are more than 20,000 species of fish, ranging in size from tiny minnows to huge whale sharks. Fish live in nearly every aquatic environment, from freshwater lakes to the bottom of the sea. Some fish even are able to survive below the ice in the Antarctic!

Fish are adapted for life in water. Like all living things, fish need to get materials from their environment. For example, fish must be able to get oxygen from water. Fish must also be able to move through water in order to find food. Fish that live in water where sunlight does not penetrate need special organs to help them find food.

Most fish move by using muscles and fins to push their streamlined bodies through water. These muscles allow fish to move more quickly than most other vertebrates. Most fish also have an organ called a swim bladder, which allows them to control the depth at which they float.

Fish have sensory organs for taste, odor, and sound. Most fish species have eyes that allow them to see well underwater. Most fish also have a sensory system unlike that of other vertebrates. This system includes an organ called a lateral line, which allows fish to sense vibrations from objects nearby without touching or seeing them.

Explore how fish breathe.

Fish, like some invertebrates, remove oxygen from water with specialized respiratory organs called gills. You can locate most fishes' gills by looking for the openings, called gill slits, on the sides of their head. You can see what gills look like in the diagram of a fish below.

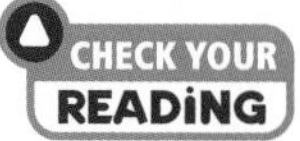


How are gills similar to lungs?

Fish gills are made up of many folds of tissue and are filled with blood. When a fish swims, it takes water in through its mouth and then pushes the water back over its gills. In the gills, oxygen dissolved in the water moves into the fish's blood. Carbon dioxide, a waste product of respiration, moves from the blood into the water. Then the water is forced out of the fish's body through its gill slits. The oxygen is transported to the fish's cells. It is a necessary material for releasing energy.

## Inside a Fish

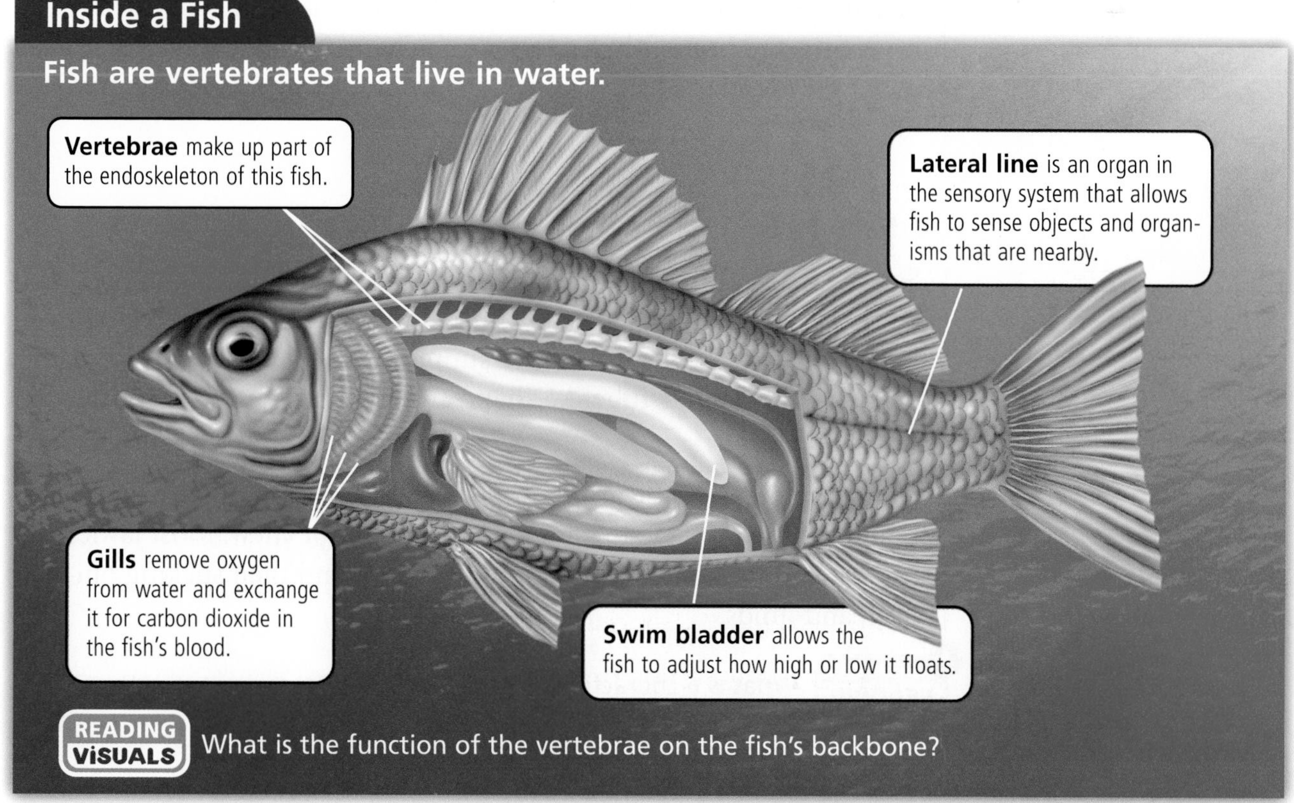

Fish are vertebrates that live in water.
**Vertebrae** make up part of the endoskeleton of this fish.
**Lateral line** is an organ in the sensory system that allows fish to sense objects and organisms that are nearby.
**Gills** remove oxygen from water and exchange it for carbon dioxide in the fish's blood.
**Swim bladder** allows the fish to adjust how high or low it floats.
READING VISUALS
What is the function of the vertebrae on the fish's backbone?

## Three Groups of Fish

Scientists usually classify fish in three groups.

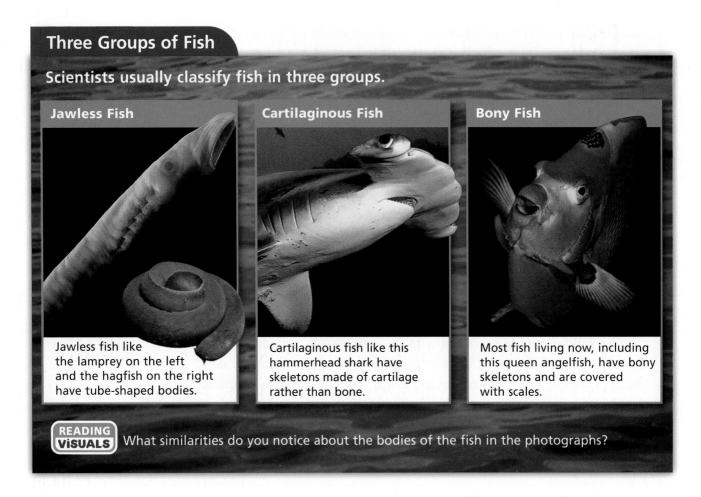

**Jawless Fish**

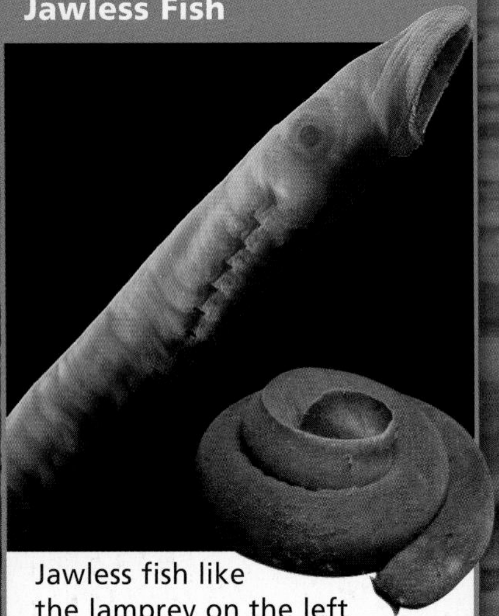

Jawless fish like the lamprey on the left and the hagfish on the right have tube-shaped bodies.

**Cartilaginous Fish**

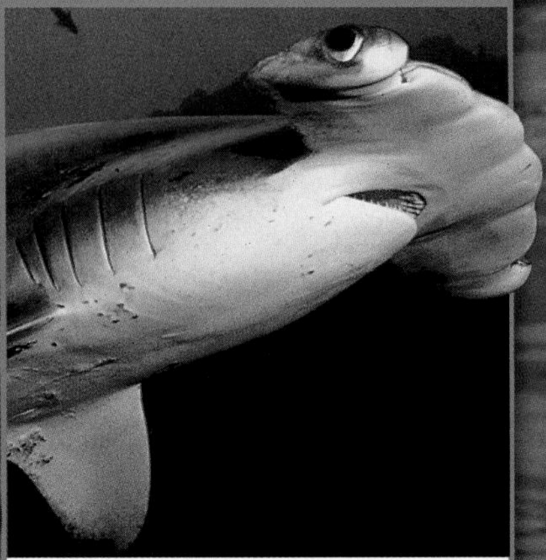

Cartilaginous fish like this hammerhead shark have skeletons made of cartilage rather than bone.

**Bony Fish**

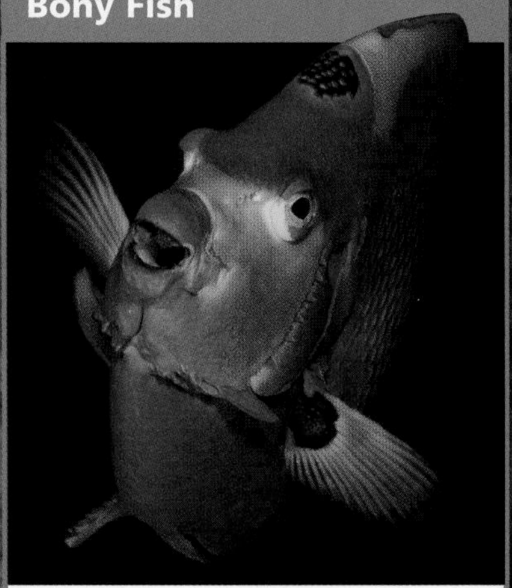

Most fish living now, including this queen angelfish, have bony skeletons and are covered with scales.

**READING VISUALS** What similarities do you notice about the bodies of the fish in the photographs?

# Fish can be classified in three groups.

Scientists classify fish into three major groups: jawless fish, cartilaginous fish, and bony fish. Each group is characterized by body features. As you read on and learn about each group of fish, look at the photographs above.

## Jawless Fish

Scientists think that fish in this group, which includes lampreys and hagfish, are the living animals most similar to the first fish that lived on Earth. Jawless fish have simpler bodies than the other fish. They have a slender tubelike shape and a digestive system without a stomach.

As the name of the group implies, these fish do not have jaw bones. Although they do have teeth, they cannot chew. Most jawless fish eat by biting into another animal's body and then sucking out flesh and fluids.

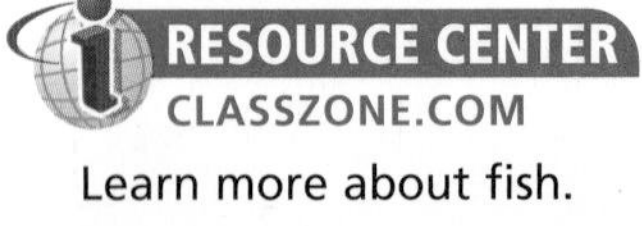

**CHECK YOUR READING** What is a characteristic of jawless fish?

RESOURCE CENTER
CLASSZONE.COM
Learn more about fish.

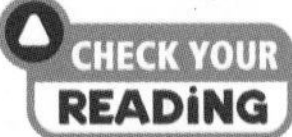

### Cartilaginous Fish

This group includes sharks, rays, and skates. Their skeletons are not made of hard bone, but of a flexible tissue called cartilage (KAHR-tuhl-ihj). Some species of sharks are dangerous to humans, but most cartilaginous fish feed primarily on small animals such as mollusks and crustaceans. Whale sharks and basking sharks, which are the largest fish on Earth, feed by filtering small organisms from the water as they swim.

Rays are flat-bodied cartilaginous fish that live most of their lives on the ocean floor. Their mouths are on the underside of their bodies. Most rays eat by pulling small animals out of the sand. A ray's flat body has fins that extend on either side of its vertebrae like wings. When rays swim, these fins wave so it looks as if the fish is flying through the water.

Describe three ways cartilaginous fish species obtain food.

### Bony Fish

Most fish species, including tuna, flounder, goldfish, and eels, are classified in this large, diverse group. Of the nearly 20,000 fish species, about 96 percent are bony fish. Bony fish have skeletons made of hard bone, much like the skeleton in your body. Most bony fish are covered with overlapping bony structures called **scales.** They have jaws and teeth and several pairs of fins.

The range of body shapes and behavior in bony fish shows how living things are adapted to their environments. Think of the bright colors and patterns of tropical fish in an aquarium. These eye-catching features are probably adaptations for survival in the fishes' natural environment. In a coral reef, for example, bright stripes and spots might provide camouflage or might advertise the fish's presence to other animals, including potential mates.

## Most young fish develop inside an egg.

Most fish species reproduce sexually. The female produces eggs, and the male produces sperm. In many fish species, individual animals select a mate. For example, a female fish might release eggs into the water only when a certain male can fertilize them. After the eggs are fertilized, the parent fish usually leave the eggs to develop and hatch on their own. Most fish reproduce this way, but there are many exceptions.

In sexual reproduction the genetic material from two parents is combined in their offspring.

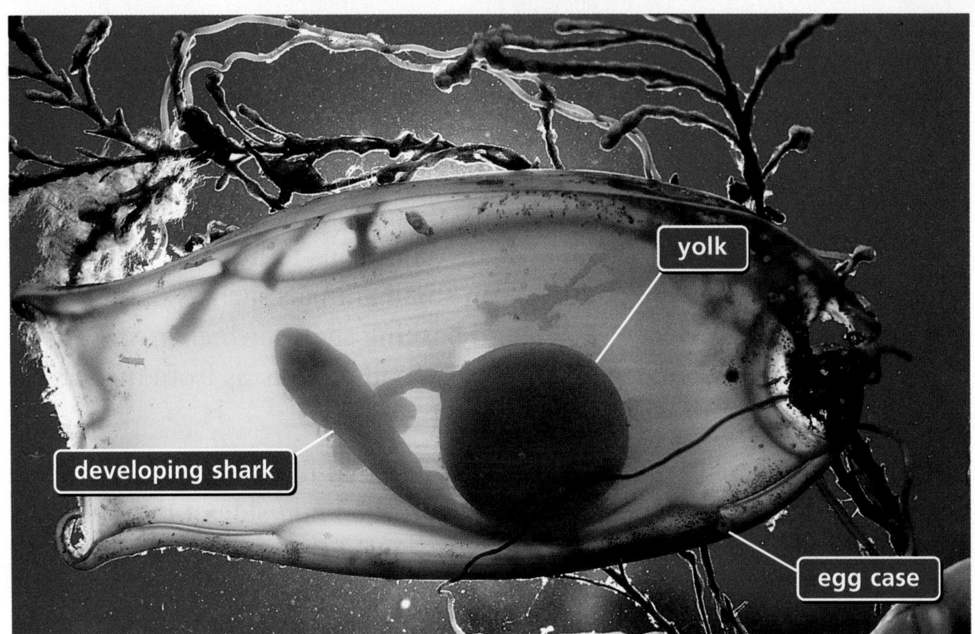


This young shark is developing from an egg that is covered by an egg case. In this photograph, light shining through the egg case allows you to see the shark and the yolk inside.

All animals and plants that can reproduce sexually produce egg cells and sperm cells. However, the structure and size of eggs vary among species. In Chapter 3, you learned that the eggs of flowering plants are found inside the seeds in fruit. In Chapter 4, you read about the eggs of different types of invertebrates. You learned that some eggs have a food supply and a protective covering. For some animals, the food supply is called yolk, and the covering is called an egg case.

**REMINDER**

An embryo is the immature form of an organism that has the potential to grow to maturity.

Most fish eggs are surrounded by a soft egg case that water can pass through. Since fish lay eggs in the water, this means that a fish embryo inside an egg gets the water and oxygen it needs directly from its surroundings. The egg's yolk provides the developing fish with food. Such eggs can develop on their own, without needing care from adults. However, many animals eat fish eggs. Fish often lay and fertilize many eggs, but few of them survive to maturity.

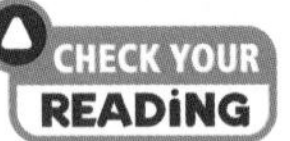

**CHECK YOUR READING** How are fish eggs different from invertebrate eggs?

## 5.1 Review

### KEY CONCEPTS

1. Why are fish classified as vertebrate animals?
2. What are three adaptations that suit fish for life in water?
3. Name a feature for fish from each of these groups: jawless, cartilaginous, and bony.

### CRITICAL THINKING

4. **Apply** If you wanted to choose tropical fish that could live comfortably in the same tank, what body features or behaviors might you look for?
5. **Infer** Some fish do not lay eggs. Their eggs develop inside the female fish. How might the offspring of one of these fish differ from those of an egg-laying fish?

### CHALLENGE

6. **Synthesize** Fossils indicate that species of fish with bodies very similar to today's sharks have lived in aquatic environments for hundreds of millions of years. What can you infer about the adaptations of sharks from this?

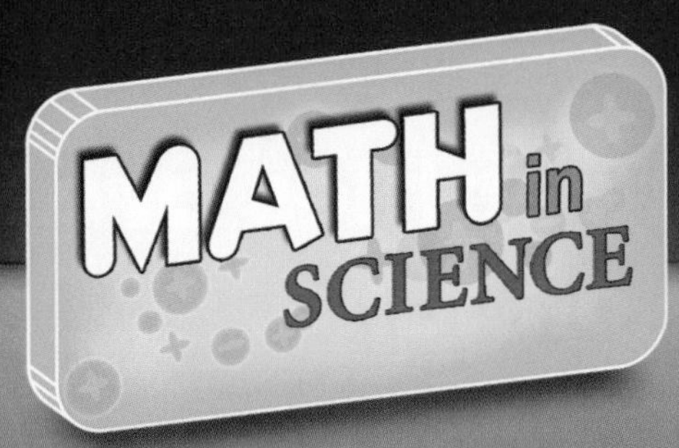


SKILL: DIVIDING BY DECIMALS

**MATH TUTORIAL**
CLASSZONE.COM
Click on Math Tutorial for more help dividing by decimals.

# Great Growth

The leatherback sea turtle is one of the largest reptiles alive. Full-grown, adult leatherbacks can weigh 880 kilograms. This huge turtle starts out life weighing just 44 grams.

## Example

**How many times heavier is the 880 kg adult than the 44 g baby?**

**(1)** Convert the units so they are all in kilograms.
$44 \text{ g} \times 0.001 \text{ kg/g} = 0.044 \text{ kg}$

**(2)** Divide 880 by 0.044 to get the answer.

**(3)** To divide by a decimal, multiply the divisor and the dividend by a multiple of 10. Since the decimal number is in thousandths, multiply by 1000.

$0.044\overline{)880000}$ $\qquad$ $\begin{array}{r} 20{,}000 \\ 44\overline{)880000} \end{array}$

**ANSWER** The adult leatherback is 20,000 times heavier than the baby leatherback hatchling.

**Answer the following questions.**

1. An adult leatherback has been measured as 1.5 m from nose to tail. The same animal measured just 6 cm as a baby hatchling. How many times longer is the adult?
2. A typical box turtle grows to 12.5 cm long. How many times longer is the adult leatherback than the adult box turtle?
3. Suppose the box turtle hatched with a length of 2.5 cm. By how many times has its length grown at adulthood?
4. How many times longer is the leatherback hatchling than the box turtle hatchling?

**CHALLENGE** What fraction of its adult weight is the leatherback hatchling in the example?

KEY CONCEPT

# Amphibians and reptiles are adapted for life on land.

**BEFORE, you learned**

- Fish are vertebrates that live in water
- Fish gills remove oxygen from water
- Most young fish develop inside eggs laid in the water

**NOW, you will learn**

- About amphibians, vertebrates that can live on land for part of their lives
- About reptiles, vertebrates that can live on land for their whole lives
- About the body temperature of amphibians and reptiles

**VOCABULARY**

**amphibian** p. 167
**reptile** p. 168
**ectotherm** p. 170

**EXPLORE Moving on Land**

### *What good are legs?*

**PROCEDURE**

1. Measure and record your height in meters.
2. Jump as far as you can, and have your partner record the distance.
3. Divide the distance you jumped by your height.
4. Some frogs can jump a distance that's equal to 10 times their body length.Calculate the distance you would be able to jump if you were a frog.

**MATERIALS**

meter stick

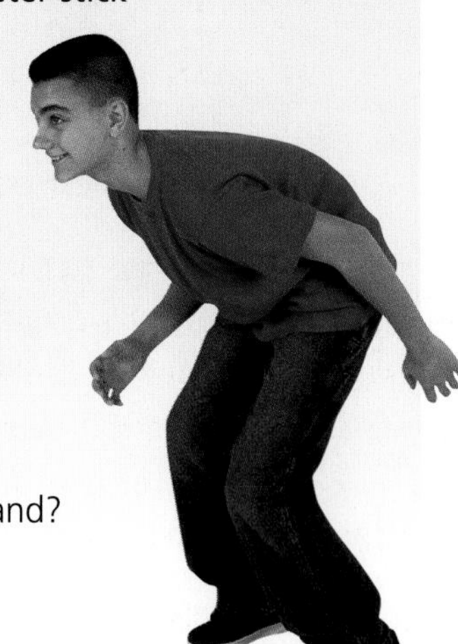

**WHAT DO YOU THINK?**

How might the ability to jump help a frog survive on land?

## Vertebrates adapted to live on land.

Most of the groups of invertebrates and all of the vertebrates you have read about so far live in water. Organisms such as plants and insects became very diverse after adapting to live on land. Some vertebrate animals adapted to live on land as well. In this section you will learn about the first vertebrates to live on land, a group called the amphibians, and the group that came next, the reptiles.

Amphibians living today include frogs, toads, and salamanders. Reptiles include turtles, snakes, lizards, and crocodiles. Some people find it hard to tell animals from these two groups apart, but there are some important characteristics that distinguish them.

More than 350 million years ago, Earth was already inhabited by many species of vertebrate animals. All of them were fish. They

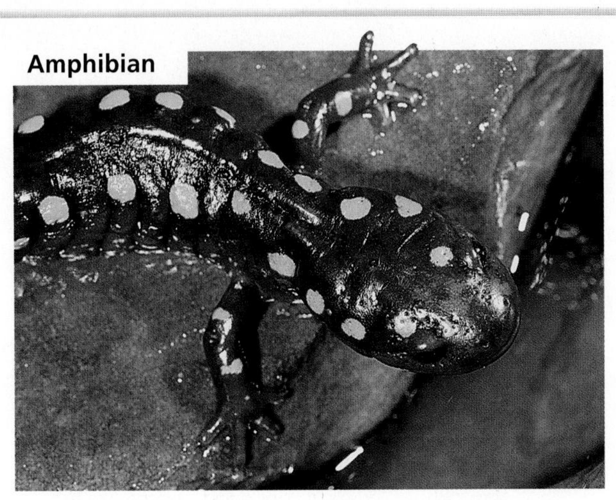
Amphibian

Reptile

READING VISUALS COMPARE AND CONTRAST Just by looking at these two animals, what physical differences can you see? What similarities do you see?

lived in salt water and fresh water, consumed other organisms as food, and obtained oxygen using specialized organs called gills.

Recall the pond you imagined in Chapter 3, when you learned that plants adapted to land. Now imagine the same pond a hundred million years later. The pond is crowded with invertebrates and fish, all competing for oxygen and food.

Suppose a period of dry weather makes the pond start to dry up. Many animals die, and food and oxygen become scarce. On the banks of the pond it might be less crowded. Invertebrates living there are sources of food. Air on land contains more oxygen than water does. Fish that could survive on land would be better off than the fish in the pond in this situation.

However, the gills of fish work only when they are wet. Fins can function to make a fish move through water, but they are not good for moving on land. Water provides more support for the body than air. Plus, fish sensory organs are specialized for detecting sounds and smells in water, not in air.

It took millions of years and many generations before different adaptations occurred and amphibians became a distinct group. These early amphibians were able to survive on land. Today there are fish that can breathe air and fish that can walk for short distances on land. There are also some modern amphibian species that have adapted to life only in water.

CHECK YOUR READING How are amphibians different from fish?

**NOTETAKING STRATEGY**
Choose a strategy from an earlier chapter or use one of your own to take notes on how vertebrates adapted to life on land.

## Wood Frog Life Cycle

**Wood frogs live in moist forest environments and breed once a year, in early spring.**

A female adult wood frog deposits a mass of eggs in a pool of fresh water.

Some of the eggs hatch and become tadpoles. Tadpoles swim and breathe like fish.

The tadpole's legs develop, and its tail shrinks. Many changes occur inside the tadpole's body as well.

The young wood frog climbs out of the water. From now on, it will live on land and breathe with lungs.

The wood frog will grow until fall and slow its activity in winter. In spring females lay eggs and the cycle repeats.

**READING VISUALS** What visible changes occur in a wood frog tadpole's body as it transforms into an adult wood frog?

## Amphibians have moist skin and lay eggs without shells.

As adults, most **amphibians** have these characteristics:

- They have two pairs of legs, or a total of four limbs.
- They lay their eggs in water.
- They obtain oxygen through their smooth, moist skin. Many also have respiratory organs called lungs.
- Their sensory organs are adapted for sensing on land.

Most amphibians live in moist environments. Their skin is a respiratory organ that functions only when it is wet. Most species of amphibians live close to water or in damp places. Some are most active at night, when the ground is wet with dew. Others live mostly underground, beneath wet leaves, or under decaying trees.

Learn more about amphibians.

Amphibians reproduce sexually. In most amphibian species, a female lays eggs in water, a male fertilizes them with sperm, and then the offspring develop and hatch on their own. Yolk inside the eggs provides developing embryos with nutrients. Like fish eggs, amphibian eggs do not have hard shells. This means developing amphibians can get water and oxygen directly from their surroundings.

How is the way most amphibians reproduce similar to the way most fish reproduce?

### Amphibian Life Cycle

The diagram shows the life cycle of one amphibian, the wood frog. When a young amphibian hatches, it is a larva. In Chapter 4 you learned that a larva is an early stage that is very different from the animal's adult form. For example, the larvae of frogs and toads are called tadpoles. Tadpoles look and behave like small fish. They breathe with gills, eat mostly algae, and move by pushing against the water with their tails.

**READING TIP**

As you read about the amphibian life cycle in these paragraphs, look at the diagram on page 166 to see what a wood frog looks like at each stage.

After a few weeks, a tadpole's body begins to change. Inside, the lungs develop and parts of the digestive system transform. The tadpole begins to have some of the external features of a frog. It develops legs, its tail shrinks, and its head changes shape.

As a young wood frog's body changes, its gills stop functioning, and it begins breathing air with its lungs. The frog starts using its tongue to capture and eat small animals. It leaves the water and begins using its legs to move around on land. Some amphibians, such as sirens and bullfrogs, remain in or near water for all of their lives. Others, like wood frogs, most toads, and some salamanders, live in moist land environments as adults.

## Reptiles have dry, scaly skin and lay eggs with shells.

**VOCABULARY**
Add a magnet word diagram for *reptile* to your notebook.

**Reptiles** evolved soon after amphibians and are closely related to them. However, animals in the reptile group have adaptations that allow them to survive in hotter, drier places than amphibians. For many millions of years they were the largest and most diverse vertebrate animal group living on land. Most of the animals classified as reptiles have these characteristics:

- They have two pairs of legs, for a total of four limbs.
- They have tough, dry skin covered by scales.
- They obtain oxygen from air with respiratory organs called lungs.
- Their sensory organs are adapted for sensing on land.
- They lay their eggs, which have shells, on land.

CHECK YOUR READING What characteristics of reptiles are different from the characteristics of amphibians listed on page 167?

### Lungs

Reptiles do not get oxygen through their skin the way amphibians do. They are born with lungs that provide their bodies with all the oxygen they need. Lungs are internal organs made up of many small lobes of thin tissue filled with tiny blood vessels. When an animal with lungs inhales, it takes air in through its nostrils or mouth and moves the air into its lungs. There, oxygen is transported across the tissues and into the blood, and carbon dioxide is moved from the blood to the lungs and exhaled.

Reptiles like these garter snakes are covered with scales and breathe through their nostrils.

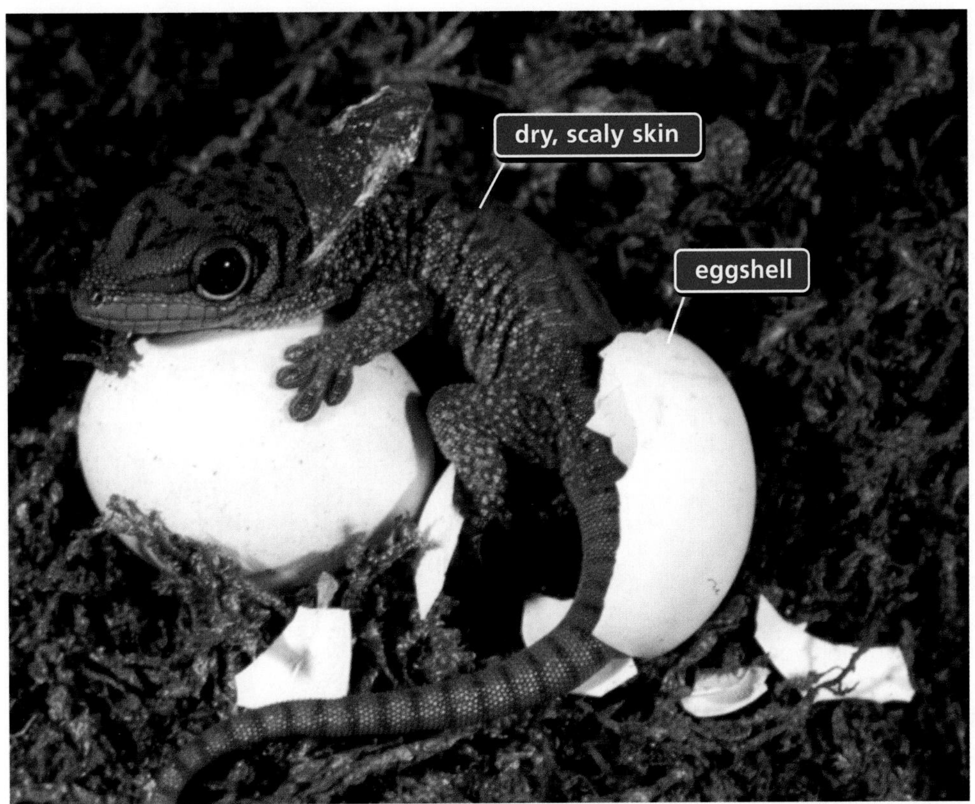


**CONTRAST** How does the egg this gecko hatched from differ from the wood frog eggs shown on page 166?

## Dry, Scaly Skin

Reptile skin is hard, dry, and covered with scales made of keratin, a substance much like your fingernails. The thick, waterproof skin of reptiles protects them from the environment and from predators. However, this means that reptiles cannot obtain water through their skin.

## Eggs with Shells

The reptile egg is an important adaptation that allows vertebrate animals to survive in hot, dry environments. The eggs of reptiles contain everything an embryo needs: water, nutrients, a system for gas exchange, and a place to store waste. Membranes separate the internal parts of the egg, which is covered by a protective shell.

Reptiles reproduce sexually. The egg cell of the female joins with the sperm cell of the male in the process of fertilization. After fertilization, a protective case, or shell, forms around each egg while it is still inside the female's body. The female selects a place to lay the eggs on land. Many species of reptiles build or dig nests. Some female reptiles, including alligators, guard their nests and care for their offspring after they hatch. Most reptiles, however, leave soon after the eggs are laid. As you can see in the photograph above, when young reptiles hatch, they look like small adults.

Find out more about reptiles.

# INVESTIGATE Eggs

**SKILL FOCUS**
Observing

**MATERIALS**
- hard-boiled egg
- plastic knife

**TIME:**
20 minutes

### *What are some of the characteristics of eggs?*

**PROCEDURE**

1. Carefully examine the outside of the hard-boiled egg. Try to notice as many details as you can. Write your observations in your notebook.
2. Gently crack the eggshell and remove it. Try to keep the shell in large pieces and the egg whole. Set the egg aside, and examine the pieces of shell. Look for details you could not see before. Write your observations in your notebook.
3. Examine the outside of the egg. Make notes about what you see. Include a sketch.
4. Use the knife to cut the egg in half. Take one half apart carefully, trying to notice as many parts as you can. Use the other half for comparison. Write up your observations.

**WHAT DO YOU THINK?**

- Reptiles, like birds, have eggs with hard shells. What structures does an egg with a shell contain?
- What might the function of each structure be?

**CHALLENGE** How might the egg's structures support a developing embryo?

## The body temperatures of amphibians and reptiles change with the environment.

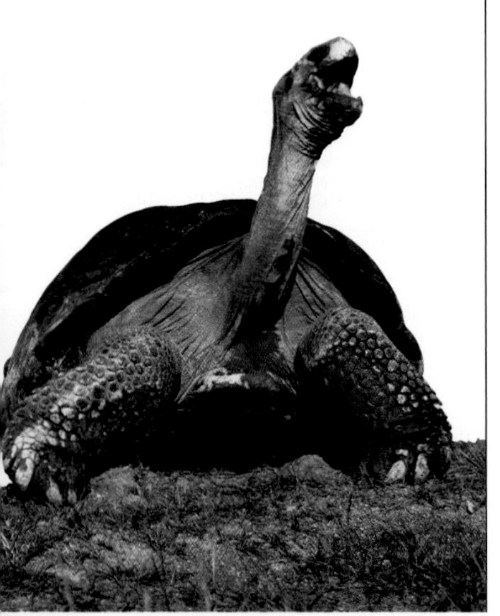

Amphibians and reptiles are **ectotherms,** animals whose body temperatures change with environmental conditions. You are not an ectotherm. Whether the air temperature of your environment is −4°C (25°F) or 43°C (110°F), your body temperature remains around 37°C (99°F). A tortoise's body temperature changes with the temperature of the air or water surrounding it. On a cool day, a tortoise's body will be cooler than it is on a hot one.

Many ectothermic animals can move and respond more quickly when their bodies are warm. Many ectotherms warm themselves in sunlight. You may have seen turtles or snakes sunning themselves. Ectothermic animals transform most of the food they consume directly into energy. Some ectotherms, even large ones such as alligators, or the Galápagos tortoise in the photograph, can survive for a long time without consuming much food.

This sand-diving lizard can reduce the amount of heat that transfers from the sand into its body by standing on two feet.

Although amphibians and reptiles do not have a constant body temperature, their bodies stop functioning well if they become too hot or too cold. Most amphibians and reptiles live in environments where the temperature of the surrounding air or water does not change too much. Others, like wood frogs and painted turtles, have adaptations that allow them to slow their body processes during the winter.

Amphibians and reptiles also have behaviors that allow them to adjust their body temperature in less extreme ways. The sand-diving lizard in the photograph above is able to control how much heat enters its body through the sand by standing on just two of its four feet. Many amphibians and reptiles live near water and use it to cool off their bodies.

## 5.2 Review

### KEY CONCEPTS

1. What are three adaptations that allowed the first amphibians to survive on land?
2. What are two adaptations reptiles have that allow them to live their whole life on land?
3. A crocodile has been lying in the sun for hours. When it slides into the cool river, how will its body temperature change? Why?

### CRITICAL THINKING

4. **Compare and Contrast** Make a diagram to show how amphibians and reptiles are different and how they are similar.
5. **Infer** Some reptiles, like sea turtles, live almost their whole lives in water. What differences would you expect to see between the bodies of a sea turtle and a land turtle?

### CHALLENGE

6. **Hypothesize** For many millions of years, reptiles were the most diverse and successful vertebrate animals on land. Now many of these ancient reptiles are extinct. Give some reasons that might explain the extinction of these reptiles.

CONNECTING SCIENCES



# Sticky Feet

Imagine having the ability to walk up a polished glass window, across ceiling tiles, and down a mirror—without using suction or glue. Small tropical lizards called geckos have this unique ability, and scientists are beginning to understand what makes these animals stick.

A gecko's foot is covered with billions of tiny hairs. Each hair branches into hundreds of smaller hairs called spatulae, and the atoms in these spatulae are attracted to atoms in the surfaces the geckos walk on.

All atoms contain particles called electrons, which constantly move around. When two atoms get very close, the motion of their electrons can change, attracting the two atoms to one another.

Spatulae 595 ×

Spatulae are over 200 times narrower than human hair. Because they are so small, many spatulae can get close enough to the surfaces geckoes walk on for their atoms to stick together.

Billions of these tiny atom-level forces combine with enough strength to suspend a gecko's body weight. Scientists call this property dry adhesion and have applied what they've learned from the soles of these small lizards to manufacturing renewable tape that never loses its ability to stick.

Shown life-size, the gecko is a reptile with tiny sticky hairs on its feet. Why are chemists and engineers interested in this adaptation?

## EXPLORE

1. **CONNECT** What are some other animals that can walk up walls or across ceilings? How do you think they do this?
2. **CHALLENGE** Do you think geckos would be able to walk up wet surfaces as easily as dry ones? Why or why not?

KEY CONCEPT

# Birds meet their needs on land, in water, and in the air.

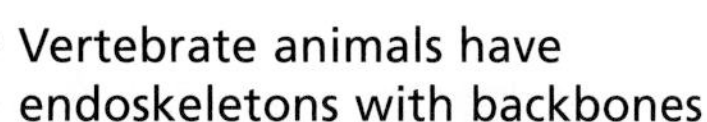

**BEFORE, you learned**

- Vertebrate animals have endoskeletons with backbones
- Amphibians and reptiles have adaptations for life on land
- Ectotherms do not maintain a constant body temperature

**NOW, you will learn**

- About birds as endotherms
- How the adaptations of birds allow them to live in many environments
- About adaptations for flight

**VOCABULARY**

**endotherm** p. 174
**incubation** p. 179

**EXPLORE Feathers**

### *How do feathers differ?*

**PROCEDURE**

1. Examine several feathers.
2. Make a list of ways some of your feathers differ from others.
3. Make a diagram of each feather, showing the characteristics you listed.
4. Compare your list and your diagram with those of your classmates.

**MATERIALS**

assorted feathers

**WHAT DO YOU THINK?**

- Of all the characteristics of feathers that you and your classmates listed, which do you think are the most important? Why?
- On the basis of your observations, what are some functions of feathers for birds?

## Bird species live in most environments.

NOTETAKING STRATEGY
Be sure to take notes on the main idea, *Bird species live in most environments.* Choose an earlier strategy or one of your own.

Penguins live in Antarctica, and parrots inhabit the tropics. Pelicans scoop their food from the water, while cardinals crack open seeds and eat the insides. Swallows skim insects from above the surface of a pond. A soaring hawk swoops down, and a smaller animal becomes its prey. There are nearly 10,000 species of the vertebrate animals called birds. Their adaptations allow them to live all over the world.

Some bird species, such as pigeons, are adapted to live in a wide range of environments, while others have adaptations that limit them to living in one place. Many birds travel long distances during their lives. Some migrate as the seasons change, and others cover long distances while searching for food.

It probably seems easy for you to recognize which animals are birds. Birds are distinguished by these characteristics:

- They have feathers and a beak.
- They have four limbs: a pair of scaly legs and a pair of wings.
- Their eggs have hard shells.

## Birds can maintain body temperature.

In the last section, you learned that the body temperature of ectotherms, such as amphibians and reptiles, changes with their environment. Birds are **endotherms,** or animals that maintain a constant body temperature. Maintaining temperature allows endotherms to live in some places where frogs, turtles, and alligators cannot.

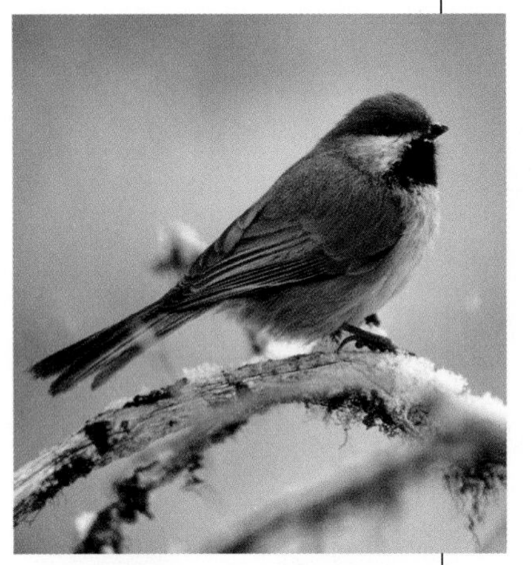

This chickadee is an endotherm. This means its body remains warm, even in very cold weather.

When an ectothermic animal's body is cool, its systems slow down and it becomes less active. A less active animal consumes little or no food and is unlikely to reproduce. It moves slowly or not at all and breathes less often. Its nervous system becomes less responsive, and its heart pumps more slowly. An ectothermic animal that stays cool for too long will die. Even if it has enough food, its body lacks the energy needed to digest the food.

All animals are affected by the air temperature of their environment and will die if they become too cold. However, birds and other endotherms can stay active in colder climates than ectotherms can. This is because endothermic animals have adaptations for generating more body heat and keeping it near their bodies.

CHECK YOUR READING How can endotherms stay alive in colder climates than ectotherms?

### Generating Heat

The energy birds produce as body heat comes from food. This means that birds and other endotherms need to eat a lot. An ectotherm such as a frog might be able to survive for days on the energy it gets from just one worm, while a bird on the same diet might starve. Also, the amount of food an endotherm needs is affected by climate. House sparrows and other birds that do not migrate need to eat more food and produce more energy to survive in winter than they do during warmer seasons.

Insulating with Down
Just as warm air trapped between down feathers helps keep geese warm, feathers in a jacket keep a student warm.
Down Feathers

### Controlling Body Temperature

Birds have soft feathers, called down, that keep warm air close to their bodies. If you have ever slept with a down comforter or worn a down jacket, you know that these feathers are good insulation, even though they are not very heavy. Other feathers, called contour feathers, cover the down on birds. In most species, contour feathers are water-resistant and protect birds from getting wet.

Birds shiver when they are cold, and this muscular movement generates heat. They also have ways of cooling their bodies down when the weather is hot. Birds do not sweat, but they can fluff their feathers out to release heat. Birds, like other animals, have behaviors for maintaining body temperature, such as resting in a shady place during the hottest part of a summer day.

## Most birds can fly.

Of all the animals on Earth today, only three groups have evolved adaptations for flight: insects, bats, and birds. Fossil evidence suggests that the first birds appeared on Earth about 150 million years ago and that they were reptiles with adaptations for flight. Scientists think that all birds are descended from these flying ancestors, even modern species such as ostriches and penguins, which cannot fly.

## Adaptations for Flight

To lift its body into the air and fly, an animal's body has to be very strong, but also light. Many adaptations and many millions of years were needed before birds' body plans and systems became capable of flight. With these adaptations, birds lost the ability to do some things that other vertebrates can. As you read about birds' adaptations for flight, match the numbers with the diagram on the next page.

**READING TIP**

As you read the numbered text on this page, find the matching number on page 177.

1. **Endoskeleton** Some of the bones in a bird's body are fused, or connected without joints. This makes those parts of a bird's skeleton light and strong, but not as flexible. A specialized bone supports the bird's powerful flight muscles.

2. **Wings and Feathers** Birds do not have hands or paws on their wings. Contour feathers along the wing are called flight feathers, and are specialized for lifting and gliding. Feathers are a strong and adjustable surface for pushing against air.

3. **Specialized Respiratory System** Flying takes a lot of energy, so birds need a lot of oxygen. They breathe using a system of air sacs and lungs. Air follows a path through this system that allows oxygen to move constantly through a bird's body.

4. **Hollow Bones** Many of the bones in a bird's skeleton are hollow. Inside, crisscrossing structures provide strength without adding much weight.

Other body systems within birds are more suited for flight than systems in other invertebrates. Instead of heavy jaws and teeth, an internal organ called a gizzard grinds up food. This adaptation makes a bird lighter in weight and makes flight easier. Birds also have highly developed senses of hearing and vision, senses which are important for flight. Their senses of taste and smell are not as well developed.

Give two examples of things that birds cannot do that relate to their adaptations for flight.

## Benefits of Flight

Flight allows animals to get food from places where animals living on land or in water cannot. For example, some species of birds spend most of their lives flying over the ocean, hunting for fish. Also, a flying bird can search a large area for food more effectively than it could if it walked, ran, or swam.

For many species of birds, flight makes migration possible. In Chapter 2, you learned that some animals migrate to different living places in different seasons. Most migratory birds have two living places, one for the summer and one for the winter.

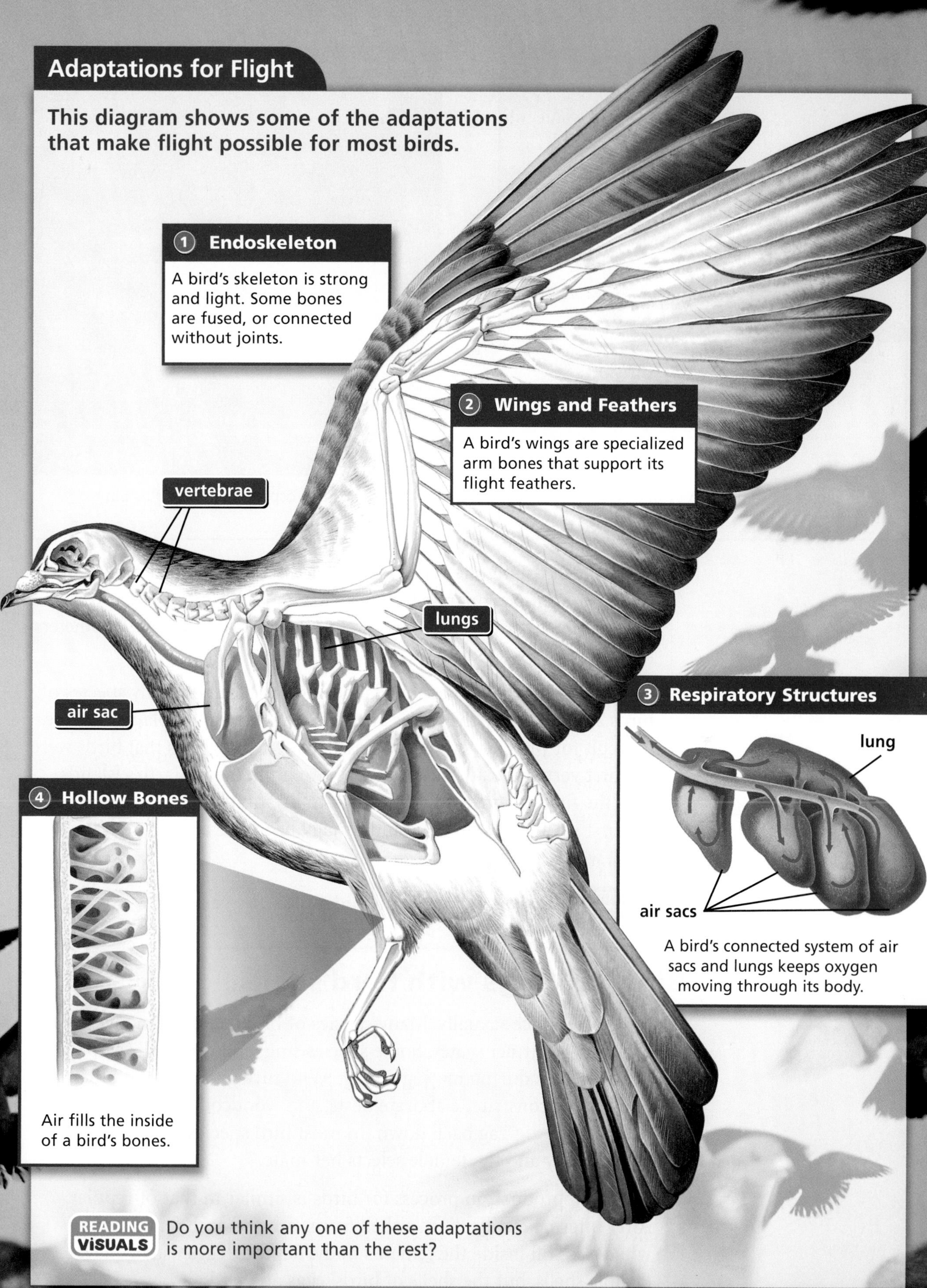
Adaptations for Flight
This diagram shows some of the adaptations that make flight possible for most birds.
1 Endoskeleton
A bird's skeleton is strong and light. Some bones are fused, or connected without joints.
2 Wings and Feathers
A bird's wings are specialized arm bones that support its flight feathers.
vertebrae
lungs
air sac
3 Respiratory Structures
lung
air sacs
A bird's connected system of air sacs and lungs keeps oxygen moving through its body.
4 Hollow Bones
Air fills the inside of a bird's bones.
READING VISUALS
Do you think any one of these adaptations is more important than the rest?

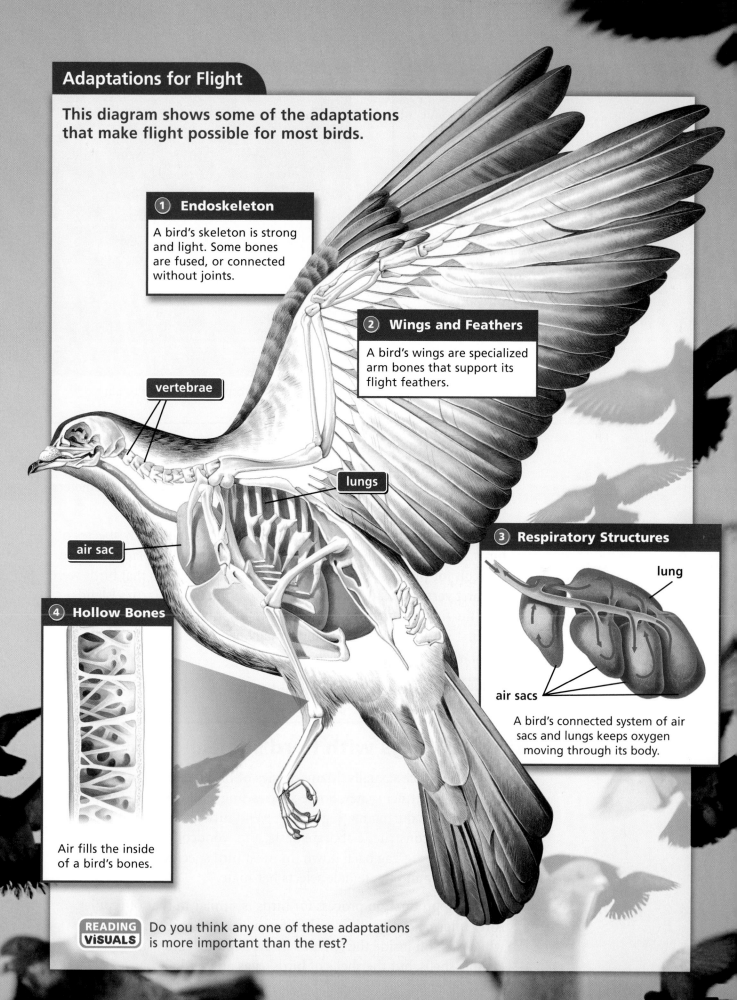

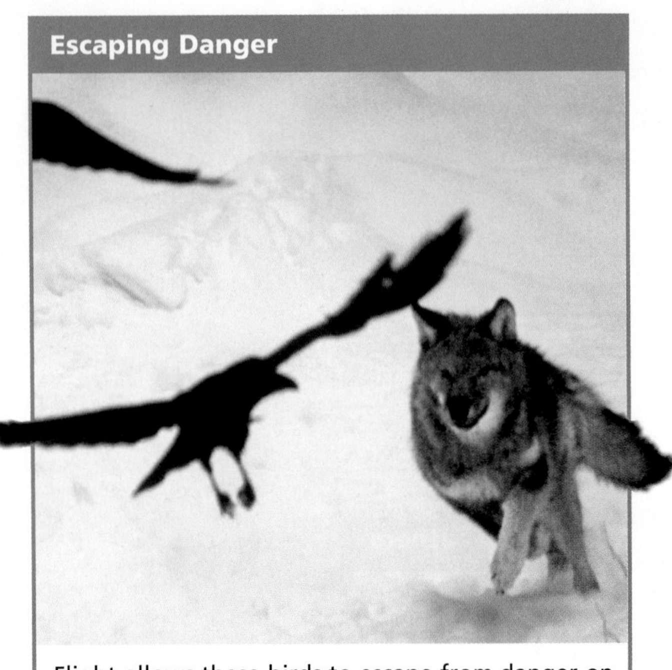

**Escaping Danger**

Flight allows these birds to escape from danger on the ground.

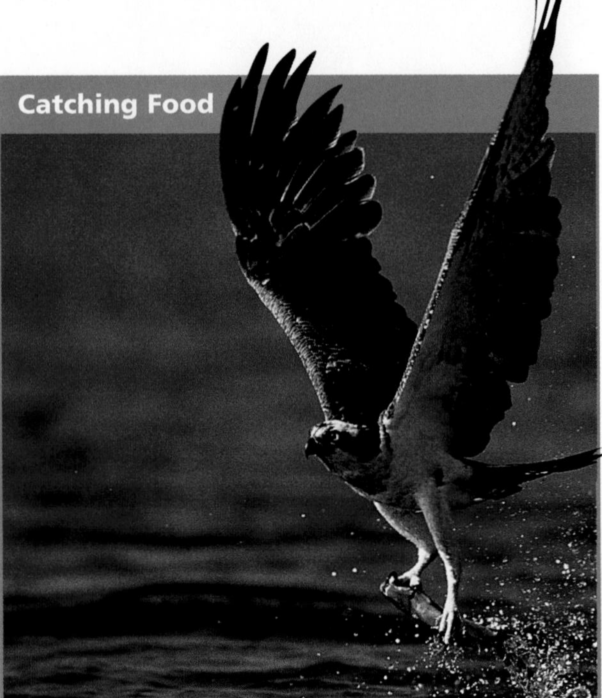

**Catching Food**

Flight allows this osprey to hunt for fish in bodies of water.

Some birds migrate very long distances. Ruby-throated hummingbirds, for example, migrate from Canada and the United States to Mexico and Central America each winter, flying nonstop 700 kilometers across the Gulf of Mexico.

By flying, birds can escape danger on the ground. Many species of birds are able to lay their eggs and raise their young in places that are difficult for predators to reach. Fossil evidence suggests that birds were the first vertebrate animal species to live on many of Earth's islands. Like the first organisms that adapted to live on land, birds that were the first vertebrates on an island usually had little competition for food, water, and living space.

How does flight benefit birds? Give three examples.

## Birds lay eggs with hard shells.

Birds reproduce sexually. Many species of birds have distinctive ways of trying to attract mates. Some species sing, and others develop colorful feathers during mating season. Wild turkeys fight each other, bowerbirds construct elaborate nests, and woodcocks fly high in the air and then zig-zag back down. In most bird species, the male animals display and the female selects her mate.

The reproduction process for birds is similar to that of reptiles. After internal fertilization, a shell forms around each fertilized egg while it is still inside the female's body. Reptiles' eggs usually have flexible shells, but the shells of birds' eggs are hard.

Usually the female bird chooses where to lay the eggs. Often this is a nest. In some bird species either the male or the female builds the nest, while in others, mated birds build a nest together. Bird eggs have to be kept at a constant, warm temperature or they will not develop. Nearly all birds use their body heat to keep the eggs warm. They sit on the eggs, which can support the adult bird's weight because the shells are hard. This process is called **incubation.** When the eggs hatch, the young birds are not yet able to fly. They must be cared for until they can meet their own needs.

These 3- to 8-day-old tanagers are being fed by both of their parents.

## Most birds take care of their offspring.

In some bird species, male and female mates care for their offspring together. This is often the case for birds, such as the tanagers in the top photograph, whose young hatch before their eyes open or their feathers grow. It takes two adult birds to provide them with enough food, warmth, and protection.

The offspring of some species, like the ducks in the bottom photograph, hatch at a later state of development, with open eyes. They are already covered with down feathers and able to walk. In such species it's common for just one adult, usually the female, to incubate the eggs and care for the young.

These 7-day-old ducklings are able to find their own food while their mother watches over them.

# 5.3 Review

### KEY CONCEPTS

1. What does an endothermic animal need to do in order to generate body heat?
2. What are two types of feathers, and what are their functions?
3. Describe three adaptations that make flight possible for birds.

### CRITICAL THINKING

4. **Compare and Contrast** How is reproduction in birds similar to reproduction in reptiles? How does it different?
5. **Synthesize** Some flightless birds live on islands or in remote places where there are few predators. Explain why, in such an environment, flying birds' bodies might have adapted and become flightless.

### CHALLENGE

6. **Hypothesize** Many species of birds begin migration while food is still plentiful in their current environment. Understanding what triggers migration in birds is an active area of scientific research. Develop a hypothesis about migration triggers in one species of bird. Describe how to test your hypothesis.

# CHAPTER INVESTIGATION

## Bird Beak Adaptations

**OVERVIEW AND PURPOSE** The beaks of most birds are adapted for eating particular types of food. In this lab you will

- use models to simulate how different types of beaks function
- infer how the shape of a bird's beak might affect the food a bird eats

### Question

Write It Up

For this lab, you will use a tool as a model of a specialized bird beak. You will try to obtain food with your beak at several different feeding stations. Each station will have a different type of food. Examine the tools that will be used for this lab, as well as the feeding stations. Then write a question about how beak shape might affect the food a bird eats. Your question should begin with *Which, How, When, Why,* or *What*. Keep in mind that you will be asked to answer this question at the end of the lab.

**MATERIALS**
- tweezers
- eyedropper
- slotted spoon
- pliers
- test tubes in rack
- water
- dried pasta
- millet seeds
- jar of rubber bands
- empty containers
- stopwatch

### Procedure

1. Make a data table like the one shown on page 181.

2. Complete the title of your data table by writing in the name of the tool you will be using.

3. Before you start collecting food at one of the feeding stations, write a prediction in your data table. Predict how well you think the tool will function and why.

4 See how much food you can collect in one minute. To collect food, you must move it from the feeding station into a different container, and you may only touch the food with the tool.

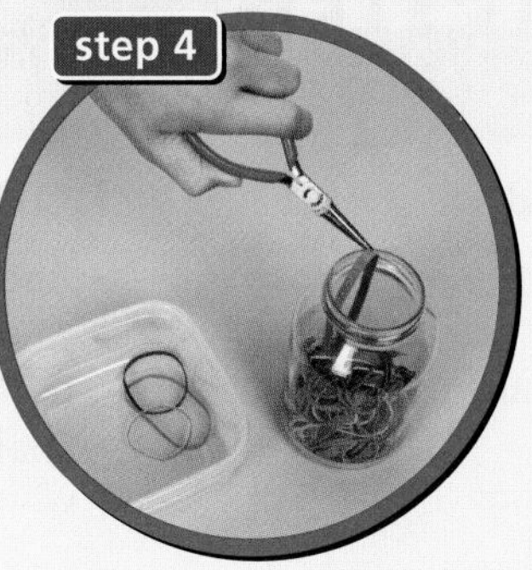


5 Describe your results in your data table.

6 Return the food you collected to the feeding station. Try to make it look just like it did when you started.

7 Repeat steps 3–6 at each of the other feeding stations.

## Observe and Analyze

Write It Up

1. **INTERPRET DATA** At which feeding station did you have the best results? Why? Explain your answer.
2. **EVALUATE** How accurate were the predictions you made?
3. **APPLY** If you could visit each feeding station again, how would you change the way you used the tool to collect food? Explain your answer.
4. **SYNTHESIZE** What environmental and physical factors can a bird actually control when it is getting food?
5. **APPLY** Examine the beaks of the birds in the photographs below. Write a brief description of the shape of each bird's beak. Then, for each bird, name one type of food its beak might be suited for and one type of food each bird would probably not be able to eat.

## Conclude

Write It Up

1. **INFER** What answers do you have for the question you wrote at the beginning of this lab?
2. **INFER** In what ways do you think the experience you had during this lab is similar to the ways real birds obtain food?
3. **IDENTIFY LIMITATIONS** What unexpected factors or problems might have affected your results?

## INVESTIGATE Further

**CHALLENGE** How are other parts of birds' bodies specialized for the environments where they live? Investigate the feet of the following birds: ostrich, heron, woodpecker, pelican, and owl.

Bird Beak Adaptations

Question:

Table 1. Collecting Food with_______

| Station | Prediction | Results |
|---|---|---|
| Water in test tubes | | |
| Dried pasta | | |
| Millet seeds | | |
| Rubber bands in jar | | |

KEY CONCEPT

# Mammals live in many environments.

**BEFORE, you learned**

- Endotherms can stay active in cold environments
- Many bird adaptations are related to flight
- Birds lay hard-shelled eggs and usually take care of their young

**NOW, you will learn**

- About mammals as endotherms
- About the diversity of adaptations in mammals
- That mammals produce milk, which is food for their young

**VOCABULARY**

**mammal** p. 183
**placenta** p. 186
**gestation** p. 186

THINK ABOUT

### *How diverse are mammals?*

Mammals have adapted to survive in many environments and come in many shapes and sizes. Whales live in the ocean, and goats may live near mountain peaks. Some monkeys live in tropical forests, and polar bears survive in frozen areas. An elephant might not fit in your classroom, but the tiny shrew shown here could fit on your finger. As you read this chapter, think about the characteristics of mammals that help them to survive in such a variety of ways.

**NOTETAKING STRATEGY**
Using a strategy of your choice, take notes on the idea that mammals are a diverse group. Be sure to include mammal characteristics.

## Mammals are a diverse group.

The group of vertebrates called mammals includes many familiar animals. Mice are mammals, and so are cows, elephants, and chimpanzees. You are a mammal, too. Bats are mammals that can fly. Some mammals, including whales, live in water.

Some mammal species, such as raccoons and skunks, have adapted to live in many sorts of environments, including cities. Others, such as cheetahs and polar bears, have adaptations for meeting their needs in just a few environments.

Mammals are a diverse animal group. Although there are less than 5000 species of mammals on Earth, mammal species come in many shapes and sizes, and have many different ways of moving, finding food, and eating. These are some of the characteristics that distinguish **mammals** from other animals:

- All mammals have hair during some part of their lives.
- Most mammal species have teeth specialized for consuming particular kinds of food.
- All mammal species produce milk, with which they feed their young.

RESOURCE CENTER
CLASSZONE.COM
Learn more about mammals.

## Mammals are endotherms.

You have learned that endothermic animals are able to stay active in cold environments. This is because endotherms maintain a constant body temperature. Mammals are endotherms. This means that they use some of the food they consume to generate body heat. Mammals also have adaptations for controlling body temperature.

### Hair

Many species of mammals have bodies covered with hair. Like birds' feathers, hair is an adaptation that allows mammals to have some control over the warmth or coldness of their bodies. Mammals that live in cold regions, like polar bears, have hair that keeps them warm. Desert mammals, such as camels, have hair that protects them from extreme heat.

Most mammals have at least two types of hair. Soft, fluffy underhairs keep heat close to their bodies, like the down feathers of birds. Water-resistant guard hairs cover the underhairs and give the animal's fur its color.

Some species of mammals also have specialized hairs. A specialized structure is one that performs a particular function. For example, whiskers are sensory hairs that are part of an animal's sense of touch. Porcupines' quills are hairs that function in self defense.

What are three functions of hair?

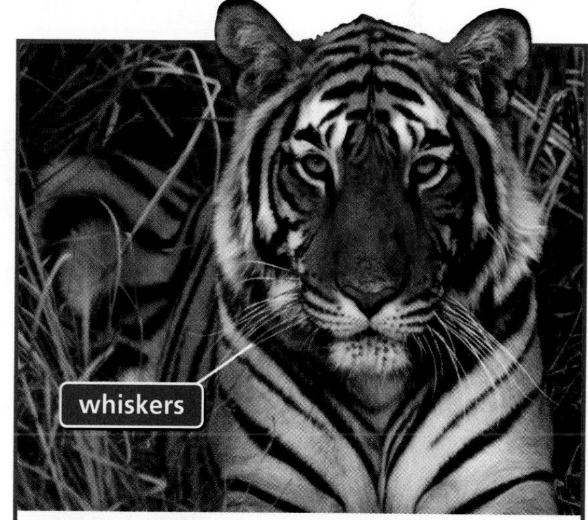

Colored guard hairs give this tiger its stripes. Its whiskers are specialized sensory hairs. It also has underhairs, which you cannot see.

This porcupine's quills are specialized guard hairs.

## Body Fat

Some mammal species that live in water, such as dolphins, have very little hair. These mammals have a layer of fat, called blubber, that plays an important role in maintaining body temperature. The blubber is located between the animal's skin and muscles, and provides its organs with insulation from heat and cold.

Body fat can also be a storage place for energy. When a mammal consumes more food than it needs, the extra energy may be stored in its fat cells. Later, if the animal needs energy but cannot find food, it can use the energy stored in the fat.

For example, animals that hibernate, such as woodchucks, may eat a lot more than they need to survive at times when plenty of food is available. This makes them fat. Then, while they are hibernating, they do not have to eat, because their body fat provides them with the energy they need.

What are two ways that body fat functions in mammals?

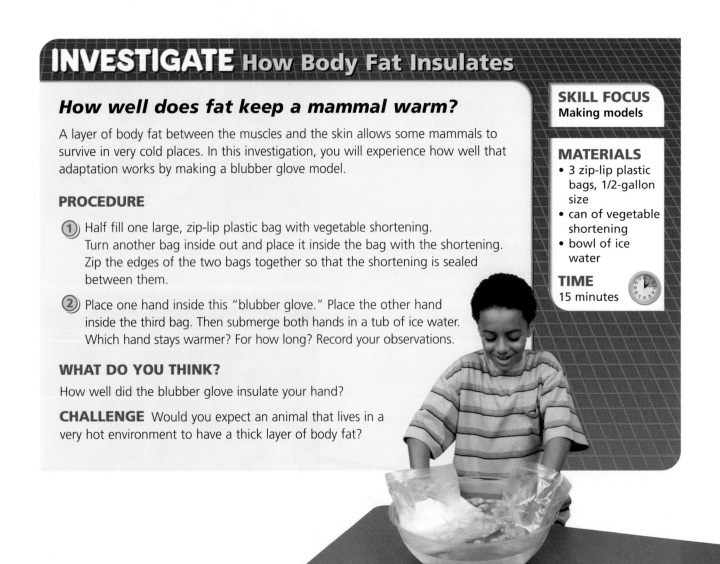

## INVESTIGATE How Body Fat Insulates

### *How well does fat keep a mammal warm?*

A layer of body fat between the muscles and the skin allows some mammals to survive in very cold places. In this investigation, you will experience how well that adaptation works by making a blubber glove model.

**SKILL FOCUS**
Making models

**MATERIALS**
- 3 zip-lip plastic bags, 1/2-gallon size
- can of vegetable shortening
- bowl of ice water

**TIME**
15 minutes

#### PROCEDURE

1. Half fill one large, zip-lip plastic bag with vegetable shortening. Turn another bag inside out and place it inside the bag with the shortening. Zip the edges of the two bags together so that the shortening is sealed between them.
2. Place one hand inside this "blubber glove." Place the other hand inside the third bag. Then submerge both hands in a tub of ice water. Which hand stays warmer? For how long? Record your observations.

#### WHAT DO YOU THINK?

How well did the blubber glove insulate your hand?

**CHALLENGE** Would you expect an animal that lives in a very hot environment to have a thick layer of body fat?

## Mammal Adaptations for a Water Environment

A dolphin's blowhole, flippers, tail flukes, and blubber are features that allow it to meet its needs in water.

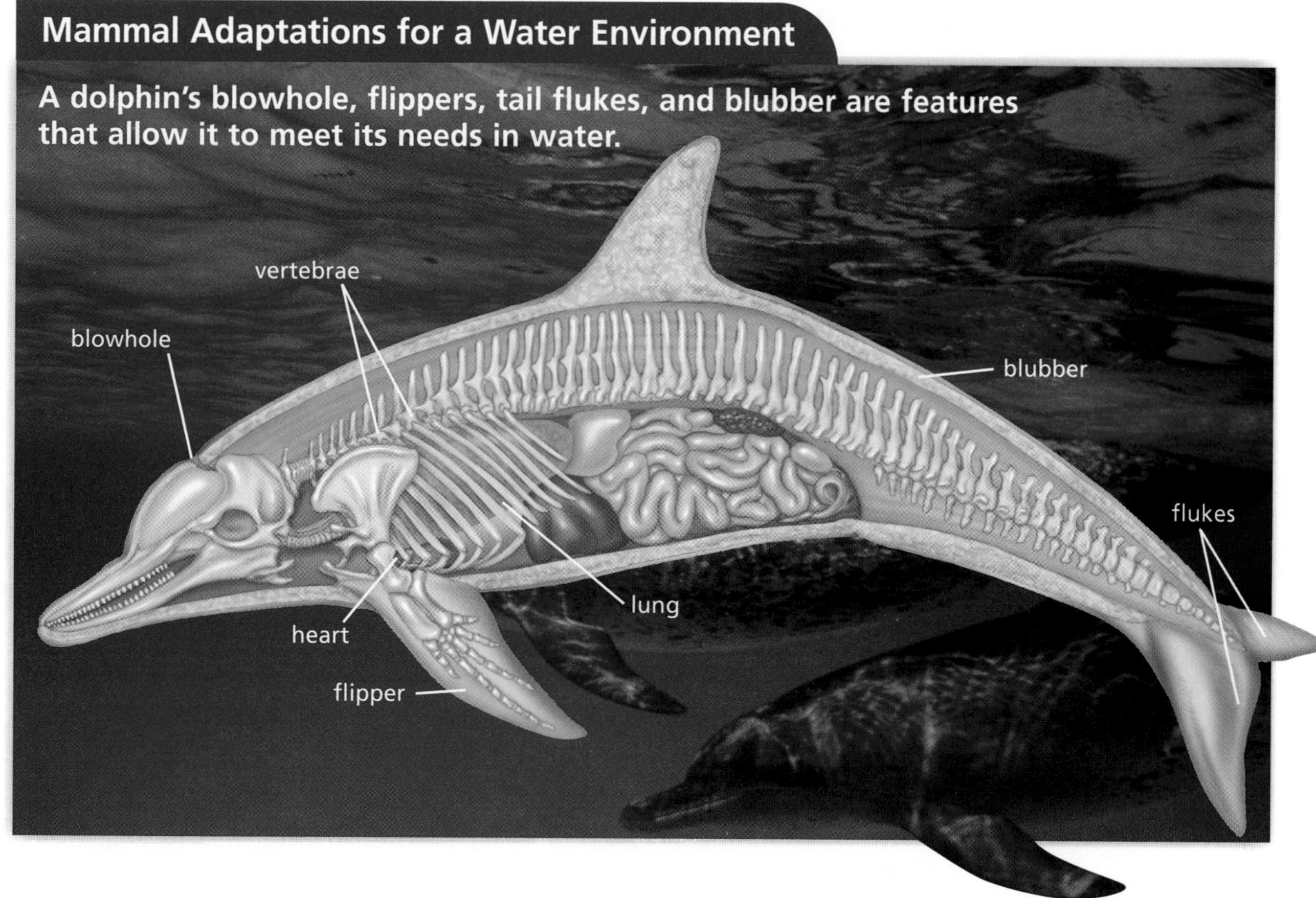


## Mammals have adapted to many environments.

Scientists think mammals appeared on Earth about 200 million years ago. Fossil evidence suggests that the first mammals were small land vertebrates with four limbs, a tail, and specialized teeth. They probably had fur and were most active at night.

Over millions of years, those early mammals adapted to live in many different environments and became the diverse group of species they are today. Moles, for example, live almost entirely underground. They have strong limbs for digging and organs specialized for sensing invertebrate prey in the dark. Spider monkeys, on the other hand, live mostly in trees. A spider monkey can use all four of its long limbs and its flexible, grasping tail to move through a forest without touching the ground.

The first mammals lived on land, but over time some species adapted to live in watery environments. Some of them, such as otters and walruses, live mostly in water but can also be found on land. Others, such as dolphins and whales, have bodies so completely adapted for life in the water that they no longer have a way of moving on land. If you look carefully at the diagram above, however, you will see that a dolphin's body plan differs in some important ways from that of a fish.

## Mammals have reproductive adaptations.

Mammals reproduce sexually. Before a mammal can produce offspring, it finds a mate. Some mammals, such as lions, live in groups that include both males and females. However, most mammals live alone most of the time. They find a mate when they are ready to reproduce. Some mammal species breed only at certain times of the year. Others can reproduce throughout the year.

### Development Before Birth

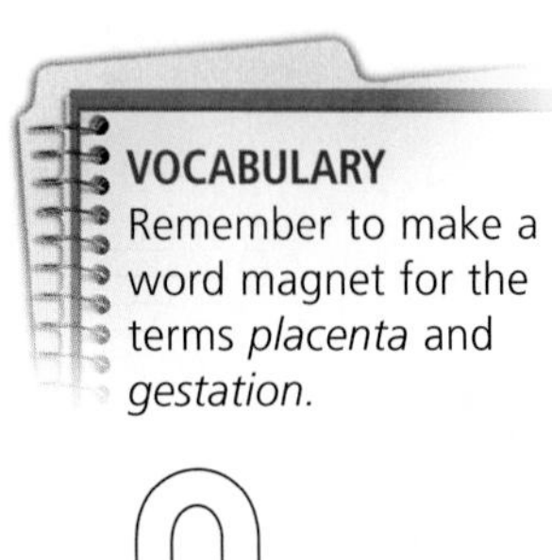


Fertilization occurs internally in mammals. In almost every species of mammal, the offspring develop inside the female's body. Many mammals have a special organ called a **placenta** that transports nutrients, water, and oxygen from the mother's blood to the developing embryo. The embryo's waste materials leave through the placenta and are transported out of the mother's body along with her waste.

The time when a mammal is developing inside its mother is called **gestation.** As you can see in the diagram, the length of the gestation period is different for different species. Gestation ends when the young animal's body has grown and developed enough for it to survive outside the mother. Then it is born.

**CHECK YOUR READING** Where do the offspring of most mammals develop before they are born?

### Length of Gestation

**The length of gestation varies greatly in placental mammals.**

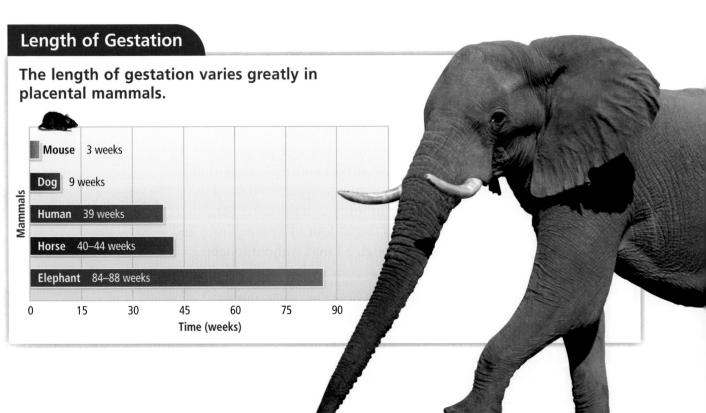

| Mammals | Time (weeks) |
|---|---|
| Mouse | 3 weeks |
| Dog | 9 weeks |
| Human | 39 weeks |
| Horse | 40–44 weeks |
| Elephant | 84–88 weeks |

Time (weeks): 0, 15, 30, 45, 60, 75, 90

Not all mammals fully develop inside their mothers. The duck-billed platypus and two species of spiny anteaters have young that hatch from eggs. Mammals in a group called the marsupials (mahr-SOO-pee-uhlz), which includes kangaroos, develop inside the mother at first but are born when they are still extremely small. Right after birth, a young marsupial climbs across its mother to a special pouch on the outside of her body. It completes its development there. Only one marsupial, the opossum, lives in North America.

## Raising Young

Milk, a high-energy liquid food full of proteins, fats, sugars, and other nutrients, is the first food young mammals consume. Each species' milk has a different combination of these ingredients.

This dog is feeding her puppies with milk.

Mammals' bodies have special glands for producing milk, called mammary glands. In almost all mammal species, only females' mammary glands function. This means that only female mammals can feed the young with milk. In most mammal species, females gestate and care for the offspring alone. However, in some mammal species, the male helps raise the young.

Different species of mammals are born at varying stages of development. Most mice are helpless, blind, and naked at birth, while giraffes can walk soon after they are born. The length of time a young mammal needs care from an adult varies. Some seals nurse their young for less than a month before leaving them to survive on their own. Some whales live alongside their young for a much longer time. However, humans may be the mammal species that takes care of their offspring for the longest time of all.

## 5.4 Review

### KEY CONCEPTS

1. Why is a bat classified as a mammal instead of a bird? Why are whales classified as mammals and not fish?
2. Name two adaptations that allow mammals to have control over body temperature.
3. How does the way that mammals feed their young differ from the ways other animals feed their young?

### CRITICAL THINKING

4. **Apply** One day on your way home from school, you see an animal that you have never seen before. What clues would you look for to tell you what type of animal it is?
5. **Synthesize** Make a Venn diagram that shows how the vertebrate animal groups you learned about in this chapter are similar and different.

### CHALLENGE

6. **Evaluate** This section begins with the statement "mammals are a diverse group." Explain what this means and why it is a true statement. How does the diversity of mammals compare to the diversity of other living things, such as bacteria, plants, arthropods, or fish?

# Chapter Review

## the BIG idea

**Vertebrate animals live in most of Earth's environments.**

## KEY CONCEPTS SUMMARY

### 5.1 Vertebrates are animals with endoskeletons.

All **vertebrate** animals have an **endoskeleton** which includes vertebrae, or backbones.

Most vertebrates are fish. Fish are adapted for life in a water environment.

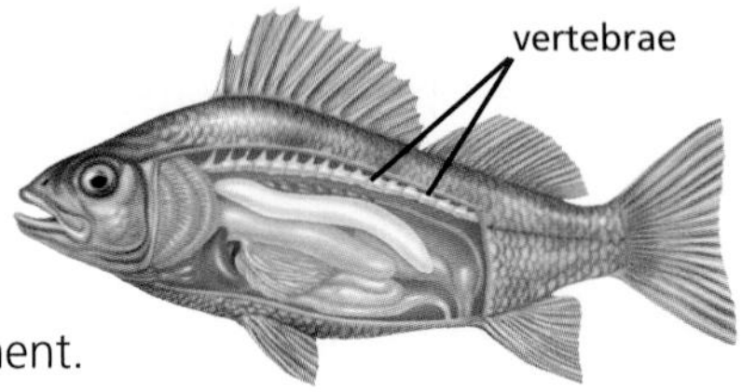

vertebrae

**VOCABULARY**
**vertebrate** p. 157
**endoskeleton** p. 157
**scale** p. 161

### 5.2 Amphibians and reptiles are adapted for life on land.

**Amphibians** and **reptiles** have adaptations for moving, getting food, and breathing on land.

Most amphibians live in moist places.

Many reptiles live in hot, dry places.

**VOCABULARY**
**ectotherm** p. 170
**amphibian** p. 167
**reptile** p. 168

### 5.3 Birds meet their needs on land, in water, and in the air.

Birds have adaptations that allow them to survive in many environments. Many of the features and behaviors of birds relate to flight.

**VOCABULARY**
**endotherm** p. 174
**incubation** p. 179

### 5.4 Mammals live in many environments.

**Mammal** species live in many environments. Mammals have adaptations that allow them to survive in cold places. They also have distinctive reproductive adaptations.

**VOCABULARY**
**mammal** p. 183
**placenta** p. 186
**gestation** p. 186

## Reviewing Vocabulary

*Place each vocabulary term listed below at the center of a description wheel diagram. Write some words describing it on the spokes.*

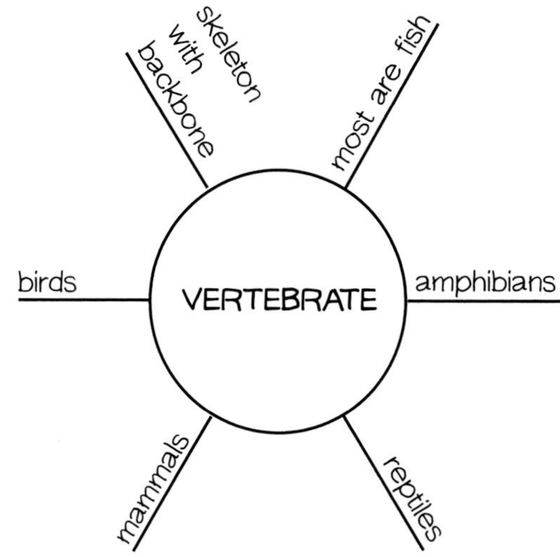


1. endotherm
2. migration
3. ectotherm
4. scale
5. incubation
6. gestation

## Reviewing Key Concepts

**Multiple Choice** *Choose the letter of the best response.*

7. The vertebrate endoskeleton differs from an arthopod's exoskeleton because it
   - **a.** supports muscles
   - **b.** protects organs
   - **c.** is inside the animal's body
   - **d.** has joints

8. Most vertebrate species are
   - **a.** fish
   - **b.** amphibians
   - **c.** birds
   - **d.** mammals

9. Fish obtain oxygen from water with structures called
   - **a.** vertebrae
   - **b.** fins
   - **c.** lungs
   - **d.** gills

10. Down feathers provide insulation for a bird's body because they
    - **a.** trap warm air between them
    - **b.** are waterproof
    - **c.** overlap each other
    - **d.** are slightly oily

11. Which organ do both fish and amphibians have?
    - **a.** lateral line
    - **b.** lungs
    - **c.** gills
    - **d.** scaly skin

12. Mammals differ from other vertebrates because mammals
    - **a.** can lay eggs
    - **b.** can produce milk
    - **c.** are endotherms
    - **d.** are able to swim

13. The two types of vertebrates that lay their eggs in water are
    - **a.** amphibians and birds
    - **b.** reptiles and fish
    - **c.** fish and amphibians
    - **d.** mollusks and fish

14. Which statement is true?
    - **a.** All birds are ectotherms.
    - **b.** All birds can fly.
    - **c.** All birds have two wings and two legs.
    - **d.** All birds have teeth and beaks.

15. The organ that transports materials between a female mammal and the offspring developing inside her body is called a
    - **a.** yolk
    - **b.** placenta
    - **c.** blubber
    - **d.** vertebrae

**Short Answer** *Write a short answer to the questions below.*

16. Describe how you would determine if an animal was a salamander or a lizard.

17. Why do bird eggs have to be incubated?

## Thinking Critically

18. **PREDICT** Imagine that you live in Mexico and you have a pen pal who lives in Iceland. Both of you want to know about animals in the other person's country. Which of you will be more likely to have seen wild reptiles? Why?

19. **APPLY** Polar bears live in an arctic environment. Jaguars live in a rain forest environment. Which animal would you expect to have more body fat? Explain.

*Refer to diagram below as you answer parts of the next two questions.*

20. **COMPARE** Birds, like all vertebrates, have internal skeletons. What functions does a bird's skeleton have in common with all other vertebrates?

21. **INFER** This diagram shows only some of a bird's body systems. Name two systems that are not shown here, including organs that belong to them and their functions.

22. **HYPOTHESIZE** Not all birds migrate. Some birds, such as pigeons and house sparrows, stay in one living place through the winter. What do you think you would find if you compared the diets of birds that migrate with those of birds that do not?

23. **MATH AND SCIENCE** Scientists studying an endangered species of rainforest salamanders estimated that only 875 of these animals were still living in 2002. If this salamander population decreases by 50 animals per year, in what year will it become extinct? Explain how you found your answer.

24. **CLASSIFY** Imagine that you move to a new place and spend a year watching nearby animals. Read each description and identify each animal described below as a fish, amphibian, reptile, bird, or mammal.
    - **a.** A scaly animal warms itself on your sidewalk when the sun is out. It has dry skin, four legs, and a tail.
    - **b.** Small animals swim in a pond near your home. They have no legs, but they do have tails. As they grow older, their tails shrink and they develop four limbs. Then they disappear from the pond.
    - **c.** A furry animal chews a hole under your porch and seems to be living there. You later see it with smaller animals that appear to be its young.
    - **d.** A pair of flying, feathered animals collect objects and carry them into an opening under the gutter of your neighbor's house. At first you see them carrying twigs and grass, but later it looks as if they are carrying worms.

## the BIG idea

25. **DRAW CONCLUSIONS** Look again at the picture on pages 154–155. What do penguins and seals have in common? What adaptations do some species of birds and mammals have that allow them to survive in cold environments like Antarctica?

26. **PROVIDE EXAMPLES** Think of an example of a species from each of the vertebrate animal groups you've learned about, and describe an adaptation that suits each to the environment where it lives. Explain your answers.

## UNIT PROJECTS

Evaluate all the data, results, and information from your project folder. Prepare to present your project. Be ready to answer questions posed by your classmates about your results.

# Standardized Test Practice

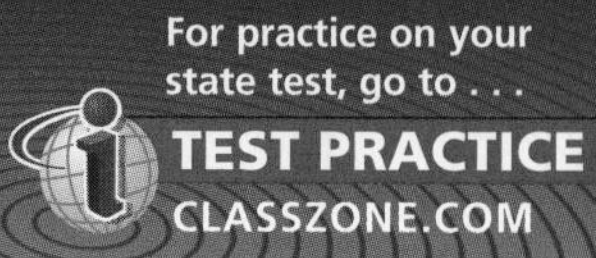


## Analyzing Diagrams

*Read the text and study the diagram, and then choose the best response for the questions that follow.*

Vertebrates, such as birds, fish, and mammals, have endoskeletons. This internal skeleton is made up of a system of bones that extends throughout the body. Muscles can attach directly to the bones, around joints—the place where two bones meet. As shown in the generalized diagram below, at least two muscles are needed to produce movement. One of the muscles contracts, or shortens, pulling on the bone, while the other muscle extends, or is stretched.

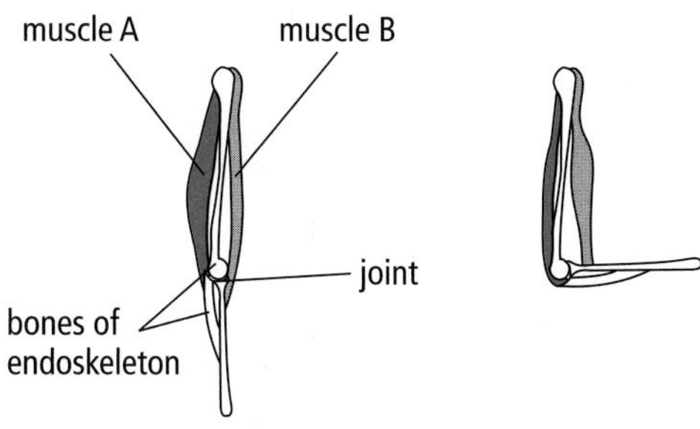


**1.** Endoskeletons are made up of
- **a.** contracting muscles
- **b.** extending muscles
- **c.** internal bones
- **d.** external bones

**2.** A muscle produces movement by
- **a.** pulling
- **b.** relaxing
- **c.** extending
- **d.** rotating

**3.** A joint is where
- **a.** one muscle connects to another
- **b.** one bone connects to another
- **c.** a muscle connects to a bone
- **d.** the bone ends

**4.** The leg in the diagram bends when
- **a.** muscle A contracts
- **b.** muscle A relaxes
- **c.** muscle B contracts
- **d.** muscles A and B contract

**5.** What is the main point of the diagram and the text above?
- **a.** Two muscles are needed to produce movement in vertebrates.
- **b.** Vertebrates have internal skeletons.
- **c.** When one muscle shortens, another muscle gets longer.
- **d.** Movement in vertebrates is the result of the interaction of muscles and bones.

## Extended Response

*Use terms from the word box to answer the next question. Underline each term you use in your answer.*

**6.** Many fish go forward by moving their tails from side to side. Describe the action of the muscles on each side of the fish as the tail moves from one side to the other.

| contract | pull |
|---|---|
| extend | muscle |

**7.** Using what you know about joints and muscles and the diagram, describe what happens to muscles and bones as you bend your leg at the knee.

UNIT D

# Motion and Forces

$F = ma$

GRAVITY

VELOCITY

# Motion and Forces
# Contents Overview

## Unit Features

FRONTIERS IN SCIENCE Robots on Mars 2
TIMELINES IN SCIENCE Understanding Forces 108

## 1 Motion 6

the BIG idea

The motion of an object can be described and predicted.

## 2 Forces 38

the BIG idea

Forces change the motion of objects in predictable ways.

## 3 Gravity, Friction, and Pressure 74

the BIG idea

Newton's laws apply to all forces.

## 4 Work and Energy 112

the BIG idea

Energy is transferred when a force moves an object.

## 5 Machines 142

the BIG idea

Machines help people do work by changing the force applied to an object.

# FRONTIERS in Science

# ROBOTS on Mars

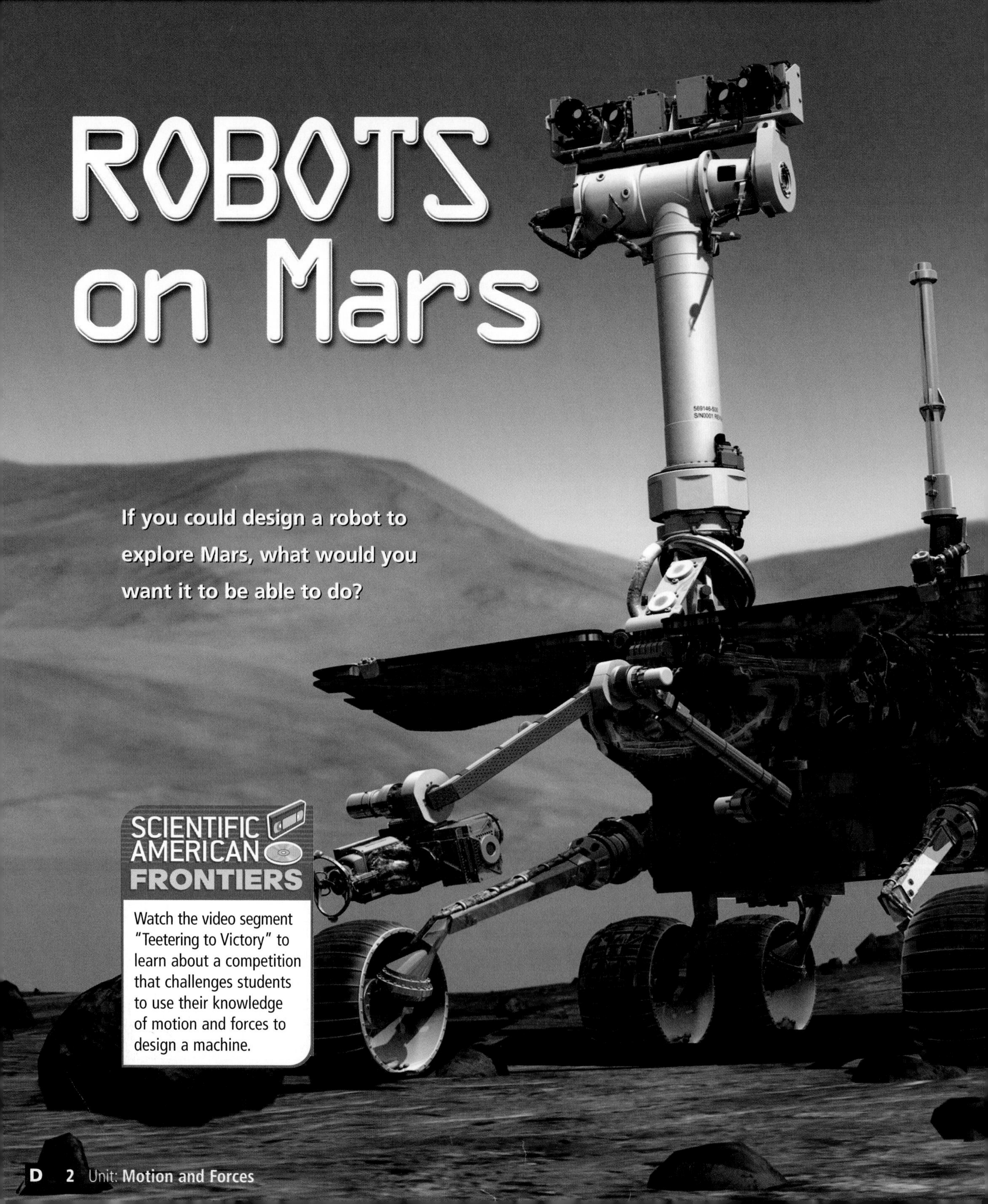

**If you could design a robot to explore Mars, what would you want it to be able to do?**

**SCIENTIFIC AMERICAN FRONTIERS**

Watch the video segment "Teetering to Victory" to learn about a competition that challenges students to use their knowledge of motion and forces to design a machine.

The surface of Mars looks rocky and barren today, but scientists have long wondered if life might have existed on Mars long ago. That would have been possible only if Mars once had water, which is necessary for all forms of life.

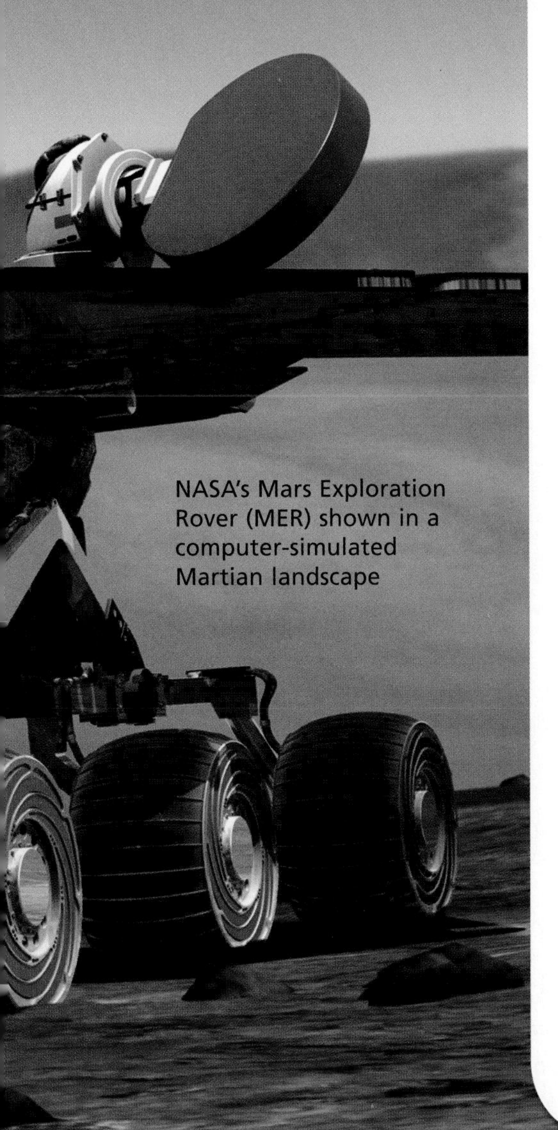

NASA's Mars Exploration Rover (MER) shown in a computer-simulated Martian landscape

## The Design Challenge

It's still not possible to send scientists to Mars to search for signs of water, but in 1999 a team of scientists and engineers began to design two robots for NASA's 2004 mission to Mars. As the team worked, they relied on their scientific understanding of motion, forces, and machines to create and test a successful design.

To identify their goals, the team started by thinking about what scientists would want to do if they could go to Mars. First they would want to look around the landscape to find good areas to study. Then they would need to travel to those areas and analyze rock samples. Finally they would use a variety of tools to analyze the rocks, interpret their data, and communicate their findings back to Earth. Those goals set the basic plan for the Mars Exploration Rovers (MERs).

As you can see in the photograph, the MER team designed a rover with cameras for viewing the surface, wheels for moving around the landscape, and an extendable arm in front equipped with tools for drilling into, observing, and identifying rocks. The rover also has a computer to process information, an antenna for radio communication with Earth, and batteries and solar panels to provide energy for everything.

As in any technology project, the MER team had to work within specific constraints, or limits. The most basic constraints were time and money. They had to design rovers that could be built within NASA's budget and that would be ready in time for launch in 2003. But the team also faced some more challenging

Members of the project team stand with a MER and a replica of the much smaller *Sojourner.*

constraints. The rover must survive a rocket launch from Earth as well as a landing on the surface of Mars. This means it must be both lightweight and compact. Engineers designed the MER to fold up into a pyramid-shaped protective compartment, which drops down onto Mars by parachute. Air bags surrounding the compartment absorb the impact, and then the compartment opens and the MER moves down the compartment panels to the planet's surface.

Scientists built on some valuable lessons learned from an earlier robot, *Sojourner,* which explored the surface of Mars for 12 weeks in 1997. At the left you see one of the MERs next to a replica of *Sojourner,* which was only about 28 centimeters (about 11 in) tall. MER's mast rises up to 1.4 meters (almost 5 ft), giving the cameras, which can be angled up or down, a view similar to what a person would see when standing on the surface of Mars.

## Testing the Model

Every part of the MER had to be tested to be sure it would work properly in the harsh conditions on Mars. For example, consider the Rock Abrasion Tool (RAT) at the end of the rover's extendable arm. The RAT is designed to grind off the weathered surface of rock, exposing a fresh surface for examination. Tests with the RAT showed that it worked fine on hard rocks, but its diamond-tipped grinding wheel became clogged with pieces of soft rock. The solution: Add brushes to clean the RAT automatically after each use.

Scientists were also concerned that the RAT's diamond grinding wheel might wear out if it had to grind a lot of hard rocks. An entry from the design team's status report explains why that turned out not to be a problem:

**View the "Teetering to Victory" segment of your Scientific American Frontiers video to learn how some students solved a much simpler design challenge.**

**IN THIS SCENE FROM THE VIDEO MIT students prepare to test their machines.**

**BATTLE OF MACHINES** Each year more than 100 engineering students at the Massachusetts Institute of Technology (MIT) compete in a contest to see who can design and build the best machine. The challenge this time is to build a machine that starts out sitting on a teeter-totter beam and within 45 seconds manages to tilt its end down against an opponent trying to do the same thing.

Just as the Mars rover designers had to consider the constraints of space travel and Mars' harsh environment, the students had constraints on their designs. They all started with the same kit of materials, and their finished machines had to weigh less than 10 pounds as well as fit inside the box the materials came in. Within these constraints, the student designers came up with an amazing variety of solutions.

The big question, of course, was how things would work under the very cold, dry, low-pressure atmospheric conditions on Mars. We put a RAT into a test chamber recently, took it to real Martian conditions for the first time, and got a very pleasant surprise. The rate at which our diamond studded teeth wear away slowed way down! We're still figuring out why, but it turns out that when you put this Martian RAT into its natural environment, its teeth don't wear down nearly as fast.

Engineers also needed to test the system by which scientists on Earth would communicate with and control the rovers on Mars. For this purpose, they built a smaller version of the real robot, nicknamed FIDO. In tests FIDO successfully traveled to several locations, dug trenches, and observed and measured rock samples.

## Goals of the Mission

Technology like the Mars Exploration Rovers extends the power of scientists to gather data and answer questions about our solar system. One main goal of the MER missions is to study different kinds of rock and soils that might indicate whether water was ever present on Mars. From the data gathered by the MERs, scientists hope to find out what factors shaped the Martian landscape. They also hope to check out areas that have been studied only from far away so that the scientists can confirm their hypotheses about Mars.

### UNANSWERED Questions

As scientists learn more and more about Mars, new questions always arise.

- What role, if any, did water, wind, or volcanoes play in shaping the landscape of Mars?
- Were the conditions necessary to support life ever present on Mars?
- Could there be bacteria-like life forms surviving below the surface of Mars today?

## UNIT PROJECTS

**As you study this unit, work alone or with a group on one of these projects.**

### Build a Mechanical Arm

Design and build a mechanical arm to perform a simple task.

- Plan and sketch an arm that could lift a pencil from the floor at a distance of one meter.
- Collect materials and assemble your arm.
- Conduct trials and improve your design.

### Multimedia Presentation

Create an informative program on the forces involved in remote exploration.

- Collect information about the Galileo mission to Jupiter or a similar expedition.
- Learn how engineers use air resistance, gravity, and rocket thrusters to maneuver the orbiter close to the planet and its moons.
- Give a presentation describing what you learned using mixed media, such as a computer slide show and a model.

### Design an Experiment

Design an experiment to determine the pressure needed to crush a small object.

- Select a small object, such as a vitamin C tablet, to use in your experiment.
- Collect other materials of your choosing.
- Plan and conduct a procedure to test the pressure required to crush the object. Vary the procedure until you can crush the object using the least amount of force.

Learn more about careers in physics and engineering.

CHAPTER

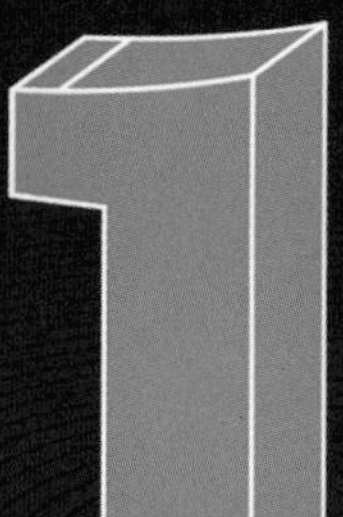

# Motion

Where will these people be in a few seconds? How do you know?

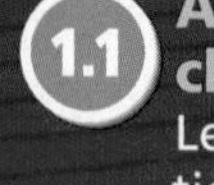

The motion of an object can be described and predicted.

## Key Concepts

SECTION

**1.1 An object in motion changes position.**
Learn about measuring position from reference points, and about relative motion.

SECTION

**1.2 Speed measures how fast position changes.**
Learn to calculate speed and how velocity depends on speed and direction.

SECTION

**1.3 Acceleration measures how fast velocity changes.**
Learn about acceleration and how to calculate it.

**Internet Preview**

CLASSZONE.COM

Chapter 1 online resources: Content Review, Visualization, Simulation, two Resource Centers, Math Tutorial, Test Practice

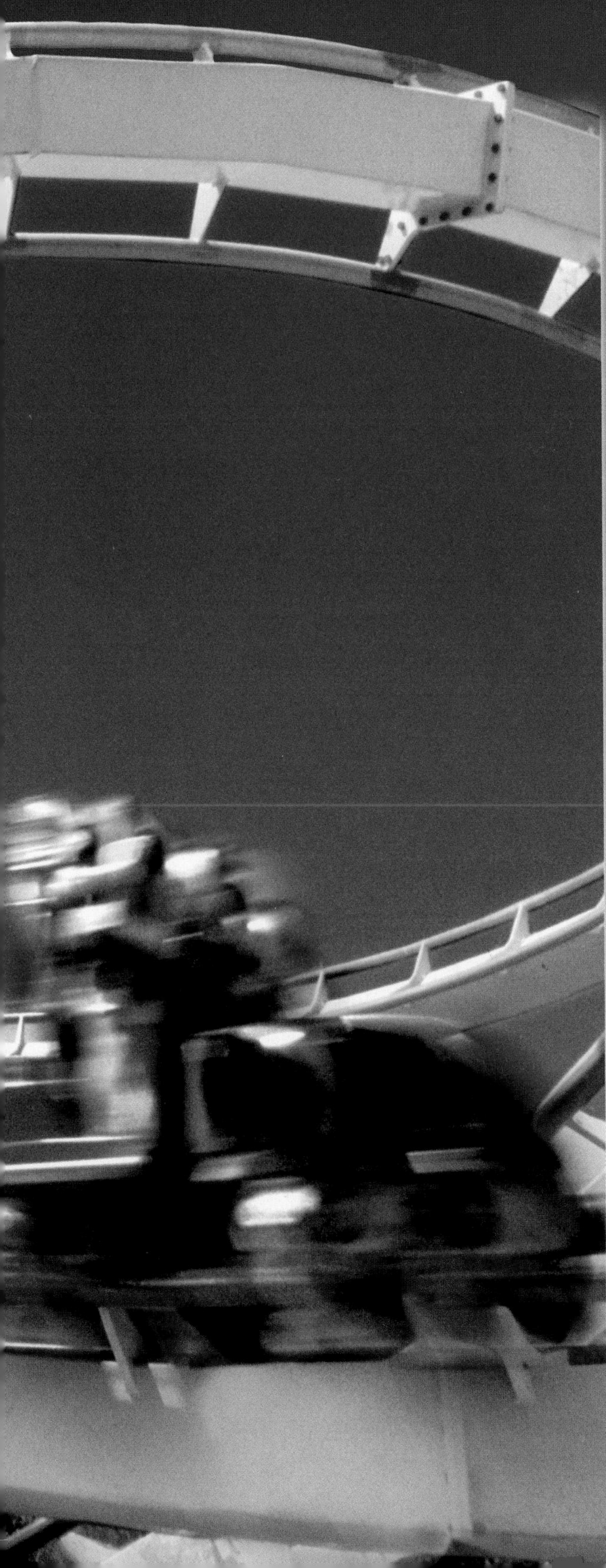

# EXPLORE the BIG idea

## Off the Wall

Roll a rubber ball toward a wall. Record the time from the starting point to the wall. Change the distance between the wall and the starting point. Adjust the speed at which you roll the ball until it takes the same amount of time to hit the wall as before.

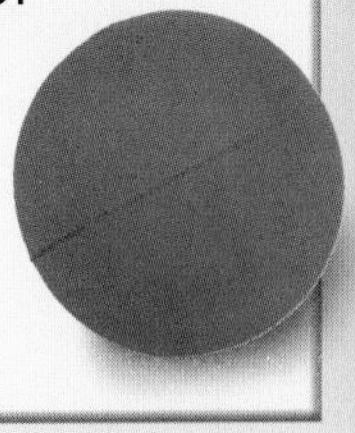

**Observe and Think** How did the speed of the ball over the longer distance compare with the speed over the shorter distance?

## Rolling Along

Make a ramp by leaning the edge of one book on two other books. Roll a marble up the ramp. Repeat several times and notice what happens each time.

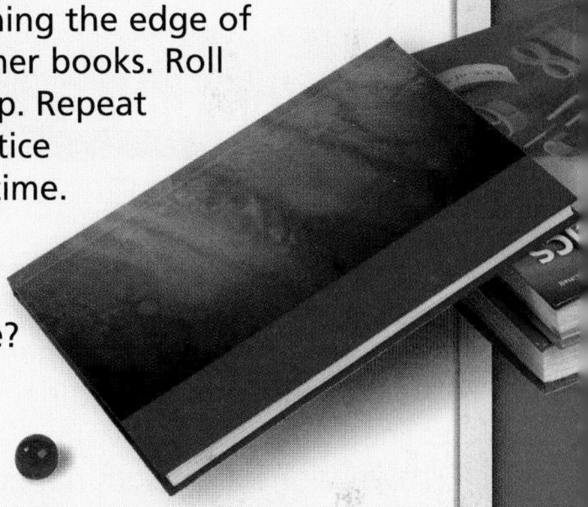

**Observe and Think** How does the speed of the marble change? At what point does its direction of motion change?

## Internet Activity: Relative Motion

Go to **ClassZone.com** to examine motion from different points of view. Learn how your motion makes a difference in what you observe.

**Observe and Think** How does the way you see motion depend on your point of view?

NSTA scilinks.org SCILINKS

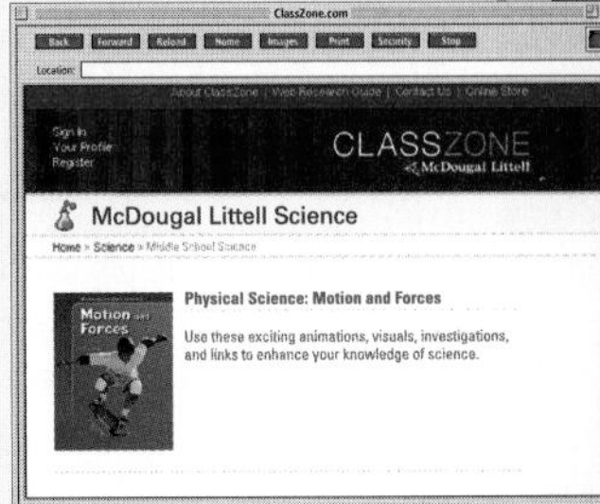

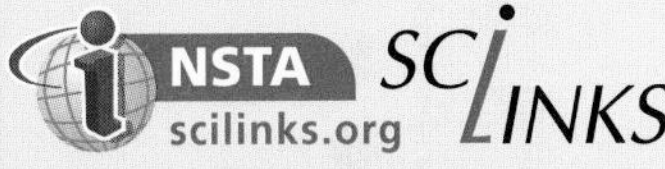

Velocity **Code: MDL004**

CHAPTER 1

# Getting Ready to Learn

## CONCEPT REVIEW

- Objects can move at different speeds and in different directions.
- Pushing or pulling on an object will change how it moves.

## VOCABULARY REVIEW

*See Glossary for definitions.*

**horizontal**

**meter**

**second**

**vertical**

CONTENT REVIEW
CLASSZONE.COM

Review concepts and vocabulary.

## TAKING NOTES

### OUTLINE

As you read, copy the headings onto your paper in the form of an outline. Then add notes in your own words that summarize what you read.

### VOCABULARY STRATEGY

Place each new vocabulary term at the center of a **description wheel** diagram. As you read about the term, write some words on the spokes describing the term.

See the Note-Taking Handbook on pages R45–R51.

SCIENCE NOTEBOOK

OUTLINE

I. Position describes the location of an object.
   A. Describing a position
      1. A position is compared to a reference point.
      2. Position can be described using distance and direction.

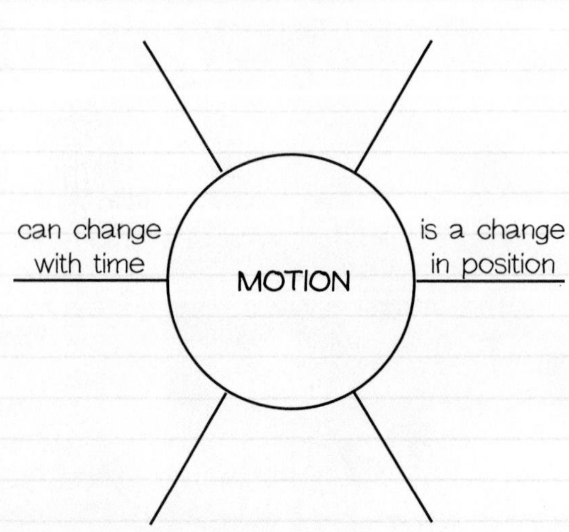

KEY CONCEPT

# An object in motion changes position.

**BEFORE, you learned**

- Objects can move in different ways
- An object's position can change

**NOW, you will learn**

- How to describe an object's position
- How to describe an object's motion

**VOCABULARY**

**position** p. 9
**reference point** p. 10
**motion** p. 11

**EXPLORE Location**

### *How do you describe the location of an object?*

**PROCEDURE**

1. Choose an object in the classroom that is easy to see.
2. Without pointing to, describing, or naming the object, give directions to a classmate for finding it.
3. Ask your classmate to identify the object using your directions. If your classmate does not correctly identify the object, try giving directions in a different way. Continue until your classmate has located the object.

**WHAT DO YOU THINK?**

What kinds of information must you give another person when you are trying to describe a location?

## Position describes the location of an object.

Have you ever gotten lost while looking for a specific place? If so, you probably know that accurately describing where a place is can be very important. The **position** of a place or an object is the location of that place or object. Often you describe where something is by comparing its position with where you currently are. You might say, for example, that a classmate sitting next to you is about a meter to your right, or that a mailbox is two blocks south of where you live. Each time you identify the position of an object, you are comparing the location of the object with the location of another object or place.

**VOCABULARY**
Make a description wheel in your notebook for *position*.

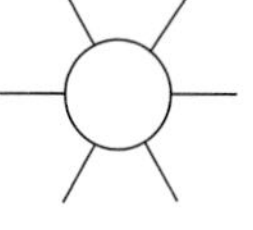

**CHECK YOUR READING** Why do you need to discuss two locations to describe the position of an object?

## Describing a Position

Learn more about how people find and describe position.

You might describe the position of a city based on the location of another city. A location to which you compare other locations is called a **reference point.** You can describe where Santiago, Chile, is from the reference point of the city Brasília, Brazil, by saying that Santiago is about 3000 kilometers (1860 mi) southwest of Brasília.

You can also describe a position using a method that is similar to describing where a point on a graph is located. For example, in the longitude and latitude system, locations are given by two numbers—longitude and latitude. Longitude describes how many degrees east or west a location is from the prime meridian, an imaginary line running north-south through Greenwich, England. Latitude describes how many degrees north or south a location is from the equator, the imaginary circle that divides the northern and southern hemispheres. Having a standard way of describing location, such as longitude and latitude, makes it easier for people to compare locations.

## Describing Position

**There are several different ways to describe a position. The way you choose may depend on your reference point.**

**① Reference Point: Brasília**

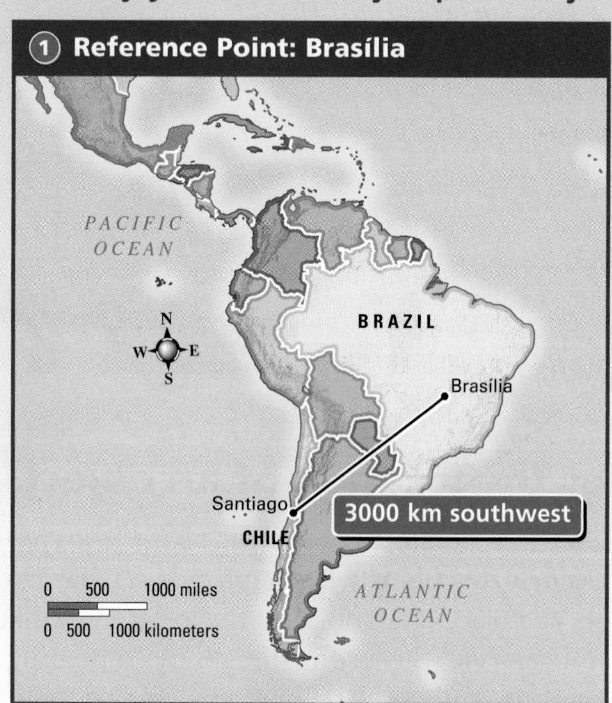


To describe where Santiago is, using Brasília as a reference point, you would need to know how far Santiago is from Brasília and in what direction it is.

**② Reference Point: 0° longitude, 0° latitude**

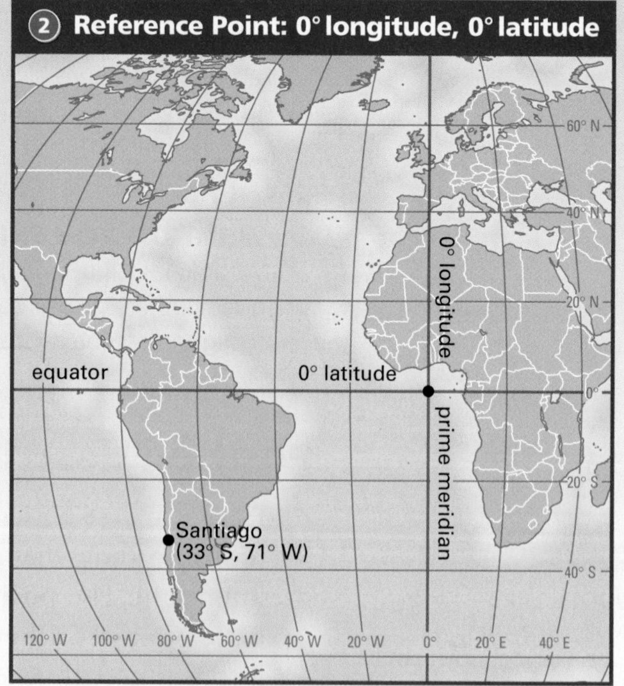


In the longitude and latitude system, a location is described by how many degrees north or south it is from the equator and how many degrees east or west it is from the prime meridian.

**READING VISUALS** Compare and contrast the two ways of describing the location of Santiago as shown here.

## Measuring Distance

If you were to travel from Brasília to Santiago, you would end up about 3000 kilometers from where you started. The actual distance you traveled, however, would depend on the exact path you took. If you took a route that had many curves, the distance you traveled would be greater than 3000 kilometers.

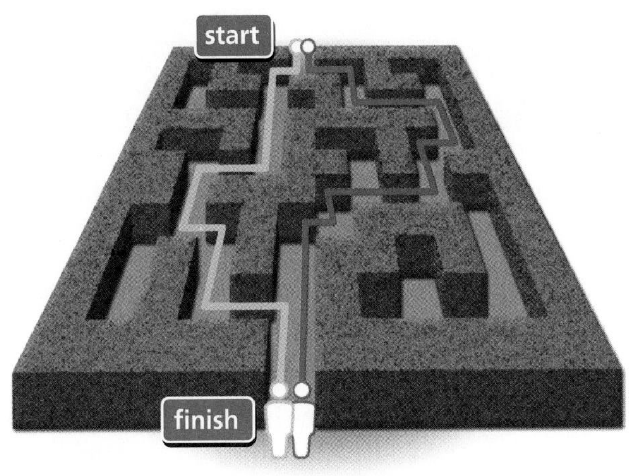


COMPARE How does the distance each person has walked compare with the distance each is from the start of the maze?

The way you measure distance depends on the information you want. Sometimes you want to know the straight-line distance between two positions. Sometimes, however, you might need to know the total length of a certain path between those positions. During a hike, you are probably more interested in how far you have walked than in how far you are from your starting point.

When measuring either the straight-line distance between two points or the length of a path between those points, scientists use a standard unit of measurement. The standard unit of length is the meter (m), which is 3.3 feet. Longer distances can be measured in kilometers (km), and shorter distances in centimeters (cm).

# Motion is a change in position.

The illustration below shows an athlete at several positions during a long jump. If you were to watch her jump, you would see that she is in motion. **Motion** is the change of position over time. As she jumps, both her horizontal and vertical positions change. If you missed the motion of the jump, you would still know that motion occurred because of the distance between her starting and ending positions. A change in position is evidence that motion happened.

REMINDER

*Horizontal* and *vertical* describe directions, as shown.

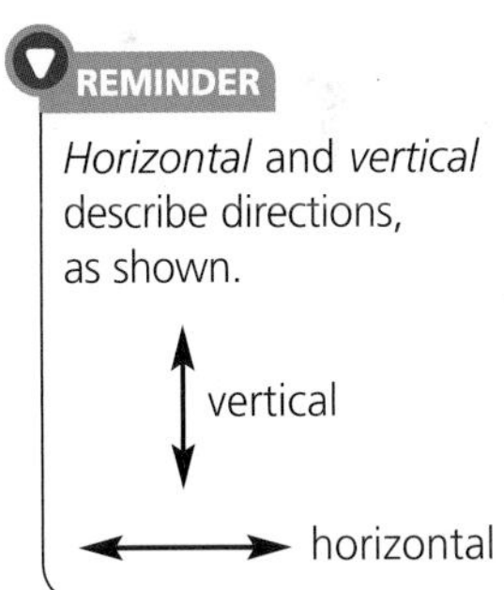

# INVESTIGATE Changing Position

## How are changes in position observed?

**SKILL FOCUS**
Observing

**MATERIALS**
- small ball
- paper
- pencil

**TIME**
20 minutes

**PROCEDURE**

1. Begin walking while tossing a ball straight up and catching it as it falls back down toward your hand. Observe the changes in the position of the ball as you toss it while walking a distance of about 4 m.
2. Make a sketch showing how the position of the ball changed as you walked. Use your own position as a reference point for the ball's position.
3. Watch while a classmate walks and tosses the ball. Observe the changes in the position of the ball using your own position as a reference point. Make a sketch showing how the ball moved based on your new point of view.

**WHAT DO YOU THINK?**

- Compare your two sketches. How was the change in position of the ball you tossed different from the change in position of the ball that your partner tossed?
- How did your change in viewpoint affect what you observed? Explain.

**CHALLENGE** How would the change in position of the ball appear to a person standing 4 m directly in front of you?

## Describing Motion

A change in an object's position tells you that motion took place, but it does not tell you how quickly the object changed position. The speed of a moving object is a measure of how quickly or slowly the object changes position. A faster object moves farther than a slower moving object would in the same amount of time.

The way in which an object moves can change. As a raft moves along a river, its speed changes as the speed of the river changes. When the raft reaches a calm area of the river, it slows down. When the raft reaches rapids, it speeds up. The rafters can also change the motion of the raft by using paddles. You will learn more about speed and changing speed in the following sections.

**APPLY** Describe the different directions in which the raft is moving.

## Relative Motion

If you sit still in a chair, you are not moving. Or are you? The answer depends on the position and motion of the person observing you. You do not notice your position changing compared with the room and the objects in it. But if an observer could leave Earth and look at you from outer space, he could see that you are moving along with Earth as it travels around the Sun. How an observer sees your motion depends on how it compares with his own motion. Just as position is described by using a reference point, motion is described by using a frame of reference. You can think of a frame of reference as the location of an observer, who may be in motion.

Consider a student sitting behind the driver of a moving bus. The bus passes another student waiting at a street sign to cross the street.

1. To the observer on the bus, the driver is not changing his position compared with the inside of the bus. The street sign, however, moves past the observer's window. From this observer's point of view, the driver is not moving, but the street sign is.
2. To the observer on the sidewalk, the driver is changing position along with the bus. The street sign, on the other hand, is not changing position. From this observer's point of view, the street sign is not moving, but the driver is.

**OUTLINE**
Add relative motion to your outline, along with supporting details.

I. Main idea
  A. Supporting idea
    1. Detail
    2. Detail
  B. Supporting idea

### Relative Motion

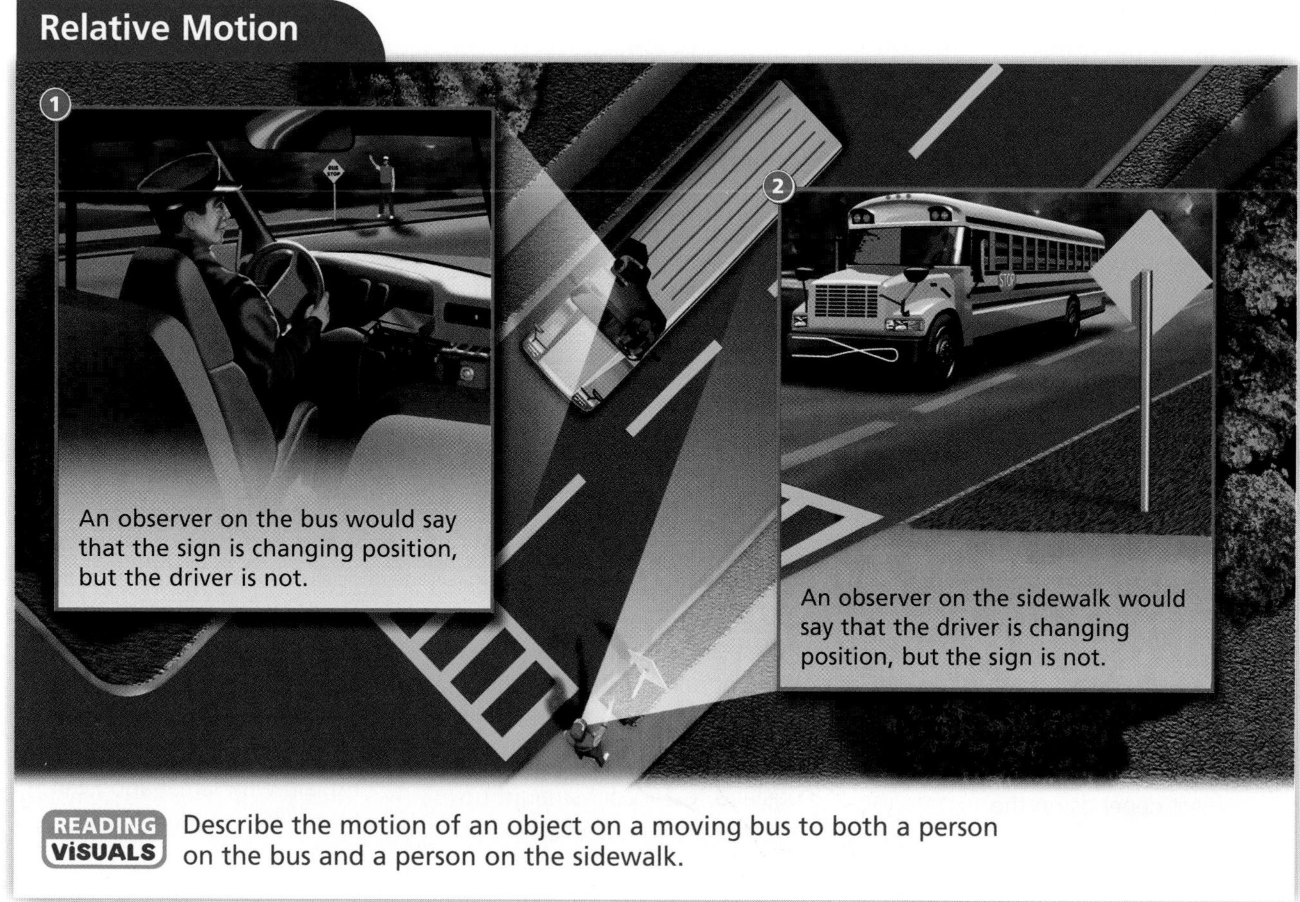


1 An observer on the bus would say that the sign is changing position, but the driver is not.

2 An observer on the sidewalk would say that the driver is changing position, but the sign is not.

**READING VISUALS** Describe the motion of an object on a moving bus to both a person on the bus and a person on the sidewalk.

APPLY In the top picture, the train is moving compared with the camera and the ground. Describe the relative motion of the train, camera, and ground in the bottom picture.

When you ride in a train, a bus, or an airplane, you think of yourself as moving and the ground as standing still. That is, you usually consider the ground as the frame of reference for your motion. If you traveled between two cities, you would say that you had moved, not that the ground had moved under you in the opposite direction.

If you cannot see the ground or objects on it, it is sometimes difficult to tell if a train you are riding in is moving. If the ride is very smooth and you do not look out the window at the scenery, you might never realize you are moving at all.

Suppose you are in a train, and you cannot tell if you are stopped or moving. Outside the window, another train is slowly moving forward. Could you tell which of the following situations is happening?

- Your train is stopped, and the other train is moving slowly forward.
- The other train is stopped, and your train is moving slowly backward.
- Both trains are moving forward, with the other train moving a little faster.
- Your train is moving very slowly backward, and the other train is moving very slowly forward.

Actually, all four of these possibilities would look exactly the same to you. Unless you compared the motion to the motion of something outside the train, such as the ground, you could not tell the difference between these situations.

CHECK YOUR READING How does your observation of motion depend on your own motion?

## 1.1 Review

**KEY CONCEPTS**

1. What information do you need to describe an object's location?
2. Describe how your position changes as you jump over an object.
3. Give an example of how the apparent motion of an object depends on the observer's motion.

**CRITICAL THINKING**

4. **Infer** Kyle walks 3 blocks south from his home to school, and Jana walks 2 blocks north from her home to Kyle's home. How far and in what direction is the school from Jana's home?
5. **Predict** If you sit on a moving bus and toss a coin straight up into the air, where will it land?

**CHALLENGE**

6. **Infer** Jamal is in a car going north. He looks out his window and thinks that the northbound traffic is moving very slowly. Ellen is in a car going south. She thinks the northbound traffic is moving quickly. Explain why Jamal and Ellen have different ideas about the motion of the traffic.

## COAST GUARD RESCUE

# Physics for Rescuers

Performing a rescue operation is often difficult and risky because the person in trouble is in a dangerous situation. Coast Guard Search and Rescue Teams have an especially difficult problem to deal with. As a rescue ship or helicopter approaches a stranded boat, the team must get close enough to help but avoid making the problem worse by colliding with the boat. At the same time, wind, waves, and currents cause changes in the motion of both crafts.

### Finding the Problem

A stranded boater fires a flare to indicate his location. The observer on the Coast Guard ship tracks the motion of the flare to its source.

### Avoiding Collision

As the boats move closer together, the captain assesses their motion relative to each other. The speeds of the boats must match, and the boats must be close enough that a rope can be thrown across the gap. If the sea is rough, both boats will move up and down, making the proper positioning even more difficult.

### Rescue from Above

The helicopter pilot determines where to hover so that the rescue basket lands on target. A mistake could be disastrous for the rescuers as well as the people being rescued.

### EXPLORE

1. **PREDICT** Tie a washer to a 30 cm piece of string. Using your hand as a helicopter, lower the rescue washer to a mark on the floor. Turn on a fan to create wind. Predict where you will need to hold the string to land the washer on the mark. Place the fan at a different location and try again. How accurate was your prediction? Does your accuracy improve with practice?
2. **CHALLENGE** Have a partner throw a baseball into the air from behind the corner of a wall. Using the motion of the ball, try to determine the position from which it was thrown. When is it easier—when the ball is thrown in a high arc or lower one?

KEY CONCEPT

# Speed measures how fast position changes.

**BEFORE, you learned**

- An object's position is measured from a reference point
- To describe the position of an object, you can use distance and direction
- An object in motion changes position with time

**NOW, you will learn**

- How to calculate an object's speed
- How to describe an object's velocity

**VOCABULARY**

**speed** p. 16
**velocity** p. 22
**vector** p. 22

**EXPLORE Speed**

### *How can you measure speed?*

**PROCEDURE**

1. Place a piece of tape on the floor. Measure a distance on the floor 2 m away from the tape. Mark this distance with a second piece of tape.
2. Roll a tennis ball from one piece of tape to the other, timing how long it takes to travel the 2 m.
3. Roll the ball again so that it travels the same distance in less time. Then roll the ball so that it takes more time to travel that distance than it did the first time.

**MATERIALS**

- tape
- meter stick
- tennis ball
- stopwatch

**WHAT DO YOU THINK?**

- How did you change the time it took the ball to travel 2 m?
- How did changing the time affect the motion of the ball?

## Position can change at different rates.

When someone asks you how far it is to the library, you can answer in terms of distance or time. You can say it is several blocks, or you can say it is a five-minute walk. When you give a time instead of a distance, you are basing your time estimate on the distance to the library and the person's speed. **Speed** is a measure of how fast something moves or the distance it moves, in a given amount of time. The greater the speed an object has, the faster it changes position.

**VOCABULARY**
Make a description wheel in your notebook for *speed*.

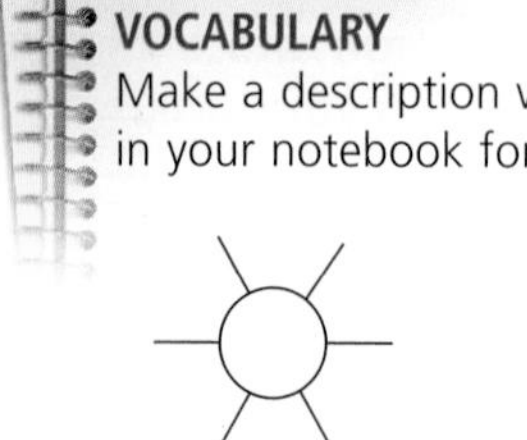

**CHECK YOUR READING** How are speed and position related?

The way in which one quantity changes compared to another quantity is called a rate. Speed is the rate at which the distance an object moves changes compared to time. If you are riding a bike to a movie, and you think you might be late, you increase the rate at which your distance changes by pedaling harder. In other words, you increase your speed.

## Calculating Speed

To calculate speed, you need to know both distance and time measurements. Consider the two bike riders below.

1. The two bikes pass the same point at the same time.
2. After one second, the first bike has traveled four meters, while the second has traveled only two meters. Because the first bike has traveled four meters in one second, it has a speed of four meters per second. The second bike has a speed of two meters per second.
3. If each bike continues moving at the same speed as before, then after two seconds the first rider will have traveled eight meters, while the second one will have traveled only four meters.

### Comparing Speed

**Objects that travel at different speeds move different distances in the same amount of time.**

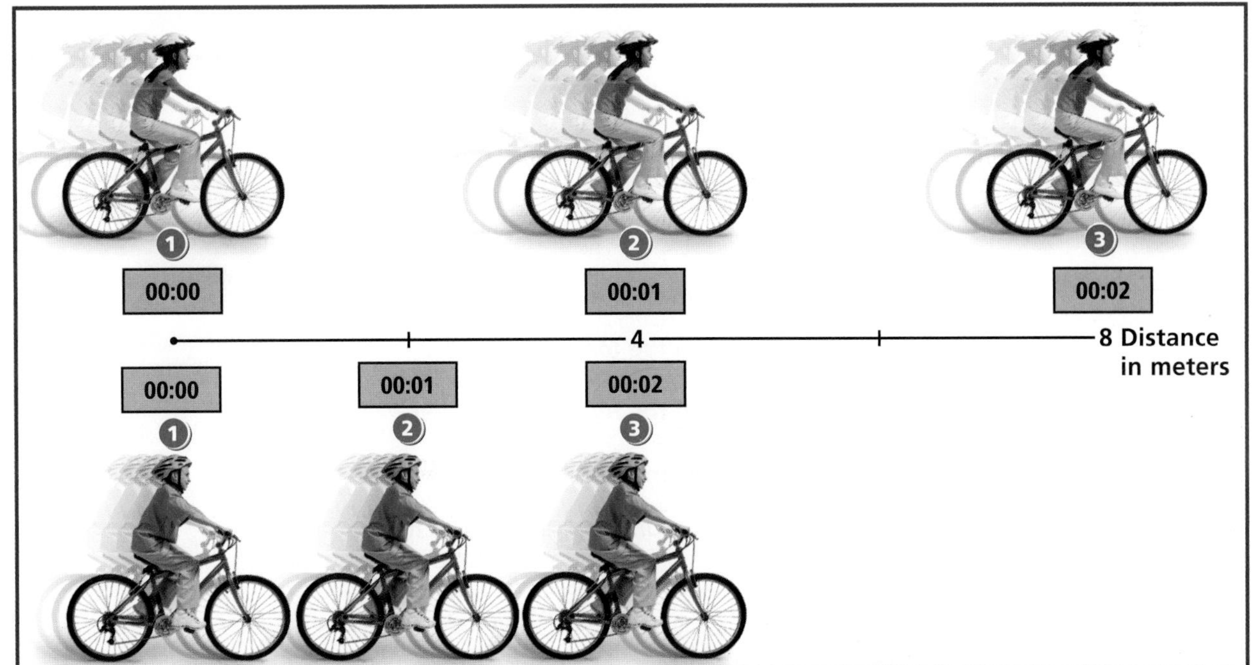


READING VISUALS How far will each rider travel in five seconds?

Racing wheelchairs are specially designed to reach higher speeds than regular wheelchairs.

Speed can be calculated by dividing the distance an object travels by the time it takes to cover the distance. The formula for finding speed is

$$\textbf{Speed} = \frac{\textbf{distance}}{\textbf{time}} \qquad S = \frac{d}{t}$$

Speed is shown in the formula as the letter *S*, distance as the letter *d*, and time as the letter *t*. The formula shows how distance, time, and speed are related. If two objects travel the same distance, the object that took a shorter amount of time will have the greater speed. Similarly, an object with a greater speed will travel a longer distance in the same amount of time than an object with a lower speed will.

The standard unit for speed is meters per second (m/s). Speed is also given in kilometers per hour (km/h). In the United States, where the English system of measurement is still used, speeds are often given in miles per hour (mi/h or mph). One mile per hour is equal to 0.45 m/s.

The man participating in the wheelchair race, at left, will win if his speed is greater than the speed of the other racers. You can use the formula to calculate his speed.

If two runners cover the same distance in different amounts of time, how do their speeds compare?

## *Calculating Speed*

### Sample Problem

**A wheelchair racer completes a 100-meter course in 20 seconds. What is his speed?**

*What do you know?* distance = 100 m, time = 20 s

*What do you want to find out?* speed

*Write the formula:* $S = \frac{d}{t}$

*Substitute into the formula:* $S = \frac{100 \text{ m}}{20 \text{ s}}$

*Calculate and simplify:* $S = 5$ m/s

*Check that your units agree:* Unit is m/s.
Unit of speed is m/s. Units agree.

*Answer:* $S = 5$ m/s

### Practice the Math

1. A man runs 200 m in 25 s. What is his speed?
2. If you travel 100 m in 50 s, what is your speed?

## Average Speed

Speed is not constant. When you run, you might slow down to pace yourself, or speed up to win a race. At each point as you are running, you have a specific speed. This moment-to-moment speed is called your instantaneous speed. Your instantaneous speed can be difficult to measure; however, it is easier to calculate your average speed over a distance.

**READING TIP**

The root of *instantaneous* is *instant,* meaning "moment."

In a long race, runners often want to know their times for each lap so that they can pace themselves. For example, an excellent middle school runner might have the following times for the four laps of a 1600-meter race: 83 seconds, 81 seconds, 79 seconds, 77 seconds. The lap times show the runner is gradually increasing her speed throughout the race.

The total time for the four laps can be used to calculate the runner's average speed for the entire race. The total time is 320 seconds (5 min 20 s) for the entire distance of 1600 meters. The runner's average speed is 1600 meters divided by 320 seconds, or 5.0 meters per second.

## INVESTIGATE Speed and Distance

### *How does design affect speed?*

**DESIGN — YOUR OWN — EXPERIMENT**

Cars are built in different shapes. How does the shape of the car affect the way it moves? Design your own car, and see how fast it can go.

**PROCEDURE**

1. Use the clay, film container lids, and toothpicks to design a car that rolls when it is pushed. The car should have a total mass of 150 g or less.
2. Using any or all of the other materials, design an experiment to measure and compare the speed of your car with the speed of someone else's car. Your experiment should be designed so that the design of the car is the only variable being tested. Write up your procedure.
3. Perform the experiment using your car and another student's car. Record the data you need to calculate the speed of both cars.
4. Calculate the speed of each car, and record which car went faster.

**WHAT DO YOU THINK?**

- What were the constants in your experiment?
- How would you improve your design if you were to repeat the experiment?

**SKILL FOCUS**
Designing experiments

**MATERIALS**
- clay
- film container lids
- toothpicks
- beam balance
- board
- books
- string
- straw
- scissors
- stopwatch

**TIME**
20 minutes

## Distance-Time Graphs

A convenient way to show the motion of an object is by using a graph that plots the distance the object has traveled against time. This type of graph, called a distance-time graph, shows how speed relates to distance and time. You can use a distance-time graph to see how both distance and speed change with time.

The distance-time graph on page 21 tracks the changing motion of a zebra. At first the zebra looks for a spot to graze. Its meal is interrupted by a lion, and the zebra starts running to escape.

**REMINDER**

The *x*-axis and *y*-axis are arranged as shown:

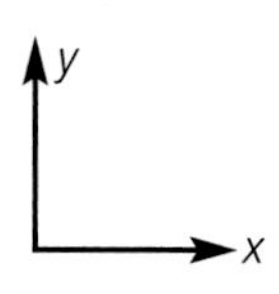


In a distance-time graph, time is on the horizontal axis, or *x*-axis, and distance is on the vertical axis, or *y*-axis.

1. As an object moves, the distance it travels increases with time. This can be seen as a climbing, or rising, line on the graph.
2. A flat, or horizontal, line shows an interval of time where the speed is zero meters per second.
3. Steeper lines show intervals where the speed is greater than intervals with less steep lines.

You can use a distance-time graph to determine the speed of an object. The steepness, or slope, of the line is calculated by dividing the change in distance by the change in time for that time interval.

### Calculating Speed from a Graph

**Sample Problem**

**How fast is the zebra walking during the first 20 seconds?**

*What do you know?* Reading from the graph:
At time = 0 s, distance = 0 m.
At time = 20 s, distance = 40 m.

*What do you want to find out?* speed

*Write the formula:* $S = \frac{d}{t}$

*Substitute into the formula:* $S = \frac{40\text{ m} - 0\text{ m}}{20\text{ s} - 0\text{ s}}$

*Calculate and simplify:* $S = \frac{40\text{ m}}{20\text{ s}} = 2\text{ m/s}$

*Check that your units agree:* Unit is m/s.
Unit of speed is m/s. Units agree.

*Answer:* $S = 2$ m/s

**Practice the Math**

1. What is the speed of the zebra during the 20 s to 40 s time interval?
2. What is the speed of the zebra during the 40 s to 60 s interval?

## Distance-Time Graph

**A zebra's speed will change throughout the day, especially if a hungry lion is nearby. You can use a distance-time graph to compare the zebra's speed over different time intervals.**

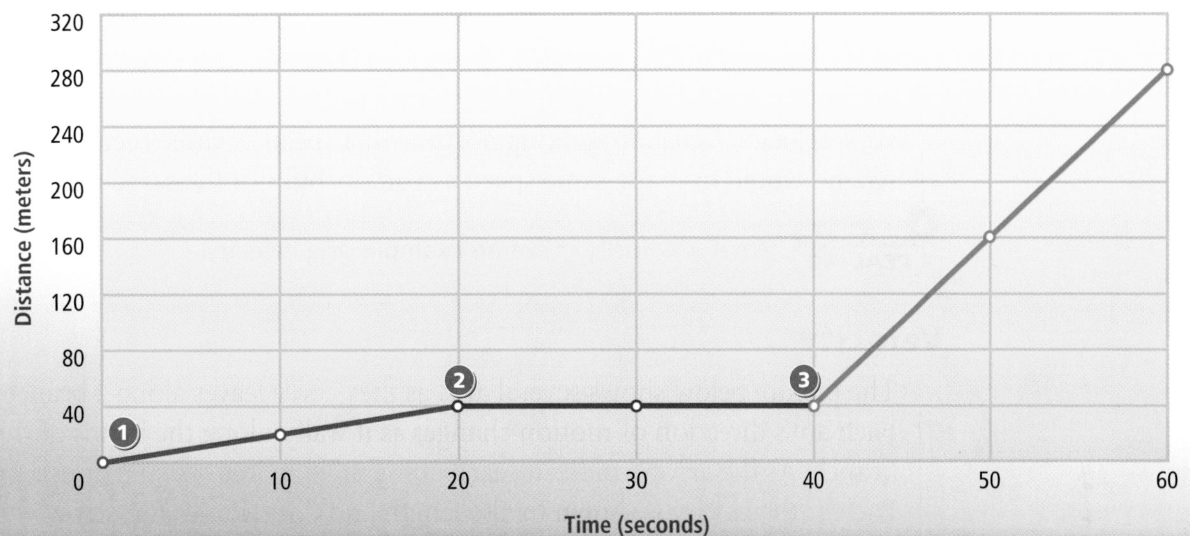


1. When the zebra is walking, its distance from its starting point increases. You can see this motion on the graph as a climbing line.

2. When the zebra stops to graze, it no longer changes its distance from the starting point. Time, however, continues to pass. Therefore, the graph shows a flat, or horizontal, line.

3. As soon as the zebra notices the lion, it stops grazing and starts to run for its life. The zebra is covering a greater distance in each time interval than it was before the chase started, so the line is steeper.

**READING VISUALS** How do the distances change over each 10-second time interval?

## Velocity includes speed and direction.

Sometimes the direction of motion is as important as its speed. In large crowds, for example, you probably always try to walk in the same direction the crowd is moving and at the same speed. If you walk in even a slightly different direction, you can bump into other people. In a crowd, in other words, you try to walk with the same velocity as the people around you. **Velocity** is a speed in a specific direction. If you say you are walking east at a speed of three meters per second, you are describing your velocity. A person walking north with a speed of three meters per second would have the same speed as you do, but not the same velocity.

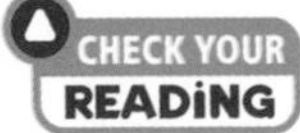


What is velocity? Give an example of a velocity.

### Velocity

The picture below shows several ants as they carry leaves along a branch. Each ant's direction of motion changes as it walks along the bends of the branch. As the arrows indicate, each ant is moving in a specific direction. Each ant's velocity is shown by the length and direction of the arrow. A longer arrow means a greater speed in the direction the arrow is pointing. In this picture, for example, the ant moving up the branch is traveling more slowly than the ant moving down the branch.

To determine the velocity of an ant as it carries a leaf, you need to know both its speed and its direction. A change in either speed or direction results in a change in velocity. For example, the velocity of an ant changes if it slows down but continues moving in the same direction. Velocity also changes if the ant continues moving at the same speed but changes direction.

Velocity is an example of a vector. A **vector** is a quantity that has both size and direction. Speed is not a vector because speed is a measure of how fast or slow an object moves, not which direction it moves in. Velocity, however, has a size—the speed—and a direction, so it is a vector quantity.

**READING TIP**

Green arrows show velocity.

A longer arrow indicates a faster speed than a shorter arrow. The direction of the arrow indicates the direction of motion.

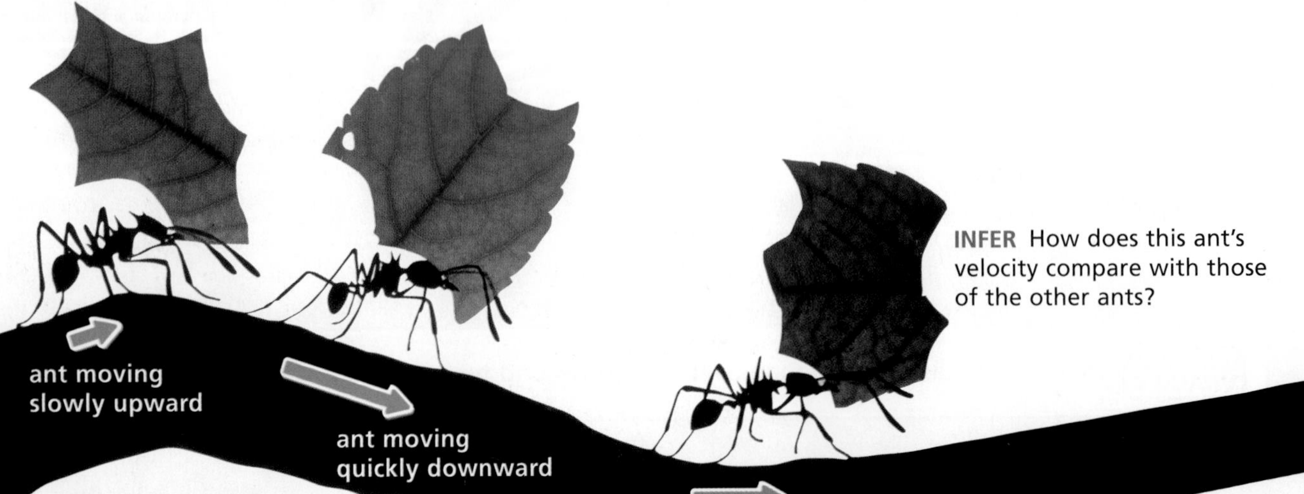


**INFER** How does this ant's velocity compare with those of the other ants?

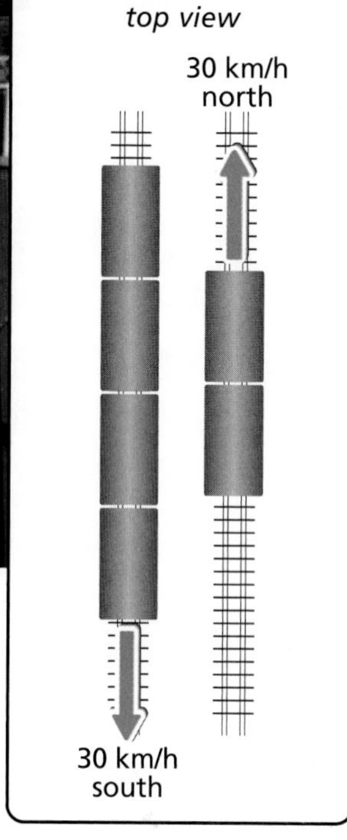


**INFER** How do the speeds and velocities of these trains compare?

## Velocity Versus Speed

Because velocity includes direction, it is possible for two objects to have the same speed but different velocities. If you traveled by train to visit a friend, you might go 30 kilometers per hour (km/h) north on the way there and 30 km/h south on the way back. Your speed is the same both going and coming back, but your velocity is different because your direction of motion has changed.

Another difference between speed and velocity is the way the average is calculated. Your average speed depends on the total distance you have traveled. The average velocity depends on the total distance you are from where you started. Going north, your average speed would be 30 km/h, and your average velocity would be 30 km/h north. After the round-trip ride, your average traveling speed would still be 30 km/h. Your average velocity, however, would be 0 km/h because you ended up exactly where you started.

Use a Venn diagram to compare and contrast speed and velocity.

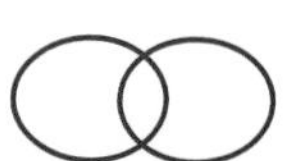

# 1.2 Review

### KEY CONCEPTS

1. How is speed related to distance and time?
2. How would decreasing the time it takes you to run a certain distance affect your speed?
3. What two things do you need to know to describe the velocity of an object?

### CRITICAL THINKING

4. **Compare** Amy and Ellie left school at the same time. Amy lives farther away than Ellie, but she and Ellie arrived at their homes at the same time. Compare the girls' speeds.
5. **Calculate** Carlos lives 100 m away from his friend's home. What is his average speed if he reaches his friend's home in 50 s?

### CHALLENGE

6. **Synthesize** If you watch a train go by at 20 m/s, at what speed will the people sitting on the train be moving relative to you? Would someone walking toward the back of the train have a greater or lesser speed relative to you? Explain.

SKILL: WORKING WITH UNITS

# Time, Distance, and Speed

If someone tells you the store is "five" from the school, you would probably ask, "Five what? Five meters? Five blocks?" You typically describe a distance using standard units of measurement, such as meters, miles, or kilometers. By using units, you help other people understand exactly what your measurement means.

When you work with a formula, the numbers that you substitute into the formula have units. When you calculate with a number, you also calculate with the unit associated with that number.

**MATH TUTORIAL**

CLASSZONE.COM

Click on Math Tutorial for more help with units and rates.

### Example

A cheetah runs at a speed of 30 meters per second. How long does the cheetah take to run 90 meters?

The formula for time in terms of speed and distance is

$$\text{time} = \frac{\text{distance}}{\text{Speed}} \qquad t = \frac{d}{S}$$

**(1)** Start by substituting the numbers into the formula. Include the units with the numbers.

$$t = \frac{90 \text{ m}}{30 \text{ m/s}}$$

**(2)** When the units or calculations include fractions, write out the units as fractions as well:

$$t = \frac{90 \text{ m}}{\frac{30 \text{ m}}{\text{s}}}$$

**(3)** Do the calculation and simplify the units by cancellation:

$$t = 90 \text{ m} \cdot \frac{\text{s}}{30 \text{ m}} = \frac{90}{30} \cdot \frac{\text{m} \cdot \text{s}}{\text{m}} = 3 \cdot \frac{\cancel{\text{m}} \cdot \text{s}}{\cancel{\text{m}}} = 3 \text{ s}$$

**ANSWER** 3 seconds

Note that the answer has a unit of time. Use the units to check that your answer is reasonable. An answer that is supposed to have a unit of time, for example, should not have a unit of distance.

**Answer the following questions.**

1. How long would it take an object traveling 12 m/s to go 60 m? What unit of time is your answer in?
2. If a car travels 60 km/h, how long would it take the car to travel 300 km? What unit of time is your answer in?
3. If a man walks 3 miles in 1 hour, what is his speed? What unit of speed is your answer in? (Use the formula on page 18.)

**CHALLENGE** Show that the formula *distance* = *speed* • *time* has a unit for distance on both sides of the equal sign.

A cheetah can reach a speed of 30 meters per second, but only in short bursts.

KEY CONCEPT

# Acceleration measures how fast velocity changes.

**BEFORE, you learned**

- Speed describes how far an object travels in a given time
- Velocity is a measure of the speed and direction of motion

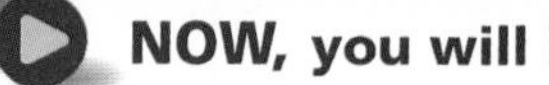

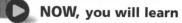

**NOW, you will learn**

- How acceleration is related to velocity
- How to calculate acceleration

**VOCABULARY**

**acceleration** p. 25

THINK ABOUT

### *How does velocity change?*

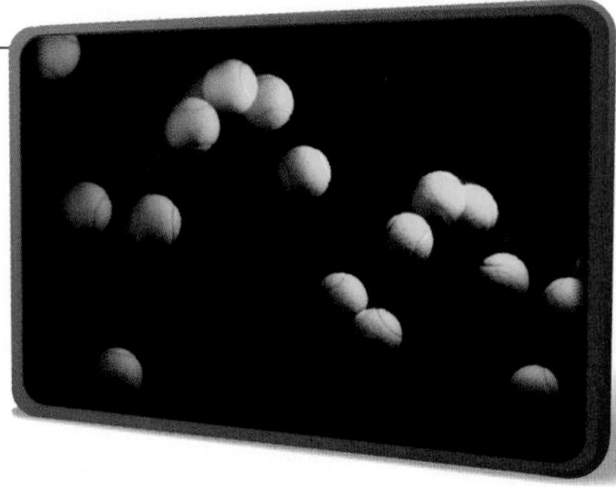

The photograph at right shows the path that a bouncing ball takes. The time between each image of the ball is the same during the entire bounce. Is the ball moving the same distance in each time interval? Is the ball moving the same direction in each time interval?

**OUTLINE**
Remember to use the blue and red headings in this chapter to help you make notes on acceleration.

I. Main idea
  A. Supporting idea
    1. Detail
    2. Detail
  B. Supporting idea

## Speed and direction can change with time.

When you throw a ball into the air, it leaves your hand at a certain speed. As the ball rises, it slows down. Then, as the ball falls back toward the ground, it speeds up again. When the ball hits the ground, its direction of motion changes and it bounces back up into the air. The speed and direction of the ball do not stay the same as the ball moves. The ball's velocity keeps changing.

You can find out how much an object's position changes during a certain amount of time if you know its velocity. In a similar way, you can measure how an object's velocity changes with time. The rate at which velocity changes with time is called **acceleration.** Acceleration is a measure of how quickly the velocity is changing. If velocity does not change, there is no acceleration.

What is the relationship between velocity and acceleration?

The word *acceleration* is commonly used to mean “speeding up.” In physics, however, acceleration refers to any change in velocity. A driver slowing down to stop at a light is accelerating. A runner turning a corner at a constant speed is also accelerating because the direction of her velocity is changing as she turns.

Like velocity, acceleration is a vector, which means it has both size and direction. The direction of the acceleration determines whether an object will slow down, speed up, or turn.

READING TIP

Orange arrows are used to show acceleration.

Remember that green arrows show velocity.

A longer arrow means greater acceleration or velocity.

1. **Acceleration in the Same Direction as Motion** When the acceleration is in the same direction as the object is moving, the speed of the object increases. The car speeds up.

2. **Acceleration in the Opposite Direction of Motion** When the acceleration is opposite to the motion, the speed of the object decreases. The car slows down. Slowing down is also called negative acceleration.

3. **Acceleration at a Right Angle to Motion** When the acceleration is at a right angle to the motion, the direction of motion changes. The car changes the direction in which it is moving by some angle, but its speed does not change.

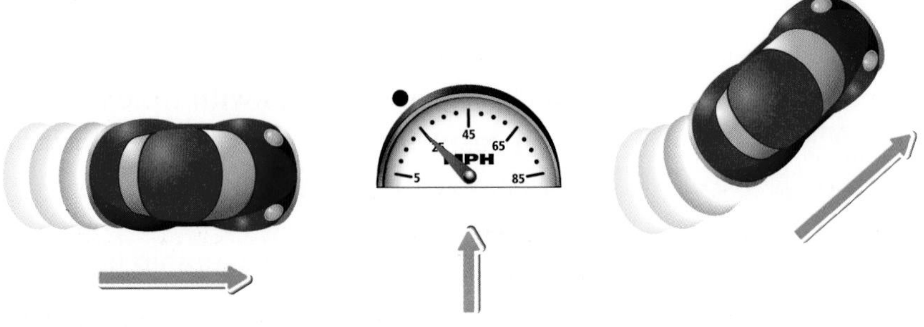


CHECK YOUR READING How does acceleration affect velocity? Give examples.

# INVESTIGATE Acceleration

## *When does an object accelerate?*

**SKILL FOCUS**
Measuring

**MATERIALS**
- template for tool
- cardboard
- scissors
- glue
- piece of string
- weight

**TIME**
30 minutes

**PROCEDURE**

1. Use the template and materials to construct an acceleration measuring tool.
2. Hold the tool in your right hand so that the string falls over the 0 m/s$^2$ mark. Move the tool in the direction of the arrow. Try to produce both positive and negative acceleration without changing the direction of motion.
3. With the arrow pointing ahead of you, start to walk. Observe the motion of the string while you increase your speed.
4. Repeat step 3, but this time observe the string while slowing down.
5. Repeat step 3 again, but observe the string while walking at a steady speed.

**WHAT DO YOU THINK?**

- When could you measure an acceleration?
- What was the largest acceleration (positive or negative) that you measured?

**CHALLENGE** If you moved the acceleration measuring tool backward, how would the measuring scale change?

## Acceleration can be calculated from velocity and time.

Suppose you are racing a classmate. In one second, you go from standing still to running at six meters per second. In the same time, your classmate goes from standing still to running at three meters per second. How does your acceleration compare with your classmate's acceleration? To measure acceleration, you need to know how velocity changes with time.

- The change in velocity can be found by comparing the initial velocity and the final velocity of the moving object.
- The time interval over which the velocity changed can be measured.

In one second, you increase your velocity by six meters per second, and your friend increases her velocity by three meters per second. Because your velocity changes more, you have a greater acceleration during that second of time than your friend does. Remember that acceleration measures the change in velocity, not velocity itself. As long as your classmate increases her current velocity by three meters per second, her acceleration will be the same whether she is going from zero to three meters per second or from three to six meters per second.

## Calculating Acceleration

If you know the starting velocity of an object, the final velocity, and the time interval during which the object changed velocity, you can calculate the acceleration of the object. The formula for acceleration is shown below.

$$\text{acceleration} = \frac{\text{final velocity} - \text{initial velocity}}{\text{time}}$$

$$a = \frac{v_{final} - v_{initial}}{t}$$

Remember that velocity is expressed in units of meters per second. The standard units for acceleration, therefore, are meters per second over time, or meters per second per second. This is simplified to meters per second squared, which is written as $m/s^2$.

As the girl in the photograph at left sleds down the sandy hill, what happens to her velocity? At the bottom of the hill, her velocity will be greater than it was at the top. You can calculate her average acceleration down the hill if you know her starting and ending velocities and how long it took her to get to the bottom. This calculation is shown in the sample problem below.

### Calculating Acceleration

**Sample Problem**

**Ama starts sliding with a velocity of 1 m/s. After 3 s, her velocity is 7 m/s. What is Ama's acceleration?**

*What do you know?* initial velocity = 1 m/s, final velocity = 7 m/s, time = 3 s

*What do you want to find out?* acceleration

*Write the formula:* $a = \frac{v_{final} - v_{initial}}{t}$

*Substitute into the formula:* $a = \frac{7 \text{ m/s} - 1 \text{ m/s}}{3 \text{ s}}$

*Calculate and simplify:* $a = \frac{6 \text{ m/s}}{3 \text{ s}} = 2 \frac{\text{m/s}}{\text{s}} = 2 \text{ m/s}^2$

*Check that your units agree:* $\frac{\text{m/s}}{\text{s}} = \frac{\text{m}}{\text{s}} \cdot \frac{1}{\text{s}} = \frac{\text{m}}{\text{s}^2}$

Unit of acceleration is $m/s^2$. Units agree.

*Answer:* $a = 2 \text{ m/s}^2$

**Practice the Math**

1. A man walking at 0.5 m/s accelerates to a velocity of 0.6 m/s in 1 s. What is his acceleration?
2. A train traveling at 10 m/s slows down to a complete stop in 20 s. What is the acceleration of the train?

**REMINDER**

Remember that velocity is the speed of the object in a particular direction.

The sledder's final velocity was greater than her initial velocity. If an object is slowing down, on the other hand, the final velocity is less than the initial velocity. Suppose a car going 10 meters per second takes 2 seconds to stop for a red light. In this case, the initial velocity is 10 m/s and the final velocity is 0 m/s. The formula for acceleration gives a negative answer, $-5\ m/s^2$. The negative sign indicates a negative acceleration—that is, an acceleration that decreases the velocity.

Learn more about acceleration.

What would be true of the values for initial velocity and final velocity if the acceleration were zero?

## Acceleration over Time

Even a very small positive acceleration can lead to great speeds if an object accelerates for a long enough period. In 1998, NASA launched the *Deep Space 1* spacecraft. This spacecraft tested a new type of engine—one that gave the spacecraft an extremely small acceleration. The new engine required less fuel than previous spacecraft engines. However, the spacecraft needed a great deal of time to reach its target velocity.

The acceleration of the *Deep Space 1* spacecraft is less than 2/10,000 of a meter per second per second ($0.0002\ m/s^2$). That may not seem like much, but over 20 months, the spacecraft could increase its speed by 4500 meters per second (10,000 mi/h).

By carefully adjusting both the amount and the direction of the acceleration of *Deep Space 1*, scientists were able to control its flight path. In 2001, the spacecraft successfully flew by a comet, sending back images from about 230 million kilometers (140 million mi) away.

**APPLY** What makes the new engine technology used by *Deep Space 1* more useful for long-term missions than for short-term ones?

## Velocity-Time Graphs

**Velocity-time graphs and distance-time graphs are related. This is because the distance an object travels depends on its velocity. Compare the velocity-time graph on the right with the distance-time graph below it.**

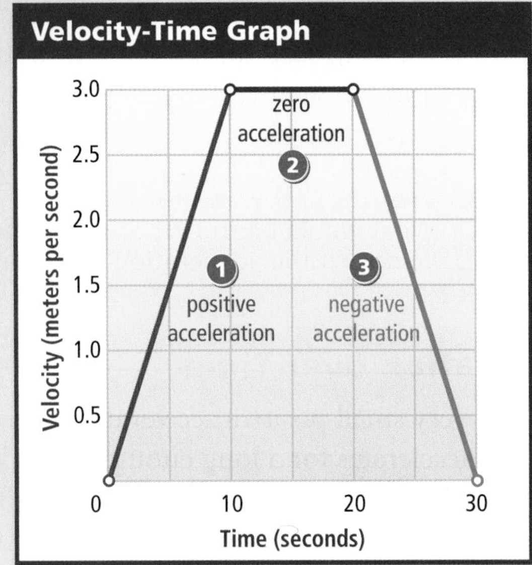

1. As the student starts to push the scooter, his velocity increases. His acceleration is positive, so he moves forward a greater distance with each second that passes.
2. He coasts at a constant velocity. Because his velocity does not change, he has no acceleration, and he continues to move forward the same distance each second.
3. As he slows down, his velocity decreases. His acceleration is negative, and he moves forward a smaller distance with each passing second until he finally stops.

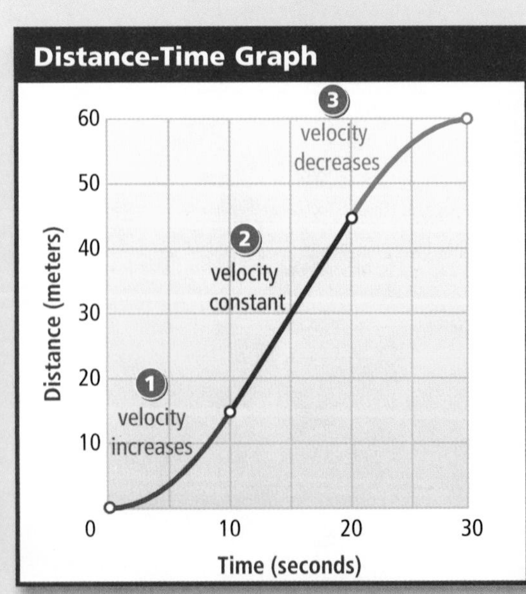


**READING VISUALS** What velocity does the student have after five seconds? About how far has he moved in that time?

## Velocity-Time Graphs

Acceleration, like position and velocity, can change with time. Just as you can use a distance-time graph to understand velocity, you can use a velocity-time graph to understand acceleration. Both graphs tell you how something is changing over time. In a velocity-time graph, time is on the horizontal axis, or *x*-axis, and velocity is on the vertical axis, or *y*-axis.

Explore how changing the acceleration of an object changes its motion.

The two graphs on page 30 show a velocity-time graph and a distance-time graph of a student riding on a scooter. He first starts moving and speeds up. He coasts, and then he slows down to a stop.

1. The rising line on the velocity-time graph shows where the acceleration is positive. The steeper the line, the greater the acceleration. The distance-time graph for the same interval is curving upward more and more steeply as the velocity increases.
2. The flat line on the velocity-time graph shows an interval of no acceleration. The distance-time graph has a straight line during this time, since the velocity is not changing.
3. The falling line on the velocity-time graph shows where the acceleration is negative. The same interval on the distance-time graph shows a curve that becomes less and less steep as the velocity decreases. Notice that the overall distance still increases.

Velocity-time graphs and distance-time graphs can provide useful information. For example, scientists who study earthquakes create these graphs in order to study the up-and-down and side-to-side movement of the ground during an earthquake. They produce the graphs from instruments that measure the acceleration of the ground.

What does a flat line on a velocity-time graph represent?

# 1.3 Review

### KEY CONCEPTS

1. What measurements or observations tell you that a car is accelerating?
2. If an object accelerates in the same direction in which it is moving, how is its speed affected?
3. What measurements do you need in order to calculate acceleration?

### CRITICAL THINKING

4. **Calculate** A car goes from 20 m/s to 30 m/s in 10 seconds. What is its acceleration?
5. **Infer** Two runners start a race. After 2 seconds, they both have the same velocity. If they both started at the same time, how do their average accelerations compare?

### CHALLENGE

6. **Analyze** Is it possible for an object that has a constant negative acceleration to change the direction in which it is moving? Explain why or why not.

# CHAPTER INVESTIGATION

## Acceleration and Slope

**OVERVIEW AND PURPOSE** When a downhill skier glides down a mountain without using her ski poles, her velocity increases and she experiences acceleration. How would gliding down a hill with a greater slope affect her acceleration? In this investigation you will

- calculate the acceleration of an object rolling down two ramps of different slopes
- determine how the slope of the ramp affects the acceleration of the object

### Problem

How does the slope of a ramp affect the acceleration of an object rolling down the ramp?

### Hypothesize

Write a hypothesis to explain how changing the slope of the ramp will affect acceleration. Your hypothesis should take the form of an "If . . . , then . . . , because . . ." statement.

**MATERIALS**
- 2 meter sticks
- masking tape
- marble
- 2 paperback books
- ruler
- stopwatch
- calculator

### Procedure

1. Make a data table like the one shown on the sample notebook page.

2. Make a ramp by laying two meter sticks side by side. Leave a small gap between the meter sticks.

3. Use masking tape as shown in the photograph to join the meter sticks. The marble should be able to roll freely along the groove.

4. Set up your ramp on a smooth, even surface, such as a tabletop. Raise one end of the ramp on top of one of the books. The other end of the ramp should remain on the table.

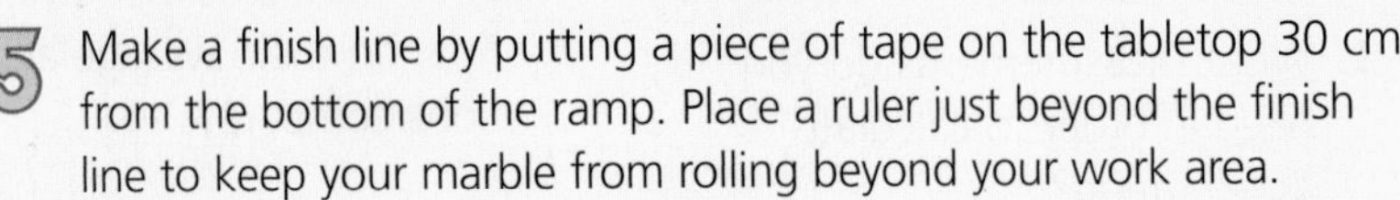

5. Make a finish line by putting a piece of tape on the tabletop 30 cm from the bottom of the ramp. Place a ruler just beyond the finish line to keep your marble from rolling beyond your work area.

6 Test your ramp by releasing the marble from the top of the ramp. Make sure that the marble rolls freely. Do not push on the marble.

7 Release the marble and measure the time it takes for it to roll from the release point to the end of the ramp. Record this time under Column A for trial 1.

8 Release the marble again from the same point, and record the time it takes the marble to roll from the end of the ramp to the finish line. Record this time in Column B for trial 1. Repeat and record three more trials.

9 Raise the height of the ramp by propping it up with both paperback books. Repeat steps 7 and 8.

## Observe and Analyze

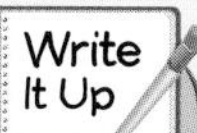


1. **RECORD OBSERVATIONS** Draw the setup of your procedures. Be sure your data table is complete.
2. **IDENTIFY VARIABLES AND CONSTANTS** Identify the variables and constants in the experiment. List them in your notebook.
3. **CALCULATE**

**Average Time** For ramps 1 and 2, calculate and record the average time it took for the marble to travel from the end of the ramp to the finish line.

**Final Velocity** For ramps 1 and 2, calculate and record $V_{final}$ using the formula below.

$$v_{final} = \frac{\text{distance from end of ramp to finish line}}{\text{average time from end of ramp to finish line}}$$

**Acceleration** For ramps 1 and 2, calculate and record acceleration using the formula below. (**Hint:** Speed at the release of the marble is 0 m/s.)

$$a = \frac{v_{final} - v_{initial}\text{ (speed at release)}}{\text{average time from release to bottom of ramp}}$$

## Conclude

1. **COMPARE** How did the acceleration of the marble on ramp 1 compare with the acceleration of the marble on ramp 2?
2. **INTERPRET** Answer the question posed in the problem.
3. **ANALYZE** Compare your results with your hypothesis. Do your data support your hypothesis?
4. **EVALUATE** Why was it necessary to measure how fast the marble traveled from the end of the ramp to the finish line?
5. **IDENTIFY LIMITS** What possible limitations or sources of error could have affected your results? Why was it important to perform four trials for each measurement of speed?

## INVESTIGATE Further

**CHALLENGE** Design your own experiment to determine how the marble's mass affects its acceleration down a ramp.

Acceleration and Slope

Problem How does the slope of a ramp affect the acceleration of an object rolling down the ramp?

Hypothesize

Observe and Analyze

Table 1. Times for Marble to Travel down Ramp

| Height of Ramp (cm) | Trial Number | Column A Time from release to end of ramp | Column B Time from end of ramp to finish line |
|---|---|---|---|
| Ramp 1 | 1 | | |
| | 2 | | |
| | 3 | | |
| | 4 | | |
| | Totals | | |
| | | Average | Average |
| | | | |
| | | | |
| | | | |

# Chapter Review

## the BIG idea

**The motion of an object can be described and predicted.**

## KEY CONCEPTS SUMMARY

### 1.1 An object in motion changes position.

Position is measured from a reference point.

Motion is measured relative to an observer.

**VOCABULARY**
**position** p. 9
**reference point** p. 10
**motion** p. 11

### 1.2 Speed measures how fast position changes.

- Speed is how fast positions change with time.
- Velocity is speed in a specific direction.

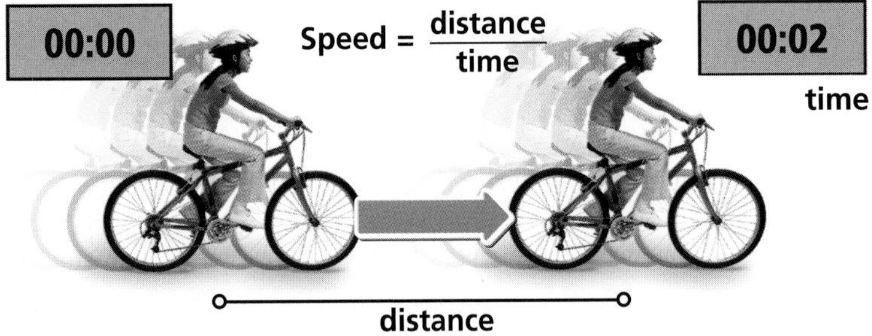


**VOCABULARY**
**speed** p. 16
**velocity** p. 22
**vector** p. 22

### 1.3 Acceleration measures how fast velocity changes.

$$\text{acceleration} = \frac{\text{final velocity} - \text{initial velocity}}{\text{time}}$$

initial velocity acceleration final velocity

**VOCABULARY**
**acceleration** p. 25

## Reviewing Vocabulary

*Copy and complete the chart below. If the left column is blank, give the correct term. If the right column is blank, give a brief description.*

| Term | Description |
|---|---|
| 1. | speed in a specific direction |
| 2. | a change of position over time |
| 3. speed | |
| 4. | an object's location |
| 5. reference point | |
| 6. | the rate at which velocity changes over time |
| 7. | a quantity that has both size and direction |

## Reviewing Key Concepts

**Multiple Choice** *Choose the letter of the best answer.*

8. A position describes an object's location compared to
   - **a.** its motion
   - **b.** a reference point
   - **c.** its speed
   - **d.** a vector

9. Maria walked 2 km in half an hour. What was her average speed during her walk?
   - **a.** 1 km/h
   - **b.** 2 km/h
   - **c.** 4 km/h
   - **d.** 6 km/h

10. A vector is a quantity that has
   - **a.** speed
   - **b.** acceleration
   - **c.** size and direction
   - **d.** position and distance

11. Mary and Keisha run with the same constant speed but in opposite directions. The girls have
   - **a.** the same position
   - **b.** different accelerations
   - **c.** different speeds
   - **d.** different velocities

12. A swimmer increases her speed as she approaches the end of the pool. Her acceleration is
   - **a.** in the same direction as her motion
   - **b.** in the opposite direction of her motion
   - **c.** at right angles to her motion
   - **d.** zero

13. A cheetah can go from 0 m/s to 20 m/s in 2 s. What is the cheetah's acceleration?
   - **a.** 5 $m/s^2$
   - **b.** 10 $m/s^2$
   - **c.** 20 $m/s^2$
   - **d.** 40 $m/s^2$

14. Jon walks for a few minutes, then runs for a few minutes. During this time, his average speed is
   - **a.** the same as his final speed
   - **b.** greater than his final speed
   - **c.** less than his final speed
   - **d.** zero

15. A car traveling at 40 m/s slows down to 20 m/s. During this time, the car has
   - **a.** no acceleration
   - **b.** positive acceleration
   - **c.** negative acceleration
   - **d.** constant velocity

**Short Answer** *Write a short answer to each question.*

16. Suppose you are biking with a friend. How would your friend describe your relative motion as he passes you?

17. Describe a situation where an object has a changing velocity but constant speed.

18. Give two examples of an accelerating object.

## Thinking Critically

*Use the following graph to answer the next three questions.*

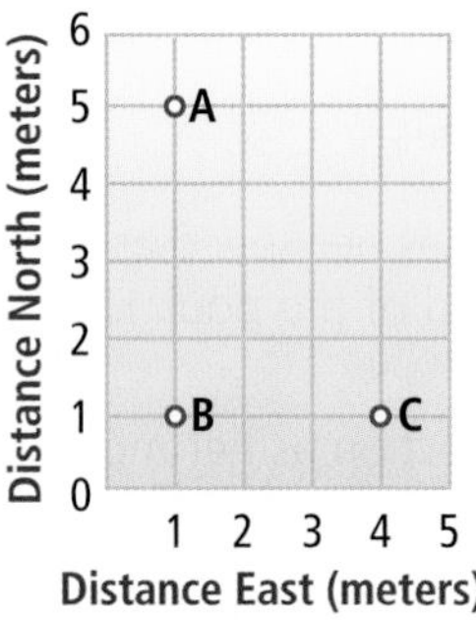


19. **OBSERVE** Describe the location of point A. Explain what you used as a reference point for your location.

20. **COMPARE** Copy the graph into your notebook. Draw two different paths an object could take when moving from point B to point C. How do the lengths of these two paths compare?

21. **ANALYZE** An object moves from point A to point C in the same amount of time that another object moves from point B to point C. If both objects traveled in a straight line, which one had the greater speed?

*Read the following paragraph and use the information to answer the next three questions.*

In Aesop's fable of the tortoise and the hare, a slow-moving tortoise races a fast-moving hare. The hare, certain it can win, stops to take a long nap. Meanwhile, the tortoise continues to move toward the finish line at a slow but steady speed. When the hare wakes up, it runs as fast as it can. Just as the hare is about to catch up to the tortoise, however, the tortoise wins the race.

22. **ANALYZE** How does the race between the tortoise and the hare show the difference between average speed and instantaneous speed?

23. **MODEL** Assume the racetrack was 100 meters long and the race took 40 minutes. Create a possible distance-time graph for both the tortoise and the hare.

24. **COMPARE** If the racetrack were circular, how would the tortoise's speed be different from its velocity?

25. **APPLY** How might a person use a floating stick to measure the speed at which a river flows?

26. **CONNECT** Describe a frame of reference other than the ground that you might use to measure motion. When would you use it?

## Using Math Skills in Science

27. José skated 50 m in 10 s. What was his speed?

28. Use the information in the photograph below to calculate the speed of the ant as it moves down the branch.

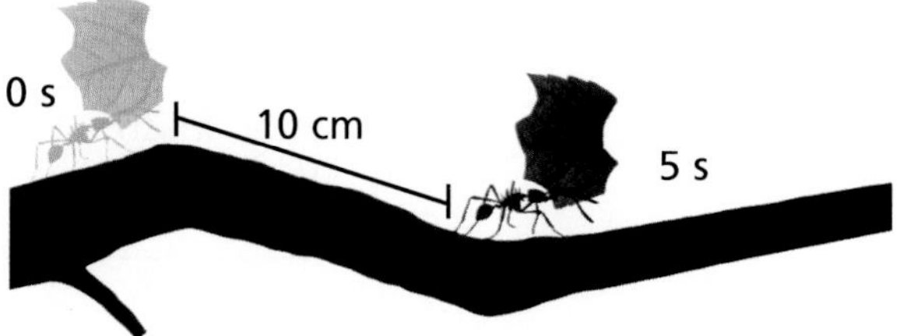


29. While riding her bicycle, Jamie accelerated from 7 m/s to 2 m/s in 5 s. What was her acceleration?

## the BIG idea

30. **PREDICT** Look back at the picture at the beginning of the chapter on pages 6–7. Predict how the velocity of the roller coaster will change in the next moment.

31. **WRITE** A car is traveling east at 40 km/h. Use this information to predict where the car will be in one hour. Discuss the assumptions you made to reach your conclusion and the factors that might affect it.

## UNIT PROJECTS

If you are doing a unit project, make a folder for your project. Include in your folder a list of the resources you will need, the date on which the project is due, and a schedule to keep track of your progress. Begin gathering data.

# Standardized Test Practice

For practice on your state test, go to . . . TEST PRACTICE CLASSZONE.COM

## Interpreting Graphs

The graph below is a distance-time graph showing a 50-meter race.

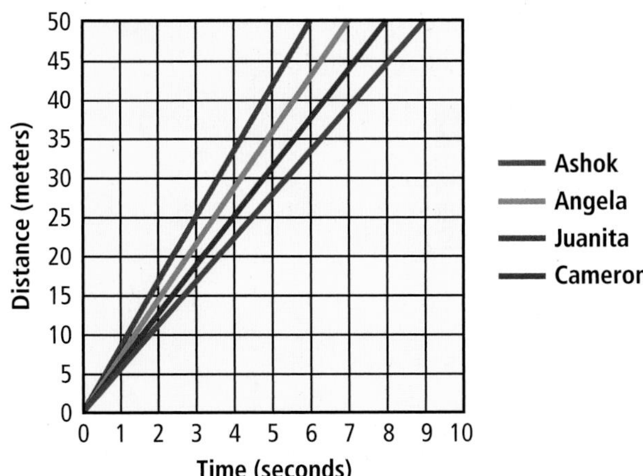


*Study the graph and then answer the questions that follow.*

**1.** Which runner reached the finish line first?

**a.** Ashok
**b.** Angela
**c.** Juanita
**d.** Cameron

**2.** How far did Juanita run in the first 4 seconds of the race?

**a.** 5 m
**b.** 15 m
**c.** 25 m
**d.** 35 m

**3.** How much time passed between the time Angela finished the race and Cameron finished the race?

**a.** 1 s
**b.** 2 s
**c.** 3 s
**d.** 4 s

**4.** Which of the following setups would you use to calculate Angela's average speed during the race?

**a.** $\frac{7\text{ m}}{50\text{ s}}$
**b.** $\frac{7\text{ s}}{50\text{ m}}$
**c.** $\frac{50\text{ m}}{6\text{ s}}$
**d.** $\frac{50\text{ m}}{7\text{ s}}$

**5.** What can you say about the speed of all of the runners?

**a.** They ran at the same speed.
**b.** They ran at a steady pace but at different speeds.
**c.** They sped up as they reached the finish line.
**d.** They slowed down as they reached the finish line.

## Extended Response

*Answer the two questions below in detail.*

**6.** Suppose you are biking. What is the difference between your speed at any given moment during your bike ride and your average speed for the entire ride? Which is easier to measure? Why?

**7.** Suppose you are riding your bike along a path that is also used by in-line skaters. You pass a skater, and another biker passes you, both going in the same direction you're going. You pass a family having a picnic on the grass. Describe your motion from the points of view of the skater, the other biker, and the family.

CHAPTER

# Forces

## the BIG idea

Forces change the motion of objects in predictable ways.

What must happen for a team to win this tug of war?

## Key Concepts

SECTION

**Forces change motion.**
Learn about inertia and Newton's first law of motion.

SECTION

**Force and mass determine acceleration.**
Learn to calculate force through Newton's second law of motion.

SECTION

**Forces act in pairs.**
Learn about action forces and reaction forces through Newton's third law of motion.

SECTION

**Forces transfer momentum.**
Learn about momentum and how it is affected in collisions.

**Internet Preview**

CLASSZONE.COM

Chapter 2 online resources: Content Review, two Simulations, four Resource Centers, Math Tutorial, Test Practice

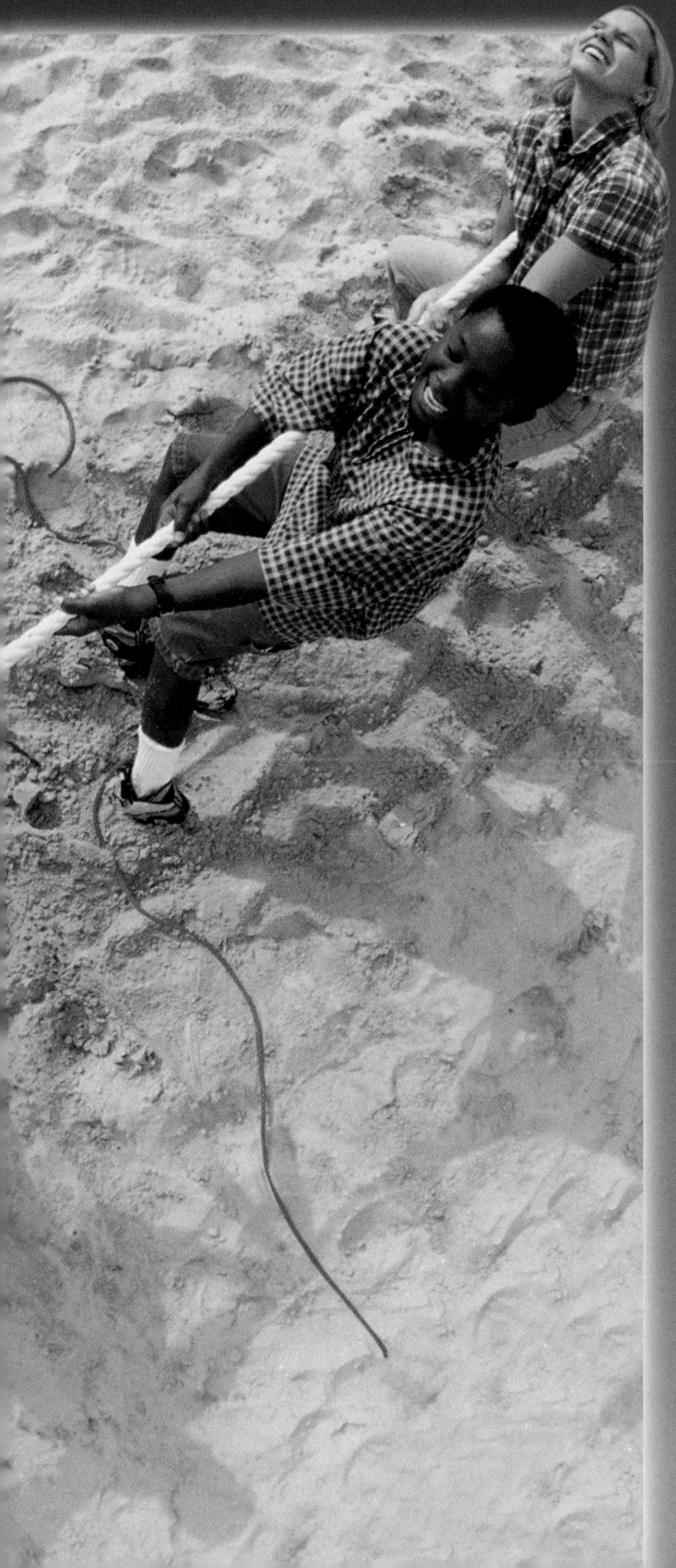

# EXPLORE the BIG idea

## Popping Ping-Pong Balls

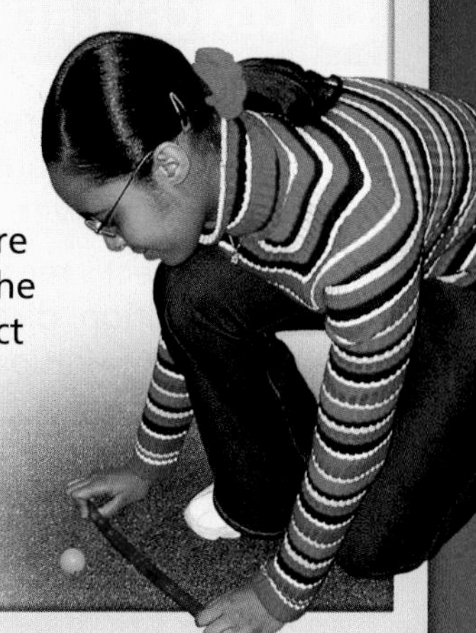

Place a Ping-Pong ball in front of a flexible ruler. Carefully bend the ruler back and then release it. Repeat with a golf ball or another heavier ball. Be sure to bend the ruler back to the same spot each time. Predict which ball will go farther.

**Observe and Think**
Which ball went farther? Why?

## Take Off!

Blow up a balloon and hold the end closed. Tape the balloon to the top of a small model car. (Put the tape around the car and the balloon.) Predict what will happen to the car when you set it down and let go of the balloon. Will the car move? If so, in what direction? How far?

**Observe and Think**
What happened to the car? If you try it again, will you get the same results? What do you think explains the motion of the car?

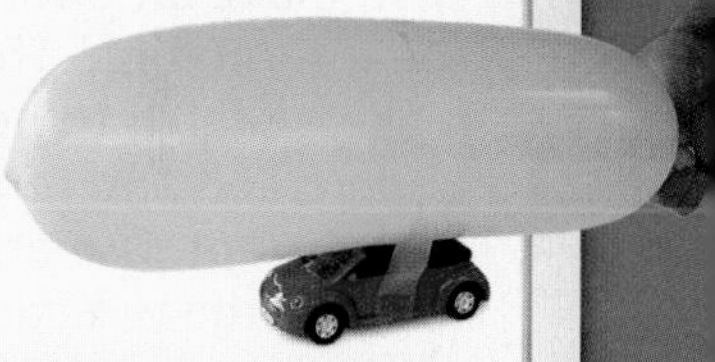

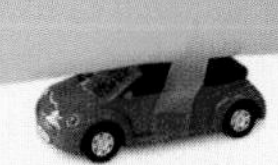

## Internet Activity: Forces

Go to **ClassZone.com** to change the sizes and directions of forces on an object. Predict how the object will move, and then run the simulation to see if you were right.

**Observe and Think** What happens if two forces are applied to the object in the same direction? in opposite directions? Why?

NSTA scilinks.org SCILINKS
Forces **Code: MDL005**

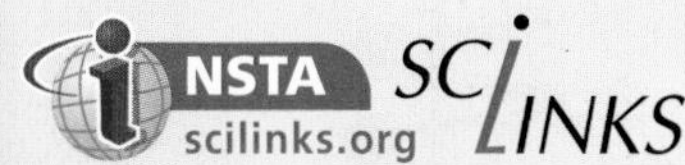

CHAPTER 2

# Getting Ready to Learn

## CONCEPT REVIEW

- All motion is relative to the position and motion of an observer.
- An object's motion is described by position, direction, speed, and acceleration.
- Velocity and acceleration can be measured.

## VOCABULARY REVIEW

**velocity** p. 22
**vector** p. 22
**acceleration** p. 25
**mass** *See Glossary.*

CONTENT REVIEW
CLASSZONE.COM
Review concepts and vocabulary.

## TAKING NOTES

### COMBINATION NOTES

When you read about a concept for the first time, take notes in two ways. First, make an outline of the information. Then make a sketch to help you understand and remember the concept. Use arrows to show the direction of forces.

### VOCABULARY STRATEGY

Think about a vocabulary term as a **magnet word** diagram. Write the other terms or ideas related to that term around it.

See the Note-Taking Handbook on pages R45–R51.

SCIENCE NOTEBOOK

NOTES

Types of forces
- contact force
- gravity
- friction

forces on a box being pushed

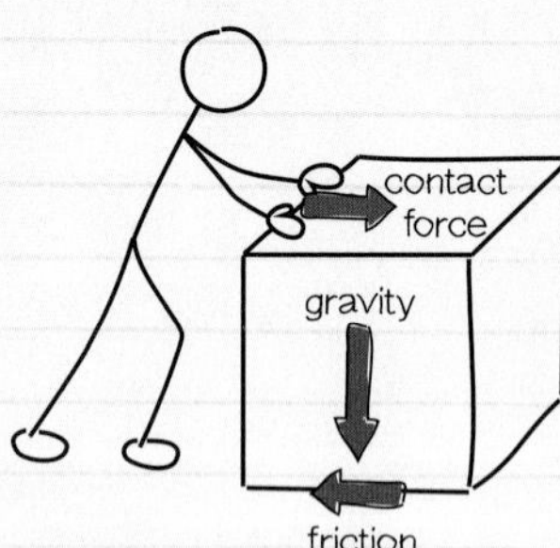


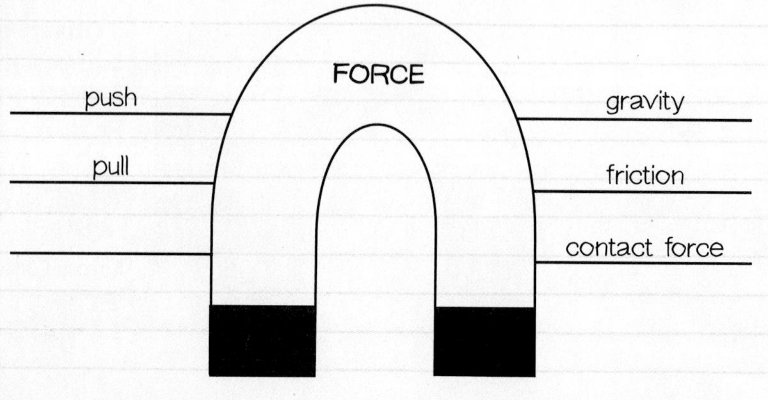

KEY CONCEPT

# Forces change motion.

**BEFORE, you learned**

- The velocity of an object is its change in position over time
- The acceleration of an object is its change in velocity over time

**NOW, you will learn**

- What a force is
- How unbalanced forces change an object's motion
- How Newton's first law allows you to predict motion

**VOCABULARY**

**force** p. 41
**net force** p. 43
**Newton's first law** p. 45
**inertia** p. 46

**EXPLORE Changing Motion**

***How can you change an object's motion?***

**PROCEDURE**

1. Choose an object from the materials list and change its motion in several ways, from
   - not moving to moving
   - moving to not moving
   - moving to moving faster
   - moving to moving in a different direction
2. Describe the actions used to change the motion.
3. Experiment again with another object. First, decide what you will do; then predict how the motion of the object will change.

**MATERIALS**

- quarter
- book
- tennis ball
- cup
- feather

**WHAT DO YOU THINK?**

In step 3, how were you able to predict the motion of the object?

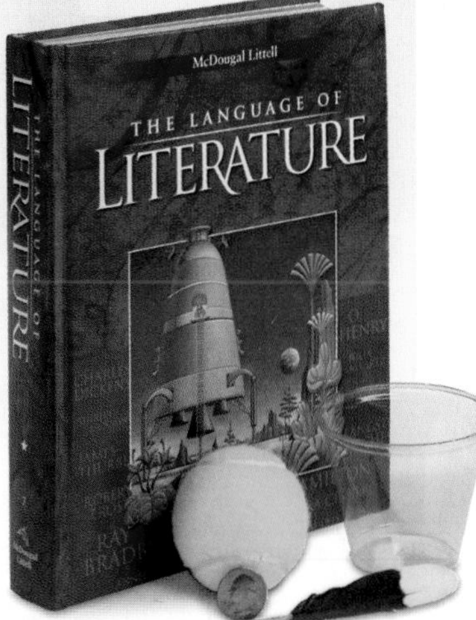


## A force is a push or a pull.

Think about what happens during an exciting moment at the ballpark. The pitcher throws the ball across the plate, and the batter hits it high up into the stands. A fan in the stands catches the home-run ball. In this example, the pitcher sets the ball in motion, the batter changes the direction of the ball's motion, and the fan stops the ball's motion. To do so, each must use a **force,** or a push or a pull.

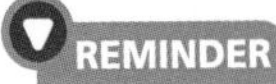

REMINDER

Motion is a change in position over time.

You use forces all day long to change the motion of objects in your world. You use a force to pick up your backpack, to open or close a car door, and even to move a pencil across your desktop. Any time you change the motion of an object, you use a force.

## Types of Forces

A variety of forces are always affecting the motion of objects around you. For example, take a look at how three kinds of forces affect the skater in the photograph on the left.

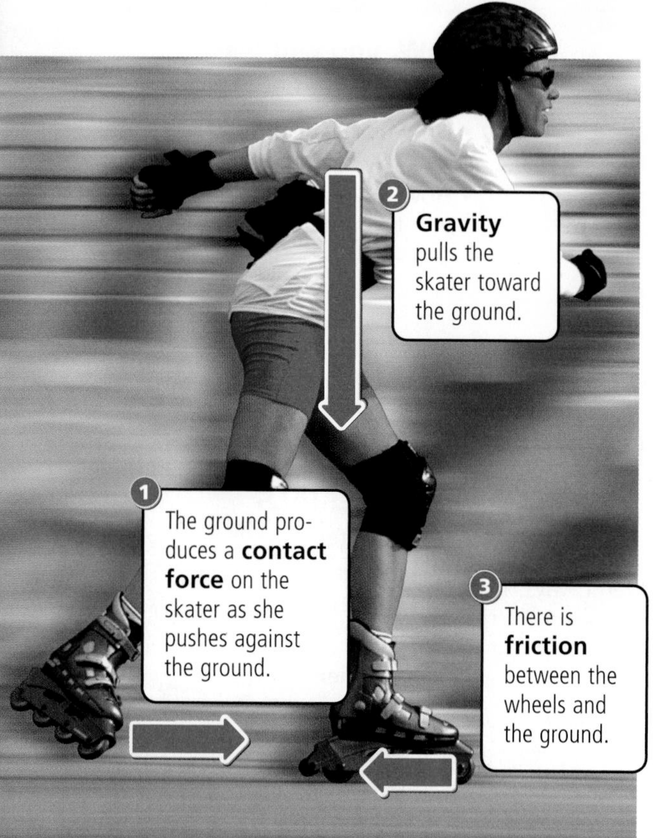

2
Gravity pulls the skater toward the ground.
1
The ground produces a contact force on the skater as she pushes against the ground.
3
There is friction between the wheels and the ground.

1. **Contact Force** When one object pushes or pulls another object by touching it, the first object is applying a contact force to the second. The skater applies a contact force as she pushes against the ground. The ground applies a contact force that pushes the skater forward.

2. **Gravity** Gravity is the force of attraction between two masses. Earth's gravity is pulling on the skater, holding her to the ground. The strength of the gravitational force between two objects depends on their masses. For example, the pull between you and Earth is much greater than the pull between you and a book.

3. **Friction** Friction is a force that resists motion between two surfaces that are pressed together. Friction between the surface of the ground and the wheels of the skates exerts a force that resists the skater's forward motion.

You will learn more about gravity and friction in Chapter 3. In this chapter, most of the examples involve contact forces. You use contact forces constantly. Turning a page, pulling a chair, using a pencil to write, pushing your hair away from your eyes—all involve contact forces.

**CHECK YOUR READING** What is a contact force? Give an example of a contact force.

## Size and Direction of Forces

Like velocity, force is a vector. That means that force has both size and direction. For example, think about what happens when you try to make a shot in basketball. To get the ball through the hoop, you must apply the right amount of force to the ball and aim the force in the right direction. If you use too little force, the ball will not reach the basket. If you use too much force, the ball may bounce off the backboard and into your opponent's hands.

In the illustrations in this book, red arrows represent forces. The direction of an arrow shows the direction of the force, and the length of the arrow indicates the amount, or size, of the force. A blue box represents mass.

**READING TIP**

Red arrows are used to show force.

Blue boxes show mass.

## Balanced and Unbalanced Forces

Considering the size and the direction of all the forces acting on an object allows you to predict changes in the object's motion. The overall force acting on an object when all the forces are combined is called the **net force.**

If the net force on an object is zero, the forces acting on the object are balanced. Balanced forces have the same effect as no force at all. That is, the motion of the object does not change. For example, think about the forces on the basketball when one player attempts a shot and another blocks it. In the photograph below on the left, the players are pushing on the ball with equal force but from opposite directions. The forces on the ball are balanced, and so the ball does not move.

Only an unbalanced force can change the motion of an object. If one of the basketball players pushes with greater force than the other player, the ball will move in the direction that player is pushing. The motion of the ball changes because the forces on the ball become unbalanced.

It does not matter whether the ball started at rest or was already moving. Only an unbalanced force will change the ball's motion.

**COMBINATION NOTES**
Make an outline and draw a diagram about balanced and unbalanced forces.

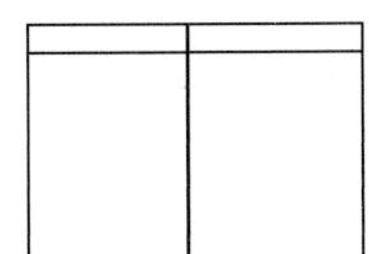

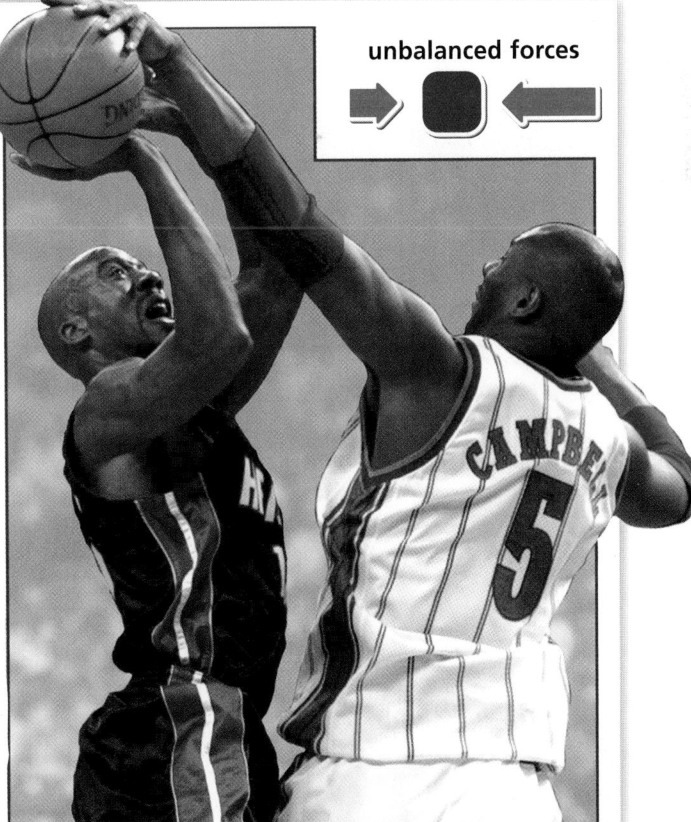


**READING VISUALS** COMPARE Compare the net force on the balls in these two photographs. Which photograph shows a net force of zero?

## Forces on Moving Objects

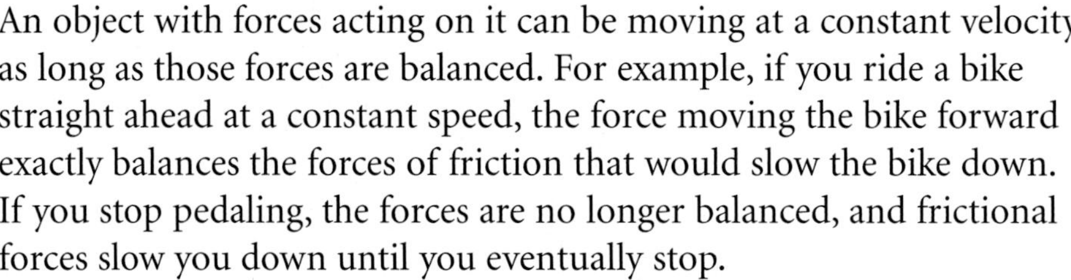

An object with forces acting on it can be moving at a constant velocity as long as those forces are balanced. For example, if you ride a bike straight ahead at a constant speed, the force moving the bike forward exactly balances the forces of friction that would slow the bike down. If you stop pedaling, the forces are no longer balanced, and frictional forces slow you down until you eventually stop.

Balanced forces cannot change an object's speed or its direction. An unbalanced force is needed to change an object's motion.

- To increase the speed of your bike, you may exert more forward force by pedaling harder or changing gears. The net force moves the bike ahead faster.
- To turn your bike, you apply an unbalanced force by leaning to one side and turning the handlebars.
- To stop the bike, you use the extra force of friction that your bike brakes provide.

**CHECK YOUR READING** What happens to a moving object if all the forces on it are balanced? Which sentence above tells you?

# Newton's first law relates force and motion.

In the mid-1600s, the English scientist Sir Isaac Newton studied the effects of forces on objects. He formulated three laws of motion that are still helping people describe and predict the motions of objects today. Newton's ideas were built on those of other scientists, in particular the Italian scientist Galileo Galilei (gal-uh-LEE-oh gal-uh-LAY). Both Galileo and Newton overturned thinking that had been accepted since the times of the ancient Greek philosophers.

The ancient Greeks had concluded that it was necessary to apply a continuous force to keep an object in motion. For example, if you set a book on a table and give the book a quick push, the book slides a short way and then stops. To keep the book moving, you need to keep pushing it. The Greeks reasoned that the book stops moving because you stop pushing it.

## Galileo's Thought Experiment

In the early 1600s, Galileo suggested a different way of interpreting such observations. He imagined a world without friction and conducted a thought experiment in this ideal world. He concluded that, in the absence of friction, a moving object will continue moving even if there is no force acting on it. In other words, it does not take a force to keep an object moving; it takes a force—friction—to stop an object that is already moving.

**READING TiP**

Contrast the last sentence of this paragraph with the last sentence of the previous paragraph.

Objects at rest and objects in motion both resist changes in motion. That is, objects at rest tend to stay at rest, and objects that are moving tend to continue moving unless a force acts on them. Galileo reasoned there was no real difference between an object that is moving at a constant velocity and an object that is standing still. An object at rest is simply an object with zero velocity.

How were Galileo's ideas about objects in motion different from the ideas of the ancient Greeks?

## Newton's First Law

Newton restated Galileo's conclusions as his first law of motion. **Newton's first law** states that objects at rest remain at rest, and objects in motion remain in motion with the same velocity, unless acted upon by an unbalanced force. You can easily observe the effects of unbalanced forces, both on the ball at rest and the ball in motion, in the pictures below.

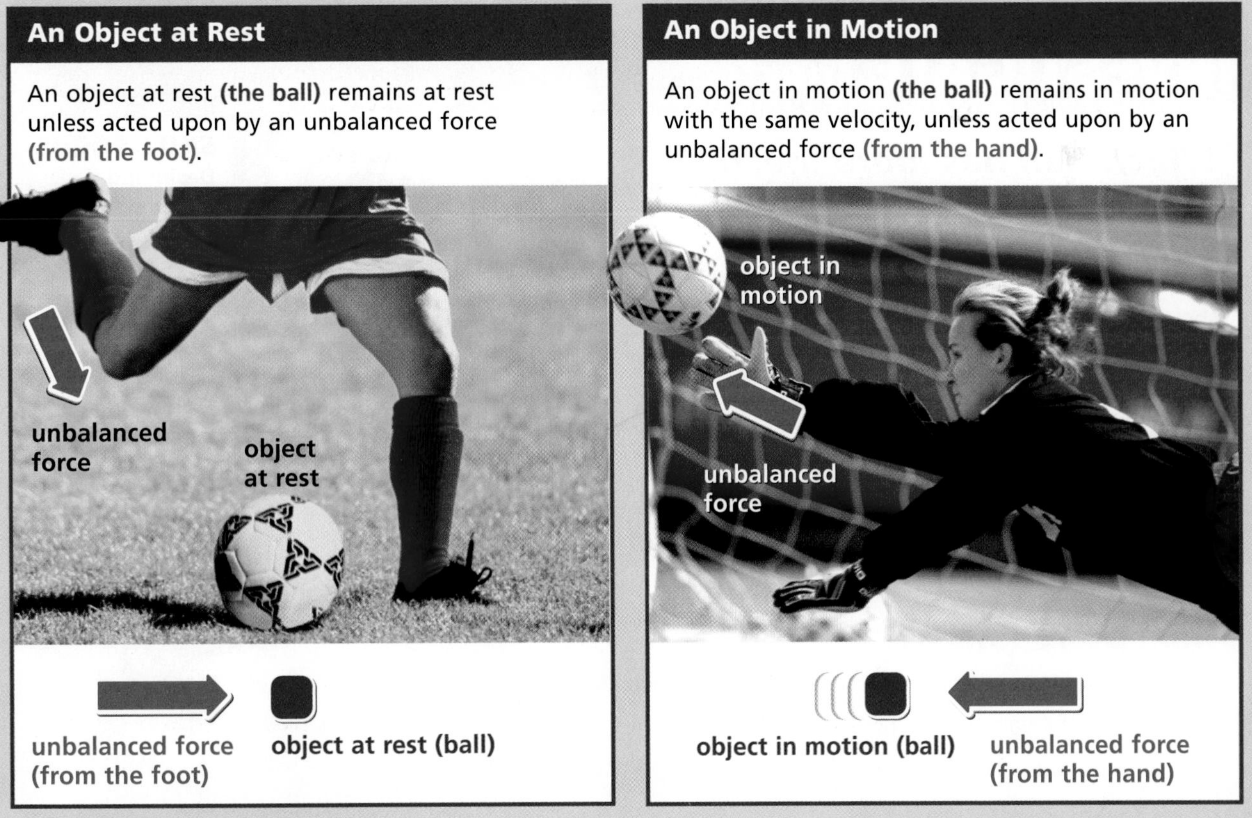

Newton's First Law
Objects at rest remain at rest, and objects in motion remain in motion with the same velocity, unless acted upon by an unbalanced force.
An Object at Rest
An object at rest (the ball) remains at rest unless acted upon by an unbalanced force (from the foot).
unbalanced force
object at rest
unbalanced force (from the foot)
object at rest (ball)
An Object in Motion
An object in motion (the ball) remains in motion with the same velocity, unless acted upon by an unbalanced force (from the hand).
object in motion
unbalanced force
object in motion (ball)
unbalanced force (from the hand)
READING VISUALS
What will happen to the ball's motion in each picture? Why?

You will find many examples of Newton's first law around you. For instance, if you throw a stick for a dog to catch, you are changing the motion of the stick. The dog changes the motion of the stick by catching it and by dropping it at your feet. You change the motion of a volleyball when you spike it, a tennis racket when you swing it, a paintbrush when you make a brush stroke, and an oboe when you pick it up to play or set it down after playing. In each of these examples, you apply a force that changes the motion of the object.

## Inertia

**VOCABULARY**
Make a magnet word diagram for *inertia* in your notebook.

**Inertia** (ih-NUR-shuh) is the resistance of an object to a change in the speed or the direction of its motion. Newton's first law, which describes the tendency of objects to resist changes in motion, is also called the law of inertia. Inertia is closely related to mass. When you measure the mass of an object, you are also measuring its inertia. You know from experience that it is easier to push or pull an empty box than it is to push or pull the same box when it is full of books. Likewise, it is easier to stop or to turn an empty wagon than to stop or turn a wagon full of sand. In both of these cases, it is harder to change the motion of the object that has more mass.

## INVESTIGATE Inertia

### *Which ball has more inertia?*

DESIGN — YOUR OWN — EXPERIMENT

Two balls have different masses and therefore different amounts of inertia. Use what you know about force and inertia to design an experiment that shows which ball has more inertia. Your procedure cannot include lifting the balls, weighing the balls, or touching the balls with your hands.

**PROCEDURE**

1. Figure out how to use the meter stick or other materials to compare the inertia of the two balls.
2. Write up your procedure.
3. Test your procedure.

**WHAT DO YOU THINK?**

- What were the results of your experiment? Did it work? Why or why not?
- What was the variable? What were the constants?
- How does your experiment demonstrate the property of inertia?

**SKILL FOCUS**
Designing experiments

**MATERIALS**
- 2 balls of unknown masses
- string
- block
- meter stick

**TIME**
30 minutes

Inertia is the reason that people in cars need to wear seat belts. A moving car has inertia, and so do the riders inside it. When the driver applies the brakes, an unbalanced force is applied to the car. Normally, the bottom of the seat applies an unbalanced force—friction—which slows the riders down as the car slows. If the driver stops the car suddenly, however, this force is not exerted over enough time to stop the motion of the riders. Instead, the riders continue moving forward with most of their original speed because of their inertia.

Find out more about inertia.

1 As a car moves forward, the driver—shown here as a crash-test dummy—moves forward with the same velocity as the car.

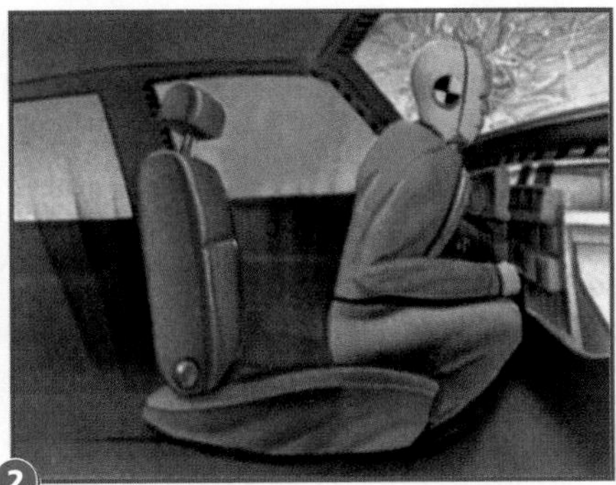

2 When the driver hits the brakes, the car stops. If the stop is sudden and the driver is not wearing a seat belt, the driver keeps moving forward.

3 Finally, the windshield applies an unbalanced force that stops the driver's forward motion.

If the driver is wearing a seat belt, the seat belt rather than the windshield applies the unbalanced force that stops the driver's forward motion. The force from the seat belt is applied over a longer time, so the force causes less damage. In a collision, seat belts alone are sometimes not enough to stop the motion of drivers or passengers. Air bags further cushion people from the effects of inertia in an accident.

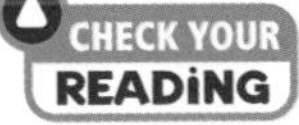


If a car makes a sudden stop, what happens to a passenger riding in the back seat who is not wearing a seat belt?

# 2.1 Review

## KEY CONCEPTS

1. Explain the difference between balanced and unbalanced forces.
2. What is the relationship between force and motion described by Newton's first law?
3. What is inertia? How is the inertia of an object related to its mass?

## CRITICAL THINKING

4. **Infer** Once a baseball has been hit into the air, what forces are acting upon it? How can you tell that any forces are acting upon the ball?
5. **Predict** A ball is at rest on the floor of a car moving at a constant velocity. What will happen to the ball if the car swerves suddenly to the left?

## CHALLENGE

6. **Synthesize** What can the changes in an object's position tell you about the forces acting on that object? Describe an example from everyday life that shows how forces affect the position of an object.

SKILL: EVALUATING HYPOTHESES

# Why Do These Rocks Slide?

In Death Valley, California, there is a dry lakebed known as Racetrack Playa. Rocks are mysteriously moving across the ground there, leaving tracks in the clay. These rocks can have masses as great as 320 kilograms (corresponding to 700 lb). No one has ever observed the rocks sliding, even though scientists have studied their tracks for more than 50 years. What force moves these rocks? Scientists do not yet know.

A playa was once a shallow lake. The water in it evaporated, leaving a dry lakebed.

## Observations

Scientists made these observations.

a. Some rocks left trails that are almost parallel.
b. Some rocks left trails that took abrupt turns.
c. Sometimes a small rock moved while a larger rock did not.
d. Most of the trails are on level surfaces. Some trails run slightly uphill.
e. The temperature in that area sometimes drops below freezing.

This rock made a U-turn.

## Hypotheses

Scientists formed these hypotheses about how the rocks move.

- When the lakebed gets wet, it becomes so slippery that gravity causes the rocks to slide.
- When the lakebed gets wet, it becomes so slippery that strong winds can move the rocks.
- When the lakebed gets wet and cold, a sheet of ice forms and traps the rocks. Strong winds move both the ice sheet and the trapped rocks.

## Evaluate Each Hypothesis

**On Your Own** Think about whether all the observations support each hypothesis. Some facts may rule out some hypotheses. Some facts may neither support nor contradict a particular hypothesis.

**As a Group** Decide which hypotheses are reasonable. Discuss your thinking and conclusions in a small group, and list the reasonable hypotheses.

**CHALLENGE** What further observations would you make to test any of these hypotheses? What information would each observation add?

Learn more about the moving rocks.

KEY CONCEPT

# Force and mass determine acceleration.

**BEFORE, you learned**

- Mass is a measure of inertia
- The motion of an object will not change unless the object is acted upon by an unbalanced force

**NOW, you will learn**

- How Newton's second law relates force, mass, and acceleration
- How force works in circular motion

**VOCABULARY**

**Newton's second law** p. 50
**centripetal force** p. 54

**EXPLORE Acceleration**

### *How are force and acceleration related?*

**PROCEDURE**

1. Tie a paper clip to each end of a long string. Hook two more paper clips to one end.
2. Hold the single paper clip in the middle of a smooth table; hang the other end of the string over the edge. Let go and observe.
3. Add one more paper clip to the hanging end and repeat the experiment. Observe what happens. Repeat.

**MATERIALS**

- paper clips
- string

**WHAT DO YOU THINK?**

- What happened each time that you let go of the single paper clip?
- Explain the relationship between the number of hanging paper clips and the motion of the paper clip on the table.

## Newton's second law relates force, mass, and acceleration.

Suppose you are eating lunch with a friend and she asks you to pass the milk container. You decide to slide it across the table to her. How much force would you use to get the container moving? You would probably use a different force if the container were full than if the container were empty.

If you want to give two objects with different masses the same acceleration, you have to apply different forces to them. You must push a full milk container harder than an empty one to slide it over to your friend in the same amount of time.

**REMINDER**

Acceleration is a change in velocity over time.

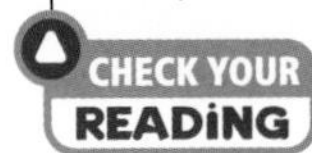

**CHECK YOUR READING** What three concepts are involved in Newton's second law?

## Newton's Second Law

Explore Newton's second law.

Newton studied how objects move, and he noticed some patterns. He observed that the acceleration of an object depends on the mass of the object and the size of the force applied to it. **Newton's second law** states that the acceleration of an object increases with increased force and decreases with increased mass. The law also states that the direction in which an object accelerates is the same as the direction of the force.

The photographs below show Newton's second law at work in a supermarket. The acceleration of each shopping cart depends upon two things:

- the size of the force applied to the shopping cart
- the mass of the shopping cart

In the left-hand photograph, the force on the cart changes, while the mass of the cart stays the same. In the right-hand photograph, the force on the cart stays the same, while the mass of the cart varies. Notice how mass and force affect acceleration.

### Newton's Second Law

**The acceleration of an object increases with increased force, decreases with increased mass, and is in the same direction as the force.**

#### Increasing Force Increases Acceleration

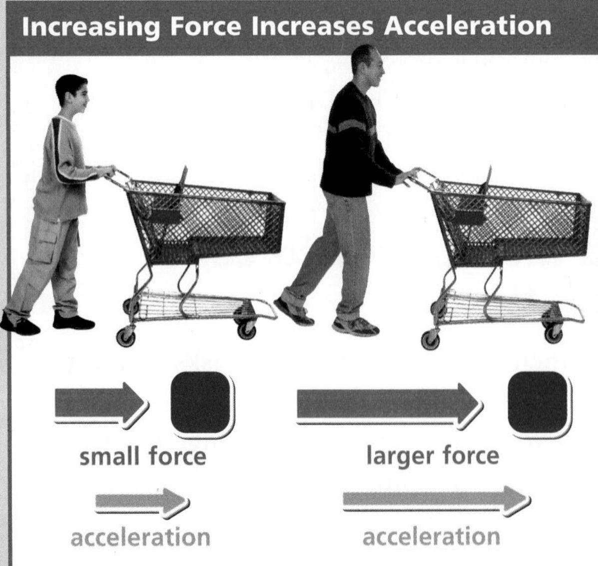


The force exerted on the cart by the man is greater than the force exerted on the same cart by the boy, so the acceleration is greater.

#### Increasing Mass Decreases Acceleration

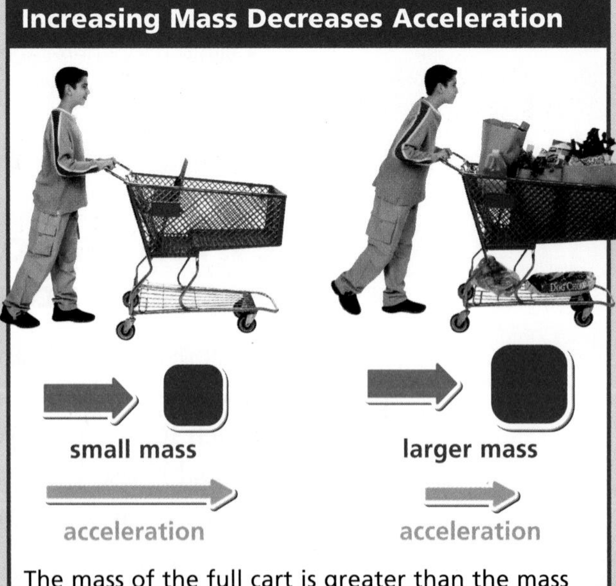


The mass of the full cart is greater than the mass of the empty cart, and the boy is pushing with the same force, so the acceleration is less.

**READING VISUALS** What do the arrows in these diagrams show?

## Force Equals Mass Times Acceleration

Newton was able to describe the relationship of force, mass, and acceleration mathematically. You can calculate the force, the mass, or the acceleration if you know two of the three factors. The mathematical form of Newton's second law, stated as a formula, is

$$\textbf{Force} = \textbf{mass} \cdot \textbf{acceleration}$$
$$F = ma$$

To use this formula, you need to understand the unit used to measure force. In honor of Newton's contribution to our understanding of force and motion, the standard unit of force is called the newton (N). Because force equals mass times acceleration, force is measured in units of mass (kilograms) times units of acceleration (meters per second per second). A newton is defined as the amount of force that it takes to accelerate one kilogram (1 kg) of mass one meter per second per second (1 $m/s^2$). So 1 N is the same as 1 kg • $m/s^2$.

**REMINDER**

*Meters per second per second* is the same as *$m/s^2$*, which can be read "meters per second squared."

**CHECK YOUR READING** If the same force is applied to two objects of different mass, which object will have the greater acceleration?

The mathematical relationship of force, mass, and acceleration allow you to solve problems about how objects move. If you know the mass of an object and the acceleration you want to achieve, you can use the formula to find the force you need to exert to produce that acceleration. Use Newton's second law to find the force that is needed to accelerate the shopping cart in the sample problem.

### Calculating Force

**Sample Problem**

**What force is needed to accelerate a 10 kg shopping cart 3 $m/s^2$?**

*What do you know?* mass = 10 kg, acceleration = 3 $m/s^2$

*What do you want to find out?* Force

*Write the formula:* $F = ma$

*Substitute into the formula:* $F = 10 \text{ kg} \cdot 3 \text{ m/s}^2$

*Calculate and simplify:* $F = 10 \text{ kg} \cdot \frac{3\text{m}}{\text{s}^2} = 30 \text{ kg} \cdot \text{m/s}^2$

*Check that your units agree:* Unit is kg • $m/s^2$.
Unit of force is newton, which is also kg • $m/s^2$. Units agree.

*Answer:* $F = 30$ N

**Practice the Math**

1. If a 5 kg ball is accelerating 1.2 $m/s^2$, what is the force on it?
2. A person on a scooter is accelerating 2 $m/s^2$. If the person has a mass of 50 kg, how much force is acting on that person?

This team of 20 people pulled a 72,000-kilogram (159,000 lb) Boeing 727 airplane 3.7 meters (12 ft) in 6.74 seconds.

The photograph above shows people who are combining forces to pull an airplane. Suppose you knew the mass of the plane and how hard the people were pulling. How much would the plane accelerate? The sample problem below shows how Newton's second law helps you calculate the acceleration.

## Calculating Acceleration

### Sample Problem

**If a team pulls with a combined force of 9000 N on an airplane with a mass of 30,000 kg, what is the acceleration of the airplane?**

*What do you know?* mass = 30,000 kg, force = 9000 N

*What do you want to find out?* acceleration

*Rearrange the formula:* $a = \frac{F}{m}$

*Substitute into the formula:* $a = \frac{9000 \text{ N}}{30{,}000 \text{ kg}}$

*Calculate and simplify:* $a = \frac{9000 \text{ N}}{30{,}000 \text{ kg}} = \frac{9000 \text{ kg} \cdot \text{m/s}^2}{30{,}000 \text{ kg}} = 0.3 \text{ m/s}^2$

*Check that your units agree:* Unit is $\text{m/s}^2$.
Unit for acceleration is $\text{m/s}^2$.
Units agree.

*Answer:* $a = 0.3 \text{ m/s}^2$

### Practice the Math

1. Half the people on the team decide not to pull the airplane. The combined force of those left is 4500 N, while the airplane's mass is still 30,000 kg. What will be the acceleration?
2. A girl pulls a wheeled backpack with a force of 3 N. If the backpack has a mass of 6 kg, what is its acceleration?

## Mass and Acceleration

Mass is also a variable in Newton's second law. If the same force acts on two objects, the object with less mass will have the greater acceleration. For instance, if you push a soccer ball and a bowling ball with equal force, the soccer ball will have a greater acceleration.

If objects lose mass, they can gain acceleration if the force remains the same. When a rocket is first launched, most of its mass is the fuel it carries. As the rocket burns fuel, it loses mass. As the mass continually decreases, the acceleration continually increases.

**APPLY** This NASA launch rocket accelerates with enough force to lift about 45 cars off the ground. As the rocket loses fuel, will it accelerate more or less? Why?

### Calculating Mass

**Sample Problem**

**A model rocket is accelerating at 2 m/s². The force on it is 1 N. What is the mass of the rocket?**

*What do you know?* acceleration = 2 m/s², force = 1 N

*What do you want to find out?* mass

*Rearrange the formula:* $m = \frac{F}{a}$

*Substitute into the formula:* $m = \frac{1 \text{ N}}{2 \text{ m/s}^2}$

*Calculate and simplify:* $m = \frac{1 \text{ N}}{2 \text{ m/s}^2} = \frac{1 \text{ kg} \cdot \text{m/s}^2}{2 \text{ m/s}^2} = 0.5 \text{ kg}$

*Check that your units agree:* Unit is kg.
Unit of mass is kg. Units agree.

*Answer:* $m = 0.5$ kg

**Practice the Math**

1. Another model rocket is accelerating at a rate of 3 m/s² with a force of 1 N. What is the mass of the rocket?
2. A boy pushes a shopping cart with a force of 10 N, and the cart accelerates 1 m/s². What is the mass of the cart?

## Forces can change the direction of motion.

Usually, we think of a force as either speeding up or slowing down the motion of an object, but force can also make an object change direction. If an object changes direction, it is accelerating. Newton's second law says that if you apply a force to an object, the direction in which the object accelerates is the same as the direction of the force. You can change the direction of an object without changing its speed. For example, a good soccer player can control the motion of a soccer ball by applying a force that changes the ball's direction but not its speed.

How can an object accelerate when it does not change speed?

## INVESTIGATE Motion and Force

### *What affects circular motion?*

**SKILL FOCUS**
Hypothesizing

**MATERIALS**
- newspaper
- paper plate
- marble
- scissors
- poster paint
- paintbrush

**TIME**
15 minutes

**PROCEDURE**

1. Spread newspaper over your work surface. Place the paper plate down on the newspaper.
2. Practice rolling the marble around the edge of the plate until you can roll it around completely at least once.
3. Cut out a one-quarter slice of the paper plate. Put a dab of paint on the edge of the plate where the marble will leave it. Place the plate back down on the newspaper.
4. Hypothesize: How will the marble move once it rolls off the plate? Why?
5. Roll the marble all the way around the paper plate into the cut-away section and observe the resulting motion as shown by the trail of paint.

**WHAT DO YOU THINK?**
- Did your observations support your hypothesis?
- What forces affected the marble's motion after it left the plate?

**CHALLENGE** How will changing the speed at which you roll the marble change your results? Repeat the activity to test your prediction.

## Centripetal Force

When you were younger, you may have experimented with using force to change motion. Perhaps you and a friend took turns swinging each other in a circle. If you remember this game, you may also remember that your arms got tired because they were constantly pulling your friend as your friend spun around. It took force to change the direction of your friend's motion. Without that force, your friend could not have kept moving in a circle.

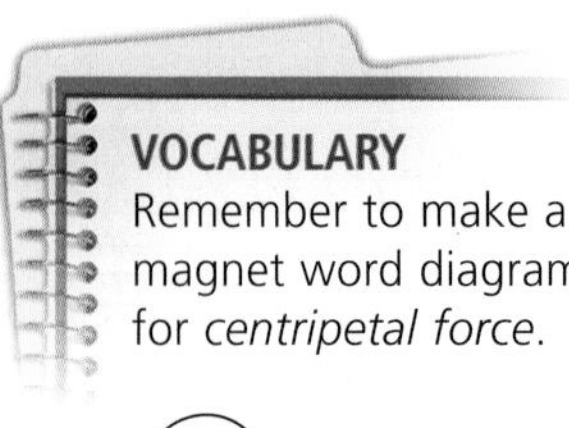

**VOCABULARY**
Remember to make a magnet word diagram for *centripetal force.*

Any force that keeps an object moving in a circle is known as a **centripetal force** (sehn-TRIHP-ih-tuhl). This force points toward the center of the circle. Without the centripetal force, the object would go flying off in a straight line. When you whirl a ball on a string, what keeps the ball moving in a circle? The force of the string turns the ball, changing the ball's direction of motion. When the string turns, so does the ball. As the string changes direction, the force from the string also changes direction. The force is always pointing along the string toward your hand, the center of the circle. The centripetal force on the whirling ball is the pull from the string. If you let go of the string, the ball would fly off in the direction it was headed when you let go.

How does centripetal force change the motion of an object?

centripetal force
top view
Centripetal force
The force that keeps the female skater moving in a circle is the pull exerted by her partner. The diagram shows the direction of the centripetal force.

## Circular Motion and Newton's Second Law

Suppose the male skater shown above spins his partner faster. Her direction changes more quickly than before, so she accelerates more. To get more acceleration, he must apply more force. The same idea holds for a ball you whirl on a string. You have to pull harder on the string when you whirl the ball faster, because it takes more centripetal force to keep the ball moving at the greater speed.

You can apply the formula for Newton's second law even to an object moving in a circle. If you know the size of the centripetal force acting upon the object, you can find its acceleration. A greater acceleration requires a greater centripetal force. A more massive object requires a greater centripetal force to have the same circular speed as a less massive object. But no matter what the mass of an object is, if it moves in a circle, its force and acceleration are directed toward the center of the circle.

CHECK YOUR
READING
How does increasing the centripetal force on an object affect its acceleration?

## 2.2 Review

### KEY CONCEPTS

1. If the force acting upon an object is increased, what happens to the object's acceleration?
2. How does the mass of an object affect its acceleration?
3. What force keeps an object moving in a circle? In what direction does this force act?

### CRITICAL THINKING

4. **Infer** Use Newton's second law to determine how much force is being applied to an object that is traveling at a constant velocity.
5. **Calculate** What force is needed to accelerate an object 5 $m/s^2$ if the object has a mass of 10 kg?

### CHALLENGE

6. **Synthesize** Carlos pushes a 3 kg box with a force of 9 N. The force of friction on the box is 3 N in the opposite direction. What is the acceleration of the box? **Hint:** Combine forces to find the net force.

MATH in SCIENCE

## SKILL: USING SIGNIFICANT FIGURES

# Meaningful Numbers

A student doing a science report on artificial hearts reads that a certain artificial heart weighs about 2 pounds. The student then writes that the mass of the artificial heart is 0.907185 kilograms. Someone reading this report might think that the student knows the mass to a high precision, when actually he knows it only to one meaningful number.

When you make calculations, the number of digits to include in your answer depends in part on the number of meaningful digits, or significant figures, in the numbers you are working with.

MATH TUTORIAL
CLASSZONE.COM
Click on Math Tutorial for more help with rounding decimals.

### Example

In an experiment to find acceleration, a scientist might record the following data.

Force = 3.1 N  mass = 1.450 kg

In this example, force is given to two significant figures, and mass is given to four significant figures.

**(1)** Use a calculator and the formula $a = F/m$ to find the acceleration. The display on the calculator shows

2.1379310345

**(2)** To determine how many of the digits in this answer are really meaningful, look at the measurement with the least number of significant figures. In this example, force is given to two significant figures. Therefore, the answer is meaningful only to two significant figures.

**(3)** Round the calculated number to two digits.

**ANSWER** acceleration = 2.1 m/s$^2$

The AbioCor artificial heart, which has a mass of about 0.9 kg, is designed to fit entirely inside the human body.

**Answer the following questions.**

For each pair of measurements, calculate the acceleration to the appropriate number of digits.

**1.** Force = 3.100 N  mass = 3.1 kg

**2.** Force = 2 N  mass = 4.2 kg

**3.** Force = 1.21 N  mass = 1.1000 kg

**CHALLENGE** Suppose a scientist measures a force of 3.25 N and a mass of 3.3 kg. She could round the force to two significant figures and then divide, or she could divide and then round the answer. Compare these two methods. Which method do you think is more accurate?

KEY CONCEPT

# Forces act in pairs.

**BEFORE, you learned**

- A force is a push or a pull
- Increasing the force on an object increases the acceleration
- The acceleration of an object depends on its mass and the force applied to it

**NOW, you will learn**

- How Newton's third law relates action/reaction pairs of forces
- How Newton's laws work together

**VOCABULARY**

**Newton's third law** p. 57

**THINK ABOUT**

### *How do jellyfish move?*

Jellyfish do not have much control over their movements. They drift with the current in the ocean. However, jellyfish do have some control over their up-and-down motion. By squeezing water out of its umbrella-like body, the jellyfish shown here applies a force in one direction to move in the opposite direction. If the water is forced downward, the jellyfish moves upward. How can a person or an object move in one direction by exerting a force in the opposite direction?

## Newton's third law relates action and reaction forces.

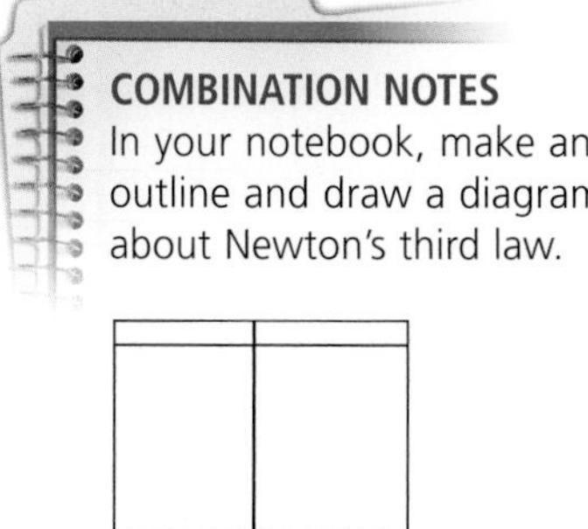

COMBINATION NOTES
In your notebook, make an outline and draw a diagram about Newton's third law.

Newton made an important observation that explains the motion of the jellyfish. He noticed that forces always act in pairs. **Newton's third law** states that every time one object exerts a force on another object, the second object exerts a force that is equal in size and opposite in direction back on the first object. As the jellyfish contracts its body, it applies a downward force on the water. The water applies an equal force back on the jellyfish. It is this equal and opposite force on the jellyfish that pushes it up. This is similar to what happens when a blown-up balloon is released. The balloon pushes air out the end, and the air pushes back on the balloon and moves it forward.

What moves the jellyfish through the water?

## Action and Reaction Pairs

The force that is exerted on an object and the force that the object exerts back are known together as an action/reaction force pair. One force in the pair is called the action force, and the other is called the reaction force. For instance, if the jellyfish pushing on the water is the action force, the water pushing back on the jellyfish is the reaction force. Likewise, if the balloon pushing the air backward is the action force, the air pushing the balloon forward is the reaction force.

You can see many examples of action and reaction forces in the world around you. Here are three:

- You may have watched the liftoffs of the space shuttle on television. When the booster rockets carrying the space shuttle take off, their engines push fuel exhaust downward. The exhaust pushes back on the rockets, sending them upward.
- When you bang your toe into the leg of a table, the same amount of force that you exert on the table is exerted back on your toe.
- Action and reaction forces do not always result in motion. For example, if you press down on a table, the table resists the push with the same amount of force, even though nothing moves.

Identify the action/reaction forces in each example described above.

## INVESTIGATE Newton's Third Law

### *How do action and reaction forces compare?*

**SKILL FOCUS**
Observing

**MATERIALS**
2 spring scales

**TIME**
15 minutes

**PROCEDURE**

1. With a partner, hook the two spring scales together.
2. Pull gently on your spring scale while your partner holds but does not pull on the other scale.
3. Observe and record the amount of force that is shown on your scale and on your partner's scale.
4. Both of you pull together. Observe the force shown on each scale.

**WHAT DO YOU THINK?**

- What happened to your partner's force as your force increased?
- What happened when you both pulled?
- Explain why you think what you observed in each case happened.

**CHALLENGE** Can you think of a way to use the scales to show Newton's first or second law?

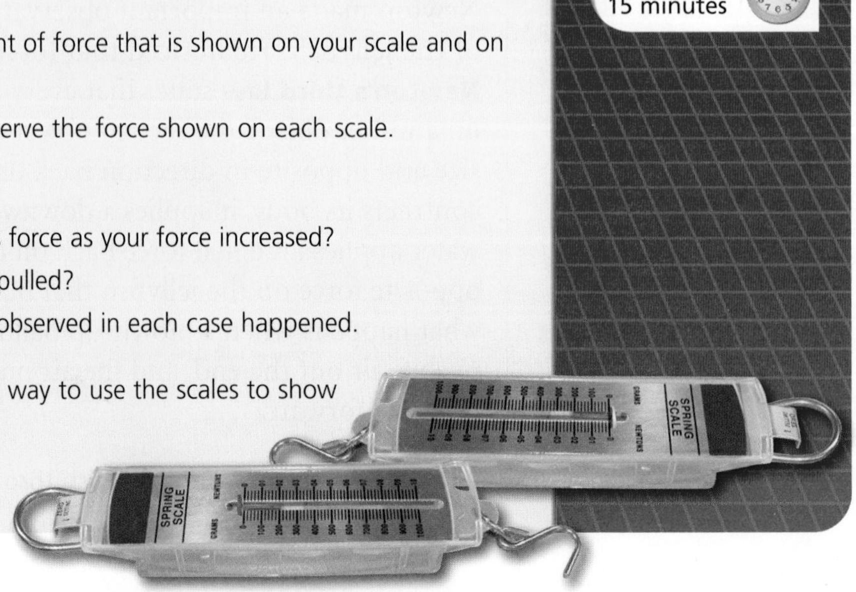

## Action and Reaction Forces Versus Balanced Forces

Because action and reaction forces are equal and opposite, they may be confused with balanced forces. Keep in mind that balanced forces act on a single object, while action and reaction forces act on different objects.

**Balanced Forces** If you and a friend pull on opposite sides of a backpack with the same amount of force, the backpack doesn't move, because the forces acting on it are balanced. In this case, both forces are exerted on one object—the backpack.

**Action and Reaction** As you drag a heavy backpack across a floor, you can feel the backpack pulling on you with an equal amount of force. The action force and the reaction force are acting on two different things—one is acting on the backpack, and the other is acting on you.

The illustration below summarizes Newton's third law. The girl exerts an action force on the boy by pushing him. Even though the boy is not trying to push the girl, an equal and opposite reaction force acts upon the girl, causing her to move as well.

### Newton's Third Law

**When one object exerts a force on another object, the second object exerts an equal and opposite force on the first object.**

**1 One Skater Pushes**

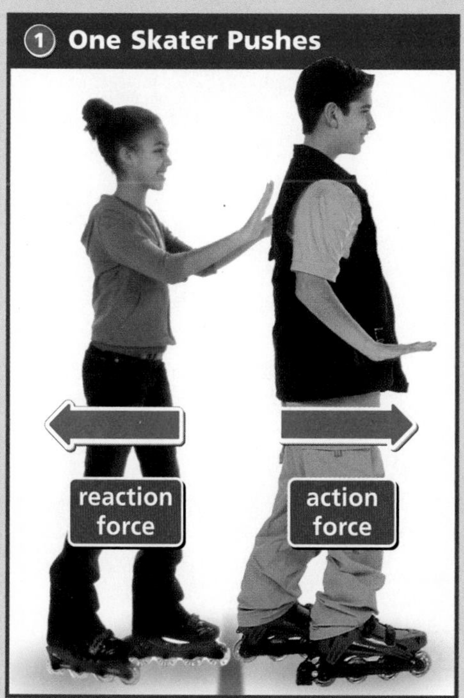


The action force from the girl sets the boy in motion.

**2 Both Skaters Move**

Even though the boy does not do anything, the reaction force from him sets the girl in motion as well.

How does the direction of the force on the girl relate to her motion?

## Newton's Three Laws of Motion

**All three of Newton's laws work together to help describe how an object will move.**

### Newton's First Law

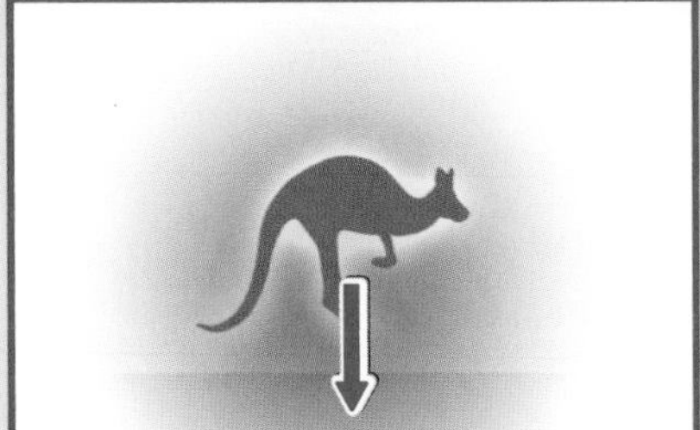

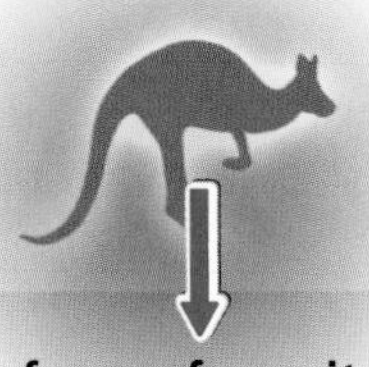


This kangaroo has jumped, setting itself in motion. If no other forces acted on it, the kangaroo would continue to move through the air with the same motion. Instead, the force of gravity will bring this kangaroo back to the ground.

### Newton's Second Law

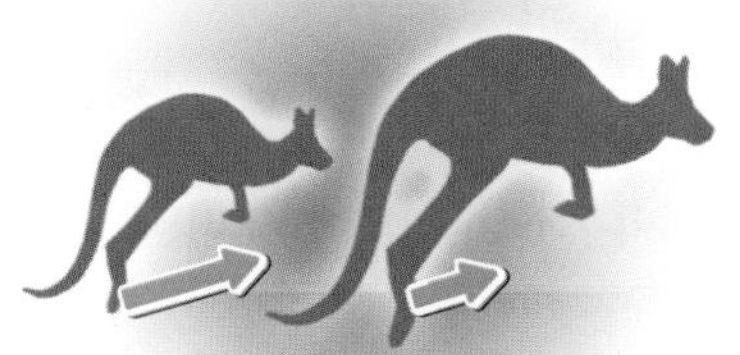


The large kangaroo does not have as much acceleration as a less massive kangaroo would if it used the same force to jump. However, the more massive kangaroo can increase its acceleration by increasing the force of its jump.

### Newton's Third Law

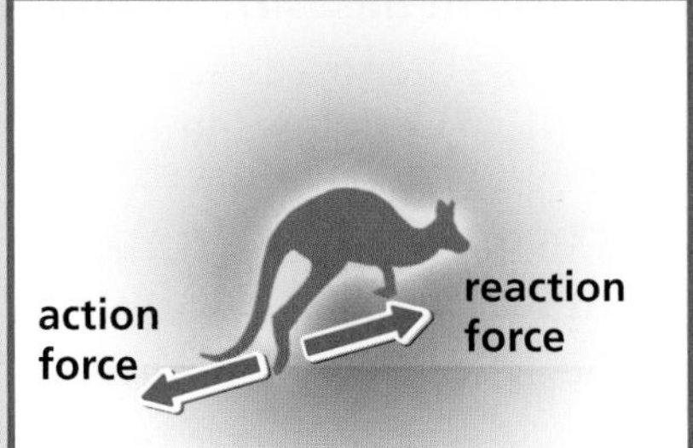

A kangaroo applies an action force on the ground with its powerful back legs. The reaction force from the ground can send the kangaroo as far as 8 meters (26 ft) through the air.

**Common Name:** Red kangaroo
**Scientific Name:** *Macropus rufus*
**Home:** Australia
**Top Speed:** 65 km/h (40 mi/h)
**Maximum Leap:** 8 m (26 ft)

AUSTRALIA

**READING VISUALS** What forces are involved in a kangaroo jump?

## Newton's three laws describe and predict motion.

Newton's three laws can explain the motion of almost any object, including the motion of animals. The illustrations on page 60 show how all three of Newton's laws can be used to describe how kangaroos move. The three laws are not independent of one another; they are used together to explain the motion of objects.

Find out more about Newton's laws of motion.

You can use the laws of motion to explain how other animals move as well. For example, Newton's laws explain why a squid moves forward while squirting water out behind it. These laws also explain that a bird is exerting force when it speeds up to fly away or when it changes its direction in the air.

You can also use Newton's laws to make predictions about motion. If you know the force acting upon an object, then you can predict how that object's motion will change. For example, if you want to send a spacecraft to Mars, you must be able to predict exactly where Mars will be by the time the spacecraft reaches it. You must also be able to control the force on your spacecraft so that it will arrive at the right place at the right time.

**COMBINATION NOTES**
Make an outline and draw a diagram showing how all three of Newton's laws apply to the motion of one object.

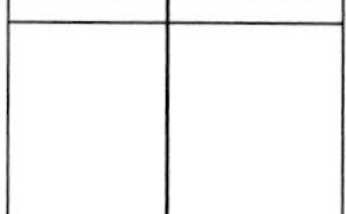

Knowing how Newton's three laws work together can also help you win a canoe race. In order to start the canoe moving, you need to apply a force to overcome its inertia. Newton's second law might affect your choice of canoes, because a less massive canoe is easier to accelerate than a more massive one. You can also predict the best position for your paddle in the water. If you want to move straight ahead, you push backward on the paddle so that the canoe moves forward. Together, Newton's laws can help you explain and predict how the canoe, or any object, will move.

## 2.3 Review

### KEY CONCEPTS

1. Identify the action/reaction force pair involved when you catch a ball.
2. Explain the difference between balanced forces and action/reaction forces.
3. How do Newton's laws of motion apply to the motion of an animal, such as a cat that is running?

### CRITICAL THINKING

4. **Apply** A man pushes on a wall with a force of 50 N. What are the size and the direction of the force that the wall exerts on the man?
5. **Evaluate** Jim will not help push a heavy box. He says, "My force will produce an opposite force and cancel my effort." Evaluate Jim's statement.

### CHALLENGE

6. **Calculate** Suppose you are holding a basketball while standing still on a skateboard. You and the skateboard have a mass of 50 kg. You throw the basketball with a force of 10 N. What is your acceleration before and after you throw the ball?

# CHAPTER INVESTIGATION

## Newton's Laws of Motion

**OVERVIEW AND PURPOSE** As you know, rocket engineers consider Newton's laws when designing rockets and planning rocket flights. In this investigation you will use what you have learned about Newton's laws to

- build a straw rocket
- improve the rocket's performance by modifying one design element

### Problem

What aspects of a model rocket affect the distance it flies?

### Hypothesize

Write It Up

After step 8 in the procedure, write a hypothesis to explain what you predict will happen during the second set of trials. Your hypothesis should take the form of an "If . . . , then . . . , because . . ." statement.

**MATERIALS**

- 2 straws with different diameters
- several plastic bottles, in different sizes
- modeling clay
- scissors
- construction paper
- meter stick
- tape

### Procedure

1. Make a data table like the one shown on the sample notebook page.

2. Insert the straw with the smaller diameter into one of the bottles. Seal the mouth of the bottle tightly with modeling clay so that air can escape only through the straw. This is the rocket launcher.

straw

clay

3. Cut two thin strips of paper, one about 8 cm long and the other about 12 cm long. Connect the ends of the strips to make loops.

4. To create the rocket, place the straw with the larger diameter through the smaller loop and tape the loop to the straw at one end. Attach the other loop to the other end of the straw in the same way. Both loops should be attached to the same side of the straw to stabilize your rocket in flight.

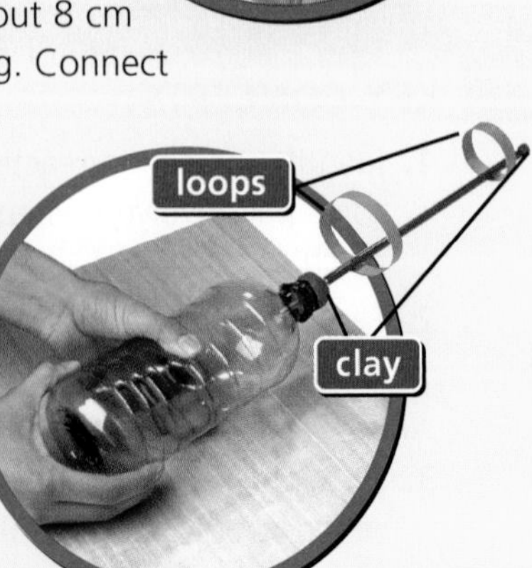

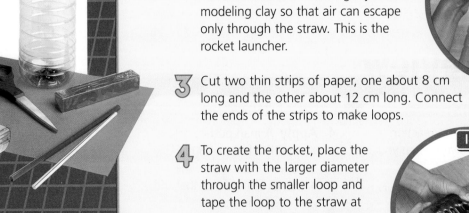

5 Use a small ball of modeling clay to seal the end of the straw near the smaller loop.

6 Slide the open end of the rocket over the straw on the launcher. Place the bottle on the edge of a table so that the rocket is pointing away from the table.

7 Test launch your rocket by holding the bottle with two hands and squeezing it quickly. Measure the distance the rocket lands from the edge of the table. Practice the launch several times. Remember to squeeze with equal force each time.

8 Launch the rocket four times. Keep the amount of force you use constant. Measure the distance the rocket travels each time, and record the results in your data table.

9 List all the variables that may affect the distance your rocket flies. Change the rocket or launcher to alter one variable. Launch the rocket and measure the distance it flies. Repeat three more times, and record the results in your data table.

## Observe and Analyze

Write It Up

1. **RECORD OBSERVATIONS** Draw a diagram of both of your bottle rockets. Make sure your data table is complete.
2. **IDENTIFY VARIABLES** What variables did you identify, and what variable did you modify?

## Conclude

1. **COMPARE** How did the flight distances of the original rocket compare with those of the modified rocket?
2. **ANALYZE** Compare your results with your hypothesis. Do the results support your hypothesis?
3. **IDENTIFY LIMITS** What possible limitations or errors did you experience or could you have experienced?
4. **APPLY** Use Newton's laws to explain why the rocket flies.
5. **APPLY** What other real-life example can you think of that demonstrates Newton's laws?

## INVESTIGATE Further

**CHALLENGE** Why does the rocket have paper loops taped to it? Determine how the flight of the rocket is affected if one or both loops are completely removed. Hypothesize about the function of the paper loops and design an experiment to test your hypothesis.

Newton's Laws of Motion

**Problem** What aspects of a model rocket affect the distance it flies?

**Hypothesize**

**Observe and Analyze**

Table 1. Flight Distances of Original and Modified Rocket

| | Original Rocket | Modified Rocket |
|---|---|---|
| Trial Number | Distance Rocket Flew (cm) | Distance Rocket Flew (cm) |
| 1 | | |
| 2 | | |
| 3 | | |
| 4 | | |

**Conclude**

KEY CONCEPT

# Forces transfer momentum.

**BEFORE, you learned**

- A force is a push or a pull
- Newton's laws help to describe and predict motion

**NOW, you will learn**

- What momentum is
- How to calculate momentum
- How momentum is affected by collisions

**VOCABULARY**

**momentum** p. 64
**collision** p. 66
**conservation of momentum** p. 67

**EXPLORE Collisions**

### *What happens when objects collide?*

**PROCEDURE**

1. Roll the two balls toward each other on a flat surface. Try to roll them at the same speed. Observe what happens. Experiment by changing the speeds of the two balls.
2. Leave one ball at rest, and roll the other ball so that it hits the first ball. Observe what happens. Then repeat the experiment with the balls switched.

**WHAT DO YOU THINK?**

- How did varying the speed of the balls affect the motion of the balls after the collision?
- What happened when one ball was at rest? Why did switching the two balls affect the outcome?

**MATERIALS**

2 balls of different masses

## Objects in motion have momentum.

If you throw a tennis ball at a wall, it will bounce back toward you. What would happen if you could throw a wrecking ball at the wall at the same speed that you threw the tennis ball? The wall would most likely break apart. Why would a wrecking ball have a different effect on the wall than the tennis ball?

A moving object has a property that is called momentum. **Momentum** (moh-MEHN-tuhm) is a measure of mass in motion; the momentum of an object is the product of its mass and its velocity. At the same velocity, the wrecking ball has more momentum than the tennis ball because the wrecking ball has more mass. However, you could increase the momentum of the tennis ball by throwing it faster.

VOCABULARY
Make a magnet word diagram for *momentum*.

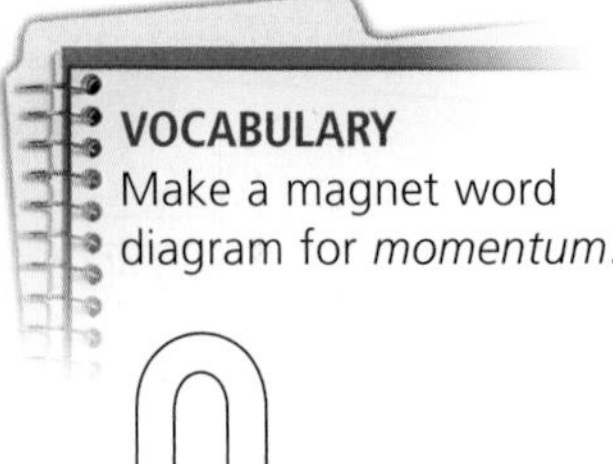

Momentum is similar to inertia. Like inertia, the momentum of an object depends on its mass. Unlike inertia, however, momentum takes into account how fast the object is moving. A wrecking ball that is moving very slowly, for example, has less momentum than a fast-moving wrecking ball. With less momentum, the slower-moving wrecking ball would not be able to do as much damage to the wall.

REMINDER

Inertia is the resistance of an object to changes in its motion.

To calculate an object's momentum, you can use the following formula:

**momentum = mass · velocity**

$$p = mv$$

In this formula, $p$ stands for momentum, $m$ for mass, and $v$ for velocity. In standard units, the mass of an object is given in kilograms (kg), and velocity is given in meters per second (m/s). Therefore, the unit of momentum is the kilogram-meter per second (kg • m/s). Notice that the unit of momentum combines mass, length, and time.

RESOURCE CENTER
CLASSZONE.COM

Explore momentum.

Like force, velocity, and acceleration, momentum is a vector—it has both a size and a direction. The direction of an object's momentum is the same as the direction of its velocity. You can use speed instead of velocity in the formula as long as you do not need to know the direction of motion. As you will read later, it is important to know the direction of the momentum when you are working with more than one object.

How do an object's mass and velocity affect its momentum?

## Calculating Momentum

### Sample Problem

**What is the momentum of a 1.5 kg ball moving at 2 m/s?**

***What do you know?*** mass = 1.5 kg, velocity = 2 m/s

***What do you want to find out?*** momentum

***Write the formula:*** $p = mv$

***Substitute into the formula:*** $p$ = 1.5 kg · 2 m/s

***Calculate and simplify:*** $p$ = 3 kg · m/s

***Check that your units agree:*** Unit is kg · m/s.
Unit of momentum is kg · m/s. Units agree.

***Answer:*** $p$ = 3 kg · m/s

### Practice the Math

1. A 3 kg ball is moving with a velocity of 1 m/s. What is the ball's momentum?
2. What is the momentum of a 0.5 kg ball moving 0.5 m/s?

# INVESTIGATE Momentum

## *What happens when objects collide?*

**SKILL FOCUS**
Observing

**MATERIALS**
- 2 rulers
- 8 marbles

**TIME**
20 minutes

### PROCEDURE

1. Set up two parallel rulers separated by one centimeter. Place a line of five marbles, each touching the next, in the groove between the rulers.
2. Roll a marble down the groove so that it collides with the line of marbles, and observe the results.
3. Repeat your experiment by rolling two and then three marbles at the line of marbles. Observe the results.

### WHAT DO YOU THINK?

- What did you observe when you rolled the marbles?
- Why do you think the marbles moved the way they did?

**CHALLENGE** Use your answers to write a hypothesis explaining your observations. Design your own marble experiment to test this hypothesis. Do your results support your hypothesis?

## Momentum can be transferred from one object to another.

If you have ever ridden in a bumper car, you have experienced collisions. A **collision** is a situation in which two objects in close contact exchange energy and momentum. As another car bumps into the back of yours, the force pushes your car forward. Some of the momentum of the car behind you is transferred to your car. At the same time, the car behind you slows because of the reaction force from your car. You gain momentum from the collision, and the other car loses momentum. The action and reaction forces in collisions are one way in which objects transfer momentum.

If two objects involved in a collision have very different masses, the one with less mass has a greater change in velocity. For example, consider what happens if you roll a tennis ball and a bowling ball toward each other so that they collide. Not only will the speed of the tennis ball change, but the direction of its motion will change as it bounces back. The bowling ball, however, will simply slow down. Even though the forces acting on the two balls are the same, the tennis ball will be accelerated more during the collision because it has less mass.

How can a collision affect the momentum of an object?

## Momentum is conserved.

During a collision between two objects, each object exerts a force on the other. The colliding objects make up a system—a collection of objects that affect one another. As the two objects collide, the velocity and the momentum of each object change. However, as no other forces are acting on the objects, the total momentum of both objects is unchanged by the collision. This is due to the conservation of momentum. The principle of **conservation of momentum** states that the total momentum of a system of objects does not change, as long as no outside forces are acting on that system.

**READING TIP**

A light blue-green arrow shows the momentum of an individual object.

A dark blue-green arrow shows the total momentum.

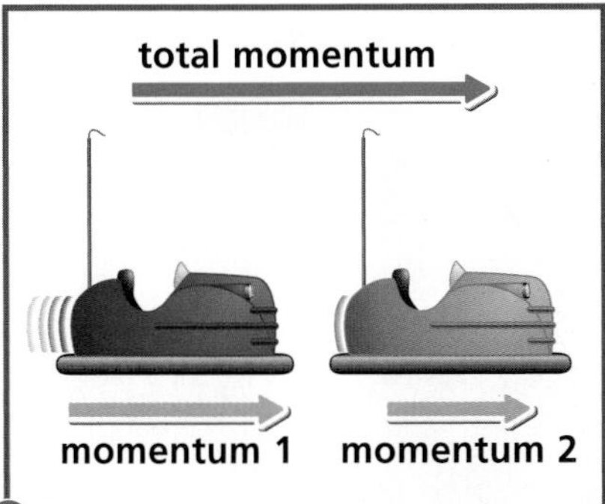


1 **Before the collision** The momentum of the first car is greater than the momentum of the second car. Their combined momentum is the total momentum of the system.

forces in collision

2 **During the collision** The forces on the two cars are equal and opposite, as described by Newton's third law. Momentum is transferred from one car to the other during the collision.

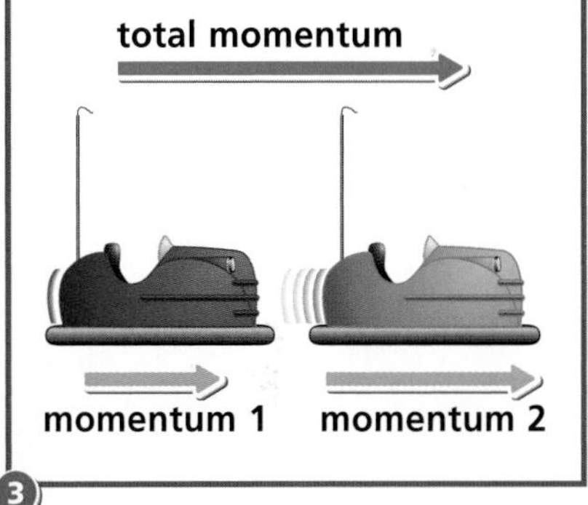


3 **After the collision** The momentum lost by one car was gained by the other car. The total momentum of the system remains the same as it was before the collision.

How much an object's momentum changes when a force is applied depends on the size of the force and how long that force is applied. Remember Newton's third law—during a collision, two objects are acted upon by equal and opposite forces for the same length of time. This means that the objects receive equal and opposite changes in momentum, and the total momentum does not change.

You can find the total momentum of a system of objects before a collision by combining the momenta of the objects. Because momentum is a vector, like force, the direction of motion is important. To find the total momentum of objects moving in the same direction, add the momenta of the objects. For two objects traveling in opposite directions, subtract one momentum from the other. Then use the principle of conservation of momentum and the formula for momentum to predict how the objects will move after they collide.

**READING TIP**

The plural of *momentum* is *momenta*.

**CHECK YOUR READING** What is meant by "conservation of momentum"? What questions do you have about the application of this principle?

## Two Types of Collisions

When bumper cars collide, they bounce off each other. Most of the force goes into changing the motion of the cars. The two bumper cars travel separately after the collision, just as they did before the collision. The combined momentum of both cars after the collision is the same as the combined momentum of both cars before the collision.

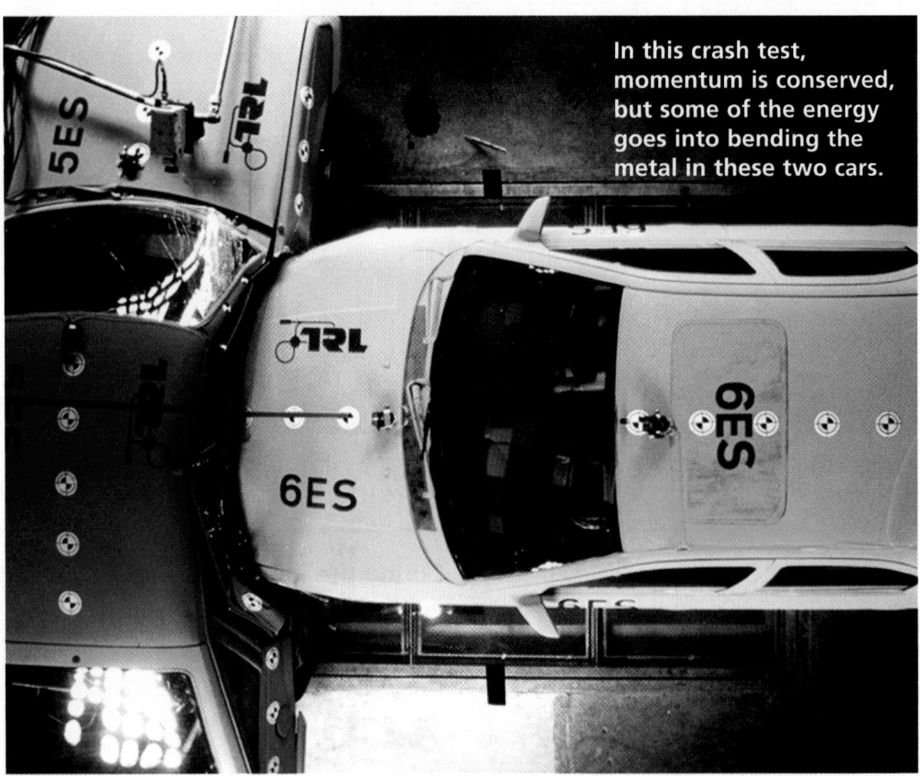


In this crash test, momentum is conserved, but some of the energy goes into bending the metal in these two cars.

When two cars collide during a crash test, momentum is also conserved during the collision. Unlike the bumper cars, however, which separate, the two cars shown in the photograph above stick and move together after the collision. Even in this case, the total momentum of both cars together is the same as the total momentum of both cars before the collision. Before the crash shown in the photograph, the yellow car had a certain momentum, and the blue car had no momentum. After the crash, the two cars move together with a combined momentum equal to the momentum the yellow car had before the collision.

Compare collisions in which objects separate with collisions in which objects stick together.

## Momentum and Newton's Third Law

Collisions are not the only events in which momentum is conserved. In fact, momentum is conserved whenever the only forces acting on objects are action/reaction force pairs. Conservation of momentum is really just another way of looking at Newton's third law.

When a firefighter turns on a hose, water comes out of the nozzle in one direction, and the hose moves back in the opposite direction. You can explain why by using Newton's third law. The water is forced out of the hose. A reaction force pushes the hose backward. You can also use the principle of conservation of momentum to explain why the hose moves backward:

Firefighters must apply a force to the water hose to prevent it from flying backward when the water comes out.

- Before the firefighter turns on the water, the hose and the water are not in motion, so the hose/water system has no momentum.
- Once the water is turned on, the water has momentum in the forward direction.
- For the total momentum of the hose and the water to stay the same, the hose must have an equal amount of momentum in the opposite direction. The hose moves backward.

If the hose and the water are not acted on by any other forces, momentum is conserved. Water is pushed forward, and the hose is pushed backward. However, the action and reaction force pair acting on the hose and the water are not usually the only forces acting on the hose/water system, as shown in the photograph above. There the firefighters are holding the hose steady.

The force the firefighters apply is called an outside force because it is not being applied by the hose or the water. When there is an outside force on a system, momentum is not conserved. Because the firefighters hold the hose, the hose does not move backward, even though the water has a forward momentum.

Under what condition is momentum not conserved? What part of the paragraph above tells you?

## 2.4 Review

### KEY CONCEPTS

1. How does increasing the speed of an object change its momentum?
2. A car and a truck are traveling at the same speed. Which has more momentum? Why?
3. Give two examples showing the conservation of momentum. Give one example where momentum is not conserved.

### CRITICAL THINKING

4. **Predict** A performing dolphin speeds through the water and hits a rubber ball originally at rest. Describe what happens to the velocities of the dolphin and the ball.
5. **Calculate** A 50 kg person is running at 2 m/s. What is the person's momentum?

### CHALLENGE

6. **Apply** A moving train car bumps into another train car with the same mass. After the collision, the two cars are coupled and move off together. How does the final speed of the two train cars compare with the initial speed of the moving train cars before the collision?

# 2 Chapter Review

## the BIG idea

**Forces change the motion of objects in predictable ways.**

## KEY CONCEPTS SUMMARY

### 2.1 Forces change motion.

**Newton's first law**
Objects at rest remain at rest, and objects in motion remain in motion with the same velocity, unless acted upon by an unbalanced force.

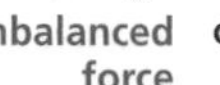

unbalanced force | object at rest | object in motion | unbalanced force

**VOCABULARY**
**force** p. 41
**net force** p. 43
**Newton's first law** p. 45
**inertia** p. 46

### 2.2 Force and mass determine acceleration.

**Newton's second law**
The acceleration of an object increases with increased force and decreases with increased mass, and is in the same direction as the force.

small force | larger force | small mass | larger mass

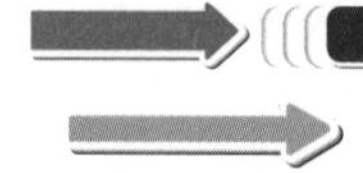

same mass, larger force = increased acceleration

larger mass, same force = decreased acceleration

**VOCABULARY**
**Newton's second law** p. 50
**centripetal force** p. 54

### 2.3 Forces act in pairs.

**Newton's third law**
When one object exerts a force on another object, the second object exerts an equal and opposite force on the first object.

**VOCABULARY**
**Newton's third law** p. 57

### 2.4 Forces transfer momentum.

- Momentum is a property of a moving object.
- Forces in collisions are equal and opposite.
- Momentum is conserved in collisions.

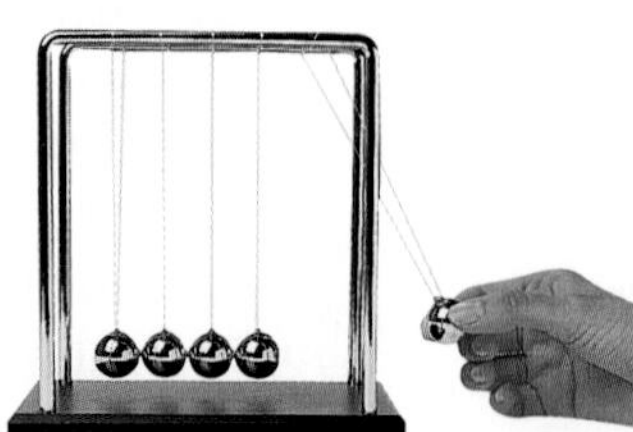

**VOCABULARY**
**momentum** p. 64
**collision** p. 66
**conservation of momentum** p. 67

## Reviewing Vocabulary

*Copy and complete the chart below. If the left column is blank, give the correct term. If the right column is blank, give an example from real life.*

| Term | Example from Real Life |
|---|---|
| **1.** acceleration | |
| **2.** centripetal force | |
| **3.** | The pull of a handle on a wagon |
| **4.** inertia | |
| **5.** mass | |
| **6.** net force | |
| **7.** Newton's first law | |
| **8.** Newton's second law | |
| **9.** | When you're walking, you push backward on the ground, and the ground pushes you forward with equal force. |
| **10.** momentum | |

## Reviewing Key Concepts

**Multiple Choice** *Choose the letter of the best answer.*

**11.** Newton's second law states that to increase acceleration, you

**a.** increase force
**b.** decrease force
**c.** increase mass
**d.** increase inertia

**12.** What units are used to measure force?

**a.** kilograms
**b.** meters
**c.** newtons
**d.** seconds

**13.** A wagon is pulled down a hill with a constant velocity. All the forces on the wagon are

**a.** balanced
**b.** unbalanced
**c.** increasing
**d.** decreasing

**14.** An action force and its reaction force are

**a.** equal in size and direction
**b.** equal in size and opposite in direction
**c.** different in size but in the same direction
**d.** different in size and in direction

**15.** John pulls a box with a force of 4 N, and Jason pulls the box from the opposite side with a force of 3 N. Ignore friction. Which of the following statements is true?

**a.** The box moves toward John.
**b.** The box moves toward Jason.
**c.** The box does not move.
**d.** There is not enough information to determine if the box moves.

**16.** A more massive marble collides with a less massive one that is not moving. The total momentum after the collision is equal to

**a.** zero
**b.** the original momentum of the more massive marble
**c.** the original momentum of the less massive marble
**d.** twice the original momentum of the more massive marble

**Short Answer** *Write a short answer to each question.*

**17.** List the following objects in order, from the object with the least inertia to the object with the most inertia: feather, large rock, pencil, book. Explain your reasoning.

**18.** During a race, you double your velocity. How does that change your momentum?

**19.** Explain how an object can have forces acting on it but not be accelerating.

**20.** A sea scallop moves by shooting jets of water out of its shell. Explain how this works.

## Thinking Critically

*Use the information in the photographs below to answer the next four questions.*

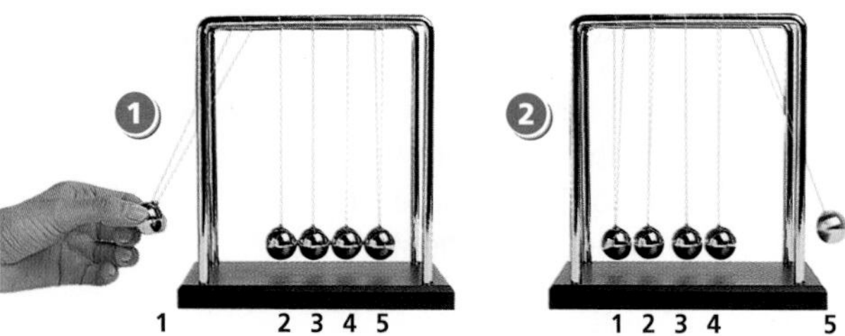


The photographs above show a toy called Newton's Cradle. In the first picture (1), ball 1 is lifted and is being held in place.

**21.** Are the forces on ball 1 balanced? How do you know?

**22.** Draw a diagram showing the forces acting on ball 2. Are these forces balanced?

In the second picture (2), ball 1 has been let go.

**23.** Ball 1 swung down, hit ball 2, and stopped. Use Newton's laws to explain why ball 1 stopped.

**24.** Use the principle of conservation of momentum to explain why ball 5 swung into the air.

*Copy the chart below. Write what will happen to the object in each case.*

| Cause | Effect |
|---|---|
| **25.** Balanced forces act on an object. | |
| **26.** Unbalanced forces act on an object. | |
| **27.** No force acts on an object. | |

**28. INFER** A baseball is three times more massive than a tennis ball. If the baseball and the tennis ball are accelerating equally, what can you determine about the net force on each?

## Using Math Skills in Science

*Complete the following calculations.*

**29.** What force should Lori apply to a 5 kg box to give it an acceleration of 2 $m/s^2$?

**30.** If a 10 N force accelerates an object 5 $m/s^2$, how massive is the object?

**31.** Ravi applies a force of 5 N to a wagon with a mass of 10 kg. What is the wagon's acceleration?

**32.** Use the information in the photograph on the right to calculate the momentum of the shopping cart.

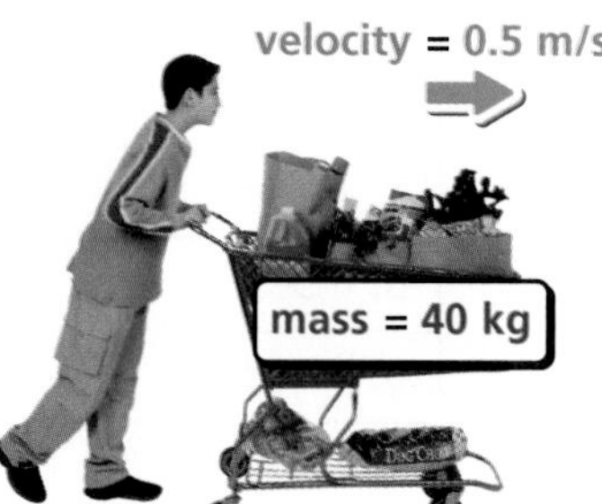


## the BIG idea

**33. PREDICT** Look again at the tug of war pictured on pages 38–39. Describe what information you need to know to predict the outcome of the game. How would you use that information and Newton's laws to make your prediction?

**34. WRITE** Pick an activity you enjoy, such as running or riding a scooter, and describe how Newton's laws apply to that activity.

**35. SYNTHESIZE** Think of a question you have about Newton's laws that is still unanswered. What information do you need in order to answer the question? How might you find the information?

## UNIT PROJECTS

If you need to do an experiment for your unit project, gather the materials. Be sure to allow enough time to observe results before the project is due.

## Analyzing Data

To test Newton's second law, Jodie accelerates blocks of ice across a smooth, flat surface. The table shows her results. (For this experiment, you can ignore the effects of friction.)

| Accelerating Blocks of Ice | | | | | | | |
|---|---|---|---|---|---|---|---|
| Mass (kg) | 1.0 | 1.5 | 2.0 | 2.5 | 3.0 | 3.5 | 4.0 |
| Acceleration ($m/s^2$) | 4.0 | 2.7 | 2.0 | 1.6 | 1.3 | 1.1 | 1.0 |

*Study the data table and then answer the questions that follow.*

**1.** The data show that as mass becomes greater, acceleration
- **a.** increases
- **b.** decreases
- **c.** stays the same
- **d.** cannot be predicted

**2.** From the data, you can tell that Jodie was applying a force of
- **a.** 1 N
- **b.** 2 N
- **c.** 3 N
- **d.** 4 N

**3.** If Jodie applied less force to the ice blocks, the accelerations would be
- **a.** greater
- **b.** less
- **c.** the same
- **d.** inconsistent

**4.** If Jodie applied a force of 6 N to the 2 kg block of ice, the acceleration would be
- **a.** 2 $m/s^2$
- **b.** 4 $m/s^2$
- **c.** 3 $m/s^2$
- **d.** 5 $m/s^2$

**5.** The average mass of the ice blocks she pushed was
- **a.** 1.5 kg
- **b.** 2.5 kg
- **c.** 3 kg
- **d.** 4 kg

**6.** If Jodie used a 3.25 kg block in her experiment, the force would accelerate the block somewhere between
- **a.** 1.0 and 1.1 $m/s^2$
- **b.** 1.1 and 1.3 $m/s^2$
- **c.** 1.3 and 1.6 $m/s^2$
- **d.** 1.6 and 2.0 $m/s^2$

## Extended Response

*Answer the two questions in detail. Include some of the terms shown in the word box. Underline each term you use in your answer.*

| | |
|---|---|
| Newton's second law | velocity |
| mass | inertia |
| gravity | balanced forces |
| centripetal force | unbalanced forces |

**7.** Tracy ties a ball to a string and starts to swing the ball around her head. What forces are acting on the ball? What happens if the string breaks?

**8.** Luis is trying to pull a wagon loaded with rocks. What can he do to increase the wagon's acceleration?

CHAPTER

# Gravity, Friction, and Pressure

## the BIG idea

**Newton's laws apply to all forces.**

## Key Concepts

SECTION

**Gravity is a force exerted by masses.**
Learn about gravity, weight, and orbits.

SECTION

**Friction is a force that opposes motion.**
Learn about friction and air resistance.

SECTION

**Pressure depends on force and area.**
Learn about pressure and how forces act on objects in fluids.

SECTION

**Fluids can exert a force on objects.**
Learn how fluids apply forces to objects and how forces are transmitted through fluids.

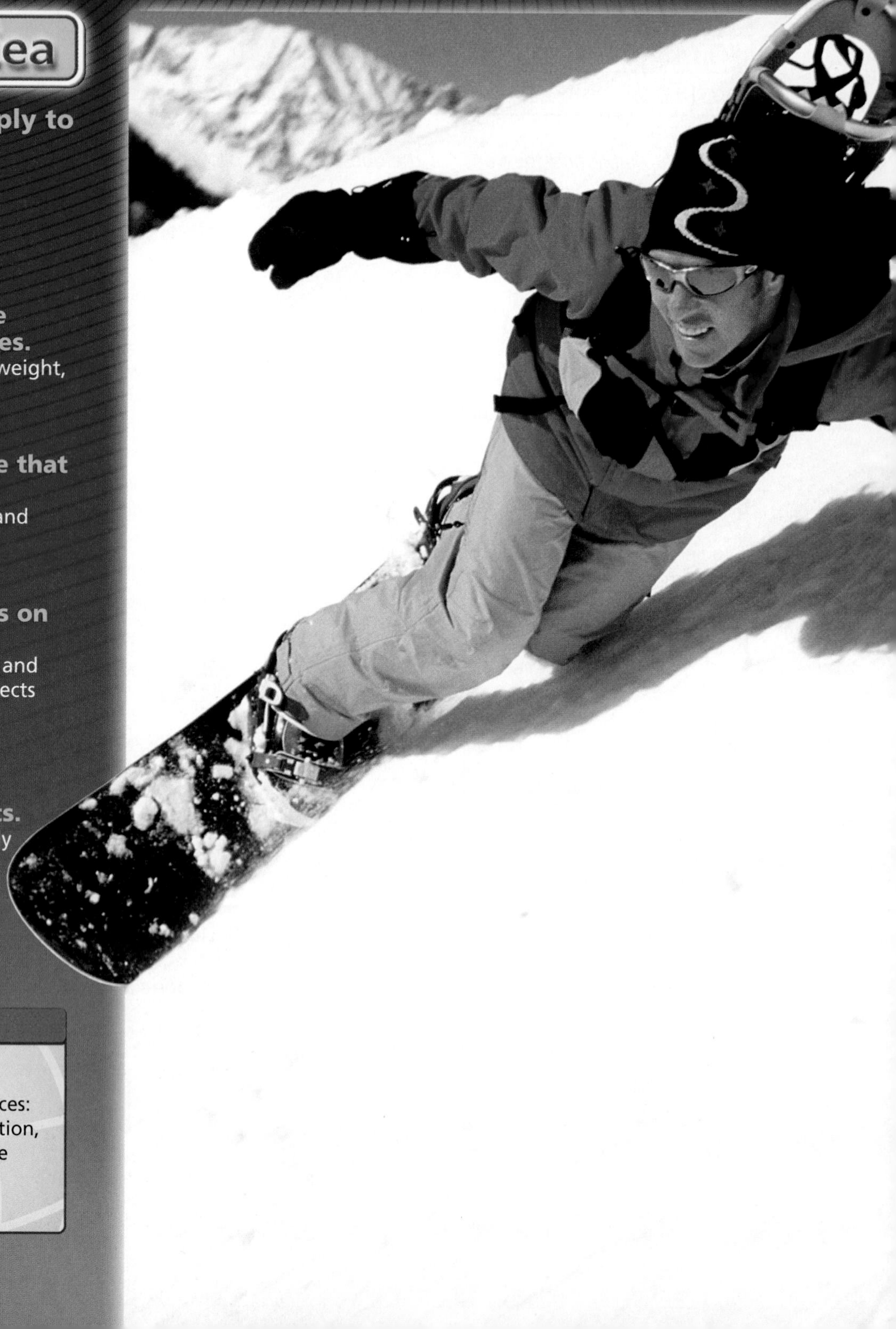

**Internet Preview**

CLASSZONE.COM

Chapter 3 online resources: Content Review, Simulation, two Visualizations, three Resource Centers, Math Tutorial, Test Practice

*What forces are acting on this snowboarder? What forces are acting on the snow?*

# EXPLORE the BIG idea

## Let It Slide

Make a ramp using a board and some books. Slide an object down the ramp. Change the surface of the ramp using various materials such as sandpaper.

**Observe and Think** What effects did different surfaces have on the motion of the object? What may have caused these effects?

## Under Pressure

Take two never-opened plastic soft-drink bottles. Open and reseal one of them. Squeeze each bottle.

**Observe and Think** How did the fluid inside each bottle react to your force? What may have caused the difference in the way the bottles felt?

## Internet Activity: Gravity

Go to **ClassZone.com** to explore gravity. Learn more about the force of gravity and its effect on you, objects on Earth, and orbits of planets and satellites. Explore how gravity determines weight, and find out how your weight would be different on other planets.

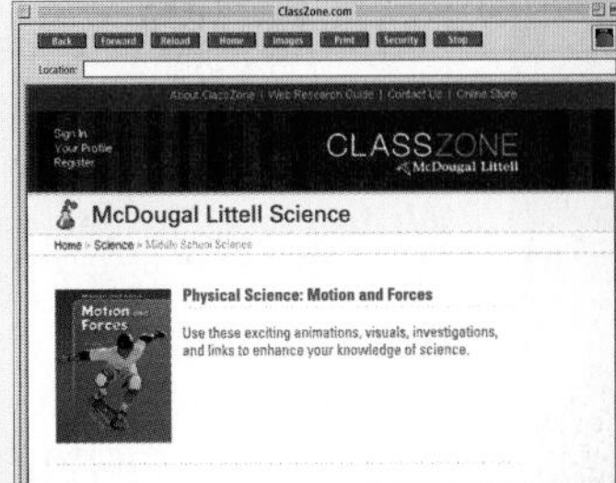


**Observe and Think** What would you weigh on Mars? What would you weigh on Neptune?

Pressure **Code: MDL006**

CHAPTER 3

# Getting Ready to Learn

## CONCEPT REVIEW

- The motion of an object will not change unless acted upon by an unbalanced force.
- The acceleration of an object depends on force and mass.
- For every action force there is an equal and opposite reaction.

## VOCABULARY REVIEW

**force** p. 41

**Newton's first law** p. 45

**Newton's second law** p. 50

**Newton's third law** p. 57

**density** *See Glossary.*

**CONTENT REVIEW**
CLASSZONE.COM
Review concepts and vocabulary.

## TAKING NOTES

### SUPPORTING MAIN IDEAS

Make a chart to show main ideas and the information that supports them. Copy the main ideas. Below each main idea, add supporting information, such as reasons, explanations, and examples.

### VOCABULARY STRATEGY

Write each new vocabulary term in the center of a **four square** diagram. Write notes in the squares around each term. Include a definition, some characteristics, and some examples of the term. If possible, write some things that are not examples of the term.

See the Note-Taking Handbook on pages R45–R51.

SCIENCE NOTEBOOK

Force of gravity depends on mass and distance.
- More mass = more gravitational force
- More distance = less gravitational force

| Definition | Characteristics |
|---|---|
| force of gravity acting on an object | • changes if gravity changes<br>• measured in newtons |
| **Examples** | **Nonexamples** |
| A 4 kg bowling ball weighs 39 N. | Mass in kg is not a weight. |

(Center term: WEIGHT)

KEY CONCEPT

# Gravity is a force exerted by masses.

**BEFORE, you learned**

- Every action force has an equal and opposite reaction force
- Newton's laws are used to describe the motions of objects
- Mass is the amount of matter an object contains

**NOW, you will learn**

- How mass and distance affect gravity
- What keeps objects in orbit

**VOCABULARY**

**gravity** p. 77
**weight** p. 79
**orbit** p. 80

**EXPLORE Downward Acceleration**

***How do the accelerations of two falling objects compare?***

**PROCEDURE**

1. Make a prediction: Which ball will fall faster?
2. Drop both balls from the same height at the same time.
3. Observe the balls as they hit the ground.

**MATERIALS**

- golf ball
- Ping-Pong ball

**WHAT DO YOU THINK?**

- Were the results what you had expected?
- How did the times it took the two balls to hit the ground compare?

## Masses attract each other.

When you drop any object—such as a pen, a book, or a football—it falls to the ground. As the object falls, it moves faster and faster. The fact that the object accelerates means there must be a force acting on it. The downward pull on the object is due to gravity. **Gravity** is the force that objects exert on each other because of their masses. You are familiar with the force of gravity between Earth and objects on Earth.

VOCABULARY
Create a four square diagram for *gravity* in your notebook.

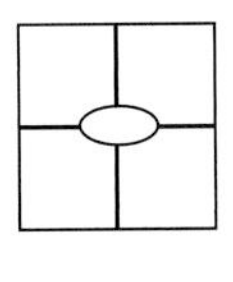

Gravity is present not only between objects and Earth, however. Gravity is considered a universal force because it acts between any two masses anywhere in the universe. For example, there is a gravitational pull between the Sun and the Moon. Even small masses attract each other. The force of gravity between dust and gas particles in space helped form the solar system.

**CHECK YOUR READING** Why is gravity considered a universal force?

## The Force of Gravity

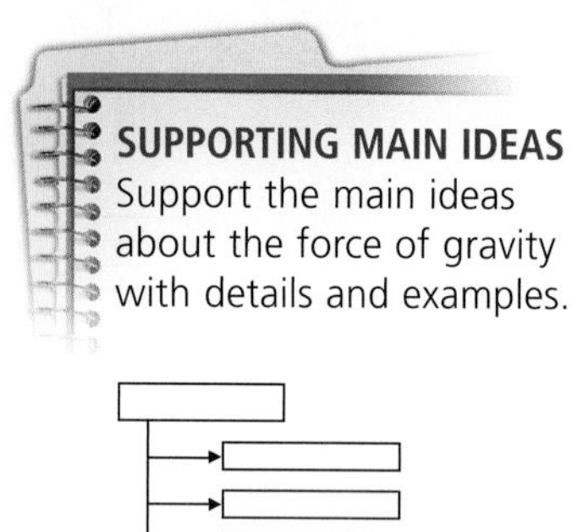

SUPPORTING MAIN IDEAS
Support the main ideas about the force of gravity with details and examples.


If there is a force between all masses, why are you not pulled toward your desk by the desk's gravity when you walk away from it? Remember that the net force on you determines how your motion changes. The force of gravity between you and the desk is extremely small compared with other forces constantly acting on you, such as friction, the force from your muscles, Earth's gravity, and the gravitational pull from many other objects. The strength of the gravitational force between two objects depends on two factors, mass and distance.

**The Mass of the Objects** The more mass two objects have, the greater the force of gravity the masses exert on each other. If one of the masses is doubled, the force of gravity between the objects is doubled.

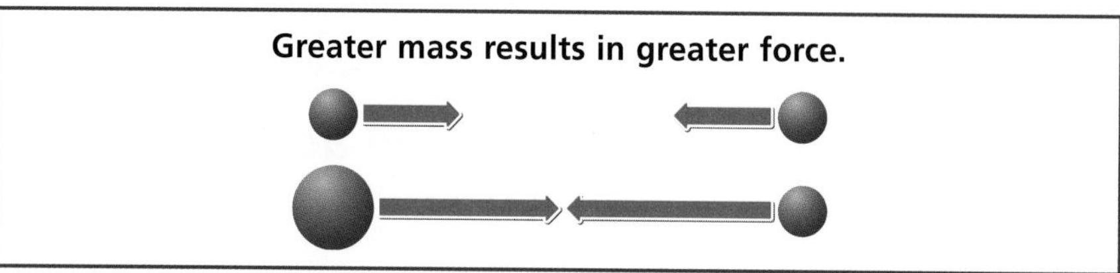


**The Distance Between the Objects** As distance between the objects increases, the force of gravity decreases. If the distance is doubled, the force of gravity is one-fourth as strong as before.

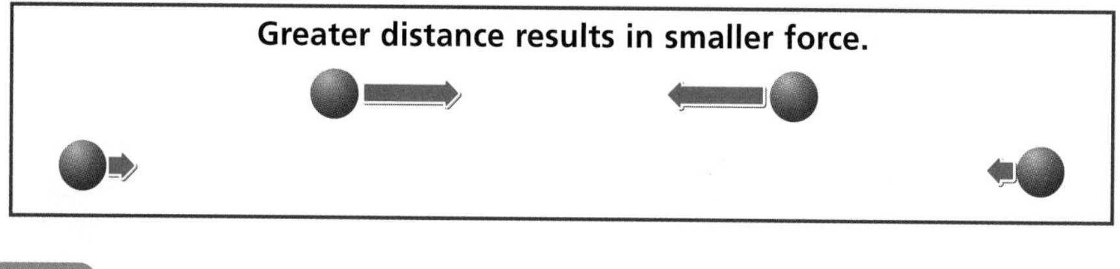


**CHECK YOUR READING** How do mass and distance affect the force of gravity?

## Gravity on Earth

The force of gravity acts on both masses equally, even though the effects on both masses may be very different. Earth's gravity exerts a downward pull on a dropped coin. Remember that every action force has an equal and opposite reaction force. The coin exerts an equal upward force on Earth. Because the coin has an extremely small mass compared with Earth, the coin can be easily accelerated. Earth's acceleration due to the force of the coin is far too small to notice because of Earth's large mass.

The acceleration due to Earth's gravity is called $g$ and is equal to 9.8 $m/s^2$ at Earth's surface. You can calculate the force of gravity on an object using the object's mass and this acceleration. The formula that expresses Newton's second law is $F = ma$. If you use $g$ as the acceleration, the formula for calculating the force due to gravity on a mass close to Earth's surface becomes $F = mg$.

## Acceleration Due to Gravity

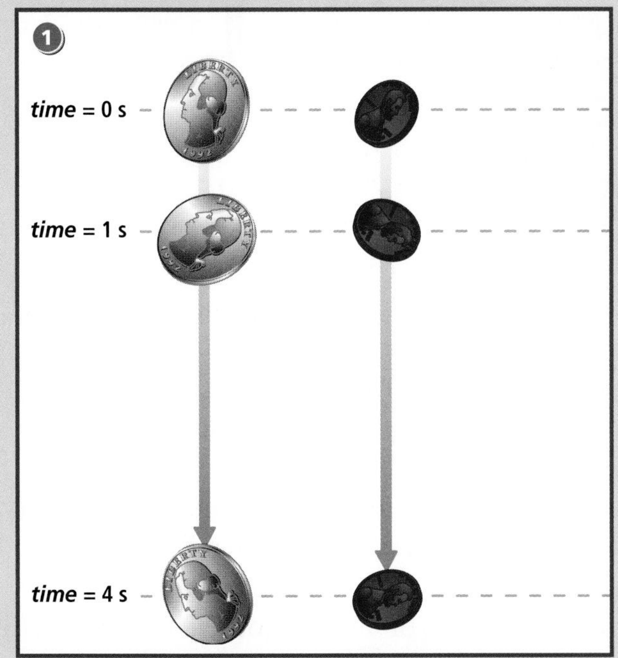


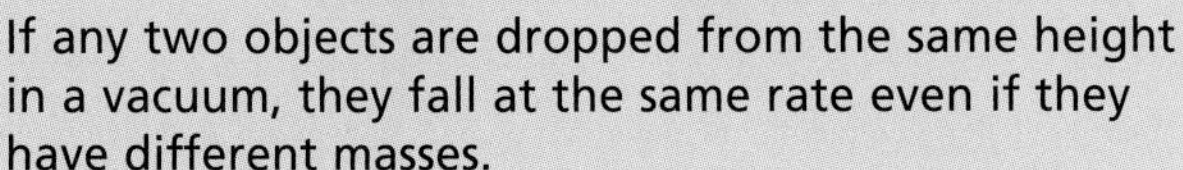
If any two objects are dropped from the same height in a vacuum, they fall at the same rate even if they have different masses.

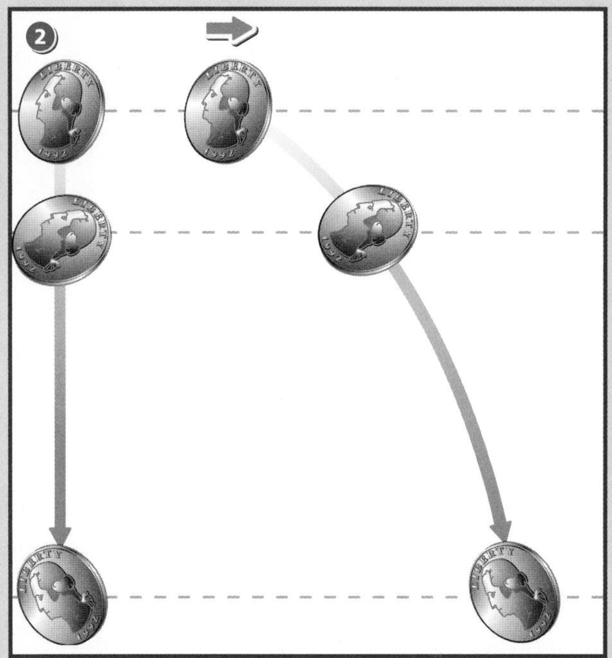


If an object has a velocity in the horizontal direction when it falls, the horizontal velocity does not change its downward acceleration.

In a vacuum—that is, where there is no air—all falling objects have the same acceleration.

1. The quarter falls at the same rate as the penny when they are dropped together. Because the quarter has more mass, gravity exerts more force on it. But greater mass also means more inertia, so the greater force does not produce a larger acceleration. Objects with different masses fall with the same acceleration.

2. A coin that is dropped falls at the same rate as one that is thrown forward. Horizontal velocity does not affect acceleration due to gravity. Because gravity is directed downward, it changes only the downward velocity of the coin, not its forward velocity.

Explore how objects fall at the same rate in a vacuum.

Compare the times it takes two objects with different masses to fall from the same height.

## Weight and Mass

While weight and mass are related, they are not the same properties. Mass is a measure of how much matter an object contains. **Weight** is the force of gravity on an object. Mass is a property that an object has no matter where it is located. Weight, on the other hand, depends on the force of gravity acting on that object.

When you use a balance, you are measuring the mass of an object. A person with a mass of 50 kilograms will balance another mass of 50 kilograms whether she is on Earth or on the Moon. Traveling to the Moon would not change how much matter a person is made of. When you use a spring scale, such as a bathroom scale, to measure the weight of an object, however, you are measuring how hard gravity is pulling on an object. The Moon is less massive than Earth, and its gravitational pull is one-sixth that of Earth's. A spring scale would show that a person who has a weight of 490 newtons (110 lb) on Earth would have a weight of 82 newtons (18 lb) on the Moon.

## Gravity keeps objects in orbit.

Sir Isaac Newton hypothesized that the force that pulls objects to the ground—gravity—also pulls the Moon in its orbit around Earth. An **orbit** is the elliptical path one body, such as the Moon, follows around another body, such as Earth, due to the influence of gravity. The centripetal force keeping one object in orbit around another object is due to the gravitational pull between the two objects. In the case of the Moon's orbit, the centripetal force is the gravitational pull between the Moon and Earth. Similarly, Earth is pulled around the Sun by the gravitational force between Earth and the Sun.

**READING TIP**

An ellipse is shaped as shown below. A circle is a special type of ellipse.

You can think of an object orbiting Earth as an object that is falling around Earth rather than falling to the ground. Consider what happens to the ball in the illustration on page 81. A dropped ball will fall about five meters during the first second it falls. Throwing the ball straight ahead will not change that falling time. What happens as you throw faster and faster?

Earth is curved. This fact is noticeable only over very long distances. For every 8000 meters you travel, Earth curves downward about 5 meters. If you could throw a ball at 8000 meters per second, it would fall to Earth in such a way that its path would curve the same amount that Earth curves. Since the ball would fall along the curve of Earth, the ball would never actually land on the ground. The ball would be in orbit.

## Orbits

**An object in orbit, like an object falling to the ground, is pulled toward Earth's center. If the object moves far enough forward as it falls, it orbits around Earth instead of hitting the ground.**

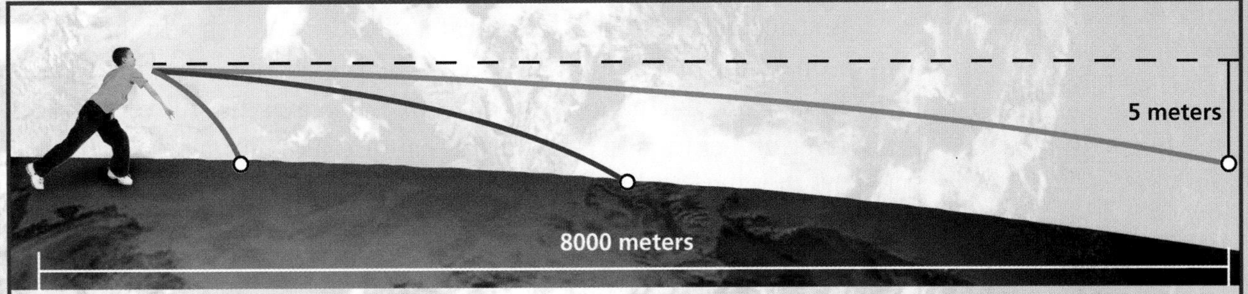


If a ball is thrown straight ahead from a 5-meter height, it will drop 5 meters in the first second it falls. At low speeds, the ball will hit the ground after 1 second.

If the ball is going fast enough, the curvature of Earth becomes important. While the ball still drops 5 meters in the first second, it must fall farther than 5 meters to hit the ground.

If the ball is going fast enough to travel 8000 meters forward as it drops downward 5 meters, it follows the curvature of Earth. The ball will fall around Earth, not into it.

A ball thrown horizontally at 8000 m/s will not hit Earth during its fall. Gravity acts as a centripetal force, continually pulling the ball toward Earth's center. The ball circles Earth in an orbit.

**Real-World Application**
A satellite is launched upward until it is above Earth's atmosphere. The engine then gives the satellite a horizontal speed great enough to keep it in orbit.

= force

= velocity

**READING VISUALS** Compare the direction of the velocity with the direction of the force for an object in a circular orbit.

## Spacecraft in Orbit

The minimum speed needed to send an object into orbit is approximately 8000 meters per second. At this speed, the path of a falling object matches the curve of Earth's surface. If you launch a spacecraft or a satellite at a slower speed, it will eventually fall to the ground.

A spacecraft launched at a greater speed can reach a higher orbit than one launched at a lower speed. The higher the orbit, the weaker the force from Earth's gravity. The force of gravity is still very strong, however. If a craft is in a low orbit—about 300 kilometers (190 mi)—Earth's gravitational pull is about 91 percent of what it is at Earth's surface. The extra distance makes a difference in the force of only about 9 percent.

If a spacecraft is launched with a speed of 11,000 meters per second or more, it is moving too fast to go into an orbit. Instead, the spacecraft will ultimately escape the pull of Earth's gravity altogether. The speed that a spacecraft needs to escape the gravitational pull of an object such as a planet or a star is called the escape velocity. A spacecraft that escapes Earth's gravity will go into orbit around the Sun unless it is also going fast enough to escape the Sun's gravity.

Did any facts in the text above surprise you? If so, which surprised you and why?

## INVESTIGATE Gravity

### How does gravity affect falling objects?

**PROCEDURE**

1. Carefully use the pencil to punch a hole that is the width of the pencil in the side of the cup, about one-third of the way up from the bottom.
2. Holding your finger over the hole, fill the cup three-fourths full of water.
3. Hold the cup above the dishpan. Predict what will happen if you remove your finger from the hole. Remove your finger and observe what happens.
4. With your finger over the hole, refill the cup to the same level as in step 2. Predict how the water will move if you hold the cup 50 cm above the dishpan and drop the cup and its contents straight down into the pan.
5. Drop the cup and observe what happens to the water while the cup is falling.

**WHAT DO YOU THINK?**

- What happened to the water in step 3? in step 5?
- How did gravity affect the water when you dropped the cup?

**CHALLENGE** Why did the water behave differently the second time?

**SKILL FOCUS**
Predicting

**MATERIALS**
- pencil
- paper cup
- water
- dishpan

**TIME**
15 minutes

## People in Orbit

Astronaut Mae Jemison is shown here working in a microgravity environment.

When an elevator you are riding in accelerates downward, you may feel lighter for a short time. If you were standing on a scale during the downward acceleration, the scale would show that you weighed less than usual. Your mass would not have changed, nor would the pull of gravity. What would cause the apparent weight loss?

When the elevator is still, the entire force of your weight presses against the scale. When the elevator accelerates downward, you are not pressing as hard on the scale, because the scale is also moving downward. Since the scale measures how hard you are pushing on it, you appear to weigh less. If you and the scale were in free fall—a fall due entirely to gravity—the scale would fall as fast as you did. You would not press against the scale at all, so you would appear to be weightless.

A spacecraft in orbit is in free fall. Gravity is acting on the astronauts and on the ship—without gravity, there could be no orbit. However, the ship and the astronauts are falling around Earth at the same rate. While astronauts are in orbit, their weight does not press against the floor of the spacecraft. The result is an environment, called a microgravity environment, in which objects behave as if there were no gravity. People and objects simply float as if they were weightless.

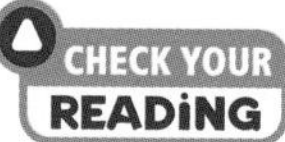

CHECK YOUR READING Why do astronauts float when they are in orbit?

## 3.1 Review

### KEY CONCEPTS

1. What effect would increasing the mass of two objects have on the gravitational attraction between them?
2. What effect would decreasing the distance between objects have on their gravitational attraction to each other?
3. How does gravity keep the Moon in orbit around Earth?

### CRITICAL THINKING

4. **Compare** How does the size of the force exerted by Earth's gravity on a car compare with the size of the force the car exerts on Earth?
5. **Apply** What would be the effect on the mass and the weight of an object if the object were taken to a planet with twice the gravity of Earth?

### CHALLENGE

6. **Synthesize** Precision measurements of the acceleration due to gravity show that the acceleration is slightly different in different locations on Earth. Explain why the force of gravity is not exactly the same everywhere on Earth's surface. **Hint:** Think about the details of Earth's surface.

EXTREME SCIENCE

GRAVITY IN THE EXTREME

# Bending Light

You know that gravity can pull objects toward each other, but did you know that gravity can also affect light? Very extreme sources of gravity cause the normally straight path of a light beam to bend.

## Going in Circles

Although Earth is massive, the effects of its gravity on light are not noticeable. However, scientists can model what a familiar scene might look like with an extreme source of gravity nearby. The image to the left shows how the light from the Seattle Space Needle could be bent almost into circles if an extremely small yet extremely massive object, such as a black hole, were in front of it.

## Seeing Behind Galaxies

How do we know that gravity can bend light? Astronomers, who study space, have seen the phenomenon in action. If a very bright but distant object is behind a very massive one, such as a large galaxy, the mass of the galaxy bends the light coming from the distant object. This effect, called gravitational lensing, can produce multiple images of the bright object along a ring around the massive galaxy. Astronomers have observed gravitational lensing in their images.

### Facts About Bending Light

- Gravitational lensing was predicted by Albert Einstein in the early 1900s, but the first example was not observed until 1979.
- The masses of distant galaxies can be found by observing their effect on light.

**Seeing Quadruple**
This gravitational lens is called the Einstein Cross. The four bright objects that ring the central galaxy are all images of the same very bright yet very distant object that is located 20 times farther away than the central galaxy.

## EXPLORE

1. **INFER** Why are you unable to notice the gravitational bending of light by an object such as a large rock?
2. **CHALLENGE** Look at the photographs in the Resource Center. Find the multiple images of the distant objects and the more massive object bending the light from them.

Find out more information about gravitational lenses.

KEY CONCEPT

# Friction is a force that opposes motion.

**BEFORE, you learned**

- Gravity is the attractive force masses exert on each other
- Gravity increases with greater mass and decreases with greater distance
- Gravity is the centripetal force keeping objects in orbit

**NOW, you will learn**

- How friction affects motion
- About factors that affect friction
- About air resistance

**VOCABULARY**

**friction** p. 85
**fluid** p. 88
**air resistance** p. 89

**THINK ABOUT**

### *What forces help you to walk?*

As a person walks, she exerts a backward force on the ground. A reaction force moves her forward. But some surfaces are harder to walk on than others. Ice, for example, is harder to walk on than a dry surface because ice is slippery. How can different surfaces affect your ability to walk?

## Friction occurs when surfaces slide against each other.

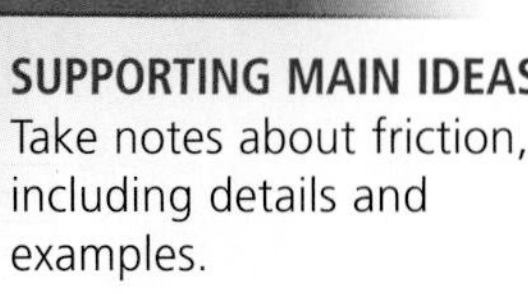

**SUPPORTING MAIN IDEAS**
Take notes about friction, including details and examples.

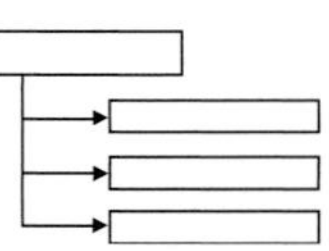

Have you ever pushed a heavy box across the floor? You probably noticed that it is easier to push the box over some surfaces than over others. You must apply a certain amount of force to the box to keep it moving. The force that acts against your pushing force is called friction. **Friction** is a force that resists the motion between two surfaces in contact.

When you try to slide two surfaces across each other, the force of friction resists the sliding motion. If there were no friction, the box would move as soon as you applied any force to it. Although friction can make some tasks more difficult, most activities, including walking, would be impossible without it. Friction between your feet and the ground is what provides the action and reaction forces that enable you to walk.

## Forces and Surfaces

Learn more about friction, forces, and surfaces.

If you look down from a great height, such as from the window of an airplane, a flat field appears to be smooth. If you were to walk in the field, however, you would see that the ground has many bumps and holes. In the same way, a flat surface such as a piece of plastic may look and feel smooth. However, if you look at the plastic through a strong microscope, you see that it has tiny bumps and ridges. Friction depends on how these bumps and ridges on one surface interact with and stick to the bumps and ridges on other surfaces. There are several factors that determine the friction between two surfaces.

REMINDER

Remember that balanced forces on an object do not change the object's motion.

**Types of Surfaces** Friction between two surfaces depends on the materials that make up the surfaces. Different combinations of surfaces produce different frictional forces. A rubber hockey puck sliding across ice has a smaller frictional force on it than the same puck sliding across a wooden floor. The friction between rubber and ice is less than the friction between rubber and wood.

**Motion of the Surfaces** You need a larger force to start something moving than you do to keep something moving. If you have ever tried to push a heavy chair, you may have noticed that you had to push harder and harder until the chair suddenly accelerated forward.

As you apply a force to push a chair or any other object that is not moving, the frictional force keeping it from sliding increases so the forces stay balanced. However, the frictional force has a limit to how

### Friction and Motion

**Before Object Moves**

When an object is standing still, there is a maximum force needed to overcome friction and start it moving. Any force less than this will be exactly balanced by the force of friction, and the object will not move.

**While Object Moves**

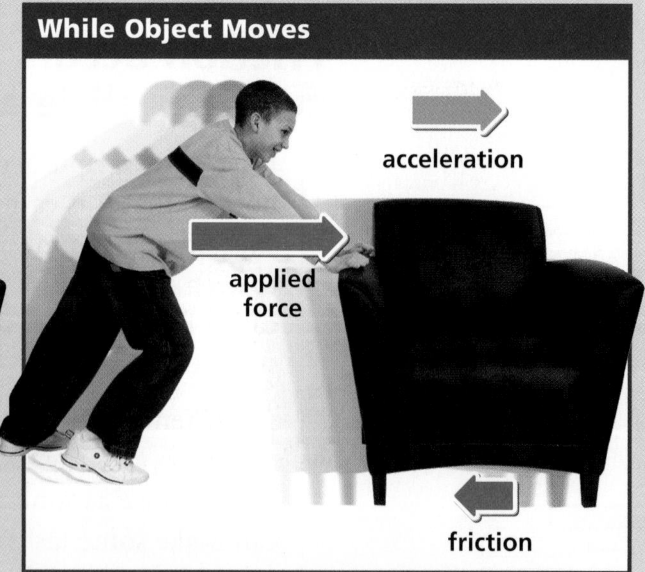


Once the object is moving, the frictional force remains constant. This constant force is less than the maximum force needed to start the object moving.

large it can be. When your force is greater than this limit, the forces on the chair are no longer balanced, and the chair moves. The frictional force remains at a new lower level once the chair is moving.

**Force Pressing the Surfaces Together** The harder two surfaces are pushed together, the more difficult it is for the surfaces to slide over each other. When an object is placed on a surface, the weight of the object presses on that surface. The surface exerts an equal and opposite reaction force on the object. This reaction force is one of the factors that determines how much friction there is.

If you push a chair across the floor, there will be a certain amount of friction between the chair and the floor. Increasing the weight of the chair increases the force pushing the surfaces together. The force of friction between the chair and the floor is greater when a person is sitting in it than when the chair was empty.

Friction depends on the total force pressing the surfaces together, not on how much area this force acts over. Consider a rectangular cardboard box. It can rest with its smaller or larger side on the floor. The box will have the same force from friction regardless of which side sits on the floor. The larger side has more area in contact with the floor than the smaller side, but the weight of the box is more spread out on the larger side.

What factors influence frictional force? Give two examples.

## Friction and Weight

### Less Weight

The force of friction depends on the total force pushing the surfaces together. Here the weight of the chair is the force pressing the surfaces together.

### More Weight

The weight of the chair increases when someone sits in it. The force of friction is now greater than when the chair was empty.

Friction produces sparks between a match head and a rough surface. The heat from friction eventually lights the match.

### Friction and Heat

Friction between surfaces produces heat. You feel heat produced by friction when you rub your hands together. As you rub, friction causes the individual molecules on the surface of your hands to move faster. As the individual molecules in an object move faster, the temperature of the object increases. The increased speed of the molecules on the surface of your hands produces the warmth that you feel.

The heat produced by friction can be intense. The friction that results from striking a match against a rough surface produces enough heat to ignite the flammable substance on the head of the match. In some machines, such as a car engine, too much heat from friction can cause serious damage. Substances such as oil are often used to reduce friction between moving parts in machines. Without motor oil, a car's engine parts would overheat and stop working.

## Motion through fluids produces friction.

As you have seen, two objects falling in a vacuum fall with the same acceleration. Objects falling through air, however, have different accelerations. This difference occurs because air is a fluid. A **fluid** is a substance that can flow easily. Gases and liquids are fluids.

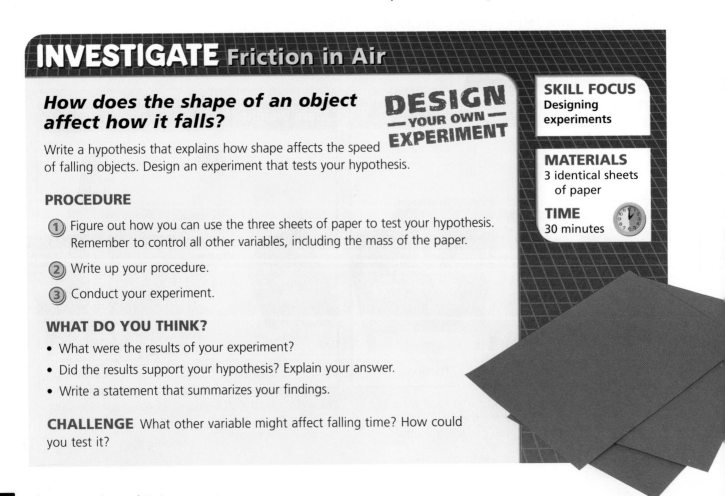

## INVESTIGATE Friction in Air

### How does the shape of an object affect how it falls?

**DESIGN — YOUR OWN — EXPERIMENT**

Write a hypothesis that explains how shape affects the speed of falling objects. Design an experiment that tests your hypothesis.

**PROCEDURE**

1. Figure out how you can use the three sheets of paper to test your hypothesis. Remember to control all other variables, including the mass of the paper.
2. Write up your procedure.
3. Conduct your experiment.

**WHAT DO YOU THINK?**

- What were the results of your experiment?
- Did the results support your hypothesis? Explain your answer.
- Write a statement that summarizes your findings.

**CHALLENGE** What other variable might affect falling time? How could you test it?

**SKILL FOCUS**
Designing experiments

**MATERIALS**
3 identical sheets of paper

**TIME**
30 minutes

When an object moves through a fluid, it pushes the molecules of the fluid out of the way. At the same time, the molecules of the fluid exert an equal and opposite force on the object that slows it down. This force resisting motion through a fluid is a type of friction that is often called drag. Friction in fluids depends on the shape of the moving object. Objects can be designed either to increase or reduce the friction caused by a fluid. Airplane designs, for example, improve as engineers find ways to reduce drag.

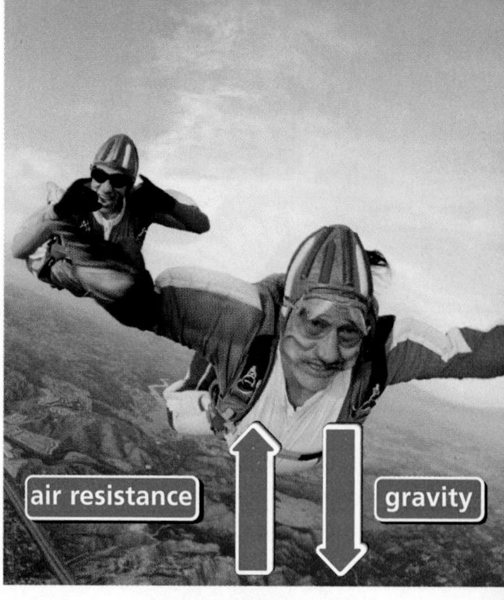


When the force of air resistance equals the force from gravity, a skydiver falls at a constant speed.

The friction due to air is often called **air resistance.** Air resistance differs from the friction between solid surfaces. Air resistance depends on surface area and the speed of an object in the following ways:

- An object with a larger surface area comes into contact with more molecules as it moves than an object with a smaller surface area. This increases the air resistance.
- The faster an object moves through air, the more molecules it comes into contact with in a given amount of time. As the speed of the object increases, air resistance increases.

When a skydiver jumps out of a plane, gravity causes the skydiver to accelerate toward the ground. As the skydiver falls, his body pushes against the air. The air pushes back—with the force of air resistance. As the skydiver's speed increases, his air resistance increases. Eventually, air resistance balances gravity, and the skydiver reaches terminal velocity, which is the final, maximum velocity of a falling object. When the skydiver opens his parachute, air resistance increases still further, and he reaches a new, slower terminal velocity that enables him to land safely.

How do speed and surface area affect air resistance?

## 3.2 Review

### KEY CONCEPTS

1. How does friction affect forward motion? Give an example.
2. Describe two ways to change the frictional force between two solid surfaces.
3. How does air resistance affect the velocity of a falling object?

### CRITICAL THINKING

4. **Infer** What two sources of friction do you have to overcome when you are walking?
5. **Synthesize** If you push a chair across the floor at a constant velocity, how does the force of friction compare with the force you exert? Explain.

### CHALLENGE

6. **Synthesize** If you push a book against a wall hard enough, it will not slide down even though gravity is pulling it. Use what you know about friction and Newton's laws of motion to explain why the book does not fall.

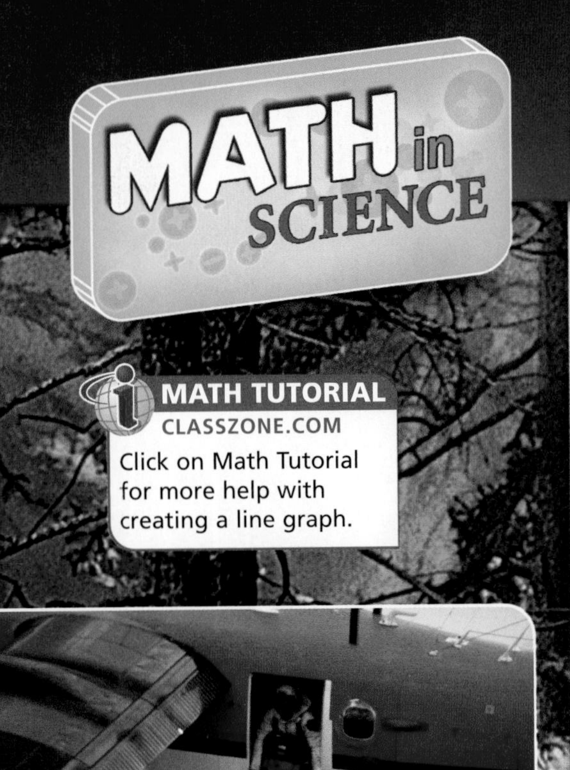


MATH TUTORIAL
CLASSZONE.COM

Click on Math Tutorial for more help with creating a line graph.

SKILL: CREATING A LINE GRAPH

# Smoke Jumpers in Action

Scientists often use graphs as a way to present data. Sometimes information is easier to understand when it is presented in graphic form.

## Example

Smoke jumpers are firefighters who parachute down into a forest that is on fire. Suppose you measured how the velocity of a smoke jumper changed as he was free-falling, and recorded the following data:

| Time (s) | 0 | 2 | 4 | 6 | 8 | 10 | 12 | 14 | 16 | 18 |
|---|---|---|---|---|---|---|---|---|---|---|
| Velocity (m/s) | 0 | 18 | 29 | 33 | 35 | 36 | 36 | 36 | 36 | 36 |

**Follow these steps to make a line graph of the data in the table.**

**(1)** For both variables, decide the scale that each box on your graph will represent and what range you will show for each variable. For the above time data you might choose a range of 0 to 18 s, with each interval representing 2 s. For velocity, a range of 0 to 40 m/s with intervals of 5 m/s each is reasonable.

**(2)** Determine the dependent and independent variables. In this example, the velocity depends on the falling time, so velocity is the dependent variable.

**(3)** Plot the independent variable along the horizontal axis, or *x*-axis. Plot the dependent variable along the vertical axis, or *y*-axis. Connect the points with a smooth line.

ANSWER

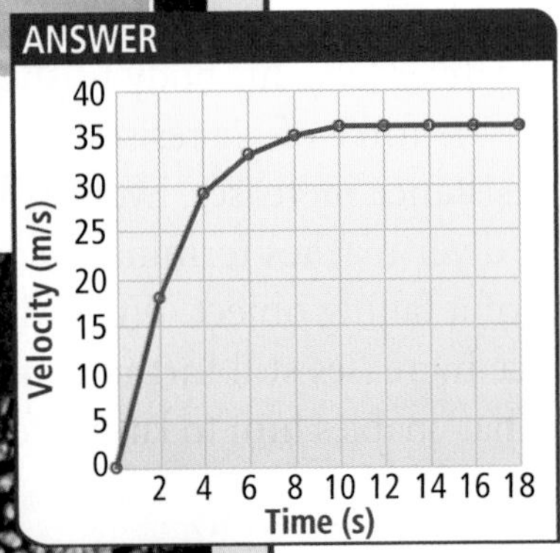


Smoke jumpers parachute into burning forests in order to contain the flames.

**Use the data below to answer the following questions.**

Suppose a smoke jumper varied the mass of his equipment over 5 jumps, and you measured his different terminal velocities as follows:

| Extra Mass (kg) | 0 | 5 | 10 | 15 | 20 |
|---|---|---|---|---|---|
| Terminal Velocity (m/s) | 36 | 37 | 38 | 39 | 40 |

**1.** Identify the independent and dependent variables.

**2.** Choose the scales and intervals you would use to graph the data. **Hint:** Your velocity range does not have to start at 0 m/s.

**3.** Plot your graph.

**CHALLENGE** How do different scales give different impressions of the data? Try comparing several different scales for the same data.

KEY CONCEPT

# Pressure depends on force and area.

**BEFORE, you learned**

- Frictional forces oppose motion when surfaces resist sliding
- Frictional force depends on the surface types and the total force pushing them together
- Air resistance is a type of friction on objects moving through air

**NOW, you will learn**

- How pressure is determined
- How forces act on objects in fluids
- How pressure changes in fluids

**VOCABULARY**

**pressure** p. 91
**pascal** p. 92

**EXPLORE Pressure**

### How does surface area affect pressure?

**PROCEDURE**

1. Place the pencil flat on the Styrofoam board. Balance the book on top of the pencil. After 5 seconds, remove the book and the pencil. Observe the Styrofoam.
2. Balance the book on top of the pencil in an upright position as shown. After 5 seconds, remove the book and the pencil. Observe the Styrofoam.

**MATERIALS**

- sharpened pencil
- Styrofoam board
- book

**WHAT DO YOU THINK?**

- How did the effect on the Styrofoam change from step 1 to step 2?
- What do you think accounts for any differences you noted?

## Pressure describes how a force is spread over an area.

**VOCABULARY**
Create a four square diagram for *pressure* in your notebook.

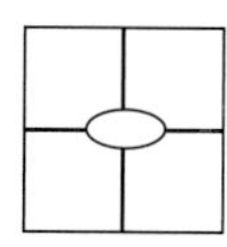

**Pressure** is a measure of how much force is acting on a certain area. In other words, pressure describes how concentrated a force is. When a cat lies down on your lap, all the force of the cat's weight is spread out over a large area of your lap. If the cat stands up, however, all the force from the cat's weight is concentrated into its paws. The pressure the cat exerts on you increases when the cat stands up in your lap.

While the increased pressure may make you feel as if there is more force on you, the force is actually the same. The cat's weight is simply pressing on a smaller area. How you feel a force when it is pressing on you depends on both the force and the area over which it is applied.

One way to increase pressure is to increase force. If you press a wall with your finger, the harder you press, the more pressure you put on the wall. But you can also increase the pressure by decreasing the area. When you push a thumbtack into a wall, you apply a force to the thumbtack. The small area of the sharp point of the thumbtack produces a much larger pressure on the wall than the area of your finger does. The greater pressure from the thumbtack can pierce the wall, while the pressure from your finger alone cannot.

The following formula shows exactly how pressure depends on force and area:

$$\textbf{Pressure} = \frac{\textbf{Force}}{\textbf{Area}} \qquad P = \frac{F}{A}$$

**READING TIP**

Notice that when a unit, such as pascal or newton, is named for a person, the unit is not capitalized but its abbreviation is.

In this formula, $P$ is the pressure, $F$ is the force in newtons, and $A$ is the area over which the force is exerted, measured in square meters ($m^2$). The unit for pressure is the **pascal** (Pa). One pascal is the pressure exerted by one newton (1 N) of force on an area of one square meter (1 $m^2$). That is, one pascal is equivalent to one $N/m^2$.

Sometimes knowing pressure is more useful than knowing force. For example, many surfaces will break or crack if the pressure on them is too great. A person with snowshoes can walk on top of snow, while a person in hiking boots will sink into the snow.

**COMPARE** How does the pressure from her snowshoes compare to the pressure from her boots?

## Calculating Pressure

### Sample Problem

**A winter hiker weighing 500 N is wearing snowshoes that cover an area of 0.2 $m^2$. What pressure does the hiker exert on the snow?**

*What do you know?* Area = 0.2 $m^2$, Force = 500 N

*What do you want to find out?* Pressure

*Write the formula:* $P = \frac{F}{A}$

*Substitute into the formula:* $P = \frac{500 \text{ N}}{0.2 \text{ m}^2}$

*Calculate and simplify:* $P = 2500 \frac{\text{N}}{\text{m}^2} = 2500 \text{ N/m}^2$

*Check that your units agree:* Unit is $N/m^2$.
Unit of pressure is Pa, which is also $N/m^2$.
Units agree.

*Answer:* $P = 2500$ Pa

### Practice the Math

1. If a winter hiker weighing 500 N is wearing boots that have an area of 0.075 $m^2$, how much pressure is exerted on the snow?
2. A pressure of 2000 Pa is exerted on a surface with an area of 20 $m^2$. What is the total force exerted on the surface?

## Pressure acts in all directions in fluids.

Explore how a fluid produces pressure.

Fluids are made of loosely connected particles that are too small to see. These particles are in constant, rapid motion. The motion is random, which means particles are equally likely to move in any direction. Particles collide with—or crash into—one another and into the walls of a container holding the fluid. The particles also collide with any objects in the fluid.

As particles collide with an object in the fluid, they apply a constant force to the surfaces of the object. This force produces a pressure against the surfaces that the particles come in contact with. A fluid contains many particles, each moving in a different direction, and the force from each particle can be exerted in any direction. Therefore, the pressure exerted by the fluid acts on an object from all directions.

The diver in the picture below experiences a constant pressure from the particles—or molecules—in the water. Water molecules are constantly hitting her body from all directions. The collisions on all parts of her body produce a net force on the surface of her body.

**CHECK YOUR READING** How does understanding particle motion help you understand fluid pressure?

### Pressure in Fluids

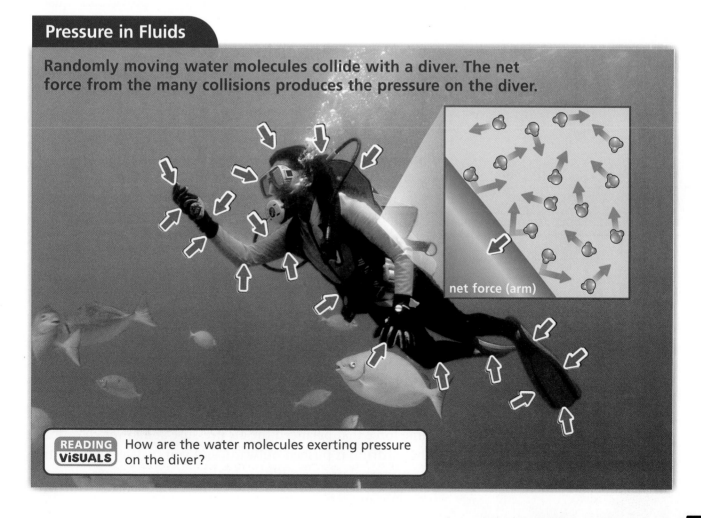

**Randomly moving water molecules collide with a diver. The net force from the many collisions produces the pressure on the diver.**

net force (arm)

**READING VISUALS** How are the water molecules exerting pressure on the diver?

## Pressure in fluids depends on depth.

The pressure that a fluid exerts depends on the density and the depth of the fluid. Imagine that you have a tall cylinder sitting on the palm of your hand. As you fill the cylinder with water, the force of the water's weight exerts more and more pressure on your hand. The force of the water's weight increases as you put in more water.

Suppose you had two identical cylinders of water sitting on your hand. The cylinders would push with twice the weight of a single cylinder, but the force would be spread over twice the area. Therefore, the pressure would still be the same. The pressure does not depend on the total volume of the fluid, only on the depth and density.

### Pressure in Air

A person at an altitude of 2000 meters experiences approximately 20 percent less atmospheric pressure than a person at sea level.

Although you do not notice the weight of air, air exerts pressure on you at all times. At sea level, air exerts a pressure on you equal to about 100,000 pascals. This pressure is called atmospheric pressure and is referred to as one atmosphere. At this pressure, every square centimeter of your body experiences a force of ten newtons (2.2 lb). You do not notice it pushing your body inward, however, because the materials in your body provide an equal outward pressure that balances the air pressure.

**Changing Elevation** Air has weight. The more air there is above you, the greater the weight of that air. As you climb a mountain, the column of air above you is shorter and weighs less, so the pressure of air on you at higher elevations is less than one atmosphere.

**Changing Density** The air at the top of a column presses down on the air below it. The farther down the column, the more weight there is above to press downward. Air at lower elevations is more compressed, and therefore denser, than air at higher elevations.

**Effects on Pressure** Pressure is exerted by individual molecules colliding with an object. In denser air, there are more molecules—and therefore more collisions. An increase in the number of collisions results in an increase in the force, and therefore pressure, exerted by the air.

As you travel up a mountain, the air pressure on you decreases. For a short time, the pressure on the inside surface of your eardrum may continue to push out with the same force that balanced the air pressure at a lower elevation. The eardrum is pushed outward, and you may feel pain until your internal pressure adjusts to the new air pressure.

## Pressure in Water

A deep-diving whale at 1000 meters below the surface experiences about 34 times more pressure than a turtle diving to a depth of 20 meters (65 ft).

Unlike air molecules, water molecules are already very close together. The density of water does not change very much with depth. However, the deeper you go underwater, the more water there is above you. The weight of that water above you produces the water pressure acting on your body. Just as air pressure increases at lower elevations, water pressure increases with greater water depth.

Water exerts more pressure on you than air does because water has a greater density than air. Therefore, the change in weight of the column of water above you as you dive is greater for each meter that you descend than it is in air. There is a greater difference in pressure if you dive ten meters farther down in the ocean than if you walked ten meters down a mountain. In fact, ten meters of water above you applies about as much pressure on you as the entire atmosphere does.

If you were to dive 1000 meters (3300 ft) below the surface of the ocean, the pressure would be nearly 100 times greater than pressure from the atmosphere. The force of this pressure would collapse your lungs unless you were protected by special deep-sea diving equipment. As scientists explore the ocean to greater depths, new underwater vehicles are designed that can withstand the increase in water pressure. Some whales, however, can dive to a depth of 1000 meters without being injured. As these whales dive to great depths, their lungs are almost completely collapsed by the pressure. However, the whales have adapted to the collapse—they store most of their oxygen intake in their muscles and blood instead of within their lungs.

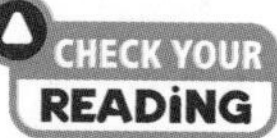


Why is water pressure greater than air pressure?

## 3.3 Review

### KEY CONCEPTS

1. How is pressure related to force and surface area?
2. Describe the way in which a fluid exerts pressure on an object immersed in it.
3. How does changing elevation affect air pressure? How does changing depth affect water pressure?

### CRITICAL THINKING

4. **Calculate** If a board with an area of 3 $m^2$ has a 12 N force exerted on it, what is the pressure on the board?
5. **Infer** What might cause a balloon blown up at a low altitude to burst if it is taken to a higher altitude?

### CHALLENGE

6. **Synthesize** During cold winters, ice can form on small lakes and ponds. Many people enjoy skating on the ice. Occasionally, a person skates on thin ice and breaks through it. Why do rescue workers lie flat on the ice instead of walking upright when reaching out to help rescue a skater?

# CHAPTER INVESTIGATION

## Pressure in Fluids

**OVERVIEW AND PURPOSE** When you put your hand under a faucet, you experience water pressure. Underwater explorers also experience water pressure. In this investigation you will

- change the depth and volume of a column of water
- determine what factors affect pressure

### Problem

Write It Up

What factors affect water pressure?

### Hypothesize

Write It Up

Write two hypotheses to explain what you expect to happen to the water pressure as you change the depth and volume of the water column. Your hypotheses (one for depth, one for volume) should take the form of "If . . . , then . . . , because . . ." statements.

### Procedure

1. Create a data table like the one shown on the sample notebook page.

2. Using a nail, poke a hole in the side of each bottle 4 cm from the bottom of the bottle.

3. Set up the materials as shown on the left. Put a ruler in the small bottle so that the lower numbers are at the bottom.

4. Put your finger over the hole so no water will squirt out. Add or remove water (by lifting your finger off the hole) so that the water level is exactly at the 12 cm mark.

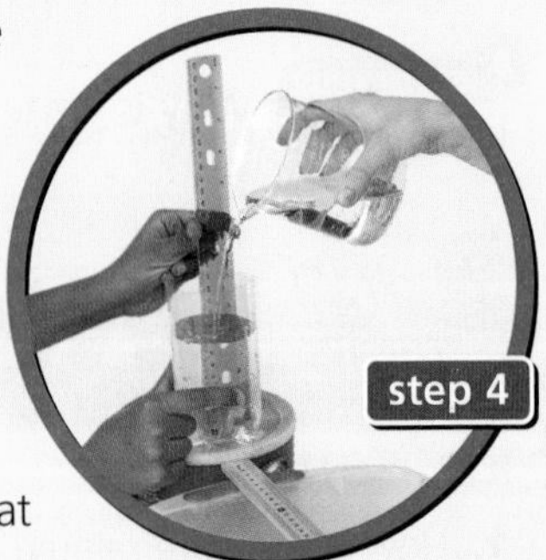

step 4

5. Release your finger from the hole, while your partner reads the exact mark where the water hits the meter stick. Cover the hole immediately after your partner reads the distance the water squirted. Record the distance on the line for this depth in your table.

**MATERIALS**
- nail
- 2 plastic bottles, small and large, with tops cut off
- ruler
- plastic container
- meter stick
- coffee can
- water

step 3

6 Add or remove water so that the water level is now exactly at the 11 cm mark. Repeat step 5.

7 Continue adding, removing, and squirting water at each whole centimeter mark until no more water squirts from the bottle.

8 Repeat steps 4–7 two more times for a total of three trials.

9 Repeat steps 4–8 using the large bottle.

## Observe and Analyze

1. **RECORD OBSERVATIONS** Be sure that your data table is complete.
2. **GRAPH** Construct a graph showing distance versus depth. Draw two curves, one for the small bottle and one for the large bottle. Use different colors for the two curves.
3. **IDENTIFY VARIABLES AND CONSTANTS** List the variables and constants for the experiment using the small bottle and the experiment using the large bottle.
4. **ANALYZE** Is the depth greater when the bottle is more full or more empty? When did the water squirt farther, when the bottle was more full or more empty?
5. **ANALYZE** Did the water squirt farther when you used the small or the large bottle?

## Conclude

1. **INTERPRET** Answer the question posed in the problem.
2. **ANALYZE** Examine your graph and compare your results with your hypotheses. Do your results support your hypotheses?
3. **INFER** How does depth affect pressure? How does volume affect pressure?
4. **IDENTIFY LIMITS** What possible limitations or errors did you experience or could you have experienced with this investigation?
5. **APPLY** Dams store water for irrigation, home use, and hydroelectric power. Explain why dams must be constructed so that they are much thicker at the bottom than at the top.
6. **APPLY** Have you ever dived to the bottom of a swimming pool to pick up a coin? Describe what you felt as you swam toward the bottom.

## INVESTIGATE Further

**CHALLENGE** Repeat the investigation using a liquid with a density that is quite different from water. Measure the distance the liquid travels, and graph the new data in a different color. Is there a difference? Why do you think there is or is not a difference in pressure between liquids of different densities?

Pressure in Fluids

Problem What factors affect water pressure?

Hypothesize

Observe and Analyze

Table 1. Distance Water Squirted with Small Bottle

| Depth of water small bottle (cm) | Trial 1 | Trial 2 | Trial 3 | Average |
|---|---|---|---|---|
| 12 | | | | |
| 11 | | | | |
| 10 | | | | |

Table 2. Distance Water Squirted with Large Bottle

| Depth of water large bottle (cm) | Trial 1 | Trial 2 | Trial 3 | Average |
|---|---|---|---|---|
| 12 | | | | |
| 11 | | | | |
| 10 | | | | |

Conclude

KEY CONCEPT

# Fluids can exert a force on objects.

**BEFORE, you learned**

- Pressure depends on force and area
- Pressure acts in all directions in fluids
- Density is mass divided by volume

**NOW, you will learn**

- How fluids apply forces to objects
- How the motion of a fluid affects the pressure it exerts
- How forces are transmitted through fluids

**VOCABULARY**

**buoyant force** p. 98
**Bernoulli's principle** p. 100
**Pascal's principle** p. 102

**EXPLORE Forces in Liquid**

### *How does water affect weight?*

**PROCEDURE**

1. Tie a piece of string to the middle of the pencil. Tie 4 paper clips to each end of the pencil as shown.
2. Move the middle string along the pencil until the paper clips are balanced and the pencil hangs flat.
3. While keeping the pencil balanced, slowly lower the paper clips on one end of the pencil into the water. Observe what happens.

**MATERIALS**

- 3 pieces of string
- pencil
- 8 paper clips
- cup full of water

**WHAT DO YOU THINK?**

- How did the water affect the balance between the two sets of paper clips?
- Did the water exert a force on the paper clips? Explain.

## Fluids can exert an upward force on objects.

If you drop an ice cube in air, it falls to the floor. If you drop the ice cube into water, it may sink a little at first, but the cube quickly rises upward until it floats. You know that gravity is pulling downward on the ice, even when it is in the water. If the ice cube is not sinking, there must be some force balancing gravity that is pushing upward on it.

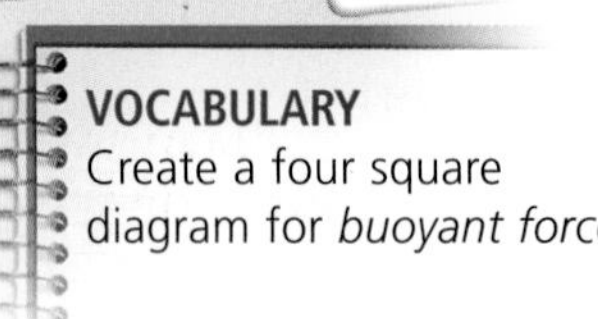

**VOCABULARY**
Create a four square diagram for *buoyant force.*

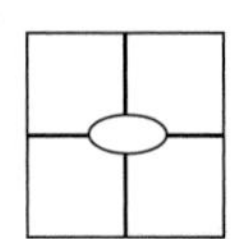

The upward force on objects in a fluid is called **buoyant force,** or buoyancy. Buoyancy is why ice floats in water. Because of buoyant force, objects seem lighter in water. For example, it is easier to lift a heavy rock in water than on land because the buoyant force pushes upward on the rock, reducing the net force you need to lift it.

## Buoyancy

The photograph on the right shows a balloon that has been pushed into a beaker of water. Remember that in a fluid, pressure increases with depth. This means that there is greater pressure acting on the bottom of the balloon than on the top of it. The pressure difference between the top and bottom of the balloon produces a net force that is pushing the balloon upward.

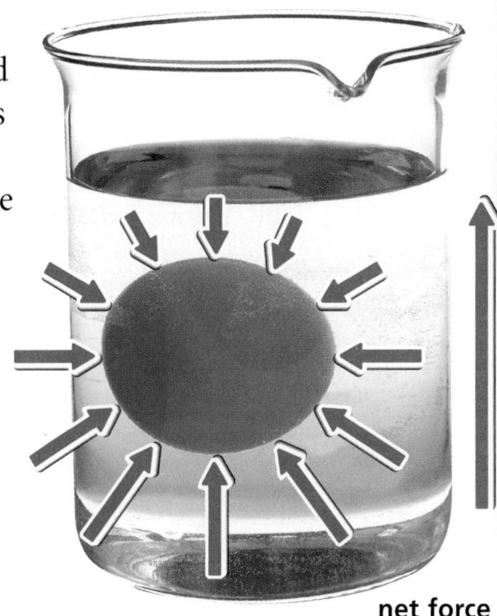


When you push a balloon underwater, the water level rises because the water and the balloon cannot be in the same place at the same time. The volume of the water has not changed, but some of the water has been displaced, or moved, by the balloon. The volume of the displaced water is equal to the volume of the balloon. The buoyant force on the balloon is equal to the weight of the displaced water. A deflated balloon would displace less water and would therefore have a smaller buoyant force on it.

**CHECK YOUR READING** Why does increasing the volume of an object increase the buoyant force on it when it is in a fluid?

## Density and Buoyancy

Whether or not an object floats in a fluid depends on the densities of both the object and the fluid. Density is a measure of the amount of matter packed into a unit volume. The density of an object is equal to its mass divided by its volume, and is commonly measured in grams per cubic centimeter ($g/cm^3$).

**READING TIP**

Remember that both air and water are fluids, and water has a greater density than air. Therefore, water has a greater buoyant force.

If an object is less dense than the fluid it is in, the fluid the object displaces can weigh more than the object. A wooden ball that is pushed underwater, as in the beaker below and on the left, rises to the top and floats. An object rising in a liquid has a buoyant force acting upon it that is greater than its own weight. If an object is floating in a liquid, the buoyant force is balancing the weight.

If the object is more dense than the fluid it is in, the object weighs more than the fluid it displaces. A glass marble placed in the beaker on the far right sinks to the bottom because glass is denser than water. The weight of the water the marble displaces is less than the weight of the marble. A sinking object has a weight that is greater than the buoyant force on it.

## The motion of a fluid affects its pressure.

The motion of a fluid affects the amount of pressure it exerts. A faster-moving fluid exerts less pressure as it flows over the surface of an object than a slower moving fluid. For example, wind blowing over a chimney top decreases the pressure at the top of the chimney. The faster air has less pressure than the slower-moving air in the fireplace. The increased pressure difference more effectively pulls the smoke from a fire out of the fireplace and up the chimney.

### Bernoulli's Principle

Bernoulli's principle, named after Daniel Bernoulli (buhr-NOO-lee), a Swiss mathematician who lived in the 1700s, describes the effects of fluid motion on pressure. In general, **Bernoulli's principle** says that an increase in the speed of the motion of a fluid decreases the pressure within the fluid. The faster a fluid moves, the less pressure it exerts on surfaces or openings it flows over.

What is the relationship between the speed of a fluid and the pressure that the fluid exerts?

## INVESTIGATE Bernoulli's Principle

### *How does the speed of air affect air pressure?*

**PROCEDURE**

1. Use the pen to mark off intervals of 1 cm along the length of one of the straws.
2. Put a drop of food coloring in the cup of water and stir it. Place the marked straw into the cup and hold it upright so that the water level in the straw is at one of the marks. The straw should not touch the bottom of the cup.
3. Position the second straw as shown. Blow across the open end of the marked straw. Observe the level of the water in the marked straw as you blow.
4. Blow harder and then softer. Observe the water level as you change the speed of the air.

**WHAT DO YOU THINK?**

- What happened to the water in the straw as you blew?
- How did the speed of the air relate to the changes you observed?

**CHALLENGE** What results would you expect if you blew over the top of a tube with a closed bottom instead of the straw? Explain.

**SKILL FOCUS**
Observing

**MATERIALS**
- pen
- ruler
- two clear straws
- clear plastic cup filled with water
- food coloring

**TIME**
15 minutes

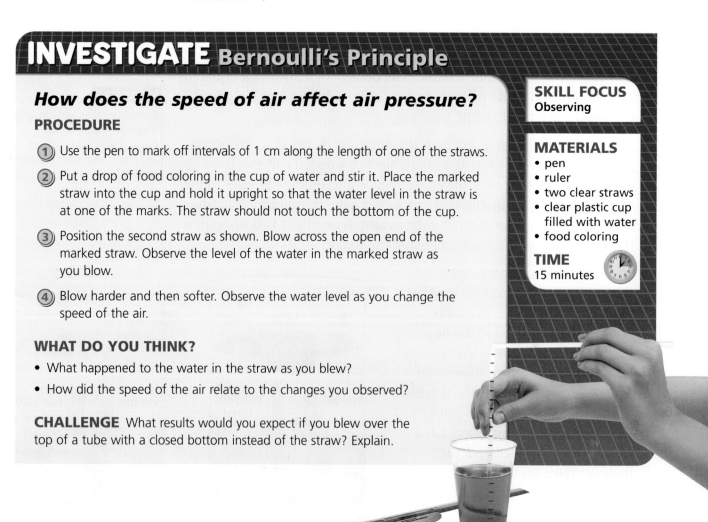

## Applying Bernoulli's Principle

Bernoulli's principle has many applications. One important application is used in airplanes. Airplane wings can be shaped to take advantage of Bernoulli's principle. Certain wing shapes cause the air flowing over the top of the wing to move faster than the air flowing under the wing. Such a design improves the lifting force on a flying airplane.

Many racecars, however, have a device on the rear of the car that has the reverse effect. The device is designed like an upside-down airplane wing. This shape increases the pressure on the top of the car. The car is pressed downward on the road, which increases friction between the tires and the road. With more friction, the car is less likely to skid as it goes around curves at high speeds.

A prairie-dog colony also shows Bernoulli's principle in action. The mounds that prairie dogs build over some entrances to their burrows help to keep the burrows well-ventilated.

1. Air closer to the ground tends to move at slower speeds than air higher up. The air over an entrance at ground level generally moves slower than the air over an entrance in a raised mound.
2. The increased speed of the air over a raised mound entrance decreases the pressure over that opening.
3. The greater air pressure over a ground-level entrance produces an unbalanced force that pushes air through the tunnels and out the higher mound entrance.

### Bernoulli's Principle in Nature

Bernoulli's principle explains why having two entrances at different heights helps ventilate a prairie-dog burrow.
1 Air moves more slowly near the ground.
2 The air over the raised entrance moves faster and has less pressure than the slower-moving air near the ground.
3 The pressure difference between the two entrances moves air through the tunnel.

## Forces can be transmitted through fluids.

Imagine you have a bottle full of water. You place the bottle cap on it, but you do not tighten the cap. You give the bottle a hard squeeze and the cap falls off. How was the force you put on the bottle transferred to the bottle cap?

### Pascal's Principle

In the 1600s Blaise Pascal (pa-SKAL), a French scientist for whom the unit of measure called the pascal was named, experimented with fluids in containers. One of his key discoveries is called Pascal's principle. **Pascal's principle** states that when an outside pressure is applied at any point to a fluid in a container, that pressure is transmitted throughout the fluid with equal strength.

You can use Pascal's principle to transmit a force through a fluid. Some car jacks lift cars using Pascal's principle. These jacks contain liquids that transmit and increase the force that you apply.

1. The part of the jack that moves down and pushes on the liquid is called a piston. As you push down on the piston, you increase the pressure on the liquid.
2. The increase in pressure is equal to your applied force divided by the area of the downward-pushing piston. This increase in pressure is transmitted throughout the liquid.

#### Pascal's Principle

**The pressure from the smaller piston is equal to the pressure pushing up the larger one. The large piston can exert more force because of its greater area.**

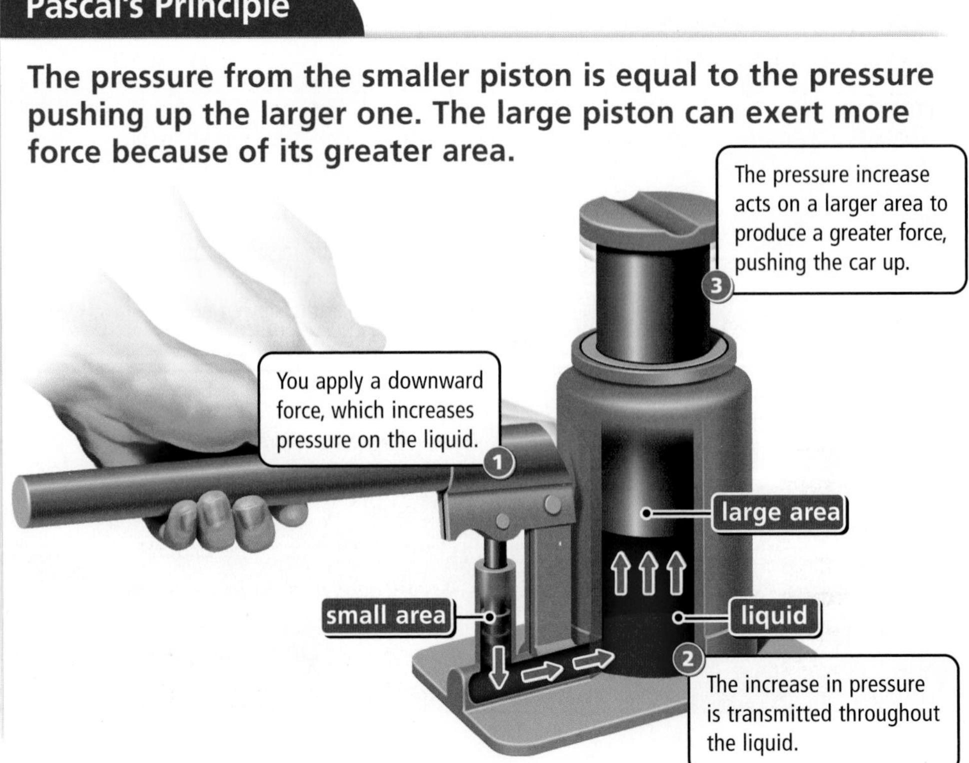
The pressure increase acts on a larger area to produce a greater force, pushing the car up.
3
You apply a downward force, which increases pressure on the liquid.
1
large area
small area
liquid
2
The increase in pressure is transmitted throughout the liquid.

3. The increased pressure pushes upward on another piston, which raises the car. This piston has a large area compared with the first piston, so the upward force is greater than the downward force. A large enough area produces the force needed to lift a car. However, the larger piston does not move upward as far as the smaller one moved downward.

Describe how pressure is transmitted through a fluid.

## Hydraulics

Machines that use liquids to transmit or increase a force are called hydraulic (hy-DRAW-lihk) machines. The advantage to using a liquid instead of a gas is that when you squeeze a liquid, its volume does not change much. The molecules in a liquid are so close together that it is hard to push the molecules any closer. Gas molecules, however, have a lot of space between them. If you apply pressure to a gas, you decrease its volume.

The hydraulic arm on the garbage truck lifts and empties trash cans.

Although hydraulic systems are used in large machines such as garbage trucks, research is being done on using hydraulics on a much smaller scale. Researchers are developing a storage chip similar to a computer chip that uses hydraulics rather than electronics. This chip uses pipes and pumps to move fluid into specific chambers on a rubber chip. Researchers hope that a hydraulic chip system will eventually allow scientists to use a single hand-held device to perform chemical experiments with over a thousand different liquids.

### KEY CONCEPTS

1. Why is there an upward force on objects in water?
2. How does changing the speed of a fluid affect its pressure?
3. If you push a cork into the neck of a bottle filled with air, what happens to the pressure inside the bottle?

### CRITICAL THINKING

4. **Infer** Ebony is a dark wood that has a density of 1.2 g/cm$^3$. Water has a density of 1.0 g/cm$^3$. Will a block of ebony float in water? Explain.
5. **Analyze** When you use a spray bottle, you force air over a small tube inside the bottle. Explain why the liquid inside the bottle comes out.

### CHALLENGE

6. **Synthesize** If you apply a force of 20 N downward on a car jack piston with an area of 2.5 cm$^2$, what force will be applied to the upward piston if it has an area of 400 cm$^2$? **Hint:** Remember that pressure equals force divided by area.

# Chapter Review

**Newton's laws apply to all forces.**

## KEY CONCEPTS SUMMARY

### 3.1 Gravity is a force exerted by masses.

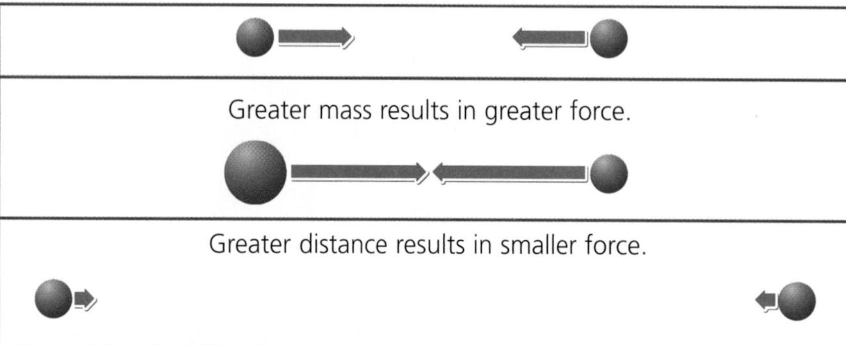

Greater mass results in greater force.
Greater distance results in smaller force.


**VOCABULARY**
**gravity** p. 77
**weight** p. 79
**orbit** p. 80

### 3.2 Friction is a force that opposes motion.

Frictional force depends on—

- types of surfaces
- motion of surfaces
- force pressing surfaces together

Air resistance is a type of friction.

**VOCABULARY**
**friction** p. 85
**fluid** p. 88
**air resistance** p. 89

### 3.3 Pressure depends on force and area.

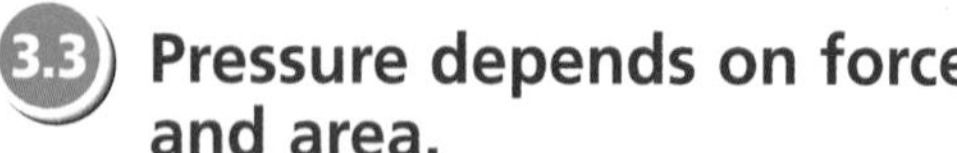

$$\text{Pressure} = \frac{\text{Force}}{\text{Area}}$$

Pressure in a fluid acts in all directions.

**VOCABULARY**
**pressure** p. 91
**pascal** p. 92

### 3.4 Fluids can exert a force on objects.

- Buoyant force is equal to the weight of the displaced fluid.
- A faster-moving fluid produces less pressure than a slower-moving one.
- Pressure is transmitted through fluids.

**VOCABULARY**
**buoyant force** p. 98
**Bernoulli's principle** p. 100
**Pascal's principle** p.102

## Reviewing Vocabulary

*Write a sentence describing the relationship between each pair of terms.*

1. gravity, weight
2. gravity, orbit
3. pressure, pascal
4. fluid, friction
5. density, buoyant force
6. fluid, Bernoulli's principle

## Reviewing Key Concepts

**Multiple Choice** *Choose the letter of the best answer.*

7. Which force keeps Venus in orbit around the Sun?
   - **a.** gravity
   - **b.** friction
   - **c.** hydraulic
   - **d.** buoyancy

8. You and a classmate are one meter apart. If you move farther away, how does the gravitational force between you and your classmate change?
   - **a.** It increases.
   - **b.** It decreases.
   - **c.** It stays the same.
   - **d.** It disappears.

9. You kick a ball on a level sidewalk. It rolls to a stop because
   - **a.** there is no force on the ball
   - **b.** gravity slows the ball down
   - **c.** air pressure is pushing down on the ball
   - **d.** friction slows the ball down

10. You push a chair at a constant velocity using a force of 5 N to overcome friction. You stop to rest, then push again. To start the chair moving again, you must use a force that is
    - **a.** greater than 5 N
    - **b.** equal to 5 N
    - **c.** greater than 0 N but less than 5 N
    - **d.** 0 N

11. How could you place an empty bottle on a table so that it produces the greatest amount of pressure on the table?

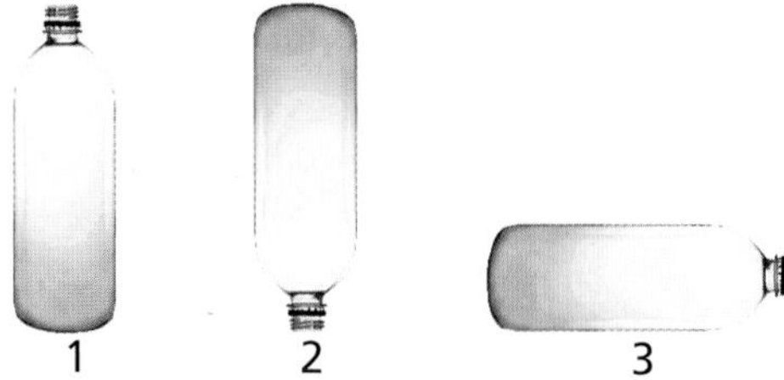


    - **a.** position 1
    - **b.** position 2
    - **c.** position 3
    - **d.** All positions produce the same pressure.

12. As you climb up a mountain, air pressure
    - **a.** increases
    - **b.** decreases
    - **c.** stays the same
    - **d.** changes unpredictably

13. If you squeeze a balloon in the middle, what happens to the air pressure inside the balloon?
    - **a.** It increases only in the middle.
    - **b.** It decreases only in the middle.
    - **c.** It increases throughout.
    - **d.** It decreases throughout.

**Short Answer** *Write a short answer to each question.*

14. How does the force of attraction between large masses compare with the force of attraction between small masses at the same distance?
15. Explain why a satellite in orbit around Earth does not crash into Earth.
16. You are pushing a dresser with drawers filled with clothing. What could you do to reduce the friction between the dresser and the floor?
17. Why is water pressure greater at a depth of 20 feet than it is at a depth of 10 feet?
18. If you blow over the top of a small strip of paper, the paper bends upward. Why?

## Thinking Critically

**19. APPLY** Explain why an iron boat can float in water, while an iron cube cannot.

**20. COMPARE** How does the friction between solid surfaces compare with the friction between a moving object and a fluid?

**21. APPLY** Explain why a block of wood gets warm when it is rubbed with sandpaper.

**22. PREDICT** The Moon's orbit is gradually increasing. Each year the Moon is about 3.8 cm farther from Earth than the year before. How does this change affect the force of gravity between Earth and the Moon?

**23. APPLY** The Moon has one-sixth the gravity of Earth. Why would it be easier to launch spacecraft into orbit around the Moon than around Earth?

*Use the photograph below to answer the next three questions.*

**24. APPLY** A skydiver jumps out of a plane. After he reaches terminal velocity, he opens his parachute. Draw a sketch showing the forces of air resistance and gravity on the skydiver after the parachute opens. Use a longer arrow for a greater force.

**25. SYNTHESIZE** Air is a fluid, which produces a small buoyant force on the skydiver. How does this buoyant force change after he opens his parachute? Why?

**26. INFER** The Moon has no atmosphere. Would it be safe to skydive on the Moon? Why or why not?

**27. INFER** When oil and water are mixed together, the two substances separate and the oil floats to the top. How does the density of oil compare with the density of water?

**28. COMPARE** Three flasks are filled with colored water as shown below. How does the water pressure at the bottom of each flask compare with the water pressure at the bottom of the other two?

## Using Math Skills in Science

*Complete the following calculations.*

**29.** How much force does a 10 kg marble exert on the ground?

**30.** A force of 50 N is applied on a piece of wood with an area of 0.5 $m^2$. What is the pressure on the wood?

## the BIG idea

**31. ANALYZE** Look again at the picture on pages 74–75. What forces are acting on the snowboarder? on the snow? Use Newton's laws to explain how these forces enable the snowboarder to move down the hill.

**32. SYNTHESIZE** Choose two concepts discussed in this chapter, and describe how Newton's laws relate to those concepts.

## UNIT PROJECTS

Check your schedule for your unit project. How are you doing? Be sure that you have placed data or notes from your research into your project folder.

# Standardized Test Practice

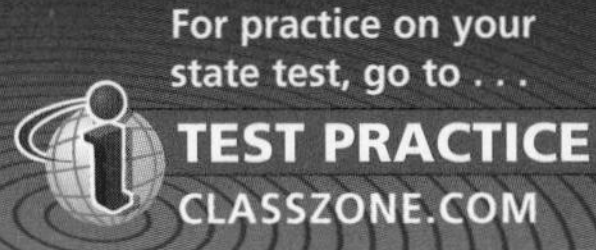


## Interpreting Diagrams

*Study the diagram and then answer the questions that follow.*

Bernoulli's principle states that an increase in the speed of the motion of a fluid decreases the pressure exerted by the fluid. The diagram below relates the movement of a curve ball in baseball to this principle. The ball is shown from above.

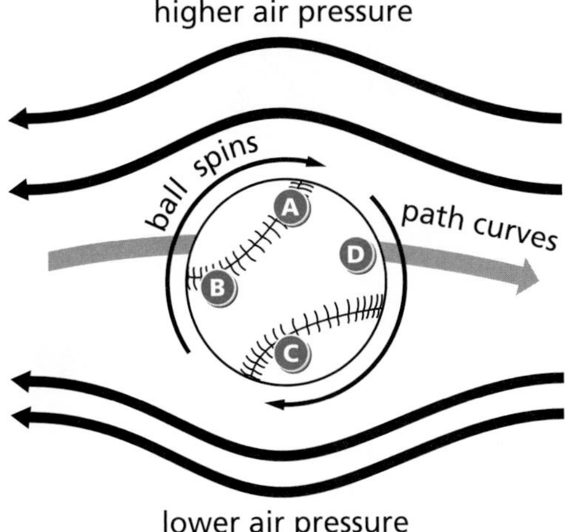


1. To which of these properties does Bernoulli's principle apply?
   a. air pressure
   b. temperature
   c. air resistance
   d. density

2. Where is the air moving fastest in the diagram?
   a. region A
   b. region B
   c. region C
   d. region D

3. Because the ball is spinning, the air on one side is moving faster than on the other side. This causes the ball to curve due to the
   a. air molecules moving slowly and evenly around the ball
   b. forward motion of the ball
   c. difference in air pressure on the ball
   d. changing air temperature around the ball

4. If the baseball were spinning as it moved forward underwater, instead of through the air, how would the pressure of the fluid act on the ball?
   a. The water pressure would be the same on all sides.
   b. The water pressure would vary as air pressure does.
   c. The water pressure would be greatest on the side where air pressure was least.
   d. The water pressure would prevent the ball from spinning.

## Extended Response

*Answer the two questions below in detail. Include some of the terms from the word box. Underline each term you use in your answer.*

| acceleration | air resistance | density |
|---|---|---|
| fluid | friction | gravity |
| mass | pressure | velocity |

5. If a feather and a bowling ball are dropped from the same height, will they fall at the same rate? Explain.

6. A balloon filled with helium or hot air can float in the atmosphere. A balloon filled with air from your lungs falls to the ground when it is released. Why do these balloons behave differently?

# TIMELINES in Science

## UNDERSTANDING FORCES

In ancient times, people thought that an object would not move unless it was pushed. Scientists came up with ingenious ways to explain how objects like arrows stayed in motion. Over time, they came to understand that all motion could be described by three basic laws. Modern achievements such as suspension bridges and space exploration are possible because of the experiments with motion and forces performed by scientists and philosophers over hundreds of years.

This timeline shows just a few of the many steps on the path toward understanding forces. Notice how scientists used the observations and ideas of previous thinkers as a springboard for developing new theories. The boxes below the timeline show how technology has led to new insights and to applications of those ideas.

350 B.C.

*Aristotle Discusses Motion*

The Greek philosopher Aristotle states that the natural condition of an object is to be at rest. A force is necessary to keep the object in motion. The greater the force, the faster the object moves.

EVENTS

400 B.C. 350 B.C. 300 B.C.

APPLICATIONS AND TECHNOLOGY

### TECHNOLOGY

**Catapulting into History**

As early as 400 B.C., armies were using objects in motion to do work. Catapults, or machines for hurling stones and spears, were used as military weapons. Five hundred years later, the Roman army used catapults mounted on wheels. In the Middle Ages, young trees were sometimes bent back, loaded with an object, and then released like a large slingshot. Today catapult technology is used to launch airplanes from aircraft carriers. A piston powered by steam propels the plane along the deck of the aircraft carrier until it reaches takeoff speed.

**250 B.C.**

*Levers and Buoyancy Explained*

The Greek inventor Archimedes uses a mathematical equation to explain how a small weight can balance a much larger weight near a lever's fulcrum. He also explains buoyancy, which provides a way of measuring volume.

**A.D. 1121**

*Force Acting on Objects Described*

Persian astronomer al-Khazini asserts that a force acts on all objects to pull them toward the center of Earth. This force varies, he says, depending on whether the object moves through air, water, or another medium. His careful notes and drawings illustrate these principles.

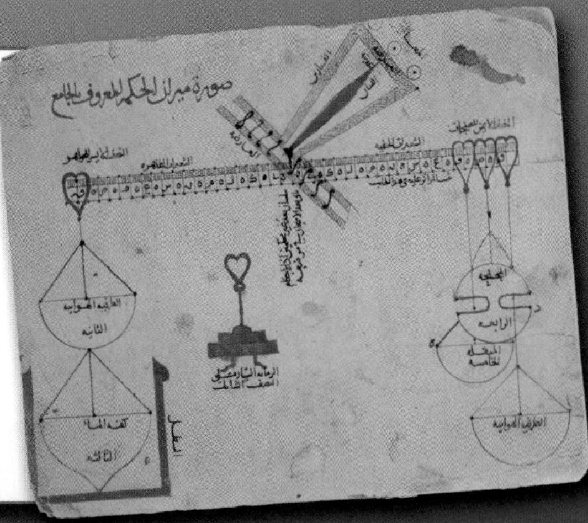

**1150**

*Perpetual-Motion Machine Described*

Indian mathematician and physicist Bhaskara describes a wheel that uses closed containers of liquid to turn forever without stopping. If it worked, his idea would promise an unending source of power that does not rely on an external source.

250 B.C. | A.D. 1100 | 1150 | 1200

## APPLICATION

### The First Steam-Powered Engine

In the first century A.D., Hero of Alexandria, a Greek inventor, created the first known steam engine, called the aeolipile. It was a hollow ball with two cylinders jutting out in opposite directions. The ball was suspended above a kettle that was filled with water and placed over a fire. As the water boiled, steam caused the ball to spin. The Greeks never used this device for work. In 1690, Sir Isaac Newton formulated the principle of the aeolipile in scientific terms in his third law of motion. A steam engine designed for work was built in 1698. The aeolipile is the earliest version of steam-powered pumps, steam locomotives, jet engines, and rockets.

1638

### *Objects Need No Force to Keep Moving*

Italian astronomer Galileo Galilei says that an object's natural state is either in constant motion or at rest. Having observed the motion of objects on ramps, he concludes that an object in motion will slow down or speed up only if a force is exerted on it. He also claims that all objects dropped near the surface of Earth fall with the same acceleration due to the force of gravity.

1494

### *Perpetual-Motion Machine Impossible*

Italian painter and engineer Leonardo da Vinci proves that it is impossible to build a perpetual-motion machine that works. He states that the force of friction keeps a wheel from turning forever without more force being applied.

1687

### *An Object's Motion Can Be Predicted*

English scientist Sir Isaac Newton publishes his three laws of motion, which use Galileo's ideas as a foundation. He concludes that Earth exerts a gravitational force on objects on its surface and that Earth's gravity keeps the Moon in orbit.

1500 1550 1600 1650 1700 1750 1800

## APPLICATION

### A New and Improved Steam Engine

Scottish scientist James Watt designed steam engines that were much more efficient, and much smaller, than older models. About 500 of Watt's engines were in use by 1800. His pump engines drew water out of coal mines, and his rotating engines were used in factories and cotton mills. Watt's steam engines opened the way to the Industrial Revolution. They were used in major industries such as textile manufacturing, railroad transportation, and mining. Watt's steam technology also opened up new areas of research in heat, kinetic energy, and motion.

**1919**

*Gravity Bends Light*

A solar eclipse confirms German-American physicist Albert Einstein's modification of Newton's laws. Einstein's theory states that the path of a light beam will be affected by nearby massive objects. During the eclipse, the stars appear to shift slightly away from one another because their light has been bent by the Sun's gravity.

**2001**

*Supercomputers Model Strong Force*

Scientists have been using supercomputers to model the force that holds particles in the nucleus of an atom together. This force, called the strong force, cannot be measured directly in the same way that gravity and other forces can. Instead, computer models allow scientists to make predictions that are then compared with experimental results.

**RESOURCE CENTER**
CLASSZONE.COM

Get current research on force and motion.

1850 1900 1950 2000

## TECHNOLOGY

### Science Propels Exploration of Outer Space

An increased understanding of forces made space exploration possible. In 1926 American scientist Robert H. Goddard constructed and tested the first liquid-propelled rocket. A replica of Goddard's rocket can be seen at the National Air and Space Museum in Washington, D.C. In 1929 Goddard launched a rocket that carried the first scientific payload, a barometer and a camera.

Many later achievements—including the 1969 walk on the Moon—are a direct result of Goddard's trail-blazing space research.

## INTO THE FUTURE

Since ancient times, scientists and philosophers have tried to explain how forces move objects. We now know that the laws of gravity and motion extend beyond Earth. Engineers have designed powerful spacecraft that can carry robots—and eventually people—to Mars and beyond. Rockets using new technology travel farther on less fuel than liquid-fueled rockets do.

Space travel and related research will continue to unravel the mysteries of forces in the universe. For example, recent observations of outer space provide evidence of an unidentified force causing the universe to expand rapidly. As people venture beyond Earth, we may learn new and unexpected things about the forces we have come to understand so far. The timeline shown here is just the beginning of our knowledge of forces.

## ACTIVITIES

### Reliving History

Bhaskara's design for a perpetual-motion machine involved a wheel with containers of mercury around the rim. As the wheel turned, the mercury would move in such a way that the wheel would always be heavier on one side—and stay in motion. Now we know that this theory goes against the laws of physics. Observe a wheel, a pendulum, or a swing. Think about why it cannot stay in motion forever.

### Writing About Science

Suppose you won a trip to outer space. Write a letter accepting or refusing the prize. Give your reasons.

# CHAPTER 4 Work and Energy

## the BIG idea

**Energy is transferred when a force moves an object.**

## Key Concepts

SECTION

**4.1 Work is the use of force to move an object.**
Learn about the relationship between force and work.

SECTION

**4.2 Energy is transferred when work is done.**
Learn how energy is related to work.

SECTION

**4.3 Power is the rate at which work is done.**
Learn to calculate power from work and energy.

***Which takes more work, lifting a box or holding a box? Why?***

**Internet Preview**

CLASSZONE.COM

Chapter 4 online resources: Content Review, Simulation, Visualization, two Resource Centers, Math Tutorial, Test Practice

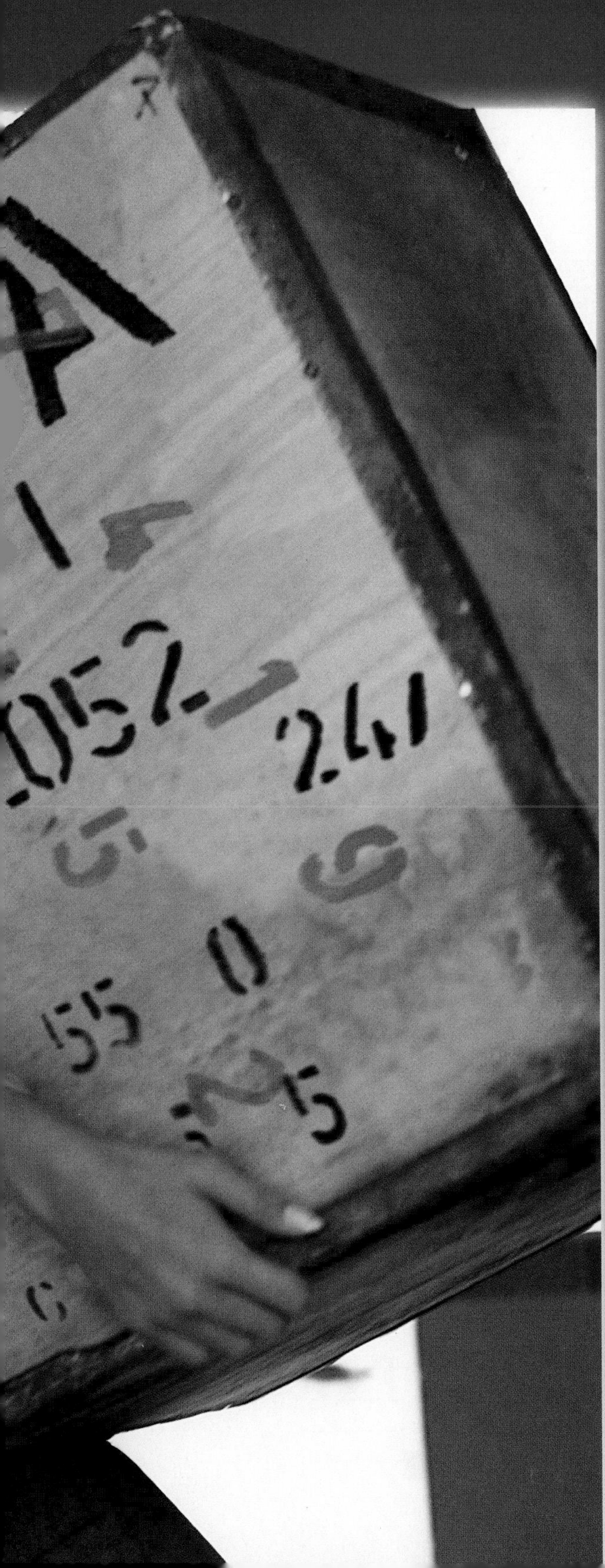

# EXPLORE the BIG idea

## Bouncing Ball

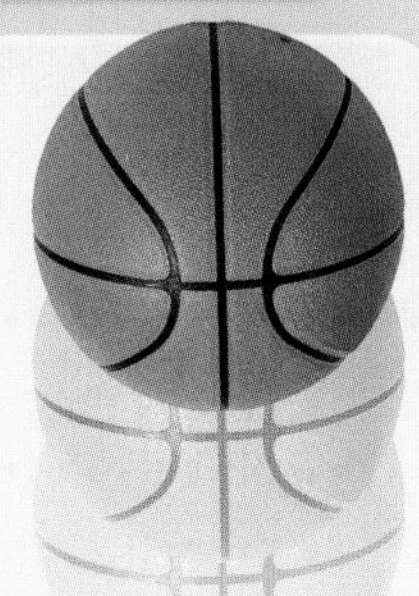

Drop a large ball on a hard, flat floor. Let it bounce several times. Notice the height the ball reaches after each bounce.

**Observe and Think**
How did the height change? Why do you think this happens? Sketch the path of the ball through several bounces.

## Power Climbing

Walk up a flight of stairs wearing a backpack. Run up the same flight of stairs wearing the backpack.

**Observe and Think**
Compare and contrast both trips up the stairs. Which one took greater effort? Did you apply the same force against gravity each time?

## Internet Activity: Work

Go to **ClassZone.com** to simulate lifting weights of different masses. Determine how much work is done in lifting each weight by watching your progress on a work meter.

**Observe and Think**
Do you think more work will be done if the weights are lifted higher?

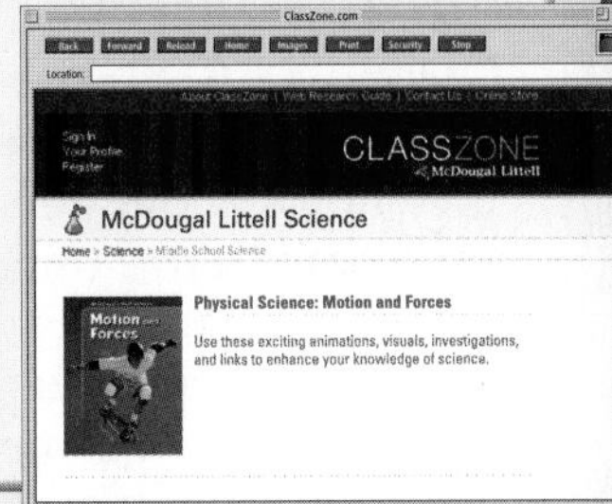

Potential and Kinetic Energy **Code: MDL007**

CHAPTER 4

# Getting Ready to Learn

## CONCEPT REVIEW

- Forces change the motion of objects in predictable ways.
- Velocity is a measure of the speed and direction of an object.
- An unbalanced force produces acceleration.

## VOCABULARY REVIEW

**velocity** p. 22
**force** p. 41

*See Glossary for definitions.*

**energy, mass**

**CONTENT REVIEW**
CLASSZONE.COM
Review concepts and vocabulary.

## TAKING NOTES

### MAIN IDEA WEB

Write each new blue heading in a box. Then write notes in boxes around it that give important terms and details about that blue heading.

### SCIENCE NOTEBOOK

Work is the use of force to move an object.

Work = Force · distance

Force is necessary to do work.

Joule is the unit for measuring work.

Work depends on force and distance.

### CHOOSE YOUR OWN STRATEGY

Take notes about new vocabulary terms using one or more of the strategies from earlier chapters—**description wheel, magnet words,** or **four square.** Feel free to mix and match the strategies or use a different strategy.

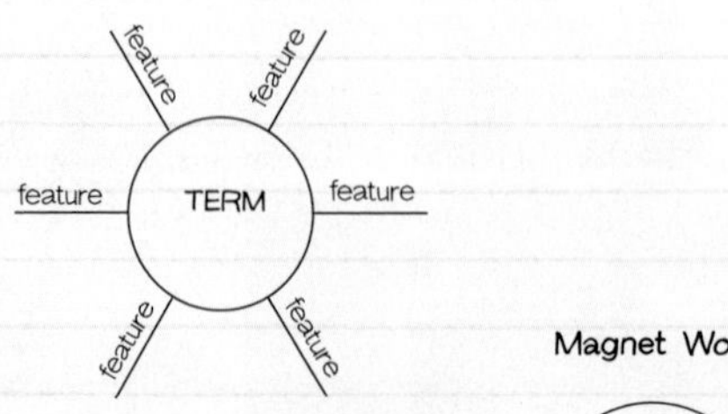


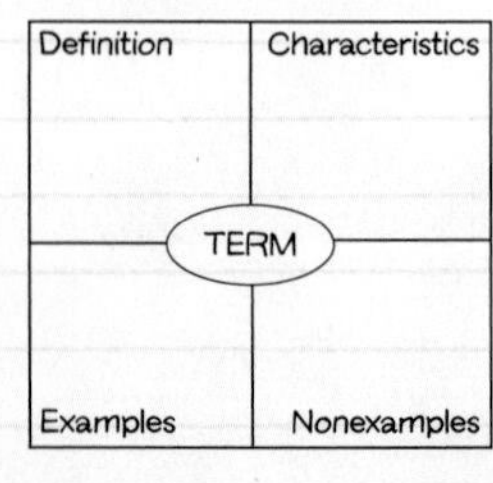


Magnet Word

TERM

related terms

related ideas

See the Note-Taking Handbook on pages R45–R51.

KEY CONCEPT

# Work is the use of force to move an object.

**BEFORE, you learned**

- An unbalanced force produces acceleration
- Weight is measured in newtons

**NOW, you will learn**

- How force and work are related
- How moving objects do work

**VOCABULARY**

**work** p. 115
**joule** p. 117

**EXPLORE Work**

### *How do you work?*

**PROCEDURE**

1. Lift a book from the floor to your desktop. Try to move the book at a constant speed.
2. Now lift the book again, but stop about halfway up and hold the book still for about 30 seconds. Then continue lifting the book to the desktop.

**WHAT DO YOU THINK?**

- Do you think you did more work the first time you lifted the book or the second time you lifted the book?
- What do you think *work* means?

**MATERIALS**

book

## Force is necessary to do work.

What comes to mind when you think of work? Most people say they are working when they do anything that requires a physical or mental effort. But in physical science, **work** is the use of force to move an object some distance. In scientific terms, you do work only when you exert a force on an object and move it. According to this definition of work, reading this page is not doing work. Turning the page, however, would be work because you are lifting the page.

Solving a math problem in your head is not doing work. Writing the answer is work because you are moving the pencil across the paper. If you want to do work, you have to use force to move something.

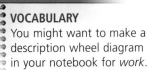

**VOCABULARY**
You might want to make a description wheel diagram in your notebook for *work*.

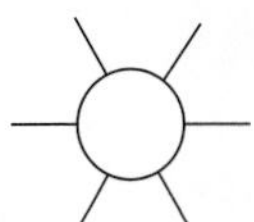

How does the scientific definition of work differ from the familiar definition?

RESOURCE CENTER
CLASSZONE.COM
Learn more about work.

## Force, Motion, and Work

Work is done only when an object that is being pushed or pulled actually moves. If you lift a book, you exert a force and do work. What if you simply hold the book out in front of you? No matter how tired your muscles may become from holding the book still, you are not doing work unless you move the book.

The work done by a force is related to the size of the force and the distance over which the force is applied. How much work does it take to push a grocery cart down an aisle? The answer depends on how hard you push the cart and the length of the aisle. If you use the same amount of force, you do more work pushing a cart down a long aisle than a short aisle.

Work is done only by the part of the applied force that acts in the same direction as the motion of an object. Suppose you need to pull a heavy suitcase on wheels. You pull the handle up at an angle as you pull the suitcase forward. Only the part of the force pulling the suitcase forward is doing work. The force with which you pull upward on the handle is not doing work because the suitcase is not moving upward—unless you are going uphill.

CHECK YOUR READING Give two examples of when you are applying a force but not doing work.

### Work

**Work is done by force that acts in the same direction as the motion of an object.**

**All of the Applied Force Does Work**

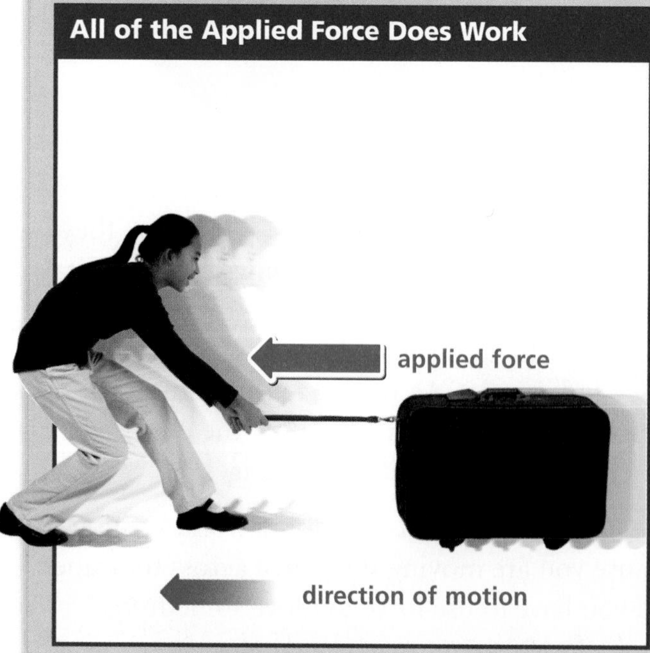


**Part of the Applied Force Does Work**

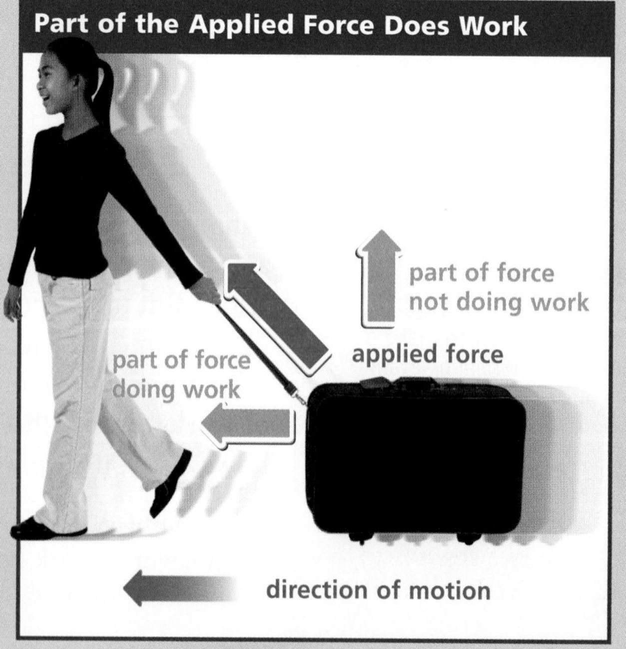


READING VISUALS How does changing the direction of the applied force change the amount of the force that is doing work?

## Calculating Work

Work is a measure of how much force is applied over a certain distance. You can calculate the work a force does if you know the size of the force applied to an object and the distance over which the force acts. The distance involved is the distance the object moved in the direction of that force. The calculation for work is shown in the following formula:

$$\textbf{Work} = \textbf{Force} \cdot \textbf{distance}$$
$$W = Fd$$

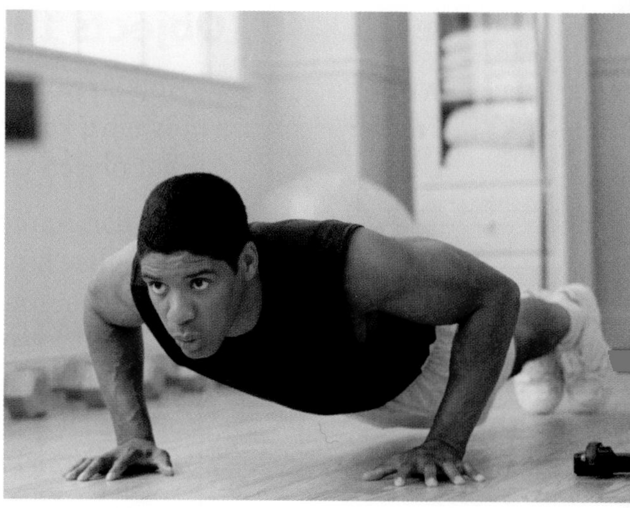

This man is doing work when he applies force to lift his body.

You read in previous chapters that you can measure force in newtons. You also know that you can measure distance in meters. When you multiply a force in newtons times a distance in meters, the product is a measurement called the newton-meter (N•m), or the **joule** (jool).

The joule (J) is the standard unit used to measure work. One joule of work is done when a force of one newton moves an object one meter. To get an idea of how much a joule of work is, lift an apple (which weighs about one newton) from your foot to your waist (about one meter).

Use the formula for work to solve the problem below.

### *Calculating Work*

**Sample Problem**

**How much work is done if a person lifts a barbell weighing 450 N to a height of 2 m?**

| | |
|---|---|
| ***What do you know?*** | force needed to lift = 450 N, distance = 2 m |
| ***What do you want to find out?*** | Work |
| ***Write the formula:*** | $W = Fd$ |
| ***Substitute into the formula:*** | $W$ = 450 N • 2 m |
| ***Calculate and simplify:*** | $W$ = 900 N•m |
| ***Check that your units agree:*** | Unit is newton-meter (N•m).<br>Unit of work is joule, which is N•m.<br>Units agree. |
| ***Answer:*** | $W$ = 900 J |

**Practice the Math**

1. If you push a cart with a force of 70 N for 2 m, how much work is done?
2. If you did 200 J of work pushing a box with a force of 40 N, how far did you push the box?

**REMINDER**

You know that $W = Fd$. You can manipulate the formula to find force or distance.
$d = \frac{W}{F}$ and $F = \frac{W}{d}$

**MAIN IDEA WEB**
Remember to organize your notes in a web as you read.

## Objects that are moving can do work.

You do work when you pick up your books, hit a baseball, swim a lap, or tap a keyboard. These examples show that you do work on objects, but objects can also do work.

For example, in a bowling alley, the bowling balls do work on the pins they hit. Outdoors, the moving air particles in a gust of wind do work that lifts a leaf off the ground. Moving water, such as the water in a river, also does work. If the windblown leaf lands in the water, it might be carried downstream by the current. As the leaf travels downstream, it might go over the edge of a waterfall. In that case, the gravitational force of Earth would pull the leaf and water down.

You can say that an object or person does work on an object, or that the force the object or person is exerting does work. For example, you could say that Earth (an object) does work on the falling water, or that gravity (a force) does work on the water.

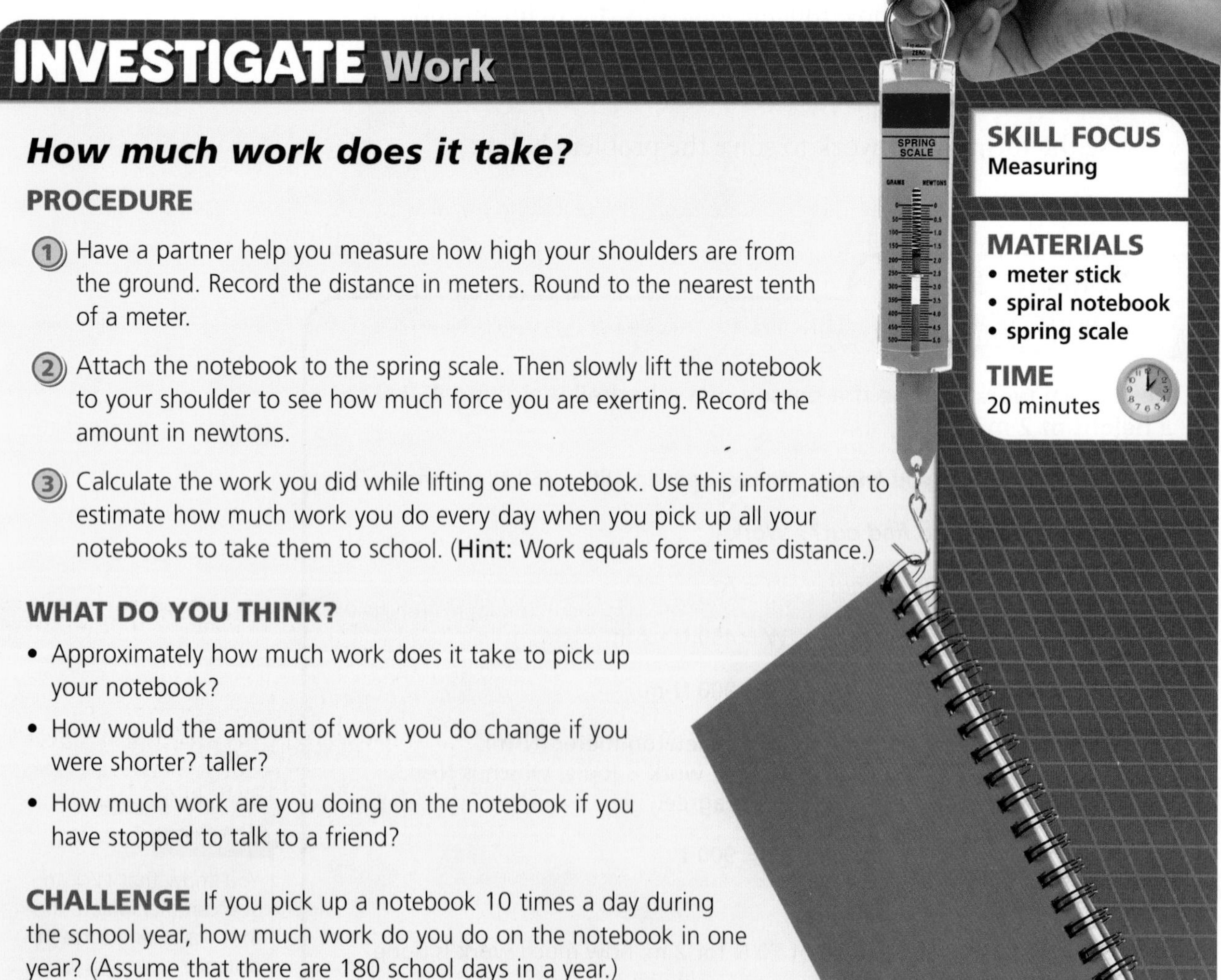


## INVESTIGATE Work

### *How much work does it take?*

**SKILL FOCUS**
Measuring

**MATERIALS**
- meter stick
- spiral notebook
- spring scale

**TIME**
20 minutes

**PROCEDURE**

1. Have a partner help you measure how high your shoulders are from the ground. Record the distance in meters. Round to the nearest tenth of a meter.
2. Attach the notebook to the spring scale. Then slowly lift the notebook to your shoulder to see how much force you are exerting. Record the amount in newtons.
3. Calculate the work you did while lifting one notebook. Use this information to estimate how much work you do every day when you pick up all your notebooks to take them to school. (**Hint:** Work equals force times distance.)

**WHAT DO YOU THINK?**

- Approximately how much work does it take to pick up your notebook?
- How would the amount of work you do change if you were shorter? taller?
- How much work are you doing on the notebook if you have stopped to talk to a friend?

**CHALLENGE** If you pick up a notebook 10 times a day during the school year, how much work do you do on the notebook in one year? (Assume that there are 180 school days in a year.)

APPLY How could you increase the work done by this water wheel?

Throughout history, people have taken advantage of the capability of objects in motion to do work. Many early cultures built machines such as water wheels to use the force exerted by falling water, and windmills to use the force exerted by moving air. In a water wheel like the one in the photograph, gravity does work on the water. As the water falls, it also can do work on any object that is put in its path. Falling water can turn a water wheel or the turbine of an electric generator.

The water wheel shown above uses the work done by water to turn gears that run a mill and grind grain. In the same way, windmills take advantage of the force of moving air particles. The wind causes the sails of a windmill to turn. The turning sails do work to run machinery or an irrigation system.

CHECK YOUR READING Describe how a water wheel does work.

# 4.1 Review

## KEY CONCEPTS

1. If you push very hard on an object but it does not move, have you done work? Explain.
2. What two factors do you need to know to calculate how much work was done in any situation?
3. Was work done on a book that fell from a desk to the floor? If so, what force was involved?

## CRITICAL THINKING

4. **Synthesize** Work is done on a ball when a soccer player kicks it. Is the player still doing work on the ball as it rolls across the ground? Explain.
5. **Calculate** Tina lifted a box 0.5 m. The box weighed 25 N. How much work did Tina do on the box?

## CHALLENGE

6. **Analyze** Ben and Andy each pushed an empty grocery cart. Ben used twice the force, but they both did the same amount of work. Explain.

MATH TUTORIAL
CLASSZONE.COM
Click on Math Tutorial for more help with finding the mean.

SKILL: WORKING WITH AVERAGES

# Eliminating Extreme Values

A value that is far from most others in a set of data is called an outlier. Outliers make it difficult to find a value that might be considered average. Extremely high or extremely low values can throw off the mean. That is why the highest and lowest figures are ignored in some situations.

## Example

The data set below shows the work an escalator does to move 8 people of different weights 5 meters. The work was calculated by multiplying the force needed to move each person by a distance of 5 meters.

4850 J 1600 J 3400 J 2750 J
2950 J 1750 J 3350 J 3800 J

**The mean amount of work done is 3056 J.**

**(1)** To calculate an adjusted mean, begin by identifying a high outlier in the data set.

High outlier: 4850

**(2)** Discard this value and find the new mean.

1600 J + 3400 J + 2750 J + 2950 J + 1750 J + 3350 J + 3800 J = 19,600 J

$$\text{Mean} = \frac{19{,}600\ \text{J}}{7} = 2800\ \text{J}$$

**ANSWER** The mean amount of work done for this new data set is 2800 J.

**Answer the following questions.**

**1.** After ignoring the high outlier in the data set, does this new mean show a more typical level of work for the data set? Why or why not?

**2.** Do you think the lowest value in the data set is an outlier? Remove it and calculate the new average. How did this affect the results?

**3.** Suppose the heaviest person in the original data set were replaced by a person weighing the same as the lightest person. What would be the new mean for the data set?

**CHALLENGE** The median of a data set is the middle value when the values are written in numerical order. Find the median of the adjusted data set (without the high outlier). Compare it with the original and adjusted means. Why do you think it is closer to one than the other?

KEY CONCEPT

# Energy is transferred when work is done.

**BEFORE, you learned**

- Work is the use of force to move an object
- Work can be calculated

**NOW, you will learn**

- How work and energy are related
- How to calculate mechanical, kinetic, and potential energy
- What the conservation of energy means

**VOCABULARY**

**potential energy** p. 122
**kinetic energy** p. 122
**mechanical energy** p. 125
**conservation of energy** p. 126

THINK ABOUT

### *How is energy transferred?*

School carnivals sometimes include dunk tanks. The goal is to hit a target with a ball, causing a person sitting over a tank of water to fall into the water. You do work on the ball as you throw with your arm. If your aim is good, the ball does work on the target. How do you transfer your energy to the ball?

## Work transfers energy.

**MAIN IDEA WEB**
Remember to add boxes to your main idea web as you read.

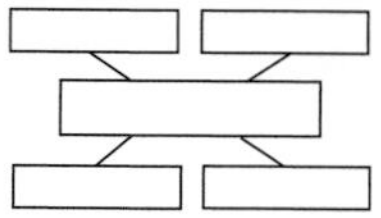

When you change the position and speed of the ball in the carnival game, you transfer energy to the ball. Energy is the ability of a person or an object to do work or to cause a change. When you do work on an object, some of your energy is transferred to the object. You can think of work as the transfer of energy. In fact, both work and energy are measured in the same unit, the joule.

The man in the photograph above converts one form of energy into another form when he uses his muscles to toss the ball. You can think of the man and the ball as a system, or a group of objects that affect one another. Energy can be transferred from the man to the ball, but the total amount of energy in the system does not change.

How are work and energy related?

## Work changes potential and kinetic energy.

When you throw a ball, you transfer energy to it and it moves. By doing work on the ball, you can give it **kinetic energy** (kuh-NEHT-ihk), which is the energy of motion. Any moving object has some kinetic energy. The faster an object moves, the more kinetic energy it has.

READING TIP

The word *potential* comes from the Latin word *potentia*, which means "power." The word *kinetic* comes from the Greek word *kinetos,* which means "moving."

When you do work to lift a ball from the ground, you give the ball a different type of energy, called potential energy. **Potential energy** is stored energy, or the energy an object has due to its position or its shape. The ball's position in your hand above the ground means that it has the potential to fall to the ground. The higher you lift the ball, the more work you do, and the more potential energy the ball has.

You can also give some objects potential energy by changing their shape. For example, if you are holding a spring, you can do work on the spring by squeezing it. After you do the work, the spring has potential energy because it is compressed. This type of potential energy is called elastic potential energy. Just as position gives the spring the potential to fall, compression gives the spring the potential to expand.

### Potential and Kinetic Energy

The boy has potential energy based on his position because gravity will pull him back down.

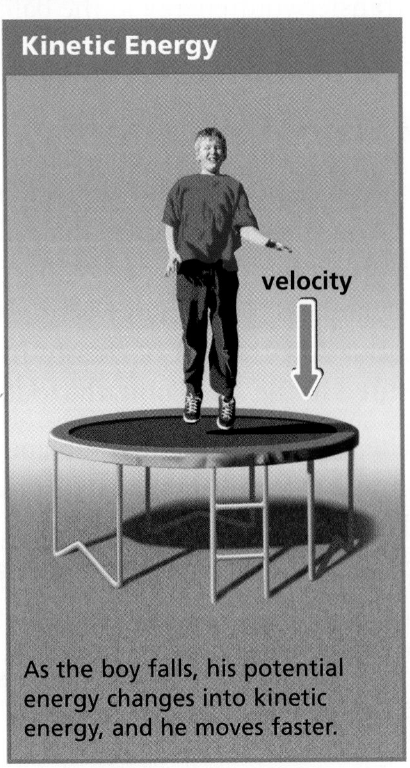


As the boy falls, his potential energy changes into kinetic energy, and he moves faster.

The trampoline has potential energy because it is stretched.

## Calculating Gravitational Potential Energy

Potential energy caused by gravity is called gravitational potential energy. Scientists must take gravitational potential energy into account when launching a spacecraft. Designers of roller coasters must make sure that roller-coaster cars have enough potential energy at the top of a hill to reach the top of the next hill. You can use the following formula to calculate the gravitational potential energy of an object:

**Gravitational Potential Energy = mass · gravitational acceleration · height**

$$GPE = mgh$$

Recall that $g$ is the acceleration due to Earth's gravity. It is equal to 9.8 $m/s^2$ at Earth's surface.

The diver in the photograph below has given herself gravitational potential energy by climbing to the diving board. If you know her mass and the height of the board, you can calculate her potential energy.

### *Calculating Potential Energy*

**Sample Problem**

**What is the gravitational potential energy of a girl who has a mass of 40 kg and is standing on the edge of a diving board that is 5 m above the water?**

*What do you know?* mass = 40 kg, gravitational acceleration = 9.8 $m/s^2$, height = 5 m

*What do you want to find out?* Gravitational Potential Energy

*Write the formula:* $GPE = mgh$

*Substitute into the formula:* $GPE = 40 \text{ kg} \cdot 9.8 \text{ m/s}^2 \cdot 5 \text{ m}$

*Calculate and simplify:* $GPE = 1960 \text{ kg m}^2/\text{s}^2$

*Check that your units agree:* $\text{kg m}^2/\text{s}^2 = \text{kg} \cdot \text{m/s}^2 \cdot \text{m} = \text{N}\cdot\text{m} = \text{J}$

Unit of energy is J. Units agree.

*Answer:* $GPE = 1960$ J

**Practice the Math**

1. An apple with a mass of 0.1 kg is attached to a branch of an apple tree 4 m from the ground. How much gravitational potential energy does the apple have?
2. If you lift a 2 kg box of toys to the top shelf of a closet, which is 3 m high, how much gravitational potential energy will the box of toys have?

**REMINDER**

A newton (N) is a kg · $m/s^2$, and a joule (J) is a N·m.

The formula for gravitational potential energy is similar to the formula for work ($W = Fd$). The formula for GPE also has a force ($mg$) multiplied by a distance ($h$). To understand why $mg$ is a force, remember two things: force equals mass times acceleration, and $g$ is the acceleration due to Earth's gravity.

## Calculating Kinetic Energy

The girl on the swing at left has kinetic energy. To find out how much kinetic energy she has at the bottom of the swing's arc, you must know her mass and her velocity. Kinetic energy can be calculated using the following formula:

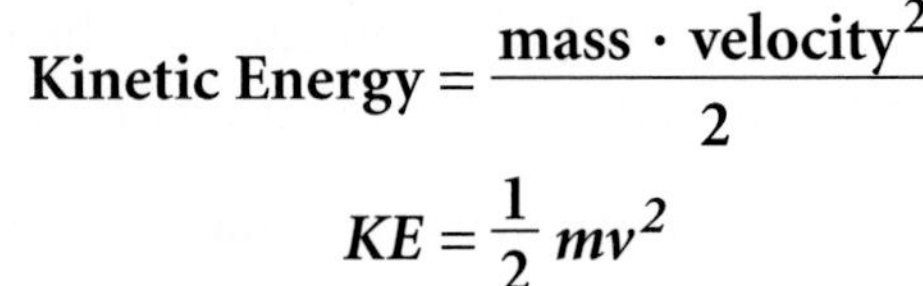

$$\text{Kinetic Energy} = \frac{\text{mass} \cdot \text{velocity}^2}{2}$$

$$KE = \frac{1}{2}mv^2$$

Notice that velocity is squared while mass is not. Increasing the velocity of an object has a greater effect on the object's kinetic energy than increasing the mass of the object. If you double the mass of an object, you double its kinetic energy. Because velocity is squared, if you double the object's velocity, its kinetic energy is four times greater.

### *Calculating Kinetic Energy*

**Sample Problem**

**What is the kinetic energy of a girl who has a mass of 40 kg and a velocity of 3 m/s?**

*What do you know?* mass = 40 kg, velocity = 3 m/s

*What do you want to find out?* Kinetic Energy

*Write the formula:* $KE = \frac{1}{2}mv^2$

*Substitute into the formula:* $KE = \frac{1}{2} \cdot 40\ \text{kg} \cdot (3\ \text{m/s})^2$

*Calculate and simplify:* $KE = \frac{1}{2} \cdot 40\ \text{kg} \cdot \frac{9\ \text{m}^2}{\text{s}^2}$

$= \frac{360\ \text{kg} \cdot \text{m}^2}{2\ \text{s}^2}$

$= 180\ \text{kg} \cdot \text{m}^2/\text{s}^2$

*Check that your units agree:* $\frac{\text{kg} \cdot \text{m}^2}{\text{s}^2} = \frac{\text{kg} \cdot \text{m}}{\text{s}^2} \cdot \text{m} = \text{N} \cdot \text{m} = \text{J}$

Unit of energy is J. Units agree.

*Answer:* $KE = 180$ J

**Practice the Math**

1. A grasshopper with a mass of 0.002 kg jumps up at a speed of 15 m/s. What is the kinetic energy of the grasshopper?
2. A truck with a mass of 6000 kg is traveling north on a highway at a speed of 17 m/s. A car with a mass of 2000 kg is traveling south on the same highway at a speed of 30 m/s. Which vehicle has more kinetic energy?

## Calculating Mechanical Energy

**Mechanical energy** is the energy possessed by an object due to its motion or position—in other words, it is the object's combined potential energy and kinetic energy. A thrown baseball has mechanical energy as a result of both its motion (kinetic energy) and its position above the ground (gravitational potential energy). Any object that has mechanical energy can do work on another object.

**VOCABULARY**
Use a vocabulary strategy to help you remember *mechanical energy.*

Once you calculate an object's kinetic and potential energy, you can add the two values together to find the object's mechanical energy.

**Mechanical Energy = Potential Energy + Kinetic Energy**

$$ME = PE + KE$$

For example, a skateboarder has a potential energy of 200 joules due to his position at the top of a hill and a kinetic energy of 100 joules due to his motion. His total mechanical energy is 300 joules.

**CHECK YOUR READING** How is mechanical energy related to kinetic and potential energy?

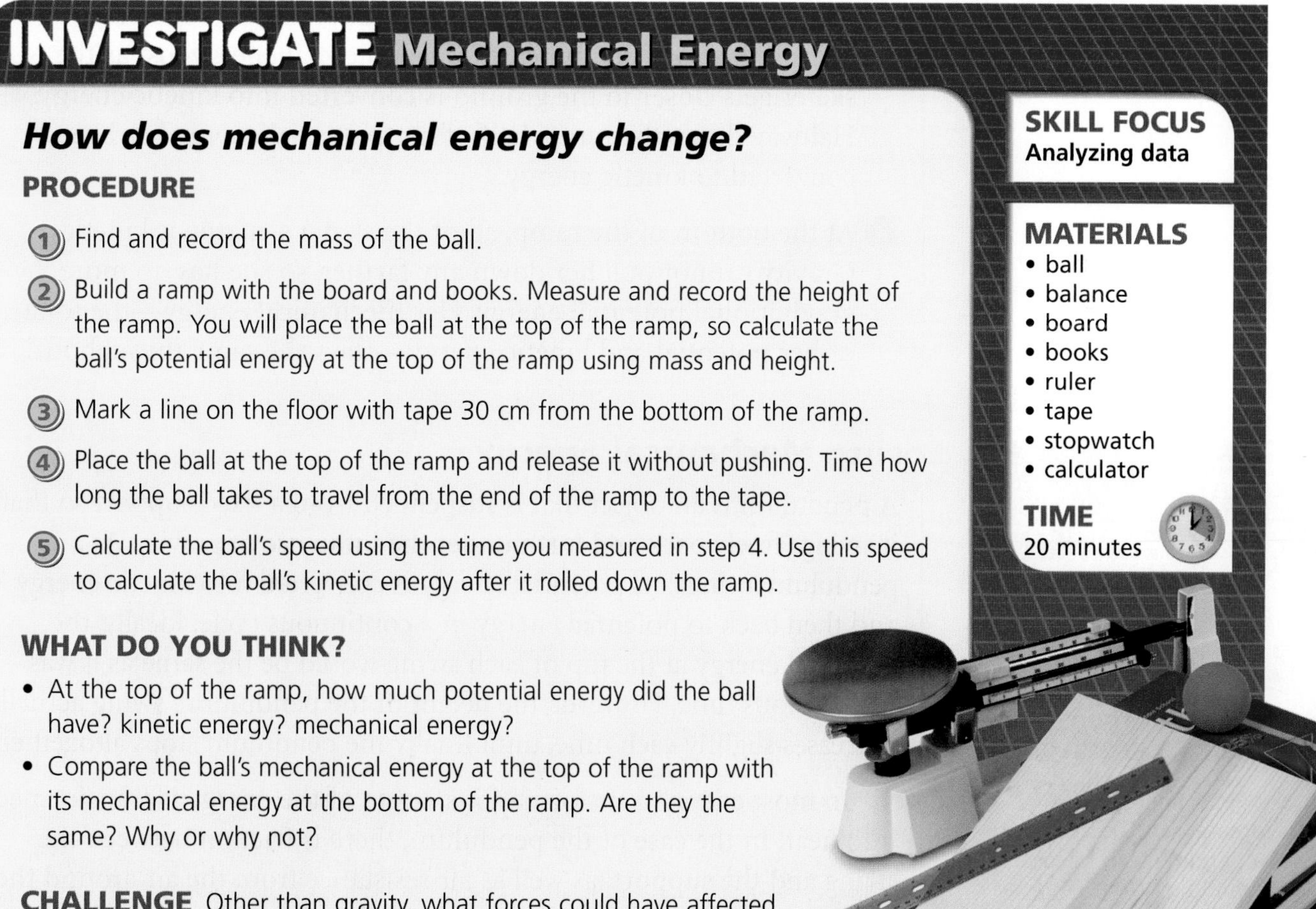

# INVESTIGATE Mechanical Energy

### *How does mechanical energy change?*

**PROCEDURE**

1. Find and record the mass of the ball.
2. Build a ramp with the board and books. Measure and record the height of the ramp. You will place the ball at the top of the ramp, so calculate the ball's potential energy at the top of the ramp using mass and height.
3. Mark a line on the floor with tape 30 cm from the bottom of the ramp.
4. Place the ball at the top of the ramp and release it without pushing. Time how long the ball takes to travel from the end of the ramp to the tape.
5. Calculate the ball's speed using the time you measured in step 4. Use this speed to calculate the ball's kinetic energy after it rolled down the ramp.

**WHAT DO YOU THINK?**

- At the top of the ramp, how much potential energy did the ball have? kinetic energy? mechanical energy?
- Compare the ball's mechanical energy at the top of the ramp with its mechanical energy at the bottom of the ramp. Are they the same? Why or why not?

**CHALLENGE** Other than gravity, what forces could have affected the movement of the ball?

**SKILL FOCUS**
Analyzing data

**MATERIALS**
- ball
- balance
- board
- books
- ruler
- tape
- stopwatch
- calculator

**TIME**
20 minutes

# The total amount of energy is constant.

VISUALIZATION
CLASSZONE.COM

Observe how potential and kinetic energy are transferred on an amusement park ride.

You know that energy is transferred when work is done. No matter how energy is transferred or transformed, all of the energy is still present somewhere in one form or another. This is known as the **law of conservation of energy.** As long as you account for all the different forms of energy involved in any process, you will find that the total amount of energy never changes.

## Conserving Mechanical Energy

Look at the photograph of the in-line skater on page 127. As she rolls down the ramp, the amounts of kinetic energy and potential energy change. However, the total—or the mechanical energy—stays the same. In this example, energy lost to friction is ignored.

1. At the top of the ramp, the skater has potential energy because gravity can pull her downward. She has no velocity; therefore, she has no kinetic energy.
2. As the skater rolls down the ramp, her potential energy decreases because the elevation decreases. Her kinetic energy increases because her velocity increases. The potential energy lost as the skater gets closer to the ground is converted into kinetic energy. Halfway down the ramp, half of her potential energy has been converted to kinetic energy.
3. At the bottom of the ramp, all of the skater's energy is kinetic. Gravity cannot pull her down any farther, so she has no more gravitational potential energy. Her mechanical energy—the total of her potential and kinetic energy—stays the same throughout.

## Losing Mechanical Energy

A pendulum is an object that is suspended from a fixed support so that it swings freely back and forth under the influence of gravity. As a pendulum swings, its potential energy is converted into kinetic energy and then back to potential energy in a continuous cycle. Ideally, the potential energy at the top of each swing would be the same as it was the previous time. However, the height of the pendulum's swing actually decreases slightly each time, until finally the pendulum stops altogether.

APPLY Energy must occasionally be added to a pendulum to keep it swinging. What keeps a grandfather clock's pendulum swinging regularly?

In most energy transformations, some of the energy is transformed into heat. In the case of the pendulum, there is friction between the string and the support, as well as air resistance from the air around the pendulum. The mechanical energy is used to do work against friction and air resistance. This process transforms the mechanical energy into heat. The mechanical energy has not been destroyed; it has simply changed form and been transferred from the pendulum.

## Conserving Mechanical Energy

**The potential energy and kinetic energy in a system or process may vary, but the total energy remains unchanged.**

### 1 Top of Ramp

At the top of the ramp, the skater's mechanical energy is equal to her potential energy because she has no velocity.

### 2 Halfway Down Ramp

As the skater goes down the ramp, she loses height but gains speed. The potential energy she loses is equal to the kinetic energy she gains.

### 3 Bottom of Ramp

As the skater speeds along the bottom of the ramp, all of the potential energy has changed to kinetic energy. Her mechanical energy remains unchanged.

Fabiola da Silva is a professional in-line skater who was born in Brazil but now lives in California.

**READING VISUALS** How do the skater's kinetic and potential energy change as she skates up and down the ramp? (Assume she won't lose any energy to friction.)

MAIN IDEA WEB
Include common forms of energy in your web.

## Forms of Energy

As you have seen, mechanical energy is a combination of kinetic energy and potential energy. Other common forms of energy are discussed below. Each of these forms of energy is also a combination of kinetic energy and potential energy. Chemical energy, for example, is potential energy when it is stored in bonds.

**Thermal energy** is the energy an object has due to the motion of its molecules. The faster the molecules in an object move, the more thermal energy the object has.

**Chemical energy** is the energy stored in chemical bonds that hold chemical compounds together. If a molecule's bonds are broken or rearranged, energy is released or absorbed. Chemical energy is used to light up fireworks displays. It is also stored in food and in matches.

**Nuclear energy** is the potential energy stored in the nucleus of an atom. In a nuclear reaction, a tiny portion of an atom's mass is turned into energy. The source of the Sun's energy is nuclear energy. Nuclear energy can be used to run power plants that provide electricity.

**Electromagnetic energy** is the energy associated with electrical and magnetic interactions. Energy that is transferred by electric charges or current is often called electrical energy. Another type of electromagnetic energy is radiant energy, the energy carried by light, infrared waves, and x-rays.

It is possible to transfer, or convert, one energy form into one or more other forms. For example, when you rub your hands together on a cold day, you convert mechanical energy to thermal energy. Your body converts chemical energy stored in food to thermal and mechanical energy (muscle movement).

### KEY CONCEPTS

1. Explain the relationship between work and energy.
2. How are potential energy and kinetic energy related to mechanical energy?
3. When one form of energy changes into one or more other forms of energy, what happens to the total amount of energy?

### CRITICAL THINKING

4. **Infer** Debra used 250 J of energy to roll a bowling ball. When the ball arrived at the end of the lane, it had only 200 J of energy. What happened to the other 50 J?
5. **Calculate** A satellite falling to Earth has a kinetic energy of 182.2 billion J and a potential energy of 1.6 billion J. What is its mechanical energy?

### CHALLENGE

6. **Apply** At what point in its motion is the kinetic energy of the end of a pendulum greatest? At what point is its potential energy greatest? When its kinetic energy is half its greatest value, how much potential energy did it gain?

Women in many countries, like this woman from Abidjan, Ivory Coast, balance heavy loads as they walk.

SKILL: ISOLATING VARIABLES

# How Do They Do It?

Some women in Kenya and other African countries walk many miles every day carrying heavy loads on their heads without an increase in their heart rate. Most have done it since they were children. Scientists have studied African women to learn how they do this.

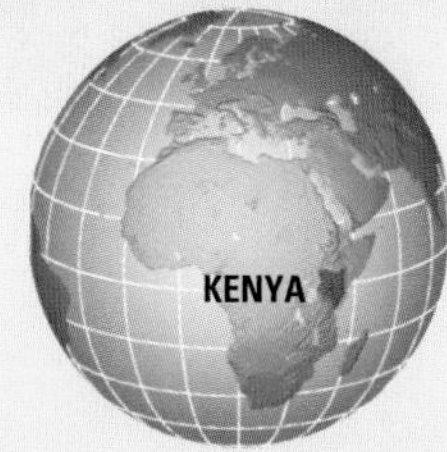


## Variables

In scientific research, variables must be chosen and tested. Variables are usually compared with a control group—that is, a group for whom all potential variables are held constant. Scientists first asked several Kenyan women to walk on a treadmill. The scientists measured the women's heart rate and how much oxygen they used while carrying different weights on their heads. They found that the women could carry as much as 20 percent of their own body weight without using extra oxygen or increasing their heart rate.

The same scientists asked subjects in a control group in the United States to walk on a treadmill. The people in this group wore helmets lined with different amounts of lead. Even the lightest load caused their heart rate and oxygen consumption to increase.

If you were studying the way these African women carry loads, what variables would you choose to isolate? What control group would you use? Here are some variables and controls to consider:

- carrying the load on the head compared with carrying it on the back
- weight of the load
- women compared with men
- African women compared with other women
- method of walking

## Isolate the Variables

**On Your Own** Design an experiment that could test one of the variables without interference from other variables. Can each variable be tested independently?

**As a Group** Discuss each variable and see if the group agrees that it can be tested independently. Can you eliminate any of the variables based on information on this page?

**CHALLENGE** How would you measure the amount of energy used for the variable you chose?

KEY CONCEPT

# Power is the rate at which work is done.

**BEFORE, you learned**

- Mechanical energy is a combination of kinetic energy and potential energy
- Mechanical energy can be calculated
- Work transfers energy

**NOW, you will learn**

- How power is related to work and time
- How power is related to energy and time
- About common uses of power

**VOCABULARY**

**power** p. 130
**watt** p. 131
**horsepower** p. 132

**EXPLORE Power**

## *How does time affect work?*

**PROCEDURE**

1. Place the cups side by side. Put all of the marbles in one cup.
2. Place each marble, one by one, into the other cup. Time how long it takes to do this.
3. Set the timer for half that amount of time. Then repeat step 2 in that time.

**WHAT DO YOU THINK?**

- Did you do more work the first time or the second time? Why?
- What differences did you notice between the two tries?

**MATERIALS**

- 2 plastic cups
- 10 marbles
- stopwatch

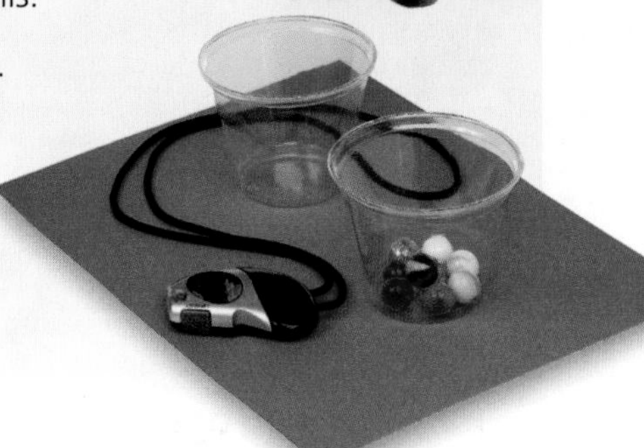

## Power can be calculated from work and time.

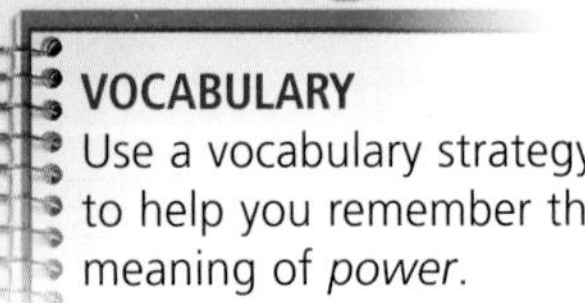

**VOCABULARY**
Use a vocabulary strategy to help you remember the meaning of *power*.

If you lift a book one meter, you do the same amount of work whether you lift the book quickly or slowly. However, when you lift the book quickly, you increase your **power**—the rate at which you do work. A cook increases his power when he beats eggs rapidly instead of stirring them slowly. A runner increases her power when she breaks into a sprint to reach the finish line.

The word *power* has different common meanings. It is used to mean a source of energy, as in a power plant, or strength, as in a powerful engine. When you talk about a powerful swimmer, for example, you would probably say that the swimmer is very strong or very fast. If you use the scientific definition of power, you would instead say that a powerful swimmer is one who does the work of moving herself through the water in a short time.

Each of the swimmers shown in the photograph above is doing work—that is, she is using a certain force to move a certain distance. It takes time to cover that distance. The power a swimmer uses depends on the force, the distance, and the time it takes to cover that distance. The more force the swimmer uses, the more power she has. Also, the faster she goes, the more power she has because she is covering the same distance in a shorter time. Swimmers often increase their speed toward the end of a race, which increases their power, making it possible for them to reach the end of the pool in less time.

Summarize in your own words the difference between work and power.

## Calculating Power from Work

You know that a given amount of work can be done by a slow-moving swimmer over a long period of time or by a fast-moving swimmer in a short time. Likewise, a given amount of work can be done by a low-powered motor over a long period of time or by a high-powered motor in a short time.

Because power is a measurement of how much work is done in a given time, power can be calculated based on work and time. To find power, divide the amount of work by the time it takes to do the work.

$$\text{Power} = \frac{\text{Work}}{\text{time}} \qquad P = \frac{W}{t}$$

**READING TIP**

*W* (in italicized type) is the letter that represents the variable *Work*. W, not italicized, is the abbreviation for watt.

Remember that work is measured in joules. Power is often measured in joules of work per second. The unit of measurement for power is the **watt** (W). One watt is equal to one joule of work done in one second. If an object does a large amount of work, its power is usually measured in units of 1000 watts, or kilowatts.

Find out more about power.

## Calculating Power from Work

**Sample Problem**

**An Antarctic explorer uses 6000 J of work to pull his sled for 60 s. What power does he need?**

*What do you know?* Work = 6000 J, time = 60 s

*What do you want to find out?* Power

*Write the formula:* $P = \frac{W}{t}$

*Substitute into the formula:* $P = \frac{6000 \text{ J}}{60 \text{ s}}$

*Calculate and simplify:* $P$ = 100 J/s = 100 W

*Check that your units agree:* $\frac{\text{J}}{\text{s}} = \text{W}$

Unit of power is W. Units agree.

*Answer:* $P$ = 100 W

**Practice the Math**

1. If a conveyor belt uses 10 J to move a piece of candy a distance of 3 m in 20 s, what is the conveyor belt's power?
2. An elevator uses a force of 1710 N to lift 3 people up 1 floor. Each floor is 4 m high. The elevator takes 8 s to lift the 3 people up 2 floors. What is the elevator's power?

## Horsepower

James Watt, the Scottish engineer for whom the watt is named, improved the power of the steam engine in the mid-1700s. Watt also developed a unit of measurement for power called the horsepower. **Horsepower** is based on what it sounds like—the amount of work a horse can do in a minute. In Watt's time, people used horses to do many different types of work. For example, horses were used on farms to pull plows and wagons.

Both the horse and the tractor use power to pull objects around a farm.

Watt wanted to explain to people how powerful his steam engine was compared with horses. After observing several horses doing work, Watt concluded that an average horse could move 150 pounds a distance of 220 feet in 1 minute. Watt called this amount of power 1 horsepower. A single horsepower is equal to 745 watts. Therefore, a horsepower is a much larger unit of measurement than a watt.

Today horsepower is used primarily in connection with engines and motors. For example, you may see a car advertised as having a 150-horsepower engine. The power of a motorboat, lawn mower, tractor, or motorcycle engine is also referred to as horsepower.

# INVESTIGATE Power

## *How much power do you have?*

**PROCEDURE**

1. Measure a length of 5 meters on the floor. Mark the beginning and the end of the 5 meters with masking tape.
2. Attach the object to the spring scale with a piece of string. Slowly pull the object across the floor using a steady amount of force. Record the force and the time it takes you to pull the object.

**WHAT DO YOU THINK?**

- How much power did you use to pull the object 5 meters?
- How do you think you could increase the power you used? decrease the power?

**CHALLENGE** How quickly would you have to drag the object along the floor to produce 40 watts of power?

**SKILL FOCUS**
Measuring

**MATERIALS**
- meter stick
- masking tape
- 100 g object
- spring scale
- string
- stopwatch

**TIME**
15 minutes

# Power can be calculated from energy and time.

Sometimes you may know that energy is being transferred, but you cannot directly measure the work done by the forces involved. For example, you know that a television uses power. But there is no way to measure all the work every part of the television does in terms of forces and distance. Because work measures the transfer of energy, you can also think of power as the amount of energy transferred over a period of time.

## Calculating Power from Energy

When you turn on a television, it starts using energy. Each second the television is on, a certain amount of electrical energy is transferred from a local power plant to your television. If you measure how much energy your television uses during a given time period, you can find out how much power it needs by using the following formula:

$$\text{Power} = \frac{\text{Energy}}{\text{time}} \qquad P = \frac{E}{t}$$

This formula should look familiar to you because it is very similar to the formula used to calculate power from work.

The photograph shows Hong Kong, China, at night. Every second, the city uses more than 4 billion joules of electrical energy!

You can think about power as any kind of transfer of energy in a certain amount of time. It is useful to think of power in this way if you cannot directly figure out the work used to transfer the energy. Power calculated from transferred energy is also measured in joules per second, or watts.

You have probably heard the term *watt* used in connection with light bulbs. A 60-watt light bulb requires 60 joules of energy every second to shine at its rated brightness.

**CHECK YOUR READING** In what situations is it useful to think of power as the transfer of energy in a certain amount of time?

## *Calculating Power from Energy*

**Sample Problem**

**REMINDER**
Remember that energy and work are both measured in joules.

**A light bulb used 600 J of energy in 6 s. What is the power of the light bulb?**

*What do you know?* Energy = 600 J, time = 6 s

*What do you want to find out?* Power

*Write the formula:* $P = \frac{E}{t}$

*Substitute into the formula:* $P = \frac{600 \text{ J}}{6 \text{ s}}$

*Calculate and simplify:* $P = 100$ J/s

*Check that your units agree:* Unit is J/s. Unit for power is W, which is also J/s. Units agree.

*Answer:* $P = 100$ W

**Practice the Math**

1. A laptop computer uses 100 J every 2 seconds. How much power is needed to run the computer?
2. The power needed to pump blood through your body is about 1.1 W. How much energy does your body use when pumping blood for 10 seconds?

## Everyday Power

Many appliances in your home rely on electricity for energy. Each appliance requires a certain number of joules per second, the power it needs to run properly. An electric hair dryer uses energy. For example, a 600-watt hair dryer needs 600 joules per second. The wattage of the hair dryer indicates how much energy per second it needs to operate.

The dryer works by speeding up the evaporation of water on the surface of hair. It needs only two main parts to do this: a heating coil and a fan turned by a motor.

1. When the hair dryer is plugged into an outlet and the switch is turned on, electrical energy moves electrons in the wires, creating a current.
2. This current runs an electric motor that turns the fan blades. Air is drawn into the hair dryer through small holes in the casing. The turning fan blades push the air over the coil.
3. The current also makes the heating coil become hot.
4. The fan pushes heated air out of the dryer.

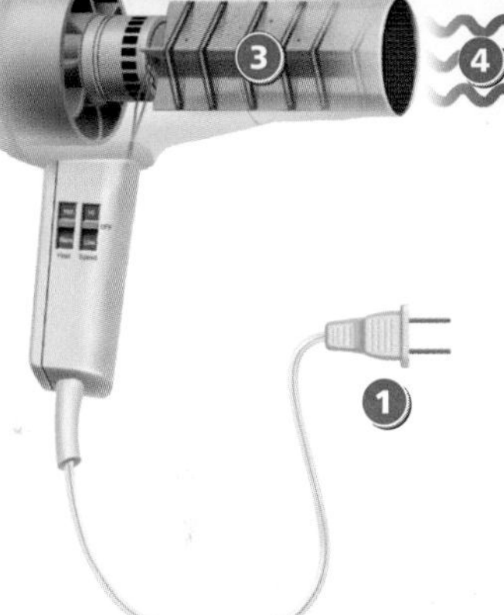


Most hair dryers have high and low settings. At the high power setting, the temperature is increased, more air is pushed through the dryer, and the dryer does its work faster. Some dryers have safety switches that shut off the motor when the temperature rises to a level that could burn your scalp. Insulation keeps the outside of the dryer from becoming hot to the touch.

Many other appliances, from air conditioners to washing machines to blenders, need electrical energy to do their work. Take a look around you at all the appliances that help you during a typical day.

### KEY CONCEPTS

1. How is power related to work?
2. Name two units used for power, and give examples of when each unit might be used.
3. What do you need to know to calculate how much energy a light bulb uses?

### CRITICAL THINKING

4. **Apply** Discuss different ways in which a swimmer can increase her power.
5. **Calculate** Which takes more power: using 15 N to lift a ball 2 m in 5 seconds or using 100 N to push a box 2 m in 1 minute?

### CHALLENGE

6. **Analyze** A friend tells you that you can calculate power by using a different formula from the one given in this book. The formula your friend gives you is as follows:
   Power = force • speed
   Do you think this is a valid formula for power? Explain.

# CHAPTER INVESTIGATION

## Work and Power

**OVERVIEW AND PURPOSE** People in wheelchairs cannot use steps leading up to a building's entrance. Sometimes there is a machine that can lift a person and wheelchair straight up to the entrance level. At other times, there is a ramp leading to the entrance. Which method takes more power?

### Problem

Write It Up

How does a ramp affect the amount of energy, work, and power used to lift an object?

### Hypothesize

Write It Up

Write a hypothesis to explain how the potential energy, the amount of work done, and the power required to lift an object straight up compare with the same quantities when the object is moved up a ramp. Your hypothesis should take the form of an "If . . . , then . . . , because . . ." statement.

**MATERIALS**

- board
- chair
- meter stick
- string
- small wheeled object
- spring scale
- stopwatch

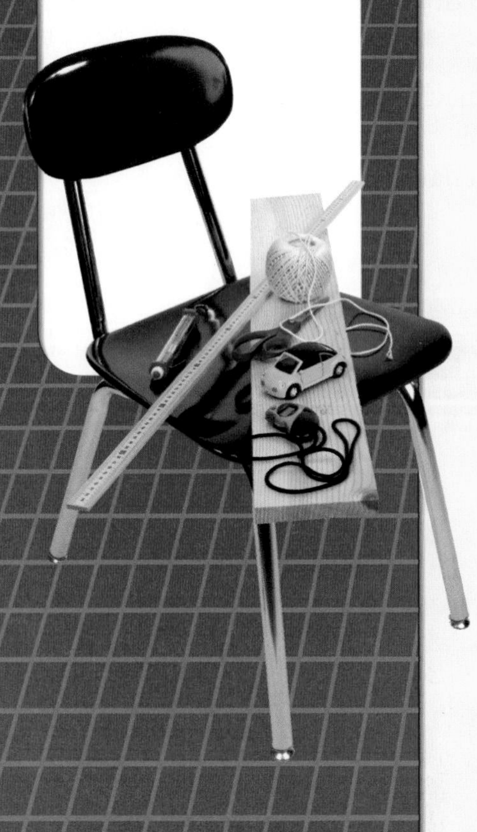

### Procedure

1. Make a data table like the one shown.
2. Lean the board up against the chair seat to create a ramp.
3. Measure and record the vertical distance from the floor to the top of the ramp. Also measure and record the length of the ramp.
4. Tie the string around the wheeled object. Make a loop so that you can hook the string onto the spring scale. Measure and record the weight of the object in newtons.
5. Lift the object straight up to the top of the ramp without using the ramp, as pictured.

6 On the spring scale, read and record the newtons of force needed to lift the object. Time how long it takes to lift the object from the floor to the top of the ramp. Conduct three trials and average your results. Record your measurements in the data table.

7 Drag the object from the bottom of the ramp to the top of the ramp with the spring scale, and record the newtons of force that were needed to move the object and the time it took. Conduct three trials and average your results.

## Observe and Analyze

Write It Up

1. **RECORD OBSERVATIONS** Draw the setup of the procedure. Be sure your data table is complete.
2. **IDENTIFY VARIABLES AND CONSTANTS** List the variables and constants in your notebook.
3. **CALCULATE**

   **Potential Energy** Convert centimeters to meters. Then calculate the gravitational potential energy (GPE) of the object at the top of the ramp. (Recall that weight equals mass times gravitational acceleration.)

   $$\text{Gravitational Potential Energy} = \text{weight} \cdot \text{height}$$

   **Work** Calculate the work done, first when the object was lifted and then when it was pulled. Use the appropriate distance.

   $$\text{Work} = \text{Force} \cdot \text{distance}$$

   **Power** Calculate the power involved in both situations.

   $$\text{Power} = \frac{\text{Work}}{\text{time}}$$

## Conclude

Write It Up

1. **COMPARE** How did the distance through which the object moved when it was pulled up the ramp differ from the distance when it was lifted straight up? How did the amount of force required differ in the two situations?
2. **COMPARE** How does your calculated value for potential energy compare with the values you obtained for work done?
3. **INTERPRET** Answer the question posed in the problem.
4. **ANALYZE** Compare your results with your hypothesis. Did your results support your hypothesis?
5. **IDENTIFY LIMITS** What possible limitations or sources of error could you have experienced?
6. **APPLY** A road going up a hill usually winds back and forth instead of heading straight to the top. How does this affect the work a car does to get to the top? How does it affect the power involved?

## INVESTIGATE Further

**CHALLENGE** Design a way to use potential energy to move the car up the ramp. What materials can you use? Think about the materials in terms of potential energy—that is, how high they are from the ground or how stretched or compressed they are.

Work and Power

Problem How does the amount of energy, work, and power used to lift an object?

Hypothesize

Observe and Analyze

Measured length of ramp = _____ cm

Height object is being lifted = _____ cm

Measured weight of the object = _____ N

Table 1. Measurements for Lifting the Object with and Without the Ramp

| | Trial No. | Force (N) | Time (s) |
|---|---|---|---|
| Straight up | 1 | | |
| | 2 | | |
| | 3 | | |
| | Average | | |
| Ramp | 1 | | |

# Chapter Review

## the BIG idea

**Energy is transferred when a force moves an object.**

## KEY CONCEPTS SUMMARY

### 4.1 Work is the use of force to move an object.

Work is done by a force that acts in the same direction as the motion of an object.

Work = Force • distance

applied force

object

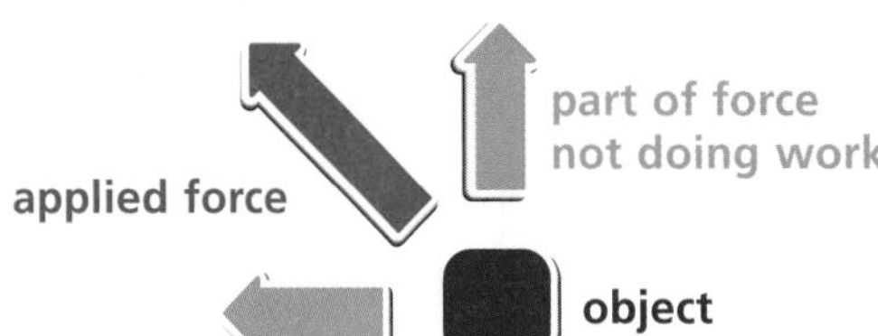

**VOCABULARY**
**work** p. 115
**joule** p. 117

### 4.2 Energy is transferred when work is done.

The amounts of potential energy and kinetic energy in a system or process may vary, but the total amount of energy remains unchanged.

$GPE = mgh$

$KE = \frac{1}{2}mv^2$

$ME = PE + KE$

**VOCABULARY**
**potential energy** p. 122
**kinetic energy** p. 122
**mechanical energy** p. 125
**conservation of energy** p. 126

### 4.3 Power is the rate at which work is done.

Power can be calculated from work and time.

$$\text{Power} = \frac{\text{Work}}{\text{time}}$$

Power can be calculated from energy and time.

$$\text{Power} = \frac{\text{Energy}}{\text{time}}$$

Power is measured in watts (W) and sometimes horsepower (hp).

**VOCABULARY**
**power** p. 130
**watt** p. 131
**horsepower** p. 132

## Reviewing Vocabulary

*Make a four square diagram for each of the terms listed below. Write the term in the center. Define it in one square. Write characteristics, examples, and formulas (if appropriate) in the other squares. A sample is shown below.*

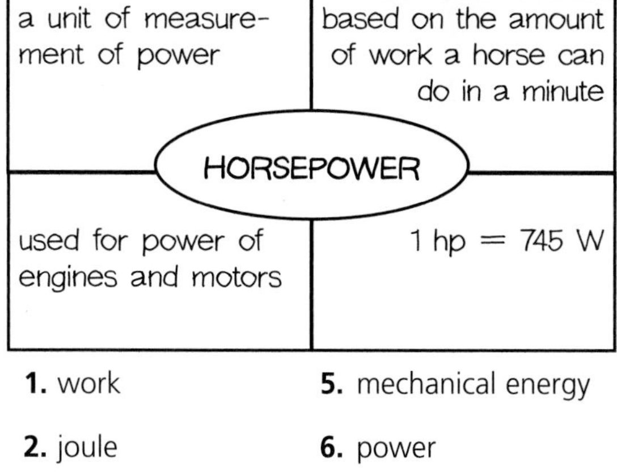


**1.** work

**2.** joule

**3.** potential energy

**4.** kinetic energy

**5.** mechanical energy

**6.** power

**7.** watt

## Reviewing Key Concepts

**Multiple Choice** *Choose the letter of the best answer.*

**8.** Work can be calculated from
- **a.** force and speed
- **b.** force and distance
- **c.** energy and time
- **d.** energy and distance

**9.** If you balance a book on your head, you are not doing work on the book because
- **a.** doing work requires moving an object
- **b.** you are not applying any force to the book
- **c.** the book is doing work on you
- **d.** the book has potential energy

**10.** Energy that an object has because of its position or shape is called
- **a.** potential energy
- **b.** kinetic energy
- **c.** thermal energy
- **d.** chemical energy

**11.** Suppose you are pushing a child on a swing. During what space of time are you doing work on the swing?
- **a.** while you hold it back before letting go
- **b.** while your hands are in contact with the swing and pushing forward
- **c.** after you let go of the swing and it continues to move forward
- **d.** all the time the swing is in motion

**12.** A falling ball has a potential energy of 5 J and a kinetic energy of 10 J. What is the ball's mechanical energy?
- **a.** 5 J
- **b.** 10 J
- **c.** 15 J
- **d.** 50 J

**13.** The unit that measures one joule of work done in one second is called a
- **a.** meter
- **b.** watt
- **c.** newton-meter
- **d.** newton

**14.** By increasing the speed at which you do work, you increase your
- **a.** force
- **b.** work
- **c.** energy
- **d.** power

**15.** A ball kicked into the air will have the greatest gravitational potential energy
- **a.** as it is being kicked
- **b.** as it starts rising
- **c.** at its highest point
- **d.** as it hits the ground

**Short Answer** *Answer each of the following questions in a sentence or two.*

**16.** How can you tell if a force you exert is doing work?

**17.** How does a water wheel do work?

**18.** State the law of conservation of energy. How does it affect the total amount of energy in any process?

**19.** Explain why a swing will not stay in motion forever after you have given it a push. What happens to its mechanical energy?

**20.** What are two ways to calculate power?

**21.** Why did James Watt invent a unit of measurement based on the work of horses?

## Thinking Critically

22. **SYNTHESIZE** A weightlifter holds a barbell above his head. How do the barbell's potential energy, kinetic energy, and mechanical energy change as it is lifted and then lowered to the ground?

23. **SYNTHESIZE** What happens when you wind up a toy car and release it? Describe the events in terms of energy.

*Use the photograph below to answer the next three questions.*

24. **APPLY** When the boy first pushes on the chair, the chair does not move due to friction. Is the boy doing work? Why or why not?

25. **ANALYZE** For the first two seconds, the boy pushes the chair slowly at a steady speed. After that, he pushes the chair at a faster speed. How does his power change if he is using the same force at both speeds? How does his work change?

26. **SYNTHESIZE** As the boy pushes the chair, he does work. However, when he stops pushing, the chair stops moving and does not have any additional kinetic or potential energy. What happened to the energy he transferred by doing work on the chair?

27. **APPLY** A bouncing ball has mechanical energy. Each bounce, however, reaches a lower height than the last. Describe what happens to the mechanical, potential, and kinetic energy of the ball as it bounces several times.

28. **CONNECT** When you do work, you transfer energy. Where does the energy you transfer come from?

## Using Math Skills in Science

*Complete the following calculations.*

29. Use the information in the photograph below to calculate the work the person does in lifting the box.

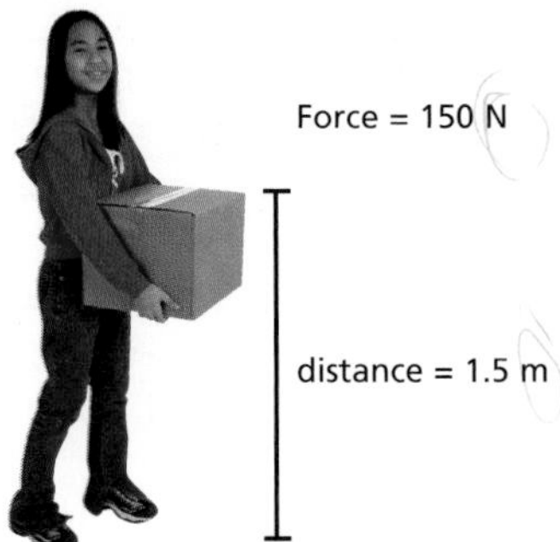


30. If you did 225 J of work to pull a wagon with a force of 25 N, how far did you pull it?

31. A kite with a mass of 0.05 kg is caught on the roof of a house. The house is 10 m high. What is the kite's gravitational potential energy? (Recall that $g = 9.8$ m/s$^2$.)

32. A baseball with a mass of 0.15 kg leaves a pitcher's hand traveling 40 m/s toward the batter. What is the baseball's kinetic energy?

33. Suppose it takes 150 J of force to push a cart 10 m in 60 s. Calculate the power.

34. If an electric hair dryer uses 1200 W, how much energy does it need to run for 2 s?

## the BIG idea

35. **SYNTHESIZE** Look back at the photograph of the person lifting a box on pages 112–113. Describe the picture in terms of work, potential energy, kinetic energy, and power.

36. **WRITE** Think of an activity that involves work. Write a paragraph explaining how the work is transferring energy and where the transferred energy goes.

## UNIT PROJECTS

If you need to create graphs or other visuals for your project, be sure you have grid paper, poster board, markers, or other supplies.

## Understanding Experiments

*Read the following description of an experiment. Then answer the questions that follow.*

James Prescott Joule is well known for a paddle-wheel experiment he conducted in the mid-1800s. He placed a paddle wheel in a bucket of water. Then he set up two weights on either side of the bucket. As the weights fell, they turned the paddle wheel. Joule recorded the temperature of the water before and after the paddle wheel began turning. He found that the water temperature increased as the paddle wheel turned.

Based on this experiment, Joule concluded that the falling weights released mechanical energy, which was converted into heat by the turning wheel. He was convinced that whenever mechanical force is exerted, heat is produced.

**1.** Which principle did Joule demonstrate with this experiment?

- **a.** When energy is converted from one form to another, some energy is lost.
- **b.** The amount of momentum in a system does not change as long as there are no outside forces acting on the system.
- **c.** One form of energy can be converted into another form of energy.
- **d.** When one object exerts a force on another object, the second object exerts an equal and opposite force on the first object.

**2.** Which form of energy was released by the weights in Joule's experiment?

- **a.** electrical
- **b.** mechanical
- **c.** nuclear
- **d.** heat

**3.** Which form of energy was produced in the water?

- **a.** chemical
- **b.** electrical
- **c.** nuclear
- **d.** heat

**4.** Based on Joule's finding that movement causes temperature changes in water, which of the following would be a logical prediction?

- **a.** Water held in a container should increase in temperature.
- **b.** Water at the base of a waterfall should be warmer than water at the top.
- **c.** Water with strong waves should be colder than calm water.
- **d.** Water should increase in temperature with depth.

## Extended Response

*Answer the two questions below in detail. Include some of the terms from the word box. Underline each term you use in your answer.*

| potential energy | conservation of energy | force |
|---|---|---|
| kinetic energy | power | work |

**5.** A sledder has the greatest potential energy at the top of a hill. She has the least amount of potential energy at the bottom of a hill. She has the greatest kinetic energy when she moves the fastest. Where on the hill does the sledder move the fastest? State the relationship between kinetic energy and potential energy in this situation.

**6.** Andre and Jon are moving boxes of books from the floor to a shelf in the school library. Each box weighs 15 lb. Andre lifts 5 boxes in one minute. Jon lifts 5 boxes in 30 seconds. Which person does more work? Which person applies more force? Which person has the greater power? Explain your answers.

CHAPTER

# Machines

## the BIG idea

**Machines help people do work by changing the force applied to an object.**

Balls move through this sculpture. What do you think keeps the balls in motion?

## Key Concepts

SECTION 5.1 **Machines help people do work.**
Learn about machines and how they are used to do work.

SECTION 5.2 **Six simple machines have many uses.**
Learn about levers and inclined planes and the other simple machines that are related to them.

SECTION 5.3 **Modern technology uses compound machines.**
Learn how scientists are using nanotechnology and robots to create new ways for machines to do work.

CLASSZONE.COM

Chapter 5 online resources: Content Review, Simulation, four Resource Centers, Math Tutorial, Test Practice

# EXPLORE the BIG idea

## Changing Direction

Observe how a window blind works. Notice how you use a downward force to pull the blind up. Look around you for other examples.

**Observe and Think**
Why does changing the direction of a force make work easier?

## Shut the Door!

Find a door that swings freely on its hinges. Stand on the side where you can push the door to close it. Open the door. Push the door closed several times, placing your hand closer to or farther from the hinge each time.

**Observe and Think** Which hand placement made it easiest to shut the door? Why do you think that is so?

## Internet Activity: Machines

Go to **ClassZone.com** to learn more about the simple machines in everyday objects. Select an item and think about how it moves and does its job. Then test your knowledge of simple machines.

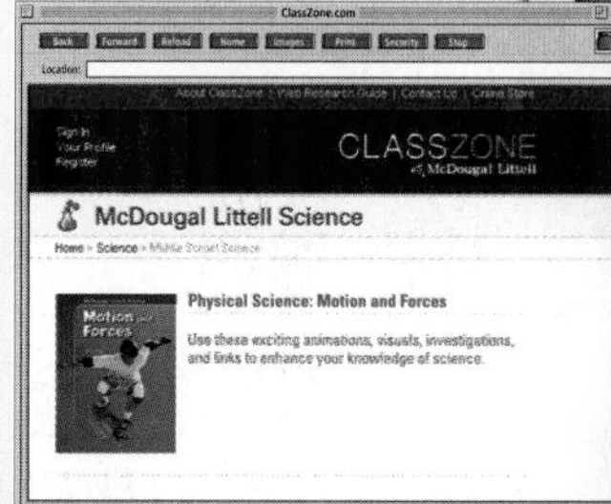


**Observe and Think**
What other objects contain simple machines?

Simple Machines **Code: MDL008**

CHAPTER 5

# Getting Ready to Learn

## CONCEPT REVIEW

- Work is done when a force moves an object over a distance.
- Energy can be converted from one form to another.
- Energy is transferred when work is done.

## VOCABULARY REVIEW

**work** p. 115

**mechanical energy** p. 125

**power** p. 130

*See Glossary for definitions.*

**energy, technology**

CLASSZONE.COM

Review concepts and vocabulary.

## TAKING NOTES

### CHOOSE YOUR OWN STRATEGY

Take notes using one or more of the strategies from earlier chapters—**outline, combination notes, supporting main ideas,** and **main idea web.** Feel free to mix and match the strategies, or use an entirely different note-taking strategy.

### VOCABULARY STRATEGY

Draw a **word triangle** diagram for each new vocabulary term. On the bottom line, write and define the term. Above that, write a sentence that uses the term correctly. At the top, draw a small picture to show what the term looks like.

See the Note-Taking Handbook on pages R45–R51.

SCIENCE NOTEBOOK

Outline

I. Main idea
A. Supporting idea
1. Detail
2. Detail
B. Supporting idea

Combination Notes

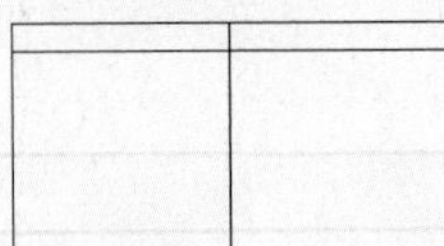

Supporting Main Ideas

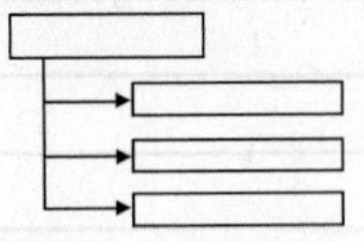

Main Idea Web

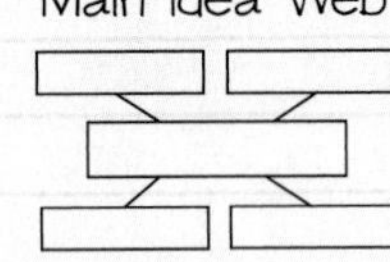

The ramp in front of our school is an inclined plane.

inclined plane—a simple machine that is a sloping surface

KEY CONCEPT

# Machines help people do work.

**BEFORE, you learned**

- Work is done when a force is exerted over a distance
- Some work can be converted to heat or sound energy

**NOW, you will learn**

- How machines help you do work
- How to calculate a machine's efficiency

**VOCABULARY**

**machine** p. 145
**mechanical advantage** p. 147
**efficiency** p. 150

**EXPLORE Machines**

### *How do machines help you work?*

**PROCEDURE**

1. Look at one of the machines closely. Carefully operate the machine and notice how each part moves.
2. Sketch a diagram of the machine. Try to show all of the working parts. Add arrows and labels to show the direction of motion for each part.

**WHAT DO YOU THINK?**

- What is the function of the machine?
- How many moving parts does it have?
- How do the parts work together?
- How does this machine make work easier?

**MATERIALS**

various small machines

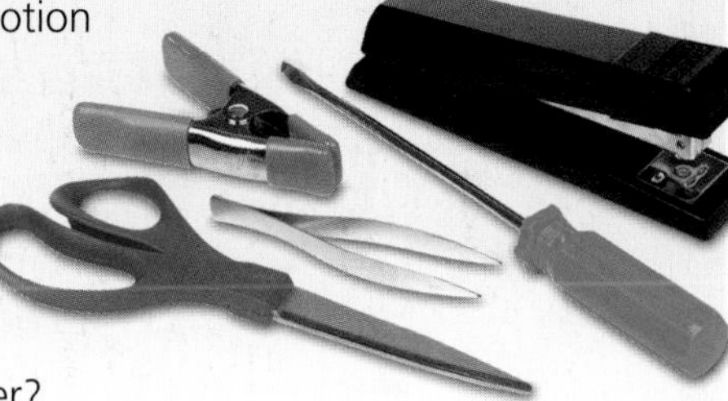

## Machines change the way force is applied.

For thousands of years, humans have been improving their lives with technology. Technology is the use of knowledge to create products or tools that make life easier. The simplest machine is an example of technology.

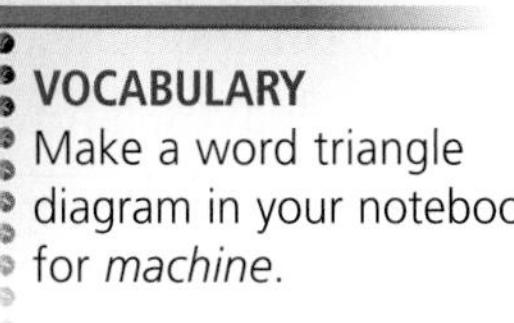

**VOCABULARY**
Make a word triangle diagram in your notebook for *machine*.

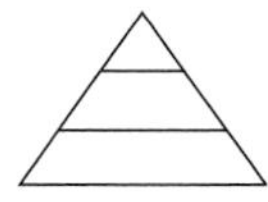

A **machine** is any device that helps people do work. A machine does not decrease the amount of work that is done. Instead, a machine changes the way in which work is done. Recall that work is the use of force to move an object. If, for example, you have to lift a heavy box, you can use a ramp to make the work easier. Moving the box up a ramp—which is a machine—helps you do the work by reducing the force you need to lift the box.

If machines do not reduce the amount of work required, how do they help people do work? Machines make work easier by changing

- the size of the force needed to do the work and the distance over which the force is applied
- the direction in which the force is exerted

Machines can be powered by different types of energy. Electronic machines, such as computers, use electrical energy. Mechanical machines, such as a rake, use mechanical energy. Often this mechanical energy is supplied by the person who is using the machine.

## Changing Size and Distance

Some machines help you do work by changing the size of the force needed. Have you ever tried to open a door by turning the doorknob's shaft instead of the handle? This is not easy to do. It takes less force to turn the handle of the doorknob than it does to turn the shaft. Turning the handle makes opening the door easier, even though you must turn it through a greater distance.

A rake is a machine that changes a large force over a short distance to a smaller force over a larger distance.

If a machine—such as a doorknob attached to a shaft—allows you to exert less force, you must apply that force over a greater distance. The total amount of work remains the same whether it is done with a machine or not. You can think of this in terms of the formula for calculating work—work is force times distance. Because a machine does not decrease the amount of work to be done, less force must mean greater distance.

A doorknob allows you to apply a smaller force over a greater distance. Some machines allow you to apply a greater input force over a shorter distance. Look at the boy using a rake, which is a machine. The boy moves his hands a short distance to move the end of the rake a large distance, allowing him to rake up more leaves.

Input force is the force exerted on a machine. Output force is the force that a machine exerts on an object. The boy in the photograph is exerting an input force on the rake. As a result, the rake exerts an output force on the leaves. The work the boy puts into the rake is the same as the work he gets out of the rake. However, the force he applies is greater than the force the rake can apply to the leaves. The output force is less than the input force, but it acts over a longer distance.

**CHECK YOUR READING** How can a rake help you do work? Use the word *force* in your answer.

## Changing Direction

Machines also can help you work by changing the direction of a force. Think of raising a flag on a flagpole. You pull down on the rope, and the flag moves up. The rope system is a machine that changes the direction in which you exert your force. The rope system does not change the size of the force, however. The force pulling the flag upward is equal to your downward pull.

A shovel is a machine that can help you dig a hole. Once you have the shovel in the ground, you push down on the handle to lift the dirt up. You can use some of the weight of your body as part of your input force. That would not be possible if you were lifting the dirt by using only your hands. A shovel also changes the size of the force you apply, so you need less force to lift the dirt.

**APPLY** How does the rope system help the man raise the flag?

## Mechanical Advantage of a Machine

When machines help you work, there is an advantage—or benefit—to using them. The number of times a machine multiplies the input force is called the machine's **mechanical advantage** (MA). To find a machine's mechanical advantage, divide the output force by the input force.

$$\textbf{Mechanical Advantage} = \frac{\textbf{Output Force}}{\textbf{Input Force}}$$

For machines that allow you to apply less force over a greater distance—such as a doorknob—the output force is greater than the input force. Therefore, the mechanical advantage of this type of machine is greater than 1. For example, if the input force is 10 newtons and the output force is 40 newtons, the mechanical advantage is 40 N divided by 10 N, or 4.

For machines that allow you to apply greater force over a shorter distance—such as a rake—the output force is less than the input force. In this case, the mechanical advantage is less than 1. If the input force is 10 newtons and the output force is 5 newtons, the mechanical advantage is 0.5. However, such a machine allows you to move an object a greater distance.

Sometimes changing the direction of the force is more useful than decreasing the force or the distance. For machines that change only the direction of a force—such as the rope system on a flagpole—the input force and output force are the same. Therefore, the mechanical advantage of the machine is 1.

NOTE-TAKING STRATEGY
Remember to organize your notes in a chart or web as you read.

## Work transfers energy.

Machines transfer energy to objects on which they do work. Every time you open a door, the doorknob is transferring mechanical energy to the shaft. A machine that lifts an object gives it potential energy. A machine that causes an object to start moving, such as a baseball bat hitting a ball, gives the object kinetic energy.

### Energy

When you lift an object, you transfer energy to it in the form of gravitational potential energy—that is, potential energy caused by gravity. The higher you lift an object, the more work you must do and the more energy you give to the object. This is also true if a machine lifts an object. The gravitational potential energy of an object depends on its height above Earth's surface, and it equals the work required to lift the object to that height.

Recall that gravitational potential energy is the product of an object's mass, gravitational acceleration, and height ($GPE = mgh$). In the diagram on page 149, the climber wants to reach the top of the hill. The higher she climbs, the greater her potential energy. This energy comes from the work the climber does. The potential energy she gains equals the amount of work she does.

### Work

As you have seen, when you use a machine to do work, there is always an exchange, or tradeoff, between the force you use to do the work and the distance over which you apply that force. You apply less force over a longer distance or greater force over a shorter distance.

To reach the top of the hill, the climber must do work. Because she needs to increase her potential energy by a certain amount, she must do the same amount of work to reach the top of the hill whether she climbs a steep slope or a gentle slope.

The sloping surface of the hill acts like a ramp, which is a simple machine called an inclined plane. You know that machines make work easier by changing the size or direction of a force. How does this machine make the climber's work easier?

As the climber goes up the hill, she is doing work against gravity.

1. One side of the hill is a very steep slope—almost straight up. If the climber takes the steep slope, she climbs a shorter distance, but she must use more force.

2. Another side of the hill is a long, gentle slope. Here the climber travels a greater distance but uses much less effort.

If the climber uses the steep slope, she must lift almost her entire weight. The inclined plane allows her to exert her input force over a longer distance; therefore, she can use just enough force to overcome the net force pulling her down the inclined plane. This force is less than her weight. In many cases, it is easier for people to use less force over a longer distance than it is for them to use more force over a shorter distance.

## Energy and Work

**To reach the top of the hill, the climber must do at least as much work as the amount of potential energy she needs to gain.**

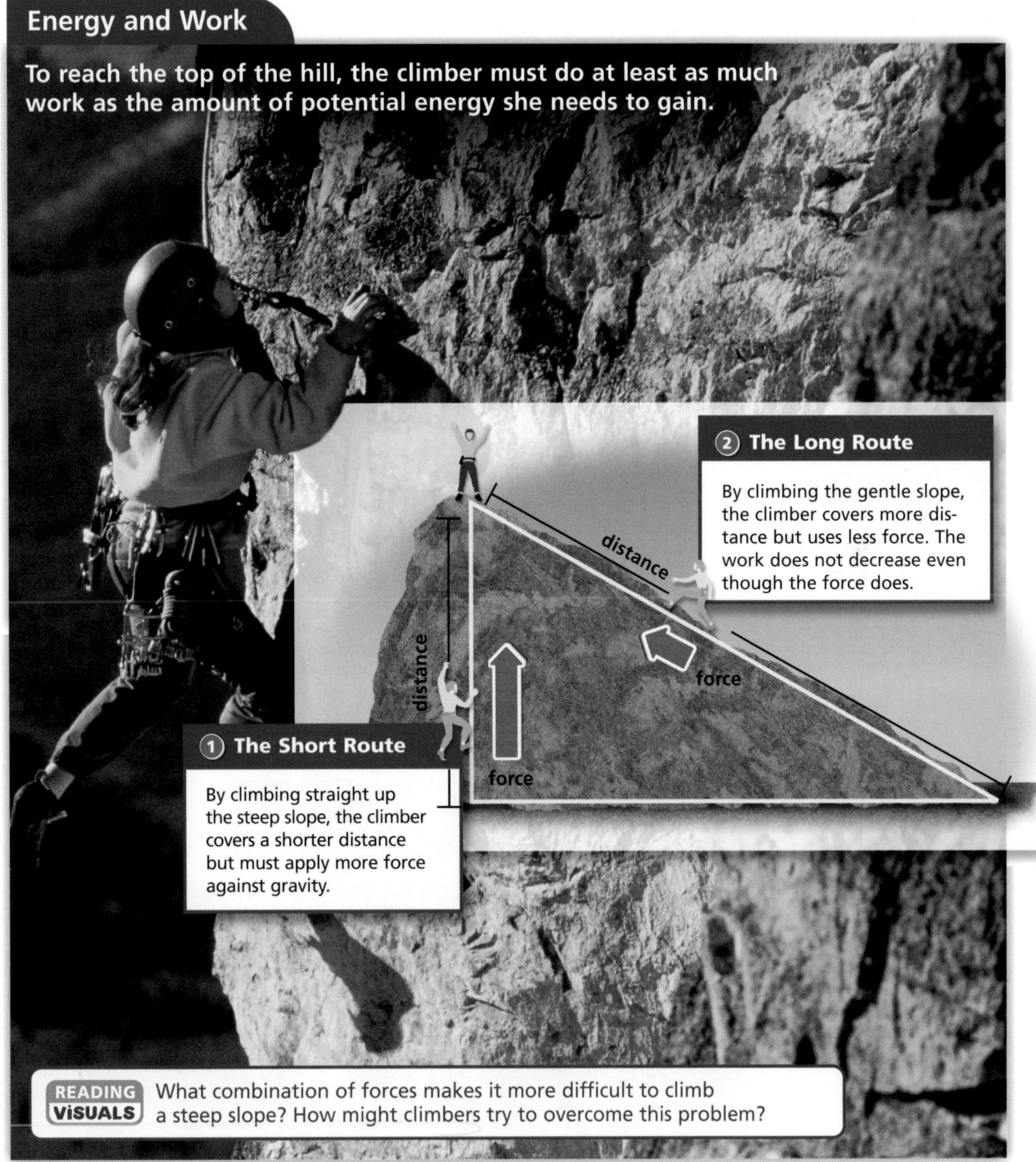


**① The Short Route**

By climbing straight up the steep slope, the climber covers a shorter distance but must apply more force against gravity.

**② The Long Route**

By climbing the gentle slope, the climber covers more distance but uses less force. The work does not decrease even though the force does.

**READING VISUALS** What combination of forces makes it more difficult to climb a steep slope? How might climbers try to overcome this problem?

## Output work is always less than input work.

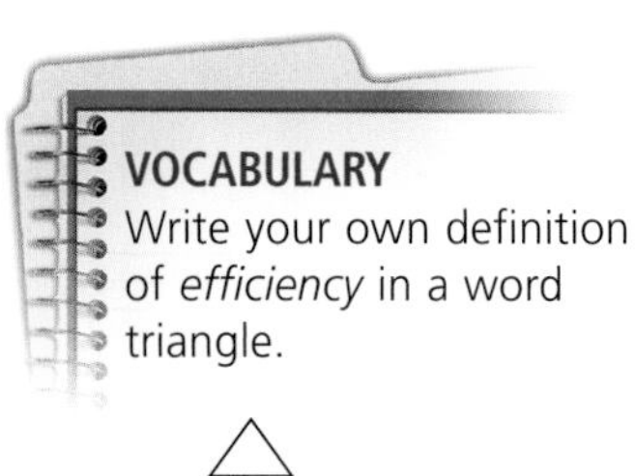

VOCABULARY
Write your own definition of *efficiency* in a word triangle.

The work you do on a machine is called the input work, and the work the machine does in turn is called the output work. A machine's **efficiency** is the ratio of its output work to the input work. An ideal machine would be 100 percent efficient. All of the input work would be converted to output work. Actual machines lose some input work to friction.

You can calculate the efficiency of a machine by dividing the machine's output work by its input work and multiplying that number by 100.

$$\text{Efficiency (\%)} = \frac{\text{Output work}}{\text{Input work}} \cdot 100$$

Recall that work is measured in joules. Suppose you do 600 J of work in using a rope system to lift a box. The work done on the box is 540 J. You would calculate the efficiency of the rope system as follows:

$$\text{Efficiency} = \frac{540\ \text{J}}{600\ \text{J}} \cdot 100 = 90\%$$

**CHECK YOUR READING** What is a machine's efficiency? How does it affect the amount of work a machine can do?

APPLY The mail carrier is riding a motorized human transport machine. Suppose the machine has an efficiency of 70 percent. How much work is lost in overcoming friction on the sidewalk and in the motor?

**Efficiency**
The work you put into a machine will always be greater than the work done by the machine. Some input work is always lost in overcoming friction.

## Efficiency and Energy

You know that work transfers energy and that machines make work easier. The more mechanical energy is lost in the transfer to other forms of energy, the less efficient the machine. Machines lose some energy in the form of heat due to friction. The more moving parts a machine has, the more energy it loses to friction because the parts rub together. Machines can lose energy to other processes as well.

For example, a car engine has an efficiency of only about 25 percent. It loses much of the energy supplied by its fuel to heat from combustion. By comparison, a typical electric motor has more than an 80 percent efficiency. That means the motor converts more than 80 percent of the input energy into mechanical energy, or motion.

Many appliances come with energy guides that can help a buyer compare the energy efficiency of different models. A washing machine with the highest energy rating may not always save the most energy, however, because users may have to run those machines more often.

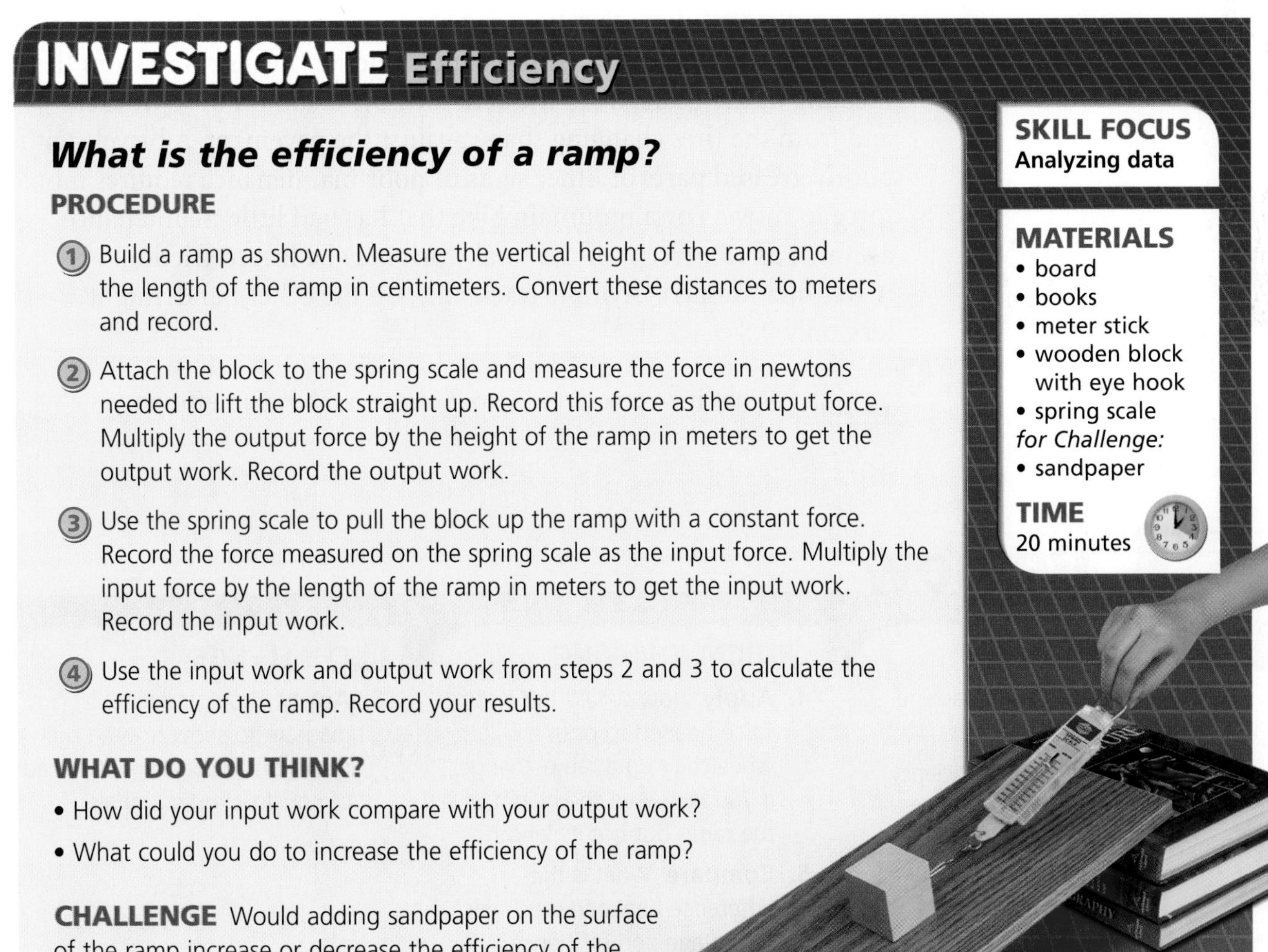

## INVESTIGATE Efficiency

### *What is the efficiency of a ramp?*

**PROCEDURE**

1. Build a ramp as shown. Measure the vertical height of the ramp and the length of the ramp in centimeters. Convert these distances to meters and record.
2. Attach the block to the spring scale and measure the force in newtons needed to lift the block straight up. Record this force as the output force. Multiply the output force by the height of the ramp in meters to get the output work. Record the output work.
3. Use the spring scale to pull the block up the ramp with a constant force. Record the force measured on the spring scale as the input force. Multiply the input force by the length of the ramp in meters to get the input work. Record the input work.
4. Use the input work and output work from steps 2 and 3 to calculate the efficiency of the ramp. Record your results.

**WHAT DO YOU THINK?**

- How did your input work compare with your output work?
- What could you do to increase the efficiency of the ramp?

**CHALLENGE** Would adding sandpaper on the surface of the ramp increase or decrease the efficiency of the ramp? Why? Test your hypothesis.

**SKILL FOCUS**
Analyzing data

**MATERIALS**
- board
- books
- meter stick
- wooden block with eye hook
- spring scale

*for Challenge:*
- sandpaper

**TIME**
20 minutes

Proper maintenance can help keep a bicycle running as efficiently as possible.

## Increasing Efficiency

Because all machines lose input work to friction, one way to improve the efficiency of a machine is by reducing friction. Oil is used to reduce friction between the moving parts of car engines. The use of oil makes engines more efficient.

Another machine that loses input work is a bicycle. Bicycles lose energy to friction and to air resistance. Friction losses result from the meeting of the gears, from the action of the chain on the sprocket, and from the tires changing shape against the pavement. A bicycle with poorly greased parts or other signs of poor maintenance requires more force to move. For a mountain bike that has had little maintenance, as much as 15 percent of the total work may be lost to friction. A well-maintained Olympic track bike, on the other hand, might lose only 0.5 percent.

What is a common way to increase a machine's efficiency?

# Review

### KEY CONCEPTS

1. In what ways can a machine change a force?
2. How is a machine's efficiency calculated?
3. Why is a machine's actual output work always less than its input work?

### CRITICAL THINKING

4. **Apply** How would the input force needed to push a wheelchair up a ramp change if you increased the height of the ramp but not its length?
5. **Compare** What is the difference between mechanical advantage and efficiency?

### CHALLENGE

6. **Apply** Draw and label a diagram to show how to pull down on a rope to raise a load of construction materials.

MATH in SCIENCE

SKILL: CHANGING RATIOS TO PERCENTS

MATH TUTORIAL
CLASSZONE.COM
Click on Math Tutorial for more help with percents and fractions.

# How Efficient Are Machines?

A hammer is used to pound in nails. It can also be used to pry nails out of wood. When used to pry nails, a hammer is a machine called a lever. Like all machines, the hammer is not 100 percent efficient.

Efficiency is the amount of work a machine does divided by the amount of work that is done on the machine. To calculate efficiency, you must first find the ratio of the machine's output work to the input work done on the machine. A ratio is the comparison of two numbers by means of division. You convert the ratio to a decimal by dividing. Then convert the decimal to a percent.

## Example

A person is doing 1000 joules of work on a hammer to pry up a nail. The hammer does 925 joules of work on the nail to pull it out of the wood.

**(1)** Find the ratio of output work to input work.

$$\frac{\text{Output work}}{\text{Input work}} = \frac{925 \text{ J}}{1000 \text{ J}} = 0.925$$

**(2)** To convert the decimal to a percent, multiply 0.925 by 100 and add a percent sign.

$$0.925 \cdot 100 = 92.5\%$$

**ANSWER** The efficiency of the hammer is 92.5 percent. This means that the hammer loses 7.5 percent of the input work to friction and other products.

No machine, no matter how large or small, is 100 percent efficient. Some of the input energy is lost to sound, heat, or other products.

**Answer the following questions.**

1. A construction worker does 1000 J of work in pulling down on a rope to lift a weight tied to the other end. If the output work of the rope system is 550 J, what is the ratio of output work to input work? What is the efficiency of the rope system?
2. If a machine takes in 20,000 J and puts out 5000 J, what is its efficiency?
3. You do 6000 J of work to pull a sled up a ramp. After you reach the top, you discover that the sled had 3600 J of work done on it. What is the efficiency of the ramp?

**CHALLENGE** If you put 7000 J of work into a machine with an efficiency of 50 percent, how much work will you get out?

KEY CONCEPT

# Six simple machines have many uses.

**BEFORE, you learned**

- Machines help you work by changing the size or direction of a force
- The number of times a machine multiplies the input force is the machine's mechanical advantage

**NOW, you will learn**

- How six simple machines change the size or direction of a force
- How to calculate mechanical advantage

**VOCABULARY**

**simple machine** p. 154
**lever** p. 155
**fulcrum** p. 155
**wheel and axle** p. 156
**pulley** p. 156
**inclined plane** p. 158
**wedge** p. 158
**screw** p. 159

**EXPLORE Changing Forces**

## *How can you change a force?*

**PROCEDURE**

1. Lay one pencil on a flat surface. Place the other pencil on top of the first pencil and perpendicular to it, as shown. Place the book on one end of the top pencil.
2. Push down on the free end of the top pencil to raise the book.
3. Change the position of the bottom pencil so that it is closer to the book and repeat step 2. Then move the bottom pencil closer to the end of the pencil you are pushing on and repeat step 2.

**MATERIALS**

- 2 pencils
- small book

**WHAT DO YOU THINK?**

- How did changing the position of the bottom pencil affect how much force you needed to lift the book?
- At which position is it easiest to lift the the book? most difficult?

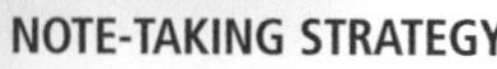

**NOTE-TAKING STRATEGY**
As you read, remember to take notes about the main ideas and supporting details.

## There are six simple machines.

You have read about how a ramp and a shovel can help you do work. A ramp is a type of inclined plane, and a shovel is a type of lever. An inclined plane and a lever are both simple machines. **Simple machines** are the six machines on which all other mechanical machines are based. In addition to the inclined plane and the lever, simple machines include the wheel and axle, pulley, wedge, and screw. As you will see, the wheel and axle and pulley are related to the lever, and the wedge and screw are related to the inclined plane. You will read about each of the six simple machines in detail in this section.

## Lever

A **lever** is a solid bar that rotates, or turns, around a fixed point. The bar can be straight or curved. The fixed point is called the **fulcrum.** A lever can multiply the input force. It can also change the direction of the input force. If you apply a force downward on one end of a lever, the other end can lift a load.

The way in which a lever changes an input force depends on the positions of the fulcrum, the input force, and the output force in relation to one another. Levers with different arrangements have different uses. Sometimes a greater output force is needed, such as when you want to pry up a bottle cap. At other times you use a greater input force on one end to get a higher speed at the other end, such as when you swing a baseball bat. The three different arrangements, sometimes called the three classes of levers, are shown in the diagram below.

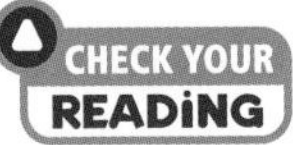


What two parts are needed to make a lever?

### Levers

**Levers can be classified according to where the fulcrum is.**

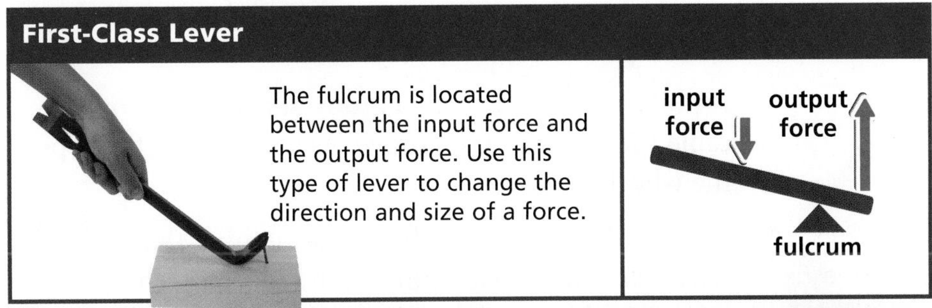

First-Class Lever
The fulcrum is located between the input force and the output force. Use this type of lever to change the direction and size of a force.
input force
output force
fulcrum


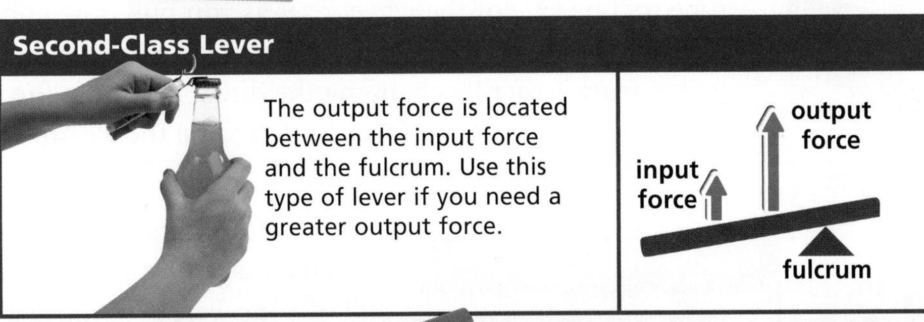

Second-Class Lever
The output force is located between the input force and the fulcrum. Use this type of lever if you need a greater output force.
output force
input force
fulcrum


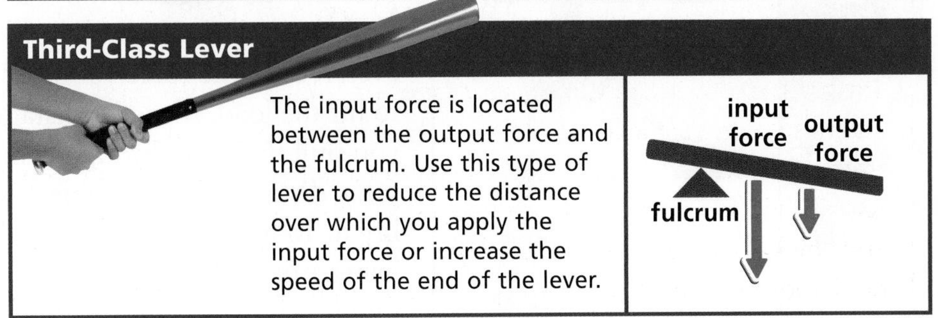

Third-Class Lever
The input force is located between the output force and the fulcrum. Use this type of lever to reduce the distance over which you apply the input force or increase the speed of the end of the lever.
input force
output force
fulcrum


**READING TiP**

The lengths of the arrows in the diagram represent the size of the force.

## Wheel and Axle

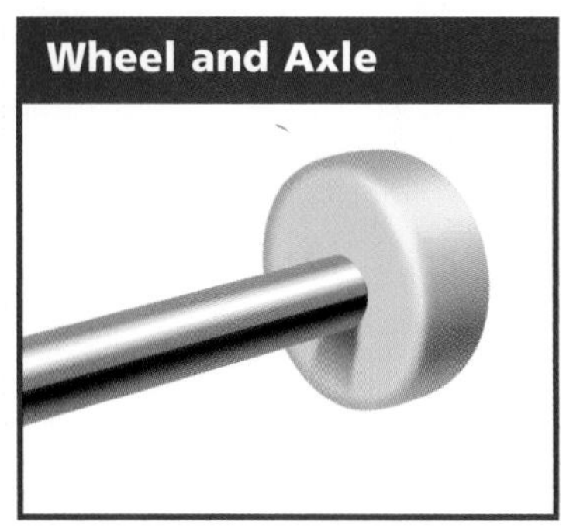


A **wheel and axle** is a simple machine made of a wheel attached to a shaft, or axle. The wheels of most means of transportation—such as a bicycle and a car—are attached to an axle. The wheel and axle act like a rotating collection of levers. The axle at the wheel's center is like a fulcrum. Other examples of wheels and axles are screwdrivers, steering wheels, doorknobs, and electric fans.

Depending on your purpose for using a wheel and axle, you might apply a force to turn the wheel or the axle. If you turn the wheel, your input force is transferred to the axle. Because the axle is smaller than the wheel, the output force acts over a shorter distance than the input force. A driver applies less force to a steering wheel to get a greater turning force from the axle, or steering column. This makes it easier to steer the car.

If, instead, you turn the axle, your force is transferred to the wheel. Because the wheel is larger than the axle, the force acts over a longer distance. A car also contains this use of a wheel and axle. The engine turns the drive axles, which turn the wheels.

Compare the results of putting force on the axle with putting force on the wheel.

## Pulley

A **pulley** is a wheel with a grooved rim and a rope or cable that rides in the groove. As you pull on the rope, the wheel turns.

A pulley that is attached to something that holds it steady is called a fixed pulley. An object attached to the rope on one side of the wheel rises as you pull down on the rope on the other side of the wheel. The fixed pulley makes work easier by changing the direction of the force. You must apply enough force to overcome the weight of the load and any friction in the pulley system.

A fixed pulley allows you to take advantage of the downward pull of your weight to move a load upward. It does not, however, reduce the force you need to lift the load. Also, the distance you pull the rope through is the same distance that the object is lifted. To lift a load two meters using a fixed pulley, you must pull down two meters of rope.

In a movable pulley setup, one end of the rope is fixed, but the wheel can move. The load is attached to the wheel. The person pulling the rope provides the output force that lifts the load. A single movable pulley does not change the direction of the force. Instead, it multiplies the force. Because the load is supported by two sections of rope, you need only half the force you would use with a fixed pulley to lift it. However, you must pull the rope through twice the distance.

**Movable Pulley**

How does a single fixed pulley differ from a single movable pulley?

A combination of fixed and movable pulleys is a pulley system called a block and tackle. A block and tackle is used to haul and lift very heavy objects. By combining fixed and movable pulleys, you can use more rope sections to support the weight of an object. This reduces the force you need to lift the object. The mechanical advantage of a single pulley can never be greater than 2. If engineers need a pulley system with a mechanical advantage greater than 2, they often use a block-and-tackle system.

## INVESTIGATE Pulleys

### *What is the mechanical advantage of a pulley system?*

**SKILL FOCUS**
Inferring

**MATERIALS**
- 100 g mass
- spring scale
- 2 pulleys with rope
- ring stand

**TIME**
20 minutes

**PROCEDURE**

1. Hang the mass on the spring scale to find its weight in newtons. Record this weight as your output force.
2. Tie the top of one pulley to the ring stand.
3. Attach the mass to the second pulley.
4. Attach one end of the second pulley's rope to the bottom of the first pulley. Then thread the free end of the rope through the second pulley. Loop the rope up and over the first pulley, as shown.
5. Attach the spring scale to the free end of the rope. Pull down to lift the mass. Record the force you used as your input force. Calculate the mechanical advantage of this pulley system. **Hint:** The mechanical advantage can be calculated by dividing the output force by the input force.

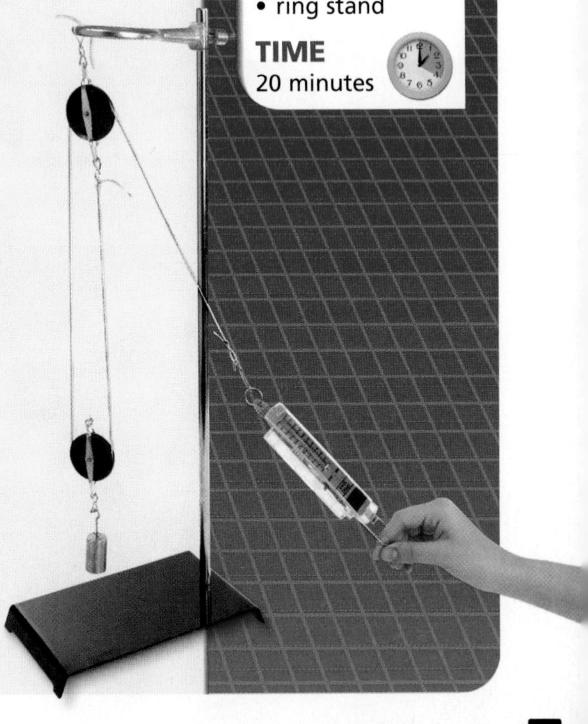

**WHAT DO YOU THINK?**

- How did your input force compare with your output force?
- What caused the results you observed?

**CHALLENGE** Explain what the mechanical advantage would be for a pulley system that includes another movable pulley.

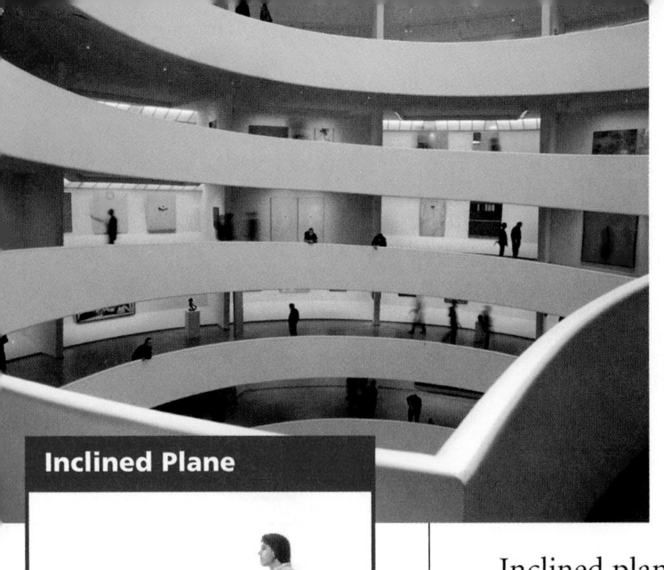

## Inclined Plane

Recall that it is difficult to lift a heavy object straight up because you must apply a force great enough to overcome the downward pull of the force of gravity. For this reason people often use ramps. A ramp is an **inclined plane,** a simple machine that is a sloping surface. The photograph at the left shows the interior of the Guggenheim Museum in New York City. The levels of the art museum are actually one continuous inclined plane.

Inclined planes make the work of raising an object easier because they support part of the weight of the object while it is being moved from one level to another. The surface of an inclined plane applies a reaction force on the object resting on it. This extra force on the object helps to act against gravity. If you are pushing an object up a ramp, you have to push with only enough force to overcome the smaller net force that pulls the object down parallel to the incline.

The less steep an inclined plane is, the less force you need to push or pull an object on the plane. This is because a less steep plane supports more of an object's weight than a steeper plane. However, the less steep an inclined plane is, the farther you must go to reach a certain height. While you use less force, you must apply that force over a greater distance.

How do inclined planes help people do work? Your answer should mention force.

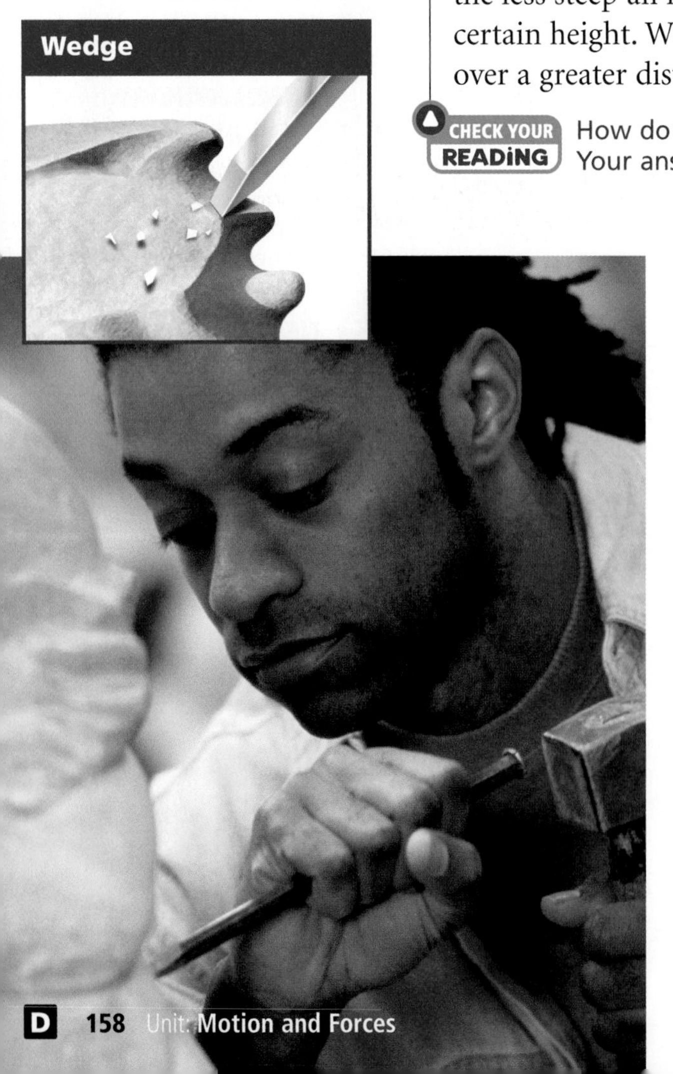


## Wedge

A **wedge** is a simple machine that has a thick end and a thin end. Wedges are used to cut, split, or pierce objects—or to hold objects together. A wedge is a type of inclined plane, but inclined planes are stationary, while wedges often move to do work.

Some wedges are single, movable inclined planes, such as a doorstop, a chisel, or an ice scraper. Another kind of wedge is made of two back-to-back inclined planes. Examples include the blade of an axe or a knife. In the photograph at the left, a sculptor is using a chisel to shape stone. The sculptor applies an input force on the chisel by tapping its thicker end with a mallet. That force pushes the thinner end of the chisel into the stone. As a result, the sides of the thinner end exert an output force that separates the stone.

The angle of the cutting edge determines how easily a wedge can cut through an object. Thin wedges have small angles and need less input force to cut than do thick wedges with large angles. That is why a sharp knife blade cuts more easily than a dull one.

You also can think of a wedge that cuts objects in terms of how it changes the pressure on a surface. The thin edges of a wedge provide a smaller surface area for the input force to act on. This greater pressure makes it easier to break through the surface of an object. A sharp knife can cut through an apple skin, and a sharp chisel can apply enough pressure to chip stone.

A doorstop is a wedge that is used to hold objects together. To do its job, a doorstop is pressed tip-first under a door. As the doorstop is moved into position, it lifts the door slightly and applies a force to the bottom of the door. In return, the door applies pressure to the doorstop and causes the doorstop to press against the floor with enough force to keep the doorstop—and the door—from moving.

## Screw

A **screw** is an inclined plane wrapped around a cylinder or cone to form a spiral. A screw is a simple machine that can be used to raise and lower weights as well as to fasten objects. Examples of screws include drills, jar lids, screw clamps, and nuts and bolts. The spiraling inclined plane that sticks out from the body of the screw forms the threads of the screw.

In the photograph at right, a person is using a screwdriver, which is a wheel and axle, to drive a screw into a piece of wood. Each turn of the screwdriver pushes the screw farther into the wood. As the screw is turned, the threads act like wedges, exerting an output force on the wood. If the threads are very close together, the force must be applied over a greater distance—that is, the screw must be turned many times—but less force is needed.

The advantage of using a screw instead of a nail to hold things together is the large amount of friction that keeps the screw from turning and becoming loose. Think of pulling a nail out of a piece of wood compared with pulling a screw from the same piece of wood. The nail can be pulled straight out. The screw must be turned through a greater distance to remove it from the wood.

Notice that the interior of the Guggenheim Museum shown on page 158 is not only an inclined plane. It is also an example of a screw. The inclined plane is wrapped around the museum's atrium, which is an open area in the center.

Explain how a screw moves deeper into the wood as it is turned.

## The mechanical advantage of a machine can be calculated.

Recall that the number of times a machine multiplies the input force is the machine's mechanical advantage. You can calculate a machine's mechanical advantage using this formula:

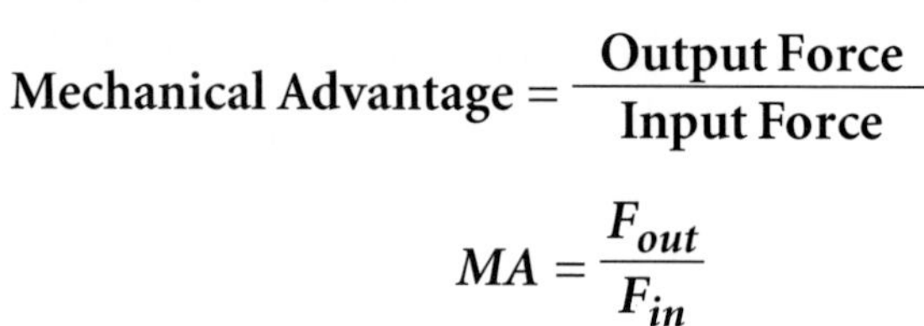

$$\text{Mechanical Advantage} = \frac{\text{Output Force}}{\text{Input Force}}$$

$$MA = \frac{F_{out}}{F_{in}}$$

This formula works for all machines, regardless of whether they are simple machines or more complicated machines.

If a machine decreases the force you use to do work, the distance over which you have to apply that force increases. It is possible to use this idea to calculate the mechanical advantage of a simple machine without knowing what the input and output forces are. To make this calculation, however, you must assume that your machine is not losing any work to friction. In other words, you must assume that your machine is 100 percent efficient. The mechanical advantage that you calculate when making this assumption is called the ideal mechanical advantage.

**READING TIP**

Scientists often consider the way in which an object will behave under ideal conditions, such as when there is no friction.

**Inclined Plane** You can calculate the ideal mechanical advantage of an inclined plane by dividing its length by its height.

$$\text{Ideal Mechanical Advantage} = \frac{\text{length of incline}}{\text{height of incline}}$$

$$IMA = \frac{l}{h}$$

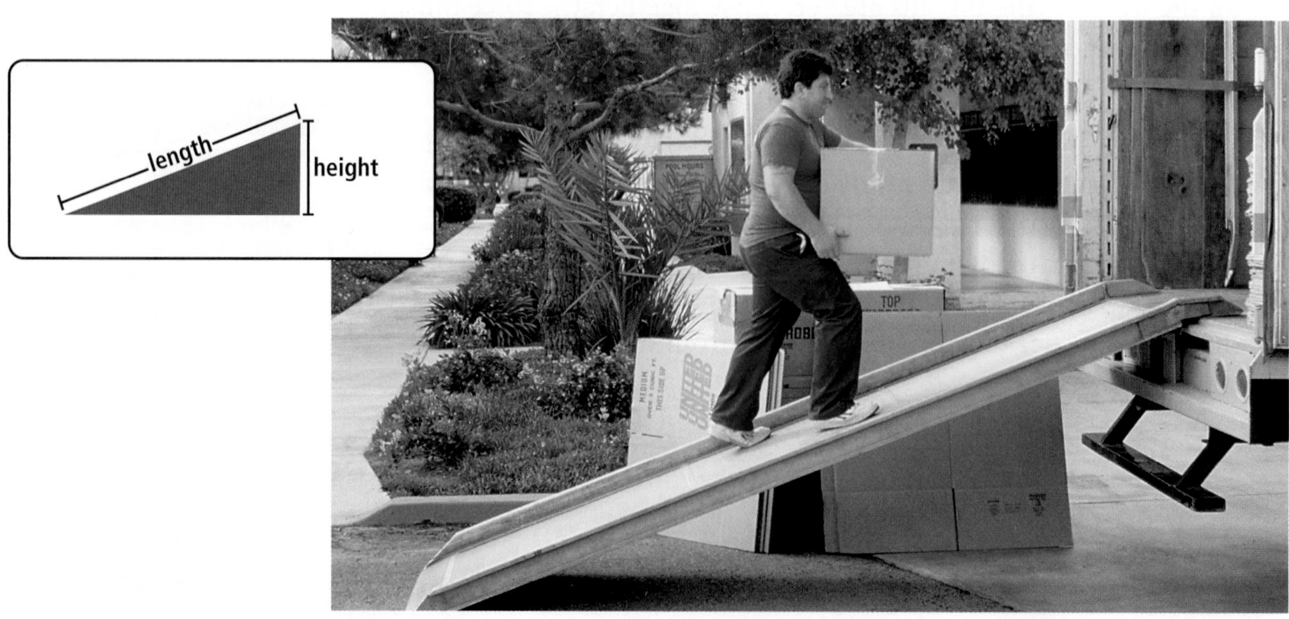

Be sure to use the length of the incline in your calculation, as shown in the diagram, and not the length of the base. If the mover in the photograph on page 160 increased the length of the ramp, he would increase the ramp's mechanical advantage. However, he would also increase the distance over which he had to carry the box.

Explore the mechanical advantage of an inclined plane.

**Wheel and Axle** To calculate the ideal mechanical advantage of a wheel and axle, use the following formula:

$$\text{Ideal Mechanical Advantage} = \frac{\text{Radius of input}}{\text{Radius of output}}$$

$$IMA = \frac{R_{in}}{R_{out}}$$

**REMINDER**

The radius is the distance from the center of the wheel or axle to any point on its circumference.

The Ferris wheel below is a giant wheel and axle. A motor applies an input force to the Ferris wheel's axle, which turns the wheel. In this example, the input force is applied to the axle, so the radius of the axle is the input radius in the formula above. The output force is applied by the wheel, so the radius of the wheel is the output radius.

For a Ferris wheel, the input force is greater than the output force. The axle turns through a shorter distance than the wheel does. The ideal mechanical advantage of this type of wheel and axle is less than 1.

Sometimes, as with a steering wheel, the input force is applied to turn the wheel instead of the axle. Then the input radius is the wheel's radius, and the output radius is the axle's radius. In this case, the input force on the wheel is less than the output force applied by the axle. The ideal mechanical advantage of this type of wheel and axle is greater than 1.

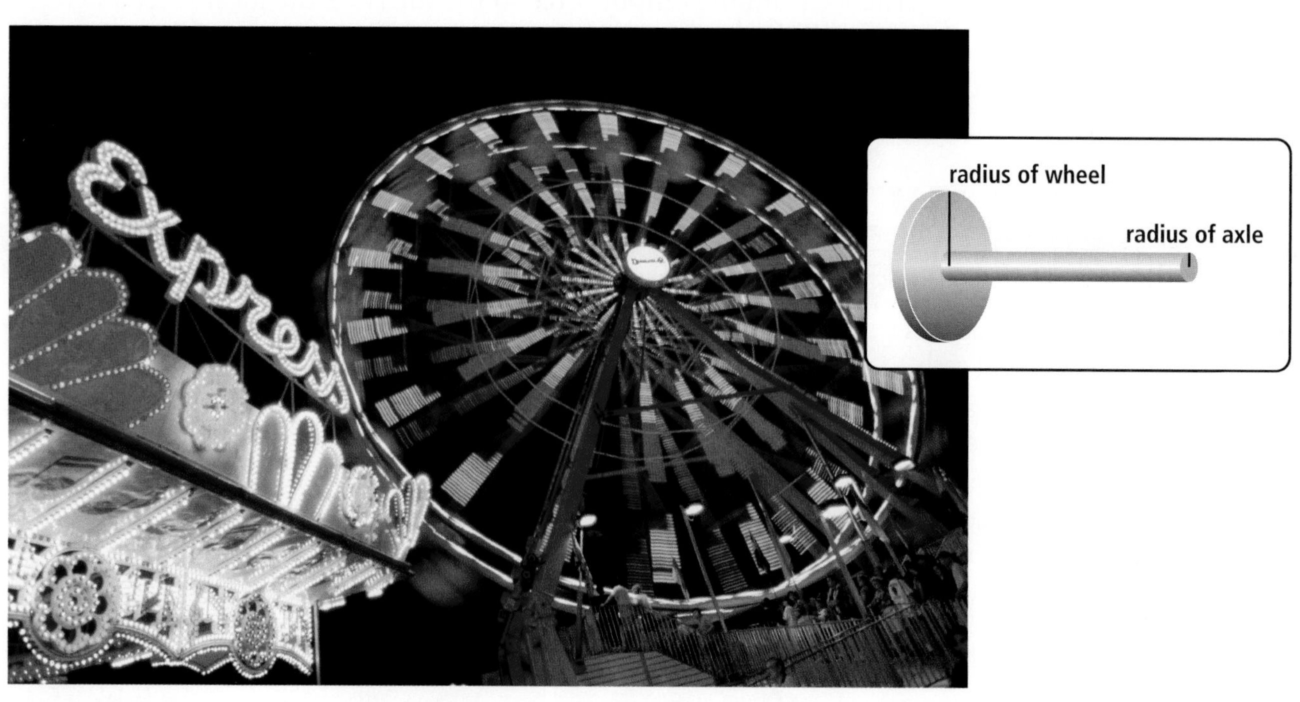

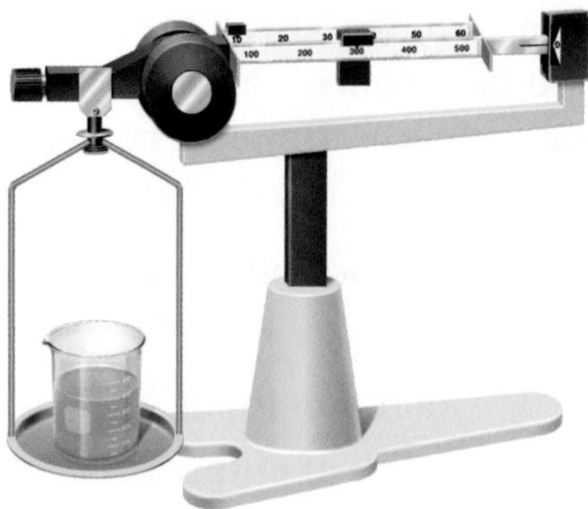

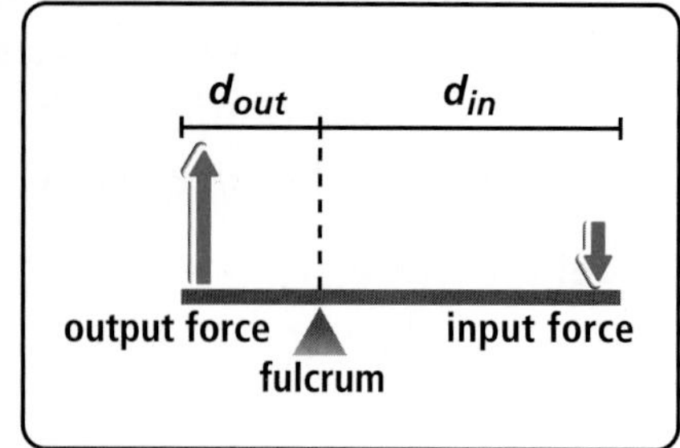


**Lever** The beam balance above is a lever. The beam is the solid bar that turns on a fixed point, or fulcrum. The fulcrum is the beam's balance point. When you slide the weight across the beam, you are changing the distance between the input force and the fulcrum. The mechanical advantage depends on the distances of the input force and output force from the fulcrum. The output force is applied to balance the beaker.

To calculate the ideal mechanical advantage of a lever, use the following formula:

$$\textbf{Ideal Mechanical Advantage} = \frac{\textbf{distance from input force to fulcrum}}{\textbf{distance from output force to fulcrum}}$$

$$IMA = \frac{d_{in}}{d_{out}}$$

This formula applies to all three arrangements of levers. If the distance from the input force to the fulcrum is greater than the distance from the output force to the fulcrum, the ideal mechanical advantage is greater than 1. The beam balance is an example of this type of lever.

## 5.2 Review

### KEY CONCEPTS

1. Name the six simple machines and give an example of each.
2. Explain how a screw changes the size of the force needed to push it into wood.
3. To calculate mechanical advantage, what two things do you need to know?

### CRITICAL THINKING

4. **Synthesize** How is a pulley similar to a wheel and axle?
5. **Calculate** What is the ideal mechanical advantage of a wheel with a diameter of 30 cm fixed to an axle with a diameter of 4 cm if the axle is turned?

### CHALLENGE

6. **Infer** How can you increase a wedge's mechanical advantage? Draw a diagram to show your idea.

CONNECTING SCIENCES

PHYSICAL SCIENCE AND LIFE SCIENCE

# A Running Machine

Marlon Shirley, who lives in Colorado, lost his lower left leg due to an accident at the age of five. He is a champion sprinter who achieved his running records while using a prosthesis (prahs-THEE-sihs), or a device used to replace a body part. Like his right leg, his prosthetic leg is a combination of simple machines that convert the energy from muscles in his body to move him forward. The mechanical system is designed to match the forces of his right leg.

## Legs as Levers

Compare Marlon Shirley's artificial leg with his right leg. Both legs have long rods—one made of bone and the other of metal—that provide a strong frame. These rods act as levers. At the knee and ankle, movable joints act as fulcrums for these levers to transfer energy between the runner's body and the ground.

## How Does It Work?

1. As the foot—real or artificial—strikes the ground, the leg stops moving forward and downward and absorbs the energy of the change in motion. The joints in the ankle and knee act as fulcrums as the levers transfer the energy to the muscle in the upper leg. This muscle acts like a spring to store the energy.
2. When the runner begins the next step, the energy is transferred back into the leg from the upper leg muscle. The levers in the leg convert the energy into forward motion of the runner's body.

The people who design prosthetic legs study the natural motion of a runner to learn exactly how energy is distributed and converted to motion so that they can build an artificial leg that works well with the real leg.

## EXPLORE

1. **VISUALIZE** Run across a room, paying close attention to the position of one of your ankles and knees as you move. Determine where the input force, output force, and fulcrum are in the lever formed by your lower leg.
2. **CHALLENGE** Use the library or the Internet to learn more about mechanical legs used in building robots that walk. How do the leg motions of these robots resemble your walking motions? How are they different?

Find out more about artificial limbs.

Other parts of the human body can act like simple machines. For example, teeth work like wedges.

KEY CONCEPT

# Modern technology uses compound machines.

**BEFORE, you learned**

- Simple machines change the size or direction of a force
- All machines have an ideal and an actual mechanical advantage

**NOW, you will learn**

- How simple machines can be combined
- How scientists have developed extremely small machines
- How robots are used

**VOCABULARY**

**compound machine** p. 164
**nanotechnology** p. 167
**robot** p. 169

THINK ABOUT

### *How does a tow truck do work?*

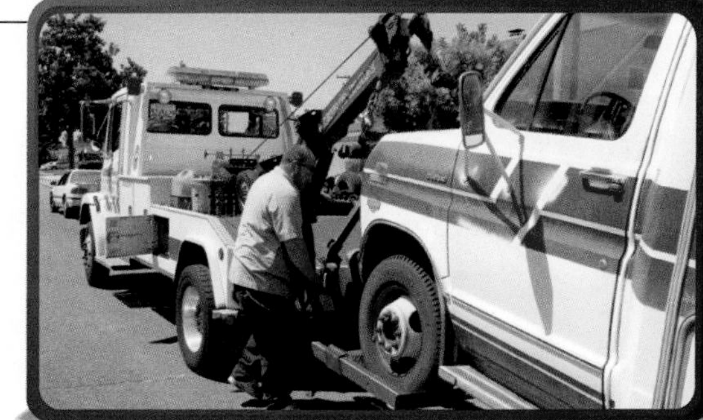

When a car is wrecked or disabled, the owner might call a towing service. The service sends a tow truck to take the car to be repaired. Tow trucks usually are equipped with a mechanism for freeing stuck vehicles and towing, or pulling, them. Look at the tow truck in the photograph at the right. What simple machines do you recognize?

## Compound machines are combinations of simple machines.

Like the tow truck pictured above, many of the more complex devices that you see or use every day are combinations of simple machines. For example, a pair of scissors is a combination of two levers. The cutting edges of those levers are wedges. A fishing rod is a lever with the fishing line wound around a wheel and axle, the reel. A machine that is made of two or more simple machines is called a **compound machine.**

**VOCABULARY**
Remember to write a definition for *compound machine* in a word triangle.

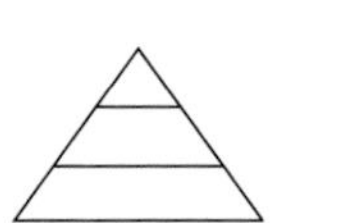

In a very complex compound machine, such as a car, the simple machines may not be obvious at first. However, if you look carefully at a compound machine, you should be able to identify forms of levers, pulleys, and wheels and axles.

How are simple machines related to compound machines?

The gears in the photograph and diagram are spur gears, the most common type of gear.

## Gears

Gears are based on the wheel and axle. Gears have teeth on the edge of the wheel that allow one gear to turn another. A set of gears forms a compound machine in which one wheel and axle is linked to another.

Two linked gears that are the same size and have the same number of teeth will turn at the same speed. They will move in opposite directions. In order to make them move in the same direction, a third gear must be added between them. The gear that turns another gear applies the input force; the gear that is turned exerts the output force. A difference in speed between two gears—caused by a difference in size and the distance each turns through—produces a change in force.

How do gears form a compound machine?

## Mechanical Advantage of Compound Machines

The mechanical advantage of any compound machine is equal to the product of the mechanical advantages of all the simple machines that make up the compound machine. For example, the ideal mechanical advantage of a pair of scissors would be the product of the ideal mechanical advantages of its two levers and two wedges.

The mechanical advantage of a pair of gears with different diameters can be found by counting the teeth on the gears. The mechanical advantage is the ratio of the number of teeth on the output gear to the number of teeth on the input gear. If there are more than two gears, count only the number of teeth on the first and last gears in the system. This ratio is the mechanical advantage of the whole gear system.

Compound machines typically must overcome more friction than simple machines because they tend to have many moving parts. Scissors, for example, have a lower efficiency than one lever because there is friction at the point where the two levers are connected. There is also friction between the blades of the scissors as they close.

APPLY What simple machines do you see in this Jaws of Life cutting tool?

## Modern technology creates new uses for machines.

Sophisticated modern machinery is often based on or contains simple machines. Consider Jaws of Life tools, which are used to help rescue people who have been in accidents. These cutters, spreaders, and rams are powered by hydraulics, the use of fluids to transmit force. When every second counts, these powerful machines can be used to pry open metal vehicles or collapsed concrete structures quickly and safely. The cutters are a compound machine made up of two levers—much like a pair of scissors. Their edges are wedges.

Contrast this equipment with a drill-like machine so small that it can be pushed easily through human arteries. Physicians attach the tiny drill to a thin, flexible rod and push the rod through a patient's artery to an area that is blocked. The tip rotates at extremely high speeds to break down the blockage. The tiny drill is a type of wheel and axle.

### Microtechnology and Nanotechnology

Manufacturers make machines of all sizes by shaping and arranging pieces of metal, plastic, and other materials. Scientists have used technology to create very small machines through miniaturization—the making of smaller and smaller, or miniature, parts. Micromachines are too small to be seen by the naked eye but are visible under a microscope. There is a limit, however, to how far micromachines can be shrunk.

**READING TIP**

*Micro*-means "one-millionth." For example, a microsecond is one-millionth of a second. *Nano*-means "one-billionth." A nanosecond is one-billionth of a second.

To develop even tinier machines, scientists needed a new approach. Scientists have used processes within the human body as their model. For example, inside the body a protein molecule carries materials back and forth within a cell on regular paths that are similar to little train tracks. The natural machines in the human body inspired scientists to develop machines that could be 1000 times smaller than the diameter of a human hair.

These extremely tiny machines are products of **nanotechnology,** the science and technology of building electronic circuits and devices from single atoms and molecules. Scientists say that they create these machines, called nanomachines, from the bottom up. Instead of shaping already formed material—such as metal and plastic—they guide individual atoms of material to arrange themselves into the shapes needed for the machine parts.

Learn more about nanomachines.

Tools enable scientists to see and manipulate single molecules and atoms. The scanning tunneling microscope can create pictures of individual atoms. To manipulate atoms, special tools are needed to guide them into place. Moving and shaping such small units presents problems, however. Atoms tend to attach themselves to other atoms, and the tools themselves are also made of atoms. Thus it is difficult to pick up an atom and place it in another position using a tool because the atom might attach itself to the tool.

**CHECK YOUR READING** Compare the way in which nanomachines are constructed with the way in which larger machines are built.

Nanomachines are still mostly in the experimental stage. Scientists have many plans for nanotechnology, including protecting computers from hackers and performing operations inside the body. For example, a nanomachine could be injected into a person's bloodstream, where it could patrol and search out infections before they become serious problems. When the machine had completed its work, it could switch itself off and be passed out of the body. Similar nanomachines could carry anti-cancer drugs to specific cells in the body.

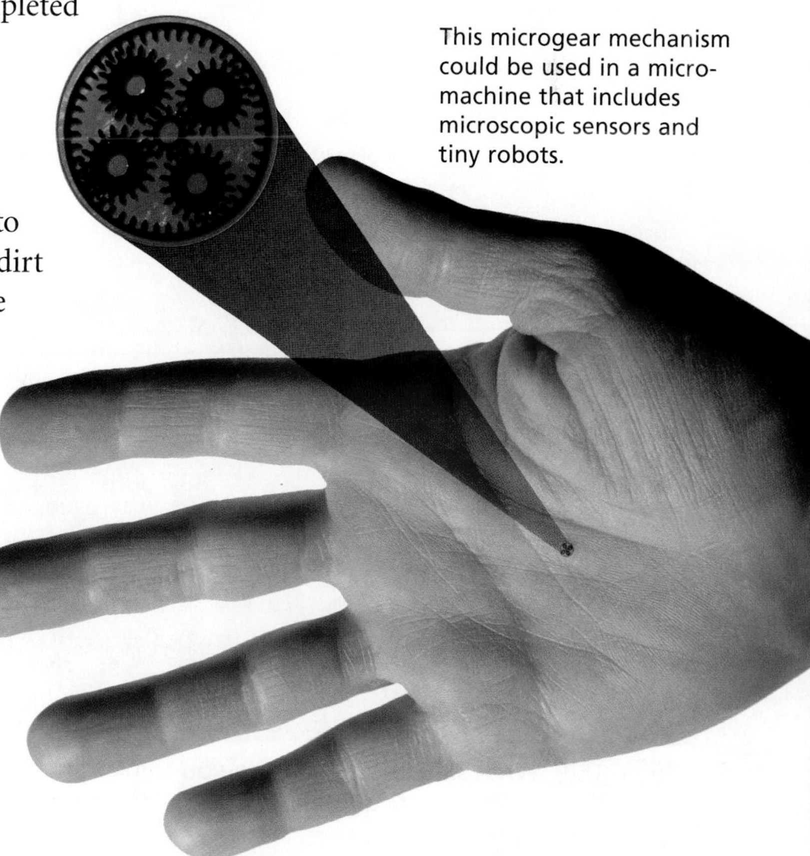

This microgear mechanism could be used in a micromachine that includes microscopic sensors and tiny robots.

Nanotechnology could also be used to develop materials that repel water and dirt and make cleaning jobs easy. Nanoscale biosensors could be used to detect harmful substances in the environment. Another possible use for nanotechnology is in military uniforms that can change color—the perfect camouflage.

In the future, nanotechnology may change the way almost everything is designed and constructed. As with any new technology, it will be important to weigh both the potential risks and benefits.

## A Robot at Work

**Scientists are using a robot to unlock the secrets of the Great Pyramid in Egypt.**

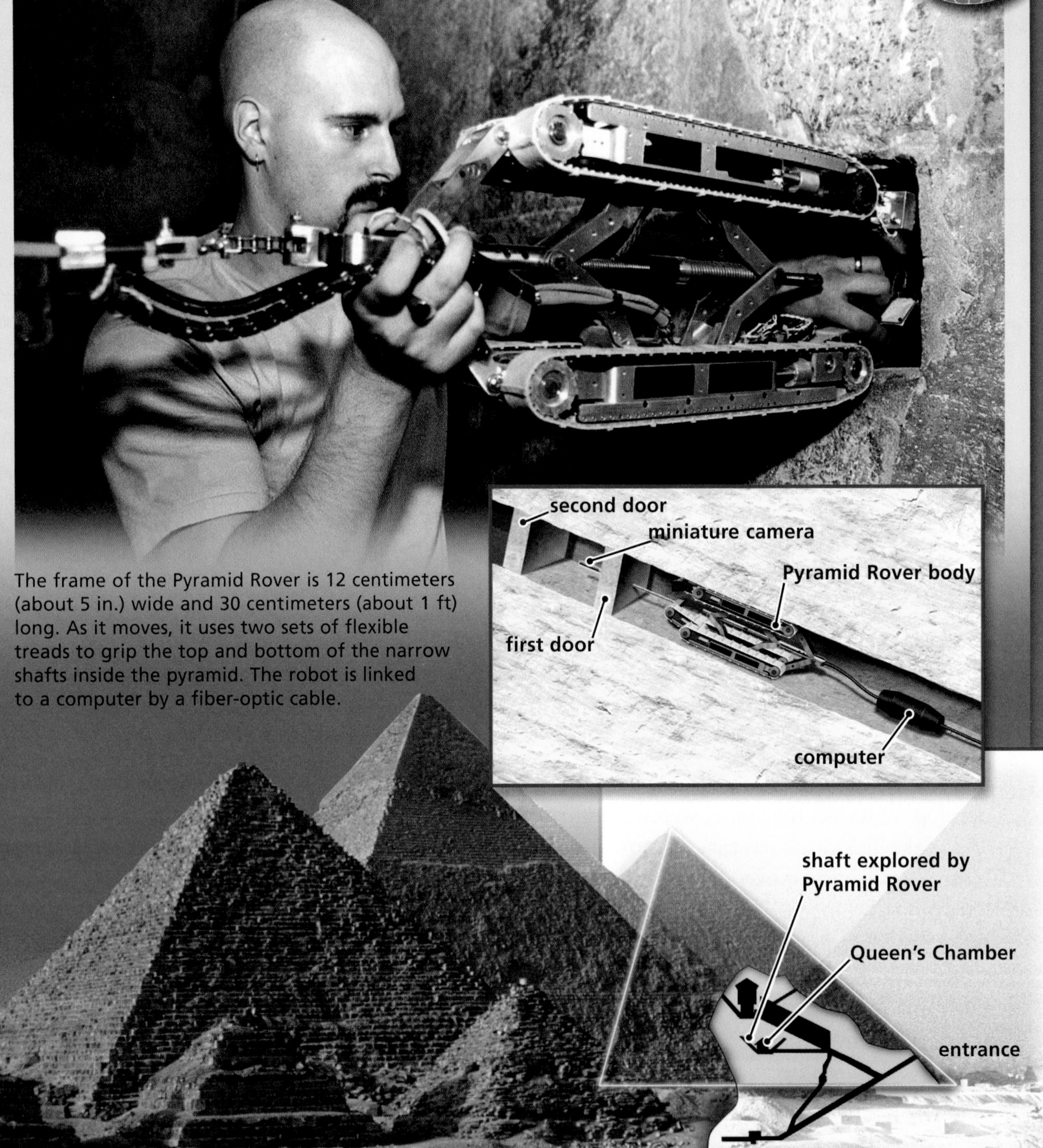


The frame of the Pyramid Rover is 12 centimeters (about 5 in.) wide and 30 centimeters (about 1 ft) long. As it moves, it uses two sets of flexible treads to grip the top and bottom of the narrow shafts inside the pyramid. The robot is linked to a computer by a fiber-optic cable.

**READING VISUALS** What simple machines do you think might be part of the Pyramid Rover?

## Robots

Humans have always taken risks to do jobs in places that are dangerous or difficult to get to. More and more often, robots can be used to do these jobs. A **robot** is a machine that works automatically or by remote control. When many people hear the word *robot,* they think of a machine that looks or moves like a person. However, most robots do not resemble humans at all. That is because they are built to do things humans cannot do or to go places where it is difficult for humans to go.

Find out more about the Pyramid Rover and other robots.

The Pyramid Rover, shown on page 168, is an example of a robot developed to go where people cannot. After a camera revealed a door at the end of an eight-inch-square shaft inside the Great Pyramid, the Pyramid Rover was sent through the shaft to explore the area. While researchers remained in the Queen's Chamber in the center of the pyramid, the robot climbed the shaft until it came to a door. Using ultrasound equipment mounted on the robot, researchers determined that the door was three inches thick. The robot drilled a hole in the door for a tiny camera and a light to pass through. The camera then revealed another sealed door!

Many companies use robots to manufacture goods quickly and efficiently. Robots are widely used for jobs such as welding, painting, and assembling products. Robots do some repetitive work better than humans, because robots do not get tired or bored. Also, they do the task in exactly the same way each time. Robots are very important to the automobile and computer industries.

How are robots better than humans at some jobs?

### KEY CONCEPTS

1. How do you estimate the mechanical advantage of a compound machine?
2. What are some uses of nanotechnology? Can you think of other possible uses for nanomachines?
3. What are three types of jobs that robots can do?

### CRITICAL THINKING

4. **Synthesize** What factors might limit how large or how small a machine can be?
5. **Infer** How do you think the size of a gear compared with other gears in the same system affects the speed of its rotation?

### CHALLENGE

6. **Apply** Robots might be put to use replacing humans in firefighting and other dangerous jobs. Describe a job that is dangerous. Tell what a robot must be able to do and what dangers it must be able to withstand to accomplish the required tasks.

# CHAPTER INVESTIGATION

## Design a Machine

DESIGN — YOUR OWN —

### OVERVIEW AND PURPOSE

Although simple machines were developed thousands of years ago, they are still used today for a variety of purposes. Tasks such as cutting food with a knife, using a screwdriver to tighten a screw, and raising a flag on a flagpole all require simple machines. Activities such as riding a bicycle and raising a drawbridge make use of compound machines. In this investigation you will use what you have learned about simple and compound machines to

- choose a machine to design
- build your machine, test it, and calculate its mechanical advantage and efficiency

### MATERIALS

- 500 g object
- 100 g object
- meter stick
- spring scale
- pulleys with rope
- board
- stick or pole

### Procedure

1. Make a data table like the one shown on page 171.

2. From among the three choices listed below, choose which problem you are going to solve.

**Carnival Game** You work for a company that builds carnival games. Your supervisor has asked you to build a game in which a simple machine moves a 500-gram object from the bottom of the game 1 meter up to the top. This simple machine can be powered only by the person operating the game.

**Video Game Contest** The marketing department of a video game company is holding a contest. Candidates are asked to submit a working model of a compound machine that will move a 500-gram object a distance of 1 meter. The winning design will be used in a new video game the company hopes to sell. This compound machine must include at least 2 simple machines.

**Construction Company** You work for a construction company. Your boss has asked you to design a machine for lifting. Your first step is to build a scale model. The model must be a compound machine with a mechanical advantage of 5 that can move a 500-gram object a distance of 1 meter. You also can use a 100-gram object in your design.

3 Brainstorm design ideas on paper. Think of different types of machines you might want to build. Choose one machine to build.

4 Build your machine. Use your machine to perform the task of moving a 500-gram object a distance of 1 meter.

If you chose the third problem, test your compound machine to determine if it has a mechanical advantage of 5. If not, modify your machine and retest it.

5 Record all measurements in your data table.

## Observe and Analyze

Write It Up

1. **RECORD OBSERVATIONS** Make a sketch of your machine.
2. **CALCULATE** Use your data to calculate the mechanical advantage and efficiency of your machine. Use the formulas below.

$$\text{Mechanical Advantage} = \frac{\text{Output Force}}{\text{Input Force}}$$

$$\text{Efficiency (\%)} = \frac{\text{Output work}}{\text{Input work}} \cdot 100$$

3. **ANALYZE**

   **Carnival Game** Add arrows to the drawing of your machine to show the forces involved and the direction of those forces. If your goal was to move the ball from the top of the game to the bottom at a constant speed, how would your machine and diagram have to be changed?

   **Video Game Contest** Does your machine change the size of the force, the direction of the force, or both? If you used a pulley system (two or more pulleys working together), describe the advantages of using such a system.

   **Construction Company** Determine whether force or distance is changed by each simple machine in your compound machine. In what ways might you improve your machine to increase its efficiency?

## Conclude

Write It Up

1. **INFER** How might changing the arrangement of the parts in your machine affect the machine's mechanical advantage?
2. **IDENTIFY LIMITS** What was the hardest part about designing and constructing your machine?
3. **APPLY** If you needed to lift a large rock from a hole at a construction site, which type of simple machine would you use and why? Which type of compound machine would be useful?

## INVESTIGATE Further

**CHALLENGE** If you made a simple machine, how would you combine it with another simple machine to increase its mechanical advantage?

If you made a compound machine, redesign it to increase its efficiency or mechanical advantage. What made the difference and why?

Draw a plan for the new machine. Circle the parts that were changed. If you have time, build your new machine.

Design a Machine

Observe and Analyze

Table 1. Machine Data

| Output force | Input force | Mechanical Advantage |
|---|---|---|
| | | |
| Output work | Input work | Efficiency |
| | | |

Sketch

# 5 Chapter Review

## the BIG idea

**Machines help people do work by changing the force applied to an object.**

## KEY CONCEPTS SUMMARY

### 5.1 Machines help people do work.

When you use a machine to do work, there is always an exchange, or tradeoff, between the force you use and the distance over which you apply that force. You can use less force over a greater distance or a greater force over a shorter distance to do the same amount of work.

**VOCABULARY**
**machine** p. 145
**mechanical advantage** p. 147
**efficiency** p. 150

### 5.2 Six simple machines have many uses.

Simple machines change the size and/or direction of a force.

**changes direction**

**changes size**

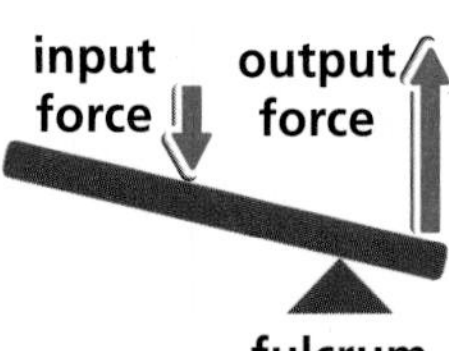


**changes both**

**VOCABULARY**
**simple machine** p. 154
**lever** p. 155
**fulcrum** p. 155
**wheel and axle** p. 156
**pulley** p. 156
**inclined plane** p. 158
**wedge** p. 158
**screw** p. 159

### 5.3 Modern technology uses compound machines.

- Compound machines are combinations of simple machines.

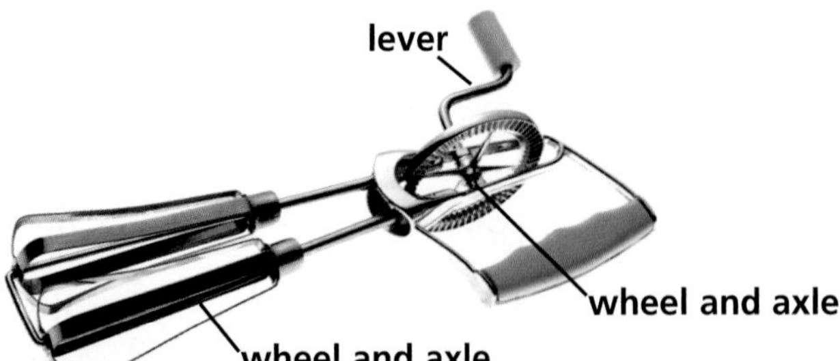


- Modern technology creates new uses for machines.
  —Microtechnology and nanotechnology
  —Robots

**VOCABULARY**
**compound machine** p. 164
**nanotechnology** p. 167
**robot** p. 169

## Reviewing Vocabulary

*Write the name of the simple machine shown in each illustration. Give an example from real life for each one.*

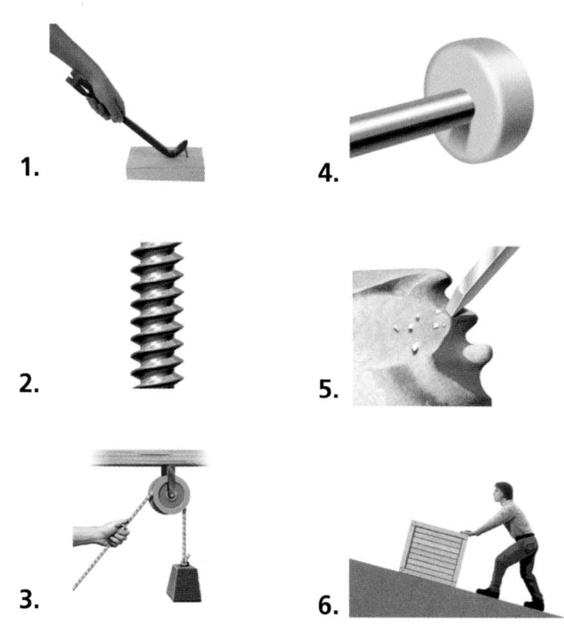


*Copy the chart below, and write the definition for each term in your own words. Use the meaning of the term's root to help you.*

| Term | Root Meaning | Definition |
|---|---|---|
| 7. machine | having power | |
| 8. nanotechnology | one-billionth | |
| 9. simple machine | basic | |
| 10. efficiency | to accomplish | |
| 11. compound machine | put together | |
| 12. robot | work | |
| 13. fulcrum | to support | |

## Reviewing Key Concepts

**Multiple Choice** *Choose the letter of the best answer.*

**14.** Machines help you work by
- **a.** decreasing the amount of work that must be done
- **b.** changing the size and/or direction of a force
- **c.** decreasing friction
- **d.** conserving energy

**15.** To calculate mechanical advantage, you need to know
- **a.** time and energy
- **b.** input force and output force
- **c.** distance and work
- **d.** size and direction of a force

**16.** A machine in which the input force is equal to the output force has a mechanical advantage of
- **a.** 0
- **b.** between 0 and 1
- **c.** 1
- **d.** more than 1

**17.** You can increase a machine's efficiency by
- **a.** increasing force
- **b.** reducing work
- **c.** increasing distance
- **d.** reducing friction

**18.** Levers turn around a
- **a.** fixed point called a fulcrum
- **b.** solid bar that rotates
- **c.** wheel attached to an axle
- **d.** sloping surface called an inclined plane

**19.** When you bite into an apple, your teeth act as what kind of simple machine?
- **a.** lever
- **b.** pulley
- **c.** wedge
- **d.** screw

**Short Answer** *Answer each of the following questions in a sentence or two.*

**20.** Describe the simple machines that make up scissors.

**21.** How do you calculate the mechanical advantage of a compound machine?

**22.** How did scientists use processes inside the human body as a model for making nanomachines?

## Thinking Critically

23. **SYNTHESIZE** How is a screw related to an inclined plane?

24. **INFER** Which simple machine would you use to raise a very heavy load to the top of a building? Why?

25. **APPLY** If you reached the top of a hill by using a path that wound around the hill, would you do more work than someone who climbed a shorter path? Why or why not? Who would use more force?

26. **APPLY** You are using a board to pry a large rock out of the ground when the board suddenly breaks apart in the middle. You pick up half of the board and use it to continue prying up the rock. The fulcrum stays in the same position. How has the mechanical advantage of the board changed? How does it change your work?

27. **SYNTHESIZE** What is the difference between a single fixed pulley and a single movable pulley? Draw a diagram to illustrate the difference.

*Use the information in the diagram below to answer the next three questions.*

28. **SYNTHESIZE** What is the mechanical advantage of the ramp? By how many times does the ramp multiply the man's input force?

29. **SYNTHESIZE** If the ramp's length were longer, what effect would this have on its mechanical advantage? Would this require the man to exert more or less input force?

30. **INFER** If the ramp's length stayed the same but the height was raised, how would this change the input force required?

## Using Math Skills in Science

*Complete the following calculations.*

31. You swing a hockey stick with a force of 10 N. The stick applies 5 N of force on the puck. What is the mechanical advantage of the hockey stick?

32. Your input work on a manual lawn mower is 125,000 J. The output work is 90,000 J. What is the efficiency of the lawn mower?

33. If a car engine has a 20 percent efficiency, what percentage of the input work is lost?

34. A steering wheel has a radius of 21 cm. The steering column on which it turns has a radius of 3 cm. What is the mechanical advantage of this wheel and axle?

35. Two gears with the same diameter form a gear system. Each gear has 24 teeth. What is the mechanical advantage of this gear system?

## the BIG idea

36. **DRAW CONCLUSIONS** Look back at the photograph on pages 142–143. Name the simple machines you see in the photograph. How do you think they work together to move balls through the sculpture? How has your understanding changed as to the way in which machines help people work?

37. **SYNTHESIZE** Think of a compound machine you have used recently. Explain which simple machines it includes and how they helped you do work.

38. **PREDICT** How do you think nanotechnology will be useful in the future? Give several examples.

## UNIT PROJECTS

Evaluate all of the data, results, and information from your project folder. Prepare to present your project to the class. Be ready to answer questions posed by your classmates about your results.

# Standardized Test Practice

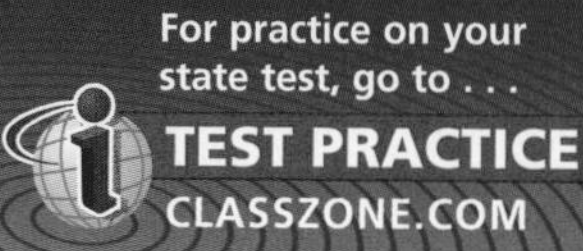


## Analyzing Graphics

The Archimedean screw is a mechanical device first used more than 2000 years ago. It consists of a screw inside a cylinder. One end of the device is placed in water. As the screw is turned with a handle, its threads carry water upward. The Archimedean screw is still used in some parts of the world to pump water for irrigating fields. It can also be used to move grain in mills.

*Study the illustration of an Archimedean screw. Then answer the questions that follow.*

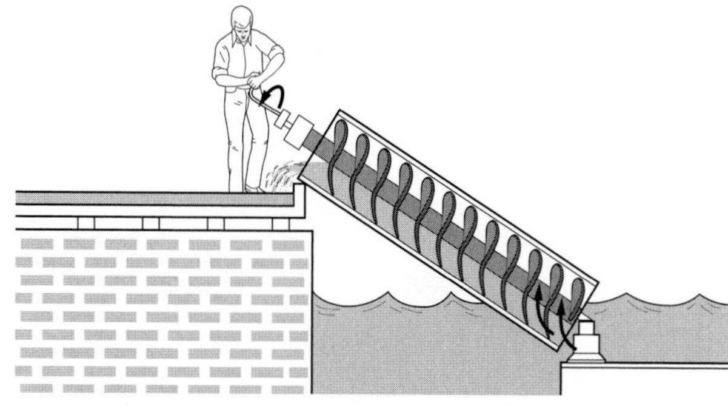

**1.** Which type of simple machine moves water in the cylinder?

**a.** block and tackle  **c.** screw
**b.** pulley  **d.** wedge

**2.** Which type of simple machine is the handle?

**a.** wheel and axle  **c.** pulley
**b.** inclined plane  **d.** wedge

**3.** What is the energy source for the Archimedean screw?

**a.** the water pressure inside the screw
**b.** the person who is turning the handle
**c.** falling water that is turning the screw
**d.** electrical energy

**4.** How is the Archimedean screw helping the person in the illustration do work?

**a.** by decreasing the input force needed to lift the water
**b.** by decreasing the work needed to lift the water
**c.** by decreasing the distance over which the input force is applied
**d.** by keeping the water from overflowing its banks

**5.** If the threads on the Archimedean screw are closer together, the input force must be applied over a greater distance. This means that the person using it must turn the handle

**a.** with more force
**b.** fewer times but faster
**c.** in the opposite direction
**d.** more times with less effort

## Extended Response

*Answer the two questions below in detail.*

**6.** A playground seesaw is an example of a lever. The fulcrum is located at the center of the board. People seated at either end take turns applying the force needed to move the other person. If one person weighs more than the other, how can they operate the seesaw? Consider several possibilities in your answer.

**7.** Picture two gears of different sizes turning together. Suppose you can apply a force to turn the larger gear or the smaller gear, and it will turn the other. Discuss what difference it would make whether you turned the larger or smaller gear. Describe the input work you would do on the gear you are turning and the output work that gear would do on the other gear.

UNIT E

# Electricity and Magnetism

magnet

ATTRACT

magnetic field

# Electricity and Magnetism Contents Overview

## Unit Features





**the BIG idea**

Moving electric charges transfer energy.



**the BIG idea**

Circuits control the flow of electric charge.



**the BIG idea**

Current can produce magnetism, and magnetism can produce current.

# Electronics in Music

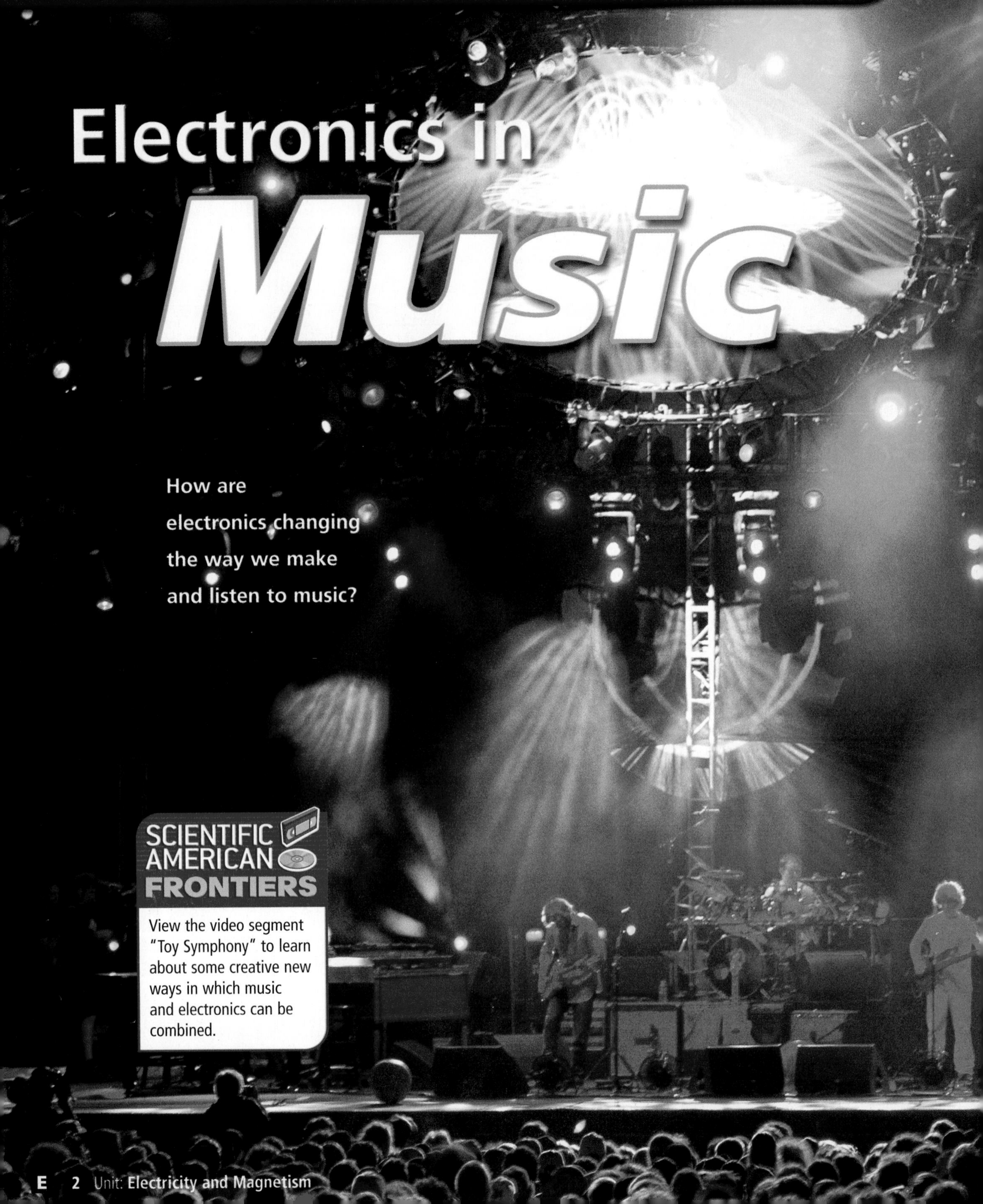

How are electronics changing the way we make and listen to music?

SCIENTIFIC AMERICAN FRONTIERS

View the video segment "Toy Symphony" to learn about some creative new ways in which music and electronics can be combined.

The quality of amplified sound waves can be controlled using electronics. Controls on this soundboard are adjusted in preparation for an outdoor concert.

## Catching a Sound Wave

Everyone knows that music and electronics go together. If you want to hear music, you turn on a radio or TV, choose a CD or DVD to play, or listen to a computer file downloaded in MP3. All of these formats use electronics to record, play, and amplify music. Some of the most recent developments in music also use electronics to produce the music in the first place. For example, the orchestral music playing in the background of the last blockbuster movie you saw may not have been played by an orchestra at all. It may have been produced electronically on a computer.

Music consists of sound, and sound is a wave. Inside your TV or stereo equipment, electronic circuits represent sound waves as analog signals or digital signals. In analog recordings a peak in the original sound wave corresponds to a peak in the current. Radio and TV broadcasts are usually analog signals. The sound wave is converted to electromagnetic waves sent out through the air. Your radio or TV set receives these waves and converts them back to a sound wave.

In digital sound recordings the system samples the incoming sound wave at frequent intervals of time, such as 44,100 times per second. The system measures the height of each wave and assigns it a number. The numbers form a digital signal. This information can then be stored and transmitted. The playback electronics, such as CD players and DVD players, convert the signal back to a sound wave for you to hear.

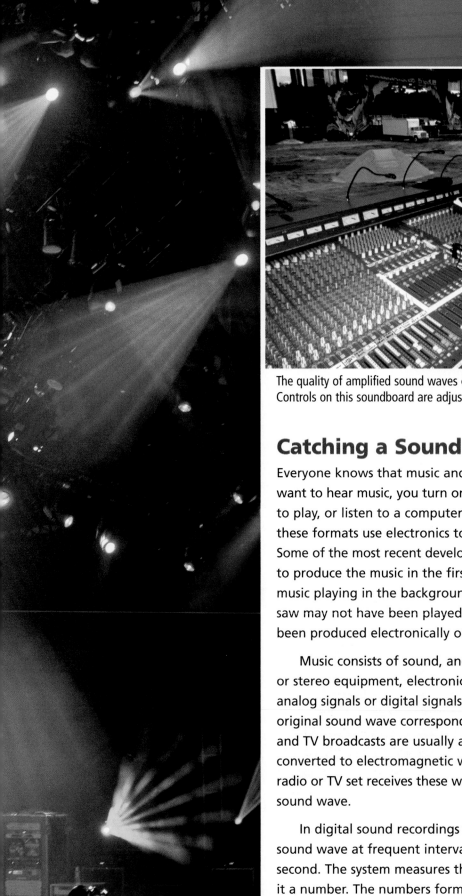

## Digital Devices

In a compact disc (CD), the numbers representing the sound wave are coded into a series of microscopic pits in a long spiral track burned into the plastic of the CD. A laser beam scans the track and reads the pits, converting the data back into numbers. This information is then converted into sound waves by an electronic circuit in the CD player. CDs can store up to 74 minutes of music because the pits are only a few millionths of a meter in size. Digital videodiscs (DVDs) often have several layers, each with a separate data track, and use even smaller tracks and pits than CDs use. As a result, a DVD can store seven times as much information as a CD.

MP3 players store digital files that are compressed in size.

The amount of computer space needed to represent a song in normal digital format is too large to store very many songs on a single device. However, the development of a compression program called MP3 decreases the size of a typical song to one-tenth its original size. This enables you to buy and download a song from the Internet in minutes instead of hours and store files on your computer or MP3 player without taking up too much space.

## Making Music

These advances in recording and playing music enables you to listen to music, whatever your taste in music happens to be. Electronic technology also allows you to change the music or even generate your own music, as shown in the video. Recording engineers used to work with large electronic consoles with hundreds of switches in order to blend different singers and background

**View the "Toy Symphony" segment of your *Scientific American Frontiers* video to learn how electronic devices allow people to interact with music in new ways.**

**IN THIS SCENE FROM THE VIDEO** **Kids play with Beatbugs at MIT's Media Lab.**

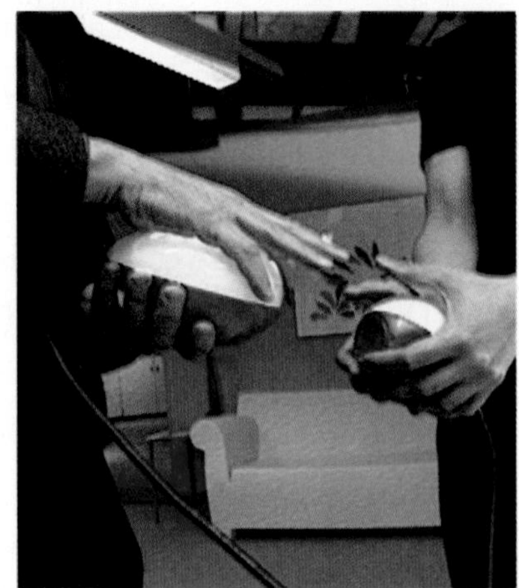

**PLAYING WITH SOUNDS** At the Massachusetts Institute of Technology (MIT) Media Lab, Tod Machover and his colleagues have invented several new musical instruments that are based on electronics. One such invention is the hyperviolin, demonstrated by concert violinist Joshua Bell. As Joshua plays the violin, a computer registers the movements of the bow and produces new and different sounds from the movements. Other musical electronic devices in the lab are designed to allow someone with little or no experience with an instrument to play and compose music.

With Beatbugs—small interactive devices—kids can play music and collaborate with others. They can also compose and edit their own music. Using new computer software, a ten-year-old boy was able to compose an entire symphony played by the German Symphony Orchestra.

Home recording studios are possible because of new electronic technology.

instruments or to add special effects such as echoes or distortion. Now this can all be done on a laptop computer, using the Musical Instrument Digital Interface (MIDI).

MIDI technology is an advancement in digital technology. Whereas CD, DVD, and MP3 files represent the sound waves themselves, MIDI files represent the instructions for another device—such as an electronic instrument—to play the music. With MIDI, you can connect an electronic keyboard directly to a computer and compose and edit your own music, layer in the sounds of different instruments, and dub in special effects. Once you understand how to use electronics to produce the sound waves you want, you can become your own favorite band.

## UNANSWERED Questions

Every year, scientists develop new technologies affecting the way we produce and listen to music. As advances in music technology are made, new question arise.

- Are there electronic sounds that no one has heard before?
- How will the development of music technology affect who is producing music?
- What type of devices will people be using to listen to music in 50 years?

## UNIT PROJECTS

**As you study this unit, work alone or with a group on one of these projects.**

### Multimedia Presentation

Put together an informative presentation that explains how electric guitars work.

- Gather information about electric guitars. Learn how they use both electricity and magnetism.
- Give a presentation that uses mixed media, such as a computer slide show, model, poster, or tape recording.

### Build a Radio

Build a working radio from simple materials.

- Using books or the Internet, find instructions for building a simple crystal radio.
- Collect the materials and assemble the radio. Modify the design of the radio to improve it.
- Demonstrate the radio to the class and explain how it works.

### Design an Invention

Design an electronic invention.

- Select a purpose for your invention, such as a toy, a fan, or a burglar alarm. Write a paragraph that explains the purpose of your invention.
- Draw a sketch of your design and modify it if necessary.
- Make a pamphlet to advertise your invention. If possible, build the invention and include photographs of it in the pamphlet.

Learn more about careers in music and computer science.

# CHAPTER 1 Electricity

## the BIG idea

Moving electric charges transfer energy.

## Key Concepts

SECTION

**Materials can become electrically charged.** Learn how the movement of electrons builds static charges and how static charges are used in technology.

SECTION

**Charges can move from one place to another.** Learn what factors control the movement of charges.

SECTION

**Electric current is a flow of charge.** Learn how electric current is measured and how it can be produced.

**Internet Preview**

CLASSZONE.COM

Chapter 1 online resources: Content Review, two Simulations, two Resource Centers, Math Tutorial, Test Practice.

*What keeps this dragon glowing brightly?*

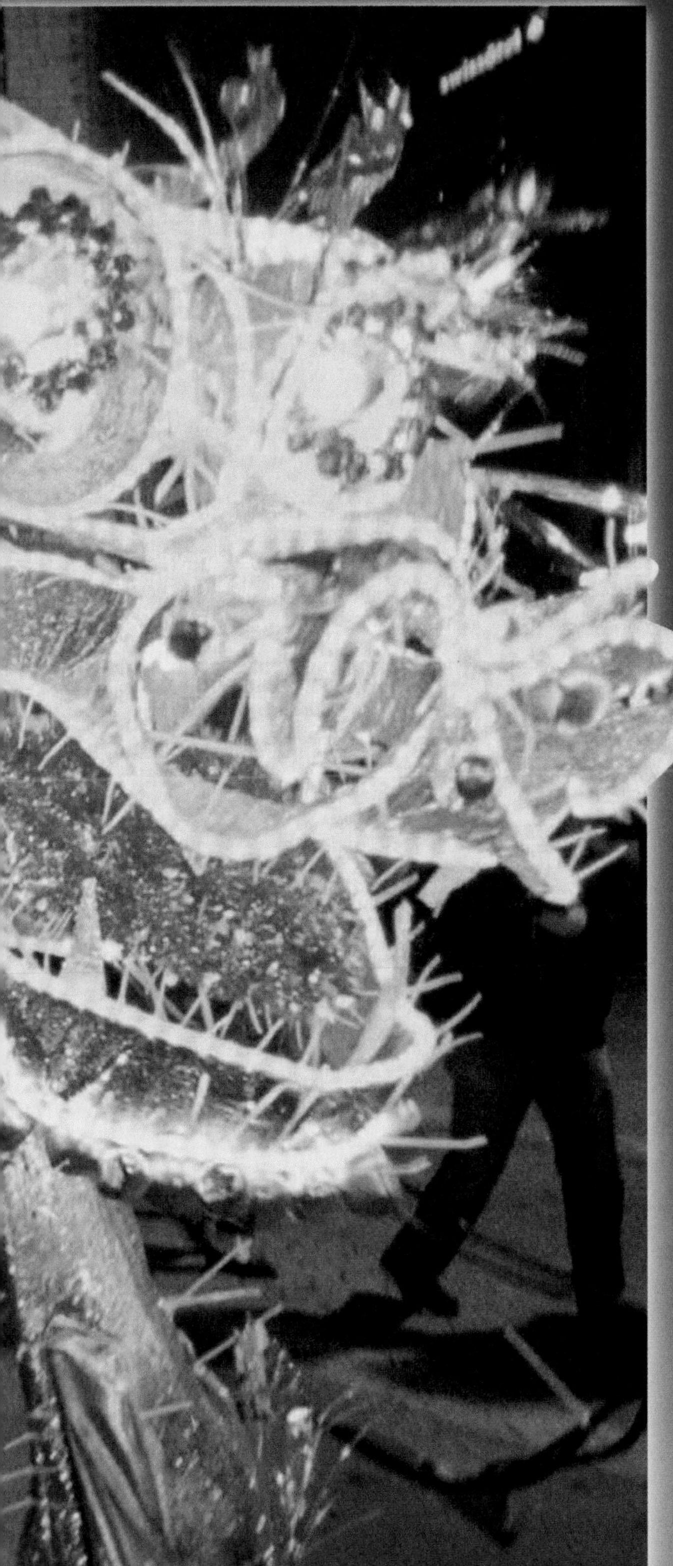

# EXPLORE the BIG idea

## How Do the Pieces of Tape Interact?

Cut three strips of tape. Press two onto your shirt. Peel them off and hold them close to each other, without touching. Observe. Hold one of them close to the third strip. Observe.

**Observe and Think**
How did the strips of tape behave in each case? Can you think of an explanation?

## Why Does the Water React Differently?

Open a faucet just enough to let flow a thin stream of water. Run a comb through your hair a few times, and then hold it near the stream of water. Observe the behavior of the water. Touch the comb to the stream of water briefly and then hold it near the stream again.

**Observe and Think** How did the interaction of the comb and the stream change after you touched the comb to the water?

## Internet Activity: Static Electricity

Go to **ClassZone.com** to learn more about materials and static electricity.

**Observe and Think** What role does the type of material play in static electricity?

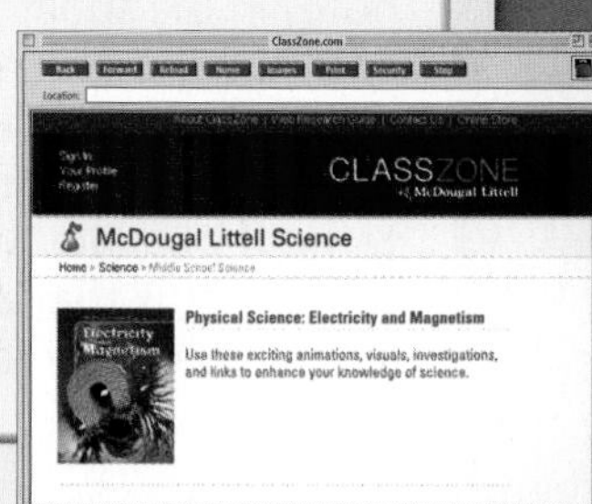

Electricity **Code: MDL065**

CHAPTER 1

# Getting Ready to Learn

## CONCEPT REVIEW

- Matter is made of particles too small to see.
- Energy and matter can move from one place to another.
- Electromagnetic energy is one form of energy.

## VOCABULARY REVIEW

*See Glossary for definitions.*

**atom**

**electron**

**joule**

**proton**

CLASSZONE.COM

Review concepts and vocabulary.

## TAKING NOTES

### COMBINATION NOTES

To take notes about a new concept, first make an informal outline of the information. Then make a sketch of the concept and label it so you can study it later.

### VOCABULARY STRATEGY

Write each new vocabulary term in the center of a **four square** diagram. Write notes in the squares around each term. Include a definition, some characteristics, and some examples of the term. If possible, write some things that are not examples of the term.

See the Note-Taking Handbook on pages R45–R51.

SCIENCE NOTEBOOK

NOTES

How static charges are built

- Contact
- Induction
- Charge polarization

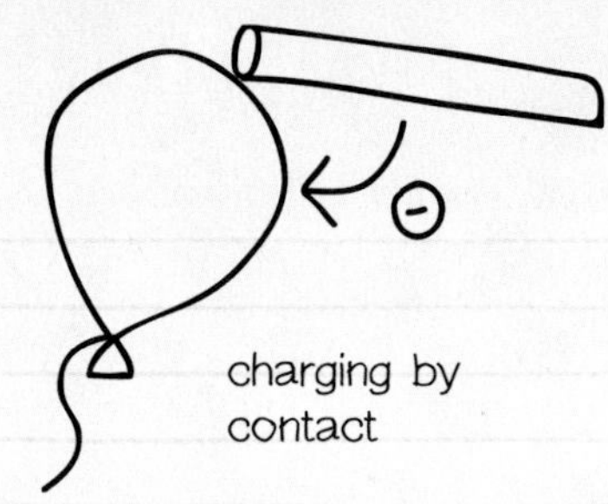


STATIC CHARGE

| Definition | Characteristics |
|---|---|
| imbalance of charge in material | results from movement of electrons; affected by type of material |
| **Examples** | **Nonexample** |
| clinging laundry, doorknob shock, lightning | electricity from an electrical outlet |

KEY CONCEPT

# 1.1 Materials can become electrically charged.

**BEFORE, you learned**

- Atoms are made up of particles called protons, neutrons, and electrons
- Protons and electrons are electrically charged

**NOW, you will learn**

- How charged particles behave
- How electric charges build up in materials
- How static electricity is used in technology

**VOCABULARY**

**electric charge** p. 10
**electric field** p. 10
**static charge** p. 11
**induction** p. 13

**EXPLORE Static Electricity**

***How can materials interact electrically?***

**PROCEDURE**

1. Hold the newspaper strips firmly together at one end and let the free ends hang down. Observe the strips.
2. Put the plastic bag over your other hand, like a mitten. Slide the plastic down the entire length of the strips and then let go. Repeat several times.
3. Notice how the strips of paper are hanging. Describe what you observe.

**MATERIALS**

- 2 strips of newspaper
- plastic bag

**WHAT DO YOU THINK?**

- How did the strips behave before step 2? How did they behave after step 2?
- How might you explain your observations?

## Electric charge is a property of matter.

You are already familiar with electricity, static electricity, and magnetism. You know electricity as the source of power for many appliances, including lights, tools, and computers. Static electricity is what makes clothes stick together when they come out of a dryer and gives you a shock when you touch a metal doorknob on a dry, winter day. Magnetism can hold an invitation or report card on the door of your refrigerator.

You may not know, however, that electricity, static electricity, and magnetism are all related. All three are the result of a single property of matter—electric charge.

**COMBINATION NOTES**
As you read this section, write down important ideas about electric charge and static charges. Make sketches to help you remember these concepts.

The smallest unit of a material that still has the characteristics of that material is an atom or a molecule. A molecule is two or more atoms bonded together. Most of an atom's mass is concentrated in the nucleus at the center of the atom. The nucleus contains particles called protons and neutrons. Much smaller particles called electrons move at high speeds outside the nucleus.

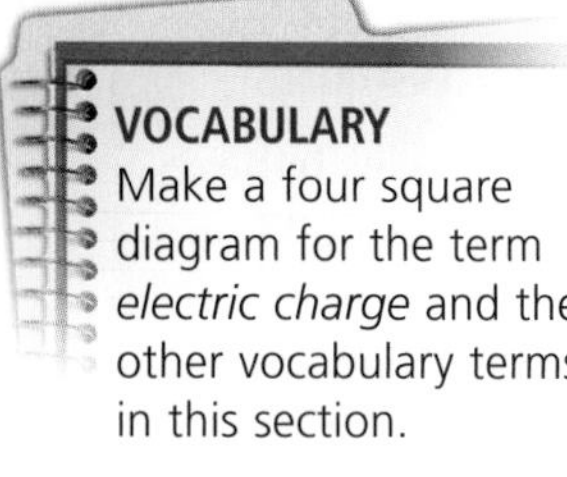

**VOCABULARY**
Make a four square diagram for the term *electric charge* and the other vocabulary terms in this section.

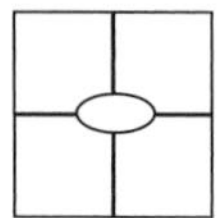

Protons and electrons have electric charges. **Electric charge** is a property that allows an object to exert an electric force on another object without touching it. Recall that a force is a push or a pull. The space around a particle through which an electric charge can exert this force is called an **electric field.** The strength of the field is greater near the particle and weaker farther away.

All protons have a positive charge (+), and all electrons have a negative charge (–). Normally, an atom has an equal number of protons and electrons, so their charges balance each other, and the overall charge on the atom is neutral.

Particles with the same type of charge—positive or negative—are said to have like charges, and particles with different charges have unlike charges. Particles with like charges repel each other, that is, they push each other away. Particles with unlike charges attract each other, or pull on each other.

## Electric Charge

**Charged particles exert forces on each other through their electric fields.**

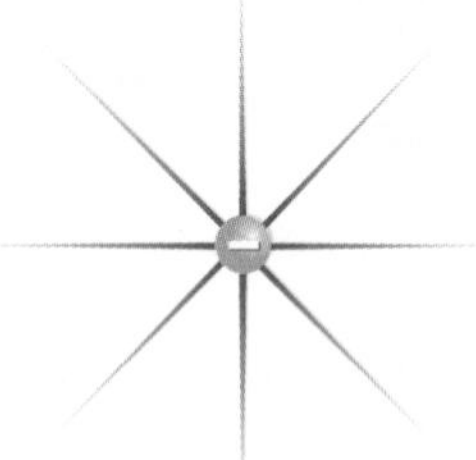

**Charged Particles**
Electric charge can be either negative or positive.

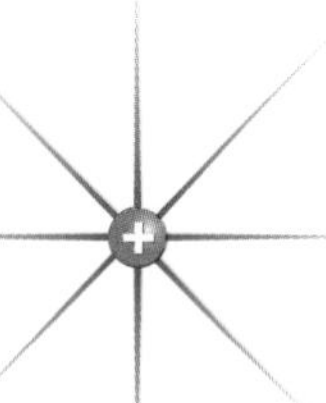

The balloon and the cat's fur have unlike charges, so they attract each other.

**① Attraction**

Particles with unlike charges attract—pull on each other.

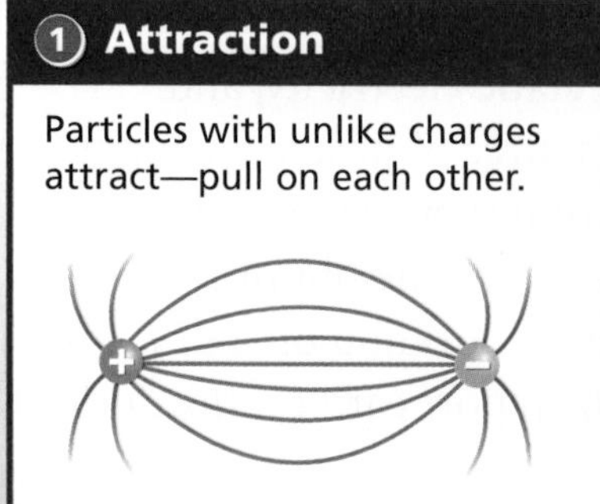

**② Repulsion**

Particles with like charges repel—push each other away.

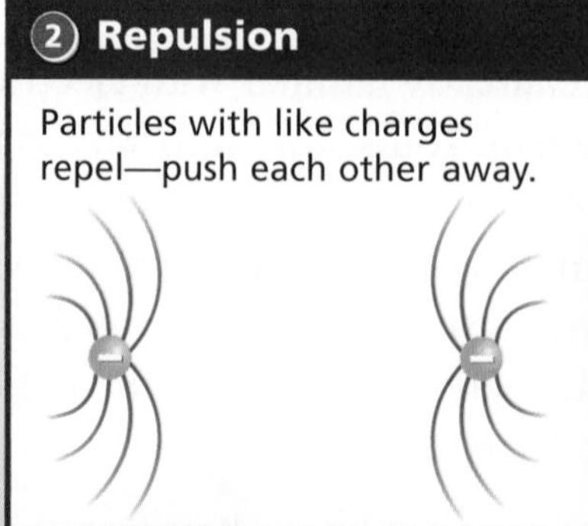

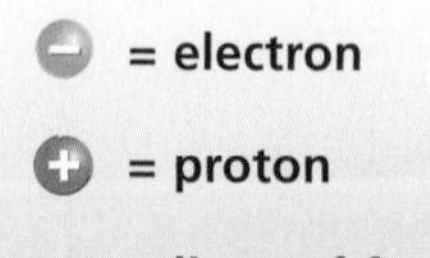


**READING VISUALS** How do the force lines change when particles attract?

## Static charges are caused by the movement of electrons.

You have read that protons and electrons have electric charges. Objects and materials can also have charges. A **static charge** is a buildup of electric charge in an object caused by the presence of many particles with the same charge. Ordinarily, the atoms that make up a material have a balance of protons and electrons. A material develops a static charge—or becomes charged—when it contains more of one type of charged particle than another.

READING TiP

The word *static* comes from the Greek word *statos,* which means "standing."

If there are more protons than electrons in a material, the material has a positive charge. If there are more electrons than protons in a material, it has a negative charge. The amount of the charge depends on how many more electrons or protons there are. The total number of unbalanced positive or negative charges in an object is the net charge of the object. Net charge is measured in coulombs (KOO-LAHMZ). One coulomb is equivalent to more than $10^{19}$ electrons or protons.

REMINDER

$10^{19}$ is the same as 1 followed by 19 zeros.

Electrons can move easily from one atom to another. Protons cannot. For this reason, charges in materials usually result from the movement of electrons. The movement of electrons through a material is called conduction. If electrons move from one atom to another, the atom they move to develops a negative charge. The atom they move away from develops a positive charge. Atoms with either a positive or a negative charge are called ions.

A static charge can build up in an uncharged material when it touches or comes near a charged material. Static charges also build up when some types of uncharged materials come into contact with each other.

### Charging by Contact

When two uncharged objects made of certain materials—such as rubber and glass—touch each other, electrons move from one material to the other. This process is called charging by contact. It can be demonstrated by a balloon and a glass rod, as shown below.

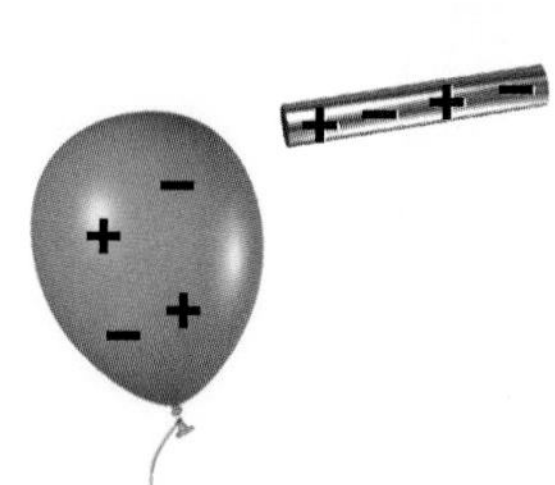

1 At first, a balloon and a glass rod each have balanced, neutral charges.

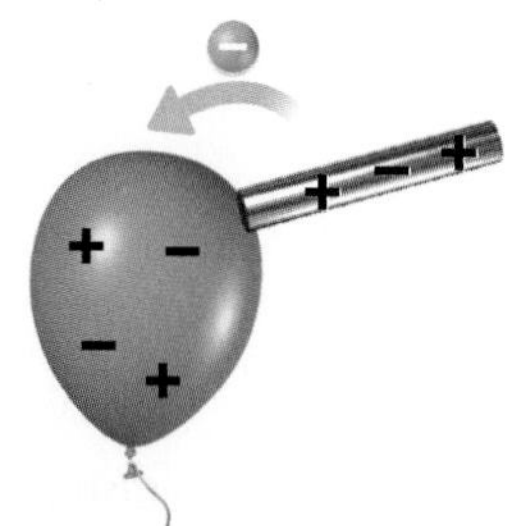

2 When they touch, electrons move from the rod to the balloon.

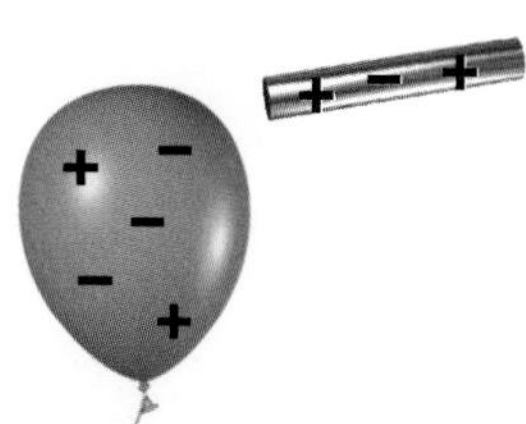

3 Afterwards, the balloon has a negative charge, and the rod has a positive charge.

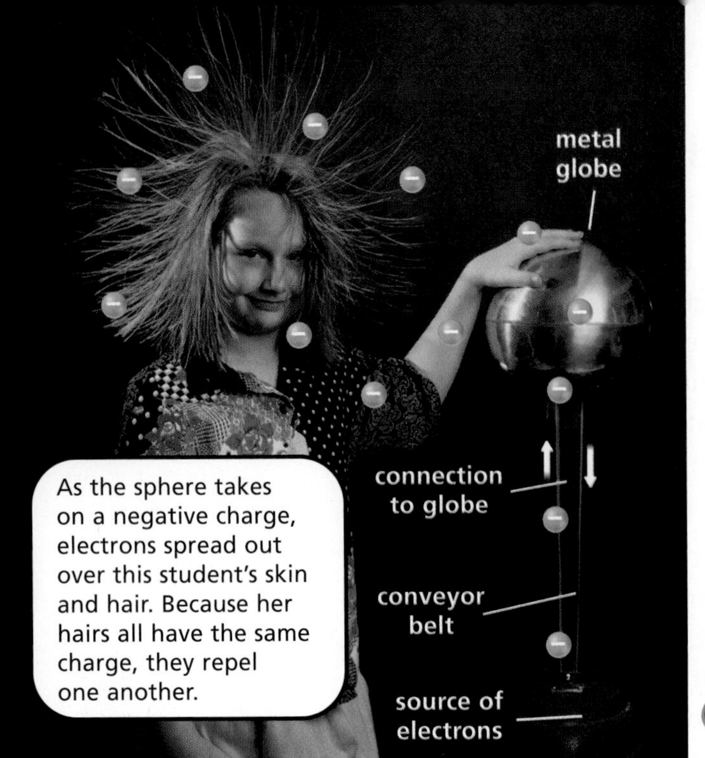


As the sphere takes on a negative charge, electrons spread out over this student's skin and hair. Because her hairs all have the same charge, they repel one another.

A Van de Graaff generator is a device that builds up a strong static charge through contact. This device is shown at left. At the bottom of the device, a rubber conveyer belt rubs against a metal brush and picks up electrons. At the top, the belt rubs against metal connected to the sphere, transferring electrons to the sphere. As more and more electrons accumulate on the sphere, the sphere takes on a strong negative charge. In the photograph, the student touches the sphere as it is being charged. Some of the electrons spread across her arm to her head. The strands of her hair, which then all have a negative charge, repel one another.

**CHECK YOUR READING** How can a Van de Graaff generator make a person's hair stand on end?

## How Materials Affect Static Charging

Charging by contact occurs when one material's electrons are attracted to another material more than they are attracted to their own. Scientists have determined from experience which materials are likely to give up or to accept electrons. For example, glass gives up electrons to wool. Wool accepts electrons from glass, but gives up electrons to rubber. The list at left indicates how some materials interact. Each material tends to give up electrons to anything below it on the list and to accept electrons from anything above it. The farther away two materials are from each other on the list, the stronger the interaction.

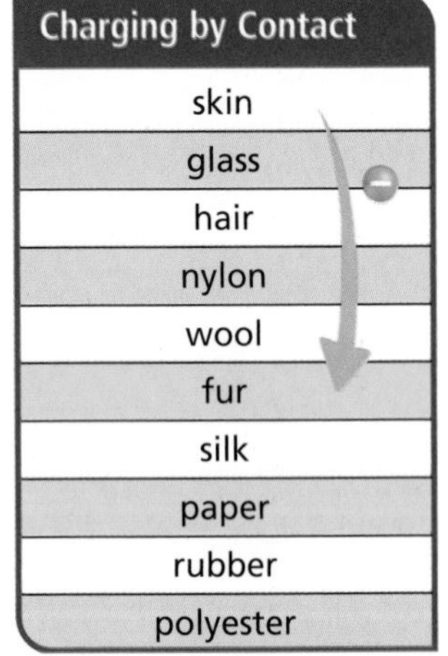

| Charging by Contact |
|---|
| skin |
| glass |
| hair |
| nylon |
| wool |
| fur |
| silk |
| paper |
| rubber |
| polyester |

Materials higher on the list tend to give up electrons to materials lower on the list.

When you walk across a carpet, your body can become either positively or negatively charged. The type of charge depends on what materials the carpet and your shoes are made of. If you walk in shoes with rubber soles across a wool carpet, you will probably become negatively charged, because wool gives up electrons to rubber. But if you walk in wool slippers across a rubber mat, you will probably become positively charged.

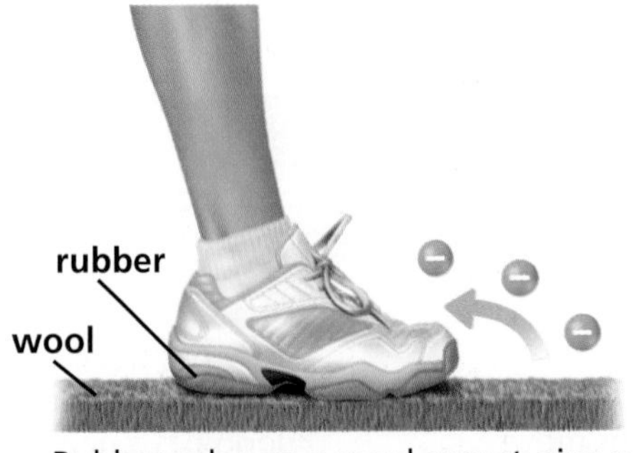


Rubber soles on a wool carpet give a person a negative charge.

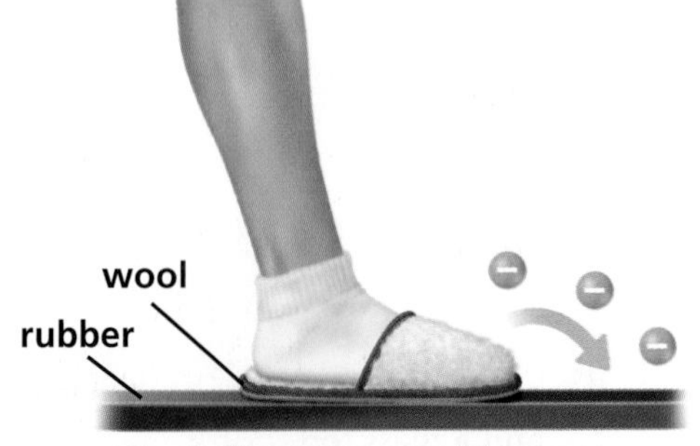


Wool slippers on a rubber mat give a person a positive charge.

## Charging by Induction

Charging can occur even when materials are not touching if one of the materials already has a charge. Remember that charged particles push and pull each other through their electric fields without touching. The pushing and pulling can cause a charge to build in another material. The first charge is said to induce the second charge. The buildup of a charge without direct contact is called **induction.**

**READING TIP**

*Induce* and *induction* both contain the Latin root *ducere,* which means "to lead."

Induction can produce a temporary static charge. Consider what happens when a glass rod with a negative charge is brought near a balloon, as shown below. The unbalanced electrons in the rod repel the electrons in the material of the balloon. Many electrons move to the side of the balloon that is farthest away from the rod. The side of the balloon that has more electrons becomes negatively charged. The side of the balloon with fewer electrons becomes positively charged. When the rod moves away, the electrons spread out evenly once again.

1. At first, the rod has a negative charge and the balloon has a balanced charge.
2. When the rod comes close to the balloon, electrons in the balloon move away from the rod.
3. When the rod moves away, electrons in the balloon spread out evenly as before.

If the electrons cannot return to their original distribution, however, induction can leave an object with a stable static charge. For example, if a negatively charged rod approaches two balloons that are touching each other, electrons will move to the balloon farther from the rod. If the balloons are then separated, preventing the electrons from moving again, the balloon with more electrons will have a negative charge and the one with fewer electrons will have a positive charge. When the rod is taken away, the balloons keep their new charges.

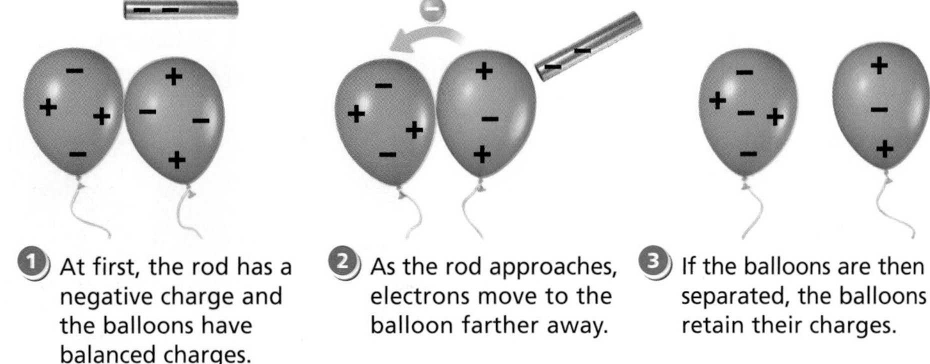

1. At first, the rod has a negative charge and the balloons have balanced charges.
2. As the rod approaches, electrons move to the balloon farther away.
3. If the balloons are then separated, the balloons retain their charges.

## Charge Polarization

Induction can build a charge by changing the position of electrons, even when electrons do not move between atoms. Have you ever charged a balloon by rubbing it on your head, and then stuck the balloon to a wall? When you bring the balloon close to the wall, the balloon's negative charge pushes against the electrons in the wall. If the electrons cannot easily move away from their atoms, the negative charges within the atoms may shift to the side away from the balloon. When this happens, the atoms are said to be polarized. The surface of the wall becomes positively charged, and the negatively charged balloon sticks to it.

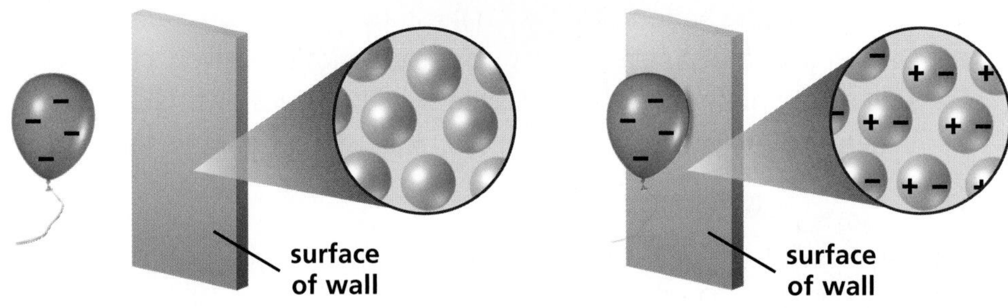


1. Before the charged balloon comes near the wall, the atoms in the surface of the wall are not polarized.
2. As the balloon nears the wall, atoms in the surface of the wall become polarized and attract the balloon.

## INVESTIGATE Making a Static Detector

### How can you detect a static electric charge?

**PROCEDURE**

1. Straighten one end of the paper clip and insert it through the hole in the cup. Use clay to hold the paper clip in place. Stick the ball of foil onto the straight end. Hang both foil strips from the hook end.
2. Give the balloon a static charge by rubbing it over your hair. Slowly bring the balloon near the ball of foil without letting them touch. Observe what happens to the foil strips inside the cup.

**WHAT DO YOU THINK?**

- What happened to the strips hanging inside the cup when the charged balloon came near the ball of foil?
- How can you explain what you observed?

**CHALLENGE** Suppose the balloon had the opposite charge of the one you gave it. What would happen to the strips if you brought the balloon near the ball of foil? Explain your answer.

**SKILL FOCUS**
Inferring

**MATERIALS**
- metal paper clip
- clear plastic cup with hole
- modeling clay
- ball of foil
- 2 strips of foil
- inflated balloon

**TIME**
20 minutes

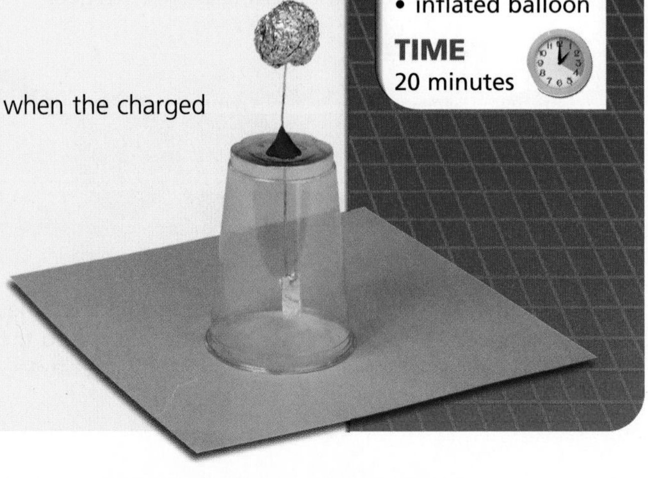

## Technology uses static electricity.

Static charges can be useful in technology. An example is the photocopy machine. Photocopiers run on electricity that comes to them through wires from the power plant. But static charges play an important role in how they work.

### How a Photocopier Works

**A photocopier uses static charges to make copies.**

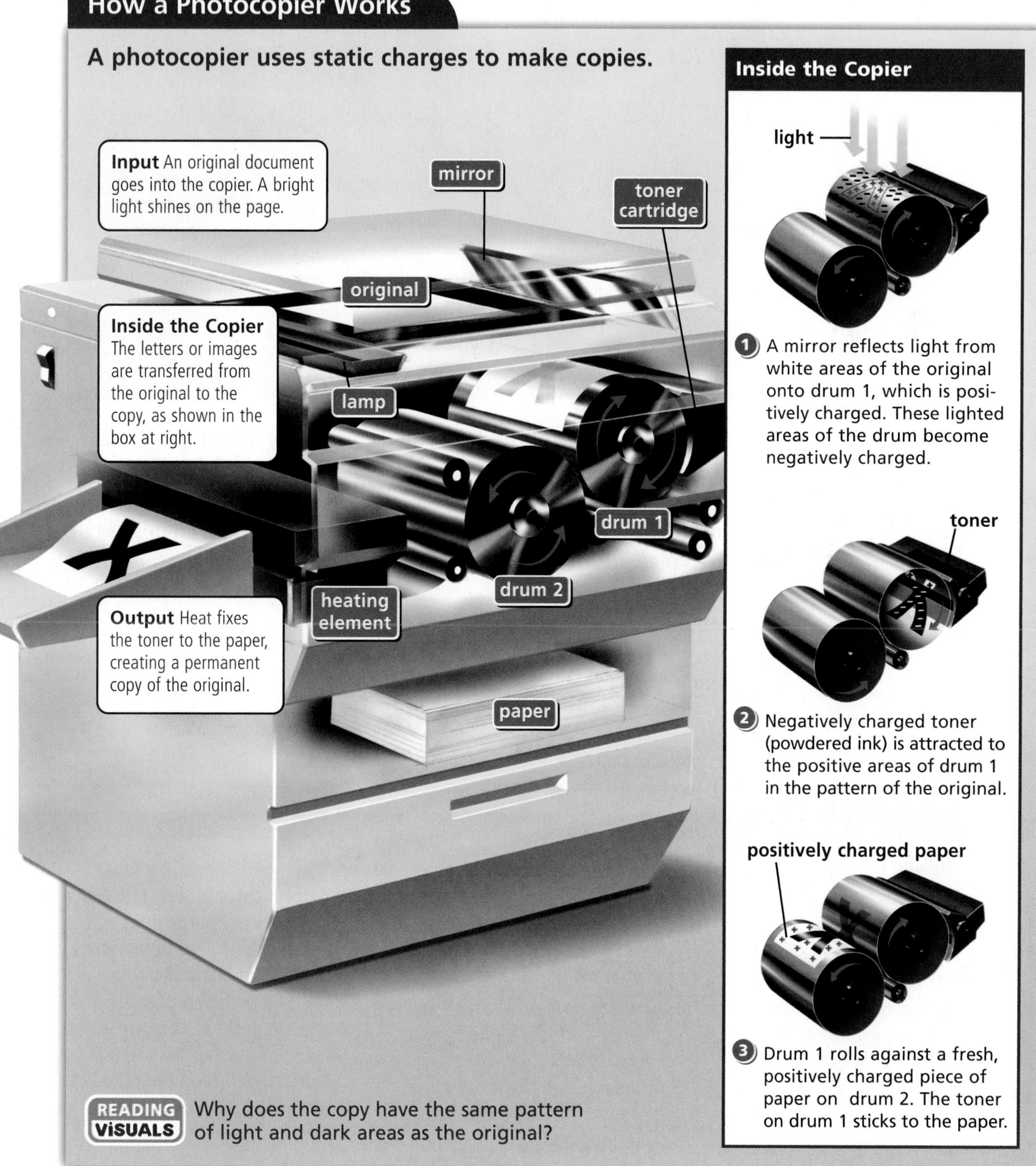

**Input** An original document goes into the copier. A bright light shines on the page.
mirror
toner cartridge
original
**Inside the Copier** The letters or images are transferred from the original to the copy, as shown in the box at right.
lamp
drum 1
drum 2
heating element
**Output** Heat fixes the toner to the paper, creating a permanent copy of the original.
paper

**Inside the Copier**

light

1. A mirror reflects light from white areas of the original onto drum 1, which is positively charged. These lighted areas of the drum become negatively charged.

toner

2. Negatively charged toner (powdered ink) is attracted to the positive areas of drum 1 in the pattern of the original.

positively charged paper

3. Drum 1 rolls against a fresh, positively charged piece of paper on drum 2. The toner on drum 1 sticks to the paper.

**READING VISUALS** Why does the copy have the same pattern of light and dark areas as the original?

Static electricity is also used in making cars. When new cars are painted, the paint is given an electric charge and then sprayed onto the car in a fine mist. The tiny droplets of paint stick to the car more firmly than they would without the charge. This process results in a coat of paint that is very even and smooth.

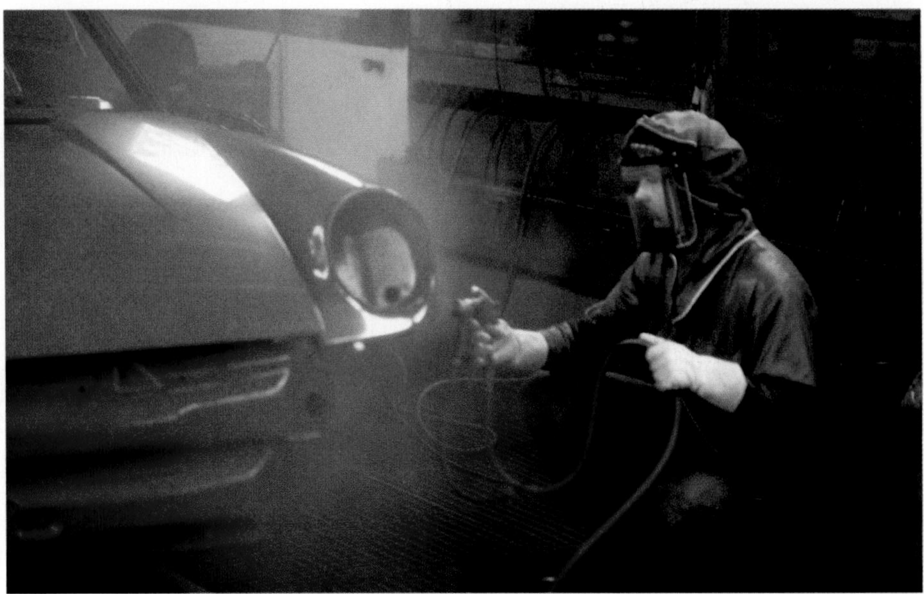

Another example of the use of static electricity in technology is a device called an electrostatic air filter. This device cleans air inside buildings with the help of static charges. The filter gives a static charge to pollen, dust, germs, and other particles in the air. Then an oppositely charged plate inside the filter attracts these particles, pulling them out of the air. Larger versions of electrostatic filters are used to remove pollutants from industrial smokestacks.

How can static charges help clean air?

## 1.1 Review

### KEY CONCEPTS

1. How do a positive and a negative particle interact?
2. Describe how the movement of electrons between two objects with balanced charges could cause the buildup of electric charge in both objects.
3. Describe one technological use of static electricity.

### CRITICAL THINKING

4. **Infer** A sock and a shirt from the dryer stick together. What does this tell you about the charges on the sock and shirt?
5. **Analyze** You walk over a rug and get a shock from a door-knob. What do the materials of the rug and the shoes have to do with the type of charge your body had?

### CHALLENGE

6. **Apply** Assume you start with a negatively charged rod and two balloons. Describe a series of steps you could take to create a positively charged balloon, pick up negatively charged powder with the balloon, and drop the powder from the balloon.

# Electric Eels

An electric eel is a slow-moving fish with no teeth and poor eyesight. It lives in the murky waters of muddy rivers in South America. Instead of the senses that most animals use—vision, hearing, smell, and touch—an electric eel uses electricity to find its next meal. Since the fish that it eats often can swim much faster than the eel, it also uses electricity to catch its prey.

## Electric Sense

An electric eel actually has three pairs of electric organs in its body. Two of them build electric charge for stunning prey and for self-defense. The third electric organ builds a smaller charge that helps in finding prey. The charge produces an electric field around the eel. Special sense organs on its body detect small changes in the electric field caused by nearby fish and other animals.

## Shocking Organs

The electric eel builds an electric charge with a series of thousands of cells called electrocytes. Every cell in the series has a positive end and a negative end. Each electrocyte builds only a small charge. However, when all of the cells combine their charge, they can produce about five times as much electricity as a standard electrical outlet in a house. The charge is strong enough to paralyze or kill a human. Typically, though, the charge is used to stun or kill small fish, which the eel then swallows whole. Electric charge can also be used to scare away predators.

### EXPLORE

1. **INFER** Electric eels live for 10 to 20 years, developing a stronger shock as they grow older. What could account for this increase in electric charge?
2. **CHALLENGE** Sharks and other animals use electricity also. Use the library or Internet to find out how.

An electric eel (Electrophorus electricus) can deliver a jolt five times as powerful as an electrical outlet.

KEY CONCEPT

# Charges can move from one place to another.

**BEFORE, you learned**

- Static charges are built up by the separation of electrons from protons
- Materials affect how static charges are built up
- Energy is the ability to cause change

**NOW, you will learn**

- How charges move
- How charges store energy
- How differences in materials affect the movement of charges

**VOCABULARY**

**electric potential** p. 19
**volt** p. 19
**conductor** p. 22
**insulator** p. 22
**resistance** p. 23
**ohm** p. 23
**grounding** p. 25

**EXPLORE Static Discharge**

***How can you observe electrical energy?***

**PROCEDURE**

1. Rub the balloon against the wool cloth several times to give the balloon a static charge.
2. Slowly bring the balloon toward the middle part of the fluorescent bulb until a spark jumps between them.

**WHAT DO YOU THINK?**

- What happened in the fluorescent bulb when the spark jumped?
- How might you explain this observation?

**MATERIALS**

- inflated balloon
- wool cloth
- fluorescent light bulb

## Static charges have potential energy.

You have read how a static charge is built up in an object such as a balloon. Once it is built up, the charge can stay where it is indefinitely. However, the charge can also move to a new location. The movement of a static charge out of an object is known as static discharge. When a charge moves, it transfers energy that can be used to do work.

**REMINDER**

Energy can be either kinetic (energy of motion) or potential (stored energy). Energy is measured in joules.

What causes a charge to move is the same thing that builds up a charge in the first place—that is, the force of attraction or repulsion between charged particles. For example, suppose an object with a negative charge touches an object with a positive charge. The attraction of the unbalanced electrons in the first object to the unbalanced protons in the second object can cause the electrons to move to the second object.

What can cause a charge to move?

## Electric Potential Energy

Potential energy is stored energy an object may have because of its position. Water in a tower has gravitational potential energy because it is high above the ground. The kinetic energy—energy of motion—used to lift the water to the top of the tower is stored as potential energy. If you open a pipe below the tower, the water moves downward and its potential energy is converted back into kinetic energy.

Similarly, electric potential energy is the energy a charged particle has due to its position in an electric field. Because like charges repel, for example, it takes energy to push a charged particle closer to another particle with a like charge. That energy is stored as the electric potential energy of the first particle. When the particle is free to move again, it quickly moves away, and its electric potential energy is converted back into kinetic energy.

When water moves downward out of a tower and some of its potential energy is converted into kinetic energy, its potential energy decreases. Similarly, when a charged particle moves away from a particle with a like charge, its electric potential energy decreases. The water and the particle both move from a state of higher potential energy to one of lower potential energy.

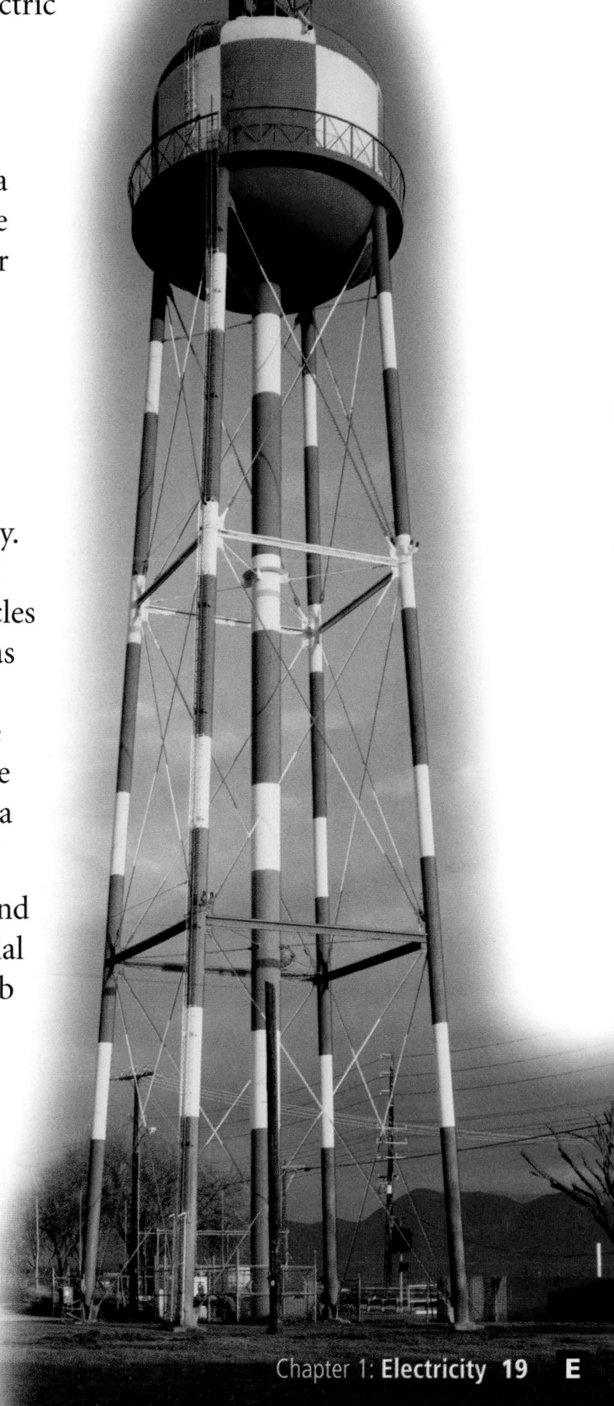

Like water in a tower, a static charge has potential energy. Just as gravity moves water down the supply pipe attached under the tank, the electric potential energy of a charge moves the charge along an electrical pathway.

## Electric Potential

To push a charged particle closer to another particle with the same charge takes a certain amount of energy. To push two particles into the same position near that particle takes twice as much energy, and the two particles together have twice as much electric potential energy as the single particle. Although the amount of potential energy is higher, the amount of energy per unit charge at that position stays the same. **Electric potential** is the amount of electric potential energy per unit charge at a certain position in an electric field.

Electric potential is measured in units called volts, and voltage is another term for electric potential. A potential of one **volt** is equal to one joule of energy per coulomb of charge.

Just as water will not flow between two towers of the same height, a charge will not move between two positions with the same electric potential. For a charge to move, there must be a difference in potential between the two positions.

## Charge Movement

When water moves from a higher to a lower position, some of its potential energy is used to move it. Along the way, some of its potential energy can be used to do other work, such as turning a water wheel. Similarly, when a charge moves, some of its electric potential energy is used in moving the charge and some of it can be used to do other work. For example, moving an electric charge through a material can cause the material to heat up, as in a burner on an electric stove.

You can see how a moving charge transfers energy when you get a shock from static electricity. As you walk across a rug, a charge builds up on your body. Once the charge is built up, it cannot move until you come in contact with something else. When you reach out to touch a doorknob, the charge has a path to follow. The electric potential energy of the charge moves the charge from you to the doorknob.

Why do you get a shock? Recall that the force of attraction or repulsion between charged particles is stronger when they are close together. As your hand gets closer to the doorknob, the electric potential of the static charge increases. At a certain point, the difference in electric potential between you and the doorknob is great enough to move the charge through the air to the doorknob. As the charge moves, some of its potential energy is changed into the heat, light, and sound of a spark.

What two factors determine whether a static charge will move?

## Lightning

Find out more about lightning and lightning safety.

The shock you get from a doorknob is a small-scale version of lightning. Lightning is a high-energy static discharge. This static electricity is caused by storm clouds. Lightning comes from the electric potential of millions of volts, which releases large amounts of energy in the form of light, heat, and sound. As you read about how lightning forms, follow the steps in the illustration on page 21.

1. **Charge Separation** Particles of moisture inside a cloud collide with the air and with each other, causing the particles to become electrically charged. Wind and gravity separate charges, carrying the heavier, negatively charged particles to the bottom of the cloud and the lighter, positively charged particles to the top of the cloud.

2. **Charge Buildup** Through induction, the negatively charged particles at the bottom of the cloud repel electrons in the ground, causing the surface of the ground to build up a positive charge.

3. **Static Discharge** When the electric potential, or voltage, created by the difference in charges is large enough, the negative charge moves from the cloud to the ground. The energy released by the discharge produces the flash of lightning and the sound of thunder.

## How Lightning Forms

**Lightning is a type of static discharge. Storm clouds may develop very large charges, each with an electric potential of millions of volts.**

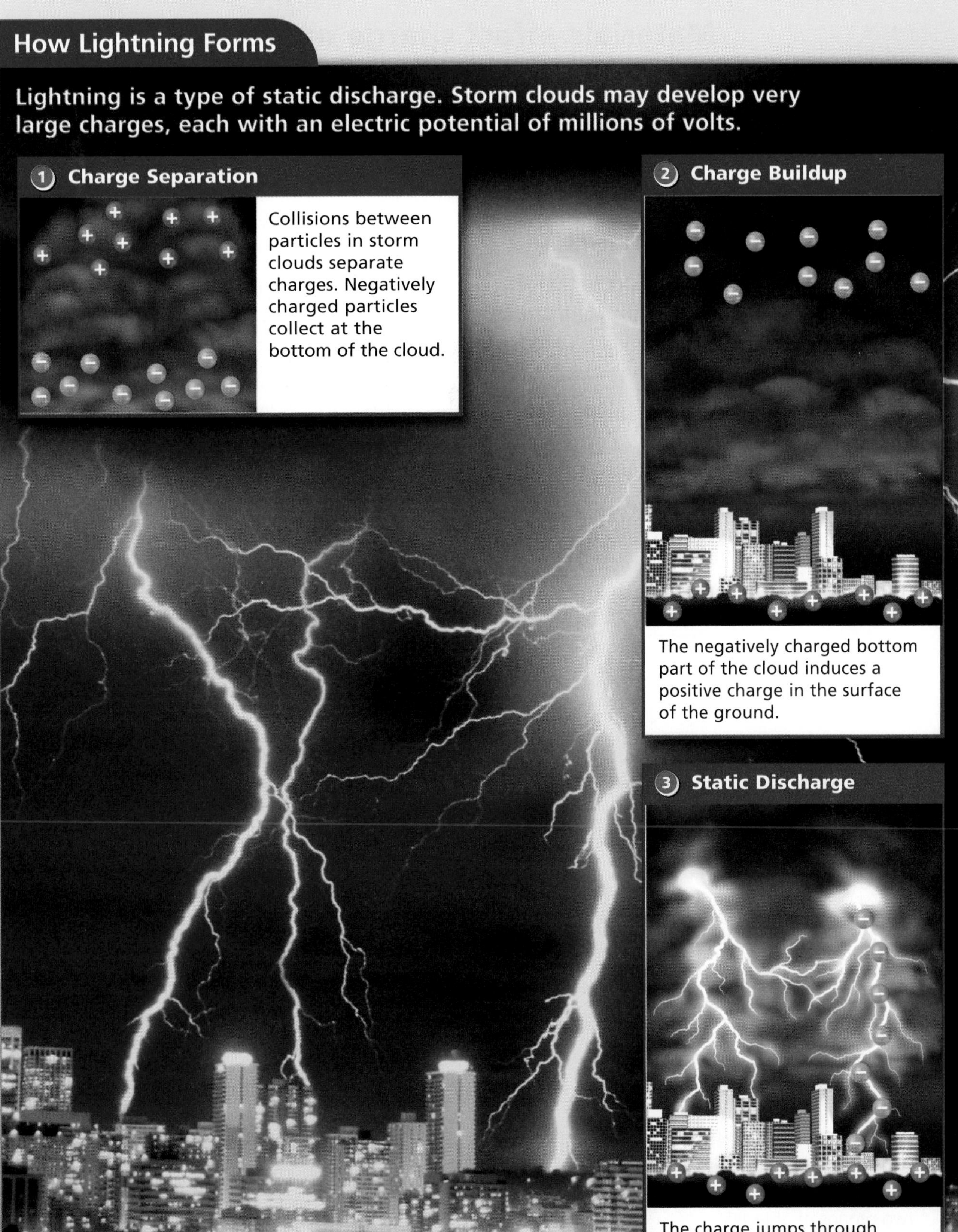

1 Charge Separation
Collisions between particles in storm clouds separate charges. Negatively charged particles collect at the bottom of the cloud.
2 Charge Buildup
The negatively charged bottom part of the cloud induces a positive charge in the surface of the ground.
3 Static Discharge
The charge jumps through the air to the ground. Energy released by the discharge causes thunder and lightning.


**READING VISUALS** How is lightning like the shock you can get from a doorknob? How is it different?

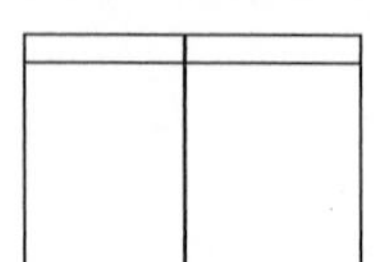

**COMBINATION NOTES** Make notes on the different ways materials can affect charge movement. Use sketches to help explain the concepts.

## Materials affect charge movement.

After you walk across a carpet, a charge on your skin has no place to go until you touch or come very close to something. That is because an electric charge cannot move easily through air. However, a charge can move easily through the metal of a doorknob.

### Conductors and Insulators

A material that allows an electric charge to pass through it easily is called a **conductor.** Metals such as iron, steel, copper, and aluminum are good conductors. Most wire used to carry a charge is made of copper, which conducts very well.

A material that does not easily allow a charge to pass through it is called an **insulator.** Plastic and rubber are good insulators. Many types of electric wire are covered with plastic, which insulates well. The plastic allows a charge to be conducted from one end of the wire to the other, but not through the sides of the wire. Insulators are also important in electrical safety, because they keep charges away from the body.

**CHECK YOUR READING** What is the difference between a conductor and an insulator?

## INVESTIGATE Conductors and Insulators

### *What materials conduct electricity?*

**PROCEDURE**

1. Use tape to connect the battery, wires, and bulb holder as shown in the photograph. Make sure that the wires connected to the battery stay in full contact with the metal parts on either end. Test the bulb and the battery by touching the free ends of wire together. The bulb should light up.
2. Test each object in turn by touching it simultaneously with both free ends of wire. Make sure the ends of wire do not touch each other.

**WHAT DO YOU THINK?**

- Which objects allowed the light bulb to light up when the wires touched them? Which did not?
- How can you explain the difference between the two groups of objects?

**CHALLENGE** Do any of the materials you tested seem to conduct a charge better than other conductors? How could you use the setup you have to compare the degree of conducting ability of materials?

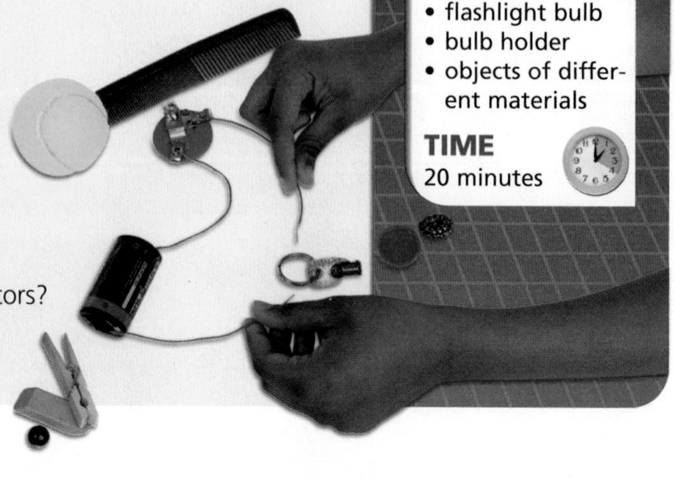

**SKILL FOCUS**
Interpreting data

**MATERIALS**
- D cell (battery)
- 3 pieces of low-voltage wire
- duct tape
- flashlight bulb
- bulb holder
- objects of different materials

**TIME**
20 minutes

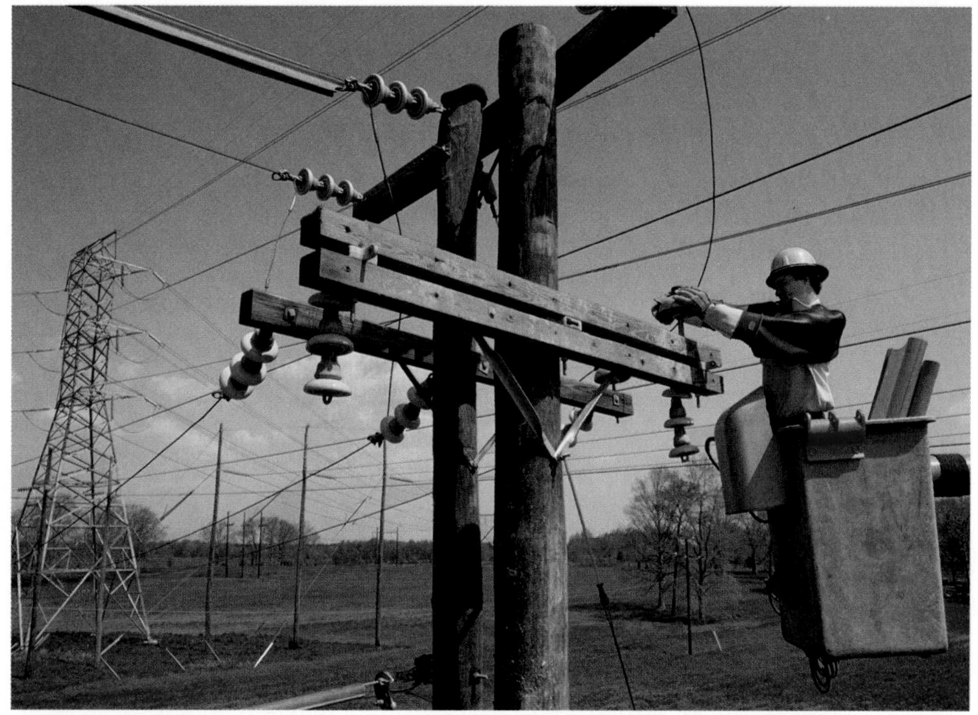

Electrons can move freely in a material with low resistance, such as the copper wire in these power lines. Electrons cannot move freely in a material with high resistance, such as the ceramic insulator this worker is putting in place or his safety gloves.

## Resistance

Think about the difference between walking through air and walking through waist-deep water. The water resists your movement more than the air, so you have to work harder to walk. If you walked waist-deep in mud, you would have to work even harder.

Materials resist the movement of a charge in different amounts. Electrical **resistance** is the property of a material that determines how easily a charge can move through it. Electrical resistance is measured in units called **ohms.** The symbol for ohms is the Greek letter *omega* (Ω).

Most materials have some resistance. A good conductor such as copper, though, has low resistance. A good insulator, such as plastic or wood, has high resistance.

Resistance depends on the amount and shape of the material as well as on the type of material itself. A wire that is thin has more resistance than a wire that is thick. Think of how you have to work harder to drink through a narrow straw than a wide one. A wire that is long has more resistance than a wire that is short. Again, think of how much harder it is to drink through a long straw than a short one.

**CHECK YOUR READING** What three factors affect how much resistance an object has?

Like a thick drink in a straw, an electric charge moves more easily through a short, wide pathway than a long, narrow one.

By taking advantage of resistance, we can use an electric charge to do work. When a moving charge overcomes resistance, some of the charge's electrical energy changes into other forms of energy, such as light and heat. For example, the filament of a light bulb is often made of tungsten, a material with high resistance. When electricity moves through the tungsten, the filament gives off light, which is useful. However, the bulb also gives off heat. Because light bulbs are not usually used to produce heat, we think of the heat they produce as wasted energy.

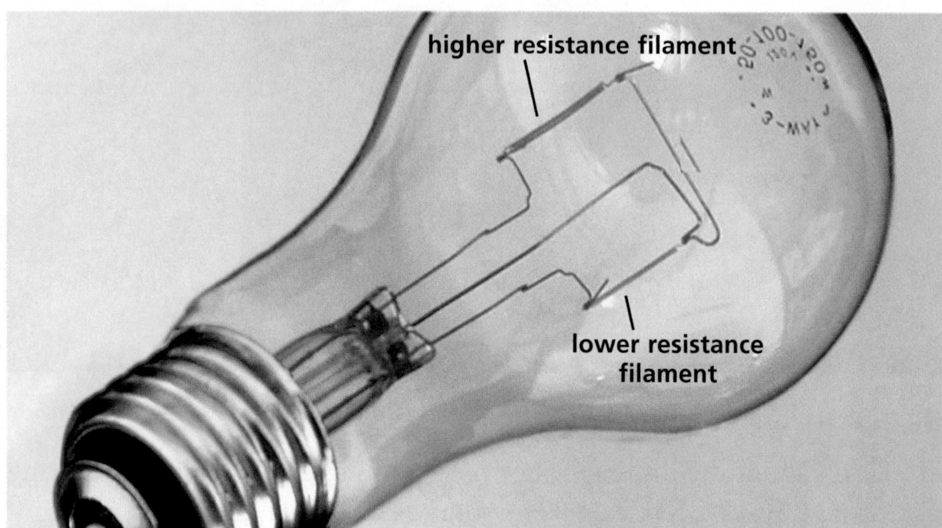


A three-way light bulb has two filaments, each with a different level of resistance. The one with higher resistance produces brighter light. Both together give the brightest setting.

A material with low resistance is one that a charge can flow through with little loss of energy. Materials move electricity more efficiently when they have low resistances. Such materials waste less energy, so more is available to do work at the other end. That is why copper is used for electrical wiring. Even copper has some resistance, however, and using it wastes some energy.

## Superconductors

Scientists have known for many years that some materials have practically no resistance at extremely low temperatures. Such materials are called superconductors, because they conduct even better than good conductors like copper. Superconductors have many uses. They can be used in power lines to increase efficiency and conserve energy, and in high-speed trains to reduce friction. Engineers are also testing superconducting materials for use in computers and other electronic devices. Superconductors would make computers work faster and might also be used to make better motors and generators.

Because superconductors must be kept extremely cold, they have not always been practical. Scientists are solving this problem by developing superconductors that will work at higher temperatures.

How much resistance does a superconducting material have?

## Grounding

If a charge can pass through two different materials, it will pass through the one with the lower resistance. This is the principle behind an important electrical safety procedure—grounding. **Grounding** means providing a harmless, low-resistance path—a ground—for electricity to follow. In many cases, this path actually leads into the ground, that is, into the Earth.

Grounding is used to protect buildings from damage by lightning. Most buildings have some type of lightning rod, which is made from a material that is a good conductor. The rod is placed high up, so that it is closer to the lightning charge. The rod is connected to a conductor cable, and the cable is attached to a copper pole, which is driven into the ground.

Because of the rod's low resistance, lightning will strike the rod before it will strike the roof, where it might have caused a fire. Lightning hits the rod and passes harmlessly through the cable into the ground.

Grounding provides a path for electric current to travel into the ground, which can absorb the charge and make it harmless. The charge soon spreads out so that its voltage in any particular spot is low.

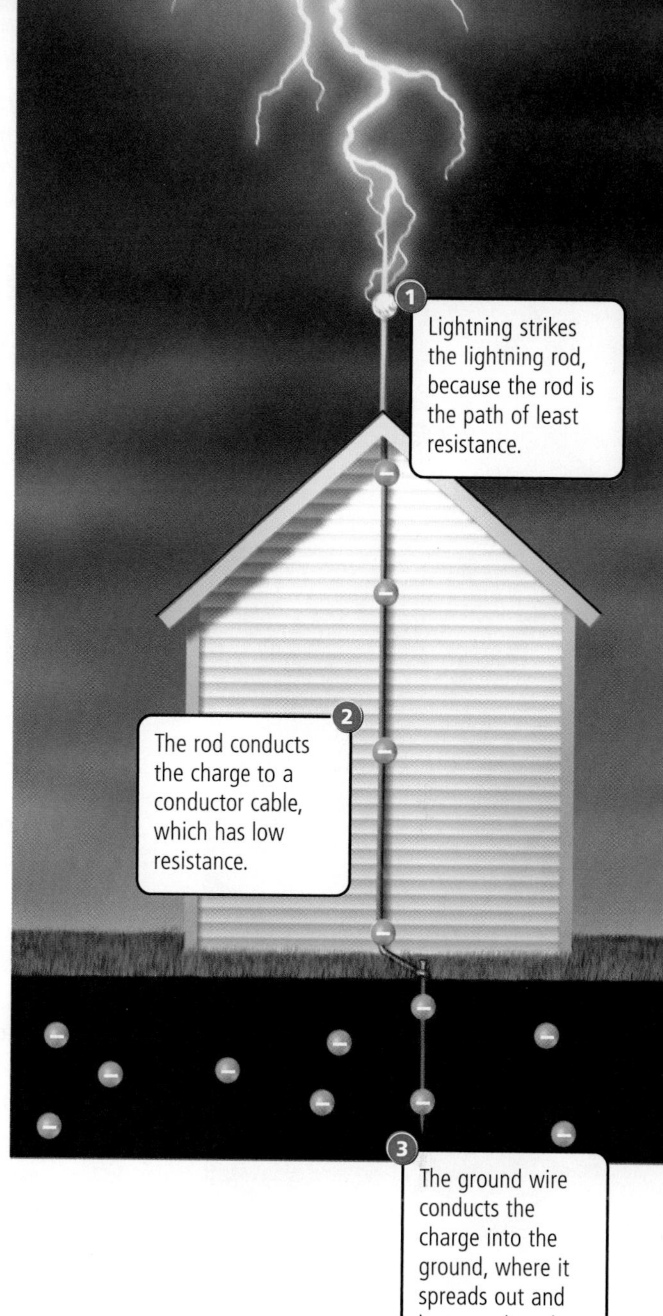
1
Lightning strikes the lightning rod, because the rod is the path of least resistance.
2
The rod conducts the charge to a conductor cable, which has low resistance.
3
The ground wire conducts the charge into the ground, where it spreads out and becomes harmless.

CHECK YOUR READING
What is a ground cable?

## 1.2 Review

### KEY CONCEPTS

1. Explain what happens when you get a static electric shock as you touch a doorknob.
2. What is electric potential?
3. What three factors affect how much electrical resistance an object has?
4. How can a lightning rod protect a building from fire?

### CRITICAL THINKING

5. **Infer** Object A has a positive charge. After Object A touches Object B, A still has a positive charge and the same amount of charge. What can you infer about the charge of B?
6. **Analyze** Why do lightning rods work better if they are placed high up, closer to the lightning charge?

### CHALLENGE

7. **Apply** Could the same material be used as both a conductor and an insulator? Explain your answer.

# CHAPTER INVESTIGATION

## Lightning

**OVERVIEW AND PURPOSE** Lightning is a form of static discharge. During storms, electric charges build up within clouds. Lightning occurs when these charges move. In this experiment, you will

- model the buildup of charges that can occur during a storm
- model a lightning strike
- use a ground to control the path of discharge

**MATERIALS**

- modeling clay
- 2 aluminum pie pans
- foam plate
- wool cloth
- paper clip

### Procedure

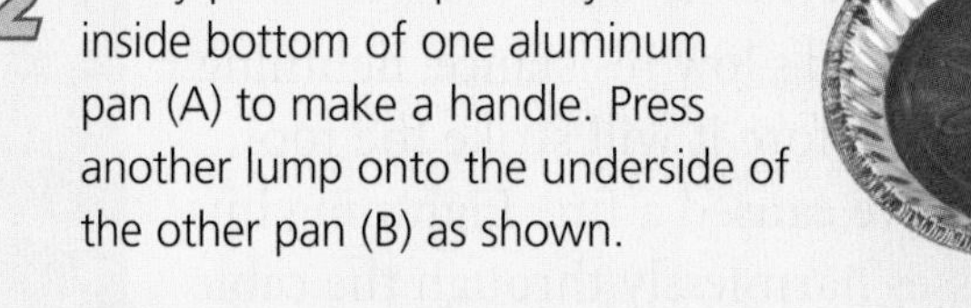

1. Draw a data table like the one on the sample notebook page.

2. Firmly press a lump of clay onto the inside bottom of one aluminum pan (A) to make a handle. Press another lump onto the underside of the other pan (B) as shown.

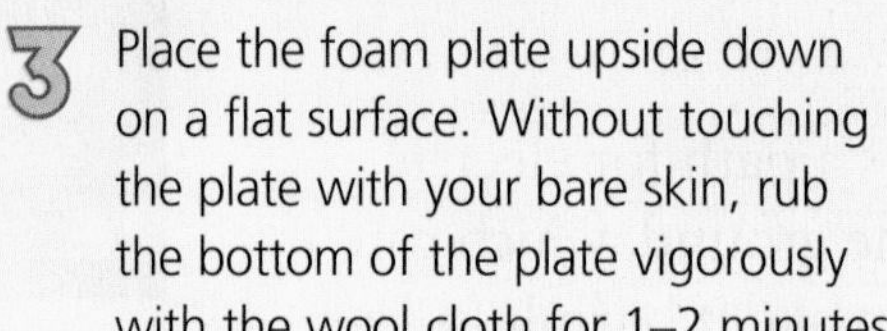

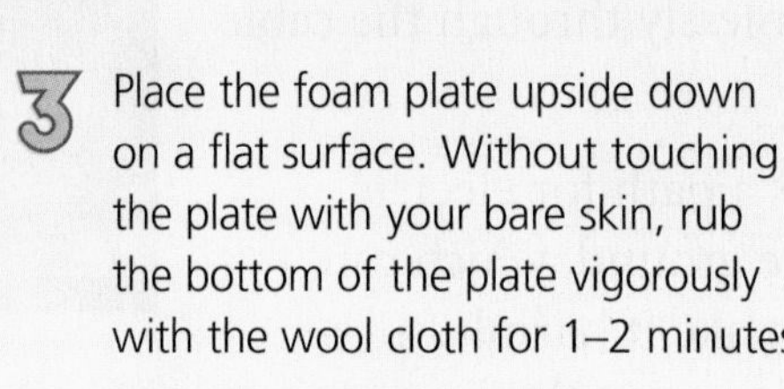

3. Place the foam plate upside down on a flat surface. Without touching the plate with your bare skin, rub the bottom of the plate vigorously with the wool cloth for 1–2 minutes.

4. Pick up aluminum pan A by the handle and hold it about 5 cm above the foam plate. Drop the pan so that it rests centered on top of the foam plate as shown. Be careful not to touch the pan or the plate.

5. Make the room as dark as possible. Slowly lower aluminum pan B over the rim of the first pan until they touch. Describe what occurs and where, in your notebook.

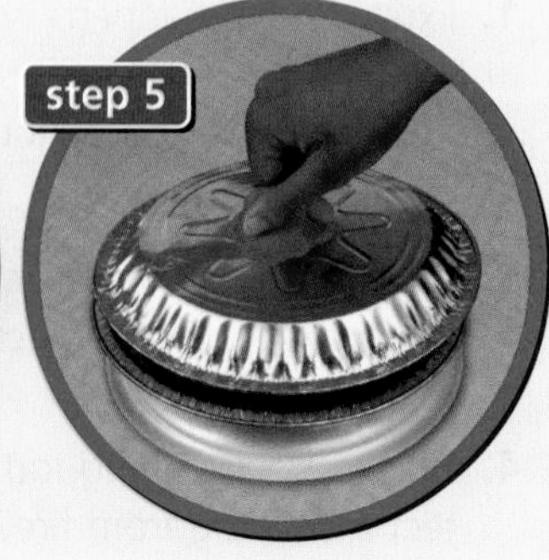

6. Repeat steps 3–5 two more times, recording your observations in your notebook.

7. Open the paper clip partway, as shown. Repeat steps 3–4. Then, instead of using the second aluminum pan, slowly bring the pointed end of the paper clip toward the rim of the first pan until they touch. Record your observations.

step 7

8. Repeat step 7 two more times, touching the paper clip to the aluminum pan in different places.

## Observe and Analyze

Write It Up

1. **RECORD OBSERVATIONS** Be sure your data table is complete. Draw pictures to show how the procedure varied between steps 5–6 and steps 7–8.
2. **ANALYZE** What did you observe in step 5 when the two aluminum pans touched? What do you think caused this to occur?
3. **COMPARE** How were your observations when you touched the aluminum pan with the paper clip different from those you made when you touched it with the other pan? How can you explain the difference?

## Conclude

Write It Up

1. **ANALYZE** Use the observations recorded in your data table to answer the following question: When you used the paper clip, why were you able to control the point at which the static discharge occurred?
2. **INFER** What charges did the foam plate and aluminum pan have before you began the experiment? after you dropped the pan on the plate? after you touched the pan with the paper clip?
3. **IDENTIFY VARIABLES** What variables and controls affected the outcome of your experiment?
4. **IDENTIFY LIMITS** What limitations or sources of error could have affected your results?
5. **APPLY** In your experiment, what corresponds to storm clouds and lightning? How did the paper clip work like a lightning rod?

## INVESTIGATE Further

**CHALLENGE** Where did the charge go when you touched the pie pan with the paper clip? Write a hypothesis to explain what happens in this situation and design an experiment to test your hypothesis.

Lightning

Observe and Analyze

Table 1. Observations of Static Discharge

| Trial | Observations |
|---|---|
| With second aluminum pan | |
| 1 | |
| 2 | |
| 3 | |
| With paper clip | |
| 4 | |
| 5 | |
| 6 | |

Conclude

KEY CONCEPT

# Electric current is a flow of charge.

**BEFORE, you learned**

- Charges move from higher to lower potential
- Materials can act as conductors or insulators
- Materials have different levels of resistance

**NOW, you will learn**

- About electric current
- How current is related to voltage and resistance
- About different types of electric power cells

**VOCABULARY**

**electric current** p. 28
**ampere** p. 29
**Ohm's law** p. 29
**electric cell** p. 31

**EXPLORE Current**

### *How does resistance affect the flow of charge?*

**PROCEDURE**

1. Tape the pencil lead flat on the posterboard.
2. Connect the wires, cell, bulb, and bulb holder as shown in the photograph.
3. Hold the wire ends against the pencil lead about a centimeter apart from each other. Observe the bulb.
4. Keeping the wire ends in contact with the lead, slowly move them apart. As you move the wire ends apart, observe the bulb.

**WHAT DO YOU THINK?**

- What happened to the bulb as you moved the wire ends apart?
- How might you explain your observation?

**MATERIALS**

- pencil lead
- posterboard
- electrical tape
- 3 lengths of wire
- D cell battery
- flashlight bulb
- bulb holder

## Electric charge can flow continuously.

**VOCABULARY**
Don't forget to make a four square diagram for the term *electric current.*

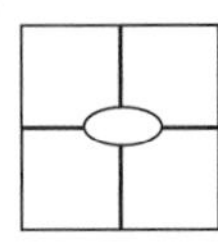

Static charges cannot make your television play. For that you need a different type of electricity. You have learned that a static charge contains a specific, limited amount of charge. You have also learned that a static charge can move and always moves from higher to lower potential. However, suppose that, instead of one charge, an electrical pathway received a continuous supply of charge and the difference in potential between the two ends of the pathway stayed the same. Then, you would have a continuous flow of charge. Another name for a flow of charge is **electric current.** Electric current is the form of electricity used to supply energy in homes, schools, and other buildings.

## Current, Voltage, and Resistance

Electric current obeys the same rules as moving static charges. Charge can flow only if it has a path to follow, that is, a material to conduct it. Also, charge can flow only from a point of higher potential to one of lower potential. However, one concept that does not apply to a moving static charge applies to current. Charge that flows steadily has a certain rate of flow. This rate can be measured. The standard unit of measure for current is the **ampere,** or amp. An amp is the amount of charge that flows past a given point per unit of time. One amp equals one coulomb per second. The number of amps—or amperage—of a flowing charge is determined by both voltage and resistance.

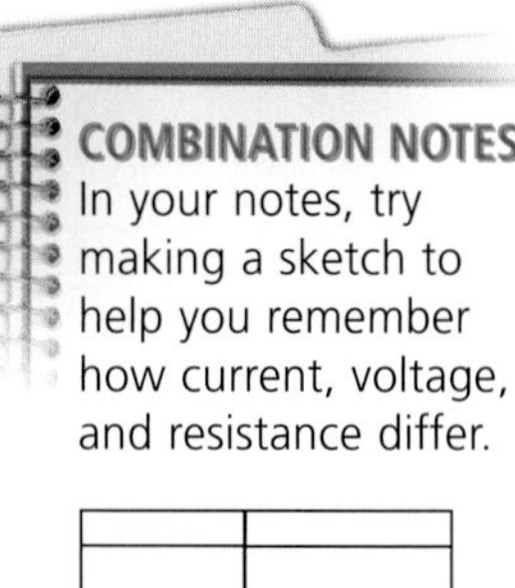

COMBINATION NOTES
In your notes, try making a sketch to help you remember how current, voltage, and resistance differ.

Electric current, or amperage, can be compared to the flow of water through a pipe. Electric potential, or voltage, is like pressure pushing the water through the pipe. Resistance, or ohms, is like the diameter of the pipe, which controls how much water can flow through. Water pressure and pipe size together determine the rate of water flow. Similarly, voltage and resistance together determine the rate of flow of electric charge.

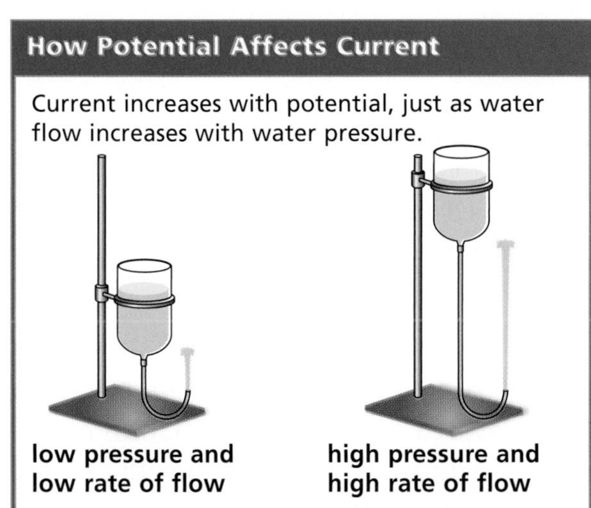


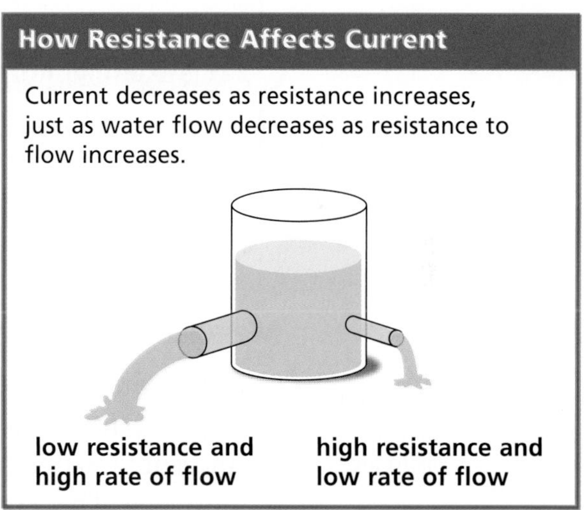


How Potential Affects Current
Current increases with potential, just as water flow increases with water pressure.

Current decreases as resistance increases, just as water flow decreases as resistance to flow increases.

## Ohm's Law

You now have three important measurements for the study of electricity: volts, ohms, and amps. The scientist for whom the ohm is named discovered a mathematical relationship among these three measurements. The relationship, called **Ohm's law,** is expressed in the formula below.

See Ohm's law in action.

$$\text{Current} = \frac{\text{Voltage}}{\text{Resistance}} \qquad I = \frac{V}{R}$$

$I$ is current measured in amps (A), $V$ is voltage measured in volts (V), and $R$ is resistance measured in ohms ($\Omega$).

What two values do you need to know to calculate the amperage of electric current?

You have read that current is affected by both voltage and resistance. Using Ohm's law, you can calculate exactly how much it is affected and determine the exact amount of current in amps. Use the formula for current to solve the sample problem below.

### Calculating Current

**Sample Problem**

**What is the current in an electrical pathway with an electric potential of 120 volts and a resistance of 60 ohms?**

*What do you know?* voltage = 120 V, resistance = 60 Ω

*What do you want to find out?* current

*Write the formula:* $I = \frac{V}{R}$

*Substitute into the formula:* $I = \frac{120 \text{ V}}{60 \ \Omega}$

*Calculate and simplify:* $I = 2$ A

*Check that your units agree:* Unit is amps.
Unit of current is amps. Units agree.

*Answer:* 2 A

**Practice the Math**

1. What is the current in an electrical pathway in which the voltage is 220 V and the resistance is 55 Ω?
2. An electrical pathway has a voltage of 12 volts and a resistance of 24 ohms. What is the current?

**READING TIP**

The terms *voltmeter*, *ohmmeter*, *ammeter*, and *multimeter* are all made by adding a prefix to the word *meter*.

## Measuring Electricity

Volts, ohms, and amps can all be measured using specific electrical instruments. Volts can be measured with a voltmeter. Ohms can be measured with an ohmmeter. Amps can be measured with an ammeter. These three instruments are often combined in a single electrical instrument called a multimeter.

To use a multimeter, set the dial on the type of unit you wish to measure. For example, the multimeter in the photograph is being used to test the voltage of a 9-volt battery. The dial is set on volts in the 0–20 range. The meter shows that the battery's charge has an electric potential of more than 9 volts, which means that the battery is good. A dead battery would have a lower voltage.

**CHECK YOUR READING** What does an ohmmeter measure?

## INVESTIGATE Electric Cells

### How can you produce electric current?

**PROCEDURE**

1. Insert the paper clip and the penny into the lemon, as shown in the photograph. The penny and paper clip should go about 3 cm into the lemon. They should be close, but not touching.
2. On the multimeter, go to the DC volts (V⎓) section of the dial and select the 0–2000 millivolt range (2000 m).
3. Touch one of the leads of the multimeter to the paper clip. Touch the other lead to the penny. Observe what is shown on the display of the multimeter.

**WHAT DO YOU THINK?**

- What did you observe on the display of the multimeter?
- How can you explain the reading on the multimeter?

**CHALLENGE** Repeat this experiment using different combinations of fruits or vegetables and metal objects. Which combinations work best?

**SKILL FOCUS**
Inferring

**MATERIALS**
- paper clip
- penny
- large lemon
- multimeter

*For Challenge*
- additional fruits or vegetables
- metal objects

**TIME**
20 minutes

## Electric cells supply electric current.

Electric current can be used in many ways. Two basic types of device have been developed for producing current. One type produces electric current using magnets. You will learn more about this technology in Chapter 3. The other type is the **electric cell,** which produces electric current using the chemical or physical properties of different materials.

### Electrochemical Cells

An electrochemical cell is an electric cell that produces current by means of chemical reactions. As you can see in the diagram, an electrochemical cell contains two strips made of different materials. The strips are called electrodes. The electrodes are suspended in a third material called the electrolyte, which interacts chemically with the electrodes to separate charges and produce a flow of electrons from the negative terminal to the positive terminal.

Batteries are made using electrochemical cells. Technically, a battery is two or more cells connected to each other. However, single cells, such as C cells and D cells, are often referred to as batteries.

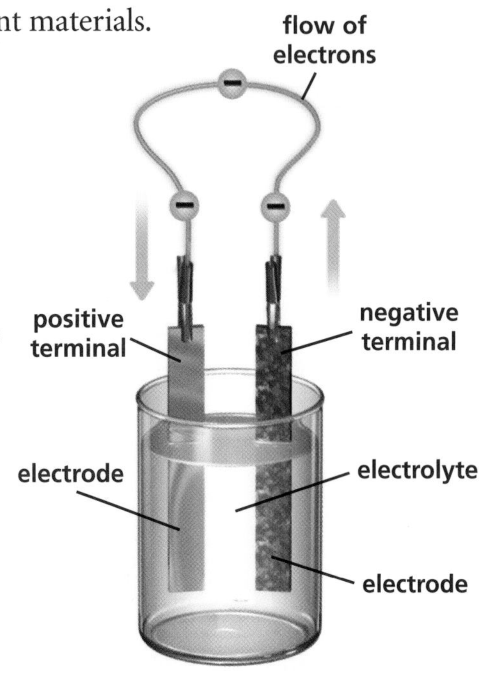

Learn more about electrochemical cells.

**Primary Cells** The electrochemical cell shown on page 31 is called a wet cell, because the electrolyte is a liquid. Most household batteries in use today have a solid paste electrolyte and so are called dry cells. Both wet cells and dry cells are primary cells. Primary cells produce electric current through chemical reactions that continue until one or more of the chemicals is used up.

The primary cell on page 33 is a typical zinc-carbon dry cell. It has a negative electrode made of zinc. The zinc electrode is made in the shape of a can and has a terminal—in this case, a wide disk of exposed metal—on the bottom of the cell. The positive electrode consists of a carbon rod and particles of carbon and manganese dioxide. The particles are suspended in an electrolyte paste. The positive electrode has a terminal—a smaller disk of exposed metal—at the top of the rod. A paper separator prevents the two electrodes from coming into contact inside the cell.

When the two terminals of the cell are connected—for example, when you turn on a flashlight—a chemical reaction between the zinc and the electrolyte produces electrons and positive zinc ions. The electrons flow through the wires connecting the cell to the flashlight bulb, causing the bulb to light up. The electrons then travel through the carbon rod and combine with the manganese dioxide. When the zinc and manganese dioxide stop reacting, the cell dies.

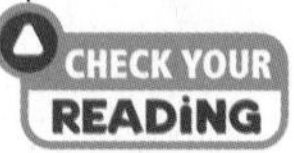

Why are most household batteries called dry cells?

**Storage Cells** Some batteries produce current through chemical reactions that can be reversed inside the battery. These batteries are called storage cells, secondary cells, or rechargeable batteries. A car battery like the lead-acid battery shown on page 33 is rechargeable. The battery has a negative electrode of lead and a positive electrode of lead peroxide. As the battery produces current, both electrodes change chemically into lead sulfate, and the electrolyte changes into water.

When storage cells are producing current, they are said to be discharging. Whenever a car engine is started, the battery discharges to operate the ignition motor. A car's battery can also be used when the car is not running to operate the lights or other appliances. If the battery is used too long in discharge mode, it will run down completely.

While a car is running, however, the battery is continually being charged. A device called an alternator, which is run by the car's engine, produces current. When electrons flow into the battery in the reverse direction from discharging, the chemical reactions that produce current are reversed. The ability of the battery to produce current is renewed.

What kind of battery can be charged by reversing chemical reactions?

## Batteries

Both primary cells and storage cells produce electricity through chemical reactions.

Flashlights use **primary cells.**

Car batteries and cell phones use **storage cells.**

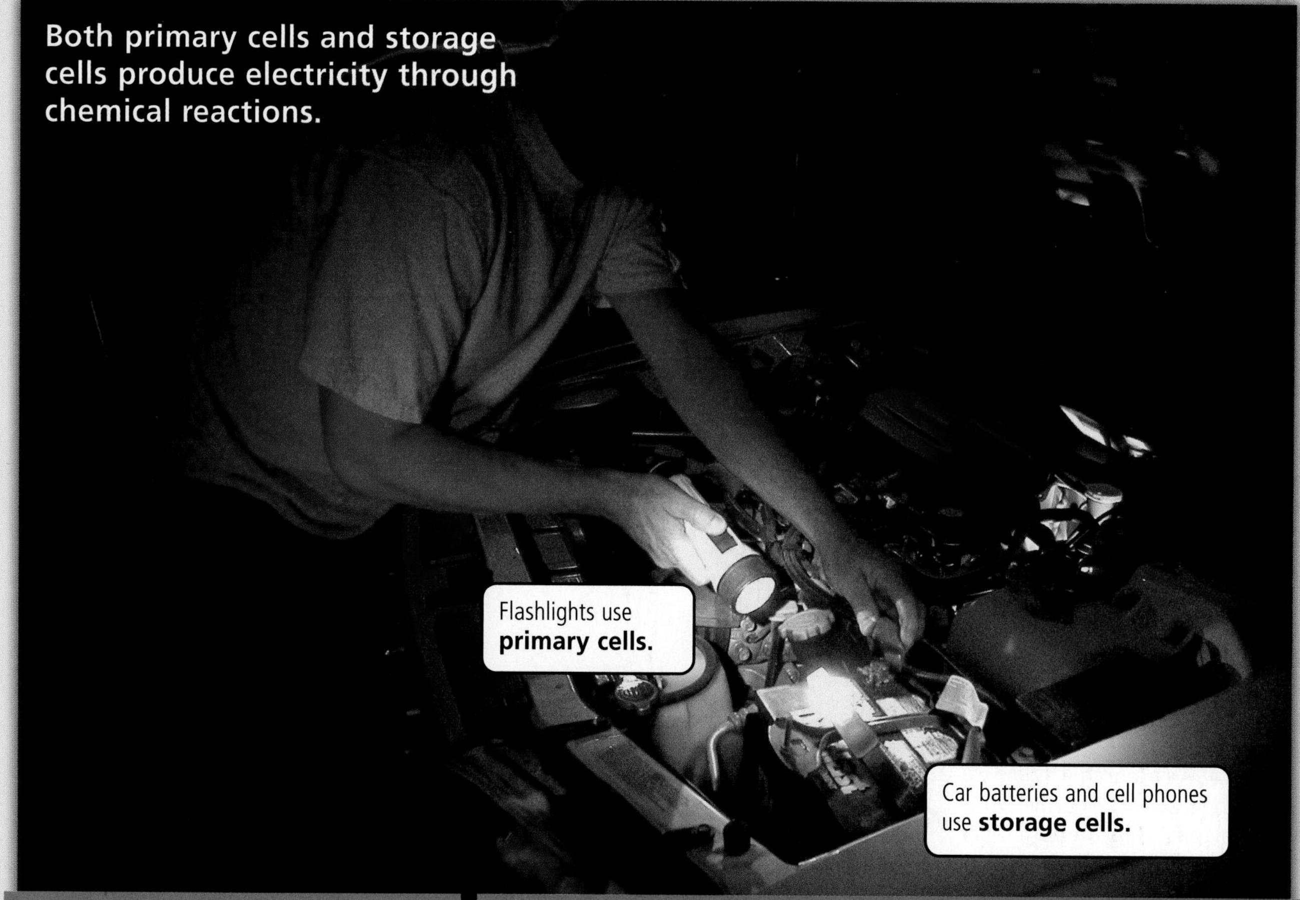

### Primary Cell

Primary cells produce electric current through chemical reactions. The reactions continue until the chemicals are used up.

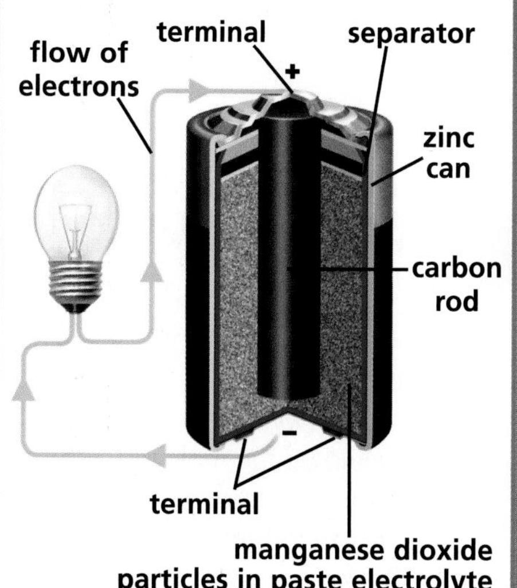


### Storage Cell

**1 Discharging** Storage cells produce current through chemical reactions that can be reversed in the battery.

**2 Charging** Sending current through the battery in the opposite direction reverses the chemical reactions.

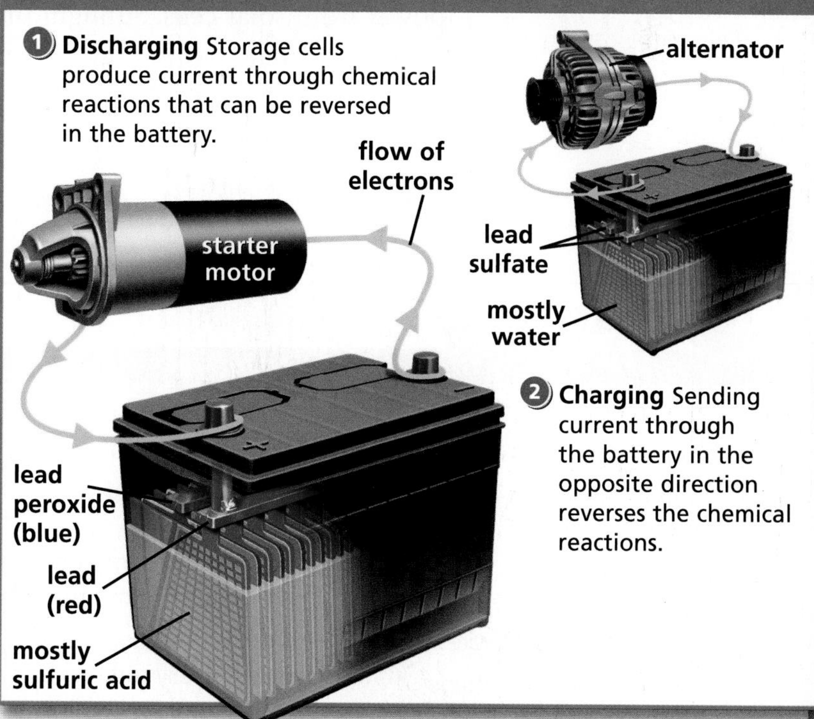


**READING VISUALS** In which direction do electrons flow when a storage cell is being charged?

**READING TIP**

The word *solar* comes from the Latin word *sol,* which means the Sun.

## Solar Cells

Some materials, such as silicon, can absorb energy from the Sun or other sources of light and then give off electrons, producing electric current. Electric cells made from such materials are called solar cells.

Solar cells are often used to make streetlights come on automatically at night. Current from the cell operates a switch that keeps the lights turned off. When it gets dark, the current stops, the switch closes, and the streetlights come on.

This NASA research aircraft is powered only by the solar cells on its upper surface.

Many houses and other buildings now get at least some of their power from solar cells. Sunlight provides an unlimited source of free, environmentally safe energy. However, it is not always easy or cheap to use that energy. It must be collected and stored because solar cells do not work at night or when sunlight is blocked by clouds or buildings.

CHECK YOUR READING Where do solar cells get their energy?

# 1.3 Review

### KEY CONCEPTS

1. How is electric current different from a static charge that moves?
2. How can Ohm's law be used to calculate the electrical resistance of a piece of wire?
3. How do rechargeable batteries work differently from nonrechargeable ones?

### CRITICAL THINKING

4. **Infer** Electrical outlets in a house maintain a steady voltage, even when the amount of resistance on them changes. How is this possible?
5. **Analyze** Why don't solar cells eventually run down as electrochemical cells do?

### CHALLENGE

6. **Apply** Several kinds of electric cells are discussed in this section. Which do you think would be the most practical source of electrical energy on a long trek through the desert? Explain your reasoning.

MATH in SCIENCE

MATH TUTORIAL

CLASSZONE.COM

Click on Math Tutorial for more help with equations.

A volume control works by changing the amount of resistance to the flow of current.

## SKILL: USING VARIABLES

# Which Formula Is Best?

A rock band needs an amplifier, and an amplifier needs a volume control. A volume control works by controlling the amount of resistance in an electrical pathway. When resistance goes down, the current—and the volume—go up. Ohm's law expresses the relationship among voltage *(V)*, resistance *(R)*, and amperage *(I)*. If you know the values of two variables, you can use Ohm's law to find the third. The law can be written in three ways, depending on which variable you wish to find.

$$I = \frac{V}{R} \qquad R = \frac{V}{I} \qquad V = IR$$

A simple way to remember these three versions of the formula is to use the pyramid diagram below. Cover up the variable you are looking for. The visible part of the diagram will give you the correct formula to use.

V

I R

### Example

What is the voltage of a battery that produces a current of 1 amp through a wire with a resistance of 9 ohms?

**(1)** You want to find voltage, so cover up the *V* in the pyramid diagram. To find *V*, the correct formula to use is $V = IR$.

**(2)** Insert the known values into the formula. $V = 1\text{ A} \cdot 9\ \Omega$

**(3)** Solve the equation to find the missing variable. $1 \cdot 9 = 9$

**ANSWER** 9 volts

**Answer the following questions.**

**1.** What is the voltage of a battery that sends 3 amps of current through a wire with a resistance of 4 ohms?

**2.** What is the resistance of a wire in which the current is 2 amps if the battery producing the current has a voltage of 220 volts?

**3.** What is the amperage of a current at 120 volts through a wire with a resistance of 5 ohms?

**CHALLENGE** Dimmer switches also work by varying resistance. A club owner likes the way the lights look at 1/3 normal current. The normal current is 15 amps. The voltage is constant at 110 V. How much resistance will he need?

# 1 Chapter Review

**Moving electric charges transfer energy.**

## KEY CONCEPTS SUMMARY

### 1.1 Materials can become electrically charged.

Electric charge is a property of matter.

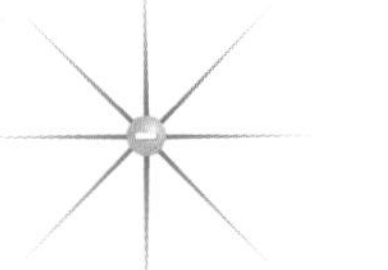

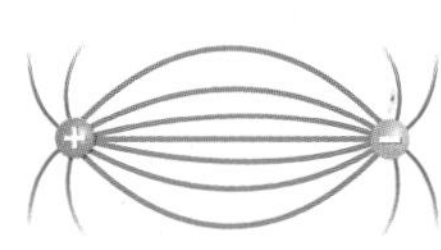

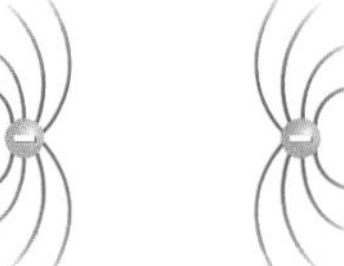

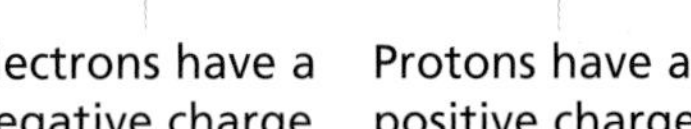

Electrons have a negative charge. Protons have a positive charge. Unlike charges attract. Like charges repel.

Static charges are caused by the movement of electrons, resulting in an imbalance of positive and negative charges.

**VOCABULARY**
**electric charge** p. 10
**electric field** p. 10
**static charge** p. 11
**induction** p. 13

### 1.2 Charges can move from one place to another.

Charge movement is affected by
- electric potential, measured in volts
- resistance, measured in ohms

A conductor has low resistance.

An insulator has high resistance.

A ground is the path of least resistance.

**VOCABULARY**
**electric potential** p. 19
**volt** p. 19
**conductor** p. 22
**insulator** p. 22
**resistance** p. 23
**ohm** p. 23
**grounding** p. 25

### 1.3 Electric current is a flow of charge.

Electric current is measured in amperes, or amps.

Ohm's law states that current equals voltage divided by resistance.

Electrochemical cells produce electric current through chemical reactions.

**VOCABULARY**
**electric current** p. 28
**ampere** p. 29
**Ohm's law** p. 29
**electric cell** p. 31

## Reviewing Vocabulary

*Copy the chart below, and write each term's definition. Use the meanings of the underlined roots to help you.*

| Word | Root | Definition |
|---|---|---|
| EXAMPLE current | to run | continuous flow of charge |
| **1.** static charge | standing | |
| **2.** induction | into + to lead | |
| **3.** electric cell | chamber | |
| **4.** conductor | with + to lead | |
| **5.** insulator | island | |
| **6.** resistance | to stop | |
| **7.** electric potential | power | |
| **8.** grounding | surface of Earth | |

*Write a vocabulary term to match each clue.*

**9.** In honor of scientist Alessandro Volta (1745–1827)

**10.** In honor of the scientist who discovered the relationship among voltage, resistance, and current

**11.** The amount of charge that flows past a given point in a unit of time.

## Reviewing Key Concepts

**Multiple Choice** *Choose the letter of the best answer.*

**12.** An electric charge is a
- **a.** kind of liquid
- **b.** reversible chemical reaction
- **c.** type of matter
- **d.** force acting at a distance

**13.** A static charge is different from electric current in that a static charge
- **a.** never moves
- **b.** can either move or not move
- **c.** moves only when resistance is low enough
- **d.** moves only when voltage is high enough

**14.** Charging by induction means charging
- **a.** with battery power
- **b.** by direct contact
- **c.** at a distance
- **d.** using solar power

**15.** Electric potential describes
- **a.** the electric potential energy per unit charge
- **b.** the electric kinetic energy per unit charge
- **c.** whether an electric charge is positive or negative
- **d.** how an electric charge is affected by gravity

**16.** A superconductor is a material that, when very cold, has no
- **a.** amperage
- **b.** resistance
- **c.** electric charge
- **d.** electric potential

**17.** Ohm's law says that when resistance goes up, current
- **a.** increases
- **b.** decreases
- **c.** stays the same
- **d.** matches voltage

**18.** Electrochemical cells include
- **a.** all materials that build up a charge
- **b.** primary cells and storage cells
- **c.** batteries and solar cells
- **d.** storage cells and lightning rods

**Short Answer** *Write a short answer to each question.*

**19.** What determines whether a charge you get when walking across a rug is positive or negative?

**20.** What is the difference between resistance and insulation?

**21.** What is one disadvantage of solar cells?

## Thinking Critically

*Use the diagram of an electrochemical cell below to answer the next three questions.*

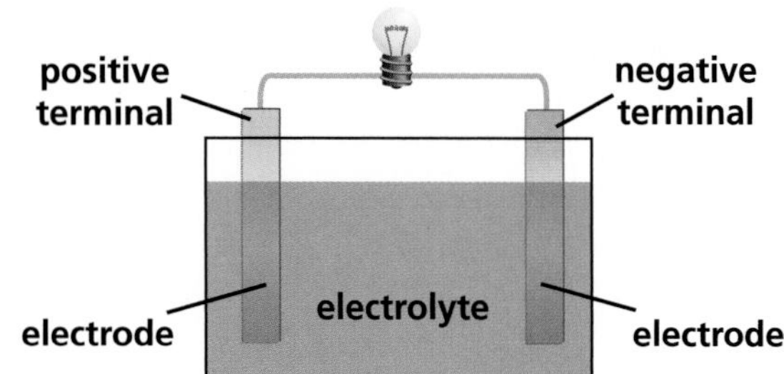


22. **ANALYZE** In which direction do electrons flow between the two terminals?

23. **PREDICT** What changes will occur in the cell as it discharges?

24. **ANALYZE** What determines whether the cell is rechargeable or not?

*Use the graph below to answer the next three questions.*

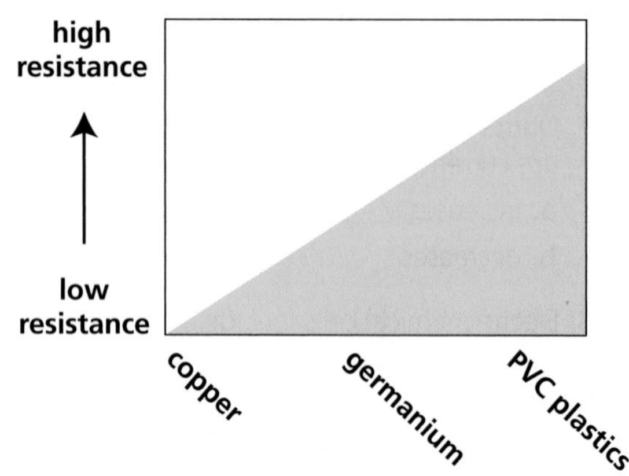


25. **INFER** Which material could you probably use as an insulator?

26. **INFER** Which material could be used in a lightning rod?

27. **APPLY** Materials that conduct electrons under some—but not all—conditions are known as semiconductors. Which material is probably a semiconductor?

## Using Math in Science

*Use the formula for Ohm's law to answer the next four questions.*

$$I = \frac{V}{R}$$

28. An electrical pathway has a voltage of 240 volts and a current of 10 amperes. What is the resistance?

29. A 240-volt air conditioner has a resistance of 8 ohms. What is the current?

30. An electrical pathway has a current of 1.2 amperes and resistance of 40 ohms. What is the voltage?

31. An electrical pathway has a voltage of 400 volts and resistance of 2000 ohms. What is the current?

## the BIG idea

32. **INFER** Look back at the photograph on pages 6 and 7. Based on what you have learned in this chapter, describe what you think is happening to keep the dragon lit.

33. **COMPARE AND CONTRAST** Draw two simple diagrams to compare and contrast static charges and electric current. Add labels and captions to make your comparison clear. Then write a paragraph summarizing the comparison.

## UNIT PROJECTS

If you are doing a unit project, make a folder for your project. Include in your folder a list of the resources you will need, the date on which the project is due, and a schedule to keep track of your progress. Begin gathering data.

# Standardized Test Practice

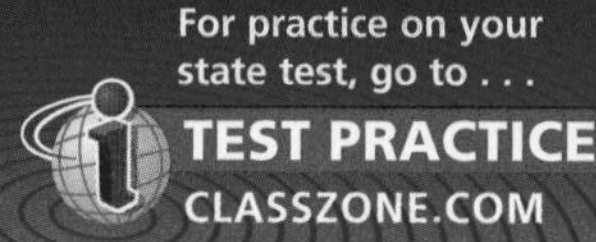


## Interpreting Diagrams

*Use the illustration below to answer the following questions. Assume that the balloons start off with no net charge.*

**1.** What will happen if a negatively charged rod is brought near one of the balloons without touching it?

**a.** The balloons will move toward each other.

**b.** The balloons will move away from each other.

**c.** Electrons on the balloons will move toward the rod.

**d.** Electrons on the balloons will move away from the rod.

**2.** What will happen if a positively charged rod is brought near one of the balloons without touching it?

**a.** The balloons will move toward each other.

**b.** The balloons will move away from each other.

**c.** Electrons on the balloons will move toward the rod.

**d.** Electrons on the balloons will move away from the rod.

**3.** In the previous question, the effect of the rod on the balloons is an example of

**a.** charging by contact
**b.** charge polarization
**c.** induction
**d.** conduction

**4.** What will happen if a negatively charged rod is brought near one of the balloons and the balloons are then separated?

**a.** The balloon farthest from the rod will become positively charged.

**b.** The balloon farthest from the rod will become negatively charged.

**c.** Both balloons will become positively charged.

**d.** Both balloons will have no net charge.

**5.** If you rub one balloon in your hair to charge it and then move it close to the other balloon, the balloons will

**a.** not move

**b.** move away from each other

**c.** move toward the ground

**d.** move toward each other

**6.** What will happen if a negatively charged rod is brought near one of the balloons, then taken away, and the balloons are then separated?

**a.** The balloon farthest from the rod will become positively charged.

**b.** The balloon farthest from the rod will become negatively charged.

**c.** Both balloons will become positively charged.

**d.** Both balloons will have no net charge.

## Extended Response

*Answer the two questions below in detail. Include some of the terms from the word box. Underline each term that you use in your answers.*

| charge separation | recharging | resistance |
|---|---|---|
| source of current | static charge | induce |

**7.** Describe the events leading up to and including a bolt of lightning striking Earth from a storm cloud.

**8.** Explain the advantages and disadvantages of storage cells over other types of electric cells.

# Circuits and Electronics

## the BIG idea

Circuits control the flow of electric charge.

## Key Concepts

SECTION

**Charge needs a continuous path to flow.**
Learn how circuits are used to control the flow of charge.

SECTION

**Circuits make electric current useful.**
Learn about series circuits and parallel circuits.

SECTION

**Electronic technology is based on circuits.**
Learn about computers and other electronic devices.

***How can circuits control the flow of charge?***

**Internet Preview**

CLASSZONE.COM

Chapter 2 online resources: Content Review, Simulation, Visualization, two Resource Centers, Math Tutorial, Test Practice

# EXPLORE the BIG idea

## Will the Flashlight Still Work?

Experiment with a flashlight to find out if it will work in any of the following arrangements: with one of the batteries facing the wrong way, with a piece of paper between the batteries, or with one battery removed. In each case, switch on the flashlight and observe.

**Observe and Think**
When did the flashlight work? Why do you think it worked or did not work in each case?

## What's Inside a Calculator?

Use a small screwdriver to open a simple calculator. Look at the circuit board inside.

**Observe and Think** How do you think the metal lines relate to the buttons on the front of the calculator? to the display? What is the source of electrical energy? How is it connected to the rest of the circuit?

## Internet Activity: Circuits

Go to **ClassZone.com** to build a virtual circuit. See if you can complete the circuit and light the bulb.

**Observe and Think**
What parts are necessary to light the bulb? What happened when you opened the switch? closed the switch?

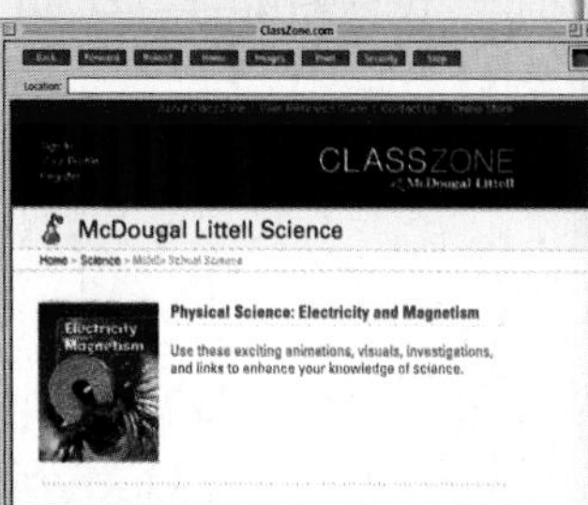

Electronic Circuits **Code: MDL066**

CHAPTER 2

# Getting Ready to Learn

## CONCEPT REVIEW

- Energy can change from one form to another.
- Energy can move from one place to another.
- Current is the flow of charge through a conductor.

## VOCABULARY REVIEW

**electric current** p. 28
**electric potential** p. 18
**conductor** p. 22
**resistance** p. 23
**ampere** p. 29

Review concepts and vocabulary.

## TAKING NOTES

### OUTLINE

As you read, copy the headings on your paper in the form of an outline. Then add notes in your own words that summarize what you read.

### VOCABULARY STRATEGY

Write each new vocabulary term in the center of a **frame game** diagram. Decide what information to frame it with. Use examples, descriptions, parts, sentences that use the term in context, or pictures. You can change the frame to fit each term.

See the Note-Taking Handbook on pages R45–R51.

SCIENCE NOTEBOOK

I. ELECTRIC CHARGE FLOWS IN A LOOP.
  A. THE PARTS OF A CIRCUIT
    1. voltage source
    2. connection
    3. electrical device
    4. switch

Electrical device

Part of a circuit

RESISTOR

Light bulb is an example

Slows the flow of charge

KEY CONCEPT

# Charge needs a continuous path to flow.

**BEFORE, you learned**

- Current is the flow of charge
- Voltage is a measure of electric potential
- Materials affect the movement of charge

**NOW, you will learn**

- About the parts of a circuit
- How a circuit functions
- How safety devices stop current

**VOCABULARY**

**circuit** p. 43
**resistor** p. 44
**short circuit** p. 46

**EXPLORE Circuits**

### *How can you light the bulb?*

**PROCEDURE**

1. Tape one end of a strip of foil to the negative terminal, or the flat end, of the battery. Tape the other end of the foil to the tip at the base of the light bulb, as shown.
2. Tape the second strip of foil to the positive terminal, or the raised end, of the battery.
3. Find a way to make the bulb light.

**MATERIALS**

- 2 strips of aluminum foil
- electrical tape
- D cell (battery)
- light bulb

**WHAT DO YOU THINK?**

- How did you make the bulb light?
- Can you find other arrangements that make the bulb light?

## Electric charge flows in a loop.

**VOCABULARY**
Use a frame game diagram to record the term *circuit* in your notebook.

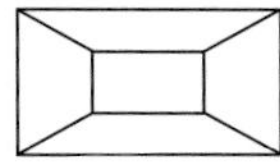

In the last chapter, you read that current is electric charge that flows from one place to another. Charge does not flow continuously through a material unless the material forms a closed path, or loop. A **circuit** is a closed path through which a continuous charge can flow. The path is provided by a low-resistance material, or conductor, usually wire. Circuits are designed to do specific jobs, such as light a bulb.

Circuits can be found all around you and serve many different purposes. In this chapter, you will read about simple circuits, such as the ones in flashlights, and more complex circuits, such as the ones that run toys, cameras, computers, and more.

**CHECK YOUR READING** How are circuits related to current?

## The Parts of a Circuit

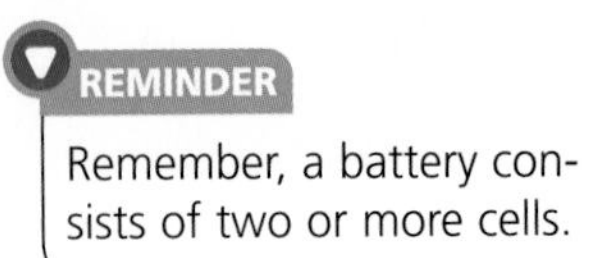


Remember, a battery consists of two or more cells.

The illustration below shows a simple circuit. Circuits typically contain the following parts. Some circuits contain many of each part.

1. **Voltage Source** The voltage source in a circuit provides the electric potential for charge to flow through the circuit. Batteries are often the voltage sources in a circuit. A power plant may also be a voltage source. When you plug an appliance into an outlet, a circuit is formed that goes all the way to a power plant and back.

2. **Conductor** A circuit must be a closed path in order for charge to flow. That means that there must be a conductor, such as wire, that forms a connection from the voltage source to the electrical device and back.

3. **Switch** A switch is a part of a circuit designed to break the closed path of charge. When a switch is open, it produces a gap in the circuit so that the charge cannot flow.

4. **Electrical Device** An electrical device is any part of the circuit that changes electrical energy into another form of energy. A **resistor** is an electrical device that slows the flow of charge in a circuit. When the charge is slowed, some energy is converted to light or heat. A light bulb is an example of a resistor.

### Circuit Parts

**The parts of a basic circuit include a voltage source, conductor, switch, and one or more electrical devices.**

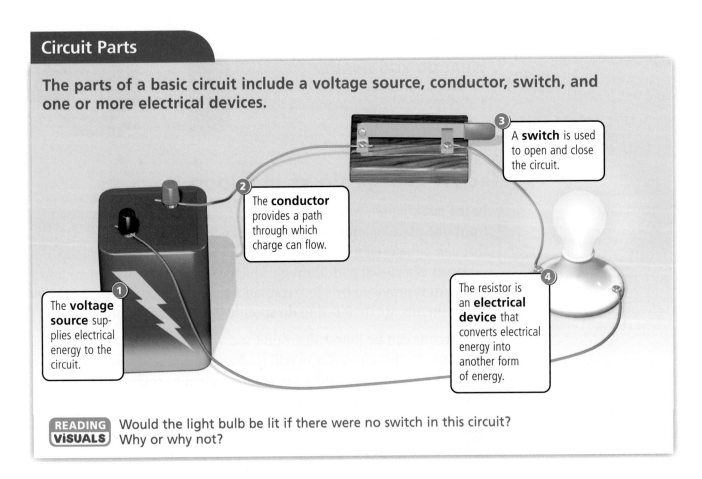

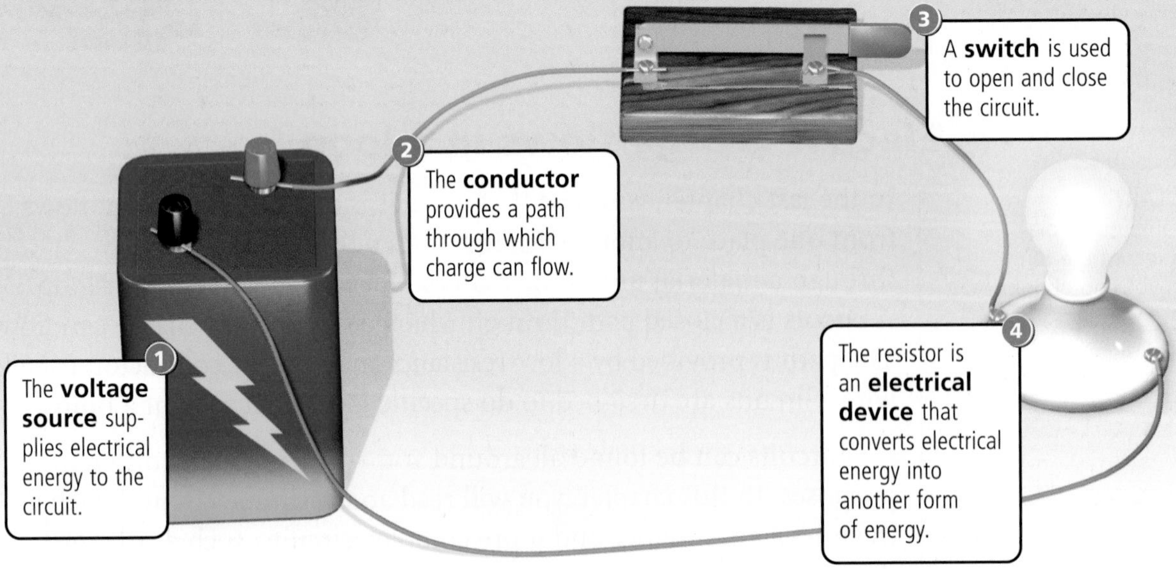

3 A **switch** is used to open and close the circuit.

2 The **conductor** provides a path through which charge can flow.

1 The **voltage source** supplies electrical energy to the circuit.

4 The resistor is an **electrical device** that converts electrical energy into another form of energy.

**READING VISUALS** Would the light bulb be lit if there were no switch in this circuit? Why or why not?

## Open and Closed Circuits

Current in a circuit is similar to water running through a hose. The flow of charge differs from the flow of water in an important way, however. The water does not require a closed path to flow. If you cut the hose, the water continues to flow. If you cut a wire, the charge stops flowing.

Batteries have connections at both ends so that charge can follow a closed path to and from the battery. The cords that you see on appliances might look like single cords but actually contain at least two wires. The wires connect the device to a power plant and back to make a closed path.

Switches work by opening and closing the circuit. A switch that is on closes the circuit and allows charge to flow through the electrical devices. A switch that is off opens the circuit and stops the current.

**REMINDER**
Current requires a closed loop.

**CHECK YOUR READING** How are switches used to control the flow of charge through a circuit?

Standard symbols are used to represent the parts of a circuit. Some common symbols are shown in the circuit diagrams below. The diagrams represent the circuit shown on page 44 with the switch in both open and closed positions. Electricians and architects use diagrams such as these to plan the wiring of a building.

**Symbols are used to represent the parts of a circuit. The circuit diagrams below show the circuit from page 44 in both an open and closed position.**

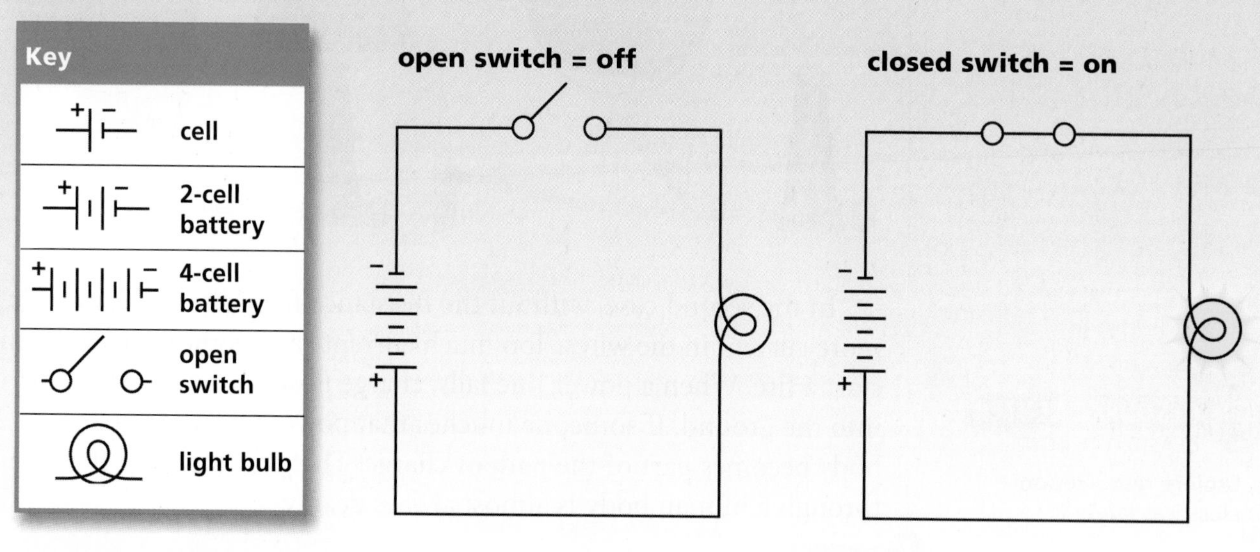


**READING VISUALS** Would charge flow through the circuit diagrammed on the left? Why or why not?

OUTLINE

Add this heading to your outline, along with supporting ideas.

I. Main idea
  A. Supporting idea
    1. Detail
    2. Detail
  B. Supporting idea

## Current follows the path of least resistance.

Since current can follow only a closed path, why are damaged cords so dangerous? And why are people warned to stay away from fallen power lines? Although current follows a closed path, the path does not have to be made of wire. A person can become a part of the circuit, too. Charge flowing through a person is dangerous and sometimes deadly.

Current follows the path of least resistance. Materials with low resistance, such as certain metals, are good conductors. Charge will flow through a copper wire but not the plastic coating that covers it because copper is a good conductor and plastic is not. Water is also a good conductor when mixed with salt from a person's skin. That is why it is dangerous to use electrical devices near water.

### Short Circuits

A **short circuit** is an unintended path connecting one part of a circuit with another. The current in a short circuit follows a closed path, but the path is not the one it was intended to follow. The illustration below shows a functioning circuit and a short circuit.

1. **Functioning Circuit** The charge flows through one wire, through the light bulb, and then back through the second wire to the outlet.
2. **Short Circuit** The cord has been damaged and the two wires inside have formed a connection. Now the path of least resistance is through one wire and back through the second wire.

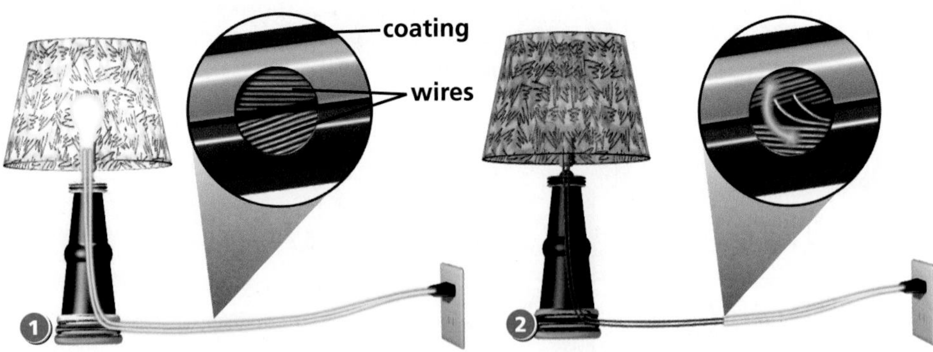


In the second case, without the resistance from the lamp, there is more current in the wires. Too much current can overheat the wires and start a fire. When a power line falls, charge flows along the wire and into the ground. If someone touches that power line, the person's body becomes part of the path of charge. That much charge flowing through a human body is almost always deadly.

Explore resources on electrical safety.

Why are short circuits dangerous?

## Grounding a Circuit

Recall that when lightning strikes a lightning rod, charge flows into the ground through a highly conductive metal rod rather than through a person or a building. In other words, the current follows the path of least resistance. The third prong on some electrical plugs performs a similar function. A circuit that connects stray current safely to the ground is known as a grounded circuit. Because the third prong grounds the circuit, it is sometimes called the ground.

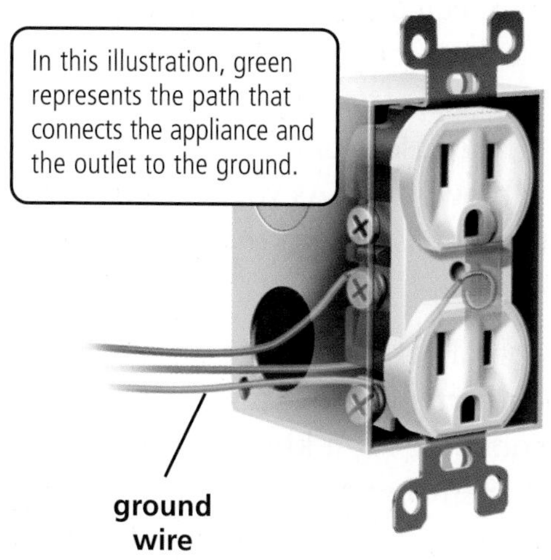


In this illustration, green represents the path that connects the appliance and the outlet to the ground.

Orange is used in this illustration to represent the path that connects the appliance's circuit to a power source and back.

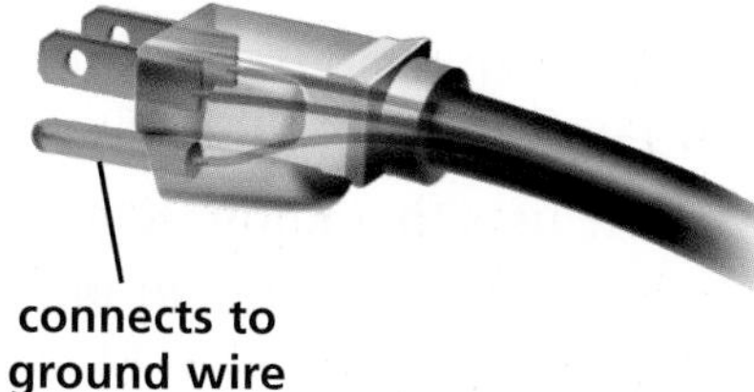


Normally, charge flows through one prong, along a wire to an appliance, then back along a second wire to the second prong. If there is a short circuit, the charge might flow dangerously to the outside of the shell of the appliance. If there is a ground wire, the current will flow along the third wire and safely into the ground, along either a buried rod or a cold water pipe.

What is the purpose of a ground wire?

**SAFETY TIPS**

- Never go near a fallen power line.
- Never touch an electrical appliance when you are in the shower or bathtub.
- Always dry your hands thoroughly before using an electrical appliance.
- Never use an electrical cord that is damaged in any way.
- Never bend or cut a ground prong in order to make a grounded plug fit into an ungrounded outlet.

# Safety devices control current.

Suppose your living room wiring consists of a circuit that supplies current to a television and several lights. One hot evening, you turn on an air conditioner in the living room window. The wires that supply current to the room are suddenly carrying more current than before. The lights in the room become dim. Too much current in a circuit is dangerous. How do you know if there is too much current in a wire?

Fortunately, people have been using electric current for over a hundred years. An understanding of how charge flows has led to the development of safety devices. These safety devices are built into circuits to prevent dangerous situations from occurring.

## How Fuses Work

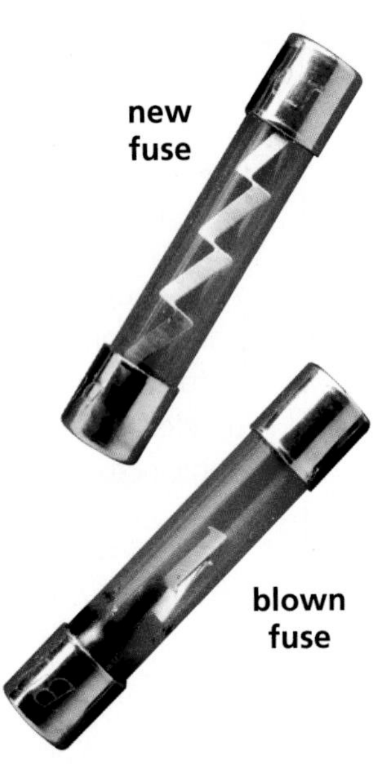


If you turn on an air conditioner in a room full of other electrical appliances that are already on, the circuit could overheat. But if the circuit contains a fuse, the fuse will automatically shut off the current. A fuse is a safety device that opens a circuit when there is too much current in it. Fuses are typically found in older homes and buildings. They are also found in cars and electrical appliances like air conditioners.

A fuse consists of a thin strip of metal that is inserted into the circuit. The charge in the closed circuit flows through the fuse. If too much charge flows through the fuse, the metal strip melts. When the strip has melted and the circuit is open, the fuse is blown. The photographs on the left show a new fuse and a blown fuse. As you can see, charge cannot flow across the melted strip. It has broken the circuit and stopped the current.

How much current is too much? That varies. The electrician who installs a circuit knows how much current the wiring can handle. He or she uses that knowledge to choose the right kind of fuse. Fuses are measured in amperes, or amps. Remember that amperage is a measure of current. If a fuse has blown, it must be replaced with a fuse of the same amperage. But a fuse should be replaced only after the problem that caused it to blow has been fixed.

## INVESTIGATE Fuses

### *How can you stop a current?*

**PROCEDURE**

1. Use the alligator clips to clip one end of each wire to the steel wool strand.
2. Place the steel wool strand in the jar. Tape the wires to the sides of the jar.
3. Clip the free end of one wire to the negative terminal of the battery.
4. What do you predict will happen when you complete the circuit? Clip the free end of the remaining wire to the positive terminal of the battery and observe the steel wool strand.

**WHAT DO YOU THINK?**

- What did you observe when you completed the circuit? Why did that happen?
- How can you stop the current?

**CHALLENGE** How is the setup in this activity similar to a fuse that would be found in a home circuit? How does it differ?

**SKILL FOCUS**
Making Models

**MATERIALS**
- 2 pieces of insulated wire with alligator clips
- single strand of steel wool
- glass jar
- tape
- 6 V battery

**TIME**
15 minutes

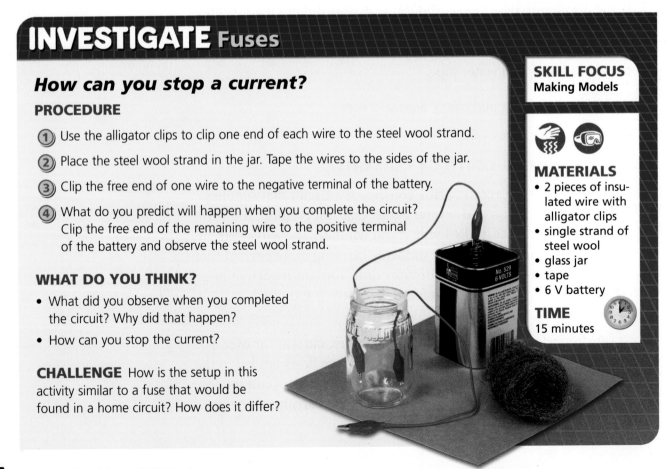

## Other Safety Devices

Most modern homes do not use fuses. Instead, they use safety devices called circuit breakers. Circuit breakers, unlike fuses, do not have to be replaced every time they open the circuit. Like fuses, circuit breakers automatically open the circuit when too much charge flows through it. If the circuit becomes overloaded or there is a short circuit, the wire and the breaker grow hot. That makes a piece of metal inside the breaker expand. As it expands, it presses against a switch. The switch is then flipped to the off position and the current is stopped. Once the problem is solved, power can be restored manually by simply flipping the switch back. The illustration on the right shows a circuit breaker.

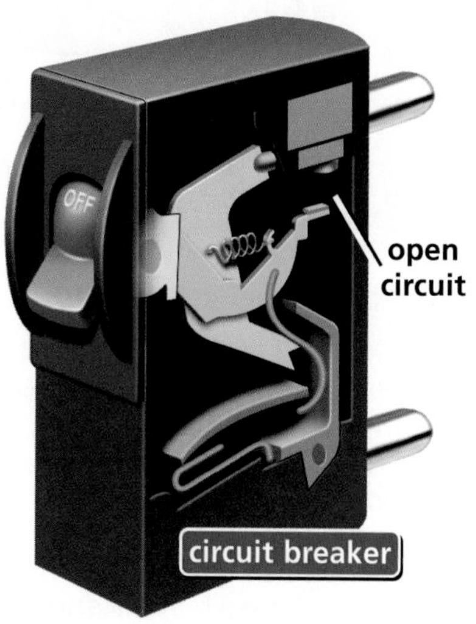

How are circuit breakers similar to fuses?

The photograph at the bottom right shows another safety device—a ground-fault circuit interrupter (GFCI) outlet. Sometimes a little current leaks out of an outlet or an appliance. Often it is so small you do not notice it. But if you happen to have wet hands, touching even a small current can be very dangerous.

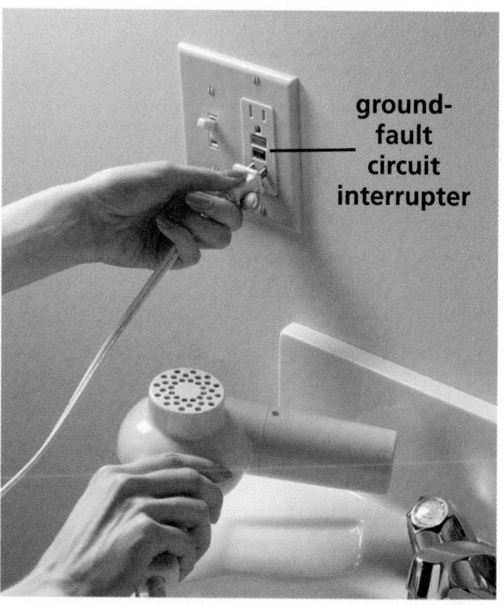


GFCI outlets are required in places where exposure to water is common, such as in kitchens and bathrooms. A tiny circuit inside the GFCI outlet monitors the current going out and coming in. If some of the current starts to flow through an unintended path, there will be less current coming in to the GFCI. If that happens, a circuit breaker inside the GFCI outlet opens the circuit and stops the current. To close the circuit again, you push "Reset."

# 2.1 Review

### KEY CONCEPTS

1. Describe three parts of a circuit and explain what each part does.
2. Explain the function of a ground wire.
3. What do fuses and circuit breakers have in common?

### CRITICAL THINKING

4. **Apply** Suppose you have built a circuit for a class project. You are using a flat piece of wood for its base. How could you make a switch out of a paperclip and two nails?
5. **Communicate** Draw a diagram of a short circuit. Use the symbols for the parts of a circuit.

### CHALLENGE

6. **Evaluate** A fuse in a home has blown and the owner wants to replace it with a fuse that can carry more current. Why might the owner's decision lead to a dangerous situation?

# SCIENCE on the JOB

## ELECTRICIAN

# The Science of Electrical Work

Electricians are the professionals who know how to control and modify electrical installations safely. They are the people who install the wiring and fixtures that deliver current to the appliances in your home. They also inspect equipment and wiring to locate and correct problems. High-voltage current can cause injuries, or even death, if not handled correctly. The electrician uses science to build and repair electrical systems safely.

### Choosing the Wire

Different types and thicknesses of wire have different amounts of resistance and can carry different amounts of current without overheating. The electrician knows which type of wire is suitable for each application.

### Installing Safety Devices

Circuit breakers shut off a circuit when the wires carry too much current. This safety device protects the wires from overheating. The electrician chooses circuit breakers with the appropriate amperage for each circuit.

### Using Circuit Diagrams

Circuit diagrams are used to map all of the circuits in a project. The electrician determines how many electrical devices each one will contain and knows how much energy those devices will use.

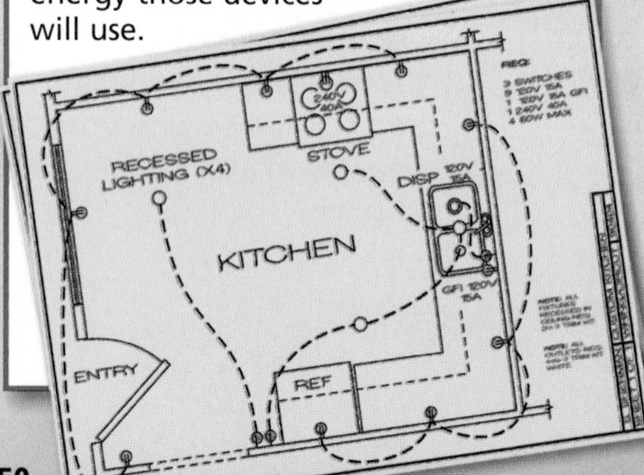


### EXPLORE

1. **INFER** Look around the room you're in for electrical outlets. Why do you think each one is located where it is? Do you think they all connect appliances to the same circuit? Explain how this is possible.
2. **CHALLENGE** Suppose you are planning the wiring for the lighting in a room. Draw a diagram of the room's layout and indicate where the wires, lighting fixtures, and switches will be located.

KEY CONCEPT

# Circuits make electric current useful.

**BEFORE, you learned**

- Charge flows in a closed circuit
- Circuits have a voltage source, conductor, and one or more electrical devices
- Current follows the path of least resistance

**NOW, you will learn**

- How circuits are designed for specific purposes
- How a series circuit differs from a parallel circuit
- How electrical appliances use circuits

**VOCABULARY**

**series circuit** p. 52
**parallel circuit** p. 53

THINK ABOUT

### *How does it work?*

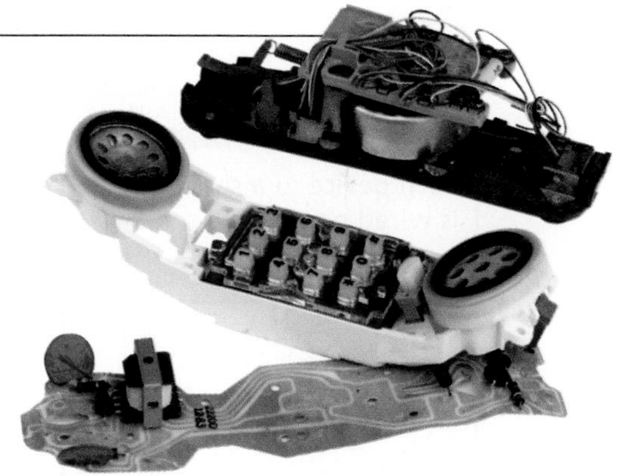

You know what a telephone does. But did you ever stop to think about how the circuits and other electrical parts inside of it work together to make it happen?

This photo shows an old telephone that has been taken apart to reveal its circuits. As you can see, there are a lot of different parts. Each one has a function. Pick two or three of the parts. What do you think each part does? How do you think it works? How might it relate to the other parts inside the telephone?

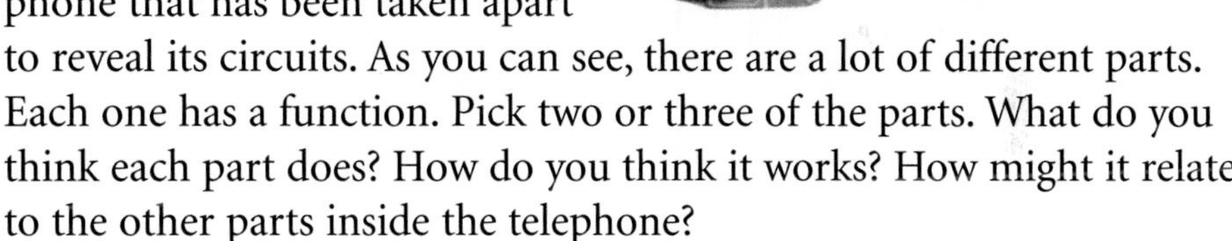

## Circuits are constructed for specific purposes.

OUTLINE
Remember to include this heading in your outline.

I. Main idea
  A. Supporting idea
    1. Detail
    2. Detail
  B. Supporting idea

How many things around you right now use electric current? Current is used to transfer energy to so many things because it is easy to store, distribute, and turn off and on. Each device that uses current is a part of at least one circuit—the circuit that supplies its voltage.

Most electrical appliances have many circuits inside of them that are designed to carry out specific functions. Those circuits may be designed to light bulbs, move motor parts, or calculate. Each of those circuits may have thousands—or even millions—of parts. The functions that a circuit can perform depend on how those parts are set up within the circuit.

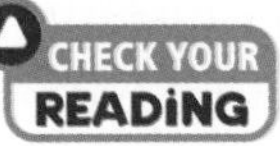

CHECK YOUR READING Why is the design of a circuit important?

## Circuits can have multiple paths.

Even a simple circuit can contain several parts. When you flip the light switch in your classroom, how many different lights go on? If you count each light bulb or each fluorescent tube, there might be as many as ten or twelve light bulbs. There is more than one way those light bulbs could be connected in one circuit. Next, you will read about two simple ways that circuits can be constructed.

### Series Circuits

**READING TIP**

The word *series* means a number of things arranged one after another.

A **series circuit** is a circuit in which current follows a single path. That means that all of the parts in a series circuit are part of the same path. The photograph and diagram below show a series circuit. The charge coming from the D cell flows first through one light bulb, and then through the next one.

**Series Circuit**

Each device in a series circuit is wired on a single path.

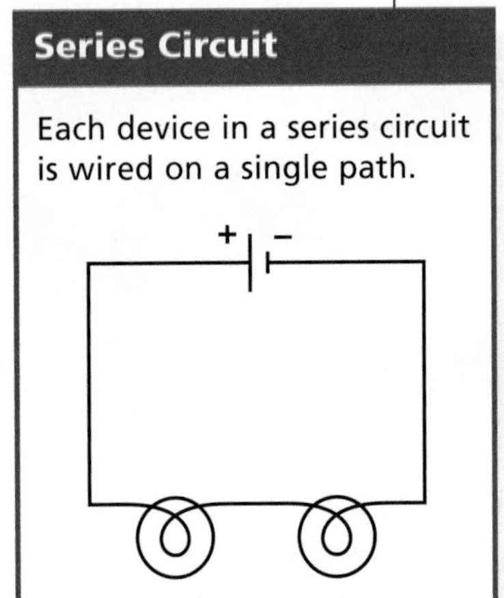


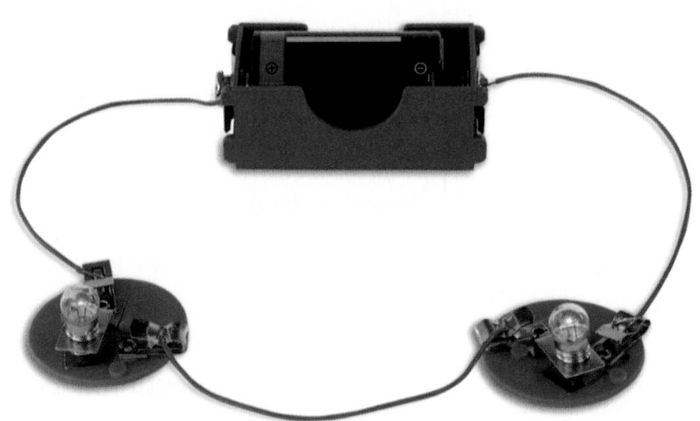

A series circuit uses a minimal amount of wire. However, a disadvantage of a series circuit is that all of the elements must be in working order for the circuit to function. If one of the light bulbs burns out, the circuit will be broken and the other bulb will be dark, too. Series circuits have another disadvantage. Light bulbs and other resistors convert some energy into heat and light. The more light bulbs that are added to a series circuit, the less current there is available, and the dimmer all of the bulbs become.

Give two disadvantages of a series circuit.

If voltage sources are arranged in series, the voltages will add together. Sometimes batteries are arranged in series to add voltage to a circuit. For example, the circuits in flashlights are usually series circuits. The charge flows through one battery, through the next, through the bulb, and back to the first battery. The flashlight is brighter than it would be if its circuit contained only a single battery.

## Parallel Circuits

A **parallel circuit** is a circuit in which current follows more than one path. Each path is called a branch. The current divides among all possible branches, so that the voltage is the same across each branch. The photograph and diagram below show a simple parallel circuit.

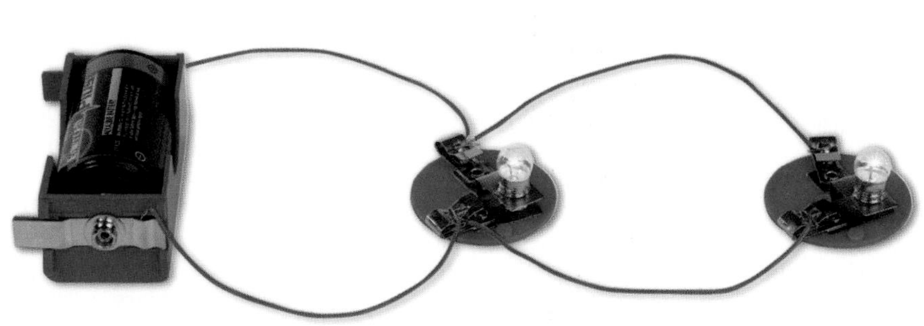

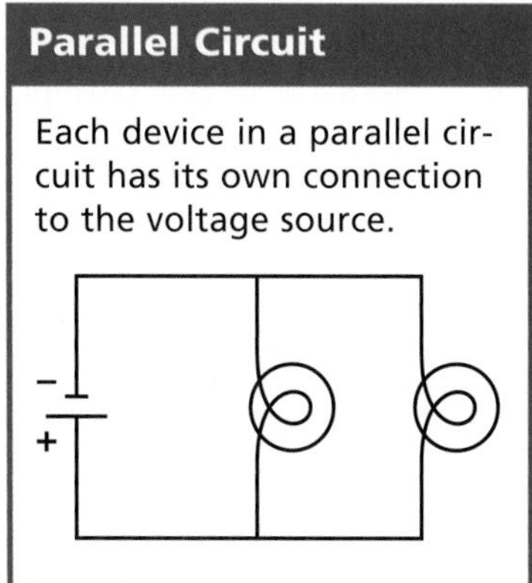


**Parallel Circuit**

Each device in a parallel circuit has its own connection to the voltage source.

Parallel circuits require more wire than do series circuits. On the other hand, there is more than one path on which the charge may flow. If one bulb burns out, the other bulb will continue to glow. As you add more and more light bulbs to a series circuit, each bulb in the circuit grows dimmer and dimmer. Because each bulb you add in a parallel circuit has its own branch to the power source, the bulbs burn at their brightest.

A flashlight contains batteries wired in a series circuit. Batteries can be wired in parallel, too. If the two positive terminals are connected to each other and the two negative terminals are connected to each other, charge will flow from both batteries. Adding batteries in parallel will not increase the voltage supplied to the circuit, but the batteries will last longer.

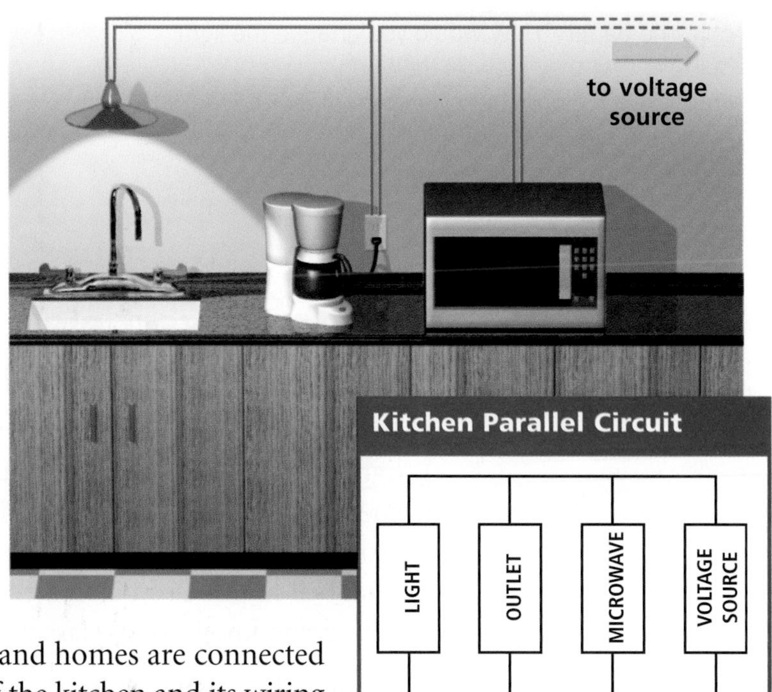


The circuits in most businesses and homes are connected in parallel. Look at the illustration of the kitchen and its wiring. This is a parallel circuit, so even if one electrical device is switched off, the others can still be used. The circuits within many electrical devices are combinations of series circuits and parallel circuits. For example, a parallel circuit may have branches that contain several elements arranged in series.

Why are the circuits in buildings and homes arranged in parallel?

# INVESTIGATE Circuits

## *How can you produce brighter light?*

SKILL FOCUS
Inferring

**MATERIALS**
- 4 insulated wires with alligator clips
- small light bulb in a holder
- 2 batteries in holders

**TIME**
15 minutes

**PROCEDURE**

1. Clip one end of a wire to the light bulb and the other end to the negative terminal of one battery to form a connection.
2. Use another wire to connect the positive terminal of the battery with the negative terminal of a second battery, as shown in the photograph.
3. Use a third wire to connect the positive terminal of the second battery to the light bulb. Observe the light bulb.
4. Remove the wires. Find a way to reconnect the wires to produce the other type of circuit.

**WHAT DO YOU THINK?**
- Which circuit produced brighter light? What type of circuit was it?
- Why did the light bulb glow brighter in that circuit?

**CHALLENGE** Suppose you wanted to construct a new circuit consisting of four light bulbs and only one battery. How would you arrange the light bulbs so that they glow at their brightest? Your answer should be in the form of either a diagram or a sketch of the circuit.

## Circuits convert electrical energy into other forms of energy.

We use electrical energy to do many things besides lighting a string of light bulbs. For example, a circuit in a space heater converts electrical energy into heat. A circuit in a fan converts electrical energy into motion. A circuit in a bell converts electrical energy into sound. That bell might also be on a circuit that makes it ring at certain times, letting you know when class is over.

Branches, switches, and other elements in circuits allow for such control of current that our calculators and computers can use circuits to calculate and process information for us. All of these things are possible because voltage is electric potential that can be converted into energy in a circuit.

Name three types of energy that electrical energy can be converted into.

A toaster is an example of an electrical appliance containing a circuit that converts energy from one form to another. In a toaster, electrical energy is converted into heat. Voltage is supplied to the toaster by plugging it into a wall outlet, which completes the circuit from a power plant. The outlet is wired in parallel with other outlets, so the appliance will always be connected to the same amount of voltage.

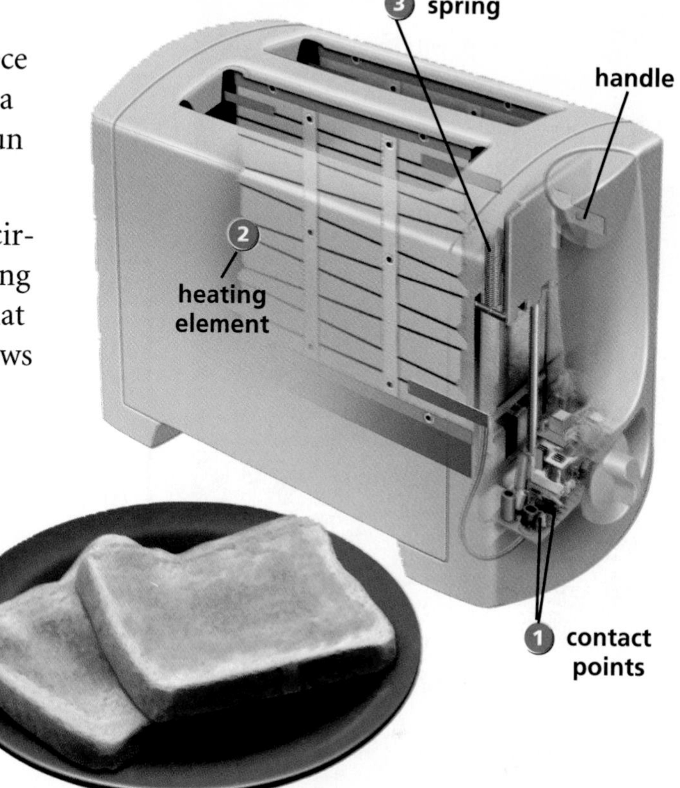


1. When you push the handle down, a piece of metal connects to contact points on a circuit board that act as a switch and run current through the circuit.
2. Charge flows through a resistor in the circuit called a heating element. The heating element is made up of a type of wire that has a very high resistance. As charge flows through the heating element, electrical energy is converted into heat.
3. The holder in the toaster is loaded onto a timed spring. After a certain amount of time passes, the spring is released, the toast pops up, and the circuit is opened. The toaster shuts off automatically, and your toast is done.

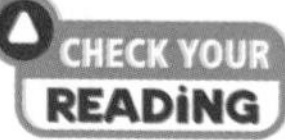


Summarize the way a circuit in a toaster works. (Remember that a summary includes only the most important information.)

## 2.2 Review

### KEY CONCEPTS

1. Explain how a circuit can perform a specific function.
2. How are series circuits and parallel circuits similar? How do they differ?
3. Describe three electrical appliances that use circuits to convert electrical energy into other forms of energy.

### CRITICAL THINKING

4. **Analyze** Why are the batteries of flashlights often arranged in series and not in parallel?
5. **Infer** You walk past a string of small lights around a window frame. Only two of the bulbs are burned out. What can you tell about the string of lights?

### CHALLENGE

6. **Apply** Explain how the circuit in a space heater converts electrical energy into heat. Draw a diagram of the circuit, using the standard symbols for circuit diagrams.

MATH in SCIENCE

SKILL: SOLVING PERCENT PROBLEMS

# Voltage Drop

A voltage drop occurs when current passes through a wire or an electrical device. The higher the resistance of a wire, the greater the voltage drop. Too much voltage drop can cause the device to overheat.

The National Electric Code—a document of guidelines for electricians—states that the voltage drop across a wire should be no more than 5 percent of the voltage from the voltage source. To find 5 percent of a number, you can set up the calculation as a proportion.

**MATH TUTORIAL**
CLASSZONE.COM
Click on Math Tutorial for more help with percents and proportions.

## Example

The lighting in a hotel includes many fixtures that will be arranged on long wires. The electrician needs to know the maximum voltage drop allowed in order to choose the proper wire. The circuit will use a voltage source of 120 V. What is 5% of 120?

**(1)** Write the problem as a proportion.

$$\frac{\text{voltage drop}}{\text{voltage}} = \frac{\text{percent}}{100}$$

**(2)** Substitute.

$$\frac{\text{voltage drop}}{120} = \frac{5}{100}$$

**(3)** Calculate and simplify.

$$\frac{\text{voltage drop}}{\cancel{120}} \cdot \cancel{120} = \frac{5}{100} \cdot 120$$

$$\text{voltage drop} = 6$$

**ANSWER** The maximum voltage drop in the wire is 6 V.

**Use the proportion to answer the following questions.**

**1.** If the voltage source is increased to 277 V, what is the maximum voltage drop in the wire?

**2.** To be on the safe side, the electrician decided to find a wire with a voltage drop that is 3 percent of the voltage from the voltage source. What is the voltage drop in the wire?

**CHALLENGE** A student wants to hang a string of lights outside and connect it to an extension cord. The voltage drop across the extension cord is 3.1 V. The outlet supplies 240 V. Does the voltage drop in the extension cord meet the code guidelines?

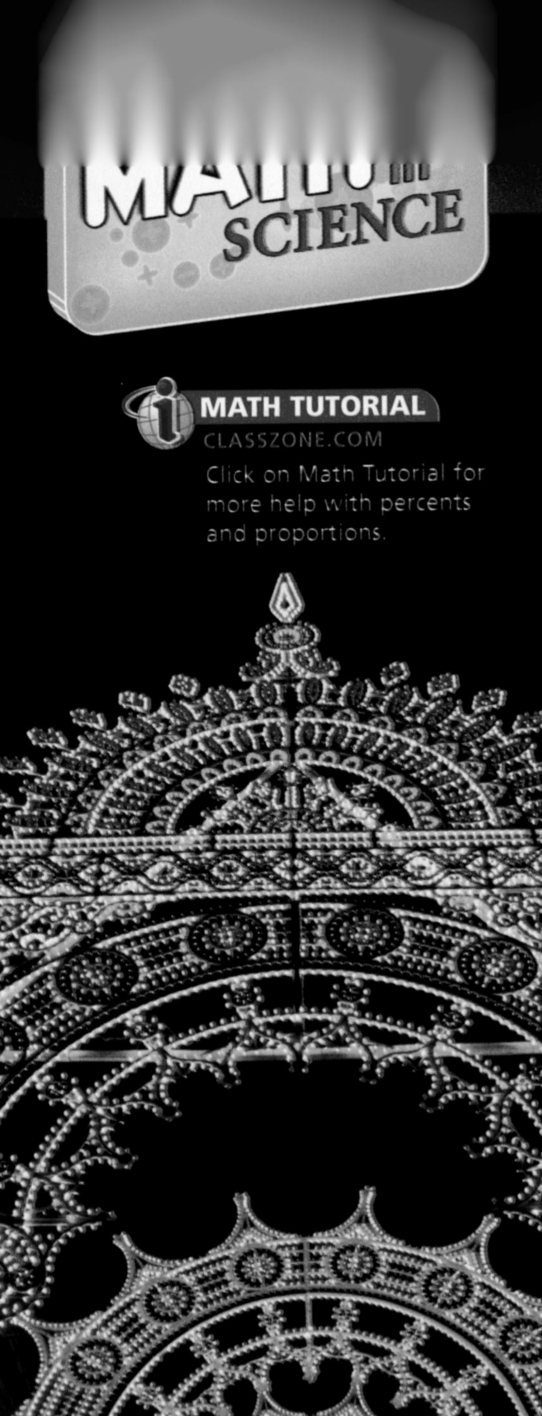

The many lights in this spectacular display in Kobe, Japan, produce a large voltage drop. The appropriate type of wire must be used to supply its current.

KEY CONCEPT

# Electronic technology is based on circuits.

**BEFORE, you learned**

- Charge flows in a closed loop
- Circuits are designed for specific purposes
- Electrical appliances use circuits

**NOW, you will learn**

- How information can be coded
- How computer circuits use digital information
- How computers work

**VOCABULARY**

**electronic** p. 57
**binary code** p. 58
**digital** p. 58
**analog** p. 60
**computer** p. 61

**EXPLORE Codes**

### *How can information be coded?*

**PROCEDURE**

1. Write the numbers 1 to 26 in your notebook. Below each number, write a letter of the alphabet. This will serve as your key.
2. On a separate piece of paper, write the name of the street you live on using numbers instead of words. For each letter of the word, use the number that is directly above it on your key.
3. Exchange messages with a partner and use your key to decode your partner's information.

**MATERIALS**

- notebook
- small piece of paper

**WHAT DO YOU THINK?**

- How can information be coded?
- Under what types of circumstances would information need to be coded?

## Electronics use coded information.

A code is a system of symbols used to send a message. Language is a code, for example. The symbols used in written language are lines and shapes. The words on this page represent meanings coded into the form of letters. As you read, your brain decodes the lines and shapes that make up each word, and you understand the message that is encoded.

An **electronic** device is a device that uses electric current to represent coded information. In electronics, the signals are variations in the current. Examples of electronic devices include computers, calculators, CD players, game systems, and more.

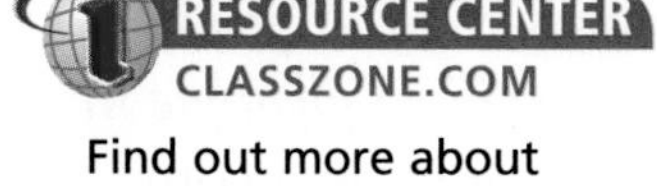


Find out more about electronics.

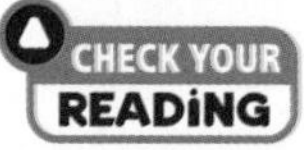


Describe the signals used in electronic devices.

## Binary Code

The English alphabet contains only 26 letters, yet there is no limit to the number of messages that can be expressed with it. That is because the message is conveyed not only by the letters that are chosen but also by the order in which they are placed.

Many electronic devices use a coding system with only two choices, as compared with the 26 in the alphabet. A coding system consisting of two choices is a **binary code.** As with a language, complex messages can be sent using binary code. In electronics, the two choices are whether an electric current is on or off. Switches in electronic circuits turn the current on and off. The result is a message represented in pulses of current.

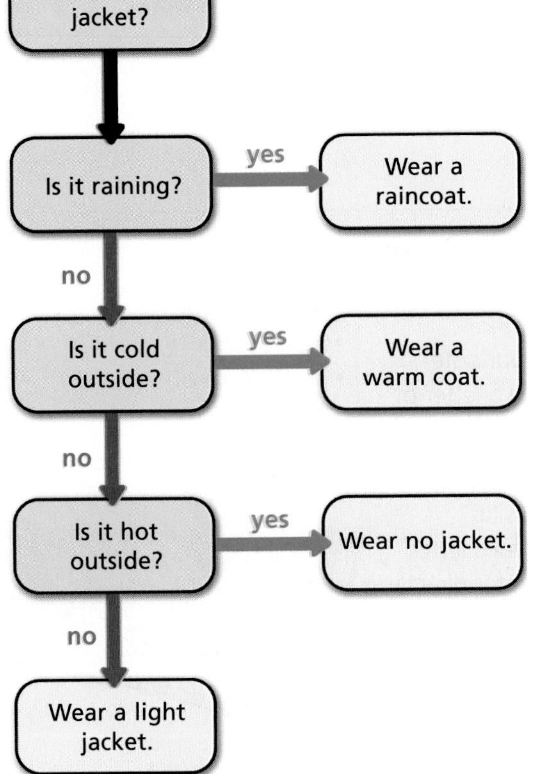


It may be hard to imagine how something as complex as a computer game can be expressed with pulses of current. But it is a matter of breaking down information into smaller and smaller steps. You may have played the game 20 questions. In that game, you receive a message by asking someone only yes-or-no questions. The player answering the questions conveys the message only in *yes's* and *no's,* a binary code.

The diagram on the left shows how a decision-making process can be written in simple steps. The diagram is similar to a computer program, which tells a computer what to do. Each step of the process has been broken down into a binary question. If you determine exactly what you mean by *cold* and *hot,* then anyone using this program—or even a computer—would arrive at the same conclusion for a given set of conditions.

How can a process be broken down into simple steps?

## Digital Information

You can think of the yes-or-no choices in a binary system as being represented by the numbers 0 and 1. Information that is represented as numbers, or digits, is called **digital** information. In electronics, a circuit that is off is represented by 0, and a circuit that is on is represented by 1.

Digital information is represented in long streams of digits. Each 0 or 1 is also known as a bit, which is short for *b*inary dig*it.* A group of 8 bits is known as a byte. You might have heard the term *gigabyte* in reference to the amount of information that can be stored on a computer. One gigabyte is equal to about 1 billion bytes. That's 8 billion 0s and 1s!

Computers, digital cameras, CD players, DVD players, and other devices use digital information. Digital information is used in electronic devices more and more. There are at least two reasons for this:

- Digital information can be copied many times without losing its quality. The 1s are always copied as 1s, and the 0s are always copied as 0s.
- Digital information can be processed, or worked with, on computers.

For example, a photograph taken on a digital camera can be input to a computer in the form of digital information. Once the photograph is on a computer, the user can modify it, copy it, store it, and send it.

Many portable devices such as game systems and MP3 players can also be used with computers. Because computers and the devices use the same type of information, computers can be used to add games, music, and other programs to the devices. The photograph at right of a watch shows an example of a portable device that uses digital information.

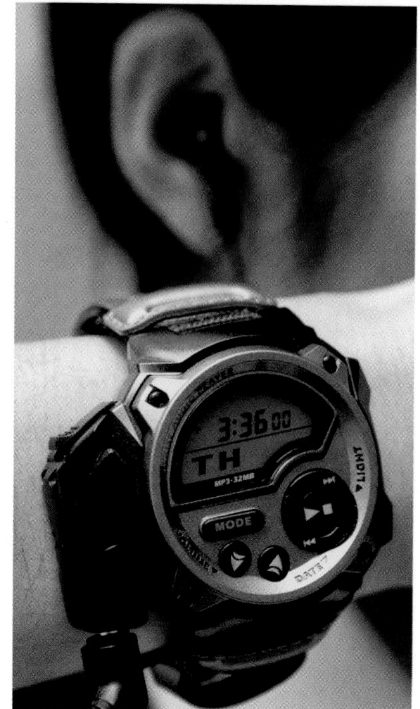


This watch also functions as an MP3 player—it can store songs as digital files.

Why is digital information often used in electronic devices?

## INVESTIGATE Digital Information

### *How can you save a drawing in 1s and 0s?*

**SKILL**
Making models

**MATERIALS**
- graph paper
- plain paper

**TIME**
30 minutes

**PROCEDURE**

1. Draw a 10-square by 10-square grid on a piece of graph paper.
2. Fill in some of the squares of the grid to draw a picture or pattern. Look at the example shown, but draw your own picture.
3. Starting in the upper left-hand corner of your grid, write 0 for every blank square and 1 for every filled-in square. Write a continuous series of 1s and 0s for all rows.
4. Exchange coded information with a partner who has not seen your picture. Draw a new grid in your notebook and fill it in using your partner's information.

**WHAT DO YOU THINK?**

- How were you able to reproduce your partner's picture?
- How is this activity similar to saving an image on a computer?

**CHALLENGE** Suppose you used three colored markers in your drawing—red, yellow, and green. How could you represent your color drawing using only 1s and 0s?

## Analog to Digital

Some electronic devices use a system of coding electric current that differs from the digital code. Those electronics use analog information. **Analog** information is information that is represented in a continuous but varying form.

For example, a microphone records sound waves as analog information. The analog signal that is produced varies in strength as the sound wave varies in strength, as shown below. In order for the signal to be burned onto a CD, it is converted into digital information.

1. The sound waves are recorded in the microphone as an analog electrical signal.
2. The signal is sent through a computer circuit that measures, or samples, each part of the wave. The signal is sampled many thousands of times every second.
3. Each measurement of the wave is converted into a stream of digits. Microscopic pits representing the stream of digits are burned onto the CD. A stereo converts the signal from digital back to analog form, making it possible for people to hear what was recorded.

### Analog and Digital Signals

**Sound is recorded as an analog signal and converted to digital information for storage on a CD.**

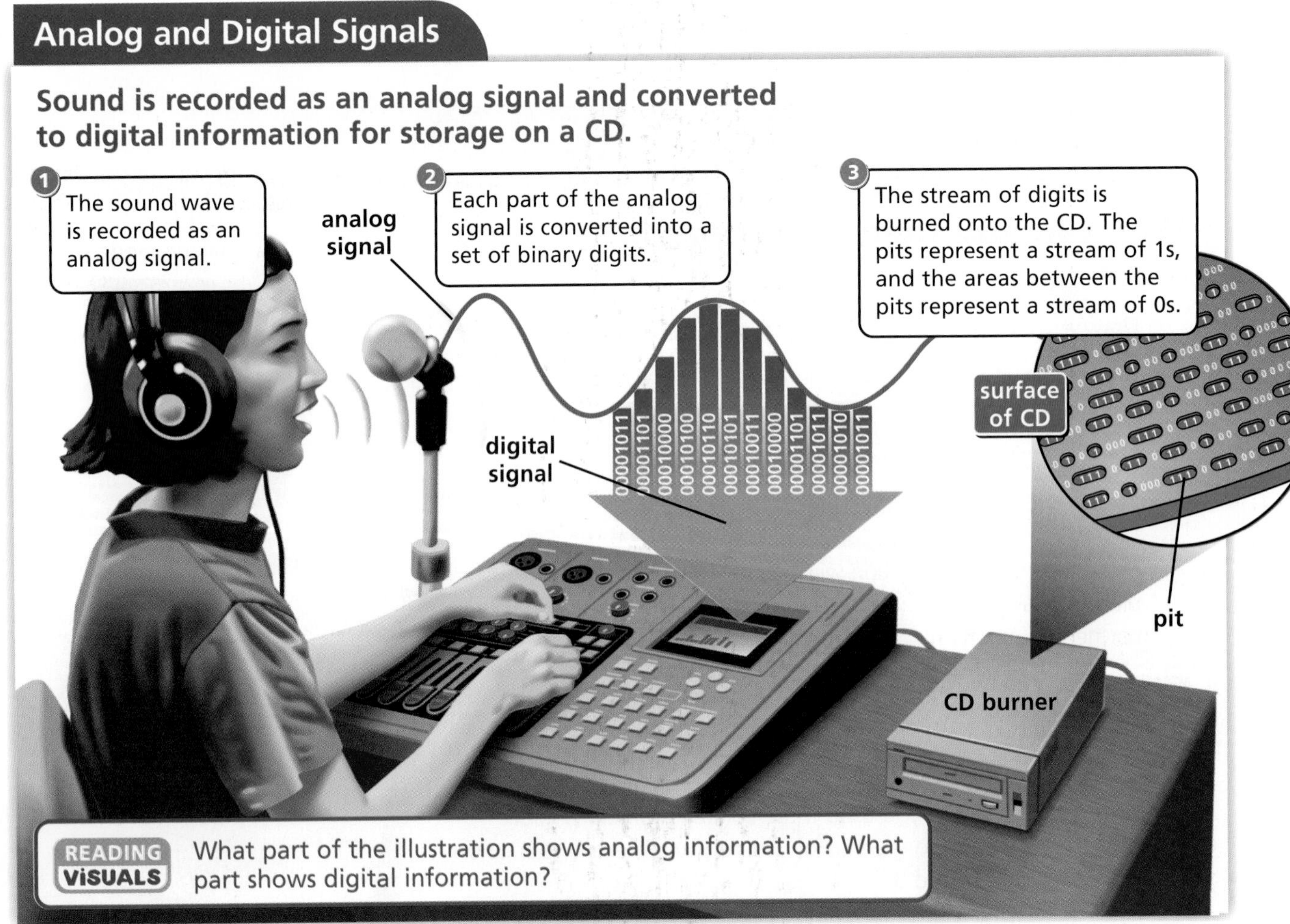

1 The sound wave is recorded as an analog signal.
analog signal
2 Each part of the analog signal is converted into a set of binary digits.
3 The stream of digits is burned onto the CD. The pits represent a stream of 1s, and the areas between the pits represent a stream of 0s.
digital signal
00001011
00001101
00010000
00010100
00010110
00010101
00010011
00010000
00001101
00001011
00001010
00001011
surface of CD
pit
CD burner


**READING VISUALS** What part of the illustration shows analog information? What part shows digital information?

## Computer circuits process digital information.

A **computer** is an electronic device that processes digital information. Computers have been important in science and industry for a long time. Scientists use computers to gather, store, process, and share scientific data. As computers continue to get faster, smaller, and less expensive, they are turning up in many places.

VOCABULARY
Remember to make a frame game diagram for *computer.*

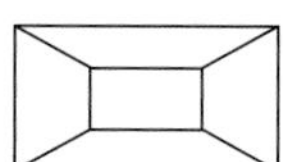

Suppose you get a ride to the store. If the car you're riding in is a newer car, it probably has a computer inside it. At the store, you buy a battery, and the clerk records the sale on a register that is connected to a computer. You put the battery in your camera and take a picture, and the camera has a computer inside it.

### Integrated Circuits

The first digital computer weighed 30 tons and took up a whole room. After 60 years of development, computers the size of a postage stamp are able to complete the same tasks in less time. New technology in computer circuits has led to very small and powerful computers.

Computers process information on circuits that contain many switches, branches, and other elements that allow for a very fine control of current. An integrated circuit is a miniature electronic circuit. Tiny switches, called transistors, in these circuits turn off and on rapidly, signaling the stream of digits that represent information. Over a million of these switches may be on one small integrated circuit!

CHECK YOUR READING How do integrated circuits signal digital information?

Most integrated circuits are made from silicon, an element that is very abundant in Earth's crust. When silicon is treated with certain chemicals, it becomes a good semiconductor. A semiconductor is a material that is more conductive than an insulator but less conductive than a conductor. Silicon is a useful material in computers because the flow of current in it can be finely controlled.

Microscopic circuits are etched onto treated silicon with chemicals or lasers. Transistors and other circuit parts are constructed layer by layer on the silicon. A small, complex circuit on a single piece of silicon is known as a silicon chip, or microchip.

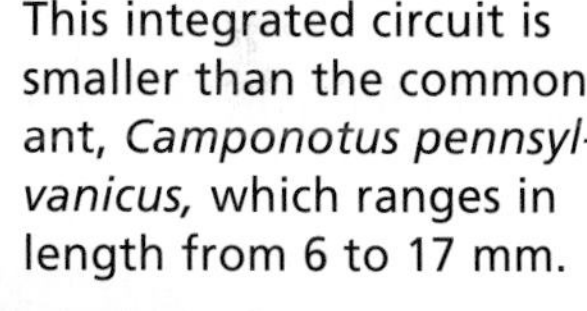

This integrated circuit is smaller than the common ant, *Camponotus pennsylvanicus,* which ranges in length from 6 to 17 mm.

**OUTLINE**
Use an outline to take notes about personal computers.

I. Main idea
  A. Supporting idea
    1. Detail
    2. Detail
  B. Supporting idea

## Personal Computers

When you think of a computer, you probably think of a monitor, mouse, and keyboard—a personal computer (PC). All of the physical parts of a computer and its accessories are together known as hardware. Software refers to the instructions, or programs, and languages that control the hardware. The hardware, software, and user of a computer all work together to complete tasks.

What is the difference between hardware and software?

Computers have two kinds of memory. As the user is working, information is saved on the computer's random-access memory, or RAM. RAM is a computer's short-term memory. Most computers have enough RAM to store billions of bits. Another type of memory is called read-only memory, or ROM. ROM is a computer's long-term memory, containing the programs to start and run the computer. ROM can save information even after a computer is turned off.

The illustration below shows how a photograph is scanned, modified, and printed using a personal computer. The steps fall into four main functions—input, storage, processing, and output.

### How a PC Works

**Digital information can move through input, processing, storage, and output devices.**

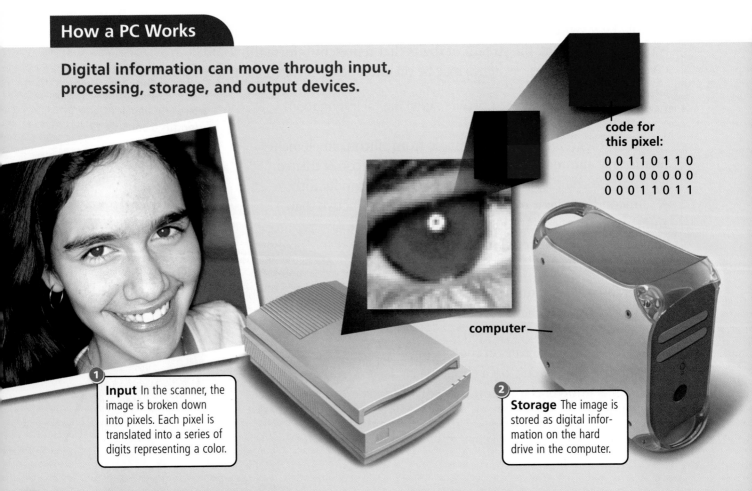

code for this pixel:
0 0 1 1 0 1 1 0
0 0 0 0 0 0 0 0
0 0 0 1 1 0 1 1

computer

1 **Input** In the scanner, the image is broken down into pixels. Each pixel is translated into a series of digits representing a color.

2 **Storage** The image is stored as digital information on the hard drive in the computer.

**1 Input** The user scans the photograph on a scanner. Each small area, or pixel, of the photograph is converted into a stream of digits. The digital information representing the photograph is sent to the main computer circuit, which is called the central processing unit, or CPU.

**2 Storage** The user saves the photograph on a magnetic storage device called the hard drive. Small areas of the hard drive are magnetized in one of two directions. The magnetized areas oriented in one direction represent 1s, and the areas oriented in the opposite direction represent 0s, as a way to store the digital information.

See how hard drives store information.

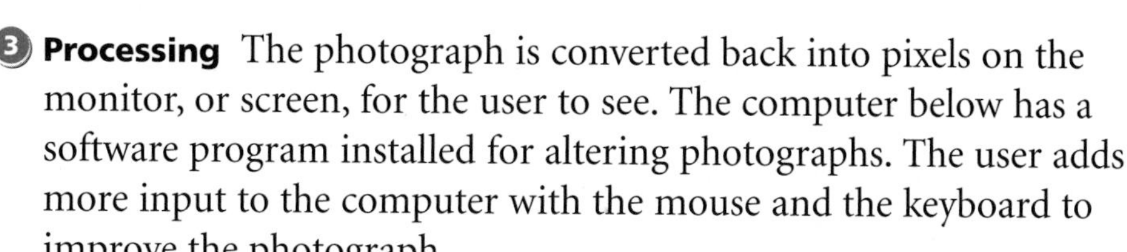

**3 Processing** The photograph is converted back into pixels on the monitor, or screen, for the user to see. The computer below has a software program installed for altering photographs. The user adds more input to the computer with the mouse and the keyboard to improve the photograph.

**4 Output** The user sends the improved photograph to a printer. The printer converts the digital information back to pixels, and the photograph is printed.

**CHECK YOUR READING** During which one of the four main computer functions is information converted into digital information?

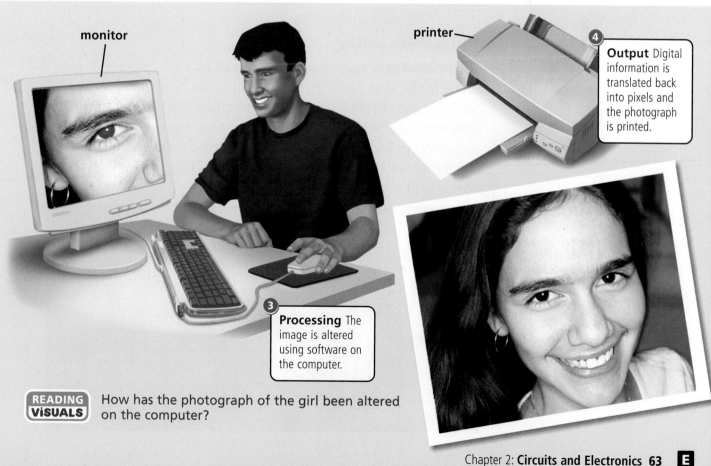

monitor

printer

**4 Output** Digital information is translated back into pixels and the photograph is printed.

**3 Processing** The image is altered using software on the computer.

**READING VISUALS** How has the photograph of the girl been altered on the computer?

## Computers can be linked with other computers.

You may have been at a computer lab or a library and had to wait for a printer to print something for you. Offices, libraries, and schools often have several computers that are all connected to the same printer. A group of computers that are linked together is known as a network. Computers can also be linked with other computers to share information. The largest network of computers is the Internet.

### The Origin of the Internet

People have been using computer networks to share information on university campuses and military bases for decades. The computers within those networks were connected over telephone systems from one location to another. But those networks behaved like a series circuit. If the link to one computer was broken, the whole network of links went down.

The network that we now call the Internet is different. The United States Department of Defense formed the Internet by linking computers on college campuses across the country. Many extra links were formed, producing a huge web of connected computers. That way, if some links are broken, others still work.

How does the Internet differ from earlier networks?

### The Internet Today

The Internet now spans the world. E-mail uses the Internet. E-mail has added to the ways in which people can "meet," communicate, conduct business, and share stories. The Internet can also be used to work on tasks that require massive computing power. For example, millions of computers linked together, along with their combined information, might one day be used to develop a cure for cancer or model the workings of a human mind.

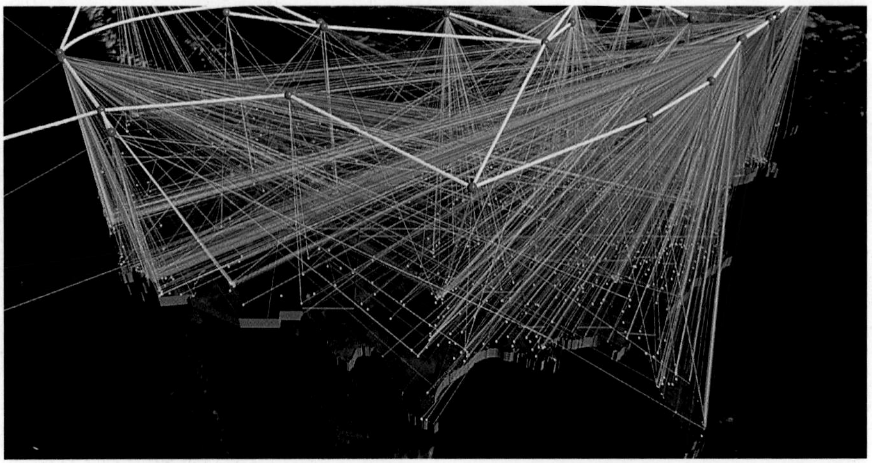

This map shows a representation of Internet traffic in the early 1990s. A map of Internet traffic now would be even more full of lines.

When you think of the Internet, you might think of the World Wide Web, or the Web. The Web consists of all of the information that can be accessed on the Internet. This information is stored on millions of host computers all over the world. The files that you locate are called Web pages. Each Web page has an address that begins with *www,* which stands for World Wide Web. The system allows you to search or surf through all of the information that is available on it. You might use the Web to research a project. Millions of people use the Web every day to find information, to shop, or for entertainment.

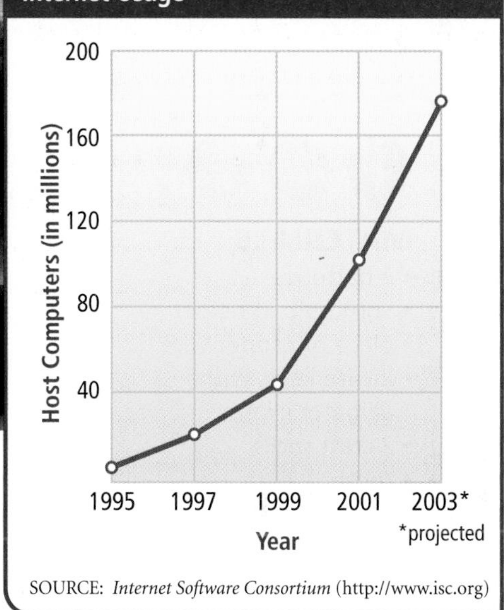


You may have heard of the Bronze Age or the Iron Age in your history class. Digital information and the Internet have had such a strong impact on the way we do things that some people refer to the era we live in as the Information Age.

## 2.3 Review

### KEY CONCEPTS

1. Describe an example of coded information.
2. What is digital information? Give three examples of devices that use digital information.
3. Give an example of each of the following in terms of computers: input, storage, processing, and output.

### CRITICAL THINKING

4. **Compare** Morse code uses a signal of dots and dashes to convey messages. How is Morse code similar to digital code?
5. **Infer** The word *integrated* means "brought together to form a whole." How does that definition apply to an integrated circuit?

### CHALLENGE

6. **Predict** Computers as we know them did not exist 50 years ago, and now they are used for many purposes. How do you think people will use computers 50 years from now? Write a paragraph describing what you think the computers of the future will be like and how they will be used.

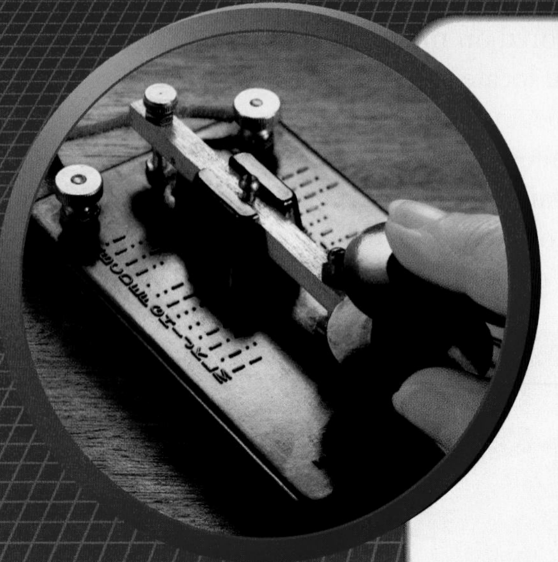

# Design an Electronic Communication Device

DESIGN — YOUR OWN —

## OVERVIEW AND PURPOSE

The telegraph was one of the first inventions to demonstrate that machines could be used to communicate over long distances. In a telegraph, messages are sent as electrical signals along a wire from a sending device to a receiver.

Like modern computers, the telegraph uses a binary code. The code is called Morse code—a combination of short and long signals—to stand for letters and symbols. In this lab, you will use what you have learned about circuits to

- design a battery-powered device that uses Morse code
- build and test your design

### MATERIALS

- 2 batteries
- light bulb in holder
- piece of copper wire
- 2 wire leads with alligator clips
- 2 craft sticks
- toothpick
- paper clip
- piece of cardboard
- clothespin
- aluminum foil
- rubber band
- scissors
- tape
- wire cutters
- Morse Code Chart

## Problem

A toy company has contracted you to design and build a new product for kids. They want a communication device that is similar to a telegraph. Kids will use the device to communicate with each other in Morse code. The company's market research has shown that parents do not like noisy toys, so the company wants a device that uses light rather than sound as a signal.

## Procedure

1. Brainstorm ideas for a communication device that can use Morse code. Look at the available materials and think how you could make a circuit that contains a light bulb and a switch.

2. Describe your proposed design and/or draw a sketch of it in your **Science Notebook.** Include a list of the materials that you would need to build it.

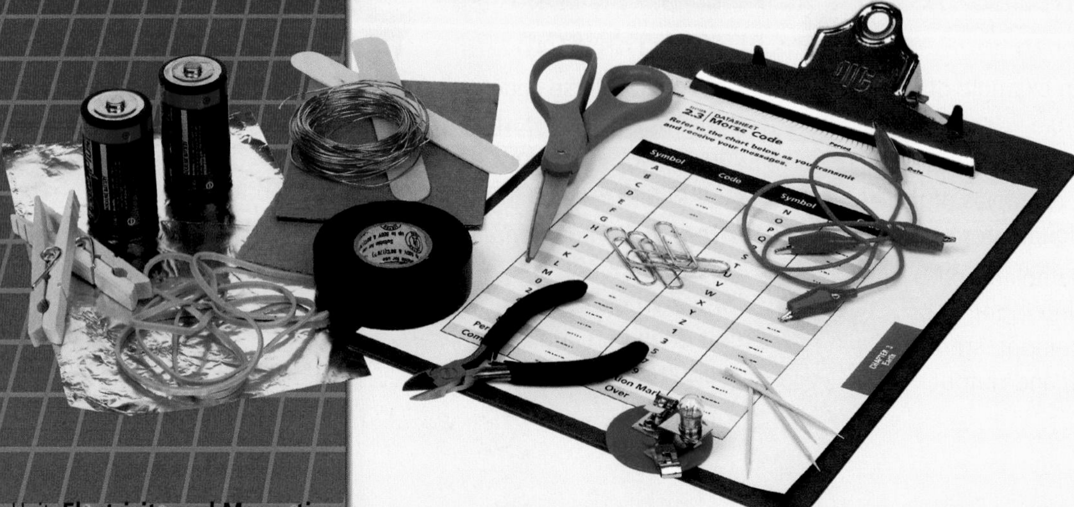

3 Show your design to a team member. Consider the constraints of each of your designs, such as what materials are available, the complexity of the design, and the time available.

4 Choose one idea or combine two ideas into a final design to test with your group. Build a sample version of your device, called a prototype.

5 Test your device by writing a short question. Translate the question into Morse code. Make long and short flashes of light on your device to send your message. Another person on your team should write down the message received in Morse code, translate the message, and send an answer.

6 Complete at least two trials. Each time, record the question in English, the question in code, the answer in code, and the answer in English.

7 Write a brief evaluation of how well the signal worked. Use the following criteria for your evaluation for each trial.

- What errors, if any, occurred while you were sending the signal?
- What errors, if any, occurred while you were receiving the signal?
- Did the translated answer make sense? Why or why not?

## Observe and Analyze

Write It Up

1. **MODEL** Draw a sketch of your final design. Label the parts. Next to your sketch, draw a circuit diagram of your device.
2. **INFER** How do the parts of your circuit allow you to control the flow of current?
3. **COMPARE** How is the signal that is used in your system similar to the digital information used by computers to process information? How does the signal differ?
4. **APPLY** A small sheet of instructions will be packaged with the device. Write a paragraph for the user that explains how to use it. Keep in mind that the user will probably be a child.

## Conclude

1. **EVALUATE** What problems, if any, did you encounter when testing your device? How might you improve upon the design?
2. **IDENTIFY LIMITS** What are the limitations of your design? You might consider its estimated costs, where and how kids will be able to use it, and the chances of the device breaking.
3. **APPLY** How might you modify your design so that it could be used by someone with limited vision?
4. **SYNTHESIZE** Write down the steps that you have used to develop this new product. Your first step was to brainstorm an idea.

## INVESTIGATE Further

**CHALLENGE** Design another system of communication that uses your own code. The signal should be in the form of flags. Make a table that lists what the signals mean and write instructions that explain how to use the system to communicate.

Design an Electronic Communication Device

Observe and Analyze

Table 1. Prototype Testing

| | Trial 1 | Trial 2 |
|---|---|---|
| Question (English) | | |
| Question (code) | | |
| Answer (code) | | |
| Answer (English) | | |
| Evaluation | | |

Conclude

# 2 Chapter Review

## the BIG idea

**Circuits control the flow of electric charge.**

### KEY CONCEPTS SUMMARY

### 2.1 Charge needs a continuous path to flow.

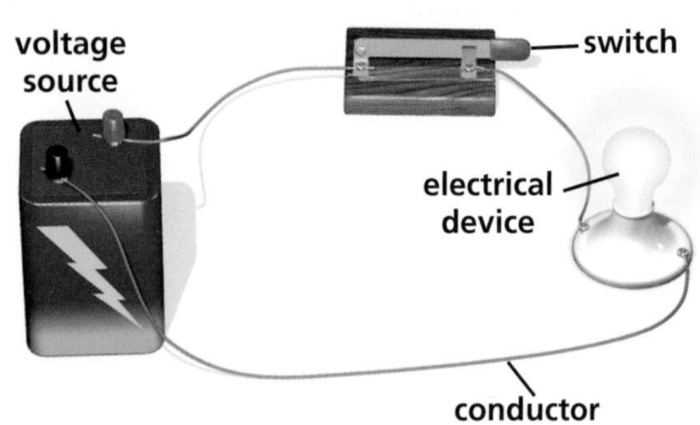


Charge flows in a closed path. Circuits provide a closed path for current. Circuit parts include voltage sources, switches, conductors, and electrical devices such as resistors.

**VOCABULARY**
**circuit** p. 43
**resistor** p. 44
**short circuit** p. 46

### 2.2 Circuits make electric current useful.

Each device in a **series circuit** is wired on a single path.

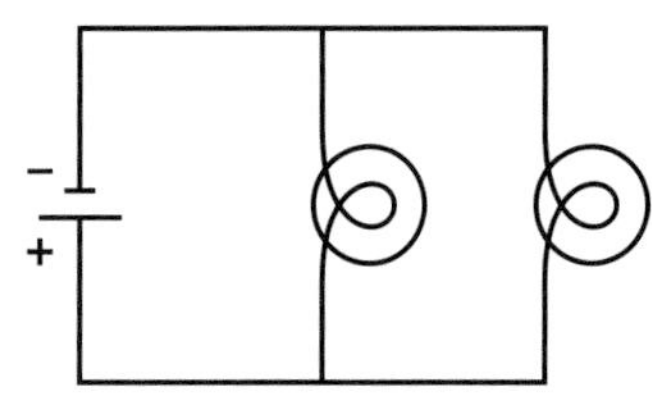


Each device in a **parallel circuit** has its own connection to the voltage source.

**VOCABULARY**
**series circuit** p. 52
**parallel circuit** p. 53

### 2.3 Electronic technology is based on circuits.

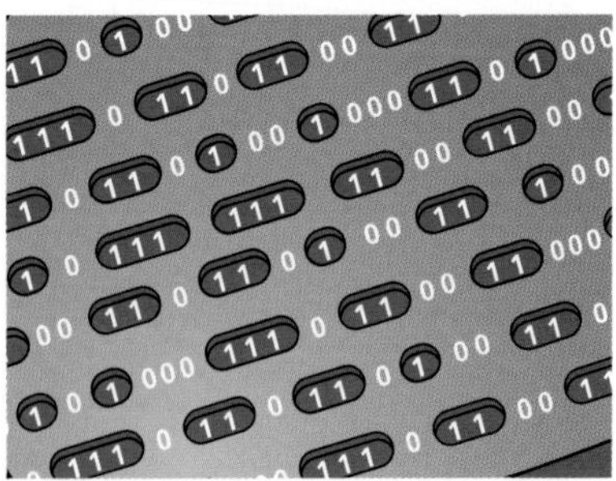

Electronic devices use electrical signals to represent coded information. Computers process information in digital code which uses 1s and 0s to represent the information.

**VOCABULARY**
**electronic** p. 57
**binary code** p. 58
**digital** p. 58
**analog** p. 60
**computer** p. 61

## Reviewing Vocabulary

*Draw a Venn diagram for each of the term pairs below. Write the terms above the circles. In the center, write characteristics that the terms have in common. In the outer circles write the ways in which they differ. A sample diagram has been completed for you.*

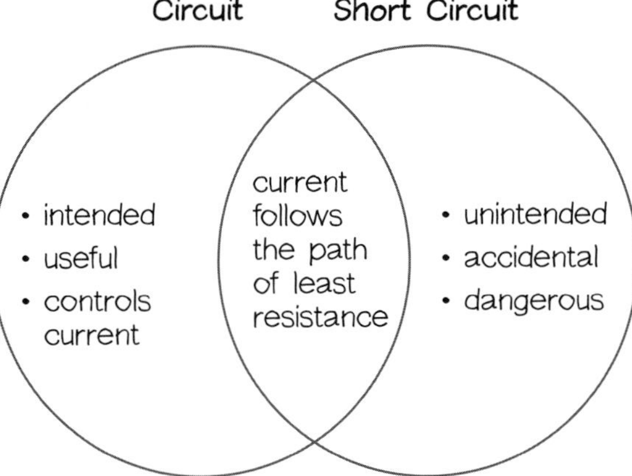


1. resistor; switch
2. series circuit; parallel circuit
3. digital; analog
4. digital; binary code
5. electronic; computer

## Reviewing Key Concepts

**Multiple Choice** *Choose the letter of the best answer.*

6. Current always follows
   - **a.** a path made of wire
   - **b.** a path containing an electrical device
   - **c.** a closed path
   - **d.** an open circuit
7. When you open a switch in a circuit, you
   - **a.** form a closed path for current
   - **b.** reverse the current
   - **c.** turn off its electrical devices
   - **d.** turn on its electrical devices
8. Which one of the following parts of a circuit changes electrical energy into another form of energy?
   - **a.** resistor
   - **b.** conductor
   - **c.** base
   - **d.** voltage source
9. A circuit breaker is a safety device that
   - **a.** must be replaced after each use
   - **b.** has a wire that melts
   - **c.** supplies voltage to a circuit
   - **d.** stops the current
10. What happens when more than one voltage source is added to a circuit in series?
    - **a.** The voltages are added together.
    - **b.** The voltages cancel each other out.
    - **c.** The voltages are multiplied together.
    - **d.** The voltage of each source decreases.
11. Which of the following is an electronic device?
    - **a.** flashlight
    - **b.** calculator
    - **c.** lamp
    - **d.** electric fan
12. Which word describes the code used in digital technology?
    - **a.** binary
    - **b.** analog
    - **c.** alphabetical
    - **d.** Morse
13. Computers process information that has been
    - **a.** broken down into simple steps
    - **b.** converted into heat
    - **c.** represented as a wave
    - **d.** coded as an analog signal

**Short Answer** *Write a short answer to each question.*

14. How can hardware, software, and the user of a computer work together to complete a task?
15. Describe three parts of a personal computer and explain the main function of each.

## Thinking Critically

*Use the illustrations below to answer the next two questions.*

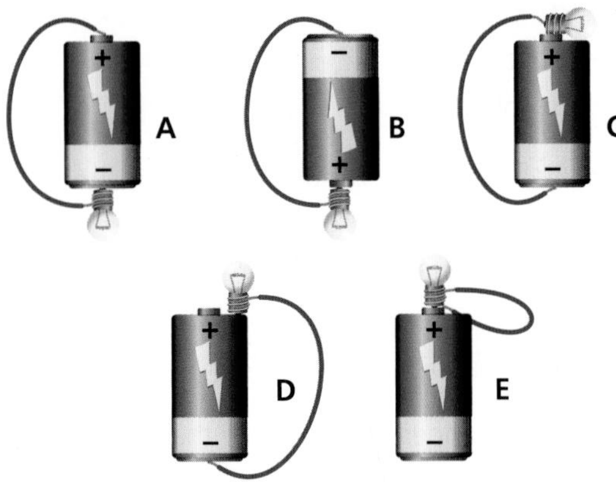


16. **PREDICT** In which arrangement(s) above will the light bulb glow? For each arrangement in which you think the bulb will not glow, explain your reasoning.

17. **APPLY** Which arrangement could be used as a battery tester? List the materials that you would use to make a battery tester.

*Use the diagram below to answer the next five questions.*

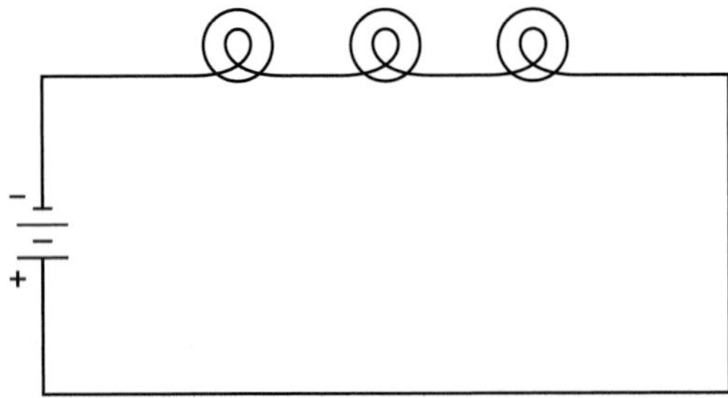

18. Is this a series circuit or a parallel circuit?

19. Explain what would happen if you unscrewed one of the bulbs in the circuit.

20. Explain what would happen if you wired three more bulbs into the circuit.

21. Draw and label a diagram of the same elements wired in the other type of circuit. Does your sketch involve more or fewer pieces of wire? How many?

22. Imagine you want to install a switch into your circuit. Where would you add the switch? Explain your answer.

23. **ANALYZE** Look for a pattern in the digital codes below, representing the numbers 1–10. What is the code for the number 11? How do you know?

    **0001; 0010; 0011; 0100; 0101;**
    **0110; 0111; 1000; 1001; 1010**

24. **APPLY** A computer circuit contains millions of switches that use temperature-dependent materials to operate lights, sounds, and a fan. How many different types of energy is current converted to in the computer circuit? Explain.

25. **ANALYZE** A music recording studio makes a copy of a CD that is itself a copy of another CD. Explain why the quality of the copied CDs is the same as the original CD.

26. **INFER** A new watch can be programmed to perform specific tasks. Describe what type of circuit the watch might contain.

27. **SYNTHESIZE** Explain how the Internet is like a worldwide parallel circuit.

## the BIG idea

28. **ANALYZE** Look back at the photograph on pages 40–41.Think about the answer you gave to the question. How has your understanding of circuits changed?

29. **SYNTHESIZE** Explain how the following statement relates to electric circuits: "Energy can change from one form to another and can move from one place to another."

30. **SUMMARIZE** Write a paragraph summarizing how circuits control current. Using the heading at the top of page 43 as your topic sentence. Then give an example from each red and blue heading on pages 43–45.

## UNIT PROJECTS

If you need to do an experiment for your unit project, gather the materials. Be sure to allow enough time to observe results before the project is due.

## Interpreting Diagrams

The four circuit diagrams below use the standard symbols for the parts of a circuit.

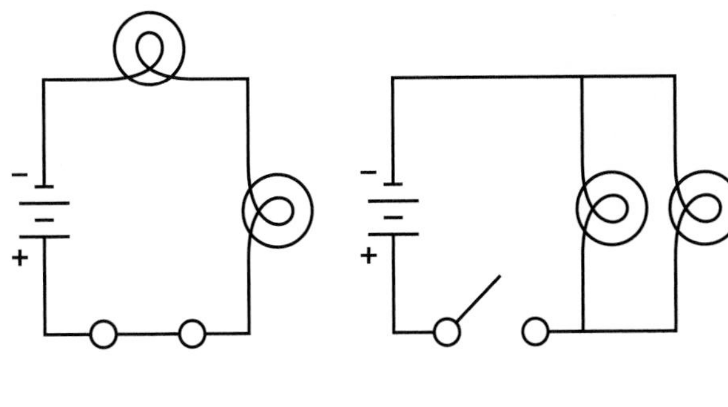

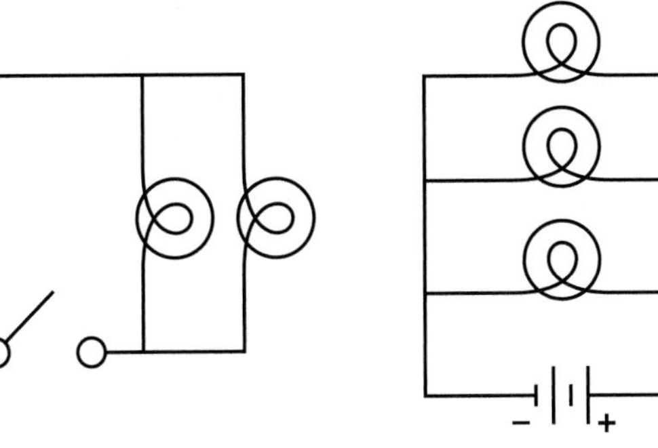

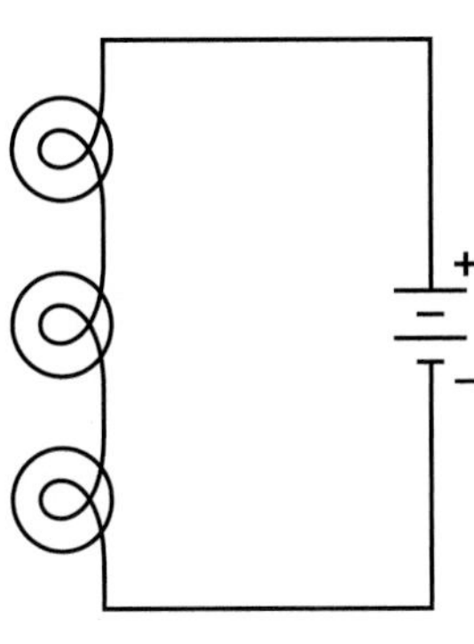

A. B. C. D.

*Study the diagrams and answer the questions that follow.*

**1.** Which diagram shows a series circuit, with one voltage source and two light bulbs?

**a.** A
**b.** B
**c.** C
**d.** D

**2.** Which diagram shows a parallel circuit powered by a battery, with three light bulbs?

**a.** A
**b.** B
**c.** C
**d.** D

**3.** The light bulbs in these diagrams limit the flow of charge and give off heat and light. Under which category of circuit parts do light bulbs belong?

**a.** switches
**b.** conductors
**c.** resistors
**d.** voltage sources

**4.** In which diagram would the light bulbs be dark?

**a.** A
**b.** B
**c.** C
**d.** D

**5.** If all light bulbs and voltage sources were equal, how would the light from each of the bulbs in diagram C compare to the light from each of the bulbs in diagram A?

**a.** The bulbs in diagram C would give less light than the bulbs in diagram A.
**b.** The bulbs in diagram C would give more light than the bulbs in diagram A.
**c.** The bulbs in diagram C would give the same amount of light as the bulbs in diagram A.
**d.** It cannot be determined which bulbs would give more light.

## Extended Response

*Answer the two questions below in detail. Include some of the terms from the word box. Underline each term you use in your answer.*

| flow of charge | electric current | binary code |
|---|---|---|
| open circuit | digital | signal |

**6.** What are two types of safety devices designed to control electric current and prevent dangerous accidents? How does each work?

**7.** Explain how an electronic circuit differs from an electric circuit. What role do electronic circuits play in computer operations?

# TIMELINES in Science

## THE STORY OF ELECTRONICS

Inventions such as the battery, the dynamo, and the motor created a revolution in the production and use of electrical energy. Think of how many tools and appliances that people depend on every day run on electric current. Try to imagine not using electricity in any form for an entire day.

The use of electricity as an energy source only begins the story of how electricity has changed our lives. Parts of the story are shown on this timeline. Research in electronics has given us not only electrical versions of machines that already existed but also entirely new technologies.

These technologies include computers. Electricity is used as a signal inside computers to code and transmit information. Electricity can even mimic some of the processes of logical reasoning and decision making, giving computers the power to solve problems.

**600 B.C.**

***Thales Studies Static Electricity***

Greek philosopher-scientist Thales of Miletus discovers that when he rubs amber with wool or fur, the amber attracts feathers and straw. The Greek word for amber, *elektron,* is the origin of the word *electricity.*

EVENTS

640 B.C. | 620 B.C. | 600 B.C. | A.D. 1740

APPLICATIONS AND TECHNOLOGY

### APPLICATION

**Leyden Jar**

In 1745 German inventor Ewald Georg von Kleist invented a device that would store a static charge. The device, called a Leyden jar, was a glass container filled with water. A wire ran from the outside of the jar through the cork into the water. The Leyden jar was the first capacitor, an electronic component that stores and releases charges. Capacitors have been key to the development of computers.

### 1752
### *Franklin Invents Lightning Rod*

To test his hypothesis that lightning is caused by static electric charges, U.S. inventor Ben Franklin flies a kite during a thunderstorm. A metal key hangs from the kite strings. Sparks jump from the key to Franklin's knuckle, showing that the key has a static charge. On the basis of this experiment, Franklin invents the lightning rod.

### 1800
### *Volta Invents Battery*

Italian scientist Alessandro Volta creates the first battery by stacking round plates of metal separated by disks soaked in salt water. Volta's discovery refutes the competing belief that electricity must be created by living beings.

### 1776
### *Bassi Gives Physics a Boost*

Italian scholar Laura Bassi, one of the first women to hold a chair at a major European university, is named professor of experimental physics. Bassi uses her position to establish one of the world's first electrical laboratories.

1760 1780 1800 1820 1840

## TECHNOLOGY

### The Difference Engine

Around 1822 British mathematician Charles Babbage developed the first prototype of a machine that could perform calculations mechanically. Babbage's "difference engine" used disks connected to rods with hand cranks to calculate mathematical tables. Babbage's invention came more than 100 years before the modern computer.

1879

### *Edison Improves Dynamo*

To help bring electric lights to the streets of New York City, U.S. inventor Thomas Edison develops an improved dynamo, or generator. Edison's dynamo, known as a long-legged Mary Ann, operates at about twice the efficiency of previous models.

1904

### *Vacuum Tube Makes Debut*

British inventor Ambrose Fleming modifies a light bulb to create an electronic vacuum tube. Fleming's tube, which he calls a valve, allows current to flow in one direction but not the other and can be used to detect weak radio signals.

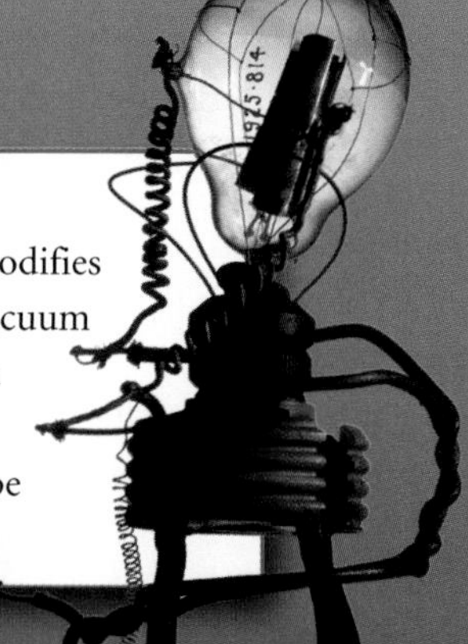

1947

### *Transistor Invented*

A transistor—a tiny electronic switch made out of a solid material called a semiconductor—is introduced to regulate the flow of electricity. Transistors, which do not produce excess heat and never burn out, can replace the vacuum tube in electronic circuitry and can be used to make smaller, cheaper, and more powerful computers.

1860 1880 1900 1920 1940

## APPLICATION

### First Electronic Digital Computer

Electronic Numerical Integrator and Computer (ENIAC) was the first digital computer. It was completed and installed in 1944 at the Moore School of Electrical Engineering at the University of Pennsylvania. Weighing more than 30 tons, ENIAC contained 19,000 vacuum tubes, 70,000 resistors, and 6000 switches, and it used almost 200 kilowatts of electric power. ENIAC could perform 5000 additions per second.

**1958**

*Chip Inventors Think Small*

Jack Kilby, a U.S. electrical engineer, conceives the idea of making an entire circuit out of a single piece of germanium. The integrated circuit, or "computer chip," is born. This invention enables computers and other electronic devices to be made much smaller than before.

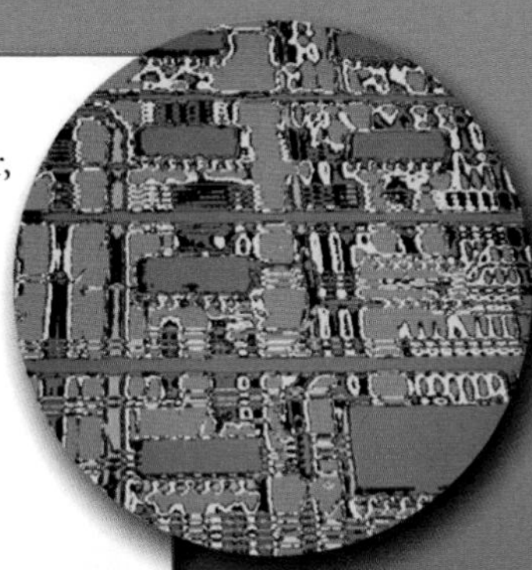

**2001**

*Scientists Shrink Circuits to Atomic Level*

Researchers succeed in building a logic circuit, a kind of transistor the size of a single molecule. The molecule, a tube of carbon atoms called a carbon nanotube, can be as small as 10 atoms across—500 times smaller than previous transistors. Computer chips, which currently contain over 40 million transistors, could hold hundreds of millions or even billions of nanotube transistors.

**RESOURCE CENTER**
CLASSZONE.COM

Explore current research in electronics and computers.

1960 1980 2000

## TECHNOLOGY

### Miniaturization

Miniaturization has led to an explosion of computer technology. As circuits have shrunk, allowing more components in less space, computers have become smaller and more powerful. They have also become easier to integrate with other technologies, such as telecommunications. When not being used for a phone call, this cell phone can be used to connect to the Internet, to access e-mail, and even to play computer games.

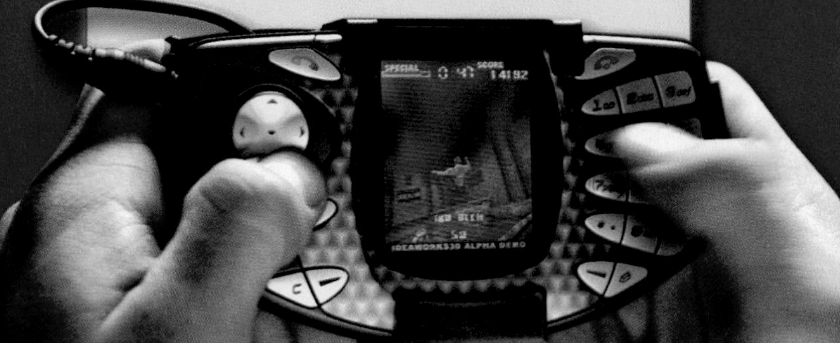

## INTO THE FUTURE

Electronic computer components have become steadily smaller and more efficient over the years. However, the basic mechanism of a computer—a switch that can be either on or off depending on whether an electric charge is present—has remained the same. These switches represent the 1s and 0s, or the "bits," of binary code.

Quantum computing is based on an entirely new way of representing information. In quantum physics, individual subatomic particles can be described in terms of three states rather than just two. Quantum bits, or "qubits," can carry much more information than the binary bits of ordinary computers. Using qubits, quantum computers could be both smaller and faster than binary computers and perform operations not possible with current technology.

Quantum computing is possible in theory, but the development of hardware that can process qubits is just beginning. Scientists are currently looking for ways to put the theory into practice and to build computers that will make current models look as bulky and as slow as ENIAC.

## ACTIVITIES

### Reliving History

Make a Leyden jar capacitor. Line the inside of a jar with aluminum foil. Stop the jar with clay. Insert a copper wire through the plug so that one end touches the foil and the other sticks out of the jar about 2 centimeters.

To test for a voltage difference between the wire and the glass, touch one end of a multimeter to the exposed wire and the other end to the glass. Run a comb through your hair several times and touch it to the wire. Test the voltage difference again.

### Writing About Science

Learn more about the current state of electronic circuit miniaturization. Write up the results of your research in the form of a magazine article.

CHAPTER

# Magnetism

## the BIG idea

**Current can produce magnetism, and magnetism can produce current.**

## Key Concepts

SECTION 3.1
**Magnetism is a force that acts at a distance.**
Learn how magnets exert forces.

SECTION 3.2
**Current can produce magnetism.**
Learn about electromagnets and their uses.

SECTION 3.3
**Magnetism can produce current.**
Learn how magnetism can produce an electric current.

SECTION 3.4
**Generators supply electrical energy.**
Learn how generators are used in the production of electrical energy.

### Internet Preview

CLASSZONE.COM

Chapter 3 online resources: Content Review, Simulation, Visualization, three Resource Centers, Math Tutorial, Test Practice

What force is acting on this compass needle?

# EXPLORE the BIG idea

## Is It Magnetic?

Experiment with a magnet and several objects made of different materials.

**Observe and Think** Which objects are attracted to the magnet? Why do you think the magnet attracts some objects and not others?

## How Can You Make a Chain?

Hang a paper clip on the end of a magnet. Then hang a second paper clip by touching it to the end of the first paper clip. Add more paper clips to make a chain.

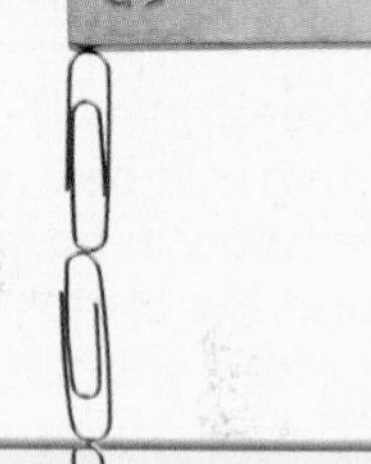


**Observe and Think** How many paper clips did you add? What held the chain together?

## Internet Activity: Electromagnets

Go to **ClassZone.com** to work with a virtual electromagnet. Explore how current and magnetism are related.

**Observe and Think** What happens when you increase the voltage?

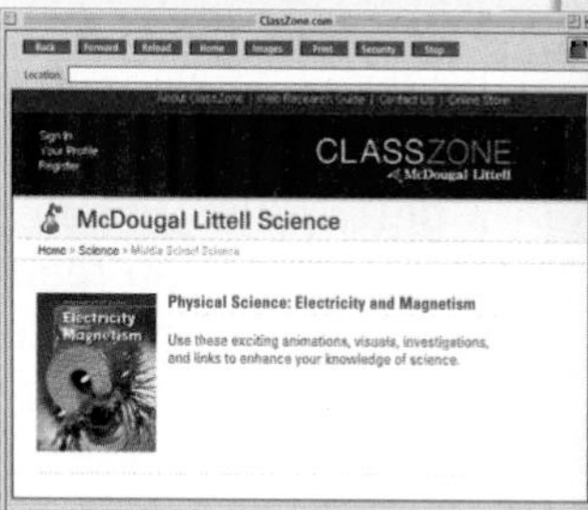

Electromagnetism **Code: MDL067**

CHAPTER 3

# Getting Ready to Learn

## CONCEPT REVIEW

- Energy can change from one form to another.
- A force is a push or a pull.
- Power is the rate of energy transfer.

## VOCABULARY REVIEW

**electric current** p. 28

**circuit** p. 43

**kinetic energy** *See Glossary.*

CONTENT REVIEW
CLASSZONE.COM
Review concepts and vocabulary.

## TAKING NOTES

### MAIN IDEA WEB

Write each new blue heading in a box. Then write notes in boxes around the center box that give important terms and details about that blue heading.

### VOCABULARY STRATEGY

Place each vocabulary term at the center of a **description wheel** diagram. As you read about the term, write some words describing it on the spokes.

See the Note-Taking Handbook on pages R45–R51.

SCIENCE NOTEBOOK

Magnetism is the force exerted by magnets.

All magnets have two poles.

Magnets attract and repel other magnets.

Opposite poles attract, and like poles repel.

Magnets have magnetic fields of force around them.

MAGNETIC DOMAINS

Magnetic fields of atoms point in the same direction.

In magnets, they line up.

Nonmagnetic materials don't have them.

Magnetic materials have them.

KEY CONCEPT

# Magnetism is a force that acts at a distance.

**BEFORE, you learned**

- A force is a push or pull
- Some forces act at a distance
- Atoms contain charged particles

**NOW, you will learn**

- How magnets attract and repel other magnets
- What makes some materials magnetic
- Why a magnetic field surrounds Earth

**VOCABULARY**

**magnet** p. 79
**magnetism** p. 80
**magnetic pole** p. 80
**magnetic field** p. 81
**magnetic domain** p. 82

**EXPLORE Magnetism**

### *How do magnets behave?*

**PROCEDURE**

1. Clamp the clothespin on the dowel so that it makes a stand for the magnets, as shown.
2. Place the three magnets on the dowel. If there is a space between pairs of magnets, measure and record the distance between them.
3. Remove the top magnet, turn it over, and replace it on the dowel. Record your observations. Experiment with different arrangements of the magnets and record your observations.

**MATERIALS**

- clothespin
- wooden dowel
- 3 disk magnets
- ruler

**WHAT DO YOU THINK?**

- How did the arrangement of the magnets affect their behavior?
- What evidence indicates that magnets exert a force?

## Magnets attract and repel other magnets.

Suppose you get home from school and open the refrigerator to get some milk. As you close the door, it swings freely until it suddenly seems to close by itself. There is a magnet inside the refrigerator door that pulls it shut. A **magnet** is an object that attracts certain other materials, particularly iron and steel.

**VOCABULARY**
Make a description wheel for the term *magnet*.

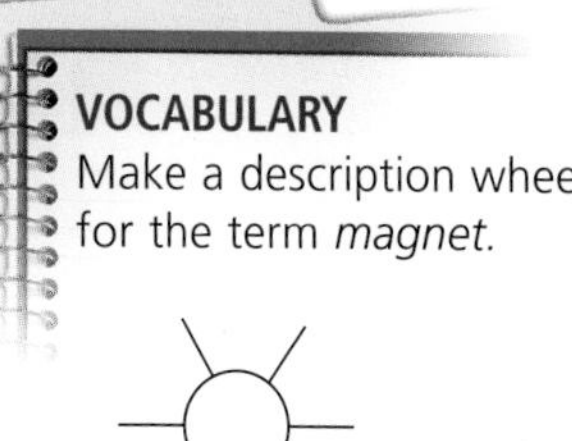

There may be quite a few magnets in your kitchen. Some are obvious, like the seal of the refrigerator and the magnets that hold notes to its door. Other magnets run the motor in a blender, provide energy in a microwave oven, operate the speakers in a radio on the counter, and make a doorbell ring.

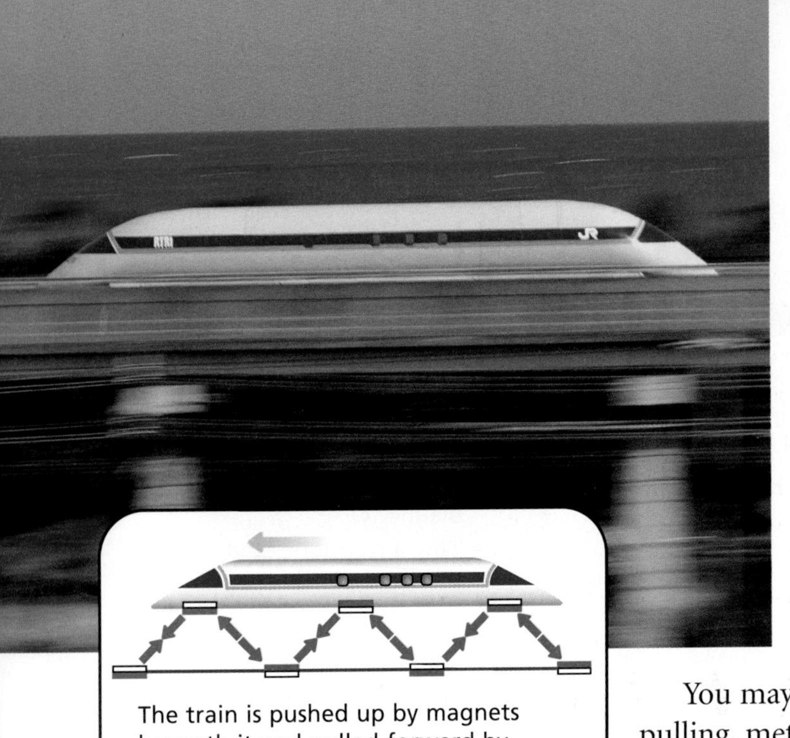

The train is pushed up by magnets beneath it and pulled forward by magnets ahead of it.

## Magnetism

The force exerted by a magnet is called **magnetism.** The push or pull of magnetism can act at a distance, which means that the magnet does not have to touch an object to exert a force on it. When you close the refrigerator, you feel the pull before the magnet actually touches the metal frame. There are other forces that act at a distance, including gravity and static electricity. Later you will read how the force of magnetism is related to electricity. In fact, magnetism is the result of a moving electric charge.

You may be familiar with magnets attracting, or pulling, metal objects toward them. Magnets can also repel, or push away, objects. The train in the photograph at the left is called a maglev train. The word *maglev* is short for *mag*netic *lev*itation, or lifting up. As you can see in the diagram, the train does not touch the track. Magnetism pushes the entire train up and pulls it forward. Maglev trains can move as fast as 480 kilometers per hour (300 mi/h).

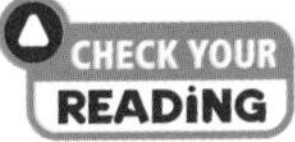


How can a train operate without touching the track?

## Magnetic Poles

Find out more about magnetism.

The force of magnetism is not evenly distributed throughout a magnet. **Magnetic poles** are the parts of a magnet where the magnetism is the strongest. Every magnet has two magnetic poles. If a bar magnet is suspended so that it can swing freely, one pole of the magnet always points toward the north. That end of the magnet is known as the north-seeking pole, or north pole. The other end of the magnet is called the south pole. Many magnets are marked with an *N* and an *S* to indicate the poles.

As with electric charges, opposite poles of a magnet attract and like poles—or poles that are the same—repel, or push each other away. Every magnet has both a north pole and a south pole. A horseshoe magnet is like a bar magnet that has been bent into the shape of a *U.* It has a pole at each of its ends. If you break a bar magnet between the two poles, the result is two smaller magnets, each of which has a north pole and a south pole. No matter how many times you break a magnet, the result is smaller magnets.

## Magnetic Fields

You have read that magnetism is a force that can act at a distance. However magnets cannot exert a force on an object that is too far away. A **magnetic field** is the region around a magnet in which the magnet exerts force. If a piece of iron is within the magnetic field of a magnet, it will be pulled toward the magnet. Many small pieces of iron, called iron filings, are used to show the magnetic field around a magnet. The iron filings form a pattern of lines called magnetic field lines.

READING TIP

Thin red lines in the illustrations below indicate the magnetic field.

**The Magnetic Field Around a Magnet**

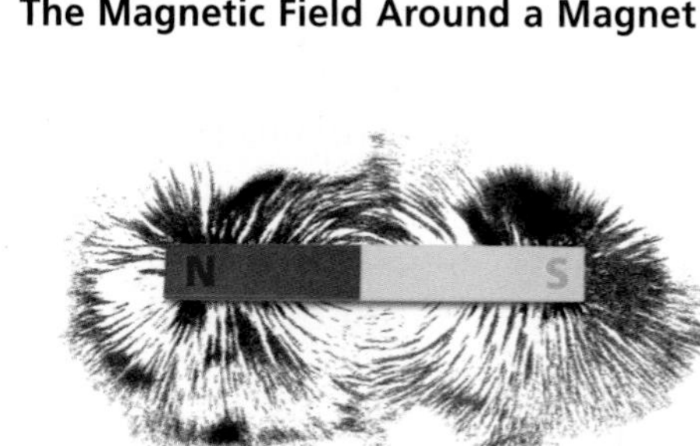


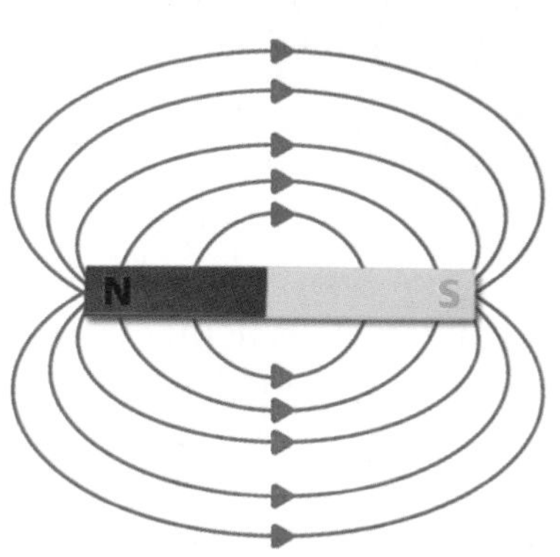


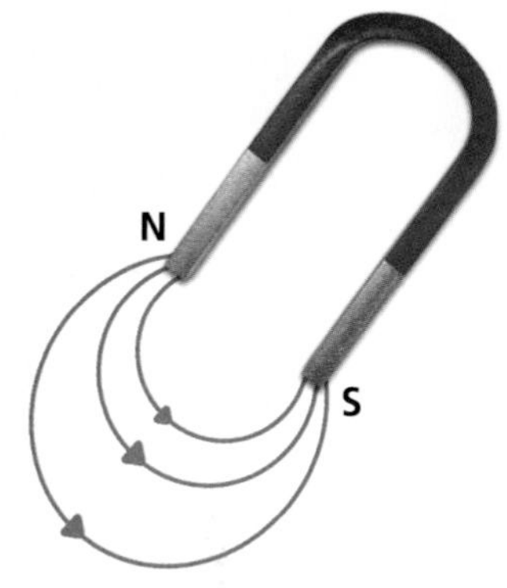


The arrangement of the magnetic field lines depends on the shape of the magnet, but the lines always extend from one pole to the other pole. The magnetic field lines are always shown as starting from the north pole and ending at the south pole. In the illustrations above, you can see that the lines are closest together near the magnets' poles. That is where the force is strongest. The force is weaker farther away from the magnet.

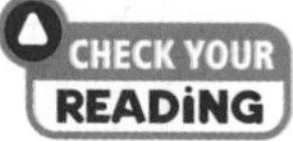


Where is the magnetic field of a magnet the strongest?

What happens to the magnetic fields of two magnets when the magnets are brought together? As you can see below, each magnet has an effect on the field of the other magnet. If the magnets are held so that the north pole of one magnet is close to the south pole of the other, the magnetic field lines extend from one magnet to the other. The magnets pull together. On the other hand, if both north poles or both south poles of two magnets are brought near one another, the magnets repel. It is very difficult to push like poles of strong magnets together because magnetic repulsion pushes them apart.

**Attraction** **Repulsion**

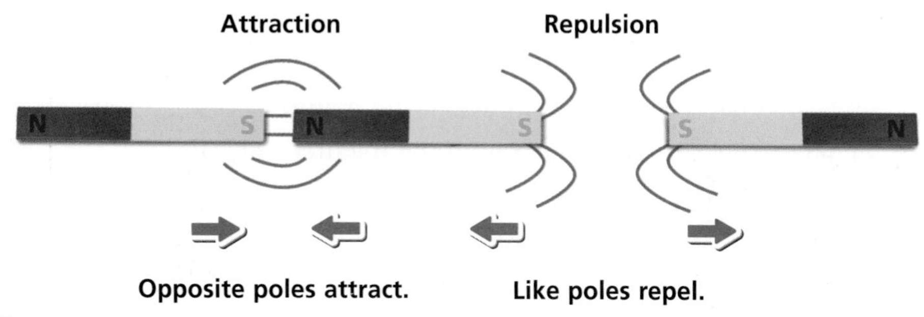


**Opposite poles attract.** **Like poles repel.**

## Some materials are magnetic.

Some magnets occur naturally. Lodestone is a type of mineral that is a natural magnet and formed the earliest magnets that people used. The term *magnet* comes from the name *Magnesia,* a region of Greece where lodestone was discovered. Magnets can also be made from materials that contain certain metallic elements, such as iron.

If you have ever tried picking up different types of objects with a magnet, you have seen that some materials are affected by the magnet and other materials are not. Iron, nickel, cobalt, and a few other metals have properties that make them magnetic. Other materials, such as wood, cannot be made into magnets and are not affected by magnets. Whether a material is magnetic or not depends on its atoms—the particles that make up all matter.

You read in Chapter 1 that the protons and electrons of an atom have electric fields. Every atom also has a weak magnetic field, produced by the electron's motion around a nucleus. In addition, each electron spins around its axis, an imaginary line through its center. The spinning motion of the electrons in magnetic materials increases the strength of the magnetic field around each atom. The magnetic effect of one electron is usually cancelled by another electron that spins in the opposite direction.

### Inside Magnetic Materials

READING TIP

The red arrows in the illustration on page 83 are tiny magnetic fields.

The illustration on page 83 shows how magnets and the materials they affect differ from other materials.

1. In a material that is not magnetic, such as wood, the magnetic fields of the atoms are weak and point in different directions. The magnetic fields cancel each other out. As a result, the overall material is not magnetic and could not be made into a magnet.
2. In a material that is magnetic, such as iron, the magnetic fields of a group of atoms align, or point in the same direction. A **magnetic domain** is a group of atoms whose magnetic fields are aligned. The domains of a magnetic material are not themselves aligned, so their fields cancel one another out. Magnetic materials are pulled by magnets and can be made into magnets.
3. A magnet is a material in which the magnetic domains are all aligned. The material is said to be magnetized.

CHECK YOUR READING How do magnets differ from materials that are not magnetic?

## How Magnets Differ from Other Materials

**Magnets, and the materials they attract, contain small regions called magnetic domains. In a magnet, the domains are aligned.**

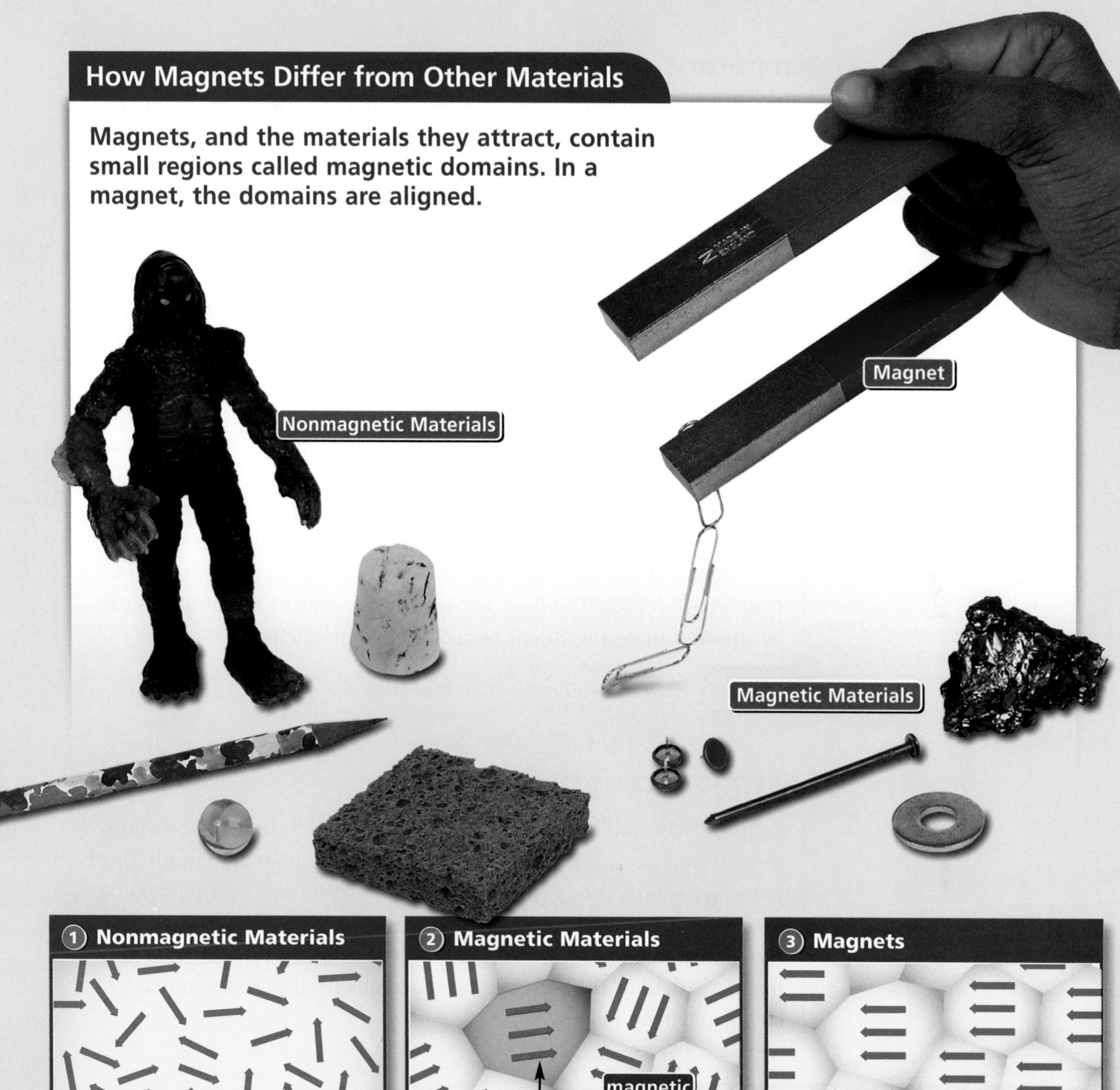


**1 Nonmagnetic Materials**

Some materials, like wood, are not magnetic. The tiny magnetic fields of their spinning electrons point in different directions and cancel each other out.

**2 Magnetic Materials**

magnetic domain

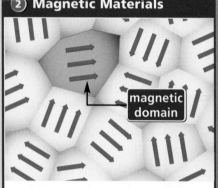

Other materials, like iron, are magnetic. Magnetic materials have magnetic domains, but the fields of the domains point in different directions.

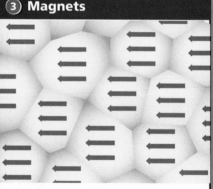

**3 Magnets**

When a material is magnetized, the magnetic fields of all the domains point in the same direction.

**READING VISUALS** Do the paper clips in this photograph contain magnetic domains? Why or why not?

### Temporary and Permanent Magnets

If you bring a magnet near a paper clip that contains iron, the paper clip is pulled toward the magnet. As the magnet nears the paper clip, the domains within the paper clip are attracted to the magnet's nearest pole. As a result, the domains within the paper clip become aligned. The paper clip develops its own magnetic field.

You can make a chain of paper clips that connect to one another through these magnetic fields. However, if you remove the magnet, the chain falls apart. The paper clips are temporary magnets, and their domains return to a random arrangement when the stronger magnetic field is removed.

Placing magnetic materials in very strong magnetic fields makes permanent magnets, such as the ones you use in the experiments in this chapter. You can make a permanent magnet by repeatedly stroking a piece of magnetic material in the same direction with a strong magnet. This action aligns the domains. However, if you drop a permanent magnet, or expose it to high temperatures, some of the domains can be shaken out of alignment, weakening its magnetism.

How can you make a permanent magnet?

## Earth is a magnet.

People discovered long ago that when a piece of lodestone was allowed to turn freely, one end always pointed toward the north. Hundreds of years ago, sailors used lodestone in the first compasses for navigation. A compass works because Earth itself is a large magnet. A compass is simply a magnet that is suspended so that it can turn freely. The magnetic field of the compass needle aligns itself with the much larger magnetic field of Earth.

### Earth's Magnetic Field

The magnetic field around Earth acts as if there were a large bar magnet that runs through Earth's axis. Earth's axis is the imaginary line through the center of Earth around which it rotates. The source of the magnetic field that surrounds Earth is the motion of its core, which is composed mostly of iron and nickel. Charged particles flow within the core. Scientists have proposed several explanations of how that motion produces the magnetic field, but the process is not yet completely understood.

What is the source of Earth's magnetic field?

## INVESTIGATE Earth's Magnetic Field

### *What moves a compass needle?*

**PROCEDURE**

1. Gently place the aluminum foil on the water so that it floats.
2. Rub one pole of the magnet along the needle, from one end of the needle to the other. Lift up the magnet and repeat. Do this about 25 times, rubbing in the same direction each time. Place the magnet far away from your set-up.
3. Gently place the needle on the floating foil to act as a compass.
4. Turn the foil so that the needle points in a different direction. Observe what happens when you release the foil.

**WHAT DO YOU THINK?**

- What direction did the needle move when you placed it in the bowl?
- What moved the compass's needle?

**CHALLENGE** How could you use your compass to answer a question of your own about magnetism?

**SKILL FOCUS**
Inferring

**MATERIALS**
- small square of aluminum foil
- bowl of water
- strong magnet
- sewing needle

**TIME**
15 minutes

Earth's magnetic field affects all the magnetic materials around you. Even the cans of food in your cupboard are slightly magnetized by this field. Hold a compass close to the bottom of a can and observe what happens. The magnetic domains in the metal can have aligned and produced a weak magnetic field. If you twist the can and check it again several days later, you can observe the effect of the domains changing their alignment.

Sailors learned many centuries ago that the compass does not point exactly toward the North Pole of Earth's axis. Rather, the compass magnet is currently attracted to an area 966 kilometers (600 mi) from the end of the axis of rotation. This area is known as the magnetic north pole. Interestingly, the magnetic poles of Earth can reverse, so that the magnetic north pole becomes the magnetic south pole. This has happened at least 400 times over the last 330 million years. The most recent reversal was about 780,000 years ago.

The evidence that the magnetic north and south poles reverse is found in rocks in which the minerals contain iron. The iron in the minerals lines up with Earth's magnetic field as the rock forms. Once the rock is formed, the domains remain in place. The evidence for the reversing magnetic field is shown in layers of rocks on the ocean floor, where the domains are arranged in opposite directions.

## Magnetism and the Atmosphere

A constant stream of charged particles is released by reactions inside the Sun. These particles could be damaging to living cells if they reached the surface of Earth. One important effect of Earth's magnetic field is that it turns aside, or deflects, the flow of the charged particles.

Observers view a beautiful display of Northern Lights in Alaska.

Many of the particles are deflected toward the magnetic poles, where Earth's magnetic field lines are closest together. As the particles approach Earth, they react with oxygen and nitrogen in Earth's atmosphere. These interactions can be seen at night as vast, moving sheets of color—red, blue, green or violet—that can fill the whole sky. These displays are known as the Northern Lights or the Southern Lights.

CHECK YOUR READING Why do the Northern Lights and the Southern Lights occur near Earth's magnetic poles?

## 3.1 Review

### KEY CONCEPTS

1. What force causes magnets to attract or repel one another?
2. Why are some materials magnetic and not others?
3. Describe three similarities between Earth and a bar magnet.

### CRITICAL THINKING

4. **Apply** A needle is picked up by a magnet. What can you say about the needle's atoms?
5. **Infer** The Northern Lights can form into lines in the sky. What do you think causes this effect?

### CHALLENGE

6. **Infer** Hundreds of years ago sailors observed that as they traveled farther north, their compass needle tended to point toward the ground as well as toward the north. What can you conclude about the magnet inside Earth from this observation?

Think SCIENCE

SKILL: EVALUATING CONCLUSIONS

# Can Magnets Heal People?

Many people believe that a magnetic field can relieve pain and cure injuries or illnesses. They point out that human blood cells contain iron and that magnets attract iron.

## Claims

Here are some claims from advertisements and published scientific experiments.

a. In an advertisement, a person reported back pain that went away overnight when a magnetic pad was taped to his back.

b. In an advertisement, a person used magnets to treat a painful bruise. The pain reportedly stopped soon after the magnet was applied.

c. In a research project, people who had recovered from polio, but still had severe pain, rated the amount of pain they experienced. People who used magnets reported slightly more pain relief than those who used fake magnets that looked like the real magnets.

d. A research project studied people with severe muscle pain. Patients who slept on magnetic pads for six months reported slightly less pain than those who slept on nonmagnetic pads or no pads.

e. A research project studied people with pain in their heels, placing magnets in their shoes. About sixty percent of people with real magnets reported improvements. About sixty percent of people with fake magnets also reported improvements.

## Controls

Scientists use control groups to determine whether a change was a result of the experimental variable or some other cause. A control group is the same as an experimental group in every way except for the variable that is tested. For each of the above cases, was a control used? If not, can you think of some other explanation for the result?

## Evaluating Conclusions

**On Your Own** Evaluate each claim or report separately. Based on all the evidence, can you conclude that magnets are useful for relieving pain? What further evidence would help you decide?

**As a Group** Find advertisements for companies that sell magnets for medical use. Do they provide information about how their tests were conducted and how you can contact the doctors or scientists involved?

**CHALLENGE** Design an experiment, with controls, that would show whether or not magnets are useful for relieving pain.

Some people believe that pads containing magnets, such as these, can relieve pain.

KEY CONCEPT

# Current can produce magnetism.

**BEFORE, you learned**

- Electric current is the flow of charge
- Magnetism is a force exerted by magnets
- Magnets attract or repel other magnets

**NOW, you will learn**

- How an electric current can produce a magnetic field
- How electromagnets are used
- How motors use electromagnets

**VOCABULARY**

**electromagnetism** p. 89
**electromagnet** p. 90

**EXPLORE Magnetism from Electric Current**

***What is the source of magnetism?***

**PROCEDURE**

1. Tape one end of the wire to the battery.
2. Place the compass on the table. Place the wire so that it is lying beside the compass, parallel to the needle of the compass. Record your observations.
3. Briefly touch the free end of the wire to the other end of the battery. Record your observations.
4. Turn the battery around and tape the other end to the wire. Repeat steps 2 and 3.

**WHAT DO YOU THINK?**

- What did you observe?
- What is the relationship between the direction of the battery and the direction of the compass needle?

**MATERIALS**

- electrical tape
- copper wire
- AA cell (battery)
- compass

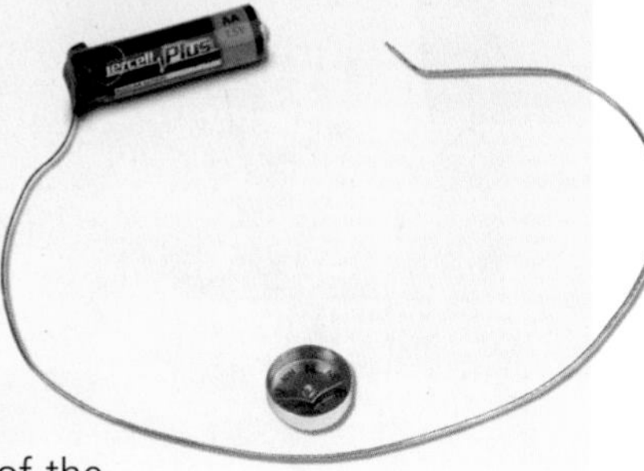

## An electric current produces a magnetic field.

**REMINDER**
Current is the flow of electrons through a conductor.

Like many discoveries, the discovery that electric current is related to magnetism was unexpected. In the 1800s, a Danish physicist named Hans Christian Oersted (UR-stehd) was teaching a physics class. Oersted used a battery and wire to demonstrate some properties of electricity. He noticed that as an electric charge passed through the wire, the needle of a nearby compass moved.

When he turned the current off, the needle returned to its original direction. After more experiments, Oersted confirmed that there is a relationship between magnetism and electricity. He discovered that an electric current produces a magnetic field.

## Electromagnetism

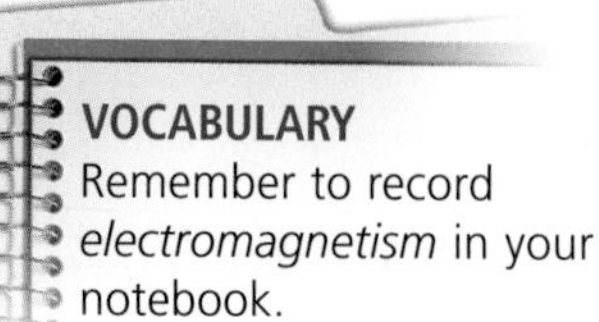


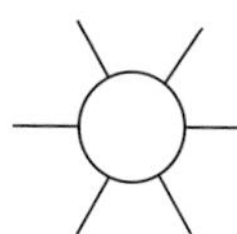

The relationship between electric current and magnetism plays an important role in many modern technologies. **Electromagnetism** is magnetism that results from an electric current. When a charged particle such as an electron moves, it produces a magnetic field. Because an electric current generally consists of moving electrons, a current in a wire produces a magnetic field. In fact, the wire acts as a magnet. Increasing the amount of current in the wire increases the strength of the magnetic field.

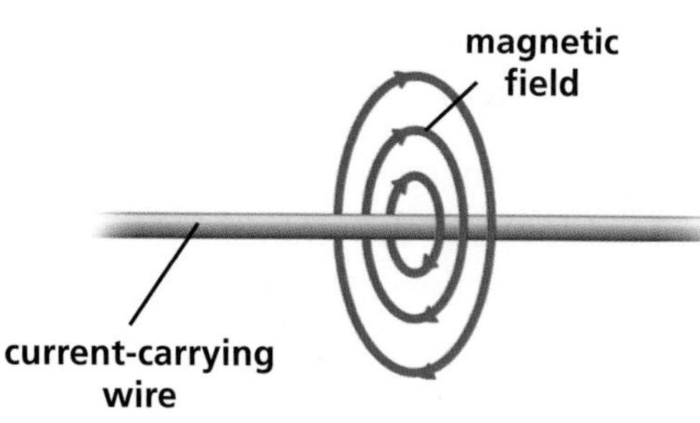


You have seen how magnetic field lines can be drawn around a magnet. The magnetic field lines around a wire are usually illustrated as a series of circles. The magnetic field of a wire actually forms the shape of a tube around the wire. The direction of the current determines the direction of the magnetic field. If the direction of the electric current is reversed, the magnetic field still exists in circles around the wire, but is reversed.

If the wire is shaped into a loop, the magnetism becomes concentrated inside the loop. The field is much stronger in the middle of the loop than it is around a straight wire. If you wind the wire into a coil, the magnetic force becomes stronger with each additional turn of wire as the magnetic field becomes more concentrated.

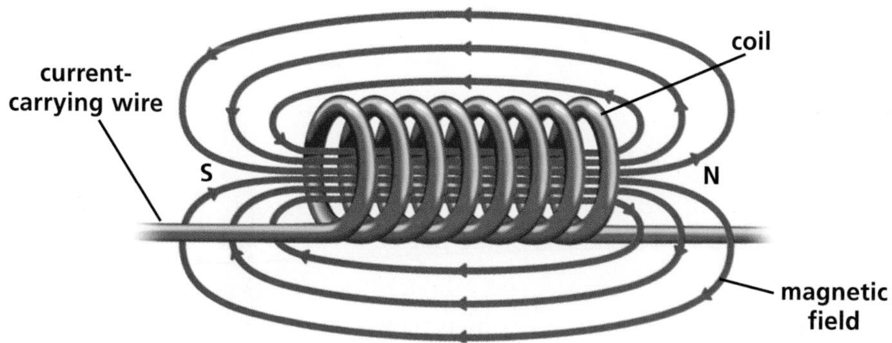


A coil of wire with charge flowing through it has a magnetic field that is similar to the magnetic field of a bar magnet. Inside the coil, the field flows in one direction, forming a north pole at one end. The flow outside the coil returns to the south pole. The direction of the electric current in the wire determines which end of the coil becomes the north pole.

How is a coil of wire that carries a current similar to a bar magnet?

## Making an Electromagnet

Recall that a piece of iron in a strong magnetic field becomes a magnet itself. An **electromagnet** is a magnet made by placing a piece of iron or steel inside a coil of wire. As long as the coil carries a current, the metal acts as a magnet and increases the magnetic field of the coil. But when the current is turned off, the magnetic domains in the metal become random again and the magnetic field disappears.

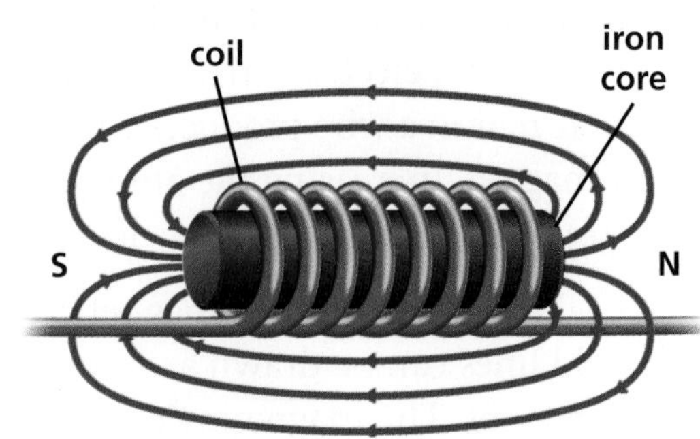


By increasing the number of loops in the coil, you can increase the strength of the electromagnet. Electromagnets exert a much more powerful magnetic field than a coil of wire without a metal core. They can also be much stronger than the strongest permanent magnets made of metal alone. You can increase the field strength of an electromagnet by adding more coils or a stronger current. Some of the most powerful magnets in the world are huge electromagnets that are used in scientific instruments.

How can you increase the strength of an electromagnet?

## INVESTIGATE Electromagnets

### *How can you make an electromagnet?*

**PROCEDURE**

1. Starting about 25 cm from one end of the wire, wrap the wire in tight coils around the nail. The coils should cover the nail from the head almost to the point.
2. Tape the two batteries together as shown. Tape one end of the wire to a free battery terminal.
3. Touch the point of the nail to a paper clip and record your observations.
4. Connect the other end of the wire to the other battery terminal. Again touch the point of the nail to a paper clip. Disconnect the wire from the battery. Record your observations.

**WHAT DO YOU THINK?**

- What did you observe?
- Did you make an electromagnet? How do you know?

**CHALLENGE** Do you think the result would be different if you used an aluminum nail instead of an iron nail? Why?

**SKILL FOCUS**
Observing

**MATERIALS**
- insulated wire
- large iron nail
- 2 D cells
- electrical tape
- paper clip

**TIME**
20 minutes

## Uses of Electromagnets

Because electromagnets can be turned on and off, they have more uses than permanent magnets. The photograph below shows a powerful electromagnet on a crane. While the electric charge flows through the coils of the magnet, it lifts hundreds of cans at a recycling plant. When the crane operator turns off the current, the magnetic field disappears and the cans drop from the crane.

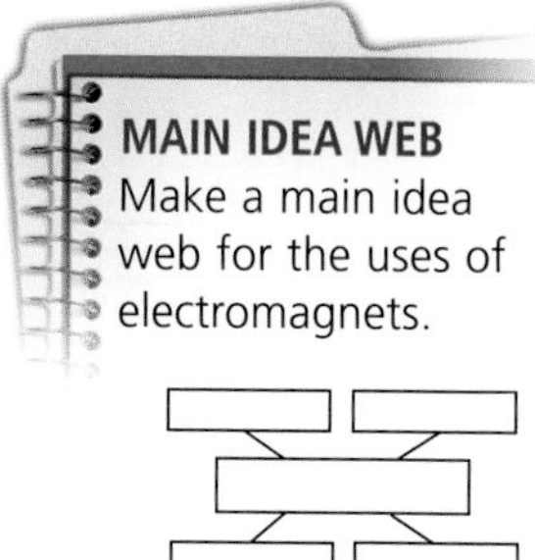

**MAIN IDEA WEB**
Make a main idea web for the uses of electromagnets.


A permanent magnet would not be nearly as useful for this purpose. Although you could use a large permanent magnet to lift the cans, it would be hard to remove them from the magnet.

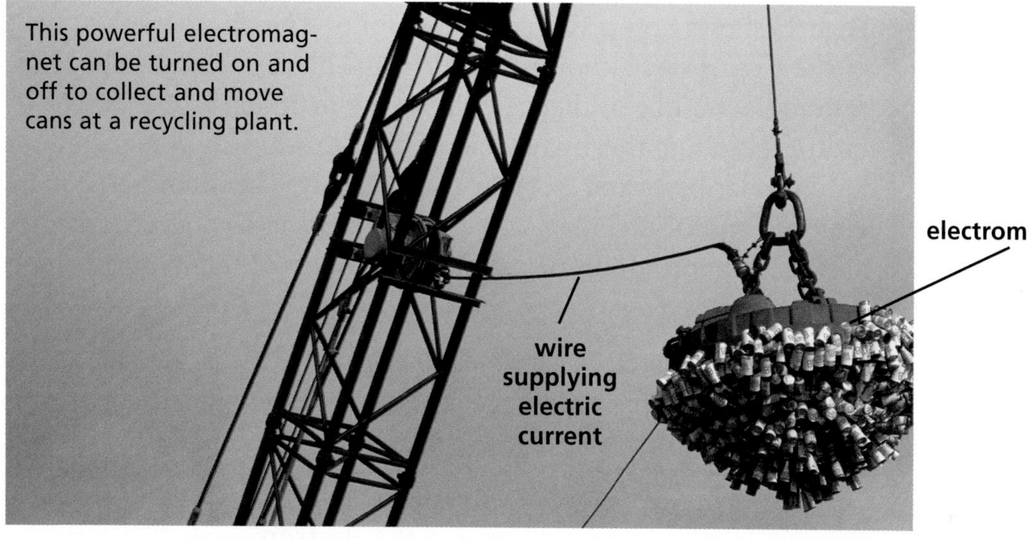


This powerful electromagnet can be turned on and off to collect and move cans at a recycling plant.

You use an electromagnet every time you store information on a computer. The computer hard drive contains disks that have billions of tiny magnetic domains in them. When you save a file, a tiny electromagnet in the computer is activated. The magnetic field of the electromagnet changes the orientation of the small magnetic domains. The small magnets store your file in a form that can be read later by the computer. A similar system is used to store information on magnetic tape of an audiocassette or videocassette. Sound and pictures are stored on the tape by the arrangement of magnets embedded in the plastic film.

Magnetic information is often stored on credit cards and cash cards. A black strip on the back of the card contains information about the account number and passwords. The cards can be damaged if they are frequently exposed to magnetic fields. For example, cards should not be stored with their strips facing each other, or near a magnetic clasp on a purse or wallet. These magnetic fields can change the arrangement of the tiny magnetic domains on the card and erase the stored information.

## Motors use electromagnets.

Because magnetism is a force, magnets can be used to move things. Electric motors convert the energy of an electric current into motion by taking advantage of the interaction between current and magnetism.

There are hundreds of devices that contain electric motors. Examples include power tools, electrical kitchen appliances, and the small fans in a computer. Almost anything with moving parts that uses current has an electric motor.

### Motors

See a motor in motion.

Page 93 shows how a simple motor works. The photograph at the top of the page shows a motor that turns the blades of a fan. The illustration in the middle of the page shows the main parts of a simple motor. Although they may look different from each other, all motors have similar parts and work in a similar way. The main parts of an electrical motor include a voltage source, a shaft, an electromagnet, and at least one additional magnet. The shaft of the motor turns other parts of the device.

Recall that an electromagnet consists of a coil of wire with current flowing through it. Find the electromagnet in the illustration on page 93. The electromagnet is placed between the poles of another magnet.

When current from the voltage source flows through the coil, a magnetic field is produced around the electromagnet. The poles of the magnet interact with the poles of the electromagnet, causing the motor to turn.

1. The poles of the magnet push on the like poles of the electromagnet, causing the electromagnet to turn.
2. As the motor turns, the opposite poles pull on each other.
3. When the poles of the electromagnet line up with the opposite poles of the magnet, a part of the motor called the commutator reverses the polarity of the electromagnet. Now, the poles push on each other again and the motor continues to turn.

coil of wire
magnet
shaft

The illustration of the motor on page 93 is simplified so that you can see all of the parts. If you saw the inside of an actual motor, it might look like the illustration on the left. Notice that the wire is coiled many times. The electromagnet in a strong motor may coil hundreds of times. The more coils, the stronger the motor.

What causes the electromagnet in a motor to turn?

## How a Motor Works

**Although motors may look different from each other, they all have similar parts and work in a similar way.**

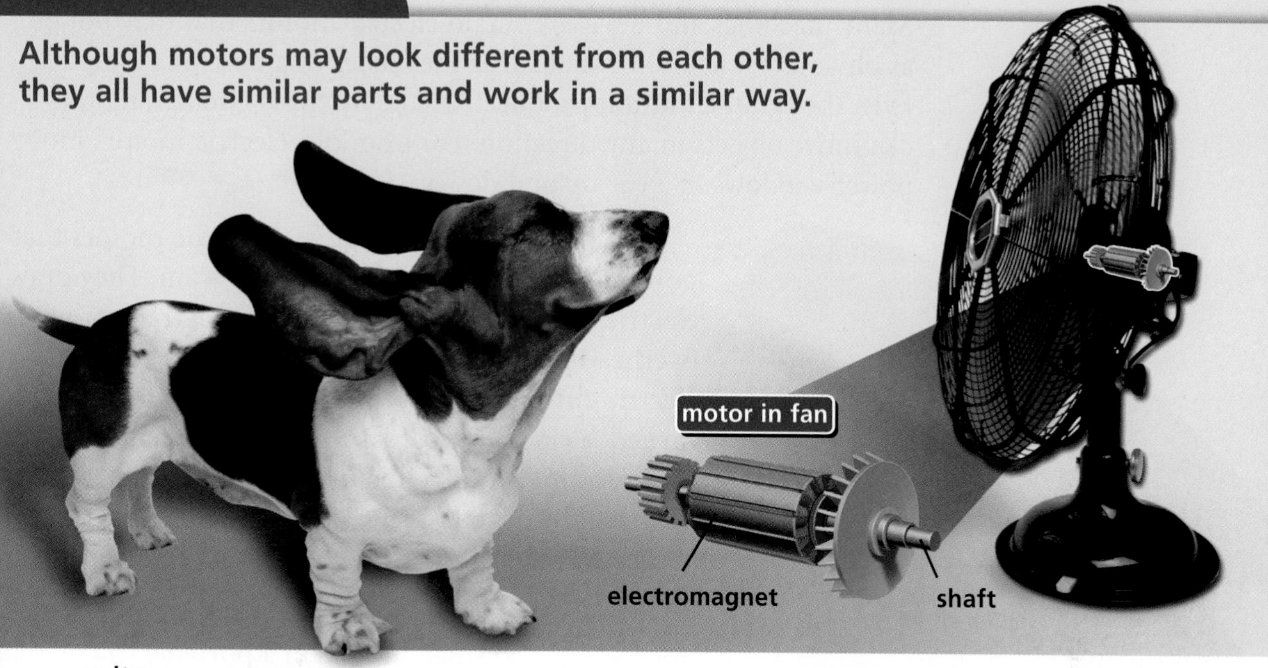


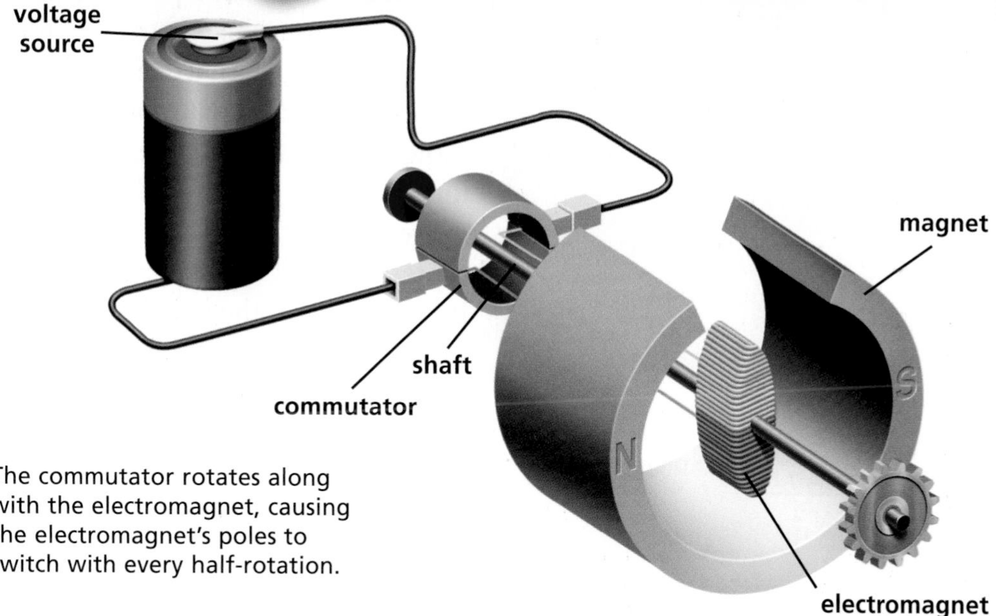


The commutator rotates along with the electromagnet, causing the electromagnet's poles to switch with every half-rotation.

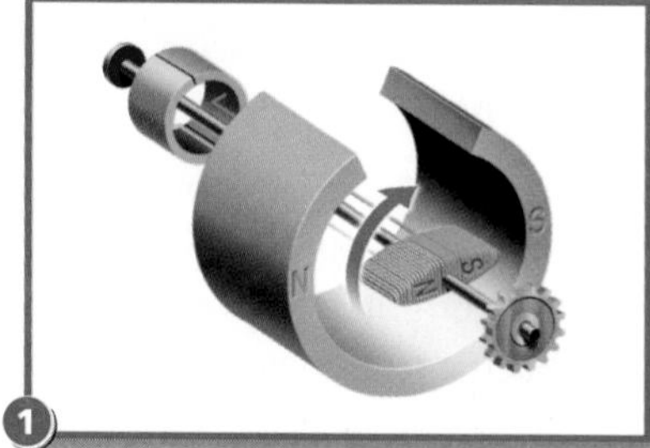

1 Like poles of the magnets push on each other.

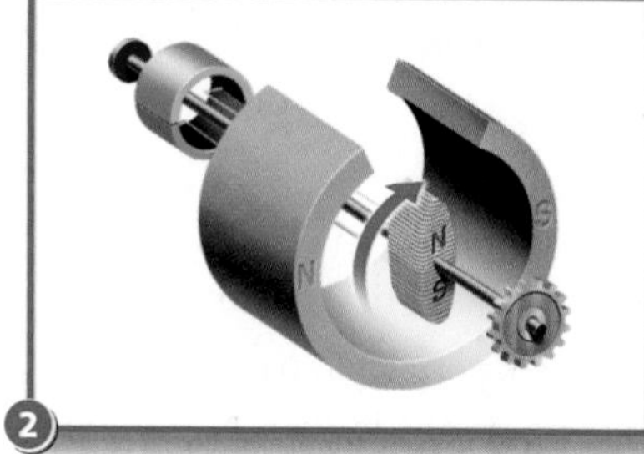

2 As the motor turns, opposite poles attract.

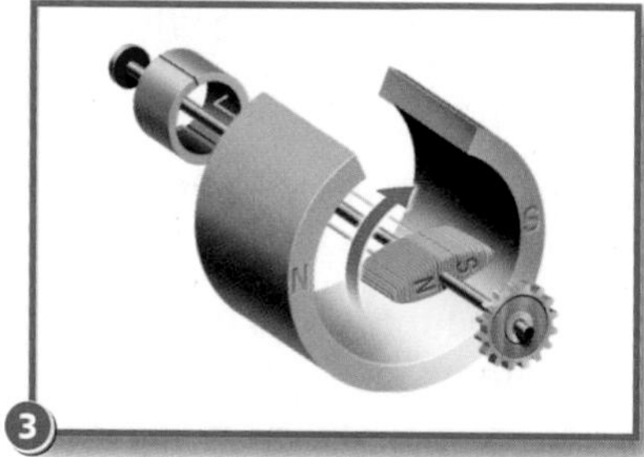

3 The electromagnet's poles are switched, and like poles again repel.

**READING VISUALS** Would a motor work without an electromagnet? Why or why not?

## Uses of Motors

Many machines and devices contain electric motors that may not be as obvious as the motor that turns the blades of a fan, for example. Even though the motion produced by the motor is circular, motors can move objects in any direction. For example, electric motors move power windows in a car up and down.

Motors can be very large, such as the motors that power an object as large as a subway train. They draw electric current from a third rail on the track or wires overhead that carry electric current. A car uses an electric current to start the engine. When the key is turned, a circuit is closed, producing a current from the battery to the motor. Other motors are very small, like the battery-operated motors that move the hands of a wristwatch.

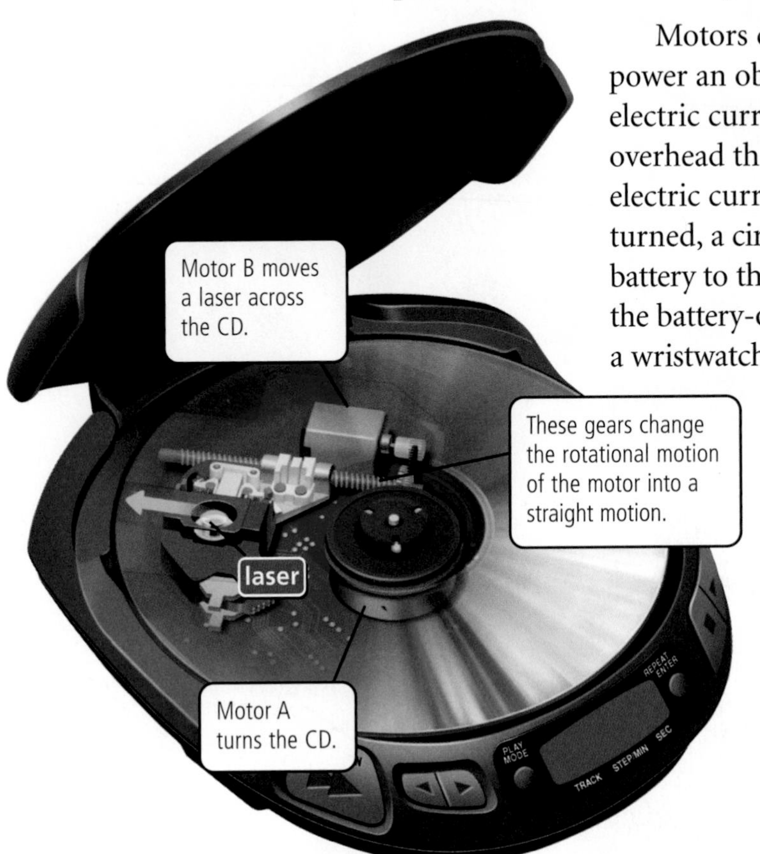

Motor B moves a laser across the CD.
These gears change the rotational motion of the motor into a straight motion.
laser
Motor A turns the CD.

The illustration on the left shows the two small motors in a portable CD player. Motor A causes the CD to spin. Motor B is connected to a set of gears. The gears convert the rotational motion of the motor into a straight-line motion, or linear motion. As the CD spins, a laser moves straight across the CD from the center outward. The laser reads the information on the CD. The motion from Motor B moves the laser across the CD.

**CHECK YOUR READING** Explain the function served by each motor in a CD player.

# 3.2 Review

### KEY CONCEPTS

1. Explain how electric current and magnetism are related.
2. Describe three uses of electromagnets.
3. Explain how electrical energy is converted to motion in a motor.

### CRITICAL THINKING

4. **Contrast** How does an electromagnet differ from a permanent magnet?
5. **Apply** Provide examples of two things in your home that use electric motors, and explain why they are easier to use because of the motors.

### CHALLENGE

6. **Infer** Why is it necessary to change the direction of the current in the coil of an electric motor as it turns?

KEY CONCEPT

# 3.3 Magnetism can produce current.

**BEFORE, you learned**

- Magnetism is a force exerted by magnets
- Electric current can produce a magnetic field
- Electromagnets can make objects move

**NOW, you will learn**

- How a magnetic field can produce an electric current
- How a generator converts energy
- How direct current and alternating current differ

**VOCABULARY**

**generator** p. 96
**direct current** p. 97
**alternating current** p. 97
**transformer** p. 99

**EXPLORE Energy Conversion**

### *How can a motor produce current?*

**PROCEDURE**

1. Touch the wires on the motor to the battery terminals to see how the motor operates.
2. Connect the wires to the light bulb.
3. Roll the shaft, or the movable part of the motor, between your fingers. Observe the light bulb.
4. Now spin the shaft rapidly. Record your observations.

**MATERIALS**

- small motor
- AA cell (battery)
- light bulb in holder

**WHAT DO YOU THINK?**

- How did you produce current?
- What effect did your motion have on the amount of light produced?

## Magnets are used to generate an electric current.

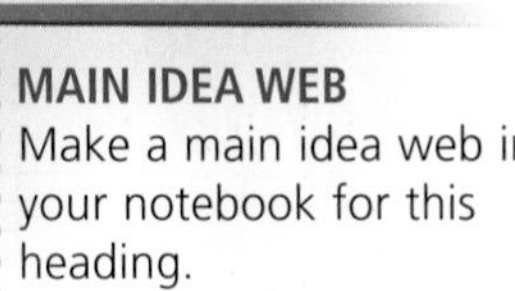

MAIN IDEA WEB
Make a main idea web in your notebook for this heading.

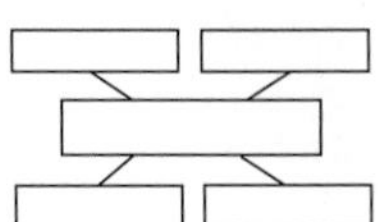

In the 1830s, about ten years after Oersted discovered that an electric current produces magnetism, physicists observed the reverse effect—a moving magnetic field induces an electric current. When a magnet moves inside a coiled wire that is in a circuit, an electric current is generated in the wire.

It is often easier to generate an electric current by moving a wire inside a magnetic field. Whether it is the magnet or the wire that moves, the effect is the same. Current is generated as long as the wire crosses the magnetic field lines.

CHECK YOUR READING What must happen for a magnetic field to produce an electric current?

## Generating an Electric Current

A **generator** is a device that converts the energy of motion, or kinetic energy, into electrical energy. A generator is similar to a motor in reverse. If you manually turn the shaft of a motor that contains a magnet, you can produce electric current.

The illustration below shows a portable generator that provides electrical energy to charge a cell phone in an emergency. The generator produces current as you turn the handle. Because it does not need to be plugged in, the generator can be used wherever and whenever it is needed to recharge a phone. The energy is supplied by the person turning the handle.

1. As the handle is turned, it rotates a series of gears. The gears turn the shaft of the generator.
2. The rotation of the shaft causes coils of wire to rotate within a magnetic field.
3. As the coils of the wire cross the magnetic field line, electric current is generated. The current recharges the battery of the cell phone.

**CHECK YOUR READING** What is the source of energy for a cell phone generator?

### How a Cell Phone Generator Works

**An emergency cell phone charger uses a generator to produce electric current.**

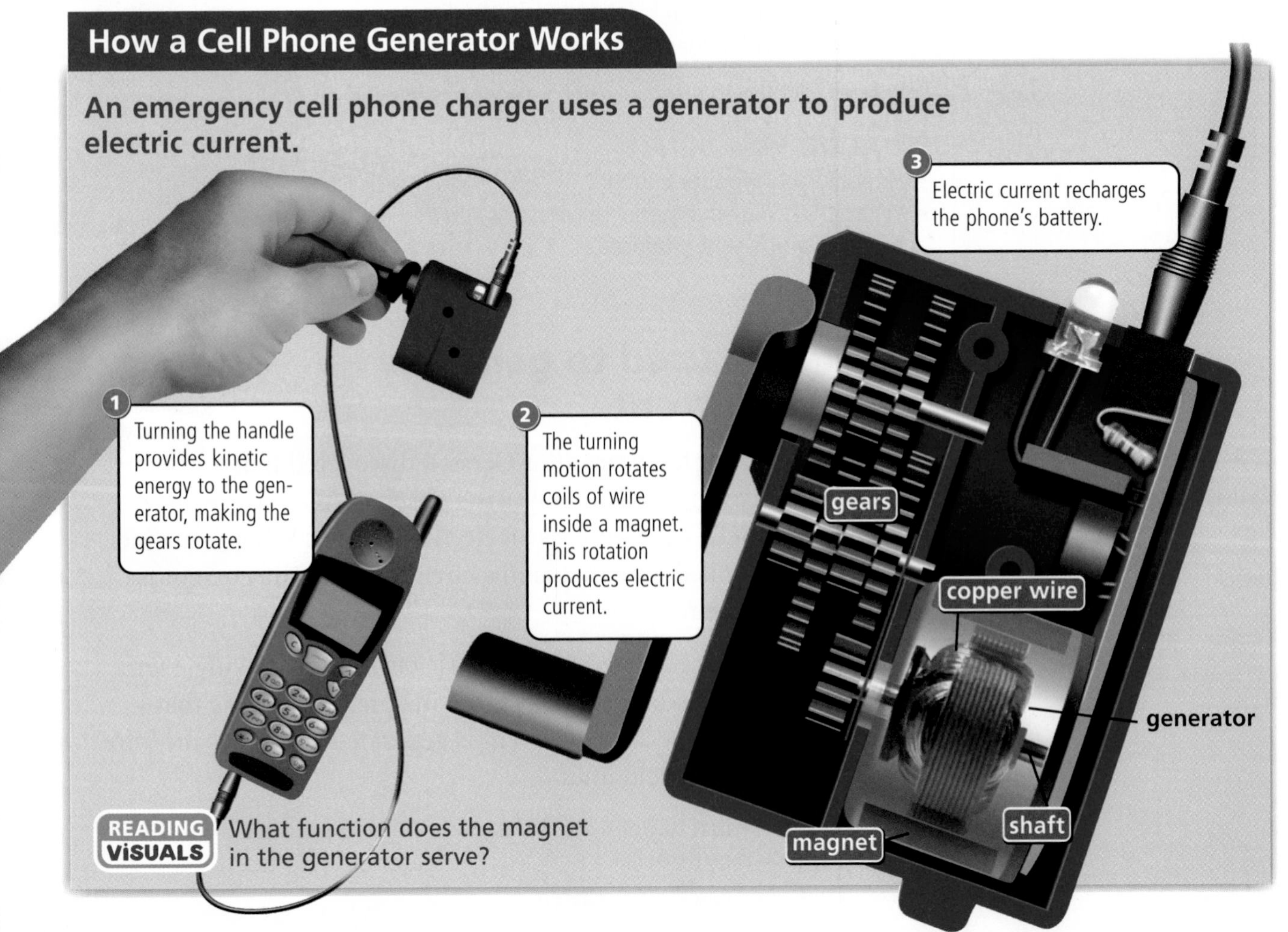

1 Turning the handle provides kinetic energy to the generator, making the gears rotate.
2 The turning motion rotates coils of wire inside a magnet. This rotation produces electric current.
3 Electric current recharges the phone's battery.
gears
copper wire
generator
shaft
magnet

**READING VISUALS** What function does the magnet in the generator serve?

## Direct and Alternating Currents

Think about how current flows in all of the circuits that you have studied so far. Electrons flow from one end of a battery or generator, through the circuit, and eventually back to the battery or generator. Electrons that flow in one direction produce one of two types of current.

- A **direct current** (DC) is electric charge that flows in one direction only. Direct current is produced by batteries and by DC generators such as the cell phone generator.
- An **alternating current** (AC) is a flow of electric charge that reverses direction at regular intervals. The current that enters your home and school is an alternating current.

CHECK YOUR READING What is the difference between direct current and alternating current?

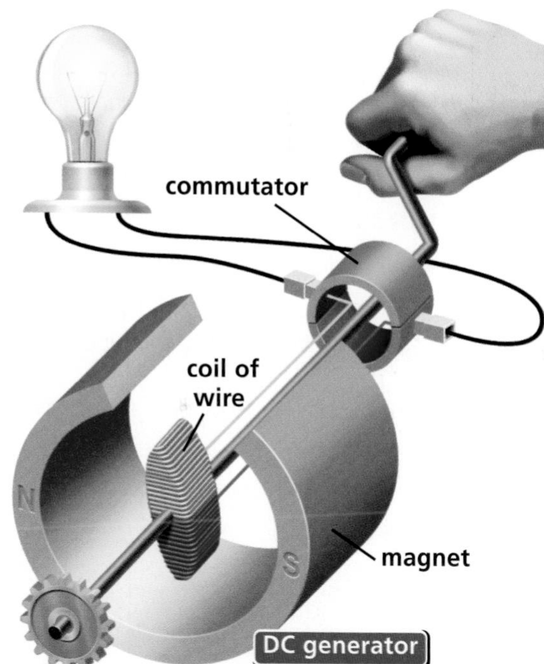

DC generator

Direct currents and alternating currents are produced by different generators. In an AC generator, the direction in which charge flows depends upon the direction in which the magnet moves in relation to the coil. Because generators use a rotating electromagnet, the poles of the electromagnet alternate between moving toward and moving away from the magnet. The result is a current that reverses with each half-rotation of the coil.

The illustration on the right shows a simple DC generator. DC generators are very similar to AC generators. The main difference is that DC generators have a commutator that causes the current to flow in only one direction.

Many things in your home can work with either direct or alternating currents. In light bulbs, for instance, the resistance to motion of the electrons in the filament makes the filament glow. It doesn't matter in which direction the current is moving.

Some appliances can use only direct current. The black box that is on the plug of some devices is an AC–DC converter. AC–DC converters change the alternating current to direct current. For example, laptop computers use converters like the one shown in the photograph on the right. In a desktop computer, the converter is part of the power supply unit.

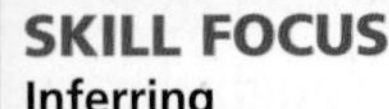

# INVESTIGATE Electric Current

## How can you identify the current?

**SKILL FOCUS**
Inferring

**MATERIALS**
- piece of wire
- compass
- ruler
- tape
- sandpaper
- D cell (battery)

**TIME**
15 minutes

**PROCEDURE**

1. Wrap the wire tightly around the middle of the compass 10–15 times. Leave about 30 cm of wire free at each end. Tape the wire to the back of the compass to keep it in place.
2. Sand the ends of the wire with sandpaper to expose about 2 cm of copper on each end. Arrange the compass on your desk so that the needle is parallel to, or lined up with, the coil. This will serve as your current detector.
3. Tape one end of the wire to one terminal of the battery. Touch the other end of the wire to the other battery terminal. Record your observations.
4. Observe the current detector as you tap the end of the wire to the battery terminal at a steady pace. Speed up or slow down your tapping until the needle of the compass alternates back and forth. Record your observations.

**WHAT DO YOU THINK?**

- What did you observe?
- What type of current did you detect in step 3? in step 4? How did you identify the type of current?

**CHALLENGE** How is this setup similar to an AC generator?

The energy that powers a car comes from burning gasoline, but the car also contains many devices that use electrical energy. Some of them are familiar—the headlights, turn signals, radio, power windows, and door locks. Others may be less familiar, such as the spark plugs that ignite the gasoline, the fuel and oil pumps that move fluids in the engine, and the air conditioner.

A car's engine includes a generator to provide current to its electrical devices. As the engine runs, it converts gasoline to kinetic energy. Some of that energy is transferred to the generator by a belt attached to its shaft. Inside the generator, a complex coil of copper wires turns in a magnetic field, generating a current that operates the electrical devices of the car.

The generator also recharges the battery, so that power is available when the engine is not running. Because the generator in most cars supplies alternating current, a car generator is usually called an alternator.

What function does a generator in a car serve?

## Magnets are used to control voltage.

A **transformer** is a device that increases or decreases voltage. Transformers use magnetism to control the amount of voltage. A transformer consists of two coils of wire that are wrapped around an iron ring.

An alternating current from the voltage source in the first coil produces a magnetic field. The iron ring becomes an electromagnet. Because the current alternates, the magnetic field is constantly changing. The second coil is therefore within a changing magnetic field. Current is generated in the second coil. If the two coils have the same number of loops, the voltage in the second coil will be the same as the voltage in the first coil.

A change in the voltage is caused when the two coils have different numbers of loops. If the second coil has fewer loops than the first, as in the illustration, the voltage is decreased. This is called a step-down transformer. On the other hand, if the second coil has more loops than the first, the voltage in the second circuit will be higher than the original voltage. This transformer is called a step-up transformer.

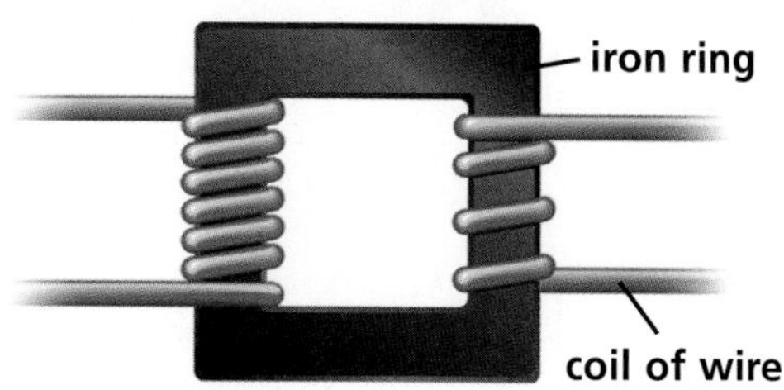

Transformers are used in the distribution of current. Current is sent over power lines from power plants at a very high voltage. Step-down transformers on utility poles, such as the one pictured on the right, reduce the voltage available for use in homes. Sending current at high voltages minimizes the amount of energy lost to resistance along the way.

## 3.3 Review

### KEY CONCEPTS

1. What is necessary for a magnetic field to produce an electric current?
2. Explain how electric generators convert kinetic energy into electrical energy.
3. Compare and contrast the ways in which direct current and alternating current are generated.

### CRITICAL THINKING

4. **Apply** Many radios can be operated either by plugging them into the wall or by using batteries. How can a radio use either source of current?
5. **Draw Conclusions** Suppose that all of the electrical devices in a car stop working. Explain what the problem might be.

### CHALLENGE

6. **Apply** European power companies deliver current at 220 V. Draw the design for a step-down transformer that would let you operate a CD player made to work at 110 V in France.

# CHAPTER INVESTIGATION

## Build a Speaker

**OVERVIEW AND PURPOSE** Speakers are found on TVs, computers, telephones, stereos, amplifiers, and other devices. Inside a speaker, magnetism and electric current interact to produce sound. The current produces a magnetic field that acts on another magnet and causes vibrations. The vibrations produce sound waves. In this lab, you will

- construct a speaker
- determine how the strength of the magnet affects the speaker's volume

### Problem

How does the strength of the magnet used to make a speaker affect the loudness of sound produced by the speaker?

### Hypothesize

Write a hypothesis that explains how you expect the strength of a magnet to affect the loudness of sound produced by the speaker, and why. Your hypothesis should be in the form of an "if . . . , then . . . , because . . . " statement.

**MATERIALS**

- 3 magnets of different strengths
- paper clip
- ruler
- piece of wire
- marker
- cup
- masking tape
- 2 wire leads with alligator clips
- stereo system

### Procedure

1. Make a data table similar to the one shown on the sample notebook page.

2. Test the strength of each magnet by measuring the distance at which a paper clip will move to the magnet, as shown. Record the measurements in your **Science Notebook.**

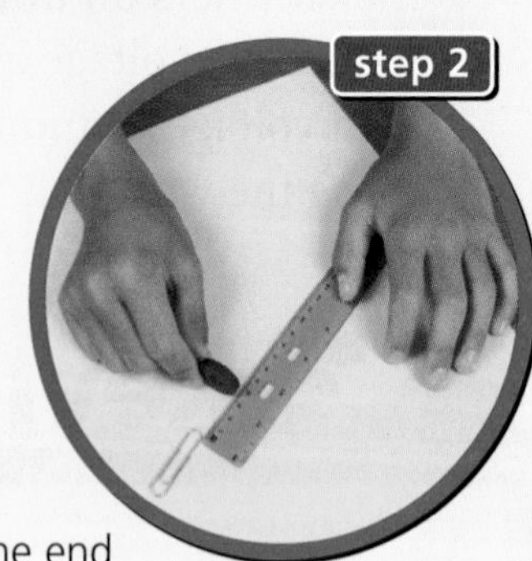

step 2

3. Starting about 6 cm from the end of the wire, wrap the wire around the marker 50 times to make a coil.

4 Carefully slide the coil off the marker. Wrap the ends of the wire around the coil to keep it in the shape of a circle, as shown.

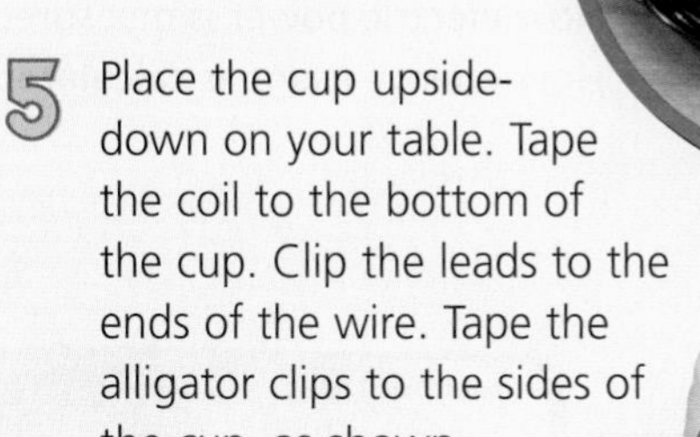


5 Place the cup upside-down on your table. Tape the coil to the bottom of the cup. Clip the leads to the ends of the wire. Tape the alligator clips to the sides of the cup, as shown.

coil

step 5

6 Take turns attaching the alligator clips to the stereo as instructed by your teacher. Place each magnet on the table near the stereo. Test the speaker by holding the cup directly over each magnet and listening. Record your observations.

## Observe and Analyze

Write It Up

1. **RECORD OBSERVATIONS** Be sure to record your observations in the data table.
2. **INFER** Why is the coil of wire held near the magnet?
3. **APPLY** The diaphragm on a speaker vibrates to produce sound. What part of your stereo is the diaphragm?
4. **IDENTIFY** What was the independent variable in this experiment? What was the dependent variable?

## Conclude

1. **INTERPRET** Which magnet produced the loudest noise when used with your speaker? Answer the question posed in the problem.
2. **ANALYZE** Compare your results with your hypothesis. Did your results support your hypothesis?
3. **IDENTIFY LIMITS** Describe possible limitations or sources of error in the procedure or any places where errors might have occurred.
4. **APPLY** You have built a simple version of a real speaker. Apply what you have learned in this lab to explain how a real speaker might work.

## INVESTIGATE Further

**CHALLENGE** In what ways might you vary the design of the speaker to improve its functioning? Review the procedure to identify variables that might be changed to improve the speaker. Choose one variable and design an experiment to test that variable.

Build a Speaker

**Problem** How does the strength of the magnet used to make a speaker affect the loudness of sound produced by the speaker?

Hypothesize

Observe and Analyze

Table 1. Strength of Magnet and Loudness of Sound

| Magnet | Strength (paper clip distance) | Observations |
|---|---|---|
| 1 | | |
| 2 | | |
| 3 | | |

Conclude

KEY CONCEPT

# Generators supply electrical energy.

**BEFORE, you learned**

- Magnetism is a force exerted by magnets
- A moving magnetic field can generate an electric current in a conductor
- Generators use magnetism to produce current

**NOW, you will learn**

- How power plants generate electrical energy
- How electric power is measured
- How energy usage is calculated

**VOCABULARY**



**THINK ABOUT**

***How can falling water generate electrical energy?***

This photograph shows the Hoover Dam on the Nevada/Arizona border, which holds back a large lake, almost 600 feet deep, on the Colorado River. It took thousands of workers nearly five years to build the dam, and it cost millions of dollars. One of the main purposes of the Hoover Dam is the generation of current. Think about what you have read about generators. How could the energy of falling water be used to generate current?

## Generators provide most of the world's electrical energy.

The tremendous energy produced by falling water provides the turning motion for large generators at a power plant. The power plant at the Hoover Dam supplies energy to more than a million people.

Other sources of energy at power plants include steam from burning fossil fuels, nuclear reactions, wind, solar heating, and ocean tides. Each source provides the energy of motion to the generators, producing electrical energy. **Electric power** is the rate at which electrical energy is generated from another source of energy.

**VOCABULARY**
Use a description wheel to take notes about *electrical power.*

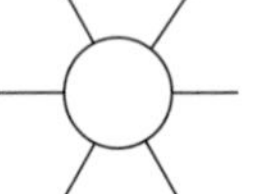

**CHECK YOUR READING** What do power plants that use water, steam, and wind all have in common?

How does the power plant convert the energy of motion into electrical energy? Very large generators in the plant hold powerful electromagnets surrounded by massive coils of copper wire. The illustration below shows how the energy from water falling from the reservoir to the river far below a dam is converted to electrical energy.

Find out more about dams that generate current.

1. As the water falls from the reservoir, its kinetic energy increases and it flows very fast. The falling stream of water turns a fan-like device, called a turbine, which is connected to the generator's shaft.
2. The rotation of the shaft turns powerful electromagnets that are surrounded by the coil of copper wires. The coil is connected to a step-up transformer that sends high-voltage current to power lines.
3. Far from the plant, step-down transformers reduce the voltage so that current can be sent through smaller lines to neighborhoods. Another transformer reduces the voltage to the level needed to operate lights and appliances.

## How Electrical Power Is Generated

**Power plants use generators to convert kinetic energy into electrical energy.**

step-up transformers

step-down transformers

shaft

turbine

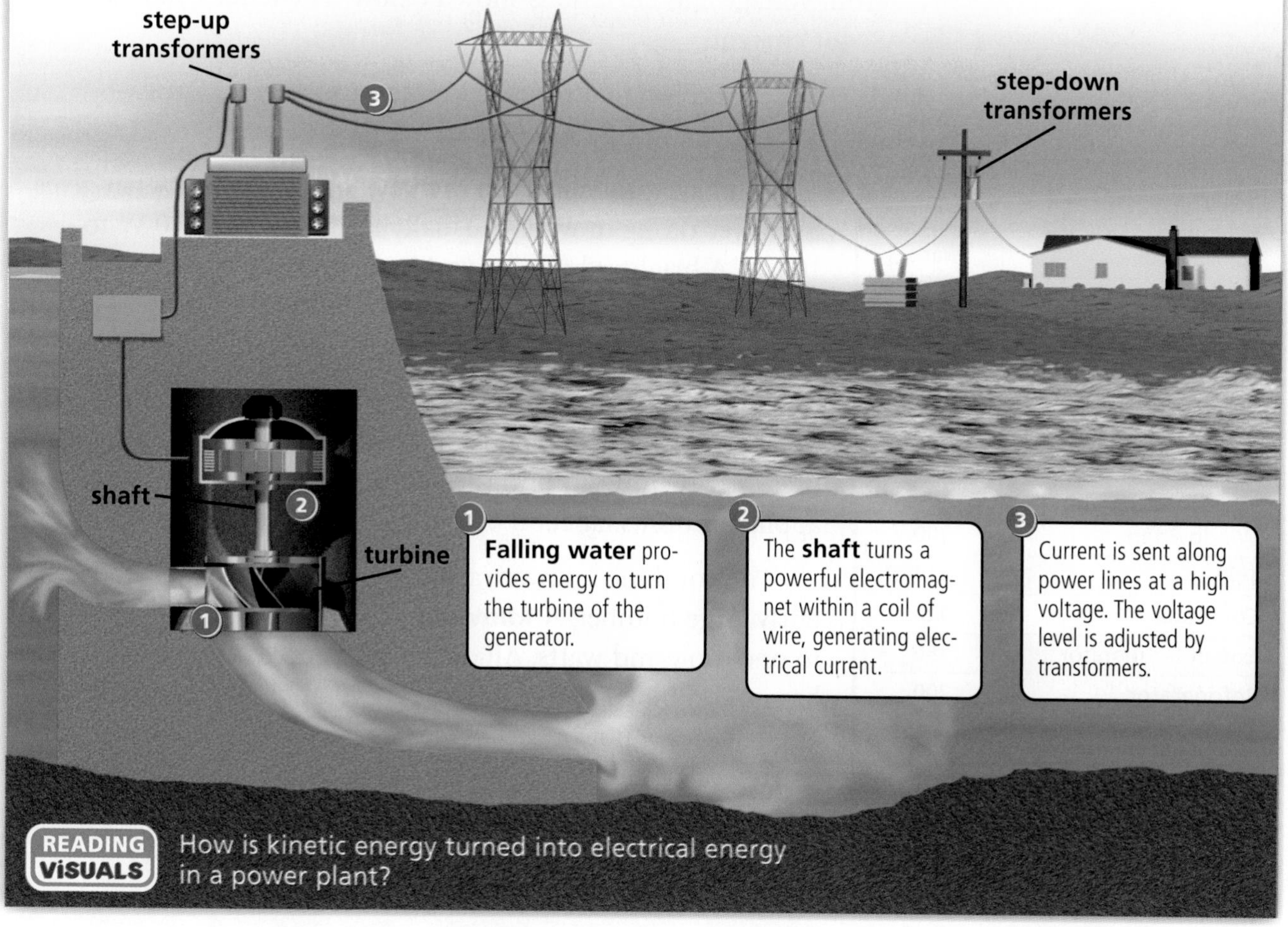

1 **Falling water** provides energy to turn the turbine of the generator.

2 The **shaft** turns a powerful electromagnet within a coil of wire, generating electrical current.

3 Current is sent along power lines at a high voltage. The voltage level is adjusted by transformers.

**READING VISUALS** How is kinetic energy turned into electrical energy in a power plant?

## Electric power can be measured.

You have read that electric power is the rate at which electrical energy is generated from another source of energy. Power also refers to the rate at which an appliance converts electrical energy back into another form of energy, such as light, heat, or sound.

Learn more about energy use and conservation.

In order to provide electrical energy to homes and factories, power companies need to know the rate at which energy is needed. Power can be measured so that companies can determine how much energy is used and where it is used. This information is used to figure out how much to charge customers, and it is used to determine whether more electrical energy needs to be generated. To provide energy to an average home, a power plant needs to burn about four tons of coal each year.

### Watts and Kilowatts

The unit of measurement for power is the **watt** (W). Watts measure the rate at which energy is used by an electrical appliance. For instance, a light bulb converts energy to light and heat. The power rating of the bulb, or of any device that consumes electrical energy, depends on both the voltage and the current. The formula for finding power, in watts, from voltage and current, is shown below. The letter *I* stands for current.

**Electric Power = Voltage • Current**

$$P = VI$$

You have probably seen the label on a light bulb that gives its power rating in watts—usually in the range of 40 W to 100 W. A brighter bulb converts energy at a higher rate than one with a lower power rating.

The chart at the left shows typical power ratings, in watts, for some appliances that you might have in your home. The exact power rating depends on how each brand of appliance uses energy. You can find the actual power rating for an appliance on its label.

**Typical Power Ratings**

| Appliance | Watts |
|---|---|
| DVD player | 20 |
| Radio | 20 |
| Video game system | 25 |
| Electric blanket | 60 |
| Light bulb | 75 |
| Stereo system | 100 |
| Window fan | 100 |
| Television | 110 |
| Computer | 120 |
| Computer monitor | 150 |
| Refrigerator | 700 |
| Air conditioner | 1000 |
| Microwave oven | 1000 |
| Hair dryer | 1200 |
| Clothes dryer | 3000 |

The combined power rating in a building is likely to be a fairly large number. A **kilowatt** (kW) is a unit of power equal to one thousand watts. All of the appliances in a room may have a combined power rating of several kilowatts, but all appliances are not in use all of the time. That is why energy is usually calculated based on how long the appliances are in use.

Explain what kilowatts are used to measure.

# INVESTIGATE Power

## How would you use your electrical energy?

**SKILL FOCUS**
Making models

**MATERIALS**
- graph paper
- colored pencils

**TIME**
30 minutes

### PROCEDURE

1. On a sheet of graph paper, outline a box that is 10 squares long by 18 squares wide. The box represents a room that is wired to power a total of 1800 W. Each square represents 10 W of power.
2. From the chart on page 104, choose appliances that you want in your room. Using colored pencils, fill in the appropriate number of boxes for each appliance.
3. All of the items that you choose must fit within the total power available, represented by the 180 squares.

### WHAT DO YOU THINK?

- How did you decide to use your electrical energy?
- Could you provide enough energy to operate everything you wanted at one time?

**CHALLENGE** During the summer, power companies sometimes cannot produce enough energy for the demand. Why do you think that happens?

## Calculating Energy Use

The electric bill for your energy usage is calculated based on the rate at which energy is used, or the power, and the amount of time it is used at that rate. Total energy used by an appliance is determined by multiplying its power consumption by the amount of time that it is used.

$$\textbf{Energy used} = \textbf{Power} \cdot \textbf{time}$$

$$E = Pt$$

The kilowatt-hour is the unit of measurement for energy usage. A **kilowatt-hour** (kWh) is equal to one kilowatt of power for a one-hour period. Buildings usually have meters that measure how many kilowatt-hours of energy have been used. The meters display four or five small dials in a row, as shown in the photograph on the right. Each dial represents a different place value—ones, tens, hundreds, or thousands. For example, the meter in the photograph shows that the customer has used close to 9000 kWh of energy—8933 kWh, to be exact. To find how much energy was used in one month, the last month's reading is subtracted from this total.

To determine the number of kilowatt-hours of energy used by an appliance, find its wattage on the chart on page 104 or from the label. Then substitute it into the formula along with the number of hours it was in use. Solve the sample problems below.

### Finding Energy Used

**Sample Problem**

**How much energy is used to dry clothes in a 3 kW dryer for 30 minutes?**

***What do you know?*** Power = 3.0 kW, time = 0.5 hr

***What do you want to find out?*** Energy used

***Write the formula:*** $E = Pt$

***Substitute into the formula:*** $E = 3.0 \text{ kW} \cdot 0.5 \text{ hr}$

***Calculate and simplify:*** $E = 1.5 \text{ kWh}$

***Check that your units agree:*** Unit is kWh. Unit for energy used is kWh. Units agree.

***Answer:*** 1.5 kWh

**Practice the Math**

1. All of the appliances in a computer lab are in use for 6 hours every day and together use 3.3 kW. How much energy has been used in 1 day?
2. How much energy is used when a 1.2 kW hair dyer is in use for 0.2 hr?

Energy prices vary, but you can estimate the cost of using an electrical appliance by using a value of about 8 cents/kWh. You can calculate how much energy you can save by turning off the lights or television when you are not using them. Although the number may seem small, try multiplying your savings over the course of a month or year.

#### KEY CONCEPTS

1. How do power plants generate electrical energy from kinetic energy?
2. Explain what watts measure.
3. How is energy use determined?

#### CRITICAL THINKING

4. **Apply** Think about reducing energy usage in your home. What changes would make the largest difference in the amount of energy used?
5. **Calculate** How much energy is used if a 3000 W clothes dryer is used for 4 hours?

#### CHALLENGE

6. **Calculate** An electric bill for an apartment shows 396 kWh of energy used over one month. The appliances in the apartment have a total power rating of 2.2 kW. How many hours were the appliances in use?

MATH in SCIENCE

MATH TUTORIAL
CLASSZONE.COM
Click on Math Tutorial for more help with rounding decimals.

SKILL: USING SIGNIFICANT FIGURES

# Energy Calculations

Significant figures are meaningful digits in a number. Calculations can sometimes produce answers with more significant figures than are accurately known. Scientists use rules to determine how to round their answers. The rule for writing an answer to a multiplication problem is shown below.

**Rule: Your answer may show only as many significant figures as the number in the problem with the fewest significant figures.**

Generally, a significant figure is any digit shown except for a zero, unless the zero is contained between two nonzero digits or between a nonzero digit and a decimal point. For example, the number 40.3 has three significant figures, but the number 5.90 has only two significant figures. The number 0.034 has three significant figures, and the number 0.8 has only one significant figure.

## Example

A computer uses 6.5 kWh of energy per day. If the computer is left on all the time, how much energy does it use in a year?

**(1)** Solve the problem.

$$E = 6.5\ \frac{\text{kWh}}{\cancel{\text{day}}} \cdot 365\ \frac{\cancel{\text{days}}}{\text{year}} = 2372.5\ \frac{\text{kWh}}{\text{year}}$$

**(2)** Look at the number with the fewest significant figures. The number 6.5 has two significant figures, and the number 365 has three significant figures. Therefore, the answer is only meaningful to two significant figures.

**(3)** Round the answer to two significant figures.

**ANSWER** $E = 2400\ \frac{\text{kWh}}{\text{year}}$

**Answer the following questions. Write your answers using the significant figure rule for multiplication.**

1. How much energy is used in a year by a computer that uses 1.7 kWh/day?
2. An energy-efficient computer uses 0.72 kWh/day. How much energy does it use in a week?
3. How much energy is used in one year if a 0.27 kW computer is on for 3 hours/day? (**Hint:** Use the formula $E = Pt$.)

**CHALLENGE** The energy usage of a computer is measured to be 0.058030 kWh. How many significant figures does this measurement have?

# 3 Chapter Review

## the BIG idea

**Current can produce magnetism, and magnetism can produce current.**

### 3.1 Magnetism is a force that acts at a distance.

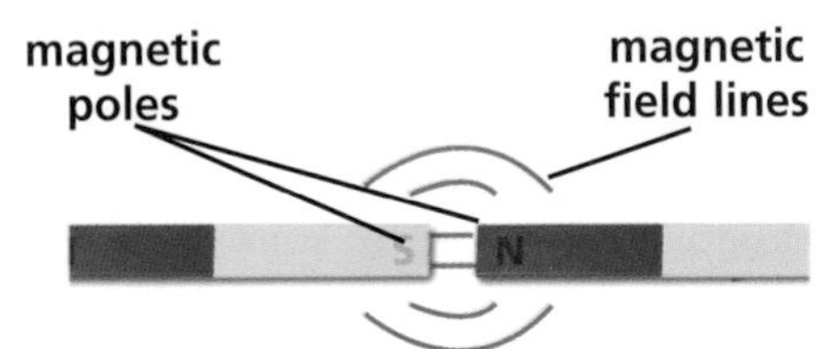


Opposite poles attract.

All magnets have a north and south pole. The like poles of two magnets repel each other and the opposite poles attract.

**VOCABULARY**
**magnet** p. 79
**magnetism** p. 80
**magnetic pole** p. 80
**magnetic field** p. 81
**magnetic domain** p. 82

### 3.2 Current can produce magnetism.

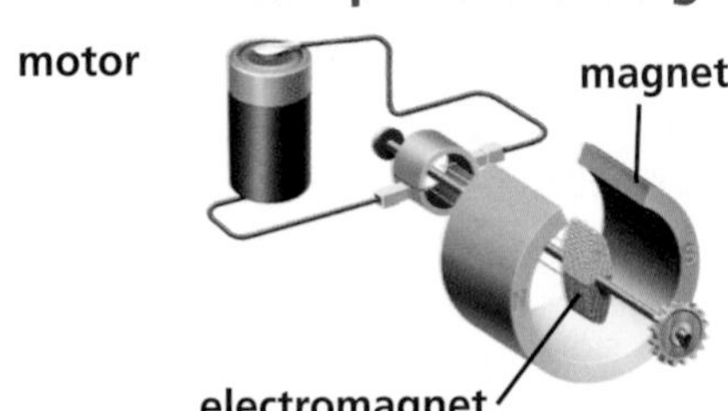


A magnet that is produced by electric current is called an electromagnet. Motors use electromagnets to convert electrical energy into the energy of motion.

**VOCABULARY**
**electromagnetism** p. 89
**electromagnet** p. 90

### 3.3 Magnetism can produce current.

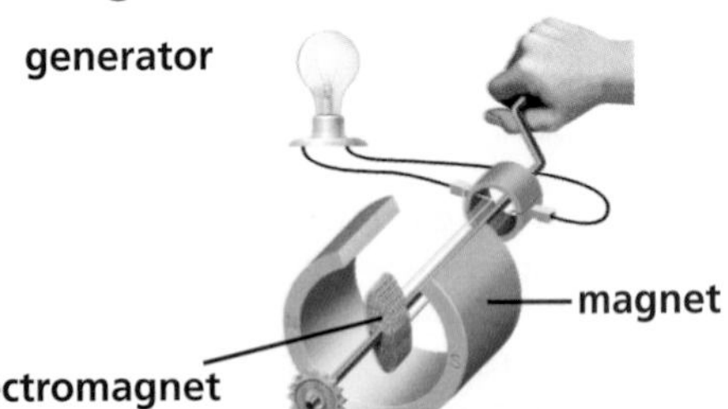


Magnetism can be used to produce electric current.
In a generator the energy of motion is converted into electrical energy.

**VOCABULARY**
**generator** p. 96
**direct current** p. 97
**alternating current** p. 97
**transformer** p. 99

### 3.4 Generators supply electrical energy.

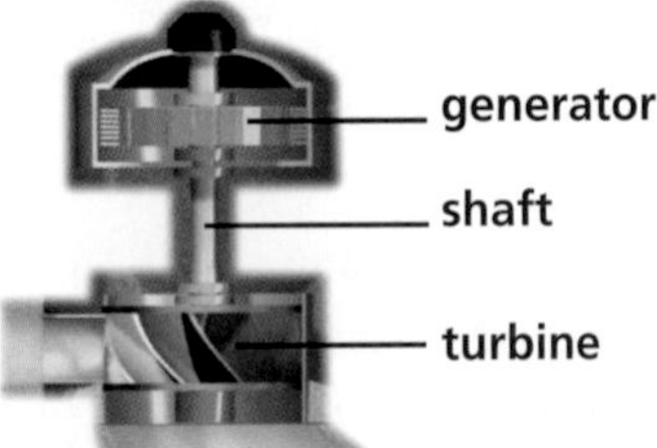


Generators at power plants use large magnets to produce electric current, supplying electrical energy to homes and businesses.

**VOCABULARY**
**electric power** p. 102
**watt** p. 104
**kilowatt** p. 104
**kilowatt-hour** p. 105

## Reviewing Vocabulary

*Draw a cluster diagram for each of the terms below. Write the vocabulary term in the center circle. In another circle, write the definition of the term in your own words. Add other circles that give examples or characteristics of the term. A sample diagram is completed for you.*

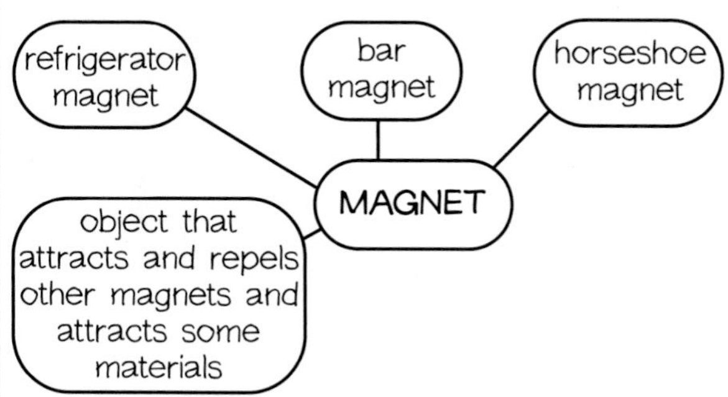


1. magnetism
2. magnetic pole
3. magnetic field
4. magnetic domain
5. electromagnet
6. generator
7. direct current
8. alternating current
9. transformer
10. electric power
11. watt
12. kilowatt-hour

## Reviewing Key Concepts

**Multiple Choice** *Choose the letter of the best answer.*

**13.** Magnetic field lines flow from a magnet's
- **a.** north pole to south pole
- **b.** south pole to north pole
- **c.** center to the outside
- **d.** outside to the center

**14.** Which of the following is characteristic of magnetic materials?
- **a.** Their atoms are all aligned.
- **b.** Their atoms are arranged in magnetic domains.
- **c.** They are all nonmetals.
- **d.** They are all made of lodestone.

**15.** The Earth's magnetic field helps to protect living things from
- **a.** ultraviolet light
- **b.** meteors
- **c.** the Northern Lights
- **d.** charged particles

**16.** To produce a magnetic field around a copper wire, you have to
- **a.** place it in Earth's magnetic field
- **b.** run a current through it
- **c.** supply kinetic energy to it
- **d.** place it near a strong magnet

**17.** An electric current is produced when a wire is
- **a.** stationary in a magnetic field
- **b.** moving in a magnetic field
- **c.** placed between the poles of a magnet
- **d.** coiled around a magnet

**18.** In a generator, kinetic energy is converted into
- **a.** light energy
- **b.** chemical energy
- **c.** electrical energy
- **d.** nuclear energy

**19.** In an AC circuit, the current moves
- **a.** back and forth
- **b.** from one end of a generator to the other
- **c.** from one end of a battery to the other
- **d.** in one direction

**20.** What is the function of the turbine in a power plant?
- **a.** to increase the voltage
- **b.** to convert DC to AC
- **c.** to cool the steam
- **d.** to turn the coil or magnet

**21.** The two factors needed to measure usage of electrical energy in a building are
- **a.** power and time
- **b.** power and voltage
- **c.** voltage and time
- **d.** current and voltage

## Thinking Critically

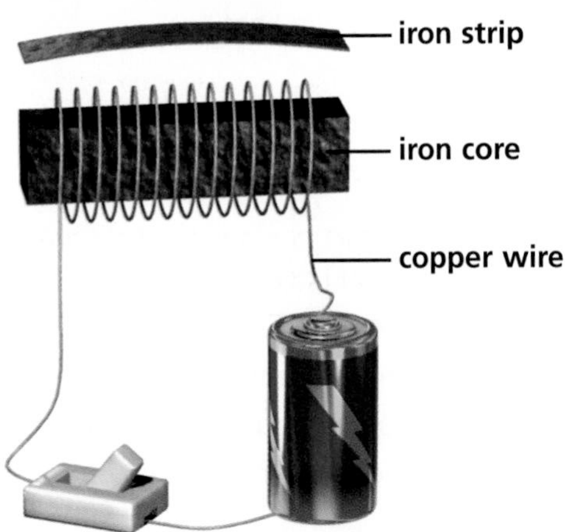


*Refer to the device in the illustration above to answer the next three questions.*

**22. APPLY** What will happen when the switch is closed?

**23. PREDICT** What effect will switching the direction of the current have on the operation of the device?

**24. CONTRAST** If the iron strip is replaced with a thin magnet, how would that affect the answers to the previous two questions?

**25. APPLY** Coal is burned at a power plant to produce steam. The rising steam turns a turbine. Describe how the motion of the turbine produces current at the plant.

**26. CONNECT** List three things that you use in your everyday life that would not exist without the discovery of electromagnetism.

**27. APPLY** A radio for use during power outages works when you crank a handle. How is the radio powered? How can it keep operating even after you stop turning the crank?

**28. HYPOTHESIZE** Use your understanding of magnetic materials and the source of Earth's magnetic field to form a hypothesis about the difference between Earth and the Moon that accounts for the fact that the Moon does not have a magnetic field.

## Using Math in Science

*Some electric bills include a bar graph of energy usage similar to the one shown below. Use the information provided in the graph to answer the next four questions.*

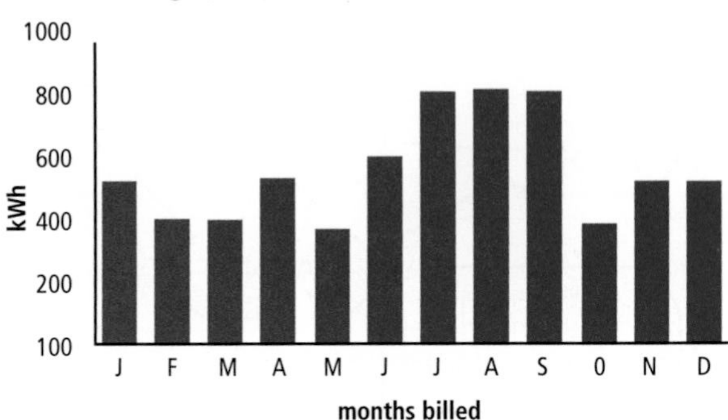


**29.** The first bar in the graph shows energy usage for the month of January. About how much energy, in kWh, was used in January?

**30.** If the appliances in the building have a combined power rating of 2 kW, how many hours were they in use during the month of March? (**Hint:** Use the formula $E = Pt$.)

**31.** The cost of energy was 8 cents per kWh. How much was charged for energy usage in May?

**32.** The most energy is used when the air conditioner is on. During which three months was the air conditioner on?

## the BIG idea

**33. ANALYZE** Look back at pages 76–77. Think about the answer you gave to the question about the large photograph. How has your understanding of magnetism changed? Give examples.

**34. SUMMARIZE** Write a paragraph summarizing the first three pages of this chapter. Use the heading at the top of page 79 as your topic sentence. Explain each red and blue heading.

## UNIT PROJECTS

Evaluate all the data, results, and information from your project folder. Prepare to present your project.

# Standardized Test Practice

For practice on your state test, go to . . .
TEST PRACTICE
CLASSZONE.COM

## Analyzing Tables

The table below lists some major advances in the understanding of electromagnetism.

| Scientist | Year | Advance |
|---|---|---|
| William Gilbert | 1600 | proposes distinction between magnetism and static electricity |
| Pieter van Musschenbroek | 1745 | develops Leyden jar, which stores electric charge |
| Benjamin Franklin | 1752 | shows that lightning is a form of electricity |
| Charles Augustin de Coulomb | 1785 | proves mathematically that, for electricity and magnetism, force changes with distance |
| Alessandro Volta | 1800 | invents battery, first device to generate a continuous current |
| Hans Christian Oersted | 1820 | announces he had used electric current to produce magnetic effects |
| André Marie Ampère | 1820 | shows that wires carrying current attract and repel each other, just like magnets |
| Georg Simon Ohm | 1827 | studies how well different wires conduct electric current |
| Michael Faraday | 1831 | produces electricity with a magnet; invents first electric generator |

*Use the table above to answer the next four questions.*

**1.** Which scientist first produced a device that allowed experimenters to hold an electric charge for later use?

**a.** Coulomb
**b.** Franklin
**c.** Ohm
**d.** van Musschenbroek

**2.** Which scientist developed the first device that could be used to provide a steady source of current to other devices?

**a.** Ampère
**b.** Faraday
**c.** Volta
**d.** Gilbert

**3.** Which scientist had the first experimental evidence that current could produce magnetism?

**a.** Gilbert
**b.** Faraday
**c.** van Musschenbroek
**d.** Oersted

**4.** Why was Coulomb's work important?

**a.** He showed that electricity and magnetism could be stored.

**b.** He showed that electricity and magnetism behave similarly.

**c.** He proved that electricity and magnetism were different.

**d.** He proved that electricity and magnetism were the same.

## Extended Response

*Answer the two questions below in detail. Include some of the terms from the word box. Underline each term you use in your answer.*

| appliance | current | generator |
|---|---|---|
| motor | coil | kilowatt-hour |

**5.** How are electromagnets produced? How can the strength of these devices be increased? How can electromagnets be used in ways that permanent magnets cannot?

**6.** Alix chats online for an average of about an hour a day 6 days a week. Her computer has a power rating of 270 watts. She has a hair dryer with a power rating of 1200 watts. She uses it twice a week for about 15 minutes at a time. Which device is likely to use more power over the course of a year? Why?

# Student Resource Handbooks

## Making Observations

An **observation** is an act of noting and recording an event, characteristic, behavior, or anything else detected with an instrument or with the senses.

Observations allow you to make informed hypotheses and to gather data for experiments. Careful observations often lead to ideas for new experiments. There are two categories of observations:

- **Quantitative observations** can be expressed in numbers and include records of time, temperature, mass, distance, and volume.
- **Qualitative observations** include descriptions of sights, sounds, smells, and textures.

### EXAMPLE

A student dissolved 30 grams of Epsom salts in water, poured the solution into a dish, and let the dish sit out uncovered overnight. The next day, she made the following observations of the Epsom salt crystals that grew in the dish.

To determine the mass, the student found the mass of the dish before and after growing the crystals and then used subtraction to find the difference.

The student measured several crystals and calculated the mean length. (To learn how to calculate the mean of a data set, see page R36.)

Table 1. Observations of Epsom Salt Crystals

| Quantitative Observations | Qualitative Observations |
|---|---|
| • mass = 30 g<br>• mean crystal length = 0.5 cm<br>• longest crystal length = 2 cm | • Crystals are clear.<br>• Crystals are long, thin, and rectangular.<br>• White crust has formed around edge of dish. |
| Photographs or sketches are useful for recording qualitative observations. | 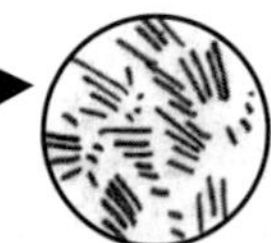 Epsom salt crystals |

### MORE ABOUT OBSERVING

- Make quantitative observations whenever possible. That way, others will know exactly what you observed and be able to compare their results with yours.
- It is always a good idea to make qualitative observations too. You never know when you might observe something unexpected.

# Predicting and Hypothesizing

A **prediction** is an expectation of what will be observed or what will happen. A **hypothesis** is a tentative explanation for an observation or scientific problem that can be tested by further investigation.

SCIENTIFIC THINKING HANDBOOK

### EXAMPLE

Suppose you have made two paper airplanes and you wonder why one of them tends to glide farther than the other one.

1. Start by asking a question.
2. Make an educated guess. After examination, you notice that the wings of the airplane that flies farther are slightly larger than the wings of the other airplane.
3. Write a prediction based upon your educated guess, in the form of an "If . . . , then . . ." statement. Write the independent variable after the word *if,* and the dependent variable after the word *then.*
4. To make a hypothesis, explain why you think what you predicted will occur. Write the explanation after the word *because*.

1. Why does one of the paper airplanes glide farther than the other?

2. The size of an airplane's wings may affect how far the airplane will glide.

3. Prediction: If I make a paper airplane with larger wings, then the airplane will glide farther.

To read about independent and dependent variables, see page R30.

4. Hypothesis: If I make a paper airplane with larger wings, then the airplane will glide farther, because the additional surface area of the wing will produce more lift.

Notice that the part of the hypothesis after *because* adds an explanation of why the airplane will glide farther.

### MORE ABOUT HYPOTHESES

- The results of an experiment cannot prove that a hypothesis is correct. Rather, the results either support or do not support the hypothesis.
- Valuable information is gained even when your hypothesis is not supported by your results. For example, it would be an important discovery to find that wing size is not related to how far an airplane glides.
- In science, a hypothesis is supported only after many scientists have conducted many experiments and produced consistent results.

# Inferring

An **inference** is a logical conclusion drawn from the available evidence and prior knowledge. Inferences are often made from observations.

SCIENTIFIC THINKING HANDBOOK

### EXAMPLE

A student observing a set of acorns noticed something unexpected about one of them. He noticed a white, soft-bodied insect eating its way out of the acorn.

The student recorded these observations.

**Observations**

- There is a hole in the acorn, about 0.5 cm in diameter, where the insect crawled out.
- There is a second hole, which is about the size of a pinhole, on the other side of the acorn.
- The inside of the acorn is hollow.

Here are some inferences that can be made on the basis of the observations.

**Inferences**

- The insect formed from the material inside the acorn, grew to its present size, and ate its way out of the acorn.
- The insect crawled through the smaller hole, ate the inside of the acorn, grew to its present size, and ate its way out of the acorn.
- An egg was laid in the acorn through the smaller hole. The egg hatched into a larva that ate the inside of the acorn, grew to its present size, and ate its way out of the acorn.

When you make inferences, be sure to look at all of the evidence available and combine it with what you already know.

### MORE ABOUT INFERENCES

Inferences depend both on observations and on the knowledge of the people making the inferences. Ancient people who did not know that organisms are produced only by similar organisms might have made an inference like the first one. A student today might look at the same observations and make the second inference. A third student might have knowledge about this particular insect and know that it is never small enough to fit through the smaller hole, leading her to the third inference.

# Identifying Cause and Effect

In a **cause-and-effect relationship,** one event or characteristic is the result of another. Usually an effect follows its cause in time.

There are many examples of cause-and-effect relationships in everyday life.

| Cause | Effect |
|---|---|
| Turn off a light. | Room gets dark. |
| Drop a glass. | Glass breaks. |
| Blow a whistle. | Sound is heard. |

Scientists must be careful not to infer a cause-and-effect relationship just because one event happens after another event. When one event occurs after another, you cannot infer a cause-and-effect relationship on the basis of that information alone. You also cannot conclude that one event caused another if there are alternative ways to explain the second event. A scientist must demonstrate through experimentation or continued observation that an event was truly caused by another event.

**EXAMPLE**

### Make an Observation

Suppose you have a few plants growing outside. When the weather starts getting colder, you bring one of the plants indoors. You notice that the plant you brought indoors is growing faster than the others are growing. You cannot conclude from your observation that the change in temperature was the cause of the increased plant growth, because there are alternative explanations for the observation. Some possible explanations are given below.

- The humidity indoors caused the plant to grow faster.
- The level of sunlight indoors caused the plant to grow faster.
- The indoor plant's being noticed more often and watered more often than the outdoor plants caused it to grow faster.
- The plant that was brought indoors was healthier than the other plants to begin with.

To determine which of these factors, if any, caused the indoor plant to grow faster than the outdoor plants, you would need to design and conduct an experiment.

See pages R28–R35 for information about designing experiments.

# Recognizing Bias

**Television, newspapers, and the Internet are full of experts claiming to have scientific evidence to back up their claims. How do you know whether the claims are really backed up by good science?**

**Bias** is a slanted point of view, or personal prejudice. The goal of scientists is to be as objective as possible and to base their findings on facts instead of opinions. However, bias often affects the conclusions of researchers, and it is important to learn to recognize bias.

When scientific results are reported, you should consider the source of the information as well as the information itself. It is important to critically analyze the information that you see and read.

## SOURCES OF BIAS

There are several ways in which a report of scientific information may be biased. Here are some questions that you can ask yourself:

1. **Who is sponsoring the research?**

   Sometimes, the results of an investigation are biased because an organization paying for the research is looking for a specific answer. This type of bias can affect how data are gathered and interpreted.

2. **Is the research sample large enough?**

   Sometimes research does not include enough data. The larger the sample size, the more likely that the results are accurate, assuming a truly random sample.

3. **In a survey, who is answering the questions?**

   The results of a survey or poll can be biased. The people taking part in the survey may have been specifically chosen because of how they would answer. They may have the same ideas or lifestyles. A survey or poll should make use of a random sample of people.

4. **Are the people who take part in a survey biased?**

   People who take part in surveys sometimes try to answer the questions the way they think the researcher wants them to answer. Also, in surveys or polls that ask for personal information, people may be unwilling to answer questions truthfully.

## SCIENTIFIC BIAS

It is also important to realize that scientists have their own biases because of the types of research they do and because of their scientific viewpoints. Two scientists may look at the same set of data and come to completely different conclusions because of these biases. However, such disagreements are not necessarily bad. In fact, a critical analysis of disagreements is often responsible for moving science forward.

# Identifying Faulty Reasoning

**Faulty reasoning** is wrong or incorrect thinking. It leads to mistakes and to wrong conclusions. Scientists are careful not to draw unreasonable conclusions from experimental data. Without such caution, the results of scientific investigations may be misleading.

### EXAMPLE

Scientists try to make generalizations based on their data to explain as much about nature as possible. If only a small sample of data is looked at, however, a conclusion may be faulty. Suppose a scientist has studied the effects of the El Niño and La Niña weather patterns on flood damage in California from 1989 to 1995. The scientist organized the data in the bar graph below.

**Flood and Storm Damage in California**

Estimated damage (millions of dollars)
2000
1500
1000
500
0
1989 1992 1995
Weak–moderate El Niño
Strong El Niño
Starting year of season (July 1–June 30)

SOURCE: *Governor's Office of Emergency Services, California*

The scientist drew the following conclusions:

1. The La Niña weather pattern has no effect on flooding in California.
2. When neither weather pattern occurs, there is almost no flood damage.
3. A weak or moderate El Niño produces a small or moderate amount of flooding.
4. A strong El Niño produces a lot of flooding.

For the six-year period of the scientist's investigation, these conclusions may seem to be reasonable. However, a six-year study of weather patterns may be too small of a sample for the conclusions to be supported. Consider the following graph, which shows information that was gathered from 1949 to 1997.

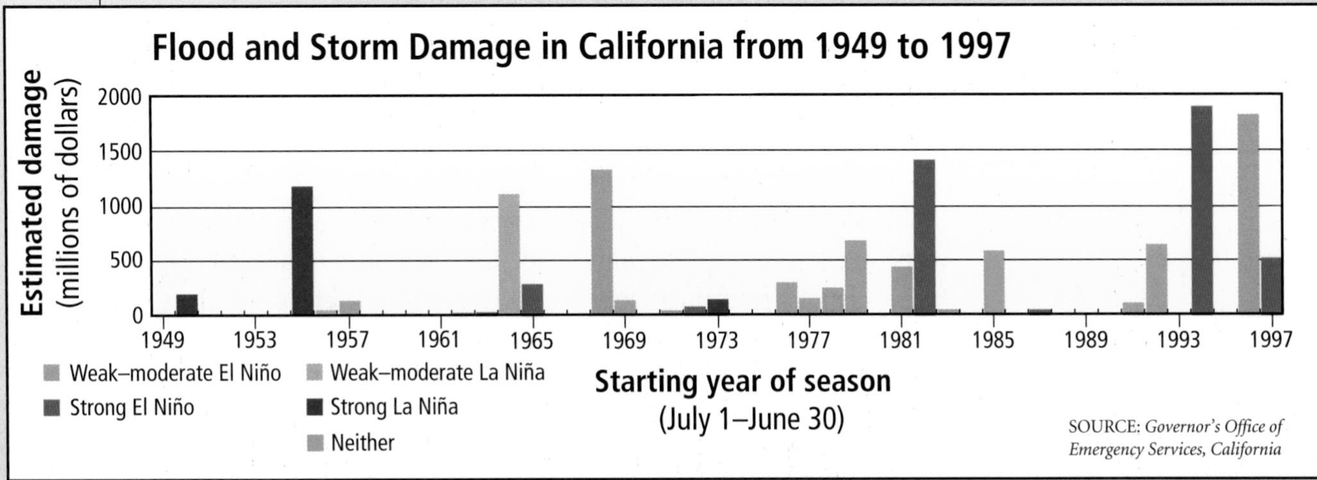


The only one of the conclusions that all of this information supports is number 3: a weak or moderate El Niño produces a small or moderate amount of flooding. By collecting more data, scientists can be more certain of their conclusions and can avoid faulty reasoning.

# Analyzing Statements

To **analyze** a statement is to examine its parts carefully. Scientific findings are often reported through media such as television or the Internet. A report that is made public often focuses on only a small part of research. As a result, it is important to question the sources of information.

## Evaluate Media Claims

To **evaluate** a statement is to judge it on the basis of criteria you've established. Sometimes evaluating means deciding whether a statement is true.

Reports of scientific research and findings in the media may be misleading or incomplete. When you are exposed to this information, you should ask yourself some questions so that you can make informed judgments about the information.

1. **Does the information come from a credible source?**

   Suppose you learn about a new product and it is stated that scientific evidence proves that the product works. A report from a respected news source may be more believable than an advertisement paid for by the product's manufacturer.

2. **How much evidence supports the claim?**

   Often, it may seem that there is new evidence every day of something in the world that either causes or cures an illness. However, information that is the result of several years of work by several different scientists is more credible than an advertisement that does not even cite the subjects of the experiment.

3. **How much information is being presented?**

   Science cannot solve all questions, and scientific experiments often have flaws. A report that discusses problems in a scientific study may be more believable than a report that addresses only positive experimental findings.

4. **Is scientific evidence being presented by a specific source?**

   Sometimes scientific findings are reported by people who are called experts or leaders in a scientific field. But if their names are not given or their scientific credentials are not reported, their statements may be less credible than those of recognized experts.

## Differentiate Between Fact and Opinion

Sometimes information is presented as a fact when it may be an opinion. When scientific conclusions are reported, it is important to recognize whether they are based on solid evidence. Again, you may find it helpful to ask yourself some questions.

1. **What is the difference between a fact and an opinion?**

   A **fact** is a piece of information that can be strictly defined and proved true. An **opinion** is a statement that expresses a belief, value, or feeling. An opinion cannot be proved true or false. For example, a person's age is a fact, but if someone is asked how old they feel, it is impossible to prove the person's answer to be true or false.

2. **Can opinions be measured?**

   Yes, opinions can be measured. In fact, surveys often ask for people's opinions on a topic. But there is no way to know whether or not an opinion is the truth.

### HOW TO DIFFERENTIATE FACT FROM OPINION

**Human Activities and the Environment**

Unfortunately, human use of fossil fuels is one of the most significant developments of the past few centuries. Humans rely on fossil fuels, a non-renewable energy resource, for more than 90 percent of their energy needs.

This careless misuse of our planet's resources has resulted in pollution, global warming, and the destruction of fragile ecosystems. For example, oil pipelines carry more than one million barrels of oil each day across tundra regions. Transporting oil across such areas can only result in oil spills that poison the land for decades.

**Opinions**
Notice words or phrases that express beliefs or feelings. The words *unfortunately* and *careless* show that opinions are being expressed.

**Facts**
Statements that contain statistics tend to be facts. Writers often use facts to support their opinions.

**Opinion**
Look for statements that speculate about events. These statements are opinions, because they cannot be proved.

# Safety Rules

Before you work in the laboratory, read these safety rules twice. Ask your teacher to explain any rules that you do not completely understand. Refer to these rules later on if you have questions about safety in the science classroom.



## Directions

- Read all directions and make sure that you understand them before starting an investigation or lab activity. If you do not understand how to do a procedure or how to use a piece of equipment, ask your teacher.
- Do not begin any investigation or touch any equipment until your teacher has told you to start.
- Never experiment on your own. If you want to try a procedure that the directions do not call for, ask your teacher for permission first.
- If you are hurt or injured in any way, tell your teacher immediately.

## Dress Code

goggles

apron

gloves

- Wear goggles when
  - — using glassware, sharp objects, or chemicals
  - — heating an object
  - — working with anything that can easily fly up into the air and hurt someone's eye
- Tie back long hair or hair that hangs in front of your eyes.
- Remove any article of clothing—such as a loose sweater or a scarf—that hangs down and may touch a flame, chemical, or piece of equipment.
- Observe all safety icons calling for the wearing of eye protection, gloves, and aprons.

## Heating and Fire Safety

fire safety

heating safety

- Keep your work area neat, clean, and free of extra materials.
- Never reach over a flame or heat source.
- Point objects being heated away from you and others.
- Never heat a substance or an object in a closed container.
- Never touch an object that has been heated. If you are unsure whether something is hot, treat it as though it is. Use oven mitts, clamps, tongs, or a test-tube holder.
- Know where the fire extinguisher and fire blanket are kept in your classroom.
- Do not throw hot substances into the trash. Wait for them to cool or use the container your teacher puts out for disposal.

## Electrical Safety

electrical safety

- Never use lamps or other electrical equipment with frayed cords.
- Make sure no cord is lying on the floor where someone can trip over it.
- Do not let a cord hang over the side of a counter or table so that the equipment can easily be pulled or knocked to the floor.
- Never let cords hang into sinks or other places where water can be found.
- Never try to fix electrical problems. Inform your teacher of any problems immediately.
- Unplug an electrical cord by pulling on the plug, not the cord.

## Chemical Safety

chemical safety

poison

fumes

- If you spill a chemical or get one on your skin or in your eyes, tell your teacher right away.
- Never touch, taste, or sniff any chemicals in the lab. If you need to determine odor, waft. Wafting consists of holding the chemical in its container 15 centimeters (6 in.) away from your nose, and using your fingers to bring fumes from the container to your nose.
- Keep lids on all chemicals you are not using.
- Never put unused chemicals back into the original containers. Throw away extra chemicals where your teacher tells you to.
- Pour chemicals over a sink or your work area, not over the floor.
- If you get a chemical in your eye, use the eyewash right away.
- Always wash your hands after handling chemicals, plants, or soil.

Wafting

## Glassware and Sharp-Object Safety

sharp objects

- If you break glassware, tell your teacher right away.
- Do not use broken or chipped glassware. Give these to your teacher.
- Use knives and other cutting instruments carefully. Always wear eye protection and cut away from you.

## Animal Safety

- Never hurt an animal.
- Touch animals only when necessary. Follow your teacher's instructions for handling animals.
- Always wash your hands after working with animals.

## Cleanup

disposal

- Follow your teacher's instructions for throwing away or putting away supplies.
- Clean your work area and pick up anything that has dropped to the floor.
- Wash your hands.

# Using Lab Equipment

Different experiments require different types of equipment. But even though experiments differ, the ways in which the equipment is used are the same.

## Beakers

- Use beakers for holding and pouring liquids.
- Do not use a beaker to measure the volume of a liquid. Use a graduated cylinder instead. (See page R16.)
- Use a beaker that holds about twice as much liquid as you need. For example, if you need 100 milliliters of water, you should use a 200- or 250-milliliter beaker.

## Test Tubes

- Use test tubes to hold small amounts of substances.
- Do not use a test tube to measure the volume of a liquid.
- Use a test tube when heating a substance over a flame. Aim the mouth of the tube away from yourself and other people.
- Liquids easily spill or splash from test tubes, so it is important to use only small amounts of liquids.

## Test-Tube Holder

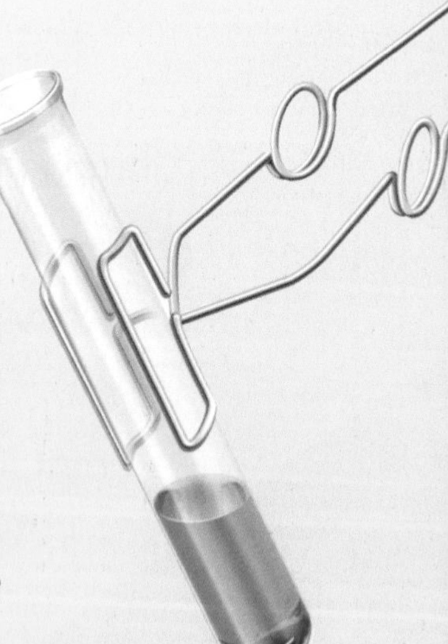

- Use a test-tube holder when heating a substance in a test tube.
- Use a test-tube holder if the substance in a test tube is dangerous to touch.
- Make sure the test-tube holder tightly grips the test tube so that the test tube will not slide out of the holder.
- Make sure that the test-tube holder is above the surface of the substance in the test tube so that you can observe the substance.

LAB HANDBOOK

## Test-Tube Rack

- Use a test-tube rack to organize test tubes before, during, and after an experiment.
- Use a test-tube rack to keep test tubes upright so that they do not fall over and spill their contents.
- Use a test-tube rack that is the correct size for the test tubes that you are using. If the rack is too small, a test tube may become stuck. If the rack is too large, a test tube may lean over, and some of its contents may spill or splash.

## Forceps

- Use forceps when you need to pick up or hold a very small object that should not be touched with your hands.
- Do not use forceps to hold anything over a flame, because forceps are not long enough to keep your hand safely away from the flame. Plastic forceps will melt, and metal forceps will conduct heat and burn your hand.

## Hot Plate

- Use a hot plate when a substance needs to be kept warmer than room temperature for a long period of time.
- Use a hot plate instead of a Bunsen burner or a candle when you need to carefully control temperature.
- Do not use a hot plate when a substance needs to be burned in an experiment.
- Always use "hot hands" safety mitts or oven mitts when handling anything that has been heated on a hot plate.

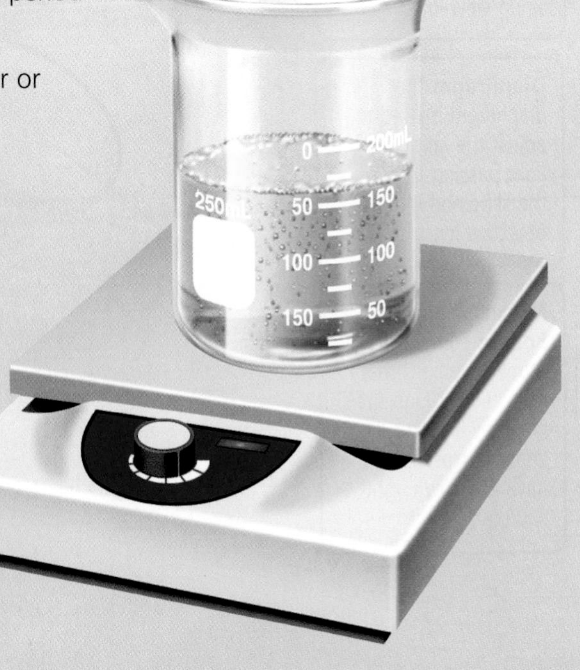


LAB HANDBOOK

## Microscope

Scientists use microscopes to see very small objects that cannot easily be seen with the eye alone. A microscope magnifies the image of an object so that small details may be observed. A microscope that you may use can magnify an object 400 times—the object will appear 400 times larger than its actual size.

**Eyepiece** Objects are viewed through the eyepiece. The eyepiece contains a lens that commonly magnifies an image 10 times.

**Body** The body separates the lens in the eyepiece from the objective lenses below.

**Coarse Adjustment** This knob is used to focus the image of an object when it is viewed through the low-power lens.

**Nosepiece** The nosepiece holds the objective lenses above the stage and rotates so that all lenses may be used.

**Fine Adjustment** This knob is used to focus the image of an object when it is viewed through the high-power lens.

**High-Power Objective Lens** This is the largest lens on the nosepiece. It magnifies an image approximately 40 times.

**Low-Power Objective Lens** This is the smallest lens on the nosepiece. It magnifies an image approximately 10 times.

**Stage** The stage supports the object being viewed.

**Arm** The arm supports the body above the stage. Always carry a microscope by the arm and base.

**Diaphragm** The diaphragm is used to adjust the amount of light passing through the slide and into an objective lens.

**Stage Clip** The stage clip holds a slide in place on the stage.

**Mirror or Light Source** Some microscopes use light that is reflected through the stage by a mirror. Other microscopes have their own light sources.

**Base** The base supports the microscope.

## VIEWING AN OBJECT

1. Use the coarse adjustment knob to raise the body tube.
2. Adjust the diaphragm so that you can see a bright circle of light through the eyepiece.
3. Place the object or slide on the stage. Be sure that it is centered over the hole in the stage.
4. Turn the nosepiece to click the low-power lens into place.
5. Using the coarse adjustment knob, slowly lower the lens and focus on the specimen being viewed. Be sure not to touch the slide or object with the lens.
6. When switching from the low-power lens to the high-power lens, first raise the body tube with the coarse adjustment knob so that the high-power lens will not hit the slide.
7. Turn the nosepiece to click the high-power lens into place.
8. Use the fine adjustment knob to focus on the specimen being viewed. Again, be sure not to touch the slide or object with the lens.

## MAKING A SLIDE, OR WET MOUNT

1 Place the specimen in the center of a clean slide.

2 Place a drop of water on the specimen.

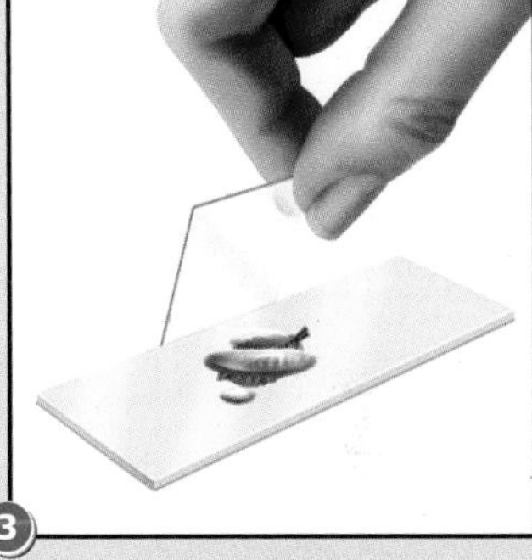

3 Place a cover slip on the slide. Put one edge of the cover slip into the drop of water and slowly lower it over the specimen.

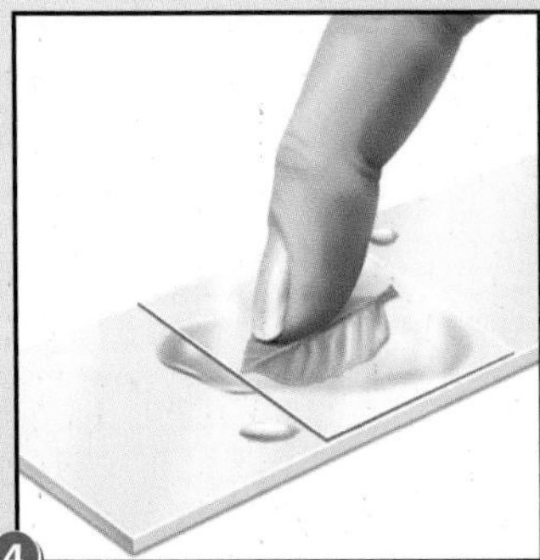

4 Remove any air bubbles from under the cover slip by gently tapping the cover slip.

5 Dry any excess water before placing the slide on the microscope stage for viewing.

## Spring Scale (Force Meter)

- Use a spring scale to measure a force pulling on the scale.
- Use a spring scale to measure the force of gravity exerted on an object by Earth.
- To measure a force accurately, a spring scale must be zeroed before it is used. The scale is zeroed when no weight is attached and the indicator is positioned at zero.
- Do not attach a weight that is either too heavy or too light to a spring scale. A weight that is too heavy could break the scale or exert too great a force for the scale to measure. A weight that is too light may not exert enough force to be measured accurately.

## Graduated Cylinder

- Use a graduated cylinder to measure the volume of a liquid.
- Be sure that the graduated cylinder is on a flat surface so that your measurement will be accurate.
- When reading the scale on a graduated cylinder, be sure to have your eyes at the level of the surface of the liquid.
- The surface of the liquid will be curved in the graduated cylinder. Read the volume of the liquid at the bottom of the curve, or meniscus (muh-NIHS-kuhs).
- You can use a graduated cylinder to find the volume of a solid object by measuring the increase in a liquid's level after you add the object to the cylinder.

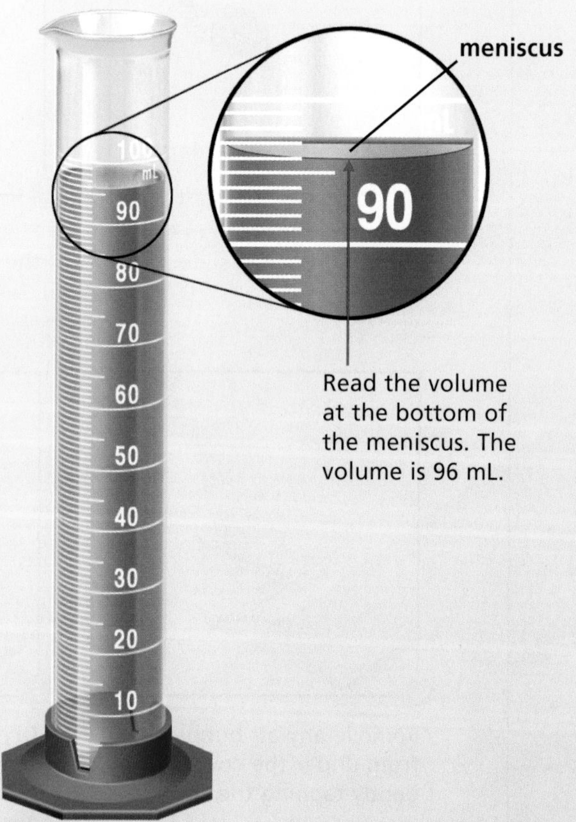


Read the volume at the bottom of the meniscus. The volume is 96 mL.

## Metric Rulers

- Use metric rulers or meter sticks to measure objects' lengths.
- Do not measure an object from the end of a metric ruler or meter stick, because the end is often imperfect. Instead, measure from the 1-centimeter mark, but remember to subtract a centimeter from the apparent measurement.
- Estimate any lengths that extend between marked units. For example, if a meter stick shows centimeters but not millimeters, you can estimate the length that an object extends between centimeter marks to measure it to the nearest millimeter.
- **Controlling Variables** If you are taking repeated measurements, always measure from the same point each time. For example, if you're measuring how high two different balls bounce when dropped from the same height, measure both bounces at the same point on the balls—either the top or the bottom. Do not measure at the top of one ball and the bottom of the other.

**EXAMPLE**

### How to Measure a Leaf

1. Lay a ruler flat on top of the leaf so that the 1-centimeter mark lines up with one end. Make sure the ruler and the leaf do not move between the time you line them up and the time you take the measurement.
2. Look straight down on the ruler so that you can see exactly how the marks line up with the other end of the leaf.
3. Estimate the length by which the leaf extends beyond a marking. For example, the leaf below extends about halfway between the 4.2-centimeter and 4.3-centimeter marks, so the apparent measurement is about 4.25 centimeters.
4. Remember to subtract 1 centimeter from your apparent measurement, since you started at the 1-centimeter mark on the ruler and not at the end. The leaf is about 3.25 centimeters long (4.25 cm – 1 cm = 3.25 cm).

LAB HANDBOOK

## Triple-Beam Balance

This balance has a pan and three beams with sliding masses, called riders. At one end of the beams is a pointer that indicates whether the mass on the pan is equal to the masses shown on the beams.

1. Make sure the balance is zeroed before measuring the mass of an object. The balance is zeroed if the pointer is at zero when nothing is on the pan and the riders are at their zero points. Use the adjustment knob at the base of the balance to zero it.
2. Place the object to be measured on the pan.
3. Move the riders one notch at a time away from the pan. Begin with the largest rider. If moving the largest rider one notch brings the pointer below zero, begin measuring the mass of the object with the next smaller rider.
4. Change the positions of the riders until they balance the mass on the pan and the pointer is at zero. Then add the readings from the three beams to determine the mass of the object.

| | |
|---|---|
| 300 g | position of largest rider |
| 90 g | position of middle rider |
| + 3 g | position of smallest rider |
| 393 g | mass of beaker |

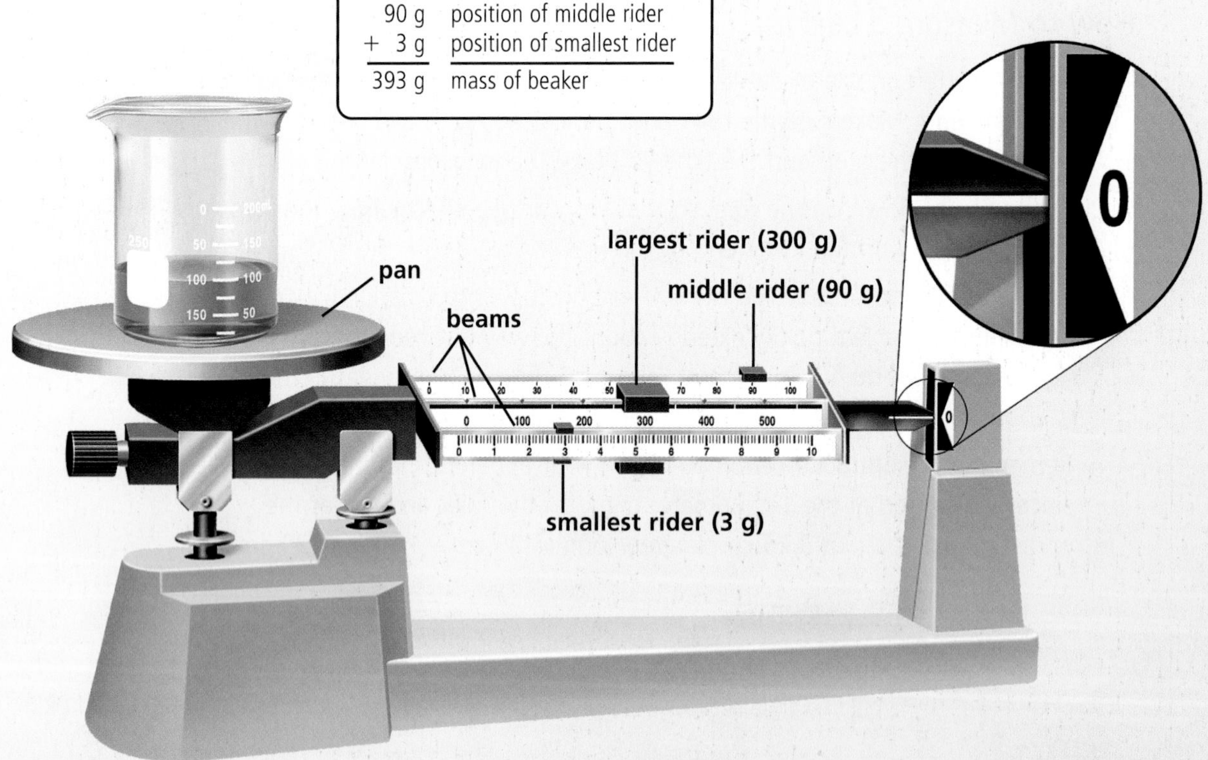

## Double-Pan Balance

This type of balance has two pans. Between the pans is a pointer that indicates whether the masses on the pans are equal.

1. Make sure the balance is zeroed before measuring the mass of an object. The balance is zeroed if the pointer is at zero when there is nothing on either of the pans. Many double-pan balances have sliding knobs that can be used to zero them.
2. Place the object to be measured on one of the pans.
3. Begin adding standard masses to the other pan. Begin with the largest standard mass. If this adds too much mass to the balance, begin measuring the mass of the object with the next smaller standard mass.
4. Add standard masses until the masses on both pans are balanced and the pointer is at zero. Then add the standard masses together to determine the mass of the object being measured.

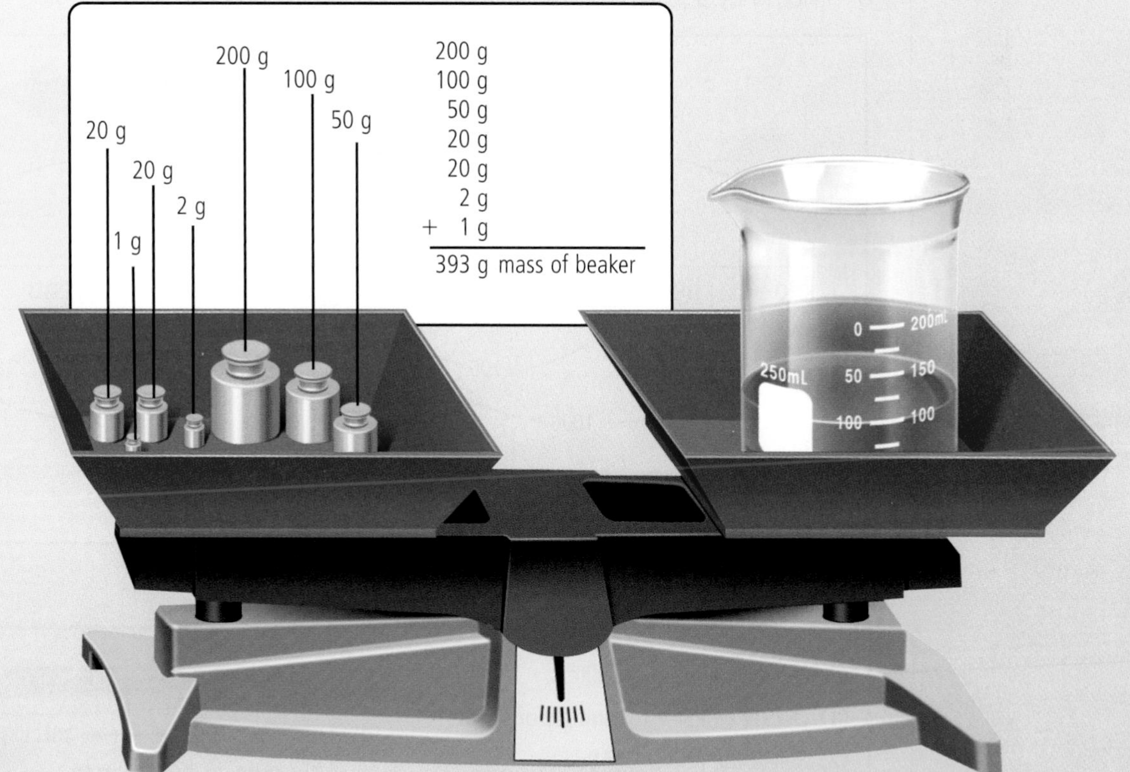


Never place chemicals or liquids directly on a pan. Instead, use the following procedure:

1. Determine the mass of an empty container, such as a beaker.
2. Pour the substance into the container, and measure the total mass of the substance and the container.
3. Subtract the mass of the empty container from the total mass to find the mass of the substance.

# The Metric System and SI Units

Scientists use International System (SI) units for measurements of distance, volume, mass, and temperature. The International System is based on multiples of ten and the metric system of measurement.

| Basic SI Units | | |
|---|---|---|
| **Property** | **Name** | **Symbol** |
| length | meter | m |
| volume | liter | L |
| mass | kilogram | kg |
| temperature | kelvin | K |

| SI Prefixes | | |
|---|---|---|
| **Prefix** | **Symbol** | **Multiple of 10** |
| kilo- | k | 1000 |
| hecto- | h | 100 |
| deca- | da | 10 |
| deci- | d | 0.1 $(\frac{1}{10})$ |
| centi- | c | 0.01 $(\frac{1}{100})$ |
| milli- | m | 0.001 $(\frac{1}{1000})$ |

## Changing Metric Units

You can change from one unit to another in the metric system by multiplying or dividing by a power of 10.

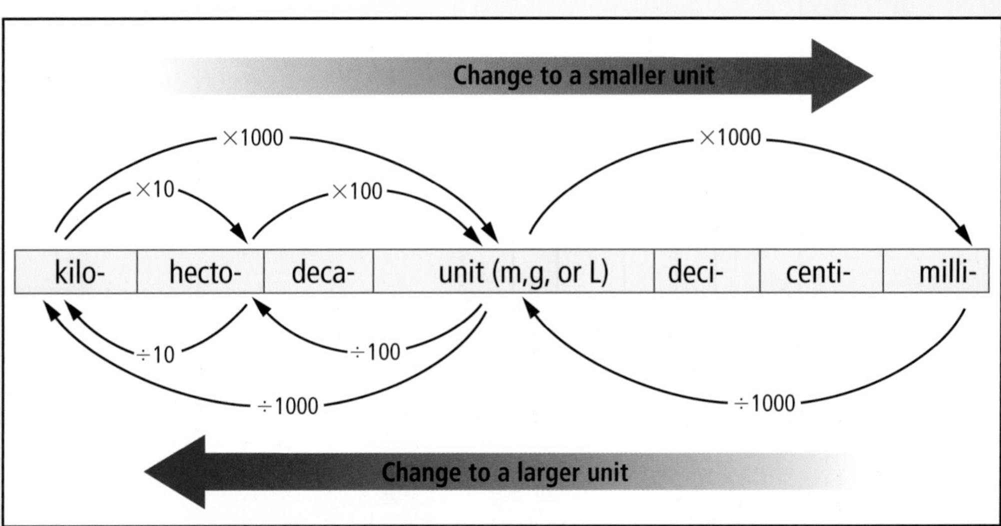


### Example

Change 0.64 liters to milliliters.

**(1)** Decide whether to multiply or divide.

**(2)** Select the power of 10.

**ANSWER** 0.64 L = 640 mL

**Change to a smaller unit by multiplying.**

L —— ×1000 ——→ mL

**0.64** × 1000 = **640.**

### Example

Change 23.6 grams to kilograms.

**(1)** Decide whether to multiply or divide.

**(2)** Select the power of 10.

**ANSWER** 23.6 g = 0.0236 kg

**Change to a larger unit by dividing.**

kg ←—— ÷ 1000 —— g

**23.6** ÷ 1000 = **0.0236**



LAB HANDBOOK

## Temperature Conversions

Even though the kelvin is the SI base unit of temperature, the degree Celsius will be the unit you use most often in your science studies. The formulas below show the relationships between temperatures in degrees Fahrenheit (°F), degrees Celsius (°C), and kelvins (K).

$$°C = \frac{5}{9}(°F - 32)$$

$$°F = \frac{9}{5}°C + 32$$

$$K = °C + 273$$

See page R42 for help with using formulas.

**Examples of Temperature Conversions**

| Condition | Degrees Celsius | Degrees Fahrenheit |
|---|---|---|
| Freezing point of water | 0 | 32 |
| Cool day | 10 | 50 |
| Mild day | 20 | 68 |
| Warm day | 30 | 86 |
| Normal body temperature | 37 | 98.6 |
| Very hot day | 40 | 104 |
| Boiling point of water | 100 | 212 |

## Converting Between SI and U.S. Customary Units

Use the chart below when you need to convert between SI units and U.S. customary units.

| SI Unit | From SI to U.S. Customary | | | From U.S. Customary to SI | | |
|---|---|---|---|---|---|---|
| **Length** | **When you know** | **multiply by** | **to find** | **When you know** | **multiply by** | **to find** |
| kilometer (km) = 1000 m | kilometers | 0.62 | miles | miles | 1.61 | kilometers |
| meter (m) = 100 cm | meters | 3.28 | feet | feet | 0.3048 | meters |
| centimeter (cm) = 10 mm | centimeters | 0.39 | inches | inches | 2.54 | centimeters |
| millimeter (mm) = 0.1 cm | millimeters | 0.04 | inches | inches | 25.4 | millimeters |
| **Area** | **When you know** | **multiply by** | **to find** | **When you know** | **multiply by** | **to find** |
| square kilometer ($km^2$) | square kilometers | 0.39 | square miles | square miles | 2.59 | square kilometers |
| square meter ($m^2$) | square meters | 1.2 | square yards | square yards | 0.84 | square meters |
| square centimeter ($cm^2$) | square centimeters | 0.155 | square inches | square inches | 6.45 | square centimeters |
| **Volume** | **When you know** | **multiply by** | **to find** | **When you know** | **multiply by** | **to find** |
| liter (L) = 1000 mL | liters | 1.06 | quarts | quarts | 0.95 | liters |
| | liters | 0.26 | gallons | gallons | 3.79 | liters |
| | liters | 4.23 | cups | cups | 0.24 | liters |
| | liters | 2.12 | pints | pints | 0.47 | liters |
| milliliter (mL) = 0.001 L | milliliters | 0.20 | teaspoons | teaspoons | 4.93 | milliliters |
| | milliliters | 0.07 | tablespoons | tablespoons | 14.79 | milliliters |
| | milliliters | 0.03 | fluid ounces | fluid ounces | 29.57 | milliliters |
| **Mass** | **When you know** | **multiply by** | **to find** | **When you know** | **multiply by** | **to find** |
| kilogram (kg) = 1000 g | kilograms | 2.2 | pounds | pounds | 0.45 | kilograms |
| gram (g) = 1000 mg | grams | 0.035 | ounces | ounces | 28.35 | grams |

# Precision and Accuracy

When you do an experiment, it is important that your methods, observations, and data be both precise and accurate.

low precision

precision, but not accuracy

precision and accuracy



## Precision

In science, **precision** is the exactness and consistency of measurements. For example, measurements made with a ruler that has both centimeter and millimeter markings would be more precise than measurements made with a ruler that has only centimeter markings. Another indicator of precision is the care taken to make sure that methods and observations are as exact and consistent as possible. Every time a particular experiment is done, the same procedure should be used. Precision is necessary because experiments are repeated several times and if the procedure changes, the results will change.

### EXAMPLE

Suppose you are measuring temperatures over a two-week period. Your precision will be greater if you measure each temperature at the same place, at the same time of day, and with the same thermometer than if you change any of these factors from one day to the next.

## Accuracy

In science, it is possible to be precise but not accurate. **Accuracy** depends on the difference between a measurement and an actual value. The smaller the difference, the more accurate the measurement.

### EXAMPLE

Suppose you look at a stream and estimate that it is about 1 meter wide at a particular place. You decide to check your estimate by measuring the stream with a meter stick, and you determine that the stream is 1.32 meters wide. However, because it is hard to measure the width of a stream with a meter stick, it turns out that you didn't do a very good job. The stream is actually 1.14 meters wide. Therefore, even though your estimate was less precise than your measurement, your estimate was actually more accurate.

# Making Data Tables and Graphs

Data tables and graphs are useful tools for both recording and communicating scientific data.

## Making Data Tables

You can use a **data table** to organize and record the measurements that you make. Some examples of information that might be recorded in data tables are frequencies, times, and amounts.

**EXAMPLE**

Suppose you are investigating photosynthesis in two elodea plants. One sits in direct sunlight, and the other sits in a dimly lit room. You measure the rate of photosynthesis by counting the number of bubbles in the jar every ten minutes.

1. Title and number your data table.
2. Decide how you will organize the table into columns and rows.
3. Any units, such as seconds or degrees, should be included in column headings, not in the individual cells.

Table 1. Number of Bubbles from Elodea

| Time (min) | Sunlight | Dim Light |
|---|---|---|
| 0 | 0 | 0 |
| 10 | 15 | 5 |
| 20 | 25 | 8 |
| 30 | 32 | 7 |
| 40 | 41 | 10 |
| 50 | 47 | 9 |
| 60 | 42 | 9 |

Always number and title data tables.

The data in the table above could also be organized in a different way.

Table 1. Number of Bubbles from Elodea

| Light Condition | Time (min) | | | | | | |
|---|---|---|---|---|---|---|---|
| | 0 | 10 | 20 | 30 | 40 | 50 | 60 |
| Sunlight | 0 | 15 | 25 | 32 | 41 | 47 | 42 |
| Dim light | 0 | 5 | 8 | 7 | 10 | 9 | 9 |

Put units in column heading.

## Making Line Graphs

You can use a **line graph** to show a relationship between variables. Line graphs are particularly useful for showing changes in variables over time.

### EXAMPLE

Suppose you are interested in graphing temperature data that you collected over the course of a day.

Table 1. Outside Temperature During the Day on March 7

| | Time of Day | | | | | | |
|---|---|---|---|---|---|---|---|
| | 7:00 A.M. | 9:00 A.M. | 11:00 A.M. | 1:00 P.M. | 3:00 P.M. | 5:00 P.M. | 7:00 P.M. |
| Temp (°C) | 8 | 9 | 11 | 14 | 12 | 10 | 6 |

1. Use the vertical axis of your line graph for the variable that you are measuring—temperature.
2. Choose scales for both the horizontal axis and the vertical axis of the graph. You should have two points more than you need on the vertical axis, and the horizontal axis should be long enough for all of the data points to fit.
3. Draw and label each axis.
4. Graph each value. First find the appropriate point on the scale of the horizontal axis. Imagine a line that rises vertically from that place on the scale. Then find the corresponding value on the vertical axis, and imagine a line that moves horizontally from that value. The point where these two imaginary lines intersect is where the value should be plotted.
5. Connect the points with straight lines.

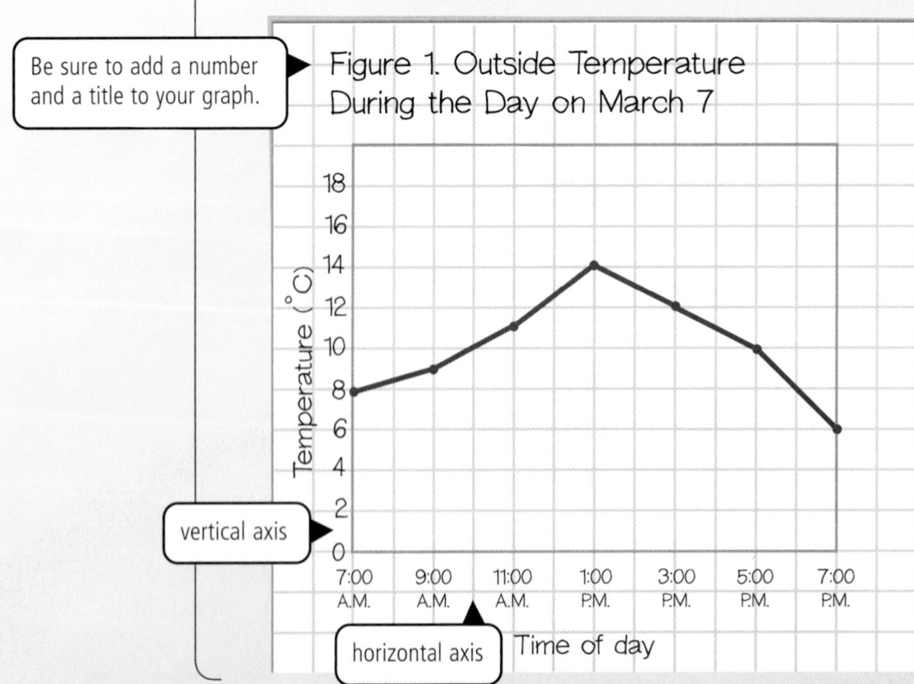


LAB HANDBOOK

## Making Circle Graphs

You can use a **circle graph,** sometimes called a pie chart, to represent data as parts of a circle. Circle graphs are used only when the data can be expressed as percentages of a whole. The entire circle shown in a circle graph is equal to 100 percent of the data.

### EXAMPLE

Suppose you identified the species of each mature tree growing in a small wooded area. You organized your data in a table, but you also want to show the data in a circle graph.

1. To begin, find the total number of mature trees.

   $56 + 34 + 22 + 10 + 28 = 150$

2. To find the degree measure for each sector of the circle, write a fraction comparing the number of each tree species with the total number of trees. Then multiply the fraction by 360°.

   Oak: $\frac{56}{150} \times 360° = 134.4°$

3. Draw a circle. Use a protractor to draw the angle for each sector of the graph.
4. Color and label each sector of the graph.
5. Give the graph a number and title.

Table 1. Tree Species in Wooded Area

| Species | Number of Specimens |
|---|---|
| Oak | 56 |
| Maple | 34 |
| Birch | 22 |
| Willow | 10 |
| Pine | 28 |

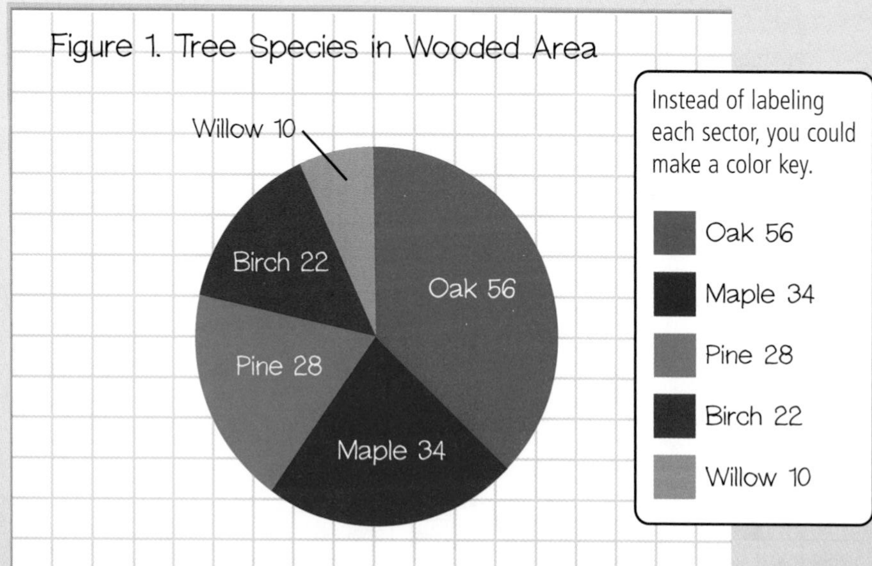


Figure 1. Tree Species in Wooded Area

Instead of labeling each sector, you could make a color key.

- Oak 56
- Maple 34
- Pine 28
- Birch 22
- Willow 10

LAB HANDBOOK

## Bar Graph

A **bar graph** is a type of graph in which the lengths of the bars are used to represent and compare data. A numerical scale is used to determine the lengths of the bars.

### EXAMPLE

To determine the effect of water on seed sprouting, three cups were filled with sand, and ten seeds were planted in each. Different amounts of water were added to each cup over a three-day period.

Table 1. Effect of Water on Seed Sprouting

| Daily Amount of Water (mL) | Number of Seeds That Sprouted After 3 Days in Sand |
|---|---|
| 0 | 1 |
| 10 | 4 |
| 20 | 8 |

1. Choose a numerical scale. The greatest value is 8, so the end of the scale should have a value greater than 8, such as 10. Use equal increments along the scale, such as increments of 2.
2. Draw and label the axes. Mark intervals on the vertical axis according to the scale you chose.
3. Draw a bar for each data value. Use the scale to decide how long to make each bar.

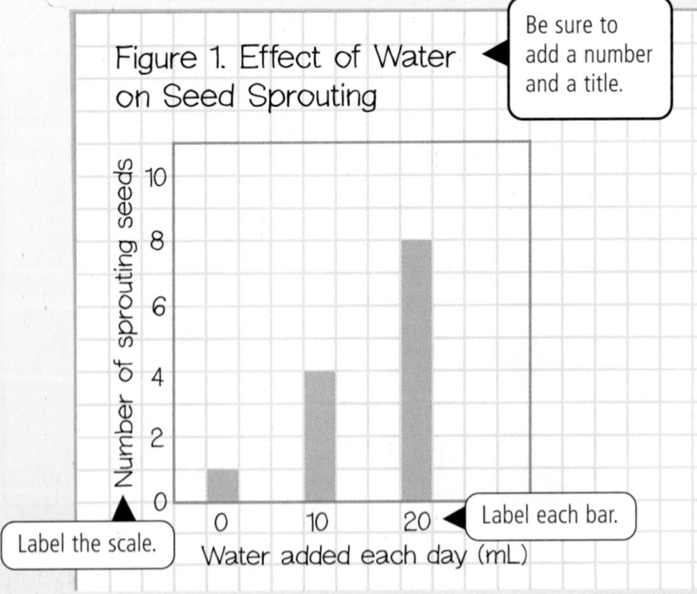


LAB HANDBOOK

## Double Bar Graph

A **double bar graph** is a bar graph that shows two sets of data. The two bars for each measurement are drawn next to each other.

### EXAMPLE

The seed-sprouting experiment was done using both sand and potting soil. The data for sand and potting soil can be plotted on one graph.

1. Draw one set of bars, using the data for sand, as shown below.
2. Draw bars for the potting-soil data next to the bars for the sand data. Shade them a different color. Add a key.

Table 2. Effect of Water and Soil on Seed Sprouting

| Daily Amount of Water (mL) | Number of Seeds That Sprouted After 3 Days in Sand | Number of Seeds That Sprouted After 3 Days in Potting Soil |
|---|---|---|
| 0 | 1 | 2 |
| 10 | 4 | 5 |
| 20 | 8 | 9 |

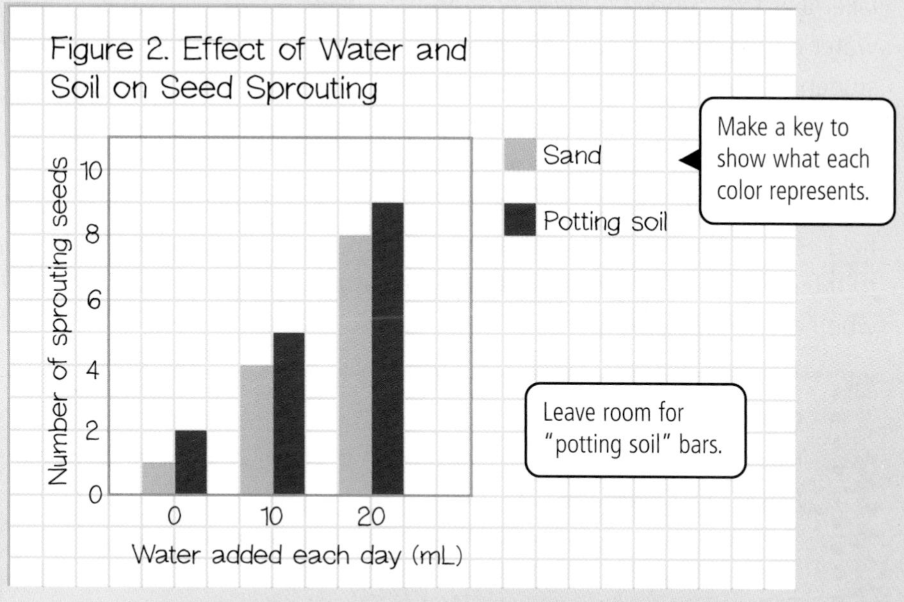

# Designing an Experiment

Use this section when designing or conducting an experiment.

## Determining a Purpose

You can find a purpose for an experiment by doing research, by examining the results of a previous experiment, or by observing the world around you. An **experiment** is an organized procedure to study something under controlled conditions.

Don't forget to learn as much as possible about your topic before you begin.

1. Write the purpose of your experiment as a question or problem that you want to investigate.
2. Write down research questions and begin searching for information that will help you design an experiment. Consult the library, the Internet, and other people as you conduct your research.

**EXAMPLE**

Middle school students observed an odor near the lake by their school. They also noticed that the water on the side of the lake near the school was greener than the water on the other side of the lake. The students did some research to learn more about their observations. They discovered that the odor and green color in the lake came from algae. They also discovered that a new fertilizer was being used on a field nearby. The students inferred that the use of the fertilizer might be related to the presence of the algae and designed a controlled experiment to find out whether they were right.

**Problem**

How does fertilizer affect the presence of algae in a lake?

**Research Questions**

- Have other experiments been done on this problem? If so, what did those experiments show?
- What kind of fertilizer is used on the field? How much?
- How do algae grow?
- How do people measure algae?
- Can fertilizer and algae be used safely in a lab? How?

**Research**
As you research, you may find a topic that is more interesting to you than your original topic, or learn that a procedure you wanted to use is not practical or safe. It is OK to change your purpose as you research.

LAB HANDBOOK

## Writing a Hypothesis

A **hypothesis** is a tentative explanation for an observation or scientific problem that can be tested by further investigation. You can write your hypothesis in the form of an "If . . . , then . . . , because . . ." statement.

Hypothesis

If the amount of fertilizer in lake water is increased, then the amount of algae will also increase, because fertilizers provide nutrients that algae need to grow.

**Hypotheses**
For help with hypotheses, refer to page R3.

## Determining Materials

Make a list of all the materials you will need to do your experiment. Be specific, especially if someone else is helping you obtain the materials. Try to think of everything you will need.

Materials

- 1 large jar or container
- 4 identical smaller containers
- rubber gloves that also cover the arms
- sample of fertilizer-and-water solution
- eyedropper
- clear plastic wrap
- scissors
- masking tape
- marker
- ruler

## Determining Variables and Constants

### EXPERIMENTAL GROUP AND CONTROL GROUP

An experiment to determine how two factors are related always has two groups—a control group and an experimental group.

1. Design an experimental group. Include as many trials as possible in the experimental group in order to obtain reliable results.
2. Design a control group that is the same as the experimental group in every way possible, except for the factor you wish to test.

**Experimental Group:** two containers of lake water with one drop of fertilizer solution added to each

**Control Group:** two containers of lake water with no fertilizer solution added

Go back to your materials list and make sure you have enough items listed to cover both your experimental group and your control group.

LAB HANDBOOK

### VARIABLES AND CONSTANTS

Identify the variables and constants in your experiment. In a controlled experiment, a **variable** is any factor that can change. **Constants** are all of the factors that are the same in both the experimental group and the control group.

**Hypothesis**
If the amount of fertilizer in lake water is increased, then the amount of algae will also increase, because fertilizers provide nutrients that algae need to grow.

1. Read your hypothesis. The **independent variable** is the factor that you wish to test and that is manipulated or changed so that it can be tested. The independent variable is expressed in your hypothesis after the word *if*. Identify the independent variable in your laboratory report.
2. The **dependent variable** is the factor that you measure to gather results. It is expressed in your hypothesis after the word *then*. Identify the dependent variable in your laboratory report.

Table 1. Variables and Constants in Algae Experiment

| Independent Variable | Dependent Variable | Constants |
|---|---|---|
| Amount of fertilizer in lake water | Amount of algae that grow | • Where the lake water is obtained<br>• Type of container used<br>• Light and temperature conditions where water will be stored |

Set up your experiment so that you will test only one variable.

## MEASURING THE DEPENDENT VARIABLE

Before starting your experiment, you need to define how you will measure the dependent variable. An **operational definition** is a description of the one particular way in which you will measure the dependent variable.

Your operational definition is important for several reasons. First, in any experiment there are several ways in which a dependent variable can be measured. Second, the procedure of the experiment depends on how you decide to measure the dependent variable. Third, your operational definition makes it possible for other people to evaluate and build on your experiment.

### EXAMPLE 1

An operational definition of a dependent variable can be qualitative. That is, your measurement of the dependent variable can simply be an observation of whether a change occurs as a result of a change in the independent variable. This type of operational definition can be thought of as a "yes or no" measurement.

Table 2. Qualitative Operational Definition of Algae Growth

| Independent Variable | Dependent Variable | Operational Definition |
|---|---|---|
| Amount of fertilizer in lake water | Amount of algae that grow | Algae grow in lake water |

A qualitative measurement of a dependent variable is often easy to make and record. However, this type of information does not provide a great deal of detail in your experimental results.

### EXAMPLE 2

An operational definition of a dependent variable can be quantitative. That is, your measurement of the dependent variable can be a number that shows how much change occurs as a result of a change in the independent variable.

Table 3. Quantitative Operational Definition of Algae Growth

| Independent Variable | Dependent Variable | Operational Definition |
|---|---|---|
| Amount of fertilizer in lake water | Amount of algae that grow | Diameter of largest algal growth (in mm) |

A quantitative measurement of a dependent variable can be more difficult to make and analyze than a qualitative measurement. However, this type of data provides much more information about your experiment and is often more useful.

## Writing a Procedure

Write each step of your procedure. Start each step with a verb, or action word, and keep the steps short. Your procedure should be clear enough for someone else to use as instructions for repeating your experiment.

If necessary, go back to your materials list and add any materials that you left out.

**Procedure**

1. Put on your gloves. Use the large container to obtain a sample of lake water.
2. Divide the sample of lake water equally among the four smaller containers.
3. Use the eyedropper to add one drop of fertilizer solution to two of the containers.
4. Use the masking tape and the marker to label the containers with your initials, the date, and the identifiers "Jar 1 with Fertilizer," "Jar 2 with Fertilizer," "Jar 1 without Fertilizer," and "Jar 2 without Fertilizer."
5. Cover the containers with clear plastic wrap. Use the scissors to punch ten holes in each of the covers.
6. Place all four containers on a window ledge. Make sure that they all receive the same amount of light.
7. Observe the containers every day for one week.
8. Use the ruler to measure the diameter of the largest clump of algae in each container, and record your measurements daily.

**Controlling Variables**
The same amount of fertilizer solution must be added to two of the four containers.

**Controlling Variables**
All four containers must receive the same amount of light.

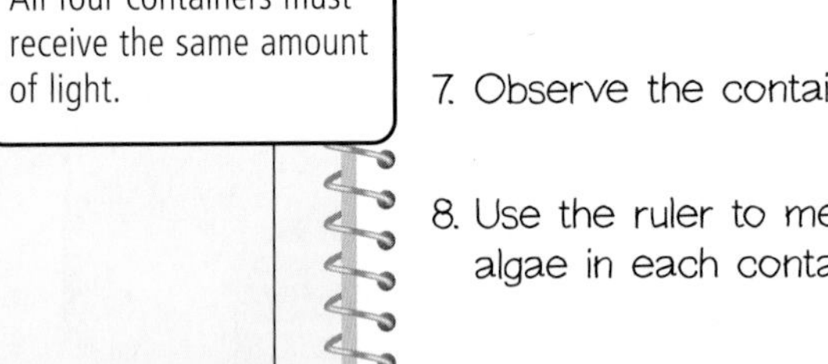

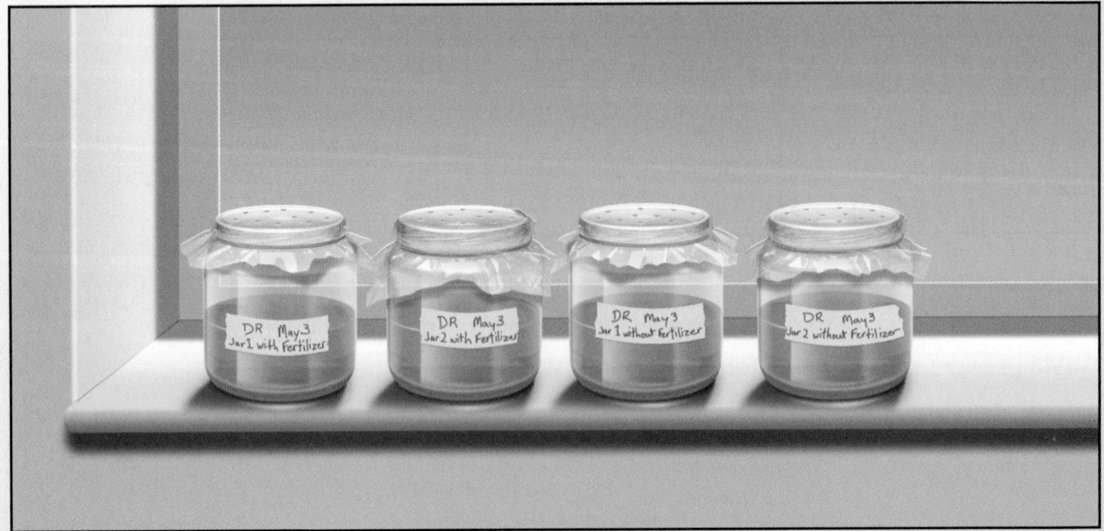

## Recording Observations

Once you have obtained all of your materials and your procedure has been approved, you can begin making experimental observations. Gather both quantitative and qualitative data. If something goes wrong during your procedure, make sure you record that too.

**Observations**
For help with making qualitative and quantitative observations, refer to page R2.

For more examples of data tables, see page R23.

Table 4. Fertilizer and Algae Growth

| | Experimental Group | | Control Group | | |
|---|---|---|---|---|---|
| Date and Time | Jar 1 with Fertilizer (diameter of algae in mm) | Jar 2 with Fertilizer (diameter of algae in mm) | Jar 1 without Fertilizer (diameter of algae in mm) | Jar 2 without Fertilizer (diameter of algae in mm) | Observations |
| 5/3 4:00 P.M. | 0 | 0 | 0 | 0 | condensation in all containers |
| 5/4 4:00 P.M. | 0 | 3 | 0 | 0 | tiny green blobs in jar 2 with fertilizer |
| 5/5 4:15 P.M. | 4 | 5 | 0 | 3 | green blobs in jars 1 and 2 with fertilizer and jar 2 without fertilizer |
| 5/6 4:00 P.M. | 5 | 6 | 0 | 4 | water light green in jar 2 with fertilizer |
| 5/7 4:00 P.M. | 8 | 10 | 0 | 6 | water light green in jars 1 and 2 with fertilizer and in jar 2 without fertilizer |
| 5/8 3:30 P.M. | 10 | 18 | 0 | 6 | cover off jar 2 with fertilizer |
| 5/9 3:30 P.M. | 14 | 23 | 0 | 8 | drew sketches of each container |

Notice that on the sixth day, the observer found that the cover was off one of the containers. It is important to record observations of unintended factors because they might affect the results of the experiment.

Drawings of Samples Viewed Under Microscope on 5/9 at 100x

Use technology, such as a microscope, to help you make observations when possible.

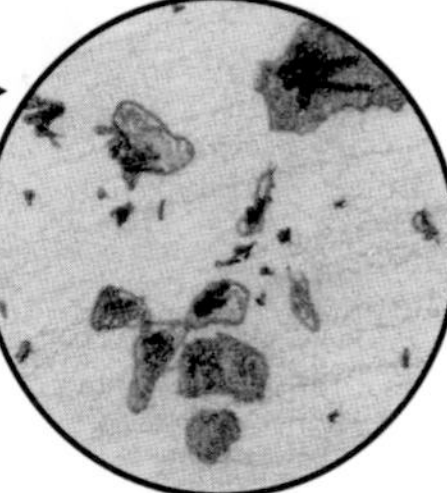
Jar 1 with Fertilizer

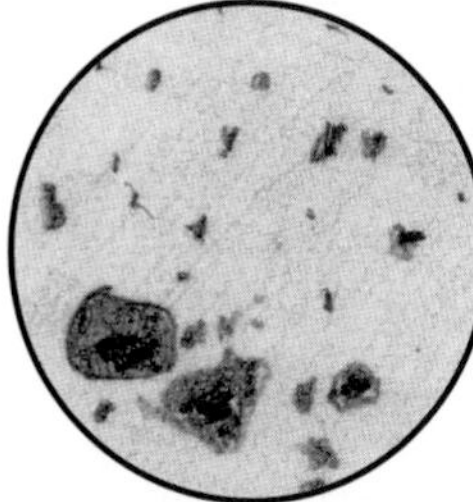
Jar 2 with Fertilizer

Jar 1 without Fertilizer

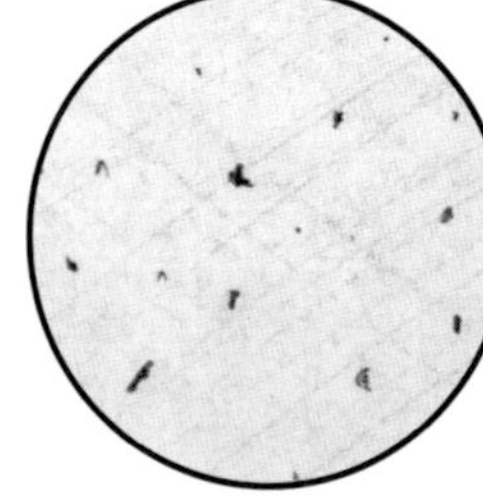
Jar 2 without Fertilizer

LAB HANDBOOK

## Summarizing Results

To summarize your data, look at all of your observations together. Look for meaningful ways to present your observations. For example, you might average your data or make a graph to look for patterns. When possible, use spreadsheet software to help you analyze and present your data. The two graphs below show the same data.

**EXAMPLE 1**

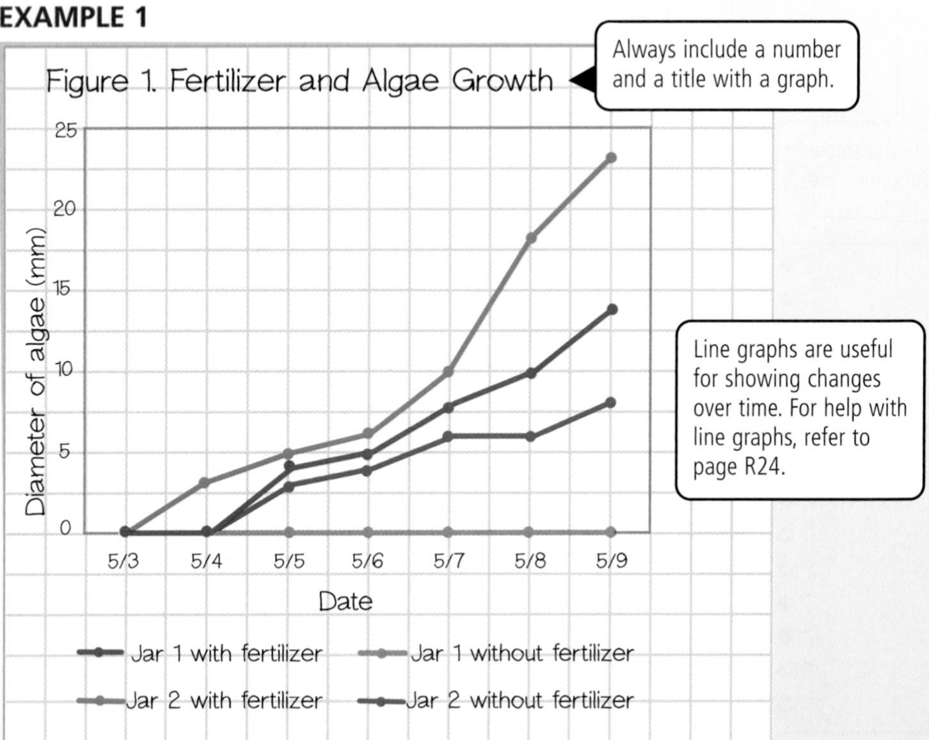


Always include a number and a title with a graph.

Line graphs are useful for showing changes over time. For help with line graphs, refer to page R24.

**EXAMPLE 2**

Bar graphs are useful for comparing different data sets. This bar graph has four bars for each day. Another way to present the data would be to calculate averages for the tests and the controls, and to show one test bar and one control bar for each day.

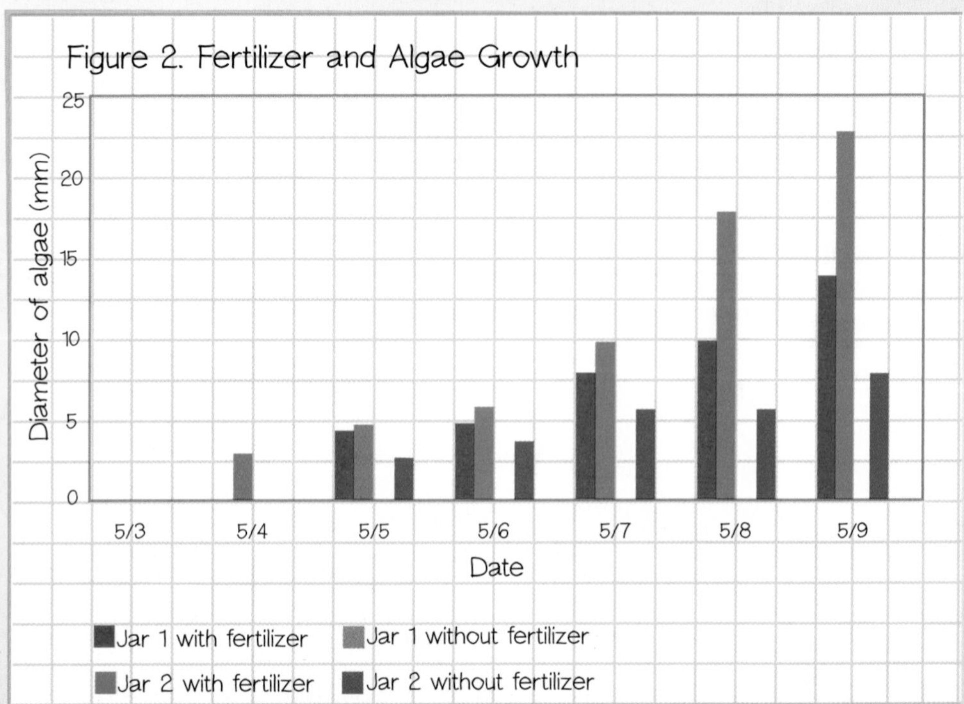

## Drawing Conclusions

### RESULTS AND INFERENCES

To draw conclusions from your experiment, first write your results. Then compare your results with your hypothesis. Do your results support your hypothesis? Be careful not to make inferences about factors that you did not test.

For help with making inferences, see page R4.

**Results and Inferences**

The results of my experiment show that more algae grew in lake water to which fertilizer had been added than in lake water to which no fertilizer had been added. My hypothesis was supported. I infer that it is possible that the growth of algae in the lake was caused by the fertilizer used on the field.

Notice that you cannot conclude from this experiment that the presence of algae in the lake was due only to the fertilizer.

### QUESTIONS FOR FURTHER RESEARCH

Write a list of questions for further research and investigation. Your ideas may lead you to new experiments and discoveries.

**Questions for Further Research**

- What is the connection between the amount of fertilizer and algae growth?
- How do different brands of fertilizer affect algae growth?
- How would algae growth in the lake be affected if no fertilizer were used on the field?
- How do algae affect the lake and the other life in and around it?
- How does fertilizer affect the lake and the life in and around it?
- If fertilizer is getting into the lake, how is it getting there?

## Describing a Set of Data

Means, medians, modes, and ranges are important math tools for describing data sets such as the following widths of fossilized clamshells.

**13 mm 25 mm 14 mm 21 mm 16 mm 23 mm 14 mm**

### Mean

The **mean** of a data set is the sum of the values divided by the number of values.

**Example**

To find the mean of the clamshell data, add the values and then divide the sum by the number of values.

$$\frac{13 \text{ mm} + 25 \text{ mm} + 14 \text{ mm} + 21 \text{ mm} + 16 \text{ mm} + 23 \text{ mm} + 14 \text{ mm}}{7} = \frac{126 \text{ mm}}{7} = 18 \text{ mm}$$

**ANSWER** The mean is 18 mm.

### Median

The **median** of a data set is the middle value when the values are written in numerical order. If a data set has an even number of values, the median is the mean of the two middle values.

**Example**

To find the median of the clamshell data, arrange the values in order from least to greatest. The median is the middle value.

13 mm 14 mm 14 mm 16 mm 21 mm 23 mm 25 mm

**ANSWER** The median is 16 mm.

## Mode

The **mode** of a data set is the value that occurs most often.

### Example

To find the mode of the clamshell data, arrange the values in order from least to greatest and determine the value that occurs most often.

13 mm 14 mm 14 mm 16 mm 21 mm 23 mm 25 mm

**ANSWER** The mode is 14 mm.

A data set can have more than one mode or no mode. For example, the following data set has modes of 2 mm and 4 mm:

2 mm 2 mm 3 mm 4 mm 4 mm

The data set below has no mode, because no value occurs more often than any other.

2 mm 3 mm 4 mm 5 mm

## Range

The **range** of a data set is the difference between the greatest value and the least value.

### Example

To find the range of the clamshell data, arrange the values in order from least to greatest.

13 mm 14 mm 14 mm 16 mm 21 mm 23 mm 25 mm

Subtract the least value from the greatest value.

13 mm is the least value.
25 mm is the greatest value.

25 mm – 13 mm = 12 mm

**ANSWER** The range is 12 mm.

# Using Ratios, Rates, and Proportions

You can use ratios and rates to compare values in data sets. You can use proportions to find unknown values.

## Ratios

A **ratio** uses division to compare two values. The ratio of a value *a* to a nonzero value *b* can be written as $\frac{a}{b}$.

### Example

The height of one plant is 8 centimeters. The height of another plant is 6 centimeters. To find the ratio of the height of the first plant to the height of the second plant, write a fraction and simplify it.

$$\frac{8\text{ cm}}{6\text{ cm}} = \frac{4 \times \cancel{2}^{1}}{3 \times \cancel{2}_{1}} = \frac{4}{3}$$

**ANSWER** The ratio of the plant heights is $\frac{4}{3}$.

You can also write the ratio $\frac{a}{b}$ as "a to b" or as $a:b$. For example, you can write the ratio of the plant heights as "4 to 3" or as 4:3.

## Rates

A **rate** is a ratio of two values expressed in different units. A unit rate is a rate with a denominator of 1 unit.

### Example

A plant grew 6 centimeters in 2 days. The plant's rate of growth was $\frac{6\text{ cm}}{2\text{ days}}$. To describe the plant's growth in centimeters per day, write a unit rate.

***Divide numerator and denominator by 2:*** $\frac{6\text{ cm}}{2\text{ days}} = \frac{6\text{ cm} \div 2}{2\text{ days} \div 2}$

***Simplify:*** $= \frac{3\text{ cm}}{1\text{ day}}$

You divide 2 days by 2 to get 1 day, so divide 6 cm by 2 also.

**ANSWER** The plant's rate of growth is 3 centimeters per day.

MATH HANDBOOK

### Proportions

A **proportion** is an equation stating that two ratios are equivalent. To solve for an unknown value in a proportion, you can use cross products.

**Example**

If a plant grew 6 centimeters in 2 days, how many centimeters would it grow in 3 days (if its rate of growth is constant)?

*Write a proportion:* $\frac{6 \text{ cm}}{2 \text{ days}} = \frac{x}{3 \text{ days}}$

*Set cross products:* $6 \text{ cm} \cdot 3 = 2x$

*Multiply 6 and 3:* $18 \text{ cm} = 2x$

*Divide each side by 2:* $\frac{18 \text{ cm}}{2} = \frac{2x}{2}$

*Simplify:* $9 \text{ cm} = x$

**ANSWER** The plant would grow 9 centimeters in 3 days.

## Using Decimals, Fractions, and Percents

Decimals, fractions, and percentages are all ways of recording and representing data.

### Decimals

A **decimal** is a number that is written in the base-ten place value system, in which a decimal point separates the ones and tenths digits. The values of each place is ten times that of the place to its right.

**Example**

A caterpillar traveled from point *A* to point *C* along the path shown.

A — 36.9 cm — B — 52.4 cm — C

**ADDING DECIMALS** To find the total distance traveled by the caterpillar, add the distance from *A* to *B* and the distance from *B* to *C*. Begin by lining up the decimal points. Then add the figures as you would whole numbers and bring down the decimal point.

$$\begin{array}{r} 36.9 \text{ cm} \\ +\ 52.4 \text{ cm} \\ \hline 89.3 \text{ cm} \end{array}$$

**ANSWER** The caterpillar traveled a total distance of 89.3 centimeters.

MATH HANDBOOK

## Example *continued*

**SUBTRACTING DECIMALS** To find how much farther the caterpillar traveled on the second leg of the journey, subtract the distance from *A* to *B* from the distance from *B* to *C*.

$$\begin{array}{r} 52.4 \text{ cm} \\ -\ 36.9 \text{ cm} \\ \hline 15.5 \text{ cm} \end{array}$$

**ANSWER** The caterpillar traveled 15.5 centimeters farther on the second leg of the journey.

## Example

A caterpillar is traveling from point *D* to point *F* along the path shown. The caterpillar travels at a speed of 9.6 centimeters per minute.

D E 33.6 cm F

**MULTIPLYING DECIMALS** You can multiply decimals as you would whole numbers. The number of decimal places in the product is equal to the sum of the number of decimal places in the factors.

For instance, suppose it takes the caterpillar 1.5 minutes to go from *D* to *E*. To find the distance from *D* to *E*, multiply the caterpillar's speed by the time it took.

$$\begin{array}{r} 9.6 \\ \times\ 1.5 \\ \hline 480 \\ 96\ \\ \hline 14.40 \end{array} \qquad \begin{array}{rl} 1 & \text{decimal place} \\ +\ 1 & \text{decimal place} \\ \hline & \\ & \\ 2 & \text{decimal places} \end{array}$$

Align as shown.

**ANSWER** The distance from *D* to *E* is 14.4 centimeters.

**DIVIDING DECIMALS** When you divide by a decimal, move the decimal points the same number of places in the divisor and the dividend to make the divisor a whole number.

For instance, to find the time it will take the caterpillar to travel from *E* to *F*, divide the distance from *E* to *F* by the caterpillar's speed.

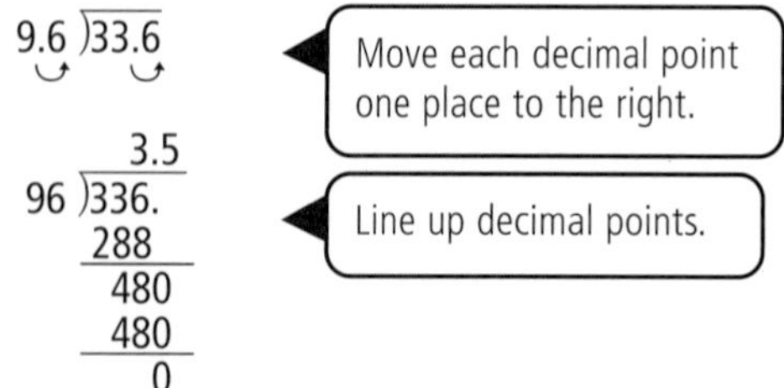

9.6 )33.6
Move each decimal point one place to the right.
3.5
96 )336.
288
480
480
0
Line up decimal points.


**ANSWER** The caterpillar will travel from *E* to *F* in 3.5 minutes.

MATH HANDBOOK

## Fractions

A **fraction** is a number in the form $\frac{a}{b}$, where $b$ is not equal to 0. A fraction is in **simplest form** if its numerator and denominator have a greatest common factor (GCF) of 1. To simplify a fraction, divide its numerator and denominator by their GCF.

### Example

A caterpillar is 40 millimeters long. The head of the caterpillar is 6 millimeters long. To compare the length of the caterpillar's head with the caterpillar's total length, you can write and simplify a fraction that expresses the ratio of the two lengths.

*Write the ratio of the two lengths:* $\frac{\text{Length of head}}{\text{Total length}} = \frac{6 \text{ mm}}{40 \text{ mm}}$

*Write numerator and denominator as products of numbers and the GCF:* $= \frac{3 \times 2}{20 \times 2}$

*Divide numerator and denominator by the GCF:* $= \frac{3 \times \cancel{2}^{1}}{20 \times \cancel{2}_{1}}$

*Simplify:* $= \frac{3}{20}$

**ANSWER** In simplest form, the ratio of the lengths is $\frac{3}{20}$.

## Percents

A **percent** is a ratio that compares a number to 100. The word *percent* means "per hundred" or "out of 100." The symbol for *percent* is %.

For instance, suppose 43 out of 100 caterpillars are female. You can represent this ratio as a percent, a decimal, or a fraction.

| Percent | Decimal | Fraction |
|---|---|---|
| 43% | 0.43 | $\frac{43}{100}$ |

### Example

In the preceding example, the ratio of the length of the caterpillar's head to the caterpillar's total length is $\frac{3}{20}$. To write this ratio as a percent, write an equivalent fraction that has a denominator of 100.

*Multiply numerator and denominator by 5:* $\frac{3}{20} = \frac{3 \times 5}{20 \times 5}$

$= \frac{15}{100}$

*Write as a percent:* $= 15\%$

**ANSWER** The caterpillar's head represents 15 percent of its total length.

MATH HANDBOOK

# Using Formulas

## A **formula** is an equation that shows the general relationship between two or more quantities.

The term *variable* is also used in science to refer to a factor that can change during an experiment.

In science, a formula often has a word form and a symbolic form. The formula below expresses Ohm's law.

**Word Form**

$$\text{Current} = \frac{\text{voltage}}{\text{resistance}}$$

**Symbolic Form**

$$I = \frac{V}{R}$$

In this formula, $I$, $V$, and $R$ are variables. A mathematical **variable** is a symbol or letter that is used to represent one or more numbers.

### Example

Suppose that you measure a voltage of 1.5 volts and a resistance of 15 ohms. You can use the formula for Ohm's law to find the current in amperes.

***Write the formula for Ohm's law:*** $I = \frac{V}{R}$

***Substitute 1.5 volts for*** V ***and 15 ohms for*** R: $I = \frac{1.5 \text{ volts}}{15 \text{ ohms}}$

***Simplify:*** $I = 0.1$ amp

**ANSWER** The current is 0.1 ampere.

If you know the values of all variables but one in a formula, you can solve for the value of the unknown variable. For instance, Ohm's law can be used to find a voltage if you know the current and the resistance.

### Example

Suppose that you know that a current is 0.2 amperes and the resistance is 18 ohms. Use the formula for Ohm's law to find the voltage in volts.

***Write the formula for Ohm's law:*** $I = \frac{V}{R}$

***Substitute 0.2 amp for*** I ***and 18 ohms for*** R: $0.2 \text{ amp} = \frac{V}{18 \text{ ohms}}$

***Multiply both sides by 18 ohms:*** $0.2 \text{ amp} \cdot 18 \text{ ohms} = V$

***Simplify:*** $3.6 \text{ volts} = V$

**ANSWER** The voltage is 3.6 volts.

# Finding Areas

## The area of a figure is the amount of surface the figure covers.

Area is measured in square units, such as square meters ($m^2$) or square centimeters ($cm^2$). Formulas for the areas of three common geometric figures are shown below.

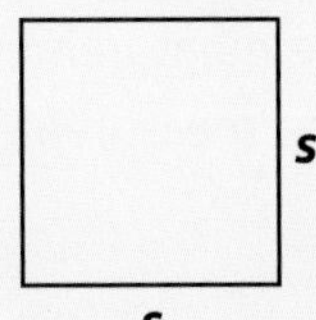


Area = (side length)$^2$
$A = s^2$

Area = length × width
$A = lw$

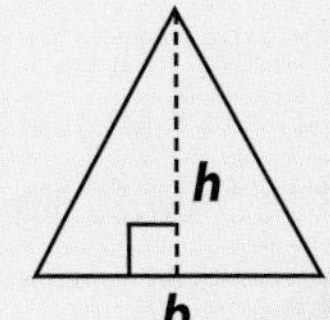


Area = $\frac{1}{2}$ × base × height
$A = \frac{1}{2}bh$

### Example

Each face of a halite crystal is a square like the one shown. You can find the area of the square by using the steps below.

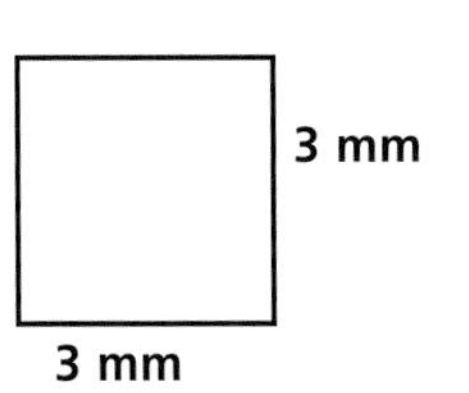


***Write the formula for the area of a square:*** $A = s^2$

***Substitute 3 mm for*** s: $= (3\text{ mm})^2$

***Simplify:*** $= 9\text{ mm}^2$

**ANSWER** The area of the square is 9 square millimeters.

# Finding Volumes

## The volume of a solid is the amount of space contained by the solid.

Volume is measured in cubic units, such as cubic meters ($m^3$) or cubic centimeters ($cm^3$). The volume of a rectangular prism is given by the formula shown below.

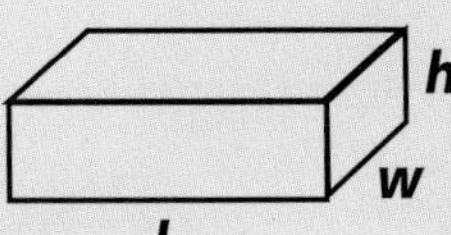


Volume = length × width × height
$V = lwh$

### Example

A topaz crystal is a rectangular prism like the one shown. You can find the volume of the prism by using the steps below.

10 mm
12 mm
20 mm

***Write the formula for the volume of a rectangular prism:*** $V = lwh$

***Substitute dimensions:*** $= 20\text{ mm} \times 12\text{ mm} \times 10\text{ mm}$

***Simplify:*** $= 2400\text{ mm}^3$

**ANSWER** The volume of the rectangular prism is 2400 cubic millimeters.

MATH HANDBOOK

# Using Significant Figures

The **significant figures** in a decimal are the digits that are warranted by the accuracy of a measuring device.

When you perform a calculation with measurements, the number of significant figures to include in the result depends in part on the number of significant figures in the measurements. When you multiply or divide measurements, your answer should have only as many significant figures as the measurement with the fewest significant figures.

### Example

Using a balance and a graduated cylinder filled with water, you determined that a marble has a mass of 8.0 grams and a volume of 3.5 cubic centimeters. To calculate the density of the marble, divide the mass by the volume.

***Write the formula for density:*** $\text{Density} = \dfrac{\text{mass}}{\text{Volume}}$

***Substitute measurements:*** $= \dfrac{8.0\ \text{g}}{3.5\ \text{cm}^3}$

***Use a calculator to divide:*** $\approx 2.285714286\ \text{g/cm}^3$

**ANSWER** Because the mass and the volume have two significant figures each, give the density to two significant figures. The marble has a density of 2.3 grams per cubic centimeter.

# Using Scientific Notation

**Scientific notation** is a shorthand way to write very large or very small numbers. For example, 73,500,000,000,000,000,000,000 kg is the mass of the Moon. In scientific notation, it is $7.35 \times 10^{22}$ kg.

### Example

You can convert from standard form to scientific notation.

| Standard Form | Scientific Notation |
|---|---|
| 720,000<br>5 decimal places left | $7.2 \times 10^5$<br>Exponent is 5. |
| 0.000291<br>4 decimal places right | $2.91 \times 10^{-4}$<br>Exponent is –4. |

You can convert from scientific notation to standard form.

| Scientific Notation | Standard Form |
|---|---|
| $4.63 \times 10^7$<br>Exponent is 7. | 46,300,000<br>7 decimal places right |
| $1.08 \times 10^{-6}$<br>Exponent is –6. | 0.00000108<br>6 decimal places left |

MATH HANDBOOK

# Note-Taking Handbook

## Note-Taking Strategies

Taking notes as you read helps you understand the information. The notes you take can also be used as a study guide for later review. This handbook presents several ways to organize your notes.

### Content Frame

1. Make a chart in which each column represents a category.
2. Give each column a heading.
3. Write details under the headings.

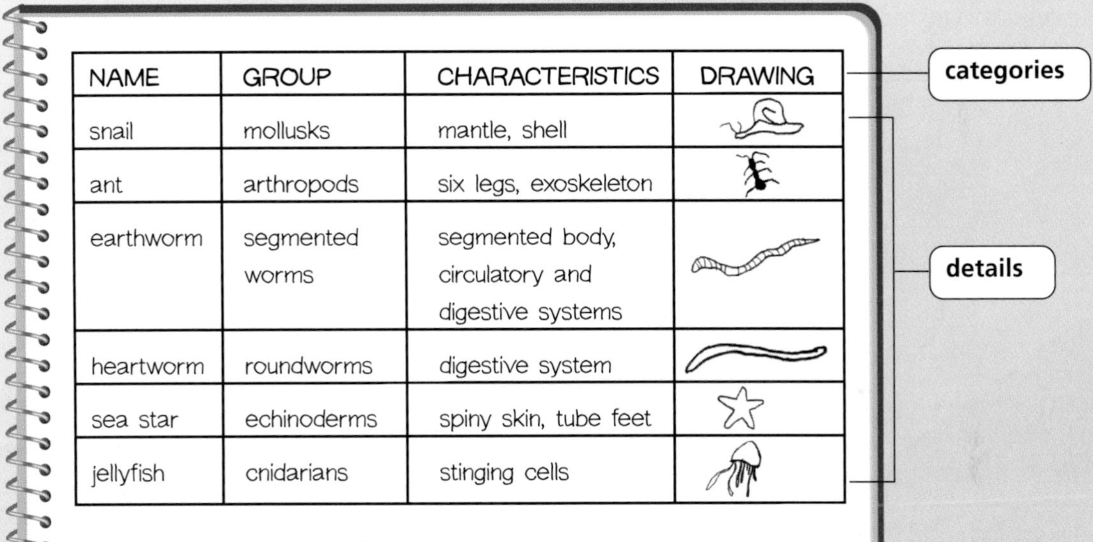

| NAME | GROUP | CHARACTERISTICS | DRAWING |
|---|---|---|---|
| snail | mollusks | mantle, shell | |
| ant | arthropods | six legs, exoskeleton | |
| earthworm | segmented worms | segmented body, circulatory and digestive systems | |
| heartworm | roundworms | digestive system | |
| sea star | echinoderms | spiny skin, tube feet | |
| jellyfish | cnidarians | stinging cells | |

categories
details

### Combination Notes

1. For each new idea or concept, write an informal outline of the information.
2. Make a sketch to illustrate the concept, and label it.

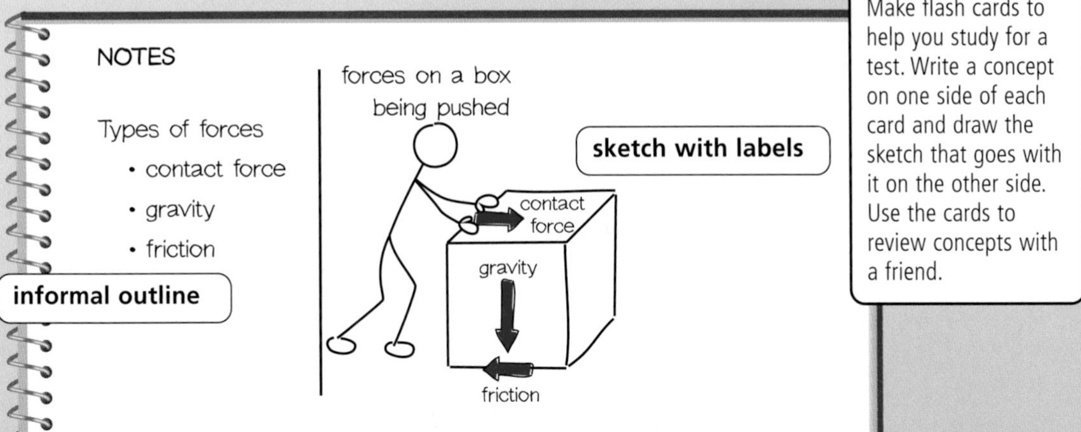
NOTES
Types of forces
• contact force
• gravity
• friction
informal outline
forces on a box being pushed
sketch with labels
contact force
gravity
friction
Make flash cards to help you study for a test. Write a concept on one side of each card and draw the sketch that goes with it on the other side. Use the cards to review concepts with a friend.

## Main Idea and Detail Notes

1. In the left-hand column of a two-column chart, list main ideas. The blue headings express main ideas throughout this textbook.
2. In the right-hand column, write details that expand on each main idea.

You can shorten the headings in your chart. Be sure to use the most important words.

When studying for tests, cover up the detail notes column with a sheet of paper. Then use each main idea to form a question—such as "How does latitude affect climate?" Answer the question, and then uncover the detail notes column to check your answer.

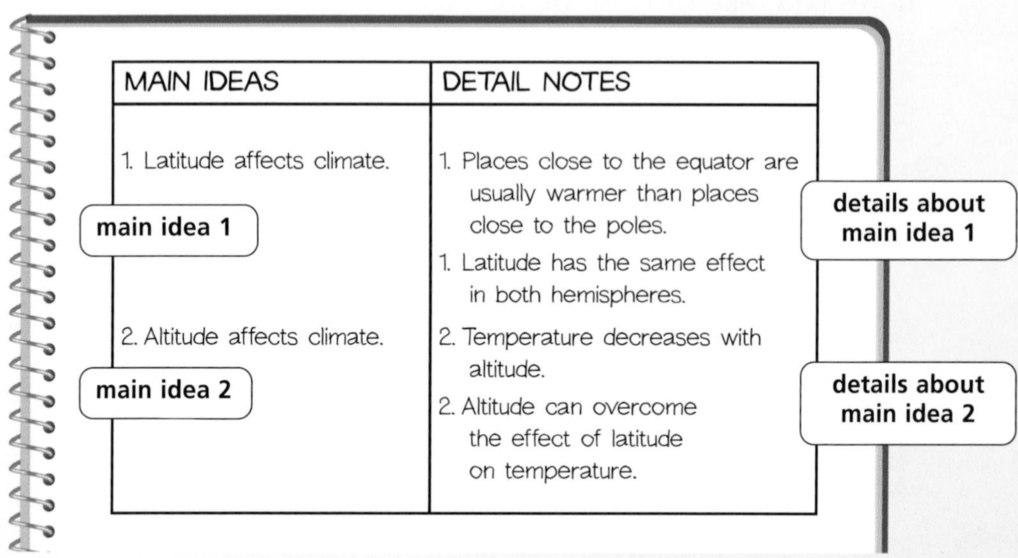

MAIN IDEAS
DETAIL NOTES
1. Latitude affects climate.
main idea 1
1. Places close to the equator are usually warmer than places close to the poles.
1. Latitude has the same effect in both hemispheres.
details about main idea 1
2. Altitude affects climate.
main idea 2
2. Temperature decreases with altitude.
2. Altitude can overcome the effect of latitude on temperature.
details about main idea 2


## Main Idea Web

1. Write a main idea in a box.
2. Add boxes around it with related vocabulary terms and important details.

You can find definitions near highlighted terms.

definition of *work*

Work is the use of force to move an object.

formula

Work = force · distance

main idea

Force is necessary to do work.

The joule is the unit used to measure work.

definition of *joule*

Work depends on the size of a force.

important detail

## Mind Map

1. Write a main idea in the center.
2. Add details that relate to one another and to the main idea.

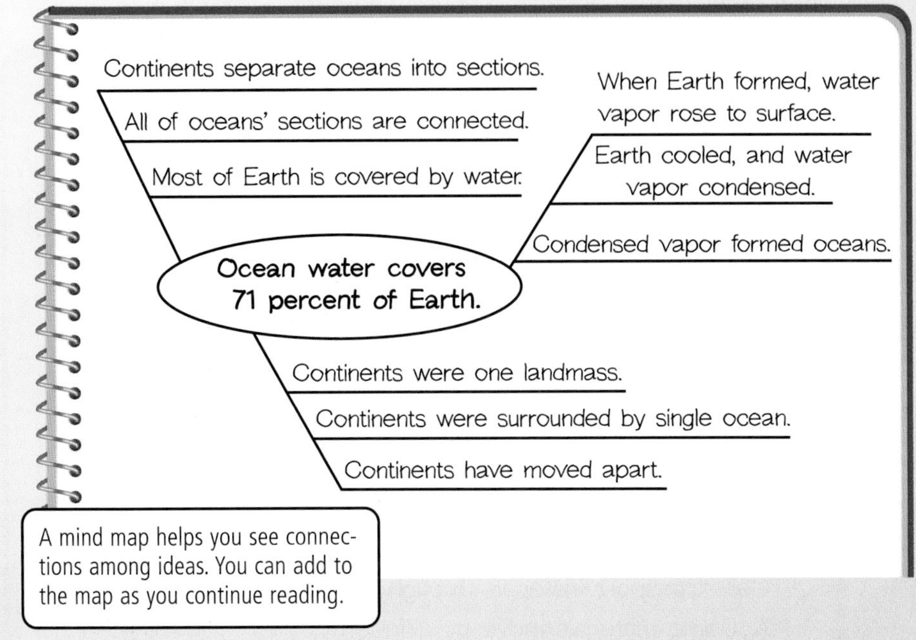


Continents separate oceans into sections.
All of oceans' sections are connected.
Most of Earth is covered by water.
When Earth formed, water vapor rose to surface.
Earth cooled, and water vapor condensed.
Condensed vapor formed oceans.
Ocean water covers 71 percent of Earth.
Continents were one landmass.
Continents were surrounded by single ocean.
Continents have moved apart.
A mind map helps you see connections among ideas. You can add to the map as you continue reading.

## Supporting Main Ideas

1. Write a main idea in a box.
2. Add boxes underneath with information—such as reasons, explanations, and examples—that supports the main idea.

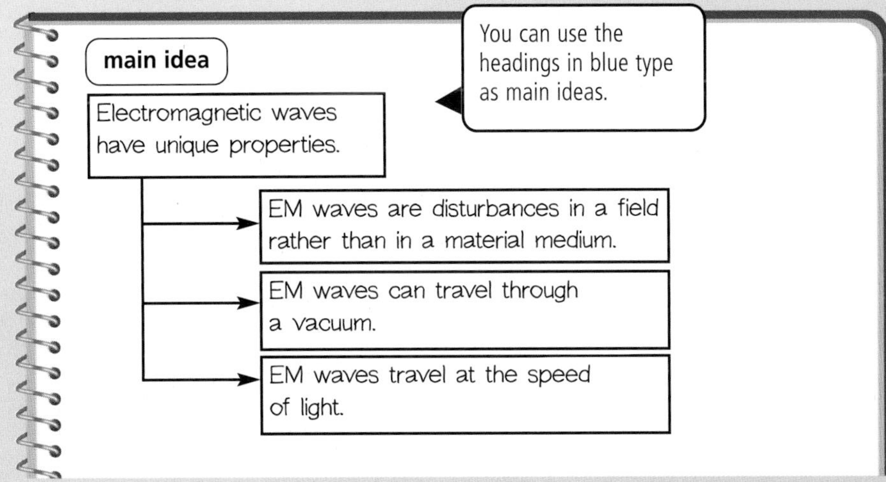

main idea
Electromagnetic waves have unique properties.
You can use the headings in blue type as main ideas.
EM waves are disturbances in a field rather than in a material medium.
EM waves can travel through a vacuum.
EM waves travel at the speed of light.

NOTE-TAKING HANDBOOK

## Outline

1. Copy the chapter title and headings from the book in the form of an outline.
2. Add notes that summarize in your own words what you read.

Cell Processes

I. Cells capture and release energy. — 1st key idea
   A. All cells need energy. — 1st subpoint of I
   B. Some cells capture light energy. — 2nd subpoint of I
      1. Process of photosynthesis — 1st detail about B
      2. Chloroplasts (site of photosynthesis) — 2nd detail about B
      3. Carbon dioxide and water as raw materials
      4. Glucose and oxygen as products
   C. All cells release energy.
      1. Process of cellular respiration
      2. Fermentation of sugar to carbon dioxide
      3. Bacteria that carry out fermentation
II. Cells transport materials through membranes.
   A. Some materials move by diffusion.
      1. Particle movement from higher to lower concentrations
      2. Movement of water through membrane (osmosis)
   B. Some transport requires energy.
      1. Active transport
      2. Examples of active transport

**Correct Outline Form**

Include a title.

Arrange key ideas, subpoints, and details as shown.

Indent the divisions of the outline as shown.

Use the same grammatical form for items of the same rank. For example, if A is a sentence, B must also be a sentence.

You must have at least two main ideas or subpoints. That is, every A must be followed by a B, and every 1 must be followed by a 2.

## Concept Map

1. Write an important concept in a large oval.
2. Add details related to the concept in smaller ovals.
3. Write linking words on arrows that connect the ovals.

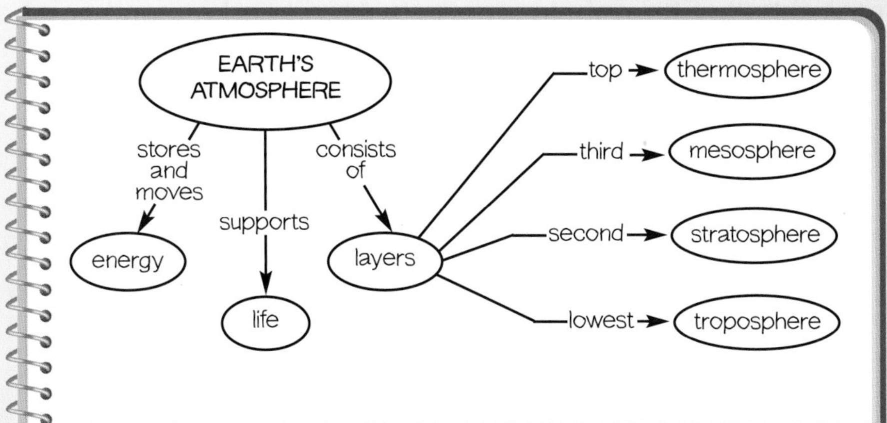


The main ideas or concepts can often be found in the blue headings. An example is "The atmosphere stores and moves energy." Use nouns from these concepts in the ovals, and use the verb or verbs on the lines.

## Venn Diagram

1. Draw two overlapping circles, one for each item that you are comparing.
2. In the overlapping section, list the characteristics that are shared by both items.
3. In the outer sections, list the characteristics that are peculiar to each item.
4. Write a summary that describes the information in the Venn diagram.

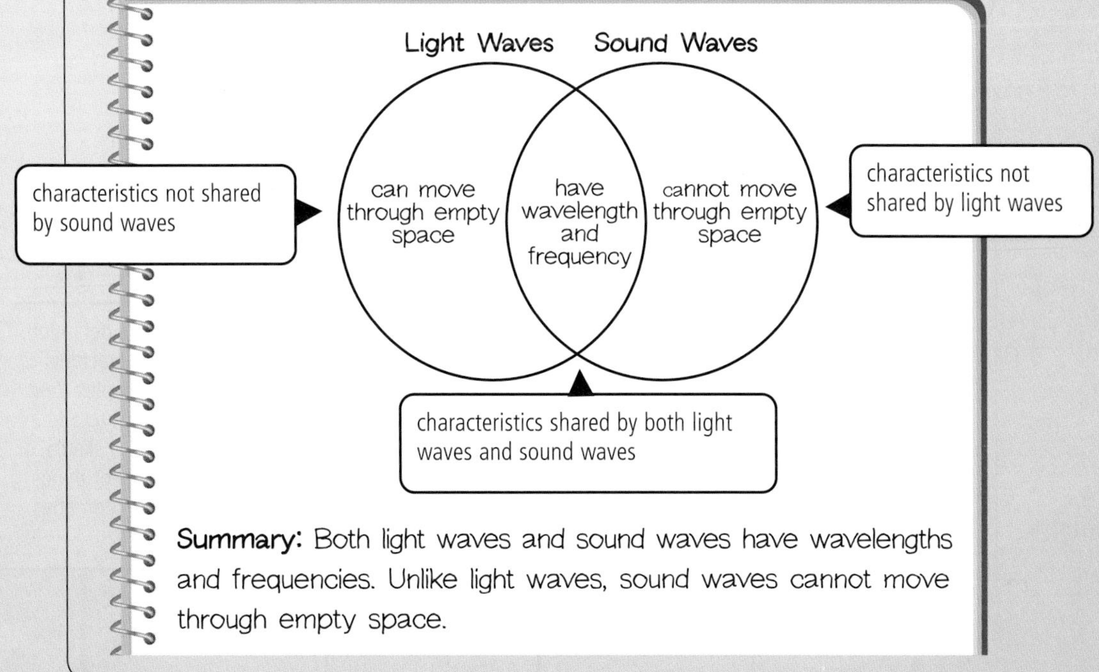


NOTE-TAKING HANDBOOK

# Vocabulary Strategies

Important terms are highlighted in this book. A definition of each term can be found in the sentence or paragraph where the term appears. You can also find definitions in the Glossary. Taking notes about vocabulary terms helps you understand and remember what you read.

## Description Wheel

1. Write a term inside a circle.
2. Write words that describe the term on "spokes" attached to the circle.

When studying for a test with a friend, read the phrases on the spokes one at a time until your friend identifies the correct term.

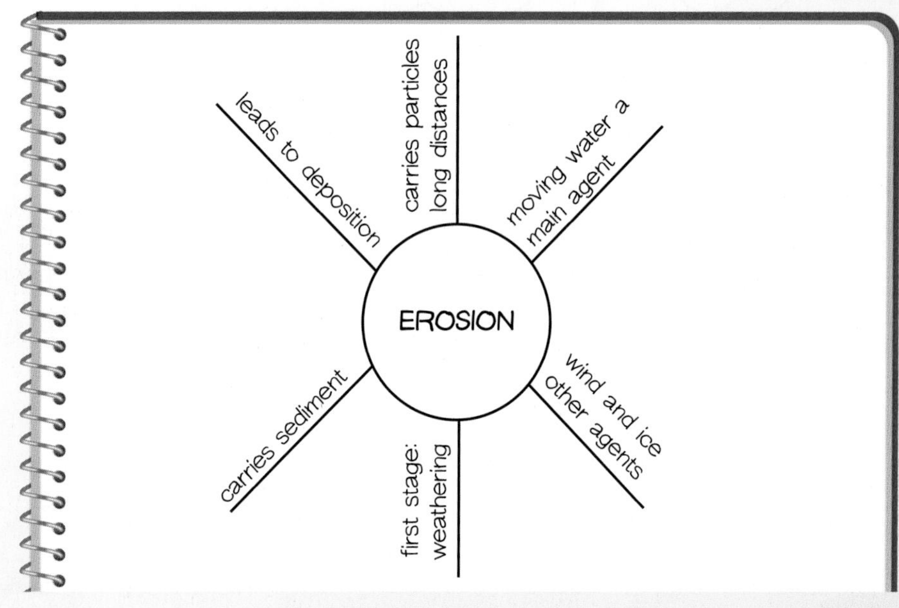


## Four Square

1. Write a term in the center.
2. Write details in the four areas around the term.

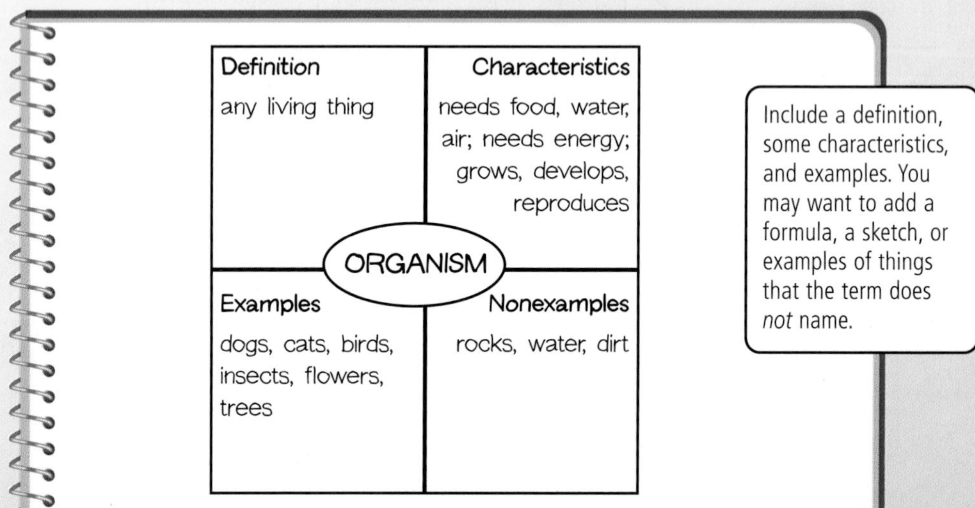


Include a definition, some characteristics, and examples. You may want to add a formula, a sketch, or examples of things that the term does *not* name.

NOTE-TAKING HANDBOOK

## Frame Game

1. Write a term in the center.
2. Frame the term with details.

Include examples, descriptions, sketches, or sentences that use the term in context. Change the frame to fit each new term.

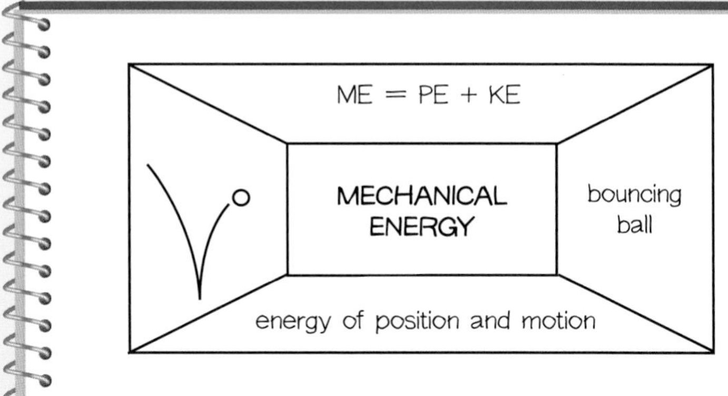


## Magnet Word

1. Write a term on the magnet.
2. On the lines, add details related to the term.

You can also use phrases or sentences on the lines.

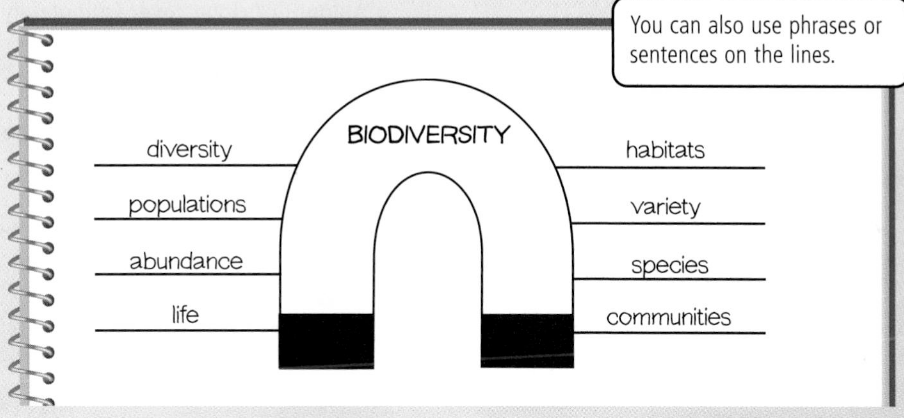


## Word Triangle

1. Write a term and its definition in the bottom section.
2. In the middle section, write a sentence in which the term is used correctly.
3. In the top section, draw a small picture to illustrate the term.

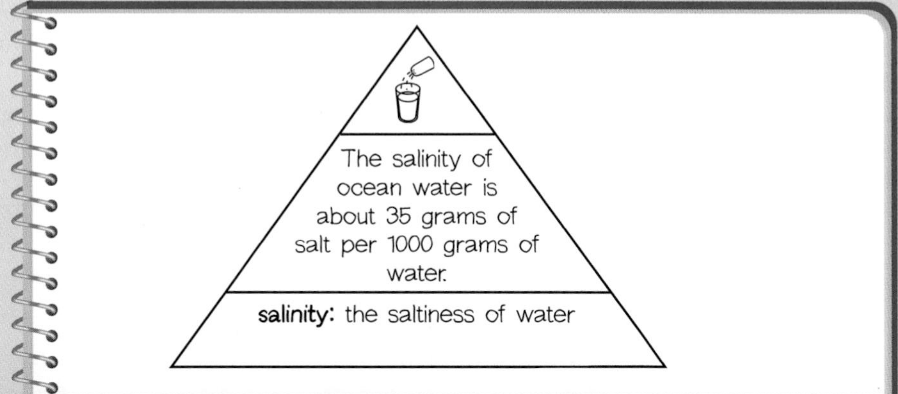


NOTE-TAKING HANDBOOK

Appendix

## Station Symbols

Meteorologists use station symbols to condense the weather data they receive from ground stations. The symbols are displayed on maps. The information in a station symbol can be understood by the meteorologists of any country.

In the symbol, air pressure readings are shortened by omitting the initial 9 or 10 and the decimal point. For numbers greater than 500, place a 9 to the left of the number and divide by 10 to get the air pressure in millibars. For numbers less than 500, place a 10 to the left and then divide by 10.

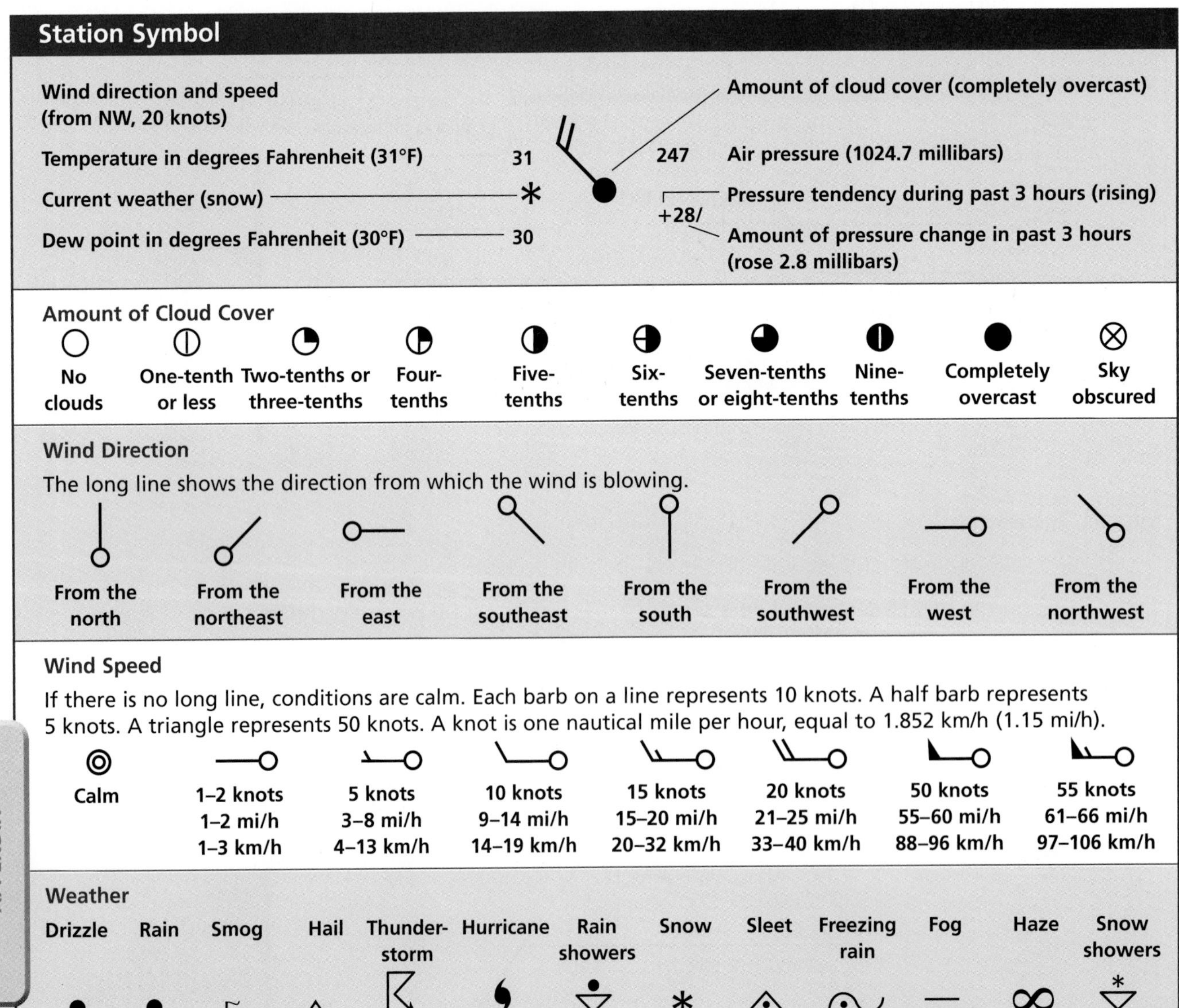


APPENDIX

# Relative Humidity

You can find the relative humidity by calculating the difference between the two readings on a psychrometer. First look up the dry-bulb temperature in the left-hand column of the relative humidity chart. Then find in the top line the difference between the wet-bulb temperature and the dry-bulb temperature.

**Relative Humidity (%)**

| Dry-Bulb Temperature (°C) | Difference Between Wet-Bulb and Dry-Bulb Temperatures (°C) | | | | | | | | | | | | | | | |
|---|---|---|---|---|---|---|---|---|---|---|---|---|---|---|---|---|
| | 0 | 1 | 2 | 3 | 4 | 5 | 6 | 7 | 8 | 9 | 10 | 11 | 12 | 13 | 14 | 15 |
| −20 | 100 | 28 | | | | | | | | | | | | | | |
| −18 | 100 | 40 | | | | | | | | | | | | | | |
| −16 | 100 | 48 | | | | | | | | | | | | | | |
| −14 | 100 | 55 | 11 | | | | | | | | | | | | | |
| −12 | 100 | 61 | 23 | | | | | | | | | | | | | |
| −10 | 100 | 66 | 33 | | | | | | | | | | | | | |
| −8 | 100 | 71 | 41 | 13 | | | | | | | | | | | | |
| −6 | 100 | 73 | 48 | 20 | | | | | | | | | | | | |
| −4 | 100 | 77 | 54 | 32 | 11 | | | | | | | | | | | |
| −2 | 100 | 79 | 58 | 37 | 20 | 1 | | | | | | | | | | |
| 0 | 100 | 81 | 63 | 45 | 28 | 11 | | | | | | | | | | |
| 2 | 100 | 83 | 67 | 51 | 36 | 20 | 6 | | | | | | | | | |
| 4 | 100 | 85 | 70 | 56 | 42 | 27 | 14 | | | | | | | | | |
| 6 | 100 | 86 | 72 | 59 | 46 | 35 | 22 | 10 | | | | | | | | |
| 8 | 100 | 87 | 74 | 62 | 51 | 39 | 28 | 17 | 6 | | | | | | | |
| 10 | 100 | 88 | 76 | 65 | 54 | 43 | 33 | 24 | 13 | 4 | | | | | | |
| 12 | 100 | 88 | 78 | 67 | 57 | 48 | 38 | 28 | 19 | 10 | 2 | | | | | |
| 14 | 100 | 89 | 79 | 69 | 60 | 50 | 41 | 33 | 25 | 16 | 8 | 1 | | | | |
| 16 | 100 | 90 | 80 | 71 | 62 | 54 | 45 | 37 | 29 | 21 | 14 | 7 | 1 | | | |
| 18 | 100 | 91 | 81 | 72 | 64 | 56 | 48 | 40 | 33 | 26 | 19 | 12 | 6 | | | |
| 20 | 100 | 91 | 82 | 74 | 66 | 58 | 51 | 44 | 36 | 30 | 23 | 17 | 11 | 5 | | |
| 22 | 100 | 92 | 83 | 75 | 68 | 60 | 53 | 46 | 40 | 33 | 27 | 21 | 15 | 10 | 4 | |
| 24 | 100 | 92 | 84 | 76 | 69 | 62 | 55 | 49 | 42 | 36 | 30 | 25 | 20 | 14 | 9 | 4 |
| 26 | 100 | 92 | 85 | 77 | 70 | 64 | 57 | 51 | 45 | 39 | 34 | 28 | 23 | 18 | 13 | 9 |
| 28 | 100 | 93 | 86 | 78 | 71 | 65 | 59 | 53 | 47 | 42 | 36 | 31 | 26 | 21 | 17 | 12 |
| 30 | 100 | 93 | 86 | 79 | 72 | 66 | 61 | 55 | 49 | 44 | 39 | 34 | 29 | 25 | 20 | 16 |

APPENDIX

# Wind Speeds

Descriptive names, such as *fresh gale,* were used by sailors and other people to describe the strength of winds. Later, ranges of wind speeds were determined. The table below lists the wind speeds and conditions you might observe around you on land.

**Beaufort Scale of Wind Speeds**

| Beaufort Number | Wind Speed | Description |
|---|---|---|
| 0 | 0 km/h (0 mi/h) | **Calm or Still** Smoke will rise vertically |
| 1 | 2–5 km/h (1–3 mi/h) | **Light Air** Rising smoke drifts, weather vane is inactive |
| 2 | 6–12 km/h (4–7 mi/h) | **Light Breeze** Leaves rustle, can feel wind on your face, weather vane moves |
| 3 | 13–20 km/h (8–12 mi/h) | **Gentle Breeze** Leaves and twigs move around, lightweight flags extend |
| 4 | 21–30 km/h (13–18 mi/h) | **Moderate Breeze** Thin branches move, dust and paper raised |
| 5 | 31–40 km/h (19–24 mi/h) | **Fresh Breeze** Small trees sway |
| 6 | 41–50 km/h (25–31 mi/h) | **Strong Breeze** Large tree branches move, open wires (such as telegraph wires) begin to "whistle," umbrellas are difficult to keep under control |
| 7 | 51–61 km/h (32–38 mi/h) | **Moderate Gale** Large trees begin to sway, noticeably difficult to walk |
| 8 | 62–74 km/h (39–46 mi/h) | **Fresh Gale** Twigs and small branches are broken from trees, walking into the wind is very difficult |
| 9 | 75–89 km/h (47–54 mi/h) | **Strong Gale** Slight damage occurs to buildings, shingles are blown off of roofs |
| 10 | 90–103 km/h (55–63 mi/h) | **Whole Gale** Large trees are uprooted, building damage is considerable |
| 11 | 104–119 km/h (64–72 mi/h) | **Storm** Extensive, widespread damage. These typically occur only at sea, rarely inland. |
| 12 | 120 km/h or more (74 mi/h or more) | **Hurricane** Extreme damage, very rare inland |

# Tornado Intensities

The Fujita scale describes the strength of a tornado based on the damage it does. The scale is useful for classifying tornadoes even though it is not exact. For example, a tornado can strengthen and then weaken before it dies out. The wind speeds are estimates of the strongest winds near the ground. Most tornadoes are F0 or F1. One-quarter to one-third of tornadoes are F2 or F3. Only a few percent of tornadoes are F4 or F5.

**Fujita Scale for Tornadoes**

| F-Scale | Wind Speed | Type of Damage |
|---|---|---|
| **F0** | 64–116 km/h (40–72 mi/h) | **Light Damage** Some damage to chimneys; branches broken off trees; shallow-rooted trees pushed over; sign boards damaged |
| **F1** | 117–180 km/h (73–112 mi/h) | **Moderate Damage** Surface peeled off roofs; mobile homes pushed off foundations or overturned; moving autos blown off roads |
| **F2** | 181–253 km/h (113–157 mi/h) | **Considerable Damage** Roofs torn off frame houses; mobile homes demolished; boxcars overturned; large trees snapped or uprooted; light-object missiles generated; cars lifted off ground |
| **F3** | 254–332 km/h (158–206 mi/h) | **Severe Damage** Roofs and some walls torn off well-constructed houses; trains overturned; most trees in forest uprooted; heavy cars lifted off the ground and thrown |
| **F4** | 333–418 km/h (207–260 mi/h) | **Devastating Damage** Well-constructed houses leveled; structures with weak foundations blown away some distance; cars thrown and large missiles generated |
| **F5** | 419–512 km/h (261–318 mi/h) | **Incredible Damage** Strong frame houses leveled off foundations and swept away; automobile-sized missiles fly through the air in excess of 100 meters (109 yds); trees debarked; incredible phenomena will occur |

# Plant and Animal Cells

Plants and animals are eukaryotes, that is, their cells contain a nucleus and other membrane-bound structures called organelles. The diagrams on page R57 show the different structures that can be found in plant and animal cells. The table below lists the functions of the structures.

| Cell Structures and Their Functions | Plant Cell | Animal Cell |
| --- | --- | --- |
| **Nucleus** | ✔ | ✔ |
| stores genetic material that enables a cell to function and divide | | |
| **Cell Membrane** | ✔ | ✔ |
| controls what comes into and goes out of a cell | | |
| **Cell wall** | ✔ | |
| tough outer covering provides support | | |
| **Ribosome** | ✔ | ✔ |
| uses genetic material to assemble materials needed to make proteins | | |
| **Endoplasmic reticulum** | ✔ | ✔ |
| manufactures proteins and other materials a cell needs to function | | |
| **Golgi apparatus** | ✔ | ✔ |
| finishes processing proteins and transports them | | |
| **Vesicle** | ✔ | ✔ |
| stores and transports materials and wastes | | |
| **Mitochondrion** | ✔ | ✔ |
| releases chemical energy stored in sugars | | |
| **Chloroplast** | ✔ | |
| uses energy from sunlight to make sugars | | |
| **Lysosome** | | ✔ |
| breaks down food particles and wastes | | |

## Plant Cell

**Found in plant cells, not animal cells:**

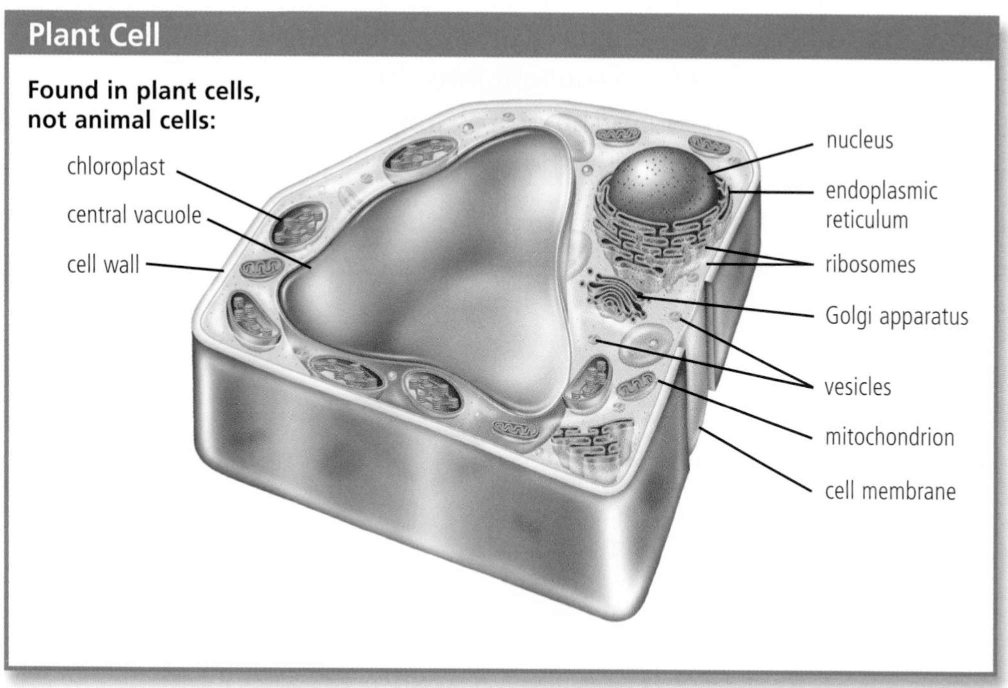


## Animal Cell

**Found in animal cells, not plant cells:**

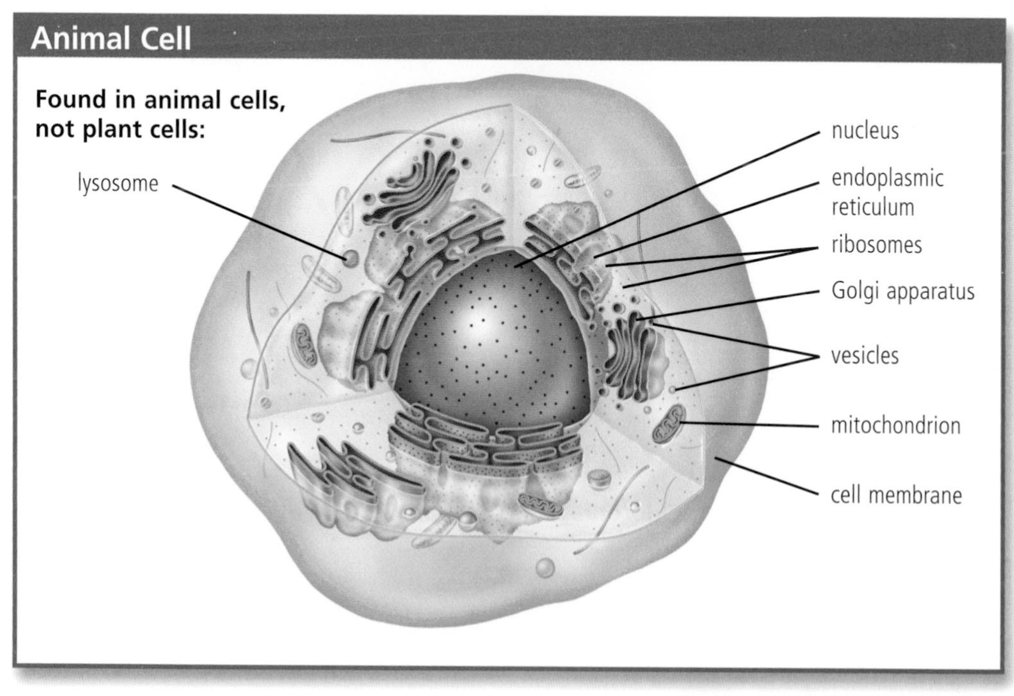


APPENDIX

# Photosynthesis and Cellular Respiration

The source of energy for almost all organisms is the Sun. Plants and other photosynthetic organisms such as algae change the energy in sunlight into a form of energy that cells can use—chemical energy. Photosynthesis is the process that changes the energy from sunlight into chemical energy and produces glucose, an energy-rich sugar. The process takes place in cellular structures called chloroplasts, found in the cytoplasm.

All cells must have energy to function. Glucose and other sugars and starches store energy, as well as serve as a source of material for cells.

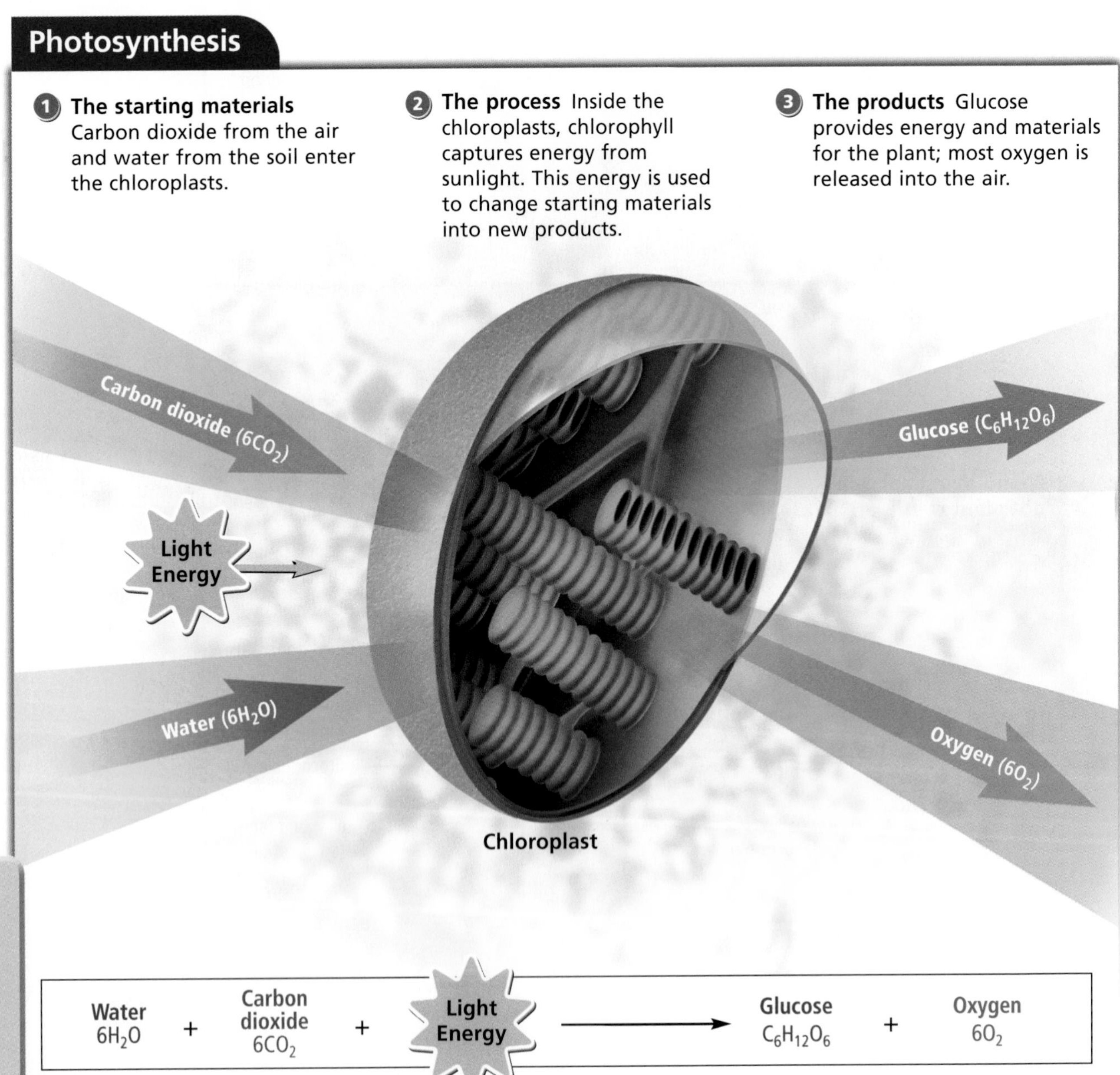

Photosynthesis
1 The starting materials Carbon dioxide from the air and water from the soil enter the chloroplasts.
2 The process Inside the chloroplasts, chlorophyll captures energy from sunlight. This energy is used to change starting materials into new products.
3 The products Glucose provides energy and materials for the plant; most oxygen is released into the air.
Carbon dioxide ($6CO_2$)
Light Energy
Water ($6H_2O$)
Glucose ($C_6H_{12}O_6$)
Oxygen ($6O_2$)
Chloroplast
Water $6H_2O$ + Carbon dioxide $6CO_2$ + Light Energy → Glucose $C_6H_{12}O_6$ + Oxygen $6O_2$
APPENDIX

Chemical energy is stored in the bonds of the sugar and starch molecules. Cellular respiration is the process that releases energy from sugars. The process takes place in cellular structures called mitochondria, found in the cytoplasm. In cellular respiration, cells use oxygen to release energy as the molecules are broken down.

Compare the starting materials and products of photosynthesis with those of cellular respiration. The starting materials of one process are the products of the other process.

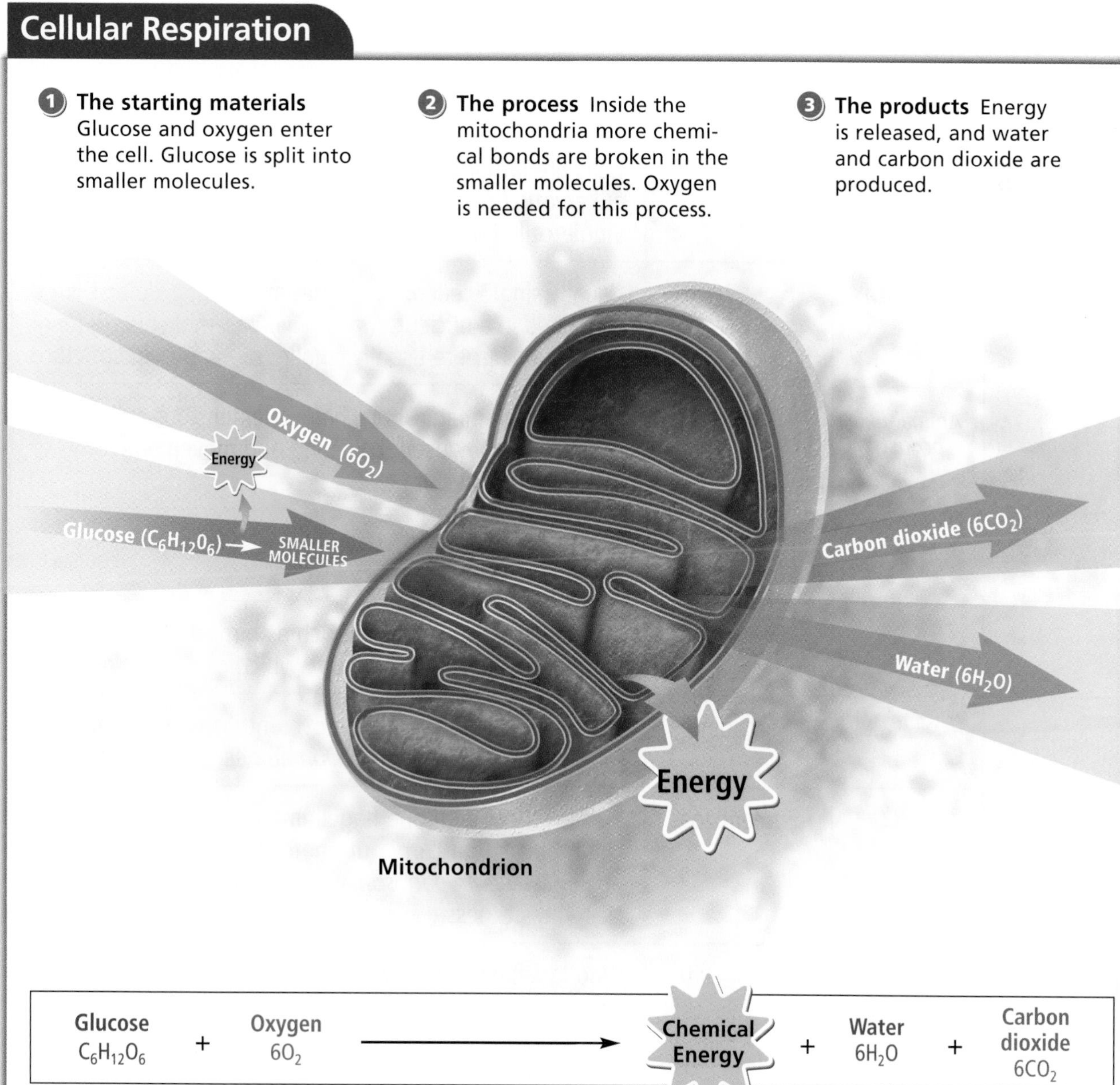
Cellular Respiration
1 The starting materials Glucose and oxygen enter the cell. Glucose is split into smaller molecules.
2 The process Inside the mitochondria more chemical bonds are broken in the smaller molecules. Oxygen is needed for this process.
3 The products Energy is released, and water and carbon dioxide are produced.
Oxygen ($6O_2$)
Energy
Glucose ($C_6H_{12}O_6$) → SMALLER MOLECULES
Carbon dioxide ($6CO_2$)
Water ($6H_2O$)
Energy
Mitochondrion
Glucose $C_6H_{12}O_6$ + Oxygen $6O_2$ → Chemical Energy + Water $6H_2O$ + Carbon dioxide $6CO_2$

# Classification of Living Things

Living things are classified into three domains. These domains are further divided into kingdoms, and then phyla. Major phyla are described in the table below, along with important features that are used to distinguish each group.

| Classification of Living Things | | | |
|---|---|---|---|
| Domain | Kingdom | Phylum | Common Name and Description |
| **Archaea** | **Archaea** | | Single-celled, with no nucleus. Live in some of Earth's most extreme environments, including salty, hot, and acid environments, and the deep ocean. |
| **Bacteria** | **Bacteria** | | Single-celled, with no nucleus, but chemically different from Archaea. Live in all types of environments, including the human body; reproduce by dividing from one cell into two. Includes blue-green bacteria (cyanobacteria), *Streptococcus,* and *Bacillus.* |
| **Eukarya** | | | Cells are larger than archaea or bacteria and are eukaryotic (have a nucleus containing DNA). Single-celled or multicellular. |
| | **Protista** | | Usually single-celled, but sometimes multicellular. DNA contained in a nucleus. Many phyla resemble plants, fungi, or animals but are usually smaller or simpler in structure. |
| | ***Animal-like protists*** | Ciliophora | Ciliates; have many short, hairlike extensions called cilia, which they use for feeding and movement. Includes paramecium. |
| | | Zoomastigina | Zooflagellates; have usually one or two long, hairlike extensions called flagella. |
| | | Sporozoa | Cause diseases in animals such as birds, fish, and humans. Includes *Plasmodium,* which causes malaria. |
| | | Sarcodina | Use footlike extensions to move and feed. Includes foraminifers and amoebas. Sometimes called Rhizopoda. |
| | ***Plantlike protists*** | Euglenozoa | Single-celled, with one flagellum. Some have chloroplasts that carry out photosynthesis. Includes euglenas and *Trypanosoma,* which causes African sleeping sickness. |
| | | Dinoflagellata | Dinoflagellates; usually single-celled; usually have chloroplasts and flagellum. In great numbers, some species can cause red tides along coastlines. |

## Classification of Living Things (cont.)

| Domain | Kingdom | Phylum | Common Name and Description |
|---|---|---|---|
| | | Chrysophyta | Yellow algae, golden-brown algae, and diatoms; single-celled; named for the yellow pigments in their chloroplasts (*chrysophyte*, in Greek, means "golden plant"). |
| | | Chlorophyceae | Green algae; have chloroplasts and are chemically similar to land plants. Unicellular or forms simple colonies of cells. Includes *Chlamydomonas, Ulva* (sea lettuce), and *Volvox.* |
| | | Phaeophyta | Brown seaweed; contain a special brown pigment that gives these organisms their color. Multicellular, live mainly in salt water; includes kelp. |
| | | Rhodophyta | Red algae; contain a red pigment that makes these organisms red, purple, or reddish-black. Multicellular, live in salt water. |
| | ***Funguslike protists*** | Acrasiomycota | Cellular slime molds; live partly as free-living single-celled organisms, then fuse together to form a many-celled mass. Live in damp, nutrient-rich environments; decomposers. |
| | | Myxomycota | Acellular slime molds; form large, slimy masses made of many nuclei but technically a single cell. |
| | | Oomycota | Water molds and downy mildews; produce thin, cottonlike extensions called hyphae. Feed off of dead or decaying material, often in water. |
| | **Fungi** | | Usually multicellular; eukaryotic; cells have a thick cell wall. Obtain nutrients through absorption; often function as decomposers. |
| | | Chytridiomycota | Oldest and simplest fungi; usually aquatic (fresh water or brackish water); single-celled or multicellular. |
| | | Basidiomycota | Multicellular; reproduce with a club-shaped structure that is commonly seen on forest floors. Includes mushrooms, puffballs, rusts, and smuts. |
| | | Zygomycota | Mostly disease-causing molds; often parasitic. |
| | | Ascomycota | Includes single-celled yeasts and multicellular sac fungi. Includes *Penicillium.* |

## Classification of Living Things (cont.)

| Domain | Kingdom | Phylum | Common Name and Description |
|---|---|---|---|
| | **Plantae** | | Multicellular and eukaryotic; make sugars using energy from sunlight. Cells have a thick cell wall of cellulose. |
| | | Bryophyta | Mosses; small, grasslike plants that live in moist, cool environments. Includes sphagnum (peat) moss. Seedless, nonvascular plants. |
| | | Hepatophyta | Liverworts; named for the liver-shaped structure of one part of the plant's life cycle. Live in moist environments. Seedless, nonvascular plants. |
| | | Anthoceratophyta | Hornworts; named for the visible hornlike structures with which they reproduce. Live on forest floors and other moist, cool environments. Seedless, nonvascular plants. |
| | | Psilotophyta | Simple plant, just two types. Includes whisk ferns found in tropical areas, a common greenhouse weed. Seedless, vascular plants. |
| | | Lycophyta | Club mosses and quillworts; look like miniature pine trees; live in moist, wooded environments. Includes *Lycopodium* (ground pine). Seedless vascular plants. |
| | | Sphenophyta | Plants with simple leaves, stems, and roots. Grow about a meter tall, usually in moist areas. Includes *Equisetum* (scouring rush). Seedless, vascular plants. |
| | | Pterophyta | Ferns; fringed-leaf plants that grow in cool, wooded environments. Includes many species. Seedless, vascular plants. |
| | | Cycadophyta | Cycads; slow-growing palmlike plants that grow in tropical environments. Reproduce with seeds. |
| | | Ginkgophyta | Includes only one species: *Ginkgo biloba,* a tree that is often planted in urban environments. Reproduce with seeds in cones. |
| | | Gnetophyta | Small group includes desert-dwelling and tropical species. Includes *Ephedra* (Mormon tea) and *Welwitschia,* which grows in African deserts. Reproduce with seeds. |
| | | Coniferophyta | Conifers, including pines, spruces, firs, sequoias. Usually evergreen trees; tend to grow in cold, dry environments; reproduce with seeds produced in cones. |

## Classification of Living Things (cont.)

| Domain | Kingdom | Phylum | Common Name and Description |
|---|---|---|---|
| | | Anthophyta | Flowering plants; includes grasses and flowering trees and shrubs. Reproduce with seeds produced in flowers, becoming fruit. |
| | **Animalia** | | Multicellular and eukaryotic; obtain energy by consuming food. Usually able to move around. |
| | | Porifera | Sponges; spend most of their lives fixed to the ocean floor. Feed by filtering water (containing nutrients and small organisms) through their body. |
| | | Cnidaria | Aquatic animals with a radial (spokelike) body shape; named for their stinging cells (cnidocytes). Includes jellyfish, hydras, sea anemones, and corals. |
| | | Ctenophora | Comb jellies; named for the comblike rows of cilia (hairlike extensions) that are used for movement. |
| | | Platyhelminthes | Flatworms; thin, flattened worms with simple tissues and sensory organs. Includes planaria and tapeworms, which cause diseases in humans and other hosts. |
| | | Nematoda | Roundworms; small, round worms; many species are parasites, causing diseases in humans, such as trichinosis and elephantiasis. |
| | | Annelida | Segmented worms; body is made of many similar segments. Includes earthworms, leeches, and many marine worms. |
| | | Mollusca | Soft-bodied, aquatic animals that usually have an outer shell. Includes snails, mussels, clams, octopus, and squid. |
| | | Arthropoda | Animals with an outer skeleton (exoskeleton) and jointed appendages (for example, legs or wings). Very large group that includes insects, spiders and ticks, centipedes, millipedes, and crustaceans. |
| | | Echinodermata | Marine animals with a radial (spokelike) body shape. Includes feather stars, sea stars (starfish), sea urchins, sand dollars, and sea cucumbers. |
| | | Chordata | Mostly vertebrates (animals with backbones) that share important stages of early development. Includes tunicates (sea squirts), fish, sharks, amphibians, reptiles, birds, and mammals. |

# Formulas

| Word Form | Symbolic Form | Purpose |
|---|---|---|
| Volume = length • width • height | $V = lwh$ | to calculate the volume of a rectangular object |
| Density = $\frac{\text{mass}}{\text{Volume}}$ | $D = \frac{m}{V}$ | to calculate the density of an object |
| Speed = $\frac{\text{distance}}{\text{time}}$ | $S = \frac{d}{t}$ | to calculate the speed of an object |
| acceleration = $\frac{\text{final velocity} - \text{initial velocity}}{\text{time}}$ | $a = \frac{v_{final} - v_{initial}}{t}$ | to calculate the acceleration of an object |
| Force = mass • acceleration | $F = ma$ | to calculate the force, mass, or acceleration of an object; called Newton's second law |
| momentum = mass • velocity | $p = mv$ | to calculate the momentum of an object |
| Pressure = $\frac{\text{Force}}{\text{Area}}$ | $P = \frac{F}{A}$ | to calculate the pressure on an object |
| Work = Force • distance | $W = Fd$ | to calculate work |
| Gravitational Potential Energy = mass • gravitational acceleration • height | $GPE = mgh$ | to calculate the gravitational potential energy of an object |
| Kinetic Energy = $\frac{\text{mass} \cdot \text{velocity}^2}{2}$ | $KE = \frac{1}{2} mv^2$ | to calculate the kinetic energy of an object |
| Mechanical Energy = Potential Energy + Kinetic Energy | $ME = PE + KE$ | to calculate the mechanical energy of an object |
| Power = $\frac{\text{Work}}{\text{time}}$ | $P = \frac{W}{t}$ | to calculate power based on work |
| Power = $\frac{\text{Energy}}{\text{time}}$ | $P = \frac{E}{t}$ | to calculate power based on energy |
| Efficiency (%) = $\frac{\text{Output work}}{\text{Input work}} \cdot 100$ | $E\,(\%) = \frac{W_{out}}{W_{in}} \cdot 100$ | to calculate the efficiency of a machine |

| Word Form | Symbolic Form | Purpose |
|---|---|---|
| Mechanical Advantage = $\frac{\text{Output Force}}{\text{Input Force}}$ | $MA = \frac{F_{out}}{F_{in}}$ | to calculate a machine's mechanical advantage |
| Ideal Mechanical Advantage = $\frac{\text{length of incline}}{\text{height of incline}}$ | $IMA = \frac{l}{h}$ | to calculate the ideal mechanical advantage of an inclined plane |
| Ideal Mechanical Advantage = $\frac{\text{Radius of input}}{\text{Radius of output}}$ | $IMA = \frac{R_{in}}{R_{out}}$ | to calculate the ideal mechanical advantage of a wheel and axle |
| Ideal Mechanical Advantage = $\frac{\text{distance from input force to fulcrum}}{\text{distance from output force to fulcrum}}$ | $IMA = \frac{d_{in}}{d_{out}}$ | to calculate the ideal mechanical advantage of a lever |
| Speed = wavelength • frequency | $S = \lambda f$ | to calculate the speed of a wave |
| Current = $\frac{\text{Voltage}}{\text{Resistance}}$ | $I = \frac{V}{R}$ | to calculate the relationships among current, voltage, and resistance; called Ohm's law |
| Electrical Power = Voltage • Current | $P = VI$ | to calculate power |
| Energy used = Power • time | $E = Pt$ | to calculate the total energy used |

APPENDIX

# Glossary



## A

### acceleration
The rate at which velocity changes over time. (p. D25)

**aceleración** La razón a la cual la velocidad cambia con respecto al tiempo.

### acid rain
Rain that has become more acidic than normal due to pollution. (p. A70)

**lluvia ácida** Lluvia que se ha vuelto más ácida de lo normal debido a la contaminación.

### adaptation
A characteristic, a behavior, or any inherited trait that makes a species able to survive and reproduce in a particular environment. (p. xxxi)

**adaptación** Una característica, un comportamiento o cualquier rasgo heredado que permite a una especie sobrevivir o reproducirse en un medio ambiente determinado.

### addiction
A physical or psychological need for a habit-forming substance, such as alcohol or drugs. (p. B145)

**adicción** Una necesidad física o psicológica de una sustancia que forma hábito, como el alcohol o las drogas.

### adolescence (AD-uhl-EHS-uhns)
The stage of life from the time a human body begins to mature sexually to adulthood. (p. B135)

**adolescencia** La etapa de la vida que va desde que el cuerpo humano empieza a madurar sexualmente hasta la edad adulta.

### adulthood
The stage of life that begins once a human body completes its growth and reaches sexual maturity. (p. B136)

**edad adulta** La etapa de la vida que empieza una vez que el cuerpo humano completa su crecimiento y alcanza la madurez sexual.

### air mass
A large volume of air that has nearly the same temperature and humidity at different locations at the same altitude. (p. A79)

**masa de aire** Un gran volumen de aire que tiene casi la misma temperatura y humedad en distintos puntos a la misma altitud.

### air pollution
Harmful materials added to the air that can cause damage to living things and the environment. (p. A27)

**contaminación de aire** Materiales nocivos añadidos al aire que pueden causar daño a los seres vivos y al medio ambiente.

### air pressure
The force of air molecules pushing on an area. (p. A43)

**presión de aire** La fuerza de las moléculas de aire empujando sobre un área.

### air resistance
The fluid friction due to air. (p. D89)

**resistencia del aire** La fricción fluida debida al aire.

### algae
Protists that live mostly in water and use sunlight as a source of energy. *Algae* is a plural word; the singular is *alga.* (p. C31)

**algas** Protistas que viven principalmente en el agua y que usan la luz solar como fuente de energía.

### alternating current AC
Electric current that reverses direction at regular intervals. (p. E97)

**corriente alterna** Corriente eléctrica que invierte su dirección a intervalos regulares.

### altitude
The distance above sea level. (p. A10)

**altitud** La distancia sobre el nivel del mar.

### ampere amp
The unit of measurement of electric current, which is equal to one coulomb per second. The number of amps flowing through a circuit equals the circuit's amperage. (p. E29)

**amperio** La unidad de medición de la corriente eléctrica, la cual es igual a un culombio por segundo. El número de amperios fluyendo por un circuito es igual al amperaje del circuito.

### amphibian
A cold-blooded vertebrate animal that lives in water and breathes with gills when it is young; as an adult, it moves onto land and breathes air with lungs. (p. C167)

**anfibio** Un vertebrado de sangre fría que vive en el agua y respira con branquias cuando es juvenil; cuando es adulto, se mueve a la tierra y respire aire con pulmones.

### analog
Represented by a continuous but varying quantity, such as a wave. In electronics, analog information is represented by a continuous but varying electrical signal. (p. E60)

**análogo** Que es representado por una cantidad variante pero continua, como una onda. En la electrónica, la información análoga se representa mediante una señal eléctrica continua pero variante.

### angiosperm (AN-jee-uh-SPURM)
A plant that has flowers and produces seeds enclosed in fruit. (p. C107)

**Angiosperma** Una planta que tiene flores y que produce semillas dentro de frutas.

### antibiotic
A medicine that can block the growth and reproduction of bacteria. (p. B81)

**antibiótico** Una medicina que puede impedir el crecimiento y la reproducción de las bacterias.

### antibody
A protein produced by some white blood cells to attack specific foreign materials. (p. B75)

**anticuerpo** Una proteína producida por algunos glóbulos blancos para atacar materiales extraños específicos.

### antigen
A particular substance that the body recognizes as foreign and that stimulates a response. (p. B78)

**antígeno** Una sustancia que el cuerpo reconoce come extraña y que causa una respuesta.

### appendicular skeleton (AP-uhn-DIHK-yuh-luhr)
The bones of the skeleton that function to allow movement, such as arm and leg bones. (p. B16)

**esqueleto apendicular** Los huesos del esqueleto cuya función es permitir el movimiento, como los huesos del brazo y los huesos de la pierna.

### archaea (AHR-kee-uh)
Single-celled organisms without nuclei that can survive in extreme environments. *Archaea* is a plural word; the singular is *archaeon.* (p. C18)

**archaea** Organismos de una célula sin nucléo que pueden sobrevivir en medios ambientes extremosos.

### artery
A blood vessel with strong walls that carries blood away from the heart. (p. B69)

**arteria** Un vaso sanguíneo con paredes fuertes que lleva la sangre del corazón hacia otras partes del cuerpo.

### arthropod
An invertebrate animal with an exoskeleton, a segmented body, and jointed legs. (p. C142)

**artrópodo** Un animal invertebrado con un exoesqueleto, un cuerpo segmentado y patas articuladas.

### atmosphere
The outer layer of gases of a large body in space, such as a planet or star; the mixture of gases that surrounds the solid Earth; one of the four parts of the Earth system. (p. A9)

**atmósfera** La capa externa de gases de un gran cuerpo que se encuentra en el espacio, como un planeta o una estrella; la mezcla de gases que rodea la Tierra sólida; una de las cuatro partes del sistema terrestre.

### atom
The smallest particle of an element that has the chemical properties of that element. (p. xxxv)

**átomo** La partícula más pequeña de un elemento que tiene las propiedades químicas del elemento.

### autonomic nervous system
The part of the nervous system that controls involuntary action and responses. (p. B107)

**sistema nervioso autónomo** La parte del sistema nervioso que controla la acción involuntaria y las respuestas.

### autotroph (AW-tuh-TRAHF)
An organism that captures energy from sunlight and uses it to produce energy-rich carbon compounds, usually through the process of photosynthesis. (p. C52)

**autótrofo** Un organismo que capta energía de la luz solar y la usa para producir compuestos de carbono ricos en energía, usualmente mediante el proceso de fotosíntesis.

### axial skeleton
The central part of the skeleton, which includes the cranium, the spinal column, and the ribs. (p. B16)

**esqueleto axial** La parte central del esqueleto que incluye al cráneo, a la columna vertebral y a las costillas.

# B

**bacteria** (bak-TEER-ee-uh)
A large group of one-celled organisms that sometimes cause disease. *Bacteria* is a plural word; the singular is *bacterium.* (p. B149)

**bacterias** Un grupo grande de organismos unicelulares que algunas veces causan enfermedades.

**barometer**
An instrument that measures air pressure in the atmosphere. (p. A46)

**barómetro** Un instrumento que mide la presión del aire en la atmósfera.

**behavior**
An organism's action in response to a stimulus. (p. C62)

**comportamiento** La acción de un organismo en respuesta a un estímulo.

**Bernoulli's principle**
A statement that describes the effects of movement on fluid pressure. According to this principle, an increase in the speed of the motion of a fluid decreases the pressure within the fluid. (p. D100)

**principio de Bernoulli** Un enunciado que describe los efectos del movimiento sobre la presión de un líquido. De acuerdo a este principio, un aumento en la velocidad del movimiento de un fluido disminuye la presión dentro del líquido

**binary code**
A coding system in which information is represented by two figures, such as 1 and 0. (p. E58)

**código binario** Un sistema de codificación en el cual la información se representa con dos números, como el 1 y el 0.

**binary fission**
A form of asexual reproduction by which some single-celled organisms reproduce. The genetic material is copied, and one cell divides into two independent cells that are each a copy of the original cell. Prokaryotes such as bacteria reproduce by binary fission. (p. C12)

**fisión binaria** Una forma asexual de reproducción mediante la cual algunos organismos unicelulares se reproducen. El material genético se copia y una célula se divide en dos células independientes las cuales son copias de la célula original. Los organismos procariotas, tales como las bacterias, se reproducen mediante fisión binaria.

**biodiversity**
The number and variety of living things found on Earth or within an ecosystem. (p. xxxi)

**biodiversidad** La cantidad y variedad de organismos vivos que se encuentran en la Tierra o dentro de un ecosistema.

**biosphere** (BY-uh-SFEER)
All living organisms on Earth in the air, on the land, and in the waters; one of the four parts of the Earth system. (p. xxxi)

**biosfera** Todos los organismos vivos de la Tierra, en el aire, en la tierra y en las aguas; una de las cuatro partes del sistema de la Tierra.

**blizzard**
A blinding snowstorm with winds of at least 56 kilometers per hour (35 mi/h), usually with temperatures below –7°C (20°F). (p. A90)

**ventisca** Una cegadora tormenta de nieve con vientos de por lo menos 56 kilómetros por hora (35 mi/h), usualmente con temperaturas menores a –7°C (20°F).

**blood**
A fluid in the body that delivers oxygen and other materials to cells and removes carbon dioxide and other wastes. (p. B65)

**sangre** Un fluido en el cuerpo que reparte oxígeno y otras sustancias a las células y elimina dióxido de carbono y otros desechos.

**blubber**
A layer of fat in some sea mammals that lies beneath the skin. It insulates the animal from cold and stores reserve energy. (p. C184)

**grasa de ballena** Una capa de tejido graso en algunos mamíferos marinos que yace bajo la piel. Aísla al animal del frió y almacena energía de reserva.

**buoyant force**
The upward force on objects in a fluid; often called buoyancy. (p. D98)

**fuerza flotante** La fuerza hacia arriba que ejerce un fluido sobre un objeto inmerso en él, a menudo llamada flotación.

# C

**capillary**
A narrow blood vessel that connects arteries with veins. (p. B69)

**capilar** Un vaso sanguíneo angosto que conecta a las arterias con las venas.

**cardiac muscle**
The muscle that makes up the heart. (p. B24)

**músculo cardiaco** El músculo del cual está compuesto el corazón.

**cell**
The smallest unit that is able to perform the basic functions of life. (p. xxxi)

**célula** La unidad más pequeña capaz de realizar las funciones básicas de la vida.

**cellular respiration**
A process in which cells use oxygen to release energy stored in sugars. (pp. B39, C53)

**respiración celular** Un proceso en el cual las células usan oxígeno para liberar energía almacenada en las azúcares.

**central nervous system**
The brain and spinal cord. The central nervous system communicates with the rest of the nervous system through electrical signals sent to and from neurons. (p. B104)

**sistema nervioso central** El cerebro y la médula espinal. El sistema nervioso central se comunica con el resto del sistema nervioso mediante señales eléctricas enviadas hacia y desde las neuronas.

**centripetal force** (sehn-TRIHP-ih-tuhl)
Any force that keeps an object moving in a circle. (p. D54)

**fuerza centrípeta** Cualquier fuerza que mantiene a un objeto moviéndose en forma circular.

**childhood**
The stage of life after infancy and before the beginning of sexual maturity. (p. B134)

**niñez** La etapa de la vida después de la infancia y antes del comienzo de la madurez sexual.

**circulatory system**
The group of organs, consisting of the heart and blood vessels, that circulates blood through the body. (p. B65)

**sistema circulatorio** El grupo de órganos, que consiste del corazón y los vasos sanguíneos, que hace circular la sangre por el cuerpo.

**circuit**
A closed path through which charge can flow. (p. E43)

**circuito** Una trayectoria cerrada por la cual puede fluir una carga.

**classification**
The systematic grouping of different types of organisms by their shared characteristics.

**clasificación** La agrupación sistemática de diferentes tipos de organismos en base a las características que comparten.

**climate**
The characteristic weather conditions in an area over a long period of time. (p. A117)

**clima** Las condiciones meteorológicas características de un lugar durante un largo período de tiempo.

**climate zone**
One of the major divisions in a system for classifying the climates of different regions based on characteristics they have in common. (p. A125)

**zona climática** Una de las mayores divisiones en un sistema de clasificación de climas de diferentes regiones, basado en las características que tienen en común.

**cnidarian** (ny-DAIR-ee-uhn)
An invertebrate animal such as a jellyfish that has a body with radial symmetry, tentacles with stinging cells, and a central internal cavity. (p. C128)

**cnidario** Un animal invertebrado tal como una medusa que tiene un cuerpo con simetría radial, tentáculos con células urticantes y una cavidad central interna.

**collision**
A situation in which two objects in close contact exchange energy and momentum. (p. D66)

**colisión** Situación en la cual dos objetos en contacto cercano intercambian energía y momento.

**compact bone**
The tough, hard outer layer of a bone. (p. B15)

**hueso compacto** La capa exterior, resistente y dura de un hueso.

**compound**
A substance made up of two or more different types of atoms bonded together.

**compuesto** Una sustancia formada por dos o más diferentes tipos de átomos enlazados.

**compound machine**
A machine that is made up of two or more simple machines. (p. D164)

**máquina compuesta** Una máquina que está hecha de dos o más máquinas simples.

**computer**
An electronic device that processes digital information. (p. E61)

**computadora** Un aparato electrónico que procesa información digital.

**condensation**
The process by which a gas changes into a liquid. (p. A56)

**condensación** El proceso por el cual un gas se transforma en líquido.

**conduction**
The transfer of heat energy from one substance to another through direct contact without obvious motion. (p. A18)

**conducción** La transferencia de energía calorífica de una sustancia a otra a través de contacto directo, sin que haya movimiento obvio.

**conductor**
1. A material that transfers electric charge easily (p. E22).
2. A material that transfers energy easily.

**conductor** 1. Un material que transfiere cargas eléctricas fácilmente. 2. Un material que transfiere energía fácilmente.

**consumer**
A living thing that gets its energy by eating other living things in a food chain; consumers are also called heterotrophs. (p. C58)

**consumidor** Un organismo vivo que obtiene su energía alimentándose de otros organismos vivos en una cadena alimentaria; los consumidores también son llamados heterótrofos.

**continental climate**
A climate that occurs in the interior of a continent, with large temperature differences between seasons. (p. A120)

**clima continental** El clima que se presenta en el interior de un continente, con grandes diferencias de temperatura entre estaciones.

**convection**
The transfer of energy from place to place by the motion of heated gas or liquid; in Earth's mantle, convection is thought to transfer energy by the motion of solid rock, which when under great heat and pressure can move like a liquid. (p. A19)

**convección** La transferencia de energía de un lugar a otro por el movimiento de un líquido o gas calentado; se piensa que en el manto terrestre la convección transfiere energía mediante el movimiento de roca sólida, la cual puede moverse como un líquido cuando está muy caliente y bajo alta presión.

**Coriolis effect** (KAWR-ee-OH-lihs)
The influence of Earth's rotation on objects that move over Earth. (p. A49)

**efecto Coriolis** La influencia de la rotación de la Tierra sobre objetos que se mueven sobre la Tierra.

**cycle**
***n.*** A series of events or actions that repeat themselves regularly; a physical and/or chemical process in which one material continually changes locations and/or forms. Examples include the water cycle, the carbon cycle, and the rock cycle.

***v.*** To move through a repeating series of events or actions.

**ciclo *s.*** Una serie de eventos o acciones que se repiten regularmente; un proceso físico y/o químico en el cual un material cambia continuamente de lugar y/o forma. Ejemplos: el ciclo del agua, el ciclo del carbono y el ciclo de las rocas.

**data**
Information gathered by observation or experimentation that can be used in calculating or reasoning. *Data* is a plural word; the singular is *datum.*

**datos** Información reunida mediante observación o experimentación y que se puede usar para calcular o para razonar.

**decomposer**
An organism that feeds on and breaks down dead plant or animal matter. (p. C19)

**descomponedor** Un organismo que se alimenta de y degrada materia vegetal o animal.

**density**
A property of matter representing the mass per unit volume. (pp. A10, D99)

**densidad** Una propiedad de la materia que representa la masa por unidad de volumen.

**dermis**
The inner layer of the skin. (p. B84)

**dermis** La capa interior de la piel.

**dew point**
The temperature at which air with a given amount of water vapor will reach saturation. (p. A58)

**punto de rocío** La temperatura a la cual el aire con una cantidad determinada de vapor de agua alcanzará la saturación.

**digestion**
The process of breaking down food into usable materials. (p. B46)

**digestión** El proceso de descomponer el alimento en sustancias utilizables.

**digestive system**
The structures in the body that work together to transform the energy and materials in food into forms the body can use. (p. B46)

**sistema digestivo** Las estructuras en el cuerpo que trabajan juntas para transformar la energía y las sustancias en el alimento a formas que el cuerpo puede usar.

**digital**
Represented by numbers. In electronics, digital information is represented by the numbers 1 and 0, signaled by a circuit that is either on or off. (p. E58)

**digital** Que es representado por números. En la electrónica, la información digital es representada por los números 1 y 0, señalados por un circuito que está encendido o apagado.

**direct current** DC
Electric current that flows in one direction only. (p. E97)

**corriente directa** Corriente eléctrica que fluye en una sola dirección.

**DNA**
The genetic material found in all living cells that contains the information needed for an organism to grow, maintain itself, and reproduce. Deoxyribonucleic acid (dee-AHK-see-RY-boh-noo-KLEE-ihk).

**ADN** El material genético que se encuentra en todas las céulas vivas y que contiene la información necesaria para que un organismo crezca, se mantenga a sí mismo y se reproduzca. Ácido desoxiribunucleico.

# E

**echinoderm**
An invertebrate sea animal with a spiny skeleton, a water vascular system, and tube feet. (p. C139)

**equinodermo** Un animal invertebrado marino con esqueleto espinoso, sistema vascular acuífero y pies ambulacrales.

**ectotherm**
An animal whose body temperature changes with environmental conditions. (p. C170)

**poiquilotermo o poiquilotérmico** Un animal cuya temperatura corporal cambia con las condiciones del medio ambiente.

**efficiency**
The percentage of the input work done on a machine that the machine can return in output work. A machine's output work divided by its input work and multiplied by 100. (p. D150)

**eficiencia** El porcentaje del trabajo de entrada suministrado a una máquina que la máquina puede devolver como trabajo de salida. El trabajo de salida de una máquina dividido por su trabajo de entrada y multiplicado por cien.

**electric cell**
A device that produces electric current using the chemical or physical properties of different materials. A battery consists of two or more cells linked together. (p. E31)

**celda eléctrica** Un aparato que produce corriente eléctrica usando las propiedades químicas o físicas de diferentes materiales. Una pila consiste de dos o más celdas conectadas.

**electric charge**
A property that allows one object to exert an electric force on another object without touching it. Electric charge can be positive or negative: positive charge is a property of the proton, while negative charge is a property of the electron. (p. E10)

**carga eléctrica** Una propiedad que permite a un objeto ejercer una fuerza eléctrica sobre otro objeto sin tocarlo. La carga eléctrica puede ser positiva o negativa: la carga positiva es una propiedad del protón mientras que la carga negativa es una propiedad del electrón.

**electric current**
A continuous flow of electric charge, which is measured in amperes. (p. E28)

**corriente eléctrica** Un flujo continuo de una carga eléctrica, el cual se mide en amperios.

**electric field**
An area surrounding a charged object, within which the object can exert an electric force on another object without touching it. (p. E10)

**campo eléctrico** Un área que rodea un objeto con carga, dentro del cual el objeto puede ejercer una fuerza eléctrica sobre otro objeto sin tocarlo.

**electric potential**
The amount of potential energy per unit charge that a static charge or electric current has. Electric potential is measured in volts and is often called voltage. (p. E19)

**potencial eléctrico** La cantidad de energía potencial por unidad de carga que tiene una carga estática o una corriente eléctrica. El potencial eléctrico se mide en voltios y a menudo se llama voltaje.

**electric power**
The rate at which electrical energy is generated from, or converted into, another source of energy, such as kinetic energy. (p. E102)

**potencia eléctrica** El ritmo al cual se genera energía eléctrica a partir de, o se convierte en, otra fuente de energía, como energía cinética.

**electromagnet**
A magnet that consists of a piece of iron or steel inside a coil of current-carrying wire. (p. E90)

**electroimán** Un imán que consiste de un pedazo de hierro o de acero dentro de una bobina de alambre por la cual fluye una corriente eléctrica.

**electromagnetism**
Magnetism that results from the flow of electric charge. (p. E89)

**electromagnetismo** Magnetismo que resulta del flujo de una carga eléctrica.

**electron**
A negatively charged particle located outside an atom's nucleus.

**electrón** Una partícula con cargada negativamente localizada fuera del núcleo de un átomo.

**electronic**
***adj.*** Operating by means of an electrical signal. An electronic device is a device that uses electric current to represent coded information. (p. E57)

***n.*** An electronic device or system, such as a computer, calculator, CD player, or game system.

**electrónico *adj.*** Que opera por medio de una señal eléctrica. Un aparato electrónico es un aparato que usa corriente eléctrica para representar información codificada.

**element**
A substance that cannot be broken down into a simpler substance by ordinary chemical changes. An element consists of atoms of only one type. (p. xxxv)

**elemento** Una sustancia que no puede descomponerse en otra sustancia más simple por medio de cambios químicos normales. Un elemento consta de átomos de un solo tipo.

**El Niño** (ehl NEEN-yoh)
A disturbance of wind patterns and ocean currents in the Pacific Ocean that causes temporary climate changes in many parts of the world. (p. A136)

**El Niño** Un disturbio en los patrones de viento y las corrientes oceánicas del océano Pacifico que causa cambios climáticos temporales en muchas partes del mundo.

**embryo** (EHM-bree-OH)
A multicellular organism, plant or animal, in its earliest stages of development. (pp. B121, C98)

**embrión** Una planta o un animal en su estadio mas temprano de desarrollo.

**endocrine system**
A group of organs called glands and the hormones they produce that help regulate conditions inside the body. (p. B110)

**sistema endocrino** Un grupo de órganos llamados glándulas y las hormonas que producen que ayudan a regular las condiciones dentro del cuerpo.

**endoskeleton**
An internal support system; such a skeleton made of bone tissue is a distinguishing characteristic of vertebrate animals. (p. C157)

**endoesqueleto** Un sistema de soporte interno, como un esqueleto formado de tejido óseo es una característica distintiva de los animales vertebrados.

**endotherm**
An animal that maintains a constant body temperature. (p. C174)

**homeotermo o endotermo** Un animal que mantiene una temperatura corporal constante.

**energy**
The ability to do work or to cause a change. For example, the energy of a moving bowling ball knocks over pins; energy from food allows animals to move and to grow; and energy from the Sun heats Earth's surface and atmosphere, which causes air to move. (p. xxxiii)

**energía** La capacidad para trabajar o causar un cambio. Por ejemplo, la energía de una bola de boliche en movimiento tumba los pinos; la energía proveniente de su alimento permite a los animales moverse y crecer; la energía del Sol calienta la superficie y la atmósfera de la Tierra, lo que ocasiona que el aire se mueva.

**environment**
Everything that surrounds a living thing. An environment is made up of both living and nonliving factors. (p. xxxi)

**medio ambiente** Todo lo que rodea a un organismo vivo. Un medio ambiente está compuesto de factores vivos y factores sin vida.

**epidermis**
The outer layer of the skin. (p. B84)

**epidermis** La capa exterior de la piel.

### evaporation
The process by which liquid changes into gas. (p. A56)

**evaporación** El proceso por el cual un líquido se transforma en gas.

### exoskeleton
The strong, flexible outer covering of some invertebrate animals, such as arthropods. (p. C143)

**exoesqueleto** La cubierta exterior fuerte y flexible de algunos animales invertebrados, como los artrópodos.

### experiment
An organized procedure to study something under controlled conditions. (p. xxxviii)

**experimento** Un procedimiento organizado para estudiar algo bajo condiciones controladas.

### extinction
The permanent disappearance of a species. (p. xxxi)

**extinción** La desaparición permanente de una especie.

### fertilization
Part of the process of sexual reproduction in which a male reproductive cell and a female reproductive cell combine to form a new cell that can develop into a new organism. (pp. B121, C48)

**fertilización** El proceso mediante el cual una célula reproductiva masculina y una célula reproductiva femenina se combinan para formar una nueva célula que puede convertirse en un organismo nuevo.

### fetus
The developing human embryo from eight weeks to birth. (p. B122)

**feto** El embrión humano en desarrollo de las ocho semanas al nacimiento.

### flower
The reproductive structure of an angiosperm, containing male and female parts. (p. C108)

**flor** La estructura reproductiva de una angiosperma, contiene las partes masculinas y femeninas.

### fluid
A substance that can flow easily, such as a gas or a liquid. (p. D88)

**fluido** Una sustancia que fluye fácilmente, como por ejemplo un gas o un líquido.

### force
A push or a pull; something that changes the motion of an object. (p. D41)

**fuerza** Un empuje o un jalón; algo que cambia el movimiento de un objeto.

### fossil
A trace or the remains of a once-living thing from long ago.

**fósil** Un rastro o los restos de un organismo que vivió hace mucho tiempo.

### fossil fuels
Fuels formed from the remains of prehistoric organisms that are burned for energy. (p. A28)

**combustibles fósiles** Combustibles formados a partir de los restos de organismos prehistóricos que son consumidos para obtener energía.

### freezing rain
Rain that freezes when it hits the ground or another surface and coats the surface with ice. (p. A68)

**lluvia helada** Lluvia que se congela cuando cae a la tierra o cualquier otra superficie y cubre la superficie con hielo.

### friction
A force that resists the motion between two surfaces in contact. (p. D85)

**fricción** Una fuerza que resiste el movimiento entre dos superficies en contacto.

### front
The boundary between air masses. (p. A82)

**frente** El limite entre masas de aire.

### fruit
The ripened ovary of a flowering plant that contains the seeds. (p. C108)

**fruta** El ovario maduro de una planta floreciente que contiene las semillas.

### fulcrum
A fixed point around which a lever rotates. (p. D155)

**fulcro** Un punto fijo alrededor del cual gira una palanca.

### gas
A state of matter different from liquid and solid, with no definite volume and no definite shape.

**gas** Un estado de la material, que no es sólido ni líquido, en el cual la sustancia se puede expandir o contraer para llenar un recipiente.

GLOSSARY

**generator**
A device that converts kinetic energy, or the energy of motion, into electrical energy. Generators produce electric current by rotating a magnet within a coil of wire or rotating a coil of wire within a magnetic field. (p. E96)

**generador** Un aparato que convierte energía cinética, o la energía del movimiento, a energía eléctrica. Los generadores producen corriente eléctrica al girar un imán dentro de una bobina de alambre o haciendo rotar una bobina de alambre dentro de un campo magnético.

**genetic material**
The nucleic acid DNA that is present in all living cells and contains the information needed for a cell's growth, maintenance, and reproduction.

**material genético** El ácido nucleico ADN, ue esta presente en todas las células vivas y que contiene la información necesaria para el crecimiento, el mantenimiento y la reproducción celular.

**geosphere** (JEE-uh-sfeer)
All the features on Earth's surface—continents, islands, and seafloor—and everything below the surface—the inner and outer core and the mantle; one of the four parts of the Earth system. (p. xxxiii)

**geosfera** Todas las características de la superficie de la Tierra, es decir, continentes, islas y el fondo marino, y de todo bajo la superficie, es decir, el núcleo externo e interno y el manto; una de las cuatro partes del sistema de la Tierra.

**germination** (JUR-muh-NAY-shuhn)
The beginning of growth of a new plant from a spore or a seed. (p. C99)

**germinación** El inicio del crecimiento de una nueva planta a partir de una espora o una semilla.

**gestation**
In mammals, the period of time spent by a developing offspring inside the mother's body. (p. C186)

**gestación** En los mamíferos, el periodo de tiempo que pasa una cría en desarrollo dentro del cuerpo de la madre.

**gill**
A respiratory organ that filters oxgen dissolved in water. (p. C137)

**branquia** Un órgano respiratorio que filtra oxígeno disuelto en el agua.

**gland**
An organ in the body that produces a specific substance, such as a hormone. (p. B111)

**glándula** Un órgano en el cuerpo que produce una sustancia específica, como una hormona.

**global winds**
Winds that travel long distances in steady patterns over several weeks. (p. A48)

**vientos globales** Vientos que viajan grandes distancias en patrones fijos por varias semanas.

**gravity**
The force that objects exert on each other because of their masses. (p. D77)

**gravedad** La fuerza que los objetos ejercen entre sí debido a sus masas.

**greenhouse effect**
The process by which certain gases in a planet's atmosphere absorb and emit infrared radiation, resulting in an increase in surface temperature. (p. A24)

**efecto invernadero** El proceso mediante el cual ciertos gases en la atmósfera de un planeta absorben y emiten radiación infrarroja, resultando en un incremento de la temperatura superficial del planeta.

**greenhouse gases**
Gases, such as carbon dioxide and methane, that absorb and give off infrared radiation as part of the greenhouse effect. (p. A24)

**gases invernadero** Gases, como el dióxido de carbono y el metano, que absorben y emiten radiación infrarroja como parte del efecto invernadero.

**grounding**
The creation of a harmless, low-resistance path—a ground—for electricity to follow. Grounding is an important electrical safety procedure. (p. E25)

**conexión a tierra** La creación de una trayectoria inofensiva, de baja resistencia—una tierra—para que la siga la electricidad. La conexión a tierra es un importante procedimiento de seguridad eléctrica.

**gymnosperm** (JIHM-nuh-SPURM)
A plant that produces seeds that are not enclosed in flowers or fruit. (p. C102)

**Gimnosperma** Una planta que produce semillas que no están dentro de las flores o las frutas.

**hail**
Layered lumps or balls of ice that fall from cumulonimbus clouds. (p. A68)

**granizo** Trozos de hielo que caen de nubes cumulonimbos.

**heterotroph** (HEHT-uhr-uh-TRAWF)
An organism that consumes other organisms to get energy. (p. C58)

**heterótrofo** Un organismo que consume a otros organismos para obtener energía.

**hibernation**
A sleeplike state in which certain animals spend the winter. Hibernation reduces an animal's need for food and helps protect it from cold. (p. C64)

**hibernación** Un estado parecido al de sueño en el cual ciertos animales pasan el invierno. La hibernación reduce la necesidad de alimento de un animal y le ayuda a protegerse del frío.

**high-pressure system**
A generally calm and clear weather system that occurs when air sinks down in a high-pressure center and spreads out toward areas of lower pressure as it nears the ground. (p. A84)

**sistema de alta presión** Un sistema climático generalmente claro y calmo que se presenta cuando el aire desciende en un centro de alta presión y se esparce hacia áreas de baja presión conforme se acerca al suelo.

**homeostasis**
A condition needed for health and functioning in which an organism or cell maintains a relatively stable internal environment. (p. B12)

**homeostasis** Una condición necesaria para la salud y el funcionamiento en la cual un organismo o una célula mantiene un medio ambiente estable e interna.

**horizontal**
Parallel to the horizon; level.

**horizontal** Paralelo al horizonte; nivelado.

**hormone**
A chemical that is made in one organ and travels through the blood to another organ. (p. B111)

**hormona** Una sustancia química que se produce en un órgano y viaja por la sangre a otro órgano.

**horsepower** hp
The unit of measurement of power for engines and motors. One horsepower equals 745 watts. (p. D132)

**caballos de fuerza** La unidad de medición de potencia para máquinas y motores. Un caballo de fuerza es igual a 745 vatios.

**host cell**
A cell that a virus infects and uses to make copies of itself. (p. C26)

**célula hospedera** Una célula que un virus infecta y usa para hacer copias de sí mismo.

**humidity**
The amount of water vapor in air. (p. A58)

**humedad** La cantidad de vapor de agua en el aire.

**hurricane** (HUR-ih-KAYN)
A tropical low-pressure system with sustained winds of 120 kilometers per hour (74 mi/h) or more. (p. A87)

**huracán** Un sistema tropical de baja presión con vientos sostenidos de 120 kilómetros por hora (74 mi/h) o más.

**hydrosphere** (HY-druh-sfeer)
All water on Earth—in the atmosphere and in the oceans, lakes, glaciers, rivers, streams, and underground reservoirs; one of the four parts of the Earth system. (p. xxxiii)

**hidrosfera** Toda el agua de la Tierra: en la atmósfera y en los océanos, lagos, glaciares, ríos, arroyos y depósitos subterráneos; una de las cuatro partes del sistema de la Tierra.

**hyphae**
Threadlike tubes that form the structural parts of the body of a fungus. *Hyphae* is a plural word; the singular is *hypha.* (p. C67)

**hifas** Los tubos, similares a hilos, que forman las partes estructurales del cuerpo de un hongo.

**hypothesis**
A tentative explanation for an observation or phenomenon. A hypothesis is used to make testable predictions. (p. xxxviii)

**hipótesis** Una explicación provisional de una observación o de un fenómeno. Una hipótesis se usa para hacer predicciones que se pueden probar.

## I

**ice age**
A period of time during which surface temperatures drop significantly and huge ice sheets spread out beyond the polar regions. (p. A135)

**edad de hielo** Un período de tiempo durante el cual las temperaturas superficiales disminuyen significativamente y grandes capas de hielo se extienden más allá de las regiones polares.

**immune system**
A group of organs that provides protection against disease-causing agents. (p. B75)

**sistema inmune o inmunológico** Un grupo de órganos que provee protección contra agentes que causan enfermedades.

**immunity**
Resistance to a disease. Immunity can result from antibodies formed in the body during a previous attack of the same illness. (p. B80)

**inmunidad** La resistencia a una enfermedad. La inmunidad puede resultar de anticuerpos formados en el cuerpo durante un ataque previo de la misma enfermedad.

**inclined plane**
A simple machine that is a sloping surface, such as a ramp. (p. D158)

**plano inclinado** Una máquina simple que es una superficie en pendiente, como por ejemplo una rampa.

**incubation**
The process of keeping eggs warm by bodily heat until they hatch. (p. C179)

**incubación** El proceso de mantener huevos cálidos por medio de calor corporal hasta que eclosionen.

**induction**
The build-up of a static charge in an object when the object is close to, but not touching, a charged object. (p. E13)

**inducción** La acumulación de carga estática en un objeto cuando el objeto está cercano a, pero no en contacto con, un objeto con carga.

**inertia** (ih-NUR-shuh)
The resistance of an object to a change in the speed or the direction of its motion. (p. D46)

**inercia** La resistencia de un objeto al cambio de la velocidad o de la dirección de su movimiento.

**infancy**
The stage of life that begins at birth and ends when a baby begins to walk. (p. B134)

**infancia** La etapa de la vida que inicia al nacer y termina cuando el bebe empieza a caminar.

**infrared radiation** (IHN-fruh-REHD RAY-dee-AY-shuhn)
Radiation of lower frequencies than visible light. (p. A23)

**radiación infrarroja** Radiación de frecuencia más baja que la luz visible.

**integumentary system** (ihn-TEHG-yu-MEHN-tuh-ree)
The body system that includes the skin and its associated structures. (p. B83)

**sistema tegumentario** El sistema corporal que incluye a la piel y a sus estructuras asociadas.

**insect**
An arthropod with three body segments, six legs, two antennae, and compound eyes. (p. C145)

**insecto** Un artrópodo con tres segmentos corporales, seis patas, dos antenas y ojos compuestos.

**interaction**
The condition of acting or having an influence upon something. Living things in an ecosystem interact with both the living and nonliving parts of their environment. (p. xxxi)

**interacción** La condición de actuar o influir sobre algo. Los organismos vivos en un ecosistema interactúan con las partes vivas y las partes sin vida de su medio ambiente.

**involuntary muscle**
A muscle that moves without conscious control. (p. B24)

**músculo involuntario** Un músculo que se mueve sin control consciente.

**isobar** (EYE-suh-BAHR)
A line on a weather map connecting places that have the same air pressure. (p. A101)

**isobara** Una línea en un mapa climático que conecta lugares que tienen la misma presión de aire.

**insulator**
1. A material that does not transfer electric charge easily. (p. E22) 2. A material that does not transfer energy easily.

**aislante** 1. Un material que no transfiere cargas eléctricas fácilmente. 2. Un material que no transfiere energía fácilmente.

**invertebrate**
An animal that has no backbone. (p. C123)

**invertebrado** Un animal que no tiene columna vertebral.

**jet stream**
A wind that flows in the upper troposphere from west to east over vast distances at great speeds. (p. A52)

**corriente de chorro** Un viento que sopla vastas distancias en la troposfera superior de oeste a este a grandes velocidades.

**joule** (jool) J
A unit used to measure energy and work. One calorie is equal to 4.18 joules of energy; one joule of work is done when a force of one newton moves an object one meter. (p. D117)

**julio** Una unidad que se usa para medir la energía y el trabajo. Una caloría es igual a 4.18 julios de energía; se hace un joule de trabajo cuando una fuerza de un newton mueve un objeto un metro.

# K

**kilowatt** kW
A unit of measurement for power equal to 1000 watts. (p. E104)

**kilovatio** Una unidad de medición para la potencia equivalente a 1000 vatios.

**kilowatt-hour** kWh
The unit of measurement for electrical energy equal to one kilowatt of power over a one-hour period. (p. E105)

**kilovatio-hora** La unidad de medición de energía eléctrica igual a un kilovatio de potencia en un período de una hora.

**kinetic energy** (kuh-NEHT-ihk)
The energy of motion. A moving object has the most kinetic energy at the point where it moves the fastest. (p. D122)

**energía cinética** La energía de movimiento. Un objeto en movimiento tiene la mayor energía cinética en el punto en donde se mueve más rápidamente.

**kingdom**
One of six large groupings of living things that have common characteristics. The kingdoms are Plantae, Animalia, Fungi, Protista, Archaea, and Bacteria. (p. C11)

**reino** Uno de los seis grandes grupos de organismos vivos que tienen características en común. Los reinos son Plantae, Animalia, Fungi, Protista, Archae y Bacteria.

# L

**larva**
A free-living early form of a developing organism that is very different from its adult form. (p. C126)

**larva** Una etapa temprana de vida libre de un organismo en desarrollo que es muy diferente a su etapa adulta.

**latitude**
The distance in degrees north or south from the equator. (p. A118)

**latitud** La distancia en grados norte o sur a partir del ecuador.

**law**
In science, a rule or principle describing a physical relationship that always works in the same way under the same conditions. The law of conservation of energy is an example.

**ley** En las ciencias, una regla o un principio que describe una relación física que siempre funciona de la misma manera bajo las mismas condiciones. La ley de la conservación de la energía es un ejemplo.

**law of conservation of energy**
A law stating that no matter how energy is transferred or transformed, all of the energy is still present in one form or another. (p. D126)

**ley de la conservación de la energía** Una ley que establece que no importa cómo se transfiera o transmita la energía, toda la energía sigue presente de una forma o de otra.

**law of conservation of momentum**
A law stating that the amount of momentum a system of objects has does not change as long as there are no outside forces acting on that system. (p. D67)

**ley de la conservación del momento** Una ley que establece que la cantidad de momento que tiene un sistema de objetos no cambia mientras no haya fuerzas externas actuando sobre el sistema.

**lever**
A solid bar that rotates, or turns, around a fixed point (fulcrum); one of the six simple machines. (p. D155)

**palanca** Una barra sólida que da vueltas o gira alrededor de un punto fijo (el fulcro); una de las seis máquinas simples.

**lichen** (LY-kuhn)
An organism that results from a close association between single-celled algae and fungi. (p. C70)

**liquen** Un organismo que resulta de una asociación cercana entre algas unicelulares y hongos.

### low-pressure system
A large and often stormy weather system that occurs when air moves around and into a low-pressure center, then moves up to higher altitudes. (p. A85)

**sistema de baja presión** Un sistema climático grande y usualmente lluvioso que se presenta cuando el aire se mueve alrededor de y hacia un centro de baja presión, y luego se mueve hacia mayores altitudes.

### lung
A respiratory organ that absorbs oxygen from the air. (p. C137)

**pulmón** Un órgano respiratorio que absorbe oxígeno del aire.

## M

### machine
Any device that makes doing work easier. (p. D145)

**máquina** Cualquier aparato que facilita el trabajo.

### magnet
An object that attracts certain other materials, particularly iron and steel. (p. E79)

**imán** Un objeto que atrae a ciertos otros materiales, especialmente al hierro y al acero.

### magnetic domain
A group of atoms whose magnetic fields align, or point in the same direction. Magnetic materials have magnetic domains, whereas nonmagnetic materials do not. (p. E83)

**dominio magnético** Un grupo de átomos cuyos campos magnéticos se alinean, o apuntan en la misma dirección. Los materiales magnéticos tienen dominios magnéticos mientras que los materiales no magnéticos no tienen.

### magnetic field
An area surrounding a magnet within which the magnet can exert a force. Magnetic fields are concentrated into a pattern of lines that extend from the magnet's north pole to its south pole. (p. E81)

**campo magnético** Un área alrededor de un imán dentro del cual el imán puede ejercer una fuerza. Los campos magnéticos se concentran en un patrón de líneas que se extienden del polo norte del imán a su polo sur.

### magnetic pole
One of two ends of a magnet where the magnetic force is the strongest. Every magnet has two poles. (p. E80)

**polo magnético** Uno de dos extremos de un imán donde la fuerza magnética es lo más fuerte. Todos los imanes tienen dos polos.

### magnetism
The force exerted by a magnet. Opposite poles of two magnets attract, or pull together, whereas like poles of two magnets repel, or push apart. (p. E80)

**magnetismo** La fuerza que ejerce un imán. Los polos opuestos de dos imanes se atraen, o jalan hacia si, mientras que los polos iguales de dos imanes se repelen, o se empujan para alejarse uno del otro.

### mammal
A warm-blooded vertebrate animal whose young feed on milk produced by the mother's mammary glands. (p. C183)

**mamífero** Un animal vertebrado de sangre caliente cuyas crías se alimentan de leche producida por las glándulas mamarias de la madre.

### marine climate
A climate influenced by a nearby ocean, with generally mild temperatures and steady precipitation. (p. A120)

**clima marino** El clima influido por un océano cercano, y que generalmente tiene temperaturas moderadas y precipitación poco variable.

### mass
A measure of how much matter an object is made of.

**masa** Una medida de la cantidad de materia de la que está compuesto un objeto.

### matter
Anything that has mass and volume. Matter exists ordinarily as a solid, a liquid, or a gas. (p. xxxiii)

**materia** Todo lo que tiene masa y volumen. Generalmente la materia existe como sólido, líquido o gas.

### mechanical advantage
The number of times a machine multiplies the input force; output force divided by input force (p. D147)

**ventaja mecánica** El número de veces que una máquina multiplica la fuerza de entrada; la fuerza de salida dividida por la fuerza de entrada.

### mechanical energy
A combination of the kinetic energy and potential energy an object has. (p. D125)

**energía mecánica** La combinación de la energía cinética y la energía potencial que tiene un objeto.

**meiosis** (my-OH-sihs)
A part of sexual reproduction in which cells divide to form sperm cells in a male and egg cells in a female. Meiosis occurs only in reproductive cells. (p. C48)

**meiosis** Una parte de la reproducción sexual en la cual las células se dividen para formar espermatozoides en los machos y óvulos en las hembras. La meiosis sólo ocurre en las células reproductivas.

**menstruation**
A period of about five days during which blood and tissue exit the body through the vagina. (p. B119)

**menstruación** Un período de aproximadamente cinco días durante el cual salen del cuerpo sangre y tejido por la vagina.

**metamorphosis**
The transformation of an animal from its larval form into its adult form. (p. C146)

**metamorfosis** La transformación de un animal de su forma larvaria a su forma adulta.

**meteorologist** (MEE-tee-uh-RAHL-uh-jihst)
A scientist who studies weather. (p. A98)

**meteorólogo** Un científico que estudia el clima.

**meter** m
The international standard unit of length, about 39.37 inches.

**metro** La unidad estándar internacional de longitud, aproximadamente 39.37 pulgadas.

**microclimate**
The climate of a smaller area within a subclimate. (p. A128)

**microclima** El clima de un área más pequeña dentro de un subclima.

**microorganism**
A very small organism that can be seen only with a microscope. Bacteria are examples of microorganisms. (pp. B148, C10)

**microorganismo** Un organismo muy pequeño que solamente puede verse con un microscopio. Las bacterias son ejemplos de microorganismos.

**migration**
The movement of animals from one region to another in response to changes in the seasons or the environment. (p. C64)

**migración** El movimiento de animales de una región a otra en respuesta a cambios en las estaciones o en el medio ambiente.

**mobile**
Able to move from place to place. (p. C130)

**móvil** Capaz de moverse de un lugar a otro.

**molecule**
A group of atoms that are held together by covalent bonds so that they move as a single unit.

**molécula** Un grupo de átomos que están unidos mediante enlaces covalentes de tal manera que se mueven como una sola unidad.

**mollusk**
An invertebrate animal with a soft body, a muscular foot, and a mantle. Many mollusks have a hard outer shell. (p. C136)

**molusco** Un animal invertebrado con cuerpo blando, un pie muscular y un manto. Muchos moluscos tienen una concha exterior dura.

**molting**
The process of an arthropod shedding its exoskeleton to allow for growth. (p. C143)

**muda** El proceso mediante el cual un artrópodo se despoja de su exoesqueleto para poder crecer.

**momentum** (moh-MEHN-tuhm)
A measure of mass in motion. The momentum of an object is the product of its mass and velocity. (p. D64)

**momento** Una medida de la masa en movimiento. El momento de un objeto es el producto de su masa y su velocidad.

**monsoon**
A wind that changes direction with the seasons. (p. A54)

**monzón** Un viento que cambia de dirección con las estaciones.

**motion**
A change of position over time. (p. D11)

**movimiento** Un cambio de posición a través del tiempo.

**muscular system**
The muscles of the body that, together with the skeletal system, function to produce movement. (p. B23)

**sistema muscular** Los músculos del cuerpo que, junto con el sistema óseo, sirven para producir movimiento.

# N

**nanotechnology**
The science and technology of building electronic circuits and devices from single atoms and molecules. (p. D167)

**nanotecnología** La ciencia y tecnología de fabricar circuitos y aparatos electrónicos a partir de átomos y moléculas individuales.

**net force**
The overall force acting on an object when all of the forces acting on it are combined. (p. D43)

**fuerza neta** La fuerza resultante que actúa sobre un objeto cuando todas las fuerzas que actúan sobre él son combinadas .

**neuron**
A nerve cell. (p. B105)

**neurona** Una célula nerviosa.

**Newton's first law**
A scientific law stating that objects at rest remain at rest, and objects in motion remain in motion with the same velocity, unless acted on by an unbalanced force. (p. D45)

**primera ley de Newton** Una ley científica que establece que los objetos en reposo permanecen en reposo, y que los objetos en movimiento permanecen en movimiento con la misma velocidad, a menos que actúe sobre ellos una fuerza no balanceada.

**Newton's second law**
A scientific law stating that the acceleration of an object increases with increased force and decreases with increased mass. (p. D50)

**segunda ley de Newton** Una ley científica que establece que la aceleración de un objeto aumenta al incrementar la fuerza que actúa sobre él y disminuye al incrementar su masa.

**Newton's third law**
A scientific law stating that every time one object exerts a force on another object, the second object exerts a force that is equal in size and opposite in direction back on the first object. (p. D57)

**tercera ley de Newton** Una ley científica que establece que cada vez que un objeto ejerce una fuerza sobre otro objeto, el segundo objeto ejerce una fuerza de la misma magnitud y en dirección opuesta sobre el primer objeto.

**nutrient** (NOO-tree-uhnt)
A substance that an organism needs to live. Examples include water, minerals, and materials that come from the breakdown of food particles. (p. B45)

**nutriente** Una sustancia que un organismo necesita para vivir. Ejemplos incluyen agua, minerales y sustancias que provienen de la descomposición de partículas de alimento.

**nutrition**
The study of the materials that nourish the body. (p. B140)

**nutrición** El estudio de las sustancias que dan sustento al cuerpo.

**ocean current**
A stream of water that flows through the ocean in a regular pattern. (p. A121)

**corriente oceánica** Un flujo de agua que se mueve a través del océano de una forma regular.

**ohm Ω**
The unit of measurement for electrical resistance. (p. E23)

**ohmio** La unidad de medición para la resistencia eléctrica.

**Ohm's law**
The mathematical relationship among current, voltage, and resistance, expressed in the formula $I = V/R$ (current = voltage/resistance). (p. E29)

**ley de Ohm** La relación matemática entre la corriente, el voltaje y la resistencia, expresada en la fórmula $I = V/R$ (corriente = voltaje/resistencia).

**orbit**
The elliptical path one celestial body follows around another celestial body. An object in orbit has a centripetal force acting on it that keeps the object moving in a circle or other ellipse. (p. D80)

**órbita** El camino elíptico que un cuerpo celeste sigue alrededor de otro cuerpo celeste. La fuerza centrípeta actúa sobre un objeto en órbita y lo mantiene en un movimiento circular o elíptico.

**organ**
A structure in a plant or animal that is made up of different tissues working together to perform a particular function. (pp. B11, C44)

**órgano** Una estructura en una planta o en un animal compuesta de diferentes tejidos que trabajan juntos para realizar una función determinada.

**organism**
An individual living thing, made up of one or many cells, that is capable of growing and reproducing. (p. xxxi)

**organismo** Un individuo vivo, compuesto de una o muchas células, que es capaz de crecer y reproducirse.

**organ system**
A group of organs that together perform a function that helps the body meet its needs for energy and materials. (p. B12)

**sistema de órganos** Un grupo de órganos que juntos realizan una función que ayuda al cuerpo a satisfacer sus necesidades energéticas y de materiales.

**ozone**
A gas molecule that consists of three oxygen atoms. (p. A23)

**ozono** Una molécula de gas que consiste en tres átomos de oxígeno.

# P, Q

**parallel circuit**
A circuit in which current follows more than one path. Each device that is wired in a parallel circuit has its own path to and from the voltage source. (p. E53)

**circuito paralelo** Un circuito en el cual la corriente sigue más de una trayectoria. Cada aparato que está conectado a un circuito paralelo tiene su propia trayectoria desde y hacia la fuente de voltaje.

**parasite**
An organism that absorbs nutrients from the body of another organism, often harming it in the process. (p. C19)

**parásito** Un organismo que absorbe nutrientes del cuerpo de otro organismo, a menudo causándole daño en el proceso.

**particulates**
Tiny particles or droplets, such as dust, dirt, and pollen, that are mixed in with air. (p. A28)

**particulados** Diminutas partículas o gotas, como por ejemplo de polvo, tierra o polen, que están mezcladas con el aire.

**pascal** Pa
The unit used to measure pressure. One pascal is the pressure exerted by one newton of force on an area of one square meter, or one $N/m^2$. (p. D92)

**pascal** La unidad utilizada para medir presión. Un pascal es la presión ejercida por un newton de fuerza sobre un área de un metro cuadrado, o un $N/m^2$.

**Pascal's principle**
A statement that says when an outside pressure is applied at any point to a fluid in a container, that pressure is transmitted throughout the fluid with equal strength. (p. D102)

**principio de Pascal** Un enunciado que dice que cuando una presión externa es aplicada a cualquier punto de un líquido en un contenedor, esta presión es transmitida a través del fluido con igual fuerza.

**pathogen**
An agent that causes disease. (p. B74)

**patógeno** Un agente que causa una enfermedad.

**peripheral nervous system**
The part of the nervous system that lies outside the brain and spinal cord. (p. B106)

**sistema nervioso periférico** La parte del sistema nervioso que se encuentra fuera del cerebro y la médula espinal.

**peristalsis** (PEHR-ih-STAWL-sihs)
Wavelike contractions of smooth muscles in the organs of the digestive tract. The contractions move food through the digestive system. (p. B46)

**peristalsis** Contracciones ondulares de músculos lisos en los órganos del tracto digestivo. Las contracciones mueven el alimento por el sistema digestivo.

**photosynthesis** (FOH-toh-SIHN-thih-sihs)
The process by which green plants and other producers use simple compounds and energy from light to make sugar, an energy-rich compound. (p. C52)

**fotosíntesis** El proceso mediante el cual las plantas verdes y otros productores usan compuestos simples y energía de la luz para producir azúcares, compuestos ricos en energía.

**placenta**
An organ that transports materials between a pregnant female mammal and the offspring developing inside her body. (p. C186)

**placenta** Un órgano que transporta sustancias entre un mamífero hembra preñado y la cría que se está desarrollando dentro de su cuerpo.

GLOSSARY

GLOSSARY

**plankton**
Mostly microscopic organisms that drift in great numbers through bodies of water. (p. C33)

**plancton** Organismos, en su mayoría microscópicos, que se mueven a la deriva en grandes números por cuerpos de agua.

**pollen**
Tiny multicellular grains that contain the undeveloped sperm cells of a plant. (p. C100)

**polen** Los diminutos granos multicelulares que contienen las células espermáticas sin desarrollar de una planta.

**position**
An object's location. (p. D9)

**posición** La ubicación de un objeto.

**potential energy**
Stored energy; the energy an object has due to its position, molecular arrangement, or chemical composition. (p. D122)

**energía potencial** Energía almacenada; o la energía que tiene un objeto debido a su posición, arreglo molecular o composición química.

**power**
The rate at which work is done. (p. D130)

**potencia** La razón a la cual se hace el trabajo.

**precipitation**
Any type of liquid or solid water that falls to Earth's surface, such as rain, snow, or hail. (p. A57)

**precipitación** Cualquier tipo de agua líquida o sólida que cae a la superficie de la Tierra, como por ejemplo lluvia, nieve o granizo.

**predator**
An animal that hunts other animals and eats them. (p. C63)

**predador** Un animal que caza otros animales y se los come.

**pressure**
A measure of how much force is acting on a certain area; how concentrated a force is. Pressure is equal to the force divided by area. (p. D91)

**presión** Una medida de cuánta fuerza actúa sobre cierta área; el nivel de concentración de la fuerza. La presión es igual a la fuerza dividida entre el área.

**prey**
An animal that other animals hunt and eat. (p. C63)

**presa** Un animal que otros animales cazan y se comen.

**producer**
An organism that captures energy from sunlight and transforms it into chemical energy that is stored in energy-rich carbon compounds. Producers are a source of food for other organisms. (p. C19)

**productor** Un organismo que capta energía de la luz solar y la transforma a energía química que se almacena en compuestos de carbono ricos en energía. Los productores son una fuente de alimento para otros organismos.

**proton**
A positively charged particle located in an atom's nucleus.

**protón** Una partícula con carga positiva localizada en el núcleo de un átomo.

**protozoa**
Animal-like protists that eat other organisms or decaying parts of other organisms. *Protozoa* is a plural word; the singular is *protozoan.* (p. C34)

**protozoarios** Protistas parecidos a los animales que comen otros organismos o partes en descomposición de otros organismos.

**pulley**
A wheel with a grooved rim that turns on an axle; one of the six simple machines. (p. D156)

**polea** Una rueda con un canto acanalado que gira sobre un eje; una de las seis máquinas simples.

# R

**radiation** (RAY-dee-AY-shuhn)
Energy that travels across distances as certain types of waves. (p. A17)

**radiación** Energía que viaja a través de la distancia en forma de ciertos tipos de ondas.

**rain shadow**
An area on the downwind side of a mountain that gets less precipitation than the side that faces the wind. (p. A129)

**sombra de lluvia** Un área viento abajo de una montaña que recibe menos precipitación que el lado de la montaña que hace frente al viento.

**red blood cell**
A type of blood cell that picks up oxygen in the lungs and delivers it to cells throughout the body. (p. B67)

**glóbulos rojos** Un tipo de célula sanguínea que toma oxígeno en los pulmones y lo transporta a células en todo el cuerpo.

**reference point**
A location to which another location is compared. (p. D10)

**punto de referencia** Una ubicación con la cual se compara otra ubicación.

**relative humidity**
The comparison of the amount of water vapor in air with the maximum amount of water vapor that can be present in air at that temperature. (p. A58)

**humedad relativa** La comparación entre la cantidad de vapor de agua en el aire y la cantidad máxima de vapor de agua que puede estar presente en el aire a esa temperatura.

**reptile**
A cold-blooded vertebrate that has skin covered with scales or horny plates and has lungs. (p. C168)

**reptil** Un vertebrado de sangre fría que tiene la piel cubierta de escamas o placas callosas y que tiene pulmones.

**resistance**
1. The ability of an organism to protect itself from a disease or the effects of a substance. (p. B153) 2. The property of a material that determines how easily a charge can move through it. Resistance is measured in ohms. (p. E29)

**resistencia** 1. La habilidad de un organismo para protegerse de una enfermedad o de los efectos de una sustancia. 2. La propiedad de un material que determina qué tan fácilmente puede moverse una carga a través de él. La resistencia se mide en ohmios.

**resistor**
An electrical device that slows the flow of charge in a circuit. (p. E44)

**resistencia** Un aparato eléctrico que hace más lento el flujo de carga en un circuito.

**respiratory system**
A system that interacts with the environment and with other body systems to bring oxygen to the body and remove carbon dioxide. (p. B37)

**sistema respiratorio** Un sistema que interactúa con el medio ambiente y con otros sistemas corporales para traer oxígeno al cuerpo y eliminar dióxido de carbono.

**robot**
A machine that works automatically or by remote control. (p. D169)

**robot** Una máquina que funciona automáticamente o por control remoto.

# S

**saturation**
A condition of the atmosphere in which the rates of evaporation and condensation are equal. (p. A58)

**saturación** Una condición de la atmósfera en la cual las tasas de evaporación y condensación son iguales.

**scale**
One of the thin, small, overlapping plates that cover most fish and reptiles and some other animals. (p. C161)

**escama** Una de las pequeñas y delgadas placas traslapadas que cubren a la mayoría de los peces y reptiles y algunos otros animales.

**screw**
A simple machine that is an inclined plane wrapped around a cylinder. A screw can be used to raise and lower weights as well as to fasten objects. (p. D159)

**tornillo** Una máquina simple que es un plano inclinado enrollado alrededor de un cilindro. Un tornillo se puede usar para levantar o bajar pesos y también para sujetar objetos.

**seasons**
Periods of the year associated with specific weather conditions. (p. A122)

**estaciones** Los períodos del año asociados a condiciones climáticas específicas.

**second** s
A unit of time equal to one-sixtieth of a minute.

**segundo** Una unidad de tiempo igual a una sesentava parte de un minuto.

**seed**
A plant embryo that is enclosed in a protective coating and has its own source of nutrients. (p. C98)

**semilla** El embrión de una planta que esta dentro de una cubierta protectora y que tiene su propia fuente de nutrientes.

**series circuit**
A circuit in which current follows a single path. Each device that is wired in a series circuit shares a path to and from the voltage source. (p. E52)

**circuito en serie** Un circuito en el cual la corriente sigue una sola trayectoria. Cada aparato conectado a un circuito en serie comparte una trayectoria desde y hacia la fuente de voltaje.

**sessile** (SEHS-eel)
The quality of being attached to one spot; not free-moving. (p. C125)

**sésil** La cualidad de estar sujeto a un punto; sin libre movimiento.

**sexual reproduction**
A type of reproduction in which male and female reproductive cells combine to form offspring with genetic material from both cells. (p. C48)

**reproducción sexual** Un tipo de reproducción en el cual se combinan las células reproductivas femeninas y masculinas para formar una cría con material genético de ambas células.

**short circuit**
An unintended and undesired path connecting one part of a circuit with another. (p. E46)

**corto circuito** Una trayectoria no intencionada y no deseada que conecta una parte de un circuito con otra.

**simple machine**
One of the basic machines on which all other mechanical machines are based. The six simple machines are the lever, inclined plane, wheel and axle, pulley, wedge, and screw. (p. D154)

**máquina simple** Una de las máquinas básicas sobre las cuales están basadas todas las demás máquinas mecánicas. Las seis máquinas simples son la palanca, el plano inclinado, la rueda y eje, la polea, la cuña y el tornillo.

**skeletal muscle**
A muscle that attaches to the skeleton. (p. B24)

**músculo esquelético** Un músculo que está sujeto al esqueleto.

**skeletal system**
The framework of bones that supports the body, protects internal organs, and anchors all the body's movement. (p. B14)

**sistema óseo** El armazón de huesos que sostiene al cuerpo, protege a los órganos internos y sirve de ancla para todo el movimiento del cuerpo.

**sleet**
Small pellets of ice that form when rain passes through a layer of cold air and freezes before hitting the ground. (p. A68)

**aguanieve** Pequeñas bolitas de hielo que se forman cuando la lluvia pasa a través de una capa de aire frío y se congela antes de caer al suelo.

**smog**
The combination of smoke and fog; a type of air pollution that occurs when sunlight causes unburnt fuels, fumes, and other gases to react chemically, often seen as a brownish haze. (p. A28)

**smog** La combinación de humo y neblina; un tipo de contaminación de aire que se presenta cuando la luz solar provoca la reacción química de combustibles no consumidos, humos y otros gases, que a menudo se ve como una bruma parda.

**smooth muscle**
Muscle that performs involuntary movement and is found inside certain organs, such as the stomach. (p. B24)

**músculo liso** Músculos que realizan movimiento involuntario y se encuentran dentro de ciertos órganos, como el estómago.

**species**
A group of living things that are so closely related that they can breed with one another and produce offspring that can breed as well. (p. xxxi)

**especie** Un grupo de organismos que están tan estrechamente relacionados que pueden aparearse entre sí y producir crías que también pueden aparearse.

**speed**
A measure of how fast something moves through a particular distance over a definite time period. Speed is distance divided by time. (p. D16)

**rapidez** Una medida del desplazamiento de un objeto a lo largo de una distancia específica en un período de tiempo definido. La rapidez es la distancia dividida entre el tiempo

**sponge**
A simple multicellular invertebrate animal that lives attached to one place and filters food from water. (p. C125)

**esponja** Un animal invertebrado multicelular simple que vive sujeto a un lugar y filtra su alimento del agua.

**spongy bone**
Strong, lightweight tissue inside a bone. (p. B15)

**hueso esponjoso** Tejido fuerte y de peso ligero dentro de un hueso.

**spore**
A single reproductive cell that can grow into a multicellular organism. (p. C67)

**espora** Una célula reproductiva individual que puede convertirse en un organismo multicelular.

**static charge**
The buildup of electric charge in an object caused by the uneven distribution of charged particles. (p. E11)

**carga estática** La acumulación de carga eléctrica en un objeto ocasionada por la desigual distribución de partículas con carga.

**stimulus**
Something that causes a response in an organism or a part of the body. (pp. B102, C55)

**estímulo** Algo que causa una respuesta en un organismo o en una parte del cuerpo.

**storm surge**
A rapid rise in water level in a coastal area that occurs when a hurricane pushes a huge mass of ocean water, often leading to flooding and widespread destruction. (p. A89)

**marea de tormenta** Un rápido aumento del nivel del agua en un área costera que ocurre cuando un huracán empuja una gran masa de agua oceánica, muchas veces provocando inundaciones y destrucción extensa.

**system**
A group of objects or phenomena that interact. A system can be as simple as a rope, a pulley, and a mass. It also can be as complex as the interaction of energy and matter in the four parts of the Earth system.

**sistema** Un grupo de objetos o fenómenos que interactúan. Un sistema puede ser algo tan sencillo como una cuerda, una polea y una masa. También puede ser algo tan complejo como la interacción de la energía y la materia en las cuatro partes del sistema de la Tierra.

# T

**technology**
The use of scientific knowledge to solve problems or engineer new products, tools, or processes.

**tecnología** El uso de conocimientos científicos para resolver problemas o para diseñar nuevos productos, herramientas o procesos.

**tentacle**
A long, slender, flexible extension of the body of certain animals, such as jellyfish. Tentacles are used to touch, move, or hold. (p. C128)

**tentáculo** Una extensión larga, delgada y flexible del cuerpo de ciertos animales, como las medusas. Los tentáculos se usan para tocar, mover o sujetar.

**terminal velocity**
The final, maximum velocity of a falling object. (p. D89)

**velocidad terminal** La velocidad máxima final de un objeto en caída libre.

**theory**
In science, a set of widely accepted explanations of observations and phenomena. A theory is a well-tested explanation that is consistent with all available evidence.

**teoría** En las ciencias, un conjunto de explicaciones de observaciones y fenómenos que es ampliamente aceptado. Una teoría es una explicación bien probada que es consecuente con la evidencia disponible.

**thunderstorm**
A storm with lightning and thunder. (p. A92)

**tormenta eléctrica** Una tormenta con relámpagos y truenos.

**tissue**
A group of similar cells that are organized to do a specific job. (pp. B10, C44)

**tejido** Un grupo de células parecidas que juntas realizan una función específica en un organismo.

**tornado**
A violently rotating column of air stretching from a cloud to the ground. (p. A95)

**tornado** Una columna de aire que gira violentamente y se extiende desde una nube hasta el suelo.

**transformer**
A device that uses electromagnetism to increase or decrease voltage. A transformer is often used in the distribution of current from power plants. (p. E99)

**transformador** Un aparato que usa electromagnetismo para aumentar o disminuir el voltaje. A menudo se usa un transformador en la distribución de corriente desde las centrales eléctricas.

**transpiration** (TRAN-spuh-RAY-shuhn)
The movement of water vapor out of a plant and into the air. (p. C88)

**transpiración** El movimiento de vapor de agua hacia fuera de una planta y hacia el aire.

**tropical storm** (TRAHP-ih-kuhl)
A low-pressure system that starts in the tropics with winds of at least 65 kilometers per hour (40 mi/h) but less than 120 kilometers per hour (74 mi/h). (p. A87)

**tormenta tropical** Un sistema de baja presión que inicia en los trópicos con vientos de por lo menos 65 kilómetros por hora (40 mi/h) pero menores a 120 kilómetros por hora (74 mi/h).

## U

**ultraviolet radiation**
(UHL-truh-VY-uh-liht RAY-dee-AY-shuhn)
Radiation of higher frequencies than visible light, which can cause sunburn and other types of damage. (p. A23)

**radiación ultravioleta** Radiación de frecuencia más alta que la luz visible que puede causar quemaduras de sol y otros tipos de daño.

**urban heat island**
The warmer body of air over a city. (p. A128)

**isla de calor urbana** La masa de aire más cálida que se encuentra sobre una ciudad.

**urinary system**
A group of organs that filter waste from an organism's blood and excrete it in a liquid called urine. (p. B53)

**sistema urinario** Un grupo de órganos que filtran desechos de la sangre de un organismo y los excretan en un líquido llamado orina.

**urine**
Liquid waste that is secreted by the kidneys. (p. B53)

**orina** El desecho líquido que secretan los riñones.

## V

**vaccine**
A small amount of a weakened pathogen that is introduced into the body to stimulate the production of antibodies. (p. B80)

**vacuna** Una pequeña cantidad de un patógeno debilitado que se introduce al cuerpo para estimular la producción de anticuerpos.

**variable**
Any factor that can change in a controlled experiment, observation, or model. (p. R30)

**variable** Cualquier factor que puede cambiar en un experimento controlado, en una observación o en un modelo.

**vascular system** (VAS-kyuh-lur)
Long tubelike tissues in plants through which water and nutrients move from one part of the plant to another. (p. C87)

**sistema vascular** Tejidos largos en forma de tubo en las plantas a través de los cuales se mueven agua y nutrientes de una parte de la planta a otra.

**vector**
A quantity that has both size and direction. (p. D22)

**vector** Una cantidad que tiene magnitud y dirección.

**vein**
A blood vessel that carries blood back to the heart. (p. B69)

**vena** Un vaso sanguíneo que lleva la sangre de regreso al corazón.

**velocity**
A speed in a specific direction. (p. D22)

**velocidad** Una rapidez en una dirección específica.

**vertebrate**
An animal with an internal backbone. (p. C157)

**vertebrado** Un animal que tiene columna vertebral interna.

**vertical**
Going straight up or down from a level surface.

**vertical** Que está dispuesto hacia arriba o hacia abajo de una superficie nivelada.

**virus**
A nonliving, disease-causing particle that uses the materials inside cells to reproduce. A virus consists of genetic material enclosed in a protein coat. (pp. B149, C14)

**virus** Una particular sin vida, que causa enfermedad y que usa los materiales dentro de las células para reproducirse. Un virus consiste de material genético encerrado en una cubierta proteica.

**volt** V
The unit of measurement for electric potential, which is equal to one joule per coulomb. The number of volts of an electric charge equals the charge's voltage. (p. E19)

**voltio** La unidad de medición para el potencial eléctrico, el cual es igual a un julio por segundo por culombio. El número de voltios de una carga eléctrica es igual al voltaje de la carga.

**volume**
An amount of three-dimensional space, often used to describe the space that an object takes up.

**volumen** Una cantidad de espacio tridimensional; a menudo se usa este término para describir el espacio que ocupa un objeto.

**voluntary muscle**
A muscle that can be moved at will. (p. B24)

**músculo voluntario** Un músculo que puede moverse a voluntad.

**voluntary nervous system**
The nerves that govern consciously controlled function and movement. (p. B107)

**sistema nervioso voluntario** Los nervios que gobiernan las funciones y el movimiento cuyo control es consiente.

# W, X, Y, Z

**watt** W
The unit of measurement for power, which is equal to one joule of work done or energy transferred in one second. For example, a 75 W light bulb converts electrical energy into heat and light at a rate of 75 joules per second. (p. D131)

**vatio** La unidad de medición de la potencia, el cual es igual a un julio de trabajo realizado o energía transferida en un segundo. Por ejemplo, una bombilla de 75 W convierte energía eléctrica a calor y luz a un ritmo de 75 julios por segundo.

**weather**
The condition of Earth's atmosphere at a particular time and place. (p. A47)

**estado del tiempo** La condición de la atmósfera terrestre en un lugar y momento particular.

**wedge**
A simple machine that has a thick end and a thin end. A wedge is used to cut, split, or pierce objects, or to hold objects together. (p. D158)

**cuña** Una máquina simple que tiene un extremo grueso y otro extremo delgado. Una cuña se usa para cortar, partir o penetrar objetos, o para mantener objetos juntos.

**weight**
The force of gravity on an object. (p. D79)

**peso** La fuerza de gravedad sobre un objeto.

**wheel and axle**
A simple machine that is a wheel attached to a shaft, or axle. (p. D156)

**rueda y eje** Una máquina simple que es una rueda unida a una flecha, o a un eje.

**wind**
The horizontal movement of air caused by differences in air pressure. (p. A47)

**viento** El movimiento horizontal de aire provocado por diferencias en la presión de aire.

**work**
The use of force to move an object over a distance. (p. D115)

**trabajo** El uso de fuerza para mover un objeto una distancia.

# Index

Page numbers for definitions are printed in **boldface** type.
Page numbers for illustrations, maps, and charts are printed in *italics*.

## A



INDEX

# B

# C



INDEX

INDEX

# D



# E



INDEX

INDEX

# F

## G

## H

INDEX

# J, K



# L



INDEX

# M

# N



# O



INDEX

# P, Q



INDEX

# R

# S

INDEX

# T



INDEX

## U



## V



INDEX

# W, X, Y, Z

# Acknowledgments

## Photography

**Cover** © David Nardini/Getty Images; i © David Nardini/Getty Images, **iii** Photograph of James Trefil by Evan Cantwell; Photograph of Rita Ann Calvo by Joseph Calvo; Photograph of Kenneth Cutler by Kenneth A. Cutler; Photograph of Douglas Carnine by McDougal Littell; Photograph of Linda Carnine by Amilcar Cifuentes; Photograph of Donald Steely by Marni Stamm; Photograph of Sam Miller by Samuel Miller; Photograph of Vicky Vachon by Redfern Photographics; **vi** © Catherine Karnow/Corbis; **vii** AP/WideWorld Photos; **viii** *bottom* © Richard T. Nowitz/Corbis; **ix** © Burke/Triolo/Artville: Bugs and Insects; **x** © Orion Press/Corbis; **xii** © Arthur Tilley/Getty Images; **xiii** © Mike Chew/Corbis; **xiv** © 2003 Barbara Ries; **xv** © Philip & Karen Smith/age fotostock america, inc.; **xx** Photograph by Ken O'Donoghue; **xxi** Photograph by Sharon Hoogstraten; **xxx–xxxi** © Ron Sanford/Corbis; **xxxii–xxxiii** © Tim Fitzharris/Masterfile; **xxxiv–xxxv** © Jack Affleck/SuperStock; **xxxvi** *left* © Michael Gadomski/Animals Animals; *right* © Shin Yoshino/Minden Pictures; **xxxvii**© Laif Elleringmann/Aurora Photos; **xxxviii** © Pascal Goetgheluck/ Science Photo Library/Photo Researchers, Inc.; **xxxix** *top left* © David Parker/Science Photo Library/Photo Researchers, Inc.; *top right* © James King-Holmes/Science Photo Library/Photo Researchers, Inc.; *bottom* Sinsheimer Labs/University of California, Santa Cruz; **xl–xli** *background* © Maximillian Stock/Photo Researchers, Inc.; **xl** Courtesy, John Lair, Jewish Hospital, University of Louisville; **xli** *top* © Brand X Pictures/Alamy; *center* Courtesy, AbioMed; **xlvii** © Chedd-Angier Production Company.

### Earth's Atmosphere

**Divider** © Bill Ross/Corbis; **A2–A3** © Bruce Byers/Getty Images; **A3** © D. Faulkner/Photo Researchers; **A4** *top left* Luiz C. Marigo/Peter Arnold, Inc.; *top center* Image courtesy Norman Kuring, SeaWiFS Project/NASA; *top right* Norbert Wu; *bottom center* © The Chedd-Angier Production Company; **A6–A7** © Peter Griffith/Masterfile frontiers; **A7** *top, center* Photograph by Sharon Hoogstraten; **A10** *top* © Didrik Johnck/Corbis Sygma; *bottom* Photograph by Sharon Hoogstraten; **A11** NASA; **A13** © Michael K. Nichols/NGS Image Collection; **A14** *top left, top right* Provided by the SeaWiFS Project, NASA/Goddard Space Flight Center, and ORBIMAGE; **A15** M. Thonig/Robertstock.com; **A16** David Young-Wolff/PhotoEdit; **A17** Photograph by Sharon Hoogstraten; **A19** © Gerald and Buff Corsi/Visuals Unlimited, Inc.; **A22, A24** Photographs by Sharon Hoogstraten; **A26** *top, bottom* PhotoDisc/Getty Images; *background* © Pulse Productions/SuperStock/ PictureQuest; **A27** Photograph by Sharon Hoogstraten; **A28** © P.G. Adam/Publiphoto/ Photo Researchers; **A29** AP/WideWorld Photos; **A30** *background, center left* PhotoDisc/Getty Images; *centerright* © Corbis/PictureQuest; **A32** © Mug Shots/Corbis; **A33** *top left, bottom left* NASA/Goddard Space Flight Center; **A34** *top left* © Still Pictures/Peter Arnold, Inc.; *left, right* Photographs by Sharon Hoogstraten; **A36** NASA; **A37** © Tom Branch/Photo Researchers; **A40–A41** © Catherine Karnow/Corbis; **A41, A45, A47** Photographs by Sharon Hoogstraten; **A54** *top left, top right* Earth Vistas; **A55** *top* NASA/Corbis; *background* © Lester Lefkowitz/Corbis; **A56** *center right* Photograph by Sharon Hoogstraten; *bottom right* © Japack Company/Corbis; **A57** © Kristi Bressert/Index Stock Imagery/PictureQuest; **A59** Photograph by Sharon Hoogstraten; **A60** GrantHeilman/Grant Heilman Photography, Inc.; **A62** *top* © John Mead/Photo Researchers; *center* © Royalty-free/Corbis; *bottom* Fred Whitehead/Animals Animals/Earth Scenes; **A63** © Tom Till; **A64** *top* © Gunter Marx Photography/Corbis; *bottom left, bottom right, center* Photographs by Sharon Hoogstraten; **A66** © Stockbyte/PictureQuest; **A67** Photograph by Sharon Hoogstraten; **A69** *bottom left* © Larry West/Photo Researchers; *bottom right* © Astrid & Hanns-Frieder Michler/Photo Researchers; **A70** © Will McIntyre/Photo Researchers; **A71** © 1990 Warren Faidley/Weatherstock; **A74** © Dorling Kindersley; **A76–A77** AP/WideWorld Photos; **A77, A81** Photographs by Sharon Hoogstraten; **A83** © PhotoDisc/Getty Images; **A86** © Stephen J. Krasemann/Photo Researchers; **A87** Photograph by Sharon Hoogstraten; **A88** Image by Marit Jentoft-Nilsen/NASA GSFC; **A89** *top, center* Courtesy of U.S. Geological Survey; **A90** Photograph by Sharon Hoogstraten; **A91** AP/WideWorld Photos; **A92, A94** *top* Photographs by Sharon Hoogstraten; *bottom left* © PhotoDisc/Getty Images; **A95** *left, center, right* © David K. Hoadley; **A96** © Reuters/New Media/Corbis; **A97** *background* © Waite Air Photos, Inc.; *top left, top right* © Fletcher & Baylis/Photo Researchers; **A98** Used with permission © January 9, 2003 Chicago Tribune Company, Chicago, Illinois. Photograph by Sharon Hoogstraten; **A101** Provided by Space Science & Engineering Center, University of Wisconsin-Madison; **A102** WSBT-TV, South Bend, Indiana; **A104** *top left* Mary Kate Denny/PhotoEdit, Inc.; *center left, bottom right* Photographs by Sharon Hoogstraten; **A105** Photograph by Sharon Hoogstraten; **A106** Image by Marit Jentoft-Nilsen/NASA GSFC; **A108** Used with permission © January 9, 2003 Chicago Tribune Company, Chicago, Illinois. Photograph by Sharon Hoogstraten; **A110** *top right* © Joel W. Rogers/Corbis; *bottom* © Dorling Kindersley; **A111** *top left* © Snark/Art Resource, New York; *top right* Matthew Oldfield, Scubazoo/Photo Researchers; *bottom* Smithsonian Institution; **A112** *top left* © Mark A. Schneider/Photo Researchers; *top right* © Bettmann/Corbis; *right center* © Roger Ressmeyer/Corbis; *bottom* © Corbis; **A113** NASA; **A114–A115** © Ferrero-Labat/Auscape International; **A115** *top, center,* **A117, A119** Photographs by Sharon Hoogstraten; **A120** *left* Tony Freeman/PhotoEdit, Inc.; *right* © Duomo/Corbis; **A123** *top left, top right* Steve McCurry/Magnum Photos; **A124** *top left* © Dave G. Houser/Corbis; *center right* AP/WideWorld Photos; *center left, bottom* Glenn Murcutt; **A125** © The Image Bank/Getty Images; **A127** *center left* © Rick Schafer/Index Stock Imagery/PictureQuest; *top left* © Gerald D. Tang; *bottom* © Photodisc/Getty Images; *center right* © Willard Clay; *top right* © Bill Ross/Corbis; *bottom left* © John Conrad/Corbis; **A130** *top left* © Mark Lewis/Pictureque/PictureQuest; *center left* Photograph by Sharon Hoogstraten; **A132** Johner/Photonica; **A133** *top right* © Photodisc/Getty Images; *bottom right* Photograph by Sharon Hoogstraten; **A137** Lonnie G. Thompson, Ohio State University; **A139** Simon Fraser/Mauna Loa Observatory/Photo Researchers.

### Human Biology

**Divider** RNHRD NHS Trust; **B2–B3** © Peter Byron/PhotoEdit; **B3** *top right* © ISM/Phototake; **B4** *top* © Wellcome Department of Cognitive Neurology/Photo Researchers, Inc., *bottom* Chedd-Angier Production Company; **B5** © Myrleen Ferguson Cate/PhotoEdit; **B6–B7** © Chris Hamilton/Corbis; **B7** *top* Frank Siteman, *bottom* Ken O'Donoghue; **B9** © SuperStock;**B10** Frank Siteman; **B11** *left* © Martin Rotker/Phototake; **B12** © SW Production/Index Stock Imagery/PictureQuest; **B13** *background* © Hulton-Deutsch Collection/Corbis, *center* © Underwood & Underwood/Corbis; **B14** Frank Siteman; **B15** © Prof. P. Motta/Dept. of Anatomy/University "La Sapienza," Rome/Photo Researchers, Inc.; **B16** © Photodisc/Getty Images; **B18** *bottom* © Science Photo Library/Photo Researchers, Inc., *bottom left* © Zephyr/Photo Researchers, Inc.; **B19** *top* © Zephyr/Photo Researchers, Inc., bottom Frank Siteman; **B20** *top left* © Stock Image/SuperStock, top right © Science Photo Library/Photo Researchers, Inc.; **B21** © Dennis Kunkel/Phototake; **B22** Frank Siteman; **B23** © Kevin R. Morris/Corbis; **B25** *background* © Mary Kate Denny/PhotoEdit, *top* © Martin Rotker/Phototake, *left* © Triarch/Visuals Unlimited, *bottom* © Eric Grave/Phototake; **B26** © Ron Frehm/AP Wide World Photos; **B27** © Jeff Greenberg/PhotoEdit; **B28** *top* © Gunter Marx Photography/Corbis, *bottom, all* Frank Siteman; **B30** © Martin Rotker/Phototake; **B31** *top* © Stock Image/SuperStock; **B34–B35** © Larry Dale Gordon/Getty Images; **B35** *top* Frank Siteman, *bottom* Ken O'Donoghue; **B37** Frank Siteman; **B38** © Amos Nachoum/Corbis; **B39** Ken O'Donoghue; **B41** *bottom left* © Michael Newman/PhotoEdit, *bottom right* © Science Photo Library/Photo Researchers, Inc.; **B43** © Kennan Harvey/Getty Images; **B44** *background* © Jim Cummins/Getty Images, *center* © Steve Casimiro/Getty Images; **B45** Ken O'Donoghue; **B47** Ken O'Donoghue; **B48** © Professors P. Motta & A. Familiari/University "La Sapienza," Rome/Photo Researchers, Inc.; **B49** © David Young-Wolff/PhotoEdit; **B50** © Dr. Gladden Willis/Visuals Unlimited; **B51** © David Gifford/SPL/Custom Medical Stock Photo; **B52** Frank Siteman; **B55** © LWA-Dann Tardif/Corbis; **B56** *top* © Myrleen Ferguson Cate/PhotoEdit, *bottom left* Ken O'Donoghue, *bottom right* Frank Siteman; **B57** Frank Siteman; **B62–B63** © Professors P.M. Motta & S. Correr/Photo Researchers, Inc.; **B63** *both* Frank Siteman; **B65** Frank Siteman; **B67** © Science Photo Library/Photo Researchers, Inc.; **B68** © Myrleen Ferguson Cate/PhotoEdit; **B69** © Susumu Nishinaga/Photo Researchers, Inc.; **B71** © Journal-Courier/The Image Works; **B72** *top left* © Michael Newman/PhotoEdit, *bottom left* Ken O'Donoghue, *center right, bottom right* Frank Siteman; **B74** Frank Siteman; **B75** *top* © Eddy Gray/Photo Researchers, Inc., *bottom* © Mary Kate Denny/PhotoEdit; **B76** © Science Photo Library/Photo Researchers, Inc.; **B77** *top* © Dr. P. Marazzi/Photo Researchers, Inc., *top right* © Dr. Jeremy Burgess/Photo Researchers, Inc.; **B78** © Science Photo Library/Photo Researchers, Inc.; **B79** Frank Siteman; **B80** © Bob Daemmrich/The Image Works; **B81** © Richard Lord/The Image Works; **B82** *background* © SCIMAT/Photo Researchers, Inc., *inset* © Vision/Photo Researchers; **B83** Ken O'Donoghue; **B84** RMIP/Richard Haynes; **B85** Frank Siteman; **B86** *top inset* © Dennis Kunkel/Phototake, *bottom inset* © Andrew Syred/Photo Researchers, Inc., *center* © Photodisc/Getty Images; **B87** *all* © Eric Schrempp/Photo Researchers, Inc.; **B88** © The Image Bank/Getty Images; **B89**

*background* © James King-Holmes/Photo Researchers, Inc., *top right* © Sygma/Corbis, *bottom right* © David Hanson; **B94** *top* © Hulton Archive/Getty Images, *bottom* © Simon Fraser/Photo Researchers, Inc.; **B95** *top* © Bettmann/Corbis, *center* © Underwood & Underwood/Corbis, *bottom* © George Bernard/Photo Researchers, Inc.; **B96** *top left* © Collection CNRI/Phototake, *top right* © Geoff Tompkinson/Photo Researchers, Inc., *bottom* © Josh Sher/Photo Researchers, Inc.; **B97** *top* © Simon Fraser/Photo Researchers, Inc., *bottom* © GJLP/Photo Researchers, Inc.; **B98–B99** © Photo Researchers, Inc.; **B99** *top* Ken O'Donoghue, *center* © Photospin; **B101** Ken O'Donoghue; **B103** RMIP/Richard Haynes; **B104** © David Young-Wolff/PhotoEdit; **B107** © Royalty-Free/Corbis; **B108** *top* © Ed Young/Corbis, *bottom* Ken O'Donoghue; **B109** *top* Frank Siteman, *bottom* Ken O'Donoghue; **B110** © David Young-Wolff/PhotoEdit; **B111** © Kwame Zikomo/SuperStock; **B112** © ISM/Phototake; **B114** Frank Siteman; **B115** © CNRI/Photo Researchers, Inc.; **B117** *left* © David Young-Wolff/PhotoEdit, *bottom right* © Glenn Oakley/ImageState/PictureQuest; **B118** Ken O'Donoghue; **B123** *background* © Yoav Levy/Phototake, *top left* © Dr. Yorgos Nikas/Photo Researchers, Inc.; **B124** © David Degnan/Corbis; **B125** *left* © Christopher Brown/Stock Boston, Inc./PictureQuest, *right* © Nissim Men/Photonica; **B130–B131** © Brooklyn Productions/Corbis; **B131** top Ken O'Donoghue; **B133** Frank Siteman; **B134** © Tom Galliher/Corbis; **B135** © Tom Stewart/Corbis; **B136** © Novastock/Index Stock Imagery, Inc.; **B138** *left* © Spencer Grant/PhotoEdit, *right* © Michael Newman/PhotoEdit; **B139** *all* from STAGE MAKEUP, STEP BY STEP. Courtesy of Quarto Publishing, Inc.; **B140** © Ed Young/Corbis; **B141** © Ronnie Kaufman/Corbis; **B142** © Photodisc/Getty Images; **B144** © Don Smetzer/PhotoEdit; **B146** © Brett Coomer/HO/AP Wide World Photos; **B147** *left* © Eric Kamp/Index Stock Photography, Inc., *top right* © Ariel Skelley/Corbis; **B148** Frank Siteman; **B149** © Mediscan/Visuals Unlimited; **B151** top left © Dr. Kari Lounatmaa/Science Photo Library/Photo Researchers, Inc., *top right* © Dr. Gopal Murti/Photo Researchers, Inc., *bottom left* © Professors P.M. Motta & F.M. Magliocca/PhotoResearchers, Inc., *bottom right* © Microworks/Phototake, *bottom right inset* © Andrew Spielman/Phototake; **B152** © Mary Steinbacher/PhotoEdit; **B153** © Srulik Haramary/Phototake; **B154** *top left* © Kwame Zikomo/Superstock, bottom left Ken O'Donoghue, *bottom right* Frank Siteman; **B155** Ken O'Donoghue; **B156** © Mediscan/Visuals Unlimited.

## Diversity of Living Things

**Divider** © Buddy Mays/Corbis; **C2, C3** © *background* Yva Momatiuk/John Eastcott/Minden Pictures; **C3** *top* © Pat O'Hara/Corbis; *bottom* © Darrell Gulin/Corbis; **C4** *top left* © Bruce Marlin/Cirrus Digital Imaging; *top right* © A.B. Sheldon; *bottom* © Chedd-Angier Production Company; **C6, C7** © Science VU/Visuals Unlimited; **C7** *top* Photograph by Frank Siteman; *center* Photograph by Ken O'Donoghue; *bottom* © Custom Medical Stock Photo; **C9** Photograph by Ken O'Donoghue; **C10** *background* © Lynda Richardson/Corbis; *inset* © Astrid & Hanns-Frieder Michler/Photo Researchers, Inc.; **C12** © A.B. Dowsett/Science Photo Library/Photo Researchers, Inc.; **C13** Photograph by Ken O'Donoghue; **C14** *right* © Dr. Gopal Murti/Photo Researchers, Inc.; *left* © K.G. Murti/Visuals Unlimited; **C15** © CNRI/Photo Researchers, Inc.; **C16** © Dennis Kunkel/Visuals Unlimited; **C17** *left* © Tina Carvalho/Visuals Unlimited; *center* © D.M. Phillips/Visuals Unlimited; *right* © CNRI/Photo Researchers, Inc.; **C18** *left* © Grant Heilman/Grant Heilman Photography; *left inset* © Dr. Kari Lounatmaa/Photo Researchers, Inc.; *center* © Roger Tidman/Corbis; *center inset* © Alfred Pasieka/Science Photo Library/Photo Researchers, Inc.; *right* © ML Sinbaldi/Corbis; *right inset* © Wolfgang Baumeister/Photo Researchers, Inc.; **C19** *left* © Jack Novak/Photri-Microstock; *left inset* © Dr. Kari Lounatmaa/Photo Researchers, Inc.; *center* © Dennis Flaherty/Photo Researchers, Inc.; *center inset* © Microfield Scientific LTD/Science Photo Library/Photo Researchers, Inc.; *right* © Dr. P. Marazzi/Science Photo Library/Photo Researchers, Inc.; *right inset* © Dr. Kari Lounatmaa/Photo Researchers, Inc.; **C20** © *background* Runk/Schoenberger/Grant Heilman Photography; *left inset* © Simko/Visuals Unlimited; *right inset* © Dwight R. Kuhn; **C21** © T.A. Zitter/Cornell University; **C22** *top* © Adam Hart-Davis, Leeds Public Health Laboraory/Photo Researchers, Inc. ; *bottom (both)* Photographs by Ken O'Donoghue; **C24, C25** Photographs by Frank Siteman; **C26** © Hans Gelderblom/Visuals Unlimited; **C27** *(both)* © Lee D. Simon/Photo Researchers, Inc.; **C28** © Bettmann/Corbis; **C29** *left* © Judy White/GardenPhotos.com; *right* © Dennis Kunkel Microscopy, Inc.; **C30** © Corbis; **C31** Photograph by Ken O'Donoghue; **C32** *left* © R. Kessel-G. Shih/Visuals Unlimited; *center* © Jan Hinsch/Photo Researchers, Inc.; *right* © Runk/Schoenberger/Grant Heilman Photography; **C33** © R. Kessel-C.Y. Shih/Visuals Unlimited; **C34** © Andrew Syred/Photo Researchers, Inc.; **C35** © Ed Reschke/Peter Arnold, Inc.; **C36** *bottom left* © Runk/Schoenberger/Grant Heilman Photography; *bottom center* © Ed Reschke/Peter Arnold, Inc.; *bottom right* © Andrew Syred/Photo Researchers, Inc.; **C38** *left* © A.B. Dowsett/Science Photo Library/Photo Researchers, Inc.; *right* © Science VU/Visuals Unlimited; **C40, C41** © Orion Press/Corbis; **C41** *top, center* Photographs by Ken O'Donoghue; **C43** © David G. Massey/AP Wide World Photos; **C44** Photograph by Frank Siteman; **C45** © Joe McDonald/Bruce Coleman, Inc.; **C46** © Michael Doolittle/ PictureQuest; **C47** *background* © Photospin; *top* © A. Mercieca/Photo Researchers, Inc.; *center* © Jim Brandenburg/Minden Pictures; *center inset* © Yva Momatiuk/John Eastcott/Minden Pictures; *bottom* © Tim Fitzharris/Minden Pictures; **C48** © Matt Brown/Corbis; **C49** *left* © Joe McDonald/Corbis; *right* © David J. Wrobel/Visuals Unlimited; **C50** © Frans Lanting/Minden Pictures; **C51, C52** Photographs by Ken O'Donoghue; **C53** *top* © Peter Dean/Grant Heilman Photography; *inset* © Pascal Goetgheluck/Science Photo Library/Photo Researchers, Inc.; **C54** *(both)* © D. Suzio/Photo Researchers, Inc.; **C55** *left* © Joel Arrington/Visuals Unlimited; *right* © Gary W. Carter/Visuals Unlimited; **C57** © Josiah Davidson/Picturesque/PictureQuest; **C58** © Yva Momatiuk/John Eastcott/Minden Pictures; **C59** *left* © Brandon Cole; *right* © Rauschenbach/Premium Stock/PictureQuest ; **C60** Photograph by Frank Siteman; **C61** *left and left inset* © Dwight R.Kuhn; *center* © Steve Maslowski/Visuals Unlimited; *right* © Belinda Wright/DRK Photo; **C62** © J. Sneesby/B. Wilkins/Getty Images; **C63** *top* © Shin Yoshino/Minden Pictures; *bottom left* © Charles V. Angelo/Photo Researchers, Inc.; *bottom right* © Fred McConnaughey/Photo Researchers, Inc.; **C64** *left* © Ron Austing/Photo Researchers, Inc.; *right* © Kevin Schafer; **C65** *left, top right* © Steve Winter/National Geographic Image Collection; *bottom right* © Brian J. Skerry/National Geographic Image Collection; **C66** Photograph by Ken O'Donoghue; **C68** © IFA/eStock Photography/PictureQuest ; **C69** *top* © Andrew Syred/Science Photo Library/Photo Researchers; *bottom* © Simko/Visuals Unlimited; **C71** *(both)* © Lennart Nilsson/Albert Bonniers Forlag AB; **C72** *top* © Bob Daemmrich/Stock Boston, Inc./PictureQuest; *bottom* Photograph by Ken O'Donoghue; **C73** Photograph by Frank Siteman; **C74** *top* © Matt Brown/Corbis; *center* © Rauschenbach/Premium Stock/PictureQuest ; *bottom* © IFA/eStock Photography/PictureQuest; **C78** *top* © Academy of Natural Sciences of Philadelphia/Corbis; *bottom* © The Granger Collection, New York; **C79** *top left, top right* © The Natural History Museum, London; *bottom left* © Photo Researchers, Inc.; *bottom right* © The Granger Collection, New York; **C80** *top left* © B. Boonyaratanakornit & D.S. Clark, G. Vrdoljak/EM Lab, UC Berkeley/Visuals Unlimited, Inc.; *top right* © OAR/National Undersea Research Program; *center* © Terry Erwin/ Smithsonian Institution; *bottom* © Emory Kristoff/National Geographic Image Collection; **C81** © Michael Bordelon/Smithsonian Institution; **C82, C83** © David J. Job/AlaskaStock.com; **C83** *(both)* Photographs by Ken O'Donoghue; **C85** Photograph by Ken O'Donoghue; **C86** *left* © Nick Garbutt/Nature Picture Library; *center* © D. Cavagnaro/Visuals Unlimited; *right* © Hal Horwitz/Corbis; **C87** © Andrew Syred/Photo Researchers, Inc.; **C88** *(both)* © Dr. Jeremy Burgess/Science Photo Library/Photo Researchers, Inc.; **C89** *background* © Donna Disario/Corbis; *top left* © Photodisc/Getty Images; **C90** © Craig K. Lorenz/Photo Researchers, Inc.; **C91** *top* © Delphoto/Premium Stock/ PictureQuest; *inset* © Unicorn Stock Photo; **C92** Photograph by Frank Siteman; **C93** *top* © Ray Simmons/Photo Researchers, Inc.; *bottom* The Field Museum of Natural History, #GEO85637c; **C94** Photograph by Frank Siteman; **C95** © Dwight R. Kuhn; **C96** *left* © Dr. Jeremy Burgess/Science Photo Library/Photo Researchers, Inc.; *inset* School Division, Houghton Mifflin Co.; *right* © Michael & Patricia Fogden/Corbis; **C97** *left* © Dwight R. Kuhn; *right* © Sylvester Allred/Fundamental Photographs; **C98** © Keren Su/Corbis; **C99** © Dwight R. Kuhn; **C100** © Martha Cooper/Peter Arnold, Inc.; **C101** *background* © Photospin; *top* © Scott Barrow/ImageState; *bottom* © Bryan Mullenix/Getty Images; **C102** Photograph by Ken O'Donoghue; **C103** © Robert Gustafson/Visuals Unlimited; **C104** *top* © Michael J. Doolittle/The Image Works; *bottom right* © James A. Sugar/Corbis; **C105** Photograph by Frank Siteman; **C106** *left* © Raymond Gehman/Corbis; *top right* © David Sieren/Visuals Unlimited, Inc.; *bottom right* © George Bernard/Science Photo Library; **C107** Photograph by Ken O'Donoghue; **C109** *background* © John Marshall; *left* © George D. Lepp/Corbis; *center* © Sergio Piumatti; *right* © Gary Braasch/Corbis; **C110** © Ed Reschke; **C111** *top* Photograph by Ken O'Donoghue; *bottom* © Custom Medical Stock Photo; **C112** *left* © Frank Lane Picture Agency/Corbis; *right* © Eastcott/Momatiuc/Animals Animals; **C113** *right* © Craig Aurness/Corbis; *inset* © Michael Newman/PhotoEdit; **C114** *background* © Lance Nelson/Corbis; *top, left* National Cotton Council of America; *right* © Mary Kate Denny/PhotoEdit; **C115** *left* © Patricia Agre/Photo Researchers, Inc.; *right* © Martin B. Withers, Frank Lane Picture Agency/Corbis; **C116** *top* © Hal Horwitz/Corbis; *center left* © Martha Cooper/Peter Arnold, Inc.; *center right* © Dwight R. Kuhn; *bottom left* © Gary Braasch/Corbis; *bottom right* © George D. Lepp/Corbis; **C117** *(both)* © Wolfgang Bayer/Bruce Coleman, Inc./PictureQuest ; **C120, C121** © Norbert Wu; **C121** *top* Photograph by Frank Siteman; *bottom* © Photospin; **C123** © Andrew J. Martinez/Visuals Unlimited; **C124** Photograph by Ken O'Donoghue; **C125** *background* © Viola's Photo Visions, Inc./Animals Animals; **C126** © Marty Snyderman/Visuals Unlimited; **C127** © Kevin Schafer/Getty Images; **C128** Photograph by Ken O'Donoghue; **C129** © Photodisc/Getty Images; **C130** *top left, bottom left* © John D. Cunningham/Visuals Unlimited; **C131** *left* © Bob Evans/Peter Arnold, Inc.; *right* © Visuals Unlimited; **C132** © Dwight R.Kuhn; **C133** *top* © Larry Lipsky/DRK Photo; *center* © A. Flowers & L. Newman/Photo Researchers, Inc.; *bottom* © Richard Kessel/Visuals Unlimited; **C134** *top* © Robert Pickett/Corbis; *bottom* Photograph by Ken O'Donoghue; **C135** *top* Photograph by Ken O'Donoghue; *bottom* Photograph by Frank Siteman; **C136** © Sinclair Stammers/Photo Researchers, Inc.; **C137** *top* © Andrew J. Martinez/Photo Researchers, Inc.; *bottom* © Konrad Wothe/Minden Pictures; **C138** *top* Photograph by Ken O'Donoghue; *bottom* © Fred

Bavendam/Minden Pictures; **C139** *top* © Andrew J. Martinez; *bottom* © David Wrobel/Visuals Unlimited; **C140** *left* © Fred Winner/Jacana/Photo Researchers, Inc.; *right* © Gerald & Buff Corsi/Visuals Unlimited; **C141** *background* © Dwight R. Kuhn; *inset* © Thomas Kitchin/Tom Stack & Associates; **C142** Photograph by Frank Siteman; **C143** *top* © Kelvin Aitken/Peter Arnold, Inc.; *bottom* © Barry Runk/Grant Heilman Photography; **C144** *background* © Corbis-Royalty Free; *top* © Tim Davis/Corbis; *center* © Steve Wolper/DRK Photo; *bottom* © George Calef/DRK Photo; **C146** Photograph by Ken O'Donoghue; **C147** *top (all)* © Dwight R. Kuhn; *bottom* © Frans Lanting/Minden Pictures; **C148** *top* © David Scharf/Peter Arnold, Inc.; *bottom* © E.R. Degginger/Color-Pic, Inc.; **C149** *left* © Science Photo Library/Photo Researchers, Inc.; *right* © Claus Meyer/Minden Pictures; **C150** *top right* © Viola's Photo Visions, Inc./Animals Animals; *center left* © John D. Cunningham/Visuals Unlimited; *bottom left* © Konrad Wothe/Minden Pictures; *bottom right* © Gerald & Buff Corsi/Visuals Unlimited; **C154, C155** © Paul A. Souders/Corbis; **C155** *top* Photograph by Frank Siteman; *center left* © Steven Frame/Stock Boston Inc./PictureQuest; *center right* © Rod Planck/Photo Researchers, Inc.; **C157** Photograph by Frank Siteman; **C158** © Corbis-Royalty Free; **C159** *background* © SeaLifeStyles Signature Series/Imagin; **C160** *background* © Colla - V&W/Bruce Coleman, Inc.; *left* © Norbert Wu; *left inset* © Brandon Cole; *center* © Georgienne E. Bradley & Jay Ireland/Bradley Ireland Productions; *right* © Brandon Cole; **C162** © David Doubilet; **C163** *left* © Kennan Ward/Corbis; *right* © Frans Lanting/Minden Pictures; **C164** *left* © Bianca Lavies/National Geographic Image Collection; *right* Photograph by Frank Siteman; **C165** *left* © Dwight R. Kuhn; *right* © Joe McDonald/Bruce Coleman, Inc.; **C166** *all* © Dwight R. Kuhn; **C168** © Francois Gohier/Photo Researchers, Inc.; **C169** © Carmela Leszczynski/Animals Animals; **C170** *top* Photograph by Frank Siteman; *bottom* © Tui de Roy/Minden Pictures; **C171** © Michael Fogden/Animals Animals; **C172** *left* ©Frans Lanting/Minden Pictures; *center* © E.R. Degginger/Color-Pic, Inc.; *right* © Science Photo Library/Photo Researchers, Inc.; **C173** Photograph by Ken O'Donoghue; **C174** © Michael Quinton/Minden Pictures; **C175** *left* © Julie Habel/Corbis; *center* © Randy Faris/Corbis; *right* © David-Young Wolff/PhotoEdit; **C177** *background* © Tim Bird/Corbis; **C178** *left* © Jim Brandenburg/Minden Pictures; *right* © Fritz Polking/Visuals Unlimited; **C179** *top* © Ron Austing/Photo Researchers, Inc.; *bottom* © S. Nielsen/DRK Photo; **C180** *top* © DigitalVision/PictureQuest; *bottom* Photograph by Frank Siteman **C181** *top* Photograph by Frank Siteman; *bottom left* © Corbis-Royalty Free; *bottom center* © Frans Lemmens/Getty Images; *bottom right* © Arthur Morris/Corbis; **C182** © Carleton Ray/Photo Researchers, Inc.; **C183** *top* © Mitsuaki Iwago/Minden Pictures; *bottom* © Don Enger/Animals Animals; **C184** Photograph by Frank Siteman; **C185** *background* © Stephen Frink/Corbis; **C186** *left* © Photodisc/Getty Images; *right* © Frans Lanting/Minden Pictures; **C187** © Comstock; **C188** *top left* © Dwight R. Kuhn; *top right* © Michael Fogden/Animals Animals; *center right* © Fritz Polking/Visuals Unlimited; *bottom left* © Frans Lanting/Minden Pictures; *bottom right* © Photodisc/Getty Images.

## Motion and Forces

**Divider** © Brett Froomer/Getty Images, **D2–D3** Courtesy of NASA/JPL/Caltech; **D3** © Stocktrek/Corbis; **D4** *top* Courtesy of NASA/JPL/Caltech; *bottom* © The Chedd-Angier Production Company; **D6–D7** © Lester Lefkowitz/Corbis; **D7** Photographs by Sharon Hoogstraten; **D9** © Royalty-Free/Corbis; **D11** © Globus, Holway & Lobel/Corbis; **D12** *top* Photograph by Sharon Hoogstraten; *bottom* © The Image Group/Getty Images; **D14** *top* © Georgina Bowater/Corbis; *bottom* © SuperStock; **D15** © Graham Wheatley/ The Military Picture Library/Corbis; **D16, D17** Photographs by Sharon Hoogstraten; **D18** © Gunter Marx Photography/Corbis; **D19** Photograph by Sharon Hoogstraten; **D21** © Tom Brakefield/Corbis; **D22** © David M. Dennis/Animals Animals; **D23** © Kelly-Mooney Photography/Corbis; **D24** © Gallo Images/Corbis; **D25** © 1986 Richard Megna/Fundamental Photographs, NYC; **D27** Photograph by Sharon Hoogstraten; **D28** © Royalty-Free/Corbis; **D29** Courtesy of NASA/JPL/Caltech; **D30** © Robert Essel NYC/Corbis; **D32** *top* © Mark Jenkinson/Corbis; *bottom* Photographs by Sharon Hoogstraten; **D34** *top* © Globus, Holway & Lobel/Corbis; *center* Photograph by Sharon Hoogstraten; **D36** © David M. Dennis/Animals Animals; **D38–D39** © Arthur Tilley/Getty Images; **D39, D41** Photographs by Sharon Hoogstraten; **D42** © John Kelly/Getty Images; **D43** *left* © AFP/Corbis; *right* © Reuters NewMedia Inc./Corbis; **D44** © Michael Kevin Daly/Corbis; **D45** *left* © Jim Cummins/Getty Images; *right* © Piecework Productions/Getty Images; **D46** Photograph by Sharon Hoogstraten; **D47** © Jeffrey Lynch/Mendola Ltd., **D48** *left, inset* © Bill Ross/Corbis; *right* Dr. Paula Messina, San Jose State University; **D49, D50** Photographs by Sharon Hoogstraten; **D52** AP/Wide World Photos; **D53** NASA; **D54** Photograph by Sharon Hoogstraten; **D55** AP/Wide World Photos; **D56** *top* Clare Hirn, Jewish Hospital, University of Louisville and ABIOMED; *bottom* John Lair, Jewish Hospital, University of Louisville and ABIOMED; **D57** © Danny Lehman/Corbis; **D58, D59** Photographs by Sharon Hoogstraten; **D60** © Photodisc/Getty Images; *background* © David C. Fritts/Animals Animals; **D62** *top* Digital image © 1996 Corbis/Original image courtesy of NASA/Corbis; *bottom* Photographs by Sharon Hoogstraten; **D64, D66** Photographs by Sharon Hoogstraten; **D68** © TRL Ltd./Photo Researchers; **D69** © Charles O'Rear/Corbis; **D70** *top* © Photodisc/Getty Images; *bottom* Photographs by Sharon Hoogstraten; **D71** © Siede Preis/ Getty Images; **D72** Photographs by Sharon Hoogstraten; **D74–D75** © Mike Chew/Corbis; **D75, D77** Photographs by Sharon Hoogstraten; **D80, D81** Photographs of models by Sharon Hoogstraten; **D80** *left* NASA; *right* © Photodisc/Getty Images; **D81** *top, bottom, background* NASA; **D82** Photograph by Sharon Hoogstraten; **D83** NASA; **D84** *left* © Royalty-Free/Corbis; *right* NASA/ESA; **D85** © John Beatty/Getty Images; **D86, D87** Photographs by Sharon Hoogstraten; **D88** *top* © Al Francekevich/Corbis; *bottom* Photograph by Sharon Hoogstraten; **D89** © Joe McBride/Getty Images; **D90** © NatPhotos/Tony Sweet/Digital Vision; *inset* © Michael S. Yamashita/Corbis; **D91** Photograph by Sharon Hoogstraten; **D92** © Wilson Goodrich/Index Stock; **D93** © Royalty-Free/Corbis; **D94** © Philip & Karen Smith/Getty Images; **D95** © Ralph A. Clevenger/Corbis; **D96** *top* © Stephen Frink/Corbis; *bottom* Photographs by Sharon Hoogstraten; **D98, D99, D100** Photographs by Sharon Hoogstraten; **D101** Photograph of prairie dogs © W. Perry Conway/Corbis; **D103** © Omni Photo Communications Inc./Index Stock; **D104** *top, bottom* Photographs by Sharon Hoogstraten; *center* © Royalty-Free/Corbis; **D105** Photograph by Sharon Hoogstraten; **D106** *left* © Joe McBride/Getty Images; *right* Photograph by Sharon Hoogstraten; **D108** *top* © Erich Lessing/Art Resource, New York; *bottom* © Dagli Orti/The Art Archive; **D109** *top left* © SPL/Photo Researchers; *top right* Sam Fogg Rare Books & Manuscripts; *bottom* © Dorling Kindersley; **D110** *left* © Victoria & Albert Museum, London/Art Resource, New York; *top right* Photo Franca Principe, Institute and Museum of the History of Science; *center right* © Scala/Art Resource, New York; *bottom right* © Dorling Kindersley; **D111** *top* © Gerald L. Schad/Photo Researchers; *bottom* NASA; **D112–D113** © Digital Vision; **D113** *top* Image Club Graphics; *center* Photograph by Sharon Hoogstraten; **D115, D116** Photographs by Sharon Hoogstraten; **D117** © Rob Lewine/Corbis; **D118** Photograph by Sharon Hoogstraten; **D119** © Reinhard Eisele/Corbis; **D120** © Roger Allyn Lee/ SuperStock; **D121** Chris Wipperman/KCPDSA; **D123** © Patrik Giardino/Corbis; **D124** © Tony Anderson/Getty Images; **D125** Photograph by Sharon Hoogstraten; **D126** © 1988 Paul Silverman/Fundamental Photographs, NYC; **D127** © Tony Donaldson/Icon Sports Media; **D129** © AFP/Corbis; **D130** Photograph by Sharon Hoogstraten; **D131** © Pete Saloutos/Corbis; **D132** © Digital Vision; **D133** Photograph by Sharon Hoogstraten; **D134** © Walter Hodges/Corbis; **D135** © Grantpix/Index Stock; **D136** *top* © David Young-Wolff/PhotoEdit; *bottom* Photographs by Sharon Hoogstraten; **D138** © Pete Saloutos/Corbis; **D140** Photographs by Sharon Hoogstraten; **D142–D143** © Balthazar Korab; **D145** Photograph by Sharon Hoogstraten; **D146** © David Young-Wolff/PhotoEdit; **D147** © Joseph Sohm/ ChromoSohm Inc./Corbis; **D149** © Brad Wrobleski/Masterfile; **D150** © Michael Macor/San Francisco Chronicle/Corbis SABA; **D151** Photograph by Sharon Hoogstraten; **D152** © Jean-Yves Ruszniewski/Corbis; **D153** © Royalty-Free/Corbis; *inset* © Felicia Martinez/ PhotoEdit; **D154, D155** Photographs by Sharon Hoogstraten; **D156** © Tom Stewart/Corbis; **D157** Photograph by Sharon Hoogstraten; **D158** *top* © David Butow/Corbis SABA; *bottom* © Peter Beck/Corbis; **D159** © Henryk T. Kaiser/Index Stock; **D160** © Tony Freeman/ PhotoEdit; **D161** © Todd A. Gipstein/Corbis; **D163** AP/Wide World Photos; **D164** © Tony Freeman/PhotoEdit; **D165** © Lester Lefkowitz/ Corbis; **D166** Hurst Jaws of Life; **D167** © David Parker/Photo Researchers; **D168** *top* AP/Wide World Photos; *bottom* © Robert Caputo/Stock Boston; *background* © Royalty-Free/Corbis; **D170** *top* © Photodisc/Getty Images; *bottom* Photograph by Sharon Hoogstraten; **D172** © ThinkStock/SuperStock; **D173** *top left* Photograph by Sharon Hoogstraten; **D174** © Tony Freeman/ PhotoEdit.

## Electricity and Magnetism

**Divider** © Nick Koudis/Getty Images; **E2–E3** © PHISH 2003; 3 © Jacques M. Chenet/Corbis; **E4** *top* © John Foxx/ImageState; *bottom* © The Chedd-Angier Production Company; **E5** © Stuart Hughes/Corbis; **E6–E7** AP/Wide World Photos; **E7, E9** Photographs by Sharon Hoogstraten; **E10** © Roger Ressmeyer/Corbis; **E12** © Charles D. Winters/Photo Researchers; **E14** Photograph by Sharon Hoogstraten; **E16** © Maximilian Stock Ltd./Photo Researchers; **E17** *left* © Ann and Rob Simpson; *right* © Patrice Ceisel/Visuals Unlimited; **E18** Photograph by Sharon Hoogstraten; **E19** © Steve Crise/Corbis; **E21** © A & J Verkaik/Corbis; **E22** Photograph by Sharon Hoogstraten; **E23** *top* © Tim Wright/Corbis; *bottom* © Leland Bobb/Corbis; **E24** © James D. Hooker/*Lighting Equipment News (UK)*; **E26** *top left* © Scott T. Smith; All other photographs by Sharon Hoogstraten; **E27, E28, E30, E31** Photographs by Sharon Hoogstraten; **E33** © Chip Simons 2003; **E34** Photo Courtesy of NASA/Getty Images; **E35** © Julian Hirshowitz/Corbis; **E36** © James D. Hooker/*Lighting Equipment News (UK);* **E40–E41** © 2003 Barbara Ries; **E41, E43** Photographs by Sharon Hoogstraten; **E48** *left* © 1989 Paul Silverman/Fundamental Photographs, NYC; *right* Photograph by Sharon Hoogstraten; **E49** © Creative Publishing International, Inc.; **E50** *top left* © Gary Rhijnsburger/Masterfile; *center left* © Creative Publishing International, Inc.; **E51, E52, E53, E54** Photographs by Sharon Hoogstraten; **E56** © Robert Essel NYC/Corbis; **E57** Photograph by Sharon Hoogstraten; **E59** *top* AP/Wide World Photos; *bottom* Photograph by

Sharon Hoogstraten; **E61** © Kurt Stier/Corbis; **E62, E63** © Gen Nishino/Getty Images; **E64** © Donna Cox and Robert Patterson/ National Center for Supercomputing Applications, University of Illinois, Urbana; **E65** AP/Wide World Photos; **E66** *top* © Sheila Terry/Photo Researchers; *bottom* Photograph by Sharon Hoogstraten; **E72** *top* © SPL/Photo Researchers; *bottom* The Granger Collection, New York; **E73** *top left* © Philadelphia Museum of Art/Corbis; *top right* © Archivo Iconografico, S.A./Corbis; *bottom* © Adam Hart-Davis/ Photo Researchers; **E74** *top* Science Museum/Science & Society Picture Library; *center left* © Bettmann/ Corbis; *center right* © Tony Craddock/Photo Researchers; *bottom* © Bettmann/Corbis; **E75** *top* © Alfred Pasieka/Photo Researchers; *bottom* AP/Wide World Photos; **E76–E77** © Philip & Karen Smith/age fotostock america, inc.; **E77, E79** Photographs by Sharon Hoogstraten; **E80** *top* © Michael S. Yamashita/ Corbis; *bottom* Photograph by Sharon Hoogstraten; **E81** Photographs by Sharon Hoogstraten; **E82** © The Natural History Museum, London; **E83** Photograph by Sharon Hoogstraten; **E84** NASA; **E85** Photograph by Sharon Hoogstraten; **E86** © Chris Madeley/Photo Researchers; **E87** © Brian Bahr/Getty Images; *inset* Courtesy of Discover Magnetics; **E88, E90** Photographs by Sharon Hoogstraten; **E91** *top* © George Haling/Photo Researchers; *bottom* © Dick Luria/Photo Researchers; **E93** © G. K. & Vikki Hart/Getty Images; **E95** Photograph by Sharon Hoogstraten; **E97** © Ondrea Barbe/ Corbis; **E98** Photograph by Sharon Hoogstraten; **E99** © Randy M. Ury/Corbis; **E100** *top* © Christopher Gould/Getty Images; *bottom* Photographs by Sharon Hoogstraten; **E101** Photographs by Sharon Hoogstraten; **E102** Bureau of Reclamation; **E104** Courtesy of General Electric; **E105** *top* Photograph by Sharon Hoogstraten; *bottom* © Maya Barnes/The Image Works; **E107** © Mark Richards/PhotoEdit; **E108** *top* Photograph by Sharon Hoogstraten.

### Backmatter

**R28** © PhotoDisc/Getty Images.

## Illustration and Maps

Accurate Art, Inc. **A75, A109, D107, D175**
Ampersand Design Group **D15, E50**
Argosy **A46, A119**
Richard Bonson/Wildlife Art Ltd. **A44, A72**
Robin Boutell/Wildlife Art Ltd. **C132, C150** *(center right)*
Peter Bull/Wildlife Art Ltd. **A99, A106, C26, C33, C34**
Steve Cowden **D122, E60, E62–E63, E68**
Stephen Durke **A17, A18, A25, A36, E11, E12, E13, E21, E25, E31, E36, E39, E44, E46, E53, E68, E103, E108, E110**
Chris Forsey **A129**
Gary Hincks **A20, A36, A48, A51**
Ian Jackson/Wildlife Art Ltd. **C67, C70, C145, C150** *(bottom)*, **C177**
Keith Kasnot, **R58, R59**
Myriam Kirkman-Oh/KO Studios **C87**
Debbie Maizels **B15, B26, B84, B90, B102, B104, B128, C45, C56** *(inset)*, **C89, C99, C101, C109, C118, C158, R57**
MapQuest.com, Inc. **A3, A14, A49, A52, A54, A55, A80, A83, A84, A85, A86, A88, A89, A93, A97, A118, A120, A121, A123, A126, A133, A134, A135, A136, A140, A143, C47, D10, D60, D129, D168**
Linda Nye **B11, B30, B46, B66, B70, B90, B92, B119, B120, B121, B122, B123, B126**
Steve Oh/KO Studios **B78, B105, C17, C27, C36**
Laurie O'Keefe **C125, C130, C159, C185**
Mick Posen/Wildlife Art Ltd. **C129**
Precision Graphics **A53, A59, A72**
Tony Randazzo/American Artists Rep. Inc. **C56** *(background)*, **D13**
Mike Saunders **A61, A69, A72**
Space Science and Engineering Center, University of Wisconsin-Madison **A84, A100, A101, A102, A106**
Dan Stuckenschneider/Uhl Studios **D102, D135, D156, D157, D158, D159, D161, D162, D165, D172, D173, E15, E33, E47, E49, E55, E92, E93, E94, E96, E97, E108, R11-R19, R22, R32**
Dan Stukenschneider based on an illustration by Matt Cioffi **D168**
UNEP-WCMC, 2002 World Atlas of Biodiversity **C81**
Raymond Turvey **A83, A106**
Bart Vallecoccia and Richard McMahon **B11, B17, B30, B32, B41, B42, B44, B46, B49, B53, B54, B58, B60, B68, B103, B105, B106, B113, B119, B120, B126**